Lone Star Rising

LONE
STAR
RISING

Lyndon Johnson and His Times
1908–1960

ROBERT DALLEK

New York   Oxford
OXFORD UNIVERSITY PRESS
1991

Oxford University Press

Oxford   New York   Toronto
Delhi   Bombay   Calcutta   Madras   Karachi
Petaling Jaya   Singapore   Hong Kong   Tokyo
Nairobi   Dar es Salaam   Cape Town
Melbourne   Auckland

and associated companies in
Berlin   Ibadan

Library of Congress Cataloging-in-Publication Data
Dallek, Robert.
Lone Star Rising :
Lyndon Johnson and His Times, 1908–1960 /
Robert Dallek.
p. cm. Includes bibliographical references and index.
ISBN 0-19-505435-0
1. Johnson, Lyndon B. (Lyndon Baines), 1908–1973.
2. Presidents—United States—Biography.
3. United States—Politics and government—1933–1945.
4. United States—Politics and government—1945–
I. Title. E847.D25 1991
973.923'092—dc20 [B] 90-39830

2 4 6 8 9 7 5 3 1

Printed in the United States of America
on acid-free paper

For Matthew and Rebecca

Preface

THE reputations of most Presidents after they leave the White House suffer an eclipse. In time, however, they make something of a comeback. Passions over controversial questions subside and achievements are balanced against shortcomings.

So far, Lyndon Johnson is a case apart. His public standing since 1969 has plummeted, and an upturn seems nowhere in sight. "Lyndon Johnson was clearly a monster of ambition, greed, and cruelty," one historian wrote in 1990. "What's not to loathe?" In the view of one journalist, "No . . . politician ever did more than he to destroy the country." There are reasons enough to dislike Lyndon Johnson: certain aspects of his private behavior offended any one with the least sense of propriety, and his public actions violated legal and democratic standards on which the American system of government is supposed to rest. But there exists a hatred of Johnson that passes the bounds of common sense and contributes nothing to historical understanding.*

We now need a balanced biography that draws on the massive documentary record and focuses less on Johnson the man and more on his larger impact. Johnson's importance in twentieth-century history is too great for us to dismiss him as little more than a contemptible character whose principal distinguishing feature was the advancement of Lyndon Johnson. He was a man of consuming ambition, but he was also a politician with considerable vision that he carried to fruition during a long career. From his earliest days in Congress he was a liberal nationalist, an advocate of Federal programs that had a redefining influence on American life. His efforts to promote the national well-being by helping the least affluent help themselves and to end racial segregation as a prelude to southern economic advance and expanded political power were acts of genuine statesmanship. They had their beginnings in Johnson's pre-presidential years reconstructed in this volume. Johnson was also a representative figure. His election campaigns, accumulation of wealth,

---

*The quotes are from reviews of Robert Caro's *The Years of Lyndon Johnson: Means of Ascent* (New York, 1990): Garry Wills in *The New York Review of Books*, April 26, 1990, p. 7; and Robert Sherrill in *The Texas Observer*, April 6, 1990, p. 14.

and manipulation of power speak volumes about the way American politics and business worked in the four decades after 1930.

The work for this book has taken over seven years. It rests upon research in over a hundred manuscript collections around the country, hundreds of oral histories, and numerous interviews. Additional years of study will precede the publication of a second volume. I hope the combined work will stand as the scholarly biography of Johnson for the foreseeable future. At the very least, I believe it represents a significant advance on where we have been in understanding the man and his times.

This is not to suggest, however, that arguments about Johnson and his historical significance will end. Quite the contrary, the materials for studying his life are so vast and his actions so controversial that we will be debating his role in national and international affairs for a long time to come. Rather than close the discussion about Johnson, then, I hope my biography will enlarge interest and become the starting point for sustained consideration of one of the most important historical figures of our time.

Los Angeles   R.D.
December 1990

Acknowledgments

ALTHOUGH books about recent American political leaders customarily ascribe authorship to one person, an army of people is needed to make such studies possible.

How far would I have gotten without the work of others who organized and opened the mass of papers housed at the Lyndon B. Johnson Presidential Library? I am indebted to Harry Middleton, the Library's Director, who is devoted to making the record of Lyndon Johnson's life and career available as quickly and fully as possible. I have also been the beneficiary of Harry Middleton's efforts to encourage Lyndon Johnson's closest associates to grant me interviews. The Library's staff was unstinting in its help: Molly Chesney, Charles Corkran, Kathy Frankum, Theodore Gittinger, Regina Greenwell, Linda Hanson, Tina Houston, David Humphrey, Lawrence Reed, E. Philip Scott, Robert Tissing, Shellynne Wucher, and Gary Yarrington. Three people have been especially kind and helpful. Claudia Anderson put her masterful command of the LBJ pre-presidential papers at my disposal. Her help was indispensable. The same was true of Michael Gillette, head of the oral history division, whose knowledge of the Johnson years is incomparable. Nancy Smith, who now works in the Office of Presidential Libraries, National Archives, Washington, D.C., helped guide my research in the crucial opening stages of the book. The Lyndon B. Johnson Foundation aided my research with two timely grants.

A number of other people and institutions helped advance my work in a variety of ways. Norman D. Brown, Robert A. Divine, and Clarence G. Lasby of the University of Texas and Louis S. Gomolak of Southwest Texas State University shared materials and insights with me. Christie Bourgeois, J. Kaaz Doyle, Craig H. Roell, and Stacy Rozek, graduate students at the University of Texas, performed a variety of tasks for which I am grateful. Larry Temple, an Austin attorney and former member of President Johnson's staff, and George Christian, LBJ's press secretary, helped arrange an interview with former Governor John B. Connally and showed me other kindnesses. No two people made my visits to Austin more satisfying than Elspeth and Walt W. Rostow. They have given new meaning to the term southern hospitality.

In Los Angeles, Ruth Behling, an undergraduate at UCLA, and Brian VanDeMark, a former graduate student at UCLA and now assistant professor of history at the U.S. Naval Academy, saved me precious time by their cheerful performance of research chores. Ruth Behling, Christie Bourgeois, and Kenneth Kurz, a graduate student at UCLA, helped by reading proof, as did Lorris Gosman. John and Sandra Brice generously shared materials they had gathered for a docudrama on LBJ. The UCLA Academic Senate and International and Overeas Programs supported my work with generous research grants. James and Geralyn Goodman have provided me with a marvelous collection of LBJ memorabilia.

The staffs of university libraries, state historical societies, and presidential libraries all over the country assisted me in the search for LBJ materials. Their contributions are reflected in the notes and sources listed at the end of the book. I wish to single out for special thanks several people who helped me gather materials: H.G. Dulany, Director of the Sam Rayburn Library, Carol Ebell at the University of Georgia, for help with the Richard Russell Papers, Gary E. Elliott, who shared his materials on Senator Alan Bible, Dr. Susan Falb, Archivist at the FBI, George D. Hedrick, who helped with the Hubert H. Humphrey Papers, Professor James H. Neal of Middle Tennessee State University, for help with the Albert Gore, Sr., Papers, Bradley S. Phillips of Munger, Tolles, & Olson, Los Angeles, who volunteered his help with an FOIA request to the FBI, Dr. Donald Ritchie of the Senate Historical Office, and Professor Athan Theoharis of Marquette University, who shared FBI materials on LBJ and gave me the benefit of his expertise.

I wish to thank the University of Virginia for permission to use material from the Harry F. Byrd, Sr., Papers and Myer Feldman for agreeing to my use of his oral history interview at the John F. Kennedy Presidential Library.

I am grateful to Ed Cray, Murray Fromson, Sam Kernell, Daniel Kevles, Stanley I. Kutler, Peter Loewenberg, and Bruce Schulman for offering me their judgments on some of my ideas. Irving Bernstein, my colleague in the political science department, was especially helpful in this respect. Edward A. Goldstein, Max Holland, Lawrence W. Levine, William E. Leuchtenburg, and Richard Weiss read and criticized the manuscript. The book is better in every respect for their generous help. I am indebted to Harold Zellman for suggesting the title.

I am particularly grateful to three other people. Lewis L. Gould has given me the benefit of his masterful knowledge of Texas history and Lyndon Johnson. He pointed me to research collections, discussed my ideas, read the manuscript with the greatest of care, and made suggestions for cuts and additions which have enriched the book. He is a scholar in every sense of the word.

Sheldon Meyer, executive vice president of the Oxford University Press, saw the virtues of publishing an LBJ biography from the moment I proposed it to him. His enthusiasm for the project matches my own. His close reading of the manuscript produced a number of excellent suggestions that have significantly improved the book. I could not ask for a more understanding and helpful publisher. Likewise, Leona Capeless gave me the benefit of her wise counsel on numerous points in the manuscript. As with an earlier book, she applied a professional standard that makes working with her a special pleasure.

Geraldine Dallek, my wife, has once again maintained a keen interest in my work that helped sustain me. She has good-naturedly listened to my repeated renderings of LBJ stories and, like me, finds LBJ so fascinating a character that she looks forward to yet another volume on his life and times. My children, Matthew and Rebecca, also shared in this project in special ways. Matthew helped with some of the research, both in Texas and Los Angeles, and along with Rebecca, read parts of the manuscript. They gave me access to the current college-age generation, which has no direct memories of LBJ. The book convinced them that Johnson deserves the extended attention I'm giving him. They now know that he made a difference in the world they inherited.

Contents

Part Four   The Majority Leader, 1955–1960

Lone Star Rising

Introduction
LBJ in History

L YNDON Johnson, the dominant political figure of the sixties who challenged us to wipe out poverty, end racial segregation, and win a morally confusing war in a remote place, has receded from our minds. Where biographical studies of FDR, Truman, Kennedy, and Nixon abound, Johnson is something of an unloved orphan. Twenty-two years after he left the White House, christened a magnificent eleven-story presidential library, and ordered the opening of thirty-two million pages of material housed there, no historian had published a major research study of his life and two journalists promising to do so had vilified him in books that only came up to the fifties, the years of his Senate career.[1]

The paucity of work alongside of other presidential biographies partly reflects the public's current low esteem for Johnson. A November 1988 Louis Harris poll on presidential performance from Franklin Delano Roosevelt to Ronald Reagan consistently ranked Johnson near or at the bottom of eleven categories. Asked which of these Presidents made people feel proudest of being an American, most inspired confidence in the White House, and could be trusted most in a crisis, respondents consistently put LBJ last along side of Gerald Ford and behind Richard Nixon. Who will history view as the best among these Presidents? Only 1 percent chose Johnson. The President best able to get things done? Three percent said Johnson, 1 percent more than said Jimmy Carter and 2 percent more than said Ford. And the President setting the highest moral standards? JFK, Reagan, and Carter, in that order, led the list. Johnson stood alone in last place, chosen by only 1 percent of the sample. Even Richard Nixon fared better with 2 percent of the vote.[2]

One biographer and historian has puzzled over the popular appeal of this negative portrait of LBJ. "Maybe Johnson has become so hated in our time that Americans want him reduced to caricature, want him presented as . . . [someone] who deceived us with his promise of the Great Society, who took away *our* idealism and *our* humanity in the flames of Vietnam. Maybe Johnson has become a scapegoat for our collective guilt over the war, and all our woes and shattered dreams that followed."[3]

Johnson's distinction as the only President in American history to have lost a war is certainly one reason for his poor ratings. Conservatives deplore his timidity in fighting a "limited war," his failure to do what needed to be done against North Vietnam. Liberals denounce his affinity for a knee-jerk anticommunism that involved us in a civil war having less to do with U.S. national security than Vietnamese aspirations to replace Western imperial control with national self-determination. Middle Americans find some appeal in both arguments, but for the most part see "Johnson's war" as a pointless exercise that took 58,000 American lives and divided and demoralized the country.

Johnson's reputation as a political operator who lied to the public and enriched himself in office by exploiting connections at the Federal Communications Commission to acquire and develop lucrative radio and television properties has also contributed to negative public feelings about him. Stories of Johnson's wheeling and dealing are legion. One of my favorites describes a visit Johnson made to Harry Truman's home in Independence, Missouri, in the fall of 1968. "Harry," Johnson said, "you and Bess are getting on in years. You ought to have an Army medical corpsman living with you in this big old house." "Really, Lyndon, can I have that?" Truman asked. "Of course, you can. You're an ex-President of the United States. I'll arrange it," Johnson replied. Six months after LBJ left the White House a reporter caught up with him one day on the banks of the Pedernales. "Is it true that you have an Army medical corpsman living here on the ranch with you?" the journalist asked. "Of course it's true," Johnson said. "Harry Truman has one."[4]

A backlash against Johnson's Great Society, and Federal social programs favoring minorities, has also taken its toll on his standing. In an article on the War on Poverty in the December 1988 issue of *The Atlantic*, Nicholas Lemann wrote: "There is a widespread perception that the federal government's efforts to help the poor during the sixties were almost unlimited; that despite them poverty became more severe, not less; and that the reason poverty increased is that all those government programs backfired and left their intended beneficiaries worse off. The truth is that the percentage of poor Americans went down substantially in the sixties." Nevertheless, it is the negative perception rather than the positive reality of the War on Poverty that currently shapes the public view of LBJ.[5]

As for the principal reforms of the Johnson presidency—Civil Rights,

Voting Rights, Medicare, Medicaid, and Federal aid to education—which most Americans see as essential to a just society, Johnson gets little or no credit for them. Only 6 percent of the Harris poll thought that Johnson's extraordinary reforms gave him claim to being the best President among the last nine in domestic affairs.

The handful of biographies appearing on Johnson since he left the White House has sent his already tarnished reputation into a free fall. I think here particularly of Ronnie Dugger's *The Politician* (1982), Robert Caro's *The Years of Lyndon Johnson* (1982 and 1990), and the revelations about Johnson in the recollections of Richard Goodwin, a Kennedy-Johnson aide. Goodwin depicts Johnson as an emotionally unstable personality. He describes him in 1965 as "paranoid" about Vietnam critics, whom Johnson called tools of the Soviets. Goodwin's concerns about Johnson's stability were so great that he consulted a psychiatrist and considered public disclosure of Johnson's troubled state of mind. Caro sees Johnson as an unprincipled scoundrel or self-serving, deceitful, power-hungry opportunist. Caro says that LBJ had "a hunger for power . . . not to improve the lives of others, but to manipulate and dominate them. . . . It was a hunger so fierce and consuming that no consideration of morality or ethics, no cost to himself—or to anyone else—could stand before it." Johnson had "a seemingly bottomless capacity for deceit, deception and betrayal."[6]

It is instructive to compare the post-presidential reputations of Richard Nixon and Lyndon Johnson. Unlike LBJ, Nixon has won a measure of public redemption. A fifteen-year campaign to convince Americans of his virtues partly explains his improved standing. The triumph of détente and the waning of the cold war, with which the Nixon presidency is closely associated, has also served Nixon's cause. But his resignation from the White House, which is seen as the worst public humiliation ever suffered by an American President, may have played the largest part. Nixon's implicit admission of fallibility has won him some degree of public forgiveness. By contrast with Nixon, Johnson did not live long enough to work at repairing his reputation. Also, the principal issues with which Johnson's presidency is primarily associated—Vietnam and the Great Society—remain in bad odor. But perhaps most important, Johnson never acknowledged any failing—never fessed up or asked forgiveness for mistakes or wrongdoing. In perhaps the greatest ironies of their careers, Nixon, the Republican, who identified with and sought to serve the interests of advantaged Americans, is seen as a sort of fallible common man. Johnson, the populist, who sincerely wished to help the poorest among us, is remembered as a man apart from the people, a kind of arrogant potentate too imperious to acknowledge weaknesses common to ordinary men.

The state of public feeling about Johnson is perhaps best caught in a drawing of him accompanying *The Atlantic* article. Dressed in a blue Napoleonic uniform with gold epaulettes, a red sash, medals, and saber at his side, Johnson sits at a dressing table smiling at himself in a mirror that reflects not only his image but that of two black cherubs holding a halo above his head. Large ears, a jutting chin, and long pointed nose accent Johnson's prominent head. A photograph of an avuncular FDR and a gold pocket watch are on the dressing table. It is a portrait of a totally self-absorbed, grandiose character intent on his image in history.

The caricature of Johnson has a basis in fact. Johnson was a larger-than-life personality who needed to hold center stage and advance himself at every turn. In 1973, when Johnson's body lay in state at the LBJ Library in Austin, Harry Middleton, a former White House aide and now Library director, told someone to keep track of how many people went by the casket. "Why are you doing that?" another Johnson associate asked Middleton. "Because," Middleton replied, "I know that somewhere, sometime Johnson's going to ask me."[7]

Johnson overwhelmed most of his contemporaries. He needed to be the best, to outdo everybody, to surpass every presidential predecessor in every way possible. As Nicholas Lemann says, Johnson "wanted to set world records in politics, as a star athlete would in sports. 'Get those coonskins up on the wall,' he would tell people around him." Above all, he wanted to surpass his mentor FDR by passing more reform legislation and winning a bigger electoral victory than Roosevelt had in 1936. Johnson's strivings to be the best extended in many directions. Presented with a set of volumes containing the Presidents' State of the Union messages, Johnson asked the editor of the books which President had delivered the longest address. Told that it was Theodore Roosevelt, Johnson replied: "You know, my recent State of the Union Address was shorter than Mr. Kennedy's 1963 speech. But everyone thought mine was longer, because I was interrupted for applause more often than he was."[8]

The caricatures of Johnson as a driven, overbearing, self-centered personality capture only part of the man. *New York Times* columnist Russell Baker remembers Johnson as "a human puzzle so complicated nobody could ever understand it." Baker, who covered the Senate for the *Times* in the late fifties, describes the upper house as filled with remarkable men. All of them, "from a writer's point of view, . . . were long magazine pieces who might at best, with plenty of coffee and cigarettes, be stretched into thin campaign biographies. Johnson was the exception. Johnson was a flesh-and-blood, three-volume biography, and if you ever got it written you'd discover after publication that you'd missed the key point or got the interpretation completely wrong and needed a fourth volume to set things right. He was a character out of a Russian novel, one of those human complications that filled the imagination of

Dostoyevsky, a storm of warring human instincts: sinner and saint, buf-
foon and statesman, cynic and sentimentalist, a man torn between hun-
gers for immortality and self-destruction."

Johnson, another journalist says, was more complex than any Mani-
chaean picture of him can convey. He was not a case of good and evil
living side by side but of "an unlovable man desperate to be loved, whose
cynicism and idealism were mysteriously inseparable, all of a piece."
This journalist quotes Robert Penn Warren's observation in *All the King's
Men:* "A man's virtue may be the defect of his desire, as his crime may
be but a function of his virtue." Lyndon Johnson was a study in ambi-
guity.[9]

Not only have we been content with one- and two-dimensional por-
traits of LBJ, we have also focused too much attention on Johnson at
the expense of larger historical themes. I am not suggesting that a Johnson biography relegate the man to a secondary role that neglects his
colorful personality and the ways in which he used the sheer force of his
character to advance himself and his ends. The means by which Johnson sought and exercised power form a fascinating story that deserves to
be told and retold. In the pages that follow, I have added a fresh body
of detail about his political skulduggery and business dealings that made
him wealthy. But when, as in the existing Johnson literature, unsavory
revelations are related with little emphasis on Johnson's contribution to
the transformation of America between 1937 and 1969, the years of LBJ's
congressional and executive service, it leaves us with an unflattering
portrait of a self-serving man who made little difference in recent American history. This, at least, is the image that seems to be reflected in the
recent Harris poll.

We would do well to remember Charles de Gaulle's comment when
he came to the United States for Kennedy's funeral in 1963. This man
Kennedy, de Gaulle said, was the country's mask. But this man Johnson
is the country's real face. It may be that Johnson tells us things about
ourselves that we are not now eager to hear. But current mood should
not define the historian's task. De Gaulle's observation has much to recommend it; Johnson is an excellent vehicle for studying America since
the 1930s.[10]

Johnson's part in the nationalization of the South and the West or his
conscious efforts to integrate the southern and western economies into
the national life is a neglected piece of American history. Johnson saw
the economic transformation of both sections as essential to their well-
being. In this he was hardly typical. Economist Gavin Wright argues in
Old South, New South (1986) that most southern congressmen and senators in the 1930s were more concerned with maintaining "the sepa-
rateness of the southern labor market . . . than with bringing federal
money into their districts" and states. Yet, Wright says, the basis for

maintaining the South's economic isolation or separation was already being thoroughly undermined. "Under the incentives established by the New Deal farm programs, plantation tenancy was disintegrating, and sharecroppers were being turned into footloose wage laborers. At the same time, federal labor policies had sharply raised the level of base wage rates in the South, effectively blocking the low-wage expansion path for regional industry. By the time of World War II, the stage was set for a rapid transformation" of the southern economy. Johnson supported all the New Deal legislation and agencies—the Works Progress Administration, the National Youth Administration, the Fair Labor Standards Act, the Soil Conservation and Domestic Allotment Act, and the Farm Security Administration—that helped transform southern economic life.[11]

Johnson was an even stronger advocate of state capitalism: New Deal policies designed to build industrial empires in the economically undeveloped South and West. Using the Reconstruction Finance Corporation, the Tennessee Valley Authority, the Public Works Administration, and the Rural Electrification Administration to foster public power and industrial development, the New Deal raised living standards and transformed the lives of southerners and westerners. During and after World War II, the Federal government made these sections the continuing recipients of its largesse through defense spending. "We no longer farm in Mississippi cotton fields," novelist William Faulkner said. "We farm now in Washington corridors and Congressional committee-rooms." No one in the House and the Senate was more active in obtaining PWA, REA, and defense funds for his district, state, and region than Johnson. In part because of Johnson, by the early 1950s, south-central Texas had been transformed into a more prosperous region by dams built on the Lower Colorado River, Texas had more air bases than any other state in the Union, and the Sunbelt was on the verge of becoming the dominant political and economic force in American life.

Johnson's role in reaching out to America's disadvantaged and combating racial segregation was perhaps his most important contribution to recent U.S. history. For all his self-serving ambition, Johnson never forgot his childhood poverty. He had genuine and extraordinary compassion for the disadvantaged—not simply when it became politically convenient in the late fifties and early sixties, but dating from the thirties when he drove himself day and night to help black, Hispanic, and poor white Texans, and secretly aided Jewish refugees from the Nazis to enter the United States. And he saw New Deal, Fair Deal, and Great Society programs as not only helping the poorest among us but also serving the national well-being by expanding the material and spiritual riches of all Americans, particularly in the South. From early in his political career, Johnson saw racial discrimination as an obstacle to southern economic advance, and as early as the 1930s he acted upon his belief.

Lyndon Johnson was much more concerned about larger issues in American life than people have generally given him credit for. As the psychiatrist Robert Coles has written, Johnson was "a restless, extravagantly self-centered, brutishly expansive, manipulative, teasing and sly man, but he was also genuinely passionately interested in making life easier and more honorable for millions of terribly hard pressed working class men and women. His almost manic vitality was purposefully, intelligently, compassionately used. He could turn mean and sour, but . . . he had a lot more than himself and his place in history on his mind." [12]

LBJ's role in the rise of the national security state also deserves more attention than it has received. From the moment he set foot in the House in 1937, Johnson was an advocate of greater defense spending. As a member of the House Naval Affairs and House and Senate Armed Services committees, he preached the importance of a strong defense and America's role in protecting "the free world." During the fifties, Johnson was an architect of bipartisan foreign and defense policies. He believed that the country must speak with one voice in meeting the Communist threat and use secret operations as Eisenhower did in Iran and Guatemala to protect itself.

Johnson was also a great believer in centralized control over foreign affairs or what Arthur Schlesinger, Jr., has called the Imperial Presidency. Johnson's conviction that decisions on overseas actions should largely emanate from the Oval Office reflected itself in his later policies toward Vietnam. His secret machinations or escalation of American involvement in Southeast Asia without a stable congressional and public consensus, a condition that played a large part in destroying his presidency, grew out of an excessively reverential attitude toward presidential power and a life-long impulse to cut political corners. Johnson viewed politics as a dirty business in which only the most manipulative succeeded. He did not come to this simply out of some flaw in his character. He learned it from the rough and tumble that characterized Texas politics in the first half of the twentieth-century, and from his early political mentors in Texas and Washington—Alvin Wirtz, Maury Maverick, Sr., Sam Rayburn, Thomas G. Corcoran, Harold Ickes, and FDR. In short, Vietnam was not simply the product of judgments about what we needed to do in Southeast Asia but also of developments in twentieth-century American politics in which Johnson had a significant part.

Because Johnson stumbled so badly in dealing with Vietnam, we have forgotten his extraordinary effectiveness as a Senate Majority Leader in the fifties. In 1957, after Johnson had led the first civil rights law through the Senate in eighty-two years, the historian C. Vann Woodward described him as having "the genius of a Henry Clay," the "Great Compromiser." A visceral New Deal liberal with a practical talent for accommodating diverse interests as no politician had since FDR, Johnson was the greatest Majority Leader in American history.

If the way other Presidents' historical reputations have fallen and recovered is any measure, Johnson's current low standing is not permanent. He seems bound to make a comeback from the almost uniformly negative view the public now holds of him. Vietnam and his affinity for backroom dealings will always dog his reputation. But once biographers begin balancing these shortcomings with greater attention to his major historical contributions, Johnson's virtues will become more evident. More important, we need to see his life not as a chance to indulge our sense of moral superiority, but as a way to gain an understanding of many subjects crucial to this country's past, present, and future.

PART ONE

The Making of a Politician
1908–1937

1

The Heritage

FROM Andrew Jackson to Ronald Reagan, the image of the self-made man has effectively served occupants of the White House. All who could, made much of their rags to riches odyssey. "When I was young, poverty was so common we didn't know it had a name," Lyndon Johnson often said. A poor boy in a remote Texas town isolated from the mainstream of early twentieth-century American life, he grew up without indoor plumbing or electricity and sometimes made do on a bare subsistence diet. The rural small towns in which he received his elementary, secondary, and college schooling did little to broaden his horizons.

Yet Lyndon came to maturity believing he was special—a young man destined for exceptional things. And he was. Fueled by his early poverty, his ambition, like Lincoln's, "was a little engine that knew no rest." It helped carry him to the U.S. House of Representatives and Senate, the vice presidency and the White House. But ambition alone did not give him the wherewithal, the inner confidence, to imagine himself in the Congress or the Oval Office. His family history gave initial stirrings to such dreams. In one of the many paradoxes that would shape his life, Lyndon was not simply an impoverished farm boy who made good, but the offspring of prominent southern families. Although he suffered painful self-doubts throughout his life, his heritage was a constant source of belief in a birthright to govern and lead. Stories told by his parents and grandparents about famous, influential ancestors were a mainstay of his early years. From the first, he thought of himself not as a poor boy consigned to a life of hardship, but as an heir of Johnsons and Buntons, Baineses and Huffmans, men and women who commanded the respect of their contemporaries and shaped public affairs.

A Texas journalist remembers how Lyndon "reveled in stories of Johnsons and Baineses who'd fought marauding Indians, of old uncles who drove cattle up the famous trails, of a hardy pioneer spirit in his genes. 'Listen, goddammit,' he once said, 'my ancestors were teachers and lawyers and college presidents and governors when the Kennedys in this country were still tending bar.' " [1]

First there were the Johnsons. They had apparently migrated from England to Georgia, where John Johnson, Lyndon's great-great-grandfather, lived in Oglethorpe County in 1795 after service in the Revolutionary War as a teenager. At his death in 1828, John Johnson owned a few hundred acres in three different counties and two female slaves he bequeathed to his heirs. Jesse Johnson, John's fourth child and Lyndon's great-grandfather, was part of the mass nineteenth-century American migration west. After the War of 1812 he was one of the first settlers in Henry County in western Georgia, where he farmed for some twenty years and served as a sheriff and a judge. In 1838, however, he moved his family further west to Randolph County, Alabama. He prospered there as a businessman and acquired seventeen slaves. But in 1846, after Texas had entered the Union, Jesse joined the flood of southern migrants from Alabama, Georgia, Mississippi, and Tennessee drawn by the lure of fertile cheap land in the Lone Star state. Jesse led his wife, eight of his ten children, four grandchildren, and several slaves in covered wagons across Alabama, Mississippi, Louisiana, and east Texas, nearly 900 miles over rutted roads and rushing rivers, to Lockhart in Caldwell County in the plains southeast of Austin. There, during the remaining ten years of his life, he acquired 330 acres of land valued at $2000 and another $740 in cattle, horses, oxen, and household goods, $525 less than the claims later made by creditors on his estate. [2]

If Jesse Johnson did not exactly prosper in Texas, his sons fared somewhat better. Andrew Jackson Johnson, Jesse Thomas Johnson, Lyndon's great uncles, and Sam Ealy Johnson, Lyndon's grandfather, migrated to Blanco County in the Hill Country west of Austin. A frontier in the late 1850s with a population of fewer than two thousand, principally Germans and Mormons, the area was notable for its infertile soil, low rainfall, springtime flooding by the Pedernales and Blanco rivers, and hostile Apache and Comanche Indians. The lure of the Hill Country for the Johnson brothers was "stock raising," the hope of making a fortune in the cattle business. The principal feature of the area then was its miles and miles of grass, "grass knee high," "grass as high as my stirrups," as two of its early settlers described it. But it was grass that had grown up over centuries on "a narrow, thin, layer of soil atop . . . limestone," and if initially the Hill Country was ideal pasture land, it would not be so for long. In the forty years after 1860, huge herds of cattle transformed the landscape. Eating the grass faster than it could grow, the stock left the land with nothing to anchor its top soil. And when periodic drenching rains washed it away, scrub brush sprang up in its place, making the hills and valleys unsuitable for grazing or agriculture of any kind.

When Jack, the oldest of the Johnson brothers, came to Blanco County in 1859, however, the region seemed like a farmer's paradise, a lush grassland where everything would grow. Settling on the north side of the Pedernales about four miles northeast of the present Johnson City, he lived there for six years, prospering as a cattle supplier for the Confederacy during the Civil War. His younger brother Tom also came to Blanco County during the war. After serving briefly in the Texas State Troops in 1864, he acquired a 320-acre spread on the Pedernales, where he began raising livestock.[3]

Sam, the youngest of the brothers, enlisted in a cavalry regiment at the age of twenty-two in 1861 and served as a private throughout the war. In 1862–63 he participated in the successful defense of Galveston Island in the Gulf of Mexico, and in the spring of 1864 he saw action in the Red River campaign, the unsuccessful attempt by Union troops to force their way up the Red River Valley, capture Shreveport, Louisiana, and carry the war into Texas. At the battle of Pleasant Hill, northwest of Natchitoches, Sam Johnson had his horse shot out from under him by Union artillery, and the 26th Texas Cavalry lost one-third of its men. Seeing "men and horses shot in every conceivable way," carrying a wounded comrade on his back from the battlefield, and holding wounded soldiers immobile during amputations, Sam Johnson never forgot what the regimental chaplain described as the "unutterable hardships and suffering . . . hunger, sickness, and unbearable toils" of the fighting in the western Louisiana parishes along the Red River.[4]

At the end of the war in 1865, Sam Johnson took up residence with his brother Tom in a log ranch house on the 320-acre spread. Circumstances now favored them as they never would again. During the war the cattle running free on the range had greatly multiplied—not only in number but also in value. A growing population in the north had increased the demand for beef. When the railroad reached Sedalia, Missouri, in 1866 and then Abilene, Kansas, in 1867, it provided a reliable means of getting livestock to the east, so the market for longhorn steers boomed. Two-dollar-a-head cattle in Texas sold for $10 in Sedalia the year after the war, and in 1867 four-dollar Texas steers brought between $40 and $50 in Abilene.[5]

The Johnson brothers aggressively joined the cattle drives north. In the years between 1867 and 1870 they made four annual five-week treks of over 600 miles along the Chisholm Trail to Abilene. Each foray was more successful than the last: despite rainstorms, stampedes, quicksand, cattle rustlers, and outlaws, the Johnsons made huge profits. By 1870 they had become the most successful trail drivers operating in Blanco,

Gillespie, Llano, Hays, Comal and Kendall Counties. That year they drove 7000 cattle to market and returned home with $100,000 in $20 gold coins stuffed in saddlebags. Flushed with success, they spent their money freely, paying some of their creditors more than they were owed, and buying thousands of acres of ranch land in Blanco, Hays, and Gillespie counties and real estate in Fredericksburg and Austin. In 1871, Tom Johnson was worth almost $17,000, making him the second largest taxpayer and property owner in Blanco County. Sam, with $15,000 in assessed value, was not far behind.

But the good times were short-lived. When the Johnsons broke camp in 1871, they headed up the trail with about 10,000 head, most purchased on credit. As in past years, the journey to Kansas was difficult— eighteen-hour days, a scarcity of water, stampedes and sleepless nights dogged them and the sixteen cowboys making the drive. But the difference this time was a glut of cattle, twice as many as had been sent up the Chisholm Trail in 1870 and four times the number driven to market in 1869, a total of perhaps 700,000. "There are not only cattle 'on a thousand hills' but a thousand cattle on one and every hill," a newspaper recorded. The result was financial disaster for the Johnsons, who sold their cattle for well below what they hoped to get. As a consequence, they could not meet their debts at home and had to sell off most of the land they had bought in the preceding five years. The following year was no better. Although sending a smaller herd to market, they suffered fresh losses. A terrible drought in the summer of 1872 coupled with a Comanche raid that cost the Johnsons between 250 and 300 horses worth about $20,000 broke their financial resources. The Blanco County property rolls for 1873 show Tom Johnson with holdings of only $180, and Sam Johnson not even on the rolls. In 1872 or 1873, Sam left the Pedernales for Lockhart and then Buda, just south of Austin, where, with his father-in-law's help, he bought a farm.[6]

Sam Ealy Johnson's in-laws were the Buntons, a family whose lustre shone more brightly than the Johnsons' and whose record of public service and political prominence was an even greater source of Lyndon's belief in his suitability for high public office. According to family lore, the line began in fourteenth-century Scotland, where several generations served in the Scottish Parliament. The first of the American Buntons was John Buntine I, who migrated to Rowan County, North Carolina, in 1758. He and three sons, John II, Robert, and James, were believed to have served in the Revolutionary War. In 1800, John II settled in Sumner County, Tennessee. His son Joseph Robert Bunton, Lyndon's great-great-grandfather, married Phoebe Ann Desha, a descendant of French Huguenots who had migrated to Pennsylvania and then Tennessee. Her brother Joseph Desha was a congressman from Kentucky for thirteen years, 1806–19, and governor of the state from 1824 to 1828.

Another brother, Robert, was a congressman from Tennessee for four years, 1827–31.[7]

The first of the Texas Buntons was John Wheeler Bunton, Joseph and Phoebe's son and Lyndon's great-great uncle. Arriving in Texas from Tennessee in 1833, John Wheeler was a central figure in the fight for independence from Mexico. Standing six feet four inches in height and holding a college degree and some training in the law, Bunton was an imposing figure, physically and intellectually. After participating in the successful siege of San Antonio in December 1835, he served as a delegate to the constitutional convention of March 1836, where he signed the Texas Declaration of Independence and was a member of the committee that wrote a constitution for the new republic. When the convention adjourned in late March, he rejoined the army and three weeks later fought in the decisive battle of San Jacinto. His "towering form could be seen amidst the thickest of the fight. He penetrated so far into the ranks of the defenders of the breastworks that it is miraculous that he was not killed. But he came out of the deadly conflict unscathed." In the painting, *The Surrender of Santa Anna*, which hangs in the Texas state capitol, John Wheeler Bunton is portrayed observing the event. Elected twice to the Congress of the new country, Bunton wrote the bill that established the Texas Rangers. But for unknown reasons he quit politics in the early 1840s and lived the rest of his life as a rancher and cotton planter in Bastrop and Hays counties, just east of the Hill Country. In the latter he built a traditional Old South mansion—a two-story house with white verandas attended by slaves and surrounded by cotton fields and pastures.[8]

Robert Holmes Bunton, John's younger brother and Lyndon's great-grandfather, did not leave Kentucky for Texas until 1858, when he was already forty years old. Like John, Robert was "a large impressive man, standing six feet and three inches in height and weighing about two hundred and sixty pounds. . . . A handsome man with fair skin, coal-black hair, and piercing black eyes," he was also "an excellent conversationalist" who was remembered best for his discourses on government and politics. After serving for four years in the Civil War, during which he won a battlefield commission as a lieutenant, Robert, like Tom and Sam Johnson, made and lost a small fortune in the cattle business. Unlike the Johnson brothers, however, Robert Bunton was a shrewd businessman who staved off ruin in the declining cattle market. Instead of continuing to raise stock for which there was little demand, he rented his pastures in Lockhart to cattlemen from south Texas who needed feeding and resting grounds for the herds they were driving north to Abilene. As a consequence, he survived the downturn of the early seventies and had enough money to help stake his daughter, Eliza Bunton, and her husband, Sam Ealy Johnson, to the farm at Buda.[9]

Eliza Bunton, Lyndon's grandmother, was eighteen when she married Sam Johnson in December 1867 and moved to the Pedernales. She was a beautiful young woman with "patrician bearing, high-bred features, raven hair, piercing black eyes, and magnolia-white skin." She took great pride in her family and loved to talk about her famous relatives—John Wheeler Bunton, Governor Joseph Desha of Kentucky, a cousin, Mary Desha, co-founder of the Daughters of the American Revolution, and her brother Joe in the Texas Rangers. She often reminded her children to be worthy of their heritage, and through her own life gave them an example with which they could identify. A "heroine" of the southwest Texas highlands, a "leading pioneer" woman, Eliza Johnson accompanied her husband on the trying cattle drives north and conquered the terrors of the frontier. Living in near isolation in a drafty log cabin in which she cooked and baked in a Texas skillet, a boiling pot hung over a fireplace, she hauled water and firewood, canned fruits and vegetables, washed, sewed, and made her own soap in an almost endless round of work days. "This life," one historian records, "was hardy, dirty, terribly monotonous, lonely, and damagingly narrow. . . . Few of the Americans who later eulogized it would care to relive it." [10]

In the six or seven years after the Civil War, it was also full of danger. In the summer of 1869, Tom and Eliza Felps of Blanco County, a young couple, were abducted and killed by Comanches. Tom was "shot, stabbed, and stripped of his clothes. Eliza Felps lay naked, the shaft of an arrow protruding from her breast. She had been scalped while still alive, but had managed to crawl some distance before dying." Sam Johnson rode with the posse that unsuccessfully chased the Indians. Eliza Johnson almost suffered a similar fate. One day while Sam was gone, Eliza sighted a party of Comanches riding toward her through the mesquite. Racing to the cabin before they detected her, she took refuge with her baby daughter, Mary, in a cellar beneath a trap door. Using a stick pushed through a crack to pull a braided rug over her hiding place, she tied a dirty diaper over the baby's mouth to keep her from crying. The Indians ransacked the cabin and stole horses from the barn before riding off. Eliza waited in the cellar until Sam returned home that night. [11]

The sixteen years beginning in 1873 that Sam and Eliza lived on the plains in Buda east of the Hill Country were less eventful. They were also a time of economic austerity when Sam barely made a living as a farmer. By 1880 he and Eliza had managed to acquire over 800 acres in property valued at $3000 and livestock worth $500. But they had only 100 acres under cultivation; the annual yield was a mere 200 bushels of corn, 100 bushels of oats, 250 bushels of wheat, and 4 bales of cotton, all worth just $560. Paying a hired hand $200, Sam and Eliza had only $360 left to support their family, which now consisted of six children.

Failing to prosper at Buda and eager to return to the Hill Country, Sam and Eliza put a down payment on a 950-acre spread along the Pedernales near Stonewall in Gillespie County in 1882. The new farm was only twelve miles from their old ranch, which had been bought by James Polk Johnson, Sam's nephew, who in 1879 laid out the town of Johnson City near its site. Eliza raised the money for the new place by selling a silver-mounted carriage and matched span of horses, which had been given to her by Sam's brother Tom as a wedding present. During the next six years the Johnsons sold off all their property in Buda. In 1889, after Sam had an altercation with a local troublemaker who had killed a number of people and now threatened him with a similar fate, he and Eliza returned with eight of their nine children to the Pedernales in Sam's beloved "mountains." [12]

Although they remained there for more than twenty-five years, the rest of their lives, it was never easy. Like their neighbors, they were subsistence farmers living with a minimum of the physical comforts other Americans had begun to enjoy in the late nineteenth and early twentieth century. To make a go of it, they mortgaged 600 acres of the farm and sold another 160 acres of it during the next twelve years. The money from the mortgage was apparently used to help build a house, outhouses, barn, smokehouse, cistern, and corrals and dig a well. Later, another house, barn, and well were added to the property some 500 yards away, where Sam's daughter Frank and her husband Clarence Martin lived for a number of years. The houses, as one writer describes them, were little more than "shanties" connected by a "dog-run," the open corridor between two cabins connected by a sagging roof in which animals relieved themselves. A poorly constructed front porch surrounded by a dirt yard that was spotted with tufts of grass and weeds and fenced by barbed wire completed the picture of the Johnson living quarters.

On 170 acres, which Sam brought under cultivation, he raised corn, wheat, and cotton, the latter being his cash crop used to purchase "staples," which were stored in the smokehouse. Except for these "staples," the farm was self-sufficient, yielding potatoes, cabbages, turnips, beans, watermelons, and peaches. Several times a year "the family butchered hogs. Bacon and hams were cured and hung in the smokehouse, while lard was rendered and sausage made and stored." There was enough to eat, but, as one of Sam's contemporaries recalled, "there was no money, and you had a hard time getting by." If cotton prices fell or you had a poor crop, there was not enough cash to buy seed and supplies and pay the mortgage and taxes. The only alternative was to go deeper into debt or lose your land, which occurred anyway if additional poor years forced you to the end of your credit. Happily for Sam, this did not happen to

him, but, as one of Lyndon's biographers, concludes, "the Johnsons arrived back on the Pedernales poor, and lived there almost thirty years—
during which they grew poorer."[13]

Sam Johnson may have been poor but he was never defeated by his
poverty. He is recalled as being gregarious, a participant in all the
neighborly gatherings, where he "met his friends with a handshake,
friendly greetings and a hearty resounding laugh." He was widely known
for his hospitality and eagerness for conversation about serious issues,
philosophy, politics, and theology. "He encouraged his children to engage in games that required them to think, such as dominoes, hearts,
pitch, and whist." He laid great value on the power of reason, the ability
to persuade others with the written and spoken word. He loved a good
debate and could be moved by a cogent argument. When a Christadel-
phian minister bested the local Baptist preacher in an all-day debate
about the Bible, Sam quit the Baptist church and became a Christadel-
phian. On matters of religion, however, he was not a strict rationalist.
He once knocked one of his sons across the room for belittling the
Scriptures.

Politics as well could arouse his passions. He had an intense interest
in current events and would ford the Pedernales every other day to get
an Austin newspaper mailed to him in Stonewall. His sense of injustice
about the plight of Texas farmers moved him to join the Texas People's
party, which had been formed in 1891. Like other Populists, he worried
about farmers losing their land. People in Blanco County remembered
the sign on an abandoned farmhouse in the drought year of 1886: "200
miles to the nearest post office; 100 miles to wood; 20 miles to water; 6
inches to hell. God bless our home! Gone to live with the wife's folks."
To aid farmers who clung to the land, Sam advocated a government
program which would help tenants buy their farms. Because he felt so
strongly about the issue, he ran for the state legislature in 1892 as a
Populist. His opponent in the campaign was Clarence Martin, his son-
in-law, who ran as a Democrat. Riding together to a speaking, Sam
would cuss Clarence as "a reactionary so-and-so" and Clarence would
call Sam a wild radical. Afterward, they would "get back on the double
buggy on the front seat and ride to the next speaking." Enraged by the
"enemies" of the farmer—railroads, bankers, and conservative gold or
tight-money Democrats like former President Grover Cleveland, who
was trying to regain the White House in 1892—Sam warned voters that
a Populist defeat would mean civil war and declared that Cleveland "ought
to be hung." Although Populist candidates for governor and lieutenant-
governor carried the Hill Country, they lost the statewide elections.
Clarence, moreover, defeated Sam two-to-one. If he were discouraged,
Sam didn't give up hope. He maintained a keen interest in politics, which

he passed along to his oldest son, Sam Ealy Johnson, Jr., who twelve years later won the seat his father had sought in the state legislature.[14]

Sam, Sr., and Eliza had nine children. The first four born between 1868 and 1875 were girls. Although Sam called them "the four prettiest little girls in ten counties," he longed for a son and greatly resented being called "Gal Johnson" by neighbors poking fun at him. He was apparently so frustrated by the birth of a second daughter in 1870 that he named her Frank. The arrival of Sam Ealy, Jr., on October 11, 1877, therefore, filled the parents with joy. Each took special pride in the boy. Eliza focused on the Bunton in him—dark eyes, black curls, and "magnolia-white" skin. She also saw evidence of the Deshas in his "quick mind, keen perception, and . . . amazing memory." As a pre-schooler, he astounded an older sister by repeating a poem of thirty-two verses she had been memorizing for a school recital.

Sam treated his son as all his own. He not only named him Sam but also dressed him as nearly as possible like himself and took Sam, Jr., with him whenever possible. Growing tall, six feet, one inch, with a large nose, "thick, bushy, black eyebrows . . . piercing eyes," "enormous ears . . . and a habit of pulling in his chin until it almost disappeared inside his collar," "Little Sam," as people came to call him, may have resembled the Buntons, but he was "Big" Sam's son. He was gregarious, friendly, outgoing. He "was the cowboy type, a little on the rough side, but he had good principles. . . . He shouted slogans when he talked." Most of all, he was fiercely competitive with an urge to dominate people. As a boy, he needed to "ride faster; plow longer, straighter rows; and pick more cotton than his companions." He "was a very persuasive man"; Congressman Wright Patman, who served with him in the Texas House of Representatives, recalled, "he would get right up to you, nose to nose, and take a firm hold."[15]

His ambition and drive were evident in his struggle to gain an education. His parents could ill afford to send him to the one-room schoolhouse in Johnson City. Not only did they need his help on the farm but they lacked the small tuition fee required to attend the public school. "Once his father gave him some cattle, saying, 'This is all I can do on your schooling this year.' " Undaunted, "Little Sam" "turned butcher, slaughtered and cut up a steer and sold steaks and soupbones to tide him over until the next 'butchering day.' " He also took up barbering. When the town barber became ill and had to retire, he bought his barber chair and tools on credit, and after practicing on friends, began giving haircuts on Saturdays and after school. Before he could finish high school, however, he was stricken by what the family called "indigestion," or some kind of nervous condition. To cure his ills, he was sent to rest on a ranch near Marfa in southwest Texas owned by Lucius Desha Bunton, his mother's younger brother. There is no record of his few months there, but when he returned to Stonewall, it was with a determination to become a schoolteacher and self-supporting. Since he had not earned a high school diploma and had no prospect of getting to a teachers' college, he set his sights on passing a state-certification exam. With thirteen books needed to prepare him in the academic subjects covered in the exam, "a bottle of pepsin pills and a sack of dried fruit (doctor's recommendation)," he took up residence with grandmother Jane Bunton, a former schoolteacher, who tutored her favorite grandson "Sammie." After only a few weeks of intensive preparation he passed the exam, scoring grades of 100 percent on the Texas and United States history sections.[16]

His teaching career was short-lived. In the fall of 1896, at the age of nineteen, he took a job in the small Hill Country community of Sandy, where he taught in a typical one-room, rural Texas school "with pupils of all sizes and ages, some older and larger than he." A second year in a school near Hye, a hamlet between Stonewall and Johnson City, persuaded him that teaching would barely allow him to earn his keep. His only strong memory of this period was of sitting around the fire in a boarding house listening to Captain Rufus Perry describe his experiences as an Indian fighter and Texas Ranger.[17]

In 1898, at the age of twenty-one, he returned to Stonewall, where he rented his father's farm and lived in his parents' house. For several years he enjoyed considerable success. Mild weather, good crops, and high cotton prices allowed him to accumulate some money, which he used to hire farmhands and successfully speculate in cotton futures. People remember him at this time as self-confident, even arrogant, with an "air of command." Like "all the Johnsons," he "strutted." And he dressed differently from the other farmers, more formally, often in the evenings wearing a suit and tie with attractive boots and hat and riding a well-groomed horse. His best friends were not local farmers and townsfolk but two "lawyers of statewide repute" and a "brilliant" engineer who would sometimes visit him at the farm.[18]

Sam, Jr., wanted to be more than a farmer. And Clarence Martin, his brother-in-law, who had defeated Sam, Sr., for the seat in the Texas House, encouraged him. After studying law and serving as a justice of the peace in Blanco and as a state legislator, Martin became a district judge in Gillespie County. At Martin's suggestion, Sam, Jr., ran successfully for justice of the peace in 1902. For two years he "married more boys and girls than any pastor in Gillespie County because he just charged $5."

In 1904, Sam, Jr., ran for the 89th District seat in the Texas House of Representatives that Martin had held from 1893 to 1895. By an unwritten rotation rule, the four counties making up the district took turns sending men to fill the seat. Since a Gillespie County man was slated to have the job from 1905 to 1907, Martin urged Sam, Jr., to stand for the position. Although he had some doubts about his suitability for the office, he ran anyway. Many persons consider it "in the nature of a joke to become a candidate and to be elected as a member of the Legislature," he announced in a campaign speech, but he viewed it as a serious undertaking. He also felt that his determination to speak for the people against the interests made him worthy of the office. Like his father before him, he saw an apocalyptic struggle between democracy and corporate power. The issue in the election, he said, was "whether the principles and tradition of a Republic shall be longer perpetuated, or whether we shall meekly surrender to the great trust combines the interests of the nation."[19]

Winning the Democratic primary and then three of the four counties in the general election, Sam went to Austin ready to do battle with the state's conservative business and financial interests. Although he found ample opportunity to vote with a minority of "agrarian liberals" supporting unsuccessful bills to tax insurance, telephone, and sleeping and dining car companies, to regulate rates charged by public utilities, to establish a pure-food standard, to levy a franchise tax on corporations, to create a juvenile court system in the state, and to give railroad workers an eight-hour day, he quickly established himself as a practical legislator guiding less dramatic bills through the House. The architect of measures to purchase and restore the historic Alamo Mission in San Antonio, to bar brutal calf-roping contests, and to exempt Blanco County from paying a bounty on every wolf shot, a charge that would have worked financial hardship on the county, Sam Johnson was described by a newspaper as one of the few legislators "who did not fail on a single measure." His political astuteness was also reflected in the fact that the 1907 legislative session, responding to a rising tide of progressism in the state, passed some of the reform legislation Sam favored. When Sam decided to break the rotation tradition by standing for a second term, he gained widespread support from local Hill Country newspapers and won the Democratic primary by such large margins in all four counties that he ran unopposed in the general election of 1906.[20]

Only twenty-nine when he won election to his second term, Sam seemed like a young man with a promising political future. But circumstances and a refusal to compromise himself or to be used by any of the interests in Austin shattered his dreams. Like his father and Uncle Tom, he went broke trying to make a fortune. Unlike them, however, he never had a lot of money. When he went to Austin in 1905, he accepted a $300 loan from a local friend, who had insisted that he go to the state capital "in style." But to remain in the legislature, he needed more. Receiving only five dollars a day for the regular sixty-day session and only two dollars a day after that, Sam could not make ends meet. What money he had, he bet on cotton futures in the rising market of 1902–05. But he lost all he made and more in 1905–06 when the market collapsed. "My daddy went busted waiting for cotton to go up to twenty-one cents a pound, and the market fell apart when it hit twenty," Lyndon later remarked. He was so broke after that he could not pay his grocery bill, which mounted to $1000; at times he had to borrow money for gas to drive to Austin.[21]

Unlike most of the other legislators, Sam would not allow himself to be bought by lobbyists who dominated the proceedings before 1907. Providing "beefsteak, bourbon and blondes," paying legislators' living expenses, and buying votes outright, which they sometimes even cast for absent members of the House, lobbyists set much of the legislative agenda. Sam would have no part of it. Not because he was a strict moralist; on the contrary, according to numerous sources, he was as ready as the next fellow to indulge his passions, drinking and whoring in the orgies that were an accepted part of the capital's life. It was more a case of being his own man. He could not bend the knee to anyone; he could not be under someone else's control. He "will bear gentle reproof, but will kick like a mule at any attempted domination," the House chaplain observed in 1907.[22]

His independence or refusal to be cowed by authority registered clearly in the most important event of the 1907 session, the reelection of U.S. Senator Joseph W. Bailey to a second term. In the era before the Seventeenth Amendment to the U.S. Constitution provided for direct election of senators, state legislatures decided who would serve in the U.S. Senate. Bailey, who began his career denouncing the money interests, had sold out to oil, railroad, and lumber companies. But he hid his corruption behind a smokescreen of rhetoric and political theater. A prominent figure in Washington, where he "dominated the Democratic minority like an overseer," he was easily the most compelling personality on the Texas political scene. His appearance and voice captivated audiences wherever he went. "This Adonis of a man with a massive brain captured my imagination and became my model," Sam Rayburn, then also a member of the Texas House, later recalled. In his "dull black frock coat, flowing tie, and big, black slouch hat," Bailey would denounce his enemies in melodious tones that "lingered in the chamber like the echoes of chimes in a cathedral." Although his honesty was clearly in question in 1907, the Texas House of Representatives would not agree to an investigation of Bailey's actions before voting on his election to another term. Under pressure from the oil and railroad interests and from Bailey himself, who rushed to Austin "to drive into the Gulf of Mexico the peanut politicians who would replace me with someone who would rattle around in my seat like a mustard seed in a gourd," the House voted 89 to 36 to return Bailey to Washington. Seven members, including Sam, were present but not voting.[23]

Although Clarence Martin was a staunch Bailey backer and the Senator had a reputation for breaking his opponents' political power and threatening them with violence, Sam urged public scrutiny of all charges before a vote was taken on Bailey's reelection. Called to Bailey's Austin hotel room, Sam refused to budge, saying that he was his friend and doubted the accusations, but believed they should be cleared up. In victory, Bailey was unforgiving. In a post-election speech before the Texas House he denounced his "enemies" as "rogues" and said that they had "made their own graves. . . . We are going to bury them face down, so that the harder they scratch to get out, the deeper they will go towards their eternal resting place. . . . I will not forgive them this side of the grave." But Sam Johnson remained unintimidated. "I did not become very badly frightened," he later said of Bailey's threats. Moreover, he stuck to his principles during the rest of the legislative session, supporting other progressive measures that would regulate lobbyists and aid cotton farmers, stock raisers, and school children. At the close of his second term, however, the need for money and the wishes of his wife, who objected to his absence in Austin, persuaded him to give up his seat.[24]

On August 20, 1907, Sam had married Rebekah Baines, whom he had met in Austin in 1906. Like the Johnsons, her line of descent provided Lyndon with a sense of inherited superiority. Indeed, the Baineses and the Huffmans, Rebekah's maternal ancestors, were formidable folk. As filtered through partial recollection and family telling, the Baineses were frontier saints. George Bains, the great-great-great grandfather, was an eighteenth-century North Carolina surveyor and planter whose "more than sixty years embodied the glorious heritage of his ancestry of Scottish kings." Thomas Baines, George's youngest son, was a Baptist minister in Georgia, Alabama, and Mississippi. The founder of numerous churches in this Deep South region, particularly in western Alabama around Tuscaloosa, he lived less than fifty years, but was "a tireless worker, an idealist, who translated his dreams into deeds."[25]

The most revered member of the clan was the Reverend George W. Baines, the offspring of Thomas. A graduate of the University of Alabama "by his own unaided efforts," he became a Baptist minister at the age of twenty-five. In 1837 he migrated to the wilderness country of Arkansas, where he organized three churches, baptized 150 people, and served a term in the territorial legislature. "Yielding to conviction of duty," he left Arkansas in 1844 for northern Louisiana. During the next six years he "became known as the foremost preacher of any denomination" in the region. In 1850, he caught the "Texas fever" after visiting the state to help set up a Baptist church at Marshall. Migrating to

Huntsville in southeast Texas, he spent the next eleven years as a pastor, church organizer, and editor of the first Baptist newspaper in the state. During this time he ministered to the spiritual needs of the Texas hero Sam Houston, whom "Brother Baines" persuaded to join the Baptist Church. Out of gratitude, Houston lent Baines $300 and subsequently forgave the interest on the loan, because "Brother" Baines's congregations lacked the "plain old fashioned honesty of paying what they subscribe." In 1861, once again "yielding to the call of his brethren," he accepted the presidency of Baylor University at Independence, a Baptist school. He resigned the post two years later, however, "on account of ruined health." Nevertheless, during the remaining twenty years of his life he continued to serve the Baptist Church, as a pastor and an agent for its State Convention and its Educational Commission. "His life was pure and blameless. Not a shadow mars the beauty of his character," one Baptist eulogy of him reads. Accepting such characterizations of "Brother Baines," the family, in the words of one later writer, viewed him as "almost . . . a figure among the prophets." [26]

Joseph Wilson Baines, George's son and Rebekah's father, was seen in much the same way. After attending Baylor University and serving in the Civil War, Joseph taught school and studied law. Opening a practice in McKinney north of Dallas, he also edited and published the *McKinney Advocate*, an influential Democratic newspaper. Between 1883 and 1887 he was Texas secretary of state under Governor John Ireland, whom he had helped elect. In 1887, at the age of forty-one, Joseph moved his family to Blanco in the Hill Country, where he practiced law, accumulated "quite a fortune," served a term in the state legislature, and was the chief pillar of the Baptist Church. But his life ended "tragically" when, according to Lyndon, in 1902 he "lost all his money on one disastrous deal." Losing the home the family had occupied for seventeen years in Blanco, he tried to repair his fortunes by starting a new law practice in the larger German community of Fredericksburg. But depressed and ill, he died two years later in November 1906. [27]

To Rebekah Baines, as she later impressed on her son Lyndon, having a father like Joseph was "most felicitous." He taught her to read, "one of the great pleasures and sustaining forces" of her life. He taught her that "a lie is an abomination to the Lord." He taught her "obedience and self-control" and "gave the timid child self-confidence." Rebekah was less devoted to her mother, Ruth Huffman. But she idealized her as well. Ruth's grandfather was a successful rancher whose breeding of short-horn cattle and Sir Archer horses in Texas made him "a man much in advance of his time." Her father, Rebekah's grandfather, was a sensitive physician whose "cruel experiences" in the Civil War caused a "nervous breakdown which occasioned his death" at the age of forty-one. Ruth Huffman herself was the "most energetic, and serenest of persons." Rebekah described herself as the "fortunate" offspring of a "happy, well-adjusted, and devoted couple."

Born in McKinney on June 26, 1881, Rebekah came to Blanco at the age of six. She remembered the small town with its "rickety wooden stores and dog-run log cabins" as a "simple, friendly, dearly loved" place that was full of "neighborliness," "delights," and "charms." She was "grateful" for "excellent teachers" and her "Baptist upbringing." Her childhood home, a white two-story stone house surrounded by "stunted mesquite . . . spindly little fruit trees," and "brown, scattered clumps" of grass, became in her memory a home with "a fruitful orchard of perfectly spaced trees, terraced flower beds, broad walks, purple plumed wisteria climbing to the roof, [and] fragrant honeysuckle at the dining room windows." However much she idealized her ancestors and up-bringing and however cynical the mature Lyndon Johnson would prove to be about principled people who failed, like his father and maternal grandfather, Rebekah's recollections must have added to Lyndon's early feeling that he had a birthright to prominence and influence over other men.[28]

Rebekah's fortitude in the face of hardships also had an impact on her son. She recalled how her father's financial reverses forced her to work in the college bookstore at Baylor to pay the costs of her final year in school. Moreover, it took all her "determination and strength of will" to adjust to the death of her father, who had been the dominant force in her life.

Before his death, Rebekah, having finished her schooling, had re-turned to Fredericksburg, where she was teaching elocution and writing for some newspapers. At her father's suggestion, she had arranged an interview with Sam Johnson, Jr., who had taken Joseph Baines's seat in the legislature. Sam was "pretty cagey" in the interview, and she re-membered being "awfully provoked with that man!" A "whirlwind courtship" began in the spring of 1907 when Sam, who "was enchanted to find a girl who really liked politics," took every opportunity to make the seventeen-mile, three-hour trip on horseback from Stonewall to Fredericksburg to visit her. He took her to the Confederate Reunion to hear Senator Joe Bailey and Governor Tom Campbell and to a session of the legislature addressed by William Jennings Bryan, the Democratic presidential candidate, whom they "admired extravagantly." When Sam asked her to marry him, she accepted after some hesitation. Although his drinking, coarse language, and lack of formal education troubled her, he was "dashing and dynamic" and, like her father, a man of "principles" who seemed destined for better things.[29]

Sam, who was almost thirty, and Rebekah, twenty-six, set up house in Gillespie County between the tiny communities of Hye and Stonewall on the north bank of the Pedernales. They occupied the old family "shack" or log-cabin dog-run, and Sam's parents moved up the road to the place where the Martins had lived. Although Rebekah had grown up in Blanco and lived for a few years in Fredericksburg, which she described as "prosy and dull," nothing had prepared her for the hardships of life on the Pedernales as a member of the last American generation of pioneer women. Rebekah later recalled that "the problem of adjustment to a completely opposite personality," and "to a strange and new way of life" compounded the normal difficulties of being a newlywed. "My early experiences on the farm were relived when I saw 'The Egg and I' "; she wrote in 1954, "again I shuddered over the chickens, and wrestled with a mammoth iron stove."

Rebekah was a romantic, delicate young woman who dressed in crinolines and lace and wore "broad-brimmed, beribboned hats with long veils." She "made a ritual out of . . . serving tea in very thin cups" and meals on tablecloths, which needed washing and ironing, rather than on oilcloth which could be wiped clean and used at the next sitting. She read poetry—Browning and Tennyson—and biographies about Texas governors, American Presidents or anyone, as long as they were about real people. One of Lyndon's earliest memories was "the sight of his mother's bed piled high with books." And she loved to talk—about ideas and the larger world of art, literature, people, and politics. "She had a great respect for books and the life of the mind," Lady Bird Johnson, Lyndon's wife, later remarked.[30]

But life on Sam's Hill Country farm afforded her few of these pleasures. Quite the contrary, it taught her that "life is real and earnest and not the charming fairy tale of which I had so long dreamed." Her home now was not the solid two-story stone house she enjoyed in Blanco but a typical early Texas shanty of three rooms, each twelve feet square: a living room-bedroom on the right and another bedroom on the left fronting a kitchen-dining area; each bedroom contained a large fireplace. The rooms were divided by a breezeway or open area dogtrot and joined by a sagging, slanting roof and front porch that included a shedroom. A back porch with a second shedroom completed the living quarters. In front of the house a barbed wire fence containing a swinging gate enclosed a yard with a few tufts of grass and a walkway to the front porch marked out by rocks and small flower beds. A rail fence bounded the back yard which contained a cistern, pump, well, barn, smokehouse, and a couple of "two-holer" outhouses. A vegetable garden and a small orchard with peach trees and a pecan grove sat on the edge of 100 acres of cultivated land and 400 acres of pastures, where forty to fifty cows grazed.[31]

Daily life was sheer drudgery. With no indoor plumbing or electricity, washing, ironing, cooking, and heating—the chores modern housewives perform with a minimum of physical exertion—were labors that taxed the strength of even the most robust woman. Wood for the fireplace over which Rebekah cooked had to be carried into the house in countless loads from piles outside. Water in seemingly endless amounts had to be pumped from the well and the four-gallon, thirty-two-pound bucket lugged into the kitchen. Each person in the house usually needed ten buckets, forty gallons, of water a day. Clothes had to be boiled in huge vats, scrubbed by hand "in hours of kneeling over rough rub-boards," and pressed with heavy flatirons that were reheated repeatedly on the stove. Three full meals a day had to be prepared for Sam and his farm-hands, and there were unceasing daily chores, sewing, feeding chickens, washing floors, canning fruits and vegetables. The work left most Hill Country women stooped and old before their time.[32]

As much as the physical strain, the cultural poverty of pioneer living worked a painful hardship on Rebekah. Her sense of isolation, of having no one to discuss ideas with except Sam, was a source of constant frustration. Sam "had lots of company," his youngest sister, Jessie, recalled. But Rebekah "didn't. . . . And it was hard on her." Her neighbors and relatives were all uneducated and barely literate. The newspapers of the time and place, the *Gillespie County News* and the *Blanco News*, testify to the limited horizons of these people. Ads to sell horses, watches, ribbons, woolens, headstones, liquors, and cigars and to provide medical, dental, and barbering services filled the pages of these weeklies. Patent medicines, like "Dr. King's New Life Pills for sick and nervous headaches" and "Electric Bitters," a curative for rheumatism, liver, kidney, stomach and bowel troubles and a suicide preventive, were evidence of the primitive state of medical care. While there were national and state-wide stories, sensational accounts of disasters aimed more at exciting the passions than informing the mind dominated the news columns. "The effect of the Russian shells and machine guns was terrific," read an account of fighting in the Russo-Japanese War of 1904–05. "The slopes of the high hills are littered with mangled bodies, severed heads and limbs." "The unfortunate girl died in horrible agony in a few minutes," the story of a young woman killed by a fallen electrical wire stated. Big city newspapers of the time were no less ready to exploit the emotions of their readers but they also carried a wider variety of more important news stories in greater detail.[33]

"I was determined to overcome circumstances instead of letting them overwhelm me," Rebekah later recalled. To an extent, she did. She was deeply in love with Sam, who, for all his crudity, remained an exciting companion. "She'd hear Sam coming home," a girl who worked for the Johnsons at the time remembers. "Her face would just light up like a little kid's, and out she'd go flying down to the gate to meet him." And quickly there was her first child. On August 27, 1908, a little over a year after she had been married, Rebekah gave birth. "The first year of her marriage was the worst year of her life," Lyndon later said. "Then I came along and suddenly everything was all right again. I could do all the things she never did."[34]

2

Childhood

REBEKAH and Sam never thought of themselves as ordinary Hill Country folks, and surviving relatives and neighbors have vivid memories of them sixty and seventy years later as a bit apart from the crowd—maybe even special: Rebekah was "a gentle, gentle woman," "a princess," "a lady," and Sam, "a swell dresser" and "proud steppin' " man. In a place and time when families struggled to make ends meet, to survive, Rebekah and Sam, remembering their heritage, had some style and dreamed of better things. It left an indelible impression on their contemporaries and had a great impact on their first-born son, who became the focus of their ambition. "We welcomed you—Daddy and I with great hope," his mother wrote thirty years later. " . . . We felt that in you we would realize dear dreams, cherished ambitions and fond hopes."[1]

Forty-six years later, Rebekah remembered Lyndon's birth as a momentous occasion: "It was daybreak. . . . Now the light came in from the east, bringing . . . a stillness so profound and so pervasive that it seemed as if the earth itself were listening." She viewed him as so special that she could never acknowledge his delivery by a midwife substituting for the local physician who only arrived several hours later. Sam was as enamored of the boy. When Otto Lindig, a neighbor, came by four hours after the birth to sell a span of horses, Sam ushered him into the house to show off his son, who he predicted would "be Governor of Texas some day." When Lindig replied, "He's certainly got his mother's head," it made Sam "mad."[2]

Rebekah and Sam viewed the boy as so extraordinary that they could not agree on a proper name. None Rebekah suggested could meet Sam's exacting standards. "Too sissy for a son of mine," he objected, or it reminded him of some rascal he once knew. After three months, Rebekah could no longer stand to have her "beautiful" child, "the most wonderful baby in the world," unnamed. One November morning, she refused to cook breakfast until they reached a decision. Sam, who had wanted to be a lawyer, now insisted that the boy be named for an attorney. "How do you like Clarence," he asked, thinking of Judge Clarence Martin, his prominent relative. "Not one bit," Rebekah answered. "Then what about Dayton?" he said, thinking now of Dayton Moses, a friend and well-known attorney. Rebekah thought it "still not quite right for this boy." Remembering a third lawyer friend, W. C. Linden, Sam suggested naming the child for this "good" and "smart" man. Rebekah agreed on the condition that she spell it *L-y-n-d-o-n*, which she thought would be more euphonious. "Spell it as you please," said Sam. " . . . We will call the baby for him and for your father." "All right," Rebekah responded, "he is named Lyndon Baines Johnson."[3]

During Lyndon's first year, Rebekah and Sam marveled at his every action. When he was nearly six months old, Rebekah penned a letter in his name to her sister-in-law: "I can sit alone now, and perform many amusing capers. My father says that I am quite an orator and translates my speech into political axioms. Mother thinks I have the studious look of a professor and is always wondering what problem I am struggling to solve." Shortly after, Sam brought home the first photo ever taken of Lyndon. Rebekah recalled how Sam "raised his hand holding the package as he saw me waiting on the porch and began to run. I ran to meet him and we met in the middle of the Benner pasture to exclaim rapturously over the photograph of our boy." Not long after, Rebekah took the baby to visit her mother in San Marcos, where Rebekah reported: "It would turn your head to hear the compliments showered on our boy. People just rave over him. . . . They think he is the sweetest baby in the whole world, as he really is of course."[4]

Relatives and friends reinforced Rebekah's and Sam's feelings about Lyndon. In the spring of 1909, when they attended a picnic near Stonewall, Lyndon greeted each neighbor with a smile and tried to climb out of his father's arms into theirs. "Sam, you've got a politician there," one of them exclaimed. I've never before seen such a friendly baby. He's a chip off the old block. I can just see him running for office twenty-odd years from now." His grandfather Johnson was also taken with the child, whom he described as "a mighty fine grandson, smart as you find them. I expect him to be United States Senator before he is forty."

Encouraged by the affection and praise and endowed with considerable intelligence, Lyndon showed himself to be a gifted child. He learned the alphabet from blocks before he was two; knew the Mother Goose rhymes and poems from Longfellow and Tennyson by the age of three; and could read and "spell almost anything that he could hear" by the time he was four. "I'll never forget how much my mother loved me when I recited those poems," Lyndon said later. "The minute I finished she'd take me in her arms and hug me so hard I sometimes thought I'd be strangled to death."[5]

Showered with so much positive attention, Lyndon had treasured memories of these earliest years and for the rest of his life he associated the Pedernales and the ranch at Stonewall with serenity and renewal. In his fifties and sixties he described himself as always eager to return to the surroundings that he knew as a child. He had especially fond recollections of himself as a boy walking along the banks of the Pedernales to his grandfather's house. "Grandfather Johnson liked to see me. . . . He had a loud laugh, and was gay and humorous." Lyndon particularly recalled the pleasure with which he listened to his grandfather's stories of cattle drives and frontier adventures: "I sat beside the rocker on the floor of the porch, thinking all the while how lucky I was to have as a granddaddy this big man with the white beard who had lived the most exciting life imaginable." Lyndon also had pleasant memories of family gatherings on July 4th and Christmas at Uncle Clarence's and Aunt Frank's big house on the river, where the children shot off firecrackers in the front yard, played with their dogs, and took presents from the chimney on Christmas eve. Other relatives recalled Sunday afternoons on "Grandpa and Grandma" Johnson's front porch, where they "sang a lot," or delightful summer evenings in big rocking chairs on Sam's and Rebekah's porch, with Sam, who "had the most beautiful voice," singing old songs.[6]

Yet all was not idyllic in Lyndon's first years. His primacy as the only child receiving his parents' undivided attention ended when he was two with the birth of his sister Rebekah and was further challenged in the next six years by the birth of three other siblings, Josefa, in 1912, Sam Houston in 1914, and Lucia in 1916. Although he remained a favored first son, he could never reclaim the exclusive hold on his parents' affections that he enjoyed in the first two years of his life. Most children adjust successfully to the birth of rivals for parental love, and in large measure Lyndon did too. But his exaggerated status as a household idol translated into a greater displacement for him than most older children usually experience.[7]

Lyndon's tension at losing center stage in the household manifested itself at age four when he began running away from home and alarming his parents, who feared he might be lost or injured. Despite warnings that he might fall in the river or run into a rattlesnake, Lyndon was always taking off for his grandfather's house or across the fields to the nearby Junction School, where he could see the children playing during recess. He also occasionally hid in the fields and refused to come out for a long time while his parents called him and his mother stood crying. In Lyndon's recollection of one of these episodes, he recounted that his mother "became very frightened when she . . . couldn't find me. She had two smaller children in the house and couldn't locate me." He also recalled that while his father searched the field for him, his "mother stood and held the baby in her arms." When asked by his father why he had run off, he found it difficult to explain. "He was not content just sitting there in the house with another baby," his cousin Ava Johnson Cox said of his behavior. "He wanted attention," Jesse Lambert, the maid working for the Johnsons at the time, believed. "He would run away, and run away, and the minute his mother would turn her back, he would run away again, and it was all to get attention."[8]

When his parents tried to solve the problem by arranging his attendance at the one-room Junction School in 1912, a year before he was supposed to enroll, the demand for attention became even more pronounced. As Lyndon and others remembered it, his mother, who was "afraid I would get in the river and drown," would lead him "with a baby in her arms" from home to the schoolhouse. There, he followed Katie Deadrich, the teacher, around all day, clinging to her skirt or "pressing up close to her and 'nuzzling' her with his shoulder." When asked if he wanted a lesson, he wouldn't reply. When he spoke, his peculiar way of rolling his r's made him difficult to understand. "Miss Kate," a teenager teaching thirty pupils with a variety of learning problems at different grade levels, turned to Rebekah for help. She advised "Miss Kate" to hold Lyndon on her lap while he read. She did, and he began trying "to master whatever Miss Kate would teach him." He also began vying for more of her attention and affection, especially with Hugo Klein, another first grader. "They always tried to outdo each other," she recalled. Lyndon would come to school dressed in a red Buster Brown suit or a cowboy outfit, including his father's Stetson hat, and Hugo would make certain to be "neat and clean." Lyndon would also approach her looking "shy and cute" and say: " 'Miss Katie, I don't *like* you one bit!' I would be so shocked. Then he would laugh and say, 'I just love you.' " Despite his success in winning Miss Kate's approval, Lyndon, as he later told Doris Kearns, when she discussed his early life with him for her biography, preferred to be home with his mother. In January, after three months at school, he came down with whooping cough and spent the rest of the school year at home.[9]

If the birth of other children forced Lyndon to compete for the parental attention freely lavished on him in his first two years, his mother's difficulties meeting the demands of several infants in a rural household compounded Lyndon's problem. In many respects Rebekah was a physically and psychologically frail person, who found the difficulties of life in Stonewall almost more than she could bear. For six years, from 1907 to 1913, she struggled with the burdens and isolation of her Hill Country existence, with the fear a historian found expressed in the diaries and letters of "a thousand separate farm wives . . . that this country would drive them mad." "She wasn't used to that kind of living," Rebekah's sister-in-law Jessie Hatcher recalled. "I used to go down and help her all the time . . . I'd go in and help her wash the dishes, sweep the floor, bathe the babies. Oh, I'd just do anything that was to be done." "We spent a long and tiresome day at Stonewall yesterday," Rebekah wrote Lyndon thirty years later. " . . . I never liked country life and its inconveniences wear me out. Don't know how I ever got along as well as I did there."[10]

To escape the primitive conditions, isolation, and poor schooling their children would receive, Rebekah and Sam agreed to move the family fourteen miles east to Johnson City in September 1913, when Lyndon was five. But life there was only marginally better. An inland town of 323 people surrounded by "an ocean of land," Johnson City, as one member of the community recalled, "had nothing there." Consisting of ten, north-south, numbered streets and eight, east-west, lettered streets, the town had a bank capitalized at $23,000, a cafe with no set hours for serving meals, a corrugated-tin cotton gin, a two-story court house, a rickety hotel with no indoor plumbing, a "sanitarium" or four-bed hospital on the second floor of "Doc" Barnwell's home, a school building housing all the local students, and a few one-story, wood stores on H or Main Street. There was no electricity, no indoor toilets, only two houses with bathtubs and running water, no place you could buy a loaf of bread or fresh meat, and almost nothing to do or any place to go.

There were no railroads through the area until after 1917, and one resident of Johnson City remembers being taken as "a great big girl" some twenty-five miles north to Marble Falls to see a train. There were no paved roads leading in and out of Johnson City, and the fifty-mile trip east to Austin or the thirty-mile journey west to Fredericksburg could be an all-day affair or longer. One resident who moved to Johnson City from San Antonio in the spring of 1912 recalls that it took "parts of three days" for his family to travel the sixty miles between the two cities. Rains often made the roads impassable, and when they could be used, flat tires were a common occurrence that made travel along Hill Country highways a test of one's endurance. When a group of Johnson City students was taken to the teachers' college in San Marcos for a debate and housed in a dormitory for the night, they did not know how to turn off the electricity in their room. They pulled down the light globes suspended on cords, put them in a dresser, and closed the draw before going to bed. When Stella Gliddon, the editor of the local newspaper, came to Johnson City from Fredericksburg in 1919, she felt as if she "had come to the end of the world."[11]

Rebekah quickly learned that moving to Johnson City was no solution to her problems. Although Sam bought her one of the nicest houses in town, a six-room, double ell, frame structure fronted by a white picket fence, she continued to lack the amenities of indoor plumbing and electricity that would have made life in a household with five far easier. The births of her fourth and fifth children in 1914 and 1916 were particularly difficult and required long periods of recovery. Two minor operations in 1917 added to her physical difficulties and occasionally after that she remained in bed for days and weeks at a time. Household chores—cooking, washing, ironing, and cleaning—had to be performed by maids and relatives, and, neighbors recall, what they didn't do remained undone. Dirty dishes piled up in the sink sometimes remained unwashed for several days, while freshly washed clothes were dumped in a bathtub, where they lay unpressed until each of the children ironed them or took them piece by piece to wear to school unpressed. Neighbors also recall that Rebekah had difficulty controlling her children when Sam was away. "We kids ran over mother," Lyndon later said. She was so ineffective in stopping their fights that she sometimes asked neighbors to intercede and spank them.

Following a pattern established by her father, Rebekah became something of a recluse in these years. Although she saw numerous people in her home and taught elocution to many local children there, she did not go out much, rarely showing up at church or meetings held at the school auditorium. Years later, when the children were in college and Rebekah and Sam had temporarily moved to San Marcos, Rebekah's memories of Johnson City made her reluctant to return. "Sam pines for Johnson City and speaks of it as if it were a regular paradise. The others of us are not so carried away with its charms. We may go back there to live, but I certainly do not look forward to the prospect."[12]

As a child, Lyndon remembered his mother as often unhappy and needing his comfort and support. One of his earliest memories, from the age of three or four, was of his mother crying at the water pump outsi their house at night. Sam was away on business, and she confided her fears of being alone to Lyndon, who promised to "take care of her." On another occasion, when Sam stayed out all night, Lyndon "woke up and heard her in the parlor crying her eyes out. I knew she needed me. With me there, she seemed less afraid. . . . I promised that I would be there to protect her always. Finally she calmed down and we both fell asleep." Lyndon also remembered that his mother's need for him made him feel "big and important. It made me believe that I could do anything in the whole world." Freud has described this state of mind as "the feeling of a conqueror, that confidence of success that often induces real success."

But the situation must have left him feeling somewhat needy and unattended. John Dollahite, one of Lyndon's high-school classmates, recalls that when Lyndon "really needed some help, he came to Aunt Clara Redford [a neighbor]. She could do for him what his mother couldn't do." Mrs. Redford had three sons and a bunch of nephews that she cared for now and then. "She was just amazing. . . . And I imagine that's the thing that affected Lyndon in going to her. He knew he could get help if possible and that there would be no complaints about it." As a boy, Lyndon read a poem in a fifth-grade reader, "Somebody's Mother," that he never forgot. It described a helpless woman, "poor," "old," "ragged," and "gray," who is aided by a compassionate young man "when her own dear boy is far away." Since it was not the literary merits of the poem that appealed to Lyndon, it was probably Rebekah's neediness that fixed the poem so firmly in his mind.[13]

Yet Rebekah's frailty and dependence were not the full measure of her personality. She was also a forceful person who asserted herself in a variety of ways. Numerous people in Johnson City remember the school plays she directed and the lessons she gave young people in her home. Boys and girls who wished to act in a play or participate in interscholastic debating came to Rebekah for free instruction in public speaking. They gathered in the Johnsons' parlor or "fireplace room," as they called it. A student would speak first and then Rebekah would show how "to put more force" in what was being said. "She was a strict teacher," one of the pupils recalls. "She was not a hard teacher, but she wanted you to do the way she thought it should be done. And she . . . was very capable. So, yes, she taught us. She really taught us."[14]

Rebekah was even more assertive with Lyndon, who later complained that her "early force feedings and attentions sometimes 'smothered' him." "There was . . . much of the ambitious stage mother in Mrs. Johnson," one of Lyndon's biographers asserts. Another describes her as a frustrated woman with a host of throttled ambitions she transferred to Lyndon. She hoped Lyndon "would fulfill the wishful dreams she had never carried out, he would become the important person she had failed to be." When Lyndon was five, she dressed him in Lord Fauntleroy suits and insisted that his long blond curls not be cut and that he take violin and dancing lessons. Later, when he showed himself to be an indifferent student and wouldn't complete his lessons, she would "devote the whole breakfast period to a discussion of what my son should have learned the night before." If there were still more to do at the end of the meal, she would walk him to the gate of the house or even all the way to school, reading the textbook assignment to him as they went.

When Lyndon defied her wishes, she was very harsh with him. "Aunt Rebekah had a way of getting under your skin that really hurt," Ava Johnson Cox recalls. After Lyndon quit violin and dancing lessons when he was eight, his mother walked around the house pretending he was dead. She wouldn't raise her voice or even scold. Ava remembers that when she was unhappy with Lyndon, she would say: " 'Now, Lyndon you have just disappointed me.' . . . Lyndon couldn't stand too much of that. . . . It hurt him." As Lyndon recalled it, she would speak to him in "a terrible knifelike voice," or greet him with an impassive stare and entirely close him off, "refusing to speak or even to look at him." His frustration at Rebekah's conditional or undependable love—an affection that depended on his conformity to her wishes—plagued him for years to come.[15]

For all Lyndon's difficulties with his mother, he felt closer to her than to his father. When Kearns discussed his early life with him, "Johnson spoke almost exclusively of his mother. When he mentioned his father, it was to enumerate his liabilities as a husband and to explain what he did to Rebekah." Lyndon's preference for his mother may already have existed by the time he was six. At the end of first grade in 1914, when he was asked to read a poem to his classmates and their parents, he selected one called, "I'd Rather be Mama's Boy."[16]

Sam, who wished to be more than a farmer or rancher and struggled to make a living for his family, was away from home a great deal in Lyndon's first years, buying and selling cattle, cotton, and real estate. When he was there, he was a demanding disciplinarian who at times drank to excess, lost control of himself, and upset his wife and children with his emotional outbursts. Lyndon recalled: "There was nothing my mother hated more than seeing my daddy drunk. When he had too much to drink, he'd lose control of himself. He used bad language. He squandered the little money we had on the cotton and real estate markets. Sometimes he'd be lucky and make a lot of money. But more often he lost out. One year we'd all be riding high in Pedernales terms, so high in fact that on a scale of A to F, we'd be right up there with the A's. Then two years later, he'd lose it all. . . . These ups and downs were hard on my mother. . . . She could never count on a stable income. When she got upset, she blamed our money problems on my father's drinking." And for Rebekah, who was so concerned with the proprieties, it must have also been a source of humiliation. One Johnson City resident remembers Sam several times coming to address the school "just lit up like a country church and have to climb up the steps on his all fours. The auditorium was on the second floor, and he would come up on his hands and knees . . . . Several times he's been at our house for breakfast and sobered up."[17]

Sam was a forceful and at times overbearing personality. "Father was a strict disciplinarian. . . . We looked on him as king," Lyndon said later. A Johnson City girl who helped Rebekah with the housework recalls that when Sam "spoke, everybody jumped. He was law and order." Ava Johnson Cox recalls Sam Ealy as a "driver. He really believed in drill. . . . He wanted you to be able to answer him right now and he didn't want to wait a second for it. . . . If he asked you what 7×9 was, you didn't say 7×9. You said 63, or you went to the end of the class."

One of Lyndon's first memories of his father was the time he cut his hair. "When I was four or five, I had long curls. He hated them. 'He's a boy,' he'd say to my mother, 'and you're making a sissy of him. You've got to cut those curls.' My mother refused. Then, one Sunday morning when she went off to church, he took the big scissors and cut off all my hair. When my mother came home, she refused to speak to him for a week." At the age of ten, when Sam went back to the legislature, Lyndon opened a shoeshine parlor in the barbershop and persuaded Rebekah to run an ad for his enterprise on the front page of the local newspaper. Although he was "very proud" of the nickels and occasional dimes he earned for his efforts, Sam "was sore as he could be" when he came home. Lyndon remembered him saying that "he didn't raise his son to be a shoeshine boy—and if he had, he didn't want to advertise it on the front page!" [18]

Sam was capable of emotional outbursts that humiliated and frightened Lyndon as a boy. One of Lyndon's boyhood friends recalls the time someone put oil of mustard in the barbershop chair Lyndon liked to sit in while reading the newspaper. "Lyndon began to turn and squirm. . . . He was on fire and he began to cry and holler. . . . He got his pants down but he didn't take them completely off and he ran out on the sidewalk. . . . His daddy heard him hollering out there. He came up out of there and . . . he took his belt off and he grabbed Lyndon by the hand and every so often he'd pop him one across the rear. . . . I thought he was the meanest man in the world." When the barbers explained what had happened, Sam "just said . . . there wasn't any kid of his that was going to run up and down the streets with his bare butt hanging out." Another time, when Lyndon accidentally threw a rock through a hardware store window, Sam "went on terribly," telling him "to go home and get a quilt and he'd take him to jail." Sam never intended to do it, "but Lyndon was very upset about it" and Rebekah had to still "the troubled waters."

Slapped and spanked repeatedly by Sam, Lyndon was afraid of his anger. "My father, he'd take a razor strap and just whip the hell out of us," Lyndon later told an interviewer. At the age of fifteen when he wrecked his father's car, he was "too frightened to know what to do. 'I knew only that I could not face my father.' " He took a bus to New Braunfels, where an uncle lived. When tracked down by his father, he " 'walked to the phone, feeling like I was going to the guillotine. I tried to keep my legs and my voice from shaking.' " Lyndon was relieved when Sam explained that he had traded in the wreck for a brand-new car and wanted him to pick it up and drive it slowly around the court house square before bringing it home. Sam wanted him to refute the " 'talk' around town . . . that my son's a coward. . . . Now I don't want anyone thinking I produced a yellow son." [19]

If Lyndon feared his father, he also entered into fierce competition with him. As a small child, he slept beside his mother when his father was away. He later remembered the " 'absolute terror' he experienced one night when he was awakened from sleep in his mother's bed by the sudden opening of the bedroom door, only to find a younger sister standing there . . . crying out for her mother." Sam Houston Johnson, Lyndon's younger brother, recalls how when he was three and Lyndon was nine, they slept together in a bedroom next to Sam Ealy's, while the girls and their mother all slept on the other side of the house. In the middle of the night Sam Ealy would call his younger son to "come in here and get me warm." Soon, after their father fell asleep, Lyndon would call Sam Houston to "come on back. I'm getting cold." If his daddy got cold again later in the night, little Sam would have to go back to his father's bed.

The overt power struggle between them continued into Lyndon's late adolescence. When Lyndon hesitated about going to college, Sam challenged him by belittling his intelligence and drive. Lyndon recalled him saying that "he just didn't believe . . . I had either the ambition or the mental equipment to take and absorb the college education. That was quite a challenge, and, by damn, I wanted to show him! . . . I remember my first grades. I took them home . . . and I threw them down in front of him and I said, 'Does that look like I've got enough sense to take a college education?' " After college, when he became a teacher, he applied his father's technique to his students: "I'd just try to run 'em under ground, just almost stomp 'em, but always would make it clear that I loved them, where they'd never run completely off. I would humiliate 'em and embarrass 'em and make fun of 'em . . . until they got to where they could take care of themselves, which they did."[20]

Lyndon's tensions with his parents may go far to explain some of his behavior as a child and adolescent. The need for attention and affection he manifested at the age of four or five remained a striking feature of his personality. During the first years in Johnson City, people remember him as aggressively demanding Rebekah's attention. Louise Casparis [Edwards], who worked for the family in 1916 after Lucia, the last child, was born, recalls Lyndon as someone who always "sort of led out" and "usually got what he wanted." Lyndon's sisters, she adds, may have been jealous of the special attention Rebekah paid to her oldest son, but they didn't show it. They demanded less, or it took less to satisfy them than to meet Lyndon's demands. A visitor in the house when Lyndon was about eleven recalled his asking his mother what a bed bug was. When "Miss Rebekah tried to shoo him out of the house," he wouldn't be put off. "He came back a second time and said, 'Until you tell me what a bed bug is I'm gonna stand right here.' " Replying simply that it is a bug that bites at night, it seemed "to satisfy him." He could be as insistent with other relatives: He once bought a little China clown for an aunt at Christmas, but not wanting it to be lost in the pile of gifts under the tree, he gave it to her weeks in advance, saying, "It cost me a dime and it's worth every penny of it."[21]

Others outside the family have similar recollections. Georgia Cammack Edgeworth, a Johnson City classmate, felt that he "was very sensitive" and "wanted so bad for people to like him. . . . He wanted to be something special." His first-grade teacher at the Johnson City school remembered him as a kind and affectionate little boy who "would crawl up in my lap and pet and pat me." By the time he reached seventh grade he commanded attention by more aggressive means. At the north end of Lyndon's schoolroom were two large blackboards flanking a door. When pupils left to go to the outhouse, they would write their name on one of the boards and erase it when they returned. Not eager to call attention to themselves, students customarily wrote their names in small letters. Except for Lyndon, he would write "Lyndon B." across the entire left side of the board and "Johnson" across the whole right side.[22]

As a boy, he also called attention to himself by being a practical joker and a tease. One of the girls who worked in the Johnson house remembers him at the age of six or seven hiding under the bed and grabbing everyone's leg when they went by. The girl who worked for them when Lyndon was nine recalls his teasing his sisters Rebekah and Josefa and his mother. "Every night when Sam came home, he would say—'Well, what has Lyndon done today?' " His mother and the girls would start to tell on him and he would hide in the kitchen behind a stove, but he always got his "seat warmed." When his mother enrolled him in Mrs. Stella Gliddon's dancing class, he spent the entire time teasing and tormenting the little girls. He was "the most mischievous little dickens you ever did see. He was always up to something, picking at you," a Johnson City contemporary recalls. Luzia Casparis, an aunt of one of Lyndon's schoolmates, remembered how "sometime we'd go on these family fishings, he would flip the hats in the water with a fishing pole." In high school, he was always cutting up and making everyone laugh. In and of themselves joking and teasing are hardly strong evidence of a heartfelt cry for attention. But in the context of Lyndon's other behavior, they are suggestive of some deep need.[23]

There is the additional fact that Lyndon's appearance—his manner of dressing—was calculated to make everyone sit up and take notice. In high school he often set himself off from the other boys, who dressed in overalls, blue jeans, knickers, and khakis, by wearing a white shirt, a necktie, and slacks. One description of him as a teenager reads: "He was something of the small-town 'jelly bean,' a sharpie who wore the only bow tie among his contemporaries and slicked back his hair." Another biographer depicts him as "sometimes outlandishly elegant" for a town like Johnson City. "By his senior year in high school, he had acquired the only Palm Beach suit and straw boater in Johnson City; on some occasions, he wore blue jeans, but wore them tucked into brightly polished boots laced up to the knee, and the shirt he wore with them was a bright yellow silk crêpe de Chine, the neck of which he kept open to display either a turtleneck dickey or an ascot; to school . . . he sometimes wore, on black hair that was painstakingly pompadoured and waved, . . . a dapper English tweed cap."[24]

Lyndon wanted people not only to notice and focus on him but also to feel sorry for him or to share his own sense of deprivation. Some commentators on his life have objected to the picture he later painted of himself in his early years as "a weak, even pitiable figure," as "the son of a tenant farmer," a "rags-to-riches" character "trudging along a dusty country road with a cardboard suitcase" in search of better things. As one of his long-time friends and associates astutely concluded, this was less an accurate reconstruction of his past than a way of disarming later critics, of getting "all those put off by his power" to feel compassion for him. But it also expressed an inner reality about his early years: he did feel needy or disadvantaged or somewhat unattended as a boy.[25]

There are numerous stories of how any injury, defeat, rejection, or reprimand brought forth exaggerated reactions aimed at arousing sympathy for his plight. When he jumped from the family barn at the age of ten and broke his leg, Cousin Ava remembers his carrying on as if he were dying: "He screamed bloody murder," and "poor old" Doc Barnwell, who was crippled, came "up that road with that little satchel just a steppin'." When he asked Lyndon how bad are you hurt, Lyndon shouted, " 'Oh, I'm killed, I'm killed.' " Although the Doctor assured him that he only had a broken leg, Lyndon continued to carry on, and Rebekah "just knew that he was gonna die." When Doc Barnwell told him that "he'd give him a shot and he would get over it . . . ol' Lyndon come up from there and . . . said, 'Oh, please Doctor don't shoot me. I want to live a while longer.' " Ava and the others present found it "funny . . . that he didn't understand what . . . [the Doctor] was going to do."[26]

Lyndon's early years were also punctuated by acts of defiance and an affinity for trouble that upset his parents. Lyndon "was the kind of little boy that his mother had to tell three or four times to get in the stove wood. He was also a boy that could be very arrogant," Stella Gliddon, a family friend, recalls. By the time he was four or five he "was too full of energy to stay still and clean without pressure from the adults or older cousins!" While the rest of the family prepared to receive special guests or to depart for a visit, a cousin was usually "given the job of guarding the active little boy until guests arrived or the Johnsons departed." As he grew, he became more difficult to control. When he was six, and once again had long curls, his mother arranged for him to recite a poem at a Confederate Reunion. Shortly before the occasion, he had his head shaved "slick as an onion." "My darling child, who did that to you?" his mother asked. "I did it myself—I got it free," he replied. Rebekah canceled their appearance at the Reunion. Lyndon also resisted his mother's demands that he wear shoes. "I don't think he wore shoes [regularly] before he was about 15 years old," Otto Lindig said. After he broke his leg, he had to stay in bed. When his cousins Ava and Margaret brought him his homework, he insisted that they play "mubble peg." When Ava observed that there was "no place to play mubble peg in here," he said, " 'That's just what you think,' and he turned around in that bed with that leg in that cast and took . . . [his] knife and stuck [it] in . . . [the] headboard of that wooden bed. . . . 'Lyndon, my daddy would just blister me good if he catch me doing something like that.' He said, 'Well, they're not gonna catch me.' And sure enough they didn't."[27]

Lyndon's defiance wasn't confined to his immediate family. Luzia Casparis, who tutored him when he was a first or second grader, remembers him as "a little tart, a real hellion. . . . Mischievous! That boy was terrible." Since he "hadn't done his homework for many days in a row," Luzia "told him he would have to miss recess. But Lyndon walked right out of the room and as he passed her screened window, he spit toward her." Luzia threw him in an ice shack, where he screamed and hollered and pushed so hard on the door that when she opened it, he fell out and bloodied his nose. "The first time I knowed him," Joe Payne said, "was back in 1917." They met in south Austin at Payne's step-grandpa's place. "Lyndon had on a pair of blue overalls and them high-top shoes, with old buckles on the side that you wrapped the string in, and a straw hat that looked like the goats had been eating on. . . . It's hard to tell who was the meanest, him or me, cause we both like to get in trouble, some kind of devilment." Stealing his grandpa's peaches, driving a bunch of black kids out of a swimming hole by throwing flint rocks at them, or getting in fistfights with the blacks were a few of the things Payne remembers their doing. When Payne visited Lyndon in Johnson City, they stayed out all night "prowling" and "loafing the town. . . . We got a couple of horses out, run 'em up and down the street, and like they got the town Marshall on us about it." When they got home in the morning, Payne's step-grandpa "took that walking stick of his to me and Mr. Sam, he kind of busted Lyndon's britches a little bit and told him not to run all over town to where he didn't know where he was at."[28]

At school as well, Lyndon was continually in trouble. At first, his academic work was good, but he received mixed grades in "deportment." In the higher elementary grades, however, he also began to have academic problems. He wouldn't do his homework, and even rebelled against going to school. One observer in the Johnson home remembers that Rebekah "had a hard time getting him up in the morning and getting him to school." A record of his school attendance from 1920 shows that out of 180 school days he was absent 50 times and was tardy on 30 of the 130 days he was present.

In 1921–22, while his family was temporarily back in Stonewall, Lyndon lived with his Uncle Tom, Sam's brother, and Aunt Kitty in Johnson City, where he began attending the high school. Tom complained to Sam that they couldn't control Lyndon, who refused to do his schoolwork, and Lyndon's teachers warned that he might be left back. To compel him to make up the work he neglected during the regular school year, Sam and Rebekah insisted that he attend a summer session at a private school in Sam Marcos, thirty miles away. In a week's time, Lyndon spent the pocket money his father had given him for the eight-week session, treating other students to candy and ice cream. When he hitched a ride home to ask for more money, Sam took him straight back to San Marcos without giving him a cent. The experience was a "very trying" one for Lyndon, who found being away from home and school work great hardships. Rebekah begged one of the teachers in the school to do all she could for her son, who needed to complete the work, and to "please pet him a little for me" when he is homesick.[29]

Lyndon's defiance—his reluctance to submit to authority—went hand in hand with a need to be top dog, to dominate, control, or bend others to his will. "Lyndon would always have to be the leader," Ava Johnson remembers. It didn't make any difference to him whose side he was on in a game, "he gonna be the leader." Louise Casparis Edwards remembers him "bossing" and being "spoiled. He wanted his way; he'd had his way at home, at least with his mother." Indeed, one of his boyhood friends recalls that he "had her in the palm of his hand. When he spoke, Mrs. Johnson jumped. Lyndon would come in and say, 'Where's my shirt, where's my britches?' and Mrs. Johnson would *run* to get his clothes." He was as overbearing with his brother and sisters. "Sometimes we'd play church and Lyndon would be the preacher," his sister Rebekah said. "I think he thought he was papa. He was always bossy." He was "overbearing," John Dollahite also says. Since Lyndon usually had the ball or glove the boys played with, he insisted on saying who was pitcher or who would play on which side. If they wouldn't let him call the shots, he would just "pick up his ball or glove and go home."[30]

He also liked to argue. "Oh, he was always arguing," Stella Gliddon says. "If he could convince you that black was white, he would try to do it. And absolutely just be tickled to death when he won his point." Emmette Redford, who would one day be the president of the American Political Science Association, says that "if there was an argument, he *had* to win. He *had* to. . . . If he'd differ with you, he'd hover right up against you, breathing right in your face, arguing your point with all the earnestness. . . . I got disgusted with him. Sometimes, I'd try just to walk away, but . . . he just wouldn't stop until you gave in." "He didn't like to be beat at nothing," Joe Payne recalls, "cause when he went into somethin' . . . he put his heart and soul into it."[31]

"It is said that famous men are usually the product of an unhappy childhood," Winston Churchill once wrote. Yet there are so many unhappy children and so few famous men. The success of the famous is surely the result of more than early unhappiness. Lyndon Johnson is a good case in point. Much in his first years—his exaggerated need for attention and sympathy, his defiance of authority and problems at school, his overbearing character and need to be first—leaves the impression of a troubled child struggling with bewildering inner tensions. In one form or another, as his adult behavior later demonstrated, Lyndon's childhood difficulties dogged him all his life. But what seems most striking in retrospect is the extent to which he identified with and drew strength from his parents and managed to convert his problems into effective means of accomplishing exceptional things and sustaining a stable family life.[32]

His relationship with his mother is illustrative. In the opinion of a number of people who observed their interaction through the years, Rebekah had an extraordinary hold on Lyndon: she endowed him with the belief that he could do anything, that nothing was too hard for him, and Lyndon reciprocated the feeling. "Anything that anybody else in the family couldn't do, she became an expert at," he said after she died. He told another interviewer: "I think except for her I might not have made it through high school and certainly not through college. . . . She was a constant, dogged, determined influence on my life." Showing a journalist in the 1960s the family genealogy his mother had compiled, Lyndon fought back tears and described her as "a saintly woman" to whom he owed everything. "My mother was everything—religion, character, and right and wrong," he told Ronnie Dugger in 1967. She was "faith, pure gold, the greatest female I have ever known, without any exceptions." "One of the things I used to like about him," Hubert Humphrey said, "was that he would get tears in his eyes when he talked about his mother."[33]

The evidence of her positive influence over him is even more striking from the words they exchanged when he was an adolescent and a man. "You can't realize the difference in the atmosphere after one of your sweet letters," he wrote her early in his college career. "Your letters always give me more strength, renewed courage and that bulldog tenacity so essential to the success of any man," he wrote when he was twenty-one. "I love; I believe in you; I expect great things of you," Rebekah wrote him when he was twenty-nine. " . . . You have always justified my expectations, my hopes, my dreams. How dear to me you are, my darling boy, my devoted son, my strength and comfort." Replying to another one of her encouraging messages a year later, Lyndon wrote: "Your thoughtful letter . . . I shall remember when I get downhearted and feel like tossing everything out the window. During the years your letters have meant more to me than I can say. They have urged me on even when I have despaired of accomplishing anything."[34]

Lyndon's father as well had a decidedly positive impact on his son's life. Although he could be painfully overbearing, drank to excess, and had an explosive temper, he was also an unusually warm, compassionate, and supportive man for whom many people felt great affection. One of the Johnson children's playmates remembers how "he would get very angry . . . but it was like a sunshine thing. It was gone in a minute and then he was always going about doing something real nice." He would come home in a bad mood and "scatter the kids coming in the door . . . send them all home and shout at 'em . . . but . . . that night there was candy for all of them or ice cream or something to make up for what he had done." There were very few people in the community who didn't like Sam Johnson, one contemporary asserts. "He was a very friendly . . . a very down-to-earth man, a man who attracted people and knew how to deal with people," a fellow state legislator recalled. Lyndon himself said that his father had a good sense of humor, loved to joke and talk and make people laugh. "He was a warm man, loved people, while my mother was sort of aloof."[35]

Sam particularly enjoyed helping others. Emmette Redford remembers his going out of his way to be kind to his grandfather, who was old, hard of hearing, and ignored by most folks. Sam became famous in the Hill Country for aiding the elderly—army veterans, retired Texas Rangers, soldiers' widows—get pensions they didn't know they deserved or how to obtain. *The Johnson City Record-Courier* said in its obituary about Sam: "There was no man in this section of Texas who has done more for the aged men and women who came to him for assistance in procuring pensions, and other favors." Wright Patman, Sam's contemporary in the Texas House and a U.S. Congressman, was even more emphatic: "Sam E. Johnson was the best man I ever knew."[36]

Sam's warmth of personality and generosity were also much in evidence at home with Rebekah and the children. He could be sensitive, nervous, impatient, and quick to voice displeasure toward members of the family, Rebekah recalls, but he was equally quick "in making amends when some word of his caused pain to another." He "adored" Rebekah, "worshipped the ground she walked on," Ava Johnson says. Others agree, remembering how much Sam respected his wife, and loved to sit and talk with her about politics, and kid her and make her laugh. It was much the same with the children. While he could be harsh and verbally abusive, he was also warm and giving. Often when he came home in the evening, he would bring something—a bag of sugar, candies, a loaf of bread—for which he would demand payment in kisses. And there was a lot of noise, laughing, and fun—"hilarious good times" that could blot out their problems and make them "a warm, happy family."[37]

He was protective of his children. Once, when a Johnson City High School teacher roughed up Lyndon for horsing around during recess in the schoolyard, Sam went after the teacher, who left town so quickly that his landlady had to mail him his belongings. On another occasion: Lyndon, after the first of two teenage car wrecks, ran away to Robstown near Corpus Christi, where he worked in a cotton gin firing a boiler, a dangerous job in which some people had been killed. Sam sent one of Lyndon's friends to get him and promised not to punish him if he would come home.[38]

Sam was also ambitious for his kids to make some mark in the world, and he tried to give them the wherewithal to succeed. Children growing up in Johnson City remember the debates and spelling bees, the arithmetic contests and competitive card games Sam put on at home. "It was our entertainment," according to one of them. Gathering around the fireplace in the winter time, they would roast marshmellows and cook popcorn while Sam engaged them in what Ava Johnson Cox calls "quick thinking. He would give you a subject . . . and you'd have three minutes to look it over and get your mind together and then get up and start talking." Should we join the League of Nations? Who was Eugene V. Debs? What was the Socialist Party? Should there be government ownership of railroads? "Those were things that were far out," Ava says. But Sam wanted you to know about them. "He wanted us to be the best. . . . He wasn't satisfied with having a bunch of Johnson kids just growing up." He wanted them to learn about the world beyond their doorstep. As a boy, Lyndon remembered being taken with other children by his father in a wagon to Austin, where the first one to spot the capitol dome would get a nickel. Later, Sam was so interested in having the kids understand the workings of the legislature that he would drive them for four hours to Austin in a model T Ford.[39]

Sam made a strong impression on Lyndon not only by his warmth of personality and his concern with his oldest son's well-being but also by being someone Lyndon could admire and wish to emulate. Between 1913 and 1920, in the seven years after Lyndon was five, when the family lived in Johnson City, Sam was a successful and prominent member of the community. He earned a good living by buying and selling real estate and cattle, investing in cotton futures, and holding a small interest in the local bank. Sam was able to afford maids for Rebekah, to drive "the biggest and most expensive car in the whole Hill Country," and make the Johnsons the best-dressed family in town. According to Lyndon, Sam was, financially and socially, among the top three men in the area.[40]

Although he had given up his seat in the legislature in 1908, Sam remained an important local political figure, a member of the " 'establishment' that made the political decisions and ruled the scene in Blanco and Gillespie counties." When prominent Texas politicians, including Governors Oscar Colquitt, (1911–15) and James E. Ferguson, (1915–17) came through Johnson City, they made a point of seeing Sam Johnson. During this time Sam also had a series of political triumphs that added to his local notoriety. In 1914 and 1916 he and Judge Clarence Martin, his brother-in-law, helped Ferguson gain the governorship by campaigning for him in Blanco, Gillespie, Kendall, and Llano counties. In 1917, after the United States entered the World War, Sam was appointed secretary of the Blanco County draft board. Later that year, when the representative to the Texas House from the 87th District resigned to report for military service, Sam announced his candidacy for the seat he had held ten years before. Since no one thought they could defeat him, he was unopposed in a special election in February 1918.[41]

In the legislature Sam's appearance, manner, and politics made him something of a stand out. Six-foot-two, with coal black hair, a big Stetson hat, hand-tooled boots, into which he tucked his pants, and a long-barreled, six-shooter on his hip, Sam was one of the few legislators who still wore a gun and looked like a cowboy. He also commanded attention by his behavior: a practical joker, loud, boastful about his family heritage, boisterous when drunk, as he often was on Saturday nights, Sam rarely went unnoticed. When he spoke to someone, he would get right up to them, nose to nose, clutching their arm, taking hold of their lapel, or wrapping his arms around their shoulders. In his politics as well he set himself off from the crowd. As in his earlier days in the legislature, he remained one of the few representatives who refused to sell out to the "interests." Though, like most other legislators, he still frequented the bars and brothels on Congress Avenue, he insisted on paying his own way.[42]

More important, he took up the cudgels for unpopular causes. He styled himself a latter-day Populist, a liberal, almost a radical Democrat who spoke for the people. But, in fact, he was more a practical idealist, a combination of shrewd politico and maverick who gained prominence in the legislature by identifying himself with the underdog. In 1914, for example, he put his support behind Jim Ferguson when professional politicians said that the tobacco spitting, suspender snapping "Farmer Jim, the Farmer's Friend," had no more chance of election "than a stump-tailed bull in fly time." Although Ferguson affected the manner of a poor, ignorant tenant farmer and called for laws limiting the amounts of cotton and grain landlords could take from their tenants, he was a well-off banker and businessman whose demagogy and corruption led to his impeachment, conviction, and removal from office in the first year of his second term. Despite Ferguson's misdeeds and antagonism to progressive Wilsonian Democrats, Sam Johnson insisted on the Governor's innocence and faithfulness to advanced ideas, describing him as a victim of rich farmers and special interests punishing him for helping the poor. Though Ferguson had sponsored laws serving the disadvantaged in the state, he also appealed to Sam by opposing Prohibition, a view Sam shared with many of his constituents.[43]

Sam's practical idealism also reflected itself in several of his political actions during 1918–20, when he served an abbreviated one-year and then a regular two-year term. During the World War, in a special "Burn the Germans" session of the legislature, Sam made his mark by opposing a sedition law providing imprisonment for anyone speaking out against American participation in the war or saying anything critical about the U.S. military or the flag. Urging patriotism tempered by common sense and justice, Sam managed to remove a provision in the bill authorizing Texans to arrest anyone considered disloyal. But the law passed by an overwhelming margin, leaving Sam as one of a few principled defenders of traditional civil liberties. If Sam's action satisfied his idealism, it also had the advantage of endearing him to German constituents, many of whom saw fit to abandon their Republican loyalties to vote for him in the next election. Similarly, Sam backed good roads, drought relief, longer free school terms, tick eradication, and cattle sale laws that were not only progressive but also clearly in the interests of his Hill Country constituents. In the most striking demonstration of his ability to be both principled and pragmatic, Sam voted to put a state constitutional amendment before the electorate on woman's suffrage and then opposed ratification of the 19th Amendment to the U.S. Constitution in the legislature after his district voted against the amendment.[44]

However forcefully Sam's shortcomings impressed themselves upon Lyndon in his first twelve or thirteen years, Sam's attributes drew the boy to his father. When Lyndon was three, he followed Sam everywhere. At the barbershop he insisted on sitting in a chair, having his face covered with lather, and, with the back of a razor, getting a shave like Sam. After the family moved to Johnson City in 1913 and Lyndon saw less of his grandfather, he grew closer to his father. After Grandpa Johnson died in 1915, "a feverish eagerness to resemble his father took possession of him." He looked to his father, Cousin Ava recalls, as a "partner, a buddy." Lyndon said later: "I wanted to copy my father always, emulate him, do the things he did. He loved the outdoors and I grew to love the outdoors. He loved political life and public service. I followed him as a child and participated in it." Lyndon "thought his daddy was a great man," a childhood friend remembers. Lyndon told him: "I want to wind up just like my Daddy, gettin' pensions for old people."[45]

Lyndon's interest in Sam's political doings were palpable. In 1914, when he was only six, he handed out literature for Ferguson and attended a rally for him in Johnson City. He also watched and listened as people visited Sam at his home to ask political advice. Sometimes he was allowed to sit with the men on the front porch or around the fireplace in the evening while they discussed local and state affairs. And if he was excluded from one of these meetings, he would hide in the bedroom next to the porch, listening through an open window to what was being said.[46]

In 1918, when Lyndon was ten, Sam began taking him to the legislature, where Lyndon would "sit in the gallery for hours watching all the activity on the floor and then would wander around the halls trying to figure out what was going on." Often, he would come on the House floor and stand or sit next to his father. Though he was not an official page, he would run errands for Sam and other members of the House. One legislator remembered him as being "a very bright and alert boy with plenty of energy and personality." He "was friendly to everyone." Another recalled how much, as a teenager, he was like Sam: Six-feet tall, skinny, dark hair and eyes, with huge ears and a large nose, he "walked the same, had the same nervous mannerisms, and Lyndon clutched you like his daddy did when he talked to you. He was a little on the rough side, too."[47]

The only thing Lyndon liked more than spending time in Austin with Sam was going with him on the campaign trail. "We drove in the Model T Ford from farm to farm, up and down the valley, stopping at every door. My father would do most of the talking. He would bring the neighbors up to date on local gossip, talk about the crops and about the bills he'd introduced in the legislature, and always he'd bring along an enormous crust of homemade bread and a large jar of homemade jam. When we got tired or hungry, we'd stop by the side of the road. He sliced the bread, smeared it with jam, and split the slices with me. I'd never seen him happier. Families all along the way opened up their homes to us. If it was hot outside, we were invited in for big servings of homemade ice cream. If it was cold, we were given hot tea. Christ, sometimes I wished it could go on forever."[48]

He was proud to be Sam Johnson's boy. After his father won reelection in November 1918, Sam took him to San Antonio for a celebration. There, in the largest city Lyndon had ever been in, they bought tamales and chili con carne from Mexican street vendors and visited the Alamo, where Lyndon saw paintings of Jim Bowie and Davey Crockett and a photo of Sam, recording the part he had played in saving the Mission.

Ben Crider, Lyndon's closest childhood friend, said: "He was very proud of his daddy's record as a member of the Texas House of Representatives. I have heard him speak of it a lot." Joe Payne recalls that when Lyndon once visited him in south Austin, they went to the state capitol, where he showed Payne Sam's picture in the House gallery.[49]

By the time Lyndon was twelve, Sam and Rebekah had ingrained more than politics in him. Although he was demanding and defiant, and particularly upset them by refusing to be a model student at the top of his class, he was in many respects the consummate expression of their wishes. Like Sam and Rebekah, he took a backseat to no one: he "was a distinctive person in the community," Emmette Redford says. "He managed to be a part of everything. . . . I used to think that if any incident occurred in town that was unusual, Lyndon would be the first person there in the front row."

Most of all, people remember his extraordinary self-confidence—his readiness to assert himself, to get up before a crowd, to take on challenges that intimidated most youngsters his age. Louise Casparis Edwards recollects that he was "always the speaker" in school. "You know, back in those days we were scared to death to get up on the stage. We were just shy little country kids. . . . I don't suppose he ever felt that way. It seemed like it was always just natural for him." When Lyndon was ten, future governor Pat Neff came to speak in Johnson City. "Ol' Lyndon went right up on the platform and shook his hand." He "had more guts than the rest of us," Tom Crider, Ben's brother, said.[50]

Ben Crider remembered that Lyndon "wouldn't run with anyone his own age. He wanted to be with older people, usually five to ten years older." Ben thinks he knew why: He was "a very brilliant young man and the boys his age wasn't his class mentally." But even the older boys couldn't hold Lyndon's attention when he could be with grown ups. Luzia Casparis remembers that "if there were some boys playing ball out in the yard and some men sittin' around whittlin' and talkin', you wouldn't find Lyndon out there with the boys. No, he'd be right in the middle of those men, listenin' and talkin'." But he wouldn't just talk; he would also argue and pontificate.[51]

Lyndon channeled some of his drive for attention and status into interscholastic debating and declamation. Although he had difficulty achieving an expressive tone because he mumbled, hopes of winning statewide acclaim made him dogged about developing his skills and preparing himself for the contests. The contrast between his commitment to school work and educating himself for public-speaking matches is striking. In 1921, when he was thirteen, he won first place in a meet in Fredericksburg for a speech on "Texas: Undivided and Indivisible," a plea against splitting Texas into several states. In high school, though members of the debating team had to get material from the University of Texas Extension Library and prepare themselves mostly in their spare time at home without the help of a teacher, it did not deter Lyndon. In 1924, his senior year, he reached the interscholastic regional finals. Defeating Blanco High in the county final by arguing against American entrance into the League of Nations, Lyndon and John Casparis, a classmate, went to San Marcos for the district final. But they were beaten there in a debate on whether the United States should withdraw its troops from Nicaragua, and Lyndon, who had dreams of winning statewide honors in Austin, "was so disappointed" that he "went right into the bathroom and was sick."[52]

Other than debate, Lyndon found few constructive outlets for his ambition and energy in his teens. Nevertheless, it was already apparent to some that he was a driven person. "He was a human dynamo," Joe Payne says. "It didn't make any difference what he was going to do. When he got ready to do it he wanted to do it right. He didn't want to wait around or poke around. In other words he was a human dynamo. I don't believe he ever got tired in his life. The time that I knowed him . . . he just never did run down."[53]

As a teenager, Lyndon also had an extraordinary ability to command approval, gain favor, and bend others to his will. Georgia C. Edgeworth, a classmate, says that "he could reason you right out of your shoes. He had a very pleasing personality and a very lovable personality. . . . If he wanted something, he knew how to go about getting it. And it wasn't fighting for it either. It was persuasion. . . . They should have named him the great persuader." Stella Gliddon believes that "there was never anyone that he wasn't friendly to. I don't care who it was. We had some codgers here absolutely chewing tobacco that could spit a mile. But Lyndon was their friend just the same." People who knew him a bit later recall similar traits. One of them emphasized the warmth of his personality; "he loved people and they loved him." Estelle Harbin, who worked with him in the early thirties, remembers him as having a divine sense of humor. "He was at his best when he was the center of attraction and telling all the stories." They would go for Sunday brunch at eleven o'clock to someone's home and most of the time they would still be there at five: "Lyndon maybe sitting on the floor in the middle of the circle, the center of attention. He would keep all of us in stitches for hours. He was great company."[54]

He had the ability to ingratiate himself with young and old alike. In high school he often convinced the girls in his class to do his math and English homework for him. When he wasn't prepared, he would get himself off the spot by distracting the teacher. Joe Crofts, one of his classmates, describes how he would divert the teacher's attention to something else, invariably bringing up a gag about which traveled the farthest the front or the rear wheel of a wagon. He was particularly adept at making older men and women like him. In his teens, he went around shaking hands with the older men and calling them by their names. He visited them when they were sick and always asked their opinions about all sorts of things. But it was the women—the mothers and grandmothers—who really took to him. He would hug and kiss them and call them grandma. "And all the women in town just *loved* him."[55]

Lyndon's characteristics were the product not only of parental influences but also of the larger community in which he grew up. Johnson City and the Hill Country played a significant part in shaping his life. Though he probably would have denied it, Lyndon had mixed feelings about the limited, parochial world of his early years. Larry L. King, a fellow Texan who knew him personally and has written about his career, believes that "he gained strength from the memory of always having led his village contemporaries in competition and from having come so far from Johnson City, and yet he privately wondered whether his potential or development had been curtailed simply because his root beginnings had not offered much in the way of day-to-day challenges. I imagine that sometimes he tossed in a sleepless bed . . . trying to balance out whether he had been all that special a duck or whether the pond simply had been too small." There is implicit confirmation of King's assertion in Lyndon's later comment to Doris Kearns: "My daddy always told me that if I brushed up against the grindstone of life, I'd come away with far more polish than I could ever get at Harvard or Yale. I wanted to believe him, but somehow I never could."[56]

Still, there was much more about the town and region that gave it a lasting hold on Lyndon's imagination. He not only often went back to visit his family and friends but also to live there. In 1957 he purchased the land and the ranch where he was born and his father and grandfather had lived. "I almost should have foreseen it," Lady Bird Johnson said in 1972, "because I think Lyndon was always heading back here." Stella Gliddon told a journalist after Lyndon's death in 1973: "I thought when I was tired of working I would move out of Johnson City. But I can't. I can't leave these people. They are so wonderful. . . . I think Lyndon felt the same way." Lyndon liked to quote Sam's remark that people in Johnson City "cared when you were sick and they knew when you died."[57]

A shared concern for each other's problems was a way of life in Johnson City. In the years between 1913 and 1927, when Lyndon spent most of his time there, it contained a homogeneous white, Anglo-Saxon, Protestant population. Though there were Baptists, Methodists, and members of the Christian Church, there was little intolerance and members of the three sects often attended a common service. In addition, there was little difference in living standards between the most and least affluent in the area. "It was a typical rural community," Emmette Redford says, and "there wasn't much social distinction." Georgia C. Edgeworth remembers the sense of community: "When you had sorrow . . . or a death in your family, it was the neighbors who went in and took care of your dead. . . . If someone was ill, some neighbor went in and sat up. . . . It was just like a big family town. That's all it was. And nobody was rich, and everybody had plenty to eat and plenty to wear, and Lyndon was no different from the rest of us. . . . I miss that little town, the feeling that you had there that everybody . . . would do anything for anybody else. . . . It was just a good, sweet country town." Some of these recollections may be partly the product of nostalgia, but they surely capture the general mood of the place and the time. It was not only Sam's example but the ethos of Johnson City that spawned Lyndon Johnson's later compassion for the disadvantaged.[58]

Much the same may be said of his ambition and life-long interest in politics. They were in the air in Johnson City. Georgia Edgeworth thought that everybody was ambitious because they didn't have much. Wilma Fawcett said that many kids dropped out of school after the eighth grade, but a lot didn't. Although the Johnson City High School was unaccredited and its graduates had to take additional work before becoming regularly enrolled college students, a considerable number of them went on to universities and became professionals—teachers, attorneys, businessmen, professors, and army officers. But hardly anyone became a scientist, and Emmette Redford believes it was because the school had no laboratories and no trained instructors that could develop an interest in science.[59]

The school and the town, however, generated an interest in government and politics. Scott Klett, the school superintendent, had attended the University of Texas Law School, was unusually well-educated for a high-school instructor, and taught a civics course that aroused great interest in Lyndon and his classmates in the workings of government. Moreover, Johnson City was the county seat, and it had a court house that attracted a great deal of attention when district court was in session and trials were being held. When Lyndon became President of the United States, reporters asked Emmette Redford, who had become president of the American Political Science Association, how a little place like Johnson City could have developed two people who achieved so much in the study and practice of government. Redford replied: "Well, there wasn't anything in town except three churches and a courthouse, and although Lyndon and I gave some attention to what was going on in the churches . . . we were more interested in what happened at the courthouse." Lyndon, of course, also had Sam's example to inspire him, but Redford's career and the active interest in public questions displayed by many of Lyndon's contemporaries suggest that it was more than Sam's influence that shaped his son's vocation. "I doubt whether there ever has been a group of kids with more intense interest in politics than the group that went through school with Lyndon," Redford believes.[60]

Ambition, charm, compassion, political concerns, and self-confidence were all parts of Lyndon's make-up, but they were muted in his early years by the preoccupations of a teenager with forging his own identity in a family beset by economic losses and reduced social status beginning in 1921. When Lyndon turned thirteen that year, he not only began the daunting rite of passage from adolescence into manhood, he also had to accommodate himself to Sam's transformation from a fairly successful family provider and member of the legislature into an economic failure and sickly man who had to give up his House seat.

In November 1919, almost three years after his mother had died, Sam had sold or mortgaged everything he owned to buy the 433-acre family farm in Stonewall from his brothers and sisters. Watching cotton prices soar to forty cents a pound in the aftermath of World War I and remembering that the farm had yielded a fair cotton crop six years before, Sam had hoped to make a financial killing. But floods in the spring and searing heat in the summer of 1920 had limited the size of Sam's cotton crop. Worse yet, a nationwide economic downturn coupled with an international cotton surplus in 1920–21 had driven cotton prices down to eight cents a pound. Instead of a financial bonanza, Sam had found himself burdened with some $40,000 in debts that forced him to sell the farm in 1922 and impoverished him until his death in 1937. Russell Morton Brown, an attorney and friend of Lyndon's beginning in the thirties, remembers that when Sam died he "had bills all over the place, and Lyndon had to pay them." A day or so after the funeral, Brown visited Lyndon in a "half-dark" office, where he sat rubbing his forehead and crying. " 'I'll never get all my debts paid,' " he said. " . . . I told him he would, and of course he did. But it wasn't easy. I remember there were tears running down his cheeks, and after I said we'd make it, he said, 'We'd better, buddy. We'd better.' "[61]

Despite his economic plight, Sam managed to remain in the legislature until the end of 1924. Moreover, during this time, he continued to make his presence felt. In 1921 he won passage of laws providing for roads in Llano County, free passes for state pensioners on railroads, and greater protection for wildlife in the Edwards Plateau region of Texas. In addition, he put himself in the forefront of a minority in the House supporting a resolution introduced by Wright Patman condemning the Ku Klux Klan. Although the Klan was weak in the Hill Country and Sam's action strengthened his standing with German-Americans in his district, he received a number of anonymous threats from "Kukluxsonsofbitches," as Sam called them, and lived with some justifiable concern for his safety. In 1923 he gave his name to the most important bill he backed during his legislative career, the Johnson Blue Sky law. To protect Texans from the sale of worthless stocks and bonds, particularly of nonexistent oil companies, Sam persuaded fellow lawmakers to add a securities division to the Railroad Commission that closely monitored the issuance and sale of public securities.[62]

Yet in spite of his success with the Blue Sky law, Sam was a distinctly secondary figure in the legislature. Someone remembered him as "a cadaverish-looking fellow with an Adam's apple," who "was never as much as a vice-chairman of a committee." Sam, in fact, was now in a bad way. To hold down expenses in Austin, he slept on a cot in a big tent he shared with thirty other legislators on the banks of the Colorado River. Hiring a cook, they managed to get by on less than a dollar a day for meals. His failure on the farm had forced him to move his family back to Johnson City in September 1922, where he was sick with an undefined illness. He was pale and gaunt and suffered from an outbreak of boils or "carbuncles" on his face. Though he managed to get up to the legislature in 1923, he came home before the session ended and took to his bed for a "good long time." Unable to earn an income, the family now began to live "from hand to mouth," "scratching to exist." People brought food to help feed the family, and Sam had to go deeper into debt to make ends meet. Unable to stay in the legislature any longer, he gave up his seat in 1924 at the age of forty-six and took the only job he could get as a two-dollar-a-day part-time game warden. He continued to spend time in Austin, where he would drink at the Driskill bar and then sleep off his drunks at a wagonyard on Congress Avenue.[63]

Sam's decline in fortunes coincided with an intensification of Lyndon's rebelliousness. The defiance he had manifested occasionally before he was a teenager now became a predominant feature of his behavior. At home he wouldn't do the chores his father assigned him, ordering his younger brother and sisters to do them for him. During meals he "ate with loud, slurping noises, violently cramming huge spoonfuls of food into his mouth" until Rebekah would burst into tears or she would make him leave the table. When Sam was away, Lyndon would ignore his orders not to use his shaving mug and ivory-handled straight razor. And when Sam was home, Lyndon would defy him by sneaking out the car after his parents had gone to sleep. Though Sam would often learn about it the next day and would punish him with a spanking, Lyndon continued to take the car without permission. "No one could boss him or persuade him to do anything he didn't want to do," Sam Houston Johnson recalls.[64]

His behavior outside of his home was similar. At school he established a reputation as an indifferent student who treated everything as a joke and scored B's chiefly because he was quicker than the other students and could fool his teachers. Despite his mother's strong ties to the Baptist Church, he defied her by joining the Christian Church. But it had more to do with a girl he fancied than with a genuine conversion. His childhood friends recall that he had no interest in religion as a boy and that he only went to Sunday School when his mother insisted. From the time he was fifteen he was more interested in running with his friends, sometimes staying out until three and four in the morning. Despite Prohibition, they bought or stole booze, got drunk, and drove recklessly. Once, they burned down a barn, and occasionally they taunted a local deputy sheriff, who was always after them. Fearing that Lyndon was turning into "a hopelessly incorrigible delinquent," Sam stormed about the house shouting: "That boy of yours isn't worth a damn, Rebekah! He'll never amount to anything. He'll never amount to a Goddamned thing!" And Grandmother Baines, a strict Christian lady, began predicting, "That boy is going to end up in the penitentiary—just mark my words!"[65]

Yet the family's concerns were overblown. Although he struggled with adolescent tensions, Lyndon was more in command of himself than his parents or grandmother believed. In May 1924, for example, he completed the eleventh and final grade of the Johnson City High School with more units than he needed to graduate. Not yet sixteen, he was the youngest member of the class and was believed to be the youngest graduate of the school. The class prophecy of the five other graduates was that he would one day become governor of Texas. However much the idea of being governor or making a great success of his life may have appealed to him, and however great the pressure from his parents and his peers at school, all of whom were going to college, he was not yet ready to embark on a fixed course toward some distant goal.[66]

Instead, he ran away to California. But even this was less the act of an incorrigible delinquent than of a defiant but ambitious teenager trying to find an alternate path to success to the one prescribed by his parents. In the spring and summer of 1924 parental pressure on him to go to college was unrelenting. Pressing him to understand that without an education he would be doomed to a life of hard physical labor, they insisted that he enroll in Southwest Texas State Teachers College at San Marcos. As best one can piece the story together from sketchy evidence, in the early summer of 1924 Lyndon entered the subcollege at S.W.T.S.T.C., where students from unaccredited high schools, like the one in Johnson City, could take the twelfth-grade courses needed for admission to the College. But it was apparently too much for him, and, as he later said, he "got kicked out of school." In a recurrent dream he remembered having at this time, he sat alone in a small cage with a stone bench and a pile of dark, heavy books. "As he bent down to pick up the books, an old lady with a mirror in her hand walked in front of the cage. He caught a glimpse of himself in the mirror and to his horror he found that the boy of fifteen had suddenly become a twisted old man with long, tangled hair and speckled brown skin. He pleaded with the old woman to let him out, but she turned her head and walked away." Waking in a sweat, he remembered muttering: "I must get away. I must get away."[67]

And so he joined a group of four Johnson City friends heading west in search of better things. Though Sam and Rebekah had refused to let him go and Sam had warned that he would yank him out of the car by his britches if he tried, Lyndon went anyway. Thoughts of adventure and an escape from hard times in Johnson City helped him rationalize his defiance of their wishes. The year 1924 was a terrible one for Hill Country farmers, and young men looking for work could find no jobs. California meant the chance to earn a living. "They thought they'd go out there and make a lot of easy money," Lyndon said later. Otho Summy, one of the boys on the trip, recalled: "They put out a report here that money was on trees out there and you would only have to reach up and get it." More than fantasy fueled their hopes: there was also the fact that Ben Crider and John Koeniger, two Johnson City friends, were working in California and that Tom Martin, an attorney, who was Clarence's son and Lyndon's cousin, was practicing law in San Bernardino.[68]

Contradictory stories about the trip abound: when Lyndon went, how long he stayed, and what he did in California. The best evidence suggests that the boys, Otto and Tom Crider, Payne Rountree, Otho, and Lyndon, left in July 1924 and spent up to ten days making the journey in a renovated 1918 Model T Ford. Traveling mainly at night to keep the car from overheating in desert heat, they followed a route across southern Texas to El Paso, over washboard and plank roads in New Mexico and Arizona, and across the Colorado River at Blythe, where they entered California with only $8 among them. Apparently Lyndon had no plan to stay very long in California. According to a Minnesota woman, a schoolteacher who made an automobile tour of the Southwest with three friends in that same summer, the boys stopped in Arizona to help them repair a spring on their car. When they agreed to drive up to the Grand Canyon together, Lyndon was "disappointed." He had promised his mother that he would be home in August for his birthday and going up to what was then called the Garden of the Gods would keep him from doing it.[69]

Circumstances put off Lyndon's return to Texas for over a year. After crossing into California, the boys went to San Bernardino, where Lyndon stayed with Tom Martin; the others headed north to Tehachapai, where Ben Crider, Otto and Tom's brother, and John Koeniger were working in a cement plant. Agreeing to have Lyndon work as a clerk in his law office and to train him to become a lawyer, Martin called Texas to obtain the consent of the Johnsons, which they gave, and then bought

Lyndon some new clothes and provided him with a room in his house. Although Lyndon enthusiastically seized the opportunity Martin offered and even persuaded him to let John Koeniger share his room and the law training Martin promised to give, the arrangement fell apart, largely because of Martin's unreliability. He told Lyndon that after studying law for a few months he would get him admitted to the Nevada and then the California bar, but Martin was making promises he couldn't keep. He was unaware that an applicant for the Nevada bar had to be twenty-one and that California required an applicant from another state to have three years' experience to qualify for a license. In addition, Nevada was in the process of setting higher standards that would have made it very difficult for Lyndon to qualify, even after four and a half years in Martin's office.[70]

Lyndon only learned about these conditions in the summer of 1925. But by then, Martin's behavior had all but convinced Lyndon and Koeniger that involvement with him might put them on the wrong side of the law. They had known that Martin had served in the Texas legislature, had won a medal as an officer in the World War, become chief of police in San Antonio, Texas, and then resigned to come to California when a grand jury considered indicting him on nineteen counts of wrongdoing ranging from consorting with prostitutes to failing to enforce Prohibition. Their trouble with Martin stemmed from a two-month drinking spree he began in the summer of 1925. While his wife and child were on vacation in Texas, he moved his mistress into his house, ran an almost continuous party, and delegated all the work of his office to Lyndon, Koeniger, and a secretary. They soon found themselves without enough money to buy groceries, so Lyndon took a part-time job as an elevator operator in the San Bernardino building in which Martin had an office. More disturbing, Lyndon and Koeniger realized that they were practicing law without a license and that, all things considered, their chances of becoming lawyers under Martin's supervision "weren't too good." When Tom's wife returned from Texas with her father-in-law in the fall of 1925, Koeniger quit to take another job, and Lyndon drove back to Texas with Clarence Martin. Although Lyndon later described his stay in California as a "vagabond life" tramping up and down the coast doing menial labor and earning barely enough to survive, the trip was a controlled experiment in adult living—a fifteen- or sixteen-month absence from home in relatively comfortable circumstances with a fixed purpose approved by his parents.[71]

Lyndon had gone to California not strictly to defy his parents but to fulfill their ambitions for him on his own terms. Although he had put geographical distance between himself and them, he remained strongly tied to home. He not only worked for Martin with their approval, he also reacted to Martin much as his mother might have. When Koeniger described Martin as a talented man, Lyndon agreed, saying "he has great ability, but his personal habits are not what they should be." He also told his Aunt Jessie that Tom Martin "charged them actresses from two to five thousand dollars to get them a divorce. . . . You know that wasn't right." Lyndon was no Puritan: he was capable of all sorts of things, then and later, that put him at odds with Rebekah's code of ethics, but he could also be as righteous as his mother. Moreover, when he wanted to come home, he called Sam for money. And when he arrived in Johnson City, he thought that his grandmother's patchwork quilt on the foot of his bed was "the prettiest sight I ever saw." [72]

He returned home, however, with mixed feelings. Although he had managed to stay away for over a year and, as he later told Ronnie Dugger, "felt on his own," he did not think of the trip as giving him the independence he craved. He came back "with empty hands and empty pockets," he said later. His cousin Ava recalls that they teased him unmercifully when he got home about having to "COD, call on dad. I'm in trouble I need money." They teased him that "he didn't come through, and we kidded him about being an elevator boy. . . . Oh, we was just mean, ornery." Worse, his parents renewed their pressure on him to go to college. But he still would not do it. Instead, he lived at home and relied on his father to get him a road construction job on the highway being built between Johnson City and Austin. Dependent on his parents for a place to live, earning only $2 or $3 a day in an exhausting job, Lyndon was more frustrated than ever. [73]

He gave vent to his tensions in a fresh outburst of rebelliousness. He became part of a group of young men called the "wild bunch." They drank, got into fights, held drag races in family cars they drove without permission, and defied the local sheriffs by stealing dynamite from the state Highway Department and setting it off in the middle of the night in town. At work, he was as defiant. One of the men he worked for complained that "he's the hard-headest thing I ever tried to work with. He could do better if he'd let you tell him something, but he won't listen." Once, he went to get some supplies for a tractor in Austin, where he apparently insulted the district highway engineer. The man showed up on the road the next day and "nearly fired everybody." Lyndon managed to stay on the job for over a year or until January 1927, when a new administration led by Dan Moody replaced "Ma" Ferguson as governor and notified all her appointees in the Highway Department, including Sam and Lyndon, that they would also be replaced. [74]

In the winter of 1926–27, Lyndon was going nowhere. He was still intensely ambitious and eager to be unique, special, someone people would notice and admire. He "always talked big . . . he had big ideas . . . and he wanted to do something big with his life," a co-worker on the road recalls. He also continued to call attention to himself by his dress and manner. He wore brightly colored silk shirts to evening dances and swaggered and strutted about the hall. But however much he might strut, at the age of eighteen and a half he was an uneducated and unskilled laborer who was about to lose his job. Moreover, on a Saturday night in February 1927, he met his "Waterloo," as Ava Johnson Cox says. He attended a dance in Fredericksburg, where his overbearing manner provoked a fight with a German farm boy who "had fists like a pile-driver" and beat him unmercifully until blood from his nose and mouth soaked his white silk crêpe de Chine shirt and Lyndon gave up. "But that was the making of it," Ava says. " . . . It made a believer out of him." It took all the wind out of his sails. It "made him realize that he wasn't cock of the walk." The next morning, after his mother cried and expressed bewilderment that "my eldest son would be satisfied with a life like this," Lyndon agreed to go to college.[75]

Lyndon left for college at age nineteen with well-defined character traits inherited from his forebears. Ambition, strivings for prominence, resentment against established authority and power, identification with the underdog, idealism and grandiosity, adaptability to changing circumstances—all, in one degree or other, were elements of LBJ's personality. But there was more to the mature Lyndon Johnson than the sum of these parts. He was not simply an offshoot of his ancestors but a distinctive person with ambivalent feelings about his parents and heritage which, combined with the influences of his environment, translated into contradictions that defy easy understanding. Yet he was no superman whose uniqueness deserves expressions of mystical regard. He was an exceptional character, but not so apart from ordinary souls that we can't make good guesses at what made him tick. As with all human beings, he exhibited patterns of behavior that repeated themselves throughout his life.

3

Student and Teacher

IN deciding to go to college Lyndon took on a substantial challenge. Although tuition, books, room, and board at Southwest Texas State Teachers College at San Marcos, where he intended to go, cost only about $40 a month, he didn't have the money. His father, who was losing his job and still in debt, could not pay his way, and Lyndon, who had almost no savings, was refused a loan at the Johnson City bank, where Sam had exhausted his credit. But like other poor youngsters in south-central Texas, who were the principal students at San Marcos, Lyndon scraped together enough money to attend. Rebekah or Sam, who had met Cecil Evans, the school's president, in Austin, arranged for Lyndon to have a twenty cents an hour, $8-a-month job on the campus clean-up squad collecting trash, removing weeds, and picking up rocks. Lyndon then persuaded Percy T. Brigham, who once worked as a law clerk for Rebekah's father and was the president of the Blanco bank, to lend him $75. Supplemented by another $25 from home, he had enough cash to meet the expenses of one term.[1]

But financing his education was just one of his problems. He also needed to satisfy the school's admission standards, and then discipline himself to do college-level work. Three years after graduation from high school, where he had never been diligent about his studies, he had reason to doubt himself. In frustration over Lyndon's refusals to enter college, Sam had told him that he didn't "have sense enough to take a college education." Sam's words now echoed in his mind.[2]

Yet his ambition to earn a college degree and make something special of his life outweighed his fears. The way he traveled from Johnson City to San Marcos reflected his determination to get ahead on his own. He refused his father's offer to drive him and hitchhiked. But instead of standing on the side of the highway thumbing a ride, he got "right out in the middle of the road," where a car would have to stop or risk hitting him. "He was a good hitchhiker," says Truman Fawcett, who saw him do it. "He knew how it was done."[3]

When he arrived at San Marcos, he went first to see Professor David Votaw, who evaluated high-school records and told college applicants what additional work they might need to gain admission. Votaw recalls that "very frequently students came with considerable fear" about proving themselves, but not Lyndon. He "sat down there and talked to me for . . . thirty or forty minutes, and there was absolutely no fear." Explaining that he had "a little bit of a roving disposition" and had been out seeing "some of the world," Lyndon expressed a wish to get an education as a way to understand government and help improve the world. "He outlined a program that he expected to follow. . . . He just about told me everything that he was going to do. . . . I was very much impressed with him. . . . He certainly appeared to know where he was going."[4]

Lyndon was putting up a brave front. When Votaw assigned him to the sub-college to prove his competency in English and math, Lyndon believed he would fail: "I thought sure it was back to the road gang for me," he said later. Although it was difficult, he satisfied the requirement in six weeks, the shortest time possible. He studied with an intensity he had never shown before and performed well in his English class, writing some themes his instructor described as "remarkable." An essay on politics impressed his teacher as stunning, and another on how society mistreated nonconformists was published in the campus newspaper. But plane geometry almost wrecked his plans. He recalled later how his mother "came to San Marcos and stayed up with me the entire night before the math exam, drilling me over and over until it finally got into my head." Even then, he made only a seventy, the lowest passing grade.[5]

On March 21, 1927, the start of the spring term, Lyndon became a regularly enrolled student. The recognition that San Marcos, as most students called the college, was a small provincial school with little standing in the world of higher education tempered his satisfaction at having gained admission. Opened in 1903 as a Normal School established to train public-school teachers, it only became an accredited four-year college in 1925. But even then, it barely met the standard. A library of 21,000 volumes and a single holder of a doctorate among its fifty-six faculty members, some of whom had no degree at all, gave it official standing in Texas as only a "third-class" college. Although it offered standard college subjects, such as biology, chemistry, economics, education, English, history, mathematics, modern languages, and physics, most of the college's twenty departments consisted of only one or two faculty members. Academic standards were lax and course requirements were closer to those of a high school than a college. Parochialism and a lack of diversity among students were other limitations. Almost all its

700 students, approximately 500 women and 200 men, were white Anglo-Saxon Protestants from south-central Texas. A handful of students with central and eastern European and Hispanic backgrounds attended, but the great majority were descendants of northern Europeans whose families lived on farms and in small towns within a hundred miles of San Marcos.

Nevertheless, to Lyndon and most of his fellow students, San Marcos had much to recommend it. Above all, it represented an opportunity to escape the rural poverty in which their parents lived. A degree promised the possibility of a better life through a career in education, business, dentistry, civil service, law, or medicine. As important, the schooling at San Marcos was inexpensive, costing generally no more than $400 for an academic year of nine months divided into three terms. Moreover, students could pay part of their way through the college by working in the school's administrative offices, book store, library, or construction and maintenance departments.

However limited its academic standing and however close to home, the college opened vistas many of the students had not glimpsed before. When Lyndon arrived in San Marcos in 1927, the campus itself, with its ten buildings, shops, laboratories, gymnasiums, and athletic fields, was an exhilarating beehive of activity. "Old Main," the principal campus structure on the highest hill in town, resembling a medieval castle with "spires, peaks and parapets," was the largest building many of the students had ever seen. A library with thousands of books, some teachers with degrees from universities as far away as New York, Chicago, and California, and visiting lecturers, theater, orchestral, and choral groups provided a measure of intellectual stimulation never before available to them. The social life and organized athletics at San Marcos had an even greater impact on boys and girls who had grown up in isolated communities. The chance to attend parties, dances, "Bobcat" basketball and football games or a movie theater showing the latest silent films, participate in an annual "Bathing Regatta" or parade on the San Marcos River, listen to groups of boys serenading coeds beneath dormitory windows, or dress like a fashionable twenties "flapper" were memorable events for San Marcos students. Southwest Texas State Teachers College was not the University of Texas, but to most of its students it was a new world in which they could grow and make a start on fulfilling what they thought of as "the promise of American life."[6]

As with so many other college freshman, Lyndon's first regularly enrolled term in college was a trial by fire. Despite his success in the subcollege, he struggled to make a creditable record. He received a "D" in debate or argumentation, an English class in which he didn't do much preparation and the teacher found him hard to handle. He also did poorly in grammar, describing himself as "a tired homesick freshman . . .

floundering in a sea of sentences in English 101." The rest of his work was passing or better, two C's and a B.

Financial worries may help account for his poor record. Having spent part of his $100 during the six weeks in the sub-college, he did not have enough money to get to the end of the term. Fortunately, Alfred T. "Boody" Johnson, a campus football hero and the boy friend of his cousin Margaret, Ava's sister, offered him a bed in a rent-free apartment Boody occupied above President Evans's garage. Clayton Stribling, another football player, who was already sharing the place with Boody, agreed to have Lyndon move in for only thirty days. Stribling, who knew Lyndon from the Johnson City high school, disliked him. He saw him as an overbearing manipulator who didn't pay his debts and got people to do his work for him. Although he knew that Lyndon "had trouble paying his board bills" and that his family was "scratching to exist," Stribling made Lyndon leave after the thirty days. He moved to a boarding house, but when Stribling left college soon after to help an ailing father run a ranch, Lyndon moved back in with Boody. The apartment had no bath and the boys had to go to the gymnasium to shower, but Lyndon viewed it as a godsend and remembered President Evans as being "very compassionate, very humanitarian" for letting them live there.[7]

Still, he found it nearly impossible to pay his way. Although he took the cheapest meal contract he could find, $16 a month for two meals a day, he still had to pay $17 a term for tuition, 75 cents a week or $3 a month for laundry, and, as he later said, "then you had to buy all your books and stuff, and so I just didn't have any money." Two meals a day weren't enough to fill him up, and he was often hungry. Fellow boarders at Mrs. Gates's boarding house on Edward Gary Street, where he took his meals, remember how he aggressively used his longer reach to take the biggest pork chop and the last biscuit he and other hungry boys jostled each other to get. The competition for the limited portions was so keen that Mrs. Gates required boarders to keep both feet on the floor when reaching across the table. Lyndon was also embarrassed at having to wear to class clothes that were too small for him.

He became so discouraged with the undistinguished school record he was making and, even more, with the constant financial pressures and deprivation he faced day to day that he laid plans to quit school and return to California. He wrote Ben Crider, who had returned there to work in a cement plant: "I just can't make it any more, I've got to drop out . . . I'm in debt over 40 or 50 dollars, I got tuition now, and I want to come out and get a job." But Ben urged him not to come. Knowing of Lyndon's discouragement, Rebekah had written Ben asking him to "help keep Lyndon in college." She also wrote Lyndon every day: "sweet cheery letters" that made him "feel so good." Although Ben told Lyndon that he could get him a job for $5 a day, he warned that it was "hell out here," a "lot of people getting lung disease" from breathing silica dust. To encourage him to stay in school, Ben sent Lyndon all his savings, $81. "I was the richest man on the campus," Lyndon recalled. "And I took that $81 and paid all my debts, and paid Dr. Evans back what I owed him, and paid my next term."[8]

Yet however much Ben's money helped, Lyndon knew it was only a temporary expedient. He needed ways to earn an income that could pay his way through each academic year. Since the eight or so dollars a month collecting trash was not enough to meet the need, Lyndon and possibly Sam or Rebekah asked Evans to find him a better paying job. Evans was an aloof, even distant figure to most students on campus, but Lyndon, living over his garage, began getting closer to him by doing things for Mrs. Evans when her husband was out of town. He and Boody would go to the grocery store for her or "move something if it was bad weather." Moreover, Lyndon worked uncommonly hard at his trash-collecting job, imagining himself in a race to clean up the most trash in the least time. Consequently, when he asked the President for a job mopping and sweeping floors in the College's buildings, a job normally reserved for athletes and paying $12 a month, Evans made him assistant to the janitor in the Science Building. Lyndon later said that he practiced debating and political oratory while pushing a broom down deserted corridors and halls late at night. "He made speeches to the walls he wiped down, he told tales of the ancients to the doormats he was shaking the dust out of," Ronnie Dugger notes. "I literally swept my way through teachers' college," Lyndon remembered.[9]

By the close of the spring term, Lyndon had decided to earn a two-year teacher's certificate as quickly as possible. This meant attending school for six straight terms or until the end of the 1928 summer term. He still could not do it, however, on $12 a month. And so, soon after getting the janitor's job, he asked Evans to make him an assistant to Tom W. Nichols, an instructor who was also the President's part-time secretary. Proposing to carry messages that, without campus telephones, had to be hand delivered, run other errands, and watch the office while Nichols was out, Lyndon persuaded Evans to make him an office boy earning $15 a month. "The first thing you want to do," Lyndon told Cousin Ava as they were walking on the campus one day, "is to know people . . . and don't play sandlot ball; play in the big leagues . . . get to know the first team. . . . 'Why, Lyndon,' she said, 'I wouldn't dare to go up to President Evans's office!' He replied, 'That's where you want to start.' "[10]

Another possibility for earning expenses was to edit the *College Star*, the student newspaper. It was one of the best paid jobs on campus—$30 a month. Although Lyndon managed to get on the editorial staff during the summer term of 1927, he was too inexperienced a journalist and too

little known on campus to become the editor. To overcome both obstacles, he began writing editorials. Exercises in stilted prose, conventional
homilies, and boosterism, Lyndon's essays celebrated fathers, courtesy,
patriotism, honesty, happiness, diligence, and Southwest Texas State
Teachers College. Father must be the "producer, the provider, and the
protector." In times of trouble, "he must square his shoulders, resolutely
grit his teeth, suppress his emotions, and with renewed courage meet
the issue." Lamenting the loss of "civilities and courtesies that were
exacted in former years," Lyndon condemned "this swiftly moving money-
mad age" and urged a return to "the demure graciousness of . . . our
grandmothers." Happiness was "a state of mind and heart" achieved
through "honest, upright lives." Defending the College bookstore against
complaints of high prices, poor service, and inferior goods, Lyndon urged
students to "boost" it. As for the College itself, it was "a splendid training school" that "not only trains, but inspires." Lyndon's essays are notable for their awkward style and familiar verities, but they effectively
served a nineteen-year-old boy aiming at a better job that could help
him earn a teacher's certificate.[11]

His appearance and determination to reach his goals made an indelible impression on fellow students, instructors, and administrators during the 1927–28 academic year. They recall a tall, lanky, "big, all bone,
Western boy," six feet three and a half inches, with black, curly hair,
and brown eyes. Described as "a slat," nicknamed "old rattle and bones,"
Lyndon had to "kind of unwind to get up" in class, where he usually
sat with his legs crossed or curled under him. Though some remember
him as handsome, he was self-conscious about his looks and took special pains with his appearance, usually dressing in a suit with a bow tie,
which became one of his trademarks. Before a date he would spend
considerable time studying himself in a mirror, "patting his hair to be
sure the waves were right" and scrunching "his neck down into his collar to make his face seem fuller." Appeasing painful doubts, he would
banter with his roommate about their irresistibility to girls.[12]

Fellow students remember his being in perpetual motion, "always in
high gallop," never resting or letting up. He was "clamoring for recognition," one classmate says. "It pained him to loaf," another recalls. He
was constantly rushing about the campus, walking "with long, loping
strides, almost like a trot." "I can see him going up the side of that hill
now," Vernon Whiteside recalls, "swinging them long arms, just walking like the seat of his britches was on fire. . . . And he always looked
busy. He could look busy doing nothing." "He was aggressive . . . had
a quick answer for everything," and left most everyone convinced that
he "was going somewhere." A close campus friend describes him as
"the only fellow I ever knew who could see around the corner." [13]

His assertiveness, an affinity for exaggeration and distortion, and an obsequiousness toward campus authorities offended some of his San Marcos contemporaries. Another of Mrs. Gates's boarders recalls how Lyndon wouldn't let other boys get a word in edgewise: "He'd just interrupt you—my God, his voice would just ride over you until you stopped. He monopolized the conversation from the time he came in to the time he left. I can still see him reaching and talking, reaching and talking." By contrast, he was unfailingly deferential and often even worshipful toward the faculty: "Words won't come to describe . . . how kowtowing he was, how suck-assing he was, how brown-nosing he was," another classmate says. Fellow students also remember how he would exaggerate his family's importance, his father's political influence, and his own successes with women, as a debater, a student, and a campus notable. "Lyndon would have you believe, if you'd listen to him, that there wasn't anybody in the Alamo except Johnsons and . . . Bainses," Vernon Whiteside says.

Some students derisively took to calling him "Bull" Johnson. Clayton Stribling says it was because he tried to "shove" and "push" people. "It was like a balking mule. . . . [He] bulled his way through." "I think they called him 'Bull' because of the amount of talk he put out," another student recalls with gentlemanly restraint. Ella Porter, a classmate and friend, who "never did call him that," associates the word with "somebody that was always talking a lot and saying a lot that maybe people didn't believe or didn't have a lot of respect for." Others are more blunt: They say it stood for "bullshit." "That was what he was generally called," one explains. "Because of this constant braggadocio. Because he was so full of bullshit, manure, that people just didn't believe him." [14]

Lyndon was overbearing, self-centered, and all too ready to ease his own self-doubts with overblown descriptions of his virtues. But he also had qualities that endeared him to most of the people he met. He was not only aggressive and ambitious but also extraordinarily personable and empathic or understanding of other people's interests and concerns. He spoke long and loud, but he also tried to amuse and please his listeners. At the boarding house he didn't simply take the floor, he entertained his tablemates with political stories and imitations of amusing characters.

He was an exceptionally warm person who made friends easily and took a genuine interest in them. Willard Deason, a classmate and lifelong associate, recalls how he and Lyndon got into a dispute while trying to outdo each other in a math class. Afterward Deason stamped out into the hall expecting a fight, but Lyndon, wrapping his long arm about Deason's shoulder, made amends and they became fast friends. "Lyndon would drape that big arm around you and he'd get his mouth about an inch from yours and look you right in the eye," another classmate remembers. He would hug and kiss the mothers of his friends and fervently clasp the hands of their fathers. "He was so warm and affectionate," Boody Johnson says. "The first time I brought him home, he grabbed my mother and hugged and kissed her, and my sisters—my father said, 'That boy you brought down here—I thought he was going to kiss *me!*' " Despite being so "aggressive and full of ambition," Lyndon "had time to talk to everyone," an admirer from San Marcos recalls. Lyndon remembered everyone's name and "was very diplomatic and . . . genuine" with them. "He was sincere in what he was doing. And you knew that," this classmate says. And so along with the drive and ambition and self-centeredness, there was a quality of caring and helpfulness. "He had a good word for everyone and something to say to everyone. And you couldn't possibly pass him without talking to him. He was just that type of person—you wanted to speak to him." [15]

At San Marcos, Lyndon was a paradox: driven, grating, self-serving, on one hand; warm, enjoyable, giving on the other. It was less contradictory than it seems. The two sides of Lyndon were comfortably linked: in return for the attention, influence, and power he craved and aggressively pursued, he gave concern, friendship, and benevolent support. "Some men," Lyndon said much later, "want power simply to strut around the world and to hear the tune of 'Hail to the Chief.' Others want it simply to build prestige, to collect antiques, and to buy pretty things. Well I wanted power to give things to people—all sorts of things to all sorts of people, especially the poor and the blacks." [16]

The ethos of the 1920s in America generally and in rural Texas in particular reinforced Lyndon's impulses to advance himself and serve the less fortunate. Lyndon's views on ambition, duty, work, sacrifice, and service were the accepted pieties of his place and time. During most of his college years, Calvin Coolidge, who "suggested the rugged honesty of the New England hills, rural virtues, clean living, religious faith, public probity," served in the White House. As the historian William E. Leuchtenburg writes, "In years when American society was changing at a frightening pace and Americans sought security by incanting their continued allegiance to older virtues at the same time that they were abandoning them, Coolidge was the most usable national symbol the country could have hoped to find." "It is not through selfishness or wastefulness or arrogance, but through self-denial, conservation, and service, that we shall build up the American spirit," Coolidge said. Such attitudes were particularly alive in "small-town Texas where," as Doris Kearns observes, "success was a reward for virtuous effort, ambition was an admired good, and there was little room for cynicism." In his eagerness to succeed and simultaneously benefit others, Lyndon was not only satisfying some inner need but also conforming to the social norms of his day. [17]

His attitudes and actions found ready acceptance from the San Marcos faculty and administrators. They viewed him as an exceptional young man, but not because of his academic performance. Although he later boasted that he got almost all A's in college—in thirty-five out of forty or thirty-eight out of forty-five courses—his school work was generally undistinguished. He told Ronnie Dugger that he had about a B— average, which is borne out by his transcript: the record shows a total of 51 academic courses with 11 A's, 22 B's, 14 C's, 4 D's, and 1 F in Physical Education, a subject in which he "displayed supreme disinterest" and one for which President Evans apparently allowed him to substitute special written assignments.[18]

His high standing with the staff rested partly on Lyndon's conscious efforts to ingratiate himself with the men and women who were judging him. He took special pains to flatter his instructors, invariably agreeing with them and often "sitting at the professor's feet." In informal bull sessions on the campus, "he would just drink up what they were saying, sit at their knees and drink it up, and they would pour out their hearts to him," one student remembers. Lyndon also made a point of lauding them in his editorials. One he wrote about President Evans in the summer of 1928 is typical: "Great as an educator and as an executive, Dr. Evans is greatest as a man. . . . With depth of human sympathy rarely surpassed, unfailing cheerfulness, geniality, kind firmness, and friendly interest in the youth of the state, Dr. Evans has exerted a great influence for good upon the students of S.W.T.S.T.C. He finds great happiness in serving others."

Lyndon "had a very high appreciation of the faculty," Professor David Votaw recalls. "Sometimes there is a sort of animosity of students against the faculty. . . . But Lyndon, . . . he thought an awful lot of Dr. Evans and of Dr. [Alfred] Nolle [Dean of the College] and in fact every faculty member that he came in contact with. . . . That was a thing that marked him in my mind. I never forgot it." On a later occasion, Votaw recalled Lyndon's "strict devotion to his assignments, to duty, his organizational ability, his attitude toward the College and society. He had a respect for the faculty and the people under whom he worked. This was quite noticeable to me and others that I have heard speak of it." Although deference and flattery helped make Lyndon a favorite with the College staff, his behavior was not strictly the product of cynical self-interest. Lyndon had a genuine regard for many of these people, as his concern and interest in them long after leaving college would demonstrate.[19]

Furthermore, deference was only one element in Lyndon's appeal to the staff at San Marcos. Were this the only or even principal side of his relations with faculty and administrators, it would have been insufficient to make him as popular as he was with them. Lots of other students also took pains to flatter their teachers. Did Lyndon act obsequiously toward the professors? an interviewer asked Vernon Whiteside. "Didn't we all?" he replied. Lyndon's characteristic ability to win the affection of older people was probably more important. "My parents loved Lyndon," Ella Porter says. " . . . Because he paid attention to them and he showed interest to older people always. I think that was one of the things that got him with . . . the faculty members that he was close with . . . I think some people have that ability, and he certainly had it, to be sort of empathetic with older people."

Lyndon's uniqueness among a student body of seven hundred was even more important. His friend and fellow student Wilton Woods recalls that Lyndon "was seeking information from any and all professors and he talked to them at length after hours about everything, but of course anything political. And there were so few [like him]. Apparently of the seven hundred at San Marcos, he was probably the only one doing that. The rest of them were interested in playing poker and a hundred other things, but not interested in politics or how people got elected. But Lyndon was." During 1928, an election year in which a President, a U.S. Senator from Texas, and a host of other national and state candidates were to be chosen, Lyndon besieged his friends with "marathon talk about political personalities and how he would run a campaign if he were a candidate." "He was a fighter," one of Lyndon's teachers recollects. "The college faculty was not accustomed to a student with such initiative." [20]

Lyndon made a lasting impression on most of his teachers, but he had a particularly strong impact on Professor of Government H. M. Greene and President Evans, the two men on campus most interested in politics. In what was to become a career pattern, Lyndon established warm relations with the two older men who, acting almost as surrogate fathers, encouraged and supported his ambitions.

Greene and Lyndon had a special affinity for each other. Neither was particularly bookish, getting information by talking and listening rather than by reading and reflecting. "I had gone through a whole lot of experiences that Lyndon went through," Greene told an interviewer in 1965. "I didn't have opportunities in school either, not even access—not even to high school. Had to pick up dirt myself. And I had to learn by listening. I didn't have time to read, but I could work at something else and listen. So, I was quite sympathetic with that attitude." Lyndon was "a carbon copy of Mr. Greene," Dean Nolle said. "Greene was not a profound scholar, you never saw him in the library, but by osmosis or something he just knew what was going on in the political world and in governmental circles. Lyndon and he had a rapport there that was just remarkable." [21]

Like Lyndon, Greene also knew how to command attention. "A short, stocky man with a thick thatch of gray hair and furrowed forehead al-

ways tinted by a green eyeshade," he cultivated a number of eccentric-
ities that made him an unforgettable character. He lived with his wife
and six children in a small frame house in the hilly part of San Marcos,
where they seldom cooked, ate out of cans, and had more books than
furniture. They were the subject of much town gossip. Spending most of
their time at a rustic cabin in the Hill Country west of San Marcos, the
family ran an experimental farm and cross-bred pigs, coming up with a
"strange strain" that became the Professor's "pride and passion." On
campus he was also a standout among the faculty. Usually dressed in a
faded khaki workshirt, worn trousers that never matched his jacket, and
an unknotted tie, he was once mistaken for "a tenant farmer in need of
employment." In class, he sat with his feet on the desk, while talking
and chewing tobacco, which he would spit into a chalk box in his desk
drawer. Most appealing to Lyndon, Green was a provocative instructor,
challenging students to debate contemporary questions and freely expressing his own liberal-populist views on the need for government policies that protected the poor from the rich. Also a fervent patriot and
democrat, he "taught love and respect" for America and preached the
conviction that "democracy is worth any price to freedom loving people."

Lyndon admired not only the way he endeared himself to an audience
but also the substance of what he said. Years later, after Lyndon had
gained high public office, he made a point of visiting Greene in San
Marcos, where he told students, "I didn't go to Harvard or Yale. But I
believe Prof. Greene knows more government than any professor up there.
When the going gets rough, I draw upon the wisdom of his teachings."
He also once brought him to Washington, D.C., where he introduced
him to President John F. Kennedy, declaring, "Here is the man who
started the fire under me. He gave me my first course in government
and my last." And Lyndon wasn't wholly exaggerating. As a student, he
worked hard to win Greene's approval and to learn all he could from
him. Greene couldn't have been more receptive. From the first, he saw
Lyndon's "reactions" as "high class," and believing that Lyndon had
"*superior*" political talents, Greene encouraged him to pursue a career
in politics rather than teaching. Occasionally, he would turn to Lyndon
in class and say, "Son, if I were headed for the political arena, I would
bear in mind that the United States Senate is one spot where a man of
integrity has a real opportunity to serve his country."[22]

Lyndon's political interests also endeared him to President Evans or
"Prexy," as he was called. The son of an Alabama probate judge and
the brother of Hiram Wesley Evans, the Imperial Wizard of the Ku Klux
Klan in the twenties, Prexy had a lifelong absorption with politics. Two
San Marcos colleagues believed politics was his hobby or diversion. But
Emmett Shelton, a graduate of the College and prominent Texas attor-

ney, thought it his vocation: he "was much more of a politician than . . . a teacher," Shelton said. As the president of the Texas teachers college closest to Austin, he became the spokesman or lobbyist in the state legislature for all the state's teachers colleges. In addition, Evans kept daily diaries, little red books full of scribbled notes on local, state, and national politics. Unlike his brother, however, Cecil Evans was a moderate Democrat with little sympathy for the Klan. Although he wouldn't commit himself publicly on the Klan issue, he privately told Hiram that he had no use for the organization. When Hiram came to San Marcos to speak to the Klan, Cecil wouldn't let him stay with him.

As with Greene, politics gave Lyndon special ties to Evans. Boldly approaching him as he walked across the campus or engaging him in conversation while mopping the hallway outside his office, Lyndon impressed Evans with his knowledge of state affairs. Soon after Lyndon became his office boy, Evans began taking him to Austin, where Lyndon would report to Evans on what occurred at committee hearings Evans could not attend. In time, he also relied on Lyndon to prepare reports to state agencies and to draft letters to legislators. Like Greene, Evans also encouraged Lyndon to become a politician rather than an educator, telling him that "A teacher is a law unto himself in the classroom. His views aren't challenged very much—you don't have to develop your full potential." [23]

Lyndon's work in Evans's office strengthened the tie between them. As Tom Nichols recalls, "Lyndon looked eagerly for assignments because he knew instinctively that service in the office was his opportunity to make the favorable impression which he was determined to create." Seated at a desk in Evans's outer office, Lyndon turned himself into an appointments secretary, announcing the arrival of visitors and encouraging the impression that people had to go through him to see the President. Also carrying messages between the President, other administrators, and the faculty, Lyndon was looked upon as a representative of the administration. To dramatize his efforts, Lyndon "would make a systematic and prompt report back to President Evans when any assignment was completed," Nichols said. "I have seen him standing at the President's elbow holding a written list of the items to which he had devoted himself, calling these off and checking with his pencil as the signal that each had been completed; and, furthermore, he frequently saw other things which he believed should be done, and made sure that these, too, had been included in the list as finished." Evans later kidded Lyndon, "you hadn't been in my office a month before I could hardly tell who was president of the school—you or me." [24]

"President Evans was attracted to Lyndon—who wasn't?" Tom Nichols said. "Lyndon was far superior to the average student who had been employed to work in the President's office." Evans himself recalled: "I was tremendously fond of him. We promoted him to increasingly responsible positions. . . . He could handle people extremely well." And none better than Evans himself, to whom Lyndon eventually felt so close that he joked with him and once even slapped him on the back in public, an expression of familiarity no other student would have dared. Sensitive to Evans's idiosyncrasies, Lyndon learned to stay on his good side. Whenever the President came back from a trip, he would be "very tired and very irritable." He would come in and immediately shout, "Get me Speck." Dean of Men Henry Speck, who "was always frail and sickly," would arrive "in agony," as if "he was meeting his maker." Evans would give him "holy hell, just chewing him out from one end to the other and he took a chunk out of me every now and then!" Nichols told Lyndon after one of these episodes. Fearful that he "was liable to get involved," Lyndon made a point of being out of the office until the President "kind of got adjusted" after a trip.[25]

Evans was a compassionate man who did all he could to help students stay in school. But he was particularly generous with Lyndon. When they needed money, Boody Johnson remembers, Evans would let him and Lyndon paint his garage, paying them forty cents an hour, twice the ordinary pay or the equal of craftsmen's wages. They did the job three times in two years, moving Evans to remark, "It might not be the best but it was certainly the most completely painted garage in San Marcos." When Lyndon graduated from the College, Prexy told the audience: "Here's a young man who has so abundantly demonstrated his worth that I predict for him great things in the years ahead. If he undertakes his tasks in the future with the same energy, careful thought, and determination that he has used in all his work in the classroom, on the campus picking up rocks, or as an assistant in the president's office, success to him is assured."[26]

Lyndon's activities during the 1927–28 school year extended not only to establishing himself as an exceptional young man in the eyes of faculty and administrators but also to participation in a number of campus clubs: the Harris-Blair Literary Society, the Schoolmaster's Club for future teachers, and the journalism society. He was also one of six students selected by Professor Greene as a member of the debate team. Beginning with the winter term 1928, Lyndon was only a sophomore, but Greene paired him with Elmer Graham, a senior, as the College's principal debaters. Traveling to other teachers' colleges in south-central Texas, Lyndon and Greene would pass the time on trips swapping off-color stories that offended Graham, who was training to become a Baptist minister. Lyndon also bothered Graham by overstating to fellow students his role in their debates. Despite their differences, they were a highly effective team, winning most of their debates and capturing the unofficial title of state champion in the spring of 1928. Graham, who had been out of school for four years preaching church sermons, was comfortable leading off with the basic argument and presenting closing summations. Lyndon's job, for which he had an impressive flair, was to answer the argument of the other team. He would calmly hammer away at opponents' weak points with jibes and sarcasm that would call into question the whole thrust of their case and sometimes would unnerve them. As his first full calendar year on campus came to a close in March 1928, Lyndon took satisfaction from having gained favor with the faculty and administration, being a successful debater, and winning election as editor of the *College Star* for the 1928 summer quarter.[27]

His failure, however, to become a Black Star, the most influential student group on campus, put a pall over his other achievements. A secret organization made up exclusively of athletes, the Black Stars initially devoted themselves to campus high jinks, breaking College rules by stealing chickens for barbecues or going to a speakeasy for a few drinks. By the mid-twenties, however, five years after it began, it had become an exclusive group enjoying special privileges and political power. As athletes, Black Star members went to the head of the cafeteria and registration lines, received the best housing assignments, and missed chapel without punishment, something other students could not do. The Black Stars also chose class officers and members of the Student Council, which selected the editors of the *College Star* and the *Pedagog*, the campus annual, and allocated student activity fees, assuring that the bulk of this money would be spent on athletics rather than debates, guest lecturers, or music and drama programs. In addition, the Black Stars associated with coeds belonging to the Shakespeare Literary Society, the leading campus social club made up chiefly of the prettiest girls.[28]

Boody Johnson, the head of the Black Stars, was Lyndon's closest college friend. They were seen together so often that people took to calling them "Johnson and Johnson." Boody tried as hard as he could to make Lyndon a Black Star. First, he urged Lyndon to go out for the baseball team, but when nothing came of that, he proposed him for membership anyway, arguing that Lyndon was close to Prexy and "could help us out if we needed it." When this didn't win Lyndon an invitation, Boody told them that Lyndon had read their secret constitution, which Boody had left lying about their apartment, and that they should admit him as a way to keep their rules secret. Both Boody and Lyndon later claimed that a single blackball, by a boy Lyndon had crossed, barred Lyndon's admission.

But others contend that the opposition was more widespread. Lyndon wasn't an athlete, and "there wasn't a chance in the world for him to get in there," Clayton Stribling says. Other Black Stars remember that they "laughed" in Lyndon's face, and told him, "You're too scrawny and skinny, and we want real men." Willard Deason and Emmett Shelton think it was more than that: "He was never very popular with his fellow students . . .," Deason says. "They thought he was arrogant. They may have been jealous of him because he had so much energy and could accomplish so much." "Lyndon was not too popular the first year or so he was down there," Shelton believes. "He was what you'd call a horse's ass. He chose his own friends, and by doing that he kind of ostracized himself from the others." The 1928 *Pedagog* echoed Shelton's point: the "Cat's Claw" or humor section of the annual included a picture of a jackass with the caption: "Lyndon Johnson—As he looks to us on the campus every day."[29]

Whatever the cause of Lyndon's exclusion from the Black Stars, it hurt him and stirred his competitive urges to outdo the people rejecting him. But an effort to square accounts had to wait another full year, until 1929-30. Continuing financial problems forced him to leave College in the fall of 1928. The $15 a month he was earning in President Evans's office wasn't enough to meet his expenses. To stay in school during the first nine months of 1928 he borrowed more money from several sources. In February, for example, he wrote a family friend that he was "in considerably straitened circumstances," that his work for Dr. Evans provided only limited funds, and that his father, who was now trying to help Rebekah, Lyndon's sister, attend San Marcos, could not help him. To make additional money, Lyndon sold "Real Silk" hose to people on campus and took a night job downtown stuffing envelopes for 25 cents an hour. Although he earned about $30 a month by these means, enough to pay his school expenses for a year, he found it impossible to live on this amount of money. In the summer of 1928 he had to borrow $2 from campus friends to pay his tuition and to persuade Mrs. Gates to let him eat on credit for three months.

During the six terms he attended San Marcos, from March 1927 to September 1928, he had indulged in luxuries he couldn't afford: clothes, expensive dates, trips to Austin, Houston, and San Antonio, frequent visits to the barber for forty-cent haircuts and twenty-five-cent shaves, and a used car on which he soon couldn't make the payments. One college friend remembered the first time Lyndon sold "Real Silk" hose on campus. He went from boarding house to boarding house waking up all the "country boys" attending the 1927 summer session. When he returned at two in the morning, he had sold over four hundred pairs of socks and had earned $42. The next day he and a friend took off for Nuevo Laredo, where they spent all the money. After he finished college, an uncle, with whom he was living in Houston, pressed him to pay off the debt he had accumulated while at San Marcos. When the uncle left town for a holiday, Lyndon went on a spree. Learning from Aunt Jessie Hatcher that Uncle George was abroad, Lyndon said, "Good . . . I'm going down here to this Pig Stand and I'm going to eat all the ice cream I can hold." And that was "instead of paying on his debt," Aunt Jessie told an interviewer. "Now, that was just as typical of him as anything on earth."

Yet if Lyndon had an affinity for self-indulgence, he was also enormously hard working and eager to earn what he spent. Consequently, during 1927–28 he had made certain to take the five education courses required for an elementary-school teaching certificate. He then arranged for a $125-a-month job beginning in September 1928 at a Mexican-American grade school in Cotulla, Texas, a town southwest of San Antonio and sixty miles north of the Mexican border near the Nueces River. At a time when the average annual salary for male teachers in Texas was $93.50 a month, Lyndon was to be unusually well paid. When he came to Cotulla, he learned why.[30]

It was "a little dried-up . . . dying" place that Lyndon remembered as "one of the crummiest little towns in Texas." The surrounding area was a flat, treeless, wilderness called the South Texas brush country, where temperatures of 110 degrees baked the summer landscape, and infrequent torrential rains turned dirt roads into muddy streams. A combination of range grass and "every type of thorny vegetation known to the Southwest" made the Nueces Plains the birthplace of the state's great cattle industry. Beginning as a cow town in the nineteenth century, Cotulla was notorious for its outlaws and gunplay. When Missouri-Pacific trains approached the town, conductors exclaimed: "Cotulla! Everybody get your guns ready." The gunplay, a chronicler of the town's history says, "would have done justice to a Western movie, only Cotulla had deadlier marksmen, with 20 townspeople and three sheriffs getting shot to death." One of the few town amusements in the early days were public hangings, which were done from a tree limb before large crowds.

When Lyndon arrived there in September 1928, the town had become more peaceful and had added certain creature comforts like running water, electricity, and fifteen paved streets in the business district. But it was still a major cattle center, with its 3000 residents making up almost half the population of LaSalle County. Three-quarters of the town's inhabitants, however, were Mexicans living in hovels or dilapidated shanties without indoor plumbing or electricity on the east side of the Missouri-Pacific railroad tracks. Treated "just worse than you'd treat a dog," Lyndon later said, the Mexicans worked at the nearby ranches and farms for slave wages. Many of the Anglos to the west of the tracks were not much better off, living in small wooden houses built on stilts to protect them from termite infestation.[31]

Despite the depressing prospect of spending the better part of the next nine months in such impoverished surroundings, Lyndon was determined to make a favorable impression that would recommend him to other school boards as an outstanding teacher. A local farmer remembers that on his first day in town he got out of his car dressed in a suit and tie and trudged through a muddy field to introduce himself as Lyndon Johnson from Johnson City, the new teacher for the fifth, sixth, and seventh grades in Welhausen Elementary School. Named after a county judge, the segregated Mexican school on the east side of the railroad tracks was housed in a relatively comfortable two-year-old red brick building. There was little else about the surroundings, however, that was attractive or calculated to encourage learning. Rows of dilapidated hovels on nearby streets, a debris-littered vacant lot in front, and a dirt-covered playground with no equipment to the rear provided the school's setting.[32]

The children themselves contributed to the feeling of deadening poverty. The twenty-eight boys and girls in Lyndon's combined class left an indelible impression on him. He remembered youngsters "mired in the slums . . . lashed by prejudice . . . [and] buried half alive in illiteracy." Most of them came to school in the morning "without any breakfast, most of them hungry," with a look in their eyes and a "quizzical expression on their faces" that asked, " 'Why don't people like me? Why do they hate me because I am brown?' " Most of them, who would only get two or three months' schooling a year, were "taught that the end of life is a beet row, a spinach field, or a cotton patch." And Lyndon later recalled lying in bed and hearing the hum of motors before daylight hauling the kids off in a truck to work on the neighboring farms in the middle of the school term.[33]

The wretched condition of his students struck a sympathetic chord in Lyndon. Where the other five teachers in the school, all local women from influential families in the town, kept their distance from the children, doing the minimum required in their jobs, Lyndon threw himself into the work with unbounded energy. "I was determined," he said later, to help "those poor little kids. I saw hunger in their eyes and pain in their bodies. Those little brown bodies had so little and needed so much. I was determined to spark something inside them, to fill their souls with ambition and interest and belief in the future. I was determined to give them what they needed to make it in this world, to help them finish their education. Then the rest would take care of itself." Though he could be terribly overbearing and intrusive with his pupils and though there was almost a desperate urgency to his desire to give them good things, as if he were filling himself with the attention and affection he so badly craved, he nevertheless provided his students with a rich, unforgettable school year.[34]

Upon his arrival in Cotulla, W. T. Donaho, the school superintendent, asked Lyndon to be Welhausen's principal as well as one of its teachers. Accepting, Lyndon "moved right in and took over." He would arrive before everyone else in the morning and be the last to leave in the evening. "He didn't give himself what we call spare time," one of his fellow teachers said. "He seemed to have a passion to see that everything was done that should be done—and that it was done right," the school's janitor remembers. As in San Marcos, he was in perpetual motion. "I used to patch his clothes," the owner of a cleaning shop recalls. "He wore blue serge trousers sharply creased. They shined like a silver dollar. And he walked so fast, it was like seeing a blur." One of his students also remembers his distinctive way of walking, "with the fast and swinging movement of his arms." [35]

At school, he was all business. When he entered class in the morning, he expected students to be ready to greet him with a song he had written to a popular vaudeville tune.

> How do you do, Mr. Johnson,
> How do you do?
> How do you do, Mr. Johnson,
> How are you?
> We'll do it if we can,
> We'll stand by you to a man,
> How do you do, Mr. Johnson,
> How are you? [36]

Students had to speak English, complete daily homework assignments, and strictly mind the teacher. Failure to comply with any of the rules resulted in prescribed punishments. Fifth-grade boys who showed up in class unprepared had their ears pinched. "He would start down the row every morning," one student remembers, "and ask, 'Did you do your lessons?' If the boy said no—yank. . . . It hurt like the dickens." Girls were spared physical punishment, but they were tongue-lashed and had to stay after school. Boys in the sixth and seventh grades who wouldn't mind Lyndon were spanked. If he heard you saying just "Buenos dias" on the playground, one of them recalls, he turned you over his knee. Years later many of the boys remembered those spankings with stems Lyndon cut from palm trees. "I could hardly sit the rest of the day," one of them said. Dan Garcia never forgot the time he got caught imitating Lyndon in front of the class when he thought the teacher was still out of the room. Lyndon grabbed him by the hand, marched him to his office, and whacked him across the rear a dozen times. [37]

Lyndon was equally demanding with the teachers under his charge. He wanted them to work as hard as he did. Seeing that they would leave the children unattended during recess, going to the bathroom to smoke, and that the students, who had nothing to do on the empty playground, would fight, Lyndon used his first pay check to buy a volleyball and a softball and ordered his five teachers to supervise play activity. But they didn't like it, and when Lyndon left town one Friday afternoon, they told the superintendent that they were going to strike. " 'Our traces are down and we have balked,' " they advised Donaho. Although they were related to the most important people in town, the mayor, the postmaster, and a leading banker, Lyndon wasn't intimidated. He went to the school board, which backed him and agreed to let him hire five new teachers from San Marcos if the strikers refused to follow his orders. Unwilling to risk their jobs, they gave in.[38]

Despite Lyndon's applying the most "stringent rules" ever set in a Cotulla school, students and teachers "were all crazy about" him. The Mexican children and their parents were astonished at an Anglo teacher who was so interested in their well-being. "He put us to work. But he was the kind of teacher you wanted to work for," one of the pupils says. "You felt an obligation to him and to yourself to do your work." "This may sound strange but a lot of us felt he was too good for us," Dan Garcia recounts. "We wanted to take advantage of his being here. It was like a blessing from the clear sky."

Lyndon gave the children a sense of importance most of them had never known before. He distributed packages of toothpaste his mother sent him and organized extracurricular activities—debate, declamation, spelling bees, band, baseball, track—and a parents-teachers association to help with after-school functions. Moreover, he encouraged all of the children to believe that they could do something better with their lives—become a teacher, a doctor, even President of the United States. Although Lyndon's version of the American dream had little relation to their reality and although he showed little regard for their own heritage when lecturing them on the virtues of speaking English and the justification for a Texas independent of Mexico and American annexations in the Mexican War, he nevertheless left them and his fellow teachers believing that he had "helped" them "tremendously." Lyndon himself felt that he was doing valuable work. In a *Star* editorial he published while in Cotulla, he said: "As the pied piper with his flute charmed the children to wander to a land beyond, so the ideal teacher leads his students into a magic land of beauty whose treasures await their grasp." The year in Cotulla sensitized Lyndon to the deprivation suffered by what would later be called America's "invisible poor." It also encouraged him to believe that people in a position of authority or power could open avenues of opportunity to the disadvantaged that would serve not only themselves but society as a whole.[39]

His sense of accomplishment sustained Lyndon through a difficult year. He felt painfully alone in Cotulla. He kept himself as busy as possible, working long days at his job and becoming the volunteer debate and basketball coach at the local high school, tutoring Welhausen's janitor in English, and taking two courses each quarter in a San Marcos extension program. Nevertheless, at times he got terribly homesick and longed to be in Johnson City with his family or back at school in San Marcos with his friends. "Sometimes Lyndon would be as serious as an old man," his landlady recalls. Instead of his characteristic friendliness and talkativeness, he would become withdrawn and wander up a hill on the edge of town, where he would stare out into the distance.[40]

His moodiness was partly the result of his separation from Carol Davis, a young woman from San Marcos he had thoughts of marrying. Although she was teaching in Pearsall, which was only thirty-five miles away, and he would visit her on weekends, there were problems with the relationship that troubled both of them. Lyndon remembered falling "in love with her the first moment we met." She was "very beautiful, tall and blonde with dark blue eyes. Her skin was pale and very soft. She was very clever and everyone admired her. . . . She seemed so much more alive than all the other girls I knew, interested in everything." But Carol's father, who was a prosperous businessman, objected to her involvement with the son of an impoverished, "no-account" Hill Country family he supposedly characterized as a "bunch . . . of shiftless dirt farmers and grubby politicians." Although Carol was much taken with Lyndon, she also had her doubts. But they were less about Lyndon's social standing than his temperament. She saw the two of them as having sharply different interests: She loved music and "picture shows," while politics, which consumed Lyndon, bored her. Lyndon also wondered about the match: " 'Miss Sarah,' " he told his landlady, " 'this girl loves opera. But I'd rather sit down on an old log with a farmer and talk.' " As status conscious as Carol's father, Lyndon was ambitious to marry well: his attraction to Carol partly rested on the advance in social standing and financial security he would have gained from marrying her. For in spite of his recognition of how ill-matched they were, he aggressively pursued the relationship until the spring of 1929 when Carol rejected him for another suitor.[41]

Fortunately for Lyndon, he returned to San Marcos in May, where he re-established contacts with friends and threw himself into a variety of activities that dulled the pain of his rejection. Returning to campus with enough money to pay his way at a rooming house, he rented a room with Boody Johnson at Mrs. Miller's on North Comanche and once again took his meals at Mrs. Gates's place. Though they lived in a small hot room with no fan and a double bed, which they divided by tying a sheet down the middle, Boody remembers that they "had a lot of fun." One source of entertainment was Vernon Whiteside, a Texan, who had just arrived on campus after two years at New York University on a track scholarship. "If you're in for a tiresome afternoon," the *College Star* advised summer students, "look up Whiteside—his line will keep you quite awake but take it with a grain of salt." In the fall, when Boody left school, Lyndon moved to Mrs. Hopper's house on West Hopkins, where he shared a "big screen porch" with three other boys, Ardis Hopper, Mrs. Hopper's son, and Elvin Reed, popular football players, and Fenner Roth, a freshman on a baseball scholarship. Since every first-year student was assigned to run errands for an upper classman, Roth became Lyndon's "freshman."[42]

Attending the summer quarter, in which he took a six-instead of a normal five-course load, Lyndon also became the secretary of the Schoolmaster's Club and the summer editor of the *Star*. Idealizing his chosen profession, he put the activities of the Schoolmaster's Club on the front page of the newspaper and celebrated the virtues of teaching in his editorials: "Though the world gives little credit to those who in . . . our schools give their lives in unselfish service to those boys and girls who go to learn, the respect and honor these teachers receive from those whom they seek to improve in mind and character is proof that, after all, it is better to carve one's name upon the hearts of men than upon marble walls." "The teacher has a great work before him," Lyndon wrote in another editorial. ". . . His task is indeed a great one fraught with wonderful opportunities for usefulness and power." Giving in to wishful thinking, Lyndon predicted that "there is a new day coming in America, when . . . great monuments will be erected to teachers as creators of significant life; when our school and university buildings will be like cathedrals in their dignity and beauty and wealth will deem itself honored to endow them."[43]

In the year between September 1929 and August 1930, when Lyndon received his B.S. degree in education and history, he worked at a feverish pace. "I never worked so hard in all my life," he said later. He squeezed twenty-three courses into four terms, including three terms of student teaching in civics and government. He particularly devoted himself to the practice teaching at the Demonstration High School in San Marcos, where one of his students remembers how alive and interesting his classes were: "He was very vivid. He walked around, and he slung his big, old long arms out and pointed and gestured," and spoke "loud" and "fast." He was "so handsome"; "all the girls had crushes on him." He had "an amazing personality"—"charming," "kind," and "humorous." As in Cotulla and during his previous year and a half on campus, he was a whirlwind of activity. He resumed his work in President Evans's office, became the president of the Press Club, rejoined the Harris Blair Literary Society, participated in Pi Gamma Mu, the national social science honor society, served on the Student Council, and remained on the *College Star* as an editorial writer.[44]

He also took a leading part in broadening control of student affairs. In the summer or fall of 1929, a group of seven or eight students, including Lyndon, organized a secret society named Alpha and Omega to challenge the exalted position of the Black Stars or football players and other athletes on campus. The initial driving force behind the idea was Vernon Whiteside and Horace Richards, particularly Richards, a born promoter, who collected money at a pep rally for nonexistent party decorations and took all the profits from labels sold by coeds boosting the football team. Whiteside and Richards were incensed at a campus tradition which discouraged the prettiest coeds from dating anyone but athletes. The Shakespeare and Idyllic clubs, both chiefly made up of the prettiest San Marcos girls, were "snooty and wouldn't invite us to their parties or special dances," says Wilton Woods, one of the original White Stars, as the group came to be called. The Black Stars and the "town" girls formed a "clique" that viewed themselves as an elite and "looked down" on the rest of us, Whiteside asserts. "They considered us all trash." Lyndon also remembered how hard it was for non-athletes to "get a date with a good looking girl," and how the "in" group monopolized control over student government and campus publications.[45]

"To get a place in the sun," as one of them put it, the White Stars, which expanded to at least thirteen members during 1929–30, launched an effort to take control of campus affairs and displace the Black Stars as the dominant force. In January 1930, at the start of the winter term, when, as at the beginning of every term, elections for class officers were held, the White Stars mapped a plan to replace Dick Spinn as senior class president with one of their own. They chose Willard Deason, a handsome, articulate boy who made himself popular on campus by remembering everyone's name and home town after one meeting. But Spinn, a football and track star who had easily won election in September, seemed almost impossible to defeat.

The White Stars, however, had the advantage of surprise, Lyndon's determination, and the resentment many students felt toward privileged athletes. Keeping the existence of their organization a secret, the White Stars operated "on the sly" and "hit them" before they knew what was happening. Their strategy was to woo student non-athletes who had never bothered to vote before, using the slogan "Brains are Just as Important as Brawn." By election eve, however, Deason was still about twenty votes short, a significant deficit in a group of fewer than 200 voters. "Most of us were ready to throw in the towel," Deason remembered. But not Lyndon. He decided to go after the YMCA group of students, which seemed certain to vote for Spinn, who was a member. But many of these students were receptive to the brains over brawn appeal and to Lyndon's "uncanny instinct" "to look a man in the eye and do a convincing job of selling him his viewpoint." Deason recalled how Lyndon began "making rounds to the dormitories and buttonholing folks. And . . .

between ten o'clock at night when we disbanded and voting time the next morning, he switched about twenty votes, and I won by a narrow margin."[46]

Encouraged by their victory, the White Stars decided to mount a broader campaign in the spring. They made an all-out push to elect their candidates to all class offices, win control of the Student Council, and choose the Gaillardians, the school's seven prettiest or most popular girls, who received special attention in the pages of the *Pedagog*. They adopted a threefold strategy in the campaign: keep the Black Stars from making an organized effort by hiding White Star activities; identify the various groups and individuals on campus who would support the White Stars; and appeal to the resentment most students felt toward a campus elite receiving special privileges. The first part of the White Stars' plan worked particularly well. According to at least one of the Black Stars, his group "wasn't ready for anything like" what the White Stars did. Had the Black Stars been better organized, Ardis Hopper said, they could have won the elections. "They had the leadership there to do whatever they wanted to do." A systematic effort to reach potential supporters also paid dividends. Lyndon recalled how he got the keys to the Registrar's office "and got all those little old yellow cards, grade cards and it was the end of the term and I got everybody that had a B average and I just invited what I thought was people with superior intellectual potentiality." In talking to these students, the White Stars were able to play effectively on their antagonism toward the "ins," "the little man's resentment of the big man."[47]

Yet for all their efforts, the White Stars believed that they would lose unless they cut some sharp corners. They "courted" or dated girls who agreed to run for class offices and Student Council and seemed likely to vote with the White Stars if elected. To assure that their candidates were chosen, the White Stars voted in the elections of all four classes. Since most students didn't attend the College for four straight years, often dropping out for a year or two to teach, it was difficult to keep track of which class anyone belonged to. Consequently, on election day, the White Stars went from one room to the next claiming to be members of the class. In addition, they steamrolled the other students who showed up. Making Horace Richards temporary chairman at each class election before anyone knew what was happening, Horace and his fellow White Stars manipulated nominations and final votes. If a popular Black Star wanted to run for class president, they nominated and elected him to lesser office, opening the way for one of their candidates to win the higher position. Moreover, Horace arbitrarily cut off nominations, shouted down efforts to keep them open, and declared all White Star candidates winners whether or not the "Ayes" for them represented a majority.[48]

Because elections of Gaillardians were campus-wide rather than by class and were more carefully scrutinized, the White Stars resorted to a different stratagem. Confident that three of their candidates would win, the White Stars won a victory for a fourth girl by forcing Ruth Lewis, a popular campus activist, out of the race. Lyndon warned her that unless she quit the contest he would expose the fact that she had once pretended to be attending the University of Texas rather than San Marcos. Threatening to write an editorial saying that she was ashamed to be identified with San Marcos, Lyndon, in the words of another White Star, "blackmailed her right out of that election."[49]

Holding a majority of Student Council seats after the spring elections, the White Stars asserted themselves in behalf of their constituents. Lyndon, who gained a seat on the Council as a representative of the junior class, remembered forty years later that he ran roughshod over his opponents. I just [took] every damn dime away from the Black Star activity. It nearly killed Strahan [the athletics director] and his outfit. I gave to the Band and I gave to the theatre, to the dramatic club, and I gave to the debaters . . . . It was a pretty vicious operation. . . . They lost everything that I could have them lose. My first real Hitler-type operation. I got them off of everything there was, and I mean I broke their back doing it. It's been broke for a good long time." Some of Lyndon's schoolmates also remembered him as being "ruthless," as ready to "cut your throat to get what he wanted." "A lot of people at San Marcos didn't just dislike Lyndon Johnson"; one of them said, "they despised Lyndon Johnson." And one biographer, elaborating on this theme, described him as having won control at San Marcos "believing in nothing—without a reform he wanted to make, without a principle or issue about which he truly cared. . . . He had demonstrated, moreover, not only a pragmatism . . . but a cynicism . . . as well. . . . A cynicism— and a ruthlessness. He didn't merely count votes; he stole them. . . . Pragmatism had shaded into the morality of the ballot box, a morality in which nothing matters but victory and any maneuver that leads to victory is justified—into a morality that is amorality."[50]

There seems little question but that Lyndon played a major part in the White Stars' underhanded seizure of class offices and the Student Council and the nasty pressure applied to Ruth Lewis to give up her bid for Gaillardians. Also, there is persuasive testimony that he measurably contributed to reallocating campus activity funds and having friends of the White Stars supplant students slated to edit the *Star* and *Pedagog* in the 1930–31 academic year. The loss of these jobs not only embittered the displaced editors but also forced one of them, who needed the salary for tuition and expenses, to leave school.[51]

Yet, at the same time, Lyndon saw a need to accommodate his opponents and create a consensus that could sustain his influence. As would be the case throughout his political career, he saw the advantages in being politic, compromising differences, and converting adversaries into supporters.

For all his later talk about overwhelming opponents and breaking backs, he in fact operated within limits. One restraining influence was H. M. Greene, who, according to Fenner Roth, Lyndon's classmate and friend, advised the White Stars "what to do and what not to do." Convinced that a democracy "is made up of strongminded men" whose "concerted action must be a compromise," Greene, Roth said, kept the White Stars "from going too far." Ardis Hopper, the captain of the football team and the president of the Student Council in the spring of 1930, believed that Lyndon's "ability to compromise and to see two sides of things probably began to develop about that time. . . . We argued for months over the distribution of the blanket tax fund," Hopper said. " . . . The way it finally turned out, we compromised it. We just kind of split it down the middle. But he didn't have to do it because he had the votes to win it." Lyndon may have liked to think of himself as doing in the Black Stars during his senior year, but the truth is his recollections were faulty. Having won the upper hand over them, he acted magnanimously, splitting student fees between athletics and other activities. It was in character with his other actions: given recognition and control, he became the benevolent patron, the *pater familias* tending to the needs of his dependent charges. It was an echo of his behavior toward the disadvantaged students at Cotulla and a prelude to what he would do in his later political career.* [52]

In the Cat's Claw section of the 1930 *Pedagog*, Lyndon's opponents roasted him for overblown rhetoric and cozying up to authority: "Believe It or Not"—"Bull Johnson cannot out talk Senator Heflin" and "Bull Johnson has never taken a course in suction." It also attacked the White Stars' role in the spring elections, depicting Lyndon and his friends surrounding a black girl—the "nigger in the woodpile," Whiteside said, referring to their manipulation of the vote. But it also recorded Lyndon's affinity for political compromise, describing a visit of "Politicus Bird" to campus to ask him: "What makes half of your face white and the other half black, Mr. Johnson?" No doubt, the question suggests a contempt for someone who was two-faced, but it also implies that Lyndon was very much the politician maneuvering between two factions with which he remained on good terms. [53]

Lyndon's affinity for politics was not confined to the San Marcos campus in 1930. In July, during his last term at the college, he involved himself in a state Senate campaign that would later open the way to his

*Why did LBJ so exaggerate what he did to the Black Stars? An impulse to overstate his importance and impact on others was characteristic of him. It also seems well to remember that his comments on crushing the Black Stars occurred in 1970 after he had lost political power and was accommodating himself to the most decisive defeat in his political career.

first job in Washington, D.C. In the summer of 1930, Pat Neff, the former governor who had made Sam Johnson a $150-a-month bus inspector, was running for election to the state railroad commission. In the rising tide of economic depression, Sam could ill-afford to lose a job that depended on Neff's return to office. A regular feature of election-year politics in south-central Texas was an all-day picnic at Henly, a crossroads west of Dripping Springs, where candidates for state and local office appealed for voter support. When the time came for Pat Neff to speak, no one came forward. Having been characterized by his opponent as a stuffed shirt who never went fishing or hunting, Neff's absence seemed to confirm the implicit charge that he was an elitist who had lost touch with the people.

Forewarned that Neff would be absent from Henly, Sam Johnson would not let him "miss this splendid opportunity to get your candidacy before the people." "Would anyone speak for Pat Neff?" Judge Stubbs, the master of ceremonies, asked the crowd. "You get up there and make a talk, Lyndon," his father said with seeming spontaneity. "I will make a speech for Pat Neff," Lyndon shouted as he pushed his way through the crowd and climbed up on the back of a wagon. Introduced as "Sam Johnson's boy," Lyndon "made the goddamn most typical speech you ever heard," a vigorous, ten-minute "arm-swinging defense" of Neff as governor and railroad commissioner. "I'm a prairie dog lawyer from Johnson City, Texas," he began. "You have heard a man say that Pat Neff doesn't hunt or fish. I want to remind you of the way these Austin sports come into your hills and shoot your cattle when they're supposed to be hunting deer," Lyndon said, referring to Neff's opponent. "I ask you if you want a city-slicking hunter who doesn't know a cow from a deer to be in charge of your railroad business and your bus line business and your oil business, or do you want a man whose character is unimpeachable?" Although the last speech of the day, given in the dark except for the light from two or three campfires, it was the "hit of the Henly picnic," receiving loud applause and whistles.

Lyndon made a particularly strong impression on Welly Hopkins, a member of the Texas Lower House running for the state Senate. "Immediately attracted and impressed," Hopkins asked the twenty-one-year-old Lyndon to become his campaign manager. "Sure I'll do it if I can call all the shots in Blanco, Hays, and Comal counties," Lyndon replied. Believing his campaign would benefit from a young man who knew "almost every man, woman and child in Blanco County and has a wide acquaintance in Comal, Kenall and Guadalupe . . . ," Hopkins turned his campaign over to him in those four counties, where "he did a magnificent job." Lyndon arranged rallies, printed and distributed literature, made speeches, and organized "a traveling claque" of White Stars who worked the crowds when Hopkins spoke, cheering and applauding until it ignited the audience to respond. He also traveled the "by-ways" with Hopkins, leading him "up every branch of the Pedernales" and into "every dry creek bed" where there was a vote to be found. Hopkins won his primary by a wide margin. Having established a reputation as a "wonder kid . . . who knew more about politics than anyone else in the area," Lyndon accepted an invitation to run Edgar Witt's fall campaign for lieutenant governor in eight Hill Country counties. Witt carried all of them.[54]

Although Hopkins took him on a week-long holiday to Mexico, Lyndon's success as a campaign manager did not translate into any other immediate return. But Lyndon hadn't assumed it would. In the spring, he had asked Uncle George Johnson, his father's brother, to help him get a teaching job in Houston. A successful high school history teacher in Port Arthur and Beaumont, Uncle George had become the chairman of the history department at the Sam Houston High School. Using his considerable influence with E. E. Oberholtzer, Houston's school superintendent, Uncle George got Lyndon an appointment in his school as a public speaking and business arithmetic teacher at $1600 a year. With the Depression forcing a freeze on hiring, however, Lyndon's job depended on a vacancy in the school. When it hadn't occurred by September, he took the only teaching job he could get—a $153-a-month position teaching government and speech at Pearsall, the town thirty-five miles north of Cotulla where Carol Davis had taught. Although he "took on the task as though the future of America depended on what he taught those children," he couldn't wait to get to Houston.

Hence, when an opening appeared there in October, he persuaded the Pearsall superintendent George Barron, whom he had not told about the Houston job, to let him go. As Barron remembered it, Lyndon "came into my office, took a seat on the corner of my desk, and abandoning all formality, he said: 'George, I look upon you as an older brother. I feel somehow that you have a kindred feeling toward me. If I didn't feel that way toward you, I wouldn't make this request.' " Describing his Houston offer, Lyndon explained that it would allow him " 'to attend night school and study law. I don't want to leave you, but what I am looking for in life will not be found in Pearsall, although I do love this little city and all of its people.' " Barron was "a bit stunned at . . . having to give up a teacher of such promise," but, not wanting to hold him back from a better job, he agreed on the condition he could find a replacement. Having anticipated Barron's concern, Lyndon proposed that his sister Rebekah and a friend take his place at the same salary the school was paying him.[55]

Houston and its central high school with nearly 1700 students and seventy teachers provided Lyndon with larger opportunities. Located fifty miles above the Gulf of Mexico with a population of almost 300,000, the largest of any Texas city, Houston was a haven for people on the make. To be sure, in the fall of 1930, the unemployed and hungry haunted the downtown streets, leaning against walls, sitting on window ledges, standing in bread lines, and waiting to eat at soup kitchens. But some Houstonites continued to prosper in the City's cotton, lumber, and oil businesses or from the millions of dollars spent by the Federal government on the construction of a shipping channel from the Gulf to make Houston a major world port. Moving into a two-story house on Hawthorne Street, ten blocks from the Sam Houston High School in the downtown area, Lyndon lived with seven relatives, his widowed Aunt Jessie (Johnson) Hatcher and her daughter, his Aunt Ava (Johnson) and Uncle John Bright, who was also a teacher, their two daughters, and his Uncle George, with whom he shared a room.[56]

Uncle George was especially helpful to Lyndon. A judicious and reserved man, except on the subject of politics, Uncle George occasionally reined in his "impetuous" nephew, whom he would caution "about the quicksands" in his job. Uncle George also fanned Lyndon's already keen interest in politics. An "old-time Democrat," who "woulda voted for a yellow dog if he were running on the Democratic ticket," Uncle George idolized Andrew Jackson, William Jennings Bryan, and Joe Bailey, whose speeches he could recite by heart. Although he had no political aspirations of his own, he loved to orate, which he sometimes did from a second-floor balcony to students assembled in the school's open courtyard. The setting and Uncle George's style of speaking reminded listeners of Italy's Benito Mussolini and won him the nickname of "Senator." George "thought Lyndon just hung the moon," and he encouraged him to think about running for something.[57]

But in the fall of 1930, when Lyndon arrived at the Sam Houston High School, his mind was focused on being the best speech and debate instructor, and maybe even the best teacher, the school had ever seen. In almost no time at all, he impressed himself on his colleagues and students as "a steam engine in pants." He worked "as if his life depended on it," a fellow teacher said. "That man is going to be a big success someday," another remarked as she watched him rush along a corridor between classes. "He'll be ahead of everybody. No one else can keep up with him." And he knew it. When the school's principal told him that Sam Houston High had never won the city debating championship, Lyndon assured him that now they would and that they would be state champions as well. Moreover, when the principal rejected his request for money to take his debaters on a trip, saying it had never been done, Lyndon replied: "Yes, but you've never had a teacher like me."[58]

He was right. Focusing his extraordinary energies on building winning debate teams, he "darn near talked debate twenty-four hours a day." Teachers and students remember him as "literally on fire," never relaxing, never attending "bull sessions" never wasting "a single moment." And the students he choose for the teams, Margaret Epley and Evelyn Lee from among the girls and Luther E. Jones, Jr., and Gene Latimer from the boys, had to live by the same standard. Insistent that they give up their leisure time and spend afternoons practicing and evenings searching in the city library for "arcane references to the jury system," the subject of that year's Interscholastic League Debates, Lyndon thoroughly dominated his debaters. How to stand, how to dress, how to use their hands, what they said, how they said it, nothing escaped Lyndon's attention. Interrupting, heckling, shouting at them until they got it right, he demanded that everything be perfect.[59]

Once he had selected his teams and "worked the life out of them" getting ready for the competitions, he scheduled an unprecedented series of fifty practice debates taking them all over south-central Texas. Crisscrossing the lower part of the state in a Model A Ford, Lyndon insisted on practice sessions even as they drove between cities and towns. Their efforts were rewarded with easy victories in all their practice contests and in the city and district competitions in April. In the finals at Austin in May, however, the bubble burst, with the girls losing in the opening round and the boys being defeated in the finals by a three to two vote. The defeat literally made Lyndon sick: he ran to the bathroom, where he threw up.[60]

By driving his debators so hard and getting them so close to a championship, he became something of a celebrity in Houston and won reappointment for a second year with a raise, one of the few given by the school board in the midst of the Depression. The success of his teams benefited the students as well as himself. It gave them great satisfaction. As with his disadvantaged pupils in Cotulla, he gave his Houston debaters a sense of shared commitment and pleasure in what they did. If he pushed them to their limits, they recognized that he brought himself to the brink of exhaustion too. Further, he did all he could to make the work enjoyable. He encouraged students to get up in front of his speech class and be silly, making noises like animals, pretending it was all a game until they could feel more comfortable about public speaking. He asked students to give a speech on "string" or the subject "spit is a horrid word." When no one took up the first challenge, he spoke on "string" for fifteen minutes. During long car rides with his debaters, he not only had them practice he also joked and sang with them, mimicked people, and regaled them with long, entertaining stories.[61]

He also made them feel accepted and valued by him. He took genuine satisfaction in their performance: "To see them stand up there and defeat the state champions, without a note in their hands on a subject with such basic and fundamental importance as maintaining a jury system, was a thrilling experience I shall never forget," Lyndon said later. "They were children just in high school with no constitutional history background and with no governmental background. The depth of their feeling that the jury was essential was impressive." During the competition he would sit in the back of the auditorium and "once in a while he opens his mouth in amazement at how clearly I am making a point," Gene Latimer remembered. "He sits up very straight and looks about in wonderment at the audience to make sure they're not missing this. And it is then he makes me think I . . . am in the process of improving on the Sermon on the Mount." "No one before or since has ever motivated me like he could motivate," Latimer added. "I guess if he told any of us to go get up on a roof . . . and jump off, we'd all pile up there and do it."[62]

He also ensured that his debaters got as much outside approval as possible. He arranged extensive coverage in Houston newspapers of their activities, persuaded the editor of the *Houston Press* to put up a $100 award for public speaking, which he divided among his four debaters, and staged pep rallies that got the high school as excited about debate as football. At one of their early debates, only seven people showed up. By the time the district and state championships had rolled around, however, the team's success and Lyndon's promotional efforts filled the auditorium, with an overflow crowd standing in the back. Despite falling short of the state championship, Lyndon also arranged a post-season banquet, where State Senator Welly Hopkins and several Houston notables came to honor Lyndon and his debaters. By the time Lyndon was done, Latimer recalled, "we were more important than the football team."[63]

Although Lyndon was determined to bring a state championship to Sam Houston in his second year, he didn't remain at the school long enough to reach his goal. In November 1931 he accepted appointment as secretary to a new U.S. congressman from the Fourteenth District in Texas. Early in the month, after Harry M. Wurzbach, the incumbent, died, Richard Kleberg, a member of the wealthy King Ranch family in south Texas, became one of eight candidates running in a special election to finish Wurzbach's term. Seeking every possible advantage in a very competitive contest, Kleberg's campaign manager, Roy Miller, a former mayor of Corpus Christi and a lobbyist for Texas Gulf Sulphur, followed Welly Hopkins's suggestion that he enlist Sam Johnson's support in Blanco and surrounding counties. Sam was "very helpful," and Lyndon apparently did a small amount of work in the brief twelve-day campaign. When Kleberg won election on November 25 by a few thousand votes over his two closest opponents, he asked Felix McKnight, a San Antonio journalist who had covered his campaign, to become his administrative assistant or secretary, as congressmen then called their aides. McKnight accepted. But Roy Miller persuaded Kleberg to offer the job to Lyndon.[64]

The day Kleberg won, Welly Hopkins wrote Miller suggesting that Lyndon be appointed to the secretary's post. His many connections in several Fourteenth District counties and his demonstrated ability as a campaigner of "very unusual ability to meet and greet the public" made him "a decided asset." "The boy is thoroughly deserving," Hopkins told Miller, "and . . . I suggest him . . . with the further idea of building up and securing Dick's political position in the future." Miller, who was already thinking about Kleberg's campaign in 1932 for a full term, liked the idea of getting a secretary who "would have a political touch in the district." Kleberg then called Lyndon at the Sam Houston High School to invite him to come to Corpus Christi for an interview. Lyndon was "so excited he didn't know what to say." After consulting with Uncle George, he called back to arrange a meeting, which took place on November 29. Making a strong impression at the interview as a "likable type of fellow" who was "agreeable" and eager "to be of personal service," Kleberg offered him the job and Miller arranged for McKnight to return to his newspaper.[65]

A few days later, after arranging a leave of absence from his teaching job, Lyndon boarded a train in Houston with Congressman Kleberg for Washington, D.C. He remembered feeling "excited, nervous, and sad. I was about to leave home to meet the adventure of my future. I felt grown-up, but my mind kept ranging backward in time. I saw myself as a boy skipping down the road to my granddaddy's house. I remembered the many nights I had stood in the doorway listening to my father's political talk. I remembered the evenings with my mother when my daddy was away. Now all that was behind me." And an extraordinary political career in the nation's capital was about to begin.[66]

4

Kleberg's Secretary

FROM the moment they began their journey to the nation's capital on December 2, 1931, Kleberg introduced Lyndon to material comforts and men of influence he had never known before. Sharing a stateroom with his "chief" and taking meals in the dining car, Lyndon had his first taste of Pullman travel aboard the *Bluebonnet*, a sleek streamliner operating between Houston and Washington, D.C. It was "a wonderful trip . . . on one of the best trains in the U.S.," he wrote a former student in Houston. In the capital they stayed at the Mayflower on Connecticut Avenue in a carpeted $13-a-day room with twin beds. Their stay at "Washington's finest hotel," drinking early morning coffee delivered by room service, and riding cabs from the hotel to the House Office Building cost Kleberg over three times Lyndon's weekly salary at the Sam Houston High School.

During their first few days in town, Lyndon met several Texas political celebrities, including Congressman John Nance Garner, a dominant Washington figure who was about to become Speaker of the House, and Senator Morris Sheppard. Lyndon and Kleberg spent over an hour with Garner, a self-contained man with "cold blue eyes and tight small mouth" who some predicted would become a Texas Coolidge. Lyndon "just listened—something hard for me to do—but quite proper for secretaries." They met Sheppard at the Occidental, "an exclusive Washington eating place," which advertised, "Where Statesmen Dine." [1]

Lyndon's taste of the good life, however, was soon over. After four days at the Mayflower, he began looking for a place to live. On Monday morning, December 7, he watched from the House gallery as Garner was elected Speaker and the Texas delegation let loose with ear-splitting war whoops and cowboy yells at the opening session of the 72nd Congress. Robert M. Jackson, an aide to another Texas congressman, remembered how "this long, tall young man came in and sat about two seats behind me and started introducing himself to everybody there. . . . He reached over a whole row of seats and shook hands with me and when I told him who I was, he wanted to know . . . where I was living and everything else. . . . I was so countrified myself, and to have someone booming out there, asking me questions . . . embarrassed me." When Jackson told him that he had a room in the Dodge Hotel, where a number of congressional aides lived, Lyndon, said, "I'll move there."[2]

An eight-story red brick structure one block south of Union Station and a few blocks north of the Capitol and the Senate and House Office Buildings, the Grace Dodge was an ideal location for aides who worked on the Hill. Although once a fine "women's" hotel with an elegant dining room and a well-appointed lobby with a large fireplace, a grand piano, chandeliers, and Oriental rugs, it had, like so much else in the Depression, fallen on hard times. To stay open, the hotel began renting basement rooms to young men on government salaries. One floor below the lobby, at the "A" level, were several "good-size" rooms with semi-private baths shared by four residents. On the lower or "B" floor, which was partly below ground, were twelve cubicles with wash basins and half-windows near the ceiling that let in a small amount of daylight. Communal toilets and showers at the end of the hall served the twenty-four occupants of these small rooms. Lyndon shared one of the "B" level rooms with Robert Jackson, paying $20 a month.

Although his starting salary was $3900 a year, more than double what he had been paid in Houston and a substantial income for a single man in the Depression, Lyndon, who sent much of his salary to his struggling parents, had a limited budget. To make ends meet, he and other congressional aides took most of their meals in cheap nearby eateries: the drugstore around the corner from his hotel, where they left nickel tips on the fountain; the All States Cafeteria on Massachusetts Avenue which served a "Fo' bitter," a filling meal for fifty cents; Child's Restaurant across from Union Station, where they got by for twenty-five cents each; or "a chili joint" behind Child's which served spicy dishes that Lyndon liked more than the other boys. Once a month, on a Sunday, they splurged and ate a one-dollar dinner at the Dodge Hotel restaurant, where a steward with a brass warming tray around his neck served them rum buns using tongs.[3]

Lyndon's hardships, however, were modest compared with those of most Americans in the winter of 1931–32, the second year of the Depression. Employed and able to help support his family in Texas, Lyndon had what millions of others in the country lacked. In December 1931, ten million Americans were unemployed, over 20 percent of the workforce, with more people losing their jobs all the time. Many who continued to work labored at miserably low wages, with industrial workers receiving 7.5 cents an hour and less. In Tennessee mills, women earned $2.39 for a 50-hour week; Connecticut sweatshops paid young girls one to two cents an hour, between 60 cents and $1.10 for a 55-hour week. Some American families forced on to relief rolls received less than $2.50 a week. People all over the country experienced "the primitive conditions of a preindustrial society striken by famine. In the coal fields of West Virginia and Kentucky, evicted families shivered in tents in midwinter; children went barefoot. In Los Angeles, people whose gas and electricity had been turned off were reduced to cooking over wood fires in back lots." But at least they had something to eat. While relatively few people starved to death, hunger was widespread. To feed themselves, some rural Americans took to eating weeds. Their urban counterparts scoured garbage cans and city dumps in search of half-rotted vegetables. "There will be a revolution in this country if nothing is done at once to create work for the unemployed or to meet their needs in some other way," a conservative labor leader declared early in 1932.[4]

In the midst of the worst economic crisis in American history, the Federal government in Washington became the focus of attention and hope. By the end of 1931, however, after three years of Hoover's presidency, few Americans had much faith that the Administration could devise ways to overcome the crisis. Doctrinaire and gloomy, the President seemed incapable of moving much beyond conventional economic wisdom or of providing the emotional boost the country needed to deal with the unprecedented collapse. Bitter jokes at Hoover's expense reflected the national mood. He was the world's greatest engineer: "In a little more than two years, he has drained, ditched and damned the United States." When told that business was improving, vaudeville comedians asked, "Is Hoover dead?"

What faith existed in the capacity of the national government to make things better fixed on the Congress, and in particular on the Democratic and progressive Republican opponents of the Administration. In the 1930 congressional elections, Republican majorities in the House and the Senate largely disappeared. The 17-seat advantage held by Senate Republicans in the first two years of Hoover's term became a one-seat margin in 1931. Moreover, when the House organized itself in December 1930, the Democrats, who had numbered a hundred fewer representatives than the Republicans, had a two-seat majority. Kleberg's election to replace Wurzbach, the only Republican congressman from Texas, had made a significant difference. Before Kleberg's victory, the count in the House had stood at 217 Democrats, 215 Republicans, one Farmer-Laborite, who seemed likely to vote with the Republicans, and two vacancies. Had the two vacant seats gone Republican, the GOP would have kept its hold on the House. But Kleberg's success ruled this out. It also expanded the power of Texas Democrats, who won control of the Speakership and five major House committees.[5]

Although Kleberg helped give the Democrats a slim majority in the House, he contributed little else to the political give and take in a government desperately seeking ways out of the collapse. A super-rich, self-indulged man, Kleberg had little taste for work of any kind. The son of Robert and Alice King Kleberg, Richard had grown up on the King Ranch founded by his maternal grandfather, a vast estate in south Texas stretching nearly a hundred miles north of the Rio Grande along the Gulf of Mexico. Consisting of 1.28 million acres, twice the size of Rhode Island, on which nearly a million cattle grazed, the Ranch, the largest in the world, made the Kings and Klebergs multimillionaires and gave "Mr. Dick," as Ranch employees and congressional aides called him, the wherewithal to be a playboy.

Mostly interested in horses, hunting, polo, golf at Maryland's Burning Tree Country Club, high-stakes poker, and entertaining himself and others on the accordion or the piano, Mr. Dick quickly established a pattern as an absentee congressman. He spent considerable time in Mexico, where he enjoyed using his expert Spanish, and when he was in Washington, he only went to his office in the late afternoon and often didn't show up at all. During his visits to Room 258, a single inside room facing the inner court of the old House—now Cannon—Office Building, Kleberg spent his time behind a partition separating him from the office staff having a drink and chatting with friends or dictating an occasional letter, usually in Spanish to acquaintances in Mexico. When he wrote in English, the letter included no punctuation, all periods, commas, colons, and semi-colons omitted. A handsome, slender, highly athletic man, five feet eleven and a half inches tall weighing 157 pounds, Kleberg at forty-four was a rich "nobleman," as one newspaper called him, who principally pursued his pleasures. "The last thing he wanted to do," Robert Jackson said, "was answer letters from constituents crying during the depression."[6]

He left the entire work of his office to Lyndon, a raw twenty-three-year-old who, for all his intelligence and energy, hadn't a clue about how to manage a congressman's business. He didn't know how to discriminate among the mass of requests for help pouring in from Kleberg's Fourteenth District or deal with the Federal bureaucracy which might answer those demands. During his first few days on the job, Lyndon relied for guidance on an experienced stenographer who had worked for several prominent congressmen. While she was able to help him give formal replies to some of the many letters that had piled up in the weeks between Wurzbach's death and Kleberg's arrival in Washington, she offered him little more than a "mechanical" approach to the mail.[7]

During his second week in the office, Lyndon initiated a systematic effort to do better. His first night at the Dodge he took four showers in the communal bathroom so that he could meet some of the other congressional aides living on the "B" floor. The next morning, to meet the rest, he washed his face and brushed his teeth five times at ten-minute intervals. At the end of the week he had identified five young men whose intelligence and experience he put in the service of his education. At the same time, he made a point of seeking out congressmen and other staff members outside of the Dodge circle who might give him a short course on how to do his job. "I met him as soon as he came up with Dick Kleberg," Texas congressman Marvin Jones, the chairman of the Agriculture Committee, recalled. "He'd come across [the hall] and talk to me and want to know just how everything was done. He wanted to find out how that big piece of machine operated. And he'd talk to all the other chairmen that had a chance to talk to him. And he learned more in six months than the average member learned in twice that length of time." R. E. Thomason, another Texas congressman, remembered how Lyndon, whose father had helped him as a young legislator in Austin, came to see him, and how Kate George, his "very efficient secretary," helped Lyndon learn his way around the Capitol.[8]

Lyndon still didn't find it easy to master the challenge. When Estelle Harbin, a young woman from Corpus Christi, began working in Kleberg's office in January 1932, she remembered how hard she and Lyndon "had to struggle to find out what to do and do it the best way we could." Watching the stacks of mail arrive at the office three times a day, Lyndon felt as if he were "going to be buried." But refusing to be overwhelmed, he took every opportunity to get on-the-job training. Arthur Perry, secretary to Tom Connally, Texas's other senator, took Lyndon under his wing and watched him "learn all he could and learn it fast. You never had to tell him anything a second time," Perry said. "This skinny boy was as green as anybody could be, but within a few months he knew how to operate in Washington better than some who had been here for twenty years before him." At lunch with other aides, he would rush to the head of the cafeteria line, select his food, hurry to a table, and wolf down his meal before the other boys arrived. "That left him free to shoot questions at us while we ate. If he didn't like the answers he got, he would argue. Lyndon was the greatest argufier any of us had ever seen," Perry recalled. "It took me a long time to catch on to the fact that most of his arguing was done simply to bring out every possible answer to his arguments. He wanted to be sure he knew all the answers."[9]

Lyndon required no instruction to know that Kleberg's success depended on satisfying the needs of his 500,000 constituents, twice as many as in most Texas districts. Many of them were veterans who stayed in the area after serving at Fort Sam Houston, the largest army post in the United States, or at one of several military air fields. In addition, cotton farmers, small truck farmers producing fruits and vegetables, cattle ranchers, and business interests in San Antonio, Corpus Christi, and Port Aransas, the district's major cities, were principal elements in the life of the area. Serving the district meant answering thousands of requests asking increased pensions, disability benefits, early payments on bonuses promised World War vets, guaranteed crop prices, appointments to government jobs, or help in refinancing farm mortgages or in getting some kind of government loan. Moved by a mix of compassion for suffering constituents and self-serving desire to keep Kleberg in office and themselves employed, Lyndon and Harbin worked their "hearts out seven days a week." "Haven't been out of the office all day," Lyndon wrote on a Sunday night in April 1932. "Didn't get up until late this morning so I was forced to rush to work and have been at it until only a few minutes [ago]. I never get time to do anything but try to push the mail out to the people back home. Received over 100 telegrams today." [10]

Recognizing that effective action needed to follow initial replies to constituent requests, Lyndon learned whom to approach and what tack to take with officials at the Veteran's Administration Bureau and the Agriculture Department, the two agencies processing most of the district's business. Unlike most other congressmen and their aides, who simply sent cases along to appropriate officials with positive recommendations, Lyndon made special efforts to get what constituents asked, carrying requests directly to supervisors or calling on the phone to ask for an affirmative response. "He was very persuasive on the telephone, as he was in person," Estelle Harbin says. "It wasn't too long, especially if he could get some old lady at the other end of the line, before he had the whole deal down hill with the wind, because he could just charm her right out of her chair." Often he wouldn't take no for an answer, doggedly pressing a case others saw as unwinnable. Relying on an instinctive feel for what would work, he alternated between harsh warnings against arousing Kleberg's displeasure and appeals to a bureaucrat's vanity that he or she was the only one who could help. Since he couldn't get Kleberg to do it himself, he often pretended to be Kleberg and had him bully or charm an official, as Lyndon thought fit. The results were impressive. During his first six months in Washington, Lyndon handled approximately 300 appeals from veterans for help. Of the 150 cases decided during this time, over 60 percent were favorable to the veterans. In addition, as the Washington correspondent for several Texas newspapers reported, Kleberg's office had been successful in filling most of the thousands of other individual requests that had landed on the congressman's desk. [11]

The assertion may have been the hyperbole of a friendly journalist, but most people in the district were, or shortly became, convinced of the claim. The office quickly developed a reputation for effective advocacy and for a keen interest in every constituent. Lyndon not only made substantive gains for people with problems, he also cultivated the art of making people feel good. Every letter coming into the office had to be answered in as personal and prompt a way as possible, meaning the same day. "It was worse than adultery to leave a letter over [night] unanswered," one of Lyndon's assistants recalled. In addition, Lyndon insisted that every correspondent be listed on a file card with as much personal detail about them as possible—the man's wife's name and his children's names and ages, for instance. Trying to get on a first-name basis with as many people as he could, Lyndon went over every county and town in the district with Kleberg to find out whom he knew well enough to address in a familiar way. In the case of a new correspondent, someone addressing Kleberg as "Dear Congressman," Lyndon would have his assistants write warm, supportive replies: "Dear Friend Jim, It was sure great to have your letter, and I'm sorry those people at Agriculture haven't been treating you right. I'm taking it up with them right now. . . . If there's anything you need, please holler." When the mail occasionally fell off, and the office was receiving "perhaps no more than double that of the usual [congressional] member," Lyndon would set his assistants to scouring the local newspapers for births, deaths, and awards, which were then noted in letters of congratulation or condolence. High-school graduates were prime targets for such letters. There were forty or fifty different versions of them, which recipients could feel had been written especially to them.[12]

Lyndon's formula for making the office function as well as it did was unstinting effort: twelve hours or more a day, seven days a week, week after week. "His energy—it is almost impossible to exaggerate," Robert Jackson says. "He was just a bundle of nervous energy—he was moving, going all the time. He would never rest." Awaking about six in the morning, he would get to the office by seven, two hours before most congressional staffs arrived. Spending an hour writing replies to letters for Harbin to type, he would begin working on the current day's mail when it came in at eight. After that, he would get on the phone or go directly to the agency dealing with pending cases. There was no lunch break. About ten-thirty he would go to the post office in the building, where postal workers would sell fifteen-cent sandwiches and ten-cent pieces of cake made by their wives. Eating at their desks, Lyndon and Harbin "kept right on working." Occasionally, on a nice spring day, Harbin would persuade him to take a brief stroll on the Capitol grounds. But Lyndon couldn't relax for long. He would begin walking faster and faster, and Harbin, who was usually dressed in a straight skirt down to her ankles and couldn't match Lyndon's long strides, would begin trotting to keep up. As they headed back to work, Lyndon would take Harbin by the hand, pulling her along as they ran across the Capitol grounds.

"He just couldn't wait to get back to that office." There, they would continue working until seven or eight in the evening, three or four hours after most offices closed. After a meal at Child's cafeteria, Lyndon would often go back to work until ten or eleven at night. If he didn't, his evening's relaxation consisted of political bull sessions with friends at the Dodge or reading government documents lying in bed.[13]

Yet however hard the staff worked, Lyndon never thought they were doing enough and tried to make the office more productive. At the end of the congressional session in the summer of 1932, when Harbin left her job, Lyndon hired Gene Latimer and Luther E. Jones, his Houston debaters. Latimer came first, at the start of the congressional term in December 1932. A good-natured little Irish kid with enormous energy, Latimer came to Washington because his fiancée had moved there and he couldn't find more than a delivery-boy's job in Houston after graduating from high school in May. To bring him, Lyndon arranged a "patronage" appointment Kleberg was entitled to make in the House Post Office at $130 a month. Since the job required only a limited number of hours delivering mail to congressmen, Latimer was largely available for typing in Kleberg's office.

The pay was modest in Washington, even by Depression standards, but Lyndon wished to use Kleberg's limited office funds to hire other assistants. Each congressman had a $5000 annual allotment for his staff and with Lyndon receiving $3900 of it, there was only $1100 left to pay additional employees. In April 1933, however, Lyndon reduced his own salary to $3050 and used the remaining $1950 to hire more help, including Jones, who joined the staff in August 1933 at $1200 a year, working first out of Corpus Christi and then coming to Washington in December. To help Latimer and Jones make ends meet, Lyndon moved them into his basement room in the Dodge, where they each paid $15 a month rent. Because he did not think he could find a job in Houston, even after two years at Rice University, Jones accepted the meager salary and hoped that Lyndon was right when he predicted that "you are going places and I'm going to help you get there."[14]

Between December 1932 and July 1935, when Latimer and Jones worked for Lyndon, they found it difficult to think about the future or anything except the day's labor. They worked phenomenally hard—fourteen-, sixteen-, often eighteen-hour days. Up at 4:30 in the morning to start his post office job at five, Latimer worked until noon. After a half-hour for lunch, he went to Kleberg's office, where he answered and typed letters until at least seven or eight at night. Jones, who had the luxury of not getting to work until seven or 7:30 in the morning, remembers often having to stay until midnight. Lyndon, who was almost always there to close the office, had no compunctions about making Latimer and Jones stay to finish the day's work or to improve on what they had done. "Lyndon Johnson was a hard man to work for," Jones said thirty-five years later, "because he insisted on perfection. Everything had to be just right, and it had to be the way *he* wanted it." When Jones first started the job, Lyndon made him rewrite and retype hundreds of letters, no matter how long it took. Lyndon's "idea of a good time," Latimer recalled, "was to pick out a holiday, and everybody go down to the office and work." On their way to work in the morning, Lyndon "could issue enough instructions in ten minutes to put a hundred people to work for a month."

One Saturday night, when Lyndon had gone to dinner, the boys rebelled and went to an early movie, leaving a note saying that they would return at nine. When Lyndon got back, he flipped through a pile of unanswered mail until he found a postcard from an unhappy constituent wondering why his previous letter had not been answered. Rushing to the theater, he made the boys come outside, where he lectured them on their duties. When Latimer pointed out that the card was from someone Lyndon was supposed to deal with, he made amends by taking them for a drink. But after five minutes of conversation, he declared, "Okay, we've been relaxing long enough, now let's get back to work, there's still three more good working hours before we fold." [15]

At times, Latimer and Jones found it nearly impossible to keep working for him. He was so demanding and occasionally so overbearing and abusive that they periodically wanted to quit. Receiving a personal phone call or taking a work break to drink coffee or smoke a cigarette was forbidden. Even going to the bathroom was frowned upon. "If he caught you reading a letter from your mother, or if you were taking a crap, he'd say, 'Son, can't you please try a little harder to do that on your own time?' " His single-minded devotion to making the office the most efficient in the Congress moved him to use a variety of devices for extracting the most work. One of his gentler techniques was to encourage competition: "It sounds like he's getting them out a little faster than you are!" he'd tell one or the other about the day's typing. And pretty soon he'd have both of them whacking away at the typewriters "harder and harder, faster and faster" in an effort to outdo each other. On the rare occasions Latimer threatened to quit, because he wasn't allowed enough time off, Lyndon sarcastically reminded him that he had little chance of getting another job and that if he left, he wouldn't be able to stay in Washington and marry his fiancée.

Toward Jones, who was better educated, much less dependent, and a prim, aloof personality, Lyndon was even more abusive. He would publicly ridicule any error he found in one of his letters, belittling his style of writing, his spelling, his typing, or any failing that put him in a subordinate position. But the worst moment in a day for Jones was when Lyndon would insist that he come into the bathroom while Lyndon sat on the toilet defecating. Jones "would stand with his head and nose averted, and take dictation." To some other, later employees, this was an example of Lyndon's "naturalness," but for Jones it was a source of humiliation and a means by which Lyndon dominated him or exercised control.[16]

Yet, as Jones and Latimer recognized, the crude, overbearing qualities represented only one side of the man. Lyndon was also "fiercely loyal" to people who worked with him. In July 1935, for example, when Latimer finally got married, Lyndon arranged a $100 gift from Kleberg, gave the couple the use of a car for a honeymoon, and arranged an excellent job for Latimer at the Federal Housing Authority, where he received $2600, "a very rich opportunity for those depression times." Similarly, when Jones wanted to begin law school in Washington in 1934, Lyndon helped by increasing his salary. Moreover, in 1935, when Jones left to attend the University of Texas Law School, Lyndon promised to help him later get a job in Washington, which he did in 1938. "Most people who had anything to do with Lyndon Johnson loved him," Jones said years later. "I'm sure he had his detractors. I know he did. But the people that worked with him liked him. He had some faults, but most people were willing to overlook them because the guy was obviously a genius in politics." Latimer echoes the point: "Biographers and news media have libelously stated that Lyndon Johnson treated his staff with demands amounting to inhumanity and brutality. . . . A reasonable statement would be that Lyndon Johnson is hard and he is tough, extremely so, but those attributes are not reserved for his staff. . . . No one under him ever worked harder than he himself. And that far from being ruthless to his employees, their welfare was very important to him."[17]

Although Kleberg was nearly twice his age, Lyndon also dominated him. Kleberg allowed him not only to run the office but also manage some of his personal and business affairs. Inattentive to family and financial matters, Kleberg left it to Lyndon to write letters to his mother and a son at the Virginia Military Institute and pay his bills. Kleberg was a free spender who lived at the Shoreham, Washington's most expensive hotel, employed chauffeurs, sent his four children to private schools, and purchased almost everything on credit. While he was exceptionally rich, much of his money was tied up in property and he didn't have "a lot of cash." Consequently, "Lyndon had to parcel out the income to keep everybody happy with a part payment. . . . Lyndon would sit him down and tell him, 'Look, I got to have so much money to pay this bill, and so much for that bill." Kleberg was so reluctant to bother with money matters that he even had Lyndon sign his name on personal checks.[18]

For a time Lyndon also became a confidant to Mrs. Kleberg, Miss

Mamie, as the staff called her. Although a charming and "handsome-looking woman" with all the social graces, she was "a somewhat neu-rotic person" with "fears and insecurities" that Lyndon "could allay." Her problems, however, were not strictly the product of her imagination. In 1932, Mr. Dick had an extramarital affair that strained the Kleberg marriage and brought him and Miss Mamie to the edge of nervous ex-haustion. Returning to Corpus Christi in May, she confided her fears and hopes to Lyndon in several letters. "I almost broke down, but I managed to conquer my feelings for I was determined to do what I could to keep Mr. Kleberg from worrying," she wrote in one of them. "It tore my heart out . . . to leave him but I knew I would never get myself straightened out up there. . . . I am so thankful that you are with him." But Kleberg was apparently too troubled to remain in Washington and he also returned to Corpus Christi. "Mr. Kleberg was on the edge of a nervous breakdown and I do not believe he could have held out much longer," she wrote Lyndon from Texas. ". . . He is so appreciative of all you have done and could not love you more if you were his own son, and I feel just like he does, Lyndon. If you had not been in Corpus the night I went all to pieces, I know I would have done something desper-ate. But all of that is behind us, thank God, and we will all three try to make something . . . worthwhile . . . of our future. . . . Love from us both—Your other Mother."

Unfortunately, the Kleberg problems did not end there. In the follow-ing year, Mrs. Kleberg told Lyndon about an anonymous letter from Mr. Kleberg's "enemies" in San Antonio threatening "political blackmail of the most vicious kind! . . . Naturally, I feel deeply humiliated over the whole thing." The Kleberg marriage outlasted the crisis. But how much of a part Lyndon played in keeping them together is unclear. A later falling out with Mrs. Kleberg, in which she accused Lyndon of being "partisan to the woman who was vamping her husband," suggests that he was less than the perfect marriage counselor.[19]

Most striking in this whole episode, however, is not the extent of Lyn-don Johnson's success in managing the Klebergs' personal problems but how quickly he altered his role in their relationship: in less than six months after becoming Kleberg's secretary, the Kleberg family de-pended on the twenty-three-year-old Johnson, an unsophisticated youngster with a limited education, for advice in handling their personal affairs. Though he always showed his boss a proper measure of defer-ence, he did not stand in the congressman's shadow: Richard Kleberg and "his genial secretary" Lyndon Johnson "were hosts to more than one hundred south Texas editors, farmers and specially invited political friends at the King ranch," a Texas newspaper reported in November 1933. When Texas congressman Wright Patman attended an American Legion convention in Corpus Christi about this time, he accepted an invitation from Lyndon to bring a number of Legionnaires to an outing on Kleberg's yacht. Lyndon was the sole host and "he impressed everyone."[20]

Lyndon also played a large part in shaping Kleberg's political actions. Nothing during his years in Kleberg's office more fully captured his attention than politics. As one of the office staff remembered, "he lived and breathed it. He woke up talking about it and he talked it during meals. . . . This was his life." L. E. Jones remembered him as "totally aware of current events." He "devoured" newspapers and weekly magazines like *Time* and *Life*. He had little appetite for recreation or anything that diverted his attention from the political: if he went to a baseball game at Washington's Griffith Stadium with friends, he "kept right on arguing politics through every inning"; in a swimming pool, he paddled around for a bit and then began a conversation; on a boat in Maryland's Chesapeake Bay, he held forth on politics while others fished. "Lyndon dropped in my office almost every day," Wright Patman remembered. ". . . He wanted to talk politics—who was doing what and what the probable outcome would be. . . . He . . . also liked to ask questions about the dirty political fighting that was part of Texas electioneering." William S. White, a young wire-service reporter from Texas, was impressed with Lyndon's "endlessly varied" questions on a single topic: "Who has the power and how is it exercised?"[21]

Lyndon told a friend at this time that there ought to be a school which taught people how government worked. He said that he had learned by doing, but he thought it would be better if there were organized training for public servants. He wished to enroll in such a program, but since there was none, he did the next best thing: he designed his own course. He attended as many of Washington's political events as time permitted: House committee hearings, speeches by White House officials, and stump talks by any political figure of note. Some time during this period, he persuaded Kleberg to let him work as a House page for a few months, though it meant a temporary pay cut. Carrying messages in and out of the House chamber, he learned about its rules and practices, became acquainted with dozens of additional congressmen, and heard Capitol gossip about their personal and public lives. To the extent possible, he enlisted Texas congressmen Patman, Garner, Jones, Thomason, Martin Dies from Lufkin, and Sam Rayburn from Bonham as his teachers. Most of them weren't eager to spend much time talking to a congressional secretary, but he spoke "so rapidly and with such vigor" that they "could not help but pay attention and remember." He got to know most of them quite well. "They thought a lot of him . . . how capable and smart he was," Robert Jackson said, and how they wouldn't be surprised if he also became a congressman one day. It wasn't long before the other congressional aides from whom he had taken initial instruction began to feel "as if we were the pupils and he were the teacher."

When Robert Montgomery, an economist from the University of Texas, and his wife spent an afternoon with Lyndon in Kleberg's office, he dazzled them with his political knowledge—the prospects of advancement for individual politicians and the chances particular bills had of winning congressional passage. He impressed them as a modern version of Plato's political animal, a man who could not explain his analytic powers, but "just *knew*" how the system worked and how political matters would turn out.[22]

And Lyndon began to develop convictions about good policy and good politics. Hoover's unresponsiveness to the nation's suffering troubled him. Refusing to believe that anyone was starving or even hungry, the President rejected appeals for federal relief or what he called "raids on the public treasury." Asked why so many people were selling apples on street corners, he replied: "Many people have left their jobs for the more profitable one of selling apples." To Lyndon, Hoover stood for "do-nothing government" that was content to let corn burn for lack of a market and cotton sell for a nickel, wheat for two bits, and calves for three cents. Hoover thought that " 'constitutional government' gave every man, woman, and child the right to starve," Lyndon said later.[23]

The plight of the Bonus Army, the approximately 15,000 World War veterans who paraded up Pennsylvania Avenue in May 1932 and encamped in the marshy flats across the Anacostia River, particularly disturbed Lyndon. Hoover refused to give any of them a hearing, and though the House passed a bill providing for immediate payment of the bonuses due them in 1945, the Senate refused to follow suit. When Kleberg had considered voting against the bonus bill because it would unbalance the federal budget, Lyndon had pounded on his desk and exclaimed, "Mr. Kleberg, Mr. Kleberg, you can't do this!" The district was fifteen or twenty to one in favor of the bonus bill, Lyndon also told him. "If you're going to have any kind of representative government, you've got to take stock of what the people want." But expediency was also involved: in a district with so many veterans, Lyndon warned that he would jeopardize his chances of getting reelected if he went against their wishes. In July, after a brief riot when District of Columbia police cleared some of the vets from an abandoned building on Pennsylvania Avenue, Hoover ordered the army to drive the veterans and their families from the city and the flats. Four troops of cavalry with drawn sabers, six tanks, and a column of infantry with fixed bayonets under General Douglas MacArthur dispersed the vets with tear gas and torched their jerry-built shacks and barracks. Lyndon later remembered seeing "the Bonus Army being driven down Pennsylvania Avenue by quirts like sheep by a man on a white horse to the flats."[24]

The timid response of Congress to the Depression also bothered Lyndon. Divided between a Republican Senate and a Democratic House, in which the Democrats were more interested in preventing Hoover's reelection than in constructing an effective program, the Congress passed little significant legislation to help the needy or revive the economy. In 1932 a majority of Democrats repeatedly sided with Republicans to defeat reform measures and balance the budget. Hiram Johnson, the progressive Republican senator from California, described the Democratic party in February "as the weak and timid echo of the Republican party in this Congress." In June, William E. Dodd, a history professor at the University of Chicago and a Wilsonian Democrat, believed there was "no doubt in the world that both political parties have been bankrupted."[25]

Huey Long, a freshman senator from Louisiana, excited Lyndon's imagination. A brilliant demagogue with a flair for political theater, Long captured national and international attention shortly after coming to the Senate in 1932. Dressing in "pongee suits with orchid-colored shirts . . . watermelon-pink ties" and "striped straw hats," he poked fun at all forms of conventionality while proposing radical solutions to the Depression that outraged his colleagues. He denounced his fellow Democrats in the Senate for cowering before Hoover like "a whipped rooster" and as afraid to confront "real" issues. He dismissed congressional interest in balancing the budget as irrelevant to current economic problems, and he called for a redistribution of wealth as the only way to head off revolution and preserve the dream of a free America. He "entranced" Lyndon, who made a deal with the Senate doorkeeper to let him know whenever Long was going to speak. "I thought he had a heart for the people," Lyndon said. "He hated poverty with all his soul and spoke against it until his voice was hoarse." "For leading the masses and illustrating your point humanly, Huey Long couldn't be beat."[26]

Lyndon never forgot an afternoon in 1932 when he watched Long, who was dressed in a "chocolate silk suit" and "bright-toned brown-and-white shoes," answer attacks on him for going into Arkansas to help Hattie Caraway, a progressive senator, retain her seat. Complaining that he had "been denounced all afternoon," Long, as Lyndon remembered, looked over at Arkansas' conservative Senator Joseph Robinson, who was the most powerful Democrat in the Senate—"a very robust man, a very rotund man, he had a great big stomach and had a cigar that he always smoked and kept in the corner of his mouth. . . . He walked right over to Joe Robinson, put his hand on his shoulder in a very affectionate and friendly way, and said, 'I wasn't in Arkansas to dictate to any human being. All I went to Arkansas for was to pull these big, pot-bellied politicians off this poor little woman's neck.'"

But it was more Long's idea for helping the poor and the South in particular that drew Lyndon to him. In February 1934, Long announced the establishment of the Share Our Wealth Society and its slogan, "Every Man a King." Through the imposition of Federal taxes, the government was to redistribute wealth: a capital-levy tax was to limit family fortunes to five million dollars; the income tax was to prohibit families from earning over a million dollars a year; and the revenue from these taxes was to guarantee every family in the country a $5000-a-year income. Long's plan was aimed at altering the relations of the various segments of the economy and of giving the Federal government a larger and permanent role in directing it. The scheme had its greatest appeal in the South, where most of the country's Share Our Wealth clubs sprang up. To Lyndon, Long's proposal was a way not only to relieve suffering but also to give the South a greater part of the national income and alter its status as the least affluent part of the United States.[27]

Lyndon believed that Franklin Roosevelt's New Deal was advancing toward the same ends, and it won Johnson's greatest enthusiasm. Although disappointed that Garner, his fellow Texan, had to settle for second place on the 1932 Democratic ticket behind FDR, Lyndon delighted in the election of New York's progressive governor to the White House and Democratic control over both houses of Congress. He later recalled attending Roosevelt's inauguration in March 1933 when people "believed that their nation had come to a dead end." But they took heart when they saw "that great man march up and hold on to that podium and say, 'The only thing we have to fear is fear itself,' " and when he "quoted from Proverbs: 'Where there is no vision, the people perish.' " Johnson said in 1964: "It gave me an inspiration that has carried me all through the years since."

Lyndon believed that special interests "particularly the moneylenders . . . and those who had the money supply and knowledge and possessions in New York, Chicago, and Boston," had caused the Depression. "They'd always been paid proportionately a far higher percentage of the total end product than they deserved. . . . They just clipped coupons and wrote down debentures we couldn't spell and stole our pants out from under us." To right the wrongs they committed, the government had to assume "the positive role of eliminating the special interests." Convinced that "neither misery nor squalor is inevitable so long as the government and the people are one," Lyndon applauded the burst of reform activism in the spring of 1933, the Hundred Days in which Congress under FDR's leadership enacted fifteen major laws that changed the course of American life. He "was deeply interested in that—in all that complex of affairs—and very smypathetic toward it, particularly in its aspects of attempting to deal with poverty and unemployment, farm mortgages, farm foreclosures—all those things very clearly engaged him personally," a journalist who knew him then recalled. The Depression and FDR's reforms convinced Lyndon that government was the great equalizer in a free market industrial system that indiscriminately injured hard-working people who, through no fault of their own, lost jobs, homes, farms, and savings. "I saw all the great reform legislation born," Lyndon said. "In the angry bitterness of the depression, we forged the vision for America."[28]

Lyndon justifiably felt that he had a small part in the creation of the New Deal. However limited Kleberg's day-to-day involvement in his duties, he had general notions about the role of government which ran counter to most everything Roosevelt and other New Dealers favored. The sort of tampering with market forces embodied in the Agriculture Adjustment Act, the National Industrial Recovery Act, the Tennessee Valley Authority, the Securities Exchange Act, and the relief and welfare measures incorporated in the Federal Emergency Relief Act and the Social Security Act impressed Kleberg as being "socialistic." Despite his identity as a Democrat and the general appeal of Roosevelt's program, Kleberg wanted to vote against all these New Deal measures. But Lyndon and Roy Miller, the lobbyist, who was as conservative as Kleberg, convinced him that it was poor politics and a meaningless gesture to boot. When Kleberg, who served on the Agriculture Committee, told them that he intended to vote against the AAA, Lyndon pointed out that mail from the district supported it by thirty to one. When Kleberg insisted on sticking to his principles, Lyndon and Miller advised him that the bill was going to pass anyway and Lyndon threatened to quit. Although Kleberg asserted himself by voting against the FERA and TVA, he gave in on the AAA and all the other major reform bills, including Social Security. When that bill was before the House in 1935, Lyndon pressed him to vote "Yes." Kleberg "genuinely believed that it [Social Security] would destroy this country. And I pled with him: 'Please, please, please go and support that measure'; and he finally did."[29]

Lyndon felt good about pressuring Kleberg to support FDR, but all the New Deal measures would have passed without Kleberg's votes. Lyndon made a larger contribution to the New Deal by helping implement the agricultural reforms of the Hundred Days. To raise crop prices and increase farm income, the AAA paid farmers to take acreage out of production and reduce surpluses. Many farmers were skeptical, however, that the government would honor plow-up contracts and they failed to see the logic of earning more by planting less. "To destroy a standing crop goes against the soundest instincts of human nature," Henry Wallace, FDR's Secretary of Agriculture, said. Even mules rebelled against the proposal: trained for years not to step on a row of cotton, they had to be re-educated to trample on the budding stalks. With enough bales already on hand to satisfy world demand, the Roosevelt administration paid out over a $100 million to farmers for destroying a quarter of the 1933 crop. And because of Lyndon, who made special efforts to sign up south Texas farmers and to assure that their contracts moved swiftly through the AAA's formidable bureaucracy, Kleberg's Fourteenth District was in the forefront of Agriculture's cotton reduction program.

Likewise, after the Roosevelt administration steered a Farm Credit Act through the Congress in June and set up a Federal Land Bank to refinance farm mortgages, Lyndon helped arrange loans to every endangered farm in south Texas. Though it had a passive junior congressman, who had given only grudging support to reform, the Fourteenth District, Robert Caro points out, fared better under the New Deal than almost any other congressional district in the nation. Its secret was "a young secretary who worked for it with a frantic, frenzied, almost desperate aggressiveness and energy."[30]

Despite his unstinting support of the New Deal, Lyndon was no liberal ideologue when he worked for Kleberg. Roosevelt's determined efforts to use the government to help people had an enduring impact on Lyndon's thinking. Yet at the same time, he was greatly impressed by the wealthy, influential men around Kleberg, with whom he readily identified. Although he "was always able to see the New Deal side of things," was "quite strong" for some of its programs, and very much taken with FDR's powers of political persuasion, one of Lyndon's friends said later, he was also drawn to the conservative businessmen and politicians with whom Kleberg associated. For a young man on the make, Kleberg's rich, successful, and powerful friends had an irresistible appeal. Roy Miller, for example, dazzled Lyndon. A handsome man with wavy, silver-gray hair and the appearance of a model southern senator in perfectly tailored suits and waistcoats, Miller was described as "perhaps the most effective single lobbyist Washington has ever known." Earning $80,000 a year, flying back and forth between Texas and Washington in a private plane, living in a luxurious suite at the Mayflower, operating with a seemingly limitless expense account, Miller commanded attention wherever he went. He was a "very distinguished looking fellow," Willard Deason said. "One of these kind of fellows when he walked into a room everybody sort of came to attention. He just had a magnetic personality." And like Kleberg, he was intensely conservative, seeing Roosevelt and the New Deal as the advance guard of a communist dictatorship which would strip privileged Americans of their wealth and power. Using Kleberg's office as if it were his own, Miller took a shine to Lyndon, who acted like his personal secretary.[31]

Lyndon also echoed a number of his ideas. "I think Lyndon's earliest orientation was on the conservative side . . . with Kleberg and Roy Miller and those people," one of Lyndon's Washington friends said. Lyndon was "not really more liberal" than Kleberg, L. E. Jones asserted. ". . . Lyndon often talked very conservative." Robert Jackson, who would argue with him in the Dodge basement, remembered how he would accuse Lyndon of being a conservative Republican. Like Miller and Kleberg, Lyndon thought that the New Deal had "brought the professors and more crackpots and dreamers to Washington than you ever saw." He also voiced their concern that Roosevelt might spend the country into bankruptcy. When Huey Long's autobiography, *Every Man a King*, appeared in 1933, L. E. Jones recalled that Lyndon "found a lot of things" in it "worth remembering, but he also was critical of the part about spending so much money— . . . just spend, spend, spend, spend. I think at this time Lyndon was reflecting Roy Miller's influence."[32]

Yet Lyndon Johnson, like so many other Americans in the early thirties, had no well-developed set of ideas about economic and social questions. He was not someone with a considered philosophy, but a young man with his eye on the main chance and an affinity for practical politics. "I don't think Lyndon was either a conservative or a liberal," Jones said. "I think he was whatever he felt he needed to be. You can't stay in politics if you don't have this philosophy. . . . Lyndon always . . . wanted to seem to be in the middle. I believe that was his nature, too," Jones added. "I think that was where he wanted to be and tried to be. . . . I think Lyndon was the happiest when he was in the center." Lyndon himself told Doris Kearns that "I never wanted to demagogue against business, Wall Street, or the power companies. I wanted a minimum of rhetoric that would inflame or incite against either business, management, or labor." Above all, he believed that "politics required reasonable discussions." And in the thirties his growing familiarity with, and regard for, "a legislative process deliberately designed to translate potentially disruptive situations into practical problems resolvable by bargaining and negotiation" added to this conviction.[33]

Most of all Lyndon was interested in being effective—in learning how to win elections, use government for practical ends, and carve out a niche for himself in the world of politics. When it came to winning elections, he learned by doing. In June 1932 he had returned to Texas to run Kleberg's primary campaign against three other Democrats. Since the Democratic nomination was tantamount to election to a full two-year term, Lyndon had spared no effort in Kleberg's behalf. Believing it essential for Kleberg to visit all of the district's eleven counties before the July primary, Lyndon laid the groundwork by crisscrossing the district and making necessary advance contacts.

Sam Fore of Floresville in Wilson County was particularly helpful in the campaign. A newspaper publisher and prominent Democrat with statewide contacts, Fore instructed Lyndon on how to proceed: "There's just two ways to do a thing—you can coast along and do it halfway with the pilot on you know, but if you want to get the job done, you got to turn on the giant burner." Although the tall, skinny, well-dressed Lyndon was a study in contrast with the 275-pound Fore, who usually wore overalls, the two men shared a common view of how to organize a campaign. An attorney and active Democrat in Seguin, the Guadalupe County seat, remembered that in 1932 Lyndon "wasn't one of those that walked into the office and sat down and wasted a lot of time. He covered not only the area around the office but all of Seguin in a whirlwind fashion, and yet he saw everybody and talked to everybody." Driving all over the district with Fore, who introduced him to local leaders, Lyndon often returned to Fore's home in the evening, where they would kick off their shoes and have what Fore called "a sock foot reunion": Lyndon lying on the floor in the living room munching cookies and both of them talking politics until late into the night. By the time Kleberg came to town, Lyndon had the political situation well in hand: They would start off down the street and Lyndon would say, "Now, Mr. Dick, don't make any mistakes, on the left is Mr. so-and-so and on the right is Mr. so-and-so." He knew them all, Fore remembered. "That's just how close and observant he was. He's an operator." Lyndon's hard work paid off when Kleberg won the primary by more than 8500 votes out of some 50,000 cast, capturing ten of the eleven counties in the Fourteenth District.[34]

The election taught Lyndon not only the value of careful grassroots' work but also how little a liberal or conservative ideology meant in such a campaign. Kleberg was more conservative than his opponents and when one of them had attacked his support of a regressive sales tax and tax exemptions for Texas Gulf Sulfur, he permitted his supporters to describe the man as a "communist." Yet despite his conservatism and smear tactics, the Citizens' League in San Antonio, a reform organization opposed to the corrupt City-County machine, backed Kleberg.

Similarly, in 1932 Lyndon worked for Maury Maverick, the offspring of a famous Texas family and a leading figure in the Citizens' League, who was running for tax collector in San Antonio. Maverick was an outspoken liberal who belonged to the American Civil Liberties Union and advocated minority rights, particularly those of the many Mexican-Americans living in the city. Lyndon, who Maverick would later praise as the "brightest secretary in Washington," took part in Maverick's campaign. He wrote radio speeches and newspaper ads, worked the crowds with Maverick in San Antonio's slums, embracing and kissing Mexican-Americans, and helped buy the election. Paying $5 a vote, Lyndon and other campaign workers handed out the money the day before the primary in a San Antonio hotel room to Mexican-American men who came in one at a time. Maverick, who complained that Washington was full of "crooked lawyers and people who want favors to which they are not entitled," taught Lyndon that winning an election in Bexar County meant buying Mexican-American votes.[35]

But Lyndon didn't need much instruction from Fore or Maverick on what it took to succeed in politics. In the spring of 1933, he made some political history of his own. In 1919, congressional secretaries had created the Little Congress, an organization modeled on the House of Representatives, where members could learn parliamentary procedures and imitate their bosses by holding debates under House rules. By 1933, the group had become an inconsequential debating society dominated by a few dozen conservative senior secretaries. Encouraged by Arthur Perry, Senator Tom Connally's assistant, who wanted to make the group a forum for prominent political leaders, Lyndon decided to run for Speaker. Learning that anyone on the congressional payroll, including elevator operators, mailmen, policemen, and typists, could vote in the election if they had paid their $2 dues, Lyndon led a quiet effort to persuade people, who had no previous interest in the organization, to come and vote for him at the group's April meeting.

Lyndon appealed to potential supporters not only by promising to attract renowned speakers but, more importantly, by making their involvement in the Little Congress an exercise in liberal reform. Excited by Roosevelt's bold innovations of the Hundred Days, Lyndon and his backers described their opponents in the Little Congress as "standpatters" and saw themselves as insurgents overthrowing an "oligarchy" that had been "dictatorial" and "reactionary." After a majority of the more than 250 people present elected Lyndon Speaker of the Little Congress, he promised them a "new deal" which would be "mindful of 'the forgotten man.' " When Lyndon gleefully reported his success to Vice President Garner, he responded: "Quit gloating and learn to heal the wounds of those you defeated. You need to have friends on both sides of the aisle, and you won't be much of a speaker if you don't." Judging from his acceptance speech, Lyndon's political instincts had already moved him to do just that: "My election tonight," he had said, "will mark . . . a new deal for all Little Congresses, and by that I mean that every one regardless of party affiliations will receive square treatment from the chair. Committees will be named on an equitable basis of membership and seniority." Since Lyndon's supporters had used harsh words in describing their opponents—words that were subsequently stricken from the record—and since some of his votes may have come from ineligible voters who had not paid their dues, he took pains to soothe the opposition, as he had in San Marcos.[36]

Lyndon's political talent registered forcefully on Garner nine months later when Lyndon outmaneuvered him in a Texas patronage fight. Democratic control of the White House for the first time in twelve years meant postmasterships for party loyalists in congressional districts all over the country. The redistricting of congressional seats in Texas in 1933, however, raised questions about which postmasterships belonged to which congressman. In the circumstances, Garner moved to clear all appointments through his office, giving one man an unprecedented hold over Federal jobs in Texas. Because loss of this patronage would seriously jeopardize Kleberg's ability to reward district supporters and hold on to his seat, Lyndon suggested that his boss put a "gentlemen's contract" before Texas's twenty-one congressmen and two senators stating that control over patronage positions in each county remain unchanged until redistricting went into effect in January 1935. Despite the agreement of the entire Texas delegation, Garner, in January 1934, nevertheless tried to take control of postmasters' jobs in all redistricted counties. In response, Lyndon leaked the "contract" to the Associated Press, and newspapers across Texas and around the nation featured the Vice President's grab for power. Embarrassed by the story, Garner publicly excluded himself from a say in Texas postmasterships. Afterward, the angry Vice President went among fellow Texans asking: " 'Who in the hell is this boy Lyndon Johnson; where the hell did Kleberg get a boy with savvy like that?' "[37]

Lyndon was learning his trade and establishing a reputation among his fellow Texans as something of a political *Wunderkind,* but politics wasn't the only thing on his mind in 1934. The first week in September he met Claudia Alta (Lady Bird) Taylor during a visit to Austin on business for Kleberg. The attraction between them was immediate, mutual, and enduring, as a ten-week whirlwind romance and more than thirty-eight years of marriage would demonstrate.

Born on December 22, 1912, in Karnack, a small town in east Texas named after the temples of Egypt by a poor speller, Claudia Taylor was the daughter of an emotionally troubled mother, Minnie Lee Patillo, and a highly successful merchant and farmer, Thomas Jefferson Taylor. The child of a wealthy Alabama planter, Minnie Lee was a bookish, cultured lady who often fled Karnack for the opera season in Chicago and the theater in Shreveport. Her daughter remembered her as a "tall, graceful" lady who "wore white quite a lot . . . went around the house in a great rush, and loved to read" Greek, Roman, and Teutonic myths, which left Claudia with a love of Siegfried. Neighbors remembered Minnie Lee as "strange," a remote, aloof lady who wandered about the woods reading novels and reciting poetry, wrapped scarfs about her head to ease the pain of migraine headaches, and often secluded herself in her room suffering from nervous exhaustion. Too ill to care for her two older sons and daughter, Minnie Lee relied on black nursemaids to attend to the children. Alice Tittle, one of the maids, gave Claudia a lifelong nickname when she described the infant "as purdy as a lady bird." In 1918, when Lady Bird was not quite six, Minnie Lee suffered a miscarriage after an accidental fall and died of blood poisoning. At first, Lady Bird was "quite sure" that her mother "was going to come back," but in time, insulated by what she later described as "some sort of protective cloak nature puts around young folks," she "quit thinking about it."[38]

Thomas Jefferson Taylor was a driven businessman who "never talked about anything except making money." Starting with practically nothing, Taylor worked ceaselessly during the first two decades of the century acquiring land, cotton gins, and general stores with signs, "T. J. Taylor—Dealer in Everything." Usually rising at four in the morning and working often until late in the evening, he became the richest man in Harrison County, accumulating approximately 65,000 acres of land. A tall, overbearing character whom whites called "Cap'n Taylor" and blacks addressed as "Mister Boss," Taylor lent money and rented land to black tenants whom he "kept in peonage." "My father was a very strong character, to put it mildly," Lady Bird said later. He was the kingpin in what she described as "a whole feudal way of life."[39]

His business concerns left him little time to think about his children. After Minnie Lee died, he kept the boys in boarding schools and took Lady Bird with him to the general store in Karnack, where she would play during the day and sleep on a second-floor cot near a stack of coffins while he worked at night. But believing this a poor way to raise his daughter, Taylor sent her to live with Aunt Effie, Minnie Lee's spinster sister in Alabama. Too busy at the store to go along, he sent her alone on a train with an identity tag on her coat and instructions for the conductor about her destination. A gentle, frail but spirited woman with a taste for books, music, and nature, Aunt Effie gave Lady Bird "many fine values." But she also left Lady Bird with the feeling that Aunt Effie was "the most unworldly human in the world," a surrogate mother with no interest in material things like arranging dancing lessons or helping a child choose attractive clothes.[40]

Lady Bird's complaint reflected painful memories of her own shyness and unworldliness as a school girl and teenager. After a year in Alabama, Lady Bird and Aunt Effie returned to Karnack to live with Lady Bird's father. For the next five years, until she was twelve, Lady Bird attended a one-room school house "on top of a red clay hill." There were usually no more than a dozen students in the school, and sometimes by the close of a school year, during which the children of white tenant farmers would leave, she was the only student left. Until she went to high school, first in the town of Jefferson and then in Marshall, the county seat, she was largely isolated from other children her age. Although a precocious student in high school, she had a limited social life: she was terribly shy, rarely dated, and had a reputation as a girl whose ambition was to be an old maid. In her last term at Marshall, the realization that she might be the valedictorian or the salutatorian of the graduating class, both of whom had to make commencement speeches, left her praying that she would stand third. "I had enough pride to want to amount to something," she recalled, "but not enough to pay the price to make a speech." To her relief, her 94 grade-point average was a half point lower than the girl who finished second in the class. Only fifteen when she graduated from Marshall, she attended St. Mary's Episcopal School for Girls, a junior college, for two years.[41]

Eugenia (Gene) Boehringer, the older sister of a high-school friend, then persuaded her to attend the University of Texas in Austin, a city she fell in love with the "moment I laid eyes on it." Gene "was one of those tremendously outgoing people who made everyone around her feel a little more alive." During their time together in Austin, she made Lady Bird feel "important for the first time" in her life as well as "friendlier" and "more confident." During her four years at the University, Lady Bird overcame much of her earlier shyness. She was active in student affairs, especially as publicity manager for the University's Sports Association, which oversaw women's athletics. She also had a lively social life, dating a number of young men. Most of all, she worked to get as much from her education as possible, earning two degrees, a Bachelor of Arts in 1933 and a Bachelor of Journalism in 1934. She remembered herself as determined to acquire the skills which could take her out of Karnack and into an interesting career. She got a second-grade teacher's certificate "with the idea of trying to get a job in some faraway romantic spot—Hawaii or Alaska." But having little desire to teach, she took typing and shorthand, courses that might have made her a good secretary and set her on the road to a successful business career. She got the degree in journalism "because I thought that people in the press went more places and met more interesting people."[42]

A career for a proper young woman from a well-to-do family, however, was out of the ordinary in 1934. And so Lady Bird, whatever her ultimate plans, decided to devote the year after earning her journalism degree to remodeling her father's house in Karnack. To that end, she went to Austin in late August to consult an architect, and while there, she met Lyndon in the Texas Railroad Commission office, where Gene Boehringer was working. Gene, who had met Lyndon through his father, had been trying to introduce Lady Bird to him for several months. When Lyndon showed up at Gene's office on that August day to keep a date with another woman, Lady Bird was also there. He invited all three young women to join him for a drink. Lyndon, who had already heard a great deal about Lady Bird, asked her to meet him for breakfast in the morning. Although she agreed, Bird was ambivalent about showing up. He was "very, very good-looking, lots of hair, quite black and wavy, and the most outspoken, straightforward, determined young man I'd ever met. I knew I had met something remarkable, but I didn't know quite what. . . . I had a sort of queer moth-and-the-flame feeling about what a remarkable man this is." She found him "a little bit scary—so dynamic and so insistent. He came on very strong, and my instinct was to withdraw."[43]

But she didn't. Though an appointment with her architect made her late for their breakfast date and though she had half a mind not to show up, she went anyway. "I dare say I was going all the time," she later said, "but just telling myself I wasn't going." During breakfast and a drive out into the country afterward, he told her "all sorts of things . . . that were extraordinarily direct for a first conversation"—about his job, his ambitions, his family, how much he earned, and how much insurance he had. "It was just as if he was ready to give me a picture of his life and what he might be capable of doing." He also asked her "the most probing questions" about herself. He talked "incessantly," seemed to be "a salesman through and through," and at first made Bird think he was "repulsive." But he was also "quite gallant" and candid, confessing that he was trying to show her his best side. She began to think him "handsome and charming and terribly bright." She was "terrifically interested and a little bit scared," both drawn and repelled at the same time. Then at the end of the day, only twenty-four hours after they had met, he asked her to marry him. She "thought it was some kind of joke."[44]

But it wasn't. Lyndon was dead serious. He felt at once that she was perfectly suited to him. She impressed him as having great common sense, reasonableness, and dependability. And to boot, like him, she was ambitious to go places, or more precisely to find a man with large dreams in which she could share. As Lyndon later put it, Lady Bird offered him "a double prize." She was not only "the one possible wife for Lyndon Johnson but also . . . the ideal helpmate for a going-places politician." And not simply because she had family money, which surely appealed to him, as some have emphasized, but because she was such a sensible, balanced person who also had her eye on larger things. Though her ambition was more muted than Lyndon's, it was plain enough to two young men who had dated her in college. One of them remembered her as outwardly submissive, but inwardly a strong person with considerable initiative and a desire only to marry someone who had "the potentiality of becoming somebody." The other boy friend saw her as "one of the most determined . . . ambitious and able" persons he had ever met in his life. She told him of "her wish to excel." But she was also a modest and cautious person who, in the social climate of the thirties, found it easier to invest her ambition in a husband than to pursue a grand career design of her own. And someone as bright, dynamic, and openly ambitious as Lyndon was as much the perfect mate for her as she was for him. "He's the only man I ever met who is taller than my daddy," she told a friend shortly after meeting Lyndon.[45]

Although no commitments were made on the day after they met, both of them began acting as if there might be. In the few days Lyndon had to spend in Texas before returning to Washington, he took Lady Bird to meet his parents and the Klebergs, and she invited him to stop in Karnack on his way north. Lyndon made his interest in Lady Bird clear to his mother, who seemed "worried about me," Lady Bird said. She wanted to reassure Rebekah that she had no intention of taking her son away from her and that even if she and Lyndon got closer, it wouldn't alter Rebekah's relationship with her son. At the King Ranch, Lyndon also made his intentions clear to Kleberg's mother, the "duchess," who privately urged Lady Bird to marry him. After their visit to Kleberg's "feudal domain," they headed for Karnack to see Lady Bird's father. "Daddy was right impressed with him," Bird recalled. "After dinner he said in a quiet moment, 'Hmmm. You've been bringing home a lot of boys. This one looks like a man.' " Lyndon, however, was concerned that he might not measure up. The next morning when Malcolm Bardwell, Maury Maverick's secretary who was driving to Washington with Lyndon and shared a room with him at the Taylor house, went downstairs in his pajamas to speak to the cook about breakfast, Lyndon exploded at him: "I'm going to marry this girl. You're going to ruin my marriage if you run around that way." Before he left, he again asked her to marry him. She wouldn't reply, but she kissed him goodbye as he stood by his car. A neighbor yelled at Lyndon, "Don't do that! Hurry up, go on—or the Ku Klux Klan will get you!"[46]

For the next seven weeks they carried on a long-distance romance by phone and mail. Although Lady Bird "didn't think of anything else . . . except him," she suggested waiting a year before they decided anything. But Lyndon had already made up his mind. "Every interesting place I see I make a mental reservation and tell myself that I shall take you there when you are mine. Why must we wait 12 long months to begin to do the things we want to do forever and ever?" he wrote shortly after getting back to Washington. "Dearest," she answered, "I've been reading [Louis Bromfield's] *Early Autumn* and am enthralled. If we were together I would read it to you. . . . There's nothing I'd like better than being comfortable in a nice cozy place and reading something amusing or well-written or interesting to someone I like. All good things are better shared, aren't they?" He fully agreed and continued to press her to act on their shared feelings for each other: "This morning I'm ambitious, proud, energetic and very madly in love with you. . . . If I had a box I would almost make a speech this minute—Plans, ideas, hopes— I'm bubbling over with them." Shortly after, in early November, he convinced her to let him come to Texas to talk about getting engaged.[47]

When he showed up at her house twenty-four hours before she was expecting him, he insisted that they get married in "two weeks from now, a month from now, or right away." But the most she would agree to was an engagement ring they drove to Austin to buy. Lyndon then went to Corpus Christi on business for Kleberg, and Lady Bird went with a friend to Shreveport to buy a trousseau. Then, she went to Alabama to consult Aunt Effie, who urged her not to marry "a strange male" she had known less than two months. "If he loves you as much as he says he does, he'll wait for you," Aunt Effie said. But Lady Bird's father disagreed. When she got back to Karnack, where Lyndon was waiting, Taylor predicted that if she waited until Aunt Effie was ready, she would never marry anyone. "Some of the best deals are made in a hurry," he told her. The next morning, November 17, she decided to discuss matters with Gene Boehringer in Austin, and agreed to let Lyndon drive her there. On the way, however, he convinced her to marry him that day: "We either do it now, or we never will," he said. "And if you say goodbye to me, it just proves to me that you just don't love me enough to dare to. And I just can't bear to go and keep on wondering if it will ever happen." Although she "realized the hazards of the future more than he did," she agreed, "because I didn't want to let him go either."[48]

Deciding to get married in St. Mark's Episcopal Church in San Antonio, Lyndon telephoned a friend and political associate, Dan Quill, the city postmaster, to arrange all the details for them. Lyndon explained that he and Lady Bird were in Texarkana, 425 miles away, and would arrive in San Antonio about six or 6:30 in the evening. He told Quill to schedule the wedding for eight and hung up before he could object. Quill, a former chief deputy county clerk, arranged for the marriage license without Lyndon's coming in person, a county requirement. He also asked the rector of the church, the Reverend Arthur K. McKinstry, to marry them. Reluctant to marry people he didn't know in what he described as a justice-of-the-peace ceremony, the Rev. Mr. McKinstry said he "wouldn't think of such a thing." But Quill, who had recently obtained a mailing permit for the church's newspaper, which saved St. Mark's about $12 a week in mailing costs, played on McKinstry's sense of obligation. Quill also invited a few of Lyndon's other San Antonio acquaintances to the wedding, including Henry Hirshberg, an attorney, who was persuaded to serve as best man. During the day Lady Bird arranged for Cecille Harrison, her college roommate who lived in San Antonio, to be the maid of honor.

When Lyndon and Lady Bird arrived at the Plaza Hotel, where Quill had reserved a room for them, Lady Bird asked Quill if he had bought a wedding ring. Although astonished that they had expected him to do this too, he ran across the street to Sears, Roebuck, where he didn't know what size ring to buy. Taking a dozen different sizes, he brought them to Lady Bird, who selected one. Quill paid $2.50 for the gold band, his wedding gift to the couple. The brief ceremony went smoothly, but as the bride and groom left the church, the Rev. Mr. McKinstry exclaimed, "I hope this marriage lasts." At a wedding supper in St. Anthony's Hotel, no one had the price of the restaurant's expensive wine. The guests toasted the couple with a bottle of sparkling Burgundy that Hirshberg supplied from home.[49]

The couple honeymooned in Mexico and then moved to Washington, where they rented a furnished one-bedroom apartment for $42.50 a month at 1910 Kalorama Road in a modest neighborhood. The day after the wedding Lady Bird had called Gene Boehringer to tell her that she and Lyndon had "committed matrimony last night." The phrase must have echoed in her mind during the first months of her marriage when she faced "a series of challenges" for which she felt "completely unprepared." Accustomed to servants, Lady Bird had no experience as a homemaker. "I had never swept a floor . . . certainly never cooked," she said later. But she was determined to learn, believing that the key to managing a household was "organization." To make her first dinner party, she "got a good cook book and just began planning it and getting everything together ready at the same time." When the Maury Mavericks showed up, Mrs. Maverick, who at thirty-five was only thirteen years older than Lady Bird, felt as if "a little girl had invited me. . . . One of the first things I saw was a Fanny Farmer cook book open on the table. Staring at me was a recipe for boiled rice. The menu included baked ham, lemon pie and of course the rice. The ham and pie were very good, but I'll never forget that rice. It tasted like library paste. To this day I connect boiled rice with library paste. But Bird was fun and a nice little hostess."[50]

An even greater challenge was mastering the demands of her imperious husband. "Lyndon is the leader," Lady Bird said later. "Lyndon sets the pattern, I execute what he wants. Lyndon's wish dominates our household. . . . Lyndon's tastes dominate our household." Calling him "Mein Herr, she danced attendance" on his every wish. She laid out his clothes in the morning, shined his shoes, filled his pens and cigarette lighters, and, along with his money and hankerchief, put them in the proper pockets of his jackets and pants. She served him coffee in bed on a tray with the morning newspaper. He also managed her dress and appearance, insisting that she wear high-heeled instead of flat-heeled shoes, that she lose some weight, change her hairstyle, wear brighter colors, and take more care with her makeup. She "became subjunctive to his objective," one of Lyndon's oldest friends recalled. Her "life melted into Lyndon's," another said. He sometimes also ordered her about in public in ways that embarrassed her and their friends. "He'd . . . just yell at her across the room, tell her to do something," yet another family friend recalls. "All the people from Texas felt very sorry for Lady Bird," and wondered "how she stands it."[51]

Lady Bird never saw it that way. As she later made clear to a journalist, her life with Lyndon meant not a loss of identity but a chance to use her endowments to the fullest, a challenge to become "a perfect wife," to stretch herself to be all she could be. For her, devotion to a difficult but extraordinary man of "indisputable talents" gave her great satisfaction. And as Doris Kearns later wrote about their relationship: "Amid the most complicated intrigues and struggles of her husband's career she remained outwardly composed and reasonable. If his incessant demands and orders . . . or his occasional abuse in front of company became too much for her to bear, she possessed, or soon developed, a strange ability to take psychic leave. . . . 'Bird,' Johnson would call out at such moments, 'are you with me?' And straight off, her accustomed alertness and competence reappeared. Without such devotion and forbearance, without a love steadily given and never withdrawn, the course of Lyndon Johnson's continuing ascent in the world of politics becomes inconceivable." And Lyndon himself came to understand this. Lady Bird "was his support, a helper in and necessary condition to his great enterprise—a figure central to his life," he told Kearns toward the end of his life.[52]

The principal question for Lyndon at the end of 1934 was how to get on with a career. After three years, the attractions of being a congressional secretary were few. He wanted to be a congressman. Now past twenty-six, more than a year beyond the qualifying age for election to the Lower House, and having essentially been the congressman from the Fourteenth District in all but name, he wished to hold an office he felt supremely qualified to fill. "I'm not the assistant type," he told a friend at about this time. "I'm the executive type." Moreover, when one of Lyndon's assistants addressed a letter over his signature to Secretary of the Treasury Henry Morgenthau, Jr., "Dear Henry," Lyndon objected. "Look, I can't call him Henry. There's going to come a day when I will, but it's not now."[53]

Lyndon now considered earning a law degree as a way to advance himself. He knew that many, if not most, congressmen were lawyers and that a law degree might make it easier for him to become one when the moment for him to run arrived.

At the same time, Alvin J. Wirtz, who had been a Texas state senator in the twenties and was now a successful and politically influential attorney in Austin, had urged Lyndon to attend law school. He had promised him a place in his law firm with the prospect of making "a ton of money" and becoming "a very powerful man." Wirtz was primarily interested in building publicly funded dams on the lower Colorado River that would prevent floods, promote conservation, and generate cheap electric power. As counsel to the Lower Colorado River Authority, a conservation and reclamation district created by the Texas legislature in 1934, Wirtz often came to Washington, where he sought the help of south-central Texas congressmen in advancing the Authority's goals. Having come to rely more on Lyndon than Kleberg in arranging entree to government officials, Wirtz saw Lyndon as an exceptionally promising young man who could serve their mutual interests by becoming an attorney.[54]

In response to these considerations, Lyndon had enrolled in the Georgetown University evening law program in September 1934. But his attendance there was brief. "I earned only a B.A. degree—for Brief Attendance," he later joked. He had neither the time nor the patience to do the required work. "I never get a chance to study. I'm working all the time, evenings as well as in the daytime," he had told Russell Morton Brown, who had sat next to him in class. He had never prepared enough to participate in class discussions. As important, the training had impressed him as too historical and impractical. When the instructor had used some latin phrases in explaining the background of English legal concepts, Lyndon had complained, "Why don't they stick to the plain English." When the teacher had covered ground he knew from watching Congress enact a law, he had muttered, "He's not telling me anything I don't know." Lyndon "was interested in going and doing and arranging and creating," Brown said. "He had scant patience for sitting down and reading an extended judicial opinion and then . . . looking up the cases they cited." Besides, as L. E. Jones remembered, his attention in the autumn of 1934 had been focused on Lady Bird. By the time Lyndon went back to Texas to get married, he had already given up on earning a law degree.[55]

He also now allowed the Little Congress to slip from his control without an all-out fight. During the almost two years since he had won the speakership, he had invested considerable energy in making the Little Congress into a more interesting organization. He had organized meetings focused on pending legislation. Aides for congressmen supporting and opposing a bill would debate each other in a prelude to what might happen on the House floor. The debates in the Little Congress had attracted large audiences, including the press, which had carried stories about them in their papers. Lyndon also had aroused interest in the organization by arranging a memorable trip to New York City for its members and fulfilling his promise to have prominent politicians address the group. The most notable example had been Huey Long, whose presence had attracted a huge crowd and given the Little Congress a measure of attention it had never received before.

Lyndon had so dominated the proceedings of the group that other congressional secretaries had begun calling him "The Boss of the Little Congress." In March 1935, however, when a group of secretaries who felt that Lyndon had become too powerful in the organization challenged his control, he did not make the sort of effort that had characterized his previous political fights. Little Congress bylaws prohibited Lyndon from seeking a second two-year term. Nevertheless, he had chosen William Howard Payne of Oklahoma as his successor and could not have been happy about the challenge to his authority led by James P. Coleman, a freshman aide from Mississippi. Coleman's campaign for the Little Congress speakership was directed less against Lyndon than Payne himself. Payne's humiliation of "a very well meaning young man from Pittsburgh" who had tried to make a speech incensed Coleman and decided him to run against Payne. Coleman recalls that others fought for him as a way to knock down Lyndon's "pretensions as boss." Although "it was a 'knock down-drag out' fight" won by Coleman, Lyndon never showed him "any resentment or acrimony." Since Lyndon's defeat revealed the embarrassing fact that some of those supporting Lyndon had not paid dues and were ineligible to vote, it is somewhat surprising that he relinquished his grip on the Little Congress without a greater struggle.[56]

But his attention was now fixed on other things. At this time, he was talking about becoming the president of Texas A&I University in Kingsville, an institution partly founded with Kleberg money and dominated by the Kleberg family. According to Luther Jones, somebody connected with the University approached Lyndon, and he began discussing plans for how he would get "better professors," do "things in agriculture that had never been done before," and turn the school into "one of the top universities in the world." Probably because he was too young and too little qualified to hold the post, it was never offered to him. Shortly after, Horatio H. Adams, the chief Washington lobbyist for the General Electric Corporation, invited Lyndon to work for him. Carrying a salary of $10,000 a year, more than two and a half times what he was earning, the job sorely tempted Lyndon. When Roy Miller explained, however, that becoming a corporate lobbyist might shorten his chances of winning a Texas election, he hesitated to accept the position. "Why don't you take it, man? You'll never get a job like that," Malcolm Bardwell, Maury Maverick's secretary, told him. "He said, 'No. No. It's not in keeping with what I want to do. Money doesn't mean everything.' "[57]

But Kleberg was forcing his hand. Mamie Kleberg had convinced Mr. Dick to dismiss Lyndon. She no longer saw him as a constructive influence on her family's life but as a threat to both her marriage and her husband's job. She had gotten hold of a letter from Kleberg's mistress to Lyndon which suggested that he favored her rival. Also knowing that Lyndon was ambitious for Mr. Dick's seat and fearing that he might run against him, Mrs. Kleberg persuaded the congressman to push Lyndon out.

Lyndon, in fact, had been building a political power base for himself in Texas. He had arranged patronage jobs for friends, advertised his part in helping district constituents, and ingratiated himself with Texas businessmen and lobbyists by arranging hotel accommodations and appointments with government officials. Yet he recognized that he could not go after Kleberg's seat unless the congressman retired or took another job. Since Kleberg enjoyed Washington's social life and the amenities of being a congressman, the first alternative seemed unlikely. The second was a greater possibility, and beginning in 1933 Lyndon had encouraged talk that Kleberg would become Ambassador to Mexico or some other Latin American country. It was soon clear, however, that Kleberg had too little standing with the Administration to receive a significant appointment of any kind. In 1935, Kleberg's Fourteenth District seat was beyond Lyndon's reach.[58]

An opportunity for a high-level appointment in the National Youth Administration answered Lyndon's hopes for a significant job. On June 26, 1935, Franklin Roosevelt issued an Executive Order establishing the NYA. Its aim was to help young people between the ages of sixteen and twenty-five stay in school or get job training. When Malcom Bardwell told Lyndon that Aubrey Williams, the head of the new agency, needed a Texas state director, Lyndon said, "I'd like that job." He and Bardwell then asked the administrative aides to Senators Connally and Sheppard to press the case for Lyndon with their bosses.

At the same time, Lyndon enlisted Sam Rayburn's help. As with President Evans and Professor Greene at San Marcos, Lyndon had begun establishing a father-son relationship with Mister Sam, as Lyndon called him. Rayburn, who had been briefly married and had no children, was drawn to the young man. Also having made his own way in politics by cultivating powerful older sponsors, Rayburn was happy to take on a protege. In addition he had warm memories of Sam Ealy Johnson, with whom he had served in the Texas legislature. By 1935, Rayburn had grown so fond of Lyndon that when the young man was hospitalized with pneumonia, he took up a vigil at his bedside and told him, "Now Lyndon don't you worry. Take it easy. If you need money or anything, you just call on me." When the NYA job appeared, Lyndon did, and Rayburn spoke to Senator Tom Connally. "One day Sam Rayburn, who had never been friendly toward me, came to see me," Connally recalled. "He wanted me to ask President Roosevelt to appoint Lyndon Johnson to run the Texas NYA, and he said he knew this fell in my patronage basket. Sam was agitated and wouldn't leave until I agreed to do this."

Lyndon also asked Maury Maverick's help, and he promised to talk to the President and Aubrey Williams. Roosevelt was reluctant to appoint someone so young, but he agreed with Maverick that Lyndon would be in a better position than someone older to understand the problems of the people he would be helping. Williams, who had already announced an appointee and then withdrew it at the advice of University of Texas Professor Robert Montgomery, was receptive to the suggestion, especially when it was reinforced by Congressman Martin Dies. In a letter to Maverick eighteen years later, Williams remembered "that the first time I ever heard of [Lyndon Johnson] . . . was one night when . . . you laid his name in my lap and said he was a good guy. Then, as I recall it he got Martin Dies to call me. The first and only time that bastard ever did me the honor. And I concluded that if Maury Maverick and Martin Dies both recommended a guy that he must be a safe bet. I have no recollection that Sam Rayburn was guilty of starting that tumble bug on his way. It was you and your buddy Martin Dies." FDR remained reluctant to appoint someone who at the age of twenty-seven would be the youngest of the state directors, but with both Texas senators amenable, leading Texas congressmen enthusiastic, and Williams recommending it, Roosevelt gave him the job.[59]

5

The Making of a
Congressman

THE National Youth Administration expressed the concern of Roosevelt's New Deal to save a generation of young people from ignorance, unemployment, and enduring hardship. When FDR took office in 1933, between a quarter and a third of America's thirteen million unemployed were sixteen to twenty-five years old. During the next two years the Civilian Conservation Corps and the Federal Emergency Relief Administration made special efforts to employ young people or help them stay in school long enough to develop marketable skills. But these were limited efforts with small impact. By the spring of 1935, 20 percent of the nations twenty-two million youngsters remained out of school and either on relief or wandering the country looking for work. "Most of those on the road nowadays are young men," a railroad policeman said, "just young fellows, just boys who don't know where they are going, or why."[1]

Some people in the Roosevelt administration urged a special effort to help the young. In May 1934, Eleanor Roosevelt declared, "I have moments of real terror when I think we may be losing this generation. We have got to bring these young people into the active life of the community and make them feel they are necessary." But how? Some like Wilson's former Secretary of War Newton D. Baker thought young people with "initiative and spirit" could find work. But the First Lady wasn't persuaded: "If you have any convincing suggestions as to how to stimulate the imagination of young people and how to direct their energies, I shall be more than grateful," she wrote Baker. "My mail is filled with pleas for help."[2]

The President himself was reluctant to single out young Americans for special help. Early in 1935 he told Eleanor that the problem of the young could not be separated from the difficulties of all the people. Appealing to the "practical politician" in her husband, Eleanor pointed out that the young would be voters one day. "There is a good deal to what you say," Franklin replied, adding he would "be glad to consider the matter." Harry Hopkins and Aubrey Williams at the WPA and Secretary of Labor Frances Perkins proposed that relief funds be allotted to provide jobs for unemployed youngsters and help students stay in school. "Do you think it is right to do this?" Franklin asked Eleanor. She did, but cautioned that critics would compare the program to Nazi efforts in Germany to bring youngsters under the control of the state. It would be described as an assault on the independence of America's schools, an unwarranted appropriation of Federal power to interfere in education. But believing that long-term benefits would exceed short-term losses, FDR decided to take the political heat. "I guess we can stand the criticism, and I doubt if our youth can be regimented in this way or in any other way," he said privately. "I have determined that we shall do something for the Nation's unemployed youth because we can ill afford to lose the skill and energy of these young men and women," he said when announcing the birth of the NYA. "They must have their chance in school, their turn as apprentices and their opportunity for jobs—a chance to work and earn for themselves."[3]

If FDR partly aimed to create a generation of Democratic voters by establishing the youth agency, Lyndon also saw political advantages in becoming head of the Texas NYA. He could build local and state-wide contacts for future campaigns. After being appointed, he told Malcolm Bardwell, "When I come back to Washington, I'm coming back as a Congressman." Lady Bird said later, "I suppose the seed had always lain dormant in Lyndon's mind that one day he would try for elective office. It seemed so utterly natural." And, she might have added, a Federal directorship of a state-wide agency was perfect for a politically ambitious young man whose goal was to represent Texas in Washington.

Like FDR, however, Lyndon's first concern was to help needy youngsters. Throughout his life, nothing in politics appealed more to him than marrying his ambition to help for the poor. Seeing the NYA as principally opening avenues of opportunity to youngsters who might otherwise never realize their potential, Lyndon was thrilled to help administer the program. Twenty-eight years later, Lady Bird remebered how much "love" and "drive" Lyndon put into his NYA work. "That was right down his alley, trying to put young people either back into schools if they could get part-time jobs or to teach them skills. At any rate, to take them off the boxcars and off the highway flagging rides and to put them to something more useful and productive. And the good effects of them [the work] have lingered through our lives to this day both in satisfactions to the spirit and in other more worldly productive ways."[4]

But making the NYA work wasn't easy. At the start of the program no one had a clear idea of how to proceed. In August 1935, nearly two months after the NYA was born, Harry Hopkins, the head of the WPA, said, "I have nothing on my mind to offer as a solution to our problems, and I know of no one else who has . . . a satisfactory program for young people. I want to assure you that the government is looking for ideas." NYA Director Aubrey Williams echoed the point: "We have no answers already written to the problems of young people. . . . To do very much about this situation may be beyond any group of people, no matter how sincere and how earnest they are."[5]

Lyndon quickly recognized that Texas had its own special difficulties. In 1935, nearly 125,000 Texans between the ages of sixteen and twenty-five were on relief, and represented approximately 5 percent of young-sters in the forty-eight states needing help. Even more daunting was the variety of conditions in Texas that had to be considered in trying to devise and administer state-wide programs: nearly one-ninth the area of the continental United States and divided into 254 counties, Texas seemed too big and varied for any single program to work effectively across the state. "Our aid problem is a big one," Lyndon told Williams shortly after starting his job, not the least of which was helping college students. New York, for example, with nearly twice the population, had only one more college than Texas, but almost half of them were concentrated in New York City. By contrast, Texas colleges were spread across 267,000 square miles, and the question of how a small staff would administer NYA programs in such a far-flung group of schools remained to be solved. Moreover, Lyndon had only half a million dollars to spend in the first year, less than 2 percent of the annual NYA budget of $27 million. "We had various choices of what to do with" needy young people in Texas, he told a group of educators in September 1935. "We could starve them to death; we could send them to school; we could kill them through war. Obviously the answer lay in sending some of them to school; giving some of them vocational training; finding work projects for others. That briefly is the work cut out for the NYA."[6]

He approached the job with ferocious energy. When Williams ap-pointed Lyndon on July 25, he asked him not to hire anyone or make any commitments until the Washington office had a clearer idea of what it wanted done. But Lyndon thought that helping thousands of high-school and college students resume classes in the fall term meant get-ting started at once. Consequently, he began publicizing the program, enlisting the help of state and local officials, recruiting a staff, and de-veloping plans to keep young people in school during his first week in office. At the Austin airport on July 31, he held a press conference, where he said his aim was to work himself out of a job. After a meeting with Governor Jimmy Allred at the state capitol, Lyndon told reporters that Allred had promised him full cooperation, and he hoped to get the same from mayors around the state. He would be flying to their cities for conferences in the coming week. When he returned, he asked L. E. Jones, who was now enrolled in the University of Texas Law School, to become an assistant director. At the same time, he outlined a four-point program for aiding college students.

Lyndon's pace was too fast for NYA headquarters in Washington. "We have been advised that a young man by the name of L. E. Jones is being described as an Assistant Director of the NYA for Texas," one of Williams's deputies wrote Lyndon on August 5. Mr. Williams "is giving no authorization to appoint an Assistant Director in your state." Lyndon was asked to wait until after a meeting of all state directors in Washington on August 18 or 19. "We have a big state, consequently a big job; and since our time is short, if we are going to put the program over, we must start moving," Lyndon replied on August 8. Attaching his four-point plan for helping needy college youngsters, he asked for a decision on it now.[7]

But Williams, under pressure to move quickly from other state directors as well, refused to act precipitously. And not because he was naturally cautious; quite the contrary, an Alabama social worker who had held a factory job at the age of six and studied philosophy at the Sorbonne with Henri Bergson, Williams was a radical who hated poverty and all those privileged Americans who acquiesced in it. As zealous as anyone to help disadvantaged young people, he wished to assure that the NYA made no false steps which could be turned against it later. But Lyndon, who thought it a mistake to wait, recruited his principal deputies and opened an office before the Washington meeting. In July, he had asked his college friend Willard Deason to take his vacation and meet him in Austin the following week. Lyndon persuaded him to devote his two-week holiday to setting up the new agency. At the end of the two weeks, he convinced Deason, who reluctantly gave up "a stepping stone toward maybe being a practicing lawyer," to take a six-month leave from his Federal Land Bank job in Houston to become an assistant. He was "just a great salesman," Deason said of his decision to accept Lyndon's offer.[8]

Jesse Kellam, another college classmate, and Sherman Birdwell, a childhood chum, also succumbed to Lyndon's wooing. Having invited both men to meet him at the Post Office Cafe in San Marcos at seven o'clock one morning, Lyndon spent a couple of hours describing the difficulties young people had staying in school or finding work and the role the NYA could play in helping them realize their dreams. Lyndon aroused their sympathy for kids who "couldn't buy pencils and paper, much less shoes," and then asked them to work for him at the NYA. Birdwell didn't need much persuading. Although he was trying to establish his own business in Austin, he agreed to take a $2200-a-year job as Lyndon's finance director. Kellam was much more reluctant. Lyndon asked him to be second in command at a $3900 annual salary. But Kellam was hesitant about leaving a good position in the state education department, which Lyndon had helped him get, for a less promising one in a new and probably temporary agency. Lyndon sold him on the idea of taking a month's leave from his current job, and subsequently convinced him to extend his leave to a year. When all three of Lyndon's assistants came to the sixth floor of the Littlefield Building in downtown Austin to begin work early on the morning of August 15, Lyndon had already been there for a while talking on the telephone.[9]

Three days later he was in Washington for the state directors' conference and a ceremonial visit to the White House, where the President gave them marching orders. The meeting with Williams put a temporary damper on Lyndon's enthusiam and that of other state directors. "Everything was so negative," Richard Brown, the head of the Colorado office, recalled. Williams rejected every plan state directors proposed, including "some very concrete" suggestions by Lyndon, as violations of Federal regulations. Brown finally said: "Well, Mr. Williams, we spent three days and three nights here trying to figure out [what to do]. All the discussions have resulted in telling us what we couldn't do. Could we have a half hour before we go home in which you tell us what we can do?" Embarrassed, Williams presided over a three-hour discussion in which people "told what they planned to do."

Though not specific about means, Roosevelt left no doubt that he wanted more than rhetoric. At the White House meeting, Lyndon's first face-to-face encounter with FDR, the President pointed out that past groups had come "to talk about education, child welfare and various things like that. They had very interesting discussions and they passed very nice resolutions. . . . Everybody went home; and little, if anything, resulted from their efforts. Our procedure is different. We have asked you here to start something. . . . It is the first time the Federal Government has attempted a great national project of this kind. It is an experiment, but we are going to get something more than mere resolutions out of it. We are going to get action." FDR, who wanted to meet the program's youngest state director, asked Lyndon to stay after the others had left. Lyndon recalled that the President said something about Maverick's part in getting him the job and "kinda petted me."[10]

Lyndon needed no encouragement to produce concrete results. He had already determined to spare no effort in behalf of the program. When he returned to Austin, he began a routine that tested his endurance and that of his most devoted co-workers. Sixteen-, eighteen-hour days, seven days a week, week in and week out became the norm. Starting usually at seven in the morning, Lyndon often worked until after midnight. He ate lunch at his desk and dinner at home with associates discussing the day's problems. At about eight, he habitually returned with them to the Littlefield office for another few hours, where they had to work by antiquated gaslight and walk down six flights of stairs in the dark because the building superintendent turned off the electricity at 10:30. Many nights they simply held staff meetings at Lyndon's house, where they reviewed the latest NYA regulations, which were changing all the time. "Along about eleven o'clock," Birdwell remembers, "we'd all be so whipped down we couldn't see. . . . About eleven or eleven-thirty Lady Bird would come in with cake and coffee," which would "renew" them for a while. When this routine became too much even for Lyndon, he and Kellam would relax by driving to San Antonio or Dallas to inspect one of their projects. But there was no let up on the road. "It was not uncommon for all of us to work all day and drive all night to start a project the next day," Birdwell said. Lyndon was totally caught up in the work, another friend recalled. "You'd ask him about the weather and he'd start talking about the projects."[11]

Recognizing how hard he drove his subordinates, Lyndon occasionally resorted to humor and an evening off to keep his people going. Deason recalls a Sunday meeting of district directors in Austin that lasted from eight in the morning until four in the afternoon. Knowing that they faced long drives home and a return to work early Monday morning, Lyndon gave them "a pep talk. He put his left hand in his left coat pocket and his right hand in his right coat pocket, and he started rattling them. He said, 'I carry Ex-Lax in this pocket to get me going. . . I carry aspirin in this one. And that's what you've got to do to get this program under way.'" Once, when Birdwell had been traveling for two weeks, he wired Lyndon: "Snow storm in Amarillo. Dust storm in Abilene. Downpour in Brownwood. . . . Tell everybody I'll report to duty tonight." When he got the telegram during a staff meeting on a Saturday afternoon, he said very seriously, "I guess we've had it." "What happened? Did somebody die?" they asked. "No, this is a weather report from Sherman," he said, and read it to them. "I think we all need to put our hats and coats on and go home. It's time when a guy starts giving us the weather reports."[12]

Humor and free time were the exceptions. The rule was unrelenting work partly inspired by Lyndon's harsh pressure. Letters had to be answered the day they arrived, dictation had to be immediately transcribed, and work performed had to be exactly as he asked. "Everything had to be done NOW!" one staff member recalled. "And he could get very, very angry if something couldn't be done immediately." "There were times when he almost drove you to the breaking point," another one said. Jake Pickle, who would later become a congressman, remembered that he would have "a hundred things for you to do during the day that you can't get done. . . . And then tomorrow he'd want to know why you didn't get through with it." But even meeting his demands was not enough to satisfy him. The flow of mail, the paperwork required by complicated and often confusing regulations, and the problems involved in implementing programs were so great that they threatened to overwhelm Lyndon and his staff. In response, Lyndon sometimes became wildly abusive of well-meaning subordinates who were already working to the limits of their capacity. He flew into rages in which he unleased a stream of curses the likes of which some in the office had never heard before. He reprimanded people both for having cluttered, sloppy desks and for clean ones, which he took as a sign of indolence. He prodded them into greater efforts with threats of dismissal and reminders of what they might face after losing their job. "Why don't I just fire you?" he shouted at one employee. "Then you can go back to making fifty dollars a month. You know why you were making fifty dollars a month, don't you? Because that's what you're worth!" "God, he could rip a man up and down," another staff member said.[13]

An individual's needs alongside the program counted little with him. Willard Deason remembers one day in San Antonio when Lyndon drove three supervisors all over the city for hours inspecting projects. "Maybe we're not going to get to eat lunch today," one of them in the back said in a stage whisper. Without saying anything, Lyndon stopped at the next drive-in restaurant, where he shouted at the waitress: "Eight hamburgers, four bottles of milk, and make it in a hurry." When Aubrey Williams came to Texas, Lyndon gave him a nonstop inspection tour. About one or two in the afternoon, Williams said, "I'm hungry." Rushing him to a restaurant, Lyndon told the waitress, "Give him a hamburger. We're in a hurry."[14]

Yet Lyndon understood that there had to be a carrot as well as a stick. He challenged people to measure up to his example. "I work seventeen hours a day," he told his staff. "All I ask you to work is sixteen, and we'll get that boy on the streetcorner a job." Driving himself mercilessly, suffering repeated colds and flus, asking no one in the office to work harder than he did, Lyndon was someone the staff not only feared but also admired. Further, impressing everyone as a man with a highly promising future, Lyndon encouraged hopes among some staff members that if they bore his pressure and abuse stoically, they might make some long-term gain. Above all, however, he inspired them with a sense that they were making history—that they were reaching out to desperate young people whose lives would be profoundly affected by what the NYA did.

Everyone in the office knew the story of the hostile San Antonio businessman at a club luncheon who told Lyndon, "All these kids need to do is get out and hustle." Having seen Mexican-American children rummaging through a garbage can behind a cafeteria from which they took grapefruit rinds to gnaw on, he answered: "Right. Last week over here I saw a couple of your local kids hustling—a boy and a girl, nine or ten. They were hustling through a garbage can in an alley." "Put them to work; get them into school!" he urged his staff. "Put them to work! Get them out of the boxcars!" he pleaded. "I never got a feeling of being driven by Lyndon Johnson," one of the staff said later. "He gave you enthusiasm for the work that you were doing, and he set some kind of vision and objective ahead of you that made you want to work just as hard as he worked." The vision included not only helping young people but also making productive citizens who would better conditions in Texas and contribute to a higher living standard throughout the South.[15]

Lyndon knew that hard work alone was not enough to assure the success of the program. Like Administration leaders in Washington, he believed that widespread public support was also essential. To that end, every director set up an advisory board to help the NYA gain acceptance in each of the states. Lyndon initially chose a five-man board representing a cross section of Texas regions and interests: Miller Ainsworth, the state commander of the American Legion from central Texas, Beauford Jester, an educator from the north, Joseph F. Myers, a labor union leader from the southeast, D. H. Perry, a spokesman for agriculture from the south, and H. J. Lutcher Stark, a wealthy businessman from east Texas, gave the NYA a spokesman in every part of the state and among every major group that might become project co-sponsors. Pressed by John J. Corson, the NYA assistant director in Washington, to select men under twenty-five years of age rather than the older people he had chosen, Lyndon objected that they would not "contribute as much as the men I have listed." When Corson continued to ask for other recommendations of "outstanding young people" and the Administration in Washington insisted on the selection of Alvin J. Wirtz as Texas advisory board chairman, Lyndon met their demands by appointing Wirtz and adding three prominent younger men to the board.[16]

At the same time, Lyndon made a point of getting the best possible publicity for the program. Cultivating businessmen, civic leaders, government officials, newspapermen, and school boards, speaking before Rotary, Lions, Kiwanis, and Optimist clubs, and issuing press releases describing their accomplishments, Lyndon and his staff blunted potential criticism of the program and persuaded almost everyone that it was doing good things. He emphasized that the NYA had no political agenda and was a program "based strictly upon American traditions." Publicity releases focused on practical achievements: on how the NYA sponsored productive work for young people contributing to the well-being of all Texans. "We have had no unfavorable news articles and no criticism through the press," Lyndon told Washington in his monthly report for

December 1935. "The papers of Texas are cooperating fully with the NYA."[17]

The approval was merited. The prodigious efforts on the part of Lyndon and his staff had helped thousands of young people get jobs and stay in school. His first concern in Austin after seeing Williams and Roosevelt in Washington had been to launch school-aid programs for elementary, high-school, and college students. Among needy young people around the United States, about half were leaving school after the eighth grade. Of those who continued, only one in five were finishing high school, and of that number, only one in five again were finishing college. In short, the great majority of poor youth in the Depression had neither much education nor training to prepare them for productive lives. In August 1935, Lyndon had a sense of urgency about keeping as many of these young people in school as possible. Reaching elementary and high school pupils in the few weeks before schools opened, however, had proved more difficult than helping college students.[18]

To explain the school-aid program, as the elementary and high school programs were called, the Educational Division of Johnson's NYA office had mailed some 4500 letters to school authorities and families and a news release to 800 newspapers. They had advised that pupils could earn up to $6 a month if they could prove that their parents were either on relief, employed by the PWA, or in the Rural Rehabilitation program. Moreover, school officials, who could help only 7 percent of the pupils enrolled in their schools, had been told to devise "useful" jobs, at hourly rates no greater than locally prevailing ones, which would not displace workers paid from other funds. With the Educational Division consisting of only four people, it quickly found itself swamped by requests from all over the state for additional information. Jesse Kellam remembered how county school superintendents bombarded the office with letters asking for detailed advice on how to proceed. But the people trying to answer the foot-high stacks of mail never seemed to make much progress.[19]

Getting the WPA to certify that families were on relief and their children eligible for school-aid programs had been a formidable problem. " 'We'll get to it as soon as we can,' " WPA officials had responded. " '. . . We're trying to get their daddies to work. . . . It's more important to get the head of the family to work than it is to get a son or daughter.' . . . But our mission wasn't to get the daddy to work," Deason explained. "We had another mission. We felt like ours should be fulfilled as quickly as the other side. . . . So naturally there was a lot of friction." Seeing the WPA folks as "can't-do people," Lyndon had pushed and shoved until they got moving. "We were just going through a shaking down period," Deason said, "with LBJ just shaking a little harder than anybody else." Part of the "shaking" had included an appeal to

Washington officials to press the Texas WPA into promptly disbursing student-aid funds. He urged that "immediate attention be given this matter. If it isn't, we are going to be in a terrible mess at a not too distant future date."[20]

Making the WPA more responsive to NYA concerns, however, did not solve all problems in the Texas school-aid program. By October 10 the Austin office had received only 1,266 student applications for part-time jobs. One difficulty was the requirement that students seeking NYA-sponsored work be 16 years of age or older. If they could include 14- and 15-year-olds in the program, Lyndon advised, it would allow them to reach many more high-school students. Further, by limiting aid to relief families, they were excluding many "worthy and needy students"—orphans, Community Chest clients, and children of farm families temporarily stricken from the relief rolls during the summer cotton-picking season. Agreeing to more relaxed requirements, the Washington office helped the Texas NYA boost enrollment in the student-aid program. By November, 8500 pupils were receiving aid. By May, the number had risen to 11,000 and by the start of the new school year in September 1936, the NYA was helping 12,342 boys and girls to continue their classwork.[21]

The college-aid program had been even more successful, reaching a greater percentage of needy students in a shorter amount of time. Dealing with fewer schools made this possible. By contrast with the 2000 elementary and high schools involved in NYA student-aid programs, there were only 83 colleges and universities, where some 5000 undergraduates had received help in the fall of 1935. Unlike lower school pupils, college students did not have to come from relief families. To receive the maximum $15-a-month NYA payment, an undergraduate had only to be declared needy by his institution and to perform "practical" work adapted to his "abilities and major interest." Although many students performed routine clerical assignments, some used the work to advance their training: agriculture students studied penetration rates of water in irrigation; budding chemical engineers assisted in experiments on hardening steel; chemistry majors removed fluoride from the water supply; geology students excavated and reconstructed fossils; government majors charted urban traffic and obedience to regulations; history majors worked in the documents division of the state archives; and aspiring sociologists returned drop-outs to public schools.[22]

Yet the college-aid program also had its share of problems. For one, there had been many more applicants for jobs than the Texas NYA could support. By the end of September 1935, some 21,766 undergraduates had applied for help. But the office only had enough money to aid 5,036 of them. Leaving the unpleasant task of choosing recipients to the individual campuses, Lyndon's office could only sympathize with the college officials responsible for the hard decisions. At Texas Tech in Lubbock, the president of the school had to pick 259 out of nearly 1500 applicants for the precious jobs. At the University of Texas in Austin, where there were over 3500 applicants for 761 jobs, the dean of students told Kellam, "I have done the most difficult job that I have ever done in my life. If I had four times as many jobs for deserving students at the University, I would still not have enough. In making these selections, I feel that I have blood on my hands." In addition, at the start of the program, the NYA had a terrible time getting students paid quickly. Because of excessive red tape, wages earned in September did not reach college students until mid-November when many of them were in dire financial straits. Appealing once again to the national office for a system that would be more responsive to student needs, Lyndon managed to simplify the procedure and expedite the distribution of funds. He found no way, however, to bring the supply of jobs into balance with the demand. By the end of the 1935–36 academic year the recipients of aid had risen, to 5,497, but so had the applications, reaching 29,000. Although the number of undergraduates being helped reached 7,123 in the following year, they still represented a small percentage of those who needed and wanted such help to remain in college.[23]

Nevertheless, the program was a boon to its participants. This was particularly true of those enrolled in Freshmen College Centers, the most innovative part of the Texas college-aid program. At a meeting on September 3 of college administrators from around the state, President Cecil Evans of Lyndon's alma mater suggested setting up freshmen centers for students who had finished high school but could not afford to attend college even with a part-time NYA job. Aimed at high-school graduates from relief families who had to stay at home and help work the family farm or support their parents and siblings, the Centers allowed these young people to take one or two tuition-free courses from instructors paid with NYA funds. As conceived by Evans, the Centers provided "a stop-gap between high school and first year college education for youths from relief families." Winning Lyndon's enthusiastic support and Washington's approval, the twenty Centers established across the state gave 900 young people their first college work during 1935–36. Located in large cities like Dallas and Houston and small towns like Brenham, Corsicana, Pittsburg, and Temple, the Centers were forerunners of the community or junior colleges that later opened the door to higher education for everyone.[24]

The Freshmen Centers as well as all the other NYA programs in Texas were a particular godsend to blacks, who were among the hardest hit by the Depression. Nationally, economic conditions for blacks in the thirties went from bad to worse. "The Negro was born in depression," one commentator on their plight observed. "It only became official when it hit the white man." In 1932, black unemployment in the United States reached nearly 50 percent, with many of those still working receiving up to 50 percent cuts in wages. Approximately 40 percent of all black workers in the thirties were farm laborers or tenants with average incomes of less than $200 a year. Among blacks over the age of twenty-five, 10 percent had not completed a single year of school; only one in a hundred held a college degree.

New Deal programs provided limited benefits to blacks. The National Recovery Administration became known among blacks as "Negro Run Around" or "Negroes Ruined Again." One historian believes that the AAA's cotton program "achieved about as much for the mass of the nearly 3 million black farm tenants as a plague of boll weevils." It was not strictly the fault of the New Dealers: they confronted Congresses in the thirties dominated by white southerners and a tradition of states' rights that made it impossible to overcome determined efforts to ignore black needs. Southern white planters, for example, had no objection to "keeping their peons alive during the slack season on pork and meal," but they wanted all relief suspended during the work season "so these niggers will be good and hungry." Yet for all that, agencies like the CCC, the Farm Security Administration, and the WPA managed to extend some help to blacks. By the late thirties over 11 percent of CCC enrollees were blacks, the FSA was giving about 23 percent of its assistance to black farmers, and the WPA was using a quota system that made the proportion of black workers on government construction projects far higher than in the private building industry.[25]

The NYA was as aggressive as any New Deal agency in helping disadvantaged blacks. Although it conformed to segregationist practices in the South, hired a disproportionate number of blacks for menial labor, and had the funds to reach only a small proportion of impoverished black youngsters, it nevertheless did more for blacks than almost any other Federal agency in the late thirties and early forties: it hired black administrators to supervise black work in all the southern states; it refused to sanction racial or geographical differentials in wages; it insisted on aid to black students in proportion to their numbers in the state populations; it employed more black administrators than any other New Deal program, including Mary McLeod Bethune, the former president of Bethune-Cookman College in Florida, as the national director of its Division of Negro Activities; and it gave up to 20 percent of its annual budget to black youngsters.[26]

In the late thirties, 855,000 blacks were living in Texas, approximately 6.5 percent of all blacks in the United States and 14.7 percent of the state's population. Black Texans between sixteen and twenty-five, however, were proportionately much greater, 27.8 percent of this age group in the state. Roughly half of them lived on farms with the rest concentrated in towns and urban centers. But regardless of locale, like blacks throughout the nation, they were among the most impoverished in the Depression. Of the 332 black families in the small town of Taylor, some twenty-five miles northeast of Austin, for example, only five had sewerage connections; every member of this black community lost an average of eighteen school or work days annually because of malaria, typhoid, dysentery, and tuberculosis.[27]

Eager to assure "just recognition" of black claims on NYA programs in Texas, the national office pressed Lyndon to appoint a black leader to his state advisory board. In August 1935, before he had gone to the conference of state directors, he had "discussed this matter thoroughly" with John Corson on the telephone and "at some length" after his arrival in Washington. Despite Lyndon's resistance to such a suggestion, Corson raised the question with him again in September: "I am sure you will feel the need of this representation in order that your Advisory Committee may be truly representative of the problem to be considered in your state," Corson wrote. After discussing the issue with "three of the most prominent members" of his board, Lyndon warned against the action that would destroy his and the NYA's credibility in the state. He predicted that such a step would force him and the nine members of his board to resign; that he "would be convicted of making a blunder without parallel in administrative circles of the state"; that "in all probability" he would be " 'run out of Texas,' " and that it would cost the NYA the cooperation of black leaders in Texas who would view such an action as likely to do more harm than good. "The racial question during the last one hundred years in Texas . . . has resolved itself into a definite system of mores and customs which cannot be upset overnight," he advised Corson. "So long as these are observed there is harmony and peace between the races in Texas. But it is exceedingly difficult to step over lines so long established and to upset customs so deep-rooted, by any act which is so shockingly against precedent as the attempt to mix negroes and whites on a common board."[28]

He also emphasized that it would destroy the good work being done for black youngsters in Texas by the NYA. He had appointed a "negro advisory board" that included prominent black Texans; it had already met in Houston and would meet again soon in Waco. Black schools across Texas had "availed themselves of the college and high-school student aid programs to the fullest extent." Plans were under way "to establish a camp for unemployed negro women from 16 to 25 years old." Efforts to provide work relief, job training, job placement, and apprenticeships were all going forward. "I feel confident that in these ways the NYA of Texas will be able to do vastly more to benefit negro youths than by setting them on the firing line of public opinion in Texas, to be shot at by the whites and dodged by the negroes," he concluded.

Persuaded by Johnson's arguments, Corson replied that he would not insist upon his request for a black board member "at this time."[29]

Johnson's response was revealing of ideas and attitudes that shaped his reactions to minority issues throughout his career. First and foremost, there were questions of political expediency: what could be done in the prevailing temper of the times and how would it affect him and the NYA? It was clear to him that a reputation as a successful state director and all that would mean for his political future partly depended on satisfying the demands from Washington for action in behalf of blacks without touching off local racial antagonisms. "Lyndon's position on blacks was purely expediency," L. E. Jones said later. " . . . If you're in politics, you've got to go the way the wind blows."

Jones's assertion takes on added meaning when one considers that Lyndon made little concerted effort as head of the Texas NYA to help "Texas Mexicans." Although they were also terribly impoverished and made up 11.7 percent of the population, Lyndon made nowhere near the effort for them he made for blacks. Since there was little, if any, pressure from Washington to help Hispanics, Lyndon could afford to ignore them. This partly reflected the realization that little sympathy existed for spending Federal funds on a group including many noncitizens.

Political considerations, however, only partly shaped Lyndon's response to Hispanic and black youngsters. He believed that Texas Mexicans, living under conditions "not unlike medieval feudalism," had a built-in primitive relief system in which landowners took care of their basic needs. Lyndon was not cynically indifferent to their plight but viewed them as in a better position than black Texans to survive the Depression without Federal help. Nor were his efforts to help blacks strictly the result of political calculation. Despite his southern roots and an attitude common to his place and time that moved him in private to speak of blacks as "niggers" and describe them in official correspondence as "negroes," he was warmly disposed to giving disadvantaged blacks opportunities for education and employment which allowed them to help themselves.[30]

His efforts to extend NYA help to blacks were similar to those he made for whites, though most of them were made behind the scenes. Soon after he had begun NYA operations in Austin, he asked for a meeting with black leaders, which took place without publicity in the basement of a black Methodist church. Advising them of his eagerness to help black youths stay in school and find jobs, he soon gave substance to his words. He appointed the separate black advisory board he described to Corson and made contact with thirteen black college presidents, who launched NYA programs at their schools. On October 12, he chaired a meeting in Dallas attended by the "Colored Advisory Committee and one hundred leaders from all parts of the state. . . . Every phase of the National Youth Administration program as it pertains to the colored people of Texas was discussed thoroughly in a session lasting all day." Following the meeting, letters from black leaders around the state demonstrated their willingness to provide "wholehearted cooperation."

By March 1936 the student-aid programs for blacks were in full swing: 887 high school and 473 college students were getting aid; while another 471 high-school graduates were enrolled in Freshmen College Centers, of which fifteen out of the twenty were set aside for blacks. The impact of the college-aid program was proportionately much greater on blacks than on whites: where 24.2 percent of all eligible black college students received help, the same was true of only 12 to 14 percent of whites. But the numbers tell only part of the story. The difficulties confronted by ambitious black students were reflected in questions raised at the Freshman Center in Houston about how they could finish their education and whether there was a place for a black person in aviation, law, medicine, or engineering. Some of these students labored to overcome additional personal handicaps that Lyndon described feelingly to Washington: there were two partially blind boys who hadn't missed a day of classes since they enrolled; there was a young widow with four children whose education had been interrupted when she married at the age of fifteen; there was a young man who had worked all night and attended high school each day with only about three hours of sleep; and there were the many "cases where the father is dead or has separated from the mother and she is the sole support of the family, which is in most cases very large."[31]

As with the plight of the Mexican-American boys and girls he taught in Cotulla, the deprivations of these young blacks moved him to special efforts in their behalf. When white colleges got donations of equipment that freed some of their NYA funds, Lyndon would pass the savings along to blacks. The bursar at the Sam Houston College for Negroes in Austin remembers how he would call up and ask: "You have any boys and girls out there that could use some money? I've got a little extra change here. Can you find a place to put it?" In an era of strict segregation he would occasionally spend a night at a black college to see how the NYA programs were doing. More than thirty years later "a venerable and distinguished Negro leader" told Doris Kearns how "We began to get word up here that there was one NYA director who wasn't like the others. He was looking after Negroes and poor folks and most NYA people weren't doing that." Lyndon's impulse to help blacks would take many twists and turns through the political cross currents of the future, but there was a strong commitment to opening doors of opportunity that revealed itself first in his leadership of the NYA and found full expression thirty years later in a different climate of opinion.[32]

In addition to school programs, work projects were also central to NYA activities in Texas. By March 1936, some 12,011 "out-of-school" boys and girls were earning between $7 and $25 a month working on "useful" NYA projects. Lyndon took great satisfaction not only in the numbers employed but also in the value obtained for the money spent. The NYA "touched the lives of over 30,000 youngsters who have been fighting for a toe-hold after the depression," Lyndon wrote in September; "yet it didn't give them one red cent they didn't work for and earn for themselves." He was painfully self-conscious about not wasting money. At the start of the works program he had made clear that he wanted no part of leaf-raking jobs, "boondoggles," as they came to be called in the thirties, that gave doles to needy people for pointless work.[33]

But the limitations on how he could proceed had made productive jobs for large numbers of young people hard to come by. The projects could not provide work that took jobs away from adults. In addition, 75 percent of all project funding had to be spent on wages. Consequently, material and equipment for most projects had to come from local and state agencies. The ideal had been to find a state-wide program that would enlist the cooperation of the state government and could be run by uniform standards. The alternative had been to start up many local programs that would require the cooperation of individual counties, cities, and towns. It had promised to be a bureaucratic nightmare that would multiply administrative costs and generate more problems than productive jobs. And Lyndon wanted no part of anything that would raise operating expenses. He "was always very conscious about this," Birdwell recalled. ". . . How much it cost us to put a boy or girl to work." Faithful to Lyndon's injunctions, Birdwell, the finance officer, sent an NYA administrator who asked for a second $1.35 office pencil sharpener a box of used razor blades wrapped in a red ribbon with a bow on it.[34]

Lyndon and his staff had gone through weeks of "interminable wrangling" over a practical works program before Gladys Montgomery, Professor Robert Montgomery's wife, gave Lyndon an idea that solved his problem—roadside parks along Texas's hundreds of miles of highways, where motorists could safely stop to rest, eat, and relieve themselves. Originally constructed without shoulders, the highways were dangerous places to stop, even briefly to change a tire. Mrs. Montgomery came up with the idea when a family of five was rammed from behind and killed while waiting out a rainstorm on the highway to San Antonio. The project won Lyndon's immediate enthusiasm: the parks could be constructed all over the state, the Highway Department could supply the building materials, the NYA the labor, and the state would have an asset that would improve road safety and make automobile travel more comfortable. Lyndon sold the idea to Gibb Gilchrist, the state's highway engineer, by pointing out the advantages not only to the state but to the boys as well: they would earn some money and learn a skill. "Your supervisors are good men," Lyndon told him, "and they can train them [the boys] to do rock . . . [and] cement work." It would "be something that no other state's doing." [35]

When Herbert Henderson, an ex-journalist and speechwriter for Maury Maverick, wrote a proposal to send to Washington, Lyndon could barely contain his enthusiasm. L. E. Jones remembers that he "drove his staff to distraction doing what had to be done. . . . One lady [in the office] . . . almost had a nervous breakdown because of the pressure she was subjected to." But the effort paid off. Administrative paperwork was completed and Washington's approval was obtained in days rather than months, and the first park was under construction in a few weeks. By the summer of 1936, there were 3600 young men building 125 roadside parks. The idea "turned out to be perfect," L. E. Jones said. Higher officials in the NYA agreed. In March, Assistant Director Richard Brown had told Lyndon that "the story of your 'pocket-sized' highway parks has spread as far as Schenectady, New York, where the Schenectady Gazette . . . suggested that they be constructed in that region." After a visit to Texas in July, the NYA's southern regional director described the parks as "excellent for our program. They have caught the imagination of the public," which was calling for "more and more projects of this type." He suggested "the possibility of permanently stamping the N.Y.A. symbol upon . . . this type of permanent construction." The parks were a source of pride to Lyndon as an example of how Texas and the South could lead the nation in advancing highway comfort and safety. The parks were still in use over fifty years later. [36]

Other highway projects followed from the decision to build the roadside rest stops. During 1936 another 2300 young men landscaped highways, planting, trimming, and cultivating shrubs, sodded slopes against erosion, widened the approaches of county roads at highway intersections, graveled areas by roadside mail boxes, making them more accessible to mail carriers, painted guard fences and road signs, constructed rural-school walks along highways, where accidents had killed or injured children, and built graveled turn-outs for school buses, allowing children to get on and off in greater safety. An even larger number of young people, nearly 4200, improved public grounds and buildings, particularly recreational areas across the state. Under prodding from Lyndon, Governor Jimmy Allred won a $50,000 appropriation from the state legislature to help construct "playground equipment such as horizontal bars, swings, double tennis courts, baseball diamonds, flower beds . . . sanitary toilets, drinking fountains, lunch tables with benches, basketball and volleyball courts, floodlights, [and] wading and swimming pools." The NYA workers also built field houses, cooperative dormitories, rural

schools, county garages, and shelters in parks. In addition, the NYA provided vocational training for unemployed and unskilled youngsters in
workshops and resident training centers, where they learned auto me-
chanics, carpentry, electronics, home economics—cooking, sewing, and
interior decorating—metal and woodworking, radio repair, and vocational agriculture. These apprentice workers honed their skills on local
NYA projects. After six to twelve months of training, NYA Guidance and
Placement Centers found regular jobs for many of the trainees.[37]

By almost any standard the NYA nationally, and in Texas particularly,
was a great success. By early 1937, after only eighteen months, it had
some 428,000 students at all levels enrolled in its programs and another
190,000 employed on work projects. Texas accounted for approximately
5 percent of the totals with nearly 29,000 young people—over 20,000
students and more than 8000 project workers—on NYA payrolls. In
Johnson's later estimate, "if the Roosevelt Administration had never done
another thing, it would have been justified by the work of this great
institution for salvaging youth." The NYA, he said in 1939, "relieved
the pressure upon our overtaxed labor market like a great dam, storing
flood waters to be released in times of thirst and drought. It . . . kept
thousands of boys and girls in high school and college, where they belonged. It . . . eased the emergency and insured youth the training
twentieth-century life demands as a requisite for success." It was "Constructive, Beneficial, American." For years afterward, Sherman Birdwell
was "amazed at the number of secretaries and dieticians and even heads
of factories who come up to me and say they got their start in the youth
program." Likewise, when Johnson gave a speech in Texas in 1967, he
found himself on a platform with a governor, a congressman, and a
chairman of the state Board of Regents who had all been in the NYA.
Moreover, he often met people around the state, "responsible and productive citizens . . . doctors, businessmen, teachers, and skilled craftsmen," who had been helped by the NYA more than 30 years before.[38]

High officials in the Roosevelt administration believed that much of
the credit for what happened in Texas belonged to Lyndon Johnson. By
the spring and summer of 1936, NYA officials were singing his praises.
Russell Ellzey, a field representative, told Dick Kleberg that "you have
the best Youth Director in the Nation in Lyndon Johnson, and he has
the finest organization in Texas of any I have seen." "All the authorities
in the Washington office feel that you boys have done a swell job," Ellzey
wrote one of Lyndon's subordinates at the same time. Garth Akridge,
the southern regional director, told Richard Brown in July that Johnson
"has developed within his organization a spirit, a devotion to duty, and
a sense of personal loyalty that is little short of remarkable. . . . The
public seems to be back of the program and the press is supporting it
almost 100%." After reading a report that 200 newspapers in Texas had

nothing but praise for the program, a skeptical NYA official in Washington asked: "Isn't that taxing one's credulity?" But a later researcher studying "newspaper articles and editorials on the [Texas] NYA from 1935 to 1937" noted that "it is indeed difficult to find criticism of the organization." In a February 1937 report that Brown passed along to Aubrey Williams, Akridge further described Johnson as "easily one of the best men directing one of the best staffs in one of the best programs with the most universal and enthusiastic public support of any state in the Union."[39]

Black officials in Washington were no less taken with Lyndon's work. Mary McLeod Bethune "held Lyndon in far greater esteem than she did some of our other southern youth administrators," Richard Brown remembered. She described Lyndon as "a very outstanding young man" who was "going to go places." Likewise, Beatrice Denmark, another black administrator in the Washington office, came away from a visit to Texas sold on Lyndon's efforts: "I have found what I have been hoping to find for colored girls. . . . I believe I know the Negro condition in the southern states, and no one would be more delighted to see them have the kind of training that Mr. Johnson is setting up in Texas. The Texas Director is doing what many of us are talking."[40]

Small wonder, then, that Aubrey Williams publicly described the Texas operation as a "first-class job," and privately called it a standing "example to other states' youth adminstrations." Also hearing about the good work being done by Johnson, Eleanor Roosevelt wrote him in January 1936 to applaud his efforts to find "employment for young people," who must "not be allowed to become so discouraged through idleness that they never acquire the ability to apply themselves diligently and consistently." She visited Texas later in the year "to find out why the Texas NYA director was doing such an effective job." She conferred with Lyndon at his headquarters on the sixth floor of the Littlefield Building and accompanied him to a vocational training center for girls on East Sixth Street in Austin and to college campuses running NYA programs. In June, when the President came to Texas to open a Centennial Exposition, Lyndon tried to arrange a stop at an eight-acre park on the Fort Worth highway five miles from Dallas. Although he got the highway department to speed completion of the project by putting 400 men on the job, the arrangement fell apart at the last minute and Lyndon had only the satisfaction of watching the President throw back his head and laugh as his motorcade drove by 155 NYA boys saluting him with shovels at present arms. When Jesse Kellam succeeded Lyndon as director in 1937, Williams called him to Washington and said, "Kellam, you haven't got but one way to go and that's down. This man Johnson was operating the best NYA program in all of the states. . . . You can't do a better job than he was doing. I hope you can do as well."[41]

The opportunity to run for Congress had decided Lyndon to resign. He had considered leaving the NYA in the spring of 1936 to try for a seat in the Texas Senate. In February, Alvin Wirtz had told Welly Hopkins that he thought "the situation might work around to where he [Lyndon] could step in and make a good showing." But nothing had come of this possibility. Moreover, Lyndon correctly believed that a young, ambitious southern liberal like himself would do better in Washington then in state politics. A seat in the Texas legislature would have meant an uphill struggle against entrenched state interests to advance himself and liberal programs like those of the NYA. In Washington, by contrast, he could share in the expanding authority devoted to changing the economic and political life of the south.

When Congressman James B. "Buck" Buchanan of the Tenth District died on February 22, 1937, Lyndon seized the chance to run for his House seat. As Buchanan's career demonstrated, once someone won election to the U.S. House of Representatives from Texas, he was likely to stay in office for over twenty years. Learning the news through a Houston paper on the 23rd, Lyndon couldn't focus on the day's work, a visit by the director of the Kansas NYA to look at Texas programs. "I kept thinking that this was my district and this was my chance. The day seemed endless. . . . I had to pretend total interest in everything we were seeing and doing. There were times when I thought I'd explode from all the excitement bottled up inside."[42]

Despite his eagerness to enter the special election, a winner-take-all contest requiring only a plurality of the votes for victory, Lyndon understood that he was not well known in the district and had only an outside chance of winning. On February 23, when the *Austin Statesman* discussed possible successors to Buchanan, Lyndon wasn't even mentioned. "You boys are talking about Lyndon Johnson," Sam Fore remembered Mayor Tom Miller of Austin telling him. "Nobody knows him. He's just a [twenty-eight-year-old] boy." He'd have to make the race against "five veteran politicians. Why he hasn't got a chance on earth." Others knowledgable about local politics echoed Miller's opinion: "He was not known at all," Dan Quill said. He was from Blanco, the smallest of the ten counties in the district, "and he wasn't known in Austin [the district's focal point] hardly at all." "Who the hell is Lyndon Johnson?" Claude Wild, the manager of Governor Jimmy Allred's successful campaign in 1934, said when asked to run Lyndon's campaign. But those who knew Lyndon well did not worry about his public obscurity at the start of the campaign. "Now, Mayor," Fore told Miller, "you're a wonderful politician, but I . . . want you to remember that on election day—you'll find how many people know him."[43]

Among the small group of Texans who believed in Lyndon's ability to succeed, none was more important than Alvin J. Wirtz. Through their contacts in Washington when Lyndon had worked for Kleberg and in Austin when they had worked together for the NYA, Wirtz, who was twenty years Lyndon's senior, had come to admire Lyndon's intelligence and capacity for hard work and to have an affection for him a father reserves for a son. Mary Rather, Wirtz's secretary, remembered one day in 1934 when she first saw Lyndon in Wirtz's Austin office. "He didn't stay long, but he turned the place upside down. He was very fast and quick and busy." He made Rather think of Josephine's first impression of Napoleon as "a tornado." She also recalled how often Lyndon began to come to the office, especially when he headed the NYA, and how he looked up to Wirtz and sought his advice and counsel. Wirtz reciprocated Lyndon's regard, calling him " 'my boy.' He was crazy about him," Mary Rather said.

Lady Bird and Wirtz were the first two people Lyndon consulted about making the campaign. Wirtz, who was characteristically soft-spoken and cautious, began by pointing out all the negatives: Lyndon would have to give up his NYA job and should he lose, he might not be able to get as good a position; his chances of defeating the older, better known, and more seasoned politicians who would run against him were small; and the cost of such a campaign would be $10,000 "just to get in the race and make a good try for it." After Lady Bird explained that she could approach her father for the money and the three of them talked the matter out, Wirtz urged Lyndon to go ahead.[44]

More than personal affection for Lyndon attracted Wirtz to his candidacy. A large, jolly, affable man with an "ever-present smile," Wirtz was a kind of "wise old uncle" whose calm, deliberate manner encouraged younger men to seek his advice and support. Although conveying the impression of an easy-going, unpretentious small-town lawyer, Wirtz was an intensely ambitious and tough-minded man with an affinity for money and power. His imposing side reflected itself in the fact that people continued to address him and refer to him as "Senator" long after he had ended his stint in the Texas Senate. He loved the position of kingmaker, and in the early thirties he had played a significant part at state Democratic party conventions, actively campaigned in the party's gubernatorial contests, and operated as a highly effective lobbyist for oil and banking interests in Austin. He had no illusions about Texas politics, believing that "no Texas election was over until the last crooks finished changing the votes in their counties." As a realist, he accommodated himself to conservative business interests at the same time he championed liberal causes. "Alvin Wirtz knew how to carry buckets of bubbling acid on both shoulders without spilling a drop," Senator Tom Connally said. "He had some of the most reactionary and ignorant Texans as his law clients, and he pursued their interests ruthlessly against a lot of helpless people. On the other hand, he loved Roosevelt and the

New Deal, and when he acted on his own, he was a champion of public power and Federal welfare programs." Like Lyndon, he saw FDR's New Deal as helping to create a more prosperous Texas and new south.

In almost every respect, Lyndon Johnson was an ideal candidate for Wirtz to back for his district's congressional seat. A highly intelligent and deferential young man with a working knowledge of congressional politics and the Federal bureaucracy, Lyndon seemed likely to be a highly effective representative for both the Tenth District and Wirtz's interests in Washington. In 1937, these included support for FDR and New Deal programs in general and additional allocations of Federal money for continued work on Lower Colorado River dams in particular. As counsel to the Lower Colorado River Authority, Wirtz believed that the dams not only would spare central Texas from destructive floods and open the way to cheaper electric power but also add to his wealth and influence in Texas and Washington.[45]

However valuable, Wirtz's backing did not eliminate several other obstacles to Lyndon's candidacy. First and foremost was the possibility that Buchanan's sixty-two-year-old widow would decide to run for her husband's seat. If she ran, one Austin newspaper predicted on February 28, none of the other potential candidates, including Lyndon Johnson, would enter the race. Sam Ealy Johnson, whom Lyndon consulted about her threat to his candidacy, advised Lyndon how to keep her from running. Accurately forecasting that she would want no part of a fight for the seat, Sam persuaded Lyndon to announce his own candidacy before she declared her intentions. Consequently, on Sunday evening the 28th, Lyndon released a statement to the press that appeared in the morning papers saying he would run.[46]

His prompt announcement also headed off opposition from the Roosevelt administration. When Aubrey Williams heard that Lyndon might run, he asked Thomas G. Corcoran, a White House aide and manipulator, to get the President to stop him. "He's my whole youth program in Texas," Williams explained, "and if he quits I have no program down there." Roosevelt was responsive to Williams's request; he wanted Professor Robert Montgomery, a prominent Texas New Dealer, to run for Buchanan's seat. Montgomery was interested in making the race. But when he heard that Lyndon had declared, like Mrs. Buchanan, he backed off. He feared that two New Dealers in the race might cancel each other out and give the seat to an anti-Roosevelt candidate. Angered at being beaten to the punch by Lyndon, however, Montgomery told him that he had also announced his candidacy. Lyndon turned white and showed palpable consternation until Mrs. Montgomery explained that her husband was kidding. Even a call from Corcoran in Washington couldn't change things: "I tried to find Johnson," he remembered, "but before I could he had quit his NYA job and filed for Congress."[47]

With Mrs. Buchanan out of the race, eight other candidates entered the competition. Five of them seemed likely to win more votes than Lyndon. The odds-on favorite was C. N. Avery, an affable fifty-eight-year-old businessman who had been Buchanan's campaign manager and secretary. A seasoned politician with a wide array of contacts in the Tenth District and a close knowledge of its interests, Avery was the heir designate. When Buchanan learned that he was dying, Avery claimed, he "asked me to run." Merton Harris of Smithville in Bastrop County southeast of Austin seemed likely to run a close second. An assistant state attorney general who had come close to defeating Buchanan in 1932, he had been working the district for several years in hopes of succeeding Buchanan. Houghton Brownlee, the district's state senator from Burnet County northwest of Austin, had acquaintances and visibility across the entire ten-county congressional district that he might translate into a substantial vote. Judge Sam Stone from Williamson County, the second largest in the district, promised to make a strong race by winning decisively in his home county. Austin attorney Polk Shelton had other advantages: he had been a star athlete at San Marcos, had served in World War I, was closely identified with the American Legion, and had a father who had been a popular Travis County district attorney. He also had a pronounced image as a New Deal supporter who entered the congressional race to oppose FDR's Supreme Court-packing plan, the President's proposal to counter the Court's nullification of New Deal legislation by appointing up to six new Justices. Alongside these five men, Lyndon Johnson, the youngest candidate, from Blanco, the smallest county in the district, seemed an able and energetic young man whose ambitions outran his political reach.[48]

Lyndon worked to perfect a campaign strategy that would allow him to overcome his opponents. A decision at the start of the race to trumpet Lyndon's identification with FDR and all his programs, including Court-packing, was central to this effort. Hoping to capitalize on Roosevelt's popularity in the district, which he had carried by a nine-to-one margin in 1936, Wirtz urged Lyndon to be "a total Roosevelt man . . . . Of course, there will be those who will be bitter at you," Wirtz advised, "but to hell with them. They're in the minority. The people like Roosevelt." Sam Fore echoed the point: "Lyndon, look, the important thing about this race is FDR. People like him, and he's in hot water over that Court-packing thing. He needs our help and we are going to come out loud and clear for him . . . . There's not going to be any halfway stuff. There's not going to be any maybe or qualifications." Wirtz and Fore understood that Roosevelt symbolized not only a way out of the Depression for Tenth District folks but a new day in the history of Texas and the south. The federal government was being put in the service of southern economic needs and was moving the region toward a more prosperous future.[49]

Lyndon was enthusiastic about the strategy. He admired FDR and believed his programs essential to the national and regional well-being. But he also knew that a strong identification with Roosevelt in general and Court-packing in particular was excellent politics. During the campaign, straw polls showed that as many as seven out of eight Tenth District voters were sympathetic to FDR's plans for Court reform. "The paramount issue of this campaign is whether the President shall be sustained in his program for readjustment of the judicial system," Lyndon said when announcing his candidacy. " . . . I have always been a supporter of President Roosevelt and I am wholeheartedly in favor of his present plan." Four days later in an opening campaign speech at San Marcos, he declared: "If the people of this District want to support Roosevelt on his most vital issue, I want to be your congressman." [50]

"The entire program of social reform instituted under President Roosevelt," Johnson said in a later speech, stood or fell with the Supreme Court. The people have told Congress in unmistakable terms [that] they want and must have certain social and economic reforms. . . . The Court has said [that] the people can't have these reforms." Johnson also identified the completion of the Colorado River control program with "what the Supreme Court may decide, and any candidate who poses as a friend of the Colorado River Authority but is against Court reform is contradicting himself." [51]

As everyone involved in the Johnson campaign understood, identifying with FDR was an obvious strategy that other candidates would adopt as well. Lyndon's aim, therefore, was to outdo his opponents in tying himself to FDR and to make it seem that he was the only one genuinely behind the President. His campaign became a celebration of FDR and an appeal to the idea that Lyndon Johnson was the single candidate in the race who would give the President unqualified support. "I'm for the President. When he calls on me for help, I'll be where I can give him a quick lift, not out in the woodshed practicing a quick way to duck," Lyndon repeatedly asserted. Campaign posters announced: "A VOTE FOR JOHNSON IS A VOTE FOR ROOSEVELT'S PROGRAM." Billboards proclaimed: "FRANKLIN D. and LYNDON B." Journalists amused by Johnson's reverential attitude toward the President in his self-aggrandizing campaign suggested the slogan: "Franklin D., Lyndon B. and Jesus C." [52]

Several of Johnson's opponents tried to counter his strategy by emphasizing their support of FDR. "C. N. Avery backs the President of the United States," one of his flyers declared. "HE HELPED ELECT ROOSEVELT . . . AND NATURALLY, C. N. AVERY will fight for the President in the Supreme Court battle." While Sam Stone stated that he would not be a " 'Yes Man' and cast aside all my convictions by following the President blindly in all matters," he nevertheless promised to "do all that I possibly can in aiding the President in working out the problems of this great

Nation." He declared himself in complete accord with Roosevelt on Court reform. Brownlee, who had voted with a majority of state senators in the Texas legislature to condemn FDR's Court plan, took pains to declare his support of New Deal programs for farmers, ranchmen, and the unemployed. Polk Shelton announced: "I yield to no man in my admiration for our great leader, President Roosevelt." Seeking to mute his open opposition to FDR on Court-packing, Shelton promised "A Progressive Program for the Tenth District." [53]

But Lyndon questioned his opponent's sincerity and commitment, calling them "eight in the dark." In a radio speech in March, he said: One opponent "has definitely announced on a platform directly in opposition to President Roosevelt's program; several have hedged and straddled the fence—one saying he will not indulge in breast-beating over the President's Supreme Court plan; another that he will have to wait before making up his mind; others have made recent records, either evasive or in opposition." Johnson stated in an address in April: "There is *only one issue* in this campaign. Are you *for* the President, or *against* him?" Roosevelt's opponents want to be sure that Buchanan's successor will be a "100 percent enemy of the President . . . . They know that there are several in this campaign they can count on . . . . They know there is *only one* who will fight them until the last dog is dead, without a compromise. They know I am that man." [54]

To give his identification with Roosevelt greater credibility, Lyndon tried to get outspoken support from prominent New Dealers. But it wasn't easy. He first went to Governor Jimmy Allred, but Allred, who opposed Court-packing and didn't want to antagonize the eventual winner of Buchanan's seat, refused to come down decisively on anyone's side. Eager nevertheless to give Lyndon some quiet help, he promised to contact all his appointees in the district and urge them to support Johnson. He also wanted to make some public gesture in Lyndon's behalf. "Where did you get that little jellybean hat?" Allred asked him during their meeting. "I got it in Washington," Lyndon replied. "Well, that's not a hat," Allred said, and he gave him a lucky Stetson that he had worn in every winning election. Lyndon featured it at all his rallies during the campaign. With help from former State Senator Welly Hopkins, he was more successful with Charles Marsh, the publisher of Austin's two major dailies, the *American* and the *Statesman*. A staunch liberal, Marsh sided with Lyndon, turning his papers into "Lyndon's harmonicas." Although making no formal endorsement, both papers gave Lyndon extensive coverage throughout the six-week campaign, usually printing the full text of his speeches. [55]

Most of all, Lyndon wanted the Roosevelt administration's direct backing. During the first week of the campaign, Welly Hopkins, who was now in Washington working as a special assistant to the U.S. Attorney General, went all out to persuade Under Secretary of the Interior Charles West to get the White House behind Johnson. He also suggested to Roy Miller that he draft a letter of support for Postmaster General James Farley's signature. But the Administration refused to risk its prestige by backing anyone openly. When Farley visited Austin in late March, he declared the contest "a local matter" and improper for him to comment on it, except to say that the district should send a "young, industrious and one-hundred percent Roosevelt man up there in this crucial hour." In April, Johnson got more direct help when Elliott Roosevelt, the President's son, wired his best wishes for "a glorious victory in your race for Congress. I feel sure that when you get to Congress the Administration will have a young vigorous and ardent supporter." The columnist Drew Pearson reported: "On the surface the Administration is keeping hands off the contest, but under cover is quietly boosting Johnson." If he won, it intended "to make heavy capital of his triumph." On April 5, five days before the election, Avery asked the President to disavow Johnson's claims that FDR was "whole-heartedly supporting him." But the only reply the White House made was "that the President is taking no part in any congressional primaries."[56]

Weak campaigns run by Lyndon's opponents added to the advantage he gained by his identification with FDR. None of the other candidates came close to matching the time and energy expended by Johnson and his supporters. Where Lyndon began campaigning on March 2, the day after he announced his candidacy, the others did not get out on the hustings until days and weeks later. Avery began on March 9, Harris on the 18th, and Brownlee did not launch an all-out effort until the Senate adjourned on March 27. Moreover, Stone campaigned almost exclusively in Williamson County, where he lived, and Avery traveled outside of Austin only once during the last two weeks of the campaign. Polk Shelton was the only competitor who came close to matching Johnson's efforts. But Shelton put voters off by his opposition to FDR's Court plan, and, according to his brother Emmett, by failing to get his supporters to the polls. "Young Johnson worked harder to win than any one of the many candidates," one local paper recorded after the election. He "spoke first, last and the loudest."[57]

Johnson even managed to turn his youth, the principal issue on which his opponents were able to score points against him, to his advantage. Concerned that voters might be reluctant to send someone only twenty-eight years old to Congress, he usually described himself as "almost thirty." "This Johnson is a young, young man," an opponent declared. "It's bad enough when you get too old a man in the Congress. But it's worse to take off the baby robe and put on the toga." Avery ridiculed him at a joint public appearance in Austin: "Every boy by the time he reaches the age of seven develops a burning desire to be a policeman, a fireman. . . . But before we entrust them with such tasks we demand that they gain a considerable amount of experience. We just can't picture a youngster with a pop-gun chasing bandits." To counter these attacks, Johnson followed his father's advice that he emphasize rather than obscure the age issue. "I'd rather be called a young whippersnapper than an old mossback—a reactionary," he began saying publicly. He persuaded Woodrow Wilson's Postmaster General Albert S. Burleson, who had been elected to Congress from the Tenth District in 1898 at the age of thirty-four, to write a statement saying that he hoped the district would "elect a young man who can develop . . . . To elect an old man is for the people to throw the office away." He also urged Johnson "to be as strong for Roosevelt and the New Deal as I was for Wilson and the New Freedom." The statement gained wide attention in the local press.[58]

To underscore the point about the virtue of having a young man represent the district and to take advantage of his underdog status, Lyndon also followed Sam Ealy's suggestion that he use cousin Ava Johnson Cox's nine-year-old son Corky to recite from Edgar A. Guest's poem, "It Couldn't Be Done." "They say I'm a young candidate," Lyndon declared on the evening Corky joined him on the platform. "Well, I've got a young campaign manager, too," he said, introducing Corky. To the delight of the crowd, the boy shouted a stanza of the poem:

> There are thousands to tell you it cannot be done,
>   There are thousands to prophesy failure;
> There are thousands to point out to you one by one,
>   The dangers that wait to assail you.
> But just buckle in with a bit of a grin,
>   Just take off your coat and go to it;
> Just start in to sing as you tackle the thing
>   That "Cannot be done," and you'll do it.[59]

The poem accurately reflected the spirit of Johnson's campaign—a never-say-die effort in every corner of the district to eclipse his better known opponents. It was a formidable job. The district stretched some 175 miles from east to west and some 100 miles from north to south. Its approximately 50,000 registered voters in a population of 264,000 were scattered across an area of almost 8000 square miles. Though 88,000 of its citizens were concentrated in Austin, the rest of the district's population lived in small towns and on farms, to which any candidate had to travel if he hoped to win a plurality in a nine-man race. "Don't ever let me be in the house where there's daylight and keep the screen locked until dark," Lyndon told Lady Bird when he began the campaign.[60]

She never had to take him up on his injunction. He drove himself night and day giving over two hundred speeches in forty-two days and traveling to every town in the district. At the edge of a town, he would get out of his car and walk its length, shaking hands with everyone he met and stopping in stores. Meanwhile, campaign workers using a loud-speaker mounted on his car would play martial music and appeal to folks to come hear Lyndon Johnson talk. The speech, usually a rousing enunciation of his eagerness to serve the district by helping Roosevelt, lasted no more than five minutes. "A five-minute speech," he later told Doris Kearns, "with fifteen minutes spent afterward is much more effective than a fifteen-minute speech, no matter how inspiring, that leaves only five minutes for handshaking." To meet as many voters in person as possible, he would stop at every filling station on the road between towns, where he would buy a gallon of gas, talk to everyone who would listen, and leave a campaign poster in a prominent spot. Every time he saw a farmer at work, he would stop his car, vault a fence, and slog through the field to shake hands and appeal for the man's vote. Johnson "swung through Bastrop county with thorough-going campaign tactics Wednesday," the *Austin American* reported on April 8, "combing the business districts of Elgin, McDade, Bastrop and Smithville and stopping at crossroads, stores and filling stations enroute from town to town."

He was at his best in a face-to-face meeting and informal talks. Grasping a man's arm with one hand and holding his hand with the other, he would get him talking about himself, his family, his work, his shared concerns with Lyndon Johnson. When he gave formal speeches, which he usually did at set rallies, his delivery was strained and awkward. He read without inflection and made little eye contact with his audience. But when it came "off the cuff" or "from the heart," as his cousin Ava described his spontaneous talks, he would look directly at his audience and "come down with that force in his voice" that conveyed a sincerity which was lost when he read someone else's words. Pounding his right hand in the form of a fist into the left, swaying as he spoke, he called his listeners to the New Deal faith, preaching the benefits of Roosevelt's programs to them, the farmers and poor folks, and the importance of helping the President now in his Court fight by voting for Roosevelt's man, Lyndon Johnson.[61]

Despite the hard work and significant gains during the first five weeks of the campaign, the outcome remained in doubt. Problems with the weather and getting people interested enough to come meet him dogged his efforts. March 1937 was "particularly raw and windy and wet," Ray Lee, one of Lyndon's campaign managers, recalls, and it discouraged people from coming to meetings. Despite advance notice to local organizers, Lyndon and his campaign workers would get to a town and only four people would show up to hear him. Even after the most intensive preparations, they might find themselves with a crowd of only a hundred people instead of the five hundred or a thousand they had hoped to get. Although an Austin newspaper survey six days before the election put Johnson and Harris in front, neck and neck, and Avery in third place, previous polls in the *San Antonio Express, San Antonio Light,* and the *Dallas News* had given Avery a substantial lead and predicted that Johnson would come in third.[62]

The uneven response to Lyndon's campaign and the initial newspaper soundings of voter opinion persuaded Claude Wild, the principal campaign manager, that they were going to have to "throw a little dirt." The Johnsons were initially reluctant. Lady Bird complained to Wild that she had helped finance this race and she "wasn't going to have her husband slinging mud. She wanted him to be a gentleman." Wild responded: "Well, do you want him to be a gentleman or a Congressman?" Lyndon also objected, saying, "No, no, if I have to do that I don't want the office." But when Wild threatened to quit the campaign and emphasized again the importance of attacking his opponents, Lyndon gave in. "Well," he said, "if it's absolutely necessary—let's mix up a little mud." He began labeling Avery a "Washington lobbyist" who had lived in an $8000-a-year hotel suite and ate caviar. "I wonder if he didn't make a mistake when he told you he paid his own expenses. . . . If he doesn't tell you who paid for it, maybe I can give you that information." He attacked Brownlee as an "economic royalist" who "has voted in favor of the special interests and power companies every time he could help them." Because the Johnson campaign was particularly worried about Harris, it tried not to build him up by calling him to public attention. Lyndon nevertheless occasionally described him as a man with no strong convictions who took a poll before staking out a position on anything. As for Polk Shelton, Lyndon said he was an attorney who "spent his life defending criminals, racketeers, and underworld characters, and turning them loose upon society as fast as the law could grab them."[63]

Subsequently his opponents charged that Johnson carried his determination to win beyond the limits of legality. Johnson campaign workers persuaded Federal officials to let Lyndon hand out parity checks to farmers, which, as Emmett Shelton said, "was of course illegal." Moreover, Polk Shelton believed that the Johnson campaign paid Elliott Roosevelt $5000 to endorse Lyndon. According to Shelton, a man he never saw again approached him during the campaign with an offer to have Elliott Roosevelt endorse him for that sum of money. Shelton said that he declined the offer but he heard later that the man "approached one other candidate who was running for Congress." Since Elliott Roosevelt endorsed Johnson, the implication of Shelton's statement is clear.

The Johnson campaign apparently had enough money to make such a payment. To begin with, there was the $10,000 Lady Bird got from her father, though $5000 of it was paid to Wild for running the campaign. Then, according to Ed Clark, Allred's secretary of state and a fund raiser for Johnson, Lady Bird's father gave an additional $25,000 "and that was damn near half of the money that we raised." He also recalled getting small donations of $5, $10, and $20 from state employees by telling them that the Governor would like them to contribute to Johnson's campaign. A considerable number of donations of between $100 and $500 were received from Austin businessmen. And larger sums came in from lobbyists close to Wirtz and Roy Miller. The total gathered, Ed Clark said, was between $75,000 and $100,000, a considerable amount of money for a congressional campaign in the 1930s.[64]

Yet if Johnson's campaign was far from a model of civic virtue, it was not much different from those of his opponents. "Mud slinging" was a commonplace in a closely contested Texas election in the first half of the twentieth century. "He is not running for office because of a genuine desire and a genuine ability to serve this district," Avery said of Johnson, "but simply because he wants to leap from obscurity to the golden glamour of the public trough." In a radio speech of April 2, Johnson complained "that the rear-guard poison-spreaders, mud-slingers and whisperers have been attacking me. . . . They are slinking around in the dark, trying to knife me without being seen. First, they tried to link me to the utilities, the sulphur interests, the power trust. . . . Next they tried to say that I changed my name—that I was born with a foreign name and was just a masquerader. Well, when they found out about my grandfather they had to try something else or be ridiculous. So they said my mother was a sister of the head of a big Texas special interest. When they found my mother had never even met this man and he had never met her, they had to change their tune."

At Smithville in Bastrop County, a debate between Emmett Shelton and Johnson "exploded . . . in a sharp exchange of oral fire." Shelton accused him of runaway expenditures in the campaign, of being backed by the sulphur interests and utilities, of never having repaid a school loan to his uncle Clarence Martin, and of being too new to the district to deserve to represent it in Congress. In an effective five-minute retort that elicited "laughter and four rounds of applause," Johnson shunned any "attempt to answer all the charges made here this afternoon by a dying, desperate candidate." Yet there was one charge he was ready "to plead guilty to—and gladly. Sure, I was born in Johnson City in the small county of Blanco." But he "didn't have any jurisdiction" in the matter. "If my mother had known that you wanted a city slicker or a ward boss for a candidate, maybe she'd been able to do something about it." He also denied getting money from special interests and described his campaign as financed by his "own meager savings."[65]

None of the candidates lacked for money in the campaign. The Sheltons, for example, spent between $40,000 and $50,000, and Robert Caro learned from unnamed "observers" that Avery and Brownlee "each spent considerably more than that figure."

Like Lyndon, Polk and Emmett Shelton used a no-holds-barred approach to the election. In an oral history interview, Emmett described himself as "ashamed" for having publicly said that Johnson hadn't paid back a loan to his Uncle Clarence. He also said that Polk "got all the Negro votes in Lee county, and that's the way we carried it. . . . We voted a lot of Negroes absentee; we voted them in that race." Johnson's distribution of parity checks was "illegal, but hell, we didn't pull any punches. Any way we'd get a vote, we did it, too." Shelton's friends "were outraged about Lyndon, the government helping him that way. Well, it outraged me, too," Emmett said, "But I thought he was smart as hell to get it done."[66]

The candidates were so distrustful of one another that when Lyndon had his appendix removed two days before the election, two of his opponents charged that it was a faked illness to win a last-minute sympathy vote. Because Lyndon feared that he would be accused of a political trick, he tried to hold off having the surgery. And when he became too ill to wait, he insisted that Senator Brownlee's brother, who was a physician, assist in the operation to counter any suggestion that it was a "put up job." Although Claude Wild thought the operation had no significant impact on the election, he believed that the unsubstantiated charges about a fake illness, which the doctors denied, backfired on Lyndon's opponents and did him some good.[67]

Lyndon's aggressive identification with Roosevelt, the stumbling campaigns of his opponents, his unrelenting efforts to become known in every corner of the district through personal appearances, newspaper ads, mailings, and radio talks gave him a surprisingly large victory margin on election day. Although he received only a shade less than 28 percent of the vote—8,280 out of 29, 943 cast—he got almost 3200 votes more than Merton Harris, his closest opponent. Polk Shelton finished third, nearly 3900 votes behind Lyndon, Sam Stone came in fourth, C. N. Avery a surprisingly poor fifth, and Houghton Brownlee, trailing by over 5200 votes, was last among the serious contenders. A breakdown of the vote by counties showed that Lyndon finished third in two, second in two, and first in six, including Travis, where he got nearly 3000 of the 10,300 votes. Unlike his opponents, who made strong showings in only one or two counties, Johnson ran well across the whole district.

A photograph of him in a hospital bed the day after the election shows him flanked by two nurses, and covered by—indeed up to his chin in— congratulatory telegrams. Though his thin unshaven face, uncombed hair, and the dark circles under his sunken eyes show the effects of his grueling six-week campaign and his recent surgery, a warm smile reflects the satisfaction of a man who had fulfilled a longstanding hope. Capturing Lyndon in an uncharacteristic moment of enforced repose, the photo is unique in the remarkable political career that unfolded over the next thirty-two years.[68]

PART TWO

The Congressman
1937–1948

6

The New Dealer

SHORTLY after his election, Lyndon was told by a friend that "some country folks near Taylor when asked who they would vote for said, 'I tank Yonson must be a pretty good Swede—I'll vote for him.' " Johnson knew that chance and peculiar circumstance would always play a part in Texas and even national politics. But from the moment he set his sights on electoral office, he operated on the assumption that political success depended primarily on planning and hard work, actions that left as little to happenstance as possible. He believed that if he were to hold his congressional seat and ultimately win a higher office, he needed to become an influential figure in Washington and effectively serve the interests of his district, state, and region.[1]

The day after his election Lyndon was eager to begin implementing his political design by answering congratulatory messages piling up at the hospital and planning the organization of his office. The campaign and his surgery, however, had left him so exhausted that he could only dictate a few conciliatory replies to defeated opponents and a thank-you note to Sam Rayburn for a "wire" that gave me a real boost." A telegram from Maury Maverick gave him one of his few happy moments during this recuperative period: "Have destroyed all copies of your picture in Austin Statesman because the general opinion is that you are lying in bed drunk. I never saw such a face. Even though you are sick you could at least wash your face or get a shave. Will be glad to furnish money for shave if you are without funds."[2]

After leaving the hospital on April 24, Lyndon stayed in Texas until May 11 to meet with the President. On April 11, the day after Lyndon's election, two Tenth District Democrats had wired Roosevelt that the outcome represented a victory for him: the six candidates favoring Court reform outpolled two opponents by a margin of almost three and a half to one. Johnson was "most outspoken for you." On April 20, after FDR had decided to combine a political junket with a fishing holiday in the Gulf of Mexico, an aide proposed that when they got to Texas, the President see the Congressman-elect. Acting as the intermediary, Governor Jimmy Allred advised Johnson that he would be invited to join the President's party at Galveston about May 10. Lyndon seized upon the invitation to ask if the President would be willing to discuss a committee assignment and pose for a photograph with him. Allred answered that the President will see you when he lands at Galveston. "You and I will ride with him to A&M College, and probably on to Fort Worth if you want to come. He was intensely interested in the details of your campaign, and himself brought up the committee matter which you and I discussed. I suggested to him that you all should have your picture made together next week, and this was entirely agreeable."[3]

On May 10, Lyndon drove in the President's open-air touring car from Houston to Galveston with Elliott Roosevelt, who had moved to Fort Worth to run the Texas State Network radio stations for Sid Richardson, a Texas oil millionaire. The next day, as the President came ashore, Lyndon stood with Allred at the foot of the gangway, where he shook Roosevelt's hand before the cameras and exchanged small talk about his fishing trip. Still very thin and pale from his recent surgery, having lost thirty of his 181 pounds, Johnson "looked like a kid fifteen years old shaking hands with President Roosevelt," one of Lyndon's boyhood friends remembered.[4]

As prearranged, on the following morning, Johnson joined Roosevelt on his special train from Galveston to College Station, where the President spoke to 3000 ROTC cadets at Texas A&M about the need for preparedness, describing it as "honestly made for defense and not for aggression." Afterwards, Johnson traveled by train with the presidential party to Fort Worth. During that day-long journey, two of America's premier twentieth-century politicians sized each other up and struck an unspoken agreement to serve their mutual interests. Roosevelt, whose worries about foreign affairs, and German, Italian, and Japanese aggression in particular, were growing, wanted to strengthen his hold over defense planning. He especially wanted to expand American naval power, which, among other things, meant having a pliable House Naval Affairs Committee. He "wanted somebody from Texas that would vote for a strong Navy," the President told Lyndon. The young man "came on like a freight train," FDR later told an aide. According to Ed Clark, Lyndon boldly asked for assignment to the Appropriations Committee, one of the two most important committees in the House and the one on which his predecessor Buck Buchanan had served as chairman. When Roosevelt said that would have to wait, Lyndon described a long-standing interest in the U.S. Navy, and raised the possibility of establishing a naval air base at Corpus Christi. He also showed the President a piece of an old paper sack on which Albert Burleson had predicted his victory in the congressional race, suggesting a shared tie to the Wilson administration in which both FDR and Burleson had served.[5]

If Lyndon was a bit obvious in his attempt to ingratiate himself, Roosevelt saw more in the young man than just another freshman congressman on the make. As Lyndon was about to leave, Roosevelt gave him Thomas G. Corcoran's telephone number in Washington and told him to call "Tommy the Cork," as his White House assistant was known, to discuss the Naval Committee assignment and any other matter on which they could be of help. Before Johnson called, the President himself telephoned Corcoran: "I've just met the most remarkable young man. Now I like this boy, and you're going to help him with anything you can." Roosevelt also told Harold Ickes, his Secretary of the Interior, and Harry Hopkins that meeting Lyndon Johnson had caused him some frustration: "if he hadn't gone to Harvard, that's the kind of uninhibited young pro he'd like to be—that in the next generation the balance of power would shift south and west, and this boy could well be the first Southern President."[6]

After Johnson left Roosevelt in Fort Worth, he flew to Washington, his first plane ride. He spent the night with Welly and Alice Hopkins, reminiscing with Welly until well past midnight about his earlier days in Washington and bubbling over with enthusiasm about the future. The next day, May 13, he took a streetcar by himself from Foxhall Village in northwest Washington, where Hopkins lived, to the Capitol for his swearing-in ceremony. In the Well of the House, with Sam Rayburn, now the Majority Leader, at his side, Lyndon took the oath of office from William Bankhead of Alabama, the Speaker. Maury Maverick asked consent to address the House for thirty seconds: "Mr. Speaker, the gentleman just sworn in, Mr. Lyndon Johnson, supported the President's judiciary plan and was overwhelmingly elected." Roosevelt's backers applauded. Facing defeat in the Senate on Court reform, they saw Lyndon's election as something to cheer about.[7]

More important to Lyndon, it immediately marked him as a strong Roosevelt man and gave him access to Administration officials who could help his congressional career. Roosevelt had already made this possible by talking to Corcoran, Ickes, and Hopkins. And they, in turn, talked to others about Johnson, especially Corcoran, who commanded extraordinary influence. A brilliant thirty-six-year-old attorney who had trained at the Harvard Law School and had drafted and maneuvered major New Deal laws through Congress, Corcoran knew how to "take care of the boy," as FDR had asked. Corcoran went to see Jim Forrestal, the Under Secretary of the Navy, to explain that "this newcomer [had] impressed the President with his interest in the administration's economic plans." Corcoran told Sam Rayburn that Roosevelt was "personally interested in his new young home-state colleague"; and he advised Carl Vinson of Georgia, the chairman of the House Naval Affairs Committee: "This is the boss's protégé." Then he went back to Forrestal to urge him to talk to Vinson about the young man. He told Senator Alban Barkley of Kentucky, who knew "the value of helping allies on the other side of the Hill, 'Now here's one of us.' "

Harold Ickes also talked up Lyndon. At lunch one day, he told Eliot Janeway, the business editor of *Time*, that he ought to meet this "new kid Lyndon Johnson." When Janeway returned to New York that evening from Washington, he had a call from Edwin Weisl, a Wall Street lawyer and personal counsel to Harry Hopkins, who wanted to know if Janeway had "ever heard of some kid called Lydie Johnson." Together, Corcoran recalls, the New Dealers created an "atmosphere, a consensus about the new boy and his immediate future in the House."[8]

Lyndon also developed contacts on his own: with James Rowe, a twenty-eight-year-old lawyer at the Securities and Exchange Commission, who in January 1938 became a White House assistant to James Roosevelt, the President's son; with William O. Douglas, thirty-eight, a former Yale law professor who had been a Securities and Exchange Commissioner since 1934 and would become an Associate Justice of the Supreme Court in 1939; with Clifford Durr, at the Reconstruction Finance Corporation, and his wife Virginia Durr, liberal Alabamans related to Senator Hugo Black; with Elizabeth Wickenden at the NYA and her husband Arthur (Tex) Goldschmidt from San Antonio, an official at the Public Power Division of the Interior Department; with Abe Fortas from Memphis, Tennessee, a brilliant twenty-six-year-old graduate of the Yale Law School who worked with Goldschmidt in the Power Division; and with Clark Foreman, the head of the Division, a Georgian, whose family owned the *Atlanta Constitution*. Lyndon formed "a natural alliance" with these men and women, all of whom lived near one another and saw each other socially on a regular basis. "In those days," Abe Fortas remembered, "it was hard to draw a line between social manners and the affairs of government." Lunches, afternoon cocktails, and spur-of-the-moment dinner parties with all these people became a fixed part of Lyndon's and Lady Bird's lives.[9]

The Johnsons made an unforgettable impression on these friends. Lyndon wasn't difficult to help, Corcoran recalled, "because he had talent and he had brains." "He was . . . long, loud and unstoppable," Corcoran adds. "Tall as a plow horse and slim as a lodgepole, he boasted a slick of black curly hair and a smile as wide as the Pedernales—a very attractive guy so cocksure of himself that he never stopped talking." He was "a tall, thin, gangling, gregarious Texan," William O. Douglas recalled. Lyndon "looked so young," Virginia Durr remembered. "He had a very boyish look. Bird was a sweet looking, dark haired, dark eyed girl

who seemed to adore her husband. . . . She talked very little and let
him do all the talking. She just looked at him . . . with worshipping
eyes and let him hold the floor, and . . . he held it very well. . . . We
used to laugh and call him 'The Drugstore Cowboy,' because he always
wore cowboy boots. . . . They were this young couple, just out of the
South, like new laid eggs . . . so young and so sweet." [10]

"This fellow really shone," James Rowe recalled. "There were a lot
of colorful, young fellows in New Deal days in the Congress and outside
the Congress. This fellow was a great operator. He stood out. And as I
look back . . . besides the drive and the energy and the doing favors,
which he did for everybody, there was a great deal of charm in this man.
. . . This was a very bright man, and . . . a very charming man, and
. . . a very ambitious man. You put them all together, you knew he was
going a long way." Elizabeth Rowe, Jim's wife, remembers that "he was
always more fun to be with than anybody else. . . . I always think of
him moving fast through a room or telling marvelous stories." Both Rowes
recalled his long monologues: "There is nothing better in the world,"
but when "he had lost his audience, he would just go to sleep, just sit
there and go to sleep. Eventually he would wake up and take the conversation over" again. "It always amused me that once he lost his audience he didn't think anybody else would say anything important so he
just slept for a while," Jim Rowe said. "But he was a great charmer." [11]

Yet not everyone Johnson met at this time was well disposed toward
him. To his New Deal friends, Lyndon "was ingratiating, gay, cocksure,
and, on occasion, hilariously funny," the journalists Rowland Evans and
Robert Novak later said. "To the rest of the world, his manner changed
with his mood and his mood was frequently overbearing." Those outside
his circle of friends remember a young man with a long, thin face distinguished by "a chin that jutted far out and slightly up from the lower
jaw . . . a large overhanging nose with wide nostrils . . . two very large
ears with long, hanging lobes," and dark, intense, "slightly menacing"
eyes. They also recall how he "chainsmoked . . . combed his glistening
hair straight back . . . fancied gabardine suits a cut too big for him . . .
[and] wore shirts with extra-long collars and exotic ties with small, hard
knots." Another journalist described the way he would lean "way over
toward you" when he spoke, and "if he wasn't smiling you'd almost
think he was Dracula." [12]

At this time, Johnson had few critics and numerous important allies.
In 1969, Jim Rowe said that as "a young man on the way up . . . he
[Lyndon] was smoother or more sensitive to the moods of the people
around him than he later became. . . . He was out to make friends. He
did it very well. You couldn't help but like him." Rowe also believed
that "he made a hardboiled judgment that the power in Washington at
the time was in the Executive Branch, which it was, not on the Hill. He

was one of the few congressmen that got to know all the young New Dealers, a lot of them through me, I may say, but he cultivated them. He quite early seemed to know where the buttons for power were." [13]

Lyndon also made special efforts to win the approval of House leaders. And he quickly convinced them that he was an effective legislator and reliable Democrat. "He made a very profound impression from the outset upon his colleagues," John W. McCormack of Massachusetts, the later Majority Leader and speaker of the House, recalled. " . . . His interest in committee work on the floor of the House clearly marked him out as one who was destined for greater responsibilities and higher honors." McCormack believed that Roosevelt's regard for Johnson was "certainly . . . helpful" to him, but "Johnson earned his position and his prestige and his standing as a result of his own contributions in committee and in the House." [14]

Lyndon's record as a congressman bears out McCormack's point, but it gives too little weight to Roosevelt's part in helping Johnson get started in the House. Not long after Lyndon had been sworn in, Fred Vinson of Kentucky, a central figure on the Ways and Means Committee, which made committee assignments, thanked Lyndon "for a good dinner" and "an excellent conversation." Vinson explained that during dinner at the White House he "kept wondering just what it was he [the President] wanted from me. I knew it was something. Finally, he said casually— oh, very casually—'Fred, there's a fine young man just come to the House. Fred, you know that young fellow, Lyndon Johnson? I think he would be a great help on Naval Affairs.' He meant the Naval Affairs Committee, you know." Vinson assured Lyndon that it would be arranged. [15]

Because he was sensitive to the importance of close working relationships with House leaders in advancing himself, Johnson made every effort to cultivate Bankhead, Rayburn, McCormack, and Fred Vinson, but particularly Carl Vinson of Georgia, who ran the Naval Affairs Committee with an iron fist.

Johnson took pains to defer to "the Admiral," as Vinson was called. Ascending to the chairmanship of the Naval Affairs Committee in 1931, after seventeen years in the House, Vinson brooked no challenge to his authority. "Well, I voted with you," a newcomer to the committee once told Vinson. "What the hell do you think I put you on this committee for," Vinson shot back. The journalist William S. White described how Vinson presided over committee hearings: He sat "front and center rather like an ancient monarch surrounded by ministers whose proximity to the throne depends upon the years that lie upon their heads." He called junior members of his committee "ensign." If they performed well, he would begin calling them "commander," and when he changes "this salutation to 'captain,' the member knows he has arrived." There was "no suggestion of power or official grandeur" about Vinson or his office.

He looked like the country lawyer he was, "and about once removed from the cracker barrel," another journalist said. "His collar is two sizes too big, his tie ordinarily has spots blotched on it, and his office spittoon is rimmed with a two-inch circle of ashes, matches and crumbled cigar wrappers." But appearances were deceptive, as some of the navy brass learned. If a new admiral asked for an appropriation without first convincing Vinson of its need, the chairman would offer some down-home, but unmistakable, advice: "Don't take your shoes off before you get to the stream, admiral." [16]

Lyndon needed only one lesson to learn what "the Admiral" expected of him. Lyndon and Warren Magnuson from the state of Washington, whose district included the Puget Sound Navy Yard and whose service on the committee also began in 1937, made the mistake of peppering witnesses with questions at their first committee hearing. "I want to see you two boys in the back room," Vinson told them afterward. "You two are nice young fellows, and I'm sure you have the interest of the Navy at heart," he said. "But we have a rule in the committee. We call it seniority. Each of you is entitled to ask only one question this whole year, and two next year." Johnson and Magnuson soon learned "how to play up to Uncle Carl. . . . Lyndon and I always called Carl Vinson Admiral," Magnuson says. "We could get around him easily after the first few years—Lyndon more easily than I because he used me as a straightman and he had the southern syrup." Vinson, whose wife was an invalid, was something of a recluse. He went home at 4:45 every afternoon to take care of her and never invited anyone to his home. Eager to hear the next morning what had occurred in the House after he had left, Lyndon and Magnuson made a habit of "filling him in." They also began telling him "dirty jokes and the details of amorous escapades, which he enjoyed with real vicarious pleasure." "Before long we were in solidly with the Admiral," Magnuson recalls.[17]

No one in the House was more important to Lyndon, however, than Sam Rayburn, his fellow Texan from Bonham in the northeast corner of the state. At the age of fifty-five, after twenty-four years in the House, Rayburn had become Majority Leader in January 1937. A short, stocky man with a bald head, broad shoulders, and a thick-set, powerful neck, Rayburn dressed in dark suits that gave him the "somber, immaculate" look of "a capable undertaker." A normally "poker-faced expression" or "stern demeanor" added to his grave appearance. A bachelor with few interests outside of the House of Representatives, which he once described as "my life and my love," Rayburn was a lonely man. On Sundays, he would awake unhappy at the prospect of a day without the excitement of the Capitol. "God help the lonely, for loneliness consumes people," he once said when facing a quiet day. Although an intensely proud man who shunned dependence on anyone, he often invited aides to join him for Sunday breakfast and fellow congressmen to spend a weekend fishing in Maryland or Virginia or go out for Sunday dinner.[18]

Lyndon and Lady Bird became his surrogate family. "No doubt the reason Rayburn was willing to put himself out for Johnson," one of Rayburn's biographers writes, "was his psychological need to have a son and a family." In 1944, when Lyndon told Rayburn that Lady Bird was expecting their first child, Rayburn, with paternal concern, asked if Lady Bird was all right. But "before Johnson could answer, he went on insistently, 'Go call her this minute and see how she's feeling.' " For Lyndon and Lady Bird the relationship not only served Lyndon's political fortunes but also rested on genuine affection and regard. Lyndon never tired of telling everyone, including Rayburn, that he was just like a daddy to him. When they met in the halls of Congress, Lyndon "would bend over and kiss him on his bald head." Rayburn, who accepted few invitations to dinner parties, and when he did, invariably announced that he had to be home by 10:00 p.m., became a regular guest at the Johnsons for dinner and Sunday breakfasts and would reciprocate by inviting them for breakfast at his apartment. On these occasions, his generally solemn, laconic demeanor would become more animated while he told political stories.[19]

The warmth of their relations extended to doings on the Hill. At the close of business every day, Rayburn invited a favored few to join him at the "Board of Education," his hideaway office directly under the House Speaker's formal office. There, they socialized and, as John Nance Garner, who originated the phrase, said, struck "a blow for liberty" with some bourbon and branch water. "Only two House members had keys and didn't have to gain admittance," Rayburn said. "I had one key; Lyndon Johnson had the other." Johnson partly reciprocated Rayburn's affection for him by arranging a surprise birthday party for "Mister Sam" at the White House in January 1939. Johnson persuaded James Rowe and Grace Tully, one of FDR's secretaries, to put the suggestion before the President as a good way to improve relations between the Administration and the House leadership. Roosevelt "thought it was a great idea." On the day of the party, the President sent word to Rayburn that he had to see him immediately at the White House. When the Majority Leader appeared, Roosevelt "scared the daylights out of him" by declaring, "You are in real trouble and I'm the fellow to tell you. . . . You are the age of [fifty-seven]," and everyone came in singing "Happy Birthday." The President gave Rayburn a big Stetson hat which Lyndon had bought with his own money and given to Roosevelt. The next day when photos of the occasion appeared in the newspapers, Lyndon was standing in the middle between the President and Rayburn. Rowe looked at the pictures and began to think he had "really met an operator." Corcoran, who was among the most effective political insiders in the Roosevelt

Administration, had a similar reaction: "That was the first time I really knew that an operator was loose." [20]

The photo partly testified to Lyndon's standing as a Roosevelt man or good New Dealer. Years later, Johnson liked to recall that before he went to Washington his father told him: "Son, measure each vote you cast by this standard: Is this vote in the benefit of the people? What does this do for human beings? How have I helped the lame and the halt and the ignorant and the diseased? See if this vote is generally for humanity." He also told him to back the President: "Now you get up there, support FDR all the way, never shimmy and give 'em hell." [21]

Johnson largely did. Like so many others who entered government service in the thirties, Lyndon's sense of participation in something larger than himself helped make him a committed New Dealer. The fact that he represented a strong pro-Roosevelt district also played a part. But his whole life experience was at the core of his identity as a southern New Dealer or liberal nationalist who aimed to integrate the South into the mainstream of American economic life. The words and deeds of Sam Ealy Senior and Junior, the instruction of Professor Greene at San Marcos, the plight of the children at Cotulla and his sense of exhilaration at being able to help them, the feelings of accomplishment when answering the cries for aid from people in Kleburg's district, the suffering caused by the Depression and the humane response of FDR's government, all made him a strong believer in using Federal power for the good of needy Americans everywhere, but especially in the South.

He gave expression to this credo through his congressional votes. On June 1, 1937, nineteen days after he entered the House, Johnson was one of only thirteen congressmen who supported FDR's veto of a bill extending veterans' term insurance for five years. More important, he voted with the President on almost every major domestic and foreign policy question between May 1937 and December 1941: to eradicate slums by creating a United States Housing Authority; to defeat a constitutional amendment requiring a national referendum on war; to create fair labor standards by establishing a minimum wage, a forty-hour week, and prohibitions against child labor; to reorganize the Executive branch of the Federal government; to help Britain and France fight Germany by adding cash and carry provisions to the Neutrality law; to institute a peacetime draft; and to create a Lend-Lease program in 1941 to keep Britain fighting. [22]

There were numerous other, less dramatic, measures on which Johnson voted with Roosevelt during these four and a half years, but it was on issues like the minimum wage and reorganization that the Administration took most careful note of where he stood. Only twenty-two southerners, including Johnson, Maverick, and Rayburn, voted with Roosevelt to force the Fair Labor Standards Act out of committee and on the floor of the House for a vote. Johnson remembered that opposition to the law was fierce: "They said it was socialism, statism, communism. . . . They said it was governmental interference, and it was. It interfered with that fellow who was running that pecan shelling plant" in which workers earned an average $1.29 a week. "It told him he couldn't pay that little widow seven cents" an hour. The bill had special meaning for the South, where workers received the lowest pay in the nation and a wages and hours bill promised to raise southern living standards and reduce the region's backwardness. Similarly, the reorganization bill, which principally aimed to make government more efficient, provoked warnings in 1938 of a coming Roosevelt dictatorship. On April 8, in the worst defeat FDR ever suffered in the House, 108 Democrats joined 96 Republicans to reject the bill, 204–196. In December, when the White House drew up a list of "dependable and loyal" House members who, among other things, had "stuck by the Reorganization Bill" and might now be appointed to the powerful Ways and Means or Rules Committee, Lyndon Johnson was one of thirty names mentioned.[23]

Yet Johnson was no cipher who consistently supported liberal initiatives. He was mindful of Sam Rayburn's conviction that a congressman needed to please the people of his district, and to do so "you must also please your colleagues in the House." In his memorable statement of the formula: "To get along, go along." But this did not mean casting a vote which would violate a man's "conscience or wreck him politically." During their first year Rayburn advised Lyndon and Magnuson to keep their "mouths shut on the floor. You won't know what the score is for a long time. Also remember, don't get involved with broad issues, because you have to get re-elected; and if you get into the big issues, the voters will think you aren't taking care of the District's problems." As Senator Russell Long of Louisiana, the son of Huey Long, later stated the point: a congressman's first obligation is to get elected; his second is to get reelected.[24]

Lyndon never overlooked the political needs of his district, state, and self. In July 1937, for example, he voted against Roosevelt and Rayburn to override a presidential veto of a bill extending loans to farmers at rates a half point below the level of other government loans. Likewise, in the 1940s, when he confronted civil rights measures to prevent lynchings of black southerners, eliminate poll taxes, and deny Federal funds for lunch programs to segregated schools, he consistently voted with his southern colleagues. He feared the political consequences of challenging the prevailing attitude in Texas on black rights. When Jim Rowe once pushed him to take an advanced position on something, Johnson objected that he could only "go so far in Texas," and invoked the example of Maury Maverick, who, after identifying himself with the most progressive elements in the House, lost his congressional seat in 1938 after only two terms. "Don't forget our friend Maury," he told Rowe. ". . . There's nothing more useless than a dead liberal."[25]

When he could operate behind the scenes for liberal causes that generated little sympathy in Texas, he went out of his way to get results. Not long after he came to Washington, he learned that black farmers in his district were not getting the same small loans given to white farmers for seed and equipment. He raised "unshirted hell" with the Farm Security Administration, and applications from blacks began to be approved. Milo Perkins, a top official in the Farm Security Administration, recalled that Johnson "was the first man in Congress from the South ever to go to bat for the Negro farmer." Johnson also worked quietly "to insure that blacks were included within the provisions of the Agricultural Adjustment Act of 1938" and to bar school lunch funds to any state with separate school systems for blacks that "did not make an equitable distribution of school lunch grants."[26]

In 1938–39, Lyndon also helped rescue Jewish victims of Nazi persecution. Hitler's seizure of Austria in March 1938 swelled the ranks of Jewish migrants seeking refuge from Nazism. Public and congressional resistance to foreigners who might land on the unemployment rolls and unstated anti-Semitism made efforts to bring Jews to the United States politically unpopular. In the spring of 1938, when Charles Marsh asked Lyndon to help Erich Leinsdorf, a brillant twenty-five-year-old Austrian Jewish musician, whose temporary visa was about to expire, Johnson was happy to comply. He was eager to please Marsh, who had thrown his Austin newspapers behind him in the campaign, but he also took great satisfaction in rescuing a highly talented young man from persecution. "You have a great art and genius to console, uplift and support you," Lyndon told him. Gaining an extension of Leinsdorf's visa for another six months, Johnson then arranged for Leinsdorf to go to Cuba, from where he could return to the United States on the Austrian quota as a "permanent resident."

The episode with Leinsdorf sensitized Johnson to the problem of others seeking refuge, and he began asserting himself quietly in their behalf. One of Lyndon's constituents in Austin was Jim Novy, a successful Russian-Jewish businessman who had come to the United States in 1913 at the age of seventeen. A leader of Austin's four hundred Jews, Jim and his brother Louis were also active in Texas politics. Contributors to philanthropic causes and Texas Democrats, the Novys had known Lyndon Johnson since he worked for Kleberg. In the spring of 1938, when Lyndon heard that Jim was planning a trip to Poland and Germany, he urged Novy to "get as many Jewish people as possible out of both countries." Attending to the necessary affidavits in Washington and calling the U.S. consul in Warsaw, Lyndon's efforts allowed Novy to arrange for forty-two Polish and German Jews, including four relatives, to come to the United States later that year.

Early in 1940, four months after the outbreak of World War II, Johnson began helping hundreds of Jewish refugees from Hitler's persecution reach Texas through Cuba, Mexico, and countries in South America. Working with Jim Novy, Jack K. Baumel, a chief engineer at the Texas Railroad Commission and an Austin Jewish leader, and Jesse Kellam, Texas director of the NYA, Lyndon and the others helped Jews get false passports and one-way visas in Latin America and then brought them to NYA training camps in Texas. Because it was illegal to house and train noncitizens at the camps, even though Novy reimbursed camp directors for all costs, *Operation Texas*, as the rescue effort was called, was kept a strict secret for over twenty years. In 1963, when Lyndon helped dedicate a synagogue in Austin, Novy declared: "We can't ever thank him enough for all those Jews he got out of Germany during the days of Hitler." As they left the temple, Mrs. Johnson recalls, "Person after person plucked at my sleeve and said, 'I wouldn't be here today if it weren't for him. He helped me get out.' "[27]

By 1938–39 some Administration leaders thought of Lyndon Johnson as the "best New Dealer from Texas." He was viewed as someone who not only backed the Roosevelt administration but also did all he could to obtain Federal benefits for his constituents, including the most needy. From the moment he arrived in Washington, he pressed the case for farmers, nationally as well as in his district. "During his year in Congress," a Burnet County newspaper declared in June 1938, "Lyndon B. Johnson . . . has demonstrated that he knows the proper interpretation of the word 'Representative.' " Johnson's "first principle . . . has been to maintain a high-income standard for the people of Central Texas. . . . Of paramount importance . . . definite steps have been taken toward permanent farm and ranch programs, to do away with sporadic relief and the recurrence of alternate periods of good times and bad times." He strongly backed passage of the Agricultural Adjustment Act of 1938, which appropriated funds for parity payments, provided farm mortgages at a low rate of interest, promoted soil conservation, and continued a program to help tenant farmers become farm owners.

In particular, Lyndon battled for cotton farmers whose large 1937–38 crops caused a precipitous drop in prices. Between March and September 1937 cotton fell nearly $4 a bale, a 10 percent decline, and threatened southern farmers with a loss of almost $80 million. A vocal member of a southern congressional delegation that visited the White House in August 1937, Johnson played a "decisive" part in persuading FDR to adopt a temporary loan program that eased the cotton farmers' plight. In 1938, moreover, he helped start a long-term relief program that included subsidies, loans and the distribution of cotton goods to needy folks on direct relief. He was "getting the farmer with cotton and the man without a shirt together," Lyndon said, and when combined with two-cent-a-bale payments and ten-cent-a-bale loan programs, the cotton farmer was "being assured his fair share of the national income."[28]

No group in Johnson's district benefited more from his actions than impoverished Hill Country farmers. Money was in such short supply in the early thirties that the area functioned as a barter economy. Moreover, with the land so unproductive—only 35,000 acres or 10 percent of Blanco County was under cultivation in 1933—New Deal programs, which paid farmers for reducing their crops, could provide little cash to the Hill Country. But Johnson found ways to help. In 1938–41, when hundreds of farmers couldn't quality for Farm Security Administration loans because they had no collateral, Johnson persuaded the FSA to waive the requirement and give each of 400 families a $50 loan. In addition, he facilitated the implementation of a "Range Conservation" program in the Hill Country that cleared thousands of acres of soil-depleting brush and increased the amount of land under cultivation by 400 percent in three and a half years. At the same time, he helped provide Federal funds for paved farm-to-market roads which facilitated the shipment of increased produce to market before it spoiled.[29]

During 1937–38 Johnson also obtained millions of dollars in WPA grants for the ten counties in his Tenth District: $70,000 for a new Federal building at Elgin; $27,000 for a sewing-room project in Bastrop County; nearly $110,000 for cutting and burning timber in a lake bed to be created by the construction of a dam; almost $20,000 for school renovations in Blanco County; $112,000 for an Austin city hall project; $33,000 for an Austin fire alarm system; $29,000 to remodel Austin's old Federal building; and grants to help fund a dormitory and student union and laboratory school buildings at his alma mater in San Marcos. In addition, he arranged radio beam service at the Austin airport to prevent accidents, increased public health services to combat an outbreak of polio in Travis County, and improved mail service for Austin. In April 1938, Lyndon advised Mayor Tom Miller of Austin to reactivate a 1933 proposal for sixteen WPA projects totaling $2.556 million. They included proposals for a new wing on the city hospital, a municipal auditorium, and a city incinerator. On June 22 the *Austin Statesman* reported that Miller had been summoned from a city council meeting to receive a call from Johnson in Washington. The congressman reported that three of the projects had been approved and that the others would be too.[30]

There were other, larger projects as well. In September 1937 the President signed the Wagner-Steagall Act creating the United States Housing Authority and making available $500 million in loans for low-cost housing. To Johnson, it meant a chance to help the building industry and poor people in his district at no expense to taxpayers. "Whenever we all unite in any program which turns business back through its natural courses, unpacking clogged money in banks, lifting the jobless off the relief rolls, unfreezing the stream of building materials and supplies . . . and putting our people in homes we have united in the best work any of us can do," Johnson said. When he returned to Texas in December 1937, Johnson told Mayor Tom Miller and other Austin leaders: "Now look I want us to be first in the United States if you're willing to do this, and you've got to be willing to stand up for the Negroes and the Mexicans." Johnson and Miller persuaded the City Council to set up an Austin Housing Authority with Alvin Wirtz and Edgar H. Perry Sr., Lyndon's allies, as members. The Austin agency then applied to the U.S.H.A. for a $450,000 loan to help finance the building of 550 rooms that would cost occupants between $3 and $5 a room a month.[31]

Lyndon then returned to Washington, where he won agreement to make Austin, along with New Orleans and New York, one of three cities to receive initial U.S.H.A. loans. Leon Keyserling, the deputy administrator of the Authority, remembered: "There was this first term congressman who was so on his toes and so active and so overwhelming that he was up and down our corridors all the time . . . . It was his go-getitness that got that first project for Austin. . . . Then he . . . called up and said, 'Lady Bird and I want you to have cocktails with us.' I said, 'How's that?' He said, 'Well, we want Austin to be announced first.' I said, 'Well, why first? Mayor LaGuardia [of New York] might not like that.' He said, 'Well, it's first in the alphabet, isn't it?' Well, we announced them all simultaneously."[32]

Some of Austin's principal realtors tried to scuttle the project. They objected to "government competition" in rental property, warning that it would discourage private building and cost the city several million dollars in business activity. Besides, they saw no need for public housing, because Austin "has no real slums. . . . There are no typical slums here," one of them said. But Johnson, Governor Allred, Mayor Miller, and other city fathers knew better. The opponents of the project, Johnson said, were "rent hogs," men who worried that decent, low-cost housing for the poor would replace slum dwellings from which they profited. "Those who are opposing this program are not only standing in the way of progress—" Allred declared, "they are opposing common decency." To back up the assertion, the Austin Housing Authority prepared maps showing that the highest concentration of juvenile delinquency, petty crime, relief families, and diseases like tuberculosis and syphilis were in the older parts of the city with the poorest housing. The areas with medium- and high-cost housing showed little evidence of these social and medical blights.[33]

On January 23, 1938, Johnson spoke on a local radio station about "Tarnish on the Violet Crown," borrowing from the writer O. Henry who, after having lived there, described Austin as "the city of the Violet Crown." Johnson recounted a walking tour he had made of Austin's slums on Christmas Day. He described housing conditions two or three blocks from Congress Avenue, the city's principal street, and the Driskill, the city's finest hotel. "Within the shadow of the Capitol," he said, "I found people living in such squalor that Christmas Day was to them just one more day of filth and misery." He saw a family of eight or ten people living in a room 20 by 25 or 30 feet, a fire hydrant from which 110 people took their drinking water, and an outdoor toilet which they all used. He added: "I found one family that might almost be called typical, living within one dreary room, where no single window let in the sun. Here they slept, they cooked and ate, they washed themselves in a leaky tin tub after hauling the water 200 yards. Here they raised their children, ill-nourished and sordid. And on this Christmas morning, there was no Santa Claus for the 10 children, all under 16, that scrambled around the feet of a wretched mother bent over her washtub, while in this same room her husband, the father of her brood, lay dangerously ill with an infectious disease."

Johnson also pointed out that Austin's housing did not measure up to national standards: 22.3 percent of all Austin homes were "either in dangerous disrepair or even unfit for habitation" compared with 18.1 percent in 64 other cities around the country. Nationally, one home out of twenty lacked running water; in Austin it was one out of six. Twice as many Austin homes lacked a private toilet as in the 64 sample cities. "If anybody says to you that the people of Austin do not need . . . [new] dwellings," Johnson concluded, " . . . take them through the blocks of slums we have, and show them conditions that are a disgrace to Americans in any city." At a public meeting in the county court house on the following night, Johnson, supported by Miller and members of the housing authority, won the unanimous consent of the audience to the slum-clearance program.[34]

During the next two years, after the U.S.H.A. increased the federal outlay to $700,000, the Austin Housing Authority constructed 186 low-cost units: 40 for Mexicans, 60 for blacks, and 86 for whites. Although the housing was strictly segregated and accommodated fewer than a thousand people, it was built for only $2100 a unit compared with a $4500 national average for similar units, and it provided the lowest rent for the same amount of space available in Texas. Returning to Austin in June 1939 to celebrate the opening of the first units, Johnson revelled in the improved living conditions of the families moving into the project. A family of seven that had been occupying a one-room hovel without indoor plumbing or electricity, now lived in a modern five-room housing unit for $15 a month plus utilities, the same rent they had been paying for their one-room hovel. Commenting that the children "already had taken two or three baths this morning," Johnson declared it "worth all the effort . . . to see the change in environment and outlook and spirit of those folks" in the project. "This country won't have to worry about isms when it gives its people a decent, clean place to live and a job," Johnson told the press. "They'll believe in the government. They'll be ready to fight for it." [35]

At the same time, Johnson supported conservation and public power through dam building on the Lower Colorado River. In this, he joined a group of self-serving altruists who used the dams simultaneously to acquire wealth and power and improve the lives of millions of Texans. Efforts at dam-building on the Lower Colorado dated from the late nineteenth century when private interests began trying to control the periodic floods that ravaged the 700-mile-long valley running from northwest Texas through Austin to the Gulf of Mexico. In the first thirty years of the twentieth century, a hundred lives and millions of dollars had been lost in three great floods that sent six-foot walls of water through the ten counties surrounding Austin. "All our fine farm land [is] at the mercy of a river" that periodically goes "berserk, on a terrible rampage," Johnson said in 1937. ". . . It sweeps over the plains. It washes away the crops in the fields. It topples the homes . . . tears fences out by the roots, levels our precious forests, [and] plays checkers with bridges and roads." By the early thirties, the Insulls of Chicago, the owners of several large utilities holding companies in the United States, had begun building dams in Texas, including the George W. Hamilton Dam in Burnet County, eighty miles northwest of Austin. A huge project employing some 1500 men, it promised to become one of the twelve or fifteen largest dams in the world with a capacity to impound a million-acre feet of water and generate hydroelectric power for the ten-county area.[36]

In 1932, however, the Depression destroyed the Insull empire and stopped work on the Hamilton Dam. Alvin Wirtz, who had become a specialist in Texas water rights and been a counsel to the Insull companies building dams on the Guadalupe and Colorado rivers, became the receiver for their holdings. In 1933, to save the Hamilton project, reduce unemployment, and build other Lower Colorado dams, Wirtz persuaded Texas state senators to pass a bill creating the Lower Colorado River Authority (LCRA), a state agency that would help finance and manage multipurpose dams. But private utility interests joined with West Texans worried about loss of water rights at the headstreams of the Colorado to defeat the law in the lower house.[37]

At the same time, Congressman Buchanan, for whom LCRA backers now promised to name the Hamilton Dam, and Joseph J. Mansfield, a south-central Texas congressman who headed the Rivers and Harbors Committee, convinced Roosevelt to support the project with a $4.5 million loan from the Public Works Administration. In November 1934, after the Administration insisted that the money go only to a public agency in Texas that would control the operations of the dam, the Texas lower house and the governor approved the establishment of an LCRA.[38]

After the Authority began functioning in February 1935, Wirtz, Buchanan, and Mansfield pressured the Roosevelt administration into increasing Federal support for dam-building on the Colorado from $4.5 to $20 million. They persuasively argued that an effective flood-control program meant constructing a small Roy Inks Dam just south of the Buchanan project and a Marshall Ford Dam, twenty-one miles northwest of Austin, where the waters from the Llano and Pedernales rivers joined with the Colorado to cause the worst floods.[39]

Despite these commitments, work on the dams proceeded slowly. Administration officials were reluctant to give the additional money. By the middle of 1937, FDR, worried that deficit spending was leading to high inflation, believed that the government needed to curb its outlays. Ickes, who had jurisdiction over the PWA, feared that money allocated to Texas dams would line the pockets of builders overcharging the government. In the summer of 1937, however, Johnson persuaded the White House to commit another $5 million to the Marshall Ford Dam, a third of the additional $15.5 million promised in 1935. The prospect of throwing some 2000 men out of work and of halting construction on a project that would ultimately save Texas millions of dollars in flood damages played a large part in the decision. Unless the Marshall Ford construction was continued, an LCRA memo warned, 80 percent of the 2500 men on the job would be fired, and floods, like one in June 1935 costing over $10 million, would continue to plague south-central Texas. On July 21, in a ceremony at the White House, James Roosevelt, the President's son and secretary, handed Johnson, who was accompanied by Wirtz and members of the LCRA Board, the President's order granting the $5 million. Joking with the delegation, Jimmy Roosevelt said that Johnson "had kept him busy so much of the time on the Texas project," that he " 'will have to catch up on his sleep' now." " 'The president is happy to do this for your congressman,' " Jimmy added. In response to repeated prodding by Johnson, the Administration provided another $14 million over the next four years to complete the network of Texas dams. The expenditure paid handsome dividends in lower unemployment, flood prevention, and more abundant and cheaper electric power.[40]

The dam-building also served Lyndon's political interests and the well-being of Brown & Root, a construction company in Austin controlled by George and Herman Brown. With Lyndon's help they won government contracts that turned a small road-building firm into a multimillion dollar business. Their success gave Lyndon a financial angel that could help secure his political future. As Tommy Corcoran put it later, "A young guy might be as wise as Solomon, as winning as Will Rogers and as popular as Santa Claus, but if he didn't have a firm financial base his opponents could squeeze him. When Roosevelt told me to take care of the boy," Corcoran added, "that meant to watch out for his financial backers too. In Lyndon's case there was just this little road building firm, Brown and Root, run by a pair of Germans."[41]

The Browns were grateful for Lyndon's help. "I hope you know, Lyndon," George wrote him in May 1939, "how I feel reference to what you have done for me and I am going to try to show my appreciation through the years to come with actions rather than words." "In the past," George wrote later that year, "I have not been very timid about asking you to do favors for me and hope you will not get any timidity if you have anything at all that you think I can or should do. Remember that I am *for* you, right or wrong and it makes no difference whether I think you are right or wrong. If you want it, I am for it 100%." For the moment, Johnson was content with automobiles the Browns provided him. "I did not hear any more from you reference to the car," George wrote in June 1939. ". . . Louis's idea was that you buy one and put a Washington, D.C. license on it. That was eliminating any question about where it came from and whom it came through. If you buy a station wagon, I will take it off your hands at your cost when you go back to Washington." When one member of the LCRA Board commented on a car Johnson was driving in the late 1930s, Johnson said that "it had been furnished him by Brown and Root." Gifts of this sort were small payment for the millions Johnson had helped the Browns make. The real payoff would come in the 1940s when Johnson needed help financing state-wide and national campaigns.[42]

In the meantime, he took considerable satisfaction from being part of a historic nation-wide movement to give rural Americans electricity. At the start of Roosevelt's first term, nine out of ten American farms lacked electric power. "Every city 'white way' ends abruptly at the city limits," one public power advocate noted. "Beyond lies darkness." "Farmers, without the benefit of electrically powered machinery," William Leuchtenburg observes, "toiled in a nineteenth-century world; farm wives, who enviously eyed pictures in the *Saturday Evening Post* of city women with washing machines, refrigerators, and vacuum cleaners, performed their backbreaking chores like peasant women in a preindustrial age." In 1933, some 90 percent of America's farmers relied on horses, mules, hand labor, and gas engines for power. Their families cooked and heated their homes with wood stoves, drew water from wells and brooks by hand, used privies, bathed and washed clothes outdoors, and lit the nights with flickering kerosene lamps. Despite repeated appeals to private power companies from country folks for power lines that would light their farms, the utilities refused to invest in what they saw as a losing proposition. Rural electrification promised a good return, but it was not as profitable as service in more densely populated urban areas.[43]

Few sections of America better illustrated the problem than the Texas Hill Country. Without electricity to pump water, heat stoves, refrigerate food, wash and iron clothes, milk cows, and light rooms at the pull of a cord or the flick of a switch, Hill Country families lived primitive lives of unceasing toil. They pumped and hauled hundreds of pounds of water and wood into the house daily, relied on sooty, erratic, wood-burning stoves that made houses unbearably hot in Hill Country summers, canned summer fruits and vegetables that refrigeration could have preserved, scrubbed clothes on washboards, rinsed them in huge vats of boiling water, wrung them by hand, pressed them with six-pound iron wedges heated on a stove, and read by dim kerosene lamps. "Living—just living—was a problem," one Hill Country woman recalls. "No lights. No plumbing. Nothing. Just living on the edge of starvation. That was farm life for us." "Work was all there was. It was a bare existence," another says. For a farm wife who had lived in a town with electricity near Corpus Christi until the Depression had forced her family into subsistence farming in the Hill Country, the change "was like moving from the twentieth century back into the Middle Ages." Appeals to Texas Power & Light, the local utilities company, to string lines to Hill Country towns and farms fell on deaf ears. T.P.&L., which was a subsidiary of a New York-based holding company, refused to provide more than one line through the Tenth Congressional District on the grounds that building more would cost far more than the company would be able to get in return.[44]

One of Roosevelt's principal aims was to bring electricity to rural America. Convinced that the private utilities companies would not do the job at rates country folks could afford, he concluded that the Federal government would have to lead the way. In 1935 he set up the Rural Electrification Administration as part of his relief program. Deciding that it should function as a lending agency which made long-term, low-interest loans to private utilities to build transmission lines in the countryside, the Roosevelt administration quickly found itself frustrated by unresponsive power companies. "There are very few farms requiring electricity for major farm operations that are now not served," their representatives declared. To overcome their opposition, the Administration urged the establishment of nonprofit rural cooperatives that would borrow money from the REA to build power lines and supply cheap electricity. In the spring of 1936, congressional leaders, rallying behind the motto "Let's electrify the country," made REA an independent agency which would principally give loans to nonprofit organizations.[45]

Alive to the hardships of rural life without electricity, Johnson was as determined as anyone to make the REA program succeed in central Texas. During his 1937 campaign for Congress, at a little out-of-the-way country schoolhouse, he told farmers that if they sent him to Congress he "would see that they got electric lights." When Sim Gideon, a later general manager of the LCRA, heard him make this pledge, he "thought . . . just how far would a man go in order to get a vote because I just didn't think they'd bring lights out 10 or 15 miles." But, as people who met him during his first term in Washington remembered, "public power was a passion with him. . . . His great ambition . . . was to get electricity into the river areas of Texas so that people could have electric lights and pumps and irrigation systems." Johnson wrote an LCRA board member in March 1938: "The first conference I held in Washington when I came here as a member of Congress last May, was to urge the PWA officials here and the CRA officials in Texas to make a power survey without further delay to determine what municipalities and areas would be potential customers . . . [when] the CRA was ready to generate and market power. In fact, I spent most of my first week in Washington on that job." [46]

During the next ten months he kept "drubbing" the LCRA to make a survey of the municipalities. But with little success. Now, he said in the spring of 1938, "the time has arrived when we are at the lick-log where we've got to decide what we're going to do." His sense of urgency rested on the knowledge that the Buchanan and Inks dams would soon be ready to generate hydroelectric power and that unless municipalities and rural cooperatives offered to buy it, it would go to private utilities that would charge all the market would bear. "The power companies will be the chief beneficiaries of this huge government investment [in multipurpose dams], supposedly made in the interest of the people of Texas," Johnson wrote an Austin newspaper editor in February 1938. "I am convinced . . . that the present high electric rates in Texas are inexcusable and beyond reason," he told the LCRA board in April. "If we have done or will do even half a job in creating our markets, we can . . . drive those rates down to within reason and within the power of our people to . . . pay for it. So far as I am concerned . . . the simple disposal of the majority of the prime power to private utilities is a crazy idea. I tell you that if we come to such an eventuality we are all likely to be run out of the state and we shall deserve what we receive in condemnation for our failure." [47]

Johnson set a campaign in motion to organize rural cooperatives and persuade Tenth District municipalities to buy the LCRA's electric power. The first task was convincing LCRA board members to join his campaign. "You and I . . . realize there are plenty of rural communities throughout the whole area, where smoky lanterns are the chief means of lighting and elbow-grease is still the main motive power, although this is the Twentieth Century and not the Middle Ages," he wrote McDonough, the general manager. "We know there are many towns in the Tenth District either entirely without electric light and power or struggling with inadequate . . . plants of their own, which supply light and power of most unsatisfactory kind at rates nothing less than blushful. There is no reason why either of these conditions should longer exist in the whole 40,000-square-mile area the Colorado River is getting ready to serve." Urging McDonough to have his office send people into the field to confer with county agents and rural leaders and address farmers' and town meetings, Johnson promised that the REA would provide "complete financing" to build service lines and wire homes and barns. He also urged LCRA officials to come to Washington with a detailed request for funds to run lines to specific towns and cooperatives.[48]

When the LCRA effectively took up the challenge in May and June by sending what one newspaper called "evangels of public power" into the countryside and by asking Washington to supply $7.35 million in grants and loans to construct transmission lines from the dams and to complete the power-generating facilities at Marshall Ford, Johnson had to persuade Federal officials to provide the money. Having obtained a little over $7 million between July 1937 and March 1938 for the Marshall Ford project and currently asking $7 million more for the dam, Johnson felt compelled to take this additional $7.35-million request directly to FDR. In addition, he hoped to persuade FDR to have the REA bend its rules on lending money to central Texas cooperatives that were springing up under LCRA prodding. Because the REA insisted that there be at least three customers for each mile of transmission line and because the limited population in the Hill Country could supply only half that number, the REA wouldn't agree to provide the funds. John Carmody, the REA's director, "was as arrogant as he could be"; Johnson recalled, "he'd already turned me down flat, had thrown me out a dozen times . . . telling me I didn't meet the standards, that he wasn't going to lend any money down there where there were only one and a half customers per mile."[49]

During the second week in June 1938, Johnson got in to see FDR, their first private meeting since the conversation on the train in May 1937. Johnson later remembered that Roosevelt put him off. Before he could get to the point, the President said: " 'Did you ever see a Russian woman naked?' And I said, 'No, but then I never have been in Russia.' And then he started telling me what Harry Hopkins, who had just been to Russia, had told him—how their physique was so different from the American woman because they do the heavy work. . . . Well, before I knew it my fifteen minutes was gone . . . and I found myself in the West Lobby without ever having made my proposition. So I had to go back and make that damn appointment all over again." Since Hopkins didn't go to the Soviet Union until much later, Johnson seems to have gotten his dates wrong.[50]

The story is revealing nevertheless of how FDR put Johnson off on a later occasion. At the June 1938 meeting, Lyndon overcame the President's token resistance to his proposal for REA funds. As Tommy Corcoran remembered the episode, Lyndon came to see him about the appointment. Corcoran told him that he had "seen many an aggressive, articulate man go in with a plan and an argument all rehearsed and never get to present it all. The President would cut him off before he got to the heart of the matter. Roosevelt was a master at sensing what someone wanted; as soon as he did, he'd start outlining the options and ramifications in his own mind while he bantered charmingly until Missy [LeHand, his secretary] poked her head in to say that time was up." Corcoran counseled Johnson to give the President pictures. "Show him what the dams will look like in that beautiful, wild country of yours. Show him what Austin will look like, growing up along the banks of a useful river that doesn't flood its banks and drive everybody into the hills every spring. Don't argue with him Lyndon, show him."

Johnson did just that. Armed with three-foot pictures of Buchanan Dam, transmission lines, and a tenant farmer's house, Johnson laid the photos before the President. But before he could say anything, Roosevelt began to "filibuster" him, going on and on about the ingenuity of multiple-arch dams. Finally, when he asked Johnson why he was showing him these pictures and what he wanted, Lyndon burst forth: "Water, water everywhere, not a drop to drink! Power, power everywhere, but not in a home on the banks of these rural rivers!" Explaining that the power companies wouldn't build transmission lines outside of the cities and that the REA's density rule would continue to deny electricity to Hill Country folks, Johnson recounted the hardships of rural life without electric power.[51]

Johnson was pushing on an open door. Had Roosevelt wanted to put him off, he certainly would have found a way. But Johnson's appeal to help promote rural electrification in central Texas and improve the living standard of its residents struck a resonant chord with the President in the spring and summer of 1938. Roosevelt now saw the South as "the nation's No. 1 economic problem" and wanted to do everything possible to reduce its poverty, including the election of southern congressmen and senators who would support New Deal programs. Citing a 1938 Administration *Report on the Economic Conditions of the South*, which described the region's poverty, Roosevelt threw his weight behind a campaign to unseat conservative southern Democrats in the 1938 primaries. In these circumstances, he was understandably receptive to an

appeal of the sort a southern liberal congressman like Johnson put before him. Roosevelt agreed to encourage the PWA to provide the $7.35
million, which it did promptly, and to press Carmody into relaxing the
density requirement for Hill Country cooperatives. While Johnson listened, the President called Carmody on the phone. After a brief conversation, in which Carmody explained the density problem, Roosevelt replied: " 'John, I know how you've got to have guidelines and rules and
I don't want to upset it, but you just go ahead and approve this for me—
charge it to my account. I'll gamble on those folks because I've been
down in that country and those folks—they'll catch up to that density
problem because they breed pretty fast."

In the following month, as Roosevelt campaigned by train across the
country in behalf of liberal Democrats, Tommy Corcoran wired Ickes,
suggesting that "Lyndon Johnson, Maury's friend . . . who has just received allotments for big transmission line from Buchanan Dam[,] come
aboard for a few minutes in Texas. Suggest it may help offset some
reports ascribed to Elliott [Roosevelt] of pro-power company speeches,
and will directly help Maury." [52]

Although persuading the Administration to back LCRA and cooperative plans for cheap public power, Johnson still had to convince Tenth
District municipalities to establish their own systems for distributing LCRA
power and farmers to join cooperatives. Texas Power and Light campaigned against municipal utilities and cooperatives as certain to jeopardize the existence of T.P.&L. and injure its many Texas customers
and stockholders. At the same time, farmers and ranchers resisted paying a $5 membership fee to join a cooperative, committing themselves
to a minimum $2.45 monthly charge, and signing easement agreements
to string transmission lines across their property. Many of them simply
didn't have the $5, or worried that they couldn't handle the monthly
charge, or thought the easement agreement might threaten the loss of
their land. Some, who had a limited understanding of how electricity
could serve them, believed that rural electrification wasn't worth the expense. "When we went out to solicit memberships in our electric co-
op," an organizer of the Pedernales Electric Co-operative recalled, "I
remember most people said they would only need enough power to run
three electric lights and a washing machine." [53]

During the summer of 1938, Johnson devoted himself to winning the
fight for public power. He joined Alvin Wirtz in having Max Starcke,
the mayor of Seguin and a successful advocate of municipal power facilities, become the operations manager of the LCRA, and Gordon
Fulcher, the editor of the *Austin American*, temporarily leave his job to
run a public-relations campaign for rural electrification. Johnson also
gave a series of talks in person and on the radio in which he emphasized

the benefits of cheap electric power and echoed current popular ideas about freeing the South from its status as an exploited "colonial economy" beholden to the industrial Northeast.[54]

In school rooms and court houses, at picnics and barbecues, he urged Hill Country folks to break the cycle of hardships they had endured hauling water and wood, scrubbing clothes on corrugated washboards, and sweating on "a hot April afternoon" while they cooked or ironed in front of "a red hot cook stove." "That river belongs to the people," he declared in speeches in Blanco and Johnson City. "The water in it belongs to the people. . . . They have a right to put it to work to do their washing and ironing. They have a right to make it light their homes, pump their water, milk their cows, bring the world into their homes by radio, and to the 1,000 other things electricity alone can do. They have a right to get that power at a decent and fair rate, a rate based upon the cost of production, rather than upon the greed and avarice of some pyramid of holding companies." We are going to get "some electric power which doesn't have to run through the cash register of a New York power and light company before it gets to our lamps," he declared at a rally in Austin. "The South has been kept in the state of a raw-material producer," he said in a commencement address at San Marcos. "It has been the looting-ground for outside investors who have exploited and plundered its natural resources." And in a radio talk beamed throughout central Texas from San Antonio, he begged municipal voters to back city "light plants" that would save them a million dollars in electric bills. In the fall of 1938, twenty-five out of twenty-six cities voted for public power, while farmers joined cooperatives in sufficient numbers to begin receiving loans from the REA.[55]

Yet it was to be another year before cheap LCRA power began to reach Hill Country towns and farms. Putting up distribution lines was slow, arduous work. Required to blast three-foot holes in the limestone surface that covered the Hill Country, labor crews usually advanced no more than twelve miles a day. One alternative to building an entirely new system of transmission and distributions lines was to buy existing facilities from T.P.&L. In September, when the company offered to sell its properties in sixteen counties for $7.4 million, the LCRA entered into negotiations that lasted several months. Demands from T.P.&L. that the LCRA agree to sell its surplus power as part of the deal and the Authority's need to borrow the $7.4 million from the RFC complicated the discussions.[56]

Fearful that any commitment to sell LCRA power to private companies would ultimately make electricity more costly in central Texas, Johnson opposed the proposal. He tried to persuade the president of T.P.&L. to drop the demand, but he couldn't. In an outburst of emotion and irritation, Lyndon said: "Well now we've tried to work with you for several months. We've waited many years to get lights in our homes, and now that we have the chance, you're going to deny us that chance, and I'm not going to try to reason with you any more . . . and so far as I'm concerned you can take a running jump and go straight to hell." Though Authority members approved Johnson's statement, Wirtz was critical: "Your conclusion wasn't very good," Wirtz told him in the privacy of his office. "It's one thing to tell a man to go to hell. It's another thing to make a man *go* to hell. . . . It took me months to get him here, and it just took you minutes to bust up the whole meeting, and now I'll have to start all over again." In a subsequent exchange of correspondence, Johnson declared: "I would rather default until '41 than suffer instant death by following the trail T.P.&L. sets out for us." "These are brave words," Wirtz replied, "but they contain more rhetoric than fact." [57]

Johnson eventually saw the wisdom of Wirtz's restrained approach to political adversaries, but he did not give in easily on the fight with T.P.&L. An agreement to pay the power company $5 million for its properties and to sell it some LCRA power satisfied him: it included provisions for the Authority to reduce sales to T.P.&L. when demand from municipalities and public agencies increased and for the power company "to pass on to the public any savings that accrue from the purchase of [LCRA] power." By October 1939, Lyndon reported to 6000 constituents that they were "now getting the benefits of cheap public power. . . . Before we put our river to work," consumers paid $1 for 10 kilowatt hours of power. Now people paid 25 percent less and got 50 percent more power: 15 kilowatt hours for 75 cents. "As you support the program of *increased use* of power at cheaper prices," Johnson declared, "other reductions may be possible. This will keep Tenth District money in the Tenth District, instead of paying big fees and dividends to officers and holding companies east of the Alleghenies." "Of all the things I have ever done," he wrote John Carmody twenty years later, "nothing has ever given me as much satisfaction as bringing power to the hill country of Texas. Today in my home county we have full grown men who have never ever seen a kerosene lamp except possibly in a movie—and that is all to the good." [58]

For his extraordinary efforts in behalf of public power, in July 1939, Roosevelt asked Johnson to become the administrator of the REA. But unwilling to give up a secure seat in Congress for an administrative job he might lose after a few years, Johnson declined. His decision neither surprised nor upset anyone in the Administration. In fact, Ickes and Corcoran had counseled against taking the job, and Corcoran had told him that FDR preferred to have him in Congress. The offer was largely a symbolic expression of regard for the man Ickes now described as "the only real liberal in Congress" from Texas. "He got more projects, and more money for his district, than anybody else," Corcoran said later. "He was the best Congressman for a district that *ever* was."[59]

Corcoran may have been right. But he can hardly be described as an objective commentator on Johnson's congressional work. For like Lyndon, Wirtz, and the Brown brothers, Corcoran's public service carried a self-serving price tag. His efforts to help Johnson with dam-building and electrification were a prelude to business ties with Brown & Root and other Texas corporations which paid his Washington, D.C., law firm handsome fees beginning in the 1940s.

The Brown brothers, whose construction firm largely built the dams that served south-central Texas so well, were even more selfish than Corcoran. PWA records are studded with complaints about their requests for "change orders," cost overruns, and labor practices that violated the spirit and the letter of the law and lined their pockets with undeserved profits. Government contracts made the Browns what some facetiously called "socialized millionaires." Though they gained substantially from the New Deal, the Browns denounced it as welfare programs for people too lazy to work. They particularly disliked the New Deal's housing and labor laws which forced them to sell slum tenements in Austin and to pay laborers a decent wage. In the late forties and fifties, they became leading advocates of anti-union legislation that allowed them to rollback some of the gains workers made in the thirties.

Wirtz and Johnson also gained personally from the Federal expenditures on the dams and transmission lines. Wirtz's law firm received substantial fees—as much $250,000, a huge sum in the 1930s—for its services. And, as with the Browns, the PWA complained loudly about the extravagant cost to the government from the charges levied by Wirtz's firm. Lyndon's return from the government expenditures was less financial than political. Though he received some payoffs from the Browns, the dams and rural electrification gave him a record of accomplishment which was invaluable in his political campaigns.

For Wirtz and Johnson, the Colorado River projects involved much more than selfish gain, however. They also took genuine satisfaction from raising living standards in south-central Texas. For them, politics meant not simply the accumulation of power and wealth but overcoming the poverty that afflicted the lives of so many Texans. Wirtz and Johnson were self-serving opportunists who used their connections to advance themselves; but they were also new breed southerners who saw the Federal government as a vehicle for advancing the interests of their state and region. They were not only shrewd operators with their eyes on the main chance but also men of vision who worked effectively for a larger good.

7

National Politics

BY the fall of 1939 Lyndon had established an almost unbreakable hold on his district. The dams, rural electrification, loans to farmers, and WPA projects had brought $70 million to his constituents and given him a reputation as a "can do" congressman. After his old friend Ben Crider had sounded out opinion in three counties in the spring of 1939, he could "truthfully say I haven't found a man against you." A district judge wrote Johnson in June 1939: "I have heard numbers of intelligent people . . . say that you have already accomplished as much in the short time you have been in Washington as Buchanan had accomplished during his many terms."[1]

During the two and a half years he had held the office, Johnson worked tirelessly for his constituents. An Austin journalist reported that Lyndon signed 258 letters in one day, all "of which had been personally dictated by him." He took special pleasure in finding jobs for youngsters who could not attend college without them. Arthur Goldschmidt, his friend from the Interior Department, remembered how he "sent every newly married couple a letter; he sent every woman with a new baby a copy of *Infant and Child Care*. He'd currycomb the material available in the Government Printing Office and see to it that the people who were interested in this or that had gotten it. . . . I don't think he could ever have been shaken out of that district because he was doing the kind of job that a congressman really ought to do."[2]

Johnson and the people around him paid a physical and emotional price for the success of the office. They worked at a breakneck pace—days, evenings, nights, often seven days a week, week after week. Sherman Birdwell, Lyndon's college classmate and NYA aide who served as his first congressional secretary, remembered arriving in Washington by car on a Saturday afternoon and going directly to Lyndon's temporary office on the first floor of the Old House Office Building. There, he worked on the mail until after midnight, slept in the office, and resumed working early Sunday morning. During his first month, though he had not been to Washington before, Birdwell never found time to walk across the street to visit the Capitol. Only when he had to carry an urgent message to Lyndon from Mayor Tom Miller of Austin did he see the inside of that building. Never getting "caught up . . . always a little behind in work that needed to be done," Birdwell left after fifteen months. Ten- and twelve-hour work days followed by evening classes in typing and shorthand drove Birdwell to the breaking point. "I had gone from 165 pounds to 130 pounds, and I was about ready to crack up," he said later.[3]

Gene Latimer, his successor, did. In the spring of 1937, Latimer was working in Washington at the Federal Housing Administration in a job that Johnson had gotten him. While Birdwell was secretary, Latimer and L. E. Jones, who was also working in the city, had helped out in the office in the evenings and on weekends. When Birdwell left, Latimer agreed to replace him, but Jones, who felt he had to get away from Johnson before he was "devoured," left town. Latimer quickly found himself with more than he could handle. Some of Johnson's staff was unreliable and the work was even heavier than it had been in Kleberg's office. Herbert Henderson, Johnson's speechwriter in the 1937 campaign, had come to Washington to perform the same function. But Henderson was an alcoholic who went off on binges for several weeks at a time, and Johnson brought John Koeniger, a Johnson City friend, into the office partly to keep Henderson from drinking. Similarly, Sam Houston Johnson, Lyndon's brother, joined Johnson's staff, where he also came and went without notice and caused Lyndon considerable grief. But the principal problem for Latimer was a work load that left him no room to breathe. "I felt I was literally working myself to death," he said later. In August 1939, "almost a year to the day" he had taken the job, "nature took its toll and I had what is commonly called a breakdown."[4]

Johnson now appointed two assistants who were more hardy and worked for him for several years. In 1938, Sam Fore, the editor from Floresville, asked Johnson to find a job for John B. Connally, an extraordinary young man from his home town who had been student body president at the University of Texas and was in law school. Arranging to have Connally work at the NYA in Austin, Johnson offered him Latimer's job in the fall of 1939. Although he had a chance to become an assistant attorney general in Texas, Connally, who had never been to Washington, accepted Johnson's offer. At the same time, Johnson hired Walter Jenkins, another UT graduate who had been recommended by the Dean and had given a good account of himself in interviews with Bill Deason, Jesse Kellam, and Johnson himself. Connally and Jenkins came to Washington together on the train and immediately found themselves working ferociously hard. During his first six weeks on the job, Connally saw nothing but the inside of the Dodge Hotel basement, where he lived, and Johnson's office, where he handled constituents and the phone during the day and answered mail at night. A friend who stayed with Jenkins in Washington for a few days recalls his returning from work one night so tired that he fell asleep in the bathtub. "Johnson was working him like a nigger slave," he said.[5]

Yet no one worked harder than Johnson. He drove himself to the limits of his endurance. Now, more than ever, everything was politics and work. On the go from early in the morning until late at night with work in the House, he nevertheless kept close tabs on his office, riding his staff by phone and showing up each day to check outgoing correspondence. "He signed every letter"; Birdwell recalled, "no one rubberstamped his name. . . . He looked at and read every letter. If we wrote something that didn't sound right, why, it was rewritten."[6]

Johnson lived with exhausting tension. "I am in terrible physical condition and I need a week or two of rest," he wrote Jesse Kellam three months after he went to Washington. He chain-smoked about three packs of cigarettes a day, and developed a nervous rash between the fingers of his right hand that cracked the skin and made it bleed. Driving himself late at night to complete the day's work, he often sat "signing mountains of letters with his . . . hand wrapped in a . . . towel to keep blood from dripping" on the paper.[7]

His tension found release in verbal assaults on his staff. "When things haven't gone well for you, call in a secretary or a staff man and chew him out. You will sleep better and they will appreciate the attention," he said. Johnson was only half joking, as his staff knew from first-hand experience. "He was relentless, almost ruthless at times," Jake Pickle, a Johnson aide and later congressman, remembered. "If you fouled up on something, . . . Johnson would ream you out . . . and the staffers would just sit there and cringe." Johnson kicked his people around, a journalist says, but "they absolutely loved the guy and they'd always come back." "There was an ugly LBJ at times. . . . ," "Pickle adds, "but the efforts to paint him as paranoid villain without character or principle is absolutely wrong." He would chew on people and then turn around and do anything in the world for them, showing "the deepest concern for their personal problems [and] their families." He frequently took new employees into live with him and Lady Bird. Once, when a new secretary became ill and had to have an operation after only a few weeks in his employ, he lent her money to pay the hospital bill and all the costs of her illness.[8]

He was a man of extremes. There were the best of times and the worst of times, but usually little in between. When he got sick, Birdwell says, "he was sicker than anybody ever had been sick in his life with a similar illness. . . . He'd just have to tell you how awful this particular illness was, just nothing like it. When he was feeling good, he felt better than anybody in the world, enthusiastic, vigorous. But when he was sick, he was next to death's door."[9]

As had been the case since his childhood in Johnson City, he needed to be the best, have the most, and command attention or impress himself on everyone he met. In taking an office in the Cannon or old House Office Building, for example, he was the first to choose the fifth or attic floor, where he had nearly double the space of other congressmen. He stayed there long after he had enough seniority to move out because it gave him something other representatives did not have. Later in his career, he "was thrilled when he was the first in Washington to have a car phone." Senator Everett Dirksen of Illinois, a friendly competitor, then got one too. When he called Johnson's limo to say that he was calling from his new car phone, Johnson replied, "Hold on a minute, Ev, my other phone is ringing." Stories about Johnson's overstated and crude behavior are legion. There was no private bathroom connected to his first congressional office, two friends of his remember. But there was a sink with running water. When he had to relieve himself, he would go behind a screen, turn on the tap, and urinate in the sink while he continued talking to whomever was there. If one of his intentions was to fix himself in people's memories, it succeeded. Those who saw him do it never forgot.[10]

Johnson's character traits not only made life difficult for himself and his staff they also put strains on his marriage. Lady Bird was a splendid complement to his volatile personality. "They love each other and are well mated," one of Lady Bird's cousins, who saw them frequently during these years, said. "Alike in ambitions, they are different in personality. He is emotional while she is restrained. He is outgoing; she is reserved. She is thoughtful and gracious; he abrupt. She is interested in literature and the arts. He isn't. Apart from Lady Bird, his only love is politics. But they have reinforced each other's strengths and blended their differences into a productive marriage."[11]

Yet the marriage worked so well partly because Lady Bird subordinated her interests and needs to Lyndon's. Although she found some of the duties of a congressman's wife as "silly as all get out," she performed them without complaint, attending innumerable weddings, teas, luncheons and paying calls. She also learned to give guided tours of Washington attractions. "The biggest word in my vocabulary, the most important, was 'constituency,' which one spelled in capitals," she later told an interviewer. Tours of the Capitol, the Smithsonian, and George Washington's Mount Vernon home became standard exercises. After two hundred visits to Mount Vernon, she stopped counting. She also disliked "the itinerant out-of-suitcase life" which they led for the first eight years of their marriage, moving into and out of ten different apartments in Washington and Austin. Several miscarriages during this time also frustrated her desire for a more stable family life. To answer this need, she proposed they buy a house. But Lyndon was reluctant. After a careful search, she found an eight-room, two-story brick Colonial off Connecticut Avenue in northwest Washington. When she interrupted a conversation at their apartment between John Connally and Lyndon to report her find, he offered no reply and resumed talking to Connally. In an uncharacteristic outburst, Lady Bird cried out, "I want that house. Every woman wants a home of her own. I've lived out of a suitcase ever since we've been married. I have no home to look forward to. I have no children to look forward to, and I have nothing to look forward to but another election." After Lady Bird's Aunt Effie agreed to provide the down payment and the owner dropped the price to $16,000, Lyndon gave in.[12]

Yet Lyndon was not so accommodating when it came to Lady Bird's feelings about extramarital affairs. Johnson developed a reputation as a womanizer. According to one journalist who knew him beginning in 1937, Lyndon had what amounted to a harem: "One way you could visualize Lady Bird is as the queen in *Anna and the King of Siam*. It worked that way; you know the scene where she sits at the table and all the babes— Lady Bird was the head wife." He had a compulsive need for conquests. In his late fifties, for example, when he was President, a White House secretary, who was described as "a very pretty young woman," claims that a flirtation between them led to casual sex on an office desk. "It was an era," one historian writes, "in which Washington valued conquest more than chastity." Mention of John Kennedy's womanizing would lead Johnson to pound on a table and shout, he "had more women by accident than Kennedy had on purpose."[13]

There was at least one long-term relationship Johnson took more seriously. It began sometime in the late thirties with Alice Glass, then the mistress and later wife of Charles Marsh, the Austin newspaper publisher. Marsh was a super wealthy man whose holdings included newspapers in twenty-seven cities across the United States, west Texas oil wells, Austin's streetcar franchise, the controlling interest in a major Austin bank, and large tracts of Austin real estate. Marsh had a town house and an office at the Mayflower Hotel in Washington, D.C., and an 860-acre estate in Culpepper, Virginia, called "Longlea," the name of an eighteenth-century English manor house after which it was modeled. Alice Glass from the Texas town of Marlin met Marsh in 1931 in Austin, where she had been working as a legislator's secretary. A strikingly beautiful woman, nearly six feet tall with long reddish-blonde hair and delicate features, Alice, according to one admirer, looked like a "Viking princess." The forty-four-year-old Marsh was so smitten that he left his wife and children to live with the twenty-year-old Alice.

Lyndon met Alice when Marsh invited him for a weekend to Longlea. Fascinated by politics and the arts, enjoying the company of famous and brilliant people, Marsh and Alice loved to entertain weekend guests at their lavish retreat. There, in what one visitor called the "most beautiful place" he had ever seen, Cabinet secretaries, leading journalists, brilliant musicians, distinguished academics, and powerful businessmen gathered to loaf in the sun, ride horseback, swim, and converse over exquisitely prepared dinners served by some of the twenty servants who ran the estate. Like so many others, Marsh took a strong liking to Lyndon, for whom he saw a great future. Marsh, in fact, was so eager to ensure Lyndon's prospects that he sold him and Lady Bird a nineteen-acre tract of land in Austin worth far more than the Johnsons paid for it. Lyndon took special pains to ingratiate himself with Marsh, asking his advice, deferring to his opinions, and making him feel as if he were a political insider. At the same time, however, Lyndon's natural talents as a storyteller and his brilliant grasp of how Washington worked made him an exciting guest to Marsh and Alice.[14]

Alice, in fact, fell in love with him. Excited by his youthfulness—he was twenty-one years younger than Marsh—and his extraordinary dynamism, Alice began an affair with Lyndon that lasted several years. Though she had two children by Marsh and risked destroying her relationship with him, she pursued the involvement with Lyndon nevertheless.

Marsh was furious when he found out. What may have tipped him off was a weekend Lyndon spent with Alice in New York. Leaving the New York phone number with John Connally, Lyndon told him not to give it out unless there was an emergency. When Marsh called and insisted on reaching Lyndon, Connally, who knew nothing of the affair, gave him the number. When Johnson returned to the office on Monday, he told Connally, "Man, you almost ruined me." One night, Marsh, after getting very drunk at his estate, complained to another guest that Alice was shacking up with Lyndon and ordered Johnson out of his house. When Lyndon returned later that evening, however, Marsh acted as if nothing had happened. Marsh and Alice eventually wed, but they had a less than perfect marriage which ended in divorce after six years.

If Alice was ready to risk her relationship with Marsh for one with Lyndon, he was unwilling to leave Lady Bird. He may have considered it, but he never acted on that impulse. For all his unfaithfulness, Lady Bird was an indispensable part of his life. "In her realm," the Washington reporter Nancy Dickerson writes, "she had no peer; she knew it, he knew it, and so did everybody else." As for Lady Bird herself, she hid

her feelings and took a detached, philosophical view of Lyndon's phi-
landering. "Bird," a friend once asked her, "how can you like so-and-
so because he's married but he's playing around with lots of other
women?" "Yes," she replied, "but that's just one side of him." Years
later, when a television producer, who was making a movie about Lyndon, boldly asked her about Lyndon's womanizing, she looked at him
"for a minute, then said, 'You have to understand, my husband loved
people. All people. And half the people in the world were women. You
don't think I could have kept my husband away from half the people?' "[15]

From Lyndon's perspective, there was also the fact that a divorce would
have been disastrous for his political career. In the thirties and forties a
divorced man had little chance to gain high political office. And Lyndon
was eager not only to stay in politics but also to go as far as his talents
and circumstances would allow. In 1939, for example, when he had been
in Congress for less than two years, he tried to gain a place on the
powerful Appropriations Committee. Although House tradition entitled
a Texas representative to fill a Committee vacancy in the 76th Congress,
Albert Thomas, another Texan with greater seniority, had a stronger
claim to it than Johnson. Despite this, Lyndon, with backing from the
White House, pressed the Texas delegation to endorse him. But it refused, inflicting what one member of the delegation described as a bitter
defeat on Johnson.[16]

Membership on the Appropriations Committee, with the greater prestige attached to it, might have tied Lyndon more firmly to the House or
at least eased his sense of urgency about moving on to higher things.
Continuing service as a congressman with modest influence increased
Johnson's desire to get to the Senate, his long-term goal. Two of Johnson's colleagues on the Naval Affairs Committee believe he had no intention of staying in the House: "He was going to go up or get out,"
Warren Magnuson said. "Lyndon and I spent a great deal of time talking about the Senate, because we both wanted to be senators." Margaret
Chase Smith of Maine said: "Anyone who got very close to Johnson
knew that he wasn't going to sit still very long." And early in 1940,
Johnson talked with George Brown about eventually running for the
Senate when either Morris Sheppard or Tom Connally, both of whom
were then in their early sixties, retired or died.[17]

The intensity of Johnson's ambition for higher office registered forcefully on George Brown in the fall of 1940. At a resort in White Sulphur
Springs, West Virginia, Brown, Marsh, and Lyndon discussed Lyndon's
need for an additional source of income that could relieve him of present and future financial pressures. Burdened by his deceased father's
longstanding debts and the need to support an extended family—his own
household, his mother, and erratic brother Sam Houston—Lyndon

struggled to pay all his bills on a $10,000 annual salary. In addition, he worried that the loss of his House seat would leave him without a live-lihood. To end his concerns, Marsh offered to sell him oil properties which he could pay for out of the annual profits produced by the wells. Worth somewhere between three-quarters of a million and a million dollars in 1940, the property increased in value over a hundred fold during the next three decades. Although the offer promised to free Johnson from all his financial worries, he turned it down. He believed that becoming a rich oil man would kill his political career. Assertions that he used his position to ingratiate himself with wealthy businessmen, who made him rich, would not only jeopardize his seat in the pro-New Deal Tenth District but would also be a liability in a state where populist antagonism to big business was a mainstay of electoral politics.[18]

In 1939–40 Johnson tied his hopes for a Senate seat to Roosevelt's continuing hold on power. It was a gamble. For FDR to remain a polit-ical force he had to run for an unprecedented third term. During the first half of 1939, no one knew if he would run again, and if he did, whether he could overcome resistance to the two-term limit. Moreover, even without the third-term question, an erosion of his popularity and influence by the seventh year of his presidency made another successful national campaign doubtful. In 1938, when he tried to defeat conserva-tive Democrats in local and state primaries, he had suffered "a humili-ating drubbing." "President Roosevelt could not run for a third term even if he so desired," one astute Washington journalist said after the 1938 elections. In Texas, the defeat by conservative opponents of Maury Maverick and W. D. McFarlane, the two most outspoken New Deal congressmen in the state, signaled the decline of Roosevelt's influence.[19]

Anti-New Deal Democrats found a rallying point in Vice President John Nance Garner. An old-fashioned rugged individualist who be-lieved in balanced budgets, limited government influence, and the sanctity of private property, Garner was antagonistic to New Deal reforms. Dur-ing Roosevelt's first term, he had largely kept his opposition to himself. In 1937, however, FDR's Court-packing bill and sit-down strikes against the automobile industry made his dissent from Administration thinking an open secret. As the President's message in support of Court-packing was read in the Senate, Garner in the private lobby behind the Chamber walked past a group of senators holding his nose with one hand and turning a thumb down with the other. In March 1939, *Time* described the FDR–Garner struggle as an "undeclared war," and quoted New Dealers, who called Garner "the leader of reaction against six years of enlightened reform."[20]

By the spring of 1939, Garner was the acknowledged frontrunner for the Democratic nomination. He was especially popular in Texas, where the state legislature passed a resolution in March endorsing "that sterling American and outstanding statesman, John N. Garner" for president. Despite Roosevelt's waning fortunes and Garner's influence in Texas, Johnson remained openly in the President's camp. In May, he joined Charles Marsh in asking Roosevelt to promote Welly Hopkins to "an important post" in the Administration as part of an effort to advance the liberal cause in Texas. In July, Texas newspapers reported a thirty-minute private conversation between Johnson and FDR in which Lyndon pressed the case for REA loans and told the President of New Deal achievements in his district. The following week Johnson released correspondence between himself and the President about the LCRA and its cooperation with Electric Bond and Share, a private utility. Shortly after, when Johnson turned down the REA job, he got White House permission to publish this exchange of letters as well.[21]

At the same time, Johnson left no doubt about his ties to the Administration when he voted against the Hatch Act, a bill designed to prevent Federal employees from actively participating in political campaigns. Garner and other anti-New Deal Democrats favored the law as a way to prevent Federal officeholders from becoming pro-Roosevelt delegates at the 1940 Democratic convention, as they had in 1936. In August, when the *Dallas Times Herald* reported the voting records of the twenty-three Texans in Congress in the session just ended, it pointed out that only six had voted with the Administration on "every important controversial measure." Lyndon Johnson was one of them. Like Maury Maverick and Alvin Wirtz, who remained staunch Roosevelt backers, Johnson saw the Garnerites as "inspired by Wall Street bankers" and unsympathetic to millions of hard-pressed Americans dependent on Federal aid for a better life, especially in the South.[22]

Johnson's loyalty to FDR found fresh expression at the end of July when Garner came under public attack from labor leader John L. Lewis. At a hearing before the House Labor Committee, Lewis blamed Garner for efforts to weaken the wages and hours law, and called him "a labor-baiting, poker-playing, whiskey-drinking, evil old man." Garner, who thought Lewis's charges might hurt his campaign, asked Sam Rayburn to arrange a public statement by the Texas congressional delegation denying the accusations. Except for Lyndon Johnson, all the Texans, who resented Lewis's assault on a respected colleague, were ready to go along. Johnson refused to sign a resolution denying that Garner was a whiskey drinker and an enemy of labor. In accounts he gave to Roosevelt and Ickes, Johnson described himself as saying: "The delegation would look foolish if such a statement were issued because everyone knew that Garner was a heavy drinker and that he was bitterly opposed to labor." After two hours of arguing, Rayburn took Lyndon into his office to "administer a spanking." But Johnson would not budge: " 'Lyndon I'm looking you right in the eye,' " Rayburn shouted. " 'And I'm looking you right back in the eye,' " Johnson replied. "Lyndon is a damned independent boy; independent as a hog on ice," Rayburn was to complain.[23]

Later the delegation—including Lyndon—agreed to a revised resolution, one that omitted specific references to Garner's drinking and anti-labor views. Instead, it expressed "deep resentment and indignation at this unwarranted and unjustified attack" on Garner's private and public life. Moreover, when the *Fort Worth Star-Telegram* asked Johnson about his attitude toward Garner's presidential campaign, he answered: "Since the Vice President has not announced his desire to become a candidate for President, I feel an announcement from a new Congressman should await, not precede, his decision."[24]

Although Johnson's differences with Rayburn and the delegation grew with each retelling, it is clear that Lyndon took his distance from Garner and worked with the White House to embarrass him. By the summer of 1939, Roosevelt's animus toward Garner was palpable. "I see that the Vice President has thrown his bottle—I mean his hat—into the ring," Roosevelt said at a Cabinet meeting. According to Corcoran, it was White House pressure that generated Lyndon's opposition to the original resolution. *"Everybody* called" Lyndon, Corcoran said. "I called him. Ickes called him. I think Hopkins called him. Maybe even Bill Douglas called him. There wasn't any doubt about what the Old Man wanted."[25]

In working for the White House, Lyndon was taking some risks. Garner's allies would certainly retaliate if he ran for state-wide office and do what they could to undermine him in his district. Ewell Nalle, the postmaster in Austin, was a friend of Garner's and by July 1939 a "vocal and bitter" critic of Johnson. Johnson had pressed Postmaster General James Farley, a Garner ally, and Roosevelt to replace Nalle with Ray E. Lee, the journalist who had worked with Johnson in the NYA. Farley told Johnson that his "enemies" in Texas did not want Nalle fired and that it was illegal anyway. Roosevelt spoke to Farley about the matter, but backed off when Farley resisted. In August, after the Lewis-Garner incident, however, Johnson pressed his case through Rowe, saying I "will not and can not go back to Texas until the President acts." Grateful for Lyndon's support, Roosevelt now wrote Rowe: "Tell the Post Office that I want this done right away for Cong. Lyndon Johnson. That it is legal and to send me the necessary papers. Tell Lyndon Johnson that I am doing it."

Although Lyndon won this fight and enjoyed strong support in his district, as demonstrated by the absence of an opponent in the 1938 election, he remained anxious about his enemies' intentions and influence. Shortly after Garner formally announced his candidacy in December 1939, Lyndon wrote Sherman Birdwell, who was now working at the NYA in Austin: "We will be fighting for our lives the next six months and I am expecting you to head up the ball team."[26]

At the same time, however, Johnson understood that his close identification with the President was doing him more good than harm, that Roosevelt probably would run again, and that even if he did not, he maintained sufficient influence to keep the Democratic party in liberal hands. The outbreak of the Second World War in September 1939 decided Roosevelt to seek another term. His problem, then, in the words of FDR biographer James MacGregor Burns, was "to be nominated in so striking a manner that it would amount to an emphatic and irresistible call to duty. This party call would be the prelude to a call from the whole country at election time." [27]

In the first months of 1940, Garner remained an obstacle to that goal, and Roosevelt wanted to send him home permanently to his 6000 neighbors in Uvalde, Texas. He gave the job to Alvin Wirtz, whom he made Under Secretary of the Interior in January 1940. Roosevelt also saw Wirtz's appointment as a way to increase the influence of New Dealers in Texas. [28]

In challenging Garner in the state, Roosevelt wished to avoid an open conflict or risk a defeat. During the last week of March he told Ickes that he did not "want any fight made for Roosevelt delegates in Texas. He thinks that Texans are unusually full of state pride and that they would resent an outside candidate coming in, even if that candidate were the President himself." In April, moreover, when the President decisively beat Garner in the Wisconsin and Illinois primaries without avowing his candidacy, and a successful German offensive in Western Europe heightened national desire for his continued leadership, FDR largely lost interest in controlling the Texas delegation to the Democratic national convention. [29]

In the spring of 1940, Roosevelt told Johnson to assure that the Texas delegation goes for Garner. FDR said: "People are proud of their leaders. If I go in there and take the people away from their leader—I don't need those votes. I'd rather John Garner have the votes. I want to be magnanimous." He proposed that the Garner delegates switch to him after the first ballot. "He was a goddamn clever fella!" Johnson said in 1968. "He makes all these boys around here now—well, look like kids." [30]

Sam Rayburn was also eager for a compromise. The Garner-Roosevelt struggle had caused him nothing but discomfort. Out of loyalty and indebtedness to an old colleague, Rayburn had supported Garner. But Rayburn had no desire to undermine his influence with FDR. He had been the Administration's principal spokesman in the House, had an interest in the vice presidency, and, barring that, wanted Roosevelt's backing for the Speakership if Bankhead retired or died in the next four years. For six weeks beginning in the middle of March, Rayburn tried to stop the intra-party strife in Texas. He got close to a settlement "several times but somebody on one side would make some foolish crack and it would all go to naught." In late April, however, as it became clear that neither New Deal nor Garner Democrats could dominate the other in Texas, both sides agreed to compromise.[31]

Roosevelt remained eager to end the in-fighting but, in doing so, he also tried to reward Johnson's loyalty. After arriving at a settlement, the factions jousted over how to publicize it. Recognizing that the compromise signaled Garner's defeat, his supporters wished to keep it quiet or give it only to the Texas press. But the New Dealers insisted that a telegram signed by Rayburn and Johnson be issued from the White House after they had conferred with the President. Although he finally agreed to the procedure, Rayburn, according to Ickes, was unhappy "that in a Texas political matter a kid Congressman like Johnson was on apparently the same footing as himself, the Majority Leader." When they came to the White House on the afternoon of April 29, Roosevelt "told them benignly that they had been good little boys and that they had 'pappa's blessing.' He treated them as political equals, with the malicious intent of disturbing Sam Rayburn's state of mind," or so Ickes believed.[32]

If Roosevelt and others in the Administration took pains to punish Rayburn, they had no intention of alienating him. He had been too valuable an ally and held too much power in the Congress for the White House to do that. Hence, when William Bankhead died suddenly in mid-September 1940, the Administration supported Rayburn's election as Speaker, which received unanimous approval in the House. Like Roosevelt, Johnson had no interest in antagonizing Rayburn. No doubt, he took great satisfaction in being recognized as an Administration spokesman in Texas, even if it irritated Rayburn. But he understood that their close personal relationship and shared perspective on the most important issues of the day would outweigh any tensions between them over Garner. Indeed, once they struck the bargain on April 29, their approach to every major political and foreign policy issue over the next six months was almost identical.[33]

The Texas political compromise satisfied both of them and they worked to hold it together. On May 1, the *Washington Post* reported Johnson's praise of "the work done by Rayburn in achieving the compromise" and "predicted he would lead the Garner-pledged Texas delegation 'with other men of liberal makeup.' " Further, when a mutual supporter wrote Lyndon to congratulate him and Sam on having "stopped a serious rupture in Texas" and expressed the wish that Sam would become the next V.P., Johnson approvingly passed the letter along to Rayburn. Moreover, though the impending fall of France kept both of them from attending the state Democratic convention in Waco on May 28, they resisted proposals that threatened to pull the agreement apart.[34]

In July, at the national Democratic convention in Chicago, Johnson strongly supported Rayburn for Vice President. When the Texas delegation divided between Rayburn and RFC director Jesse Jones, Lyndon, who chaired the Texas caucus on the issue, pressed the case for Mister Sam. But Roosevelt frustrated Johnson and a vocal minority of other delegates by choosing Secretary of Agriculture Henry Wallace. Lyndon found it "unbelievable" that the President would select a man many described as "an ex-Republican with little political savvy and a reputation for mysticism." Nevertheless, Johnson and Rayburn, who accepted FDR's request that he give a seconding speech for Wallace, supported Roosevelt's choice. Nearly three hundred delegates, including many from Texas, opposed Wallace, greeting speeches for him with hisses, jeers, and catcalls. But when FDR threatened to decline the nomination and one of his supporters moved among the delegations asking, "Do you want a President or a Vice-President?," the convention gave in, choosing Wallace over Bankhead, the choice of party conservatives, by a vote of 628 to 329.[35]

During the spring and summer of 1940, however much energy Johnson and Rayburn put into politics, it absorbed only part of their attention. The dangers to American national security from Nazi victories in Europe also concerned them. Hitler's conquest of Denmark, Norway, Holland, Belgium, and France in the two and a half months between April 9 and June 22 aroused widespread fears in the United States that Britain would also fall victim to Nazi arms, that Hitler would control the British fleet, and that Germany would dominate the eastern approaches to our shores. Roosevelt publicly warned that unless the United States now quickly expanded its military might, it could become like a prisoner "handcuffed, hungry, and fed through the bars from day to day by the contemptuous, unpitying masters of other continents." In response to Roosevelt's appeals, the Congress approved the first peacetime draft and appropriated $17 billion to build a modern mechanized army, a two-ocean navy, and a 50,000-plane air force. Johnson and Rayburn gave their voices and votes to all these measures.[36]

But Lyndon, following popular and congressional sentiment and worried about antagonizing German-Americans in his district, spoke out against American involvement in the war. "The ability of the American people to think calmly and act wisely during a crisis is going to keep us out of a war," he told his constituents in June. Alvin Wirtz, who strongly disagreed, pressed Lyndon to see the light. When Colonel Charles Lindbergh, the prominent aviator and isolationist, returned to the United States from Germany in May 1940, Wirtz wrote Lyndon: "I suppose you want to decorate . . . Lindbergh, but I think he should be interned or sent back to Europe where he belongs. . . . The Colonel is preaching your doctrine: just don't bother Hitler and he won't bother you. . . . There is no pacifist sentiment in your District unless it is around Brenham and they are not going to come out in the open down there. . . . I will admit you are a whiz on domestic problems but I still think that on international problems you should listen to the elder statesmen." [37]

As Wirtz understood, for all Johnson's willingness to vote with the Administration on defense measures, he, like most Americans in 1940, was reluctant to see the United States become enmeshed in foreign affairs. He was sensitive to defending the country from external threats, but he saw military expenditures as meant for defense and not of-fense.

Johnson's view of arms expenditures, moreover, was principally in-formed by what it meant to central Texas—defense contracts that would expand employment, raise general living standards, and serve the inter-ests of Brown & Root in particular. In August 1940, for example, he urged Secretary of War Henry Stimson to see central Texas as an ideal location for new defense plants. Because the area was "reasonably se-cure from long range bombing" and satisfied a variety of other "tech-nical requirements," Lyndon's efforts produced substantial results. Lyn-don "sensed what was ahead of us better than anybody I know," a pioneer in the Texas air industry recalled. "And he wanted Texas to have a major role in it. . . . It was a matter of plants and production as well as installations for training and for the operation of the air forces and the naval air armament." Carl Vinson said that Johnson "played a domi-nant role in setting up the Naval Air Base in Corpus Christi, the Naval Air Training Station near Dallas, and shipbuilding facilities in southeast Texas, Houston and Orange. He was instrumental in organizing ROTC units at the University of Texas . . . Southwest Texas State College, and . . . Southwestern University in Georgetown." For Lyndon, defense partly meant giving the South and Texas in particular additional Federal grants for improving the region's economic life. [38]

The Corpus Christi Naval Air Station was central to Lyndon's efforts and put Brown & Root "on another plateau." "We all helped Brown and Root bid on the contract to build the Corpus Christi base. . . ," Tommy Corcoran recalled. "We advised them how to bid, what to offer, who to talk to and all the rest of it." The contract was given not to the lowest bidder but was made on a "cost plus" or "negotiated" basis in June 1940. The largest "cost plus" agreement awarded by the Federal government up to that time, it called for initial expenditures of $24.5 million, including a profit of $1.2 million for the contractors doing the work. As the need for navy pilots ballooned in the next few years, the size and cost of building the base increased fourfold. [39]

Johnson's success in getting defense plants and contracts for Texas partly rested on his close ties to the Administration. Word went out in Washington, Corcoran remembered, that Federal contracts in Texas were to go to "Lyndon's friends." By helping them "stay solvent," Lyndon's opponents could not "starve him out of politics, or squeeze him out of the next campaign." As Corcoran told FDR in September 1940, it also helped "crystallize a new leadership in Texas around your man, Lyndon Johnson." "Local control of the Texas situation is desperately important," Corcoran added. "Mutual acrimonies splitting the Texas crowd" offered "an extraordinary opportunity to get control. . . . The two growing points in the Texas situation are Rayburn and Johnson, who, with his sponsor, Wirtz, has taken over all the strength Maury Maverick once had on a much more intelligent plane. . . . Johnson went 'down the line' on the Vice Presidency and Rayburn likes him. Rayburn, therefore, will not get in the way and will rather get behind any attempt to strengthen Johnson's position. The natural place to build up Johnson and to 'recognize' Texas in the national party picture is as Secretary of the National Democratic Committee."[40]

The principal reason for making Johnson Committee Secretary was to give him a position from which he could work to sustain the Democratic party's control of the House. By the beginning of September 1940, party leaders anticipated losing their majority in the lower house in the November elections, even if FDR won a third term. Although the Democrats held a 92-seat advantage, seventy-five of them seemed in jeopardy. The defeat of only 47 Democrats would mean Republican control of the House, likely disruption of Administration plans, and Rayburn's loss of the Speakership. Since the Republicans enjoyed a considerable advantage over Democrats in campaign funds and could capitalize on anti-war and anti-New Deal sentiments, the Democrats had good reason to fear that the next House of Representatives would have a Republican majority for the first time in 10 years.[41]

Because Lyndon's appointment promised to improve party prospects in the House and give Johnson both greater national visibility and increased influence in Texas, Roosevelt considered supporting it. But recognizing that senior party officials would not take kindly to so independent a role for a young congressman and eager not to be seen as trying to dictate the outcome of congressional elections, the President turned aside the suggestion. Lyndon, however, refused to take no for an answer. On October 1, he wrote FDR: "My own youth and inexperience may be in error, but I feel tonight that we do stand in danger in the lower house. I know in your wisdom you will work it out." Adding that "we may lose fifty close House seats" in cities and districts with less than 200,000 population, Johnson urged him to "call on me for anything at any time. P.S. We lost eighty-two seats in 1938. The present forty-five margin gives me the night-sweats at three a.m."[42]

When Rayburn and majority Leader John W. McCormack pressed Roosevelt to make Lyndon "congressional campaign manager for the House," the President gave in. After Rayburn warned that losing Congress "would tear him to pieces just like it did President Wilson after 1918," Roosevelt called Johnson to the White House. There is no record of their conversation on October 9, and Lyndon came away from the meeting with no formal title for his assignment. But it is clear that Roosevelt wanted him to proceed without any special title or public fanfare that could identify him as working for the President. Lyndon was described as simply assisting the Congressional Campaign Committee. In fact, he now began to play a significant part in national political affairs.[43]

Three hours after he saw Roosevelt, Lyndon had rented a one-room office in downtown Washington on the third floor of the old, narrow Munsey Building at 1329 E Street, NW. Furnishing it with a desk and swivel chair, three other chairs, a divan, a telephone, and a typewriter, Johnson, helped by John Connally and Herbert Henderson, began working fifteen- to eighteen-hour days.[44]

His first concern was how to help House Democrats threatened with defeat. Everyone agreed that a good many Democrats were going to get beat unless they got money for aggressive campaigns. Lyndon, however, had not conceived of his job as "raising and expending funds." And as late as October 9, House Democratic leaders believed that the Democratic National Committee (DNC) would give House candidates the money. Wayne Johnson, the party's finance chairman, had told Rayburn on the 2nd that he hoped to provide "some substantial help," but he did not know when it might be available. On the 10th, therefore, after the DNC gave the Congressional Campaign Committee a check for only $10,000, a tenth of what Rayburn had asked, hopes were dampened.[45]

Fund-raising now became Lyndon's highest goal. Most incumbents in 1940 could run an effective campaign for under $5000. In large cities like New York, the cost was more than double that amount, but in many places around the country it was no more than $2000. Yet finding the $2000 to $5000 was not easy for many House Democrats. Traditionally, the party had depended on a limited number of big donors to supply congressional and presidential campaign funds. But the introduction of progressive income, gift, and inheritance taxes in the thirties reduced the number of contributors willing to make five- and six-figure donations. The passage of the Hatch Act in 1940 also limited party funds by restricting annual individual contributions to $5000. The Republicans had managed to overcome the problem by hiring a professional fund-raiser who had systematically built up a large war chest for the 1940 campaign. By contrast, informality and confusion characterized Democratic fund-raising: a handful of individuals operated independently of the party's National Committee which had little say over how the money would be spent.[46]

During his first days in the Munsey Building, Johnson, helped by

Rayburn, devoted himself exclusively to raising cash. Having been encouraged by George Brown not to show "any timidity" in asking a return on the favors done for Brown & Root, Johnson now drew on this account. He asked the Browns to make a significant contribution to a congressional campaign fund. At the same time, Rayburn urged Clint W. Murchison and Sid Richardson, both independent oil men, and E. S. Fentress, Charles Marsh's partner, to provide some support. The response exceeded all expectations. Although Federal law prohibited corporations from contributing to political campaigns, and individuals from giving more than $5000, the Browns arranged for Lyndon to receive $30,000 in Brown & Root money by October 18. Sending the money through six business associates, George Brown wired Lyndon on the 19th, "You were supposed to have checks by Friday. . . . Hope they arrived in due form and on time." They had: "All of the folks you talked to have been heard from," Lyndon answered on the 21st. "Many, many thanks. I am not acknowledging their letters, so be sure to tell all these fellows that their letters have been received. . . . I'm on a 20-hour schedule but can't hold up to it very long. . . . The thing is exceeding my expectations." Johnson collected an additional $15,000 from Rayburn's sources. On October 21, Lyndon told Swager Sherley at the National Committee: "We have sent them more money in the last 3 days than Congressmen have received from any committee in the last 8 years." [47]

But it was not enough to do the job. There were 101 House Democrats "in trouble," Johnson also told Sherley, 29 in the Mid-West, 26 elsewhere who had won by only a few hundred votes in 1938, 21 whose margin had been only a few thousand votes, and 25 who were in "real danger." Lyndon believed that saving these congressmen from defeat required more than $45,000. On the 22nd, he wired Rayburn, who was in Texas, that a careful check showed 105 Democrats needed money, but that the "Barrel has been scraped." He now asked the Garment and the United Mine Workers unions, Wall Street investment bankers, and Charles Marsh to help. At the same time, he urged Rayburn to press on "our friends down there" the importance of being helpful. [48]

All of these contributors, north and south, added thousands of dollars to the party's war chest. Though some of them, like the UMW and independent oil producers Rayburn went to see in Dallas and Fort Worth, had little use for Roosevelt, they had selfish reasons for wanting a Democratic Congress. The Mine Workers wished to preserve New Deal gains made by unions, while the Democrats had arranged special tax advantages for the oil men. "Bring in a Republican Congress, with a new Speaker and new committee chairmen," Rayburn told them, "and they'll tear your depletion allowance and intangible-drilling write-offs to pieces." [49]

Just how much these different people contributed is impossible to know. Some, like Charles F. Roeser, an independent petroleum producer in Fort Worth, followed his meeting with Rayburn by sending a check directly to Johnson. But others, who had already reached the $5000 annual limit, skirted the law by giving cash that Rayburn and others carried to Lyndon and the Congressional Committee in Washington. Rayburn accepted the money, two of his biographers write, "apparently without qualms. . . . Campaign laws then were . . . largely unenforced. Rayburn appears to have been as willing as the next public official to exploit the loopholes, although there was never the slightest hint that he gained personally from it." As one of Rayburn's Texas political friends described it: "Someone like [oilman Arch Rowan] could come up and visit him and say, 'Now, Sam, you are going to need money to get somebody elected in Idaho. Here is $2,000 in cash.' Of course, that is not a bribe in any sense of the word. Mr. Rayburn put it in his pocket and when the time came he got to Washington he would give it to somebody to go help the guy in Idaho get elected." One go-between for Texas oil money asserted that Sid Richardson gave as much as $100,000. Richardson himself said, "I was the big factor in raising $70,000" in 1940.[50]

Yet however great the flood of money, it was not enough to finance more than a hundred congressional races. To Lyndon, the objective was not simply to give money indiscriminately to Democratic candidates, but to support those with a good chance to win. To this end, he consulted with party leaders across the United States. He also made painstaking analyses of past votes and current conditions in various districts. On October 15, he sent a questionnaire to 77 candidates. "Is [your] district normally Democratic or Republican?" he asked. What was your district's vote in 1938? Who is your opponent? Is he "stronger than your 1938 opponent?" What sort of campaign is he making and what principal issues is he raising? Lyndon also asked for three suggestions on how to help.[51]

Because the bulk of the money he got was distributed by the Congressional Campaign Committee, Lyndon needed to ensure that it went to the people he chose. He asked contributors making recorded donations to send him a letter saying that the "money be expended in . . . the campaign of Democratic candidates for Congress as per list attached." Lyndon drew up the lists and determined the amounts each candidate received. In addition, to ensure that the Committee followed his lead and that candidates learned of his help to them, Lyndon sent them telegrams: "As result my visit to congressional committee few minutes ago, you should receive airmail special delivery letter from them." In letters he sent on October 24th, he was able to make his role even more explicit: "Because I knew you needed and deserved assistance . . . , I contacted some of my good Democratic friends in Texas and obtained a contribution for you. I personally gave to the Democratic National Committee today $400 [the amount varied in each letter], with directions to send this to you airmail special delivery. . . . I want to see you win. . . . I am devoting my entire time to an attempt to co-ordinate and expedite assistance for you. . . . Call on me, at any hour of the day, by phone, wire or letter." [52]

The money, generally in amounts between $200 and $500, was what the candidates needed most. Some, like two Ohio congressmen, said they wanted nothing else. But most asked for other things as well: a visit to their home area by the President or other prominent public figures, endorsements from Democratic leaders who had wide name recognition among their constituents, or help with getting public works projects for their districts approved before election day.

Lyndon tried to satisfy their requests. He could not make specific commitments for FDR visits, but through Jim Rowe he was able to ask. "You told me to have Lyndon Johnson, who is helping Democratic Congressmen, clear his reports through me," Rowe advised the President on October 18. " . . . He has been on the telephone talking to Congressmen from Illinois, Indiana and Missouri. . . . Every single Congressman urged upon him the necessity of your appearing in Illinois or Indiana. . . . They insist money, projects and nothing else can help them; only the President. Some of the best New Deal Congressmen are in this group." Projects were easier for Lyndon to arrange. He and Rowe prodded the WPA into approving pending grants. "Johnson and I have got a number of projects through already to help some of the Congressmen," Rowe told the President in the same memo. [53]

At the same time, Lyndon worked hard to get speakers and endorsements for various congressmen. He found prominent black, Italian, Jewish, Polish, and farm leaders to speak in districts where their voices would have particular resonance; he also paid traveling expenses and broadcasting costs for local radio. At the same time, he devised brief endorsements Administration leaders could use to voice support for particular congressmen. [54]

Nan Wood Honeyman from Portland, Oregon, who was trying to regain a seat she had lost in 1938, was a recipient of Lyndon's help. She had been one of the few women in the House, and Lyndon was particularly eager to have her return. " . . . Having you back here with us . . . would really tickle me," he wrote her. " . . . If you don't write, wire, or phone me any time there is anything—big or little—I can do for you, I am going to be awfully mad at you." He not only sent her $500 out of his initial donations, he also arranged endorsements from Rayburn, McCormack, liberal Senator George W. Norris of Nebraska, Congressman John Rankin of Mississippi—like Honeyman a public power

advocate—and Senator Claude Pepper of Florida, a favorite with reti-
rees on Social Security. Best of all, Lyndon got her a warm personal
letter from the President she could release to the press.[55]

Word of Lyndon's efforts, coupled with a telegram sent on October
26 asking candidates to "suggest any service we can render," produced
a flood of requests for money during the closing days of the campaign.
But the pleas for funds once again exceeded Lyndon's capacity to help.[56]

He and Sam Rayburn met with the President on October 27, ten days
before the election, to discuss the problem. In a letter to Swager Sherley
the next day, Lyndon reported that $76,000 was needed to help 82 can-
didates and maintain control of the House. If the DNC would give
$50,000, "I will raise the additional 26 necessary. . . . The Boss said in
his conference with the Speaker and me . . . that he thought the Committee should give us at least 50 thousand in order to save this situation." To get the $26,000, Lyndon went back to the Browns, and Ray-
burn to his Texas oilmen. Two Brown & Root corporate officials sent
$2500 each, and the firm's general manager called on Wilton Wood,
Lyndon's college friend, to deliver an envelope to Lyndon's office and
to "handle it carefully." Five oilmen gave on-the-record contributions
of $14,000. Because the DNC didn't provide the $50,000, Lyndon had
to parcel out the money more carefully than he had planned. Although
a number of the candidates got the modest $200 and $300 sums they
requested, a few received larger amounts, and some, whose prospects
seemed bleak, were frozen out entirely.[57]

The result in the congressional races was better than even Lyndon
dared hope. He bet Jim Rowe that the Democrats would lose fewer than
thirty House seats. Rowe, reflecting the White House view, thought it
would be thirty or more. But Lyndon, like other close observers at the
time, anticipated a close contest, even for the President, who accurately
foresaw that this was going to be his toughest race. The day before the
election Lyndon wired Missy LeHand, FDR's secretary, "We have been
keeping in close contact with 175 congressional candidates throughout
the country. Today I . . . requested they wire me as early as possible
Tuesday evening concerning the results of their campaign and the national picture. If I feel the information received is of sufficient interest,
I will take the liberty to call the President." Remembering that bearers
of bad tidings won no favor, Lyndon only planned to call with good
news. It was also his way of suggesting that for an early read on the
congressional elections, the President might want to call him.[58]

He did. About midnight, after Roosevelt learned that he would receive
a third term, he called Johnson and Rowe, who were together at a party
in Georgetown, where Lyndon had been getting reports from his Munsey office on the House races. Although Roosevelt beat Willkie by five
million votes, it was only half the margin he had won by in 1936 and

the smallest plurality of any winner since 1916. Also recalling party losses in 1938, Roosevelt feared a further reduction in Democratic majorities. The President asked Lyndon "how many seats are we going to lose." Using figures compiled by Walter Jenkins in the bedroom of the Georgetown house, Johnson replied: "We're not going to lose. We're going to gain.' " "It *was* impressive," Jim Rowe said. ". . . And it impressed the hell out of Roosevelt. I remember that." The fact that the Democrats gained six House seats, especially while they were losing three Senate seats, impressed a lot of other people as well, including particularly the candidates Johnson had helped. They sent him warm expressions of gratitude for his part in saving them from defeat.[59]

Their words pleased Johnson, but none more so than those of columnists Drew Pearson and Robert S. Allen, who wrote in their widely syndicated "Washington Merry-Go-Round": "To the boys on the Democratic side of the House of Representatives, many of them still nervously mopping their brows over narrow escapes, the hero of the hair-raising campaign was no big shot party figure. . . . In the House all the praise is for the youngster whose name was scarcely mentioned. . . . The Democrats' unknown hero was Representative Lyndon Baines Johnson, a rangy, 32-year-old . . . who . . . has political magic at his finger tips. . . . How Johnson took over the Democratic congressional campaign, when it looked as if the party was sure to lose the House . . . is one of the untold epics of the election."[60]

The Pearson-Allen column was part of a campaign Johnson unleashed to make himself the head of a party organization that would finance and run congressional campaigns beginning in January 1941. In the four weeks immediately after the election, Lyndon wrote all the party's leaders, including Roosevelt, Wallace, Rayburn, McCormack, Harry Hopkins, and Ed Flynn in New York thanking them for letting him get in "my few licks." "I know some of our Democratic brethren would have been utterly out in the cold except for your good offices," he told FDR. "You made it possible for me to get down where I could whiff a bit of the powder, and this note is to say 'Thank You.' It was grand. The victory is perfect."[61]

To persuade party leaders that he should lead a full-time congressional campaign effort, he got columnist Robert Allen to write Rayburn a letter, which Allen also sent to FDR: Johnson "should be made head of the Congressional Campaign Committee and given a free hand: first, to set up a full-time paid staff. . . ; and second, to start building up a campaign fund." Johnson also enlisted Ickes's support. In a discussion on November 29, Johnson told him that he had raised $100,000 in the recent campaign which had been of significant help to Democrats in doubtful districts. "He thinks that this work ought to be continued, and, obviously, he would like to be in charge of it. I know of no better man,"

Ickes recorded in his diary. Roosevelt, who was genuinely grateful to Lyndon, was ready to hear his proposal. During a two-hour lunch at the White House on December 1, he told the President that "some sort of an organization ought to be set up at once looking to the Congressional elections two years from now," that he and Tommy Corcoran could raise $300,000 between them, and that "every democratic Congressman in a doubtful district in 1942" should receive $2500. Lyndon asserted that "if these Congressmen knew that they were going to be helped the way they were during the last campaign," it "would mean an influential bloc upon which the President could depend."[62]

Lyndon had the impression that Roosevelt "thought well of his suggestions," but he would not act on them. He shared Lyndon's interest in ensuring continued Democrat control of the House. But an investigation of campaign finance laws begun on November 26 by Attorney General Robert H. Jackson probably made Roosevelt reluctant to encourage a significant fund-raising effort just then. Swamped by complaints that the $3 million limit on campaign expenditures had been "violated or evaded" by both parties, Jackson convened Federal grand juries in five cities, including Washington, D.C., to study the charges.[63]

Roosevelt also worried that partisan actions of the sort Johnson proposed would undermine immediate national needs. In particular, Roosevelt foresaw a difficult period of debate over foreign affairs. In the winter of 1940–41, the country remained sharply divided over America's proper stance toward the European war. Should the United States give Britain additional aid in its struggle with Hitler? And if so, how much? Was it more important to assure the defeat of Nazism or to stay out of the fighting? Roosevelt knew that controversy would greet his every action toward the conflict, especially his response in December to Britain's inability to keep paying cash for desperately needed war supplies. Eager to make the United States an "arsenal of democracy," as he shortly called it, and convinced that sustained commitments abroad depended on a consensus at home, he wished to avoid anything that increased domestic divisions. Lyndon's plan, especially with a central part for Tommy Corcoran, one of the most controversial New Dealers, threatened to cause political problems that Roosevelt wanted to avoid.[64]

In the winter of 1940–41 there were enough political conflicts without adding to them. In December, the Congress threatened to override Roosevelt's veto of the Walter-Logan bill, a conservative-backed law to restrict the powers of executive agencies. The Administration and its congressional allies were so convinced that a combination of Republicans and anti-New Deal Democrats would successfully defy the President that they decided not to put up a fight. But Tommy Corcoran, refusing to accept defeat, pressed McCormack, Ickes, Rayburn, and Johnson into an all-out effort that succeeded. "Is my face red. Rayburn and Lyndon Johnson too," Jim Rowe told Corcoran in a congratulatory telegram. "God love the Irish."

Two days later, Roosevelt had Lyndon back in the White House, where they discussed not fund-raising and the 1942 campaign but how to promote better relations with House Democrats. The urgency of the assignment, Johnson wired John and Nellie Connally, would compel him to miss their wedding. Consulting with Rayburn and McCormack, Johnson drew plans for the President to meet with the 267 House Democrats. Lyndon suggested seven after-dinner sessions with about forty members each, the Speaker and Majority Leader, four or five Assistant Secretaries and Under Secretaries, and some White House assistants. The President asked an aide to keep Lyndon's list in case he decided "to see some of these Congressmen later on." He also began cooperating more closely with the House leadership. But he neither acted directly on Lyndon's proposal nor gave him a larger formal role in national party affairs.[65]

Roosevelt's pay-off to Johnson for his loyalty to the Administration came in the spring and early summer of 1941 when he ran for a Senate seat. On April 9, Morris Sheppard, the senior senator from Texas, died after a brief illness. Walter Jenkins called Lyndon at seven in the morning to give him the news. Lyndon "was immediately interested in that," Jenkins recalled, "I mean immediately." A special election to complete Sheppard's term meant that Lyndon could run without giving up his House seat. Lyndon made a beeline for his office, where he began making some calls, including one to Alvin Wirtz, who urged Lyndon to make the race.[66]

Lyndon wished to give the impression that he was reluctant to run. It was a ploy for getting Administration backing. "Lyndon does not much take to the idea of making the race, but I believe he would if his friends convinced him that he has a chance," Wirtz wrote a potential supporter on April 12. Lyndon gave Ickes the impression that "he didn't . . . care whether he ran for senator or not. . . . I had the impression that if the President would send for him matters might be worked out." James Rowe pressed the same point on Roosevelt: "Lyndon Johnson will run for the Senate if the Administration helps him." "Lyndon has practically decided not to make the race," he told Roosevelt four days later. "He feels no great enthusiasm has been shown by you. . . . I think you ought to call him to the White House and talk to him, if you are interested."[67]

Although Lyndon had doubts about winning, he never hesitated about running. On April 11, Wirtz, Charles Marsh, and Harold Young, a Texas attorney on Vice President Henry Wallace's staff, laid plans for Lyndon's campaign. They discussed getting Texas Governor W. Lee O'Daniel to make him interim senator until the special election on June 28, when and how FDR should endorse him, and the themes Lyndon would sound in the race.

By April 17, Lyndon had begun raising campaign funds. He had arranged with the Brown brothers to make the first of many hidden contributions. Convinced that Lyndon would have more influence on defense spending as a senator than he would as a congressman, the Browns were eager to support a campaign that promised to serve their long-term interests. They also saw a means of making it serve their immediate ones as well. On the 17th, a check for $6000 was given to D. G. Young, the secretary of Brown & Root. It was listed in the corporation's records as a bonus authorized on December 27, 1940, and as an expense deduction in Brown & Root's tax returns. In fact, on the same day Young received the check, he gave $5,270 in cash to Lyndon's campaign.[68]

Lyndon, Wirtz, and the Browns had no overt concerns about violating campaign and tax laws. Federal investigations of campaign law violations in 1940 had concluded in February with no indictments. It apparently persuaded them that they had nothing to fear from Federal authorities. Moreover, they believed that if their campaign stayed within the $25,000 limit allowed by Federal law, it would mean certain defeat. Since a state-wide radio talk cost $1300, a highway billboard ad $200–300, a small newspaper ad $25–50, it was an unspoken assumption of the campaign that anyone making a serious bid for the office would exceed the $25,000 limit many times over.[69]

Lyndon's first concern in the two weeks after Sheppard died was not campaign financing but Roosevelt's public blessing. The defeat of congressional candidates FDR had endorsed in the 1938 primaries made him reluctant to take a stand in the Texas Senate race. But Rowe assured him that Johnson would avoid "the mistakes of the 1930 'purge,' " and advised him that the alternatives to Johnson were "too frightful for contemplation." Rowe believed that the President would boost the morale of New Dealers and liberal control of the Democratic party by getting behind Lyndon's campaign. Ickes told Roosevelt much the same thing. The alternatives to Johnson were "anti-administration, anti-New Deal, and particularly anti-Roosevelt. . . . By inspiring and encouraging [Lyndon], the President may . . . help the liberal cause."[70]

Roosevelt, who had thoughts of getting Johnson on the Senate Military Affairs Committee, agreed on the condition that Lyndon first return to Texas to assess his political strength. In a speech to a joint session of the Texas legislature on April 21, Lyndon urged support of FDR's defense and foreign policies. A standing ovation from the legislators served Johnson's efforts to get the President's backing.

After his speech, Johnson met privately with O'Daniel, who assured him that he had no intention of running for Sheppard's seat. Having resisted suggestions that he resign the governorship and let Lieutenant Governor Coke Stevenson appoint him interim senator while he campaigned for a six-year term, O'Daniel seemed to be operating in good faith. Later that day, when he appointed eighty-six-year-old Andrew Jackson Houston, Sam Houston's son, O'Daniel eliminated the advantage of incumbency from the campaign. Houston, who would die on June 26, two days before the election, was too frail to think of running for a regular term. Houston's appointment also left open the possibility that O'Daniel would later join the race. The fact that O'Daniel had coupled his appointment of Houston with an appeal to Texans for "advice, prayers, and suggestions" on whether he should seek the job convinced many observers that he would run. Lyndon took him at his word and assumed he would not.[71]

Lyndon flew back to Washington that night and met with the President the next day. On the White House steps, Johnson declared himself in the race and his intention to fight for democracy "under the banner of Roosevelt and unity." At a press conference, the President said that "I can't take part in a Texas primary. . . . If you ask me about Lyndon himself, I can't take part in his election. I can only say what is perfectly true,—you all know he is a very old and close friend of mine. Now that's about all. Now don't try to tie those things together!" The transcripts of his remarks noted: "(the President brought the house down with laughter)." Newspaper accounts in Washington and Texas left no doubt that Roosevelt was endorsing Johnson. They described the journalists' hilarity over the President's injunction not to tie his description of Lyndon as an old friend to the Texas campaign, and they carried headlines like one appearing in the Texas *Taylor Times:* "F.D. Tosses Lyndon's Hat for Senate."[72]

In backing Johnson, Roosevelt was betting on a long shot. A statewide poll published on April 21 showed Lyndon with only 5 percent of the vote. O'Daniel commanded support of 33 percent of the state's voters, while Gerald C. Mann, the Texas attorney general, had 26 percent and Martin Dies, the east Texas congressman from Orange, had 9 percent. Twenty-seven candidates entered what some national magazines would call the "Screwball Election in Texas" or the "Screwy Texas Race." A special election open to anyone paying a $100 filing fee, the race drew publicity seekers of all kinds: a Baptist preacher with an alcoholic press agent urging Prohibition; two bearded gentlemen, who claimed power of prophecy as their qualification for office; a self-styled "Commodore" demanding a five-ocean navy; an ex-bootlegger; an admitted kidnapper; a promoter of goat-gland medicines promising rejuvenation; a laxative manufacturer offering a free mattress at each of his rallies to the couple with the most children; and a Naval Academy graduate urging an immediate declaration of war against Japan.[73]

In late April, with O'Daniel undeclared, Lyndon's principal opposition came from Mann and Dies. Both were better known, as the initial voter survey showed, and both seemed able to mount campaigns that

Lyndon would have difficulty matching. Johnson was a "David" facing one and possibly two Goliaths, one newspaper said. Outside of two congressional districts, "Johnson is not known in Texas," a report reaching James Rowe through Attorney General Robert Jackson concluded. In the Dallas area, where "the vast majority of the votes of Texas originate, I doubt if 5% of these voters have ever heard of Johnson," Jackson's source reported. He also believed that in a three-way race between Johnson, Dies, and Mann, Dies would "attract a large number of the voters," but not merely as many as Mann. "If the elections were today [May 2] . . . Mann would sweep the field." [74]

Mann, who declared his candidacy on April 12, had demonstrated in earlier statewide campaigns that he was the second most popular public official in Texas after O'Daniel. Raised in the small northeast Texas town of Sulphur Springs, Mann had gained fame at Southern Methodist University in Dallas as an all-conference quarterback. Mann was also known as religious and honest. He had earned a Harvard law degree while working as the pastor of the Congregational Church in Gloucester, Massachusetts. After serving as an assistant attorney general and secretary of state of Texas, he had won election to the attorney general's office in 1938 at the age of thirty-one. In 1940, he had refused appointment as chief justice of the state Supreme Court to run unopposed for a second term. He compiled an exemplary record, strictly enforcing state anti-trust laws and waging "a continuous war" against racketeers, loan sharks, and tax cheats. His personal credo, inscribed on a plaque hanging in the attorney general's office, was: "I sacrificed no principle to gain this office and I shall sacrifice no principle to keep it." [75]

Dies's appeal was more emotional and narrower. At forty, he was a ten-year veteran congressman with a national reputation as the chairman of the House Un-American Activities Committee. A superpatriot who played on people's fears of Communism and Nazism, he warned against subversion in Texas, reminding people that a fifth column had helped destroy Belgian independence in 1940. He also declared that a secret foreign army outnumbered the American army, and that foreign-controlled parties in America had seven million members. He predicted that his elevation to the Senate would enhance his anti-subversion work: "I feel certain that Texas will endorse the program I have outlined to rid this country of traitors," he told one campaign supporter. Although he had opened a gulf between himself and the White House by alleging widespread Communist penetration of New Deal agencies, he strongly supported the President's defense programs. He said that Roosevelt needed him in the upper house, and urged against sending Johnson, "a yes-man, [the inexperienced Mann] a green man, or [O'Daniel] a showman" to the Senate. Blessed with a fine speaking voice, Dies impressed many voters as sounding more like a senator on the radio than any other candidate.[76]

At the beginning of May, O'Daniel seemed certain to become a candidate and the odds-on favorite. A superb actor and salesman, O'Daniel had established himself as the most successful vote-getter in Texas political history. In 1927, at the age of thirty-seven, he had come from Kansas to Fort Worth, where he became the sales manager for a flour manufacturer. He increased sales by advertising the company's Light Crust Flour on a local radio station. A country and western band played and sang sentimental and religious tunes he had composed. "Marvelous Mother of Mine," "Shall We Gather at the River," and "Sons of the Alamo" typically set the backdrop for the sermons he delivered on mother's virtues, the Ten Commandments, and the greatness of the Lone Star state. Calling himself "Pappy," O'Daniel was introduced at the start of each show by a woman asking him to "Please pass the biscuits, Pappy."

In 1935 he opened the Hillbilly Flour Company. He sold the flour in sacks stamped with a picture of a billy goat, the words, "Pass the biscuits, Pappy," and a rhyme he had composed: "Hillbilly music on the air,/ Hillbilly flour everywhere;/ It tickles your feet—It tickles your tongue,/ Wherever you go, its praises are sung." By 1938, Pappy had organized a band consisting of his two sons and a daughter which made personal appearances with him around the state. His radio show had begun reaching millions of Texans on a state-wide network. "At twelve-thirty sharp each day," a national magazine reported, "a fifteen-minute silence reigned in the state of Texas, broken only by mountain music, and the dulcet voice of W. Lee O'Daniel."

That year, he asked listeners if he should run for governor, and when more than 50,000 wrote to say, "yes," he declared himself a candidate. Although his opponents pointed out that he was a wealthy businessman and not an ordinary, poor citizen, as he claimed to be, that he had no political experience, and no way to deliver on a promised thirty-dollar a month old-age pension, which would cost the state four times its current annual budget, Texas voters nevertheless flocked to his standard. An evangelist in politics preaching the Ten Commandments and the Golden Rule, O'Daniel won 573,000 votes or 51 percent of the 1.1 million cast for thirteen candidates in the Democratic primary. In 1940, despite his failure to deliver on his pension promise, his vote in the primary climbed to 645,000, some 54 percent of the total against 46 percent won by his six opponents. If O'Daniel entered the Senate race, he seemed certain to win.[77]

Lyndon believed that he had only an outside chance of beating O'Daniel, Mann, and Dies. If Congressman Wright Patman from Texarkana in the northeast corner of the state joined the campaign, as he wanted to, Lyndon saw his chances dropping to almost zero. A staunch liberal, Patman would split the New Deal vote and benefit O'Daniel. Although Patman acknowledged this, he saw his consistent support of the Administration and eight years of House seniority to Lyndon entitling him to FDR's support. Sam Rayburn and W. R. (Bob) Poage, another liberal Texas congressman, tried to convince Patman otherwise, but during the first ten days of May he refused to stand aside.

A survey of voter opinion completed on May 3 showed Lyndon with little chance of winning. Thirty-three percent favored O'Daniel, who was still not an avowed candidate, 28 percent preferred Mann, and a like number supported Dies, while only 9 percent chose Johnson. When O'Daniel was removed from the race, Mann led with 41.9 percent, trailed by Dies and Lyndon with 40.4 percent and 14.6 percent respectively.[78]

Lyndon's first week on the campaign trail confirmed his doubts. Between May 3 and 10 he traveled over 2000 miles across the state giving thirty six speeches, five of them on statewide radio. His talks were all high-minded appeals for unity and sacrifice in time of crisis: "For two weeks I waited to announce in the hope some candidate would have the courage to commit himself to all-out support for the President and his foreign policy. This was not done. Therefore, I am in the race. . . . National defense is *the* job. War is near our borders. . . . Our prayer is that America can remain at peace. But more than we . . . love peace, we love liberty. . . . The job now [is] to save America. . . . If you select me as your Senator, it will be because you have acted with the thought in mind of unity and the welfare of the country." Emphasizing his own readiness to serve the nation, he declared that "if the day ever comes when my vote must be cast to send your boy to the trenches, that day Lyndon Johnson will leave his Senate seat to go with him."[79]

To be "senatorial—statesmanlike and dignified," Lyndon initially took a high road in the campaign. "I entered this race with malice toward none and good will for all," he said in his opening speech. "I hope they will let me end it that way." He tailored his appearance to match his rhetoric: he dressed in dark blue suits with a vest, a starched white shirt with gold cufflinks, a neatly folded handkerchief in his breast pocket and matching tie, and a fedora instead of a Stetson. He carried a briefcase containing the text of a speech he read to his audience.

The results were disappointing. Although campaign organizers arranged for large and enthusiastic audiences, Lyndon's formal talks bored his supporters. By the close of his speeches only small crowds remained applauding mechanically. Posed photos of him on placards distributed at the start of his campaign also struck the wrong note. "Please get me some placards with a good, serious, clear-cut, honest to God, straight-looking photograph on it and leave the B. out on Lyndon's name . . . ," a campaign worker wrote John Connally. " . . . These Hollywood poses won't go in West Texas."[80]

By May 10, Lyndon's poor prospects in the race had shaken his confidence. The polls "made me feel mighty bad when my mother and wife told me I was the last man in the race. I know that my throat got bad on me, and I had to spend a few days in the hospital." In fact, it was closer to two weeks. The likelihood of losing threw him into a fit of depression or "nervous exhaustion," as Harold Young described it. Compounded by a throat infection or what John Connally called pneumonia, Johnson had to break off his campaign. His temporary incapacity and thoughts of giving up the race made him irrational. When Connally, who had become his principal assistant, and Gordon Fulcher, an Austin journalist who was handling publicity, wanted to tell the press about his hospitalization, Lyndon resisted. Connally said: "For God's sake, you've got a week's schedule of speaking engagements." Johnson replied that they could have a stand-in. When Connally and Fulcher asked how they were going to explain another speaker and Johnson's "being incommunicado for several days or a week . . . he just threw a fit, went into a tirade, ordered us out of the house, said he never wanted to talk to us again."[81]

During his first ten days in the hospital, matters went from bad to worse. Although he managed to hide his illness for a few days by entering a clinic some sixty miles outside of Austin, the *Austin American* reported his throat ailment on May 14 and his temporary inability to give scheduled talks. On the 20th, the newspaper revealed Johnson's hospitalization at the Scott and White clinic in Temple, and described him as "getting a much needed rest and isolation from campaign and congressional worries." If these accounts added to his upset, it must have been nothing along side of the news that the FBI was investigating him. On May 14, Alvin Wirtz, who had resigned as Under Secretary of the Interior to run Lyndon's Senate race, phoned Oscar Chapman, an Assistant Secretary in the Department, to report that an FBI agent had come to Johnson's office to interview him. Wirtz shielded Lyndon from questioning by explaining that he was in the hospital. He at once asked Ickes to "find out from the Department of Justice what this is all about." An inquiry from Ickes to Francis Biddle, the Solicitor General, produced a memorandum from FBI Director J. Edgar Hoover explaining that Johnson was being investigated for campaign violations in 1940. Five days after this fell on Johnson, O'Daniel announced that he was coming into the race.[82]

Lyndon's supporters took the bad news as an inducement to try harder. Charles Marsh called Harold Young to Austin to help "rearrange" the campaign and to go to Temple "to cheer up [Lyndon] a bit." John Connally persuaded Sammy Baugh, the Washington Redskins quarterback, to send a letter supporting Lyndon to football coaches in Texas, while another aide convinced former Detroit Tigers outfielder Ty Cobb to give radio talks for Lyndon. Others in the campaign pressed Lyndon's case with black and Mexican voters. More important, despite heavy spring rains that flooded parts of the state, forced rallies indoors, and kept other candidates off the campaign trail, a number of stand-ins fulfilled Lyndon's speaking commitments. Connally, Wirtz, Roy Hofheinz, a Houston County judge, and Everett Looney, one of Ed Clark's law partners, gave a series of talks that were more pleasing to audiences than Lyndon's and went far to boost his voter appeal. A new opinion survey published on May 19 showed that Lyndon had nearly doubled his support to 17.6 percent of the vote, while O'Daniel, who was still uncommitted when the poll was taken, fell ten points to 22 percent. Mann and Dies were deadlocked with 26 percent each.[83]

The poll buoyed Lyndon, and he came out of the hospital on May 23 with renewed hope. Mounting evidence that the Roosevelt administration was giving him considerable aid especially pleased him. In early May, Roosevelt send word to Johnson through Jim Rowe that three officials in the Agriculture Department would "be of help in the Texas situation." Another official advised Wirtz that the Farm Security Administration, "the most powerful" Federal agency in Texas, could undermine O'Daniel if its principal employees would just "get out and produce some results for the . . . administration."

FDR also put pressure on Jesse Jones of Houston, now the Secretary of Commerce, to have his Texas newspapers and radio stations back Lyndon. "Every other department and agency of the Government are cooperating 100% behind Johnson, but nothing has been heard from the Secretary of Commerce," Rowe wrote the President on May 5. "In fact, the reverse seems to be true. . . . The question is, whether Jesse Jones is above the Administration or takes orders like the rest of us." Roosevelt sent Rowe's memorandum to Jones and asked: "How can I answer this?" In addition, Roosevelt told Rowe and others that "whatever Johnson wants in terms of projects to be announced, whatever the government can do, they will do it." And they did: in late May, Lyndon was able to tell folks all over the state that hundreds of thousands of dollars in WPA funds would be used to build airports, school buildings, and roads and to improve streets and disposal plants. Roosevelt also asked Robert Jackson and Henry Morgenthau, Jr., to have Justice and Treasury Department officials in Texas support Lyndon's campaign. At the same time, he convinced Wright Patman not to enter the race.[84]

Ickes was also a big help to Lyndon. He carried word to Jackson and Morgenthau about the President's wishes, and when Morgenthau showed himself reluctant to get "in on anything like that," Ickes reminded Roosevelt "to give a tip to Henry Morgenthau that you are interested in the election of Lyndon Johnson in Texas." "H.M. Jr., Do what you can!" the President scrawled on Ickes's note and sent it to Morgenthau. More important, Ickes apparently helped kill the FBI investigation of Johnson's campaign violations. "Thank you for your note of May 22 to which was attached a memorandum from Mr. Hoover with reference to the 'investigation' of Lyndon Johnson," Ickes wrote Francis Biddle on May 23. "People certainly can get excited during a campaign. I would not have gone to the trouble to call you up if Under Secretary Wirtz had not requested that I do so by long-distance telephone." Nothing more was heard of the "investigation" after Ickes's exchange with Biddle.

Ickes also took up the cudgels against Martin Dies, whom he despised. He tried to get information on Dies's property taxes that could publicly embarrass him, and he put Wirtz in touch with an insurance agent in Texas whom Ickes consulted. Cautious about saying too much over the long-distance telephone about politics, the agent subsequently sent Ickes a letter saying that he was "just as strongly opposed to Dies as ever and will be glad to assist you in any way I can to retire him to private life." "The defeat of Dies . . . will be balm of Gilead so far as I am concerned," Ickes confided to his diary.[85]

O'Daniel was more of a concern to Johnson. Speaking on the radio from the governor's mansion every day at noon and on Sundays at six in the morning, he described his platform as "one hundred percent approval of the Lord God Jehovah, widows, orphans, low taxes, the Ten Commandments, and the Golden Rule." Although he was unable to make his first campaign appearance until June 2, O'Daniel's traveling road show promised to be as much a magnet to voters as in his gubernatorial campaigns. It featured a bus topped by a loudspeaker in the form of the state capitol, a hillbilly band that included O'Daniel's three children, Pat or "Patty Boy," a fiddler, Mike or "Mickey Wickey," a banjo player, and Molly, a vocalist, who complemented Leon Huff, the "Texas Songbird" and "Texas Rose," another singer. The principal attraction at these rallies, however, was O'Daniel himself. He appealed to fundamentalist religious and family values and spoke to fears of impoverishment, especially among the elderly. He touched the emotions of his rural audiences as few politicians ever had in Texas history.[86]

Johnson and Wirtz mapped a campaign to overcome the advantages of O'Daniel, Mann, and Dies. Their first goal was to raise a large campaign fund which would allow them to finance a better traveling circus than O'Daniel's and to blitz the state with campaign material that would make Johnson a household name. In addition, they planned to emphasize Johnson's ties to FDR, cultivate black and Mexican voters, and publicize the weaknesses of the three frontrunners.

Raising large sums of money proved to be easier than Johnson and

Wirtz had thought possible. "We never were in danger of running out of money," Herman Brown later told Eliot Janeway, "but we damn near ran out of names," or ways "to allocate the money." "It was rather a customary way of doing business in Texas politics to take money wherever you could get it," a participant in the campaign said. "You needed all you could find. . . . So no one certainly would blame Lyndon for taking money from anybody. It didn't make any difference." It did to one San Antonio attorney, who complained afterward to members of the Texas House and Senate that "business men, corporations, oil and utility companies, and United States Government contractors . . . [were] high-jacked out of large sums of money to buy the senatorial election. I have been informed and believe . . . that this election was the most corrupt, disgraceful debauchery of an election ever undertaken in Texas, or probably elsewhere."[87]

No one could tell from official campaign reports that massive amounts of money were spent by all the leading candidates. Like Johnson, O'Daniel, Mann, and Dies had large contributions from business interests. O'Daniel also had the support of great numbers of small contributors. Possibly millions of dollars were collected over the years at O'Daniel's rallies by his children passing small barrels labeled "Flour; not Pork" in which people would drop nickels, dimes, and quarters. The contributions not only helped pay for O'Daniel's campaigns they also gave people a stake in his election and increased the likelihood that they would turn out to vote.[88]

Yet no candidate outdid Lyndon in attracting financial support. The campaign "was Brown & Root funded," Lyndon told Ronnie Dugger in 1967. The Browns gave nearly $300,000. Bonuses of $150,800 listed in fraudulent minutes of December 27, 1940, were paid to key corporate officers in the spring of 1941 and then transferred in checks and cash to Johnson's campaign. According to a 1944 Internal Revenue Service report, another $19,600 in phony attorneys' fees, some of them from Victoria Gravel Company, a Brown & Root subsidiary, ran "from the taxpayer to the Johnson Campaign Fund." A $100,000 bonus paid by the W. S. Bellows Construction Company, another Brown & Root subsidiary, also found its way into Johnson's Senate race. A petty cash account or "slush fund" at Brown & Root was tapped as well for campaign money. There was more: perhaps another $200,000 came in from northern labor unions and businessmen, independent Texas oil men, and Charles Marsh. There may have been other secret contributions, but "perjury on the part of officers and employees of the taxpaying corporation [Brown & Root] and refusal of witnesses not employed by the corporation to testify" make it difficult to know.[89]

Alvin Wirtz made certain that there was no exact record of contributions and expenditures. Wilton Woods, who managed and paid the ex-

penses of the Austin campaign office, kept a financial record of his activities in a little black book. When Wirtz heard about it, he called Woods
in and asked to see the book. "This is money that went to the campaign?" he asked. "Yes, sir," Woods replied. " . . . We had an agreement that there wasn't going to be any bookkeeping," Wirtz said. "Don't
you remember that?" Wirtz tore the book "into a hundred pieces. So
there wasn't any accurate record kept in that portion of the campaign." [90]

The Johnson campaign used some of its money for a traveling road
show that outdid O'Daniel's. As soon as O'Daniel entered the race, the
Johnson managers looked for ways to turn their rallies into something
more than set speeches by the candidate. At first they tried a "Band
Concert and Rally" that featured a speech by Lyndon identifying him
with Roosevelt's "defense of democracy against aggression." They next
tried a mix of songs, poems, and local speakers in a "Program" emphasizing America's, Roosevelt's, and Johnson's virtues in this time of crisis.
Things only came together, however, when they turned to Harfield
Weedin, a Houston radio personality and advertising executive. Agreeing to pay him $1000 a week, put airplanes at his disposal, and use his
ad agency, the Johnson people accurately foresaw that Weedin could
make their rallies exciting enough to attract large crowds and put votes
in Lyndon's column.[91]

"We finally decided that if you couldn't beat 'em, you might as well
join 'em; so we got ourselves a band and we had ourselves a starlet,"
Lady Bird Johnson later said. In fact, under Weedin's direction, they
staged a lavish two-hour carnival in all parts of Texas during the last
three weeks of the campaign. Advertised as a "Patriotic Rally," "All-
Out Patriotic Revue," or "International Revue," when presented in south
Texas, the show invariably featured a huge canvas backdrop picture of
Lyndon and the President shaking hands with the words underneath:
"ROOSEVELT AND UNITY—ELECT LYNDON JOHNSON UNITED
STATES SENATOR." It was an enlarged and altered version of a 1937
photo that included Lyndon, FDR and Governor Jimmy Allred; the 1941
pictured "blocked out" the governor. The show began with a twenty-
three piece jazz band designated the "Johnson Swingsters" or the "Pa-
triots" attired in white dinner jackets with red carnations and blue pants.
After a couple of ear-splitting numbers, two vocalists treated the audience to patriotic, Texas, southern, and cowboy songs. Sophia Parker, the
285-pound "Kate Smith of the South," dressed in a white, tent-like evening gown decorated in red, white, and blue, sang "I Am an American,"
"Dixie," and "The Eyes of Texas Are Upon You." Mary Lou Behn, a
shapely torch singer, rendered her versions of "I Want To Be a Cowboy's Sweetheart" and "San Antonio Rose." Johnny Landy, a harmon-
ica player, concluded the half-hour of musical entertainment.

A half-hour performance by Harfield Weedin followed. Styled after a popular radio and movie newscast, "The March of Time," Weedin's show was a musical pageant of recent history titled "The Spirit of American Unity" or "The Spirit of '41." Weedin's melodramatic narrative described the Depression, Roosevelt's defeat of Hoover, New Deal triumphs, the war in Europe, and the President's courageous response to the world crisis: "When Roosevelt became President the banks were popping like popcorn"; patriotic unity was essential against "the monster that raised itself up to gaze with covetous and fiendish eyes upon the democracies." Weedin said: "I can't emphasize . . . how effective this little thirty-minute show . . . was in taking . . . people who didn't know Lyndon from anybody and getting them involved in it and wanting to see this man that Franklin D. Roosevelt thought so much of."

By the time Lyndon was introduced the audience had been brought to fever pitch. Weedin had never "seen anything other than a religious meeting get an audience so worked up." As Weedin and the entire cast stood marching in place and singing "God Bless America," Lyndon came on stage for a half-hour set speech followed by his "country-boy style of talking," "extemporaneous" remarks that had been rehearsed and were delivered in a "very stiff, very uncomfortable" way. Though his speaking style dampened crowd enthusiasm, a closing lottery in which Defense Bonds and Stamps were given away kept the audience to the end of the rally.[92]

Johnson's well-publicized ties to Roosevelt and his focus on meeting the dangers of the world crisis more than offset his failings as a speaker. Ads, posters, mailings, and radio talks convinced voters that Lyndon was FDR's choice in the race and that Johnson, like the President and much of the nation, was primarily concerned about the growing threat to American security from Nazi victories. Additional German military gains in the Balkans, the North Atlantic, and North Africa in the spring of 1941 made all Americans particularly conscious of foreign affairs.[93]

On May 31, four days after Roosevelt had declared a national emergency, Johnson cabled him: "If my Commander-in-Chief needs me during the next four weeks in my Congress seat will you please command me and I will come at once." The reason for his wire, Johnson told Missy LeHand, was that other candidates were urging his return to Washington to help the President and that he was "being called a slacker to an old and trusted friend." To answer these demands and underscore his unity with the President, Wirtz drafted a reply to Johnson which FDR agreed to send:

I have declared a national emergency because the seriousness of the present emergency warrants it. However, we should not lose sight of our ultimate objective which is the defense of our demo-

cratic way of life. The people of Texas by taking part in the election
. . . of a United States senator thereby present a convincing demonstration of our democratic process at work. . . . The people of
Texas are entitled to be informed of the issues by the candidates
for that office and I can think of no better way to present the issues
than through personal appearances by all the candidates.

Therefore I suggest that you stay in Texas during the campaign
unless conditions change so radically that your presence in Washington is necessary. If that happens I will send for you. Please return immediately after election.[94]

When Hitler invaded the Soviet Union on June 22, a week before the
election, it gave added meaning to Johnson's warnings about Nazi plans
for world-wide conquest and strengthened his appeal as a candidate who
understood the dangers from abroad. To ensure that every voter got the
message, Johnson's campaign had hired popular music composer Irving
Caesar to write an adaptation of "Tea for Two" for broadcast on Texas
radio stations:

UN-I-TY - FROM YOU AND ME - IS NEEDED BY DEMOCRACY
AND THAT IS WHY WE ALL NEED *LYNDON B.*—

. . .

HE HAS BRAIN - AND HE HAS HEART-
SO SPREAD THE WORD AND DO YOUR PART-
AND LET'S BE SMART AND VOTE IN HARMONY—-
MISTER ROOSEVELT DOES AGREE—
THAT *UN-I-TY* AND *LYNDON B.*
WOULD HELP *DEFENSE* AND HELP *DEMOCRACY!*[95]

Crowd reactions and statewide polls demonstrated the effectiveness of
Johnson's campaign. In early June, when Supreme Court Justice William O. Douglas, who was motoring crosscountry with his family, pulled
into Big Spring in west Texas, a town of 10,000 people, Lyndon was
"pouring it on" to an audience of 3000. "Every time he mentioned your
name," Douglas wrote FDR, "the crowd cheered. Every time he mentioned [Charles] Lindbergh the crowd booed. It was an enthusiastic
Roosevelt crowd." A voter survey published on June 8 showed that Lyndon still trailed his three principal rivals, but his share of the vote had
risen to 19.4 percent; he was only 7.6 percent behind Gerald Mann, who
led O'Daniel by about one percent and Dies by almost 3.5 percent. By
June 21, however, Johnson was in a virtual deadlock with O'Daniel and
Mann for the lead. "Lyndon Johnson had achieved a remarkable rise
from a young and relatively unknown Central Texas Congressman to
one of the top favorites in the contest," the pollsters reported. "He now

stands at practically even stature with Gerald C. Mann and W. Lee O'Daniel."[96]

Lyndon's rise in the polls was the product not only of his identification with FDR and a popular defense policy but also of less appealing campaigns by his opponents. Martin Dies had run a particularly weak race, focusing almost exclusively on the subject of un-American activities. He was quickly seen as a Johnny-one-note who could excite an audience of superpatriots but had limited appeal to most people around the state. By the last week of the campaign he had fallen into fourth place.[97]

Mann had made a vigorous state-wide effort, but he could not match Johnson in hoopla or substantive appeal. Though he hammered on his favorite theme of integrity and persuasively attacked interference by Federal officials and the expenditure of vast sums of money in Johnson's behalf, he had his own honesty effectively called into question by allegations about his financial backers and campaign tactics. Ties to oil interests, including an assistant attorney general who had worked for Standard Oil, support from the Congress of Industrial Organizations (CIO), which he attacked for helping Johnson, lukewarm backing for FDR's 1940 campaign, and a broken promise not to run for another office during his second term as attorney general undercut his credibility with the electorate. The last opinion survey published on election day showed that Mann had dropped to 25.2 percent of the vote against 31.2 and 26.7 percent for Johnson and O'Daniel respectively.[98]

Although O'Daniel remained Johnson's principal competitor, his Senate race had been less effective than his gubernatorial campaigns. This was partly because he faced a more formidable field of competitors than in his earlier races. But he had other campaign problems as well. Tied to Austin by a legislature that refused to adjourn, O'Daniel found it impossible to get out on the hustings until the last two weeks of the election. When he did, his personal touch was as powerful as ever, but it was not enough to offset Johnson's ties to FDR or Johnson's emphasis on the idea that O'Daniel was a well-intentioned governor who should be kept in Texas, where he could do people in the state the most good.

O'Daniel's attitude toward FDR and the Federal government was even more of a problem for him. Telegrams from FDR to Johnson extolling his support of New Deal farm and social security programs cut into O'Daniel's backing from farmers and the elderly. The implied message that Johnson was a modern politician who would effectively serve state and regional interests and that O'Daniel was a local leader with limited vision gave Lyndon an important advantage in their contest. In response, O'Daniel tried to identify himself with FDR. He declared that he had written a song for him in 1932, had voted for him in 1936, and had even offered a radio prayer for him. "So onward, noble President, we pledge our faith in you. 'Cause when we see your smilin' face, we never can feel blue." He also said that when he got to Washington he would help rescue the President from the "professional politicians" or the "pussyfooting, pusillanimous politicians who were not fit to run a peanut stand." Johnson pressed O'Daniel to say whether he considered Roosevelt one of these politicians and whether he considered Sam Rayburn, Senator Tom Connally, Jesse Jones, and members of the Texas delegation in the House part of this group. Johnson further turned the "professional politican" remark against him by urging voters to keep O'Daniel in Texas, where he could protect the people from them and fulfill his promise to get old folks larger pensions. To counter Johnson's argument, O'Daniel said that he would be keeping a wary eye on the Texas legislature while he was in Washington, and his hillbilly band played, "I'll Be with You When I'm Gone." Yet try as he might, O'Daniel could not generate the same enthusiasm he had aroused in past campaigns.[99]

Twenty-four hours after the polls closed on Saturday June 28, with 96 percent of the vote counted, Lyndon led O'Daniel by 5,150 votes. The next day the Texas Election Bureau and newspapers around the state declared Johnson the unofficial winner. Johnson campaign workers were jubilant, parading around the Stephen F. Austin Hotel with Lyndon on their shoulders. Lyndon was so confident of victory that he "practically hired a staff." When he and Wirtz spoke to Harold Ickes in Washington on Sunday, they "were absolutely sure that, on the basis of the ratio of the voting in the different sections of the state, Johnson could not fail to win." Jim Rowe in Washington shared in the merriment. He wired Lyndon: "O'DANIEL WENT INTO THE LYNDON DEN HE MET THE SAME FATE AS DIES AND MANN. HE WENT FROM BAD TO WIRTZ. OUR LYNDON IS THE NERTS. HEIGH HO LADY BIRD."[100]

But Johnson and Wirtz underestimated the resourcefulness of a coalition of political forces determined to put O'Daniel in the Senate, or more precisely, to get him out of the governor's chair. Two days before the election, Mayor Tom Miller of Austin told Charles Marsh that Lyndon had a lead in the race, but "gambling, horse racing and whiskey-beer combination will throw behind O'Daniel to get him out of state. [Coke] Stevenson [the lieutenant governor] may become Governor and stop prohibition drive which O'Daniel started last week." Supported by former Governor Jim (Pa) Ferguson, who had become general counsel to the Texas Brewers Association, and some state legislators, this combination of forces was so confident of their ability to shape the outcome of the vote that on Monday morning, when one of O'Daniel's aides spoke with him at the governor's mansion, he remarked that Johnson's 5000-vote lead did not " 'make any difference.' He said that Coke Stevenson had told him that he [O'Daniel] would come out ahead." The same day, with Lyndon still in the lead, another O'Daniel confidant said privately: "The election of O'Daniel is in the bag." [101]

Their confidence rested on knowing how many votes they needed to win and how to get them after the polls were closed. During the campaign, Johnson and his principal advisers had taken pains to assure the support of the San Antonio machine and the south Texas political bosses, the Knaggs boys in the Winter Garden area, the Guerra brothers in Starr County, Ed Vela, the mayor of Hidalgo, E. B. Reyna in the La Joya district, Judge Bravo, Sheriff Sanchez, and Manuel Cuellar in Zapata County, Judge Raymond in Webb County, and the best-known of the south Texas bosses, George Parr, the Duke of Duval County, as he was called. J. C. Looney, an attorney in the south Texas area along the Rio Grande known as "The Valley," was Johnson's district manager for the region. In the Valley, Looney said, "you had a good deal of what you might call bloc-voting . . . areas where a comparatively few people were able to influence a substantial number of voters in a statewide race." Indeed, the Valley was notorious for selling its votes to the highest bidder, with the buyer usually receiving over 90 percent of the ballots. In 1941, the Johnson campaign outbid O'Daniel, who had carried the area in 1940. Horace Guerra assured Lyndon that he could "depend on my and my friends' wholehearted support. I predict Starr County will give you a substantial majority." [102]

It did. The question for the Johnson campaign on election day was not whether it would win the south Texas vote but when to report it. Usually waiting to see how much they needed from the Valley to offset an opponent's advantage in another area, a candidate commonly instructed south Texas machines to hold back the count until other parts of the state had reported. Johnson, however, wanted the Valley votes "in early so it would look like he was leading." It was a mistake. "As soon as they all reported," John Connally said later, "the opposition knew our total. The thing began to erode. . . . It was a question of the opposition *knowing*." [103]

On Sunday, the 29th, with some 18,000 rural east Texas votes still to be counted, the anti-O'Daniel beer and liquor interests conspired with fifteen state senators to put enough of these ballots in O'Daniel's column to give him the election. In these east Texas counties, where initial results had shown a plurality for Dies, O'Daniel suddenly became the leading vote-getter. Once it was clear that Dies could not win, Ferguson's and Stevenson's allies in the area shifted some of the Dies's votes to O'Daniel. In a confidential analysis of the vote that pollster Joe Belden sent John Connally on July 11, he described O'Daniel's "sudden jump in the late returns" as "somewhat unnatural; every trend measured by the surveys for two months before the election . . . pointed to a Johnson victory." A post-election survey of east Texas voters by Belden revealed "an amazing change of votes" from the reported count, especially from Dies to O'Daniel. In Angelina County, for example, where election officials reported Dies and O'Daniel with 44 and 34 percent of the vote respectively, Belden's post-election survey of voters showed that the count should have been 52 percent for Dies and only 22 percent for O'Daniel. The fraudulent returns did the job. By Monday night, June 30, Lyndon's lead had fallen to 77 votes and by Tuesday evening O'Daniel held a 1,095-vote advantage.[104]

When the Johnson campaign heard what was happening, they tried to find effective counter measures. Governor Jimmy Allred was the first to report the news: "I'm listening to the radio," he told Carroll Keach over the telephone. "They're stealing this election in East Texas!" After a conference with his principal staff people, Johnson called George Parr in Duval to see if he could send in more votes. But official returns had already been reported from south Texas and neither Parr nor anyone else in the Valley would risk trying to alter the result.[105]

The Johnson camp then appealed to Roosevelt for help. On Monday evening, June 30, the President, who was in Hyde Park, "got an intimation," as he told some reporters the next day, " . . . that Lyndon Johnson's friends were all 'het up' because the—there is such a thing, you know,—this is off the record—of withholding returns. I don't of course say what the motive is, but Texas law has been withholding the returns." When a reporter pointed out that 18,000 to 20,000 votes were still out, Roosevelt said "that steps are being taken to police it. Is that a polite word? You had better find out from Washington, but the intimation last night is that they were going to police the thing." "State police?" one of the reporters asked, and they all laughed. In fact, the Administration was sending in the FBI to intimidate county judges and force an honest return from East Texas that would allow Lyndon to hold on to his lead. Johnson "thinks that if the ballots are honestly counted and reported from the non-Johnson counties," Ickes noted in his diary, "Johnson will turn out the winner after all. To throw the fear of the Lord into some of the politically minded and not over-scrupulous county judges who are in charge of the election machinery in Texas, some FBI men have been sent into the State. They are going to scrutinize the returns and ask the county judges to explain the great reversal in the delayed vote returns."[106]

The tactic failed, however. The investigation didn't get off the ground until July 3, two days after the result had been turned in O'Daniel's favor. Moreover, under pressure to report quickly, the agents were unable to be very thorough in sorting out the facts in twenty-four counties or do much about getting records of any long-distance telephone calls Coke Stevenson and three other alleged conspirators made on June 29 and 30. Consequently, after only six days, the investigation turned up no evidence of a conspiracy or agreement to violate Federal election laws. To be sure, the investigators found that many people without poll tax receipts were permitted to vote and that in rural communities election officials counted "incomplete" and "mutilated" ballots, but that "no evidence of any unlawful intent on the part of any election officials" counting these ballots had been disclosed. Having failed to inhibit altered returns for O'Daniel by this preliminary investigation, the Johnson campaign opposed the suggestion of doing more. Lyndon told his staff that he did not want to contest the election. Worried that an evenhanded inquiry would reveal the many violations of campaign finance and elections laws by his supporters, Lyndon told his brother, " 'I hope they don't investigate *me.*' " His objective was to survive to fight another day.[107]

He put the best possible face on his defeat. Lady Bird remembered how he looked when he walked off to catch a plane for Washington, "very jaunty, and putting extra verve into his step. His head was high, and he was stepping along real spryly. I know how much nerve and effort were now required for him to keep up that courageous appearance." In fact, he was "in a very black mood," and even Roosevelt could not cheer him up. The President "kidded the hell out of him": " 'Lyndon, up in New York the first thing they taught us was to sit on the ballot boxes.' " What partly kept him going was the thought of another go round: "Did you ever see a shooting gallery with its circular, rotating discs with lots of pipes and rabbits on the circuit?" he asked Tommy Corcoran. "Well, when you miss one the first time, you get a second chance. And the sonofabitch who trimmed you will always come up again. And then you can get him." [108]

The elections of 1940 and 1941 had reminded Lyndon that Texas and national politics were not for the fainthearted. The violations of campaign finance laws and ballot box manipulations were hardly revelations to him. But the 1940 House victories and the 1941 Senate defeat had convinced him as never before that politics was a dirty business in which a willingness to be more unprincipled than your opponents was a requirement for success. It was a lesson which would have echoes throughout the rest of his political career. Likewise, the fact that his identification with FDR as a new South politician had gone far to give him an edge over O'Daniel strongly impressed itself on him. The popularity of Roosevelt's domestic and defense programs in Texas was something he filed away for use in a future state-wide race.

8

Politics, Patriotism, and Personal Gain

LYNDON described the months after his defeat as "the most miserable in his life. I felt terribly rejected, and I began to think about leaving politics and going home to make money." To cheer him up, friends echoed his own hope that his "day of triumph" was "only delayed." Senator Claude Pepper of Florida wired him: "I know what has happened and why it has happened. But I know too that the people will avenge their wrongs. You can count on that." While thoughts of eventually serving in the Senate buoyed him, Lyndon saw more immediate and larger reasons to get back into political harness after the Senate race. "In the end, I just couldn't bear to leave Washington," he later told Doris Kearns, "where at least I still had my seat in the House. Besides, with all those war clouds hanging over Europe, I felt that someone with all my training and preparedness was bound to be an important figure." [1]

In the summer of 1941 he believed it essential for the United States to enter the war. Like 85 percent of the American public, Johnson saw recent British defeats in the Balkans, North Africa, and the Atlantic as compelling U.S. participation. But unlike most Americans, who remained ambivalent about fighting, Johnson thought it imperative to enter the conflict as soon as possible or before it was too late to aid Britain. Where some Americans saw Hitler's invasion of the Soviet Union on June 22 as easing the need for U.S. involvement, Johnson called it further evidence of America's need to combat Nazi plans for world conquest. Political considerations were also part of Johnson's thinking. Because preparedness was an issue on which most Texans agreed, Lyndon intended to put it at the center of a 1942 campaign against O'Daniel. [2]

During the summer Lyndon was reluctant to see the President about another Senate race. "When I came back up here," he wrote Jimmy Allred in early August, "I did not call the President. I felt that I had written too many checks on my rather wobbly account. I had overdrawn, and I did not want a check to bounce back in my face." He had, however, sent Roosevelt a note of appreciation in late July saying that he had been "glad to be called a watercarrier" for the President during his Texas campaign: "I would be glad to carry a bucket of water to the Commander-in Chief any time his thirsty throat or his thirsty soul needed support, for you certainly gave me support nonpariel. One who cannot arise to your leadership shall find the fault in himself and not in you!"

Although Roosevelt shared Johnson's disappointment at losing the Senate seat to O'Daniel, the President continued to see Johnson as a valuable ally with a rosy political future. "General Watson, I want to see Lyndon," Roosevelt scrawled on Johnson's note of July 21. Their meeting on July 30, ten days before FDR met British Prime Minister Winston Churchill at the Atlantic Conference off Newfoundland, "was probably the happiest half-hour I ever spent with" the President, Lyndon wrote Allred. Roosevelt said "he was happy about the campaign—he thought we had actually won a major victory," and they "discussed plans which he [FDR] brought up." In response to Jim Rowe's recommendation, Roosevelt asked Lyndon to be the keynote speaker at a national convention of Young Democrats in late August in Louisville, Kentucky. FDR, who would also speak there, wanted to focus the meeting on foreign affairs and national defense. Johnson could help set the meeting's agenda. At thirty-two, he was still "a Young Democrat" and his speech would be " 'right' on foreign policy." Indeed, as Lyndon remembered the episode twenty-four years later, the President told him, "I have already prepared your speech for you."[3]

They also discussed the selective service law. In September 1940 the Administration had persuaded Congress to enact the first peacetime draft in American history. Attacked by isolationists as certain to put American boys in foreign wars and "slit the throat of the last great democracy still living," the law had put Roosevelt on the defensive in his 1940 presidential campaign. Although the required year's service from 900,000 men could hardly be a prelude to offensive action, Roosevelt had felt compelled to justify the program as "defensive preparation and defensive preparation only." In June 1941, Roosevelt had concluded that the national security required an extension of service by selectees for the duration of the emergency. On July 21, he had sent a strongly worded recommendation to Congress warning against the "tragic error" of allowing the "disintegration" of America's comparatively small army. With an opinion poll showing that only 51 percent of the public supported extended military service and the Senate approving only an eighteen-month extension or a maximum thirty-month tour of duty, the Administration faced a hard fight in the House. "In forty years on the Hill," one congressional secretary reported, "he had never seen such fear of a bill." Organized opposition to extension brought trainloads of demonstrators to Washington, who picketed on Capitol Hill and packed the House gallery. Draftees complaining that a solemn promise was being broken scrawled OHIO on latrine walls—Over the Hill in October.[4]

Roosevelt asked Lyndon's help with the Selective Service bill. Johnson urged him to have Secretary of State Cordell Hull, a former member of Congress who enjoyed "enormous good will there and enormous private respect," make the final appeal. Lyndon became one of Rayburn's principal lieutenants in a sharply contested fight. On August 8, four days before a vote, Lyndon made an emotional appeal on the House floor. Breaking a habit of not making extended on-the-record remarks, Lyndon said: "I am confident that, at this time, every American knows his country is an island in a world of danger. . . . If we vote down this proposal . . . we will . . . send two-thirds of our present Army home. . . . It is just reaching a point where we may begin to think of it as approaching adequacy." He urged his colleagues not to sell out the welfare of the United States for the sake of a few votes.[5]

Yet despite Lyndon's urgings and more formidable appeals from Secretary of War Henry Stimson, Secretary of the Navy Frank Knox, Hull, and the country's military chiefs, the House remained closely divided. The President, who had secretly left Washington for his meeting with Churchill, was unavailable for last-minute appeals to wavering congressmen. The burden fell on Sam Rayburn, who wielded an iron fist to drive the bill through the House by one vote. Using a parliamentary maneuver to freeze a vulnerable 203 to 202 majority, Rayburn, in the words of one journalist, "literally played the role of dictator within the framework of representative government, for the safety and good of the government itself."[6]

Lyndon saw the episode as a good example of how American politics really worked, as opposed to textbook depictions of democracy. Political candidates trying to gain or hold office, or a government uncertain about majority support for policies serving the national security, ignored the democratic niceties and simply did what needed to be done. Democrats trying to keep control of Congress in 1940, Pappy O'Daniel fighting to win a Senate seat, and Rayburn determined to sustain the draft in 1941 bent existing rules to get their way. It all reinforced Lyndon's thinking that his own transgressions in 1937 and again in 1940–41 were no more—indeed were less—than what other high officials did to win a political fight. He noted the lesson for future use.

After the victory in the House, Lyndon took to the stump to alert the country to foreign dangers. On August 21, in his speech before the Young Democrats, he issued an appeal for selfless sacrifice in behalf of democratic beliefs. "Shall we, the young who must fight this war and live the peace to come afterwards, passively become a part of a Nazi empire? . . . Shall we submit to Nazi slavery, or will our American youth demand the perpetuation of this free government?" He described German youth as "fired from childhood with Nazi zeal," and he urged America's young people to align themselves with equal passion behind American ideals. The time had come for them to preach "the gospel of winning this war now" and arranging "a peace of liberty and justice" afterward. "It is *your* war and it will be *your* peace," he concluded. "I call you now to both flags." Lyndon repeated the message throughout the fall in central Texas. He complained that American industry was devoting only one out of every eight hours to war production and that too many workers were short-changing the national interest by going on strike. He predicted that the country would eventually have to get into the fighting and that the time for all-out preparedness was now.[7]

Lyndon's support of a defense buildup served not only the national interest but also his personal political ends. He effectively publicized the millions of dollars he helped bring into the state for Army camps and defense plants. "It is essential for small Texas manufacturing plants to have a share in defense production not only because maximum production is needed for this country's protection," he told Texas editors in a news release, "but in order to bolster those firms which have been producing only for civilian needs. . . . Texas not only wants to do everything it can for defense, but it foresees the need for preserving and expanding its manufacturing plants for normal demands of the future." Lyndon's appeal resonated across the South. Where before 1941 southern state governments saw white supremacy and social stability as their primary goals, after that, encouraged by a Roosevelt administration which saw the war partly as a chance to transform the southern economy, business and industrial development became their central purpose.

Lyndon also scored political points in Texas by pressing for higher oil prices. In a memorandum that went to the Office of Price Administration, he argued that a ten-cent rise in a barrel of oil to $1.25 "would have very slight, if any, effect on the retail market," but would encourage exploration to meet the sharply increased demands coming from the army, navy, and Lend-Lease programs. Because they lacked incentive, U.S. oil producers had supplied only 2.5 of the 4 billion barrels used during the last three years. Unless they received a greater return, the oil companies would not increase production, and the country faced the possibility that it would run out of gas in the middle of the emergency.[8]

Support of defense spending and high oil prices was partly a prelude to another Senate race against O'Daniel. Pappy had made himself vulnerable to attack by opposing draft extension and a more active American role abroad. Throughout the summer and fall people close to Lyndon assumed that he would run again in 1942. "Your real friends in Texas are taking it for granted that you will be a candidate for the Senate next year and are now getting set for the campaign," Willard Deason wrote him at the end of July. Lyndon did nothing to discourage the idea. He discussed possible campaign strategies with supporters and encouraged Texas newspaper accounts that he was running.[9]

He also worked through Jim Rowe to assure continued White House backing. In September, Rowe told Lyndon about a pollster who could "break down your [Texas] counties by precincts, [and] . . . show where you have to do your work next year." Shortly after, when Gerald Mann tried to see the President, Roosevelt refused until he met again with Lyndon Johnson. When Roosevelt saw Lyndon, they discussed "the picture in Texas and the real friends of the Administration that have always gone to . . . bat when needed." Further, at the end of the month, when Governor Coke Stevenson was about to see the President, Lyndon sent word through Rowe that Stevenson had "long been anti-Administration" and was "a personally pleasant Bourbon." Johnson "hoped you could give Stevenson some indication that he, Lyndon, is still *persona grata* at the White House." Roosevelt, who was troubled by complaints from friendly senators and congressmen that the Administration was ignoring them and that he needed to improve relations with the Hill, did nothing to alienate one of his strongest supporters in the House. On December 6, Lyndon asked FDR for another appointment to discuss "His own future as to where he can best serve the President" and the "Congressional elections in Texas."[10]

While holding open the possibility that he would run, Lyndon was uncertain. "I do not have any idea what my personal plans are and do not plan to come to any definite conclusion immediately," he wrote on November 30. "I haven't any plans for the summer as yet but am going to continue sending out [press] releases periodically," he told a journalist in Corpus Christi two days later.[11]

His ambition for the Senate seat had in no way diminished, but he saw reasons to avoid another campaign in 1942. John Connally, who was practicing law in Texas, advised him that some of your supporters would not "go all out" in another race next year. Johnson replied: "I could hardly expect . . . anyone . . . to go as all-out as they did for me last time. It costs too much aside from there being the great personal strain." He also thought it would be difficult to raise the money for the campaign. Charles Marsh tried to persuade him that a successful race could be made with only $25,000. But Lyndon was unconvinced.[12]

He was also wary about exposing himself and Lady Bird to what Connally called "a smear campaign . . . principally from O'Daniel sources."

Connally advised him that he would be attacked for having used insider information to let Lady Bird make $75,000 in a stock deal and for letting his campaign take a questionable contribution from United Mine Workers president John L. Lewis. Lyndon denied that there were "stock deals or any other kind of deals." But he expected another contest with O'Daniel to produce charges and countercharges about 1941 that might damage both of them.[13]

More important, a Senate race would jeopardize his long-term political career. If he ran against O'Daniel in 1942, he would have to give up his House seat and risk not winning it back in 1944. As he told Austin Postmaster Ray Lee in the fall of 1941, "I think our very future is at stake. . . . Like a great many other Congressmen, we are degenerating. The thing that has put us where we are has fallen off. We are short on accomplishments, on contacts." Despite rules against partisan politics by postal employees, Lyndon wanted Lee to spend some time with Connally and Wirtz "and particularly with the people out in the ten counties, and we will start rebuilding again." In December, when Connally told him that O'Daniel "will be much harder to unseat than it was to defeat him for the unexpired term," Lyndon largely abandoned plans for another Senate race in the following year.[14]

The Japanese attack on Pearl Harbor on December 7 and American involvement in the fighting largely shifted Johnson's focus from politics to winning the war. "Until this war is won and the evil forces of dictators are crushed, Americans will have no time for politics," he wrote a Texas friend on December 17. This was partly rhetoric on Johnson's part. His political future never totally left his mind, as his wartime actions demonstrate. Nevertheless, the surprise attack on the United States made him boil with patriotic fervor. "I'm glad the Japs have struck," he declared in a public statement on December 8. "Our job is now clear. . . . All one hundred thirty million of us will be needed to answer the sunrise stealth, the Sabbath Day Assassins."[15]

Lyndon had already prepared to serve the country by obtaining a commission as a U.S. Naval Reserve. In the spring of 1940, when Nazi victories in Europe made it seem that the United States might eventually be drawn into the war, he applied for a commission. Although he "had not trained a day to qualify for it," as he told Harold Young, and had several physical problems—chronic tonsilitis and sinusitis, a kidney ailment, and skin rashes brought on by nervous tension—he received his naval appointment as a lieutenant commander. A paucity of volunteers and connections with high Navy Department officials facilitated his request. Walter Jenkins recalls that James Forrestal, a Wall Street investment banker who became Under Secretary of the Navy in August 1940, recruited Lyndon. Forrestal "came to our office and told Mr. Johnson that he would like to see him take a commission in the naval reserve, that they needed young, able, aggressive men. Mr. Johnson indicated an interest in it, although the application was a major job." Jenkins filled it out, and the Navy promptly granted Lyndon's request. John Connally and Jenkins then also were offered commissions, though Jenkins refused his and was later drafted into the army as a private.[16]

Following Pearl Harbor, Lyndon, remembering his promise during the 1941 campaign, "urgently" asked the President to assign him "immediately to active duty with the Fleet." Although he became one of the first members of Congress to enter the armed services, he had no preparation for combat and the navy refused to assign him to a warship. Warren Magnuson, Lyndon's colleague on the Naval Affairs Committee, who was also a Naval Reserve officer, was given the same response to his request for sea duty. Magnuson, however, appealed to Carl Vinson, who persuaded the navy that the Naval Affairs Committee would profit from having a member with combat experience. Magnuson served for five months on an aircraft carrier that participated in battles off the Solomon Islands.

Lyndon did not appeal the navy's decision but chose instead "to work on production and manpower problems" that were slowing the output of ships and planes. Forrestal assigned him to the Under Secretary's office, where he took responsibility for war production in Texas and on the West Coast. It was an assignment for which he was well qualified. Columbia University professor J. W. Barker, Forrestal's assistant for labor problems, considered Lyndon a godsend. Barker described him as "just the man to be assigned as my assistant." He thought that Johnson could attend to "employment problems, labor-market situations, pre-employment training programs . . . on-the-job and up-grading training" facing navy contractors in the Southwest and West. "Thank God for our wisdom in grabbing Lyndon Johnson to work in the Navy. He's going to be a grand 'goad' stuck into everyone's side including me," Barker said. "He's a live-wire of the first water."[17]

After Pearl Harbor, bottlenecks in the production of warships, troop transports, and merchantmen jeopardized the war effort. During the second half of 1941, despite plans for expansion, fewer navy and cargo ships were produced than in the first half of the year. When the President delivered his State of the Union message to Congress on January 6, 1942, he stressed the need to strain every existing arms-producing facility to the maximum, asking, for example, that merchant ships increase nearly sixfold from 1.1 million tons in 1941 to 6 million tons in 1942 and to 10 million tons in 1943. A lack of transports that would inhibit major troop movements for the next two years informed the President's goals. Similarly, shortages of skilled labor and the inefficient use of available manpower created production tieups that plagued the country throughout the nearly four years of fighting.[18]

Characteristically, Johnson threw himself into his war work with unbridled energy. For four months beginning at the end of December he spent most of his time traveling in Texas, California, and the state of Washington, trying to assess the labor needs of war production plants and to suggest answers to their problems. Everywhere he went he found a variety of administrative and technical difficulties that reflected what he saw as a deeper problem, namely, that Americans weren't yet sure what the war was about: "The fact that they don't *know* is in evidence in every plane plant—on every ship way," he wrote Sam Rayburn in February. "Their physical appearance shows lack of understanding. Their lack of mental concern is evident on every facial expression. Their complacency, indifference, and bewilderment are an open invitation to direction of some sort." In particular, Johnson complained of a division of authority that immobilized attempts to get the most from available resources. "The word 'conference' is coming to mean lost man hours," he said in a memo. "Conferences between agency heads, conferences between division heads, conferences with advisory committees, conferences with special groups—conferences with minority groups, conferences of Regional Labor Supply Committees—local conferences, state conferences, regional conferences, national conferences—too damn many conferences. It is time to quit 'conferring' and to go to work. Decision must replace indecision. Action must replace inaction. The road to hell is paved with indecision and inaction. Results are the only things that count in a crisis, and that is where we are *today—now.*"[19]

To give substance to his words, Lyndon formulated a series of proposals that could assure the availability of sufficient numbers of trained workers for war production. At a meeting with officials of the Lockheed Aircraft Corporation in Burbank, California, on January 4, 1942, for instance, he gave what one participant described as "a brilliant (I mean it) symposium of factors in the procurement of an adequate labor supply for defense industries." His general answer to the problem was to create a single Man-Power Agency that would recruit and supply men not only to the armed forces but also to all war industries. Recalling his experience in the NYA, he also suggested the appointment of a national director and forty-eight state directors responsible for war-worker training.[20]

As for the navy itself, he emphasized the need to identify where it would find sufficient numbers of workers to staff jobs in navy yards and how to make them more productive. He proposed that laborers be drawn from pre-draft-age men, men with dependents who would not be called, men deferred because of physical disabilities, and women who could not only do clerical jobs but also work on assembly lines and in repair shops as well as or even better than men. Productivity of these workers could "be astonishingly increased" if the navy were to set up a "Job Production Analysis Division" and "the best plant production specialists in this country should be drafted for it." Johnson also proposed that the National Youth Administration and the Civilian Conservation Corps be merged into a single agency that would set up War Work Centers to train 150,000 youngsters every ninety days for jobs in navy yards.[21]

Though some of Lyndon's proposals, particularly on the NYA and CCC, found a ready response from the Administration and the navy, his frustrations trying to provide effective answers to the navy's labor and production problems outran his successes. His old friends Arthur and Elizabeth Goldschmidt remember a Sunday morning visit from him during a trip back to Washington, D.C. "He had an absolute sure-fire solution to the West Coast labor trouble. . . . He strode up and down our living room trying to sell me his solution." When Arthur told him it wasn't "worth a tinker's dam," he exploded: "Oh, you're just a goddamned radical." When Elizabeth told him that his idea had been tried and had failed in England and that someone who had just been in England to look at the matter was in town, he immediately called his hotel and went off to see him. However frustrated that his brainstorm was imperfect, he was instantly off and running "to find the solution, not his solution, but a solution" to the problem.[22]

Above all, he was convinced that if he had enough authority, he could spark the enthusiasm and find the organizational means to meet the President's war production goals. Although he got in to see the President at the end of January 1942, it brought no change in his position. At the end of February, he complained to one of Forrestal's aides that he saw "great need [everywhere] of positiveness, leadership, and direction. There is much that I should be doing that I am not. One does not function well without authority and responsibility. When and if you or the Boss [Forrestal] run into a problem that requires energy, determination, and a modicum of experience give me the word." And in handwriting, he added: "I need more work."[23]

It was not more work but *more important* work that he wanted. In early March he wrote FDR's secretary Grace Tully from San Francisco: "Things are very dull here with me. How I yearn for activity and an assignment where I can be reasonably productive. I hope sometime you run across something that you think I can do well 24 hrs. per day." Alvin Wirtz had tried to get it for him. Wirtz had raised the matter with Roosevelt's aide "Pa" Watson during a conversation in February: "Watson does have in mind that you should be more active in Washington, and I suggested that you be made Admiral and given the same comparative job in the Navy that [William S.] Knudsen has in the Army." A former president of General Motors and a member of the Office of Production Management which Roosevelt had set up early in 1941 to spur industrial mobilization, Knudsen was made a lieutenant general and charged with expediting output for the army. "I can appreciate how you feel and how much you would like to get more power to get things done," Wirtz also told Lyndon, "but I am doubtful whether it would be altogether advisable for you to be called into the White House before summer and before you have seen more active service. All of us have to do the things we can do, and we can't all be Roosevelts and Mac-Arthurs." [24]

In seeking a larger arena for his talents, Lyndon hoped to serve his political interests as well as the war effort. He and Wirtz believed that a future successful bid for higher office would partly depend on a record of significant war service. "I think that Johnson would be more useful in Congress than in the Navy," Harold Ickes wrote in his diary on December 14, 1941, "but he feels—probably somewhat for political reasons—that he ought to take this step." After Jonathan Daniels, a journalist and aide to the President, met Lyndon for a drink at the Carlton Hotel in Washington in the spring of 1942, he concluded that Johnson was "an energetic and intelligent Texas Congressman . . . [who] wants for sake of political future to get into danger zone[,] though realizes talents best suited for handling speakers and public relations." [25]

His departure for the navy, however, created a problem about his immediate political prospects. It was clear to him and Wirtz and Connally that it would be very difficult, if not impossible, for him to run for the Senate seat while he was in the service. Charles Marsh thought otherwise, but he was in a distinct minority among Johnson's friends, and during the first three months of 1942 Lyndon had concluded that he would do well just to hold on to his House seat. When he left for the navy, he had not resigned from Congress but taken a leave of absence approved by the House. His dilemma was to convince Tenth District voters that he should be continued in office despite being on indefinite leave in the service. His fertile political imagination produced a highly successful answer to the problem. He brought Lady Bird in to run the congressional office. They "believed that the people of the District would feel a closer bond to their Congressman if his wife [rather than some staff person] served as 'a kind of liason' between them," Lady Bird said later. Lyndon urged her to talk to anyone who called the office, to "watch the hotels for people from Texas whom you should call; read every paper for births, deaths, weddings, for a letter over your signature," and "find something to send all of our editors every ten days or two weeks over your signature." "If you could spend all day in the office," Lyndon wrote her from the West Coast, "it wouldn't be long until we would be invincible. Think of the effect it would have if 2,000 of our best friends in the District had personal notes from you written at the rate of 25 a day for sixty days." [26]

After Lady Bird had done the job for four months, Lyndon and Wirtz were convinced that she could be elected if he didn't run. But Lyndon's preference was to have the district draft him for another term. He, Wirtz, and Lady Bird arranged for Mayor Tom Miller and Jake Pickle, who left a job at the NYA, to get 75 percent of district voters to sign petitions asking that Lyndon place his name on the ballot and that Lady Bird "be the acting Congressman while her husband was off in war." Although Pickle and other campaign workers quickly concluded that it would take too long to reach the 75 percent goal, they managed to get 20,000 of the almost 40,000 Democratic voters in the district to sign in just a month's time. Lady Bird's effective management of the office and the strong showing in the petition campaign assured Lyndon an uncontested victory in the summer primary.[27]

It also freed him to seek the larger role in the war that he believed could serve both the nation and himself. In March he tried to arrange appointments with the President and Harry Hopkins, who had become the Lend Lease Administrator, to discuss "where I go and what I do after I get back that way." But nothing could be set up until late April. This frustrated him and Charles Marsh, who wrote him: "Get your ass out of this country at once where there is danger, and then get back as soon as you can to real work. If you can't sell the Navy on ordering you out, you are not as good as I think you are." The last week of April, Lyndon got in to see Thomas McCabe, one of Hopkins's aides, and then the President at the White House on the 26th. "Lyndon Johnson is anxious to get out some place where the bombs are dropping," McCabe wrote Hopkins. "Do you have any reactions on the desirability of trying to get him detailed from the Navy to Lend-Lease, giving him a cram course here and then shipping him out to the Lend-Lease Mission in Australia?"[28]

Before Hopkins could answer, the President gave Lyndon an assignment to his liking. According to handwritten notes Lyndon made of his conversation with FDR, the President first discussed the manpower situation and said: "We must have a young man who will attend. Want you to represent Navy and stand up and fight for me. Have talked to Jim Forrestal who will attend first meeting and then quit going. You will then sit with boards." Roosevelt next told him: "Will send you to Southwest Pacific on job for me re our men there. We may need to take additional steps for their health and happiness. You won't need to stay at Pearl Harbor but a couple of days then you can go to Australia New Zealand etc.—I'll get word to Jim." Finally, they discussed "Congressional Campaign: We agreed—1. Person must be his man but selected by Rayburn, McCormack et al.; 2. gen. education campaign; 3. No open telegrams and endorsements. Nothing until you return from Southwest Pacific." Number 1 referred to the person who would run against O'Daniel in the party primary; 2 related to the 1942 congressional elections; and 3 indicated the President's intention to avoid a public role in the campaign and to refrain from assigning behind-the-scenes activities of the sort carried on in 1940 until Lyndon came back from his mission.[29]

It is difficult to know what Roosevelt intended in sending Johnson to the Southwest Pacific. It simply may have been his way of accommodating Lyndon's wishes. But he also could have wanted a firsthand report from a loyal subordinate on the state of morale among America's fighting men in the area. When they talked in late April, Allied fortunes against the Japanese were at low ebb. Guam and Wake Island, Burma, the Philippines, the Malay Peninsula, including Singapore, the Dutch East Indies, and some of New Guinea and the Solomon Islands had fallen, or were about to fall to Japanese arms. The victories opened Australia, New Zealand, and India to invasion and put Japan on the verge of what Roosevelt called "a dominating position from which it would prove most difficult to eject her." Despite promises of help to General MacArthur, first in the Philippines and then in Australia, where he had taken command of all Allied forces in the Southwest Pacific in March, Roosevelt had found it impossible to send men and materiel in the numbers MacArthur had requested. By sending Lyndon Johnson, Roosevelt may have been offering MacArthur and his staff a small gesture of concern to help sustain morale until desperately needed aid could begin to arrive in the region.[30]

Whatever Roosevelt intended, Lyndon aimed to get firsthand information on America's fighting men in the Pacific and a taste of combat that tested his courage and gave him something to advertise in future political campaigns. Bryce Harlow, who was on General George C. Marshall's staff in 1942, remembered that Lyndon was one of four congressmen in the service for whom he arranged "a special escort through a combat area. . . . So then they would be veterans who had served in combat, so they could approach the voters unassailably the following election year. It was really, of course, a political charade."

But it was more than that. In the midst of an unbroken string of military reverses inflicted on the United States by Japan, America's ability to stem and reverse the tide deeply concerned Johnson. George Brown remembered him at the time as "very worried about our fortunes over there . . . very alarmed." Although the political gain from getting close to the action was a central consideration with Lyndon, he also hoped to advance the war effort by assessing conditions on the front line.

The mission had an air of unreality to it. His destination was MacArthur's headquarters in Melbourne, Australia, where he would learn about army and army air force, not naval, activities. Moreover, he had no military expertise to make competent judgments on the nature of MacArthur's efforts in the Southwest Pacific. As Jonathan Daniels noted when he saw him on the eve of his mission, "Slim and curly-haired, joking and laughing, he looked less like the conventional portrait of a congressman than the equally conventional picture of a movie actor in seagoing costume. I left him to go to realism in the White House." Home movies made with a 16 mm camera during the trip by Lyndon underscores Daniels's impression of a handsome young congressman playing a role. The mission was a temporary exposure to danger calculated to satisfy Johnson's personal and political wishes, but it also represented a genuine effort on his part, however misplaced, to improve the lot of America's fighting men.[31]

Leaving Washington, D.C., on May 2, it took him six days to reach Honolulu. He stayed there for five days waiting to fly to Auckland, New Zealand, with Vice Admiral Robert L. Ghormley, who was to command a force preparing an attack on the Solomon Islands. An eight-day journey through Palmyra Island, Canton Island, Suva in the Fiji Islands, and Noumea on New Caledonia to Auckland initiated Johnson's survey of American forces in Pacific outposts. On the last leg of the trip he met Lt. Col Samuel E. Anderson and Lt. Col. Francis R. Stevens of the Operations and Plans Division of the War Department General Staff in Washington. Anderson was Army Air Force and responsible for air-planning in the Southwest Pacific, and Stevens was U.S. Army and charged with ground-force operations. They were on their way to MacArthur's headquarters in Melbourne and a look at front-line conditions in New Guinea. They rode with Johnson on Ghormley's plane from Noumea to New Zealand. After learning about their respective missions, they agreed to carry out their assignments "almost as a team."[32]

After three days in Auckland, they flew to Melbourne, where they saw MacArthur on May 25. MacArthur was less than pleased by the visit: "What did you want to see me about?" he asked Johnson after shaking hands. "I have a message from the President," Lyndon replied. MacArthur was unimpressed. He told the two colonels: "There might have been a reason, but"—he said turning to Johnson—"God only knows what you're doing here."[33]

A four-page memo Johnson subsequently made of the conversation reflected a very different tone. He described MacArthur as "the number one hero of World War II," and as "extremely cordial and, I think, glad that we came." MacArthur was "immaculately attired—medals and all." He promised to help them "see all," and then treated them to a two hour-and-ten-minute exposition unequaled in Johnson's experience: "Perfect organization, a forceful presentation, and a rhetoric most pleasing, colorful, and descriptive." Beginning with a summary of Australian conditions, MacArthur depicted the country as "totally unprepared to face war—even more unprepared than our beloved country." Their soldiers lacked discipline and were led by a former chief of police of Melbourne, who was not a professional soldier. The Australians also had a distinct lack of air power and plans were being made to utilize the country's capacity for plane production. As for America's military capacity, on which he dwelled at length, he explained that the Japanese had "progressed at will and taken what they wanted because of only one thing: [Our] Inadequate Sea Power." Specifically, military gains in the region depended on heavy ships supported by air cover. "Why do we have some of our best carriers in the Atlantic? Why is [British] Admiral [James] Somerville with three carriers and several battleships in the Indian Ocean instead of here with us?" MacArthur also stressed the lack of planes sent to his command, with inadequate provisions for repairs and replacements. These limitations compelled his troops to be more a defensive than an offensive force. American ground forces consisted of only two unseasoned divisions with limited training.[34]

MacArthur's concerns were echoed by his staff, all of whom were ordered to give *"Congressman*—not Lieutenant Commander—Johnson . . . VIP treatment."* Evidence of MacArthur's directive was reflected in the fact that William F. Marquat, a brigadier general, was assigned to escort three officers of distinctly subordinate rank. Sometime at the start of his month-long visit to Australia, Johnson convinced MacArthur, through conversations with his subordinates, that he shared his perspective and could be a useful spokesman in Washington for the warnings the General had been sending that a continuing dearth of men and supplies in the southwest Pacific forestalled effective resistance to the Japanese and threatened the safety of Australia. Roosevelt's commitment to a Europe- or Atlantic-first strategy could not fully withstand the effectiveness of the Japanese and MacArthur's pressure. By the end of 1942, contrary to Washington's fundamental war plans, nine of the seventeen army divisions and nineteen of the sixty-six air groups that had gone abroad were in the Pacific.[35]

As he toured the region, hearing and witnessing the military problems facing United States forces, Johnson became a ready convert to Mac-Arthur's viewpoint. Johnson's subsequent comments on conditions in the Southwest Pacific leave no doubt that he saw a genuine need for stepped-up efforts there. But his advocacy of more men and supplies for the area was also a device for convincing MacArthur and his staff to let him participate in a combat mission. If he were to "see personally for the President just what conditions were like," or if he were to make an effective case for MacArthur's demands, he implicitly told Marquat, he needed to take part in a bombing run against the Japanese. Though Marquat himself thought it unwise and warned Johnson about the considerable risks involved, MacArthur's headquarters gave direct orders to let Johnson and his two colleagues from the War Plans Division go on a raid against Japanese forces in Lae, New Guinea, on June 9. They were also given priority over other officers, who were barred from going as observers because of limited space on the planes.[36]

Johnson's insistence on observing the air raid was reckless. The attacks by American B-25 and B-26 medium bombers against Japanese bases in Rabaul on New Britain Island and Lae on New Guinea had cost American air forces heavy casualties in men and planes. Lacking effective fighter cover for the bombers and unable to match the quality of the Japanese Zero fighters and the skill of the Japanese pilots at this early stage of the war, American raiders sometimes lost a quarter of their planes and crews on a mission. The raid on June 9 against Lae consisted of three B-17 heavy bombers attacking from 30,000 feet, followed by twelve B-25s that were to draw off the Zeros at 18,000 feet while twelve B-26s were to drop their bombs from only 10,000 feet. They flew early on the morning of June 9 from Gargutt Field at Townsville in northern Australia to an airfield seven miles outside of Port Moresby, New Guinea. Johnson initially boarded the "Wabash Cannonball," one of the B-26s. Leaving the plane briefly to urinate before they took off, Johnson found his place taken by Colonel Stevens when he returned. He asked the captain of the "Heckling Hare," another B-26, if he could go with him, and was invited aboard. Amazed that Johnson voluntarily came on such a dangerous mission, Harry G. Baren, the tailgunner, told him he was "crazy" and urged him to "do like everybody else does—wait until you get back and get it from intelligence." When Johnson explained that he wanted "to see it for myself," Barens said, "You're nuts. There's no milkruns. You're outa your goddamn mind." [37]

During the one-hour flight to the target Johnson was all over the plane seeing everything he could. As they approached Lae, two dozen Zeros broke off their engagement with the B-25s to attack the B-26s before they made their bombing run. The "Wabash Cannonball" was quickly hit by cannon fire and crashed into the ocean killing Colonel Stevens and the entire crew. A call of nature had saved Lyndon's life. Meanwhile, Lyndon's plane, the "Heckling Hare," had lost power in one engine and couldn't make the final approach to the target. Instead, Walter Greer, the pilot, had to drop out of formation, jettison his bombs, and turn for home. Eight Zeros came after the crippled plane. Going into a weaving, skidding dive to escape the pursuers, Greer managed to keep from being shot down. But not without absorbing hits on the wings and fuselage from the attacking Zeros. As Johnson watched, "cool as a cucumber," according to one crew member, Baren shot down the only Zero destroyed by the bombers on the mission. "It's rough up here, isn't it," Johnson yelled to one of the gunners, who only nodded. When the Zeros broke off the attack, the relief inside the B-26 was enormous. "I sure am glad to be back on this ground," Johnson exclaimed after they landed. "It's been very interesting," he told the crew as he left. He was "as cool as ice," one of them remembered. In bed that night, he had trouble sleeping: "Couldn't get my mind off Steve . . . and other fine boys," he recorded in a diary. [38]

Other adventures marked Johnson's return to Melbourne. On June 10 he flew from Port Moresby to Darwin on the north central coast of Australia to inspect an airbase that had been under repeated attack from the Japanese. Early the next morning the VIP party took off for a flight across the central Australian desert on the way to Melbourne. After four hours of flying, they learned that the navigator's equipment had failed and that they were "completely lost." Despite having three generals and an Australian air marshall aboard, who tried to help, they roamed for four hours. With their fuel running low, they decided on a forced landing. A "very tense" hour followed while the pilot tried to find a clearing with solid ground and no gully or ravine that would smash up the plane and spill his brass all over central Australia. Locating a couple of white houses, where they might be able to get help after landing, the pilot sent all his passengers to the tail of the plane and made a three-point landing at Carris Brook farm, a ranch forty miles from the city of Winton. Greeted by Australian ranchers, Lyndon immediately began "shaking hands all around . . . . Pretty soon he knows all their first names, and they're telling him why there ought to be a high tariff on wool." To his fellow Americans, he described the Australians as "real folks—the best damn folks in the world, except maybe the folks in his own Texas. . . . He swung that county for Johnson before we left," one of the observers noted. After an uncomfortable night and morning with little sleep, plenty of mosquitoes, and no bath, Johnson asked that someone write a song dedicated to him, "I Wish I Were Still on Capitol Hill."[39]

On June 12, they got back to Melbourne and "civilization," where he spent a week. On the 18th he had another meeting with MacArthur. In notes he made later, Johnson described him as "very sad. Head down—Low voice, 'Glad to see you two fellows here where three were last. It was a mistake of the head to [go] on combat mission but it did justice to your heart. It was just what I would have done.'" Colonel Anderson remembered that MacArthur expressed astonishment that Johnson had gone on such a risky mission. When he explained that he wanted to give the President first-hand information and also show his fellow Texans among the airmen he met that he was ready to share the same dangers they faced, MacArthur dropped the subject. After listening to an hour-long report, MacArthur concluded the meeting by announcing that Colonel Stevens was being awarded a Distinguished Service Cross and that Stevens, Anderson, and Johnson would each receive a Silver Star. The other crew members who died on the "Wabash Cannonball" received only Purple Hearts, while Johnson was the only one on the "Heckling Hare" who got a medal for the June 9 mission.[40]

It is difficult not to suspect political backscratching. Lyndon went home with a "war record" and a medal and MacArthur had a new vocal advocate in Washington with some access to the President and more to Congress and the press. Indeed, even before Johnson left Melbourne,

American newspapers carried stories about his participation in the raid on Lae and how he "got a good first-hand idea of the troubles and problems confronting our airmen." [41]

Lyndon was self-conscious about getting a medal. In a draft letter he showed Tommy Corcoran but never sent, he wrote: "My very brief service with these men and its experience of what they do and sacrifice makes me all the more sensitive that I should not accept a citation of recognition for the little part I played for a short time in learning and facing with them the problems they encounter all the time." He left Harold Ickes with the impression in July that he had refused a medal: "MacArthur offered to give a decoration to Johnson but Johnson declined," Ickes noted in his diary after seeing Lyndon.

Yet the temptation to play the hero was too great. Johnson not only kept the medal he also made more of it in future political campaigns than the facts warranted, repeatedly exaggerating what had actually happened. As one journalist later wrote, Johnson's medal was "one of the least deserved but most often displayed Silver Star in American military history." Yet Johnson could at least feel that MacArthur got an instant return for the honor the General bestowed on him. When Robert Sherrod, a correspondent for *Time,* asked Johnson to help him bypass the military censors by carrying an article critical of MacArthur back to his editors, Lyndon agreed. But after reading the story, he never passed it on. [42]

Johnson's return journey to the United States was almost as harrowing as the mission to Lae or the forced landing near Winton. Coming down with a 103.6° fever that forced his hospitalization in Suva for five days, he was delirious part of the time. When he finally reached Pearl Harbor, Admiral Chester Nimitz offered him a seat on his plane going to San Francisco. But Lyndon decided to remain in Honolulu for ten days until July 6. His decision may have saved his life. He later told Ronnie Dugger that Nimitz's plane had turned over in San Francisco Bay and "the Lieutenant who had taken my seat had drowned." [43]

Lyndon was now eager to leave the navy and return to Congress, where he saw important war work. He was sensitive to the political danger in such a move. "There are a good many people who . . . would think it all right for a congressman to give up his seat and to stay in active service," Jesse Kellam wrote him. Lyndon asked Sam Rayburn to assure that his return to Congress would not open him to criticism. In turn, Rayburn convinced FDR to issue a directive placing all members of Congress serving in the Armed Forces "on inactive duty July 1, 1942 . . . except those who wish to remain on active duty for the duration of the war." Under further prodding from Rayburn, FDR revised his order to eliminate the exception. Congressmen and senators who remained in the service had to resign their seats. It guaranteed that the House and the Senate would not operate with fewer members than normal. It also reduced the likelihood that Lyndon would be one of the few congressman in the service returning to the House. "Sam assured me," Lady Bird wrote George Brown "that the orders about members returning, the phrasing of which was so objectionable, have been at Sam's urging changed. They are now quite all right."[44]

Even then, only four of the eight House members in the service decided to return to Washington. Consequently, Lyndon took pains to emphasize how important it was for him to come back. Lyndon wanted Roosevelt to announce that he was placing congressional members on inactive duty because "the Congress at this time has before it a heavy program of vital legislation . . . necessary to a successful war effort, and it is imperative that all members of Congress be available until this program is completed."[45]

Lyndon saw Roosevelt's direct stamp of approval as politically essential. On July 13, three days after he got back to Washington, he asked Grace Tully to get him "a moment with my Boss . . . before the Navy puts me overboard or I resign from Congress." He intended to "sit at home" until he received word of an appointment, "because if I go to the Hill or the [Navy] Department it means a barrage of questions and I do not know what *my* Boss thinks I must do." Getting in to see FDR "off the record" on the 15th, the President agreed with his decision to return to Congress. Even then, Lyndon got Secretary of the Navy Knox to write him a letter saying that "the President has determined that your services to the nation in this critical period are more urgently required in the performance of your duties as a member of the House . . . than as an officer on active duty with the Navy." Lyndon genuinely believed that he would perform more important national service in the House, particularly on industrial mobilization, than in the navy, but he wanted no hint of a suggestion that he had left the fighting and dying to other men. It was a case of both patriotism and politics: more politics than patriotism, to be sure, but the well-being of the country also bulked large in Johnson's concerns.[46]

Once he was back in the House, his first goal was to get word out on problems facing America's fighting men in the Southwest Pacific. "I've seen a lot of unpleasant things in the past few months," he wrote a friend in Texas on the 15th. "We've got a bigger job on our hands than a lot of people think" He tried to make the same point to the President, telling him that the American planes being sent to MacArthur's command were "far inferior" to those flown by the Japanese, that U.S. airmen were reluctant to fly them without improvements, and that officers from the rank of captain up were fighting the war "from the ground or from behind a desk" while inexperienced junior officers were leading squadrons in combat missions. Although Lyndon spent an hour telling

FDR " 'what I could,' " he did not get very far. " 'You know how it is when you are trying to tell something to the President,' " Lyndon told Ickes. " 'He is always trying to tell something to you.' From this I gathered that the President did not have an inquiring mind when he had a chance to get this report from Lyndon," Ickes noted. Having heard more about MacArthur's problems than he cared to, Roosevelt drowned out Lyndon's report with talk of his own.[47]

But Lyndon was determined to be heard. And characteristically, he tried to serve both national and selfish political interests at the same time. He hoped to advance the war effort by publicizing military and civilian problems. He also believed his outspokeness would advance his career. His model was Senator Harry S. Truman of Missouri who in 1941 had become the head of an oversight subcommittee of the Senate Military Affairs Committee. Disturbed by rumors of waste in the rearmament program and complaints from constituents about geographical allocations of defense work that short-changed Missouri contractors, Truman won agreement from fellow senators to look into defense spending. Eager to head off a similar investigation by an unfriendly member of the House, the Administration endorsed Truman's proposal. The committee traveled to army camps around the country to make on-the-spot inquiries and quickly turned up $100 million in waste in the camp-building program.[48]

Truman did not fully come into his own as a national figure until 1943, when he appeared on the cover of *Time* and *Look* named him one of the ten most useful civilians to the war effort in Washington. By the second half of 1942, however, Lyndon and other congressmen saw how much could be gained for the nation and themselves by heading a House version of Truman's committee. When Lyndon approached Sam Rayburn about such an appointment, Rayburn put him off, saying that such an assignment encroached on the preserves of Andrew J. May and Carl Vinson, heads of the Military and Naval Affairs committees.[49]

Rayburn's discouraging response did not deter Lyndon from mounting a private campaign to streamline America's war machine. On July 16, he sent Under Secretary Forrestal a memo about the "critical" need for 6800 additional experienced men if the Pacific Fleet were to operate efficiently. He also provided a twelve-point program for significantly improving the war effort in the Southwest Pacific, including a clearer military plan for the region and "greater cooperation and coordination *within* the various commands and *between* the different war theatres."[50]

He was no less critical in public, where he hoped not only to advance the war effort but also call attention to himself as a potential Secretary of the Navy. On July 26, in a radio report carried throughout Texas, in which Rayburn and Wright Patman, another Texas congressman, asked him what the country was going to do about the "many problems and many weaknesses in our setup," Lyndon demanded that "indecisive, stupid, selfish and incompetent generals, admirals and others in high military positions" be removed at once and that the country give its fighting men more and better equipment than they presently have. "We must make it clear that it is no longer a crime to cut red tape," he added. "We are going to have to give our men leadership and equipment superior to that of any in the world."[51]

On August 19, in the largest radio hookup he had ever had, Lyndon criticized military and industrial chiefs. He urged a purge of "indecisive, unimaginative, nonaggressive" military leaders. He also pointed out that American industry was operating at somewhat less than 70 percent of capacity, and he denounced "selfish groups," especially the steel, aluminum, rubber, and oil industries "for their 'business as usual' policy" and their excessive interest in profits.[52]

Mindful that a congressional election was less than three months away and that a Democratic victory in the House was essential to any remaining hopes he had of a significant committee assignment, Lyndon gave free rein to his partisanship, attacking industrialists in his speech as "the same boys who during the Hoover depression were saying 'prosperity is just around the corner.' " When he returned to Washington in the fall, Lyndon pressed the case for a vigorous campaign to preserve the party's House majority. In conversations with Rayburn, McCormack, and Jonathan Daniels, he proposed that the President and party leaders overcome political apathy among voters by emphasizing the symbolic importance of a democratic election in the midst of a war against totalitarian states. Lyndon also suggested that the leadership identify thirty men who would collect $5000 each for the congressional campaigns of 150 Democrats.[53]

Roosevelt wanted no part of it. Early in 1942 he had told a press conference that people needed to wake up to the fact that "this is war. Politics is out. Same is true in Congress." When Eleanor Roosevelt told him that the Democratic party was beginning to creak from disuse, the President replied that the Republicans creaked more, and when he took Willkie, their titular head, into the government, they would be in even worse shape. Roosevelt's attitude registered on Lyndon and Jonathan Daniels when they went to see him on October 15 about their plans "to help in the re-election of Democratic Congressmen." Although the President had told Lyndon to draft a plan, he was unreceptive to hearing about it. As they waited to get into the Oval Office, "Pa" Watson told them that "the President hasn't anything to say to you," and after consulting with him, Watson reported that Roosevelt thought it would be better to see them later. After Lyndon left "in a pique," Marvin McIntyre, FDR's appointments' secretary, described him to Daniels as "one of those thin skinned Southern gentlemen" and Rayburn, who was also angry with the President for being ignored, as "swell-headed."[54]

After the Republicans gained forty-four seats in the election, cutting the Democrats' advantage in the House to thirteen, Lyndon complained to Daniels that "all the boys who went down were Roosevelt men . . . who have voted with him come Hell or high water." Lyndon was particularly worried that the Republicans might run the House with the help of some conservative Democrats and that while Democrats would chair committees, the Republicans might actually control them. Shortly after the election McIntyre sent Lyndon a copy of a letter from a defeated liberal Democrat in Nebraska, who complained that "Reaction is now in the saddle, riding hell-bent for election—in 1944." For the time being Lyndon felt there was "nothing that we can or should do about the matter."[55]

His discouragement partly related to concern that an Internal Revenue Service investigation of Brown & Root might lead to criminal indictments against the Browns for income tax evasion and mean the destruction of his political career. In the fall of 1941 two deputy IRS collectors advised intelligence agents in Washington that Brown & Root "had unlawfully evaded a large part of its income taxes for the year 1940 and was expected to use the same method in evading larger tax liability for the year 1941." Since Brown & Root held a number of war contracts, the Treasury Department directed that B & R be included among a group of other tax-paying corporations doing war work and "be examined without delay." The allegations against the Browns were passed on to revenue agents in Texas "with instructions to watch for evidence of fraud in their routine inquiries." Their audit of B & R in June 1942 aroused further suspicions and led to inquiries about the "business expenses," "attorneys' fees," and "bonuses" that had in fact gone into Johnson's Senate campaign. Advised by Johnson and Wirtz that "Internal Revenue agents were going all through Texas stirring up political trouble for 'our crowd,'" James Rowe sent the President a memorandum during the summer "saying that they [the Revenue agents] were after the 'third term crowd' who had done the job in Texas, that they were going to all the banks and to the lawyers checking up on political contributions and that if it weren't stopped we wouldn't have a friend left in Texas." FDR spoke to McIntyre, who asked Assistant Secretary of the Treasury John Sullivan to look into the matter. After doing so, Sullivan assured Rowe that the investigation of B & R was routine and that the case had been closed.[56]

In fact, the probe had only just begun. On September 4 the IRS concluded that a "full investigation" was necessary and agents were assigned to the case. In October, after they questioned B & R attorney

Edgar Montieth about a profit distribution to him that had helped pay part of Johnson's campaign expenses, Guy Helvering, Commissioner of Internal Revenue in Washington, received complaints that the probe was hindering B & R's war work. At the same time, Alvin Wirtz and George Brown came to Washington to see Johnson about the case. Johnson and Brown then invited Rowe to meet with them at a Brown & Root town house at Sheridan Circle. During their conversation, which Rowe insisted take place on the street, where they wouldn't be vulnerable to bugs the IRS might have planted, Johnson, who seemed "worried," asked Rowe to kill this "politically inspired" investigation.

Shortly after, Rowe sent Grace Tully a memorandum repeating his belief that anti-New Dealers in Texas had inspired the probe. He said that no one was looking into the contributions of the Garner, Tom Connally, Jim Ferguson, and Coke Stevenson people who had "spent a great deal more money in the last couple of years to try to stop the Roosevelt men than have we." Rowe also reported that he had gone to Helvering, "knowing he was the President's man," and he had suspended the investigation. But Secretary of Treasury Morgenthau, who Rowe said "has no political sense," wanted to continue the inquiry. "I am completely convinced that this is political persecution," Rowe told Tully. "I do not think I have been 'sold a bill of goods.' I know I would not sell my President one for any one else." Although the pressures to end the investigation produced a two-month suspension in late November, the evidence against B & R was so telling and Morgenthau so committed to the rule of law that the probe resumed in January with instructions to agents only to be "diplomatic" and limit their interviews to people in the B & R organization.[57]

In the fall of 1942 the possibility that the investigation would lead to his political demise moved Lyndon to consider an alternative career and means of support. Yet even if he remained in Congress, he wanted to cash in on the booming war economy, as many others in Texas and around the country were, to build a nest egg for his family. "People in Texas were getting rich, very rich indeed . . . ," Lyndon's biographer Merle Miller notes, "and they did not hesitate to display their opulence—mink coats, diamonds, huge ranches, Cadillacs. It was said that in Texas you did not ask what kind of car you were going to buy. They asked only, 'What color?' "

"Boss" Taylor, Lyndon's father-in-law, was one of those who had become "very rich." In the five years since Lyndon had gone to Congress, Taylor had presided over a construction company that had made handsome profits from government contracts. He had also received $70,000 from the sale of 7,804 acres of land to the Federal government on which it built an ordnance plant. Taylor was well on his way to becoming a millionaire.

Lyndon aspired to similar wealth. Jonathan Daniels glimpsed Lyndon's taste for the good life when in December 1942 he visited his "hideaway office on the top floor of the old House office Building, room 544: the green burlap and wood screen around the basin where the pretty blonde secretary in red mixed drinks and made coffee; dark red steel filing cases; green figured carpet; black leather couch with red satin pillow on it; big red desk with Congressman's feet on it; statuette of a fighting Irishman, labeled 'I'm Dimocrat'; photographs of politicians on the walls; hat stand with light gray Texas hat on it; green steel wastepaper basket; monk's cloth curtains; Scotch and soda bottles behind monk's cloth curtains on the book cases."[58]

Lyndon was also eager to find an outlet for Lady Bird's considerable talents. Like him, she had strong ambitions. And until the fall of 1942 she had largely channeled them into Lyndon's career. Jonathan Daniels described her at this time as "the sharp-eyed type who looks at every piece of furniture in the house, knows its period and design—though sometimes she is wrong. She is confident that her husband is going places and in her head she is furnishing the mansions of his future." Her effective handling of his congressional affairs while he was in the navy demonstrated her potential for a successful career of her own. After he returned to Washington, she was left at loose ends with little to do. Several miscarriages had deprived her of children and the satisfaction of raising a family. To meet their mutual desire for larger earnings and Lady Bird's gainful employment, they considered buying a newspaper, a prospect that especially appealed to Bird, whose interest in journalism dated from her college years. An inheritance from her mother's estate of $41,000 paid in seven annual installments between 1937 and 1942 gave them the financial wherewithal. Although Lyndon had some discussions about buying the Waco *News-Tribune*, opposition from Charles Marsh, who didn't want Lyndon to own a competing paper, and the asking price killed the deal.[59]

Instead, Lyndon and Lady Bird decided to go after KTBC, a failing radio station in Austin. Established in 1939 by Dr. James G. Ulmer, whose Texas Broadcasting Company owned a half-dozen other stations, KTBC was beset by problems from the start. The Federal Communications Commission (FCC) had limited it to 250 watts of power, daytime broadcasts, and transmitting wave lengths shared with the college radio station at Texas A & M. KTBC could reach only a small audience. Consequently, Ulmer sold the station to three buyers, including Robert B. Anderson, a future Secretary of the Treasury. Unable to persuade the FCC to increase the station's capabilities, the three owners offered it to James West, a conservative self-made millionaire whose newspaper, the *Austin Tribune*, was notable for its opposition to Roosevelt and the New Deal. West assumed that he could convince the FCC to let him acquire and increase the transmitting power of the station, but he ran into a stone wall.[60]

Established in 1934 as an agency that would regulate the use of the airwaves and eliminate the audio chaos caused by unregulated radio operations, the FCC was also supposed to be a nonpolitical agency which would act in the "public interest." To assure against its outright politicization, the 1934 legislation provided that no more than four of the seven Commissioners shall be from the same political party. Despite this provision, political considerations shaped FCC actions from its inception. James L. Fly, FCC chairman in the early 1940s, was a staunch Texas New Dealer, who reflected FDR's concern that conservative newspaper owners were monopolizing public channels of communication by controlling more than one-third of the radio stations in the United States. West's application for ownership of KTBC impressed Fly as a prime case in point, and the Commission blocked West's acquisition of the station by refusing to act on his request. West died in 1942, and his option to buy KTBC passed to his sons, James, Jr., and Wesley, and E. G. Kingsbery, a conservative Austin businessman who James, Sr., directed should have a half-interest in the station.[61]

At this time, friends in Austin told Lyndon about KTBC and suggested that he and Lady Bird buy it. Although Lyndon didn't "know anything about running a radio station," he quickly recognized, as West and others had before him, that favorable rulings from the FCC could turn the station into a profitable business. Unlike West, however, he had good reason to believe that the FCC would be responsive to his requests. By the fall of 1942, when the KTBC proposition came to his attention, he already knew his way around the FCC. During 1941 he had helped Roy Hofheinz, a county judge in Texas and supporter in the 1941 Senate campaign, win a license for a radio station in Houston.[62]

Lyndon's principal contact at the FCC was his friend Commissioner Clifford Durr, the brother-in-law of Supreme Court Justice Hugo Black. When the possibility of buying KTBC arose, Lady Bird spoke to Cliff Durr, asking his advice on whether it would be a good investment. Durr, according to his own recollection, urged her to go ahead: "I told her that . . . if she could get that station on its feet and get it well managed, it ought to be a very good investment. That was my connection with it. Now there wasn't any skulduggery that I ever saw at the FCC. It was more or less the routine approval of the purchase of a station." Yet Durr also remembered that the Johnsons' acquisition of KTBC would have a salutary political effect on Texas politics. Lady Bird emphasized to him her concern over the "vicious attacks on President [Homer] Rainey" of the University of Texas, who was then in the midst of a struggle with reactionary Regents eager to limit academic freedom and dismiss Rainey. "She was hoping if they could get that station on its feet, they could give him [Rainey] a fair break. I remember her mentioning that," Durr said twenty-two years later. Durr's encouragement signaled what the Johnsons already knew—that unlike a James West, good New Deal folks like Lyndon and Lady Bird would receive a friendly hearing from the FCC.[63]

Lyndon needed to get the option to buy the station from Kingsbery and the Wests. Kingsbery didn't need much convincing. Over eggnogs a few days before Christmas 1942, Johnson reminded him that he had helped his son enter the Naval Academy the previous year. Kingsbery agreed to relinquish his option, but it then reverted to Wesley and Jim West, Jr., whom Lyndon "was afraid to talk to" for fear "they would brush him off" as "too far to the left." Lyndon wanted George Brown to buy the station from the Wests and then sell it to him. But George urged him to get it on his own. In a four-hour meeting arranged by Brown, Lyndon, applying all his powers of persuasion, convinced the Wests that he was "a pretty good fellow" with an appealing "philosophy of life." The Wests agreed to give him exclusive rights to their option. Alvin Wirtz then negotiated the sale from the Anderson group to Lady Bird for $17,500. Although the station had almost $30,000 in assets, it had a debt equal to Lady Bird's offering price and had lost $7,500 in the previous year. In January 1943, Lady Bird filed an application with the FCC to buy KTBC. To avoid charges of influence peddling and skirt an FCC requirement of "full time" attention to station business, Lyndon made Lady Bird the sole purchaser. She listed assets of $64,322 in cash and real estate and her work in Lyndon's office as evidence of past business success, another FCC requirement. The FCC quickly approved the sale.[64]

Lyndon privately acknowledged that political considerations were involved. When Elliott Roosevelt, FDR's son, who was in the radio business with Sid Richardson in Texas, heard that the Johnsons had bought KTBC, he sent word through John Connally that they were going to take business away from his stations by keeping KTBC alive and that he intended to retaliate in any way he could. The Johnsons replied that their acquisition of KTBC prevented its purchase by "enemies of the Congressman, enemies of Elliott and enemies of the President. It was purely and simply a question of having a friend or a foe operating the other station. It was not a question of the station going out of existence at all."[65]

During the first six months they had the station, Lady Bird spent much of her time in Austin working to turn the station into a profitable enterprise. Consisting of largely "obsolete" and "barely workable" equipment and a poorly paid, demoralized staff of nine, KTBC was losing over $600 a month. "The staff was infected with a sense of failure and uncertainty, and sloppiness had become a way of life," Lady Bird recalled. She armed herself with a broom, a mop, and a pail and cleaned the station until it sparkled. "I think it kind of improved everybody's spirits. It certainly did mine." More important, she began improving the quality of programs which increased the size of KTBC's audience and share of local radio advertising. In May, she and Lyndon persuaded Harfield Weedin, an experienced radio and advertising man who had served Lyndon so well in the 1941 campaign, to become station manager. At the same time, they moved the station into more spacious quarters in the Brown Building in downtown Austin. According to Weedin, they assured him that the station would soon shift from a daytime to a day and evening schedule, have its own frequency, and increase its power to 1000 watts. Although their application for these changes did not go to the FCC until the end of June, they were confident in May that they would be approved, suggesting, as Weedin assumed, that Lyndon had already arranged it. As with their initial request to buy the station, the FCC promptly agreed to modify KTBC's operating conditions. By August, the station operated in the black for the first time, showing an $18 profit.[66]

Although Lyndon made every effort to avoid public identification with the station, he was deeply involved in its operations. Between February and September, Lady Bird played the largest role in running KTBC. By the fall, however, she was beginning the second trimester of another pregnancy, and Lyndon's part in managing the station increased. According to Weedin, Lyndon was "tremendously interested" from the start: "he wanted to see the books and everything else when he came to town." He also arranged an affiliation with the Columbia Broadcasting System (CBS). He went to see William Paley, the president of CBS, in New York. Paley's secretary said that "there was a very tall Texan waiting out there in a big hat and boots who said he was a Congressman." Paley politely explained that CBS had affiliates in Dallas and San Antonio, but he sent Johnson to see Frank Stanton, a young man on his staff who managed network affiliations. Armed with letters gathered by Weedin from people in Austin complaining that they couldn't tune in KTSA, the 5000-watt CBS station in San Antonio, Lyndon persuaded the network to sign a contract in September making available to KTBC, "at least thirty-five hours per week of network sustaining and sponsored programs."[67]

At the same time, he sought advertisers for the station. "I managed to hit a lick here and there on the radio station," he wrote Jesse Kellam after he visited Austin in June. Ed Clark, Lyndon's longstanding political ally who practiced law in Austin, was a prime mover in helping him get ads. "Take time out and write me your impressions on the general operation and reception of the station," Lyndon wrote him in October. Clark sent Lyndon the names of key business people in a dozen different enterprises from whom he might want to solicit ads. Clark did some of it for him: he asked an Austin grocery-chain owner to "contact the advertisers whose products he sells at his stores." Clark arranged for General Electric's popular "World News Today" to be heard over the station, and he assured Lyndon that it "will add to the listeners for KTBC." Lyndon agreed, describing it as "the most important thing that has been accomplished lately" at the station. Lyndon occasionally went to New York in search of ads. Edwin Weisl, Sr., a Wall Street attorney who had met him through Harry Hopkins, remembered that after "Mrs. Johnson purchased the radio station, and it was having quite a difficult time to survive," Lyndon would come to the city "to promote his interests in his radio station" by getting national companies to place ads or "to work through the home office to induce local people to advertise." [68]

Lyndon also sought business for KTBC through Tommy Corcoran, who had set up a law practice in Washington after leaving the Administration in 1941. Lyndon drew up lists of forty-one CBS daytime programs that were not heard on KTBC and forty-seven CBS programs heard in Dallas but not in Austin. He wanted Corcoran to get the advertisers of these programs to pressure CBS into putting them on KTBC: The Austin station "is not now getting our program," the advertiser was to say. "Many of the people in the Capitol City of the biggest state in the Union do not now hear Columbia programs because of the weak coverage of the Columbia stations." The agency representing the advertiser was to ask CBS to add KTBC to the stations carrying its program.[69]

That Johnson wanted to enrich radio programming in Austin sat well with city residents. But his involvement in a business that largely depended on the actions of a Federal agency for its success created a clear conflict between his private interests and public position. Although he later insisted that he had never lobbied the FCC in behalf of KTBC and that he had never cast a congressional vote on a controversial radio or television issue, he was less than candid. His close identification with the Roosevelt administration and ties to FCC commissioners played a part in the uniform and rapid consent Lady Bird won for all her requests. Moreover, the fact that he was a well-connected congressman could hardly have been lost on the various businessmen he or, in most cases, his agents pressed for commitments to KTBC.

In acquiring and turning KTBC into a profitable enterprise, Lyndon was walking a thin ethical line. No doubt he took comfort from the thought that others in Congress were doing the same thing. But as his friend Supreme Court Justice William O. Douglas later wrote: "Among the great plums in the Washington, D.C., pudding has been the granting of radio and TV licenses. The contests have been tremendous and many political allies have been marshaled in the cause. Even some members of Congress obtained licenses for themselves or their families while in office—a practice that should be forever barred as being beyond the ethical line." [70]

Lyndon never saw it that way. To him, the chance to acquire the radio station was essentially a reward for public service well done. In his eyes he was doing no more than seizing an opportunity in a free enterprise system to make a lot of money by hard work and aggressive business practices. Initially, however, it meant even more to him—the possibility for an alternative livelihood should his political career come to a sudden end. And during 1943, as the IRS investigation of Brown & Root went forward, this remained a serious concern. In the ten months after the inquiry resumed in January, the IRS had concluded that fraud had been committed and that Brown & Root owed back taxes of approximately $1,161,000, including about $300,000 in fraud penalties. In addition, criminal charges for alleged fraud and perjury by B & R officers and employees made it a possibility that some people would go to jail.

In early November, after Morgenthau had resisted renewed pressure to kill the investigation, Alvin Wirtz asked for an off-the-record appointment with the President to discuss "a matter which I think is important to the Administration, as well as myself." Following conversations with Wirtz on November 8 and 10, the President called Morgenthau to ask why he was "going after these people in Texas, and . . . why not somebody like O'Daniel." Roosevelt said that the people involved wanted to pay up, and he asked Morgenthau to see Wirtz, which he did on November 12. Although Wirtz urged a speedy conclusion to the case and explained that his clients wanted to pay anything they legitimately owed, Morgenthau refused to give the case special consideration and expressed confidence that the President would not ask him to do so. [71]

When IRS investigators pressed their inquiry in December and January and one B & R employee refused to answer questions on grounds that "it might incriminate him," Johnson and Wirtz went to see the President together. On January 11, Lyndon left word for "Pa" Watson that he was "very anxious to see the President, as quickly as he possibly could. He says it is not a 'Sunday School' proposition." Though Lyndon later denied that he and Wirtz discussed the Brown & Root matter with Roosevelt during visits to the White House on January 13 and 17, the fact that Assistant Secretary of the Treasury Elmer Irey was asked to report on the case to the President on the 14th and that a new IRS agent took over the investigation on the 17th suggests otherwise. Moreover, the fact that this investigator quickly recommended against prosecution, because there was not "quite enough evidence" and it would undermine B & R's war work, further demonstrates that Roosevelt wanted to satisfy demands from his Texas friends for a speedy and well-circumscribed end to the case. Consequently, on February 15, the IRS chief of intelligence ordered that the case be concluded on the "basis of the facts now in hand." When the principal Texas agent in the case argued against ending the inquiry, he was told emphatically to follow the order of February 15. Though the Texas field office now recommended an additional tax payment of $1,649,916, including penalties, the IRS ultimately made Brown & Root pay only $372,000 in back taxes.[72]

At the same time the IRS investigation posed a threat to Lyndon's congressional career, a shift to the right in Texas and nationally also made him doubt his political future. At the end of 1942, Jonathan Daniels noted that the war had solved the economic problems of most people, who no longer felt a need to fight for the New Deal. Though Roosevelt remained a "master politician," Daniels saw him as "not interested in party politics now." Lyndon shared Daniels's view, complaining that the political situation was now "pretty bad" and predicting in December that there was "practically not a member of the Texas delegation who wouldn't be defeated if he came up for re-election now."[73]

Lyndon partly responded to the downturn in his political prospects by investing time in the radio station. But politics remained his first love, and he tried to serve his political future by coming to terms with the change in public mood, particularly resentment toward rationing and bureaucratic red tape, symbols of heavy-handed Federal authority. In a speech on December 7, 1942, at the scrapping of the battleship *Oregon* in Portland, Oregon, Lyndon aligned himself with the nation's more conservative climate of feeling. "What about the scrapping jobs to be done elsewhere?" Johnson asked. ". . . What about over-staffed, overstuffed government that worried along like a centipede—too good in the production of limbs and not good enough in the production of arms? . . . What to do about rationing that has gone irrational, about administrators who spend too much time laying down the law to us and not enough time in reading up on the law? . . . Many of the weapons we once took up in a war against depression have now outlived their usefulness. With our shoulders to the wheel of war against foreign enslavement, these old domestic museum pieces, the PWA, the FHA and WPA are in the way. . . . The social gain that we are very busy preserving at this moment is our status as free men in a free nation." At the same time, however, he declared the need for a new progressive approach to world affairs—one that would shun the failed isolationism of the past and assure an enduring peace.[74]

The speech put Lyndon on the right side of public opinion in Texas, where it received considerable attention. But it also aimed to advance the war effort and reiterate Lyndon's capacity for a larger role. "Lyndon Johnson: Next Secretary of the Navy?" one Texas newspaper asked in response to his address. It was a reasonable question. His speech clearly reflected White House thinking. Before he spoke, Lyndon discussed his talk with the President and showed it to James Rowe, who called the "first part good and the last part excellent." Tommy Corcoran and William O. Douglas had also approved the speech. In fact, according to Charles Marsh, they had arranged for Lyndon to give the talk and saw it as part of a campaign to bring the Administration into line with the more conservative mood in the country. Marsh believed it was all part of a plan to dump Wallace as Vice President in 1944 and replace him with Douglas, who would appeal to the revived conservativism in the party and the nation. Roosevelt gave credence to Marsh's belief in 1943 when he said that "Dr. Win the War" needed to replace "Dr. New Deal." [75]

The Oregon speech set a pattern for Lyndon's approach to public affairs during 1943: to promote a more effective war effort at home; to identify himself with the country's more conservative wartime temper; to advance long-term liberal domestic and foreign policies which he believed would hold center stage in postwar affairs; and to win a position of greater authority in the government as a prelude to a U.S. Senate seat.

To advance three of these ends he launched a campaign at the start of 1943 to use American manpower more effectively in the war effort. Like a clear majority of Americans, Lyndon opposed the selfish actions of labor unions hindering war production. In 1942, when labor leaders insisted on a forty-hour week and time and a half for overtime, Lyndon privately denounced workers who wished to profit at the expense of the national interest. "I am no alarmist," he told Sam Rayburn, ". . . nor do I want to see the rightful gains of Labor snatched away by those who have forever held Labor in Bondage, but these are practical times with practical problems which must be solved—and solved quickly." He saw no constitutional guarantee of individual rights that "ran counter to the national welfare." [76]

To meet wartime needs for the rational distribution of manpower between the civilian and military sectors and among competing industries in the United States, Roosevelt had established the War Manpower Commission in April 1942 under Paul V. McNutt, a former Indiana governor and current director of the Federal Security Agency. Scarcity of skilled workers, absenteeism, and unessential work by men deferred from military service moved Roosevelt to put the Selective Service System under the authority of McNutt's Commission in December 1942. McNutt then issued a "work or fight" order in January that limited deferments to men engaged in essential war work. His directive, which offended labor and the Congress as too authoritarian and likely to demoralize workers, had to be withdrawn before the end of 1943. [77]

Lyndon, however, who had been advocating a more regimented use of manpower for over a year, liked McNutt's directive and introduced "work or fight" measures of his own. In January 1943, *Time* magazine reported that absenteeism at American factories and shipyards was seriously impairing the country's output of planes, ships, tanks, and munitions. Inquiries by Lyndon into the facts of the matter convinced him that this was a serious problem needing corrective legislation. A host of statistics he put before the House made the point: absenteeism at navy yards in January 1943 amounted to 9.4 percent of the total workforce, an increase from 8.9 percent in the previous April; 12.7 million manhours had been lost to the construction and repair of naval vessels through absenteeism in December 1942 alone, with the figure rising to 23.25 million for the month if maritime shipbuilding programs were included; the loss to the war effort amounted to one aircraft carrier, or 2 light cruisers, or 11 destroyers, or 21 destroyer escorts, or 15 submarines, or 50 sub-chasers, or 42 Liberty ships that could have carried 336,000 tons of planes, guns, and tanks.[78]

Lyndon's answer to the problem was an amendment to a pending Navy Department bill requiring shipyards to file quarterly reports with local draft boards on absenteeism. Shortly after, the Naval Affairs Committee approved a broader proposal from him for reports on absenteeism from all war industries. This more comprehensive bill provided that any request to a draft board for deferment of an employee as an "essential worker" had to be accompanied by his absentee record. Since the Selective Service law required a renewal on all deferments every six months, the Johnson bill assured that "deferred" absentees would not escape scrutiny for long.[79]

Although key Administration figures, including Secretary of the Navy Knox, Under Secretary of War Robert Patterson, and War Shipping Administrator Emory S. Land, supported the bill, it ran into a storm of criticism. Labor leaders objected that it would violate the Constitution by establishing involuntary servitude, convert the military service into a penal institution, give employers the power to inflict distasteful working conditions on labor by threatening to report them for absenteeism should they strike, and generate resentment and demoralization among war workers. Secretary of Labor Frances Perkins opposed the Johnson bill as "almost certain not" to correct the problem and as likely to "result in delaying practical solution by industry and labor." *Time* reported that absenteeism was a complicated problem that defied easy solution and could not be laid at labor's door alone. When the House Labor Committee complained that the Naval Affairs Committee had preempted a matter properly in its jurisdiction, the Rules Committee tabled Johnson's bill.[80]

The objections did not convince Lyndon. He defended his bill as throwing a "cloak of protection" over the vast majority of workers by shielding them from a violent anti-labor reaction that would follow the accentuation of the problem. He denied that he was anti-labor. Yet in

June 1943, when Congress responded to a coal miners' strike with a War Labor Disputes Act that empowered the President to seize any strike-bound plant, mine, or facility useful to the war effort, Lyndon joined the anti-labor majority passing the bill. Further, when Roosevelt vetoed the law as going too far in setting back the rights of labor, the Congress, with Lyndon again among the majority, overrode his veto. Lyndon cast his vote with an eye on the rising anti-unionism in Texas.[81]

Lyndon's appointment in January 1943 to chair a Naval Affairs sub-committee to investigate whether personnel in the Navy Department and other "naval Establishments" were pursuing the war effort "efficiently, expeditiously, and economically" partly relieved his frustration over the defeat of his absenteeism bill. Although a limited budget and agenda inhibited him from converting this assignment into something resembling the Truman Committee, he made more of the job than House leaders could have guessed. To get the kind of staff a successful investigating committee needed, Lyndon borrowed Naval Reserve officers from the Navy Department who, as noncareer reservists, were more interested in advancing the war effort than in protecting the navy from criticism. Johnson made Donald C. Cook, a former assistant director at the Securities and Exchange Commission, the subcommittee's chief counsel. As a first-rate attorney and a non-Jew, which Lyndon saw as a precondition for avoiding traditional navy anti-Semitism, Cook perfectly suited Lyndon's needs.[82]

So did Gene Latimer, his former assistant who was serving as a second-class petty officer in Chicago. Lyndon transferred him to his staff, and assured himself a loyal subordinate. Latimer's job "was to help run part of the committee office, but in civilian clothes in order not to confuse any captains or other high ranking officers of whom I might ask questions." Latimer stayed with the Chief and Lady Bird at their home, "and things were pretty much as in the old days, except that every two weeks I put on my dress whites with petty officer ensignia and reported to the disbursing officer long enough to draw my pay check, then slipped back into civies and resumed investigating personnel of the Navy Department."[83]

Characteristically, Johnson drove himself and the subcommittee staff as if the whole war effort depended on their work. During 1943, the subcommittee investigated deferments of civilian employees in the Navy Department, the use of over 4000 able-bodied seamen in Washington clerical positions, the work of naval personnel in the Office of Censorship, the operations of the Navy Department's Incentives Division, which was responsible for "the stimulation of production of war materials," the work of the navy's Procurement Division in overseeing its Bureau of Supplies and Accounts, and the working conditions and production at shipyards and naval air training stations. Although the Johnson subcommittee uncovered a number of problems that the navy corrected to the benefit of the war effort, its achievements were unspectacular and did little to advance Lyndon's claim on higher office, particularly as Navy Secretary. When Frank Knox died suddenly of a heart attack in April 1944, there was some talk that Lyndon might succeed him. But Roosevelt promptly appointed Under Secretary Forrestal to the post.[84]

It is conceivable that Lyndon's investigations had cost him some influence with the Administration, which had grown resentful of congressmen trying to check the drift of power from Capitol Hill to the White House by monitoring the defense program and Executive agencies. Specifically, staunch New Dealers like Charles Marsh and James Rowe noted Lyndon's drift to the right and gave him hell for it. After his Oregon speech, Marsh took him to task for "swimming" or "float[ing] out on the tide" and being "a Representative for the tired Liberals," who feared they would "have no home in the cold." James Rowe objected to Lyndon's absenteeism bill as causing "great bitterness in the ranks of labor. . . . Its net effect is to promote disunity and hurt production not help it." He also attacked Lyndon's vote for a deficiency appropriation bill in May 1943 which included a provision against paying the salaries of three Federal officials accused of subversion by Martin Dies's Un-American Activities Committee. Roosevelt signed what he saw as an essential appropriations bill under protest, and Rowe sent Lyndon, "without much hope," a protest against a "lynch law." "I hope the name of the 78th Congress will become as infamous for this day's work . . . as is the name of [A. Mitchell] Palmer, an Attorney General held in disrespect by all lawyers." Three years later the Supreme Court ruled that Congress had punished the three men without a trial and violated the constitutional ban on bills of attainder.[85]

Yet the White House never saw Lyndon as a fallen away New Dealer. His words and deeds in behalf of liberalism during 1943–44 were more in evidence than his flirtations with the conservatives. In May 1943, for example, he made a state-wide appeal in Texas for postwar internationalism that closely reflected Administration thinking. Predicting that scientific advances spawned by the current war would make future conflicts yet more devastating, he asserted that "what we do to rule out future wars . . . will be as vital as what we are doing to win this war. . . . We shall have to join with other peoples of the world as willingly in peace as we have joined with them in war." America's future safety and peace now depended on a national consensus for cooperation with other nations intent upon "a new world freedom—freedom from war."

At the same time, in 1943, when a conservative coalition in Congress of southern Democrats and Republicans began an assault on the "social gains of the last ten years" by liquidating the NYA and the National Resources Planning Board, cutting the budget of the Farm Security Administration, and threatening to weaken the Securities and Exchange Commission and the Holding Company Act, Lyndon was one of a handful of congressmen asked by Administration leaders to hold the line and win support for tax and other legislation it wished to steer through Congress.[86]

Still warmly disposed to liberal nationalism, Lyndon was receptive to the appeal, particularly when it came to checking big business and assuring Americans in general and servicemen in particular of a postwar economic bill of rights. During the second half of 1943 he was an outspoken critic of war contractors who wanted to do away with the Renegotiation Act which required defense industries to amend their contracts with the government when they began making excess profits. During hearings before the House Naval Affairs Committee, and in interviews and speeches, Lyndon defended the law as saving the government $4 billion that would have created a class of war millionaires. The law, he said, does not take the war contractor's "leg or his arm or his blood. It does not take his life." It "says to him only, you shall not build a personal fortune out of the misfortune and miseries of this total war."[87]

"I'm for free enterprise," Lyndon told the Texas legislature in January 1944. "I'm for local self-government. I'm against centralizing power in Washington." But after visiting wounded veterans in a Texas hospital, he said he "thought about free enterprise and about concentrating powers of government in Washington and about local self-government. And I reached this conclusion: I want to substitute for free enterprise *equal opportunity*. Every man who has gone through a living Hell for you and for me, and comes out with scars on his body and his soul to show for it, shall have an equal opportunity to get a job when this is over." He was happy to leave it to the local community to assume this responsibility, but if it failed to act, he intended "to vote for whatever legislation is necessary to let the Federal Government do it. If that be enlarging the power of the Federal Government, and if that be centralizing more power in Washington, make the most of it."

Eight days after Johnson's speech, in what historian James Mac-Gregor Burns describes as "the most radical speech of Roosevelt's life," the President declared the need for a strong program of economic stabilization and an economic bill of rights. He called for a tax on all unreasonable profits, a continuation of the Renegotiation Act, and "a useful and remunerative job" for all Americans. In February, when the Congress passed a tax bill that raised $2.3 billion in new revenues instead of the $10.5 billion FDR asked, Lyndon voted against the substitute measure. Moreover, when FDR vetoed the bill as providing relief "not for the needy but for the greedy," Lyndon was one of only ninety-five House members voting to sustain the President's veto.[88]

His opposition to wartime profiteering carried over into his actions toward the oil industry. In June 1943, the Federal government terminated a contract with Standard Oil of California for the operation of the Elk Hills naval oil reserve in Kern County, California. The House Naval Affairs Committee then appointed a subcommittee headed by Lyndon to determine what arrangements at Elk Hills would better serve the national interest. Despite being from Texas, "where oil and gas was king in a real, real sense," Donald Cook said, Johnson "didn't flinch from doing what needed to be done." He helped persuade the Naval Affairs Committee that the interest of the United States in conserving its oil reserves and of Standard Oil in exploiting them amounted to an incompatible difference requiring the exclusion of Standard and other private interests from the Elk Hills reserve. The Committee recommended that all naval oil reserves should strictly serve the needs of the Fleet. Lyndon opposed big oil again in June 1944 by voting with a narrow majority in the House against a thirty-five-cent rise in the price of crude oil. A report from the Office of Price Administration predicting that the increase might cause serious inflation and cost the country billions of dollars convinced Lyndon to join Mike Monroney of Oklahoma as one of only two Southwest congressmen choosing national over parochial interests.[89]

Johnson's support of Administration policies aroused opposition to him in his district and raised the likelihood of a fight to keep his seat. Convinced that the OPA had to keep the lid on basic commodities like oil, beef, poultry, and dairy products, Lyndon backed rationing and price controls as essential to the national well-being. In a report to his district, he declared that "winning the war must and does come first." He had no love of rationing and price controls and looked forward to the day when they would end, but as long as the war continued, he shared the view of the country's military and political leaders that they "were essential."[90]

Yet he worried that his loyalty to the Administration and its stabilization policies would lead to his political demise. "Lyndon sees only disaster ahead for the Democrats," Harold Ickes recorded in November 1943. ". . . He doubted whether he could win in his own district in Texas. . . . While everyone else has deserted the President and the New Deal, he continues to back the Administration." Mayor Tom Miller of Austin wanted Lyndon to denounce gasoline rationing for Texas, saying "that the state was swimming in oil." Instead, Lyndon made a speech in which he denounced "those people in Texas who would withhold petroleum from our armed forces in order to use it at home." Repeated reports from friends in Austin during the fall of 1943 that either Mayor Miller or a Joe Carrington representing the Chamber of Commerce would run against him for failing to fight OPA regulations and support the special interests of his constituents upset and depressed Lyndon. "Lyndon was very downhearted about the political situation in Texas," Ickes noted in December. "He had just had a long letter from Wirtz. Johnson doesn't think that he can hold his own district, and Wirtz was so pessimistic as to say that Roosevelt might not be able even to carry Texas." Wirtz and Ed Clark compounded Lyndon's concern in January by reporting that the state's oil interests, which were already trying to beat Sam Rayburn, were now intent on finding "a worthy opponent" to run against you.[91]

Attacks on him for having bought KTBC and a luxurious duplex at 1901 Dillman Street in Austin with money supplied by special interests also discomfited Lyndon. He vehmently denied any improprieties. The money for these purchases had come from Lady Bird's inheritance, but the possibility in the winter of 1943–44 that the facts uncovered in the Brown & Root investigation or FCC favoritism for KTBC might become public added to his political worries.[92]

The likelihood of facing a formidable opponent in the 1944 Democratic primary led Lyndon to abandon the Administration on the "soldier vote" in February and March. Eager to assure that the nine million servicemen, who polls showed favored the Democrats, would vote in 1944, the Administration supported a bill to simplify absentee voting: eliminating a requirement that soldiers request a ballot from their local registrar, it proposed instead that a Federal ballot automatically be sent to all servicemen overseas. Seeing the Administration bill as an assault on states' rights, including the power of southern states to limit the enfranchisement of black servicemen, southern Democrats joined with Republicans in amending the law to keep control over absentee voting in the hands of the states. Lyndon voted with the conservatives to alter the Administration's bill.[93]

By April, however, he was more confident about the political future. He told Ickes that a trip across his district, in which he had gone "to bat for the President and the New Deal," convinced him that he would have no significant opposition and that FDR would be reelected, though the Republicans might win control of Congress. Although Buck Taylor, a sixty-year-old World War I veteran and former committee clerk in the state legislature, had entered the race against him with the backing of conservatives or Democratic party "regulars," Taylor did not seem a formidable opponent. "The kindest thing that could be said of Buck," one of Lyndon's associates later said, "was that he was a nobody. His obvious function was to be a mouthpiece for the anti-Roosevelt faction."[94]

In April 1944, other Texas New Dealers shared Lyndon's optimism about Roosevelt's prospects in their state. A March opinion survey showed 65 percent of Texas voters in favor of FDR. But as Wirtz later told Ickes, the friends of the Administration or "real Democrats were asleep. . . . It seemed that everybody in [the state's party leadership] was for Roosevelt." But, in fact, party regulars were establishing "a far-reaching organization, all without publicity and in utmost secrecy," to reassert conservative control over the Democratic party in Texas and throughout the South and, if possible, to defeat FDR. Led by Commerce Secretary Jesse Jones, Senator O'Daniel, Will Clayton, an Assistant Secretary of State, and oilmen and bankers from Dallas, Fort Worth, Houston, and San Antonio, party regulars appealed to widespread frustration with price controls on oil and agricultural products, fear of a fourth term with liberal Vice President Henry Wallace as the successor, and antagonism to expanded civil rights, particularly a 1944 U.S. Supreme Court decision denying that the Texas Democracy was a private organization which could bar blacks from voting in party primaries.[95]

Holding a nine to seven majority of delegates at the state party convention in May, the regulars sponsored resolutions that provoked an all-out fight with liberals. The regulars favored an uninstructed delegation to the national convention in Chicago. They also insisted that the convention restore the two-thirds rule for presidential nominees, assuring the South a veto in selecting the party's candidate. If the Chicago convention rejected this change, the state's presidential electors would not be bound to vote for the party's nominee. After losing a preliminary test of strength on who would serve as temporary chairman of the state convention, Wirtz and the liberals demanded a vote on requiring Texas presidential electors to vote for the candidate with the largest popular vote in the November election. Wirtz's motion provoked derisive cries from opponents and fistfights erupted between pro- and anti-New Dealers. When Lyndon mounted the platform to quiet the delegates, Texas regulars became more agitated, shouting, "Get that yes-man off the platform" and "Throw Roosevelt's pin-up boy out of there."[96]

When order was restored, the convention tabled Wirtz's motion by a 952–695 vote. The former head of the Austin League of Women Voters then proposed that the President's friends withdraw from the state Senate chamber, where the convention was meeting, and reconvene in the House chamber. As nearly 300 pro-Roosevelt delegates marched from the room behind a labor leader carrying a four-foot picture of FDR, the regulars booed and hissed while an organist played "Good Night, Ladies" and "God Be with You Till We Meet Again." Although he followed the bolters across the hall, Lyndon viewed the split in party ranks as a mistake and tried to heal the breach. He also thought that Roosevelt supporters would be in a weak position to contest the regulars at the national convention unless they forced a vote on the question of pledging support to the party's nominee. "Before we go off half-cocked," he told the bolters, "it's extremely important that we give every Democrat and every so-called Democrat another opportunity to say whether they expect to vote for the party nominee in November . . . When I bolt a

convention it's going to be a Hoovercrat Republican convention," he
said.[97]

Wirtz convinced the bolters to ask the regulars for an up or down vote
on support for the party's nominee. The regulars rejected the proposal.
In response, Lyndon and the liberals denounced the regulars as reactionaries intent on robbing the people of their franchise if they voted for
FDR. Lyndon also attacked these "pseudo-Democrats" for agitating
Americans with false rumors that the Roosevelt administration intended
to change the country's form of government with a "bloodless revolution."

The actions of the Texas regulars also incensed FDR. A letter from
Wirtz to Ickes saying that the Texas reactionaries hoped to have other
southern states withhold their electoral votes from the President, throw
the election into the House of Representatives, and set up a fascist state
disturbed Roosevelt. He confronted Jesse Jones, whom he privately called
"Jesus" Jones, with Wirtz's allegations. Jones denied "any connection
with the whole business," but Roosevelt pressed him to remember that
the split in the Democratic party in 1860 had helped bring on the Civil
War: "The people in Texas were out to destroy the party system." To
combat their influence, the party leadership in Chicago divided the forty-
eight Texas seats at the convention evenly between the regulars and FDR
loyalists. Eager to prevent Wallace's renomination as Vice President and
to replace him with Harry Truman, the party's leaders refused to seat
only loyalists, who would have favored another Wallace term.[98]

Although Lyndon was appointed deputy sergeant-at-arms and given
a room with his name on the door, he decided not to attend the convention. Sam Rayburn made the same decision, though he was in the running for the vice-presidential nomination. Convinced that the division
among Texas Democrats had already killed his chances, Rayburn ignored the advice of some die-hard supporters that he come to Chicago.
He also had more compelling business in Texas. The national convention began three days before the Texas primaries. Locked in hard-fought
renomination campaigns for their House seats, Rayburn and Johnson
believed it a sign of overconfidence to leave their districts before election
day.[99]

In 1944, both Sam and Lyndon felt that they were fighting for their
political lives. Targeted by Texas reactionaries as principal advocates of
Roosevelt's drive to replace free enterprise and political liberty with socialism and dictatorship, Rayburn and Johnson were subjected to the
strongest attacks they had yet experienced in their public careers. In a
campaign costing nearly $200,000—which Rayburn said was more than
had been spent on an election in the Fourth District "in the past 30
years combined"—Rayburn's opponent, a Texas state senator, saturated
the district with charges that the Speaker favored "creeping socialism"

and the Fair Employment Practices Commission (FEPC), a "Negro controlled" Federal agency. Pointing to the extraordinary gains his north Texas constituents had made during his sixteen terms in the House and especially under the New Deal, Rayburn won, but only by 6000 votes out of the 43,000 cast.[100]

Although the challenge to Johnson proved to be less substantial, Lyndon had to take it seriously. "Yesterday my opponent carried almost a full-page ad in *The Houston Post,*" Johnson wrote Jim Rowe in May. The Christian American outfit [a right-wing group] is financing him and I may have a lot of trouble before it is over. . . . Outside of the fear we have of not being reelected everything else goes well." Johnson's campaign strategy was to hide his concern and publicly ignore Taylor's challenge. Aside from some form letters to his constituents reminding them of his accomplishments, private meetings, and last-minute telephone calls to voters, Lyndon left the campaigning to his friends. Johnson's low-keyed response provoked Taylor and his supporters into shrill attacks that did Lyndon more good than harm. By appealing to racial antagonisms with assertions that Johnson favored the destruction of the "white primary" and the creation of the FEPC, calling him a "millionaire," and describing him as friendly to labor racketeers and hostile to war veterans, they aroused indignation in Johnson's favor. Carrying nine of the ten counties in his district, Lyndon beat Taylor by a margin of almost two and a half to one.[101]

Taylor's campaign greatly agitated Lyndon. Some of his concern surfaced in assertions that he had publicly opposed the FEPC, consistently favored the poll tax, and voted repeatedly against strikes, labor racketeers, and the "John L. Lewis dictatorship." But he did not give full expression to his anger until after the campaign when he told the *Houston Post* that the attack on him, which was financed wholly from outside his district, was "the most bitterly vituperative, the most poisonous . . . and the slimiest . . . on an official within his memory." He was no less angry in private, telling Roy Miller: "old-timers say it was the dirtiest campaigning they have ever seen. The lies and insinuations reached a new low . . . and all of his [Taylor's] speeches, circulars and funds originated down in Houston."[102]

Despite the hard knocks, Johnson, Wirtz, and Texas New Dealers ended the 1944 campaign season in high spirits. Taking advantage of the peculiar Texas tradition of another state Democratic party convention in September, when the governor announced his program and the delegates elected a state party chairman and executive committee, Wirtz organized a grassroots campaign that gave pro-Roosevelt delegates control of the convention. Using this majority to select New Deal supporters to party offices, Wirtz also replaced conservative presidential electors with men friendly to FDR. When the Texas secretary of state refused to confirm this new slate of electors, Wirtz won a favorable ruling from the Texas Supreme Court, which he described to FDR as "a great victory for democratic government, the people, and Franklin D. Roosevelt. . . . It will be confirmed by the electorate in November, when the nation will overwhelmingly draft you for another term." Although the regulars now organized a third party and asked voters to insert the name of any Democrat other than Roosevelt on the ballot, the President confirmed Wirtz's prediction in Texas and around the nation. Roosevelt, with Truman as his running mate, defeated New York Republican Governor Thomas Dewey by nearly an eight to three margin in Texas and by 432 to 99 electoral votes. The addition of 22 House seats and the loss of only one Senate seat extended the party's control over the Congress.[103]

Lyndon entered 1945 in an upbeat mood. He was particularly pleased at the birth of his and Lady Bird's first child. After nearly ten years of marriage, during which three miscarriages had deprived them of children and caused them much sadness, Lady Bird gave birth to a healthy girl in March 1944. Lyndon wanted to name her Lady Bird to keep the family initials intact, but Lady Bird resisted and they compromised on Lynda Bird. Five days before the baby arrived Lyndon told a friend "how nervous I am about this." His anxiety didn't abate after the baby came home. When Lynda developed colic, Lyndon thought she was dying and wanted to rush across the street to ask help from FBI Chief J. Edgar Hoover, his neighbor. But reminded by Lady Bird that Hoover was a bachelor, they turned to another neighbor, the wife of a doctor who calmed their fears. The child was a source of great happiness to both of them. "I wish you could see Lady Bird—being a mamma is really very becoming to her," he wrote Sherman Bridwell shortly after the birth. "Little Lynda is growing very fast and always has the spotlight over at my place," he wrote in October.[104]

At the same time, he took great satisfaction from the progress of his political and business fortunes. The settlement of the Brown & Root tax case coupled with his and the party's victories in 1944 rekindled his hopes for a higher elected or appointed office. The wartime success of Brown & Root also promised to serve his political ambitions. Having helped B & R win over $350 million in shipbuilding contracts, Lyndon knew he could rely on their financial support in any future campaign. He was also greatly pleased with the course of events at KTBC. At the end of July 1944 he had told Harfield Weedin, who had joined the navy, that "the radio station has been progressing very nicely." In October, he had told Jesse Kellam that the station was "doing fine . . . . We have great plans for the future and at this stage I am rather optimistic." In March 1945, after a trip to Austin, during which he "did a great deal of visiting around in the radio station," he reported that he "was well pleased with developments." His optimism largely rested on the station's balance sheet: by February 1, 1945, KTBC had an operating profit of $42,491 and a net profit of $11,885 for the previous six months.[105]

Lyndon's hopes of increasing the return at KTBC were closely tied to having FDR and other political friends in control of national affairs for another four years. In December 1944, for example, when the President appointed Paul Porter chairman of the FCC, it promised Lyndon the likelihood of a sympathetic hearing for any radio business he might bring before the Commission. An attorney and New Deal administrator who had served in the Agriculture Department and the OPA, Porter was Lyndon's good friend and neighbor. Part of the Corcoran, Fortas, Rowe circle that would gather on Lyndon's back porch for informal suppers and wide-ranging discussions, Porter rode to work in Lyndon's car on a regular basis during the war.

Lyndon also wanted to assure himself of access to Porter's principal assistant. W. Ervin "Red" James, an Alabaman who had served as Cliff Durr's legal assistant at the FCC and then as assistant secretary of the Commission, remembered that at the end of his war service in the navy he was invited to become the legal assistant to the chairman of the FCC. " 'We are waiting for you to come back here,' " Porter's secretary told James when he returned to Washington. " 'You're slated to be the legal assistant to the new chairman.' . . . 'Well, I think I know who started that,' " James replied. "I was correct; it was LBJ." At the end of 1946 when James decided to go back to Alabama to practice law, Lyndon, with whom he had become very friendly, proposed that they go into the radio and television business in Alabama and Texas. " 'Between the two of us we can get some grants, and we can build some stations and we can make a lot of money,' " Lyndon told him. But James didn't have the money, and "we never did do that."[106]

In 1945, Lyndon's political fortunes remained closely tied to FDR's presence in the White House. Despite some differences with the Administration in the war years, Johnson continued to be seen, especially in Texas, as an unqualified pro-Roosevelt man. Although Lyndon had never been a White House insider the way Corcoran or Rowe had been, he was nevertheless an ally with meaningful ties to the President that would echo through the rest of his political career. When Lynda was born, a White House car had dropped off a baby gift at the Johnsons' residence, a book about FDR's dog Fala with the inscription, "From the master—to the pup." Later in the spring, when the Texas Democrats had openly split into pro- and anti-Roosevelt factions, the President had asked Lyndon's advice on whether he should call on Jones and Clayton for a frank discussion. In June, before the Democratic convention in Chicago, Lyndon had been "burning up to tell the President about the Texas situation," and had made an off-the-record visit to the White House.[107]

It was his last meeting with FDR. On April 12, 1945, at the close of the day's business in the House, Lyndon wandered into Sam Rayburn's hideaway office, shortly after Vice President Harry Truman, who had also stopped by for a drink, had been called to the White House. As Lyndon remembered, Rayburn answered his phone. "He didn't say anything at all that I could hear—just a kind of gulp. Then he hung up and looked at me. Finally, he said the President was dead."[108]

Like so many other Americans, Johnson was devastated. He had a profound sense of loss. As he told a reporter later that day, " 'I was just looking up at a cartoon on the wall [of Rayburn's office]—a cartoon showing the President with that cigarette holder and his jaw stuck out like it always was. He had his head cocked back, you know. And then I thought of all the little folks, and what they had lost. He was just like a daddy to me always; he always talked to me just that way . . . . I don't know that I'd ever have come to Congress if it hadn't been for him. But I do know I got my first great desire for public office because of him— and so did thousands of other young men all over the country.' "

A secretary remembered that Lyndon's "grief was just unreal. He just literally wasn't taking phone calls and he just literally shut himself up. His grief was vast and deep and he was crying tears. Manly tears, but he actually felt . . . that it was just like losing his father." The day of Roosevelt's funeral he was so upset he went to bed. And his grief lasted for weeks and months. Sam Houston Johnson remembered that Lyndon "lost some of his drive, periodically pausing in the middle of his still-crowded work day to stare out the window with a troubled look in his eyes. He might spend a half hour that way." Jim Rowe, who was in the Pacific in the navy, couldn't bring himself to write anyone in Washington for two months after the President died. "All the charm and idealism that once peopled that town seemed to die with the Boss and the less I heard about it or from it the more pleased I was," he wrote Lyndon in June. "Never have I felt a greater need for your presence than I felt during the weeks that followed April 13th . . ." was Johnson's reply in July. "It is a different town today. . . . There is little to stimulate one to doing unbelievable things and such accomplishments as we are likely to make will be of the routine type."[109]

Roosevelt's passing engendered a profound sense of loss in millions of Americans, but it did not mean the end of the ideas and programs launched in the preceding twelve years. Johnson, like others in and out of the government, was a bearer of the New Deal legacy. Although he would tack back and forth between liberalism and conservatism in the next fifteen years, positioning himself to run for the Senate and the presidency, he never forgot the lessons learned from the Roosevelt era: a sound economy, social justice, and national security depended in large measure on a wise use of Federal power by the White House and the Congress. The states, localities, and private enterprise all had a significant role to play in assuring the national well-being, but Federal action was a requirement of change and progress. This was especially true for the South, which Johnson believed had the most to gain from Federal economic and racial policies. And though he cautiously felt his way on these matters from 1945 to 1960, often letting expediency guide him into actions which angered progressive Democrats, he was a liberal nationalist biding his time until circumstances favored a new round of activism that would carry the country beyond where it had been when FDR passed from the scene.

9

The Liberal As
Conservative

ROOSEVELT'S death opened up a period of uncertainty in Johnson's life that lasted for three years. The day after the President died, Dorothy Nichols, one of Lyndon's secretaries, asked: " 'He's gone; who do we have now?' And Johnson said, 'Honey, we've got Truman.' I don't remember what I said, but he said, 'There is going to be the damnedest scramble for power in this man's town in the next two weeks that anybody ever saw in their lives.' " Three months later, he was still uncertain about where things were heading, either generally or in his own career. "What line his [Truman's] subordinates follow has yet to be developed," Johnson wrote Jim Rowe. ". . . Most of our old friends are bewildered and I think that is true, generally speaking, of the people who have acquired responsibility and power so quickly. . . . My own course in political affairs is yet to be charted. We are giving serious thought to going back to the Hill Country in Texas and making our contribution to a better world from that spot." [1]

Say what he might, Lyndon was glued to Washington. He remained as ambitious as ever for a powerful voice in public affairs, particularly on the nation's future course abroad. On April 13, he counseled Sam Rayburn to go on one of the radio networks to steady "the nerves of a lot of excited people" and "hit hard" at how the Congress is prepared to help the new President, especially with postwar international relations. Lyndon himself issued a statement to Texas newspapers describing Roosevelt's passing as "a shock from which we will not soon recover" and his successor as a sound, steady, and solid man who would carry on in the Roosevelt tradition.

Jim Rowe was not so sure: "I am afraid Truman will get the temporary backing of the pressure-groups and the business men and professional politicians (an epithet I reserve for those servants of the people who don't hold my opinions!) and in so doing will lose the backing of the people, those people your father used to tell you about and whom I think you still understand. . . . I hope . . . that Truman's moves are consciously calculated to achieve a decent peace because right now that is all I am interested in."[2]

International relations were also high on Lyndon's agenda. When Germany surrendered in May 1945, he was eager for an assignment that would enlarge his part in postwar planning. Mindful that a controversy had erupted at the end of World War I over the disposition of naval supplies abroad, Lyndon persuaded House leaders to let him chair a five-man subcommittee evaluating how U.S. "Naval properties" could be used to meet the need for a strong postwar defense. Although Sam Rayburn had decreed that House members not go abroad, he made an exception for Lyndon's subcommittee. Johnson convinced him that it was "extremely important" to decide what matériel would be integrated into "the Navy of tomorrow" and what would be sent to the Pacific, where most Americans believed a great deal of hard fighting remained.[3]

The subcommittee's trip, which began on May 14, a week after Germany surrendered, and lasted until June 12, proved to be little more than a congressional "junket." The conclusion of the fighting in the Pacific in August made the transfer of naval forces and equipment unnecessary, but even if the war had lasted longer, a total of only $47 million in surplus naval supplies in Europe made the subcommittee unnecessary. Rear Admiral Donald J. MacDonald recalled: the "first question that came out of [General Dwight D.] Eisenhower's staff" in the European Theater of Operations when they heard about the Johnson committee's trip was, " 'What are they doing here?' And we couldn't produce any real answer except just a trip to see, but one thing we found out . . . they wanted . . . to get up on the front lines and maybe see a couple of their constituents."

Lyndon had a different view of the mission. As Donald Cook, his principal aide on the trip, remembered: "There may have been some members of the congressional party who regarded it as a frolic . . . but that wasn't Johnson's attitude. . . . He knew when he got back to Washington he had to have a report for Carl Vinson and it better have some meat in it. And . . . I had a report ready the day we landed." Johnson was also "very conscious of the fact that dealing with war matters . . . he had to have a solid record and unless he . . . [did], he'd be vulnerable to a great deal of criticism."[4]

Secretary of the Navy Forrestal praised the report Johnson and Cook produced. Forrestal was "grateful for the appreciation of the navy planning that went into the operations in Europe," and he cited the report as evidence of "the cooperation that should and can exist between the Executive and legislative branches of government." While he also commended the committee for its "carefully considered criticism," Forrestal was offering no more than a polite nod to Johnson and Cook for a well-drawn report of no real consequence; it was quickly buried in Navy Department files.[5]

Although little, if anything, came from the committee's work, Lyndon found the trip exciting and instructive nonetheless. Never having been to Europe or North Africa, he had his first exposure to Bermuda, the Azores, London, Paris, Bremen, Naples, Rome, Palermo, Oran, Rabat, Casablanca, Marseilles, Cannes, Edinburgh, and Reykjavik, in that order. It was not the usual tourist attractions that made the strongest impression on him, however, but the devastation from nearly six years of fighting. A detailed log of the committee's journey captured the horrors of the time: the many areas of London that had been smashed by German V-1 and V-2 rockets and made block fronts on many streets look "like the mouth of a small boy with missing front teeth"; the Normandy beaches littered with damaged landing craft and tanks; the city of St.-Lô which, from the air, seemed to consist only of skeleton buildings; the shortages of food, electricity, and transport afflicting Paris; the lifeless piles of rubble in the Ruhr; the gutted city of Bremen, where nothing remained standing in its central area except a few walls in "crazy patterns" and "the smell of death" from thousands of people buried in the wreckage "hung heavy in the air"; the caves outside Rome in which the Germans had massacred 325 Italians; the poverty and filth of Palermo, where 2000 hungry Sicilians ate a thick soup made from the garbage of U.S. military mess halls; and the squalor which seemed to be everywhere in North Africa.[6]

However unforgettable the devastation, it was men and politics—the subjects of greatest interest to Johnson—that made the strongest impressions on him during the trip. In Rheims, France, where the surrender documents had been signed two weeks before, Eisenhower charmed Lyndon and his colleagues. The General patiently briefed the delegation on European conditions, encouraged them to go anywhere they wished, and telephoned an aide to assure that they had "a very pleasant and wonderful visit." By the end of the meeting "he had all the congressmen just eating right out of his hand." A 45-minute private meeting with Pope Pius XII at the Vatican made an even stronger impression on Johnson: the Pope "projected a personality that was at one and the same time austere, understanding, sympathetic, magnetic, almost ethereal and then finally no-nonsense." He read a statement of welcome in English that he had typed on a portable typewriter that morning. He and Johnson discussed "the sadness of the struggle, the terrible consequences of

the war, the necessity for peace and rehabilitation and the drawing together again of mankind to the extent that it was possible." [7]

There is no record of how these people regarded Johnson. But Donald
Cook remembers Lyndon's masterful manipulation of people during the
trip. Convinced that a successful job depended on the agreement and
support of all the committee's members, the two Republicans as well as
the two Democrats, Johnson took account of each man's strengths,
weaknesses, and idiosyncrasies and did "whatever was necessary to keep
them in the right frame of mind." When F. Edward Hebert of Louisiana, who was "sort of the playboy of the western world," wanted to visit
a "house of ill-fame" or pick up a case of Scotch in Edinburgh, which
they freely drank throughout the trip, or play some poker, or attend the
Folies Bèrgèrè, Lyndon did not object. Johnson "really wanted to make
a contribution to ending the damn war, and if it took permitting a few
frolics along the way . . . okay . . . . It was all for a good cause," Don
Cook said. Lyndon was "very, very likable. And . . . we had a lot of fun
on the trip," Hebert recalls. Describing how they rolled a bottle of Scotch
from one end of their big DC3 to the other so everyone could have a
drink, Hebert told an interviewer: "I'm telling you these things to show
how human he was . . . . I mean he was one of the boys, [one of the]
gang. Now shut that [tape recorder] off," Hebert said before relating
something indiscreet. The report the committee produced may not have
made much difference, but Johnson knew how to make its members
speak with one voice. It was a political strength he turned to good advantage repeatedly during his career. [8]

The two most important impressions Johnson carried away from the
trip were the military's profligacy and the "Communist threat." In Naples the congressmen and their aides had dinner with Adm. William A.
Glassford, commander of Mediterranean forces. The Admiral was living
in a "fabulous villa" with a magnificent view of the Bay. The variety
and quality of the food, wine, and entertainment made Cook and the
others feel not "within fifty years of war. It was unreal and . . . in incredibly bad taste . . . . Within a hundred yards [of the villa was] the
most abject poverty"—a "fantastic juxtaposition of poverty . . . and op-
ulent splendor." Later, Lyndon smiled at Cook and said, "those military
cats really live. . . . They had airplanes to go out and pick up antiques
to furnish the chateaus. They had the best food, the best everything that
was available. Of course, they were putting their lives on the line, so
maybe that's part of the compensation for doing it. But not many of the
dogfaces were invited guests at Glassford's villa." The experience underscored something Lyndon never forgot—most of America's military
chiefs were as self-serving as everyone else. [9]

A constant refrain Johnson and the others heard in France was the danger of a Communist take-over. By May 1945, troubles with the Soviets over Poland had made talk of a "barbarian invasion of Europe" or the spread of Communism to the West a clearly sounded theme in the United States. In France, where there was a well-organized and powerful Communist party, fear existed that unless the United States restored the country's transportation system to distribute coal and food and stimulate employment, France would become a satellite of the Soviet Union. Warned by American Ambassador Jefferson Caffery in Paris of these dangers, seeing the woeful conditions under which so many Europeans were living, and hearing from GIs in Germany that they had had enough of war and wanted to come home, Johnson developed a powerful fear of Communist expansion throughout Western Europe. Cook said later that "all of our work was worthless" on the trip, "except maybe some of the observations that we had on the . . . importance of preventing the spread of communism."[10]

From the summer of 1945 to the spring of 1946 domestic affairs were more important to most Americans than the Communist threat. They feared that the sudden curtailment of military production would cause massive unemployment and a return to the economic conditions of the thirties. Some economists, however, predicted that the postwar problem would not be a recession or a depression but runaway inflation. A scarcity of consumer products and huge wartime savings threatened to make large demand and limited supplies a principal feature of the postwar economy. But in August, when a *New York Times* story predicted that 5 million Americans would lose war production jobs and 1.8 million people were laid off in the first ten days after the Pacific fighting ended, fears of depression eclipsed forecasts of unprecedented inflation.

Truman responded to the economic slowdown by calling for the economic bill of rights Roosevelt had announced in 1944. On September 6 the President put a twenty-one point domestic program before the Congress that included a full employment bill, assuring all job seekers of work, expanded unemployment benefits, a higher minimum wage, housing and hospital construction programs, permanent farm price supports, massive new public works, lower taxes, and a permanent Fair Employment Practices Commission.[11]

The announcement of the twenty-one-point program struck a resonant chord with liberals, but it represented only one side of Truman's thinking and spoke to a distinct minority in the country and Congress. While Truman went to bat for liberal reform, he also made clear that his primary concern was not an all-out fight for liberal advance but a smooth shift from a war-based to a peacetime economy, a reconversion program that would satisfy conservatives as well as liberals and keep Democrats in power. As historian Alonzo Hamby puts it, above all Truman was "a professional politician, for whom party regularity was a way of life." He was "hardly a liberal crusader. Most of his best friends were the moderates and conservatives of the Senate 'Establishment.' " Truman reflected these leanings in his appointment of moderate and conservative Democrats to government jobs: Fred M. Vinson of Kentucky, a middle of the road, practical New Dealer, as Secretary of the Treasury; the moderate Tom Clark of Texas, an early Truman supporter for the vice presidency, as Attorney General; and the conservative Missouri banker John Snyder as director of the Office of War Mobilization and Reconversion. Truman had little affinity for what he called "intellectual" or "nonpolitical" liberals. As he told one aide, he wanted no part of the "crackpots and lunatic fringe" that had been close to FDR and had put the country through the "experiments" from which it now wanted a rest. At the same time, however, Truman considered himself "a legatee of the New Deal . . . a liberal of sorts." Although he did not want to be called a "liberal" or a "progressive," he was happy to be thought of as "forward-looking." [12]

Although Lyndon had initial doubts about Truman, they had a lot in common. Johnson was delighted that the President followed the advice of the Texas delegation, including his, that Tom Clark replace Francis Biddle, a prominent liberal, as Attorney General. "I want you to be the first I write since the nomination," Clark notified Lyndon in Europe. Clark described himself as "ever grateful" for his help and "flabbergasted" when Truman offered him the job. "As I tried to leave through a window (instead of the door) he [Truman] said 'up to your old tricks eh!' I had confused a large window for the door." Fred Vinson's cabinet post also pleased Lyndon: It "gives all new hope and it may be that he will lead us out of the wilderness," Johnson wrote Rowe.[13]

Lyndon also liked Truman's liberal policy statements. The President's call for a full-employment bill in September coincided with Lyndon's discussion of postwar reconversion in his congressional district. By organizing an all-day meeting in an Austin hotel on August 31, Johnson brought together five hundred Federal, state, and local officials and leading private citizens to discuss how war workers and returning veterans could be absorbed into the economy and how every man, woman, and child could find the means for an independent and happy life in the postwar era. Lyndon outlined a program in which "private business and venture capital would be given [the] first opportunity to absorb the services and abilities of every person looking for work." But if private enterprise was "unable to take up the unemployment slack," public agencies were to plan building programs that would do the job and preserve communities from "the necessity of feeding hungry men through the expediency of 'leaf-raking' projects or the dole or soup lines." "We're going to try to make our system work," Johnson told the audience,

"—but we're not going back to 1933. I know that hungry, sick, jobless, illiterate men lead nations into war. I'm for local self-government, but a hungry man can't eat it. I'm for state's rights, but you can't feed that to a starving baby." Federal programs for people in need, the liberal nationalism Lyndon had warmly supported in the thirties, remained his answer to potential economic ills after the war.[14]

Johnson's response to a series of Administration measures that came before the House during the next eight months was of a piece with his reconversion conference in Austin. Although the House, with Truman's acquiesence, watered down the full-employment bill, Lyndon joined the majority in voting for what he and the White House viewed as a qualified victory. Omitting a commitment to full employment, the law nevertheless promised government support of *maximum* employment and set up a potentially important Council of Economic Advisors. Further, Lyndon spoke and voted for bills that aimed to allieviate the housing shortage caused by a wartime moratorium on home construction. He supported legislation providing 100,000 temporary housing units for distressed families of servicemen and for steps "to insure the availability of real estate for housing purposes at fair and reasonable prices." He also voted to continue price control and stabilization laws that would prevent a reoccurrence of the boom and bust cycle that followed World War I. He declared himself for a farm program of "highlines and highways to our farms, high soil productivity, and high but stablized farm prices"; in short, rural electrification, farm to market roads, soil conservation, and generous price subsidies.[15]

On no issue did Johnson speak more eloquently during this time than Federal assistance to health care. In a speech on the House floor favoring a five-year $375 million appropriation to assist states in building hospitals, he pointed out that physical and mental defects had barred one out of every four men from military service. In the South, the ratio had been even higher. This information, Johnson said, is "a proper predicate for a bill" that would "raise the level of man's physical well-being" by helping local communities build hospitals. "This is no attempt to federalize the Nation's hospitals," he added. Nor was it a step toward socialized medicine. Rather, it was a measure to alleviate the acute shortage of hospitals, doctors, and nurses in the country and, by so doing, improve the health of all Americans: "The fly which eats at the open privy of a slum area has no scruples about carrying polio to the child in the silk-stocking area. The health of a community can be no better than the health of those least able to afford medical and hospital care . . . . That, then, is the bill. It proposes to spend in one year much less than the cost of one day of war. It proposes to make these expenditures, not that men shall die but that men may live. It is rooted in the sound American doctrine of local government." Johnson's support of what became the Hill-Burton Act was a prelude to later efforts to ensure affordable medical care for the elderly. The hospital construction program particularly served the South, where more than 40 percent of the health facilities built under Hill-Burton were located.[16]

In the immediate postwar period Johnson also continued to urge ideas about world affairs that had informed liberal thinking during the war. In particular, he identified himself with people like Dr. Robert Montgomery of the University of Texas, who warned that another war in an atomic age would mean the end of humankind. "We've got to live in a brotherhood of man," Montgomery declared. "I don't like the idea, either, of being brothers to Russians. And Africans, and Republicans. And some Democrats. But that's the way it is . . . . We've got to have peace. We probably have to have one world government. A United States of the world." Paul Bolton, the news director at KTBC, reported Montgomery's speech on Johnson's station: "He is preaching salvation, yours and mine," Bolton said. " . . . If he doesn't convince you that we must have a brotherhood of man, he'll . . . scare the living hell out of you." Johnson placed Bolton's remarks about Montgomery's "most impressive presentation of the necessity for world cooperation in the atomic age" in the *Congressional Record*.[17]

In the first half of 1946 Johnson urged continued cooperation with the U.S.S.R., opposed mounting anticommunism in the United States, and supported a plan by financier Bernard Baruch for control of atomic power. His trip to Europe had aroused fears in him of Communist expansion, but his initial solution to the problem was a reaffirmation of FDR's cooperative approach to the Russians. In January, he told the League of Women Voters in Austin that we've got to continue to get along with Russia. He favored giving the secret of the atomic bomb to Moscow. "Those people who seek to breed hate and distrust may kill millions of their own boys," he said. In 1945, he was absent when the House voted first to establish a permanent standing committee on un-American activities and then to fund it. In May 1946, he was one of only 81 House members voting against continued funding for the Committee's work. In the summer, after Baruch unveiled his plan for international control of atomic energy with the words "We are here to make a choice between the quick and the dead," Lyndon declared himself in favor of "putting the atomic bomb under international control under the United Nations if a secure system could be worked out." He warned that without some kind of agreement to prevent the proliferation of atomic weapons, "civilization is going to be wiped out."[18]

Johnson's espousal of government activism in behalf of the disadvantaged and of international cooperation for peace reflected what liberal Congresswoman Helen Gahagan Douglas characterized as the warm, humane, populist side of LBJ. "He cared about people; was never cal-

lous, never indifferent to suffering. There was a warmth about the man"
that moved liberals to forgive him his occasional votes against some of
their most passionately held ideas. Yet it was not simply idealism ani-
mating Johnson's actions. The liberal measures he supported in 1945–
46—employment, housing, farm electrification, road building, conservation, and hospital construction bills—were all calculated to serve the
continued economic expansion of the South. His identification with
southern interests was also reflected in anti-labor and anti-civil rights
votes.

Like Truman and millions of Americans in 1945–46, Johnson had
little sympathy for strikes by unions demanding higher wages to meet
price increases and to make up for reduced work hours. He shared the
President's perception that union wage demands were excessive and were
putting the Administration's reconversion plans and the country in jeopardy. Early in 1946, after Truman asked the Congress to set up fact-
finding boards to investigate labor disputes and compel laborers to return
to work while the boards deliberated, Johnson voted with the President.
Further, in May, when strikes by two railway unions threatened to shut
down the railroads, disrupt the American economy, and interrupt relief
shipments to Europe, Truman asked congressional authority to draft
strikers. Despite bitter criticism from liberals, Johnson joined the House
majority approving the President's request. In June, moreover, after
Truman rejected a permanent antiunion law that was too strong for him,
Johnson voted with 255 other House members unsuccessfully trying to
overturn the President's veto.[19]

Similarly, in 1945–46, Johnson uniformly sided with southern opponents of anti-lynching, anti-poll tax, and FEPC laws. Johnson said that
he was not "against" blacks but rather for states' rights. He further justified his votes by asserting that these bills would not pass anyway, and
he did well to vote with southerners on civil rights as a way to command
their help on other important issues. Some of this was just rhetoric. While
Johnson genuinely wished to see greater opportunities and improved
conditions for blacks that would ultimately serve all southerners, he also
shared conventional southern attitudes toward blacks.

Beginning in the mid-1940s, Robert Parker, a black sharecropper's
son, worked for Johnson part time as a servant at private dinner parties
in Washington. He remembers it as a "painful experience." Grateful to
Johnson for getting him a job at the post office and work at cocktail and
dinner parties of other prominent Washington officials, Parker feared
Johnson "because of the pain and humiliation he could inflict at a moment's notice. . . . In front of his guests Johnson would often 'nigger'
at me. He especially liked to put on a show for [Mississippi] Sen. [Theo-
dore G.] Bilbo, who used to lecture: 'The only way to treat a nigger is to
kick him.' . . . I used to dread being around Johnson when Bilbo was

present, because I knew it meant that Johnson would play racist. That was the LBJ I hated. Privately, he was a different man as long as I didn't do anything to make him angry. He'd call me 'boy' almost affectionately. Sometimes I felt that he was treating me almost as an equal. . . . Although I never heard him speak publicly about black men without saying 'nigger,' I never heard him say 'nigger woman.' In fact, he always used to call his black cook, Zephyr Wright, a college graduate who couldn't find any other work, 'Miss Wright' or 'sweetheart.' "[20]

Like his attitude toward blacks and civil rights, personal background and experience partly shaped Johnson's anti-unionism. In October 1945, after the Lower Colorado River Authority refused to consider requests from electrical workers to bargain collectively, the men walked off the job. Threatening to disrupt power and water supplies to central Texas towns, the strike brought a sharp public reaction from Johnson: "The sick in hospitals are endangered. Farm products will spoil . . . . The people of my district will not countenance this action. I do not know the things in controversy, but I do know that Texans will not tolerate this stoppage or sabotage." The workers, incensed at Johnson for speaking without knowing the facts, complained that he seemed to place "no responsibility on management," which was treating employees like "peons."

If he had second thoughts about his attack on the LCRA workers, an attempt by the Communications Workers of America (CWA) to unionize KTBC ended them. When station employees announced a strike and began picketing, Lyndon issued a statement declaring himself mystified by the action: The station had no reason to think that employees were discontented; they had no complaints about a $1 minimum wage, which was more than double the Federal standard, year-end bonuses, two-week vacations, and two-week sick leaves. He believed his votes on recent labor legislation to be the source of the problem: "If a union, or anybody else who dislikes my vote, elects to measure out my punishment—well, I won't stand for being pushed around. I don't like it any better than any other American citizen." When he heard rumors that the CWA planned to destroy KTBC's transmitter, he persuaded some old friends to guard the station with shotguns. No attack occurred, and the attempt at unionization failed. Nevertheless, the strike pained him. When Eliot Janeway wrote to say that descriptions of him as anti-labor were "unfair and irresponsible," Lyndon was grateful for his "thoughtful and understanding letter."[21]

Johnson's anti-civil rights and anti-union actions in 1945–46 were less an expression of genuine antagonism to these groups than an attempt to position himself to make state-wide races in Texas—first for the governorship and then for a U.S. Senate seat. Convinced that he needed to appease conservatives or alter his image as a staunch Roosevelt Democrat, he now aggressively identified himself with widespread feelings in

Texas against Federal civil rights legislation and unions. "On many important votes," Helen Gahagan Douglas said, "it was impossible to know why he had voted a certain way, whether it was from conviction or political considerations. He was willing to make the compromises necessary . . . to guarantee that he stayed in the Congress. In fact, he made fun of those who refused to bend at all to conditions stacked against them . . . . He wanted to stay on top in Congress and to stay in politics. And he wanted to play an active role at the head of the majority, not at the head of the minority."[22]

By the spring of 1946, however, he concluded that his shift to the right might not be enough to assure him a victory in a state-wide race. Although he encouraged rumors beginning in April 1945 that he would become a gubernatorial candidate, he was ambivalent about making the race. In the fall of 1945, when Sam Rayburn told him that Truman would ask Tom Connally, who was chairman of the Senate Foreign Relations Committee, to become Ambassador to the United Nations, Lyndon gave priority to running for Connally's Senate seat. After Connally rejected Truman's offer, however, Lyndon again considered running for governor. He wrestled with the decision until March 1946, when he decided not to risk it. Straw polls in twenty-three cities across the state gave him a five-point lead over his nearest rival, but he had only 22 percent of the vote, with the rest of the electorate divided among six other candidates. The survey raised serious doubts about whether he would win. "A lot of people . . . are now saying 'We hate to see Lyndon get into this Governor's race,' " the pollster wrote Johnson in February. " 'There is some chance he will get beat and it will hurt him for the real job that Texas needs him for.' There seems to be a feeling that you could go to the Senate against O'Daniel in two years from Congress better than from the Gov.'s office. From studying this thing . . . damn if I am not coming to the same feeling."[23]

Another House race, in which he had no significant opposition, had special appeal to Lyndon in early 1946. Having been sick with flu and then hospitalized for pneumonia in January, he wished to avoid a strenuous election contest. Moreover, by 1945–46, at the age of thirty-seven, he had lost some of his drive and grown a little complacent about his hold on his congressional seat. In December 1944, Harold Ickes noted "that he is toning down a bit. He is not so young and exuberant, as he used to be, at least he does not appear to be." In February 1946, after his bout with pneumonia, he wrote his cousin Oriole Bailey in Texas that he looked forward "to the day when I can settle in Austin and lead a normal existence without being pulled this way and that by hundreds of people everytime I go home."

Throughout his political career, Johnson saw politics as a matter of giving and taking. But the incessant giving sometimes exhausted him.

Twenty-five years later, after Johnson retired, the governor of Texas asked to visit him at his ranch. "What did the Governor want?" an aide asked Johnson. "Damned if I know," Johnson replied. "He came with his wife and daughter and sat around my living room all afternoon but never said what he wanted. Maybe he wanted me to kiss his ass. After all, that's the business I've been in for the last forty years."

It particularly bothered Lyndon in 1946 when people in his district criticized him for giving more time to "big shots" than "little shots." Since he spent 95 percent of his time in Austin seeing ordinary folks with everyday problems, he wrote Wirtz, he could see only two explanations for the discontent: either constituents enjoyed the privlege of "saying anything any time about him"—"one of the prices a person pays for public service"—or he had been lax about pressing the case for himself in the district lately. "I have found that age has probably mellowed me some, because in my younger days I didn't hesitate to charge hell with a bucket of water or ask a man to move out of his own house if it would help me. Now I am a little more considerate and those things are a little more distasteful to me." [24]

Wirtz gently prodded him to be more aggressive about the coming election. On February 27, he told Johnson that an unknown Brenham woman had filed to run against him and predicted that he would have other opponents. "I am not telling you this to alarm you. . . . But I do think the situation will require that you devote some time to visiting and hand-shaking over the District. . . . I think you and your friends had just as well prepare to put on a real old-fashioned campaign and let them know that when they get into a race against you it is like going rabbit hunting and jumping a bear." [25]

During the next six weeks, when the same "oil boys out of Houston" who tried to defeat him in 1944 prepared another no-holds-barred campaign, Lyndon was ready for them. At the beginning of April, he wired the editor of the *Austin American* that his opponents were trying to persuade war veterans to announce against him in each of the ten counties of the Tenth District. At the last moment nine were to withdraw and throw their support to the tenth. "Each candidate is promised liberal, and I mean liberal, support by the same oil crowd that tried to defeat me two years ago. This is a barefaced contemptible attempt to manipulate the veteran vote as it is done by big city bosses. . . . I hope you see fit to publish this telegram." [26]

Johnson's opponents chose Hardy Hollers, a forty-five-year-old much-decorated army colonel and attorney, to run against him. Hollers also had the distinction of having helped Supreme Court Justice Robert Jackson prepare the Nuremberg trials against Nazi war criminals. Despite Hollers's formidable credentials, Johnson was convinced that he would be little more than a front man for the Texas regulars. [27]

Anticipating a dirty campaign in which he would have to give as good as he got, Johnson asked Tommy Corcoran to get somebody in Washington to give him Hollers's service record. "Col. Harvey Hollers . . . has announced against Lyndon Johnson . . . for Congress on the ground that Hollers is a great war hero and the guy who really prepared the Nuremberg trials for Bob Jackson," Corcoran wrote his contact in the War Department. "Could we look at his record to see how great a war hero he really is?" After obtaining the record, Corcoran reported to Johnson that "There is no actual evidence that this officer participated in actual engagements with the enemy." In addition, his work at Nuremberg "was a very narrow lawyer's job of sitting in a chair and sifting through documents—nothing more." Lyndon told John Connally, who managed his campaign, that Hollers was a Judge Advocate General (JAG) officer. "There is no record of a JAG ever having even an ear drum punctured by the sound of combat . . . . I should think a young war veteran could point this out very nicely in Austin." However much Hollers may have embellished his service record, Corcoran and Johnson had broken Federal regulations to acquire the information.[28]

Hollers nevertheless had a more impressive war record than Johnson, and he emphasized the point in the opening speech of his campaign. "It was a vicious speech," Connally wrote Johnson. " . . . He hit the war record, yours and his, pretty hard." But Connally thought this would not carry much weight in a two-and-a-half-month campaign: "people are going to be awfully sick of a man publicly and blatantly patting himself on the back about what a great hero he is." Attacks on Johnson for having enriched himself in office worried Connally more: "His insinuations about your affluence and the enrichment of your friends will have some effect and will eventually have to be answered by someone." Connally urged Johnson to bide his time and let Hollers's overstatements and accusations undermine his credibility as a sensible candidate for high office.[29]

Over the next ten weeks, Hollers mounted an attack that made Johnson fear for his political life. Hollers hammered on the issue of "honesty in government," or whether Johnson had used his congressional job to help enrich relatives, principal supporters, and himself. According to Hollers, Thomas Jefferson Taylor, Lyndon's father-in-law, had gone into the construction business shortly after Johnson entered Congress and had made several hundred thousand dollars by building, among other things, rural electrification systems, a matter of central concern to the congressman. Taylor had also made a healthy profit on land sold to the Federal government for an ordnance plant. Why the government chose Taylor's land for the ordnance works and why he received about twice as much money per acre for his land as other nearby landholders were unanswered questions.

Hollers said that Johnson friends had also profited from the congress-man's position and influence: Alvin Wirtz had received $90,000 in fees from the LCRA, an agency beholden to Johnson; Herman Brown, "the war-rich construction man," who headed the firm of Brown & Root, had built the Corpus Christi Naval Base and received numerous other de-fense contracts while Johnson "was a member of the House Naval Af-fairs Committee"; several of Johnson's former secretaries and associates had received a license from the FCC to build KVET, a competing radio station in Austin that would broadcast over KTBC's transmitter, an unheard-of arrangement for competing radio stations; and numerous postmasters and civil servants held their government jobs by working for Lyndon Johnson, who had set up a "political machine" that was "only one step ahead of the Gestapo system they had in Germany."

Hollers complained that the advantages received by Johnson's rela-tives and friends were minor alongside of those accruing directly to Johnson. KTBC was given longer hours and increased power, advan-tages denied its previous owners, shortly after the Johnsons acquired the station. Advertisers on the station received government contracts and hard-to-get wartime materials. An owner of "one of the war-rich Austin contracting firms . . . boasted that he contributed $100,000 to his [Johnson's] campaign for the United States Senate." After he was de-feated, Johnson "threatened to contest the election. But a gentle hint that there might be an investigation into his campaign silenced his pro-tests." Johnson purchased a luxurious house on Dillman Street in Aus-tin from W. S. Bellows, a B & R partner, and in eight days paid off an eight-year $10,000-note in cash. Johnson was so busy with his business interests in Austin, Hollers said, that he was on the job in Congress only 40 percent of the time in 1945. Finally, on two occasions, Johnson em-issaries had offered Hollers "a fat government job" if he agreed to drop out of the race. But Hollers "told them I was in this race for keeps. I told them that Lyndon Johnson, by his own official acts and conduct as a Congressman, had proven himself UNFIT to hold public office. I told them that I HADN'T REACHED THAT LOW DEPTH where I would barter the rights of the men and women of the 10th Congressional District" for the kind of self-serving arrangement Johnson himself typically made.[30]

In the face of so many charges, Johnson had to respond. As he told one supporter in late June, "Enough has been said about me and my wife and my baby and my wife's father, and I am going to justify every-thing." Johnson sent Hollers a letter saying he would refute the charges one by one.[31]

"No person to my knowledge has ever offered you any Government job . . . , and certainly no one with my knowledge or consent made any such statements." Since it was simply Johnson's word against Hol-lers's, the matter of whether Johnson tried to get him out of the race with a job offer remained in dispute. "No Austin contractor or any other contractor ever gave me $100,000 or $1,000 or $1." Johnson challenged Hollers to provide proof that someone had. Since the IRS investigation of Brown & Root was not known or available to Hollers, he had only hearsay evidence to support his charge. Further, because he had made no public statement, as Hollers said he had, about contesting the 1941 election, Johnson effectively denied that he had ever considered doing it.

As for Taylor's business ventures and profits, Lyndon simply denied that he had anything to do with them. He also sent a telegram to Assistant Secretary of War Howard Peterson asking him to investigate the purchase of Taylor's land for $23 an acre and explain why other landowners received only $13 per acre. He challenged Peterson to bring forth any information showing that he had any part in Taylor's dealings with the War Department. None existed, and it is conceivable, as Walter Jenkins later asserted, that Taylor was a "very strong-minded" businessman who never consulted Johnson about any of these business matters. But the timing and circumstances of Taylor's gains and the general knowledge that Johnson had quietly served Brown & Root so effectively left substantial questions about whether he had also helped his father-in-law. Johnson was on stronger ground when he denied that he had a record of absenteeism from the House in 1945. He was able to show that he had been present 79 percent of the time.[32]

Johnson's answers to allegations that he had Tenth District postmasters in his pocket, had a self-serving interest in the success of KVET, and had bought the house on Dillman Street with Brown & Root money left the first two issues on the table. His response to the postmaster charge was particularly vague: "You have stated that . . . I had built up a 'big wartime political machine' . . . ," he wrote Hollers. "If you mean that friends who support my cause belong to a machine, then I am sure you will find out on July 27th that we have about three-fourths of the citizens of the district riding in it." In fact, postmasters in the district were not only indebted to Johnson for their jobs, they also violated the Hatch Act by secretly working to keep Johnson in office. In February 1946, for example, Ray Lee, the postmaster at Austin, informed Lyndon about the volume of mail being received by a "Mr. R . . . . I thought you would want to know. Now throw this away." In Brenham, Postmaster T. A. Low, Jr., "Brother Low" to Lyndon, organized contacts with Johnson voters in Washington County during the 1946 campaign, for which Johnson was most grateful: "You are doing a top job," Lyndon wrote him. "Let's carry Washington County overwhelmingly." Eager to use Federal employees throughout his district to the fullest possible extent in the '46 campaign, Johnson had Walter Jenkins and Don Cook, who was now with the Justice Department, gather information on how much the Hatch Act limited the political activities of civil servants.[33]

Questions about Johnson's associations with KVET remained a source of controversy throughout the campaign. The fact that ten of Johnson's friends, all World War II veterans, including John Connally, Ed Clark, and Jake Pickle, received a license for a competing radio station moved Hollers to suggest that Johnson was using them as a front for his ownership of the station and his monopolization of Austin radio. Although Johnson defied Hollers to prove that he had any investment in KVET or that he had any part in the FCC decision to approve the application for the station, the absence of any competition for the license and the likelihood that KVET would cooperate rather than compete with KTBC made even the most trusting soul doubt that Johnson had no involvement with KVET.

Some of Hollers's suspicions were justified. By 1945–46, KTBC had become a lucrative investment for the Johnsons, and Lyndon was determined to protect its future growth and profitability. In the summer of 1945, when a friend had asked whether Johnson had an interest in selling KTBC, he had replied: "I have talked to Bird about your letter. . . . The answer is 'no.' That's our old age pension." But it was more than that. In the fall of 1945, they had won approval from the FCC to increase the station's power to 5000 kilowatts and its primary listening audience to 2.5 million people. The station's after-tax profits for 1945 had reached nearly $40,000 and by May 1946 its net worth was $115,500. Should Lyndon have been forced out of office, he would have had a lucrative business to run. To keep it that way, however, he wished to assure that an inevitable third Austin station would not undercut KTBC.

In February 1946 he learned that "a bunch of Texas regulars" had made an application for an Austin radio station that would be an NBC affiliate. Lyndon asked Tommy Corcoran to find out if NBC actually planned to do this, and if they did, he told Corcoran in a telephone conversation, "then I'm going to get my hat on my head and get up there" to New York. Whether he ever interceded with NBC is unknown, but he took other steps to assure that a competing radio station in Austin would not undermine KTBC or would provide what he called "responsible competition." If somebody has got to have a competing radio station, he told FCC Chairman Paul Porter, "I would rather have it with my friends than with my enemies." Consequently, he helped John Connally and the nine other vets win a license from the FCC for KVET and arrange a desirable wave length, which a San Antonio station agreed to relinquish. He also assisted in getting the Civil Aeronautics Administration to drop an objection to a 211-foot KVET broadcasting tower. In return for Johnson's aid, the new station accommodated itself to KTBC by focusing its programming on sports and news. In 1955, for example, when the St. Louis Cardinals and Budweiser announced an agreement to broadcast games on "100-plus radio stations," Bill Deason, the general manager of KVET, told Walter Jenkins: "We are very much interested in carrying these games in case KTBC is not. Please see what you can find out." Johnson may not have owned any part of KVET, but he assured that it did nothing to jeopardize the success of KTBC.[34]

Johnson was particularly aggressive about answering questions relating to the Dillman Street property. Though he had bought the duplex apartment building from W. S. Bellows, the Brown & Root partner, there was no skulduggery involved. Bellows had built the apartment for a mistress, who had been living in it when she committed suicide in 1943. Eager to get rid of the property, Bellows sold it to the Johnsons for $15,490, which they paid in cash from Lady Bird's inheritance. Because he was on solid ground in answering this charge, Lyndon made a great deal of the accusation in the campaign. At his opening rally, he announced that he was making financial records available to disprove the charge and invited anyone who wished to see them to come forward at the close of his speech. He also announced that canceled checks and legal papers in connection with the purchase of KTBC, their home in Washington, D.C., and the Dillman street house "are open to your inspection at the Capital National Bank" in Austin.[35]

Because Johnson was unable to answer some of the charges leveled against him, Hollers's campaign angered and provoked Lyndon and his closest associates. They did not think that Hollers could beat Johnson, but they believed he was undermining Lyndon's standing as a leading candidate for a Senate seat in 1948. What particularly galled Lyndon and his supporters was their conviction that Hollers, who was "holier than thou" in his attacks on the Johnsons, was himself a bought man. "Everybody knew that you were going to have opposition," John Connally had written Lyndon in May. "It was just a question of who was a big enough political whore to succumb to the seduction of the Houston oil men and it wasn't to Hardy's credit that he was about the 12th political prostitute who was propositioned." Johnson and his friends believed that the oil interests had paid Hollers up to $25,000 to enter the campaign, and were spending thousands more to win the primary.[36]

As a seasoned politician, Johnson understood that a big victory, which could make him a frontrunner for the Senate in 1948, partly depended on exciting interest in the campaign. The first requirement was to get out on the hustings and "press the flesh." Lyndon organized a seventeen-day schedule that took him through all ten counties in his district, where he gave fifty-one speeches and shook hands with thousands of constituents. Johnson "prides himself on being able to outwalk anybody in Austin," one of his campaign handouts read. "He's been walking fast tonight, too. His suit is already drenched through and the perspiration is running down his forehead. They say that in a single day the young Tenth District Congressman can greet by NAME several hundreds of the home folks of his district."[37]

The carefully orchestrated efforts of campaign aides assured that Johnson spoke to large crowds. His organizers in Austin informed local leaders of when Johnson would come to their town. A few days before his appearance, voters received a postcard inviting them to hear the speech. Newspaper ads, posted handbills, and telephone calls on the day of the speech reminded voters of the coming event. Two hours before his arrival, "Johnson's Hill Billy Boys," a four-piece band, rode around town playing music and urging folks to hear Lyndon speak. There was more: in some places, notices that they would give away ice cold watermelons and that movie star Gene Autry would entertain drew large crowds. Having helped get Autry into the Air Transport Command during the war and speed up his discharge at the end of the fighting, Lyndon accepted an offer from him to work in the campaign. Singing the hit tune, "I'm Back in the Saddle Again," Autry would shout, "Let's put my friend Lyndon back in the saddle again, because that's where he belongs." In a time before television brought entertainers like Autry into people's homes, seeing a movie star up close had tremendous appeal. Also using hoopla to combat the charges of wrongdoing against him, Lyndon's "Hill Billy Boys" sang, "A Man who'll fight/ For what is right/ Let's vote for Lyndon Johnson./ A man who's fair/ And on the square/ Let's vote for Lyndon Johnson./ He'll be your voice/ The people's choice/ Let's vote for Lyndon Johnson./ . . . For he's one guy/ No one can buy/ Let's vote for Lyndon Johnson."[38]

Humor was also an effective weapon against Hollers. "This mudslinging and mire reminds me of a story," Lyndon told his audiences. "One fellow said to another, 'Say, did you hear about Smith making $100,000 on wheat?' The other said, 'Yes and no.' The first one asked, 'What do you mean, yes and no?' 'Well,' said the second, 'It's true and it isn't true. His name wasn't Smith, it was Jones. It wasn't wheat, it was rye. It wasn't $100,000, it was just $10. And he didn't make it, he lost it.' " "And everybody just howled," Jake Pickle recalled, "because he said, 'Now, that's what they've been saying about your congressman; that he has been involved in all of these things. It wasn't Johnson, it was the Magnolia Oil Company. It wasn't a commodity, it was oil. And he hasn't been making it for himself, he has been making it for you.' "[39]

Yet all the mudslinging, hoopla, and humor were secondary to the fact that Johnson had a nine-year record of accomplishment for the district which he made the centerpiece of his campaign. His slogan, printed across handbills passed out at every rally, was: "I Remember, and I Know You Have Not Forgotten." His constant refrain was "the hard times that we had during the thirties: the banks going broke; people not having anything to eat or any jobs; how we had built back up now; how we have saved democracy." As Jake Pickle remembered the campaign, Johnson pulled at people's heartstrings by tying New Deal accomplishments and his role in them to a popular song of the day, "Did you ever see a dream walking? Well, I did." "His was a dream," Pickle remembered Johnson saying, "where people could work; people could have a job; people could get an education; where there would be no poverty." And to make this dream come true, he had worked successfully for Colorado River dams, rural electrification, soil conservation, stable farm prices, farm to market roads, low cost loans to farmers, expanded opportunities for vocational and all other education, slum clearance, veterans' housing, and a G.I. Bill of Rights. "What he was saying then," Pickle told an interviewer, "was he had seen a dream, and he was trying to make that dream come true for all the people. I've often remembered just how dramatic he could be on that one point, and it sold good, too."[40]

Johnson won a decisive victory on July 27. Carrying all ten counties in the district, he beat Hollers by a margin of two and a half to one, 42,672 to 17, 628 votes. "I should say this was the time for Holley to holler!" Tommy Corcoran wrote Lyndon. ". . . As for the result—you know you never kidded me that there was any doubt of it." But Lyndon, who felt "pretty well beat out from the campaign," never saw the outcome as predictable. "Since I won by a big majority," he wrote Elizabeth Rowe, "I am having a hard time convincing my Washington friends how bad the situation was before I came down here and hit the trail day and night for the last three weeks. Really I wasn't crying 'wolf'."[41]

Johnson understood that by the second half of 1946 his campaign was something of an anachronism. An emphasis on New Deal programs was largely out of vogue around the country, but especially in the South. When Harold Ickes resigned from the Cabinet in February and Truman fired Henry Wallace in a dispute over foreign policy in September, it signaled the demise of New Deal influence in the White House. "The New Deal as a driving force," the *Chicago Sun* declared, "is dead within the Truman administration." But Truman's separation from old New Dealers was not enough to put him in sync with the new conservative mood. Weariness with government controls and mounting hysteria over Communist expansion and subversion put the Democrats in general and Truman in particular on the defensive. The Democratic Congress and the Truman administration were blamed for meat and housing shortages, strikes, inflation, Communist gains in Eastern Europe and China, and spy rings in Canada and the United States. Whereas 87 percent of Americans approved of Truman shortly after he took office in 1945, only 32 percent gave him their endorsement a little over a year later. "To err is Truman," became a popular quip of the day.[42]

The President's fellow Democrats couldn't escape the onslaught. "Had enough?" Republican candidates for Congress shouted in 1946. "Got enough meat?" an Ohio Republican running for the House asked. "Got enough houses? Got enough OPA? . . . Got enough inflation? . . . Got enough debt? . . . Got enough strikes? . . . Got enough Communism?" Voters replied by ending the Democrats' twenty-eight-year hold on both houses of Congress. The Republicans won a six-seat margin in the Senate and a fifty-eight-seat advantage in the House. "November 5th was a terrific licking and even though we were all mentally prepared for it, it still comes as a shock when we get it," Jim Rowe wrote Lady Bird. "I often wonder if the last ten years was worth all the effort we put into it—though I know in my calmer moments it was—and I could see the same unspoken thought on your everloving husband's face while he was in Washington."[43]

The Republican victory seemed to mark a sea change in American politics and persuaded Johnson that he could not get to the Senate now unless he showed himself as more in harmony with the current mood. An Associated Press interview and a planted story carried in Texas newspapers in April 1947 outlined Johnson's approach to a 1948 campaign. "The term 'New Dealer' is a misnomer," he told the A.P. He still supported water power, the REA, and all-weather roads. "But I believe in free enterprise, and I don't believe in the government doing anything that the people can do privately." According to Tex Easley, a reporter in Washington for several Texas newspapers, there were three false assumptions about Lyndon Johnson: that he had lost the great influence he had in Washington during FDR's term; that he was still a strong New Dealer; and that he had given up all intention of running again for the U.S. Senate. In fact, Easley asserted, Johnson had strong ties to HST and was particularly close to most of his Cabinet members. Further, the New Deal tag no longer applied, and though it meant risking a secure House seat and eventual appointment as chairman of the powerful House Armed Services Committee, Johnson was very much a contender for O'Daniel's seat in 1948.[44]

Johnson's principal concern was to establish a conservative track record on labor, civil rights, and off-shore or tideland oil that would sit well with Texas voters in a Senate campaign. All were highly visible and emotional issues in 1947–48 that could turn powerful corporations and the majority of white voters against a candidate for state-wide office in Texas. Between 1945 and 1948 union demands supported by work stoppages fueled anti-labor sentiment throughout the state. A four-month survey of ten dominant metropolitan newspapers in late 1945 revealed 295 editorials hostile to labor and only four that were pro-labor. Another study showed that weekly newspapers around the state freely published anti-labor columns and cartoons sent by the National Association of Manufacturers. None of the papers indicated the source of their material. During the first half of 1947 the state legislature, with Governor Beauford Jester's acquiesence, passed nine major anti-labor laws that included an anti-union or anti-closed shop right-to-work bill and an anti-mass-picketing law. A principal architect of this legislative attack on labor was Lyndon's friend and supporter, Herman Brown of Brown & Root.[45]

During the first month of the Eightieth Congress, representatives and senators introduced over a hundred bills regulating labor, including one sponsored by Lyndon limiting bonus and profit-sharing payments to workers.

The Taft-Hartley bill, which aimed to limit the advantages given labor unions under the Wagner Act of 1935, was the most significant of the anti-labor bills. As passed by the Congress on June 9, the law maintained the right of workers to join unions, bargain collectively, and strike, but it prohibited the closed shop, allowing states to legislate against union membership as a prerequisite for employment. It also empowered the President to declare a threatened strike a peril to the national safety and to seek court injunctions requiring an eighty-day cooling-off period before an industry-wide shutdown could occur. Truman biographer Robert J. Donovan describes the bill as "a dividing line between liberal and conservative, New Dealer and anti-New Dealer, friend of labor and foe of labor." At the beginning of June, Lyndon joined 102 Democrats and 217 Republicans in approving the bill. Later in the month, he voted with 105 Democrats and 225 Republicans to override Truman's veto. When the issue generated the greatest volume of mail ever received by Johnson's office, most of it favoring his support of Taft-Hartley, he answered that his vote served the interests of all the people and that he shared the widespread desire to control "irresponsible, racketeering, self-inflated labor leaders."[46]

On civil rights as well he unequivocally went along with the opposition of most Texas voters. During his congressional career he had kept a low profile over the issue of black rights, shunning all controversy. Conditions in 1946–48, however, changed this. Anti-black violence in the South coupled with defections of black voters to the Republican party in 1946 moved Truman to appoint a civil rights committee that would propose Federal means of defending the rights of all Americans. In October 1947, the committee's book-length report, *To Secure These Rights*, provided detailed recommendations for stronger legal machinery to protect civil rights and broaden equality of opportunity. On February 2, 1948, Truman sent a "Special Message to the Congress on Civil Rights," an unprecedented act for an American President. He asked for anti-lynching and anti-poll tax laws, a permanent Fair Employment Practices Commission, a permanent Commission on Civil Rights, and a Joint Congressional Committee on Civil Rights to consider the need for other

legislation. The President's message touched off an explosion of southern opposition that made civil rights questions a litmus test for office
seekers throughout the South. "I am certain that I express the attitude
of Texas when I state that I am unequivocally opposed to this fantastic
federal idea of Negro-white social equality," one Austin citizen wired
Johnson.[47]

In private, Johnson was ready to acknowledge that "there is much that
can be said for their [the black, pro-civil rights] viewpoint." He also
described himself as horrified by lynching and opposed to a poll tax. "I
have no racial or religious prejudices," Johnson wrote in a form letter
he sent to all advocates of the President's civil rights program. "I have
always defended, and shall continue to defend, the right of every citizen,
regardless of race, color, or creed, to all the liberties guaranteed by our
Constitution." But that same Constitution, he argued, inhibited the
Federal government from appropriating the rights of the states to legislate against lynching and other crimes and on the qualifications of voters. Nor did the Federal government have the constitutional power to
say whom an individual had to hire, no more than it had the right to
say for whom an individual had to work. Opponents of the President's
program who wrote Johnson received no lecture on constitutional principles; only assurances that he had "voted against all anti-poll tax, anti-
lynching, and all FEPC legislation since I came to Congress and expect
to continue to do so."[48]

The growing influence of the oil industry in Texas, state revenues produced by offshore oil fields, and a resurgent concern with states' rights
made the tidelands oil question another matter on which a state-wide
candidate had to take a stand. In September 1945, Truman issued a
proclamation claiming Federal jurisdiction and control over offshore oil.
Led by the South and California, the Congress passed a joint resolution
in the summer of 1946 nullifying the proclamation and asserting state
control. The President vetoed the resolution, saying the Supreme Court
should decide the question, and the House narrowly sustained his veto.
Away in Texas for his primary fight with Hollers, Johnson conveniently
took no position on the issue. In April 1948, after the Supreme Court
had decided that the Federal government had paramount rights to the
tidelands, the House overturned the Court's ruling by affirming the states'
title to submerged lands and natural resources three miles off their shores.
Lyndon voted with the 93 Democrats and 163 Republicans approving
the bill. Although it died in the Senate, his vote insulated him from
potential political attacks.[49]

While Johnson adopted conservative positions on highly visible labor,
civil rights, and tidelands issues, he remained staunchly liberal in his
congressional votes on other matters that were less controversial in Texas.
In February 1947, when the Republican-controlled House approved a

constitutional amendment limiting a President to two terms, an act of revenge against Franklin Roosevelt, as some called it, Johnson joined 119 other representatives, all Democrats, voting no. He was in the minority again two weeks later when he opposed a resolution setting a ceiling on Federal expenditures for the fiscal year 1948. He also lost in March when a coalition of Republicans and conservative Democrats included a local option in a rent-control bill to allow local boards to raise rents and deny tenants the right of appeal to Federal authorities.

In June and July, Johnson voted against Republican-sponsored tax reduction bills that favored the wealthy. He was one of only 99 House members opposing a bill giving a 60 percent increase in take-home pay to the 1400 taxpayers in the country earning $300,000 or more a year and only a 5 percent increase to the 46 million taxpayers earning less than $5000 a year. Two weeks later, 134 House Democrats, including Lyndon, gave the President a rare victory when they sustained his veto of the bill. In July, however, the House overrode another presidential veto of a second tax reduction bill that was somewhat less favorable to wealthy Americans. Johnson once again voted with the liberal minority. Moreover, in the first half of 1948, he warmly supported additional funding for the REA in a speech on the House floor titled, "Break the Bottleneck in REA Line Building—They Have Waited for Lights Long Enough." At the same time, he supported other traditional New Deal programs for housing and roads. By 1948, Texas voters may have held a new image of Johnson as a conservative southern congressman, but his voting record demonstrated that he had not strayed far from the New Deal fold.[50]

If there was substantial expediency in Johnson's conservative labor, civil rights, and tidelands votes, he was genuinely in tune with patriotic and nationalistic impulses in postwar Texas that favored greater Federal spending for national defense. Between the end of the war in 1945 and the spring of 1948, Johnson had remained vitally interested in national security affairs, serving on the Naval Affairs Committee, the Armed Services Committee, which replaced the Naval and the Military Affairs committees in 1947, and the Joint Committee on Atomic Energy. His contributions to their work gave him great satisfaction and allowed him to strike a resonant chord with most Texans.[51]

Lyndon was not shy about advertising his national defense work. In the spring of 1946, he arranged to have Assistant Secretary of War for Air Stuart Symington, with whom he had established a warm friendship, come to Texas, where there were the largest number of air bases in any state. Symington's inspection of air fields and luncheon and dinner talks, which Lyndon hosted, served the congressman's political standing in his home district and throughout the state.[52]

The same applied at the end of 1946, when he openly protested the

efforts of Standard Oil of California to amend its contract with the Navy
Department for the development and operation of the Elk Hills Naval
Petroleum Reserve. Despite differences with Carl Vinson, who found
Standard's request reasonable, Johnson publicly objected that the contract changes "are unrelated to the conservation of oil in the Elk Hills
Reserve and would be detrimental to the financial interest of the United
States." Putting his case in a statement to the Naval Affairs Committee
and in letters to President Truman and Secretary Forrestal, Johnson
won praise from some citizens. "The Congressman was from a state that
had a very big stake in oil," Donald Cook later said, "and yet when he
had the choice to make—namely between an oil company orientation
and being a true patriot in every sense of the word—he made what I
regarded . . . as the right choice."

But Lyndon wasn't quite as heroic on the Elk Hills dispute as Cook
believed. If his outspokeness pitted him against Standard Oil of California, it had no direct impact on Texas oil companies. It also sat well with
most Texas voters, who shared Johnson's genuine concern to put the
national security of the United States above the interests of any single
corporation, oil or otherwise.[53]

As tensions with the Soviet Union mounted in Europe and the Near
East in 1947, Johnson became more attentive to foreign affairs. On one
hand, he was genuinely concerned about a Communist threat to national security, and on the other, he was sensitive to what would serve
him best in a 1948 Senate campaign. The near collapse of the British
economy under the weight of a record cold snap in the winter of 1946–
47 confronted Washington with a new crisis. Unable to continue the
financial and military support it had been giving Greece and Turkey
against Communist subversion, Britain warned the Truman administration that unless it assumed responsibility for the independence of these
countries the whole Near and Middle East and northern Africa might
be lost to Communist control. Since there were no appropriations to
support Greece and Turkey and since the Republican-controlled Congress was proposing to cut $6 billion from the President's budget, the
Administration launched a campaign to persuade Congress to provide
the funds. In a speech at Princeton University in February, Secretary of
State George C. Marshall sounded a warning against the country's impulse to relax "now that an immediate peril is not plainly visible . . . .
Many of our people have become indifferent to what I might term the
long-term dangers to the national security."

On March 6, Johnson lent his voice to the Administration's campaign.
In remarks on the House floor, he warned against a return to the sort of
isolationism after 1918 that helped bring on the Second World War:
"There is a budget hysteria on foot now to sink our ships, ground our
planes and reduce the size of our army. . . . We listened to these 'Bud-

geteers' before . . . and found ourselves in a bitter war a generation later." He predicted that the "Budget politicians . . . would give us the second best Army, Navy and Air Force," and quoted Air Force General Ira Eaker's remark that " 'having the second best air force is just like having the second best poker hand.' "[54]

On March 12, the President weighed in with his Truman Doctrine speech before a joint congressional session. He asked the Congress to appropriate $400 million in aid to Greece and Turkey and to authorize sending some military personnel and equipment to each country. He warned that America's failure to help free peoples "may endanger the peace of the world." On May 7, Lyndon backed the President in a speech to the House. He recounted the history of appeasement before World War II and asserted that "we have fought two world wars because of our failure to take a position in time." He called former Vice President Henry Wallace's contention that Truman's request might provoke a war with the Soviet Union "absurd," and said it was time to stand up to Moscow: if "Russia is not willing to stop with the land she has taken away from Poland, Finland, and Czechoslovakia; is not willing to get out of Austria, but insists on a foothold in the Mediterranean . . . , then now is the time for us to decide whether we will meet her there and meet her now. . . . When democracy lays down before any other ideology, there is no more democracy."[55]

After Congress approved the aid bill to Greece and Turkey in May, the Administration turned its attention to the rehabilitation of Western Europe. Having made a far slower recovery from the war than anticipated, the European democracies remained vulnerable to Communist subversion. Their economic weakness also undermined their ability to buy American exports and threatened to precipitate a recession in the United States. In a speech at Harvard University on June 5, the Secretary of State proposed a massive aid program for Europe that became known as the Marshall Plan. After sixteen nations responded by forming the Committee for European Economic Cooperation, the Truman Administration asked the Congress to appropriate $17 billion to fund a four-year recovery program.[56]

Lyndon warmly supported the plan. In the fall of 1947, he told the Austin Kiwanis Club that there was only one major problem facing the country: "It is to preserve the system under which we have grown to be the greatest nation in the world." The question Americans had to consider was whether they wanted to spend a modest amount of money "over the next four years in an attempt to stop the spread of Communism or to spend 300 or 400 billions in another war from which nobody would emerge the winner. . . . We must apply to Dictator Stalin the same doctrine that we should have applied to the Kaiser and to Hitler.

. . . Nobody else can do it. We want peace. We can't have it unless we're prepared to underwrite the cost."[57]

Johnson was as outspoken about maintaining an American lead in nuclear weapons. In the fall of 1947, almost three months after he had been appointed to the Joint Congressional Committee on Atomic Energy, he told an audience in San Antonio that the country had to shoulder the cost of nuclear research. If it didn't, "something a lot worse than bankruptcy is going to happen to us. . . . I did not become a member of the Atomic Energy Committee to liquidate the atomic bomb and make America the vassal of another power."

Johnson's contribution to the development of nuclear power went beyond mobilizing public opinion. David E. Lilienthal, the head of the Atomic Energy Commission, saw Johnson's appointment to the Joint Committee as "a good break[,] for that committee can make or break us." Johnson, whom he described as "an able young man, definitely liberal and shrewd, full of savvy," counseled Lilienthal on how to involve Committee members in the Commission's work and assure appropriations from a tight-fisted Republican Congress.[58]

Johnson's greatest efforts in behalf of preparedness revolved around issues that served not only the nation's defense but also the economic well-being of Texas and his political standing in the state. Synthetic rubber and expanded oil and natural gas production were cases in point. As a member of House Armed Services subcommittees concerned with the country's future capacity for industrial mobilization, Johnson fought against rubber industry demands for elimination of government-owned synthetic rubber plants, which were principally located in Texas and the South, and for government incentives to oil and natural gas producers to increase their exploration and supplies. Convinced that rubber and energy shortages would bedevil the nation in another war unless careful planning was done now, Johnson also saw great advantages to Texas and himself from such plans: "In the new day of decentralizing industry," he said, "Texas will gain most from development of synthetics. In an age of synthetics, Texas—as the fountainhead of natural gas and oil—may easily become the kingpin state in a new industrial age." In a discussion of how to increase U.S. oil supplies, he urged Federal financial support of private oil exploration, the allocation of scarce materials to companies doing this work, and "special tax relief on income from new production."[59]

Lyndon got some notoriety for his preparedness work in 1947, but European tensions in March 1948 allowed him further to emphasize his service to the nation and Texas in behalf of national defense. During the month, a Soviet-sponsored coup brought Czechoslovakia firmly into the Communist camp, and Soviet-American tensions mounted over plans to create an independent West German state aligned with the West. After the West European nations signed a collective defense agreement in Brussels, President Truman asked a joint session of Congress to restore the draft, pass a Universal Military Training law, and fund the Marshall Plan. Lyndon sent Truman an approving letter, and urged him to suspend the "sale at sacrifice prices [of] various plants and housing projects constructed during the last war . . . because . . . [they] may be urgently required in a matter of days." Releasing his letter to the press and radio, it "received wide use," and encouraged one of Lyndon's aides to suggest that he hold a press conference: "it would be a good opportunity to get some wide play in Texas at this time."[60]

The President, seeing Lyndon's letter as a chance to put some additional pressure on Congress for his requests, replied: If the Congress had acted on the measures he had asked for since November 1945, "there would be no necessity for any world emergency." He advised Lyndon to "put his shoulder to the wheel and help get those measures I asked for on the statute books." Lyndon assured him that "my shoulder will always be at the wheel of preparedness," and renewed his appeal for suspending the sale of war assets. The correspondence and the Administration's subsequent decision to declare a moratorium on the sale of war plants received wide newspaper coverage and enhanced Lyndon's image as a staunch proponent of national security.[61]

On no issue did Johnson push harder in the spring of 1948 than a 70-group air force of 12,441 planes. Johnson became the chief House advocate of the program. In private letters, public speeches, the press, before the Armed Services Committee, and on the floor of the House, he urged a rapid and sustained buildup of air power that would assure America's safety from air attack and secure the peace. "Mr. Chairman," he told the Congress, "I have not dramatized, exaggerated, or emotionalized the facts about our air power. In each of your offices are the reports from the authentic agencies which will verify the urgency, the terrifying urgency, of our situation." Although the House voted $822 million for 70 air groups, the Senate, fearful of "the impact of the cost of the program on the national economy," preferred a less expensive 66-group air force. Johnson attacked the proposed reduction as a "deception and sham." Arguing that 70 groups was the minimum needed for security, Johnson told the House that "if we refuse to modernize and give this country a 70-group modern Air Force, there may not be any security for ourselves or for our dollars." He said that 66 groups insure nothing more than a second rate air force for this country." A genuine anxiety about the communist threat, which he saw as a renewal of the dangers posed to the democracies by Hitler in the thirties, partly accounted for his insistence on greater air power.[62]

Yet the advantages to Texas and himself also shaped his rhetoric. "What was the Seventy Group Air Force?" Bryce Harlow, a professional staff member of the House Armed Services Committee in 1947, later said. "Nobody knew. . . . It could be as big or as little as 'group' meant. It was a slogan superbly drawn up by the air force and merchandised beautifully by [Stuart] Symington."

Seventy groups meant Federal money serving the Texas economy: "The House passed a 70-group Air Force appropriation just the other day, and I have hopes that it will be successful in passing the Senate," Johnson wrote the manager of the Brownwood, Texas, Chamber of Commerce. "Once this 70-group program becomes a law, then we can anticipate an expansion in the Air Program in the State of Texas." In a press release, Lyndon announced his intention to confer with Defense Secretary Forrestal about the production of jet engines at Fort Worth aircraft factories, the establishment of our Air Force Academy at San Antonio, the shift of additional defense plants to Texas, and Federal legislation to increase fuel supplies for the 70-group air force.[63]

Much of what Johnson did in 1947 and the first four months of 1948 was calculated to help him in a Senate race. But until May he was not sure that he would run. Unlike 1941, a Senate bid now meant giving up his House seat and a possible end to his political career. Such an outcome, however, did not put him off entirely. In 1947 Lady Bird had given birth to Lucy Baines Johnson, their second child, and the thought of managing their lucrative radio business, acquiring a television station, and spending more time with his family were alternatives with which Lyndon believed he could live. Yet politics remained his vocational passion, and he could not easily accommodate himself to the thought of giving up his House seat. When he first considered making another Senate race, he later told Doris Kearns, "I just could not bear the thought of losing everything."[64]

Lyndon's caution was well advised. There was much to suggest that he would not win. In the spring of 1947, Joe Belden, the Texas pollster, took initial soundings on the 1948 Senate race. In a contest between Johnson and Pappy O'Daniel, Johnson was projected as a clear winner: 64 percent of the sample said they would vote for Johnson. The poll demonstrated what Texas political observers already knew—namely, that O'Daniel's performance in the Senate, particularly appeals for isolation from world affairs and bitter attacks on unions and Federal officials as setting up a Communist dictatorship, had alienated Democratic colleagues and limited his ability to represent Texas. Further, revelations of highly profitable business dealings shattered his reputation as a man of the people and assured that he would not win a second term.

O'Daniel's political vulnerability, however, was small comfort to Lyndon. Former Governor Coke Stevenson and incumbent Governor Beauford Jester, two other potential candidates, defeated O'Daniel by three-to-one margins and seemed likely to beat Johnson in a Senate race. A decision by Jester not to run did not help Johnson much. A June 1947 opinion survey pitting Coke, Pappy, and Lyndon against each other gave Stevenson 55 percent of the vote, with Johnson and O'Daniel receiving 24 and 21 percent respectively. Another poll in October that included eleven candidates put Lyndon in a three-way tie for third with only 11 percent of the vote. Asked who their second choice would be for the Senate seat, should their first choice not run, only 8 percent named Johnson.[65]

In the first four months of 1948, Johnson saw some hopeful signs in the polls. Although Stevenson and George E. B. Peddy, a Houston attorney, announced their candidacies in January and Johnson refused to declare, Stevenson showed no gain in the opinion surveys and Peddy commanded only one percent of the vote. In February and March, Stevenson's lead over Johnson vacillated between 25 and 30 points. Moreover, some deeper probing suggested that Johnson had some advantages over Stevenson which he might be able to exploit in the primary. Asked whether someone with experience in Congress, as governor, or none in public office would make the best Senator, 45 percent of Texas voters chose a person with congressional experience, 27 percent preferred a governor, and 16 percent selected a political novice. Asked if they wanted a senator who was nearer forty, fifty, or sixty years of age, 48 percent preferred a forty-year-old, Johnson's age in 1948, to 5 percent for a sixty-year-old, Stevenson's age. When voters were asked if they thought it would be better to have someone in the Senate "who has been strongly in favor of the New Deal, or one who has not been so strongly in favor of the New Deal," a plurality wanted the latter: 39 percent chose a weak New Dealer, 31 percent said a strong New Dealer, and the remaining 30 percent preferred someone in between or had no opinion.[66]

John Connally saw good news in the polling data, but others were not as optimistic. "I do not want to be a wet blanket," Maury Maverick wrote Lyndon in April, "but frankly I think anybody with any brains— such as you—. . .would have little chance of election. I consider you a Master Politician (besides being a first-class man) but I . . . think it would be very difficult for you to be elected to the Senate now. Truman has everybody in as big a state of confusion as he is himself, and although the Generals are about to get us in a war and they are fundamentally unpopular, nevertheless superficially they mislead the people enough in some sort of curious way that some bum like O'Daniel or Stevenson has a chance of election." "Thanks much for your letter . . . ," Lyndon replied. "It doesn't sound very optimistic, but I guess we will have to get the campaign under way before our folks really get pepped up. . . . I don't know yet when or where we will go. . . . 'I am more confused than Truman.' "[67]

Johnson genuinely feared losing and had substantial reservations about making the physical and emotional sacrifices tied to a Senate race. Yet, as he later told Kearns, feeling that "something was missing from [his] life" and wanting, as one friend remembered, "to be Senator more than anything else in the world right then," he quietly planned a campaign in the spring of 1948. He announced his candidacy at an afternoon press conference in the Driskill Hotel on May 12.[68]

Although he viewed his decision as possibly marking the end of his political career, he exuded confidence to the assembled journalists and friends. He deserved to be a Senator, he said. He had actually won the seat in 1941 against O'Daniel but his opponents had altered the tally to deprive him of the victory. "I was urged to contest that result, but I tried to be a good sport. Lots of people said they'd support me next time, but the war intervened . . . . I know the fair-minded people of Texas will help me win that promotion to which I came so close before." He emphasized that his long service in the Congress, his youthfulness and energy compared with that of his opponents, his accomplishments in helping raise the living standard of all his constituents, his experience on the Armed Services and Atomic Energy committees, where he had schooled himself in the great issues of war and peace, all made him the best candidate for the office and demonstrated that he would be a highly effective senator. His announcement began a political struggle that would echo through the rest of his public career.[69]

10

Texas Elects a
Senator

JOHNSON'S decision to run for the Senate triggered an explosion of activity. With less than eleven weeks to go before the July 24 election, Lyndon faced a formidable challenge. Winning over a majority of the more than 1.2 million Democrats who would vote in the party primary seemed too much to achieve in so short a time. If he could hold Stevenson under 50 percent, while he ran a close second, he could force a one-on-one run-off that would give him another month to overcome Stevenson's lead.

The campaign was a decisive moment in his career: he would either become a U.S. Senator or lose his House seat and the eleven years of seniority and influence that went with it. Johnson launched the most energetic, all-consuming drive for office he had ever made. After he announced on the afternoon of May 12 his decision to run, he returned to his Dillman Street residence, where, with the help of a secretary, he made calls from 5:00 p.m. to midnight on two telephones in his backyard. The next morning at seven they were at it again, "getting county people; getting district leaders; [and arranging] finances . . . the initial onslaught," Dorothy Palmie, the secretary working with him, called it.[1]

A week after Lyndon announced, Pappy O'Daniel declared himself out of the running. Facing the likelihood of a crushing defeat, O'Daniel departed the political wars with advice to the public that if it disliked the Senate candidates, it should write in the name of someone it preferred. One Texas newspaper called his decision to retire "the one most constructive act" of his ten-year political career. It partly testified to the fact that anti-government and pro-isolationist ideas did not enjoy a strong hold on the popular imagination in Texas. The dependence of the state and the South generally on federal largesse for its prosperity made someone like Johnson a more appealing candidate than O'Daniel.

Johnson publicly applauded O'Daniel's retirement, and described it as a first step in the elimination of the two men, O'Daniel and Stevenson, who had deprived him of the Senate seat he had legitimately won in 1941: "One of the twins is out. Now we stand one down and one to go." Predictions that O'Daniel's anti-New Deal support would go largely to Stevenson and Peddy blunted Johnson's satisfaction. It increased the possibility that Stevenson might exceed 50 percent of the vote in a first primary.[2]

A health crisis put Johnson's candidacy in even greater jeopardy during the next two weeks. Johnson scheduled an opening campaign address at Wooldridge Park in downtown Austin for Saturday night May 22. In the week before the speech, Paul Bolton, a journalist and broadcaster at KTBC, and Warren Woodward, a recent University of Texas graduate and new member of Johnson's staff, helped write the speech and arrange the rally. Late in the afternoon of the 22nd, Bolton drove the two miles from campaign headquarters in downtown Austin to Dillman Street to deliver a final copy of the speech. Letting himself in the front door, Bolton met Dr. William Morgan, Lyndon's physician, on the stairs to the second floor. "Is someone sick here?" Bolton asked. Morgan gave no reply, but Bolton needed none when he entered Johnson's bedroom. The Congressman had an excruciatingly painful kidney stone. Having had stones before and quickly passed them, Johnson anticipated the same outcome. But this stone was not so cooperative. It was causing severe pain—for which Dr. Morgan had given him several shots that day—and there was an infection accompanied by a high fever with chills and sweating.[3]

On Saturday, Johnson gamely went ahead with his speech. After two fiddle bands had warmed up an overflow crowd, Johnson, dressed in a well-tailored navy blue suit and accompanied by his mother and Lady Bird in white dresses, bound forward to the band shell in the center of the park. There, he took off his expensive Stetson hat and sailed it out into the audience, announcing, "I throw my hat in the ring." One boy in the crowd remembered it as "the corniest thing I'd ever seen."[4]

Johnson's speech was a brilliant piece of bombast. Delivered in loud raucous tones meant to convey the urgency of the issues being addressed, the speech focused on international and domestic concerns and shrewdly combined conservative and liberal ideas about current events. Preparedness, peace, and progress were the "bold signposts" marking the road "toward a better tomorrow." "Communism surges forward in a blood-red tide," which only an America with a strong industrial system, the world's most powerful air force, an army and navy adequate to any task, and a commitment to continued scientific development could

contain. The goal of this preparedness, however, was not war but peace—
a peace less the result of unbridled U.S. strength than international cooperation. "Conceived and born in America, the United Nations is our
greatest hope for maintaining the peace," Johnson said. Similarly, reciprocal trade agreements or a free flow of international trade were essential to overcome the war-breeding conditions of squalor, poverty, hunger, and disease.

Preparedness and peace would mean progress at home. But only if
the Federal government played its proper role. It needed to support
farmers with parity payments, electrified homes, and conservation; aid
education by helping states increase teacher pay; assure elder citizens a
decent standard of living by raising Social Security payments; improve
the nation's health by building hospitals and helping train more doctors
and nurses; and protect labor's recent gains by guaranteeing reasonable
working hours and minimum wages. At the same time, however, government needed to be a strong ally and not a foe of free enterprise and
state's rights. Johnson decried needless red-tape, union excesses, socialized medicine, and the civil rights program, which "is a farce and a
sham—an effort to set up a police state in the guise of liberty." The
emphasis on federal programs was meant to contrast Johnson's liberalism with Stevenson's opposition to governmental activism. Johnson's
closing remarks also put him on the side of the anti-government, anti-
union, anti-civil-rights sentiments Stevenson had effectively identified
with as Governor.[5]

Limited newspaper coverage of his opening address upset Johnson,
and he worked on the problem the next day when he and Bolton and
Woodward flew to Amarillo in the northwest panhandle via San Angelo,
Abilene, and Lubbock. At each of the stops, though they had only five
or ten minutes on the ground, he called local newspaper publishers to
talk up his campaign.

Although he said nothing about his health to Bolton or Woodward
and spent three days campaigning in and around Amarillo, by Tuesday
night he was very sick. Despite taking aspirin and other pain killers
prescribed by Dr. Morgan, he was so feverish and perspired so freely
that he went through six or seven shirts a day and had to spend Tuesday
evening in bed before boarding an overnight train to Dallas.

The journey was a nightmare. Bolton got off the train in Wichita Falls,
where Johnson was scheduled for a speech on Wednesday evening, while
Woodward and the Congressman continued on to Dallas. During the
night, Johnson alternated between freezing chills and burning fever. "One
moment he was just as hot as could be and in the next moment he was
as cold as could be." When he shook with chills, Woodward piled blankets on him and even crawled into his bed to give him body warmth.
When the fever took over, he would throw off the blankets and holler

for Woodward to yank down his Pullman window. Woodward was so worried about his condition and so attentive to Johnson's every need that he never got a moment's sleep.[6]

At the hotel in Dallas, Johnson rejected Woodward's advice that they call a doctor and inform others of his condition. Instead, he rested in bed and prepared to meet with Secretary Symington, who was in Dallas for a speech, to discuss making Sheppard Air Force Base at Wichita Falls a permanent base. He also intended to fly to Wichita Falls for an evening meeting and talk. By the time he met with Symington, however, "his face was gray and he was obviously in terrible pain." Symington remembered that "he showed great courage in being able to get up at all." He now felt so badly that he canceled his trip and agreed to call a doctor. The doctor insisted that he go to the Medical Arts Hospital in downtown Dallas. Johnson agreed on the condition that his illness be kept a strict secret. At the hospital, where he began to feel even worse, he gave Woodward a tongue lashing for leaving his side for five minutes. While Woodward had been filling out admittance papers, Johnson threw up in a corridor on the way to his room. "Don't ever leave me again," he said to Woodward when he returned. ". . . You left me, and I needed you and you weren't there." He was "possessive of his people," Woodward later recalled. ". . . In his moments of personal trial he wants his people around him." He now instructed Woodward to inform John Connally of his whereabouts, but insisted that Connally say nothing to the press and explain his absence from Wichita Falls as a result of bad weather.[7]

Connally refused. He thought it "ridiculous" to try to hide Johnson's hospitalization, so he gave the story to the press. "Well, if I can't run my own campaign," Johnson told Woodward, ". . . I might as well withdraw." Dictating a statement to Woodward, Johnson asked him to release it to the press. But convinced that Johnson was delirious from his high fever and not rational, Woodward persuaded him to wait until Mrs. Johnson, who was flying to Dallas, arrived. She took over completely, soothed Lyndon, convinced him to put aside the statement and concentrate on getting better, and freed Woodward to get some desperately needed sleep.[8]

The doctors recommended removing the stone by abdominal surgery that would have incapacitated Johnson for about six weeks. "You're telling me I'm losing this campaign before I get started," Johnson said to the doctors. "Well, that's what you'll have to do," they replied. Stuart Symington suggested an alternative: Jacqueline Cochran, a well-known aviator and a good friend of the Johnsons, could fly them to the Mayo Clinic in Rochester, Minnesota, where doctors had treated her husband for the same problem with a new technique: an instrument that reached up through the urethra and pulled out the stone if it were not too high.

It required no incision, and if it succeeded Johnson would be able to resume campaigning in about a week.[9]

Although the doctors in Dallas opposed the plan, the Johnsons saw the Mayo procedure as the only chance to save Lyndon's campaign. "Our departure from that hospital was funny," Lady Bird recalled, "it was almost like an escape from a penitentiary." Lady Bird was surprised that the hospital even lent them a stretcher to carry Lyndon to the ambulance for his trip to the airport. Lyndon was so concerned that Texans would resent his leaving the state for treatment, he arranged with Cochran to make it seem he had been pressured into going. Pretending she had had no prior discussion with the Johnsons, Cochran told Woodward how Lyndon could be helped at Mayo Clinic and that she intended to take him there. When Woodward informed Johnson, he replied: "No, I'm not gonna do that. . . . They'll just say that Texas doctors are not good enough for me. . . . The Texas doctors can handle this situation. I don't need to go up there." When Woodward gave Johnson's reply to Cochran, "she just wouldn't accept that for an answer" and insisted on speaking to Mrs. Johnson. Woodward believed that their conversation and further discussions with local doctors convinced the Johnsons to go. If anyone in Texas complained about Johnson's limited confidence in local doctors, Woodward could describe Lyndon's great reluctance to leave the state.[10]

On May 27, Cochran and a co-pilot flew the Johnsons and Woodward to Rochester, where, as the Mayo staff recalled, Lyndon became the Clinic's "leading pain in the ass." He installed three telephones in his room, from which a nurse claims he made sixty-four calls in one day. He also turned part of the Clinic into a temporary campaign headquarters, from where he constantly monitored the work of his aides in Texas and pressed doctors into issuing optimistic statements about his condition. His ten-day stay at the Clinic seemed like a year to some staff members.

During his first two days there the staff ran a series of tests, brought his fever under control, and listened to Johnson's pleas to purge the stone without surgery. In hopes of jarring it loose, Johnson took car rides on rough back roads and climbed up and down the hospital's back stairs. On his fourth day, with no change in his condition, the doctors performed the special procedure they had developed. Although the stone was as far up as it was possible for them to go and still get it, the doctors removed it in less than an hour. One of the few early successes the Clinic achieved with the procedure, it later displayed the surgical instrument in its museum.[11]

Compelled to remain in the hospital for another five days to recover, Johnson chafed under the restraint. Jim Rowe, knowing how frustrated he was, wired Lady Bird: "Tell Lyndon to stop loafing. Doesn't he know there is a campaign going on in Texas. Delighted to hear he is feeling better."

While he recovered, Lyndon kept tabs on the campaign. He sent Woodward to Houston to gather information on how Johnson's illness was viewed and arrange the details of a June 7 speech. Johnson also monitored developments in Austin through Roy Wade, a public relations expert who tracked press opinion and activities in Stevenson's headquarters. Wade received information from a campaign worker that Stevenson planned an attack on Johnson beginning June 1.[12]

Johnson learned from his aides that public interest in the election, which was still nearly two months off, was small. If they tried to stage an outdoor rally in Houston's Hermann Park, it might attract only a small crowd that would embarrass him. Instead, they decided to squeeze fifty or so people into Roy Hofheinz's small radio station for a state-wide talk. Making sure that Johnson's studio audience would be a "noisy vociferous group," Woodward was able to create the impression that the Congressman was speaking before a large enthusiastic crowd.

Johnson's speech emphasized his liberal nationalism and differences with Stevenson. He asked Stevenson whether he shared his commitment to aiding education, rural electrification, farm to market roads, parity payments to farmers, rural area hospitals, better housing, reciprocal trade agreements, the Taft-Hartley law, fifty-dollar-a-month pensions for the elderly, the Marshall Plan, and an increased program of preparedness. Shouting to emphasize his points and arouse his audience to the urgency of the issues, Lyndon asked them "to join us in this fight . . . to reaffirm your faith in our Americanism. It's your Government and mine we're talking about. It's your America and mine. It's your campaign. . . . Write me tonight. Write and say, 'Lyndon, I'm with you. . . . Lyndon, we'll get this job done.' "[13]

Johnson understood that to get his name and message before the electorate and overcome Stevenson's lead in the polls required something more dramatic than campaign rhetoric. He and John Connally hit on the idea of using a helicopter. An uncommon aircraft in 1948, it seemed certain to draw a crowd wherever Johnson went. In addition, it promised to give Johnson greater capacity to speak in more towns in a shorter period of time than if he traveled on commercial airlines between major cities and drove from one town to another. At the beginning of May, even before he had announced his decision to run, he had Woodward investigate the possibility of using such a machine. Working through Stuart Symington and General Robert Smith, a former airline executive, Johnson decided to lease a Sikorsky S51 three-passenger craft that could travel a hundred miles an hour and cover 250 miles without refueling. To avoid having the daily $250 rental cost charged to his primary campaign, which was limited by law to $10,000 in direct spending, Johnson invented the fiction that the Dallas Veterans for Johnson committee rented the craft. Naming his machine the Johnson City Windmill, Lyndon announced a plan on June 12 to go to every town in northeast Texas, and see folks who rarely met a candidate for state-wide office."[14]

On June 15, Johnson launched his helicopter blitz of Texas that carried him to 118 cities and towns in the next seventeen days. Crisscrossing northern and central Texas, from Lubbock in the western panhandle to Texarkana on the Arkansas border and Austin in the south, Johnson reached over 175,000 people. On Sunday the 14th—after ordering that a loudspeaker be fastened to one of the landing gear struts and that his name be painted in large white letters on the sides—Johnson and "a retinue of about 14 people" had the first of what would become weekly strategy sessions on how to proceed during the next seven days. They agreed to have campaign workers reach each town before Lyndon and attend to the details of a successful visit. "I don't think we consciously realized we were starting a brand new era of advance men," Woodward later said. But it occurred because Johnson wanted everything to go just right at each of his stops.[15]

For the campaign to work as planned, the advance men had to get to a town well ahead of Johnson's arrival. There, they arranged for a safe landing site at least 250 by 400 feet in size and free of electric cables and other possible obstructions. They distributed circulars; hired a telephone operator to inform everyone in town about the time and place of Johnson's visit; organized a reception committee to meet the helicopter; and assured that high octane gasoline would be available to refuel the aircraft. To keep ahead of the helicopter, the advance men drove at speeds of seventy and eighty miles an hour between towns. Automobiles must be carefully checked each night, campaign headquarters instructed the advance men. Otherwise, they might not reach their scheduled stops before, as one observer described it, "Lyndon and that damn thing came into Hillsboro going sideways at a thousand miles an hour."[16]

Lyndon quickly established a routine with the helicopter that effectively served his campaign. It not only allowed him to reach a larger audience, it also gave him an unprecedented means of capturing voter attention and fixing his name in their minds. Flying a few hundred feet above the ground, Johnson had the pilot hover over communities not on their itinerary, where he would shout over a loudspeaker, "Hello, down there. This is Lyndon Johnson; your candidate for the U.S. Senate." While he added a little spiel appealing for their votes, aides showered startled folks below with campaign leaflets. To make it easier to throw them out and reduce the temperature inside the craft, Johnson had the doors removed. Occasionally, Johnson had the pilot make unscheduled landings, where he would greet amazed onlookers personally. Aides also compiled lists of people in small towns between stops who at one time or another had written the Congressman. As they flew over them, Johnson said: "Hello, there, Mr. Jones. This is your friend, Lyndon Johnson. I'm sorry we can't land today, but I want you to know that I'm up here thinking of you and appreciate your kind letter and comments. I just want you to be sure and tell your friends to vote for me at election time." The business of talking over the loudspeaker to folks between towns became so routine that Johnson had one of his aides or the pilot do it while he rested. Handing the microphone to one of them, Johnson would say, "Tell them about me." [17]

The campaigning at each town also settled into a pattern. Before landing, the helicopter circled while aides threw out leaflets and Lyndon, using the loudspeaker, urged everyone to come meet him. As they hovered over the landing site, Lyndon appeared in the doorway of the helicopter, where he waved his Stetson to the crowd before tossing it out. Aides ran to retrieve the hat or gave a dollar to anyone who did. On the ground, Lyndon exchanged greetings with the local reception committee before talking to the crowd. Drawn by the fascination with seeing a helicopter, the music and songs of the Beau Jesters, a barbershop quartet from Dallas who drove with the advance men, and the possibility of winning a savings bond, the gathering often included the entire town.

Lyndon shunned set speeches, which never showed him at his best. Instead, he gave impromptu talks in which he sounded themes of his earlier addresses. Like a performer who sensed the mood of his audience, he spoke for only fifteen or twenty minutes, thirty at most, relating his experience in the war, showing concern for their local problems, describing how he intended to serve them and the country, and making fun of Stevenson. He told how he had sent home the belongings of his friend killed on the mission over New Guinea, and emphasized the need for greater preparedness to prevent another war. He vowed to raise the living standards of all Texans with Federal help, and belittled Stevenson's ideas about government aid. One of his aides reported to state headquarters on the "manner in which the candidate is selling himself to the folks. His approach is easy, relaxed, optimistic and enthusiastic. He is talking their language—language they can understand." At the end of his talk, he stayed to shake hands, look people "in the eye and touch them on the shoulder." [18]

Nothing at these campaign stops, however, was left to chance. Warren Woodward had responsibility for arousing crowd enthusiasm. Most of the time there was no need, but if the Congressman came up against an unresponsive audience, Woodward, who regularly wandered through the crowd, began clapping at predetermined points in the speech until "everybody would pick it up." At the end of a talk, a few people invariably approached the Congressman with special requests. Woodward, who always had a notebook and pencil handy, jotted down the person's name and problem. Even though these people were not in his district, Johnson ensured that something was done about each request.[19]

During his time on the road, Johnson usually worked a twenty-hour day. He arose at five in the morning to make a local radio broadcast to farmers at six or 6:15. He then campaigned until noon when he took a three-hour break to clean up, eat lunch, and rest. Dirty and sweaty from the dust flying in the open doors of the helicopter and the summer heat, he showered, ate lunch in his pajamas, and took a brief nap before picking up his afternoon schedule. Often, though, the nap lost out to pressing phone calls, or meetings with staff and local people. The evening offered no pause from the hectic pace. Banquets and receptions followed by meetings to review the day's activities, especially the unexpected foul-ups, and the next day's schedule lasted most nights until two or three in the morning. One aide remembered that Johnson "even worked in the bathtub! You'd be in a little hotel in this little town, and you'd get a summons to come into the bathroom to talk to the Congressman. You'd go in and he'd be in the tub, and he would talk to you and two or three secretaries would come in and take letters. He never stopped. . . . The conversation would go on during supper and right up to bedtime." Dorothy Nichols, Dorothy Plyler, and Mary Rather, his three secretaries, were unable to keep the pace for more than a week at a time and rotated, going on the road every third week.

Johnson himself barely held up. Dorothy Plyler recalled that by the end of the third week on the road Johnson could "hardly stand." At a reception in Lubbock he "was literally propped against the wall . . . with somebody on each side of him, because he was just at the point of total exhaustion." Too tired to speak, he greeted folks lined up to meet him by extending "his left hand with the little life that was still in it." Flying between towns during the day, he often fell asleep with his body stretched out and wrapped around the controls of the helicopter.[20]

The helicopter gave Johnson something new and special in the campaign, and judging from the numbers of people who turned out to hear him, it was a great success. "We were getting a thousand people in a town of a thousand," Walter Jenkins said. On a Wednesday night in Paris, northeast of Dallas, Johnson drew 5000 people: "Traffic was jammed and the crowds were all over the streets." In the smaller town of Commerce, forty miles to the south, 1000 people heard him speak on a Friday at noon. Seventy-five to a hundred miles further south in Athens and Jacksonville between 1400 and 1500 people turned out at each stop. By the middle of July Johnson's campaign headquarters estimated that he had spoken to over 175,000 people. The campaign also included broadcasts of Johnson's speeches all over the state as a means of reaching voters, but it was the helicopter that generated the most excitement and attracted the attention of Texans everywhere. High winds that grounded the helicopter in Waco for a couple of days brought home forcefully the extent of its appeal. Traveling by automobile between towns on those days, Johnson lost his crowds. A campaign official, who called the pilot to ask when he could get the machine back in the air, reported: "The only people he [Johnson] talks to are a couple of old people that can't get out of the square and a few old dogs that are running around. There just aren't any people around."[21]

"Johnson's 1948 Senate race was the first modern mass media campaign in Texas," one Johnson biographer says. True enough. But it wasn't radio and advertising, a helicopter and opinion polling alone that made Johnson effective. It was also his phenomenal hard work and readiness to combine the new with the old, the reliance on modern technology to communicate with traditional small town Texans about their current concerns. The helicopter itself probably didn't get any votes, Johnson felt, "but it gave him an opportunity to try to get . . . votes." Johnson supporters believed that what he said and how he said it was what really made the difference in the campaign. Johnson's emphasis on the differences between himself and Stevenson, between a modern politician and an old-fashioned anti-government conservative struck resonant chords with lots of people who valued government programs that contributed so much to their prosperity.[22]

Underwriting Johnson's whole enterprise was a lot of money: "the mother's milk of politics," as Jess Unruh, a California state assembly leader, later described it. Texas campaign laws permitted candidates to spend up to $10,000 in a primary—$8000 in the initial contest and $2000 in a run-off. But the law had a huge loophole. The $10,000 limit applied only to the candidate himself or the organization directly under his control. Campaign committees that "voluntarily" sprang up in support of a candidate could also spend money in his behalf. The Dallas Veterans for Johnson committee, which supposedly contributed the helicopter to the campaign, was one case in point. Claude Wild, Johnson's campaign manager in 1941, and "Chairman of the Johnson-for-Senate committees'" in 1948 was another. John Connally was the "campaign manager" and Wild headed up a group of so-called "independent" committees that spent a lot of money. "A technicality," Johnson aide Horace Busby told Walter Jenkins, "but it avoids embarrassment with the law."

Former Congressman Martin Dies briefly entered the Senate race at the end of May, but withdrew in June when he couldn't persuade Texas Attorney General Price Daniel to increase the spending limit to $60,000 or convince himself that Daniel would strictly enforce the law. Dies complained that candidates spent hundreds of thousands of dollars without jeopardy of prosecution. He contended that political office in Texas "is sold to the highest bidder on public auction, with buyers owning the candidates who win. . . . It cost me $1,500 to make the single [state-wide] broadcast I made while I was in the race," he said. "Multiply that by twenty-five broadcasts and see if the politicians are staying within the $10,000 expenditure limit."[23]

Convinced that certain defeat awaited anyone who tried, Johnson and Stevenson spent hundreds of thousands of dollars in their fight for the nomination. Stevenson later complained that Johnson "spent more than a million dollars." Stevenson also said that in 1926 Samuel Insull con-tributed $125,000 to a Republican primary candidate for U.S. Senator in Illinois. "Mr Insull's $125,000 was chicken feed compared to what several single individuals spent for Mr. Johnson in Texas." Johnson spent $30,000 in phone bills alone, someone inside the Johnson campaign later told Ronnie Dugger. Johnson's spending on radio broadcasts must have exceeded that figure. During just 23 days in July, there were talks on local rural stations, regular 15-minute broadcasts every morning in Dallas, Wichita Falls, San Antonio, Houston, and Austin and seven state-wide night broadcasts. If it cost Dies $1500 for his one state-wide radio speech, what did it cost the Johnson campaign for all the radio time it consumed?

Stevenson didn't lag far behind in his spending. Why should he follow the $10,000 legal limitation while Stevenson ignored it with impunity? Johnson asked during the campaign. "Who is paying for the $1100 [full-page] newspaper ads and the $330 billboard posters for Stevenson on the highways?" Johnson wanted to know. "In a twenty-five-mile stretch from Sugarland to Houston, there are seven such Stevenson billboards." "I'm thankful I don't have to have $1100 advertisements saying I can't be bought," Johnson added. Big oil supported Stevenson. The major oil companies, despite Johnson's recent conversion to defending Texas oil interests through advocacy of an increased depletion allowance and state control of tidelands oil, preferred the more conservative Coke Steven-son.[24]

Who financed Johnson's campaign? There were numerous backers: George and Herman Brown, Sid Richardson and Wesley West, inde-pendent oil producers; Amon Carter, the Fort Worth newspaper pub-lisher and oilman; Houston Harte, the publisher of a dozen Texas news-papers; Maco Stewart, a Galveston insurance millionaire; Gus Wortham, the head of American General Insurance Companies in Houston; Hob-art Taylor, Sr., a black Houston businessman and civic leader; the air-craft industry generally, and Hughes Aircraft in particular; and synthetic rubber producers. Attorney General Tom Clark, Washington lawyers Abe Fortas and Paul Porter, and Wall Street attorney Ed Weisl arranged contributions from wealthy New York attorneys and movie people like George Skouras of Twentieth Century-Fox and Howard Hughes of RKO. "We will very shortly send you a small contribution from each of us in the [law] firm here," Paul Porter wrote Johnson at the start of the campaign. "However, I recognize that this sentimental and personal interest is but an inadequate expression in a fight where extensive financial commitments are involved."[25]

The exact cost of Johnson's campaign is unknown. It is clear, however, that he received large contributions, especially from Sid Richardson, Gus Wortham, and the Browns. Richardson's support was in return for valuable help Johnson gave him in his business dealings with the Federal government and out of fondness for Johnson, whom he would fly to his privately owned island in the coastal Gulf for weekend socializing. An exceptionally charming conversationalist and a lonely bachelor, Richardson sought out others with the gift of gab like Johnson for companionship. "I think you are well aware of Mr. Richardson's relation with Mr. Johnson, and I can assure you that his organizations will do all they can for Mr. Johnson's candidacy," W. F. Matheny, a vice president of one Richardson company, wrote Walter Jenkins in June 1948.

Richardson was particularly grateful to Johnson for having helped arrange the purchase of a carbon black plant in Odessa, Texas, from the War Assets Administration. At the same time that Johnson complained about government sales at bargain prices of surplus war plants that might be essential to the national defense, he pressed the case for Richardson to pay only $4.3 million for one of the largest munitions facilities built during the war, a complex of 447 buildings on 426 acres with fifty miles of pipelines and the capacity to produce 45 million pounds of carbon black a year. Johnson then proposed that the government designate carbon black a critical material and store it at Richardson's plant. He also helped Richardson's company ward off a government anti-trust suit which alleged collusion between Richardson Carbon Company and the United Carbon Company.[26]

Gus Wortham's ties to Johnson are more obscure. Wortham was close to Judge Roy Hofheinz in Houston, whom Johnson had helped obtain a license from the FCC for a radio station. Hofheinz was in charge of Johnson's campaign in about thirty-five counties in southeast Texas. Wortham told W. Ervin "Red" James, former counsel at the FCC and friend of both Wortham's and Hofheinz's, that "Roy Hofheinz was the difference in that 1948 campaign between victory and defeat. It was Roy Hofheinz that pulled that victory in 1948." Wortham was also a business associate of George and Herman Brown. Hofheinz and the Browns may have persuaded Wortham to back Johnson, but whatever the reason, Wortham, according to James, "probably spent as much in the 1948 campaign as anybody else, maybe except George Brown, I don't know. But he spent a bunch."[27]

As in 1941, the Brown brothers were the biggest contributors to Johnson's 1948 nomination fight. Did you help Johnson in the 1941 campaign? an interviewer asked George Brown in 1969. " 'I did everything I could to help him get elected' " Brown replied. " '. . . You were raising money for him?' " the interviewer asked. " 'I didn't raise any money for him. I spent money of my own. . . .' 'Then in the future campaigns, did you also help Lyndon Johnson again?' 'Yes, in '48'," Brown answered. " 'In much the same way?'," the interviewer asked. " 'In the same way'." The Browns had more reason than ever to help in 1948. They were indebted to him not only for wartime ship-building contracts but also for two postwar deals that opened new opportunities for growth and profit. In 1946, when Johnson was a member of a House subcommittee on U.S. governance of former Japanese-controlled islands, the Browns won part of a $21 million Defense Department contract to build navy and air force bases on Guam. The contract, which increased nearly fivefold in cost during the next four years, helped Brown & Root raise its net worth in the twelve years after 1942 from $5.3 million to $27.5 million.[28]

The Browns profited even more from the acquisition of government-owned oil and natural gas pipelines built during World War II. They joined with Charles I. Francis, a Houston oil and gas attorney, Gus Wortham, and twenty-four others to form the Texas Eastern Transmission Company. It bought the Big Inch and Little Big Inch pipelines in February 1947 for $143 million, $12 or $13 million over what a competing group represented by Tommy Corcoran offered. Nine months later the twenty-eight original investors turned a $150,000 investment into a paper profit of $9,825,000, a 6,550 percent return. The pipelines carried crude oil and natural gas from east Texas to the northeastern United States and played a central part in helping Texas Eastern multiply its worth tenfold to $1.4 billion in the next twenty years. Charles Francis later told Ronnie Dugger that "Lyndon took no part in helping out with the original sale. I talked to Lyndon. He said, 'Charley, I can't do that. Tommy Corcoran is on the other side.' " But Francis wasn't certain about Johnson's role: There could have been "something that I didn't know. George Brown and he were awfully close." Speaking more generally of Johnson and the Browns, Francis told Dugger: "I was close to the Browns. I just believe that Johnson helped them get contracts. I *know* he did, and I don't know it either."[29]

Circumstantial evidence suggests that Johnson helped the Browns acquire the pipelines. Donald Cook, Johnson's principal aide on several of his naval subcommittees, played a significant role, at Johnson's behest, in helping Sid Richardson fend off the anti-trust suit against his carbon black company. According to Francis, he also did all the necessary research for Texas Eastern in buying the pipelines. Further, in early June 1947, Herman Brown wrote Sam Rayburn to say how much he enjoyed his visit with him and Lyndon in Washington. "I want to thank you for your help with Chairman [of the House Committee on Interstate and Foreign Commerce Charles] Wolverton as he certainly went ahead and held a hearing [on the pipelines]. If the Committee will now report it out so that we can get some action, it will certainly help us in consummating our deal with the Government. It will save months of time for both the Government and ourselves in closing the matter." Brown or Rayburn sent Lyndon a copy of the letter. Almost a year later, Johnson wrote Tommy Corcoran: "If I can get George Brown and his enthusiasm this time as much as it was in 1941, there won't be a second primary. One U.S. Senator for the next 30 years is worth more than two Big Inches."[30]

Yet however much Johnson had helped the Browns, they were reluctant, after their donations to the 1941 campaign almost got them indicted for tax fraud, to take similar risks in 1948. Nor did they want to put up Brown & Root funds or contribute money that came out of their own pockets and gave no significant tax reductions to any of their corporations. "There are only 45 days left," Johnson also said in his note to Corcoran, "and two weeks have just passed when I haven't had the kind of help I need. He [George Brown] just must sign himself up to this Senate thing because this is the crisis. I am either in the Senate or I'm out completely. God knows that the one man that I need to depend on is he."[31]

Brown signed himself up, but only to a point. For what many people inside Johnson's campaign vividly remember was not the abundance of money which allowed the candidate to fly around in a helicopter, give numerous radio talks, buy newspaper and billboard ads, and distribute literature through the mails, but the shortage of funds to pay for all these things. "My God, we spent . . . the majority of our time, it seems to me, just raising money," John Connally says. "And it was an expensive campaign. . . . We were constantly scrambling for money." Dorothy Nichols recalled that at one point Connally had to ask a supporter in Taylor, Texas, for $1000 to pay the rent on the Austin headquarters. "The campaign as a whole was run on less money I suppose for what we did than any campaign I've ever seen," Charlie Herring, an attorney and Johnson activist said. ". . . We . . . didn't have any money, it was hard to get. The public seemed to think that Governor Stevenson was going to win . . . and money was a difficult thing to raise."

Herring remembered trying to escape one bill collector in Austin by climbing out of an upstairs' window. Warren Woodward recalled paying a hotel bill in Paris, Texas, by selling campaign literature to a supporter who then raised local money to pay himself back. According to Walter Jenkins, Johnson replaced the Sikorsky with a smaller two-passenger Bell helicopter for the last three weeks of the campaign in July to save money. No longer able to pay the bills on the Sikorsky, Johnson largely compensated Bell Aircraft by advertising their machine. A secretary in the Austin office also recalled how uncertain they always were about when they would get paid. Since most of the office staff had no other income, they often relied on one secretary, who received regular disability checks from the army, to feed all of them. Johnson's campaign received plenty of money, but they spent more than they could raise.[32]

The operating principle was: spend not within the limits of what you had but whatever it would take to win. And this meant convincing all sorts of special interests and the public en masse that Johnson was in tune with their needs and Stevenson was not. It meant lavish spending to sell Johnson to the public as a doer who understood what people wanted from the government and knew how to get it for them better than Stevenson. A number of pro-Johnson newspapers around the state picked up the theme: "Johnson knows Texas needs and can do something about them," the *Brownwood Bulletin* declared. "Lyndon Johnson is the go-getter of Washington. He did so much for the entire state that he has become known as Texas Congressman-at-large," the *San Antonio Light* said. The Beau Jesters carried the message around the state, singing to the tune "Is It True What They Say About Dixie?," "Is It True What They Say About Johnson?"

> Is it true what they say about Johnson?
> Has he done what he said he would do?
> He brought electrification and brought it here to stay
> And won our admiration when he served the U.S.A.
> Is it true when he's sent back to Congress
> That he'll keep right on fighting for you.
> Is there work to be done up in Washington, D.C.?
> If it's true, vote for Lyndon B.[33]

Johnson didn't miss a beat in trying to identify himself with numerous interest groups in the state who benefited from the liberal nationalist policies he favored. Through his speeches, mass mailings, and personal contacts, he enlisted support from farmers, who shared his enthusiasm for government agricultural programs; Federal workers, for whom he endorsed a pay raise; teachers, who liked his stand on Federal aid to education; the elderly, who lobbied legislators for the $50 a month guaranteed pension he backed; veterans, who enjoyed the G.I. benefits he supported; doctors, who wanted the modern hospitals he promised in every Texas county; professional women, who applauded his advocacy of women's service in the regular branches of the armed forces; local leaders, whom he informed about Federal defense spending in their communities; and blacks and Hispanics, whom he privately courted with promises of greater equality of treatment.

Paul Bolton and John Connally tried to reflect the diversity of Lyndon's campaign by having representatives of various interests on the platform with him when he spoke. For one speech they got a banker, a ranch spokesman, a small businessman, a teacher, a doctor, and five disabled veterans, one of whom was blind and "a guy with one leg." The vets also had to represent the army, navy, and marines. One evening during the campaign, Joe Mashman, the Bell helicopter pilot, expressed admiration for Johnson's ability to make the content of his speeches fit the group and locale he was addressing. "Joe," Johnson said, "you have to speak to people in a language that they understand and . . . it's going to change from person to person, community to community. A successful politician is a person that is able to do that and that's essentially what I'm trying to do here in this campaign."[34]

Johnson's endorsement of government backing for various special interests was highly appealing. But not simply because it served group interests. He identified Federal programs as essential to the national well-being and attacked critics of the national government such as Stevenson and Peddy as unpatriotic. In a state-wide broadcast on July 20 he "lashed out" at "politicians who build campaigns on suspicion and mistrust of their own government. . . . These self-serving critics, these wily insinuators, forget to tell you that our government whipped the greatest depression and won the greatest war in history. . . . I call upon Texans to shame those who cannot find one praiseworthy word for our United States of America. I cry shame upon them, just as in May 1947, I cried shame on Henry Wallace when he sought to undermine his native land by going abroad to criticize our foreign policy." Johnson denounced "as a fraud, a sham and a smokescreen the . . . cry of state's rights against any move to help the people. Why do you turn to the federal government for help in solving your community's difficulties when all local means are exhausted?" he asked. "Is it not because you have nearly always met with a NO response in Austin?"[35]

Johnson shrewdly extended the point to national defense. He depicted opponents of Federal power as old-fashioned isolationists reluctant to spend money on preparedness and international obligations, and warned against outdated thinking that could get the country in another war. He reminded audiences of past errors through appeasement and pointed to the crisis in Berlin, where in June the Soviets had begun a blockade of the western sector of the city and the United States had responded with an airlift of supplies. Since the issue might be nothing less than war or peace in the next six years, Johnson urged voters to see his eleven years dealing with foreign and military affairs in Congress as reason alone to make him their Senator.[36]

The decision of the American Federation of Labor (AFL) in Texas to endorse Coke Stevenson also served Johnson in the July primary. On June 22, at their convention in Fort Worth, AFL leaders broke a fifty-year tradition by taking sides in an election. Incensed at Johnson's recent voting record on labor issues and particularly at his strong support of the Taft-Hartley law, the AFL convention came out against Johnson as one who had "disqualified himself in the eyes of the working people of Texas." Johnson responded: "I have voted for many bills that benefited the working man." He explained his vote for Taft-Hartley as "AGAINST anyone who thought he was bigger than the people and the government, whether big labor bosses or big business." He warned that Stevenson may have promised to support repeal of Taft-Hartley in return for AFL backing. Johnson also reminded voters that Stevenson had consistently refused to take a stand on the Taft-Hartley law and had allowed "the most vicious Labor bill ever passed by the Texas legislature" to become a law.[37]

Johnson effectively countered the AFL action. Tommy Corcoran in Washington contacted a leading official in the Railroad Brotherhoods, who agreed that Stevenson's overall record was "far more anti-labor" than Johnson's and promised to get "a favorable word . . . down to the Railroad Brotherhoods in Texas before Lyndon began to hit the big labor populations in the last weeks of his campaign." Corcoran then had dinner with Joe Keenan, an AFL executive. Corcoran emphasized Johnson's liberal record, his need to support Taft-Hartley in Texas to save his political skin, and Sam Rayburn's belief that the liberal cause in Texas required Lyndon's election. Keenan promised to "do his best to soften up the effect of the [AFL] endorsement." Robert Oliver, the regional director for Texas of the Congress of Industrial Organizations (CIO), received a call from Walter Reuther, a CIO official in Washington and a friend of Johnson's, urging CIO support of Johnson in the race. The best Oliver could get was "a no-endorsement policy."[38]

For Stevenson, the AFL endorsement was a mixed blessing. While he wanted the support of organized labor, he did not want to be too closely identified with unpopular Texas labor leaders. After he received word of the AFL endorsement, Stevenson sat in a car with Charles Boatner, a Fort Worth journalist, for ten minutes without saying a word. Finally, he said, "Well, I'm going to accept it; it will do me less harm to accept it than fight it. . . . Is that your opinion?," he asked Boatner, who replied: "I'm no politician, that's your problem." And it was.

For the next month Johnson hammered on the idea that Stevenson, who had been anti-union, had made a deal with labor. He also taunted Stevenson for not saying where he stood on Taft-Hartley. When Stevenson refused to make an unequivocal statement on the law, it began to look like he "was trying to hoodwink somebody" or that he was a fence straddler incapable of making up his mind.[39]

Stevenson's waffling on Taft-Hartley fit perfectly with Johnson's overall effort to encourage a view of him as "a do-nothing candidate who refuses to say what he stands for." Anticipating the theme that would serve Truman so well in his autumn presidential campaign against New York governor Thomas Dewey, Johnson identified Stevenson with the "do-nothing government of the Hoover days," which "sat on its heels and cooled things off while millions of people were thrown out of their homes and off their farms . . . and honest men trudged the streets looking in vain for work so that they could feed the hungry mouths at home." Like Hoover, Stevenson was "a do-nothing, sit-it-out candidate, both platformless and promiseless."[40]

Stevenson had begun the campaign as a highly popular public figure. "Coke Stevenson was just like the Coca-Cola," a state legislator said. "He was a state-known product. Everybody knew who he was. And the *Dallas News* had built up his image as 'our cowboy governor'." He was the "household word of conservatism . . . the old Texas goat rancher."

Born in a log cabin in Kimble County in west-central Texas in 1888, Stevenson was a self-made man. Studying law while he worked in a bank as a janitor and a cashier, he built a successful law practice, became a county judge, entered the Texas House in 1928, and became its Speaker in 1933. His election as lieutenant governor in 1938 and 1940 made him governor when Pappy O'Daniel won the 1941 special election for senator. His five and a half years in the state house was a time of general prosperity, allowing him to turn a $30 million state deficit into a $35 million surplus. His personal characteristics joined with his successful management of state affairs to make him the most appealing Texas politician of his time. A strong, silent cowboy type, he was most comfortable at his ranch outside of Telegraph on the Llano River, 150 miles west of Austin, where he loved to chop cedar, herd cattle, and hunt deer. He was so slow-moving, slow-talking, and deliberate that journalists dubbed him "Calculating Coke." When asked a question, he would light and puff on a pipe for a few minutes before giving a measured reply. Asked in 1947 to recall his greatest decision, he said: "Never had any." Describing himself as "just not fitted for the Washington pattern," he nevertheless decided to run for the Senate on a platform of less government, lower taxes, states' rights, and "the complete destruction of the Communist movement in this country."[41]

Yet Stevenson was not as benign as his popular image made him appear. Sam Rayburn called him a "mountebank politician," and liberals viewed him as a reactionary who partly built a budget surplus by slashing state services. He reduced funds for river authorities, starved schoolteachers, and abolished the Old Age Assistance Special Fund, which supported the aged, the blind, and dependent children. The Texas writer and liberal J. Frank Dobie said, "Coke stands for dollars and he does not stand for civilized life as it is furthered by schools, hospitals, and other institutions that must be promoted at public expense." Stevenson was also a racist who denounced the Supreme Court's 1944 decision on black voting rights in Texas as a "monstrous threat to our peace and security." He refused to take any action against a wartime lynching in Texarkana, saying in private that "certain members of the Negro race from time to time furnish the setting for mob violence by the outrageous crimes which they commit." He was more tolerant of Mexicans. When he agreed to set up a Good Neighbor Commission to improve relations with Mexico, he said, "Meskins is pretty good folks. If it was niggers, it'd be different." In 1944, when a reactionary Board of Regents fired University of Texas president Homer Rainey for holding unpopular views, Stevenson fled the capital and refused to intervene. "No hole was too small for him to crawl through," one critic claimed. Stevenson was also an isolationist. In 1947 he opposed the Marshall Plan and said that some of the European nations were "beggars" and ought to do more for themselves. Dobie believed that Stevenson knew "as much about foreign affairs as a hog knows about Sunday."

The Johnson campaign recognized that Stevenson's personal style and politics could be turned against him in 1948. Johnson pressed a case against him as too cautious. Using a song, "Let the Coffee Cool," Johnson's Beau Jesters sang,

> My friends, please make me Senator.
> I was your calculating governor.
> I'm sure you know my steadfast rule
> Of always let the coffee cool.
>
> All through my office term just past
> Were controversies thick and fast.
> And when the matters came to me,
> I solved 'em all with 'Leave 'em be.'
>
> You got to let the coffee cool.
> Then you'll be safe from ridicule.
> Don't ever touch a subject when it's hot.
>
> . . .
>
> You got to let the coffee cool,
> Courage is for dangerous fools,
> Don't never ever touch a boiling pot.

When capital and labor fight
I always find that both are right.
Whenever wets and drys collide
I just wait and choose the winning side.[42]

Johnson also scored points against Stevenson as too wedded to the past and too old. Johnson pretended to interview him in front of rural crowds. First taking the part of a journalist, he would ask: "How do you stand on the 70-Group Air Force?" Then putting a corn cob pipe in his mouth and lowering his voice to imitate Stevenson, he would reply, "I believe in a constructive government." "What do you think about Federal aid for teachers, veterans, etc.?" "Well, I don't want to move the County Court House to Washington." With his hands on his hips, Lyndon would stroll back and forth across the platform and mutter through the pipe stem, "I'm for states' rights; I'm for states' rights." Lyndon also emphasized that Stevenson was sixty years old, "that a man past 60 starts going down," and that if Stevenson got to the Senate, he would never be able to stay long enough to gain the seniority that would make him effective.[43]

Stevenson's campaign style underscored Johnson's picture of him as an indecisive and undynamic figure who was stuck in the past with no clear vision for the future. He traveled around the state in an old Plymouth driven by his nephew, "one-arm" Bob Murphey, a twenty-six-year-old law graduate. Although he traveled over 50,000 miles and shook over 200,000 hands in 211 counties, Stevenson ran a very poor campaign with little or no organization and no overall plan. "He was the worst campaigner that I ever saw in my years of observing politics," Bob Murphey later said. "He had none of the talents for a fast handshake and a quick grin and a slap on the back . . . . He was . . . a reserved man . . . a very quiet man." If Stevenson had a plan, Murphey "never knew it. He campaigned just like he always had, person to person, get in the car, drive to the county seat, go in the courthouse, shake hands with the elected officials, walk around the square, shake hands, make a noon speech to one of the civic clubs, this type of campaign. No glamour, no great advertising or publicity campaigns." When reporters asked him why he didn't fly around the state or get a helicopter like Johnson, he said that "he'd lived a pretty long time and . . . in his lifetime . . . he could not recall ever riding in anything that sooner or later he didn't have to get out and push."

Some people in Stevenson's campaign urged him to become more aggressive and be more decisive in his statements. But Morris Robert, the campaign manager, and Stevenson's brother, Pearce, both of whom were also very "easy-going," opposed the idea. When, after much deliberation, Stevenson issued a "Bill of Particulars" to make his views more specific, he largely stuck to generalities. "You can't get Coke to take a stand on anything controversial," one newspaper complained. "Coke stands first and last for votes for Coke. Beyond that he is the sphinx of Kimble County." "It reminds me," Johnson said of his "Bill of Particulars," "of the Mother Hubbards our grandmothers used to wear. It covers everything and touches nothing." [44]

Despite the slow-moving campaign, Stevenson and his closest advisers hoped that they would win a majority of the vote on July 24 and avoid a run-off. In his 1942 and 1944 primary campaigns for Governor, Stevenson had won by record-setting margins and avoided run-offs. But his campaign against Johnson was a different matter. Running as an isolationist for a Senate seat was not the same as running for Governor. Polls of June 20 and July 3 showed Stevenson with 46.6 and 46.5 percent of the vote. Johnson was a strong second in both polls, 36.8 percent in the first and 38.2 percent in the second. To reach 50 percent, the Stevenson forces encouraged the idea that George Peddy, who received only a 12 percent share in the June poll and 11 percent in July, had no chance to win or even come in second and that his supporters, who preferred Stevenson to Johnson, should vote for Stevenson now and save themselves the trouble of voting for him later in a run-off. But Peddy, who refused to concede, stepped up his campaign in the closing days of the race and raised his share of the vote to 14.5 percent in a poll published on July 21. The survey showed Johnson trailing Stevenson by only 4.4 percent, 38.8 to 43.2 percent. [45]

The election on July 24 frustrated all three of the front runners. Stevenson, who won 477,077 of the 1.202 million votes or 40 percent, was forced into more campaigning in a five-week run-off. Peddy, who received 237,195 votes or a surprising 20 percent, was knocked out of the race. And Johnson, who won 405,617 votes or 34 percent, faced an almost insurmountable challenge. He trailed by over 71,000 votes, had won only 72 counties to Stevenson's 168 and had placed third behind Stevenson in all of the 14 Peddy counties. Lyndon needed to capture 200,000, or nearly two out of three, of the 320,000 votes cast for Peddy and the eight other minor candidates. "We thought we were going to come out of it winning or be real close to the top," Lady Bird said, "and we were overwhelmingly, vastly, horribly behind. . . . It looked hopeless."

Lyndon's best showing was in six of the state's nineteen congressional districts, where he won between 40.4 and 64.8 percent of the vote. These included the two central districts where he was best known: the Tenth, his own, and the Eleventh, immediately north surrounding Waco. The Fourteenth and Fifteenth south Texas districts, with heavy Mexican populations, gave him strong support, and so did the Thirteenth and Nineteenth districts in northcentral and northwest Texas, where he had campaigned extensively in his helicopter. His focus now, however, was not on areas of support but on the other thirteen congressional districts all over the state where he mustered only between 21.9 and 39.4 percent of the vote.[46]

The day after the election, a Sunday, Lyndon and Lady Bird met in the backyard of their Dillman Street house to discuss the run-off with their closest friends and supporters John and Nellie Connally, Alvin Wirtz, Everett Looney, Willard Deason, Charlie Herring, and Claude Wild. Lady Bird remembered it as "one of the gloomiest days we ever lived through." Lyndon was physically exhausted, fearful that most of Peddy's vote would go to Stevenson, and depressed at the thought of another five-week campaign that would probably end in defeat. Others were ready to throw in the towel. But some, including Lady Bird, urged him not to quit. "I must say that was one time that I was very determined and tough, even belligerent about it," she recalled, "and I told Lyndon I'd rather put in our whole stack, borrow anything we could, work 18 hours a day, and lose by 60,000, than to lose by 70, or maybe we could hew it down to 50, or maybe we could even conceivably win."[47]

However strong the momentary letdown, Johnson had no intention of quitting. If we work hard enough, we can win, he told his friends, and they all immediately resumed the campaign. Lyndon took a plane to Washington, where Truman had called a special session beginning on July 26 to put urgent business before the "do-nothing" Republican-controlled Eightieth Congress. Johnson returned to the capital not only for congressional business but to guard against any advantage Coke Stevenson might gain by coming to Washington. A few days before the July 24 vote, Stevenson had announced that he would go to Washington during the special congressional session to see Federal officials and get information about foreign policy. He was eager to demonstrate that he was not an isolationist and to counter assertions that Johnson's knowledge of foreign affairs made him a better candidate for the Senate.[48]

It was a mistake. Traveling by train, rather than plane as Johnson had, Stevenson confirmed Johnson's picture of himself as a modern leader doing battle against a slow-moving, old-style, parochial politician. Further, photos in Texas newspapers of Stevenson pointing to a seat in the U.S. Senate chamber antagonized some voters, who thought it presumptuous of him to act as if already elected. Although Stevenson received positive publicity for meetings with Secretary of Defense James Forrestal, Under Secretary of State Robert A. Lovett, and Senators Tom Connally and Arthur Vandenberg of the Foreign Relations Committee, he opened himself to ridicule for taking "the shortest short course in history on international affairs." "He will need to cram considerably to get ready in five weeks for the exam for which I have been studying for eleven years," Johnson said.

At the same time, after conferring with Secretary Forrestal, Johnson announced that he had persuaded the Secretary to increase Defense Department spending and expand the workforce from 11,000 to 14,000 employees at the Fort Worth Consolidated-Vultee aircraft plant. He also reported the President's willingness to move two Missouri-based anhydrous ammonia plants to the Houston area, where they would supply synthetic rubber plants that the Congressman had singlehandedly kept open. The actions of the Truman administration made clear its preference for Johnson over Stevenson. No one at the White House doubted that Lyndon would be much more in harmony with its domestic and foreign policies than Coke, who was identified with the reactionary Texas regulars.[49]

Stevenson's presence in Washington also gave Johnson the chance to use the Capitol press corps against him. "We did our best to manage his [Stevenson's] appearance in Washington," Walter Jenkins later said. Johnson "briefed them [the journalists] thoroughly" on what to ask Stevenson, Jake Pickle recalled. Johnson "had many friends who were willing to help him, or . . . to counsel with him . . . about questions to ask—the things that would give them a briefing on this man Coke Stevenson whom they had never heard of and never seen." Drew Pearson remembered: "When Coke Stevenson came up here, Lyndon tipped me off and I arranged a press conference . . . and had a question asked of him by one of my assistants about the Taft-Hartley Act." At the conference Stevenson refused to take a forthright position on the law, and Pearson told readers of his column: "Ex-Governor Coke Stevenson of Texas . . . on a recent trip to Washington evaded more issues and dodged more questions than any recent performer in a city noted for question dodging." The press corps, like the Administration, saw Johnson as certain to be a more progressive and constructive senator than Stevenson.[50]

Johnson continued to make Stevenson's indecisiveness and old-fashioned resistance to Federal programs a point of attack in the run-off campaign. In a speech recorded in Washington and broadcast across Texas on July 29, Johnson declared that "their Senator must be willing to take a stand; that he cannot dodge or duck . . . . That a Senator must answer Yes or No." He challenged Stevenson to come down on one side or the other of the Marshall Plan, Taft-Hartley, cost-of living increases for pensioners, and Federal support of increased pay for teachers, farm subsidies, rural electrification, farm to market roads, and hospital construction. He asked the help of all Texans who wanted "an end to the era of evasion" and a return "to forthright, straight-talking public officials who are willing to stand up and be counted."

The Johnson campaign held on to this theme throughout the run-off. At a Johnson rally in Mineola in east Texas on August 6, Stevenson was attacked as "Silent Coke." Referring to Calvin Coolidge, the conservative Republican President of the twenties, the speaker said: "The day of Silent Cal or Silent Coke in Texas and the nation, for that matter, is past." On August 25, three days before the election, the *Austin American*, an unqualified Johnson supporter, depicted Stevenson as a man faithful to the concept "that government was for the protection of property and the status quo," an idea "fixed before two world wars brought new complexities into American life." Stevenson's "philosophy cut him off from many modern problems and is responsible for his sketchy and inadequate contact with national affairs and world conditions. He has been, with all his public service, denied the training and background to meet the acute problems facing Congress in the world of today."[51]

The case for Johnson, the modern leader running against an outdated politico trying to hide his limited understanding of current events, had considerable appeal. But Johnson and his advisers recognized that they would have to make more people aware of him and his message than they had in the first primary. In addition, they would have to make him more attractive to the many Texans who wanted not only a modern man in the Senate but also someone who spoke to their intense concerns about the "Communist threat" and "self-serving" labor unions.

To reach a greater number of voters, Johnson abandoned the helicopter, which had been so effective in rural areas, and concentrated instead on the 30 percent of the vote in seven major cities and counties, where he had fared poorly in the first primary. In the counties containing Amarillo, Beaumont, Dallas, Fort Worth, Galveston, Houston, and San Antonio, Johnson had averaged only 27 percent of the vote against Stevenson's 49.6 percent. Except for Austin, he hadn't done enough in the major cities, Johnson told reporters on August 2. "Everywhere I spoke and visited I led the ticket. . . . I plan to spend considerable time in the big cities during the next month." It was belated recognition on his part that 62 percent of the state's population, up from 45 percent in 1940, now lived in cities, with many of those folks concentrated in eleven metropolises of over 100,000 each.

As evidenced by his opening speech of the run-off on August 6, which he gave at Center in Peddy's east Texas home county, Johnson had also decided to make a special effort to attract Peddy's conservative supporters. Peddy is a man he "liked and admired," Johnson told his Center audience. He and I "thought alike on the main issues."[52]

At the same time Johnson committed himself to a more aggressive campaign in major cities, he also tried to increase his rural support. They "organized a lot of automobile caravans . . . ." Jake Pickle recalled. "We'd go out with Lyndon Johnson signs on our cars and with a P.A. system that played band music on top. And we'd drive into a town and people would get out of the cars, say fifty to a hundred people in a town of two thousand or three thousand. That really made an impression. We'd shake hands and tell people why we were for Lyndon and hand out literature . . . . It was really very effective."

To expand its efforts in the cities and maintain its momentum in the small towns, the campaign had a larger, more active staff than in June and July. Charlie Herring remembered that "in the headquarters office we did a good deal more telephoning and keeping up with people throughout the state and all the counties and precincts that we could and used the telephone night and day . . . to try to keep people active and . . . cause them to work harder in the second primary than they did in the first."[53]

Claude Wild believed that Johnson could not beat Stevenson unless he also avoided errors he had made in the first primary. "In your efforts to sell yourself to the people as a man big enough to be United States Senator," Wild wrote him on July 31, "many people are getting the impression that you are trying to get over as a 'big shot.' " Attired in silk monogrammed shirts with gold cuff-links, two hundred-dollar hand-made suits, and calfskin shoes, Johnson offended some plain folks who preferred the less pretentious Coke Stevenson. Wild also warned Johnson against being facetious; bragging about his limited war record, which angered some veterans; emphasizing Stevenson's age, which many people did not think was too old; acting too impatient with county and district campaigners, at whom he sometimes exploded in public; or having female aides in his hotel rooms late at night. "In the smaller cities the people are not accustomed to women secretaries being in men's bedrooms at all hours. I realize that this is delicate, but it has hurt." Others saw Johnson as altogether too hyper. He was "a sight to see," one newsman said. "While talking, he may, among other things, move from chair to chair around the room, pace the floor, puff cigarettes endlessly, rub salve on his hands, take a digestion tablet, gulp water, and use an inhaler in his nose. He's just too nervous to remain still."[54]

Curbing these "errors" impressed Johnson as less important than finding specific means of drawing new voters to his side. Consequently, he "made a deal" with James E. McDonald, the Texas Commissioner of Agriculture, "a man with one of the biggest political followings in Texas." A few days after the first primary, McDonald sent Walter McKay, the chief entomologist in the Agriculture Department, to see Arthur Stehling, an attorney in Fredericksburg who knew Johnson and shared ownership of a radio station with McKay. McKay asked Stehling to put a proposition before Johnson. McDonald and the Georgia Commissioner of Agriculture were under Federal indictment for violating the Federal lobbying law. If Johnson would use his influence to get the indictment dismissed, McDonald promised to switch his political support from Stevenson to Johnson. Told of the proposition by Stehling, who flew to Washington to see him, Johnson exploded: "Arthur, you tell that

S.O.B. to go straight to hell." After Johnson apparently reconsidered, he said to Stehling: "Tell him that, as he well knows, Stevenson cannot be of any help to him whatsoever under the present administration. I can help him more as a Senator than as a Congressman. I know McDonald has at least a hundred thousand votes in his hip pocket that he can deliver but I just don't want to obligate myself."

McDonald met Stehling at the Austin airport to get Johnson's reply. Johnson and McDonald then apparently met several days later in Austin, where they "made a deal." According to McKay, McDonald met his part of the bargain by passing word to 500 cotton inspectors and other employees in his Department "to support Johnson and to press all of the cotton farmers and all other persons they came in contact with to do likewise." Stehling believes that in return for McDonald's support, Johnson used his influence to delay a trial of the case against McDonald. Although there is no direct evidence that Johnson intervened in the case, McDonald never came to trial and the charges in Federal court against him were still on the court docket when he died in 1952.[55]

Yet however valuable a "deal" with McDonald might be, Johnson believed that he could not win the run-off without appealing to intense anti-Communist and anti-labor sentiment. By August, the successful Communist coup in Czechoslovakia, the ongoing confrontation with Moscow in Berlin, Communist military victories in China, and the House Un-American Activities Committee investigation of a prewar Communist spy ring in Washington that allegedly included Alger Hiss, the current head of the Carnegie Endowment for International Peace, had brought anti-Communist sentiment to fever pitch. Defending America against the "Red Menace" became an irresistible tactic in the campaign. On July 31, Wild urged Johnson to begin hammering on "the defense program, the Taft-Hartley Bill and Communism. I would come out progressively to the people with this idea . . . that you have watched the growth of these evils as they are attempting to overpower or undermine this Government. That you have stood for your defense program in order to be strong enough to withstand the onslaught of Russian imperialism and their Communist propaganda." Wild also urged him to emphasize the danger not from labor unions, which he had supported, but from "labor bosses" who aim "to take over the Government of this country from behind the scenes." These people "are now supporting my opponent. The issue, therefore, in this race is whether or not the people of Texas are going to yield to this unseen group of bosses, many of them outside of the state of Texas, in the election of our public officials."[56]

Johnson followed Wild's advice. On August 8 the *Dallas News* carried a full-page ad for Johnson praising his "courageous and outspoken championship of the Taft-Hartley Law which halted the labor bosses who had all but throttled private industry and enterprise in this state and nation. . . . The same labor bosses which Lyndon Johnson helped to force into the raiment of Americanism are now down here in Texas, using Coke Stevenson. . . . If Lyndon Johnson is defeated, every CIO-PAC-AFL labor boss in the country will hail the victory . . . and the march of decentralized industry to Texas . . . will stop—while Calculatin' Coke calmly lights his pipe." In a state-wide radio broadcast three days later, Johnson declared that "my opponent hasn't ever said whether he favors curbing the power of this country's John L. Lewises and Caesar Petrillos [James C. Petrillo, head of the musicians' union]. . . . He's absolutely refused to comment on the law which would run the Communists out of the labor unions. . . . And a lot of those big labor bosses have refused to take the pledge that they are not members of the Communist Party. But did my opponent tell you that he didn't want the support of those labor bosses who have refused to take the non-Communist pledge? Oh, no." Johnson promised to maintain the Taft-Hartley provision requiring labor bosses to sign a pledge that they are not Communists. He wondered whether Stevenson, who had an AFL endorsement, would do the same.[57]

In the "Johnson Journal," a publication sent to rural voters, the campaign depicted Stevenson as a pawn of northern Communist labor bosses. "The big Northern labor unions, with their leadership which includes admitted Communists . . . have aligned their forces against Lyndon Johnson and in favor of Coke Stevenson." The "Journal" warned that the Communists, "many of them leaders in the big national labor unions . . . favor the election of isolationist candidates . . . . That's why the big shot labor bosses up North are trying to put Stevenson in office . . . . Wake up Texans! Don't let the Reds slip up on you by any such cunning plot!" Quoting Johnson, the "Journal" described northern labor bosses as "the same Communists who would confiscate the farms of Texas and place Texas farmers under the lash of a commissar's whip . . . ."

At the same time, retired Air Force General Ira Eaker, who now worked for Hughes Aircraft, campaigned in west Texas for Johnson. Stating that Russia had already declared war on the United States, Eaker urged Texans to serve their country by recognizing the danger to national security and selecting wise leaders like Lyndon Johnson who stood for preparedness and the destruction of the subversive Communist fifth column in the country.[58]

To make a Stevenson tie to northern labor more convincing, the Johnson campaign asked Welly Hopkins, now a principal attorney for John L. Lewis's United Mine Workers Union, to issue a statement favorable to Stevenson. While on a family visit in Gonzales, a town southeast of Austin, the press asked Hopkins to explain his presence in Texas. Hopkins replied that it was strictly personal; the UMW had no members in Texas and no interest in Texas politics. Seeing the news item the next day, Wirtz drew up a statement which John Connally carried by plane to Gonzales, where he caught Hopkins at the airport. Connally explained that "the race was close," and asked Hopkins to sign a statement that he was an old friend of both candidates, but "judging by the official record and platform of the two men, I have no hesitancy in saying that if John L. Lewis and the United Mine Workers were taking any interest in Texas politics, they would support Coke Stevenson." Hopkins refused, saying the statement "was an untruth." [59]

At the same time Johnson was doing everything possible to identify Stevenson with unpopular labor leaders, he courted them behind the scenes. He sent word to unions that if elected he would give "careful consideration" to "amendments or corrections" of Taft-Hartley. Influential Washington friends also made the case for him. Attorney General Tom Clark, Congresswoman Helen Gahagan Douglas, and Tommy Corcoran quietly persuaded four transportation brotherhoods to endorse Lyndon. Corcoran told Harold Ickes on August 11 that he "had a terrible time straightening out labor" in the Johnson campaign, "but it is finally straightened out." That Lyndon was effectively courting all sides in the campaign was not lost on the *Dallas News*, a conservative Stevenson paper. The editors complained on August 21 that "a variety of business tycoons, left-wing laborites, corporation lawyers, New Dealers, anti-New Dealers, etc." were all riding Johnson's band wagon. [60]

Stevenson's campaign was no model of civic virtue or consistency either. Although justifiably calling Johnson's accusations "political clap-trap," Stevenson also appealed to public fears by describing Johnson as insensitive or indifferent to the Communist threat. In a speech on August 18, Stevenson asked: "Did the other candidate for the United States Senate, in any of his eleven years in Congress, ever introduce a bill which would make a contribution to controlling activities of the Communists? Did he ever sponsor a measure which would help cut down on the dangerous efforts of spy rings to obtain valuable information?" In fact, Stevenson asserted, on three separate occasions Johnson had voted against measures that would have stopped the Communists. Echoing this theme in subsequent talks, Stevenson asked whether Johnson's lavishly financed campaign was getting money from Henry Wallace's leftist backers, and complained that Johnson had joined with "Vito Marcantonio of the Harlem District," meaning the Communist congressman representing New York City's black ghetto, in resisting the appropriation of funds for HUAC, which investigated spying, and a ban on aid to countries dominated by Russia. [61]

Convinced that they were locked in a tight race, both sides reached for every possible advantage in the final days of the run-off. On August 25, Johnson accused Stevenson of opposing actions favored by Secretary of State Marshall and Senators Connally and Vandeberg and supporting another opposed by J. Edgar Hoover and the FBI. Also warning that Soviet actions had darkened "the war clouds on the American horizon" and that "it may be later than you think," Johnson urged Texans not to elect an isolationist to the U.S. Senate On the same day, Stevenson raised questions about Johnson's honesty: he invoked a section of the Texas election law that allowed him to appoint supervisors to monitor the vote in Webb County in south Texas, where Johnson had received 6,476 votes to 531 for Stevenson and 61 for Peddy in the first primary. He also associated Johnson with Federal efforts "to tell the white people of Texas that they must send their children to the same schools attended by colored children."[62]

Lyndon and Lady Bird stretched themselves to the limit in the last two days of the campaign. Lyndon's "voice was a sore-throat croak, his eyes were black-circled and deep inside their sockets, and his face seemed to be skin stretched over long bones." Lady Bird also ended the race physically drained. Traveling with him often during the second primary, she described herself as "a recorder, a message carrier, a thanker, a suitcase packer, a small speechmaker at women's groups, [and] small town groups." On the last evening of the run-off she planned to join Lyndon at a rally in San Antonio, where she was slated to make her first radio speech. That afternoon, she and Marietta Brooks, the head of the Women's Division in the campaign, drove from Austin to a reception in Seguin. On the way their car skidded and landed in a ditch. Brooks had to be hospitalized, but Lady Bird, who was badly shaken, went to the reception, having borrowed clothes from her hostess to replace her muddy dress and torn stockings. Afterward, despite what she later called "some of the worst bruises you can imagine," she went to San Antonio. She did not mention the accident to Lyndon. When he noticed her bruises as she undressed later that evening, he thought her performance "the most wonderful, courageous, exciting thing that he'd ever heard of anybody doing." She ignored her injuries, and spent the next day in Austin with her mother-in-law and Lyndon's three sisters dividing up the phone book and calling people to ask for their votes.[63]

Lyndon spent election morning campaigning in San Antonio. He saw the city as one key to his election. In the first primary, Stevenson had led him by over 12,000 votes in Bexar County, but Paul Kilday, San Antonio congressman, promised Stuart Symington, who went "as far as I could" in pleading for Kilday's help, that the results this time would be "interesting and better." Leaving nothing to chance, the Johnson campaign had united the city's normally antagonistic Kilday and Maverick factions behind Lyndon. Lyndon also wanted to ensure that San Antonio Mexican political bosses would stay bought. According to the Fort Worth journalist Charles Boatner, Johnson's backers had paid off three local Mexican leaders in the first primary, but when Stevenson's people gave them more money they had switched to Stevenson. On election day, Johnson accompanied James Knight, the county clerk, around the San Antonio polls. Knight later told Ronnie Dugger that the Johnson people gave him $1000 in one dollar bills, which he distributed to Johnson supporters who had been "drumming up votes [and] putting up posters." The effort in San Antonio paid handsome dividends. In Bexar County, Johnson beat Stevenson in the second primary by 99 votes, 15,610 to 15,511.[64]

The overall result, as one opinion poll earlier in the week had forecast, was so close that no one could be sure who won. The initial returns on election day, Saturday, August 28, favored Stevenson. According to the Texas Election Bureau, an unofficial agency run by Texas newspapers, Stevenson led at midnight by 2,119 votes out of 939,468 counted. "Well, it looks like we've lost," Lady Bird told Dorothy Nichols on the phone. "I guess we'll just have to get real busy and work real hard in the radio business now." But Stevenson's lead evaporated the next day. By 9:00 p.m. Sunday Lyndon held a 693-vote edge out of 979,877, with an estimated 11,000 votes yet to be counted. By Monday evening, Stevenson had swung back into the lead by 119 votes with 400 ballots still uncounted. The following day, the 31st, the lead increased to 349 votes. When the Bureau gave its final unofficial return on September 2, Stevenson's lead stood at 362 votes.[65]

During the five days after the election, both sides had jockeyed to ensure a favorable outcome. Recognizing that the greatest possible vigilance was essential in so close a contest, the Johnson and Stevenson camps monitored each other's actions. Remembering how early reporting of pro-Johnson counties in 1941 had told O'Daniel's men how many votes they needed to win and how a failure to watch east Texas counties closely had turned Lyndon's victory into a defeat, Johnson backers now withheld final official tallies in several of his counties for as long as possible and kept close watch on ballot boxes all over the state. Walter Jenkins recalled that in 1941 Johnson aides had reported strong Johnson counties early so that the headlines would say he had won. "In 1948 we learned better, and we didn't rush the people in the counties where we had strong votes. We rather hoped that they would hold back, so if there was . . . any sort of fraud" Stevenson wouldn't know how much he needed to win.

At the same time, Johnson supporters arranged to have ballot watchers everywhere. Two weeks before the election, at a meeting in Beeville in south Texas near Corpus Christi, Sam Houston Johnson told a group of Johnson campaigners, "Stevenson controls the machinery of the party. We've got to have poll watchers. If you don't do these things, Stevenson people are going to steal the election." A week before the balloting a directive from Johnson headquaters to county campaign chairmen emphasized the importance of getting a prompt read on all ballot boxes and of getting people friendly to Johnson to stand guard at the polls."[66]

Not anticipating so close a result, Stevenson had been more relaxed about monitoring the vote. On Sunday, however, after seeing how close the contest was, he rushed to Austin, where he had better radio and telephone means of following the returns. Calling his county managers all over the state, he asked them to check the results closely. On Sunday night he told a supporter in San Antonio that his canvass of the state showed they had won the election, but that Johnson would now try to change the outcome by altering the final, official returns, especially in south Texas.[67]

Both sides were well advised to watch the other. But in the last-minute manipulation of votes, the Stevenson campaign was no match for Johnson's. Bob Murphey, Stevenson's nephew and driver during the campaign, later told an interviewer: "We've got 254 counties in this state, and if you didn't change but 10 votes per county, you're talking about over 2,500 votes. And this was the strategy of the Johnson forces. We knew that. We had information, and it's kind of like fighting a war there. Both sides had lines of information coming from one another. We had our people who were letting us know what they were doing, and I'm confident that they had people letting them know what we were doing. As a result, we knew what their plan was. Here is where Mr. Stevenson's more or less loose organization took a beating. . . . At this critical point of the campaign during this battle for ballots, after the election was over, Mr. Johnson's refined organization and the lieutenants that he had who were experienced in this type of activity shot us out of the water, just to be perfectly frank about it."[68]

The Johnson camp, seeing itself as "fighting fire with fire," put Johnson in the lead when the official returns came in to the state Democratic Executive Committee in Austin on September 3 and 4. To keep the Stevenson campaign from altering too many votes, the Johnson people monitored telephone calls coming into Stevenson headquarters. Every time they got a call from one of their county managers saying "We think we can pick up a few votes here," a Johnson representative sped to the scene to look over the officials' shoulders. The Johnson people, however, couldn't stop the Stevenson campaign from making some favorable adjustments to their total. But "every time the Stevenson forces would come through with some votes," a Johnson insider later said, "Connally would top it." Having instructed Johnson supporters in various counties to undercount Lyndon's vote and hold back final official returns, Connally now had Johnson backers send in higher tallies.

The "corrected" returns on September 3 reduced Stevenson's total by 205 votes and increased Johnson's by 174, giving him a 17-vote lead. The biggest single shift had come from the town of Alice in Jim Wells

County in south Texas, where Johnson received an additional 202 votes and Stevenson one. Other "corrections" from around the state the next day increased Johnson's lead to 162.[69]

The altered results generated charges of fraud. On September 3, Stevenson complained that "it is becoming increasingly obvious that a concentrated effort is being made to count me out of this Senate race." On the following day the *Dallas News* called for an investigation of the election by the state Senate Investigating Committee, saying, "Let's Clear Texas's Good Name." Anticipating accusations against his campaign, Johnson had taken the offensive on August 31 when he told the press that corrected totals from a west-central Texas county and from two Gulf coast counties had given Stevenson 338 more votes. "I'm sure that all of the mistakes have been honest mistakes," Johnson said, "but nevertheless, Stevenson has been kept in the running by those mistakes . . . . In 1941, I lost this office by 1,311 votes, and I was counted out on Wednesday [four days after the election]. In 1941 the same men were involved. I lost the senatorial race by 1,311 votes and Coke Stevenson won the governorship by 1,311 votes." On September 2, when the Election Bureau's unofficial result had given Stevenson the victory, Johnson had declared himself the winner. After he got the lead and the *Dallas News* asked an investigation, he questioned whether Stevenson's old cronies in the Texas state Senate could be fair and suggested asking the FBI.[70]

Stevenson, convinced that he had won the actual election and that Johnson's victory rested on the superior ability of his campaign to manipulate final returns, tried to discredit the results in south Texas, an area notorious for boss rule, bloc voting, and doctored ballots. Like every close observer of Texas politics, Stevenson knew that south Texas counties had managed elections and that George Parr, the "Duke" of Duval County, was famous for arranging landslides for his chosen candidates. The heir to a political dynasty or political machine his father Archer had established early in the century, George was the patron of the county's Mexican-Americans, who outnumbered Anglos by two to one. He ensured that county jobs went almost exclusively to "Latins" and acted as a kind of local welfare bureau for them from his offices in San Diego, the county seat. Parr also paid the poll taxes of the county's Mexicans and told them how to vote. In three of his state-wide races Stevenson had been the beneficiary of Parr's largesse, receiving majorities in Duval County of 3,643 to 141; 2,936 to 77; and 3,310 to 17. Committed to no ideology, except the survival of his machine, Parr favored and opposed politicians according to his needs. Unfriendly to Beauford Jester and the Pat Neff family, Parr gave Jester and Pat Neff, Jr., zero votes in their respective 1946 races for governor and attorney general. Their opponents each received the same total—1,735 votes. In 1944, when John

Lyle ran for the congressional seat that included Duval County, Parr called to say he would support him. When Lyle said he would campaign in the county, Parr asked, "What for? . . . I told you that we were going to support you." Duval gave Lyle a lopsided majority.[71]

During his last gubernatorial term, Stevenson crossed Parr. In 1943 the state district attorney for the judicial district including Laredo in Webb County resigned to enter the army. Pressured by the War Department to clean up the vice that surrounded the Laredo Air Force Base, Stevenson ignored the recommendation of Manuel Ramon, Parr's ally in Webb, and appointed S. Truman Phelps to complete the unexpired term. Stevenson told Phelps that he would never be elected to the office by the local voters and urged him to satisfy the War Department's demand for a house cleaning. Aware that the appointment meant the end of Parr's and Ramon's support, Stevenson assumed that he could win any future race without it. Nevertheless, in 1947, Stevenson went through the motions of asking for their help. At a meeting in Laredo with Ramon and other local political bosses, Stevenson received a direct reply. "Coke, you know we can't support you and . . . we're going to have to be all out against you." They explained that losing control over local appointments could destroy their political organizations and couldn't be ignored. "We like you. We're not against you personally, but we've got to do this," they said.[72]

Stevenson believed that south Texas was a vulnerable chink in the Johnson campaign's manipulation of final returns. Parr himself would not stand up well under close scrutiny in an election contest. He had been convicted of income tax evasion in 1934 and been sent to jail for nine and a half months in 1936 for probation violations; Parr and his lieutenants would not carry spotless reputations into a law court. Moreover, Parr presided over a financial empire that included two banks, a construction company, and a 57,000 acre ranch with a private racetrack, a two-story mansion, a swimming pool, and servants' quarters. Parr was reputed to have made his fortune through the manipulation of county contracts and on the backs of unskilled Mexicans earning $16 a week.[73]

The Stevenson people viewed the results in Duval and Jim Wells counties as particularly open to suspicion. Returns from Duval on election day showed Johnson ahead, 4,197 to 40. The following day—during which Johnson turned an over-all 2,119-vote deficit into a 693-vote lead—Duval added 425 ballots to his total. The additional 203 votes from Box 13 in Alice in Jim Wells County, where Parr had one of his banks and a close alliance with Ed Lloyd, the local boss, seemed even more suspicious. In the corrected result given on September 3, six days after the election, the Alice officials had increased the total vote by nearly 25 percent, from 825 to 1,028. Since the local official had been given only about 600 ballots for Box 13 and only 499 votes had been cast for gubernatorial candidates and 501 for U.S. Senate contestants in the first primary, it was an astonishing total vote.[74]

Stevenson tried to enlist the aid of state and Federal officials in challenging the results in south Texas. But almost no one was willing to help. Governor Beauford Jester, who was out of the state at the time, showed no inclination to get involved. Price Daniel, the attorney general, said he had no authority to investigate or prosecute alleged election fraud. Senator Tom Connally, who was away in Europe, was "truly glad" to avoid the unpleasant recriminations over the Senate contest. O'Daniel rejected a plea from the U.S. Senate Elections Committee for help with an investigation requested by Stevenson people. He said he had no interest in the matter and didn't "give a damn about either Johnson or Stevenson." J. Edgar Hoover of the FBI turned aside pleas for an investigation by saying a request had to come from U.S. Attorney General Tom Clark, and Clark delayed doing anything by turning the matter over to subordinates, who simply waited on events. Most of these officials probably shared the feeling of a San Antonio attorney that all an investigation would produce would be "damage and injustice to the . . . state": he told Senator Tom Connally that the inevitable charges and countercharges would undermine the confidence of citizens in their government and would satisfy only "the enemies of our party both in Texas and throughout the nation."[75]

Johnson tried to discourage an investigation by making clear that it would force Texas and Federal officials to confront publicly the widespread manipulation of ballots in a Texas election. Gathering a file on thirty "possible election irregularities which benefited Coke Stevenson," Johnson used a radio address on September 6 to mention some of these and put other political leaders on notice that a challenge to his election would embarrass them as well. Good-naturedly describing himself as "Landslide Lyndon," Johnson reminded listeners that he had not protested the questionable outcome in 1941, and by enumerating instances of bloc voting for Stevenson across the state he countered attacks on his "bloc votes in one county." He also wondered why it had "taken so many years" for a "hue and cry" to develop over the vote in Jim Wells County. Despite the fact that Stevenson and a long list of "distinguished Texans who have served in high judicial and executive posts" had received lopsided majorities in that county since 1924, nothing was said until the Jim Wells vote gave him his lead.[76]

Stevenson believed he had nothing to lose and everything to gain from pressing a challenge. On September 7, he sent Kellis Dibrell, a former FBI agent and attorney in San Antonio, and Callan Graham, a close friend and fellow attorney from Junction, to Alice, the Jim Wells County seat 140 miles south of San Antonio. Their objective was to investigate the 203-vote "correction" in Box 13 reported on September 3. What

they suspected, but could not prove, was that after Stevenson had regained the lead on Monday, August 30, Johnson representatives asked
Parr to find more votes for their side. Saying he had done all he could
in Duval, where he had used all the names on the poll tax list, he promised to do what he could in Jim Wells. According to Luis Salas, Parr's
ally and the election judge for Box 13 in Alice, Parr ordered him to add
200 votes to Johnson's column by using the names of people from the
poll tax list who had not voted. Salas had two aides add 202 votes for
Johnson and one for Stevenson. They made the mistake of putting the
additions in alphabetical order and in a different color ink from the
names legitimately on the voting list.[77]

Salas later claimed that Johnson was at the meeting in Parr's office,
and others said that Johnson made calls to Parr at this time. Johnson
knew Parr and acknowledged that over the years they had had a number
of conversations. Johnson loved to "imitate Parr calling in on his old-
fashioned telephone. 'Can you hear me, Lyndon, can you hear me?,'
LBJ the mime would quaver, holding up an imaginary two-piece phone.
Then Johnson would act out his own role. 'Yes, yes, go ahead, George.'
And sure enough, the Duke would report another election landslide for
his chosen candidates, Lyndon being one." Years later, referring to the
week after the 1948 election, Johnson said: "I never saw George Parr."
Walter Jenkins and others confirmed that Johnson never left Austin during
the week of August 29. Moreover, it seems unlikely that Johnson even
spoke directly to Parr. He knew that the post-election alteration of vote
totals would generate controversy and that it would be difficult for Stevenson to mount a successful challenge unless, as one attorney later
wrote, "it could be clearly shown that he [Lyndon] is personally responsible for, or at least party to, some fraud or skulduggery." Johnson apparently steered clear of direct meetings or conversations with Parr and
his subordinates in Alice. Nevertheless, according to what John Cofer,
one of Lyndon's attorneys, later told Ronnie Dugger, Johnson was at a
meeting in Austin when Johnson campaign managers decided to accept
the "corrected" Alice total and announce the altered Jim Wells result
on the 3rd.[78]

On the drive to Alice from Austin, Dibrell and Graham discussed what
to do. Warned not to wear suit coats so that no one would suspect them
of hiding guns, they were "a little uptight" about their safety. They agreed
to go see Tom Donald, the Democratic county chairman and manager
at Parr's Alice National Bank. They asked him for the voting list, which
every citizen had a right to see. But Donald refused to open the vault in
which he had put Box 13. Dibrell and Graham then called Stevenson—
who decided to come to Alice with James Gardner, another ex-FBI agent
from San Antonio, and Frank Hamer, an ex-Texas Ranger famous for

having helped track down Bonnie and Clyde. While awaiting Stevenson's arrival, Dibrell and Graham enlisted the help of Harry Lee Adams, the incoming county chairman, who was neutral in the Johnson-Stevenson contest.

When the Stevenson party went back to the bank to see Donald, two groups of armed men stood in the street. In a confrontation reminiscent of the old West, Hamer faced them down. Approaching a group of riflemen standing across from the bank, Hamer pointed down the street and said just one word: "Git." Then Hamer walked to the front of the bank, where he ordered the other gunmen to "Fall Back." As they did, Stevenson and his party entered the bank. Though Donald refused to let Stevenson or any of his men see the voting list, he agreed to let Adams, who was now responsible for it, enter the vault for five minutes. Following the suggestion of Stevenson's people, Adams scanned the last 203 names on the list, making note of the last name that preceded them, the first and last names of the two hundred plus additional voters, and nine others.[79]

Adams now told the Stevenson group about the change in ink color and the alphabetical listing of the last 203 names. He also gave them the twelve names he had managed to copy. When they questioned the last man to vote before the 203 added to the list, he said that he had come to the polls as they were locking the doors. Of the eleven people questioned among the 203, none had actually voted. Some said they had been out of town, some of them were sick, and some simply hadn't bothered to vote.[80]

Dibrell and Graham had stayed in Alice for several days to find and question these people. In the middle of one night, Clarence Martens, the secretary to the County Executive Committee, called them at their hotel. Worried that he might get into trouble for signing a false election certificate, he asked for a meeting on a back country road. Dibrell and Graham convinced him to come back to their hotel to sign a corrected certificate saying the September 3 report was in error. Before Graham could finish typing the document, however, a man burst into their room and dragged Martens out into the hall, where Ed Lloyd, the local Parr boss, was standing. Apparently informed by Martens's wife that he had gone to the hotel, Lloyd arrived in time to keep him from signing a new certificate.[81]

On another night, Dibrell and Graham had a call from Hap Holmgreen, the county clerk, who described himself as friendly to Stevenson. Inviting them to his office at the courthouse after dark, he said he had to meet someone and left them alone in his office for thirty minutes. After he left and locked them in, they discovered that his vault door was open. Inside they found an unlocked box with the Precinct 13 ballots in it. Luis Salas's signature was on the backs of all of them. But a different handwriting and a different color ink were distinguishing features of the last 203 ballots.[82]

Following these events from Austin, the Johnson camp was particularly alarmed by the possibility that a new Jim Wells County Executive Committee, which was due to meet on Friday morning, September 10, might throw out the revised September 3 result. Taking the matter to a state judge in Austin, Johnson's lawyers asserted that the Stevenson group was conspiring to have the Alice vote "thrown out on grounds of fraud and irregularity," and that Frank Hamer was using "threat and intimidation" on Committee members to force a change in the vote. The judge issued an injunction forbidding any alteration in the September 3 report of the vote, and ordered a hearing on the matter in the Alice district court on Monday, September 13.[83]

The Stevenson people realistically had little hope that an Alice judge, who was a Parr ally, would allow a recanvass of the vote. Instead, they focused their attention on the State Democratic Executive Committee meeting on September 13 and the party's state convention on September 14 in Fort Worth. Under party rules the Committee was responsible for counting statewide primary returns from the counties and certifying the nominees for the fall elections. Because the outcome of the Senate contest was so close, Robert W. Calvert, the Committee's chairman, set up a subcommittee to count the vote composed of three members appointed by him, two by Stevenson, and two by Johnson.

At about midnight, on Sunday the 12th, in a Fort Worth hotel, Calvert ran into Vann Kennedy, the state party secretary, who had the county ballot reports. " 'Do you want to know who's won the Senate race?',' Kennedy asked Calvert. " ' . . . Yes, I'd be curious,' " he replied. " 'Well, Johnson has it won by eighty-seven votes. All hell's going to pop tomorrow,' " Calvert said.[84]

The fireworks began in the subcommittee. After it totaled the result on an adding machine, Stevenson's representatives objected to the inclusion of the amended Box 13 return, and were able to pass, 4 to 3, a resolution eliminating Lyndon's 202 last-minute Alice votes. The minority report included them and recommended Johnson's certification as the party's Senate candidate. Later that day, the party chairman from Harrison, Lady Bird's home county, advised Calvert that he had sent in an erroneous certificate with about 250 too many votes for Johnson. He wanted to file an amended return. But when Calvert warned that it might expose him to an indictment for perjury or false swearing, he let the original certificate stand.[85]

The full Executive Committee met that night in the ballroom of Fort Worth's Blackstone Hotel. The meeting was jam-packed, with every seat taken, and people standing against the walls. The tension in the room was explosive. Lyndon and Lady Bird sat in the front row facing the Committee with Stevenson seated ten feet away puffing on his pipe. Kennedy read the majority and minority resolutions, and an hour and a half debate over whether to approve the pro-Johnson one followed. The exchanges were vicious. Presenting the evidence gathered in Alice, one Stevenson lawyer shouted: "I am here to prevent the stuffing of the ballot box." Johnson's lawyers ridiculed Stevenson's claims, said they could give two examples of fraud for every one Stevenson presented, and attacked Dibrell, Graham, and Gardner as Stevenson's "goon squad" that had "threatened those poor Mexican people and intimidated them at the point of a gun" into signing affidavits that they hadn't voted.[86]

The Committee vote added to the drama. As it was tallied, Jake Pickle's heart pounded so hard he "could hardly write." One of Lyndon's ballots was a proxy from an Austin attorney who had had a heart attack in the hotel lobby and had signed over his vote before going to the hospital. The fifty-six Committee members in the room divided 29 to 27 in favor of Johnson. But before Kennedy could verify the result, a woman delegate from Conroe County reversed herself, producing a 28-28 tie. As chairman, Calvert had the right to cast a tie-breaking vote. He was "convinced absolutely" that the additional votes for Johnson in Box 13 were a fraud. But knowing that a state Supreme Court decision in 1932 had denied the Committee the right to go behind the ballots or do anything except count and abide by the reported return, he intended to endorse Johnson's 87-vote victory. Unwilling to vote, however, until six absent Committee members were given a last chance to cast ballots, Calvert asked Kennedy to call their names one more time. None of the first five responded, but as Kennedy shouted the name of Charlie Gibson of Amarillo, the last one on the list, Gibson, who some claim was drunk and had to be rushed to the ballroom, ran in the back of the hall, climbed on a chair, and asked what motion was being considered. After being told, he cast the deciding vote for Johnson. The hall erupted in cheers and boos, while someone kicked over Gibson's chair.[87]

Stevenson wouldn't give up his fight for the nomination. Since the party convention the next day had the power to reject the Executive Committee's report, Stevenson hoped to win a majority of the 2000 delegates to his side. A head count by one Johnson supporter gave Lyndon only a twelve-vote edge, and last-minute absences and vote shifts could defeat him. But the factor of a larger intraparty struggle between pro- and anti-Truman forces ensured his victory. Texas Democrats, like other southerners, were torn in 1948 between backing Truman, the party's presidential candidate, and Governor Strom Thurmond of South Carolina, who had bolted the party over its support of civil rights to organize the States Rights party or Dixiecrats. To ensure party loyalty to the national ticket, Truman Democrats refused to seat pro-Thurmond delegations from Dallas, Fort Worth, and Houston. Since most of the Thurmond people were also pro-Stevenson, their removal from the convention gave Johnson an easy victory in the vote to confirm the Executive Committee's recommendation.

The pro-Thurmond, pro-Stevenson delegates left in a huff. The Houston contingent marched out under Thurmond banners with one of them shouting; "You can't put me in bed with Truman and his Commiecrats." The Fort Worth group, which had paid for the rental of the convention hall and all the equipment, took everything with them—tables, chairs, desks, typewriters, and adding machines. They even cut off the electricity and the pipe organ. Their moving men carted off a table Sam Rayburn was sitting at on the platform, and when he got up to protest, they took his chair. Remaining delegates collected rent money for the hall by passing several hats among themselves. With Johnson's friends in control of the convention, he was asked to address the delegates. Promising to go all out to be a good senator, he also thanked George Parr, whom Rayburn had called to the platform. Rayburn described Parr as "the hero of the Democratic party in Texas," and Parr received Johnson's tongue-in-cheek praise as "the man that casts more Democratic votes than anybody else in the state." [88]

The fight for the nomination was still not over. After the convention endorsed Johnson's nomination, Stevenson went to court. Very early on the morning of September 15, after an all-night drive to Caddo Lake on the Louisiana border, two of Stevenson's representatives reached the rural residence of T. Whitfield Davidson, Federal district judge for North Texas. As he drank coffee on his front porch, Davidson read a petition from Stevenson asking a temporary restraining order against putting Johnson's name on the November ballot. Persuaded that Stevenson was entitled to a hearing, Davidson issued the order at 6:25 a.m. and scheduled a court date for September 21 in Fort Worth.

Johnson suspected a conspiracy. Connie Renfro, one of the men who delivered Stevenson's petition, was, according to a Johnson attorney, "very, very close to Judge Davidson." Johnson and his lawyers thought that the proper jurisdiction for the case was the state courts. But no state court would have barred Johnson's name from the ballot without first attempting to throw out illegal votes from all counties. In their view, the result of such a review would have been an even larger margin of victory for Johnson. Instead, Stevenson had chosen to put his case before a Federal judge who was a conservative anti-New Dealer and a friend. Stevenson and his attorneys contended that a state-wide recount could not have been completed in time to get Stevenson's name on the November ballot. In addition, the fradulent votes in Alice for a Federal office constituted an invasion of his civil rights which a Federal court should protect. [89]

Convinced that there were no accidents in politics and that Stevenson's petition to Davidson was a good case in point, Johnson and his advisers felt free to engage in some skulduggery of their own. Having learned from someone in Stevenson's camp that he planned to appeal to Davidson, Johnson, Alvin Wirtz, former Governor Jimmy Allred, and the Brown brothers had asked J. R. Parten, a liberal oilman, to talk to Myron G. Blalock, a former Davidson law partner, to "see if he wouldn't use his influence to help Lyndon." Though Blalock tried, nothing came of his effort.

After Davidson issued his ruling, Johnson's attorneys unsuccessfully appealed to the state Supreme Court. While that was taking place, one pro-Johnson lawyer suggested an appeal to Chief Justice Fred Vinson of the U.S. Supreme Court. He also proposed "that Mr. Rayburn and Mr. [Alben] Barkley [Truman's 1948 running mate] could be present or get in touch with Judge Vinson, that might get some help." There is no evidence that any one approached Vinson. Instead, the Johnson group prepared itself for the hearing in Davidson's court. They learned from a Stevenson legal aide that "they were going to have some of the election officials and a number of others as witnesses from Jim Wells County in court." When these people came to Fort Worth, a Johnson aide kept track of their phone calls through a hotel switchboard operator.[90]

Johnson's nine attorneys mapped strategy to overcome Stevenson's challenge. Their first line of defense was to argue that the Federal court had no jurisdiction in the matter, and they drew up a motion citing twenty-two reasons why Davidson should throw out Stevenson's petition. Since they were not optimistic about persuading Davidson, they debated what their next step should be. On September 18, former Attorney General Francis Biddle, Thurman Arnold, and Paul Porter, three of the most prominent attorneys in Washington, advised Wirtz that if they lost their case before Davidson, they should immediately appeal to the Fifth Circuit Court of Appeals in Atlanta. It was also possible for them to bypass the Appeals Court and go directly to the U.S. Supreme Court, but they thought it would probably be best to try the Circuit Court first. Johnson's lawyers could not agree on how to make a successful appeal in the shortest possible time. Knowing that Abe Fortas was in Dallas taking depositions in another case, Lyndon asked him to join the discussion in Fort Worth. Luther Jones, Lyndon's former secretary and now one of his lawyers, remembered how Fortas dealt with the problem: "Abe was a brilliant lawyer, and this Federal civil procedure was his speciality. It was a thing of beauty to watch the way he handled it. He listened to all of them for perhaps an hour, took all their work, got a secretary, and in ten minutes, came back with a one-page opposition . . . a very brief one. It was just exactly what was needed." Fortas advised going to the court of appeals first and then to Associate Justice

Hugo Black, who was responsible for the Fifth Circuit, as the surest way to succeed quickly.[91]

As they had anticipated, Johnson gained no satisfaction in Davidson's court. Seeking to assure the parties to the case that he would decide the issue strictly on its merits, Davidson took note of "my friend John Cofer," one of Lyndon's attorneys, in the courtroom and of ties to Lady Bird's father, who had been Davidson's "continuous client." "If this case is to be decided on friendship, we don't think the complainants would have very much standing in court," Davidson said. But he assured them that "real Justice is blind." As soon as Wirtz heard Davidson's remarks, he leaned over and said: "Lyndon, I'm leaving for New Orleans," where he would file an appeal with Joseph C. Hutcheson, chief judge of the Fifth Circuit. Wirtz's assumption, as Lady Bird recalled, was that "if you're going to deal somebody a very severe blow, you're likely . . . to try to say something nice about them."

Davidson rejected Johnson's request to dismiss the case on jurisdictional grounds and invited both sides to submit evidence in behalf of their arguments. Stevenson submitted affidavits to demonstrate fraud in Jim Wells, Duval, and Zapata counties. Johnson's attorneys filed a petition generally denying all of Stevenson's allegations, complained that he did "not come into court with clean hands," and promised to show in "the proper forum" that the complainant was the beneficiary of illegal votes. Unwilling to be specific, however, lest they concede Stevenson's right to have the case heard in Federal court, Johnson's lawyers refused to answer the charges against him in detail. Walter Jenkins recalled how frustrated Jimmy Allred was at not being able to respond. He kept jumping up in court and one of the other lawyers kept pulling him down by his coattail.[92]

Davidson suggested settling the dispute by putting both Johnson and Stevenson on the November ballot. Lyndon's lawyers debated the merits of the proposal, but Lyndon himself refused to accept it. He cursed Davidson, said he had won the election, would not temporize one bit, and insisted that his lawyers "proceed accordingly." On September 22nd, after they rejected the compromise, Davidson granted Stevenson's request that the temporary injunction against certifying Johnson as the Senate candidate remain in force and that Special Masters hold hearings in Duval, Zapata, and Jim Wells counties on the allegations of fraud and report their findings to him before he tried the case on its merits.[93]

Johnson's lawyers now appealed to Judge Hutcheson. Luther Jones flew on a twin-engine Brown & Root plane to New Orleans with a 28-page brief asserting that Davidson had no jurisdiction in the case and that his injunction should be vacated. On September 24, Hutcheson ruled that a single judge had no power to issue a stay while the Circuit Court was in recess, that he would not convene an emergency session, and that they would have to wait until October 14 for a hearing in Atlanta. By then, it would have been too late to get Johnson's name on absentee ballots and difficult to print ballots in time for the November election.

The next day, September 25, Paul Porter, Abe Fortas, and Thurmond Arnold "convened the greatest collegium of legal talent that Washington could supply" in their office. Ben Cohen, Tommy Corcoran, Hugh Cox of the Covington firm, Francis Biddle, and Joe Rauh were some of the other lawyers present. They drafted a motion to put before Hugo Black. Arnold and Porter decided to file the pleadings personally. They drove to the Supreme Court, where the clerk refused to take the documents, saying that he could not receive a matter still pending before the Fifth Circuit and that they lacked a docket number. "Take any number from one to ten," Arnold said. Remembering an obscure device in common-law pleading, Porter simply left the papers on the clerk's desk and said that he was "effectuating a lodgement." The next day, the 26th, Black's clerk called to say that the Justice would hear them on the 28th in open court provided counsel for Stevenson was present. Former Governor Dan Moody, Stevenson's chief counsel, agreed to fly up for the hearing.[94]

While the attorneys took the case before Black, Johnson met with President Truman. The President and Clark Clifford, a top White House aide shaping Truman's campaign strategy, continued to see Johnson as a politically more congenial senator from Texas than Stevenson. "I am overjoyed at your wonderful victory and I consider it a great result not only for Texas but for the entire country," Clifford had written him on September 14 after the state convention endorsed his nomination. Answering for Lyndon, Horace Busby wrote Clifford on the 20th that Johnson was in Fort Worth to contest Stevenson's injunction, but that they saw little hope for a quick end to "the see-saw fight over this election." Busby emphasized to Clifford that Johnson's failure to overcome the injunction "might mean the election of a Republican Senator—or a Dixiecrat." White House sympathy for Lyndon was reflected in "some kind of conversations [Clifford had] with Abe Fortas" about Johnson's contested election and Johnson's appearance with Truman and Clifford on September 27 as they campaigned in Texas. Coming aboard the President's train in San Antonio, Johnson, as Jonathan Daniels remembered, looked "like the damnedest tramp I ever saw in my life. He couldn't have shaved in at least two days and he looked sick as hell." Having been through a very close reelection campaign of his own for the Senate, Truman, Daniels believed, "had a great deal of sympathy for Lyndon in his unshaven, worn-looking condition." As the train made its way north to Dallas, Truman urged Texans to vote for Johnson.[95]

With the hearings in Duvall, Zapata, and Jim Wells counties beginning on September 27 and Justice Black slated to hear Johnson's appeal

on the 28th, no one could predict what the outcome of all these deliberations would be. Jonathan Daniels remembered how up in the air
everything was on the 27th when Lyndon came on the train. "At that
point he was going to be just another Texan or a great guy. And he
didn't know and nobody else knew which it was going to be. . . . If he
lost at that point, he was pretty well licked for the rest of his life." Lady
Bird remembered the experience as "similar to what goes on in a concentration camp under prolonged questioning or prolonged tension."[96]

Parr and his allies, M. B. Bravo in Zapata and Ed Lloyd in Jim Wells,
did everything possible to cover their tracks during three days of hearings conducted by Davidson's Special Masters. Bravo reported that no
poll tax lists existed and that one of the precinct returns had disappeared. In Duvall, only eight out of fifty witnesses called to testify could
be located and no county official could produce any precinct returns. In
Jim Wells, where the hearing focused on Box 13 in Alice, evidence was
also scarce. Tom Donald, the former county chairman, who had allowed
Harry Lee Adams, his successor, a brief look at the Box 13 votes, was
away in Mexico. Clarence Martens, who had been dragged off as he
was about to sign an affidavit declaring the revised certificate with the
additional 203 ballots incorrect, testified that he had refused to sign
anything without seeing evidence of voting irregularities and that Graham had never shown him anything. Luis Salas, the precinct judge responsible for Box 13, denied any wrongdoing, and testified that he had
had two copies of the voting record, but one had been lost and the other
stolen from the trunk of his car along with everything else in it. The
original returns were supposed to be in the Precinct 13 ballot box. When
William Robert Smith, the Special Master, ordered the ballot boxes
brought into court and Box 13 opened, they found nothing except a few
blank ballots and some trash.[97]

Everett Looney, one of Lyndon's attorneys, was convinced that Stevenson's lawyers got so little from the hearings that they were glad to
call them off. He told John Cofer, a co-counsel in the case, "that they
were absolutely able to show nothing fradulent. There were some suspicious circumstances in connection with the disappearances of the poll
lists and tally lists, but Stevenson's men were as much under a cloud as
Johnson's." Smith, the Special Master, did not see it that way. He later
said that he found Salas's testimony "pretty hard to believe I
thought at the time he was lying." To Smith, "the most potent fact in
the whole case" was the failure of the Johnson forces to bring in the
official poll records of Precinct 13. "That would have been a perfect way
to refute the allegations of Stevenson. But they never did . . . it and
they kept telling about how those poll tax lists had been stolen and misplaced."[98]

A Court order from Black saved Johnson from a trial in Davidson's courtroom and his likely replacement on the ballot by Stevenson. Johnson had the law on his side in halting Stevenson's appeal to a Federal court. "With all respect to Coke Stevenson and his lawyers," Abe Fortas said, "there really was no question about the merits of the case. The injunction was improvidently entered; that is, the federal judge enjoining the state election under these circumstances was just plain wrong." Black saw it that way. Stevenson should have brought his suit in a state court, and if there wasn't time to get a ruling before the election, as he asserted, he could have presented his case to the U.S. Senate, which has the right to determine its own membership. On the 29th, when Black's order reached Davidson, he suspended the south Texas hearings and Johnson's name went back on the ballot.[99]

Did someone in the Administration or close to Truman intercede with Black to help Johnson? Truman himself, Sam Rayburn, and Abe Fortas were all later described as having done so. But no one ever produced evidence to support these assertions, and when Ronnie Dugger asked Black if Rayburn spoke to him, he denied it. It is clear, from the approach to Davidson through Blalock and the suggestion that Rayburn and Barkley approach Chief Justice Vinson, that people in the Johnson camp weren't above considering such an idea.

Attorney General Tom Clark, who was strong for Lyndon and was shunning any investigation of the primary at this time, might have taken on the job. He later said, "I knew that they had filed a petition . . . that they had asked Justice Black . . . to pass on it, and I being a student of the Supreme Court, of course I had kept up with it pretty carefully; and being a friend of Mr. Johnson I was naturally interested in it." Hardly an admission that he had lobbied Black, but given the fact that Clark was indebted to Lyndon for helping him become Attorney General and that Lyndon's political future was hanging by a thread, something of the kind might have occurred. A detailed record of the controversy over the run-off primary Clark compiled as it developed and a later expression of appreciation from Lyndon to Clark for all he did in helping him get back to Washington add to the possibility that Clark interceded with Black. Later observers of the Johnson presidency who wondered over his selection of Ramsey Clark, Tom's son, as Attorney General might find part of the answer in Tom's help to Lyndon in 1948.[100]

Joe Rauh, one of Lyndon's attorneys, "always thought that Tom Corcoran had spoken with Black before the hearing." In 1970, perhaps emboldened by his success in 1948, Corcoran, according to the *New York Times*, "visited [Supreme Court] justices, all old friends, on behalf of El Paso Natural Gas Company, a client desperate to secure a reversal of an adverse court ruling." On that occasion, all "the justices showed 'Tommy the Cork' the door." But it is reasonable to assume that Black, a political friend of Johnson's, would have listened to Clark's and Corcoran's private pleas. Twenty years later, when the U.S. Senate debated Abe Fortas's confirmation as Chief Justice of the Supreme Court, Black, now a strong opponent of Fortas's, secretly persuaded Alabama Senator Lister Hill to vote no. Black was not above committing an impropriety. Justice William O. Douglas believed that political considerations influenced Black's thinking in Johnson's 1948 appeal.[101]

Although Black's decision greatly relieved Johnson, he worried that fresh challenges might still defeat him. According to a conversation reported to Johnson on the 29th, Dan Moody believed that the Texas election was not settled by any means. The Fifth Circuit Court in New Orleans had the power to endorse or dispute Black's ruling. And Harold Ickes, who had been corresponding with Lyndon in September about his court fight, wanted to do something to ensure that the Supreme Court remained on Lyndon's side. "The net result of all this court fighting over my nomination will probably be a Republican Senator from Texas—if I am kept off the general election ballot," he wrote Ickes on September 28. "I am delighted with Justice Black's decision . . . . On October 1, Ickes replied: "Of course Stevenson will doubtless continue to press for your seat . . . . Let me know if there is the least thing that I could do." Sometime in the next five days Ickes spoke with Tommy Corcoran about Lyndon's problem. "I wouldn't do anything until the Circuit Court of Appeals . . . decides the merits of the case—as it is expected to do this week—in Lyndon's favor," Corcoran wrote Ickes on October 6. "Then it won't be the lousy Supreme Court but Joe Hutcheson of Texas who makes the decision." To Johnson's satisfaction, on the following day, the Circuit Court endorsed Black's order to dismiss Stevenson's petition.[102]

Now that he was securely on the ballot, Lyndon fixed his attention on the November election. Normally, a Republican had no chance for a Texas Senate seat. There had never been a Republican senator from Texas, and Johnson's people expected the tradition to hold in 1948. Yet the long drawn-out primary contest had convinced the public that there was fraud and raised the possibility of a Democratic defeat on November 2. A Stevenson decision to support Jack Porter, the Republican nominee, compounded the problem. Nevertheless, most observers thought Johnson would win, but that he would face future problems: because half of his party's voters opposed him, he would be a one-term Senator. To counter these difficulties, Johnson publicly emphasized that he was going to be the next senator, that he "was an innocent victim of circumstance about vote fraud," and that *next time* he will win by a lop-sided majority all over the state." His headquarters launched an extensive letter-writing campaign to friends and supporters across the state saying that the election was over and that " 'There ain't gonna be no run-off in 1954'." Through a limited number of speeches and personal appearances, Lyndon also tried to shift the focus from the primary contest to substantive issues on which he and the public shared common ground.[103]

Yet Stevenson and Porter made it difficult for him to leave the vote fraud issue behind. On October 18, Stevenson made a radio speech in which he reviewed recent events and challenged Johnson's right to be on the ballot. Porter took advantage of the dispute by distributing flyers citing evidence in Davidson's court showing fraud in Johnson's primary campaign. Johnson felt compelled to refute the charges: on October 19, he asked Jimmy Allred to make a speech answering Stevenson, and on the 28th, he gave his own reply in a state-wide radio address. Declaring himself the victim of "malice and hate" heaped upon him by "poor losers," he described the allegations against him as "mis-statements and half-truths" by "parrots of special privilege" intent on electing a Republican senator. When Lynn Landrum, a columnist for the conservative *Dallas Morning News*, repeatedly accused Johnson of fraud in six articles in October and urged him to save his honor by forgoing the nomination, Lyndon replied in an emotional letter on October 31. He decried "the biased and polluted columns of the *Dallas News*," which catered to "Johnson haters" with grossly distorted accounts of the facts, and refused to step aside and let an "oilcrat, Republican" take the Senate seat.[104]

Despite the sharp exchanges in the closing days of the campaign, Johnson was confident that he would win. While he fought Porter and Stevenson, he took time from his campaign to help raise some badly needed money for Truman's election. In early October, he persuaded Wright Morrow, a Houston oilman and party official, to contribute $10,000 of the $39,000 needed for a Truman radio talk. In the middle of the month, he carried an Administration request to five Texans, including the Brown brothers, for funds that he was to deliver to Louis Johnson at the Democratic National Committee in New York. The money helped Truman score an upset victory over Dewey in the election and restore Democratic control over both houses of Congress. Lyndon beat Porter two to one, 702,985 to 349,665. But alongside of Truman, who received 750,000 votes in Texas, and Democratic Governor Beauford Jester, who won 320,000 more votes than Johnson, it was a disappointing showing and raised concerns about Lyndon's chances for reelection in six years.[105]

There were more immediate worries, however, about a Senate investigation that might still bar him from getting a first term. In early October, he began moving to counter a possible Stevenson effort in the Senate to deny him the seat. He contacted potentially helpful members of Congress and discussed having "our good friend [Tom Clark] the Attorney General . . . assign some able member of his staff, and, of course, a loyal Democrat, to brief the rules, procedure, and generally 'roundup' the handling of such a case as our enemies may contemplate

. . . before any committee of the Senate or Department of the Government." On October 20, after the Senate Committee on Rules and Administration received a request from Stevenson for an investigation, its subcommittee on Privileges and Elections sent two investigators to south Texas armed with subpoenas asking officials in five counties to produce ballots and records. Donald Cook, who became Johnson's Washington counsel in the matter, asked the subcommittee to obtain ballots and records from all counties, but especially from eight counties, where Johnson alleged fraud favorable to Stevenson.

Although the investigators managed to impound ballots from seven counties—Jim Wells, Starr, Zapata, and four Johnson had cited—they learned that the Duval County courthouse janitor had burned the August 28 primary ballots on October 19. According to the county's Democratic chairman, he had asked the janitor to get 39 ballot boxes from the courthouse basement so that some of them could be lent to Jim Wells' officials for use on November 2. When he did, the janitor emptied them in a trash container in a vacant lot and burned the contents "in broad daylight." According to Parr associates, Johnson or somebody speaking for him called to ask that the ballots not be burned, explaining that it would reflect badly on him. "To hell with you," Parr is supposed to have replied. "I'm going to protect my friends." [106]

Worried that Stevenson and the Republican-controlled subcommittee had cooked up a plot to take away his seat, Johnson confronted the issue with its chairman, Republican Senator William Jenner of Indiana. Citing three secret conferences between Stevenson's counsel and subcommittee lawyers, Johnson mentioned rumors about a trade "between your Party and Stevenson" that had produced "his endorsement of your Party's candidate and your endorsement of his smear battle." Johnson "refused to believe those rumors even though Stevenson, a Democratic office holder for 30 years, endorsed the Republican nominee and your investigators simultaneously started making headlines." If there were such an agreement, the election of a Democratic majority in the Senate made it irrelevant after November 2. On the 8th, Jenner announced that despite information "of sufficient seriousness to warrant a full investigation" into the Texas primary election, his subcommittee would leave the job to the Eighty-first Congress. The *Dallas News* believed the announcement removed all doubt that Johnson would be seated. Styles Bridges, Republican senator from New Hampshire, "has been personal friend enough to guarantee that the Jenner group will do nothing to hurt at this end," Tommy Corcoran wrote Sam Rayburn. "For the record," Corcoran told Lyndon, "Styles Bridges got this formal action taken for us. Remember that some day." [107]

Despite the Democratic victory, Stevenson didn't give up. He released a statement on November 12 expressing faith in the Senate, Democratic

or Republican, not to countenance "open dishonesty." Denying Johnson's assertions that "there was election crookedness all over the state,"
Stevenson described it as concentrated in Duval, Jim Wells, Starr, and
Zapata counties, where it had gone on for a long time. Yet "this is the
first instance in recorded history," he said, "that those bloc-voting counties have determined the outcome of a state-wide election. And more
than that, this is the first time that the manipulators of the voting in
those counties were not content with all-out bloc voting, but re-opened
the boxes in secret long after the election had closed and stuffed them
with a directed number of ballots." [108]

Stevenson was naïve, or simply too emotional about his defeat to accept political reality and give up the contest. After Stevenson's announcement of November 12, Johnson went to see Senator Tom Connally at a hotel in Marlin, Texas, south of Waco. He reported that
Stevenson had been to see Senator Robert Taft of Ohio and some other
leading Republicans about denying him his seat, and asked Connally to
"do all he could to stop that. . . . 'Well, now, Lyndon, that's just nothing to worry about at all,' " Connally said. " 'The Democrats have control of the Senate. As long as we've got control of the Senate, you're
going to be seated. Stevenson's just wasting his time going up there
talking to Taft about a matter like that. Don't worry. We'll all do everything we can.' " And he did. On January 3, he released a statement
prepared by Johnson's lawyers decrying Stevenson's "deliberate attempt
to overrule the will of the people" by bringing "a flimsy, discredited
charge" against Johnson before the Senate.[109]

The Democratic-controlled subcommittee on Privileges and Elections
was as accommodating. Francis Myers of Pennsylvania, the chairman
of the subcommittee, also issued a statement on January 3 dismissing
the charges against Johnson. "I was a member of the Republican-
dominated sub-committee which dispatched a corps of investigators
around the country before the November elections to assist GOP candidates by embarrassing and intimidating Democratic nominees for the
Senate. These so-called investigators failed even to find enough for one
good front page headline in their examination of Lyndon Johnson's
nomination in Texas. . . . It would be a waste of time to give these
charges any further consideration here in the Senate." Compelled
nevertheless to investigate and report on the second or run-off Texas
primary, the sub-committee of Myers, Guy Gillette, a Democrat from
Iowa, and William Knowland, a California Republican, allowed Johnson's lawyers to shape their 32-page report. In March, Charles I. Francis
and Alvin Wirtz drew up an outline of what they "thought would be the
proper approach for the Committee." Sending it to Lyndon "for your
consideration and that of your Washington advisers," Francis said: "this
suggested report presents a method of approach which . . . should lead

the Committee to dismiss the requested investigation." It did in June when it declared that "no evidence has been disclosed which would establish Stevenson's allegations" and that Johnson was "a duly elected Senator of the United States from the State of Texas." [110]

After he had won the election in November and his title to the seat was confirmed in the Senate, Lyndon developed a kind of gallows humor about the controversy. "Nearly anything can happen in a Texas election—and most of it did this year," he wrote fellow senator J. William Fulbright of Arkansas. Although he told Harold Ickes that he wished he had won by 87,000 votes instead of 87, he could laugh at being dubbed "Landslide Lyndon." He also loved to tell the joke about a little Mexican boy in Alice sitting on the curb crying. A passerby asked him: " 'Son, are you hurt?' He said, 'No, I no hurt.' . . . 'Are you sick?' . . . 'No, I no sick.' . . . 'Are you hungry?' . . . 'No, I no hungry.' " The passerby asked: " 'What's the matter? What are you crying for?' He said, 'Well, yesterday, my papa, he been dead four years, yesterday, he come back and voted for Lyndon Johnson, didn't come by to say hello to me.' "

Almost twenty years later, when Ronnie Dugger, the journalist and aspiring Johnson biographer, interviewed him in the White House, Johnson suddenly excused himself to find a photograph. Returning after five or ten minutes, he handed it to Dugger with evident delight. It was a photograph of five men sitting on the hood or standing in front of a car with a 1948 Texas license plate. A small can with "PRECINCT 13" lettered on it rested on the hood. The five men included Givens Parr, George's cousin, and Ed Lloyd, the Jim Wells boss. When Dugger asked Johnson to tell him about the time, occasion, and identity of the men in the photograph, he offered nothing but an amused grin. [111]

Yet Johnson was not always so whimsical about the controversy which heavily contributed to his enduring reputation as a consummate political wheeler dealer. Several journalists remember that whenever the issue came up in the 1950s, Johnson became angry and defensive. The Stevenson people "tried to steal the '48 election like they stole the '41 election," he would reply. Unfounded allegations generated by Sam Smithwick, a deputy sheriff in Alice, Texas, particularly distressed him. Smithwick was an unbalanced personality who killed a local radio commentator in 1950 for saying critical things on the air about him and his family. In March 1952, Smithwick wrote Coke Stevenson from the penitentiary, where he was serving a life term. Asserting that the "main cause" of his troubles with the man he killed was the missing Precinct 13 ballot box, Smithwick offered to "produce" it if Stevenson would come visit him at the prison. Three weeks later—as Stevenson was on his way to visit him—Smithwick was found hanged in his cell. Evidence that Smithwick's dispute with the murdered man had nothing to do with the '48 election and that Smithwick had been having hallucinations and had killed himself did not prevent allegations that Parr was responsible for Smithwick's death. Nor did it stop Stevenson from releasing the letter to the press and saying it vindicated his complaint about election fraud in 1948. According to Johnson, in 1956, Governor Allan Shivers of Texas accused *him* of having had Smithwick murdered. The charge understandably enraged Johnson.[112]

In July 1977, more than four years after Johnson died, the 1948 election dispute surfaced again. Luis Salas, saying he wanted "peace of mind," acknowledged that he had lied in 1948 and that the complaints about 203 fraudulent Box 13 votes were accurate. Salas's assertions, however, that Johnson was present at a meeting in Parr's office when they decided to add the votes and that he, Parr, Ed Lloyd, and Lyndon saw President Truman on his campaign train, where they enlisted the President's help with Justice Black, raised fresh questions about Salas's credibility. After Salas spoke out, a number of people came forward to deny that Johnson ever went to south Texas in the week after the election or that any of these people other than Lyndon ever saw Truman on his train. Almost no one disputed, however, that the additional votes in south Texas gave Johnson his narrow, last-minute victory.[113]

Was Coke Stevenson, then, actually entitled to the nomination? No one will ever be able to answer with any certainty. The historian George Norris Green believes it "possible that if the vote count had been honest and accurate across the state, Johnson might have won the primary anyway, but the preponderance of evidence indicates that the victor should have been Coke Stevenson." When the Austin attorney Creekmore Fath asked Austin mayor Tom Miller who really won the 1948 election, Miller replied: "They were stealin' votes in east Texas . . . . We were stealin' votes in south Texas. Only Jesus Christ could say who actually won it."[114]

If it is impossible to say with any certainty who received the larger vote, it is reasonably clear that three things had allowed Johnson to overcome Stevenson's 71,000-vote lead in the run-off. For one, Johnson's emphasis on the differences in their ideas about government policies convinced some Texans who had voted for Stevenson or Peddy that he would make a more suitable national representative than Coke. Stevenson's isolationism, for example, rallied support for Lyndon among veterans and their families. Second, the fall off in the voter turnout of some 200,000 in the second primary hurt Stevenson more than Johnson. Many of them were Peddy supporters who would have more likely voted for Stevenson than Johnson had they gone to the polls. And third, a run-off in the Rio Grande valley between Lloyd M. Bentsen, Jr., and Philip Kazen for a House seat directly benefited Lyndon. Both men supported Johnson over Stevenson, and their higher respective totals in the run-off translated into more votes for Johnson. Lyndon surely made every conceivable effort in the Valley and across the entire state to increase his

vote total in August by fair means and foul. But to see his enlarged
support as simply the product of skulduggery gives too little weight to
his characteristic resourcefulness as a politician and the changed conditions from the first to the second primary.[115]

Yet tainted means had played a significant part in giving Lyndon his
victory. Had they simply been his secret, he might have taken pleasure
from having outsmarted the competition. But the ballot manipulation
was there for all to see, calling into question his legitimate claim on his
seat, and driving him to justify his presence in the Senate. Had he entered the Senate without suspicions of vote fraud, he still would have
challenged himself to be the best senator Texas ever had. His ambition
would have required nothing less. But the cloud which hung over his
election intensified his determination to make a mark that would equal
and, if possible, eclipse what the most distinguished members of the
Senate had accomplished in the preceding one hundred and sixty years.
At the end of his term, he wished to be remembered as one of the greatest members of the upper house in U.S. history.

PART THREE

The Senator
1949–1954

11

"The Best
Possible Senator
for . . . Texas"

FORTY years of age when he entered the U.S. Senate in January 1949, Johnson was a well-known figure among Washington insiders. He had lived in the capital for fifteen of the last seventeen years and was more at home in Washington than in Texas. Moreover, his election to the Senate gave him an ideal locus for his interests and talents. Prominent Federal officials, past and present, who knew Johnson well, expected his presence in the "Club," as many called the 96-member upper house, to benefit both Texas and the nation. Those who knew him best believed that his knowledge of national politics and congressional operations made him better prepared than almost any other member of the lower house to become a United States senator.

Yet opinion about Johnson at the start of his Senate term was not uniformly enthusiastic. As was the case throughout his life, Johnson appealed greatly to some people and offended others. All agreed on one thing, however: he was a memorable character. At six feet three and a half inches, with long arms, big ears, a prominent nose, and outsized personality to match, Johnson left a lasting impression on everyone he met. Interviews about him done twenty, thirty, and even forty years after 1949 are fresh and vivid, as if people were describing yesterday's events. Bryce Harlow, a counsel to the House Armed Services Committee and a Special Assistant to President Dwight Eisenhower, remembers encounters with Lyndon as memorable: "they were searing; they were big; they were tough; they were exciting; they were out of the ordinary, because he was bigger than life."[1]

The recollections of Johnson from his Senate years provide a portrait of a large, powerful figure who defied easy understanding. George Reedy, a principal aide on Johnson's Senate staff, described Lyndon as a Jekyll-and-Hyde character: "a magnificent, inspiring leader" one minute and "an insufferable bastard" the next. But that characterization doesn't really do Johnson justice, Reedy says. We would do better to read Luigi Pirandello's drama, *Six Characters in Search of an Author.* The play leaves "you with the most baffled wonderment as to whether there really were six characters in search of an author or whether the whole thing was a figment of somebody's imagination . . . Johnson would leave you like that." Johnson was an example of what the Japanese call the contradiction of opposites. Driven, tyrannical, crude, insensitive, humorless, and petty, he was also empathic, shy, sophisticated, self-critical, witty, and magnanimous. "He was a man of too many paradoxes," Reedy adds. "Almost everything you find out about him you can find out a directly contrary quality immediately, and your problem is always which quality was real and which was assumed. Or maybe neither quality was real. Or maybe both were real, who knows."[2]

Johnson was a man of so many faces because it served his deepest need: to assert himself effectively, come out on top, and exercise control. He was a very good actor who used his talents to fill the stage and dominate an audience. Some of this was consciously done in order to manipulate people, but much of his acting was a spontaneous device for winning approval and establishing control.

Nothing was more important to Johnson than being seen and heard. He did outlandish things to fix himself in people's memories and, if possible, intimidate them. The historian Arthur Schlesinger, Jr., remembers Johnson as a character Mark Twain and William Faulkner could have invented. Several years after Johnson had established himself in the Senate he had Schlesinger to his office. As Harvard economist John Kenneth Galbraith tells the story, Johnson spent a whole morning with Schlesinger. "Johnson went over every member of the Senate—his drinking habits, his sex habits, his intellectual capacity, reliability, how you manage him. Arthur said, 'Most informative morning I ever spent. Never got a word in edgewise.' " Not long afterwards, Johnson told Galbraith, " 'I've been meeting with your friend, Arthur Schlesinger. Really had a very good meeting. We had a long talk. He's a right smart fellow. But, damn fellow talks too much.' "[3]

Bryce Harlow, who watched Johnson operate over several years in the House and Senate, describes him as someone who appeared to be moving even when seated. "Wherever he'd sit down there was a cloud of dust. Something was happening all the time, even if he were seated in the committee room. He was talking to the guys next to him. . . . He was getting up; he was sitting down. . . . His alarm clock watch, which he just loved to harass people with. . . . It was a stunt . . . he always set it off at some propitious time to attract attention to himself. He couldn't stand not being the cynosure of all eyes. He had to be at the head of the table. . . . And people had to do what he thought they should do. And ordinarily he made them do it. How many people do you know like that? None. You never know anybody like that, because they don't make them. But, yes, they do, once in a millennium. That's Lyndon."[4]

Harlow recalls that as soon as Johnson entered the Senate he went out of his way to make a mark. At a House-Senate Armed Services committee conference, Harry Byrd, Sr., of Virginia, "an institution, as patrician a patrician" as ever served in the Senate, denounced the Seventy Group Air Force as "an advertising slogan of the Secretary of the Air Force." Johnson, the most junior member of the committee attending his first conference as a senator, demanded an apology from Byrd for impugning the character, motives, and intelligence of Seventy Group supporters, of whom he was one. Though Byrd assured him that he had no desire to "malign" the motives of any member of Congress, Lyndon insisted on an apology and threatened to take the matter to the floor of the Senate unless Byrd withdraw his remarks. A "flustered" Harry Byrd, wishing to get on with the business at hand, gave in. "Lyndon had made his first big move to the leadership of the Senate," Harlow asserts. "He had faced down Harry Byrd. He hadn't been in the Senate long enough to warm his seat. That's Lyndon. No other Senator could possibly have done it. No other Senator could have gotten away with it."[5]

Part of the legend Johnson created for himself revolved around his work habits. Work was a huge part of his life: it was as essential to him as breathing; he was a workaholic, an addict who needed a regular fix. And like everything he did, he tried to be the best at it and use it to impress people with his uniqueness. "My husband was always a taut, driving perfectionist who lived with constant tension," Mrs. Johnson said. Hubert Humphrey, liberal senator from Minnesota who entered the upper house with Johnson in 1949, remembered his total absorption with politics. "He knew all the little things that people did. I used to say he had his own private FBI. If you ever knew anybody, if you'd been out on a date, or if you'd had a drink, or if you'd attended a meeting, or you danced with a gal at a night club, he knew it! It was just incredible! I don't know how he was able to get all that information, but he lived and breathed and walked and talked politics. . . . He was just totally immersed in it." Donald Cook, Johnson's House Naval Affairs Committee aide, remembered that at the start of Johnson's Senate term, "despite the passage of ten very hard, vigorous years—in which I know he was working night and day, Saturdays, Sundays, holidays, nothing stood in the way of things that he felt he had to do . . .—he still had the same energy; he was just as vigorous, just as dynamic, just as sharp, just as thoughtful."[6]

People who worked for Johnson became extensions of himself and his ambition. "One of the things about him that goes along with his tremendous power and vehmence is that he is sometimes all-absorptive," Senate aide Harry McPherson says. "He consumes people, almost without knowing it. He wants, once the deal is made, once the friendship is established, he really wants that person to be a Johnson man and it takes a long time of being with him, around him, to free yourself. There's a period in which it's almost suffocating."[7]

Once someone was on his staff or worked with him on something, he imposed on them at any time of the day or night. Telephone calls at six o'clock in the morning or midnight were commonplace. "He'd wake up at five o'clock and he never fully appreciated why people were oftentimes so sour when he woke them up at six with a phone call," Horace Busby, who came to work for him in 1948, says. Ed Clark remembers that at election time in Texas Johnson would call him every morning at six o'clock. "I'd tell my wife, 'This is LBJ. Go get me a cup of coffee and bring it in here. . . .' And I'd talk to him thirty minutes or an hour." Charles Boatner, a journalist who became a Johnson assistant, lived with him and Lady Bird for a while. Boatner found himself on constant call. At night, Lyndon would summon him to his bedroom, and Boatner quickly learned to take a pad and pencil whenever so called. He only left when Johnson fell asleep. "The next morning, just as regular as rain, at five o'clock there'd be a knock on the door, 'Charlie, are you awake? . . . I was down in the kitchen fixing me a cup of Sanka, and I just made you a cup of coffee.' He'd bring the coffee on in and . . . sit down on the bed and drink his Sanka. I'd take my coffee and put it on the night stand next to my bed and pick up my pencil and note pad, because I knew I was never going to drink that coffee."[8]

Johnson established a reputation as a maniacal taskmaster. He thought nothing of yelling at an aide in public for an omission or slip up. Once, when a reporter asked a question he couldn't answer and George Reedy couldn't supply the needed facts, Johnson bawled the hell out of him in front of everybody. Felix McKnight, a Texas journalist, remembers his doing the same thing to Mary Rather, his secretary, who "left the room, not crying, but a little beaten." He could be just as hard on his peers. After one senator gave a poor account of himself on the Senate floor, Johnson "just reamed him out like he was a bad boy in the family." One of his aides counseled him against speaking to a fellow senator that way. "But he's a stupid bastard," Johnson replied. Johnson's demands on himself and others for "a kind of nose-to-the-grindstone puritanical devotion to duty and work all the time" added to his image as a larger than life character.[9]

Johnson also had a more subtle side. He had an extraordinary capacity to read other people and to put himself in their place; he had super sensitive antennae that allowed him to get into other people's skins. "He is the fastest learner of personality that I have ever encountered in my life," Harry McPherson says. "Abe Fortas once told me, when he and I were lamenting the fact that Johnson didn't like somebody that we liked, that he thought Johnson was wrong in this case, but that generally speaking he was the best judge of character he had ever seen. And I must say that I have been immensely impressed by his capacity to judge people." George Reedy believes that Johnson had a remarkable capacity to understand people with different backgrounds. Johnson's popularity with garment workers born in Jewish ghettos, with the "broad masses of Negroes," and the Mexicans in Texas could be ascribed to "his almost uncanny insight into their psychology." June White felt that "he could read people almost on meeting them. . . . It's almost as though he knew their assets, their plusses and their negative points, so that he could go . . . to their plus points and use them, even helping them to use themselves to their best advantage."[10]

It gave Johnson a talent for touching vital chords in people and moving them to agree or accept his lead on controversial questions. In Reedy's words, "the man had a remarkable capacity for persuading people to work together even when they didn't like each other very much. He was equally at home with conservative [Senator] Richard B. Russell of Georgia and liberal [Senator] Stuart Symington of Missouri; with [Senator] Leverett Saltonstall, a Massachusetts Republican, and [Senator] Warren Magnuson, a Democrat from the other side of the continent." As chairman of a Senate committee dealing with "some very controversial subjects," he "succeeded in achieving unanimous report after unanimous report." Johnson's persuasiveness partly rested on a capacity to become, in some undefinable way, a physical and psychological extension of someone else. A shared perspective or an affirmation of someone else's thinking complemented the grabbing and holding, the chest to chest, nose to nose closeness for which he was famous.[11]

His appeal to fellow senators and others also depended on his considerable charm and humor. June White remembers "a fascinating, charming evening" with him during which he spoke about himself: "impressions weaving in and out, humor weaving in and out. He was in a very, very good mood. There was no greater experience in life than spending time like this with Lyndon Johnson. . . . You could see people, particularly when they were meeting him for the first time, just be charmed out of their wits." Harry McPherson heard numerous people, "very distinguished people," say after leaving a small meeting with Johnson, "My God, if people could only see him that way." He was "at his best" in such a setting, where he could be "damned near irresistible." He had a talent for storytelling and mimicry. George Reedy believes that he "could easily have made his living on the vaudeville stage. His caricatures of people he did not like . . . were cruel but irresistibly comic." If the person were someone he was fond of, the portrayal could be very sympathetic. Busby remembers him as "marvelous at one-man theater." At one of their first meetings he reenacted for Busby the drama in Sam Rayburn's hideaway office the day FDR died. He played all the parts, Truman, Rayburn, himself, moving back and forth across the room, speaking their lines, imitating their voices. He got so caught up in the drama, so emotional, that his eyes were moist when he finished.[12]

In a more formal social setting, at a reception or a cocktail party, Johnson often felt awkward and shy. At one time during his Senate career, he hired an aide whom he wanted to attend these parties and functions and always go two steps in front of him. "There was a streak—and people will think, anybody that ever reads or hears this will think I'm out of my mind—there was an enormous streak of shyness in him," Busby says. "He was always so afraid that in a graceful social setting that he wouldn't be mannered properly. Now he took over any party he went to . . . because if he didn't take it over it might bite him, in manners." His need to be number one or the focus of attention was probably the key to his social unease.[13]

Johnson was also a highly intelligent and sophisticated man. "The Johnson IQ took a back seat to very few others—perhaps even to none," Reedy contends. "His mind was magnificent—fast, penetrating, resourceful." McPherson believes that when he dealt with sophisticated men, he was their equal, and that this goes far to explain why he enjoyed the support of so many prominent Washington attorneys and officials over the years. Abe Fortas said he "had one of the brightest, ablest minds I have ever encountered. . . . He had a great power to retain information," which he could retrieve "accurately and effortlessly." Several people who worked for Johnson told Darrell St. Claire, the assistant secretary of the Senate in the fifties, that "he was the most extraordinary person they have ever known in their lives, that he had a mind that you would not believe." June White knew many of Washington's most talented men, including Dean Acheson, whose brillance she thought did not outshine Lyndon's. "Lyndon Johnson," she says, "had a fantastic mind."[14]

And he had a notable capacity for self-criticism and self-control to go with it. McPherson remembers his having "the most devastating capacity for self-analysis I have ever seen." As they sat looking at some photographs of him one night, Johnson said, " 'Have you ever seen a phonier smile in your life?' " When McPherson agreed, Johnson added, " 'That's the way I always look when I don't want to. When I don't feel sincere, I try all the harder to look sincere and it looks all the worse every time.' " Though McPherson and others had known that about him, McPherson had not realized that Johnson did too. At other times, when McPherson offered critical observations to him, Johnson was "thoughtful" about what he said, valuing such comments from people who were genuinely concerned about him, as he knew McPherson was.[15]

Although Johnson could be terribly overbearing and vindictive toward his adversaries and anyone who had resisted him, he also operated with a strong sense of limits. Toward the end of his House career, Johnson had arranged through Attorney General Tom Clark for William Lewis, the general counsel of the Naval Affairs Committee and Carl Vinson's principal aide, to get a top job in the Justice Department. Lewis knew nothing of it until Johnson called him to his office one day and said: "Bill, I have been observing you very closely, I have decided to make you an LBJ boy." Johnson then revealed that he had arranged Lewis's appointment under Clark. But Lewis, who preferred to remain where he was, turned Johnson down, and Lyndon never forgave him. For the next twenty-five years, whenever they saw each other in the Congress and spoke, "the conversation always ended in one way. It was Lyndon Johnson leaning over, looking at me and almost rubbing his nose against my nose . . . and thumping me on the chest and saying, 'Remember, Bill, you had your chance.' He never got over the fact that I said no."[16]

While he never forgave Bill Lewis for refusing to become "an LBJ boy," Johnson did not try to drive him out of government or blackball him in the Congress. McPherson remembers how hard he could press people to do things, but when they directly said they couldn't, he would "become almost tender" with them, and "he's let them alone. . . . And he hasn't gone out to try to ruin them later. . . . He has a considerable respect for such men." One journalist, who later turned down an offer from Johnson to work for him as a press secretary, recalls that whenever they met after that Johnson always got his name wrong. But, as with Lewis, Johnson did nothing to interfere with his government career.[17]

The benign picture of Johnson drawn by some of his associates needs qualifying. People like Lewis and the journalist were too inconsequential for Johnson to bother bringing down. When he was up against powerful enemies who had harmed him or could harm him, he did what he could to punish them. As he gained power in the Senate, and later, during his presidency, he arranged some rough treatment for opposing politicians and journalists. When he believed that someone had crossed him, he felt free to give as much as he got. He saw politics as a rough game in which the most successful sometimes wrote their own rules.

However self-centered and self-serving Johnson could be, he also had a sense of being involved in matters that were larger than himself. Horace Busby remembers that he was always talking about being "close to history," to the memorable events or shaping moments in the life of the nation. Undoubtedly, it gave him a sense of personal importance to be at the center of American politics, but he also recognized that he was doing things which went much beyond himself and for which he would be accountable to history or future generations. Journalist Hugh Sidey believed that Lyndon Johnson was a case of "corrupt means for noble ends. . . . There is a group of politicians, for which Johnson may qualify, who have come out of the seamy regions of American life . . . but have also held a certain reverence for the system and it goals. Ultimately, they may have produced more good than their critics." [18]

At the start of his Senate term, if he were to play the larger role in American affairs he envisioned for himself, Johnson needed to convince Texas voters that he had a legitimate claim to his seat. A farmer and ranchman from Floydada, Texas, undoubtedly spoke for many in the state when he wrote Senator Tom Connally on December 30, 1948: "There exists in my mind a doubt that the matter [of the contested election] has been properly closed. From the large number of Democrats who voted for a Republican candidate in Texas, it can be presumed that there is doubt in the minds of a lot of good people in Texas. The good name of Lyndon B. Johnson should be cleared of this cloud. He cannot make a good senator to all the people of Texas without their confidence." [19]

Lyndon was mindful of the challenge. But he knew that nothing would effectively eliminate the question about who had genuinely won the runoff primary. "We can write explanations, defenses and rebuttals from now until 1960," he wrote Paul Bolton in October 1949, "and they won't pick up a single friend or lose a single enemy." To assure his reelection in six years, Lyndon had a well-developed three-pronged strategy: first, avoid identification with issues that Texans saw as controversial and could intensify the image of him as a disputatious, troublesome character; second, establish himself as an effective spokesman for Texas interests and concerns; and third, make himself a significant figure in the national Democratic party and the Senate. In short, he aimed to set up a contrast to Pappy O'Daniel, the irresponsible crank who had done little for Texas and held no influence in the party or the upper house. [20]

Johnson shunned anything that seemed controversial. In December 1948, when Barefoot Sanders, the president of the University of Texas student body, asked Johnson's view of an 18-year-old-vote, Warren Woodward replied: "Off the record, Barefoot, I think you understand Mr. Johnson's position. He has just been through a bitter campaign and is hesitant to take on any more controversial issues. . . . For the present I am sure it is best that he refrain from entering into this dispute."

In January, Jack Anderson, columnist Drew Pearson's associate, confronted Johnson with the details of the Brown & Root tax case, including the laundered money put into Johnson's 1941 campaign and the Johnson-Wirtz visits to FDR. Lyndon denied any wrongdoing, described the meetings with Roosevelt as relating to other business, and begged Anderson to understand that if the story was published it would mean the return to the Senate of Pappy O'Daniel or someone like him. "My feelings on this case are mingled," Anderson wrote Pearson. "The circumstantial evidence, at least, is overwhelming against Lyndon. At the same time, he gave me such a sales talk that I can't help believing he is so much better than the crowd fighting him that I hate to play into their hands. . . . On the whole, Lyndon's record has been far better and more progressive than the average Texan. We also run the risk of embittering some of our best friends who are close to Lyndon. Yet as I told him, I believe in treading the straight and narrow as nearly as possible even if it means stepping on some friendly toes." Anderson and Pearson waited seven years to publish the story.[21]

During the first two years of his Senate service, Johnson took pains not to come under suspicion of involvement in self-serving business deals. In the summer of 1949, the attorney Everett Looney asked Johnson's help with a business arrangement that could net his law firm a considerable return. Looney had heard that the Budweiser beer distributorship in Austin would change hands, and he wanted Lyndon to help Dave Bassist, a client, win control of the franchise. Since Looney assured him "that your name has not and will not be mentioned to Dave or anyone else," Johnson made an immediate inquiry which indicated that there was nothing to Looney's information. When Jake Pickle wrote to ask if Johnson had heard about a possible change in the Budweiser distributorship, Johnson answered no, and declared: "And if there should be, I am sure you know I would have nothing whatever to do with the arrangements." In February 1950 Stuart Long, a broadcaster at KVET and representative to the State Democratic Committee from Austin, advised Lyndon of rumors that Johnson and the Austin newsman Gordon Fulcher would sell a $400,000 parcel of land to the Post Office for a million dollars. Johnson quickly replied: "I know absolutely nothing about the new Post Office contract, what sites have been offered, who owns them, or how much the bids are. There is one more paragraph to that sentence. I don't care to know, because I don't want to become involved in it, and, even if I wanted to, I could not, since the decision is made wholly by the Post Office Department and the Public Buildings Administration."[22]

However eager he remained to increase his own financial worth, Johnson temporarily shunned private business dealings that could distract him from being an aggressive and effective advocate of Texas interests. "Right now, I'm trying to get my feet on the ground and be the best possible Senator for all the people of Texas," he told the *Amarillo Times* in January. By the fall the *Houston Chronicle* could report that "Johnson has not made much noise or many headlines, but he has been a hardworking behind-the-scenes operator who knows how to get things done."

As a senator from the fourth most populous state in the Union, with over 7.5 million people, Johnson confronted a heavy burden of demands which he met with one of the largest and most efficient staffs in the Senate. Employing a sixteen-member workforce, which was twice the size of the average Senate office and seven more than fellow Texas Senator Tom Connally's, Johnson crowded his people into 321 of the Senate Office Building, a three-room suite previously occupied by Pappy O'Daniel. Denied occupancy of one of the 45 four-room suites available to senior senators, Johnson pressed a case for more space. Within a matter of weeks he persuaded Carl Hayden of Arizona, the ranking member of the Rules and Administration Committee, to give him an additional single room on another floor. Believing that his office would function more effectively if it conducted most of its business on the telephone, he also convinced Hayden to give him a fourth telephone line, one more than freshmen senators normally received.[23]

Johnson's staff was young, intelligent, hard working, idealistic, and loyal. Fourteen of its sixteen members were under thirty-one years of age, including John Connally, whom Johnson had persuaded to come temporarily to Washington to organize the office. Connally had gone back to Austin in 1946 to run radio station KVET and build a successful business career. Horace Busby remembers him at this time as "unfairly handsome" with a "lavish personality" that made him an immediate center of attention wherever he went. Busby first met him in 1948 in an Austin restaurant, where it took Connally fifteen minutes to cross the room as he greeted friends and acquaintances. Although he held no office, it was "an article of faith" among people who knew him that Connally would become a senator or governor. Busby instantly liked him, seeing him as "an accomplished, well-turned-out, tremendously intelligent, articulate guy." Sam Rayburn and Stuart Symington shared Busby's feelings. Rayburn "had an extravgant, very high opinion of John Connally," who he thought "had more natural ability than any man of his age that he'd ever known." Symington considered him "one of the brightest and most able people I've known." Viewed as "more charismatic than LBJ" and as "in a class by himself," Connally, during nine months as Johnson's administrative assistant, turned a staff including Walter Jenkins, Mary Rather, Dorothy Nichols, Glynn Stegall, Warren Woodward, and Busby into what one newspaper called "a well-oiled machine."[24]

Johnson and Connally put the office on a twenty-four-hour-day that allowed them to respond quickly and effectively to constituents. The watchword of the office was unceasing work. "You don't know what it's like to be exhausted until you've worked here," one staff member told a journalist. "An eight-hour man ain't worth a damn to me," Johnson said. He wanted married couples on his payroll, because he didn't "want some wife at home complainin' that the cornbread's gettin' cold while her husband's doin' somethin' for *me.*" Johnson himself set the pace, usually working "from 6:30 A.M. to the small hours of the next day . . . arguing, listening, 'needling,' explaining, compromising, chain-smoking and chain-telephoning." At some time during each shift, he would come dashing through the office, urging on the staff: "C'mon, let's function . . . let's function." [25]

At first, no amount of effort seemed to meet the demands on the office. "This has been a mad-house since I first arrived," Connally complained in January. "I am hoping that it will settle down very shortly." By the end of February nothing had changed. "These past two months have been most hectic," he wrote a friend in Texas. ". . . If the damn mail doesn't quit being so heavy I assume I will be here from now until I die, because I can't even go home at night." Jenkins wrote in mid-March: "We have been so snowed under with work the last few weeks that we hardly know whether we are coming or going." The chief problem was the mail. Johnson saw a huge flow of correspondence between his office and Texas as essential to his success. He wanted his staff to handle up to 650 letters, 500 phone calls, and 70 visitors a day. "Johnson was a man to solicit mail," Walter Jenkins said. "He just told everybody everywhere he went to write him. . . . And they did." Sometimes between 1000 and 1200 letters arrived in a day. Usually, it was about 300 a day coming in and another 300 going out. Johnson was so attentive to this correspondence that the office compiled data on who wrote what from where. [26]

The pressure on staff people from Johnson was always heavy, but it was particularly intense in his first Senate years when he was trying to prove himself. Congressman Jake Pickle remembers how "relentless, almost ruthless" he could be. When a secretary came down with stomach ulcers, a visitor to the office asked another employee, "Doesn't the Senator ever get ulcers? He doesn't get 'em. He just gives 'em," was the reply. Johnson demanded total commitment from his staff. When one bright young man who had worked for him published a successful novel, Johnson wanted to know if he had written the book while he was in his office. The author explained that he had done his writing at nights and on weekends. "You ought to have been answering my mail," Johnson said. [27]

Some couldn't stand the abuse and quickly left his employ. Others, who wanted a larger career of their own, also left. John Connally, for example, went back to Texas in September 1949 to practice law. Yet more stayed than left, and some spent years on Johnson's staff. Above all, there was Walter Jenkins. Years later, Tommy Corcoran, who followed Johnson's rise to power from day one as a congressman in Washington, praised Jenkins as the single most important person outside of Lyndon and Lady Bird in ensuring Johnson's success. To achieve his goal, "Lyndon needed thousands at his service," Corcoran wrote Jenkins. "And only *you* gave *them* to *him*. It was only *through* you, as his 'power train,' that in every step in his struggle upward he had those thousands at his service." Bill Moyers, a later staff member, echoes Corcoran: "When they come to canonize political aides, he [Jenkins] will be the first summoned, for no man ever negotiated the shark-infested waters of the Potomac with more decency or charity or came out on the other side with his integrity less shaken. If Lyndon Johnson owed everything to one human being other than Lady Bird, he owed it to Walter Jenkins. When others of us wandered back and forth, flirting with first one career, then another, fickle Doubting Thomases of a sort, Jenkins stayed and kept it all together. And Johnson loved him."

The support Jenkins and others gave was not simply the product of selfless devotion to Lyndon's needs. Gifts and flattery, especially lavish descriptions of the person's indispensability to Johnson's success as a senator, motivated staff members. There was also a sense of excitement about working for Johnson. It was "very interesting to be around Johnson," Horace Busby says, and there was always the feeling that he was going places and that you were part of something larger than yourself. To Dorothy Nichols, "the magic of Mr. Johnson as boss, the participation in the things he was trying to accomplish for the country, the feeling he gave you that you yourself were saving the country every day, was irresistible." [28]

As important, Johnson's employees were never simply office staff who worked *for* the Senator and saw him socially at the annual Christmas party or office picnic. Once they came into Johnson's orbit, they were "family," whose lives became entwined in his and Lady Bird's. In December 1948, while Connally and his family drove to Washington, Lyndon rented an apartment for them and Lady Bird remembered how she bought "beds, dressers, chairs, [a] dining table, and . . . a large portion of cheap china and cooking utensils. . . . They arrived and we had the most marvelous Christmas. All the staff was there, as they very frequently were. . . . Everybody's children around the Christmas tree." Lyndon found a live Santa Claus to come to their house at 30th Place. In the fall of 1949 when Lady Bird went to Texas with the two girls, Walter Jenkins and his wife and two small children moved in with Johnson. Two years later, when Willie Day Taylor came from Texas to work for him, Lyndon and Lady Bird took her "out to their house where I stayed through the Christmas holidays. . . . Lucy [the Johnson's younger, three-year-old daughter] and I fell in love with each other on first sight." They had a lovely family Christmas with most of the staff there. One of "the great human qualities about Johnson," Charles Boatner recalled, "was trying to keep up with what was happening to people, the little town aspect of him." Even after they left his employ, he wanted to know about "their jobs and their sorrows and their sicknesses and their crop failures and their accidents—he still wanted to know." [29]

From the start of his Senate term, Johnson cultivated an image as the man "who gets things done." Whenever he persuaded a Federal agency to spend money in Texas, he issued a press release tying his name to the accomplishment. Since there were limits to these instances of Federal largesse, however, his office also released stories about Johnson's concern with everything from agricultural subsidies to veterans' rights. In the spring of 1950, he also began making weekly radio broadcasts about Washington events that affected the fortunes of Texas. [30]

At the same time he reached out to the mass public, he also took pains to establish good relations with Texas officials and political leaders. He was eager to be of service whenever possible, he told Lieutenant Governor Allan Shivers in February 1949, and asked his views on all matters of mutual interest. "I shall need the help of fellows like you . . . to be the kind of a Senator Texas deserves." Texas's large congressional delegation was not ignored: Unlike Tom Connally, who antagonized Texas representatives by taking exclusive credit for Federal projects, Johnson made a habit of including congressmen in his press releases. He also had his staff "flatter them" by saying how "good" he thought their weekly newsletters were and how eager he was for copies. He wrote to every postmaster in the state offering his "cooperation and assistance." And he made Jake Pickle in Austin his political eyes and ears in Texas, asking him to advise the Washington office "on who we should write and what we should say or do." When Pickle "ran across" I. J. Cernosek, a leading citizen in the south Texas town of Schulenberg, who spoke highly of Johnson, Lyndon told Pickle: "it would be worth a million dollars to me if you would write me more letters about people like this friend Mr. Cernosek." [31]

In the spring of 1950 former Governor Jimmy Allred gave Lyndon the "good news" that no one in south Texas had anything negative to say about him. "I am afraid you are going to have to content yourself with no news being good news," Allred told him. But Johnson was unwilling "to let well enough alone when folks were apparently disinterested." In fact, he was "alarmed that folks aren't saying anything one way or the other." [32]

Lyndon wanted recognition and enthusiatsic appreciation for the numerous Federal projects coming to the state. Before he had even begun his term, he had lobbied for committee assignments that could help him serve Texas and win a large favorable vote in 1954. Although he knew that "freshmen Senators usually eat off the second table" when it came to committee appointments, he asked for assignment to the influential and prestigous Appropriations Committee. Membership on Appropriations would have given him not only a say in the distribution of "federal loaves and fishes" but also a leg up on the national prominence he craved.[33]

Since it usually took six years to get on Appropriations, Lyndon's request was not taken seriously. In November 1948, when he went to see Tom Connally about Stevenson's challenge to his seat, Johnson had raised the possibility of serving on the committee. Connally put the upstart in his place: Chewing on a "big cigar" and pulling "his glasses over his nose," Connally said: " 'Now, wait a minute, Lyndon, wait a minute!' He pulled out a book of committees, and he said, 'Now let's see. Here's the Agriculture Committee. You could get on that. You could always be hollering about what you're going to do for the farmers. . . . You're for the farmers, ain't you, Lyndon?' " When Johnson agreed, Connally went on: " 'Well, I thought I heard you say something about it during the campaign.' And his eyes were just twinkling, Connally's were. And then he said, 'Oh, yes, the Armed Services Committee. Get on it, and you can always holler about what you're going to do for A&M. . . . And then'—and he threw his hands out in the air—'after you have been in the Senate for some time, and they've stopped all this talk about the close election, then you can get on the Atomic Energy Commission, or the Foreign Relations Committee, and render a real public service.' " John Connally and Frank Oltorf, a state legislator, who were in the room, found it so comical that they had to keep themselves from laughing.[34]

Johnson wasn't deterred. He went directly to Kenneth McKellar of Tennessee, the Appropriations Committee chairman. McKellar advised him to see Scott Lucas of Illinois, the new Majority Leader, Carl Hayden of Arizona, a senior member of the Democratic Steering Committee, which controlled committee assignments, and Alben Barkley of Kentucky, who was leaving the Senate to become Vice President. Lucas and Hayden were sympathetic, but Barkley brushed him off. Johnson then enlisted Rayburn and Attorney General Tom Clark in his campaign, and asked Millard Tydings of Maryland, another senior senator on Appropriations, for support; but all to no avail. Johnson had to settle for the Armed Services and Interstate and Foreign Commerce committees.[35]

Despite his disappointment, the two committees gave him ample means to serve Texas. Armed Services made decisions about Texas air bases, and Commerce shaped legislation affecting Texas oil and natural gas

interests. Picking up where he had left off in the House, Johnson successfully promoted the maintenance and reactivation of Air Force bases,
the passage of the Wherry Housing bill, which generated construction
of military housing at bases around Texas, Federal subsidies to the tin
smelting industry in Texas City on Galveston Bay in the Gulf of Mexico,
an R.F.C. loan to support the Lone Star steel plant in northeast Texas,
the sale of war assets to the University of Texas to facilitate research on
government contracts, and R.F.C. home loans to veterans. "There are
Fifty-Four Billion Dollars in home loans outstanding at this time," the
Texas oilman Clint Murchison wrote him in March 1949, "and if the
average is $7,000 per loan and each loan carries two votes, it seems to
me like this is 14,000,000 votes. Can you hear me?" "I can hear you!"
Johnson replied.[36]

Johnson's effectiveness in catering to state needs broadened his base
of support. In the words of one Texas business leader, Johnson's efforts
for the state brought "recalcitrant and hardened Ag'inners [in]to the
fold of 'I told you so' supporters." Another Texas businessman told
Johnson that he heard "such nice things . . . all over the state . . . .
People are delighted with the response they are getting out of your office
and . . . [don't] see how you manage to do such a tremendous job."
When Air Force General Hoyt Vandenberg spoke to Fort Worth's leading businessmen, he praised the state for electing fine representatives to
Congress. "Texas and the Air Forces are especially fortunate in having
sent this man Lyndon Johnson to the United States Senate. I have seen
him stand up and fight for Texas and for the Air Forces and I can tell
you that he is a very able man." The people in the audience were Coke
Stevenson, Dixiecrat, and Republican voters, one of Lyndon's friends
wrote him. "In other words, they were the Chamber of Commerce crowd
. . . but I am almost certain that I saw in their eyes the dawn of understanding."[37]

The report was music to Johnson's ears. As a liberal nationalist who
continued to believe in using Federal authority to serve the disadvantaged as well as local and state interests, he assumed that New Deal–
Fair Deal Texans would continue to support him. To win reelection
however, he needed to appease the rising tide of conservatism in the
state or to overcome the image conservative Democrat E. B. Germany
and others held of him as "the very essence of New Dealism and a
stalwart of the philosophy of government which has brought this Nation
to the brink of disaster. During all these years," Germany said, "he
[Johnson] sat close to the thrones of those who determined our national
and international policies. . . . He helped sow the seed for the harvest
we now are reaping . . . [of] communists, fellow travelers, pinkos, and
traitors to the American way of life firmly entrenched in . . . power."[38]

Conservatives shamelessly exploited public fears in the 1940s and 1950s to identify liberals and their policies of the previous twenty years with Communist subversion. Johnson knew these accusations were largely a political device for Republicans and conservative Democrats to regain power. But he also understood that such rhetoric appealed to the Texas electorate and that he could not afford to dismiss the state's conservatism without jeopardy to his political future. Consequently, in 1949–50 he went out of his way to identify himself with anti-civil rights, pro-oil, and anti-Communist groups and actions. About this time Johnson told H. Roy Cullen, a conservative Houston oil millionaire, that his debt to the Roosevelt family and the New Deal had been paid and that his "vote in the Senate would please all good conservative Texans."

Yet at the same time, he tried not to cut himself off from his old New Deal allies. If he simply aligned himself with southern conservatives, he would have been identified as a regional senator with little national standing. On the other hand, the road to Senate influence and national prominence was partly through southern powerbrokers: Richard Russell and Walter George of Georgia, Tom Connally of Texas, James Eastland and John Stennis of Mississippi, Lister Hill of Alabama, Harry Byrd of Virginia, and Allen Ellender of Louisiana. They were crucial allies for anyone eager to rise in the Senate hierarchy and shape national policies. But Lyndon also needed to take his distance from them if he were to have any credibility as a broad-based national leader. As Hubert Humphrey later put it, "Johnson did not consider himself a southerner and he knew that he could not be its captive. . . . He was a Democrat and a Texan, enjoying the benefits of southern hospitality, southern power, southern support, but who carefully avoided the liabilities of being clearly labeled a Southerner."[39]

Although his first priority in 1949–50 was to establish his bone fides as a conservative, Johnson avoided doctrinaire positions that would make him seem like a clone of the southern bloc. His initial reaction to President Truman's announcement in his January State of the Union message of a Fair Deal program is a case in point. After Truman's stunning victory over Dewey in November 1948 and liberal success at the beginning of January 1949 in stripping the House Rules Committee of power to bottle up reform bills, the President outlined a program of liberal goals: progressive tax reform, repeal of Taft-Hartley, a 75-cent minimum wage, expansion of Social Security, increased public power, national medical insurance, Federal aid to education, housing programs, and civil rights. An Administration effort to apply cloture to filibusters against motions to take up bills tested Truman's power to drive Fair Deal measures through the Congress. Senate rules allowed two-thirds of those present on the floor to end a filibuster against pending legislation, but cloture was not applicable to debate on motions to consider a bill. At the beginning of March 1949, the White House tried to push a rule change through the upper house to clear the way for its civil rights program.[40]

To defeat Truman's cloture proposal and his whole civil rights program, senators from the former eleven Confederate states organized themselves into a southern caucus and met to map strategy. Twenty of the twenty-two southerners attended. Only Lyndon and freshman senator Estes Kefauver of Tennessee did not show up. Unwilling to identify himself as simply another southern-bloc senator or, as he put it to Jim Rowe, to "be indicted with 'guilt by association,' " Johnson stayed away from the southern strategy meeting. Yet at the same time, he wished to assure Texans that he stood with the South on civil rights. When an Associated Press reporter ran into him while the caucus was meeting and asked why he was absent, Johnson refused to answer and fled to his office, where he locked the door and cursed the "goddam so and so" for trying to get a story that could embarrass him. Behind the scenes, Johnson left no doubt with southern senators where he stood. On March 7, eight days after the cloture fight had begun, John Stennis of Mississippi wrote a Texas supporter: "Senator Lyndon Johnson is cooperating fully with us in this fight to prevent the adoption of the cloture rule."[41]

Johnson's first Senate speech two days later opposed cloture as an unacceptable limitation on free speech that could undermine the rights of all minorities. "When I say minority," Johnson declared, "I do not limit the term to mean only the South. . . . The filibuster is not a Southern creation; it belongs to all the Nation, and to all the minorities—racial, religious, political, economic, or otherwise—which make up this nation." If a southern minority were deprived of open-ended debate or "free speech," all minorities would be the losers. Johnson did not limit himself to a discussion of cloture and shun the real issue of civil rights legislation: "When we strip away the trappings of rhetoric and theory and legend which surround the arguments here against the filibuster, we have left the simple fact that we are debating the so-called civil-rights legislation."[42]

Johnson emphasized that his opposition to civil rights reform was not racist: "No prejudice is so contagious or so dangerous," he said, "as the unreasoning prejudice against men because of their birth, the color of their skin, or their ancestral background. . . . When we of the South rise here to speak against this resolution or to speak against the civil-rights proposals, we are not speaking against the Negro race. We are not attempting to keep alive the old flames of hate and bigotry." Nor, Johnson announced, did he believe in the poll tax or have anything but contempt for "the shameful crime of lynching." Johnson said he had no quarrel with the aims of civil rights advocates, only their methods: Federal laws would not accomplish what they intend. He saw the surest path to ending poll taxes and lynchings through state reform and changes in local attitudes. In Texas, for example, lynching was "virtually non-existent." [43]

Johnson's arguments convinced no civil rights supporters. Liberal Houston banker Walter Hall wrote to say he was "sorry you think more of your right to speak without limit than you do another man's right to vote." Jim Rowe described the speech as "reasoned and temperate" and without "the demagoguery on this issue that the South had indulged in for so many years." Moreover, Rowe said he had no strong feelings on cloture, but he did feel strongly about southern reasons for wanting to keep the filibuster—namely, as a means for consigning blacks to an inferior position. He believed that Lyndon was wrong to lend his support to what he called "the crime of America." "Your old friends, who remember the high stepping, idealistic, intelligent young man who came here as a bright young Congressman in 1938 expect more of you than that." Blacks in Texas felt the same way: "The Negroes who sent you to Congress are ashamed to know that you have stood on the floor against them today," the secretary of the Houston NAACP wired him. "Do not forget that you went to Washington by a small majority vote and that was because of the Negro vote. There will be another election and we will be remembering what you had to say today." [44]

Black Texans had been more supportive of Johnson than Stevenson, but when it came to votes, Johnson believed that the speech did him far more good than harm. "The mail on the speech has been quite large, overwhelmingly favorable except for NAACP telegrams," he wrote Paul Bolton. "Quite a number of prominent Fort Worth and West Texas folks who were against us last summer have written highly gratifying comments on the speech," Johnson told newspaper publisher Amon Carter. [45]

Although he took satisfaction from the political gains he made through his anti-civil rights stand, suggestions that he was insensitive to the well-being of minorities and that he had all but abandoned his old New Deal faith upset him. He also had little patience with the "bomb throwers," as he called them, radicals on the Left and Right who saw no room for compromise or failed to see that the road to progress was along a middle path that quieted passions, promoted consensus, and assured civic order. To help chart a moderate course on the cloture issue, for example, Johnson had asked Jim Rowe to write his speech. When Rowe refused and criticized what he said, Johnson answered: "I think all men are created equal, I want all men to have equal opportunity. Yes, I even think your civil rights slogans are eloquent and moving. But when you and [Hubert] Humphrey . . . reach the point of translating your humanitarian spirit into law you seem always to lose any sense of charity, faith in your fellow man, or reasonableness." Johnson complained that Truman's civil rights bills were not "benevolent" but "almost sadistic." At the 1948 Democratic convention "you saw two blind unreasoning minorities collide. Both of them, judging from what I know of their character, are cruel, ruthless, and vicious. Justice, to their way of thinking, carries a cat-o'-nine tails in one hand and salt in the other. You may think that characterization applies only to my Dixiecrat friends; I believe it applies to both sides equally."[46]

Johnson was also eager to answer black Texans who attacked his anti-civil rights stand. When a Houston man wrote to complain, Johnson replied: "It has been a matter of profound regret to me that many Negro citizens of Texas have viewed my speech in the Senate as an affront to them. I did not and would not make a speech in that spirit." A delegation of Houston blacks traveled to Washington to see Johnson. But the meeting went badly: heated words were exchanged and the blacks left unsatisfied.[47]

Johnson did better with Hispanics. Since they made up nearly 20 percent of the population in Texas, almost twice the number of black Texans, he was especially concerned not to offend them. He considered hiring "a talented and goodlooking Mexican or Spanish American girl" as a receptionist or secretary to show his "appreciation of the support" given him by "this estimable class of Texas citizens." But an opportunity at the beginning of 1949 to do a highly visible public service for a Texas Hispanic family made the point and overshadowed his anti-civil rights stance. In early January, Hector Garcia, the head of a veterans organization in Corpus Christi, informed Johnson that the only funeral home in Three Rivers, a south Texas town, would not handle the interment in the town's all-white cemetery of Felix Longoria, a Mexican-American soldier killed in the Philippines during World War II. Incensed at this blatant bigotry against a war hero and alert to the possibility of showing "how he felt about the Latins," Johnson arranged to have his body buried at Arlington National Cemetery. Though some white Texans saw his actions as a cynical publicity stunt and some Texas legislators launched an unsuccessful campaign to whitewash the town and discredit Johnson, he was sincerely outraged by the incident and able to turn it to good political account. He received positive notoriety on the front page of the *New York Times* and elsewhere as a politician who had the courage of his convictions.[48]

Johnson wasn't simply posturing for the sake of political advantage. He genuinely wanted to improve the lives of black and Hispanic Texans, many of whom lived in poverty. He didn't see the path to this advance, however, through civil rights laws. Instead, as he told Jim Rowe, the country needed a "frontal assault on the 'ill-housed, ill-clad, ill-fed' problem facing part of our nation. Until this problem is met, all your other legislation is built upon sand. That is the end of the problem I hope I can grab hold of and do something about during my years in the Senate." Fearful that Federal civil rights laws, or attempts "to force people to do what they are not ready to do of their own free will and accord," would lead to a "wave of riots" across the South, Johnson supported efforts "to equalize the opportunity and reward of all Americans through better housing, better schooling, better health, and all those things which are the true rights of first-class citizenship."

In supporting Federal programs that eased poverty and increased opportunity, Johnson had the southern experience in mind. As a result of minimum wage laws and outside public and private spending and investment in the South, the per capita income had shown a dramatic increase in the 1940s. At between 50 and 60 percent of the national average in 1940, by the end of the decade it had risen to between 60 and 80 percent. Lyndon believed correctly that continued Federal spending on defense and agriculture and expanded programs to house, educate, and improve the health care of southerners would increase the region's prosperity and bring it closer to the national standard than it had been at any time since the Civil War. He also believed that civil rights advances would follow from improved living conditions. The economist Gavin Wright thinks Johnson was correct: writing in 1986, Wright saw the fundamental economic changes in the South in the forties as the prelude to "the success of the civil rights revolution of the 1950s and 1960s."[49]

Lyndon would not support Truman on civil rights in 1949, but he favored many of his other reforms. "You speak of the President's program of 'social reform' and imply that it has been killed by some arbitrary coalition," he wrote a liberal Texan in April 1949. "The President's program . . . embodies a good deal more than the Civil Rights legislation. Rent control, expanded social security, housing, agricultural assistance—all those subjects, and more, are in the program and they are by no means dead." After a majority of conservative Republicans and southern Democrats had defeated the Administration's cloture reforms in March, Johnson aligned himself with the White House and voted for extended rent control; the first significant aid-to-education bill, which proposed to equalize educational opportunities among the states; additional low-rent public housing; a higher minimum wage; and expanded Social Security benefits. While all these bills, with the exception of aid to education, became law, most of Truman's Fair Deal proposals fell victim to a conservative coalition in Congress that wanted no part of further economic or social change in American life.[50]

Johnson's votes for Fair Deal measures did not go unremarked in Texas. One Texas businessman hammered at him for backing rent control and pressed him to fight legislation weakening the Taft-Hartley labor law. When several revisions of Taft-Hartley were proposed in June 1949, Johnson consistently voted with the conservatives. He also defended his vote on rent controls by pointing out that the law allowed state and local officials the option to remove them. "I believe private enterprise to be the keystone in our democratic system, and that it should not be weakened, ignored or taken away." He assured this businessman that he would "oppose those measures which I believe will tend to socialize our economy or push us toward a communistic system." At the same time, however, he continued to see a major role for Federal authority in the regulation of economic and social affairs. When a Fort Worth industrialist wrote to complain about wasteful government expenditures, Johnson challenged him to get specific: "Would you have the government repudiate the national debt so that five billion dollars could be saved? . . . Would you scrap all our programs of Veterans' benefits and throw the Veterans recklessly on to the labor market, compounding the chaos of unemployment?" Johnson also wondered whether he wanted to eliminate the courts, the FBI, Federal meat and food inspection, the Public Health Service, nuclear weapons research, and military defense. "Perhaps you think we can get along without any government at all. If that is what you think, then you and I disagree fundamentally."[51]

Johnson's support of Federal authority did not extend to regulation of the oil and natural gas industries. Like Sam Rayburn, he "knew what a rapacious bunch of people the big oil companies were," but he felt that a senator from Texas had little choice other than to represent their interests. "A lot of my friends who didn't like LBJ," D. B. Hardeman, Rayburn's principal aide, says, "thought he was a pawn of the oil and gas companies. . . . Certainly he befriended them. He helped them a whole lot. There's no question about that. But I don't think he could have remained in the Senate and done otherwise. I don't think he could have been re-elected if he had followed another path." Texas had "hundreds of thousands of landowners who had a direct stake in the oil business through their leases . . . And then you had many people in Texas—workers, all the way from roughnecks to the people in the oil well supply houses, people in banks . . . who were dependent on the oil industry for a livelihood." The fact that state law required oil companies to turn a percentage of their profits over to public schools also made it difficult for any elected official in the state to oppose the industry. Johnson "was never a friend of the oil and gas industry," Harry McPherson says. But support for them "was a fact of life for any Texas Senator. You simply could not oppose that and stay alive as a political figure in Texas."[52]

Johnson himself described the pressure on him to speak for oil, gas, and other conservative interests in a December 1948 conversation with Bobby Baker, the Senate's twenty-year-old principal page, who had a reputation for knowing "where the bodies are buried." Mindful that Baker's job was to assist the Senate Democratic leadership, Johnson wanted him to understand the political constraints under which he had to operate. "My state is much more conservative than the national Democratic party. I got elected by just eighty-seven votes and I ran against a caveman. . . . I cannot always vote with President Truman if I'm going to *stay* a senator." When Baker asked which issues would likely give him the most trouble, Johnson answered: Taft-Hartley and oil. "Labor's not much stronger in Texas than a popcorn fart. . . . I ran on a ticket that says we like the Taft-Hartley Act; we're not going to repeal it. . . . I'm for the natural gas bill and for the tidelands bill. Frankly, Mr. Baker, I'm for nearly anything the big oil boys want because they hold the whip hand and I represent 'em. Yeah, I represent farmers and working men and when I can help President Truman help 'em, I'll do it. But the New Deal spirit's gone from Texas and I'm limited in what I can do." Johnson was emphatic about Taft-Hartley and oil: "I don't want you bothering my ass on the two issues." [53]

Three oil and gas issues were under consideration during Johnson's first Senate term: reduction of the 27.5 percent depletion allowance to oil producers on their taxes, Federal versus state ownership of the tidelands, and deregulation of natural gas production. Johnson had least difficulty with the depletion allowance. Believing that it encouraged domestic exploration and that the country's national security depended on self-sufficiency or the widest possible development of all our domestic oil reserves, he viewed reduction of the allowance in the late forties and fifties as "unthinkable." Although the Truman administration saw the 27.5 percent allowance as excessive and its reduction as a good way to raise Federal revenues, tax reform had little congressional support in 1949. And even when tax increases were voted in 1950 and 1951, the 27.5 percent allowance remained untouched. We could have taken a 5 or 10 percent figure," Tom Connally said, "but we grabbed 27.5 because we were not only hogs but the odd figure made it appear as though it was scientifically arrived at." An amendment to the Revenue Act of 1951 proposing to reduce depletion allowances on gas and oil wells from 27.5 to 15 percent of gross income lost in the Senate by 71 to 9. [54]

Tidelands or offshore oil was a more controversial matter. In 1947, after Truman had vetoed a 1946 congressional resolution vesting control of the tidelands in the states, the Supreme Court had ruled that the Federal government had paramount rights to the submerged lands off of California. Because Texas had been "a sovereign nation" before it came into the Union, state officials believed it had a stronger claim to its tidelands than California. States' rights and money from offshore oil production for public schools made the tidelands a "burning issue" in Texas. The state's land commissioner urged Texas to secede from the Union before surrendering its territory. Attorney General Tom Clark, who filed the suit against California, received "scurrilous telephone calls" saying he was "a thief and a rascal" and a renegade who had "betrayed" his own state (Texas). In 1950, when the Supreme Court also ruled against Texas, renewed cries for secession arose and some Texans urged Austin to exercise its unique right to divide into five states, adding eight additional senators who could vote for state control of the tidelands.

In private, Johnson told friends that he favored Federal control of the submerged lands. But publicly he aligned himself with state feeling. "I do not have to repeat to you my personal determination to do all that I can as senator to keep the Tidelands of Texas away from Federal control," he wrote the chairman of the state's Special Committee on Tidelands in December 1948. "You well know my sentiments with reference to tidelands legislation and that I will do everything I consistently can to help in connection with it," he wrote Governor Allan Shivers in December 1950. In 1951–52, Johnson helped pass bills granting forty-seven states control over three miles of offshore lands and Texas, with its special history, ten and a half miles. Truman vetoed the bills calling them "robbery in broad daylight."[55]

Johnson added to his reputation as a defender of Texas oil and gas interests during a well-publicized fight in 1949–50 to restrict Federal Power Commission (FPC) regulation of natural gas production. Until 1945 natural gas had been a relatively unimportant resource. But the construction during the war of pipelines from the Southwest to the Northeast made gas an alternative to coal for home heating, and gas production a big business. Moreover, until after the war the FPC saw no authority in the 1938 Natural Gas Act to regulate prices charged by independent producers or any company not described as a utility. In 1947, however, the Supreme Court ruled that the Commission had authority to regulate all gas sold in interstate commerce. Believing that the Congress had never intended the 1938 law to be read that way, representatives and senators, led by members from gas-producing states, urged legislation denying the FPC power to set prices for independent natural gas companies.

Senator Robert Kerr, an Oklahoma Democrat and member of the 1949 freshman class, made deregulation his first priority. The owner of an estimated $100 million in natural gas reserves that gave him an annual $12 million gross income, Kerr had a huge personal interest in passing such legislation. A Baptist teetotaler with an evangelical faith in free enterprise, Kerr openly acknowledged his stake in deregulation and made no apologies for a law which he thought would serve the national well-being, the natural gas industry, and himself. A brillant orator and debater, Kerr put his talents to good effect in behalf of the legislation. Inviting opposing journalists to his office for heart-to-heart talks, Kerr tried to preserve them from "evil and untruth," sometimes quoting passages from the Bible to support his arguments. His initial approach to fellow senators was a soft sell, amiably pointing to misinformation they may have received on his bill and graciously asking their support or, at least, neutrality. When aroused by opposition, however, he used his "razor-sharp mind" against opponents with devastating effect. "He was frightening on the floor and he had full command, almost in an eighteenth-century way, of political invective," Harry McPherson remembers. Wallace Bennett of Utah recalled: "We used to call him 'the King of the Senate.'" Kerr thought of himself as "an invincible debater and I don't think many people wanted to mix with him. He could be very scornful, very cutting . . . and it wasn't a pleasant experience."

When Republican Homer Capehart of Indiana angered him, Kerr described him in a Senate speech as "a rancid tub of ignorance." The next day Capehart objected to being called "a rancid cup of ignorance." Kerr replied that Capehart was mistaken; he had said "tub" not "cup." "Anyone who can observe the corpulence of the Senator from Indiana will see how ridiculous it would be to . . . [say] that the Senator from Indiana was 'a rancid *cup* of ignorance.'" When columnist and radio commentator Drew Pearson opposed his bill, Kerr declared: "No wonder American Broadcasting Co. puts Airwick on the air for 15 minutes after he gets through. . . . Do they need it."[56]

Johnson became Kerr's strong right arm in the fight. Mindful of how much good it could do him in Texas, Johnson became the chair of an Interstate and Foreign Commerce subcommittee reporting on the bill and publicized his support of the legislation. He spoke on the floor of the Senate, welcomed newspaper articles about his leadership, and urged oil and gas lobbyists to get the word out on the "vital and affirmative way" in which he was battling for the law. But his support was not just an exercise in political cynicism. He disputed critics who predicted that deregulation would lead to higher gas prices and bigger producer profits. He stated that deregulation would not affect FPC authority to prevent price increases, that profits on natural gas principally went to distributors or pipeline owners, that coal producers and the United Mine Workers were self-serving opponents of the legislation, and that deregulation of independents would increase natural gas production, reduce prices, and serve the national security by decreasing American dependence on foreign supplies. He and Kerr convinced forty-two other senators to vote with them and fourteen more to absent themselves, winning passage of their bill in March 1950 by a 44–38 margin. Yet Kerr, Johnson, and Rayburn, who managed a two-vote victory in the House, could not sell the White House on the benefits of the law. "Certainly the reason the natural gas companies want to escape Federal regulation," Drew Pearson wrote, "isn't to reduce prices." Apparently agreeing, Truman vetoed the law.[57]

The closeness of the congressional vote and the influence of powerful groups aligned against the legislation had made Johnson doubtful that the bill would become law. However much Texas oil and gas interests might appreciate his efforts for deregulation, then, they would come away from this fight without clear evidence that Johnson was actually effective in their behalf. And in the first year of his Senate career he wanted something which could emphatically make this point. He found it in Truman's request for the reconfirmation, as required by law, of Leland Olds to the Federal Power Commission. A prominent liberal who had been a radical journalist in the twenties, a member of the FPC since 1939, and a leading spokesman for extensive and tough Federal regulation of power interests, Olds was a hero to consumer advocates, labor unions, and all who believed in an enlarged role for Federal control of private enterprise.

Taking on Leland Olds appealed to Johnson on several counts. First, Texas oil and gas interests and anyone who saw those industries as synonymous with the well-being of the state viewed Olds as an unmitigated foe who would give the FPC an anti-industry and anti-Texas majority for several years. In April 1949, before Truman publicly recommended Olds's reappointment, Charles I. Francis, the Houston oil and gas attorney, advised Lyndon that practically all the state's oil and gas executives opposed Olds and that he and others in Texas could not understand why the President would want to punish "one of our most important Texas industries" by recommending Olds's return to the FPC. Second, keeping Olds off the FPC would serve Johnson's biggest financial booster, Brown & Root, whose share of Texas Eastern Transmission made them keenly interested in anything affecting oil and gas. Third, it was likely that Olds's reappointment could be defeated. A clear majority of senators, who either wanted to defend local interests, attack expanded Federal regulatory power, or punish Olds for deliberately defying the expressed intent of Congress in the 1938 natural gas law, opposed his return to the Commission. Finally, Olds's radical background made him an attractive target for a Texan who wanted to align himself with the general swing toward conservatism in the state.[58]

Johnson chaired an Interstate and Foreign Commerce subcommittee that orchestrated Olds's defeat. Supported by Senate leaders on both sides of the aisle, by former Secretary of Interior Ickes and his Under Secretary Abe Fortas, both of whom wanted to settle old scores with a bureaucratic adversary, Johnson allowed witnesses to pillory Olds for ideas and associations dating back twenty and thirty years. They pointed to Olds's service as an editor at the radical Federated Press and cited fifty-four articles published by *Labor Letter*, a radical journal in the twenties. South Texas congressman John Lyle denounced Olds for sneering at the fourth of July, calling the church "a handmaiden of the capitalist system," advocating nationalization of the coal, railroad, and utility industries, preaching the Communist doctrine of class struggle, and praising "the Russian system as the coming world order." Olds replied that he had never favored Communism and that he had changed his mind about Russia. His critics, however, focused on his reply to Johnson that he still held to the positions he had taken in the twenties, though he would "write some of those articles in a somewhat different way today."[59]

While newspapers across the country denounced the hearings for smear tactics serving oil and gas barons, Johnson avidly joined in the red-baiting. At a time when the Soviet Union had exploded its first atomic device, a Communist regime had taken power in China, former State Department official Alger Hiss was under suspicion of espionage, and eleven American Communist party officials were on trial for advocating the overthrow of the government, anticommunism held an irresistible appeal for some politicians trying to make headlines. At the hearings Johnson established that Olds had shared a platform with Communist party leader Earl Browder in 1924. Johnson also wrote a letter to the *Denver Post* saying that Truman had nominated Olds for another term in order to win favor with the pro-Communist American Labor party. When Truman wrote Senator Edwin Johnson of Colorado, the Commerce Committee's chairman, urging Olds's appointment as "a matter of public interest," Johnson described Lyndon's subcommittee as "shocked beyond description by the political and economic views expressed by Mr. Olds some years ago. We cannot believe that a person under our democratic capitalistic system holding such views is qualified to act in a quasi-judicial capacity in the regulation of industry." Ed Johnson reported that the subcommittee had voted seven to nothing against the nomination. The full Commerce Committee opposed it by a vote of 10 to 2.[60]

The one-sided committee votes made clear that the Senate would not confirm Olds's nomination. Despite this, Lyndon took the floor two days before the Senate vote to hammer home the case against him, or, more to the point, to publicize Lyndon Johnson's pro-oil, anticommunist views in Texas. Olds should be rejected, Johnson argued, because of his "life-long prejudice and hostility against the industries he now regulates." His "record is an uninterrupted tale of bias, prejudice, and hostility, directed against the industry over which he seeks now to assume the powers of life and death." Olds was the spokesman of special interests who favored his high-handed arrogation of powers Congress never intended him or any FPC Commissioner to have over gas producers. Furthermore, Olds was not a loyal member of the Democratic party, but a former member of the American Labor party, which he left in 1938 for reasons of political expediency. "I do not charge that Mr. Olds is a Communist," Johnson said. ". . . I realize that the line he followed, the phrases he used, the causes he espoused, resemble the party line today," but that did not make him a Communist. Still, Johnson said, the issue before the Senate is: "Shall we have a Commissioner or a commissar?" On October 14, the Senate decisively rejected Olds's reappointment by a vote of 53 to 15.[61]

The attack on Olds outraged Lyndon's liberal friends. Joseph L. Rauh, an organizer of the progressive Americans for Democratic Action (ADA) and Washington attorney who had helped him in his legal battle for his Senate seat, saw Lyndon's handling of the Olds nomination as "a pre-Joe McCarthy campaign . . . really vicious. . . . That was one of the dirtiest pieces of work ever done." The way in which Johnson helped "end the career of the number one power advocate in America was a shocking thing, and it must be on Johnson's conscience," Rauh said. James Rowe and Tommy Corcoran "were very critical of the way he [Lyndon] was smearing Olds. He was not just against him, he was saying he was a commie, I assume it was to make himself a hero with the oil men . . . in Texas. We did everything we could to change his mind, we couldn't budge him." Rowe thought it would have been legitimate for Johnson to have gone after Olds for "fighting *my* people in Texas," but instead "he got this damn commie thing and he ran it into the ground for no reason anybody could see. . . . And he was made damn uncomfortable about it, because a lot of his old friends attacked him for it."[62]

Johnson's attack on Olds helped him to shed his reputation as a staunch New Dealer, establish himself as an uncompromising defender of Texas interests, and align himself with the conservative political mood in the state. When the president of a Dallas life insurance company said that Johnson's stand on Olds had converted him from an opponent to a supporter, Lyndon replied: "It is always good to have new friends, and I hope I shall always justify myself and my actions in your eyes." Senator Richard Russell of Georgia told Johnson of sharp criticism in his state for their defeat of Olds. "We may be assassins over in Savannah," Lyndon answered, "but we're saviors in the Southwest." Although he denied assertions that he was now in the pocket of oil and gas men, he also told Russell: "Cloture is where you find it, sir, and this man Olds was an advocate of simple majority cloture on the gas producers."[63]

After he had established himself as a savior among Texas energy interests and conservatives more generally, Johnson was eager to appease liberals. He asked a south Texas newspaper publisher who complained about Johnson's attack on Olds to understand that "the Olds fight was not the black and white case it appears to be when presented by the columns and the commentators. More especially, I want you to understand that Si Cassidy [liberal Texas Democrat] has a world more 'influence' on me than any lobby you or I could name." Replying to similar complaints from a liberal El Paso journalist, Johnson urged him to see the Olds battle as " 'bygones.' I'll be fighting for you more than I fight with you, I'm sure." When liberal journalist Jack Anderson spoke to Lyndon about the Olds case, he convinced Anderson that he had been fair in the hearings and was not beholden to the oil and gas industry. "Lyndon is also far from the worst Senator on the Hill," Anderson told Drew Pearson. "He has gone down the line for the Fair Deal, except for his votes on labor, civil rights and tidelands oil." Moreover, when Truman nominated Mon Wallgren, a former Washington senator and governor with "a rather liberal record," to replace Olds on the FPC, Johnson helped him win confirmation with all-out support.[64]

From day one in the Senate, Johnson is supposed to have set his sights on larger things—leadership of the upper house, the vice presidency, even the presidency. According to all his biographers, as soon as he took his seat, he tried to distinguish the "whales" from the "minnows," the powerbrokers from the ordinary Senate members, and to cultivate the most important leaders, like Richard Russell. Johnson himself encouraged the idea that he had control of the Senate in mind as early as 1949 and intended to do it by allying himself with the principal leaders: "I knew there was only one way to see Russell every day," Johnson told Doris Kearns, "and that was to get a seat on his committee. Without that we'd most likely be passing acquaintances and nothing more. So I put in a request for the Armed Services Committee—and fortunately, because of all my work on defense preparedness in the House, my request was granted."[65]

Johnson unquestionably made conscious efforts to learn about and establish himself in the good graces of Senate leaders. " 'I want to know who's the power over there, how you get things done, the best committees, the works,' " he told Bobby Baker at their first meeting. "He solicited opinions of, and thumbnail sketches of, senators little known to him; he peppered me with keen questions for a solid two hours. I was impressed," Baker recalls. "No senator had ever approached me with such a display of determination to learn, to achieve, to attain, to belong, to get ahead. He was coming into the Senate with his neck bowed, running full tilt, impatient to reach some distant goal I then could not even imagine." But then neither could Johnson. Typically trying to master the new surroundings in which he found himself, ensure his success, and, in some undefined way, make himself a dominant, outstanding figure in the upper house, Johnson threw himself into his Senate work with unrestrained energy.[66]

Yet Johnson's principal goal in 1949 was not to become Majority Leader but to ensure his reelection by making himself a highly regarded Texas, southwestern, and nationally minded Senator. His objective was to reach out to as many constituencies as possible. Getting on the Armed Services Committee, for example, not only meant getting close to Richard Russell but also ensuring Texas, the South, and the West of the largesse that came from military spending, and the nation of the best national security its money could buy. He aimed to build a long Senate career on a reputation as one of the most effective senators Texas, the Southwest, and the nation had ever seen. If this led to larger things, he would be ready to seize the opportunities. But he needed first to lay the groundwork for a successful stay in the Senate by winning the widest possible approval that political calculation and fortune would allow.

He now performed what journalists Roland Evans and Robert Novak called "tightrope walking" or a "balancing act." First, he allied himself with the powerful southern leaders, but especially with Russell. "The power of this inner club was evident at once to the entering freshman," Doris Kearns writes. "Its members ate lunch at a special table, where, others believed, they discussed and determined how and when various issues would come to the Senate floor." Allen Ellender of Louisiana said, Johnson "knew whom to talk to. He knew who had a little influence. . . . Among the first he tackled for assistance was Richard Russell of Georgia." [67]

Russell's exceptional influence in the Senate made him important to Johnson. But more than power considerations attracted Johnson. There was much about Russell that Johnson genuinely admired. He was a man of uncommon talent who had been the youngest governor in Georgia's history and had served in the Senate since 1932. His knowledge of American history and politics was legendary. He had a "towering intellect," George Reedy says, and a detailed grasp of politics across the United States that astonished other senators. He often had a greater understanding of another senator's state than the senator. Reedy remembers him at a NATO parliamentary conference where he demonstrated a knowledge of the internal politics of the European countries that exceeded that of the specialists briefing the American delegation. Johnson and Russell also shared an affinity for many New Deal Social programs, an antagonism to labor "bosses," a military able to defend American global interests, and Federal spending that boosted their state and regional economies. Russell had a reputation as a staunch conservative, but he had helped create the Rural Eletrification Administration and the Farmers Home Administration. "I'm a reactionary when times are good," Russell once said. "In a depression, I'm a liberal." Although Russell was much more southern and committed to racial segregation than Johnson, they both opposed Federal activism in behalf of civil rights in the early fifties. More important, they both worked for the fuller integration of the South and the West into the nation's economic and political life. They wanted both regions to gain a larger share of the national wealth and power than they had controlled during the first half of the century. [68]

Russell had many supplicants for his attention and support. But none succeeded as well as Johnson in gaining his affection and backing. The two men were very different in temperament and personality. Quiet, courtly, aloof, and introspective, Russell "dressed like a small-town banker and worked in an austere office devoid of any token of power or wealth." Johnson was flamboyant, earthy, and intimate, with a taste for plush surroundings and an inclination to self-promotion that Russell shunned. In his first Senate years, Johnson toned down his behavior to court Russell. Whereas he called other senators by their first names and aggressively barged into their offices without even a "how d'ya do," he always referred to Russell as "Senator Russell" and made polite overtures before entering his office. He impressed Russell as being "quiet and gentle" and doing "everything . . . with great deliberation and care."

As important, Lyndon was "thoughtful and attentive" toward Russell, who was a lonely bachelor. Johnson "took pains . . . to make his family Dick Russell's family," often having lunch with him at the Senate on Saturdays and inviting him home for weekend meals. To the Johnson daughters, he became "Uncle Dick." By November 1949, the two men had become so close that Russell spent part of the Thanksgiving holiday with Lyndon in Texas. "Ever since I reached home I have been wondering if I would wake up and find that I had just been dreaming that I had made a trip to Texas. Everything was so perfect that it is difficult to realize that it could happen in real life," he wrote Johnson. Lyndon replied: "As the most wide-awake man in the Senate, you need not worry that you were dreaming about your trip to Texas. It is all real and it is here 365 days a year waiting for Dick Russell to return and enjoy it."[69]

Johnson got close to Russell, but he consciously strove to avoid becoming "a profesional Southerner" like Russell. Hubert Humphrey remembered Russell as "smarter than others, shrewd in the ways of the Senate, brillant in tactics and parliamentary maneuver, and . . . constructive on most matters of foreign policy and on many domestic issues." But "his tremendous ability was weakened and corroded by his unalterable opposition to the passage of any legislation that would alleviate the plight of the black man throughout the nation. He was the victim of his region, the victim of a heritage of the past, unable to break out of the bonds of his own slavery." Russell himself told Harry McPherson, he "just let the twentieth century pass him by." Johnson wouldn't let that happen to him. As a liberal nationalist who wanted to rise above a regional identification, Lyndon put some distance between himself and Russell. Their relationship "intrigued" Hubert Humphrey. Johnson "was a close friend of Dick Russell's; a close associate of Walter George, who was a powerful senator from Georgia; he was on good working relationships with every southerner, but he wasn't quite southern. He was a different cut. He worked with them on all the issues they were interested in, the depletion allowances, and in the early days on civil rights. . . .

But the relationship was never what I considered an emotional one, it was a pragmatic one which later on was fully demonstrated, that it was very pragmatic." [70]

As part of Johnson's effort to be more than just a "southern" Senator, he established a relationship with Humphrey. A leading civil rights advocate who had alienated southerners by ramming a tough civil rights plank through the 1948 Democratic convention, Humphrey met a frosty reception from the conservative southerners who dominated the Senate. "My actions at the Democratic Convention," Humphrey recalled, "had elicited bitterness and antagonism far beyond what I expected. I was treated like an evil force that had seeped into sanctified halls." One afternoon as Humphrey walked from the Senate chamber past a group of southern senators, Russell said loud enough for Humphrey to hear: "Can you imagine the people of Minnesota sending that damn fool down here to represent them?" Vice President Alben Barkley was quoted as saying: "Minnesota is a great state—first they sent us their Ball [Senator Joseph Ball, 1940–49], then they sent us their Thye [Senator Edward Thye, 1946–59], and now they've sent us their goddam ass." Humphrey "was crushed. . . . Never in my life have I felt so unwanted as I did during those first months in Washington."

Humphrey's "apprenticeship of isolation" lasted about a year, or until "I got to know Lyndon Johnson, and that changed my role in the Senate." Taking up a suggestion from Russell Long of Louisiana that he start having lunch in the Senate dining room, where the Democrats dined at a community table and enjoyed a relaxed social hour without political discussion, Humphrey began to develop "a spirit of friendship" with southern Democrats, especially Lyndon. Johnson began inviting Humphrey to his office to talk about the Senate and legislation over a drink. Sometimes another Senator, usually Russell, would be present. Johnson and Russell now started to think of Humphrey as "a more pragmatic fellow" who "wanted to learn how to live with people." Similarly, Humphrey began to think of Johnson as not "a real conservative" but "a pragmatic moderate." While Humphrey's little group of twenty-five or so liberal Senators remained very suspicious of Johnson, Humphrey "looked upon him with more friendship . . . [and] felt that he was a lot more liberal . . . than he ever acted." For liberals in 1964 who wondered about Humphrey's willingness to become Johnson's Vice President, the explanation begins here in 1950. [71]

Johnson also made special efforts to maintain good relations with the White House. Although he had opposed the President on civil rights, natural gas legislation, and the Olds nomination, he had also voted for several pieces of Fair Deal legislation and demonstrated the kind of practical political savy and flexibility Truman understood and admired. At the same time, Lyndon cultivated a relationship with Clark Clifford,

the White House counsel, occasionally having him to dinner with Abe
Fortas to talk about political issues and problems. "It was during that
period," Clifford says, "that I remember breaking the ice by inviting
him to sit in at 'the poker game.' " Though Johnson took little pleasure
in the eight-handed poker Truman liked to play every other week, "he
enjoyed the contact with the President," especially the meal times on
summer weekends aboard the President's yacht floating down the Potomac. In the company of Truman, Clifford, Chief Justice Fred Vinson,
Senator Clinton Anderson of New Mexico, George Allen, Truman's close
friend, and occasionally, former Ambassador Averell Harriman, or Senator Robert Kerr, Johnson would listen to "Truman's marvelous reminiscing" and swap political gossip.[72]

White House affinity for Johnson also rested on a shared desire for
an effective military buildup against Communist expansion. In the summer of 1949, when strong navy advocates, in what the press called the
"Revolt of the Admirals," launched an attack on proponents of larger
air forces, including Air Force Secretary Stuart Symington, Johnson helped
defend the expansion of air power. In August and September, when the
Administration tried to appoint Carl Ilgenfritz, a U.S. Steel vice president, chairman of the Army-Navy Munitions Board, Johnson joined Harry
Byrd of Virginia and Wayne Morse of Oregon in leading a successful
fight against him. Truman's Secretary of Defense Louis Johnson and
Senate Armed Forces chairman Millard Tydings of Maryland wanted
Ilgenfritz to receive his $70,000 a year corporate pay instead of a $14,000-
a-year government salary. Johnson and 21 other Democrats and 18 Republicans objected that the arrangement would produce a conflict of
interest and hurt the defense program by undermining public support
and barring U.S. Steel from bidding on defense contracts. In addition,
Johnson took a leading part in fighting for a variety of defense appropriations, rubber and tin production programs, and absentee voting by
members of the armed forces. "You were the tower of strength on so
many pieces of legislation that it is hard to single out any one item as
the one for which you should receive the most thanks," Defense Secretary Johnson wrote him at the end of 1949.[73]

Shaken by Moscow's acquisition of an atomic bomb and the Communist takeover in China, the White House valued congressional leaders who shared its concern to strengthen the country's capacity to cope
with the Communist threat. Publicly urging the development of guided
missiles, Johnson declared, "For push-button war, we have neither the
push nor the button." He called for a recognition of the need to make
full use of the country's scientific and technological resources to defend
itself and of the reality that "the period of challenge will last many years."
Although some of his criticisms were directed against the Administration for being too slow to push defense needs, most of what he said

echoed White House concern to convert the Congress and the country to more defense spending. In National Security Council (NSC) 68, the blueprint for a twenty-year Cold War initialed by Truman in April 1950, the Administration committed itself to a long-term struggle against Communism and the creation of a domestic consensus for higher taxes to pay for hydrogen bombs and a buildup of conventional forces that could protect U.S. interests without atomic war. As a member of the Armed Services Committee, Johnson was privy to and in close harmony with Administration thinking.[74]

Johnson also fully supported the Administration's decision to fight in Korea. On June 25, Communist North Korea launched an attack across the 38th parallel which separated it from the American-supported Republic of South Korea. Truman believed that the attack represented a challenge to the free world reminiscent of Hitler's aggression against Czechoslovakia in 1938. He was also convinced that Western security and the principle of collective security embodied in the United Nations required a firm response. Truman announced his determination to meet force with force. Although he called his decision a "police action" and made no request for a congressional declaration of war, which he feared might produce "endless criticism" and a "derogation of presidential power," his commitment to fight in Korea received almost universal approval in the United States; conservatives and liberals alike rallied to the President's side. "I have lived and worked in and out of this city for 20 years," the journalist Joseph C. Harsh wrote in the *Christian Science Monitor* on June 29. "Never before in that time have I felt such a sense of relief and unity pass through the city. . . . Mr. Truman obviously did . . . almost exactly what most individuals seemed to wish he would do."[75]

"The President's decision was courageous and essential and I support it," Lyndon announced. "History may prove that this was the turning point of the Cold War. The world has expected the United States to lead the free nations unafraid and unbullied. Now we are showing that we mean what we say." He also wrote Truman to express "my deep gratitude for and admiration of your courageous response to the challenge of this grave hour." Johnson pledged to make his work on the Armed Services Committee "contribute to the success of our undertaking." Truman's reply was a brief but warm expression of appreciation for Lyndon's "assurance of helpfulness in our undertaking to champion liberty wherever the tyranny of communism is the aggressor."[76]

The Korean War presented Johnson with a dual opportunity. On one hand, it meant a chance to press Americans to recognize what he saw as the terrible dangers facing the country. On the other, it opened the way to a larger role for himself in national affairs that would make it difficult for anyone to dislodge him from his Senate seat. Convinced that "the survival of the ruling clique in Russia depends upon conflict" or that "Russia needs . . . and wants war," Johnson described the Korean attack as part of a Soviet design for world domination. In a Senate speech sixteen days after Truman committed American forces to fight in Korea, Johnson said: "Never before, during my experience, has the nation been in such grave peril as it is at this moment." Although he counseled against recrimination over who had brought the country to this state of affairs, he sharply attacked the Administration's stinginess with the military which had left the country with only "50 percent of the military might we need" to fight in Korea. He urged an end to the policy of "delay—defeat—retreat" through the immediate call up of all National Guard and Reserve units and the "full mobilization of our industrial capacity." "We are presently in the midst of a grave national emergency," he declared on July 17. "In the minds of all of us there is at least the strong possibility that we may be approaching World War III." [77]

As his contribution to the war effort, he wished to chair a watchdog committee similar to the one Truman had presided over during World War II. After consultations with Russell and Millard Tydings, the Armed Services Committee chairman, Johnson won approval for the creation of such a subcommittee on July 17.

His assumption that he would become the subcommittee's chair ran into opposition during the next ten days. Tydings's seniority gave him first claim to the chairmanship. Since the position seemed likely to give its recipient considerable public attention, Tydings considered taking it. In the first half of 1950, after Republican senator Joseph McCarthy of Wisconsin had issued a series of sensational charges about Communists in the State Department, the Senate had set up a committee under Tydings to investigate. When Tydings demonstrated that McCarthy's charges were bogus, McCarthy attacked him as a Red stooge who was part of a plot to clear subversives in the State Department. Although a conservative, anti-New Deal Democrat whom FDR had tried to purge in 1938, Tydings was thrown on the defensive and saw the chairmanship of Johnson's subcommittee as an effective means to serve a reelection campaign in 1950. Fearful that Johnson might use the subcommittee too aggressively against the Administration, the White House also favored having Tydings in the chair. When Tydings learned, however, that McCarthy planned to campaign actively against him in Maryland, he gave up thoughts of chairing the subcommittee and devoted himself instead to an unsuccessful reelection fight. [78]

Journalists, Johnson aides, and the White House all saw political motives behind Johnson's creation and leadership of the subcommittee. "Because an obscure Senator named Harry Truman parlayed an innocuous resolution for similar policing of World War II into the Presidency of the United States," Doris Fleeson wrote in the *St. Louis Post Dispatch*, "unusual interest attaches both to the subcommittee's plans and the personality of its chairman." When Leslie Carpenter published an article in *Collier's* about Johnson early in 1951, the lead sentence described him as "a likely Democratic Vice-Presidential nominee for 1952. His war-investigating subcommittee may do for him what it did for ex-Senator Truman." Years later, when interviewers asked Walter Jenkins and Gerald Siegel, another aide, whether Johnson considered the political implications of his assignment, they were certain he had: "I'm sure he did," Walter Jenkins said. "No question, no question about that," was Siegel's reply.[79]

Truman saw similar motives at work. When Defense Secretary Louis Johnson told the President about an upcoming meeting with Lyndon's subcommittee, Truman replied: "I am returning the letter from Lyndon Johnson, together with the subjects he desires to cover. Apparently he has never read about the conduct of the war in the 1860s." Truman was referring to a joint congressional committee on the conduct of the Civil War that had caused Lincoln problems by interfering with military strategy and operations; Truman wanted Lyndon and his subcommittee to understand that they could do more harm than good. In fact, he saw no need for either Johnson's Senate subcommittee or one being set up in the House under Emanuel Celler of New York. In a letter to Celler, Truman said that his World War II committee had been established to help meet the emergency for military construction in the United States. "We are confronted with an entirely different situation now— . . . we have no major construction jobs which the Government will have to undertake. . . . We have the Military Branch of the Government on a completely coordinated basis. . . . Of course, it is not for me to tell the Congress what to do . . . but it seems to me that the Standing Committees of the House and the Senate . . . are perfectly capable of carrying on such investigations as are necessary."[80]

Lyndon largely disarmed White House antipathy by informing Truman of his plans. At the beginning of August, he sent Matthew Connelly, the President's secretary, a statement of subcommittee intentions with particular paragraphs marked for the President's attention. These included promises not to hunt headlines or "exploit the sensational," or become "a Monday morning quarterback club, second-guessing battle-front strategy." Lyndon followed this up by requesting a private off-the-record discussion with the President. Their meeting on August 8 was an exercise in mutual stroking. Johnson won Truman's backing by pointing out that the special subcommittee would forestall the Government Operations Committee, on which Joe McCarthy sat, from investigating the war effort. Johnson "asked for advice and assistance, discussed staff leadership, pitfalls, and received an invitation to bring the full committee to the White House at any time." Truman "heartily" approved the subcommittee's statements "as some of the finest ever to be made by a

Senate committee." Truman urged him to "go right ahead, on the charted course; if anything is wrong, come and tell him about it and it will be remedied." Johnson described the session as " 'the finest meeting' that could 'possibly be had.' "[81]

Johnson's direction of the subcommittee during the next five months won him national approval and projected him into the forefront of the Democratic party. His success rested on a genuine commitment to advancing the war effort with little regard for partisan considerations. Although his anxieties about a world-wide Communist threat seem much overdrawn in retrospect, they were sincere and spurred him to press the case for a more effective mobilization of resources to fight the war. Between August and January, the subcommittee produced the first four of what eventually would be forty-four reports. They criticized the Administration and Federal agencies for "paperwork preparedness," a "siesta psychology," and "business as usual" attitude. Specifically, they complained about a government Munitions Board which continued to sell "critically-needed surplus property" to industry, including synthetic rubber plants, and failed to make effective plans to stockpile sufficient amounts of rubber, nickel, tin, and wool.[82]

The four reports, as with the subsequent forty, received unanimous support from the seven subcommittee members and widespread national praise. Although consisting of four Democrats, Johnson and three other freshman senators, Virgil Chapman of Kentucky, Lester Hunt of Wyoming, and Estes Kefauver of Tennessee, and three senior Republicans, Styles Bridges of New Hampshire, Wayne Morse of Oregon, and Leverett Saltonstall of Massachusetts, Johnson was able to maintain a consensus among them. The three Democrats and Saltonstall were amenable to Johnson's bipartisan leadership. But Bridges and Morse were more independent and needed special attention to ensure their support of subcommittee investigations and conclusions. In their meeting on August 8, Truman had warned Johnson that Bridges was unfriendly to the Administration and could be a problem, but he "could be handled by 'buttering him up' and letting him get some headlines." More important to Bridges, Johnson never tried to whitewash the Administration, and according to Walter Jenkins Bridges "worked hand in glove with Mr. Johnson." Morse, who was notoriously independent and combative, also enthusiastically supported Johnson's readiness to get at the "facts" and follow wherever they led.[83]

Even the White House acknowledged that Johnson's subcommittee was acting in the national interest and readily accepted its proposals. In September, after Truman read the subcommittee's first report, which criticized Hubert E. Howard, Munitions Board chairman, for ineffective administration and singled out the Board's failure to stockpile enough rubber to supply the military and hold down civilian prices, the President fired Howard and ordered an increase in synthetic rubber production. Quoting Morse, Johnson wrote Truman, "You have set a magnificent example for all components of the government in cooperating with this committee." Johnson also thanked the President for replacing Howard, saying "it should provide a timely shot in the arm for that agency's service to the nation."[84]

To Johnson's great satisfaction, he now reaped a harvest of nationwide praise in the press. Led by columnist Arthur Knock in the *New York Times*, newspapers and magazines across the country lauded Johnson, the subcommittee and its able staff headed by Donald Cook, the vice chairman of the Securities and Exchange Commission. Krock called the first report "a model of its kind in that (1) it is unaffected by partisan or political considerations; (2) goes to the heart of the subject of military surplus disposal and rubber stockpiling; and (3) gives specific instances of sleeping bureaucracy and the successful methods used to awaken it. . . . The seven Senators . . . are all practicing politicians. . . . But in this first report . . . there is not a trace of the political animation by which, for example, Democratic Executives are 'taken care of' by Democratic legislators and their lapses are magnified by Republican legislators." By December, a memo on subcommittee prospects for 1951 concluded that it had "benefited from an unprecedented display of confidence in the national press."[85]

The bipartisanship and favorable press response that surrounded the subcommittee's actions masked the intense political maneuvering that went on behind the scenes. However eager most Democrats and Republicans may have been to suspend normal political combat in the midst of a national crisis, neither side could resist the opportunities for partisan advantage. At a meeting on June 25 among Truman and his advisers, Under Secretary of State James Webb suggested that they "talk about the political aspects of the situation. We're not going to talk about politics," the President snapped. "I'll handle the political affairs." The next day, before Truman announced his decision to fight, Republican Senators Bridges and William Knowland of California attacked the indecisiveness of the Democratic administration. The President's decision to use force quieted these voices temporarily, but conservatives in both parties, led by Joe McCarthy, and Pat McCarran of Nevada on the Democratic side, kept up a steady drum beat of criticism about the Administration's weak response to the Communist threat. "American boys lie dead in the mud of Korean valleys," McCarthy wrote Truman in July, because the congressional program for Korea "was sabotaged." In September, McCarran pushed an Internal Security bill through Congress that assaulted traditional civil liberties in the name of anticommunism.

Despite Truman's veto and grave reservations in Congress about the constitutionality of the law, congressmen and senators, who believed their political lives at stake, overrode the President's veto.[86]

Johnson was no less mindful of the political gains and losses that could be had from the war crisis. His committee was a vehicle for advancing not only the war effort but also his political ambition. "Some consideration should be given to how the office will henceforth handle contacts with various agencies which will come under the jurisdiction of my committee," Johnson said in a memo to his staff about constituent problems with defense agencies. "Extreme caution will be used in 'following up' . . . on decisions made on contracts. . . . It would be most embarrassing if the subcommittee's investigation led to examination of a file showing that the chairman had apparently insisted upon favoritism or other than routine regular action on the merits," Johnson said. He was intensely concerned at the end of 1950 to preserve the positive image his subcommittee had created. "Today the Committee is unchallenged—in the public mind—as the official 'watch dog,'" a staff member concluded. Yet a serious challenge to the subcommittee's "accuracy, its methods, or its purposes, either from within the government or from without is surely inevitable." To fend off such charges, the staff member suggested that the subcommittee hold more hearings to prevent the individuals and agencies being criticized from complaining that they were "not being heard." To justify itself, the subcommittee also would eventually have to uncover "an individual crook." "If this committee doesn't catch a 'crook,' some other Committee may and that is going to hurt this Committee," especially if the individual turned up in an agency the Johnson subcommittee was overseeing.[87]

The initial success of the preparedness subcommittee partly came from an identification with American military victories in the first five months of the war. After halting the North Korean advance in July, American forces under General Douglas MacArthur landed behind North Korean lines at Inchon in mid-September. By October, North Korean troops had been cleared from the South and MacArthur's forces had moved above the 38th parallel with the intention of conquering North Korea and unifying the peninsula under South Korean control. Despite warnings from Peking that it would not allow the fall of North Korea and the creation of a hostile state on its Manchurian border, American troops advanced to the Yalu River. On November 26, two days after MacArthur had announced an end-the-war offensive, 200,000 Chinese troops crossed the Yalu into North Korea and began a rout of American forces that lasted almost two months and drove them back below the 38th parallel.

The intensification of the war inspired renewed militancy in the United States. The Administration declared a state of national emergency, proposed a nearly fourfold rise in the defense budget, increased the size of the army by 50 percent to 3.5 million men, and hinted at the use of atomic weapons. Johnson now deplored the nation's failure to adopt permanent mobilization policies during the previous six months, saying "we have thrown up a chicken-wire fence, not a wall of armed might." "Makeshift mobilization" and Washington "doubletalk" would no longer satisfy the American people who wanted effective action. Johnson urged an overall global plan that outlined America's diplomatic and military aims for the next twenty years. Further, he proposed full mobilization of the nation's manpower and economic resources. The country would require wage and price controls for the forseeable future and would have to reduce government domestic programs for the sake of defense spending. If "our Nation, our civilization, our world" were to avoid "being engulfed by a gathering darkness," there would have to be a period of sacrifice with more guns and less butter.

Johnson's appeal for an expanded war effort was sincere. But he also saw it as good politics. However much the country was behind the government in the Korean fighting, there was a growing frustration with the Administration. This excited Republican hopes for renewed control of Congress and the White House, and made numerous Democrats reluctant to be too closely identified with Truman's policies. In the November 1950 congressional elections, even before the reversal of battlefield fortunes, the Democrats had lost twenty-eight seats in the House and five in the Senate, where a twelve-seat advantage had shrunk to two. Scott Lucas, the Democratic party's Majority Leader, Francis Myers of Pennsylvania, the party Whip, Millard Tydings, chairman of the Armed Services Committee, and Elbert D. Thomas of Utah, chairman of the Labor Committee, had all gone down to defeat. Richard Nixon had won an open seat in California by labeling liberal congresswoman Helen Gahagan Douglas the "pink lady."[88]

The election results and Johnson's political effectiveness catapulted him into running for party Whip. Lister Hill of Alabama had resigned the job in January 1949 to put some distance between himself and a Democratic administration sponsoring civil rights reforms. Since both the Democratic Leader and Whip had been defeated in 1950, many saw appointment to either party office as more of a liability than a prize. When Bobby Baker suggested to Johnson that he become Whip, Johnson answered, laughing, "You'll destroy me, because I can't afford to be identified with the Democratic party right now." But this was truer for Ernest W. McFarland of Arizona, who became the new Majority Leader in 1951, than for Johnson. A fairly conservative Democrat who had voted against the FEPC and shown few qualities of leadership in his ten-year Senate career, McFarland was Richard Russell's choice. With only two years to go in his term and a poor chance for reelection, McFarland was a sort of sacrificial lamb. He lost his seat in 1952.[89]

By contrast with Lister Hill, Scott Lucas, Francis Myers, and Mc-Farland, Johnson could afford to be a party leader or take the Whip's job without fear of defeat. His opposition to Truman's civil rights proposals and Leland Olds and his support of natural gas deregulation and all-out mobilization against the Communist threat made him popular in Texas. "People in Texas are *bitter* in their criticism of the administration, and especially Truman," Jake Pickle wrote him on December 26, 1950. But everyone Pickle talked to thought Johnson was "really on the ball. They give you high praise for having the courage to be the 'voice in the wilderness.' They think you have proven your . . . grasp of international matters—and the people strongest against you in 1948 are your big backers now." [90]

Other circumstances had come together to make Johnson a leading candidate for party Whip. A conservative-liberal split among Democratic senators made a moderate with a foot in each camp a way to hold the party together. Although McFarland had voted against the FEPC and some other Fair Deal measures, he claimed an 85 percent party regularity in his votes and was acceptable to the White House. Johnson had also established himself as a party centrist. His anti-civil rights stand and militant anticommunism gave him credibility with conservatives, while his support of domestic social programs redeemed him with liberals like Humphrey. "Despite his deviations from the administration program," Leslie Carpenter wrote in *Collier's* in February 1951, "Johnson is, generally speaking, a Fair Dealer." [91]

Robert Kerr and Richard Russell saw the wisdom of making Johnson party Whip. Kerr, who was eager to become a party kingmaker, initially urged Clinton Anderson of New Mexico for the post. But when Anderson showed no interest, Kerr made Johnson his candidate. Russell was reluctant to have two men from the Southwest as formal party leaders, but Lyndon's attributes outweighed this disadvantage. Because McFarland, a heavy-set, easygoing man, was not very energetic, Russell believed that Johnson "would make up for whatever deficiencies there might be in McFarland. . . . Russell was a very shrewd man," George Reedy says. "I think . . . he realized that Johnson would work much harder simply because it could be regarded as an advancement. He had very correctly gauged Johnson as the kind of a man who would work his head off if he were presented with a new challenge." In addition, Russell now saw Johnson as "a man of tremendous competence, ability, [and] patriotism." According to Donald Cook, the "remarkable" work that Johnson did on the preparedness subcommittee won him the admiration of Russell and other senators. [92]

Johnson was eager to take the job. John Stennis of Mississippi remembers that Lyndon called him in Mississippi to ask his support. Stennis was candid: "Lyndon, you might have known that I wasn't just going to promise a whole lot out of the clear sky . . . Senator Russell and I are very close and . . . I would naturally consult with him before I would give a final answer to anyone." Johnson answered: "You must think that I am foolish . . . I wouldn't have been calling you or anyone else about voting for this position unless I already had a firm position from Dick Russell that I am the man." Though liberal senators made some bows in the direction of Alabama's John Sparkman, on January 2, 1951, by acclamation, Johnson became the youngest Whip in party history.[93]

During his two years in the Senate, Johnson had moved quickly to establish himself in the front rank of his colleagues. It was part of a strategy for winning reelection in 1954. It was typical of him to seek a lead role; but in this instance he also saw it as essential for his political survival. When combined with the benefits he brought Texas from his service in the upper house, he expected his national and party prominence to erase the shadow of his 87-vote victory in 1948 and make him a shoo-in for another term.

12

For Country, Party, and Self

LYNDON'S election as majority Whip in January 1951 encouraged a belief among Washington insiders that he was a rising star in the Senate and Democratic party. In the first five months of the year, articles in *Collier's* and *The Saturday Evening Post*, two mass-circulation magazines, described him as a political phenomenon, a standout in the "star-packed Freshman Class of 1948." A fellow senator called him "the most effective freshman he has seen in . . . eighteen years." One high ranking Administration official dubbed him a "man of destiny," while the magazines described him as "just about the hottest young senator in the Capitol," a lifetime senator, if he wanted to be, and a leading vice-presidential candidate in 1952 or 1956. Since Johnson had entered the Senate, the *Post* pointed out, "twelve young Texans have been hopefully named Lyndon. . . . Today, like twelve smiling young apostles, their photographs hang from the senator's office wall, silent testimony to the fact that his influence already has passed into another generation."

Johnson relished the notoriety. Journalist and later Johnson biographer Alfred Steinberg remembers an interview with him in the spring of 1951 when Johnson tried to persuade him to write an article not on congressional leaders but "a whole big article on just me alone." In the lavishly furnished President's Room off the Senate floor, where Presidents since Lincoln had come when visiting the Senate, Johnson "sat with his knees pressed against mine, a hand clutching my lapel, and his nose only inches away from my nose. When he leaned forward, I leaned back at an uncomfortable angle. 'What would the pitch of an article on you be?' " Steinberg asked. " 'That you might be a Vice-Presidential candidate for 1952?' . . . 'Vice President hell!' he whispered. 'Who wants that? . . . President! That's the angle you want to write about me. . . . You can build up to it by saying how I run both houses of Congress right now.' " Steinberg asked for an explanation of this extraordinary claim: " 'Well, right here in the Senate I have to do all of Boob McFarland's work because he can't do any of it.. . . . And then every afternoon I go over to Sam Rayburn's place. He tells me all about the problems he's facing in the House, and I tell him how to handle them. So that's how come I'm running everything here in the Capitol,' he finished, gripping me above the knee." [1]

Johnson was a master of self-promotion and loved the attention he won so quickly in the Senate. Yet at the same time, he was not as confident about his future as his conversation with Steinberg made it appear. For all his bravado about running the Congress and being presidential timber, he remained uncertain about his political career, even fearing that something unexpected might jeopardize his Senate seat. He knew that men of consuming ambition like himself who cut corners to get ahead and made both powerful enemies and friends could just as quickly be brought down as elevated to higher station. Instead of seeing the *Post* article, for example, as a boost to his career, he puzzled over its value. He objected to the *Post*'s characterization of him as "The Frantic Gentleman from Texas," who is "taut as a bowstring," and the suggestion that he had his eye on the vice presidency. His reaction amazed, "flabbergasted," and "baffled" George Reedy, who saw the piece as the sort of thing highly paid public-relations men would have turned somersaults to arrange. [2]

Johnson was also of two minds about his election as Whip. Although he had pushed hard to get the job, he doubted its worth. When his old friend Justice William O. Douglas wrote to congratulate him, he replied: "I don't know whether you should congratulate or commiserate with me on my selection as Majority Whip. I think you will grant it is a moot question—perhaps a 5 to 4 decision is indicated." To be sure, the job carried no real power. The Whip was little more than a front man for the party's power brokers, a sort of honorary clerk or messenger who collected information for the party Leader on how Democratic senators would vote. "The whip's job is a nothing job," Johnson told Steinberg. "Skeeter Johnston [secretary to the Senate Majority Leader] can keep track of the way the Democratic senators are going to vote without wasting any of my time." The Whip also had to spend more time in Washington away from constituents than other senators, and that had contributed to Francis Myer's defeat in November 1950. Financier and prominent Democrat Bernard Baruch told Johnson that being Whip also might limit his freedom as chair of the preparedness subcommittee to criticize the Administration's defense programs.

Yet for Lyndon the job offered more plusses than minuses. A one-room hideaway office in the Capitol and a front row center aisle desk on the Senate floor when McFarland was absent were two advantages. The job also widened his contacts with other senators and the White House, where he was now included in legislative conferences. In the words of *Newsweek* journalist Sam Shaffer, "it lifted him out of the rut of freshman senator," and allowed him to "be noticed." Most important, it enlarged his reputation in Texas, where newspapers carried stories about his "remarkable recognition" after only two years in the Senate as "one of the most powerful men in the Capital." State pride in his accomplishment was bound to help his chances of reelection.[3]

Much could happen, however, in the four years before he would face the voters. He took nothing for granted. Another Senate term required continuing attention to constituent needs and the nation's security. He particularly wished to serve the Korean war effort through the work of his preparedness subcommittee. Leadership of an investigative committee was, more than ever, an excellent vehicle for building his political reputation. The first session of the 82nd Congress devoted more time and money to investigations than any Congress in American history. One hundred and thirty committee probes into everything from Communism and crime to government waste appealed to legislators on both sides of the aisle as surefire means of commanding public attention and advancing political careers.[4]

Mobilizing military manpower topped Lyndon's agenda in 1951, an issue he had spoken to forcefully, if with limited impact, during World War II. The Korean fighting had renewed public interest in the problem. In 1948, the Congress had passed a draft law requiring nonveterans between the ages of nineteen and twenty-six to serve for twenty-one months. The military, however, inducted only about 30,000 men during the next two years. When the Korean war began, the United States had only one and one-third divisions at home and some understrength and undertrained occupation forces in Japan. To ensure that the country would not be caught short in a future military crisis, the Truman administration in the summer of 1950 had proposed a revision of the draft law to include eighteen-year-olds and extend the term of service to 27 months. It also asked for a program of Universal Military Training (UMT), requiring all young men to serve six months' active duty and seven and a half years in the reserves. Opponents of a UMT law cited dangers to traditional freedoms from a standing army.[5]

Johnson shared the Administration's belief that a revised draft and universal military training would do more to save the country's freedom than endanger it. In August 1950, after the Senate Armed Services Committee had suspended hearings on draft revision and UMT, Richard Russell asked Johnson's preparedness subcommittee to draft a law covering both matters. Working closely with the Administration, Johnson steered a bill through his committee and the Senate in the spring of 1951. Truman, Secretary of Defense George Marshall, and Russell praised him for doing "a whale of a job," and a United Press story from Washington marveled at Johnson's skill in getting the UMT part of the draft bill, a measure "loaded with controversial issues," through the Senate with only five votes against it.

On June 19, Johnson was in the front rank of White House guests as the President signed the act into law. The bill, however, was significantly watered down from its original form. The draft-age was lowered to only 18 ½, the term of service extended to only 24 months, and UMT could become a reality only after a national commission had developed a more detailed work plan. Although 60 percent of Americans favored implementation of the UMT program and leading members of the Senate, including Johnson, wanted prompt action, the House shelved a bill to set up a national commission in the spring of 1952. Opposed by a vocal minority, the measure impressed House members as too hot to handle in an election year.[6]

Convinced that recommendations for a more efficient use of military manpower would advance the war effort and receive widespread support, Johnson devoted a substantial amount of subcommittee time to the question in 1951. In June the subcommittee reported that sixteen military indoctrination centers had enough superfluous "housekeeping jobs" to create three to five combat divisions. The subcommittee's thirty-first report in October identified six navy and marine corps training centers, where men were being misused in the performance of "minor duties." The following month the subcommittee made headlines across the country when it described Washington, D.C., as top heavy with admirals, generals, and civilian administrators. In 1951 the armed forces consisted of some 3.5 million men compared with more than 12 million in 1945. Yet the number of admirals and generals had dropped only about 10 percent from 397 to 361 and civilian Defense Department employees only some 8 percent, from 98,000 to 91,000. In its fortieth report in 1952, the subcommittee urged the Secretary of Defense to create a civilian panel that would recommend "the more efficient and economical use of military personnel."[7]

By 1952, the subcommittee's attention had shifted to Johnson's long-standing concern, air power. In November 1951, when the preparedness subcommittee issued a report on defense production, it warned that "deliveries on . . . planes, tanks, ships, and guns have fallen dangerously behind schedule. . . . We are not achieving as rapidly as possible the minimum necessary force essential for the security of the United States." Although aircraft production was ahead of other arms deliveries, it was running almost two years behind what Johnson and others believed would match Soviet air power in 1952. Military chiefs, however, disputed

Johnson's findings, contending that original estimates of Soviet strength were exaggerated and that a 1954 target of 95 air wings would satisfy the national security. In March 1952, when the Administration announced a further postponement of its airpower goal from 1954 to 1955, Johnson declared his intention to make a full review of American air forces, especially comparing U.S. and Soviet air production and quality of aircraft.[8]

The inquiry over the next two months, the most extensive ever made by the subcommittee, further alarmed Johnson and his colleagues. Testimony from the nation's highest ranking officers indicated that the "most serious possible danger to the United States" from Soviet air strength was likely to be in 1954. Yet the Administration was content to achieve "full Air Force readiness" in 1955, while the House of Representatives was proposing to "further stretch out Air readiness from 1955 to 1957." To influence current deliberations on air force appropriations, Johnson's subcommittee rushed out a report in June citing the Joint Chiefs' view that 1954 was "the crucial year," described the "stretch-out" on an air buildup as strictly for "budgetary" and "not military reasons," and warned that "a further stretch-out would reduce our defenses below sane levels and be an invitation to disaster." Whatever the problems facing the air buildup, "they must be solved because the alternative is extinction of our way of life." In a final "definitive report on aircraft production and air preparedness" issued in August, the subcommittee characterized the Administration's air power program as "abuse, misuse and disuse of power."[9]

Both then and later some government officials and journalists saw Johnson's air power assessments and his overall view of the dangers to American security as greatly exaggerated. Members of a Senate-House production committee and high Defense Department officials did not share Johnson's anxieties about the state of the country's defenses and praised Administration leaders for "an outstanding job of defense mobilization." Johnson himself knew that some of his concerns were questionable. George Reedy had told him that a November 1951 subcommittee report saying arms deliveries were behind schedule and "too much production was going into luxuries and not enough into military necessities" had rested on pretty thin evidence. The subcommittee had no precise schedules behind which production had fallen and was unable to point to specific examples of defense materials being diverted to nonessential production.[10]

Journalist and LBJ biographer Ronnie Dugger sees Johnson's views on defense issues in 1951–52 as "a Strangelovian transport of patriotism and military desperation." Johnson believed "a final showdown with the Reds" was inevitable: "Someday, somewhere, someway, there must be a clear-cut settlement between the forces of freedom and the forces of communism," he declared in a speech in Texas. "It is foolish to talk of avoiding war. We are already in a war—a major war. The war in Korea is a war of Soviet Russia." He believed it essential for Americans to understand and the Soviets to assume that the United States would not fight other police actions against Russian satellites while Moscow got off scot-free. He told a luncheon of civic leaders in Dallas that he favored a declaration to the men who sit behind the walls of the Kremlin—" 'We are tired of fighting your stooges. . . . The next aggression will be the last. We will strike back not at your satellites—but you. . . . and it will be a crushing blow.' "[11]

Johnson's concerns were exaggerated and his solutions now seem unthinkable. But they reflected what most of the country and its highest officials believed at the time. And they appealed to Lyndon as good politics, especially in Texas, where anticommunism remained at fever pitch. A series of Gallup polls in 1950–52 found that 81 percent of the American people saw Russia as "trying to build herself up to be the ruling power of the world"; 55 percent thought Korea meant we were already in World War III; nearly 75 percent wished to see a doubling of defense expenditures; two-thirds favored using atom bombs on Russia first or before they used them on us in an all-out war; 82 percent opposed any drop in defense spending after the Korean war ended; 56 percent saw Russian threats to peace as the most important problem facing the country; and 51 percent were ready to see the United States use the atom bomb on military targets in Korea.[12]

American political leaders shared and encouraged the public's militant anticommunism. President Truman privately speculated on an all-out war with Russia and China in which the major cities and manufacturing centers of both countries would be "eliminated." Liberal senator Hubert Humphrey paid tribute to Johnson's leadership of his preparedness subcommittee, and liberal economist Eliot Janeway found stirrings wherever he went "in constructive response to the warnings of the Johnson Committee. It has become *the* leadership organ of our national defense program," Janeway told a Texas journalist, "and Senator Johnson himself is rapidly growing into one of our major national figures. I assume that you are aware of the close and sympathetic attention which the editors of *Newsweek* constantly give his work."[13]

However much Johnson's hawkishness stirred and reflected national fears, he did not relish an unwinnable war with the Soviet Union and China that would leave all the belligerents devastated by atomic bombs. Consequently, in April 1951, when President Truman dismissed General Douglas MacArthur for publicly challenging Administration policy of limiting the war to Korea, Johnson sided with the President.

MacArthur's repeated insubordination had provoked Truman's action. In August 1950, in defiance of a presidential decision that Chinese

Nationalist forces not be used in Korea or unleashed to invade mainland China from Formosa, MacArthur had publicly urged such actions. In January 1951, MacArthur had asked permission to blockade the China coast, launch air attacks on Chinese military and industrial installations, and bring Nationalist troops into the fighting. Truman rejected the plan as likely to lead to a wider war. Undeterred, in late March, MacArthur had publicly urged the Chinese military commander to discuss surrender terms with him and warned of direct attacks on Chinese territory. On April 5, Republican House leader Joe Martin had read a letter from MacArthur decrying the limits on his freedom to fight the Korean war and saying: "There is no substitute for victory." On April 11, Truman relieved MacArthur of his command, citing the constitutional requirement of military subordination to civil authority.[14]

MacArthur's dismissal provoked an outpouring of sympathy for the General and antagonism to the Truman administration equal to any explosion of public feeling in American history. Tumultuous crowds and rhetorical hyperbole greeted MacArthur's return to the United States. On April 17, a half-million people cheered his arrival in San Francisco. He received "an almost hysterical welcome" at the Washington, D.C., airport and moved people to tears with his address to a joint session of Congress on the 19th. Recalling a refrain from a popular barracks ballad of his days at West Point, he declared: "Old soldiers never die; they just fade away." Overwhelmed by the moment, one Harvard-educated congressman said: "We saw a great hunk of God in the flesh, and we heard the voice of God." Herbert Hoover considered MacArthur the "reincarnation of St. Paul into a great General of the Army who came out of the East." An estimated 7.5 million people, nearly twice the crowd cheering Eisenhower's return from Europe in 1945, turned out for MacArthur's visit to New York City.

At the same time, MacArthur's supporters excoriated the Truman government. Republican senator William Jenner of Indiana said it had placed the country "in the hands of a secret inner coterie . . . directed by agents of the Soviet Union." He urged Truman's impeachment and the revelation of "the secret invisible government which has so cleverly led our country down the road to destruction." Senator Richard Nixon called MacArthur's dismissal appeasement of world communism; Senator Joseph McCarthy believed it a prelude to the loss of Asia, the Pacific, and Europe to communism; and the Republican Policy Committee declared it preparation for a "super-Munich" in Asia.[15]

Johnson's initial reaction to MacArthur's recall was a clear statement of support for Truman. Although he regretted MacArthur's dismissal, he believed it "essential that civilian control over the military be maintained. . . . The basic issue is whether American policy shall be made by the elected officials of the government who are responsible to the people or by military leaders who are responsible only to their immediate superiors." His viewpoint was not popular with most Texans and other Americans who wrote him and other senators. Three days after Truman's action, an aide reported that the Senate postoffice was receiving the largest flow of mail in its history, an estimated two million letters. Walter Jenkins recalled that the MacArthur controversy produced "the largest single mail that we ever had on one issue." Most of it was favorable to the General and called for Truman's impeachment. Johnson's initial attempt to answer these correspondents with an expression of regard for MacArthur but support for Truman subjected him to angry abuse. "Nuts!" one woman scribbled across his reply, and declared his letter "only Acheson propaganda." Another resented the "insult [to] my intelligence by a parrot-like repetition of the refrain adopted by the administration bootlickers." [16]

The powerful emotional response favoring MacArthur troubled Johnson. When Clint Murchison, the Texas oil man, wrote to warn that MacArthur was "going to cause disunity among the people . . . [and] sink the Democratic Party into oblivion for the next twenty years," Johnson replied: "I am trying my best to think this whole thing through. Seeing and hearing MacArthur yesterday in his magnificent performance [before the Congress] convinces me that it is more important than ever that the MacArthur movement not be allowed to 'roll over the American people.' Frankly, I don't think I have got the answer figured out as yet." [17]

Others in the Administration and the Congress found an effective solution to the problem, which Johnson fully endorsed. Immediately after MacArthur's dismissal, Republican congressional leaders had called for an investigation of the Administration's foreign and military policy and a chance for the General to present his views. The Democrats seized upon the idea as a means of exhausting public interest in the debate and mounting a political counterattack against him. Hearings conducted jointly by the Senate Foreign Relations and Armed Service committees with Richard Russell in the chair seemed like a fine way to give MacArthur his day in court and demonstrate to the country that his strategy would have risked a wider war. [18]

Johnson played a significant part in the hearings. He lent his aides George Reedy and Gerald Siegel to the joint committee for the laborious staff work involved in the investigation. Committee members believed that national security considerations dictated against open hearings. But some felt that the prompt release of substantial information was essential if the country were to understand just how questionable MacArthur's ideas were, and they used Reedy to release sanitized testimony to the press. The committee's promptness in making information available surprised and pleased reporters. At the same time, Reedy and Siegel spent nights formulating questions for committee members to ask the next day. Siegel remembered that Johnson and "Don Cook would take the product of our night work and brief Senator Russell in the early part of the morning before the next day's hearings began." These questions showed that MacArthur was "wrong in his analysis of the policies that should have been implemented in the Korean War." How could he know how Moscow and Peking would respond to aerial attacks and a blockade of China? Would America's allies and the United Nations join us in a wider war, and if not, could we defend Europe and Asia without them? If Chinese Nationalist forces were brought into the fighting, could we rely on them? Were we prepared to make an effective defense of Japan? How wide a war did he consider acceptable? [19]

During the hearings, Johnson exposed MacArthur's questionable ideas. As one journalist wrote, he "tried hard to get General MacArthur to admit that he didn't know too much about our responsibilities in Europe and cared less." Johnson also asked his opinion of UMT. MacArthur said that he had never given the subject "the slightest thought." Johnson's questions suggested that MacArthur had given little consideration to problems confronting the United States beyond the Far East, particularly the capacity of the United States to fight a wider war. Johnson also asked him what the United States should do if the Chinese retreated across the Yalu and then refused to sign a treaty. Although MacArthur refused to see this as a likely outcome, Johnson effectively made the point that Chinese intransigence would require the United States to maintain a large force on the Yalu to protect our position. In reply to a Johnson question, Secretary of Defense George Marshall said " 'that the global consequences [of MacArthur's strategy] have not been entirely apparent to him.' " Johnson asked Marshall: If MacArthur " 'were here and looking at the whole world and the reports that were received on it, might he arrive at an entirely different conclusion?' 'I think that is quite possible,' " Marshall answered. Johnson then drew him out on the harmony among American defense chiefs on the Administration's approach to the Korean fighting and their unwillingness to abandon it for MacArthur's strategy. [20]

In his public statements on the hearings, Johnson offered no judgments on the dispute, focusing instead on how MacArthur and the Administration differed. It was a means of getting people to draw their own conclusions about MacArthur's ideas. By the close of the investigation, Reedy recalls, it had become clear to the public that MacArthur "was indulging in pipe dreams." The probe confirmed some people in the belief that MacArthur had been right all along, but, according to one student of the controversy, it showed "many Americans that MacArthur might not be right after all." Later in the summer, after the hearing, MacArthur attended a baseball game at the Polo Grounds in New York. He left before the game ended, walking across the diamond to the centerfield exit while the loudspeaker blared "Old Soldiers Never Die." When an irreverent fan shouted, "Hey Mac, how's Harry Truman?" the crowd exploded in laughter.[21]

To Lyndon, the MacArthur hearings were partly an object lesson in the politics of foreign policy. Although never saying so publicly, the Democrats had a hidden agenda to undermine MacArthur's hold on the public imagination. The hearings showed Lyndon that political leaders accepted the necessity of manipulating public opinion for the sake of a "good" foreign policy and the advantage of their party.

Johnson gained considerable political capital from the MacArthur hearings and the work of his preparedness subcommittee. His biographer Merle Miller writes: Placed in "a prominent spot . . . just one seat down [from Russell during the MacArthur hearings], assiduous in his preparation and prompt in his attendance, [Johnson was] never far from the eye of the camera or the notepad of the nearest reporter." Roswell L. Gilpatric, an Assistant Secretary of the Air Force in 1951, remembered that Johnson took over "the leadership of what had been the old Truman Committee, and was attempting to make it as much of a force as it had been during World War II." In November 1951, Johnson had Don Cook give *Newsweek* an advance copy of his subcommittee's guns and butter report. In return, *Newsweek* gave him the cover of its magazine. This, according to George Reedy, angered economics writers in Washington: "they all set out to prove the report was a phony, and they did."

Democratic Senator Harley Kilgore of West Virginia marveled at Johnson's skill in winning headlines for "the piddling work of the Preparedness Subcommittee." Kilgore believed that the appropriations subcommittee on the Defense Department's budget, of which he was a member, did much more effective work in conjunction with the Government Accounting Office in identifying and countering wasteful defense spending, but it lacked the public relations skills Johnson's committee commanded.[22]

Kilgore's committee did not have George Reedy, a highly skilled publicist. Numerous memos to Johnson from Reedy in 1951–52 demonstrate a concerted effort to build a positive public image of the subcommittee's work. In February 1952, for example, Reedy cited the need for "a major project" to sustain press interest and public attention. "Whatever the major project," Reedy added, "it should be planned *from the beginning* in conjunction with public relations. This should be true of all major Committee activities." Shortly after, when a House committee counterpart headed by Congressman F. Edward Hebert, "stumbled on a major source of military waste," and began "taking the play away from us on the waste question," Reedy urged Johnson to "swing into action with something responsible and significant fairly soon." Otherwise, "we might find both ourselves and the Hebert Committee [which had overstated its case] backed off the map." [23]

Because Johnson was so aggressive about tracking down wrongdoing in the country's defense programs, he took pains to ensure that no hint of corruption attached to his committee. When Jimmy Roosevelt, FDR's son, asked him to help a construction company win an army contract, Lyndon replied: "Ever since I was made Chairman of the Preparedness Subcommittee, I have followed a policy of not taking up the problems of individual companies with the military authorities. . . . I think you can understand why." Similarly, when George Brown approached him about air force contracts for Brown Engineering, Johnson suggested seeing Air Force Under Secretary John McCone. At the same time, he filed a memo on a conversation with McCone in which he urged the Under Secretary only to consider the matter on its merits. "I just don't want the files to reflect that I am trying to influence the decision. If any of my staff call or write a letter, please don't consider it as anything more than a request for information or for consideration on its merits." [24]

Yet this written record hardly reflects the full story of Johnson's influence in behalf of George Brown. During the 1950s, Brown & Root was one of several prime contractors that built nine NATO air bases in France costing over $200 million and four U.S. air force bases and a U.S. naval base in Spain for some $350 million. Johnson's ties to the company were so widely assumed that in 1960, after John F. Kennedy became the country's first Catholic President, the following story made the rounds in Texas: "Now, Lyndon," Kennedy is supposed to have said, "I guess we can dig that tunnel to the Vatican." "Okay," Johnson said, "so long as Brown & Root get the contract." As one B & R competitor noted, Johnson's influence registered on contract decisions in indirect ways. In the summer of 1952, when Maury Maverick and a J. H. Blackaller of the H. B. Zachry Co. made the rounds of Defense Department offices in behalf of overseas construction contracts, Blackaller made notes on a meeting with a "John P. H. Perry, Civilian Assistant to Assistant Secretary of the Air Force Huggins, and the man who is reputed to have given the nod to Brown & Root-Bechtel-Raymond in France. . . . I formed the opinion that he was the fall guy for any criticism which had been handed out over the Bechtel-Raymond-Brown & Root deal in France. I also got the impression that possibly Bechtel & Raymond Concrete Pile were given the nod due to being old time friends, and that Brown & Root was pulled in on the deal to allay investigation similar to [one of] North African [air bases under construction] which was ramrodded by Linden [sic] Johnson's investigating committee." [25]

Try as they might, it was impossible for Johnson and his subcommittee to avoid public controversy. In September 1951, columnist Drew Pearson complained about the Senate's refusal to investigate graft in the sale of American war supplies to Nationalist China and the sale of tin to Communist China by Chiang Kai-shek's relatives. After Pearson exposed the details of these transactions, he asserted that Johnson's subcommittee "has had some of these facts for months" without doing anything about them. Dubbing Johnson, "Lyin'-Down Lyndon," Pearson said that "in keeping with his Texas nickname, he laid down on the job." Eager to mute rather than increase public interest in the charge, Johnson waited three and a half weeks before answering Pearson. It also gave him time to construct an effective reply: His committee had investigated the charges, Johnson said, and concluded "no violations of United States laws had been found in the transaction." Because his committee lacked the resources for an investigation "with world-wide ramifications extending far beyond the Department of Defense," the air force and the FBI had made an exhaustive study of the matter and neither agency had found any wrongdoing by a United States official. He dismissed Pearson's accusations against his committee as baseless. Pearson's readiness to single out Johnson for timidity in pursuing a defense-related scandal partly stemmed from his growing disenchantment with him for being an opportunist who was "lyin'-down" on liberal causes and accommodating himself to conservative influences in Texas and the nation.[26]

Yet despite the growing perception of Johnson in 1951–52 as a conservative convert, he had not entirely broken with his liberal past or quit voting for selective liberal measures. In January 1951 the Administration set up a Civil Defense Administration, and Mary McLeod Bethune, head of the Office of Minority Affairs for the National Youth Administration (1936–44), saw an opportunity to do the same "type of thing we did in NYA"—advance the well-being of blacks by setting up a minority affairs office in the CDA. She asked Lyndon to help her. "Tell him," Bethune said in a telephone message, "I leave my blessings, and want him to go until I come to see him some day in the White House." Similarly, in the following month, his New Deal friends Tommy Corcoran and Jim Rowe called to tell him that Texas oil interests had managed to appoint one of their people as head of the Interior Department's Natural Gas Section, but that they had "succeeded in stopping it." "He has stayed out of this particular fight because he has friends on both sides," Rowe told Walter Jenkins, "and I would think he would want to continue to stay out of it." "Tell him this too—" Corcoran said in his message to Johnson, "I ain't asking him to do nothing. I don't ask any help myself, but just please don't help that bear."[27]

At the same time that old liberal friends saw him as still receptive to their appeals, Johnson continued to vote for social and economic measures favored by New Dealers and Fair Dealers. He supported increased Federal assistance for the aged, blind, and disabled under Social Security; greater funding for vocational education; more money for flood control and soil reclamation; a continuation of price, wage, and rent controls; an excess profits tax; and exemption of the Public Health Service, National Cancer Institute, and National Institutes of Health from a 5 percent across-the-board spending cut in Federal domestic programs. When an aide pointed out how much the excess profits tax could handicap new enterprise, Johnson agreed, but said that "coming out against the excess profits tax [in the midst of a war] would be like coming out for gangsters." He impressed this aide as "being an intensely practical, goal-oriented type person who was very much interested in principles and consistency but not where it was a waste of time, where there would be no fruits, either immediate or long range.[28]

Hubert Humphrey also remembered him as a practical liberal. "You see Johnson was essentially . . . a Rooseveltian, and he was a westerner at heart and he understood agriculture's needs. Of course he always used to rub my nose in it a little bit. He'd say, 'Well now, you see, I go for you for 90 percent of parity, why don't you come with me for oil depletion? . . . When it comes to dairy products, Humphrey, when it comes to that corn and that wheat you want the whole world, but when it comes to my little oil men down there you want to push them down in the ground. You don't want to give them anything.' "[29]

Yet it was not Johnson's liberalism but his accommodation with conservatives on the most visible issues of the day that came across to people at this time. In September 1951, for example, when Hubert Humphrey tried to close one of the "inexcusable loopholes" in the tax laws by reducing the depletion allowance on oil and gas from 27.5 to 15 percent, Johnson led the opposition. He argued that "it would strike a direct blow at the Nation's preparedness program" by reducing incentives to increased oil production, which would be essential in an all-out war. Johnson persuaded 70 out of 79 senators voting on the measure to stand with him. Calling Johnson's Senate address "one of the greatest speeches" on the oil industry "that I have ever heard," one producer declared: "Every man in the oil industry owes you a debt of gratitude." "I take my hat off to you," another said.[30]

Johnson was as vocal about the tidelands issue, which commanded greater public attention in 1951–52. In the fall of 1951, when newspapers reported that the Interior Department might try to issue Federal leases on tidelands, Johnson told a Dallas audience that seizure of Texas's tidelands "was illegal, unethical and immoral." Shortly after, he wrote the President urging against such action at a time when the Congress was considering legislation clarifying title to the tidelands: "It would be an unthinkable display of contempt for Congress and for the States." In his reply, Truman reaffirmed his determination "to see that the whole United States profits from the national ownership of Tidelands oil," and promised never to stop working on the issue "until clear title to all the

Tidelands is vested in the United States of America." Johnson won the argument with Truman in the Congress, where a bill he co-sponsored returning the tidelands to state control passed in April 1952. The President, however, had the last word: Truman vetoed the law, and its advocates lacked the votes to override him. Rather than have another defeat on the record, they decided to wait until a new President, who might be more sympathetic to state control, entered office.[31]

If liberals could understand and even forgive Johnson's defense of oil interests, they were less accepting of his conservative response to other issues vital to them. In the fall of 1951, Walter White, executive secretary of the National Association for the Advancement of Colored People, denounced Johnson's stand on civil rights at a meeting of the Texas NAACP in Austin. "The grievous disappointment of Johnson's lining up with the Dixiecrats against civil rights," he said, "makes it imperative that by 1952 the Negro registered vote in Texas be raised as close as possible to its full potential of 600,000."[32]

Johnson also offended liberals by attacking Truman's seizure of the country's steel mills in April 1952 as a mistaken action which "smacks of the practices that lead toward a dictatorship." The President's move followed a refusal by steel producers to accept a Wage Stabilization Board recommendation on pay raises and fringe benefits for labor without a price increase of $10 to $12 a ton. The Administration believed that the steel industry had a sufficient profit margin to absorb the increased labor costs with only a $2.50 to $4.00 a ton price rise. The White House insisted that producers accept a settlement and avoid a strike that could cripple the country's war production. When the industry wouldn't give in, Truman ordered a seizure of the steel mills and their continued operation under Federal control. Some liberals shared conservative reservations about such a drastic exercise of presidential power. But most believed that the President "had struck a justifiable blow at an arrogant and unpatriotic corporate power." Johnson thought it essential for the steel industry to maintain production, and so voted for a bill giving the President temporary power to seize the mills. But only eleven other senators voted with him, and he opposed a law giving the President "a permanent seizure authority." Johnson's strongest preference was for the use of the Taft-Hartley Act to compel labor to stay on the job for 80 days while the dispute was mediated. The Administration and liberals, however, rejected this alternative as unfair to labor. When the Supreme Court ruled the seizure unconstitutional, the Administration agreed to a settlement giving industry a $5.65 a ton increase.[33]

Johnson further antagonized liberals by his votes on restrictive internal security and immigration laws. In September 1950, he had joined 69 Senate colleagues in voting for the McCarran Act, an antisubversion law requiring registration of all Communist party members, forbidding their employment by the Federal government, and allowing deportation of alien Communists. With American military forces directly fighting Communism in Korea, the country engaged in an anticommunist outburst that even most liberals in Congress found impossible to resist. Only twenty House members and seven senators mustered the courage to vote against what Truman described as a fundamental assault on traditional American freedoms embodied in the McCarran Act. Despite an eloquent statement of libertarian principles in his veto message, Truman could persuade only forty-eight representatives and ten senators to sustain his veto. Johnson was not one of them, but Helen Gahagan Douglas was, and she soon found herself out of Congress. Immediately after voting against the McCarran bill she went to the House dining room, where she joined a group of fellow Democrats who had begged her to save her political life by voting for the law. One of them said: "Helen, how does it feel to be a dead statesman. It feels just fine to be a live politician."

If there was some politicial expediency in Johnson's vote on the McCarran bill that liberals in the Congress could forgive, they were less sympathetic to his support of the McCarran-Walter Act of June 1952. A reaffirmation of the discriminatory national-origins quota system of 1924 and an expansion of arbitrary exclusion and deportation powers, the law reflected the xenophobia that was part of the anticommunist mood dominating the country in the early fifties. Johnson joined the majority in a 57 to 26 override of the President's veto, one vote more than the required two-thirds.[34]

Johnson's pro-oil and anti-civil rights stands, hard line anticommunism, and rise to prominence in the Senate in only four years made him a likely shoo-in for another six-year term in 1954. But he continued to believe that politics includes few givens, especially in the early fifties when scandals in the Truman administration and Communist witchhunting destroyed many careers. Drew Pearson's widely publicized attack on him in 1951 for "lyin' down" on an investigation and the criticism of his November 1951 guns-and-butter report as lacking substance had fueled his anxiety about his political future.

Alvin Wirtz's sudden death of a heart attack at a University of Texas football game in October had greatly saddened him and added to his worries. Wirtz was only sixty-three at his death, and it reminded Johnson of his own family's history of heart disease and stroke and his vulnerability to a crippling attack or early death. It had also heightened his sense of political uncertainty. Wirtz's death "was kind of the end of an era . . . one of the final blows that ushered us into having to stand on our own," Lady Bird recalled. He was an "advisor and mentor and friend and sort of court of last resort." Wirtz's passing meant that "there was nobody to go to really." Walter Jenkins remembered what "a vacuum" Wirtz's death created for Johnson: "He depended on Senator Wirtz I

think more than anybody in his life for real sage advice, counsel. . . .
Mr. Johnson leaned on him till the end." [35]

Wirtz's death removed a constant from Johnson's life that could not
be replaced. And for someone who craved an inner sense of surety it
was a painful loss. As much as ever, Johnson was a man plagued by a
sense of emptiness that overeating, heavy smoking, womanizing, and
frenzied work schedules could not appease. "Lyndon was the biggest
eater I ever watched," Florida senator George Smathers said. "He would
eat two large meals and gulp them down as if he were starving. Nobody
could slow him down." He needed constant talk and motion, as if his
very existence depended on conversation and the mastery of a current
challenge that forced him to work day and night. Telephones to keep
him in touch with everyone and everything were an essential part of his
daily life. He had phones everywhere, Steinberg says: "The walls of his
Washington and Austin homes were studded with telephone outlets. . . .
One of the trees in his back yard in Austin was wired for sound with a
thirty-foot extension-corded telephone." At the Dallas airport one day,
Horace Busby found him pacing back and forth before three phone booths.
"Watch those phones!" Johnson shouted. "I've got a long-distance call
working in each." [36]

The greatest anchor in his life was Lady Bird. Although he rarely
spent a relaxed evening at home and often devoted Sundays to political
talk with house guests, Lady Bird provided him with a kind of sanctuary
from himself, a well-organized household where her calm balanced his
volatility. With the help of Zephyr Wright, a black cook recruited from
Texas, and Helen Williams, a housekeeper, Lady Bird managed to attend to his every need and provide gracious hospitality to an almost
endless stream of guests he brought home for dinner at a moment's
notice. "Gosh, how that woman let the storms roll over her back and
kept everything on an equilibrium!" one family friend recalled. "When
you went over to their house . . . instead of eating dinner at 7 o'clock
or 8 o'clock in the evening, maybe you didn't eat until 12 or whatnot.
She'd never let anything ruffle her." No single thing contributed more
to Lyndon's success than "her great good judgment and advice and her
serenity, her sweetness, and her ability to just roll with the punches . . .
to take things big and little, good and bad" as they came. [37]

The Johnson girls—Lynda Bird, seven, and Lucy Baines, four in 1951—
were on the periphery of Lyndon's attention. Although he took great
satisfaction in watching them grow and progress, he largely left their
rearing to Lady Bird and some of the women on his staff, particularly
Willie Day Taylor, a clerk in his office, whom the girls called "Wil-
Day." Absent often from early in the morning until late in the evening,
he saw them on Sundays or during a cocktail hour at home when they
were "introduced nicely to the elders," and would do a little bit of serv-

ing before going to bed. During their early school years, they spent the first semester in Austin, living in an apartment with Willie Day, and the second semester at home in Washington. Sleep-away camp in Texas filled their summers.[38]

Shortly before Wirtz died, Johnson had acquired a new fixture or stabilizing force in his life that gave him considerable satisfaction. In 1951 he bought the property on the Pedernales between the communities of Hye and Stonewall, near where he had been born and lived the first five years of his life. He had been thinking about buying the LBJ Ranch, as it came to be called, for at least three years and probably longer. Lyndon's Aunt Frank and Uncle Clarence Martin, Sam Ealy's sister and brother-in-law, had owned the property since the early years of the century, and they had willed it to Tom and Lela Martin, their son and daughter-in-law, on the condition that they care for them until they died. Tom and Lela, who had returned from California in the thirties, had upheld their part of the bargain through the years, moving onto the Martin ranch in 1940, four years after Clarence had passed away. Tom Martin died in 1948, and a year later, Aunt Frank, who was seventy-seven years old, went to court to break the agreement with Lela Martin and establish her sole claim to the property. The best available evidence suggests that Lyndon was behind the lawsuit, promising Aunt Frank the use of his boyhood home in Johnson City and an annual annuity for the rest of her life in return for the 243-acre ranch. Lela Martin was also promised compensation for her loss of the property. Her refusal led to a court fight that Aunt Frank won in 1951, which allowed Lyndon to buy the ranch.[39]

Lyndon's desire for a ranch, and more especially the Martin ranch, was partly political. As a state-wide officeholder, he needed something more than the duplex apartment he owned in Austin, where he could demonstrate his Texas roots and entertain guests in a style more befitting someone of his station. It was a mark of status among Texas millionaires and many senators to have a ranch or "spread," where they could retreat on vacation and throw lavish parties. In the view of one Texas columnist: Johnson "created the hill country ranch as the proper home setting of a Texan in Washington. Mr. Johnson is not intrinsically a Texas rancher, either in outlook or behavior. . . . He is seen in his real self in the midst of political strife and controversy in Washington. . . . He is like the ancient Romans. The historian Will Durant says they could not wait to get to their country seats, but, once there, paced the atrium until they could leap into their chariots to return to Rome."[40]

But the ranch meant more to Lyndon than that: "I almost should have foreseen it," Lady Bird said during an interview at the ranch in 1972, "because I think Lyndon was always heading back here. . . . It enabled us to have a big, comfortable house that meant a lot to him, to his spirit and his heart." Lyndon himself said: "I had no regrets about going to Washington and spending a good part of my life there, but I've always found it possible and almost necessary to return to Texas. This country has always been a place where I could come and fill my cup, so to speak, and recharge myself for the more difficult days ahead. Here's where we come to rest our bones and to collect our thoughts and to lay our plans." The historian Paul Conkin asserts: "It would be impossible to overestimate the place of the ranch in Johnson's self-concept, its crucial role in his later life. He loved it. When he bought it he knew next to nothing about ranching. . . . But, almost at once, Johnson took on the identity of a western rancher, down to the expensive boots and cowboy hats. The ranch became his only real toy, his one avocation. In the midst of his busy, often frustrating life in Washington, he could always escape, at least in fantasy, to the ranch. . . . It symbolized peace, simplicity, honest friendship, a manageable world, one colored by nostalgia and embellished by romantic sentiments."[41]

Lyndon did not see the ranch as a money-making proposition. Quite the contrary, the construction of a commodious house and general improvements on the property to make it a working ranch required thousands of dollars. But by 1951–52, the Johnsons could afford it. KTBC, which in 1947 Lady Bird had signed over to a company she called the Texas Broadcasting Corporation, had increased in value to $488,000 by March 1952, with an after-tax profit of $57,983 for 1951. Moreover, in the spring of 1952, the Johnsons looked forward to the possibility of significant financial gains from the acquisition of an FCC license to construct the only Very High Frequency (VHF) television station in Austin. Between 1945 and 1948 the FCC had allocated only 106 television stations for the entire country. In 1948, as pressure built for new allocations, the FCC had declared a moratorium on issuing new licenses and launched a four-year study of where and how many new stations should be constructed across the United States.[42]

As early as the spring of 1948, Lyndon and Lady Bird had considered entering the television business—both as a broadcaster and a distributor in the Austin area for the Dumont network and TV manufacturer. But they were hesitant. The cost of setting up a station was considerable and the long-term prospects for the industry were uncertain. The existing stations in Texas were losing money, and Lyndon believed it might take ten years before a new station could turn a profit. But Leonard Marks, the Johnsons' attorney, and Edward Joseph, an Austin businessman and family friend, urged them to go ahead. "It would be just exactly like it was with your radio station," Joseph told Lyndon. "It got off the ground the first week you took it over. You have enough connections, national connections, that you can just make this pay right from the start." "Well that's something to think about," Lyndon replied. As others put it, Johnson could have made "a success of a television station in the Gobi Desert."[43]

By July of 1952, however, when the FCC lifted its freeze and began allocating 1,945 new television stations, it was reasonably certain that acquisition of a VHF station promised a large return. "Because of the tremendous value that is attributed to a television license, . . . we think it would be an understatement to say that competition for channels will be keen," an FCC report stated. The Interstate and Foreign Commerce Committee anticipated that over the next two years the television industry would generate $3 billion in new business.[44]

Given how lucrative a VHF station seemed likely to be, it is surprising that Lady Bird's Texas Broadcasting Company had no competition for the one VHF channel allocated to Austin. As one of the applicants for a less desirable Ultra High Frequency (UHF) station in Austin in 1952 explained it: "Lyndon was in a favorable position to get that station even if somebody contested it. Politics is politics."[45]

Yet Johnson and many of his associates emphatically denied that politics played a part. He never voted in Congress on any radio or television controversy, and he never went near the FCC in behalf of KTBC radio or KTBC-TV, they contended. "He scrupulously avoided any contacts with the Federal Communications Commission because he felt that in his position as an official of the Senate he would not want to be involved in discussions," Leonard Marks said. One FCC Commissioner told Marks: " 'Leonard, you should feel very complimented because the file at the Commission which has been most thumbed and most scrupulously examined is that of KTBC. Newspaper people, professional politicians, those who thought they might be able to find some hint of influence or pressure have just examined that file from page one to the end.' At no time has anyone ever been able to find anything that was improper," Marks added. In a 1959 letter to Governor James P. Coleman of Mississippi, an old friend, who asked Johnson for help at the FCC, Johnson himself said: "Unfortunately, the Federal Communications Commission is one area in which I cannot move. As you know, my wife has interest in television and radio, and I have made it a strict rule not to intervene in any way with the Commission. I have not set foot in the Commission offices. I have never asked the Commission to do anything either for me or for a constituent." Johnson couldn't bring himself to send this false denial. Instead, he called Coleman to say that "his family is in the radio-television business and contact with the FCC is a delicate matter."[46]

It is not surprising that few traces of Johnson's actions at the FCC showed up in the Commission's files. Johnson was too shrewd and subtle to have left a clear record of his influence at the FCC. As the attorney W. Ervin "Red" James, who had known Johnson since the thirties and had served at the Commission, put it: "Johnson learned early, when he was a young Congressman, you don't go down and ask Harold Ickes, the Secretary of the Interior, to do something. You reach over in the Bureau of Indian Affairs, or the Forest Service or whatever, National Park Service, one of the bureaus of the Interior Department, and you find some guy in there who is a bright guy that knows what the hell he's doing, and you talk to him about getting it done. You start it up from that way and not fool with these people at the top." Johnson had strong connections at the FCC, particularly to Clifford Durr, a Commissioner from 1941 to 1948; Paul Porter, the chairman of the Commission for fourteen months between 1944 and 1946; Rosel H. Hyde, who served for over twenty-three years beginning in 1946; and Robert T. Bartley, Sam Rayburn's nephew from Texas, who sat on the Commission for twenty years from March 1952 to June 1972. Durr, Porter, and Bartley shared identification with Johnson as Democrats, and Hyde, a Republican, was indebted to Johnson for persuading the Truman White House to appoint him.[47]

Johnson knew that he could count on a friendly reception for Lady Bird's requests from certain commissioners, but his efforts to influence the Commission did not stop there. In September 1945, for example, when the movie star Gene Autry asked him "to put in a plug" with Paul Porter for a radio license in Tucson, Arizona, Lyndon replied: "There is not much I can do on the matter you mentioned but you can count on me putting in a good word for you." He was not so coy with Tommy Corcoran, who in November 1945 asked him on the telephone to help block an application for a New York radio station. Corcoran said: "I want you to get hold of your good friend . . . and tell him that everybody in New York would consider it a most unfortunate act if an application . . . for a new station in New York on 620 were granted." Johnson said he understood. In February 1946, when Lyndon wanted to know if NBC was planning to go into Austin, Corcoran, who had close contact with Charles Denny, who was about to become FCC chairman, assured Lyndon that he knew "how to do that" and promised to "find that out for you." Lyndon, of course, had his own contacts at the FCC, one of whom in 1946 let him read the application from the "Texas Regulars" for a competing radio station in Austin. He also had a well-developed knowledge of how to make things happen at the FCC.[48]

When Arthur Stehling, an old friend and collaborator on REA matters, came to see him in the late forties about an application for radio station KNAF in Fredericksburg, Texas, Johnson was eager to help. Stehling was in competition for the 1340 frequency with two men who had asked the Commission to license a station in Austin. Since helping Stehling meant eliminating potential competition for KTBC, Johnson told him how to push his application through the Commission. " 'Go see Commissioner A, tell him you know Senator Wirtz and mention the

Senator's goats—the Commissioner thinks they are something. See Commissioner B. He's from Oklahoma. Tell him you feel he is really the Commissioner representing us Texans. See Commissioner C. Simply tell him you are my friend. See Commissioner D. He's already for you. Say nothing except to call his attention to the pending application and express your hope that the Commission will act on it soon. Don't see Commissioner E. He will resent your approaching him.' . . . I had instructions in respect to every member of the Commission." A week after Stehling followed Johnson's advice, the FCC granted him a license.[49]

Johnson's influence at the Commission also extended to assuring that KTBC-TV would enjoy a " 'monopoly' on television broadcasting in Austin" throughout the fifties. Where the Dallas–Fort Worth area received five VHF stations, Houston four, and San Antonio four, Austin got only one. The FCC contended that technical considerations about signal interference and population were the determining factors in these allocations. Yet in 1952, Corpus Christi, with a population of 108,000 compared with Austin's 132,000, got two stations and a license for a third in 1959, which could not be used to start broadcasting for five years because of signal interference. The two existing stations in Corpus Christi had objected that their city could not support a third station and suggested that it be put in Austin. The FCC rejected their proposal. Moreover, Amarillo, a city with a population only 60 percent the size of Austin's in the late fifties, had three stations compared with Austin's one. By the early sixties, there were 107 single-channel communities in the United States. Unlike Austin, however, most of them were "located in 'overlap' areas where advertisers can reach the set owners via other nearby stations." KTBC's monopoly allowed it to charge higher advertising rates. One "overlap" community, Rochester, Minnesota, a city of comparable size to Austin, received $325 an hour for network programming in 1964. The rate for Austin was $575 an hour.[50]

When asked if the FCC was "politicized," John Connally, who had a rich knowledge of the radio business in Texas and remained close to Johnson through the fifties, answered: "Oh, yes, no question. . . . The Federal Communications Commission would deny there was any politics to it. But, nevertheless, he [Johnson] was fortunate in that the FCC designed the coverage areas . . . to where Austin just happened to be without competition in . . . the profitable band of television in those days."[51]

When it came to ensuring the business success of the radio and TV stations, Johnson did not miss a beat. During 1951, KTBC radio suffered a slump in early morning advertising revenues, slipping from $6000 to $2000 a month. Johnson sent Horace Busby to Austin, Marble Falls, and Johnson City to reverse the slide.

In August 1952, after receiving the television license, Johnson arranged affiliations with all three networks, ABC, CBS, and NBC. "Theodore Granik called from New York City and said he has been lunching with some NBC Vice President's (sic) and that one stated he had just left a meeting with you," George Reedy told Johnson. ". . . The reaction was extremely favorable. He, himself, thinks your affiliation with the network would be a wonderful thing since 'everybody admires' you as a man who is doing a marvelous job for the country and who always stands by his word. Granik . . . said he is very happy to volunteer his services for your current transactions."

Johnson aggressively managed the radio and television stations. "No one in recent years has had any dealings with KTBC without being aware that the driving force behind the operation was Lyndon Baines Johnson," Life magazine said in 1964. "A former KTBC employee recalls that during the 10 years he worked for the station, it was Lyndon Johnson himself who presided over meetings of department heads." Another employee described Johnson as "a powerful person. Whenever he came into the station, he set things buzzing. Frankly he scared hell out of a lot of people." Johnson's attentiveness to his radio and television interests paid large dividends. By the end of February 1953, the Texas Broadcasting Company had assets of $734,220, with excellent prospects for more growth as additional homes in the greater Austin community acquired television sets.[52]

Johnson, believing that television stations would pay high returns in the next decade, expanded the holdings of Texas Broadcasting beyond Austin to other Texas cities. At the same time he captured control of Austin's only station, he launched an effort to win part ownership of the sole VHF channel in Waco, a smaller city 98 miles north of Austin.

In December 1951, KWTX Broadcasting Company, the owner of a radio station in Waco, asked permission to build Waco's TV station. The Waco Television Corporation submitted a competing application. In January 1952, the KWTX attorney asked Johnson for information about "the procedural pattern followed by the Federal Communications Commission," and described the attributes of KWTX stockholders, including those of two "with whom, of course, you are acquainted." Johnson passed the request along to the Commission. In March, Paul A. Walker, the Commission's new chairman, wrote Lyndon recommending that his correspondent acquaint himself with FCC criteria for a license by reading published reports of its decisions. Since the correspondence seemed to serve no intrinsic purpose, one may assume that Lyndon was signaling his interest in KWTX's application. More than a year later, on April 30, 1953, with the matter of which applicant would get the license still unresolved, Johnson wrote again, enclosing a resolution from the Waco Board of Commissioners, and asking "serious consideration to this problem, based on its merits."[53]

Nineteen months later the FCC granted KWTX's application. At the same time, in December 1954, Johnson's Texas Broadcasting Company won approval to buy KANG, Waco's UHF TV station, for $25,000 and assume its rapidly growing debt of $109,000. The rationale for this surprising decision registered on KWTX owners almost at once. When KWTX tried to complete arrangements with CBS for a network affiliation, CBS abandoned the negotiations, explaining that it was afilliating with KANG. In May 1953, ABC had preceded CBS in choosing to affiliate with the unpromising UHF station, KANG, rather than wait for the VHF station to begin operations. NBC affiliation with a nearby Temple, Texas, station, which beamed its programs into Waco, precluded negotiations with that network. Texas Broadcasting further undermined KWTX's prospects in April 1955 when the FCC approved an application to increase KTBC-TV's power from 100 kilowatts to 247 kilowatts. Attorneys for KWTX now asked the Anti-Trust Division of the Justice Department to consider action against Texas Broadcasting and petitioned the FCC to hold hearings on the merits of increased power for KTBC-TV.[54]

The KWTX lawyers submitted a fifty-page brief to the FCC describing KTBC-TV's monopolistic practices and the injury being done to KWTX by them. Through its operation of KTBC-TV in Austin and KANG-TV in Waco, the network affiliations of these stations, and FCC approval of KTBC-TV's request for more broadcasting power, the Texas Broadcasting Company was violating the Sherman Act and the Clayton Antitrust Act and the Commission's announced policies against undue concentration of control and for the widest possible public choice of television programming. Texas Broadcasting had used KANG "to expand KTBC-TV's monopoly in a larger service area" by preventing KWTX-TV from securing a network affiliation. The network decisions were a "conspiracy"—"not motivated by ordinary business judgment"— to advance the interests of KTBC-TV at the expense of KWTX-TV. The increase in KTBC-TV power to 247 kilowatts meant that instead of a 91-square-mile overlap, where KTBC-TV and KWTX-TV jointly reached 1,493 people, KTBC-TV would now be able to broadcast in 740 square miles of KWTX-TV's territory with an audience of 21,307 people. The networks and Texas Broadcasting "categorically and unequivocally" denied all the allegations.[55]

Before the issues could be adjudicated, however, KWTX-TV withdrew its protest to the FCC on May 16, 1955, eighteen days after it had been filed. Negotiations between the two companies, including three discussions between Johnson and one KWTX-TV attorney and stockholder, had decided KWTX-TV to drop its complaints against Texas Broadcasting. In return, ABC was to shift its affiliation from KANG to KWTX-TV. Since an ABC affiliation did not promise long-term success for the Waco station, the two sides negotiated a more comprehensive agreement that gave Johnson's company 29.05 percent of all KWTX holdings.

In return, Texas Broadcasting dissolved KANG and transferred its assets and CBS affiliation to KWTX.[56]

It is difficult to believe that all these events favoring Johnson's interests simply happened. The FCC choice of KWTX over Waco Broadcasting, Johnson's purchase of KANG-TV, the amazing network affiliations with a UHF station that would command a small fraction of Waco's audience, the FCC approval for KTBC-TV's increased power and expanded coverage meant that KWTX-TV would have to make significant concessions to Texas Broadcasting to survive. Was there a secret, unrecorded deal between Johnson and some of the KWTX-TV owners? Probably. The overt events suggest the following: In return for string-pulling at the FCC by Johnson to assure the assignment of Waco's VHF station to KWTX, Johnson was to receive a piece of the station. The cooperation of high CBS and ABC officials was essential, but it is hardly inconceivable, especially since they would end up with what they wanted anyway—namely, affiliation with Waco's VHF station. There is no smoking gun to prove these assertions, but the circumstantial evidence seems persuasive enough to warrant these conclusions.[57]

During the next four years, Johnson's Texas Broadcasting made additional direct and indirect acquisitions and gains. In 1955–56 the FCC granted KTBC-TV another increase in power to 316 kilowatts, allowed Texas Broadcasting to change its name to the LBJ Company and to acquire part of KRGV-TV and radio in the Rio Grande Valley town of Weslaco. Shortly after, the FCC agreed to an increase in KRGV-TV's transmitting power from 28.8 kilowatts to 100 kilowatts, and the station won network affiliations with ABC and NBC. During this time, KWTX bought a half ownership in KBTX-TV, a Bryan, Texas, educational station that the FCC, in an exception to its rule, allowed to convert to commercial use. At the end of April 1956, the LBJ Company had assets of $1,534,381. Nearly three years later, on March 31, 1959, the company's value had reached $2,569,503.[58]

In advancing his business interests, Johnson was doing what came naturally to most aggressive entrepreneurs. His principal vocation as a high ranking elected official and his use of that office to serve his private interests, however, made some, if not most, of his business dealings improper. He had no illusions about what he was doing, as his efforts to hide his close involvements with the radio and television properties demonstrate. But enduring anxieties about losing his office allowed him to rationalize his actions. The possibility that his livelihood might one day depend exclusively on the radio and television stations was never far from his mind. And the fear that this could happen in 1954 remained very much a concern throughout 1951–52.

A report in March 1951 by syndicated columnist Robert S. Allen that Johnson had led a faction in the Senate Democratic Policy Committee advocating an end to Tennessee Senator Estes Kefauver's investigations of syndicated crime "before it wrecks the whole Democratic Party" had upset him. Aware of how popular Kefauver's probe was and how "explosive" opposition to it could be, Johnson immediately called Allen to deny that any such discussion had occurred. He said: "Now, Bob, no such talk ever took place. I never took such a position. . . . My position is to Hell with the Democratic Party, Kefauver ought to do whatever ought to be done." Further, in the spring of 1952, when Sam Smithwick's letter to Coke Stevenson and Smithwick's subsequent suicide revived questions about the 1948 election, it shook Johnson's confidence in his political standing. He took pains to refute the accusations and ensure that a report on Smithwick by state officials would conclusively demonstrate that there was "no evidence of foul play" and that the man was "deranged." Adding to these concerns was a state poll in February 1952 showing that only 55 percent of Texas voters could identify Johnson as a U.S. Senator and that when people went to the polls they often voted without knowing much about the candidate or his record.[59]

Possible scandals and voter ignorance weren't the only things threatening Johnson's reelection in 1954. A possible bid for his Senate seat by Governor Allan Shivers, an ultraconservative who controlled the Texas Democratic party in 1952, worried him as much. The youngest state senator in Texas history and a World War II army hero, Shivers had been elected lieutenant governor in 1946 and succeeded to the governorship when Beauford Jester died of a heart attack in 1949. Determined to dominate the state Democratic party, Shivers hired Jake Pickle, then in the public-relations business, to organize the state party convention in September 1950. With Pickle's help, Shivers purged liberals from the party's hierarchy and filled the Executive Committee with Shivercrats. By the summer of 1951, Shivers was laying plans to "be damned sure that I am in charge" of the state party convention in the spring of 1952 and that the Texas delegation to the national convention would not be pledged to any candidate opposing state control of tidelands oil. In a powerful demonstration of his political muscle, Shivers arranged for Attorney General Price Daniel, who shared his views on the tidelands, to run for the U.S. Senate against Tom Connally. When statewide polls in the first months of 1952 showed that Connally, after thirty-five years in the Senate, had lost his appeal to Texas voters and that Daniel would beat him handily in a primary, Connally announced his retirement.[60]

Beginning in 1951, Lyndon worked to keep Shivers from running against him in 1954. In the fall of 1951, when liberal or "loyal" Democrats met in Austin to work for a Truman-instructed delegation at the 1952 national convention in Chicago, Johnson rejected their invitation to attend, saying he would either have to be in Washington or Dallas.

Further, when Daniel announced his candidacy, Johnson adopted a hands-off position toward the contest. As soon as Connally withdrew from the race, however, Johnson gave Daniel his backing.[61]

At the same time, Johnson tried to act as an intermediary between Shivers and Sam Rayburn. Rayburn, who saw Shivers as more of a Republican than a Democrat, privately declared his partiality for "loyal" Democrats, and persuaded liberal former assistant attorney general Ralph Yarborough to run for governor against Shivers. Despite his encouragement to Yarborough, Rayburn was cautious about openly fighting Shivers. Shivers was also eager to avoid an open break with Rayburn. The Speaker was slated to be permanent chairman of the national convention and would have a large say in whether the Shivercrats or "loyal" Democrats were seated in Chicago. Fearful that a split with the national party during his primary fight with Yarborough for the Democratic gubernatorial nomination might be disastrous, Shivers tried to appease Rayburn.

Although he had every intention of breaking with the party if Truman or another liberal became its nominee in 1952, Shivers encouraged the Democratic leadership, and especially Rayburn, to think otherwise. During the spring and early summer, Lyndon took Shivers at his word and tried to convince Rayburn that a "complete understanding" between him and Shivers was likely. He assured Rayburn that Shivers would not bolt the party, that in a deadlocked convention Shivers would support Rayburn's nomination for the presidency, and that it was essential for the good of the party in Texas and nationally to avoid an embarrassing fight. When Shivers came to Washington in early June, Johnson took him to see party leaders and subsequently urged them to believe that the governor would stay in the party. Johnson wasn't the only one making the case for Shivers. Houston attorney Charles I. Francis sent Rayburn the same message.[62]

At the convention in Chicago, Johnson led a successful campaign to seat the Shivercrats instead of Maverick's loyalists. He arranged a meeting between Shivers and Rayburn in the latter's hotel room, where apparently Shivers promised to support the convention's nominees if his delegation were seated. Johnson also argued Shivers's case with some members of the convention's credentials committee. By his help to Shivers, Johnson hoped to head off a contest between them for the Senate seat in 1954.[63]

It also served an agreement Johnson had made with Richard Russell to support him for President. Truman's decision in March not to run for another term had opened up the race for the Democratic nomination. Shivers also favored Russell. But where Shivers's support was ideological, Johnson's was more practical. Russell had promised Johnson that if he failed to win the presidential nomination, he would back Johnson for

Vice President. Since Russell was seen as too much of a sectional candidate to command a national following, Johnson seemed likely to get the better of this bargain. He had no illusions about Russell winning the nomination, but he believed a strong showing by him essential for Russell to have significant "trading strength" at the convention. Consequently, Johnson was ready to "hustle for Russell," as his backers urged party activists to do. Johnson asked George Reedy to map out a strategy for Russell's campaign; provided a statement singing Russell's praises; advised Russell on what to say about the Taft-Hartley law to attract labor support; instructed John Connally and Walter Jenkins to work for Russell at the convention; and, in the words of William Darden, Russell's secretary, "did his darnedest to get the nomination for Senator Russell."[64]

Russell's campaign was doomed from the start. He did poorly in the primaries and ran third behind Estes Kefauver and Governor Adlai Stevenson of Illinois on the first ballot at the convention. Kefauver's unpopularity with northern party bosses, who resented his investigation linking politicians to organized crime figures, and with southern Democrats, who disliked his moderate views on race, caused him to lose the nomination to Stevenson on the third ballot.

Johnson fared no better than Russell. The Georgia senator had no say in the selection of a vice-presidential candidate, and Johnson received no serious consideration. According to Sam Rayburn, the vice-presidential decision was made at night after Stevenson was chosen. Truman, Stevenson, Democratic National Chairman Frank McKinney, Senate secretary and Truman adviser Leslie Biffle, and Rayburn conferred in a little room behind the convention platform. Stevenson wanted Alben Barkley, Truman's Vice President, but Stevenson felt he was too old, especially if they were going to make an issue of Eisenhower's age in the campaign. Kefauver's large party following recommended him, but Stevenson wanted a Vice President "who could help get my program through the Senate." "Then you damn sure don't want Kefauver!" Truman said. "He doesn't have a single friend in the whole damn Senate unless it's Paul Douglas." They narrowed the choice to John Sparkman of Alabama and Senator Mike Monroney of Oklahoma. Eager for a southerner with a record of party regularity, Stevenson chose Sparkman. In Rayburn's account, Johnson was never even mentioned.[65]

The 1952 presidential campaign in Texas became a political minefield for Democratic office holders eager to keep faith with their party. General Dwight D. Eisenhower's announcement in January 1952 that he was ready to accept a call to higher duty moved William and Oveta Culp Hobby, owners of the *Houston Post*, and Jack Porter, Lyndon's Republican opponent in 1948, to organize an Eisenhower-for-President committee in the state. Joined by conservative Democrats alienated from Truman's policies on race and the tidelands, the Eisenhower Republicans battled the reactionary wing of the party favoring Senator Robert Taft of Ohio for President. When the Republican national convention in June seated the Eisenhower rather than the Taft delegation from Texas, it opened the way to Eisenhower's nomination on the first ballot.[66]

Despite his pledge to the contrary, Shivers bolted Stevenson for Eisenhower and took a majority of the Democrats in the state with him. On August 23, Shivers visited Stevenson in Springfield, Illinois, where Stevenson bluntly supported Federal ownership of the tidelands. In response, Shivers and Price Daniel announced their preference for Eisenhower, who favored state control of offshore minerals. At the Democratic party state convention in early September, Shivers won majority votes for resolutions backing Eisenhower and Richard Nixon, his running mate, and denouncing "the Federal larceny of our tidelands" and Federal exploitation of minority groups through "class legislation" labeled "civil rights." Funded by state oil interests, Republicans saturated the state with ads showing Adlai Stevenson sneering at a classroom of children, saying "Tideland funds for those kids? Aw, let them pick cotton." The Republicans also assailed the Truman administration for corruption and weakness in fighting Communism. They threw the Democrats on the defensive in Texas and threatened to win the state for the first time since 1928.

The response of loyal Democrats was ineffective. Although Sam Rayburn took control of the state campaign for Stevenson, he was unable to carry many other Democratic office holders and party officials with him. As two of Rayburn's biographers write, "Democratic politicians scattered like doves in hunting season. . . . Some state officials hid out, incommunicado, in the New Mexico mountains or in hospitals." In November, Eisenhower defeated Stevenson by more than six million votes nationally and won Texas by 131,000 votes, 1.1 million to 969,000.[67]

Johnson had taken a measured, middle-of-the road course in the campaign. As a national party figure genuinely committed to most Democratic views on Federal power, Johnson had come out for Stevenson. The unpopularity in Texas of Stevenson and Democratic liberalism, however, discouraged Johnson from enthusiastic support. Stevenson's forthrightness on the tidelands had upset Johnson. He had worked out a very careful statement on the subject which Stevenson had failed to use. "Boy, it was a beaut!" George Reedy Says. "It didn't say anything!" According to Sam Houston Johnson, Lyndon called Stevenson a "goddamn fool" for letting "Shivers go up there and trap him on tidelands." He worried that support of Stevenson would "crucify" him. Moreover, he didn't think Stevenson had a chance against Eisenhower, and he "wanted to duck it [the campaign] completely, but . . . he came around to the realization that if he did he would have no future whatsoever in the Democratic party." [68]

He also believed that Stevenson would make a better President than Ike and that a Democratic victory would be better for Texas and the nation. In a private conversation with a conservative Republican friend of Herbert Hoover's, Johnson said: "If you want to get Ike elected, you should have him travel around the country and smile and say nothing for every time he opens his mouth he will lose more votes than get them." He disagreed with Stevenson on Taft-Hartley, the FEPC, and the tidelands, Johnson said, but Eisenhower's positions on these issues, except for the tidelands, differed little from Stevenson's. On most other questions affecting the country's peace and prosperity, Johnson thought Stevenson and the Democrats would do better than Eisenhower and the Republicans. Johnson continued to believe that the well-being of Texas and the South depended on the Federal activism of the thirties and the forties that had transformed southern economic life. [69]

After weighing all the factors, Johnson had announced for Stevenson. In a statement to the press on August 28, he had declared his support of the party's nominees. He thoroughly disagreed with Stevenson on the tidelands, but Stevenson's error here did "not automatically make Eisenhower right on all other issues." Johnson reminded people of the many years of suffering endured by the state after it had deserted the Democrats for Herbert Hoover in 1928, and he warned that Texas had more to lose by deserting the Democrats than it had to gain from the Republicans. Johnson's statement produced a cordial exchange of letters with Stevenson. A state-wide radio address on October 13, a three-day speaking tour beginning on the 14th, public appearances with Stevenson on the 17th and 18th, and an appearance with Alben Barkley in Austin on the 29th followed. Under prodding from Senator J. William Fulbright of Arkansas, Johnson also had urged Richard Russell to speak out for the Democratic ticket or "at least to make a show of supporting" the party's nominee. [70]

Johnson's support of Stevenson, however, was most notable for its restraint. At the end of September, Dallas oil man Clint Murchison warned him that the current campaign was becoming so "hot" that people would not forget it for years to come and that unless he drew back from Stevenson it was "going to definitely impede your political future." When Rayburn asked him to meet and introduce Stevenson at Fort Worth, Johnson phoned Shivers to ask his advice and fret about how it might affect his reelection campaign in 1954. Shivers urged him to go ahead, but cautioned Johnson not to go overboard. Johnson heeded the advice. His state-wide radio speech was a strong plea for the Democratic party, but made no mention of Stevenson. His introduction of Stevenson at

Forth Worth moved the candidate to say: "I thought when he got through he was going to introduce Ben Franklin. A little flattery is all right—as long as you don't inhale." Liberals complained of Johnson's tepid support. Drew Pearson reminded readers of Johnson's nickname, "Lyin' down Lyndon," and related how Senator Fulbright "exploded into unspecified profanity" over Johnson's reluctance to make much of an effort for the ticket. They also complained that Johnson spent more time campaigning in Stuart Symington's Senate race in Missouri than in Texas speaking for Stevenson.[71]

Yet however limited Lyndon's efforts for Stevenson in Texas, they excited conservative determination to get even with him in 1954. One Fort Worth man wrote to say that "patriotic Democrats who place loyalty to their state and to their nation above any party label" had "committees in ten of the largest cities in the state and will expand a lot in the next two years." Unless Johnson announced a change of heart and came out against Stevenson, the group was going to launch "a quiet and vigorous campaign seeking to deny you the senatorial nomination in '54." Although there was no such organization, Johnson worried that there might be, and in February 1953, he had a Dallas friend check up on the man. On November 7, the day after Texas newspapers had carried a story saying Johnson had no apologies for supporting his party's candidate, an anonymous citizen from Vernon had sent him a clipping of the article with a note: "We won't forget Lindie. . . . It won't be too long before Texas will have a chance to get rid of one of Harry's boys in our state. We won't forget. You'll be up for reelection before we forget!!!"

A state-wide Belden poll in November found that Johnson's stand for Stevenson had caused a "reversal in his previously growing popularity in Texas." His approval rating, which had reached 60 percent during 1952, had dropped back to 50 percent and made him "vulnerable to defeat by a strong opponent" in 1954. The strong opponent, as the *Dallas Times Herald* reported on November 12, might be Allan Shivers, who was "leaving all political doors open—including that of running for the U.S. Senate in 1954."[72]

Johnson's principal political concern after the 1952 election was not simply to regain lost ground in Texas but to heighten his appeal to more of the state's voters. He told Booth Mooney, a campaign manager for Coke Stevenson in 1948 and new member of Lyndon's staff, that "about half the voters of Texas were against him," and he needed "to make a dent in that large body of citizens before 1954." He did not think he could use his preparedness subcommittee to appeal to voters because he expected a quick end to the Korean war. Truce talks beginning in the summer of 1951 and an Eisenhower promise during the '52 campaign to go to Korea had raised hopes of an end to the fighting in 1953. To improve his state-wide standing, Johnson planned to seek a leadership role in the Senate and cooperate with the Eisenhower administration on conservative legislation palatable to Texas voters.[73]

His plan stemmed from the results of the 1952 Senate elections. The Democrats dropped to 47 seats, and the Republicans were able to organize the upper house. Democratic Majority Leader Ernest McFarland of Arizona was one election casualty, losing to Barry Goldwater, a conservative department-store owner. Although the last two Democratic leaders, Lucas and McFarland had lost their seats in 1950 and 1952 respectively, Johnson decided to try for the job. Unlike Lucas and McFarland, Johnson would not have to carry the burden of unpopular liberal programs advanced by a Democratic President. Rather, as a Minority Leader working with a popular President espousing less controversial conservative measures, Johnson could establish a reputation as a Democrat who put country above party and served the wishes of the Texas majority who liked Ike.

For almost two months, from November 5, the day after the election, to January 3, the day Senate Democrats met to elect their leaders, Johnson devoted himself to winning the Leadership post by the largest possible vote. He first went after Richard Russell's backing, which promised additional southern support. The exact sequence of events by which Johnson brought Russell and other senators to his side is difficult to reconstruct. Those who helped make Johnson Minority Leader have different recollections of how it occurred. It is clear, however, that Johnson himself masterminded the campaign. The day after the election he called Bobby Baker and several Democratic senators from his ranch. He arranged for Baker to have Senator Burnett Maybank of South Carolina, Baker's original sponsor, send Lyndon a telegram promising support if Russell didn't want the job. Baker promptly spread word of Maybank's endorsement to other southern senators and friendly journalists.[74]

In the meantime, Johnson urged Richard Russell to take the post. Johnson promised to do the work and let Russell be the boss. But Russell refused. He did not want to be a Minority Leader with little opportunity to lead; nor did he want to abandon his role as Armed Services Committee chairman or as an opponent of civil rights legislation. Moreover, his identification as an anti-civil rights spokesman would have made him unacceptable to northern and some border-state Democrats.

Lyndon then asked Russell to support him. Russell told an aide: "Lyndon came to me and asked me to support him, and he said, 'I don't believe I can be elected—reelected to Senator in Texas without the prestige of this office,' and so I've committed myself to support him." Russell already had a high opinion of Johnson, but a speech Lyndon gave on November 5 in San Antonio to rural electrification officials strengthened Russell's belief that Johnson would make a fine party Leader. Lyndon said that Eisenhower's victory was not the end of the world, and predicted that the American people would insist on continuing New Deal programs. After Russell agreed to support him, Lyndon asked Russell to move his Senate seat behind his, where he could easily turn to him for advice.[75]

Lyndon immediately began rounding up other support. Most of the southerners were ready to follow Russell's lead, especially after Bobby Baker called to warn them that Hubert Humphrey might get the job if Johnson didn't. According to Sam Houston Johnson, the prospect of Humphrey also brought conservative Texans to Lyndon's side. Stories that Humphrey was running for the job moved the *Dallas Morning News*, Fort Worth newspaper publisher Amon Carter, Sid Richardson, and George Brown to press Lyndon to take the position. Johnson's expressions of concern that Allan Shivers might run against him in 1954 and that he would need to spend too much time in Texas to become Minority Leader evoked assurances that Shivers would not run. Johnson himself approached Shivers about his intentions. He asked Shivers's advice on the Leadership post, and said he didn't want to have the same experience the two most recent Democratic leaders had of losing their Senate seats. Shivers saw Johnson's call as his way of "softening" him up and getting assurances that he did not intend to run.[76]

Lyndon pressed his case with other senators as well. Ernest McFarland remembered that "as soon as I was defeated, he [Johnson] called me up. And he had me call all my friends boosting him." Border and western state senators and the six freshman Democrats also received phone calls from Johnson. Earle Clements of Kentucky, a staunch liberal, Robert Kerr of Oklahoma, J. Allen Frear of Delaware, freshman John F. Kennedy of Massachusetts were all wooed successfully. Clements was asked to become party Whip, and Kennedy was flattered with attention from Johnson, a party leader. The call to a surprised Kennedy came at dawn, just after his election was confirmed. "The guy must never sleep," Kennedy said to an aide.

The key figure in Johnson's selection, however, was Russell. He moved lightning fast to make Lyndon the new party Leader. On November 10, only five days after Lyndon had launched his campaign for the job, Russell noted on his desk calendar: "Saw L. Johnson & buttoned up leadership for him." A week later he conferred with Lyndon and Clements in his office and then ate supper in Lyndon's room at the Mayflower Hotel.[77]

Although Russell and Johnson expected the Democratic caucus in January to produce a comfortable victory for Lyndon, they also knew that liberals led by Humphrey, Paul Douglas of Illinois, Guy Gillette of Iowa, and Fulbright would make it less than unanimous. On November 13, Jim Rowe had called Johnson to say that "some of the liberals are getting ready to try to knife you." William Fulbright and Drew Pearson had arranged a luncheon at Pearson's house, where they agreed "to put the heat on Lister Hill [of Alabama] to run." Although Hill wanted no part of the idea and was happy to see Lyndon become party Leader, seven or eight liberals forged ahead. Paul Douglas's secretary called around complaining that Lyndon had lost Texas for Stevenson by refusing to make more of a fight in the state, and Jim Murray of Montana agreed to be the liberal candidate. Drew Pearson than published a column on the 20th saying that "some Democratic Senators aren't at all happy about" the prospect of Johnson as Leader. "They figure that 'Lyin'-down' . . . will follow a pro-Republican line and there won't be much Democratic opposition to GOP policies."[78]

Johnson was eager to launch his term as Leader with the greatest possible party harmony; he asked liberals not to oppose him. He called Hubert Humphrey at home and expressed regret over Hubert's opposition "because he was considering me for the minority whip job." Though the suggestion exhilarated Humphrey, he was more interested in "better committee assignments, [and] more power for liberals on the steering and policy committees of the Senate Democratic caucus." Johnson made clear to Humphrey that under his Leadership the Policy Committee would represent "different viewpoints," and he raised the possibility of putting two liberals, including Humphrey, on the Foreign Relations Committee. Hubert said he couldn't endorse Johnson publicly and intended to stick with Murray, but promised "to do all he can to minimize a fight and try to make it [the vote] unanimous." Johnson reported this to Adlai Stevenson in a phone call, and urged Stevenson to steer clear of the fight lest the press say that he was "telling the Senate what to do." To Johnson's satisfaction, Stevenson said it was "the last thing" he wanted to do "to get in any way entangled with the selection." Moreover, Stevenson wanted to minimize disagreements in the party, because "it is going to make the Democrats look as if they were incapable of governing."[79]

After Humphrey discussed Johnson's telephone call with other liberals, he, Douglas, Lester Hunt of Wyoming, and Herbert Lehman of New York approached Johnson about trading their support for committee assignments. Johnson was in no mood to make concessions and "politely but curtly" sent them away. Johnson then called Humphrey, asking him to come alone to his office. Johnson wanted to know how many votes Humphrey thought he had. When Humphrey said, "anywhere from thirteen to seventeen," Johnson gave him a lesson in political nose counting. "First of all, you ought to be sure of your count," Johnson said. "That's too much of a spread. But you don't have them anyway. *Who* do you think you have?" As Humphrey went down the list of senators and checked some off, Johnson shook his head on most of them. "You don't have those senators. I have personal commitments that they're going to vote for me. You ought to quit fooling around with people you can't depend on." Shifting to a friendlier tone, Johnson praised Humphrey for being a straightshooter and asked him to come back after the caucus to discuss "what we're going to do. I want to work with you and only you from the bomb throwers."[80]

When the caucus met on January 2, 1953, Humphrey found that Johnson "was just as right as day." Richard Russell, in what one Johnson aide called "a very wonderful speech," nominated Lyndon, at forty-four, to become the youngest Leader in Democratic party history. He pointed to Johnson's record of party loyalty, his "human values," peerless qualities as a conciliator, and championship of party unity. Russell expressed "complete confidence" in Johnson's ability to serve the "party to which we adhere & [the] country & people we seek to serve." In a show of unity, Theodore Francis Green of Rhode Island, speaking for the East, and Dennis Chavez of New Mexico, speaking for the West, seconded the nomination. The opposition, represented by Murray's candidacy, got just five votes. Only Douglas, Hunt, and Lehman voted with Humphrey and Murray. Humphrey then proposed that the nomination be unanimous, because he "didn't want Jim Murray to be humiliated."

Before Johnson left the meeting, he invited Humphrey to come see him. Their discussion was "brief and to the point." Johnson agreed to put Murray on the Democratic Policy Committee, though he thought it was "a damned fool selection." Murray was "too old," and Johnson predicted that he would go along with everything Johnson wanted. Humphrey gave Johnson other requests for liberal representation on the party's Steering Committee and the Senate Finance, Judiciary, Commerce, and Appropriations committees. Johnson agreed to all of them and sent a message to the liberals through Humphrey: Tell them "that you're the one to talk to me and that if they'll talk through you as their leader we can get some things done."[81]

Johnson had made his first major move toward consolidating his power as Democratic Leader and restoring the position to the importance it had under Joe Robinson of Arkansas in the 1930s.

13

Bipartisan Politics

JOHNSON delighted in the national attention, party influence, and Senate power given him by the Minority Leadership. After only four years, he was on the Senate's center stage, though not yet in the lead role. That part had fallen to Robert Taft of Ohio, the Majority Leader. The son of a former President, a third-term senator, a man described as "Mr. Republican," Taft dwarfed Lyndon in national reputation and prestige. And Lyndon couldn't stand it. When Taft, as he often did, ignored Lyndon's existence, Johnson would lean across the center aisle, pretending he had forgotten his reading glasses, and ask Taft to read the fine print in a bill or committee report to him. When journalists Johnson courted gave Taft more newsprint, Johnson privately referred to them as "piss-ant reporters." He sarcastically told his friend Bill White, who in early 1953 understandably wrote more stories about Taft than Johnson: "This is Lyndon Johnson [calling], the Minority Leader of the Senate, you may remember. I would take it very kindly if I could have an appointment with the Senate correspondent of the *New York Times*. Now, of course, I don't want to put you out—I would be glad to meet you in Senator Taft's office." [1]

Becoming Minority Leader gave Lyndon a greater sense of self-importance. But he did not seek the job simply for its prestige. He saw the post as carrying responsibilities he welcomed. As a key party figure and a Senate leader, he mapped a strategy that could restore Democratic control of Congress and serve the well-being of the country. Two days after the election, even before he had won the Leader's post, he had asked George Reedy to consider means of achieving these goals. Reedy wrote a memo, which Johnson showed "to everybody in sight," recommending that the Democrats "vote as a united party wherever possible" and cooperate with Eisenhower, who would likely be in greater agreement with Senate Democrats than Senate Republicans. The outcome would be Republican infighting, "a dignified but pointed record on all issues where the Democratic party is . . . strongest—REA, soil conservation, power, housing," and "a record that would be very potent campaign ammunition" in the 1954 and 1956 campaigns.

Sam Rayburn had reached much the same conclusion. Immediately after the 1952 election, he had decided to accept the House Minority Leadership and use bipartisanship for both national and self-serving political ends. "Any jackass can kick a barn down, but it takes a good carpenter to build one," he said. He told Eisenhower: "I'll help you on international affairs and defense, if you can get a majority of your own party to go along." Further, if the President wished to extend any existing Democratic program, Rayburn promised to help. Any attempt to jettison New Deal–Fair Deal programs, however, would be resisted. When the majority proposed unacceptable legislation, he intended "to take the bad parts out and put good parts in."[2]

Johnson saw the wisdom of the Reedy-Rayburn approach. He was one of a very few people who realized that Eisenhower's 1952 election provided a chance to "convert the fractionalized Democratic Senate group into a cohesive whole" and advance American interests at home and abroad. Our objective should be party harmony, he told a Senate Democratic caucus on January 2. Together, they should fight for a positive program—"a program geared NOT just to opposing the majority but to serving America." At the beginning of February, when Eisenhower called for "true bipartisanship" in foreign and defense policies, Johnson declared his party "ready and eager to consult with the President." In a speech at a Jefferson-Jackson dinner later that month, Johnson asked his fellow Democrats to shun "the politics of partisanship" for "the politics of responsibility." It was only through the latter that "we can offer leadership to the American people that will be accepted," and that would help assure the survival and future well-being of the United States. Always more comfortable in the middle as a consensus builder accommodating opposing factions than as an unqualified partisan, Johnson relished the role of bipartisan leader.[3]

The first and most essential condition of Democratic success under a popular Republican President was party unity. Johnson was mindful of Will Rogers's observation: "I am not a member of any organized political party. I am a Democrat." He also remembered the old saw that a Democrat would rather fight a Democrat any time than fight a Republican. In the winter of 1953, the Democrats seemed more divided than ever among conservatives, liberals, and moderates: segregationists like Harry Byrd of Virginia and Richard Russell of Georgia seemed incapable of cooperation with southern and midwestern liberals like Estes Kefauver of Tennessee, Paul Douglas of Illinois, and Hubert Humphrey of Minnesota. These competing factions could swamp senators in the middle like Johnson. All the Senate Democrats, except for Russell, were "very, very skeptical of the Johnson leadership. Johnson did not get the leadership because anybody thought he could handle it," George Reedy says. "But there was just nobody else. No liberal could have stepped into that position at that point without tearing the Democratic party to pieces, and no conservative could have stepped into it at that point." Democrats, *Time* magazine said in 1953, were members of "a party which is looking for an excuse to fly to pieces."[4]

Johnson enlisted the support of other moderates and reformed party institutions to advance Democratic unity. He asked Earle C. Clements of Kentucky to become party Whip with expanded responsibilities. Clements was a southern patrician with unassailable liberal credentials. As someone from an influential southern family who had served his state as a congressman and governor, Clements was accepted into the Senate club or oligarchy as soon as he came to the upper house in 1951. As someone who had compiled a liberal voting record praised by organized labor and middle-class consumers and had gone all out for Stevenson in 1952, Clements was attractive to Senate liberals. Eager to take advantage of Clements's standing with both wings of the party, Lyndon made him party Whip, gave him a special office and staff, and relied on him to round up party members for legislative votes. "Clements had a great sensitivity to what Johnson was trying to do," an aide recalled. "When a particular action of some kind was coming up, Johnson would explain to Clements in three sentences what he wanted, and Clements would just get the full picture. It might take him an hour to give me my orders—I was leg man for the whip—but three sentences were enough from Johnson."[5]

Johnson also turned the Senate Democratic Policy Committee into a unified party voice on legislation. Originally created in 1947 to formulate the party's legislative positions, the Committee did little more than keep track of each senator's voting record. Moreover, southern dominance of the party had largely made the Committee a preserve of conservatives. Lyndon changed both conditions. He broadened the composition of the Committee to consist of four conservatives, two moderates, and three liberals, and he made it an effective party voice on legislation. To ensure that differences among committee members did not turn into open fights on the Senate floor, he won agreement to a "unanimous consent rule"—90 percent of Committee members had to support legislative recommendations. Liberals were not entirely happy with the Committee's power to prevent controversial bills from coming before the Senate. Lyndon believed that calling up unpassable bills that provoked Democratic infighting was unwise. "Why should we cut each other up and then lose after the bloodshedding?" he said to Bobby Baker. Privately, Johnson complained about damned fool liberals "who'd rather piss into the wind than with it." [6]

Johnson also convinced a more representative Senate Democratic Steering Committee to consider criteria other than seniority for committee assignments. The Steering Committee's principal function was to name party members to the Senate's various committees. Under the senority system, the longest serving Democrats, which usually meant southern conservatives, received the best committee assignments. Johnson believed that party harmony partly depended on altering that tradition. It required skillful manipulation on his part. With six of the fifteen places on the Steering Committee vacant, Johnson appointed three liberals and three conservatives. Then he prevailed upon Richard Russell to make the criteria for committee assignments a senator's interest and aptitude and party harmony rather than simply seniority.

Russell believed that such a reform would help restore Democratic control over Congress and advance Johnson's prospects for the presidency. "Russell made no bones whatsoever—he was quite open with me—" George Reedy recalls, "that he thought the only way to ever really put an end to the Civil War was to elect a southerner president. And he could not see any southerner that could get elected president except LBJ. He talked about that to me as early as 1953." Reedy doesn't know whether Johnson seriously believed in 1953 or later that he could become President, but he is certain that Johnson used that possibility as a way to buy "elbow room from the southern Democrats" in establishing rapport with liberals. [7]

With Russell's backing Johnson made a convincing case to the Steering Committee for relaxation of the seniority rule. Johnson used an anecdote about two boyhood friends to persuade his colleagues: Ben and Otto Crider were brothers and Lyndon's neighbors in Johnson City. Ben, the older of the two, was more outgoing and popular. One weekend, when Lyndon invited Otto to spend the night at his house, Mrs. Crider said, "No." " 'But mama,' " Otto protested, ". . . 'Ben, he's already been twowheres, and I ain't never been nowheres.' " As Lyndon told Adlai Stevenson, "We have old members who have everything, and want more, and the younger, abler men sit under the trees and do nothing. We are opening up 9 to 10 committee assignments for the younger men." Hubert Humphrey and Mike Mansfield of Montana went on the coveted Foreign Relations Committee; Stuart Symington of Missouri joined the Armed Services Committee; John F. Kennedy of Massachusetts was assigned to Labor and Public Welfare; Price Daniel to Interior; Russell Long of Louisiana to Finance; Albert Gore of Tennessee to Public Works; and George Smathers of Florida to Interstate and Foreign Commerce. The consequence of these appointments, Johnson told Adlai Stevenson, was that "we have more unity among the Senate Democrats than we have ever had during my service here."[8]

Lyndon also promoted unity by muting ideological differences between liberals and conservatives. Hubert Humphrey was a principal case in point. By appointing Humphrey to the Foreign Relations Committee, Lyndon recognized his worth, flattered his ego, and inhibited Humphrey from agitating domestic issues that divided Senate Democrats. Humphrey had to resign from the Labor and Public Welfare and Agriculture committees to accept Foreign Relations. He was reluctant to do it. " 'My gosh, Mr. Leader, you know at home my constituency is Democratic farmer-labor party. You're asking me to give up labor. You're asking me to give up . . . Agriculture.' . . . 'Now listen,' " Johnson told him, " 'this is one time where you're going to serve your country and your party. . . . You've just got to take another look at yourself here. You can fight for the farmers down here on this [Senate] floor and you can fight for the laboring man, but we've got some serious foreign policy issues coming up and they're going to be major.' "

Humphrey could help stop Secretary of State John Foster Dulles from scuttling the Roosevelt-Truman foreign policies, or so Lyndon said. Actually, he principally wanted to divert Humphrey's attention from domestic affairs. When Adlai Stevenson told Johnson that Humphrey was "modulated" and "doesn't seem to be breathing the same kind of extreme fire that he used to," Johnson replied: "I tried to explain to him that we could not have a completely labor party, and if he would stop making about 40 speeches for the CIO every week, . . . we might bring some of these things together. He is doing that." Humphrey agreed to take the Foreign Relations seat on the condition that he be returned to Agriculture in the future.[9]

Similarly, Johnson kept Albert Gore, another liberal, from agitating divisive civil rights issues by keeping him off the Judiciary Committee. Johnson assigned Olin D. Johnston of South Carolina, a segregationist, and Thomas Hennings of Missouri, a manageable liberal, to the Committee, and put Gore on Public Works, where he could compile a liberal record on roads, dams, and public buildings but not arouse passions over civil rights. Johnson's maneuvers helped assure that civil rights legislation would make no gains in 1953. In January, a proposal to revise the cloture rule as a first step toward civil rights reform failed after limited debate by a 70–21 vote.[10]

To promote Democratic unity in 1953, Lyndon had to tame not only Humphrey and Gore but also Wayne Morse and the tidelands issue. Morse was a maverick Republican from Oregon who supported Stevenson in the 1952 campaign. Morse promised to vote with the Republicans in organizing the Senate if they let him stay on the Armed Services and Labor committees. But Taft didn't need his vote. Morse's defection to the Democrats would have produced a 48–48 tie, which Vice President Richard Nixon could have broken. Liberal Democrats were ready to take Morse into their party. But Johnson refused. Morse would have replaced deserving Democrats on Armed Services and Labor and seemed certain to become an unmanageable liberal.

Johnson's decision angered Morse, who now had to serve on the Public Works and District of Columbia committees. Although Morse declared himself the Independent party of the United States, he had to sit on the Republican side of the aisle, where they harassed him with nasty cracks. Morse asked permission to sit with the Democrats, but Johnson, who wanted to hold him at arm's length, left the decision to the Rules Committee. When it rejected the request, Morse focused his frustration on Johnson, telling Paul Douglas that he intended to campaign against Johnson in Texas the following year. Johnson relished the possibility of Morse's intrusion into his Texas campaign. As *Time* reported the story, when Douglas, who lobbied for Morse's addition to the party, related Morse's threat to Johnson, Lyndon replied: "You aren't trying to argue that we should give in to political blackmail, are you?" [11]

During the first five months of 1953 Johnson also had to fend off threats to Democratic unity from the tidelands dispute. In January, Price Daniel introduced a bill restoring control over submerged lands to the states. The Republicans, having promised to support such legislation, embraced Daniel's proposal. It helped blunt sharp Democratic differences on an explosive issue and created tensions between Republican senators and the White House. Instead of attacking their party colleagues supporting the bill, liberal Democrats went after the Republicans as the "give-away boys." Most Republicans were ready to support a bill affirming state control over nine statute miles of offshore lands. But Herbert Brownell, Eisenhower's Attorney General, wished to limit state property rights to three miles or to maintain Federal ownership and let the states reap the benefits of offshore oil drilling. His opinion angered proponents of Daniel's bill and forced the Administration to explain its position. Although Lyndon openly supported Daniel, he was able to leave most of the public maneuvering against a twenty-seven-day filibuster to Taft. After a five-week debate, the Senate passed the Daniel bill restoring state control over nine miles of offshore lands. The measure increased Johnson's popularity with the 74 percent of Texans who favored it and did little to damage his influence with Democratic opponents of the law. [12]

Yet Johnson's success in muting Democratic divisions was not complete. Columnist Drew Pearson, who in November had attacked Johnson as unlikely to offer strong minority leadership against Eisenhower, criticized him in January for betraying the Democratic party and committing acts of corruption. Pearson went after Johnson for personal and political reasons. In early January 1953, Pearson had asked Johnson to help stop Joe McCarthy from attacking him as a Communist. Pearson and McCarthy had been fighting publicly since McCarthy had begun his anti-Communist crusade in 1950. Later that year, at a party in the posh Washington Sulgrave Club, McCarthy physically attacked Pearson, kneeing him in the groin and slapping him repeatedly across the face. "When are they going to put you in the booby hatch," Pearson shouted at him. Three days after the attack, McCarthy began denouncing Pearson on the Senate floor as "the voice of international communism." " 'Lyndon, you know that I'm not a Communist,' " Pearson told him. " 'You were good enough when running against Coke Stevenson to express your appreciation to me, and I assume that I might have a little help from you . . . showing that I'm not a Communist.' And he looked at me with considerable disapproval and said, 'Drew, you've not been kind to me lately.' So that ended the interview." But not the pressure from Pearson, who pressed Johnson to have a Democratic caucus condemn McCarthy. Incensed at being called "Lyin'-down Lyndon" and convinced that it would be "suicidal" for the Democrats to take on McCarthy in 1953, Johnson refused.[13]

Pearson then began a series of broadcasts and columns that blasted Johnson's politics and ethics. First, he accused Johnson of having made a deal with Taft to throw one Democratic vote to the Republicans every time Wayne Morse voted with the Democrats, and he reported a comment from Republican Senator Karl Mundt of South Dakota that Johnson could be relied on to vote with the Republicans six out of seven times. He then accused Johnson of suppressing Preparedness subcommittee reports on "General Motors for pyramiding profits on defense contracts" and on crime on the New Jersey waterfront that cost the U.S. government a lot of money. He also complained that Johnson had fired the two investigators who had brought him the "facts" on waterfront racketeering. Pearson thought that Johnson "considered General Motors too big to tackle," and that he had sat on the crime investigation because his and Senator Russell's friends had been "dickering" for the support of New Jersey delegates at the 1952 Democratic Convention in Chicago.[14]

The charges enraged Lyndon, who complained that Pearson was "blackmailing" him and that "this dirty son of a bitch is mad at me because I won't bail him out with McCarthy." Although the controversy caused Johnson considerable discomfort, it died out quickly. At the end of January, Jim Rowe went to see Pearson in Lyndon's behalf. After Rowe argued against Pearson's allegations with information provided by Johnson and pointed out that Lyndon had created more unity among Senate Democrats than there had been for years, Pearson described himself as "an old friend of Johnson's" and as planning to write "some nice things in the future about Lyndon Johnson." Rowe accurately predicted that Pearson was "now going to shut up." However painful the episode, it did little to loosen Johnson's hold over his party in the Senate."[15]

Along with party unity, Johnson considered a bipartisan foreign policy essential for renewed Democratic majorities in the Congress and the well-being of the country. Opposing Eisenhower on foreign affairs at the start of his term would have been political suicide. Besides, Old Guard, isolationist Republicans were going to do it for the Democrats, and allow them to score political points by backing Ike. Lyndon saw this as not only good politics, but also good national policy. He gave public backing to bipartisanship early in 1953 and sent copies of what he said to columnists and Republican party leaders. In April, after conservative Republicans had made foreign affairs an issue between themselves and the Administration, Johnson wrote Maury Maverick, "We cannot allow the Republicans to jump off the cliff, because they will carry the nation with them."[16]

Eisenhower considered Democratic support of his foreign and defense policies essential. In his State of the Union message on February 2 he called for bipartisanship; and in a private meeting with Republican legislators on February 16, he insisted that it be "firmly established as soon as possible," or before "a major crisis came along." The President then introduced regular defense briefings for Democratic and Republican congressional leaders. At the first of these on February 19, Dulles and the Joint Chiefs described Administration policy to eleven Democrats, including Lyndon, and fifteen Republicans. Lyndon said little during the meeting, leaving most of the talking to Administration spokesmen.[17]

In his State of the Union message, Eisenhower "hammered" the Democrats for having made secret agreements at Yalta in 1945 which permitted Soviet "enslavement" of Eastern Europe. His remarks implied that he would ask Congress to repudiate the Yalta commitments. But a resolution he sent to the Hill on February 20 only criticized the Soviet Union for interpreting Yalta "to bring about the subjugation of free peoples." Isolationist Republicans led by Joseph McCarthy attacked Eisenhower's failure to repudiate the agreements and called for action to free Eastern Europe. Eisenhower urged Republican leaders not to amend his statement. He feared that repudiation would cancel American occupation rights in Berlin and Vienna and alienate the Democrats, who saw it as an attack on FDR.[18]

When it became clear that the Republican Old Guard would not back down, Lyndon made the Democrats the defenders of a constructive Eisenhower foreign policy. On February 24 the Democratic Policy Committee commended the President's resolution as containing "no trace of the partisanship that could lead to discord and disunity." The Committee urged unanimous Senate approval as a demonstration of united American opposition to Soviet tyranny. Taft tried to end the controversy among Republicans by amending the resolution to say it did "not constitute a determination by the Congress as to the validity or invalidity" of the Yalta agreements. The Foreign Relations Committee approved the amended resolution by a vote of 8 to 6, and Dulles tried to persuade Johnson and the Democrats to go along. But Lyndon, backed by his Democratic colleagues, wouldn't budge. He told Dulles that the amendment undermined the objectives the President had in mind. "We start off by saying we refuse to admit there are any understandings and then give them [the Soviets] hell for perverting those understandings. . . . How can we criticize the Russians for perverting understandings if we refuse to admit their validity?" Unable to find a way out of the dilemma and eager to end a controversy that served the Democrats, the Administration used Stalin's death on March 5 to shelve the question.[19]

Conservative Republican opposition to Charles Bohlen's appointment as Ambassador to the Soviet Union afforded Johnson and the Democrats another chance to back Eisenhower on foreign policy. A career Foreign Service officer with a rich knowledge of Soviet affairs, Bohlen was an excellent choice. But having served during the Roosevelt administration and helped draft the Yalta agreements, which he refused to repudiate, Bohlen became an object of McCarthy's wrath. Although Eisenhower defended Bohlen as "the best-qualified man for that post that I could find," McCarthy insisted that secret FBI reports would demonstrate otherwise. Refusing to release the FBI materials as a violation of Executive privilege, the White House allowed Senators Taft and Sparkman to examine the file. After doing so, they reported that it contained nothing damaging and urged Bohlen's confirmation.

Johnson, who liked Bohlen and thought he would make a fine ambassador, defended him on the Senate floor. He cited the President's support and the absence of any evidence indicating that Bohlen was a security risk. Johnson then described opposition to Bohlen as tantamount to questioning the integrity of Eisenhower, Taft, and Sparkman. Johnson also denied that Democrats were gleeful over the Republican infighting, as Illinois senator Everett Dirksen said they were. Although genuinely convinced that Bohlen's appointment by a 74-to-13 vote on March 27 was in the country's interest, Johnson also took satisfaction from the political advantage the controversy gave the Democrats.[20]

Johnson was more circumspect on the Administration's efforts to end the Korean war. Although Eisenhower came under considerable pressure from Republican hardliners to free North Korea from Communist control, he refused. A visit to Korea in December 1952 convinced him to end the war as quickly as possible. He saw little prospect of gain from either a new offensive against the North or a continuing stalemate in which the United States took additional casualties. When right-wing Republicans attacked Ike over renewed armistice talks with the Chinese and North Koreans in the spring and summer of 1953, Johnson took no part in the debate. He believed that a negotiated end to the conflict was in the best interests of the United States, but was reluctant to argue with hardline anti-Communists on an issue that might cost him politically in Texas and the nation. Johnson, however, responded critically to an armistice signed on July 26. He attacked the agreement as merely releasing aggressive armies to attack elsewhere and urged that retaliation against Moscow should follow any future aggression by a Soviet satellite.[21]

A proposal from Republican senator John Bricker of Ohio to amend the Constitution provoked another foreign policy controversy. Bricker urged limits on Executive authority to make treaties in order to prevent future "Yaltas." Executive and other agreements were not to become the "supreme law of the land" until Congress passed legislation making them so. In January 1953, his amendment won the support of sixty-two senators, two short of the two-thirds needed for passage.[22]

No one knew what the Bricker Amendment meant. Eisenhower called it "an addition to the Constitution that said you could not violate the Constitution. How silly." The President quickly became "sick of the Bricker Amendment" and wanted to scotch it. But the measure enjoyed widespread support in the Republican party and throughout the country. George Reedy said that in all the years he was in Washington the Bricker Amendment was the most controversial issue to come before Congress. "Nobody was quite certain what it would do. . . . Proponents were convinced that it would prevent American boys from having their hands chopped off in Saudi Arabia, and being sentenced to five years in solitary confinement in France. And all the antagonists were absolutely convinced that . . . it would make complete hash out of American foreign policy. . . . It was customary to receive sometimes several thousand letters a day on this one issue. It got to the Senate, and it became apparent . . . that it could not be defeated on a straight-out vote. No one could vote against the Bricker Amendment with impunity, and very few could vote against it and survive at all—at least, so they thought."[23]

Lyndon shared this concern and declared himself an initial supporter of the Amendment. Yet, like Eisenhower, he had no desire to see it pass. "It's the worst bill I can think of," he told Bobby Baker. "It ties the president's hands and I'm not just talking about Ike. It will be the bane of every president we elect. . . . We've got to stop the damn thing, and I think we can. We don't want to go putting that idea up on billboards, though." During 1953 the White House managed to tie up the Amendment in hearings. At the same time, Lyndon half-truthfully told a state-wide Texas radio audience that he favored an amendment which would ensure against a loss of constitutional rights through any treaty and a loss of presidential power to conduct foreign affairs effectively.[24]

Eisenhower and Johnson had to confront the issue at the start of 1954: Bricker and his supporters pushed the Amendment through the Judiciary Committee and on to the Senate floor for a vote. In response, Eisenhower mounted an aggressive opposition campaign, saying it would unduly limit a President in foreign affairs. When a number of senators agreed to abandon Bricker's Amendment, the President gave his support to an innocuous substitute saying that an international agreement could not override the Constitution. To identify Democrats with the President's substitute, Johnson persuaded Walter George of Georgia, the chairman of the Foreign Relations Committee, to present a substitute resolution much like Ike's. Bricker parried this by introducing a revised version of his proposal, and William Knowland of California, the Majority Leader since Taft had succumbed to cancer in 1953, introduced his own amendment.[25]

Since Eisenhower and Johnson wanted no limitation on presidential powers, they arranged the defeat of all three proposals. At the end of February, the Senate rejected Bricker's revised amendment by 50 to 42 and then voted 61 to 30 to substitute the George resolution. When the final tally was taken on the George amendment, however, it failed to win a two-thirds majority by a 60-to-31 count. Although Lyndon was one of the sixty, he was able to reflect the wishes of his Texas constituents without fear that the amendment would pass. According to the fullest study of the Bricker Amendment, "one should not read too much significance into the fact that the George Amendment fell just one vote short of . . . approval, for there are some indications that the measure's opponents had a few votes in reserve that could have been called upon if necessary." A State Department official later revealed that a handful of senators who voted yes for political reasons had been ready to vote no if their support had been needed to defeat the amendment.[26]

The vote on the George substitute was characteristic of Johnson's Senate leadership. He relied on Clements and Bobby Baker, whom Johnson had made assistant secretary to the Senate minority, to calculate every senator's vote. In addition, he encouraged senators "who need to vote against us [to] go ahead and do that if it causes no harm. That way, we'll have a little something in the bank for future uses," he told Baker. "If we'll be understanding when senators are in a bind and have to go against us for the record, then we can press 'em a little harder on another issue when the going is really tough." Since Knowland favored passing an amendment, Johnson played the crucial role in defeating the George substitute. He later claimed that he had foreseen the 60–31 result. He "had engineered this cliff-hanging vote . . . in order to make the Administration sweat." No doubt he had accurately estimated the final tally, but had not anticipated some last-minute dramatics. At the end of the voting the count stood at 60 to 30, enough for the George substitute to pass. The missing vote was liberal West Virginia Senator Harley Kilgore, who apparently had too much to drink and was sleeping it off or still imbibing at a local tavern. Hustled to the Senate floor at the end of the roll call, Kilgore cast the deciding "no" vote.[27]

As in the selective service fight in 1941 and the MacArthur hearing in 1951, Lyndon saw the battles over Yalta, Bohlen, the Korean truce, and the Bricker Amendment as ways to serve the country's international needs and score points for the Democrats by hidden, highhanded means.

Domestic affairs was a less promising arena for Johnson's bipartisan strategy. As George Reedy observed, "Eisenhower was an economic conservative and, on domestic legislation, his heart belonged to the moderate right wing of the Republican party." With the exception of a Labor Secretary who had been head of the plumbers' union, the President principally appointed conservative businessmen to his Cabinet, including three men tied to the automobile industry. *The New Republic* described the Cabinet as "Eight millionaires and a plumber," and Adlai Stevenson complained that "the New Dealers have all left Washington to make way for the car dealers."

Yet even on domestic issues, Johnson made it seem that the President and the Senate Democrats were joined in a struggle against reactionary Republicans. Johnson held "Democratic" legislation to a minimum, and turned Eisenhower's bills into "New Deal-ish" laws with amendments spawned by the Democratic Policy Committee. By leaving Eisenhower's stamp on the bill, Johnson accurately calculated that the President wouldn't intervene in the Senate debate or veto the measure. "It also meant," Reedy says, "that the Senate Democrats were pitted solely against Senate Republicans and, as the Democrats were fighting only for amendments, the picture before the public was that of a Republican president and a Democratic Senate cooperating in the service of the nation while a small group of GOP partisans were trying to throw sand in the gears."[28]

The shift in Republican Senate leadership from Taft to Knowland in 1953 partly made this possible. Taft himself was unsympathetic to much of what Eisenhower proposed at the start of his term. When the President told Taft at a White House meeting in April that his first budget would be $5.5 billion in the red, the Senator pounded his fist on the Cabinet table and shouted: "With a program like this, we'll never elect a Republican Congress in 1954. You're taking us down the same road Truman traveled. It's a repudiation of everything we promised in the campaign."

Knowland was even more of a problem. Former governor of New

Hampshire Sherman Adams, who had become "Assistant to the President," said, "It would have been difficult to find anyone more disposed to do battle with much of the President's program in Congress" than Knowland. In addition to being so conservative, he was also inept. In the view of one Democratic senator, Knowland "possessed little skill or finesse" for the Majority leader's job. "The blustery Knowland was a man of principle, to the point of bullheadedness. So often did he cross paths with his president's program, that Dwight Eisenhower soon found he could work more comfortably with the Senate's Democratic leader than with the Republican Knowland." In a note to a friend, Eisenhower himself said of Knowland: "It is a pity that his wisdom, his judgment, his tact, and his sense of humor lag so far behind his ambition." As time passed, Eisenhower became even more more critical of him: "In his case," the President confided to his diary, "there seems to be no final answer to the question 'How stupid can you get?' " Republican senator Styles Bridges of New Hampshire once told Johnson, "Don't think you can pull the wool over my eyes the way you do with Bill Knowland."[29]

In the summer of 1953, after Congress adjourned, Lyndon publicly emphasized that the President's real friends on domestic legislation were the Democrats. He described the session as "a shakedown cruise" and said that its principal bills were extensions of New Deal–Fair Deal measures: the Reciprocal Trade Agreements Act—"the monument to the Great Democratic statesman, Cordell Hull"—was extended for a year; a grant of authority to reorganize executive agencies was "the same authority granted to predecessor Presidents"; and the excess profits tax represented a six-month extension of an existing law. Yet "a majority of the basic issues" had been put off until the next session with the agreement of the President. Johnson described the outstanding feature of the first session as the responsibility displayed by the minority Members of both Houses. "The great majority of the President's program was put through only because of Democratic support." Most of the opposition came from "the ranks of his own party." The Democrats had "acted upon the conviction that the future of the Nation was far too important to be jeopardized for the sake of a narrow partisan gain."[30]

And "through a strict adherence to the politics of responsibility, the Democrats achieved almost unprecedented heights of unity during this session." Johnson's Democratic colleagues agreed with him. As *Time* reporter John L. Steele told his New York office, "Congress ended on the sweet note of unity. Everyone loved everyone else." Tennessee's Albert Gore lauded Johnson for having " 'unified the Democratic party in the U.S. Senate as I have not seen it unified in 15 years.' The remarkable note in the praise was that it came from every section of the Democratic party. Fair-Dealing Herbert Lehman noted that in January 'the Democratic party was a divided party . . . but . . . the area of agree-

ment we have reached today is far greater than the area of differences.' "
Conservatives George Smathers of Florida and Ed Johnson of Colorado
"joined the praise. Even 'go it alone' Pat McCarran [of Nevada] joined
what he called 'this love feast.' "[31]

Johnson used some of this praise in his 1954 reelection campaign,
which began early in 1953. Even with the prestige of the Minority Leader's job and his effective cultivation of former opponents in Texas, Johnson worried about the outcome. He had some reason for concern. An
article in the January 20, 1953, issue of *The Reporter* had drawn a less
than flattering picture of a "politician's politician" whom Senate colleagues admired rather than liked. Described as "stern to the point of
ruthlessness" and strictly intent on the acquisition of power, Johnson
came across as an opportunist eager to shed the image of "a Dixiecrat
in Washington and a Communist in Texas."

Johnson and Reedy believed that a host of Democrats, including Shivers, were preparing to compete for Lyndon's seat. "You had more people getting set to run against Lyndon Johnson for the Senate than you
had voters in the average Texas precinct," Reedy recalled. ". . . There
was quite a bit of thought that Johnson would be meat in '54." In June
1953 a message reached Johnson's office that Coke Stevenson had met
with some Republicans and "Republicrats" at his ranch to find "a man
to beat Lyndon Johnson. Now while all this is still rumor," Johnson's
informant said, "the party telephone lines and similar sources are seldom wrong." At the same time, the Republicans, led by Jack Porter,
Lyndon's opponent in '48, were also looking for a strong candidate who
would use Eisenhower's popularity to challenge Johnson. The President
endorsed the idea in a memo to Attorney General Brownell.[32]

At the start of 1953, Johnson had asked Reedy and others to begin
knocking down potential opponents. When Governor Shivers visited
Washington in February, Sam Houston Johnson had arranged a luncheon for him with the Texas congressional delegation. Sam Houston
had also included the Texas press, and asked Sam Rayburn to award
Lyndon a testimonial plaque. After the Speaker presented it with "a
flow of eloquent praise," Shivers, who assumed the luncheon was off-
the-record, outdid Rayburn in complimenting Lyndon. When Texas
newspapers printed Shivers's remarks with a photo of him embracing
Johnson, the governor's chief aide complained: "Goddamn it. Allen should
have known better than to get boxed in like that in Lyndon's own backyard. He'll never be able to squeeze out of this one." Lyndon gave Sam
Houston the plaque, telling him: "You're the one who won it."[33]

During the first nine months of the year, Johnson's office did not miss
a beat in polishing his image. In June, *Time* put him on its cover and
described him as a possible presidential nominee in 1956: "I'm not smart
enough to make a President," Lyndon said. "I come from the wrong

part of the country. I like the Senate job. . . . I want to stay here."
Shortly after, columnist Joseph Alsop wrote a flattering editorial. Weekly
radio reports and occasional television appearances coupled with a steady
flow of photographs to newspapers kept Lyndon before the Texas public.
Reedy was attentive to the smallest detail: "The newsreel shot of you
was excellent." But "you should have been wearing a dark suit" with a
"light pastel colored" shirt and "a solid color tie." As in his early House
days, Johnson's Senate office sent out congratulatory letters to every high
school graduate across the state, and publicized Federal spending in
Texas, especially by the air force.[34]

Yet all this positive publicity did not convince Johnson that he was a
safe bet for reelection. He wanted a bold stroke that would discourage
any one of importance from running against him and would give him a
landslide. "To knock out the opposition before it became opposition,"
Reedy proposed that Johnson run a two-and-a half-month fifth-year
campaign in the fall of 1953. The objective was to launch a whirlwind
tour of the state in which Johnson could shake thousands of hands and
talk "to every single person that would stand still long enough to listen
to him." Since he would have no competition in the fall of 1953, he
could create enough momentum for himself to discourage any serious
opposition in 1954.[35]

Beginning in September for three months, Johnson went into every
congressional district in Texas, where he spent almost every waking hour
of every day speaking. He gave between 13 and 17 speeches a day to
groups of 25 to 300 people and shook some 200,000 hands. It was a
potent means for winning a state-wide race. Cecil Burney, a Corpus
Christi attorney and longtime supporter, remembered picking Johnson
up early one morning in Gonzalez and working their way south to Corpus Christi. "We talked to every school and Rotary club," in the area.
"We'd drive along the road, and there'd be a little country store along
the roadside; and he'd say, 'Stop, Cecil; stop, Cecil! I've got to go in
here.' So he'd jump out . . . and run in there and shake hands with
everybody in the store, and then run and jump back in the car and away
we'd go. And the little country crossroads would tell everybody that ever
came in that store that Senator Johnson had been there the day before.
It was the greatest advertising you could ever get."

The campaign paid off handsomely. The tour was "absolutely breathtaking," George Reedy says, and at the end of it "nobody wanted to run
against him." To have challenged him at that point "would have been
absolute madness."[36]

Yet mindful of how quickly political fortunes can change, Johnson
worried that his strong standing might erode during 1954. The congressional session promised to be far more difficult for the Democrats than
the previous one. Controversial legislative issues left over from 1953 would

test bipartisanship, and the upcoming congressional elections would provoke constant jockeying for political advantage. A ten-seat Republican majority in the House and a 48-to-48 Senate deadlock following Taft's death and replacement by a Democrat put both houses up for grabs. Democrats anticipated a campaign emphasizing Ike's need for a Republican Congress and a renewal of 1952 charges of Democratic corruption and weakness on Communism.[37]

At the start of the 1954 session, liberal Democrats demanding a legislative program separate from Ike's challenged bipartisanship. In early January, Lyndon reiterated his commitment to the strategy that had worked so well in 1953. "We Democrats are going to take the only prudent course through which we can truly serve. It is to examine the President's program item by item and take our stand on the basis of the national interest." Lyndon called it the "politics of responsibility" and suggested that the popular Eisenhower would do better with a Democratic than a Republican Congress: "We understand the Republican National Committee has opened a drive to elect a Republican Congress. . . . It is rumored that the President contends privately this is an anti-Eisenhower plot."[38]

When Eisenhower presented a "forward-looking" legislative program that appealed more to Democrats than Republicans, Johnson saw ever greater sense in the bipartisan strategy. "Lyndon has determined upon a policy of 'responsibility' for the Democratic party," John Steele told his editors, "because he is confident it not only is good for the country but also damned good politics." Lyndon was confident that Republicans would tear themselves apart as Ike's legislative program advanced. Some of Johnson's colleagues, "nettled by Republican attacks and facing tough re-election campaigns," wanted "more of a 'give 'em hell approach.' " But "despite any reports to the contrary, he is thus far in complete control of the situation within his own party and in day-to-day activities he can pull the plug on Bill Knowland any time he wants."[39]

Although Steele described Johnson as "cool, confident, even cocksure," Lyndon in fact was worried about liberal attacks on his Leadership that could divide the party and undermine it in the 1954 congressional elections. An editorial in the Louisville (Kentucky) *Courier-Journal* in early February complained that Senate Democrats were being "led into the bondage of timid, calculating and narrow politics . . . to save the skin of a single colleague." According to the *Courier-Journal*, Johnson needed to lie low to prevent wealthy Texas reactionaries from opposing his reelection. The newspaper pointed out that Johnson had won two Senate votes in January by uniting southerners and Republicans against a majority of Democrats. Johnson was not leading the Democrats but dividing them, and "the division so created amounts practically to repudiation." A few days later when Drew Pearson attacked Johnson's integrity and weak support of Stevenson in 1952, Lyndon had Reedy write a defensive memo that reiterated the virtues of Democratic unity and predicted a party pay off in November from Johnson's leadership.[40]

Liberal criticism of Johnson for bipartisanship convinced him that Democratic party unity required some kind of response to right-wing Republican attacks. Joseph McCarthy asserted in February that the Democrats were guilty of "twenty years of treason." Johnson responded that "irresponsible statements" by Republicans might endanger bipartisanship. Eisenhower then asked Republicans to "tone down" their attacks. Lyndon praised Ike as "a gentleman and an American" who had to "rebuke" his own party.[41]

Despite his eagerness for some confrontation with the Republican right, Johnson did not think an all-out Democratic assault on McCarthy wise. He viewed McCarthy as "a Republican party problem" that ultimately would drive a wedge between the Republican right and the Eisenhower administration. Lyndon told John Steele: "why put on the brave act, beat one's chest, and net 25 votes against Joe, and in turn get smeared and unite the Republicans behind Joe." With fewer than three Americans in every ten disapproving of McCarthy and his approval rating up sixteen points in the previous six months, Johnson correctly saw him as a no-win issue in February 1954. Other senators agreed. When a $214,000 appropriation for McCarthy's permanent subcommittee on subversion came before the upper house that month, only William Fulbright of Arkansas voted against it. Liberals Douglas, Humphrey, Kefauver, and Lehman all voted "aye." Eisenhower himself refused to challenge McCarthy directly, never mentioning McCarthy by name in his request for less strident attacks by Republicans.[42]

Johnson saw safer ground on which to fight. When the country went into a mild economic recession in the first months of 1954, Lyndon attacked the Republicans as "still Republicans. Like the Bourbons of France," Johnson told a Democratic audience, "they have learned nothing—and have forgotten nothing—since the days of McKinley and high-button shoes." The Republicans had promised a balanced budget and tax cuts, but during fiscal 1954 the budget would be "9 billion dollars out of whack," and the Republicans were planning to cut taxes "for the big fellow who didn't need it" and to keep them "high for the little fellow. Maybe this Administration believes that since the little fellow has already lost all his overtime pay [in the recession] he won't have so much taxes to pay anyway."

The Republican farm program received Johnson's strongest fire. Eisenhower and Secretary of Agriculture Ezra Taft Benson believed that Democratic price supports for basic crops had caused farm surpluses and wasted tax dollars. They wanted reduced payments and a return to a free agricultural market. But they were running against the national tide. Most Americans favored price supports for farmers. Lyndon, relishing the chance to revert to the New Deal experience, attacked the Eisenhower farm program as a " 'bold dynamic forward-looking' retreat from Democratic gains of the past twenty years." The Republican "cure for falling prices," Lyndon said, "was to push prices down even further." Benson's "flexible price support is a simple plan. It gives the farmers an umbrella when the sun is out and takes it away when it rains."[43]

Johnson also turned a proposal for Hawaiian statehood, a divisive question for Democrats, into an issue with party-wide appeal. Southern and northern Democrats differed on bringing the multiracial islands into the Union. Johnson tried to blunt the difference by supporting commonwealth status instead of statehood, but that motion failed 60 to 42. Johnson then attacked Knowland and the Republicans for unilaterally scheduling a Senate night session on the question. Shifting the focus from Hawaiian statehood to the prerogatives of the Democratic minority, Johnson united the party behind him in a vote on adjournment. Winning by a count of 48 to 45, Johnson had the support of 46 Democrats, populist-Republican William Langer of North Dakota, and Independent Wayne Morse. After the vote, Johnson's fellow Democrats flocked around to congratulate him. Knowland complained that he was "a Majority Leader without a majority." Johnson said he had a worse predicament: he was "a Minority Leader *with* a majority." Although a bill granting statehood to Hawaii and Alaska passed the Senate on April 1, controversy among Democrats had been drained from the issue and the bill died in conference later in the session.[44]

During April and May, Johnson found three other opportunities to promote party unity. One was over French defeat in Vietnam. During the first four months of 1954, after an all-out battle began with the Communist Vietminh at Dien Bien Phu, French forces confronted a decisive defeat. Paris asked Washington to use American planes and troops to save French power in Indochina. Since the French would not promise independence to Vietnam in return for American help and since the British would not agree to the use of Anglo-American air power or even a joint resupply effort, Eisenhower refused to commit American forces. Yet he was desperately concerned not to lose Indochina to the Communists. Therefore, as a French collapse became increasingly likely, he mapped a strategy that could save part of Vietnam and contain Communism in Asia. He publicly declared that the loss of Vietnam could have a "domino" effect, with all of Southeast Asia falling to Communism. A Communist victory in Vietnam would be the "beginning of a disintegration that would have the most profound influences." Anticipating a division of the country into Communist and pro-Western parts, he saw his remarks as a prelude to American support for a non-Communist South Vietnam.[45]

Eisenhower also worried about the political repercussions to his Administration and the Republican party from French defeat. He had campaigned against the Democrats as soft on Communism and promised "rollback" or "liberation" from Communist control of "enslaved" areas. Now he expected right-wing and Democratic questions about "Who lost Vietnam?" To keep this to a minimum, on April 2, he had Dulles ask congressional leaders of both parties for discretionary authority to use American air and sea power against Communist aggression in Southeast Asia. As Eisenhower expected, the congressmen, led by Senator Russell and supported by Lyndon Johnson, rejected the idea unless America's allies joined in and the French promised independence to Vietnam.[46]

Eisenhower's maneuver threw part of the responsibility on Congress for American nonintervention in the fighting. But it did not insulate the Administration from a Democratic attack. On May 6, the day before Dien Bien Phu fell, Johnson expressed the Democratic point of view at a party dinner. He decribed the *"new dynamic foreign policy . . .* New York advertising hucksters and TV experts have merchandized," as a failure: "What *is* American policy in Indo-China? It is apparent only that American foreign policy has never in all its history suffered such a stunning reversal. . . . Our friends and allies are frightened and wondering, as we do, where are we headed. We stand in clear danger of being left naked and alone in a hostile world." He belittled Vice President Nixon's comment of a few months before that it was wonderful to have a Secretary of State who stood up to the Communists, and concluded: "This picture of our country needlessly weakened in the world today is so painful that we should turn our eyes from abroad and look homeward." By 1954, taking advantage of a foreign policy loss for political gain had become a well-developed part of post-1945 party competition.[47]

Johnson also won liberal approval and avoided strife among Democrats by his handling of a proposal for Taft-Hartley revision and his response to *Brown v. Board of Education of Topeka, Kansas,* the May 1954 landmark case abandoning the fifty-eight-year-old "separate but equal" doctrine justifying racial segregation in public schools. In 1953 the Eisenhower administration had flirted with relaxing some of the anti-labor provisions of the Taft-Hartley law that allowed union busting. When Eisenhower reneged on proposing such legislation, however, Secretary of Labor Martin Durkin resigned. Moreover, at the start of the 1954 session, the Administration proposed strengthening anti-labor provisions in the law. With the backing of liberals and the support of southerners who were content to leave Taft-Hartley intact, Johnson had the bill sent back to committee, where it died. Jim Rowe wrote labor lawyer Arthur Goldberg, "to ask, in a somewhat sardonic fashion . . . what comments you had on my friend Lyndon Johnson's performance in knocking off the Taft-Hartley amendments for you." Although Rowe expected Goldberg to say that "Lyndon and the southerners were against the amendments for the wrong reasons," he urged him to remember "that results are what count."[48]

At the same time, when the Court handed down its *Brown* decision, Lyndon gained the approval of liberals by separating himself from many southern politicians who appeased constituents with extreme segregationist rhetoric. In Texas, three out of every four adults disapproved of the Court's decision. Nevertheless, Johnson publicly declared that "however we may question the judgment of the men who made this ruling, it . . . cannot be overruled now, and it is probable that it can never be overruled." Although Johnson believed that the "separate but equal" doctrine had allowed both races to make "enormous strides over the years in education" in Texas, he saw "no point in crying over spilt milk. . . . I have unlimited confidence in the ability of our people to work this matter out within the boundaries of the Supreme Court decision and in a manner that will be satisfactory to both races." His statement was in sharp contrast to Eisenhower's, who refused to make any public endorsement of the decision. When the Judiciary Committee responded to the *Brown* ruling with a number of bills calculated "to weaken the Court's position," Lyndon plotted the strategy to kill all of them. A sharp debate over the Court's decision impressed Lyndon as likely to open deep divisions in the country and Democratic party. He hoped the South would find constructive ways to accommodate itself to the Court's action. Indeed, he believed that in the long run southern acceptance of desegregation was essential to the region's economic advance. Until it gave blacks the chance to improve their lot and adopted racial attitudes more in line with the rest of the nation, the South would not attract the sort of investment that could put its living standard on a par with other sections of the United States.[49]

Johnson's differences with the Administration on agricultural price supports, Hawaiian statehood, Vietnam, Taft-Hartley, and the *Brown* decision hardly meant the end of bipartisanship. To the contrary, Eisenhower's legislative agenda included a number of measures Johnson and most Senate Democrats helped pass: Social Security expansion, a public housing law, a vocational rehabilitation program, an unemployment compensation bill, reciprocal trade extension, the outlawing of the Communist party, a tax revision bill, and excise tax reductions.[50]

Likewise, on foreign policy, despite his criticism of the Administration's Indochina policy, Johnson maintained a bipartisan stand. He was especially supportive of the Administration's use of the Central Intelligence Agency to topple the regime of Jacobo Arbenz in Guatemala. Elected president in 1950, Arbenz had antagonized the Eisenhower administration by tolerating the Guatemalan Communist party and nationalizing some of the American-owned United Fruit Company's vast idle acreage. In May 1954, after Eisenhower had ordered the CIA to replace Arbenz with a pro-American regime, the Arbenz government received a shipment of artillery pieces and small arms from Communist Czechoslovakia. CIA warnings about Arbenz's pro-Communist leanings were subverting the Guatemalan military, and Arbenz wanted the arms to create a people's militia free of army control. Eisenhower and Secretary of State Dulles, however, viewed the arms shipment as threatening Communist domination of all Central America. The Eisenhower administration saw the area, with its extremes of wealth and poverty, as a breeding ground for Communism, and Arbenz as an opening wedge for Communist subversion throughout Latin America. "My God," Eisenhower told his Cabinet in June, "just think what it would mean to us if Mexico went Communist!"

On June 19, an American-supplied force of 150 men under Carlos Castillo Armas, an exiled colonel, launched what the American government and press called an "invasion" of Guatemala. After advancing six miles into the country, Armas and his men encamped in a church and waited for Arbenz to resign. When he didn't and the Guatemalan army refused to take sides between Arbenz and Armas, the White House authorized bombing raids against Guatemala City by two planes given to Armas and U.S. bombers flown from Managua, Nicaragua, by CIA pilots.[51]

During these events, Johnson introduced a resolution in the Senate endorsing the Administration's view that the Communists were seeking to establish a beachhead in the Americas. "The Communist penetration of the Western Hemisphere . . . is intolerable from every standpoint and must not be permitted to happen. There is no question here of United States interference in the domestic affairs of any American state," Johnson said. "We are concerned only with external aggression." Like the White House, Johnson saw a secret operation by the CIA to block a Communist advance as entirely justified. In the face of what he considered a genuine threat to the national security, he had no qualms about violating Guatemala's self-determination or proceeding without congressional and public approval in the United States. He shared a growing conviction among government officials that saving American democracy meant ignoring some of its rules. The success of the Guatemala operation encouraged Johnson's attraction to this unfortunate proposition.

Johnson biographers later concluded that his resolution, which passed 69 to 1, was an attempt to make it appear that Senate Democrats forced Eisenhower to do something about Guatemala. But, in fact, the resolution didn't pass the Senate until after Arbenz had resigned from power on June 27. Moreover, it had the approval of Senate Republicans and the Administration. On June 26, Knowland told Dulles that he "thought the resolution good," and "thought it a good idea" for the Secretary to tell Johnson so. In a telephone conversation with Johnson, Dulles thanked him for his resolution, and "said it was very timely and a good demonstration of united support at a good time." Two days later, after Dulles told Johnson of "the favorable break in Guatemala," Lyndon asked Dulles to call two Republican senators "to emphasize getting the resolution through with as close to a unanimous vote as possible." Johnson's resolution scored political points for the Democrats not by showing themselves more patriotic than the Republicans but by demonstrating once again that they were a "responsible" opposition which put cooperation for the good of the country above partisanship.[52]

The toughest challenge to Johnson's strategy of promoting party unity and bipartisanship at the same time came over the Atomic Energy Revision Act. The law embodied Administration opposition to public power projects in general and supported government-financed atomic research by private corporations in particular. Lyndon's longstanding commitment to public power moved him to support liberal amendments limiting Administration goals. He backed unsuccessful attempts to bar the Atomic Energy Commission from entering into contracts with Dixon-Yates, private southern power companies, to build power plants for the federally owned Tennessee Valley Authority. He and liberals succeeded, however, in amending the bill to require that "public bodies and cooperatives" have first claim on atomic power generated by government-owned plants. Despite this amendment, liberals were opposed to a law that turned atomic energy production and control over to private power interests. Consequently, they conducted an eleven-day filibuster that put Johnson on the side of the Administration. Concerned that the filibuster was damaging the image of the Democrats as united and "responsible" and might persuade the Senate to liberalize the rule for invoking cloture, Johnson joined southern Democrats and Republicans in ending the filibuster and passing the bill. When it came back to the Senate from a conference committee with the liberal amendments deleted, however, Johnson helped restore them to the bill.[53]

At the close of the congressional session, Johnson was happy to hear it described as the "can do" Congress. He said it clearly demonstrated differences between Democrats and Republicans, which voters would consider when voting in November, but he gave greater emphasis to its bipartisanship: "on the whole, it was not an acrimonious session," he said. When conservative journalist Fulton Lewis, Jr., described Johnson's leadership as "middle of the road," Johnson replied: "I have always liked to walk in the middle of the road because I believe that is where the majority of the American people are and those are the kind of policies that I think the Democratic Party should follow."[54]

During the congressional session, Johnson had kept a close eye on developments in Texas. After his fall 1953 campaign swing, he had every reason to believe that he would have no significant opposition in 1954. A Houston friend had told him in January: "As of now the vast majority of voters in the county approve of your conduct as senator and as minority leader and would vote for you against any opponent except the Governor." Still, he had cautioned Lyndon against relaxing: holding on to the advantage would require "keeping balance on a very tight wire."

By the beginning of February, remarks by Wayne Morse in Austin had strengthened Johnson's position in the state. Speaking to the liberal Americans for Democratic Action, Morse spent five minutes praising FDR, twenty-five minutes "castigating" Johnson and Price Daniel, and an hour "telling what a great man he himself is." In a press conference, Morse said: "Texas ought to elect itself two senators. You have none now. One represents the oil interests and the other represents Lyndon Johnson—and when I say that I am engaging in the height of senatorial courtesy." Morse asserted that Johnson had "the most reactionary record in the Senate. . . . If he should ever have a liberal idea, he would have a brain hemorrhage." Morse's attack aroused widespread sympathy for Johnson: Morse's "loose talk at Austin must be as palatable to the vast majority of Texans as a dose of castor oil," the *San Antonio Express* said. "Morse helped more than he hurt," Herman Brown wrote Lyndon. "If my mail is any indication, you are certainly right," Johnson replied. "It is running about 98% for me and 2% for Morse." [55]

By the end of February, however, other developments had eroded Johnson's confidence that he easily would win the July primary. In January and February, George Parr, "the Duke of Duval County," had begun making headlines when he got into "a bloody court house corridor brawl at Alice" with two Texas Rangers. Governor Shivers, Texas Attorney General John Ben Sheppard, and U.S. Attorney General Herbert Brownell had given Parr more bad publicity by announcing that a joint state-federal investigation of his tax returns and his use of public funds soon "would bear fruit." Everett Looney, Lyndon's old friend in Austin, warned that the Parr case "could very well affect you quite adversely. This Parr business has been resurrected to the point where it is now the hottest it has ever been." Looney feared that Sheppard might use the case to run for Lyndon's Senate seat: Sheppard would point to what he had "done to clear up the mess in Duval County, without which, he will say, you would not have been elected in 1948." The *New York Herald Tribune* and *Newsweek* ran stories saying that the Parr dispute might affect Johnson's chances of reelection. Looney urged him to ensure that "no one—no one at all—by any scheme or ruse, gets you into public print on the Parr matter." Another acquaintance in San Antonio wrote Lyndon that "Your name has certainly been used in a bad way as regards the present investigation. And it is surprising how many people, who voted for you in 1948, now state they are in a state of indecision."[56]

In February, a confidential survey by the Texas Poll had indicated that Johnson had lost significant ground with voters in the previous two months. Where a November–December 1953 survey had shown that 60 percent approved of Johnson, 15 percent disapproved, and 25 percent were undecided, the February poll had registered 47 percent in favor, 15 percent against, and 38 percent without an opinion. Although the pollsters could not say whether it was Morse's attack, the Parr issue, a hostile column by Drew Pearson, or all combined that had done the damage, they were certain that Johnson's public standing had slipped.[57]

It encouraged Dudley T. Dougherty, a thirty-year-old, first-term state legislator from Beeville in south Texas, who had declared his candidacy in mid-February. An eccentric millionaire who had been the largest single contributor in Texas to Adlai Stevenson in 1952, Dougherty had decided that only a McCarthy-style campaign could allow so young and unknown a candidate to beat Johnson in 1954. When he had announced for Johnson's seat, he had called himself an isolationist, urged U.S. withdrawal from the U.N. and a break in relations with Moscow, and described FDR and Truman as mentally incompetent pro-Communists and Eisenhower as no better. He introduced an anti-Communist bill in the legislature shortly after which banned voting, office holding, and free speech for all "subversives," including Puerto Rican nationalists, if any should ever come to Texas. Although it was immediately clear that Dougherty "had absolutely no concept of campaigning, no concept of politics," and "was impelled only by an extreme right wing ideology," his candidacy threatened Johnson. Having lost to O'Daniel in 1941 and possibly to Coke Stevenson as well in 1948, despite his 87-vote victory, Lyndon feared that Dougherty might somehow use the extreme anti-Communist mood in Texas to portray him as a dangerous radical and force his defeat. There was also the possibility that Dougherty would lose but embarrass Johnson by making a strong showing.[58]

Johnson mapped a careful campaign against Dougherty. Every Sunday he gave a report from Washington on the Texas State Network, describing his efforts to serve Texans and asking people to send him their ideas on how to proceed in the current congressional session. At the same time, he publicized a letter urging that he not campaign in the state during the spring and summer but instead attend to the "many important questions" before Congress. Although friends in Texas told him throughout the spring that Dougherty himself admitted he couldn't win and was only in the race for the publicity, Johnson continued to run an aggressive campaign from Washington. He sent a regular newsletter to 25,000 Texans, a column of support appeared in 200 newspapers, Jake Pickle pressed district and county men to advance Johnson's candidacy, and fellow senators wrote influential Texans praising Johnson's party leadership and service to the country. Johnson also asked Reedy to keep Dougherty from making "a lot of trouble" by piling up a sizable vote. Reedy planted letters in Texas newspapers asking Dougherty to say where he stood on sensitive issues, arranged replies from Johnson men to potentially harmful charges by Dougherty, and worked to demonstrate Johnson's competence for the job and Dougherty's incompetence.[59]

Dougherty cooperated in demonstrating his unsuitability for high office. Described by sophisticated political observers in Texas as "a sincere nut," "a political screwball," and someone without "all his marbles," Dougherty's rambling comments on public questions alienated whites, blacks, liberals, conservatives, and most everyone in the state who wasn't already firmly opposed to Johnson. "Lyndon Johnson's the luckiest sonofabitch in the world," Maury Maverick told liberal Austin attorney Creekmore Fath. ". . . Dougherty called Eleanor Roosevelt 'an old witch.' And that is only the beginning." During the three months before the July 24 primary, Johnson's Texas friends assured him that he was a shoo in and would probably win two-thirds or more of the vote. Political observers across the state saw no contest and believed it a waste of Johnson's time and money to campaign. They reported that many people didn't know Lyndon had an opponent.[60]

Yet Dougherty said a number of things that upset Johnson and aroused him to mount an aggressive response. Charges that he was soft on Communism, had enriched himself in office, was a messenger boy for Brown & Root, and deserved to be in jail for breaking campaign spending laws put Johnson on the defensive. Lyndon requested and received information on Dougherty from the FBI which was used to block Dougherty from publishing a last-minute "libelous" attack on Johnson. He asked Nevada's fiercely anti-Communist Senator Pat McCarran for a letter praising Johnson's "staunch Americanism," and he had Herman Brown send the Committee for Constitutional Government, a right-wing organization supporting Dougherty, a letter emphasizing Johnson's anti-Communism. Johnson also solicited a letter from Houston conservative Roy Cullen lauding Johnson's public stand against admitting Communist China to the U.N. Reedy sent a seven-page response to Dougherty's charges to a San Antonio newspaper editor who would "know what to do with it."[61]

Johnson's staff tried to put Dougherty on the defensive. They showed that Dougherty had missed seven out of every ten roll-call votes in the state legislature. They called in tough questions during 24-hour Dougherty talkathons, and wrote to ask where it said in Dun and Bradstreet that Johnson was worth over a million dollars. They explored possible violations of the Texas elections laws by the Committee for Constitutional Government and tried to locate a letter from Herman Brown asking Johnson to help Dougherty get out of the army during World War II. As a concluding shot in his campaign, Johnson arranged an interview with the Washington columnist Joseph Alsop. On July 6, Alsop published a column praising Johnson as an exceptionally able Senate Leader who had united the Democratic party behind moderate goals and restored the Senate to its original function of legislating rather than investigating.[62]

Johnson's campaign was largely superfluous. He received 529,000 more votes than Dougherty, beating him 883,000 to 354,000. Johnson won a decisive 71.37 percent share of the vote. There had been no need for him to campaign beyond what he had done publicly in the fall of 1953. He had arrived in American politics as an unusually talented senator, and only his own inner doubts had driven him to bother fighting so weak a challenger as Dougherty. As Reedy had told him in June, "Dougherty is just a screwball . . . and I think we have got to equate him with no opposition at all." It was inconceivable to Joe Alsop that Texas voters would have rejected as talented a senator as Lyndon Johnson. After spending a morning together, Alsop wrote him: "I have never before learned so much about the practical processes of the American government in so short a time. You are far more brilliant and impressive than Jimmy Byrnes when you can bring yourself to talk about the true character of your big assignment—and I can think of no higher praise than that for I have always regarded Jimmy as the prime teacher of government in the real sense of that much misused word."[63]

Johnson's one-sided victory freed him to be less attentive to the conservative impulses dominating Texas politics. This registered most immediately in his efforts to have the Senate repudiate Joseph McCarthy. As a party leader, Johnson had been under pressure to do something about McCarthy. By the end of 1952, McCarthy had become a formidable and disturbing force in American politics. His irresponsible charges about Communists in high places exploited national anxieties about the nation's security in the Cold War. No one was immune from his attacks: he had called President Truman "a son of a bitch" counseled by advisers drunk on "bourbon and benedictine," and he had charged General George C. Marshall, a national symbol of patriotism and integrity, with "a conspiracy so immense and an infamy so black as to dwarf any previous such venture in the history of man."

Republican control of the Senate in 1953 had made McCarthy chairman of the Government Operations Committee and its Permanent Subcommittee on Investigations. He had used his position in 1953 to attack the State Department's Overseas Information Program and the Central

Intelligence Agency as infiltrated by subversives. At the same time, J. B. Matthews, his Committee's chief investigator, had published a magazine article saying that the "largest single group supporting the Communist apparatus in the United States today is composed of Protestant clergymen." At the beginning of 1954, McCarthy had launched an investigation of the army. He charged that officers at Camp Kilmer, New Jersey, were "shielding Communist conspirators," because they permitted an army dentist to resign with an honorable discharge after he had refused to sign a loyalty oath.[64]

As McCarthy had widened his circle of attack, Johnson had come under increasing pressure to oppose him. *New York Times* journalist William S. White, who worried about McCarthy's destruction of civil liberties, told Lyndon, "You really must do something about this damned fellow." Party liberals particularly had pressured Johnson to get after McCarthy. In 1953, Herbert Lehman had asked Johnson to support a Senate condemnation of McCarthy for his attack on the State Department. In February 1954, Hubert Humphrey had written Senator Olin D. Johnston of South Carolina: "The Gallup Poll shows that about 74% of the people still believe that the government has Communists within it. . . . The fact is that the public has been sold that the Democrats are soft on Communism and Commies were in the government by the hundreds and that Ike had to clean house." Humphrey had asked Johnston to "take this up with Lyndon Johnson and the Policy Committee." "Somebody is going crazy," Maury Maverick had written Lyndon in April 1954, "and as the leader of the Senate Democrats I hope you will do your part to stem the tide. Everybody in the Government is scared to death. . . . There is nobody in Washington to take up for any part of the Constitution for anybody."[65]

McCarthy's actions had distressed Johnson as much as the liberals. McCarthy's abuse of General Marshall, especially his success in getting Eisenhower to drop a laudatory remark about Marshall from a speech in Wisconsin during the 1952 campaign, had angered Johnson and Rayburn. "Joe will go that extra mile to destroy you," Lyndon had said. Johnson had some first-hand evidence that McCarthy saw him as a potential victim. Arthur Stehling, Lyndon's friend from Fredericksburg, remembered being introduced to McCarthy in Washington by a lobbyist who helped McCarthy speculate in commodity futures. Over dinner, after he had learned of Stehling's friendship with Johnson, McCarthy asked Stehling "about how Johnson made his money, how he treated his office help, and whether he trifled on his wife. Had I known the answers to these questions," Stehling later wrote, "I would not have answered them anyway."[66]

Johnson believed that the way to beat McCarthy was to wait until he attacked conservative institutions and individuals. As Hubert Humphrey recalled: "Lyndon kept saying that we had to wait until McCarthy began attacking the more conservative, the respected, the senators of what you might call the old school." Johnson had also warned Humphrey to keep away from McCarthy. "He just eats fellows like you. You're nourishment for him. . . . The only way we'll ever get Joe McCarthy is when he starts attacking some conservatives around here, and then we'll put an end to it." Johnson had told Maury Maverick that he deplored the "hysteria around the country and in the Government," but "you have got to realize that atmosphere can be dispelled only by letting it run its course so that people can see for themselves what is really behind all the noise." McCarthy is "the sorriest senator up here," Johnson had told Bobby Baker. "Can't tie his goddamn shoes. But he's riding high now, he's got people scared to death some Communist will strangle 'em in their sleep, and anybody who takes him on before the fevers cool—well, you don't get in a pissin' contest with a polecat." [67]

In 1952–53, Johnson had seen the beginnings of McCarthy's downfall when he clashed with Senators Carl Hayden of Arizona and Harry Byrd of Virginia, two senior conservatives. In the spring of 1952, McCarthy had attacked Darrell St. Claire, the chief clerk of Hayden's Rules Committee, for actions he had taken as a member of the State Department's loyalty board. Hayden objected on the Senate floor that St. Claire "has been dragged into this dispute without any basis of fact at all." McCarthy, who regarded Hayden "as an old, blind, deaf fuddy-duddy," hit back at him. "God," George Reedy said later, "that was a stupid thing for him to do." McCarthy "didn't know that Carl Hayden was one of the toughest creatures that ever walked the face of this earth." That night Lyndon told some reporters, "Joe has made a lifelong and powerful enemy in Carl Hayden, and Carl is not a man who forgets easily." The following year in July, when McCarthy's aide Matthews attacked the Protestant clergy and the Methodist Bishop of Washington, D.C., G. Bromley Oxnam, in particular, it angered Harry Byrd, Oxnam's friend. Lyndon told Hubert Humphrey that Matthews's attack was "a fatal mistake" for McCarthy. "You can't attack Harry Byrd's friends in this Senate, not in this Senate," Johnson said. "Mark my words, Hubert, he's in trouble." Byrd challenged McCarthy on the Senate floor for appointing Matthews as his chief investigator. With the help of the three Democrats on McCarthy's subcommittee and Republican Charles E. Potter of Michigan, Byrd engineered Matthews's dismissal by a vote of four to three. [68]

McCarthy's political demise, however, came with his 1954 assault on the army. Attacks on Brigadier General Ralph W. Zwicker, a much decorated World War II hero and commandant of Camp Kilmer, and Eisenhower's Secretary of the Army Robert Stevens provoked an Administration reaction. In February 1954, at a subcommittee hearing in New

York, McCarthy berated Zwicker as "not fit to wear that uniform" and as lacking "the brains of a five-year-old child." When Stevens deplored the "humiliating treatment" and "abuse" of Zwicker and ordered him not to appear again before the subcommittee, McCarthy told Stevens that he would "kick the brains out of anyone who protects Communists." The following week McCarthy and sympathetic Republican senators tricked Stevens into signing a statement he hadn't fully agreed to: the fine print committed Zwicker to testify again and give McCarthy the names of everyone involved in the promotion and honorable discharge of the Camp Kilmer dentist. Stevens and the Administration now counterattacked by releasing a list of charges against McCarthy and Roy M. Cohn, an aide. Stevens accused them of trying to intimidate army officials into giving an army inductee, G. David Schine, Cohn's close friend and co-worker, special treatment. McCarthy accused the army of trying to "blackmail" him into calling off his "exposure of Communists." His subcommittee now agreed to have Republican Karl Mundt of South Dakota, an ardent McCarthyite, chair an investigation of the charges by and against McCarthy.[69]

Johnson believed that daily public exposure would go far to undermine McCarthy's credibility; he urged John McClellan of Arkansas, the senior Democrat on the subcommittee, to insist on televising the proceedings. Johnson had concluded that "the newspapers alone and two minutes a night on television during the Army hearings wasn't enough" to hurt McCarthy. Fuller exposure day after day "would make people see what the bastard was up to." Johnson asked Wall Street attorney Ed Weisl, to convince American Broadcasting Company chairman Leonard Goldenson, his client, to televise the hearings. Known as the third network, ABC was eager for programs that could enlarge its audience. Goldenson saw the Johnson-Weisl proposal as such an opportunity. When McClellan agreed to Johnson's suggestion and persuaded McCarthy to go along, the stage was set for a public confrontation that went far to break McCarthy's hold on public opinion.[70]

For thirty-six days from April to June, McCarthy performed before millions of television viewers. Although Mundt was the ostensible chairman, McCarthy dominated the proceedings. Interjecting frequent points of order that Mundt allowed, McCarthy used "doctored photographs, phony FBI reports, and memoranda lifted from Pentagon files" to blunt charges against himself and Cohn and remind his audience of the omnipresent Communist threat. But McCarthy's appearance—his dark beard and nasal monotone—combined with evidence of his underhanded tactics worked to defeat him.

Most of all, though, he was no match for Joseph N. Welch, the army's sixty-three-year-old special counsel, a life-long Republican and man of transparent integrity. Welch's understated studiousness presented a sharp

contrast to McCarthy's harshness and stridency. A memorable showdown between them occurred on June 9 when McCarthy tried to sidetrack Welch's questioning of Cohn with an accusation against Fred Fisher,
a young attorney in Welch's law firm. McCarthy falsely asserted that
Welch had tried to make Fisher a counsel to the subcommittee and
revealed that Fisher had been a member of the National Lawyers Guild,
a leftist organization McCarthy described as once "the legal bulwark of
the Communist Party." McCarthy then sanctimoniously lectured Welch
on the danger of the Communist threat. Welch candidly acknowledged
Fisher's brief association with the Guild and a decision not to have him
assist in the hearings for fear he would be unjustifiably attacked. "Little
did I dream you could be so reckless and so cruel as to do an injury to
that lad," Welch told McCarthy. ". . . If it were in my power to forgive
you for your reckless cruelty I would do so. I like to think that I am a
gentle man, but your forgiveness will have to come from someone other
than me."[71]

The audience in the Senate hearing room cheered Welch, and so did
much of the country. Republican leaders across the United States believed it was time to repudiate McCarthy before he dragged them down
to defeat. In Ohio, a conservative Republican candidate for the Senate
described McCarthyism as "a synonym for witch-hunting, star-chamber
methods, and the denial of those civil liberties which have distinguished
our country in its historic growth." In Texas, where McCarthy had enjoyed substantial support, a June opinion poll showed people disapproving of him by about a six-to-four margin. The survey largely mirrored
national sentiment as reported by the Gallup poll.[72]

Two days after the hearings closed on June 17, Vermont Republican
Ralph Flanders, a symbol of New England integrity, introduced a motion to remove McCarthy from his chairmanships. McCarthy was justifiably confident that the Senate would not go along with such an assault
on its seniority system. "They should get a net and take him to a good
quiet place," McCarthy said. On June 30, Flanders substituted a simple
censure resolution for his original motion, asking that McCarthy be condemned for actions which were contrary to senatorial traditions and tended
to bring the Senate into disrepute. During the next month the Senate
struggled privately over how to deal with the Flanders resolution. On
July 29, the day before the motion came up for a vote, Johnson called a
meeting of the Democratic Policy Committee. The Committee met for
nearly four hours, its longest session of the year, in Johnson's third floor
Senate office. Inviting five liberal nonmembers of the committee to participate in the discussion, Johnson successfully persuaded his colleagues
that the Policy Committee should not take a stand. The committee concluded that it would play into McCarthy's hands and put him back in
the good graces of the Republican party if it did. The committee an-

nounced the party's neutrality on the resolution and recommended that each senator vote his own conscience.[73]

Eager to avoid even the appearance of an impropriety in condemning McCarthy and to wait until after the fall elections, the Senate voted 75 to 12 on August 2 to appoint a special committee of three Democrats and three Republicans to recommend a response to Flanders's resolution. Lyndon had been discussing this idea for a year and a half. "If I were the Majority Leader," he told some journalists early in 1953, ". . . I'd appoint a bipartisan select committee, and I'd put on our side the very best men we have, men who are above reproach, the wisest men I know in the Senate and the best judges, and I'd ask 'em to make a study of McCarthy and report to the Senate." To support his position, Johnson had gathered information on the historical precedents for such action. In the summer of 1953, shortly after the Matthews-Oxnam episode, Johnson had discussed the appointment of a select committee with Hubert Humphrey. Months before the Flanders resolution came up for consideration, Johnson had sent Bobby Baker secretly to talk with "key senators" about this procedure for condemning McCarthy. "We [also] consulted with Chief Justice Earl Warren of the Supreme Court and with President Eisenhower's congressional liaison man, General Jerry (Slick) Persons," Baker recalls.[74]

Johnson "spent a lot of time and a lot of thought and a lot of conversation in naming" the members of the committee. He felt that "these charges ought to be heard by the most judicious and fairminded men in the Senate—men who would not be partisan in the least." Lady Bird remembered that he viewed this as "a very solemn thing that had to be done . . . I never saw him try harder to create a committee that would be above reproach, of balanced Democrats and conservatives and somebody deeply versed in the Constitution." Liberals wanted "people of ideological purity," but Johnson believed "that would be . . . just grist for McCarthy's mill." He wanted conservatives who had been offended by McCarthy's abuse of Senate standards and could not be accused of being Communist dupes. On the Democratic side, he wanted Walter George or Richard Russell of Georgia. But neither would accept the assignment. "They're afraid of sticking their heads in the noose," Johnson told Bobby Baker. "They say McCarthy's still strong medicine down in Georgia and they've just got no stomach for it." On the Republican side, another staunch conservative, Eugene Millikin of Colorado, who was ill, also refused the job.

Lyndon found other conservatives who were ready to accept. Ed Johnson, a Democrat from Colorado who was close to southern senators, had a reputation for integrity, and was known as the least partisan man in the Senate, relished the assignment. He told Lyndon that he hated McCarthy, who had done something nasty to a friend. If he could knife

him, he intended to "put it in and twist it north, east, south and west."
Democrats John Stennis of Mississippi and Sam Ervin of North Carolina, both men of impeccable conservative credentials and judicial backgrounds, also agreed to serve.[75]

Lyndon then chose the Republican committeemen. "Knowland theo-
retically appointed the Republican members," William S. White says,
"but Johnson appointed every one of them. . . . I was present in his
[Knowland's] office . . . when they had their final conference on this."
Johnson "would fix on some Republican he knew Knowland detested.
He'd say, 'Now, Bill, I'm sure you want so-and-so.' Knowland would
say, 'Oh, no! Good God, no, I don't want so-and-so!' And he'd wind up
naming the man Johnson wanted." For chairman, Knowland and Johnson agreed on Arthur Watkins of Utah, a "thin, gray, sternly upright,
shy ascetic," "painfully ethical Mormon." A "regular" Republican,
Watkins was devoted to the Eisenhower administration McCarthy was
assaulting. Next in seniority was Frank Carlson of Kansas, a deliberate,
incorruptible Baptist of Swedish background who was also thoroughly
committed to Eisenhower. Finally, there was Francis Case of South Dakota, a Methodist teetotaler whose steady conservatism matched his lack
of Senate influence.[76]

Since this was only the third time in Senate history that a special
committee considered the censure of a member, it was a foregone conclusion that McCarthy would be found guilty. Nine days of hearings
between August 31 and September 13 led to a recommendation on September 27 that McCarthy be "condemned" for breaking Senate rules
and abusing General Zwicker. After the congressional elections in November, the Senate reconvened to debate the special committee's report.
On November 29, three days before the Senate voted, George Reedy
drafted a reply to Clint Murchison, the Texas oil baron, who wanted
Johnson to oppose the resolution. "The decision was made last summer
when the whole question was put in the hands of men like Ed C. Johnson, John Stennis, Sam Ervin, and Watkins," Reedy wrote. ". . . As the
resolution is now drawn it does not touch upon McCarthy's activities as
an anti-Communist but goes only to his methods. Pro-McCarthyites would
resent it bitterly but cannot use it conscientiously as ammunition to further divide the country. Anti-McCarthyites will be satisfied for the time
being and may relax their efforts which are splitting the country." On
the Senate floor, Johnson declared that his vote on the resolution reflected his view of appropriate Senate behavior. He condemned Mc-
Carthy's characterization of Watkins as "stupid" and "cowardly," and
of the committee as having "done the work of the Communist party."
"The words . . . used in describing these men do not belong in the
pages of the *Congressional Record,*" Johnson said. "They would be more
fittingly inscribed on the wall of a men's room."[77]

Johnson set his party's tone; most Democrats said little during the Senate debate. Behind the scenes, however, they all, but one, agreed to vote for McCarthy's condemnation. The exception was John Kennedy, who was recovering from back surgery in a Boston hospital and saw good political reasons not to vote. (Massachusetts had the highest proportion of McCarthy supporters of any state in the nation.) A 67-to-22 margin for the resolution included not a single Democrat for McCarthy.

The vote signaled McCarthy's eclipse as an influential figure in the Senate and the country. In the three years before he died in 1957, he deteriorated into an alcoholic who was barely recognizable as the man who had dominated public discussion in the first four years of the decade. "He never recovered," Harry McPherson says. ". . . I would just see him lurch down the halls in the mornings, and he had a kind of bloated face with heavy jowls; he really looked terrible. And he would make those long, awful, incomprehensible speeches, seconded by other Republican drunks. He was clearly finished." George Reedy saw McCarthy on a Washington, D.C., street a few months before he died. "It took me about thirty seconds to realize that this was the remnant of Joe McCarthy—unshaven, needing a bath, bloated from too much booze, almost inarticulate."

Although most liberals had doubted Johnson's approach to the McCarthy problem at the time, many in retrospect saw him as an architect of McCarthy's demise. "Johnson was splendid on McCarthy," Paul Douglas declared thirty years later. "He got every single Democrat, including Jim Eastland, to vote for, not censure, but disapproval of McCarthy, and combined with one-half of the Republicans, that gave a three-quarters vote for censure of McCarthy and was the beginning of his downfall." McCarthy "was checked in one of the most delicate operations in modern political history," George Reedy wrote in 1982. "It was Lyndon Johnson at his highest level of skill." Johnson "never had anything but contempt for McCarthyism," Harry McPherson says. But he felt compelled to wait until the moment was ripe to strike at him. As Johnson told Elizabeth Rowe, " 'You see, you always wanted me to hurry, to speed it up, but I kept telling you, you can't speed it up. You have got to know when the time has come for you to win. Now I was right, wasn't I? We've done it. We've got him. He's finished.' " [78]

Was Johnson right? Probably. Had the Democrats tried to get McCarthy before the Republicans were ready to join in the attack, it would have sustained his Republican backing and extended his influence. Although Johnson and other Democrats, including Truman, had contributed to the excessive fears of Communism in the United States that gave McCarthy his chance to become a dominant political figure for a time, the principal culprits were all those Americans who gave in to irrational fears of subversives who didn't exist. Johnson's role in ending

McCarthy's influence should not be exaggerated. Though he played a major part in arranging McCarthy's demise, it was McCarthy's own excesses and the good sense of the country that ultimately made the difference in repudiating his methods and ideas. Johnson was a facilitator of the process but the nation's affinity for centrist politics was the deciding force in bringing him down.

The repudiation of McCarthy paralleled Johnson's efforts to reestablish Democratic control over both houses of Congress. With only a five-seat disadvantage in the House and an evenly divided Senate, the Democrats had seemed likely to convert the normal off-year congressional gains into House and Senate majorities. Moreover, the economic slowdown in 1954, internal Republican differences between conservatives and moderates, and resurgent Democratic unity engineered by Johnson and Rayburn had added to favorable Democratic prospects. Countering these, however, had been Eisenhower's continuing popularity, which Republican leaders had hoped would rub off on congressional candidates, and continuing anxieties about the Communist threat, which Republicans had hoped to exploit once again. In the Senate, several more Democrats had been up for reelection than Republicans, reducing the likelihood that the Democrats would gain the one seat needed for control of the upper house.[79]

Johnson's principal objectives in the campaign had been to maintain Democratic unity, deny the Republicans exclusive identification with anti-Communism, and refute suggestions that a Republican Congress would serve Eisenhower better than a Democratic one. By winning Democratic agreement not to make McCarthy a party issue, Johnson had reduced Republican freedom to use anti-Communism as a talking point. In August, in conjunction with Hubert Humphrey, who had worried that questions about his devotion to anti-Communism might jeopardize his reelection, Johnson had helped lead a bill through the Senate outlawing the Communist party. Every liberal Senate Democrat had become a co-sponsor of the bill. Republican John Marshall Butler of Maryland had proposed a law empowering the Attorney General to investigate any organization believed to be "Communist-infiltrated." Organized labor had seen the bill as a device for union busting. Humphrey had viewed Butler's measure as another Republican attempt to turn voters against liberal Democrats. In what two columnists called a "cleverly conceived, ruthlessly executed and politically adroit" maneuver, Humphrey and fellow liberals had substituted the proposal to ban the Communist party. Because Republicans couldn't afford to appear less anti-Communist than the Democrats, the bill had passed 85 to 0. Humphrey later said, "It's not one of the things I'm proudest of."[80]

The liberals' maneuver had not deterred Vice President Nixon from questioning their patriotism during the campaign. Nixon "threw himself into the campaign with his usual enthusiasm and recklessness," a biographer writes. Nixon had believed that a victory in 1954 was crucial to the long-term success of the Republican party, and had gone after the Democrats as hard as he could. In June, he had blamed the loss of China, the war in Korea, and the dangers in Indochina on "the Acheson policy." During forty-eight days in the fall, on a thirty-one-state tour, he had said that the Democrats had either misunderstood or ignored the Communist threat, and had "covered up rather than cleaned up" the Communist infiltration of the government. He had complained that the Americans for Democratic Action had taken over the Democratic party: "this clique is notoriously soft on the Communist threat at home and is blatantly advocating socialization of American institutions."[81]

Adlai Stevenson, Sam Rayburn, and Johnson had answered Nixon's charges. Stevenson had declared that Nixon was off on an "ill-will tour" and that he represented "McCarthyism in a white collar." Rayburn had called attacks on Democratic patriotism "mean, untrue and dastardly." He had described Nixon as "the next thing to McCarthy in the United States," and as "very cruel" and "the meanest face I've ever seen in the House." Privately, Johnson had said that Nixon was "a fascist." After the election, he told John Steele that " 'people are getting mighty fed up with cheap politics. . . . Ike's relations with Congress were not helped at all by the tone of the Republican campaign, particularly the Nixon line. . . . Many Democrats deeply resent charges and unjust accusations made in the campaign, namely that a Democratic victory would mean that leftwingers would take control of the next Congress.' Johnson rolled off his tongue with obvious relish the list of committee chairmen 'leftwingers' such as Byrd, George, [Allen] Ellender [of Louisiana], etc." Johnson had made the same point publicly during the campaign: Democratic control of the Senate would mean "mature, prudent and patriotic leadership. These men are progressive without being radical, prudent and conservative without being reactionary. Their record of service is a repudiation to extremism of either the left or the right. They . . . are a demolishing answer to the frantic last-minute smears of the Republican Old Guard."[82]

While Nixon had attacked the Democrats, Eisenhower had hung back from an active role in the campaign. Behind the scenes, he had ordered Executive agencies to "step up expenditures to stimulate industrial activity." Moreover, at the end of September, he had sent Nixon a private message praising "the result of your intensive—and I am sure exhaustive—speaking tour. Please don't think that I am not unaware that I have done little to lighten your load." In October, however, after polls had showed a strong Democratic trend and he had received warnings that a Republican defeat would mean "extreme right wing" efforts to recapture control of the party, Ike had joined the campaign. He traveled

10,000 miles and made forty speeches in behalf of moderate Republicans. Although he had generally taken "the high road, emphasizing Republican accomplishments," he had also felt compelled to scare people by warning that a Democratic Congress would start "a cold war of partisan politics." In response, Johnson and Rayburn sent Eisenhower a telegram reminding him of how much the Democrats had done "to cooperate with your Administration and to defend your program from attacks by members and leaders of your own Party. . . . We assure you that there will be no cold war conducted against you by the Democrats when we gain control of either or both Houses of the Congress."[83]

Because his own election had been assured, Johnson had made only two appearances in Texas. On October 5, he had spoken to the Mid-Continent Oil and Gas Association in San Antonio. His speech had left no doubt that he intended to continue serving the state's oil and gas interests: He had underscored his opposition to unnecessary and confusing government regulation, and had declared it "the duty of all of us to keep this industry as a vital force for the preservation of our Nation." Then he had gone to Uvalde, Texas, to see former Vice President John Nance Garner. Garner had opposed Johnson in 1948, but Lyndon had won him over by making his nephew Uvalde's postmaster. With Johnson at his side, Garner had declared to a reporter, " 'Can anybody think of any good, patriotic or party reason why Lyndon B. Johnson should not be reelected to a second term in the Senate? That's all. The rest is off the record. Let's go strike a blow for liberty,' and he went and started to pour the liquor." The story swept Texas and got big headlines everywhere.[84]

Johnson's principal effort in the campaign had been a ten-day speaking tour of eight western states to support House, Senate, and gubernatorial candidates. In Washington and Utah, where there had been only House races, and in Nevada and New Mexico, where Democratic senators Alan Bible and Clinton Anderson held safe seats, Johnson had done little more than show the flag. But in Wyoming, Montana, Minnesota, and Arizona, Johnson had done useful work. Joseph O'Mahoney in Wyoming, who had lost a bid for a sixth term in 1952, was running again, and in Montana, seventy-eight-year-old liberal Jim Murray was in serious danger of losing his seat. Both men had come under attack from right-wingers for being weak on Communism. In both states, Johnson rebutted the accusations effectively by saying, "They're trying to tell you there are nothing but a bunch of Communists among the Democrats in Washington. I suppose they mean that good old red Communist Harry Flood Byrd. . . . Do you think that Walter George of Georgia is a Communist? . . . Do you think that Dick Russell is a Communist or Big Ed Johnson?"

When Johnson and O'Mahoney appeared on the same platform in

Cheyenne, O'Mahoney offered an hour-long discourse on why he had served as a counsel for the accused in a well-publicized government "loyalty" case. Amazed at O'Mahoney's failure to discuss what he would do for Wyoming if voters returned him to the Senate, Johnson had muttered aloud, "Joe, for God's sake, shut up." William S. White, who had been covering Johnson's campaign swing for the *New York Times,* remembered that "Johnson did everything but get up and drag him down."

When Johnson's turn came to speak, he delivered the campaign address O'Mahoney should have given. He reminded voters of how Democrats had served the well-being of average Americans and of westerners in particular. Secretary of Defense Charles Wilson, who had described the interests of the country and General Motors as synonymous and likened the poor to "kennel-fed dogs," was Johnson's foil. "A Secretary of Defense, who has made his department safe for General Motors, says there are too many kennel dogs. Personally, I think there are too many 'fat cats.' " Before the election was over, Charley Wilson was "going to find out that there are many breeds of dogs," including bulldogs like Joe O'Mahoney who always showed tenacity in fighting for the people of Wyoming and the West. "His brains and driving energy have shaped the face of this land—have transformed it into a better world for all who live in Wyoming." In the two years since he had been out of the Senate, however, "the Democratic party—whose eyes have always been on the West—is no longer in a Majority where it can carry out the development of our nation." For the sake of the region, the state, and the average citizen, it was time to return O'Mahoney and a Democratic majority to the Senate. If the words Texas and South were substituted for Wyoming and West, Johnson could have been describing his own achievement.

In Minnesota, Johnson and Humphrey had gotten "along beautifully," and Lyndon had made a good speech. But Humphrey had been running against a moderate Republican, who had refused to use McCarthyist tactics against him, and Humphrey had an excellent campaign organization that had assured him of reelection by a comfortable margin. Johnson had been of greater help in Arizona, where former Senator Ernest McFarland had been in a very tight race for governor, and Johnson was able to assure voters that McFarland had many important friends in Washington who could help him serve the interests of the state.[85]

The November elections had given the Democrats renewed control of Congress. In Nixon's estimate, poor candidates and weak organization had defeated his party. "There were just too many turkeys running on the Republican ticket," he said at a Cabinet meeting. In the House, the Democrats had gained seventeen seats and Sam Rayburn had been assured of becoming Speaker again. The Senate had a much closer result. Although O'Mahoney and Murray won close races and Humphrey and Johnson had landslides, the Democrats ended up with forty-eight Senate seats, the same number they had before the elections. The Republicans also had the same number of seats, forty-seven. Now, however, Wayne Morse of Oregon, the former Republican who had declared himself an Independent in 1953, promised to vote with the Democrats. Calling Morse "one of the abler members of the Senate," Johnson told reporters, "I don't know what he may want, but whatever he wants he's going to get it, if I've got it to give." In return for his vote, Morse wanted a seat on the Foreign Relations Committee. Since Lyndon had it to give, the Democrats assured themselves of a 49 to 47 edge and Lyndon of election at the age of forty-six as the youngest Majority Leader in Senate history.[86]

Johnson was clear on how he would use his new position. Even before the deal with Morse had been sealed, Johnson had announced that bipartisanship or cooperation with the Administration for the good of the country would continue to be his primary goal. In a meeting with journalists on November 6, four days after the election, Johnson, "a silky smooth symphony in blue called in reporters . . . to coo words of harmony into waiting ears. . . . 'My Daddy,' Lyndon told the fifteen newsmen, 'got all us kids around the table when there was a decision to be made. He'd start off with words from Isaiah—"Come now, let us reason together." ' That admonition . . . Lyndon said, would serve the Congress and the nation well today. . . . Chain-smoking cork-tipped Winstons, and occasionally wiping his sharply tapered hand over his angular face . . . Johnson stated a half dozen times that the Democrats are ready to cooperate with the President."[87]

Johnson was genuinely eager for cooperation. When Ike invited Democratic leaders to attend a bipartisan legislative conference at the White House on November 17, Johnson described it as a step in the right direction, and added: "True bipartisanship is the goal we seek, whether we achieve it or not depends primarily on the Chief Executive." The price Lyndon wanted for cooperation was a direct say in major decisions: "The Democratic party can't be asked to bear responsibility for decisions in which it has no part," he said.

Johnson's relations with leading Republicans like Nixon and Karl Mundt had demonstrated that bipartisanship wasn't simply political rhetoric on his part. During the campaign, Johnson had invited Nixon to spend a night at his ranch. Nixon had accepted, but when Texas Republicans had heard he was coming to the state, they had put the heat on him to talk at a fund raising dinner instead. "As you can imagine," Nixon wrote Johnson, "I would much rather have come out to your place for the night but under the circumstances I was unable to resist the pressure of the poverty-stricken Republicans! One condition that I insisted on in making the speech was that I not have to endorse the Republican candidates for the House and Senate in Texas. You can be sure that nothing I say will be in any way uncomplimentary as far as the Minority Leader is concerned!" Similarly, Mundt had written him at the same time about a commemorative commission he hoped they would serve on together, and closed: "Trusting that you Democrats in Texas are doing as well as we Republicans in South Dakota." [88]

Lyndon's attraction to bipartisanship rested on personal preference and shrewd political judgments. At heart, he remained a liberal nationalist who saw a broad consensus for a strong defense against external threats and for domestic programs that eased the problems of an advanced industrial society and particularly served the economic needs of the South. Since moderate Republicans like Ike shared a commitment to ensuring the national security, and were willing to leave most New Deal gains in place, Johnson had good reason to join hands with them. In 1953–54, cooperation with the White House had yielded a constructive legislative record in domestic and foreign affairs. To be sure, the Congress did not break new ground for liberal measures, but it had extended earlier ones and resisted some backward steps that would have ill-served the nation at home and abroad. Perhaps most important, the Senate had played a large part in bringing down McCarthy and restoring an element of sanity to the debate on the "Communist threat," though its support of the Guatemalan intervention and the ban on a Communist party did it or Lyndon in particular little credit. Bipartisanship had also gone far to give the Democrats control of Congress in 1954 and open the door to Lyndon's election as Majority Leader. It was a highly effective means for advancing national, southern, and party designs—as well as Johnson's personal ambitions for an ever larger role in American political life.

PART FOUR

The Majority Leader
1955–1960

Family gathering, ca. 1914. *(Seated)* Eliza Bunton Johnson; *(standing behind to the right)* Sam Ealy Johnson, Sr. Sam Ealy, Jr., and Rebekah Baines Johnson are at the far left and right respectively. Others unknown. *(LBJL)*

Sam Ealy Johnson, Jr., ca. 1930. *(LBJL)*

Rebekah Baines Johnson, 1917. *(LBJL)*

LBJ at eighteen months, 1910. *(LBJL)*

LBJ at seven and a half years, 1915, on front porch of Johnson City home. *(LBJL)*

LBJ in May 1924, three months before turning sixteen, graduated from high school. *(LBJL)*

Claudia Alta (Lady Bird) Taylor in 1934, a few months before marrying Lyndon. *(LBJL)*

L. E. Jones, Jr., LBJ, and Gene Latimer, 1933, Washington, D.C., taking a rare break from their work in Kleberg's office. *(LBJL)*

Congressman Richard M. Kleberg, "to my tried and loyal friend." *(LBJL)*

FDR, Governor Jimmy Allred, and LBJ, at Galveston after LBJ won his congressional seat. *(LBJL)*

LBJ greeting FDR during a visit to Amarillo, July 11, 1938. *(LBJL)*

Alvin J. Wirtz, 1940, inscribed photo to Lyndon, "of whom I am both fond and proud as if he were actually my own son." *(LBJL)*

LBJ in his congressional office. *(LBJL)*

LBJ in his office with John B. Connally, Dorothy Nichols, Herbert Henderson, and Walter Jenkins, ca. 1939–40. *(LBJL)*

George Brown, LBJ, and Tommy Corcoran; the figure behind LBJ may be Herman Brown. *(LBJL)*

LBJ speaking in Waco during the 1941 Senate campaign. *(LBJL)*

George and Herman Brown, ca. 1942, whose company, Brown & Root, prospered with Lyndon's help. *(LBJL)*

Maury Maverick, Gene Autry, Speaker Sam Rayburn, Herman Jones, and Wright Patman (standing next to LBJ), May 3, 1945. *(LBJL)*

Brig. Gen. Harry Vaughan, Postmaster Gen. Robert Hannegan, Sec. of the Treasury Fred M. Vinson, LBJ, Reconversion chief John W. Snyder, Pres. Truman, and Sec. of Agriculture Clinton P. Anderson at a Truman stag party aboard a Coast Guard cutter, September 22, 1945. *(UPI)*

LBJ campaigning by helicopter in San Angelo, June 30, 1948. *(LBJL)*

Lynda Bird, age four, Lady Bird, Lucy Baines, age two, and Lyndon on election day of the second primary in August 1948. *(LBJL)*

Coke Stevenson (with the cigar) and others at the Box 13 hearings in Alice. *(LBJL)*

LBJ and Attorney General Tom Clark, who may have lobbied Justice Hugo Black in Lyndon's behalf, September 27, 1948. *(LBJL)*

Sen. Richard Russell congratulates LBJ on becoming Minority Leader, January 1953. *(UPI)*

LBJ and family at the ranch, September 1954. *(LBJL)*

LBJ in his Senate office, November 1954, discussing the Senate's reprimand of Senator Joseph McCarthy. *(LBJL)*

Vice President Richard Nixon visits LBJ at the Bethesda Naval Hospital after his heart attack, July 30, 1955. *(LBJL)*

Sam Rayburn, LBJ, and Adlai Stevenson, September 29, 1955, hold a press conference at LBJ's ranch. *(LBJL)*

LBJ and Sen. Hubert Humphrey at the Democratic Convention in Chicago, August 14, 1956. *(UPI)*

Sen. Estes Kefauver, HST, presidential nominee Adlai Stevenson, and LBJ at the Democratic Convention in Chicago, August 17, 1956. *(LBJL)*

LBJ in Senate Office after vote on jury trial amendment to the civil rights bill, August 5, 1957. *(LBJL)*

LBJ and President Eisenhower after a breakfast meeting at the White House, August 26, 1957. *(Wide World Photos)*

George Reedy, Booth Mooney, Lady Bird, and LBJ speaking to an AFL/CIO group in LBJ's office, March 4, 1958. *(LBJL)*

LBJ, HST, John Nance Garner, and Rayburn on the occasion of Garner's 92nd birthday, November 2, 1958. *(LBJL)*

LBJ and JFK at a breakfast given by the Pennsylvania delegation to the Democratic Convention, Los Angeles, July 11, 1960. *(UPI)*

JFK and LBJ campaigning in Dallas, September 13, 1960. *(LBJL)*

LBJ campaigns from the back of the LBJ Special, Culpepper, Virginia, October 10, 1960. *(LBJL)*

LBJ and Lady Bird face a hostile crowd in Dallas, November 4, 1960. *(LBJL)*

14

The Making of a
Majority Leader

IN January 1955, Johnson's election as Majority Leader promised few advantages. True, the post gave him national prominence as a spokesman for the Democratic party, but party misadventures could be laid at his doorstep, and with a popular Republican in the White House, Lyndon's danger of negative publicity was considerable. Moreover, if past experience was any guide, the Leader's job would be a source of frustration and a burying ground for hopes of higher office. Most earlier Senate Leaders had faced insurmountable difficulties in effectively bringing other senators into line on party programs. While senators usually have a strong party identification, and party affiliation has a major influence on voting behavior, they are much more beholden to their constituents than to party leaders. "Senators are like a hundred barons," one observer of the upper house said. "They do not owe each other a damned thing. Except insofar as they find it expedient to work together, they are completely independent of one another." One former Senate Leader complained: "I didn't have anything to threaten them with, and it wouldn't have worked even if I had tried . . . sure as hell, someone would have gotten up on the floor and accused me of trying to become a dictator."[1]

Only one Senate Democratic Leader in the twentieth century, Joseph T. Robinson of Arkansas, had made much of a mark. Oscar Underwood of Alabama, the first formally to hold the post, from 1920 to 1923, quit out of frustration with Senate rules and a desire to run for President. Robinson, his successor, held the position for fourteen years, but only asserted himself effectively from 1933 to 1937, when the Democrats enjoyed large majorities and FDR's New Deal proposals had widespread national appeal as an answer to the Depression. Alben Barkley of Kentucky became Vice President after eleven years as Senate party Leader, but his legislative victories were few and far between. Scott W. Lucas and Ernest McFarland, Lyndon's two immediate predecessors, lost their seats after each served two unproductive years. The party's most powerful senators in the fifties, Walter George and Richard Russell, wanted no part of the assignment.[2]

Lyndon's effectiveness as Minority Leader suggested that he might prove to be a cut above earlier Majority Leaders, but the slim two-vote Democratic margin in the Senate and a popular Republican President added to the normal limitations a Democratic floor leader faced in making much of a legislative record. Political and personal problems at the start of Lyndon's term further limited his influence over fellow senators. In mid-November 1954, the Waco *Tribune-Herald* reported a conversation between Texas Governor Allan Shivers and Truman's Secretary of State, James Byrnes of South Carolina. When Shivers suggested Johnson as "a compromise presidential candidate in 1956," Byrnes described him as "a young upstart." Although Byrnes and Shivers denied the story, it embarrassed both of them, and Lyndon as well. In a telephone conversation with Shivers, Lyndon expressed "not the slightest interest" in becoming a candidate, saying, "what I have got here on my hands now is of course about as difficult a situation as any human could. I imagine it will be blown up 40 times before" the next campaign. Lyndon told the press the same thing, hoping to convince fellow senators that he was not taking his success as Majority Leader for granted and looking past the current challenge to 1956. The discussion of his candidacy seemed certain to discourage other ambitious senators from helping him build a record as Leader on which he could run for the White House.[3]

In December, Johnson's standing with other senators suffered further when Adlai Stevenson installed Paul Butler of Indiana as Democratic National Committee chairman. Although Johnson and Rayburn tried to delay a vote on the chairmanship until January, the Committee meeting in New Orleans elected Butler by a decisive margin. Butler at once began attacking the Eisenhower administration and urging a separate Democratic legislative agenda. Convinced that outright opposition to Eisenhower would identify the Democrats as more interested in party advantage and presidential politics than in national needs, Johnson publicly reiterated his desire for bipartisanship and "a program geared to the best interests of our people." The Democratic congressional leadership would not surrender its authority to anybody, Johnson told the press. Privately, he predicted that the party's nominee would fare better in 1956 if he could point to a Democratic record of "principled stands on principal issues" rather than one "too much concerned with partisan tactics." Butler and other party liberals, however, were not convinced, and their unmanageability embarrassed Johnson, whose leadership was openly called into question.[4]

Lyndon also stumbled in his first legislative fight of the new congressional term. In January 1955, Sam Rayburn proposed a $20 across-the-board tax cut for every man, woman, and child in the country. Complaining that a 1954 Republican-sponsored tax bill had favored corporations and wealthy individuals, Rayburn urged a tax reduction that would benefit the mass of Americans—and give Democrats a talking point in the 1956 campaign. The Administration complained that Rayburn's bill was "some kind of a height in fiscal irresponsibility"; it would cost the government $2.3 billion a year and unbalance the budget. After a sharp fight in the House, Rayburn's bill passed on February 25 by only five votes, 210 to 205. The Senate refused to go along. Conservative southern Democrats Harry Byrd and Walter George joined with seven Republicans on the Finance Committee to defeat the proposal, 9 to 6.[5]

Despite the likelihood of defeat, Lyndon sponsored a modified version of Rayburn's plan. As a sop to party liberals, the principal advocates of tax reform, Lyndon proposed a less far-reaching tax cut: a $20 tax credit for heads of households, $10 for dependents, and nothing for spouses. In addition, he proposed making up for lost revenues with corporate and excise taxes and the elimination of provisions for accelerated depreciation allowances. The changes did not win any conservative votes, and the debate in the Senate divided along ideological lines. Liberals filled the Chamber with talk of "trickle down theory," relief for the rich, neglect of the poor, and help for the underdog. Conservatives denounced the Johnson bill as a "hoax" based on a "fiscal numbers racket" that would add to the Federal deficit. In a vote on March 18, five conservative Democrats joined forty-five Republicans to defeat Lyndon's tax plan, 50 to 44.[6]

Surgery at the Mayo Clinic had adversely affected Lyndon's ability to lead a tax cut through the Senate. On January 18, after several weeks of severe back pain, he took a train to Rochester, Minnesota, for treatment of a kidney stone. Unable to talk the doctors out of operating, Lyndon spent eleven days at the Clinic and another twelve days at his Texas ranch recovering. He found the inactivity unbearable, and only pleas from Eisenhower and close friends kept him from returning to the capital before mid-February.

Hearing, however, that things were not going well without him and that Earl Clements, his temporary replacement, had made "a rather poor impression on some members of the press," Lyndon, who was corresponding with party leaders, went back to the capital on February 12. Two weeks of continuing discomfort made him return to Mayo's. With the problem finally taken care of, he came back to Washington on

March 6 "a little shaky," but full of stories about the stone he had "re-posing in a jar" and wearing a corset he showed anyone who asked about his health.[7]

Yet rumors of his presidential ambitions, liberal control of the Democratic National Committee, defeat on the tax cut, and temporary physical problems were minor impediments to Lyndon's leadership of the Senate. In the midst of these setbacks, he established a system of control over the upper house that made him the most effective Majority Leader in Senate history. Why did he succeed when others had failed? Bryce Harlow, Ike's aide, says that Johnson had a special gift, an undefinable talent for leadership that created fear, admiration, and a desire in others to follow. His leadership consisted of intellectual force, discipline, and indefatigability. It was a mixture of being like other people and different from or superior to them at the same time. "You're one of the boys, but you're bigger than any of them. You're different from them." Above all, it was Lyndon's unequaled "domination of people by sheer force of personality. Never seen his equal," Harlow says, "and I've rubbed up against the greatest people this country has produced for twenty years running." Johnson's presence in the Senate, Florida senator George Smathers recalls, was like "a great overpowering thunderstorm that consumed you as it closed around you."[8]

Central to Johnson's power were the political debts owed him by other senators, particularly for coveted committee assignments. Since a senator "makes his reputation with his colleagues and leaves his mark on legislation" in committees, his place in the "committee caste system" is of paramount importance. First as Minority and then Majority Leader, Lyndon chaired the Democratic Steering Committee, the body responsible for committee appointments. Having increased the seats on major committees—by reducing the number on minor ones—and having guaranteed one good committee assignment to each senator, regardless of seniority, he was able to create a set of political IOUs that came due during future legislative struggles.[9]

In making committee appointments in 1955, Johnson reached out to nearly all Democratic senators. Operating from a back room in the Capitol, he made over 200 phone calls, touching all bases and conferring especially with Russell, George, Symington, and Humphrey. According to John Steele of *Time*, when Johnson finished, he had covered himself "with glory by throwing (for a second time) strict seniority rules to the wind and parcelling out committee assignments in a manner to please." All Democratic newcomers got at least one good appointment, while Alben Barkley and Joe O'Mahoney, former senators who had regained their seats and could have been treated like freshmen, got exactly what they wished. "The move not only was magnanimous," Steele said, "it was smart politics—and Lyndon excels at both. An angry, hurt Barkley

. . . would have provided a potential rallying point for any northern liberals who chaff under Johnson's reins this year. But now Alben is in Lyndon's corner and he's acting kittenish." The same was true of O'Mahoney. When another journalist complained about Johnson's appointments in a syndicated column, Hubert Humphrey suggested that he compare the Republicans' "miserable record with the Democratic leadership's action. . . . I worked day and night for better than ten days with Senator Johnson and others on these committee assignments. I can honestly say that . . . the Senate Democratic liberals were given a mighty good deal." Sam Rayburn agreed, writing Lyndon to say what a wonderful job he had done on committee appointments. "You have shown real leadership." [10]

Lyndon made certain to tell senators what he had done for them. Telephone calls reporting Steering Committee decisions were a way of driving home the point. If he didn't reach the senator, his wife would do as well. When he called John Stennis to report his appointment to the Appropriations Committee and Mrs. Stennis said he wasn't there, Lyndon laid it on thick: John had received a great honor, and the Senate had honored itself by selecting "a great American" and one of its finest members to this high post. Lyndon also sent each senator a laudatory press release about their committee appointments with a note saying they were free to distribute it in any manner they considered advantageous. Wayne Morse, for one, found it "very helpful" and put it to use in Oregon, where the press now, unlike 1954, had "difficulty in belittling" his committee assignments. [11]

Lyndon had to disappoint some, but he usually found alternative means to satisfy them. When he couldn't appoint Jack Kennedy to Appropriations, Foreign Relations, or Finance, he wrote a placating letter saying he couldn't "overcome seniority completely" and promised future amends. When he denied liberal Illinois senator Paul Douglas a slot on Finance, he made him chairman of the Joint Economic Committee. With Tennessee's Estes Kefauver, however, who was a Johnson rival and an uncooperative liberal, Lyndon was not so forthcoming. In January, after Kefauver asked to be on the party's Policy Committee, Lyndon bluntly told him: "I have never had the particular feeling that when I called up my first team and the chips were down that Kefauver felt he ought to be . . . on that team. If you feel you . . . want to be, it is the best news I have had. I will meet you more than 50% of the way. I will push you into every position of influence and power that you can have." In short, when Kefauver was ready to become a "Johnson man," Lyndon would be more receptive to his demands. Kefauver preferred to remain his own man. [12]

Lyndon's acquisition of political debts extended to other favors valued by senators. Help with getting a bill passed was one. As chairman of the

Democratic Policy Committee, Lyndon had the power to initiate a legislative fight when and on the terms he wanted. Several requests a day came into the Leader's office from senators asking that he speed up or delay a legislative proposal. And Lyndon mastered the tactics for doing both. "Timing can make or break a bill," he told Doris Kearns. "The first weeks provide the best opportunity to fight off a filibuster, the last weeks to avoid a conference committee, and the middle weeks to explore the issue. Sometimes the best tactic is delay—allowing time for support to build up and plunge—moving immediately to take advantage of momentum. Still other times the best timing inside the Senate depends on what's going on outside the Senate, such as primaries or elections or marches or something." [13]

Johnson also used his control over legislative scheduling to choose between competing bills and select the one that caused senators the least political problems. As one Senate aide described it, "No Southern Senator—except perhaps the two from Alabama—can afford to vote for a public housing bill. The Northern Democrats can't afford to vote against one. You can't ask a Senator to slit his own throat. So you bring up the bill in such a way that the Southerners can vote for it because it provides less housing than the alternative (or because it does not contain an FEPC provision) and the Northerners vote for it because it is better than nothing." Senator J. William Fulbright of Arkansas remembers Lyndon as very cooperative in helping pass bills coming out of the Foreign Relations Committee. Johnson "used to say, if anything came out of the committee, just let him know, and he would see that it was passed, and he pretty well did. . . . He was the manager of the Senate. He could make it function. He got action!" Stuart Symington recalled, "If he knew somebody wanted a dam badly, or a new military installation, he would tell him he would do his best to help him get it." But ultimately a favor was expected in return: He would say later, " 'I would like you to help me.' He was a master inside negotiator with his colleagues on such matters." [14]

Offices and parking spaces also counted with senators. One chief Senate clerk called them "the keys to happiness. Morale in the Senate depends on those two things." Recognizing their importance as a source of influence, Johnson shifted authority for making office and parking assignments from the Rules Committee to the Majority Leader. The first one he satisfied with his newly acquired power was himself. Grover Ensley, the executive director of the Joint Economic Committee, remembered how Lyndon came to visit the attractive offices of his committee one evening in January 1955. "I had the fire going in the fireplace. I was getting ready to go home about quarter til six . . . and the door opened. Lyndon Johnson came in. . . . He looked around the office— he noted the beautiful chandelier, the john, and the view from the windows. He sat down and we visited a while. He was always looking around the office." The next day Ensley received word that Johnson needed the offices. Ensley then spoke to all the Democrats on the committee, John Sparkman, Paul Douglas, Fulbright, and O'Mahoney. Lyndon had already seen each of them. In return for giving him the Joint Committee's offices, Johnson gave Sparkman an additional hideaway office; Douglas the chairmanship of the Joint Committee; Fulbright a promise of help to become chairman of Foreign Relations; and O'Mahoney a seat on the Joint Committee that five other Democrats had superior claims to. Ensley said later: "Lyndon Johnson had covered *every* possible angle on securing the space!" [15]

Committee and office assignments and help with legislation went far to establish Johnson's influence. But there was a host of other favors and courtesies that his colleagues valued as well: appointments to special committees and as delegates to international conferences, appropriations for subcommittees, information about the consequences of a bill for a senator's constituents, and help in finding an administrative assistant, scheduling a Senate speech, or identifying a pair on a particular bill. Recording the birth of William Knowland's fourth grandchild in the *Congressional Record,* attending the funeral of a senator's relative, noting birthdays and wedding anniversaries, passing along an expensive box of cigars, all were courtesies that were not forgotten and strengthened Johnson's influence.

De facto control of the Senate Democratic Campaign Committee gave Lyndon additional leverage with his party colleagues. But Republicans were not neglected. "I have always been told that no man can be a successful Leader unless he has personal friends on both sides of the aisle," Johnson wrote Republican Karl Mundt of South Dakota in April 1955. Maine's Republican senator Margaret Chase Smith recalled that Johnson played fairly with the membership, whether it was Republicans or Democrats. "He learned what they wanted, what they were interested in. It might be some little bill that affected their district or their state. It might be some personal thing. It might be of little importance to the Senate generally." But it counted with individual senators, who responded by forgetting about party line and ideology when Lyndon needed their help. [16]

All Johnson's wheeling and dealing in behalf of other senators was a prelude to his exercise of personal influence—daily, constant efforts to persuade colleagues to follow his lead. The "only real power available to the leader is the power of persuasion," Lyndon said in 1960. "There is no patronage; no power to discipline; no authority to fire senators like a President can fire [Cabinet] members." Lyndon made persuasion into a science that played the largest part in passing laws. Under his direction, Senate legislation became less a matter of floor debate or open argument and more a case of behind-the-scenes arrangements. Historian Paul Conkin points out that Johnson "had little sympathy for those who wanted to air points of view, to use speeches as a vehicle of public education. Debate tended to sharpen differences or allow senators to posture for audiences back home. . . . Success required a masking of issues, not sharpening them through debate." Johnson worked "through informal personal techniques and numerous small caucuses to build the temporary alliances necessary to pass a bill. These alliances were often years in the making, were tied to numerous small revisions or excisions in ever more complex bills, and in the end reflected numerous bargains or trade-offs among senators. Johnson was a master at bringing this complex process to a final climax at the exact time he had the majority required for victory." [17]

Johnson used what journalists called "the treatment" to deal effectively with individual senators and small caucuses. Evans and Novak described it as "supplication, accusation, cajolery, exuberance, scorn, tears, complaint, the hint of threat. It was all of these together. It ran the gamut of human emotions. Its velocity was breathtaking, and it was all in one direction. Interjections from the target were rare. Johnson anticipated them before they could be spoken. He moved in close, his face a scant millimeter from his target, his eyes widening and narrowing, his eyebrows rising and falling. From his pockets poured clippings, memos, statistics. Mimicry, humor, and the genius of analogy made The Treatment an almost hypnotic experience and rendered the target stunned and helpless."

Benjamin Bradlee of the *Washington Post* compared it with going to the zoo. "You really felt as if a St. Bernard had licked your face for an hour, had pawed you all over. . . . He never just shook hands with you. One hand was shaking your hand; the other hand was always someplace else, exploring you, examining you. And of course he was a great actor, bar fucking none the greatest. He'd be feeling up Katharine Graham and bumping Meg Greenfield on the boobs. And at the same time he'd be trying to persuade you of something, sometimes something that he knew and I knew was not so, and there was just the trace of a little smile on his face. It was just a miraculous performance." Hubert Humphrey said: "He'd come on just like a tidal wave. . . . He went through the walls. He'd come through a door, and he'd take the whole room over. Just like that. . . . There was nothing delicate about him." [18]

Doris Kearns believes that "the treatment" was more calculated and subtle. Johnson usually designed his approaches to other senators to seem wholly spontaneous—an accidental encounter in a Senate corridor leading to a private talk. In fact, they were carefully planned. He "would practice his intended approach, often in the presence of one of his aides. He sorted out in rambling fashion the possible arguments pro and con, experimented with a variety of responses, and fashioned a detailed mental script from which he would speak . . . when the meeting took place." The physical contact was "the product of meticulous calculation": it created a sense of genuine and benign intimacy and affection. Johnson's rhetoric was also carefully scripted to create an illusion that the outcome of the pending legislation depended on the actions of this one senator. "Johnson's argument invoked country and party, loyalty to the leadership, reminders of past services and hints of future satisfactions—but always in a form that disavowed any intention that there was a debt to be paid or trade being offered. There was the welfare of the Senate to be considered and a casual mention of certain powerful interests. All of these mingled arguments were set forth as if they constituted a unitary motive for action, and this was all presented as if Johnson's object were not persuasion, but to 'reason together' in hopes of clarifying the considerations that would help a man to make his own informed decision." [19]

Johnson himself discounted the descriptions of "the treatment" as "nonsense" perpetrated by "intellectuals." He complained that they pictured him performing "a back-alley job . . . holding the guy by the collar, twisting his arm behind his back, dangling a carrot in front of his nose, and holding a club over his head. It's a pretty amazing sight when you think about it. I'd have to be some sort of acrobatic genius to carry it off, and the Senator in question, well, he'd have to be pretty weak and pretty meek to be simply standing there like a paralyzed idiot." Johnson contended that his powers of persuasion rested on his talent for debate and the extensive preparation that went into it. [20]

Great preparation unquestionably preceded Johnson's conversations with his colleagues. He made certain to master the details of the bill under consideration and to marshall the facts either for or against the measure. More important, he knew "every personal interest of every member of the Senate just like he knew the palm of his hand," William Fulbright said. "He knew how to bring people together, because he could appeal to their different interests." Johnson took account of the power groups in each senator's state and who supported and opposed him. According to Henry Jackson, "He understood fully . . . the philosophy, the ideologies, of the senators. He was keenly aware of what would fly with them and what would not." [21]

Johnson told the journalist Sarah McClendon that he had "a complete study made of the life of each senator. He knew everything about them, their weaknesses, their good and bad things. And this he needed, he felt, to work with those men and to get along with them." Doris Kearns says that Johnson "shaped a composite mental portrait of every Senator: his strengths and his weaknesses; his place in the political spectrum; his aspirations in the Senate, and perhaps beyond the Senate; how far he could be pushed in what direction, and by what means; how he liked his liquor; how he felt about his wife and his family, and, most important, how he felt about himself." Johnson told Kearns: "When you're dealing with all those Senators—the good ones and the crazies, the hard workers and the lazies, the smart ones and the mediocres—you've got to know two things right away. You've got to understand the beliefs and values common to all of them as politicians, the desire for fame and the thirst for honor, and then you've got to understand *the* emotion most controlling that particular Senator when he thinks about this particular issue." [22]

"He knew his colleagues so well," Clark Clifford said "—what their ambitions and goals were. I got the feeling after a while that he played the Democrats in the Senate the way a skilled harpist would play a harp. He knew which string to pull at a particular time and how he could bring a fellow along." Johnson aid Gerald Siegel agrees: "He knew them better than they knew themselves. Depending upon the issue and depending upon the particular individual, he shaped his message." And tone. "Demure with Richard Russell, he could swagger and swear with Robert Kerr. A populist with liberals, he could be a gas and oil man with the conservatives." [23]

Johnson himself described how he applied the technique to journalists. Because William S. White of the *New York Times* admired subtlety, Johnson tried to be subtle with him. Because columnist Stewart Alsop cared "a lot about appearing to be an intellectual and a historian," Johnson played down "the gold cufflinks which you play up with *Time* magazine, and, to him, emphasize your relationship with FDR and your roots in Texas. . . . You learn that Evans and Novak love to traffic in backroom politics and political intrigue, so that when you're with them you make sure to bring in lots of details and colorful description of personality. You learn that Mary McGrory likes dominant personalities and Doris Fleeson cares only about issues, so that when you're with McGrory you come on strong and with Fleeson you make yourself sound like some impractical red-hot liberal." [24]

To Johnson, information was power. His "search for information was ceaseless," Kearns says. "Each encounter, whatever its purpose, was also a 'planned interview,' in which Johnson probed, questioned, and directed the conversation according to *his* ends. Whether in the office or the cloakroom, over lunch or over drinks, Johnson somehow made others feel that every conversation was a test in which they were expected not only to come up with the answers but to score 100 percent, resulting in a tension that often brought forth additional information." Johnson would frequently get staff people together from different Senate committees and pick their brains. He wasn't going around their bosses, William Darden, Richard Russell's aide, remembered, but just getting them to report on the current state of things in their respective committees.

Mostly, however, Johnson depended on what the journalist Stewart Alsop called "the biggest, the most efficient, the most ruthlessly overworked and the most loyal personal staff in the history of the Senate" for intelligence gathering.[25]

The principal figure in this operation was Bobby Baker. Johnson made him secretary to the Senate Majority Leader. At the age of twenty-six, Baker had a matchless knowledge of Senate operations and its members. One senator, who "never liked him very much," said that "if you wanted to know what was going on, Bobby was the guy you called. He had the head count. He knew who was drunk, who was out of town, who was out sleeping with whom. He knew who was against the bill and why, and he probably knew how to approach him to get him to swing around. Bobby was it." George Reedy says that the senators "liked Bobby because he was useful, very useful. He'd trade information back and forth. . . . He could deliver money to them during political campaigns. . . . He'd count votes. God, he could count votes. . . . The most important part of Johnson's operation was really sort of an intelligence operation that kept feeding in things with a scale and an efficiency the CIA never dreamed of. Bobby was a very important element of that operation."[26]

Some marveled at Baker's success in mastering so much information. Baker himself said there was no "magic in it. I was industrious, hard working, ambitious . . . I was not bashful in seeking Senators out to ask their views on bills and issues, to learn who influenced who. It was simply a matter of watching, listening, and doing one's homework." But there was more to it than that. Baker haunted the Senate Democratic cloakroom, which he called "the Central Intelligence Agency of the Senate." It was the place where "senators opened up their heads and their hearts—especially as the day wore on and flasks were nipped. . . . It was here I first heard direct from the horse's mouth what senators were considered to be for hire, and to what extent, and to whom." Baker catalogued their preferences and dislikes, their jealousies, class differences, and clashing personal goals. He paid special attention to Senate staffers, read committee reports, and provided senators with numerous favors. "You'd go down in Bobby's office," a member of the Capitol police force recalls, ". . . and on his desk were stacks of money. On his desk. Drawers full of money." Campaign contributions, help in arranging Senate junkets, or in getting a particular desk on the Senate floor, "the mule work," as Baker called it, stored up "residues of goodwill for the future."[27]

While Baker was at the beck and call of all Democratic senators, he was principally Lyndon's man. "We were so well atuned to each other, we could almost read each other's minds," Baker told an interviewer. Some called him the "ninety-seventh Senator," but most referred to him as "Lyndon, Jr." or "Little Lyndon." When he wanted something, Baker would often say, "We want" or "Lyndon wants." And Johnson valued him greatly. "Thank you for sending me the 'run-down' on Democratic Senators," he wrote Baker during a period of indisposition in 1955. "I'm going to be needing more and more as time goes on. I haven't had such a complete round-up of the news in a mighty long time." [28]

Johnson's mastery of the Senate came not only from knowledge of other senators but also a skillful use of Senate rules. Unanimous consent agreements, aborted quorum calls, night sessions, and periods of inaction alternating with bursts of frenetic activity were Johnson's principal weapons in driving bills through. Consent agreements set a time limit on debate; drawn-out quorum calls that replaced traditional brief recesses and were suspended when Johnson was ready to have the Senate resume gave him time to cut deals in the cloakroom; night sessions and stop and go legislating exhausted senators, discouraged prolonged debate, and promoted backroom agreements as the principal device for passing laws. Johnson told reporters that he "talked less and passed more bills than anyone else." [29]

And the outcome was a Senate following Lyndon's lead. On bill after bill, resolution after resolution, Lyndon dominated the 84th Congress. Successful opposition on January 6 to a proposal for changing the Senate rule on curbing filibusters gave a first hint of his mastery of Democratic colleagues and the upper house. Eighteen liberal Democrats, led by Herbert Lehman of New York, met to discuss a rules' fight. Hubert Humphrey argued against "a frontal assault." He urged liberals to "abandon the devil theory of history" that made all southern senators their enemies and to give Lyndon "a chance to see what he could do with the South." Humphrey persuaded fellow liberals to fight for civil rights legislation through the regular committee route. "Behind Humphrey," John Steele told his editor, "stood the off-stage figure of Lyndon Johnson, who wants nobody and nothing to rock the Democratic cockle-shell." Walter White, the head of the NAACP, publicly complained that "shrewd horse trading over committee memberships . . . caused abandonment of the proposed change of Senate rules." Although Humphrey denied it, he told White that "the liberal position on the committees this year is far better than it has been in recent years." He sent Lyndon copies of his correspondence with White and asked if he had "any room in Texas for a displaced liberal." [30]

Although Lyndon's absence at the Mayo Clinic muted his role in passing a Senate Resolution giving the President authority to defend Formosa and the Pescadores Islands in the South China Sea, he nevertheless played a significant part. In January 1955, when the Chinese Communists publicly described an invasion of Formosa as "imminent" and Chiang Kai-shek warned of an attack on Quemoy and Matsu, islands off the mainland, Eisenhower submitted the Resolution. Eager to avoid the kind of criticism Truman received for entering the Korean war without congressional authority, Eisenhower asked for an unprecedented congressional commitment to freedom of action in a foreign crisis. The President consulted with all congressional leaders, including Lyndon, before making his request. The House immediately approved on January 24. But the Senate began four days of debate, which John Steele felt could have been avoided if Lyndon had been present. Nevertheless, on January 28, the Senate passed the Resolution with Lyndon's backing by a vote of 83 to 3. In 1964, after Johnson became President, he remembered the Senate's action as a precedent for asking similar freedom to deal with Vietnam.[31]

The Resolution did not intimidate the Chinese Communists, who continued to speak and act as if they would attack all the islands in Nationalist hands. Conservative supporters of Chiang in the United States, led by Senator Knowland of California, "the Senator from Formosa," demanded that the Administration commit itself to defend not only the Pescadores and Formosa but also Quemoy and Matsu. Eisenhower was eager to fudge the question of whether the United States would defend the offshore islands, saying only that he would act if an attack on them represented a prelude to an assault against Formosa. Most Senate Democrats shared the President's reluctance to make an unqualified commitment. "I have had about enough of Asia, and of special laws passed to take care of Asia . . .," John Stennis wrote Lyndon on February 8. "If you are gone too long, when you get back we may be annexed to Formosa and be purely a subsidiary of 'Knowland's Asia.' " Lyndon agreed, and issued a statement criticizing the "war party" and identifying Senate Democrats with the President's opposition to commitments that could lead to war.[32]

In March, when Eisenhower and Dulles announced their readiness to use tactical atomic weapons in case of war in the Formosa Strait, Lyndon warned against "an irresponsible adventure for which we have not calculated the risks." By discussing a possible use of atomic bombs, the President aimed to intimidate the Chinese Communists and appease the right wing of his party. Lyndon's outspoken opposition helped the President follow a more restrained policy. Convinced that Ike was operating "under heavy pressure from his own political right wing," and confident that he would act with appropriate restraint if left to his own devices, Lyndon lined up Democratic opposition to defending Quemoy and Matsu unless it was "absolutely" needed to save Formosa. In April, partly because of Lyndon's actions, Eisenhower told his principal advisers that a war with China over Quemoy and Matsu would be unwise; it would lead to a wider conflict in which public opinion at home and abroad would largely oppose America's decision to fight. Later in the month, when the

Chinese Communists declared their desire for peace with the United States and for the liberation of Formosa by peaceful means, the President gave a conciliatory response.[33]

Lyndon also supported Eisenhower in June when Joseph McCarthy tried to limit the President's freedom to negotiate at a Big Four—American, Russian, British, French—meeting in Geneva in July. After Ike had agreed to the summit, McCarthy introduced a resolution opposing attendance at the conference unless the Soviets agreed to discuss the status of their East European satellites. Such an arbitrary invasion of a President's foreign policy prerogatives was doomed to defeat in committee. But in order to embarrass the Republicans, Lyndon forced McCarthy's resolution onto the Senate floor, where it provoked an angry debate among them before being decisively voted down. "It's no longer McCarthyism," Eisenhower said, "it's McCarthywasm." Pointing to the Senate's support of Ike's Formosa and Geneva policies, Lyndon said that "the crowning achievement of the session was to unite the Nation behind a policy designed to protect our freedoms and preserve peace." The Senate actions were also a political triumph for the Democrats, who once again showed themselves to be more reliable supporters of Ike's foreign policy than the Republicans. Despite pronouncements then and later about having politics end at the water's edge, partisan advantage in foreign affairs was never far from Lyndon's mind.[34]

The bills passed during the 1955 session demonstrated Lyndon's masterful leadership. Although meeting twenty days and two hundred hours fewer than the first session of the 83rd Congress, the initial meeting of the 84th passed nearly two hundred more bills than the 83rd. In addition, the first session of the 84th Congress had no filibusters or heated exchanges over several days that engendered long-term feuds. At the same time, it tackled and passed some of the most controversial legislation the Congress had confronted in seven or eight years. As a memorandum celebrating Lyndon's achievement put it, despite the Democrats' slim, two-vote advantage, "as long as Lyndon was on the Senate floor, the Democrats lost only one party vote during the entire session—and that was the Tax Bill which burst upon the Senate while Johnson was in the hospital."[35]

There was some hyperbole in Lyndon's claims. The first half of 1955 witnessed an economic boom that discouraged the creation of new Federal programs. Moreover, as Eisenhower biographer Stephen Ambrose says, "the combination of a Democratic Congress and a Republican administration meant that precious little in the way of domestic legislation could be passed. Both parties were jockeying for position for the 1956 presidential election; neither party was willing to give the other credit for major legislation." Nevertheless, Lyndon skillfully drove more than

1300 bills through the Senate, including major trade, wage, and housing laws.[36]

A three-year extension of the Reciprocal Trade Agreement Act was the product of considerable horse-trading on Lyndon's part. The original bill submitted by the White House gave concessions to protectionists and free traders. But it also antagonized many in both camps. Extended negotiations in the Senate Finance Committee produced a bill by the beginning of May that established an "armed truce" between warring factions. To keep the "uneasy" agreement from coming unstuck, Johnson needed "to ram it through the Senate as rapidly as possible . . . with the least number of roll call votes" that could embarrass various senators. To do so, Lyndon invoked a rarely used "constitutional gimmick" requiring a roll call only when one-fifth of members present asked for it, and arranged a unanimous consent agreement limiting debate to two hours for each amendment and four hours for final passage of the law. With most senators "damned agreeable to voting quickly and with as little pain as possible," the bill, which normally would have been debated for several weeks, passed the Senate after only three days on a 75-to-13 vote.[37]

An increase in the minimum wage, which had not been changed in six years was also the product of Johnson's maneuvering. Organized labor called for an increase from 75 cents an hour to a $1.25 minimum wage and its extension to all retail and service workers. The Eisenhower administration proposed 90 cents an hour and some expanded coverage. Southern Democrats accepted the 15-cent rise to 90 cents but opposed any wider coverage. Working closely with Robert Oliver, lobbyist for the CIO, Lyndon concluded that a 25-cent increase to $1 an hour without any broader coverage was the best they could get. He pushed this compromise through the Labor subcommittee against the wishes of its chairman, Paul Douglas, by warning that amendments to the bill, extended debate on the Senate floor, or a roll-call vote would jeopardize passage.

Oliver remembers that for days after the subcommittee reported the bill Johnson left it untouched. Then one day in June he suddenly began buttonholing people "in a very animated fashion." He rushed the bill to a vote when its principal opponents were absent, and won passage on a voice vote after only an hour's debate. The whole thing happened so fast that Alabama's Lister Hill, the Labor Committee chairman, was in the cloakroom when the vote took place. Herbert Lehman, a liberal eager to urge a higher wage and expanded coverage, arrived on the floor as the vote concluded. "What's the vote on?" Lehman asked. The reply that the Senate had just passed his committee's bill left him speechless. Spessard Holland of Florida, the bill's leading opponent, was in the Senate dining room at the time of the vote. When he returned to the Senate floor and learned what had happened, he began "jumping, screaming, and hollering and pounding the desk. Johnson said, 'Well, Spessard, I had a little quorum call. If you fellows aren't on the job around here, I've got legislation to pass.' " Hubert Humphrey recalled, "He just slipped right on through there. Zip! Oh boy, they were furious with him."[38]

Lyndon's greatest triumph in the session was the passage of a public housing bill. In 1954 the Republican-controlled Congress had essentially ended federally financed housing, and prospects for a major housing law in 1955 were dim. Nevertheless, Lyndon encouraged the Senate Banking Committee to report a bill authored by Alabama's John Sparkman providing for 135,000 housing units over three years. Homer Capehart of Indiana, speaking for the Eisenhower administration, offered an amended bill authorizing 70,000 units over two years. Lyndon publicly expressed little hope of beating Capehart, and the liberal Americans for Democratic Action (ADA) blasted Johnson for "affably acquiescing to the Republican assault upon liberalism." "Lyndon," Capehart told him, "this is one time I've really got you. I'm going to rub your nose in it!"

Initial tallies showed that southern Democrats would vote with the Republicans for Capehart's amended bill. But Lyndon concocted a strategy that beat Capehart. He called in a favor from one western Republican and persuaded four other northern Republicans to serve their constituents by voting with Sparkman. Southern Democrats were urged to follow their natural political bent and vote against both the Capehart and Sparkman bills. When most of them agreed, an eight-vote victory for Capehart turned into a six-vote defeat, 44 to 38. Hubert Humphrey was predictably one of the 44, but only because Lyndon had taken special pains to arrange his timely return from Minnesota, where he had been speaking. Delayed by bad weather on the flight from Minneapolis to Washington, Humphrey's plane was stacked up over National Airport as the Senate began voting. Calling the control tower at National to arrange priority landing and sending a Capitol police car to speed Humphrey back to the Senate Lyndon got him there in time. As the final count was announced, Capehart "was a slumped down hulk . . . And Bill Knowland, his face a fiery red, stared stunned at the . . . tally sheet in front of him." George Reedy remembers that "the press gallery nearly collapsed out of sheer shock, because they'd all written stories that morning predicting that this would be a major defeat for Lyndon Johnson as Democratic leader." Once the Capehart bill was out of the way, the Republicans, who agreed on the need for some kind of housing bill, grudgingly backed the Sparkman alternative, which passed by a vote of 60 to 25.

"Johnson plays the Senate like a well trained violin virtuoso," John Steel declared. When it was ready to vote Lyndon's way, he planted Alan

Bible of Nevada in the presiding officer's chair and directed the Senate's every move. "His baggy-cut, almost zoot suit coat flys open. He raises his right hand in the air circling with his index finger like an airport mechanic signaling a pilot to rev up his motors—the meaning, speed. He's got the Senate tally clerks trained so they can do a slow roll call while waiting for stragglers to come in or speed it up to get a vote out of the way before enemies enter or the Senate's voting mood is lost. . . . It's incredibly hard . . . grubby painstaking work. But it's how you pass a bill in the Senate." Paul Douglas told Johnson about the Housing bill, "I didn't think you could do it, and I will never know *how* you did it, but you did it, and I'm grateful." [39]

Johnson's success in leading a closely divided Senate through a productive session stimulated discussion of his suitability for higher office. In June and July 1955, *Newsweek, The New Republic,* and the *Washington Post* speculated on his nomination for the presidency in 1956 or 1960. A *Post* column described him as "the first party leader in modern times to tame the independent Senate," and as a man who was riding "a presidential boom." Grace Tully, an FDR secretary, reported that one political activist traveling in upstate New York had heard repeated suggestions of Johnson for the number two spot on the ticket in 1956. Asked on network television whether he thought Johnson would have support for the presidential nomination "next time," Richard Russell replied that Johnson would make a great President of the United States but doubted that he was running in 1956. Columnist Joe Alsop told George Reedy that Adlai Stevenson would probably offer Lyndon the vice presidential nomination in 1956. If he accepted and the Democrats lost, Stevenson would support Johnson for the presidency in 1960. Convinced that any boom for him a year in advance of the Democratic convention would give newspaper columnists a target to shoot at and would impede his work in the Senate, Lyndon denied any intention of running. [40]

A serious heart attack in the summer of 1955 also discouraged talk of his running for higher office. The attack had been in the making for a long time because of the furious pace he set during the first half of 1955. "$E = mc^2$ is Albert Einstein's world-shaking formula for energy," one journalist wrote. "But in Washington, D.C., there is a simpler, more understandable formula. In that city of energetic men, energy in its purest political form is expressed in the letters $E = LBJ$." [41]

Johnson's day usually began at six-thirty, when he ate breakfast in bed while skimming the previous day's *Congressional Record.* Dressing in a silk suit and a monogrammed shirt with French cuffs and long pointed collars, he often left for the Capitol at seven-thirty in a chauffered limousine, reading the *New York Times* and *Washington Post* en route. Arriving at his office about eight, he ordinarily conferred with

Bobby Baker and Walter Jenkins about the day's schedule. Committee meetings and telephone calls to other senators, especially committee chairmen, filled his morning. Beginning at noon, he would spend the afternoon in the Senate managing the Chamber's activities. Back in one of his offices by six or visiting with Sam Rayburn in his Speaker's office for drinks, he would often stay until ten preparing for the next day's work.

Lunches were eaten on the run and dinners late at night after several drinks had eased the tensions of the day. Often he would bring several people home with him for late night suppers that Lady Bird and Zephyr Wright, the Johnson's cook, would prepare. Bobby Baker remembers that he would then eat "like a starving dog," wolfing down "God-awful platters of the heavy southern cooking he preferred." Supplied with fresh memos, mail, and staff reports delivered by a Capitol messenger around midnight, Johnson would read himself to sleep. Sometimes waking in the middle of the night with concerns that he might forget pressing tasks, he would telephone assistants at two or three in the morning to put assignments on their calendars. Some senators remember calls from him before daylight about Senate business with requests for early morning meetings.[42]

Johnson's stressful schedule, terrible eating habits that drove his weight up to 225 pounds, and three pack-a-day cigarette habit were a formula for disaster. On Saturday, June 18, he ate lunch with Florida senator George Smathers in the Senate dining room, where "he ate his usual double meal and gulped the food." Later in the afternoon, on the way to George Brown's estate in Middleburg, some forty miles from the District, Lyndon grasped his chest and complained of indigestion. A coke and bicarbonate of soda didn't relieve the discomfort. Although he said he felt better the next morning, Smathers didn't think he looked any better and urged him to see a doctor when he got back to town. A cursory exam by the Capitol physician on Monday morning turned up nothing and Lyndon resumed his normal schedule. In fact, he had suffered a heart attack and was on the verge of a more severe one.[43]

During the next two weeks, Lyndon felt continuously tired. On Friday, July 1, he put in a hectic day at his office, holding discussions with numerous senators about legislation they wanted passed before the summer adjournment. In the evening he went to dinner with Sam Rayburn and Senator Stuart Symington of Missouri. He was very tense throughout the evening, and incessantly discussed politics. Noticing how tired he looked, Rayburn urged him to slow down and take some time off. Lyndon said he would at the close of the session, when he planned to go hunting. After they dropped Lyndon off, Rayburn told Symington and his wife, "He just can't think, eat or drink anything except the problems he has as Majority Leader. He won't relax."[44]

The following day, Lyndon held an early afternoon press conference with three wire-service reporters to emphasize accomplishments and describe plans for the rest of the session. Tired, irritable, and eager to get away to George Brown's Virginia estate for the July 4th weekend, Lyndon was in no mood for a reporter's probing questions. John Chadwick, a veteran Associated Press journalist, pressed him to explain why the McCarran-Walter immigration law would not be amended in the current session. Lyndon's reply that he couldn't do anything about a bill that was still in the Judiciary Committee irked Chadwick, who pointed out that Johnson had just discussed the fate of other bills still in committee. Was the Majority Leader really for alterations in the law? Chain-smoking throughout the conference to soothe his jangled nerves, Lyndon now exploded with invective, tongue-lashing Chadwick so severely that his colleagues defended him. Embarrassed by his loss of restraint, Lyndon abruptly ended the conference.[45]

Johnson then left the Senate in his limousine to visit Walter George at the Mayflower, where he was recovering from a respiratory infection. It was almost five o'clock before he began the trip to Virginia. Since it was Lucy's birthday and she was sick with a high fever, Lady Bird stayed in Washington, promising to follow Lyndon when she could. Shortly after crossing the Potomac, Lyndon broke out in a cold sweat and suffered terrible pain in his midsection and chest. He thought he had indigestion from a heavy lunch of hot dogs and beans. He tried to relieve his nausea by throwing up, but couldn't, and when he arrived at Brown's place at about six o'clock, he went to a downstairs bedroom to rest. George Brown gave him some anti-acid, which didn't help, and then a shot of whiskey, which relieved his discomfort a little. When the symptoms returned a few minutes later, Brown, who now suspected that Lyndon might be having a heart attack, gave him some digitalis, which Brown used for a heart murmur. None of this helped, and in fact the digitalis could have killed him.[46]

Brown now told Frank Oltorf, Brown & Root's Washington lobbyist and another weekend guest, to find a local doctor. In the meantime, Senator Clinton Anderson, who had had a heart attack, arrived at the house. On hearing Lyndon's complaints, he shouted, "My God, man! You're having a heart attack!" When the doctor who had been called by Oltorf arrived, he quickly reached the same conclusion and called an ambulance in order to rush Lyndon to the Bethesda Naval Hospital. When the ambulance—which doubled as a hearse in Middleburg—arrived, the doctor sat in front with the town undertaker, who was driving, and Lyndon stretched out in the back, with Oltorf sitting beside him. On the way, Lyndon suffered terrible pain and asked for a shot. But the doctor advised against stopping to administer it. Fearing he would die before he got to Bethesda, Lyndon reached up to Oltorf and told him where his will was and his wish that Lady Bird get everything. Despite his pain and fear, "he was extremely courageous and brave." Nor had his sense of humor deserted him. "Will I ever be able to smoke again if this is a heart attack?" he asked the doctor. "Well, Senator, frankly, no," the doctor replied. ". . . He gave a great sigh and said, 'I'd rather have my pecker cut off.' "[47]

When they arrived at the hospital, Lady Bird, Walter Jenkins, and George Reedy were already there. When hospital attendants carried him in on a stretcher, Lady Bird was greatly relieved "because he looked just like himself." Lyndon handed her his wallet and keys, asked that she call his mother, and then told Jenkins where his will was. He instructed Reedy to tell Earle Clements that he would have to take over the Senate for him, and the press that his heart attack was "a real bellybuster." He asked for a cigarette, and when a doctor urged against any more smoking, he agreed, but said he wanted just one more. Lady Bird remembers that "it was very sensuous . . . he looked at it like, 'This is the dearest thing.' " As they wheeled him into an elevator for the ride to his room on the seventeenth floor, he remembered that he had been fitted for two suits, a brown and a blue, by a Washington tailor that morning. Tell him "to go ahead with the blue," Lyndon said. "I'll need it whichever way it goes." As they put him in an oxygen tent, he went into shock and turned gray, "just about the color of pavement." He was "motionless as stone and cold to touch. His blood pressure dropped to zero over forty." He had suffered a coronary occlusion and the doctors gave him a fifty-fifty chance of survival.[48]

His condition was touch and go for the next forty-eight hours, but by Wednesday, the fourth day after his attack, prospects brightened. During the next month, he struggled to adjust to the limitations imposed on him by his heart disease—a ban on smoking, a strict diet to reduce weight, and a period of relative inactivity. Lady Bird called it the "Battle of Patience," and though she thought Lyndon might "get along all right, I don't know whether I'll make it or not." The thought of breaking the smoking habit and following a "dismal low-calorie/low-fat diet" filled him with a sense of deprivation. Walter Jenkins remembered how after his recovery "he would take a cigarette and lick it or hold it in his mouth" without lighting it, and Lyndon later told Lady Bird that he had missed smoking every day of his life. He despised the hospital food and Lady Bird had to bring him some of Zephyr Wright's home-cooked meals. He took to eating a lot of cantaloupe, which is low in calories, and he satisfied his craving for desserts with tapioca. "I'm either going to have to turn registered chemist or jump out of the window," Lady Bird told a reporter.[49]

In general, Lyndon did "a wonderful job" of making peace with his new regimen, but he had to fight his way through a period of depression. He was quiet and sober and spoke a lot about having to retire not only from the Leadership but from politics entirely. Walter Jenkins remembered him as so despondent that he required medication for his depression. Jenkins feared that "he would kind of give up, maybe wouldn't really make the effort to [recover.]" George Reedy remembers his just lying in bed and sulking, showing no affect, as if "he wasn't there." Lady Bird recalls his depression as very hard on "everybody around him because he would just sit and stare into space." [50]

But the outpouring of sympathy and encouragement from family, friends, political colleagues, journalists, and the public buoyed him. On July 5, his Senate colleagues took to the floor of the Chamber to praise him and pray for his recovery. They followed up with personal letters saying how beloved and respected he was. "It just isn't the same around here without you," Hubert Humphrey said. ". . . I miss having you get after me. I miss your good humor. Yes, we are just lonesome for you. It's a strange thing—one never appreciates what he really has until it is absent. . . . Once you have recovered, God only knows what will happen around this town! Lyndon Johnson tired was a ball of fire; Lyndon Johnson rested will make the atom bomb obsolete!" Newspapers across the United States, regardless of political coloration, expressed appreciation for his leadership. On the day after Lyndon was hospitalized, one reputedly tough, unsentimental journalist called the Johnson home "crying so he could hardly talk." [51]

Johnson was genuinely touched and grateful for the attention and warmth of feeling. A letter from President Truman made Lyndon "perk up right away. . . . He has kept it by his bedside constantly since it arrived," Lady Bird wrote HST. He became "absolutely obsessive" about the get-well messages flooding the hospital, George Reedy recalls. "He was just basking in those letters. He'd read them over and over and over again. . . . There was sort of an unspoken yearning of his that could be felt all the way down to the Senate for that kind of reassurance, and he got it." [52]

With the help of these expressions of affection and concern, Johnson's thirst for activity quickly returned. After the oxygen tent was taken away, he had a radio brought to his room, and he listened to news broadcasts, switching from station to station to get full coverage. He had Lady Bird turn her next door room into an office, where she answered his mail. Soon Jenkins and Reedy were on constant call, consultations with Earl Clements occurred, and visits from other political leaders, including President Eisenhower and Vice President Nixon, were arranged. After a Republican senator had come for a talk, Lyndon's doctor said he had had his quota of visitors for the day. "Oh, now look, doctor," Johnson protested, "you're not going to count Republicans are you?" On July 22 he gave an interview to *Newsweek*, and shortly after a group of reporters came to see him. When they all remarked on how thin he was, Johnson ordered Sarah McClendon, the one female journalist in the room, to turn her back while he dropped his pants to show the boys how thin he really was. On August 7 he left the hospital for his Washington home, where he received a stream of visitors, whom he regaled with the details of his illness and his regimen for recovery. He also began peppering reporters and Senate colleagues with reminders of what had been accomplished in the recent session and told them that he planned to complete his recovery in Texas and then have another session of accomplishment in 1956.[53]

On August 25th he flew from Washington to Fredericksburg on Texas millionaire Wesley West's plane. Lady Bird, Willis Hurst—Lyndon's cardiologist at Bethesda—Sam Houston Johnson and his wife, and Zephyr Wright accompanied him. Several local physicians, who were to confer with Dr. Hurst, and Mary Rather, who was to handle Lyndon's correspondence at the ranch, met the plane. "He was the thinnest thing you have ever, ever seen, and his clothes were just hanging on him. And of course, Mrs. Johnson looked bad, too," Mary Rather recalled. The party immediately went to the Stonewall ranch seventeen miles away, where Lyndon settled into a new routine. He woke up at dawn to the mooing of a milk cow, ate breakfast under the trees while reading the morning newspapers, and then took "a half-mile walk down the road with a view of my fat cows grazing on the one side and my beautiful river flowing on the other." A ride around the ranch, a walk in the plowed fields, "just to feel the dirt under my feet," stops at a tenant house and swimming pool under construction, lunch, an afternoon nap, a little reading in histories and biographies, dinner, and a game of dominoes filled out the day.[54]

Although he described it as "an ideal life," he couldn't stand the inactivity. "It was way out in the country and it was so quiet and still," Mary Rather said later. "The awareness of his very bad heart attack made it such a long, sad time. . . . He had slowed down so much and the days were so long because we took very few phone calls. We had hardly any visitors, and you knew that this worry about his health was on his mind and Lady Bird's mind every day, plus the big decision about what to do about being a member of Congress and what to do with his life if he didn't return to Congress."

He channeled his enormous energy into an exercise program, walking a mile to and from his cousin Oriole's house, and maintaining a strict diet that brought his weight down from 220 to 177 pounds. "He became the goddamndest diet fanatic that ever lived," George Reedy says. When Lady Bird served him some watermelon that had more calories than cantaloupe, "you would have thought that the world had come to an end." "Bird! Bird!" he would shout into an intercom from a chaise alongside the swimming pool. "When this is over," she told a friend, "I want to go off by myself and cry for about two hours." He also became obsessed about the swimming pool, supervising every detail of its construction, which drove the builder to distraction. When Dorothy Palmie, a former secretary, came by to visit, she found him "going full-blast. Mary Rather and Lady Bird were beating their brains out with all these little details and tasks and chores. . . . They [had] set up shop in the living room." [55]

Politics and thoughts of running for President continued to preoccupy him and helped spur his recovery. In September, he began urging Senate colleagues to visit him at the ranch, and on the 24th, news that Eisenhower had suffered a heart attack fixed his attention on the President's health. He spoke to James Hagerty, Ike's press secretary, two or three times a day for the first three days, and then Jerry Persons, the White House staff man for congressional relations, called Lyndon once a day. Eisenhower's illness opened up a five-month period of uncertainty about who would be the Republican nominee for President in 1956. George Reedy at once sent Lyndon a series of memos on how the President's illness might affect the Democrats, and Lyndon in particular. [56]

A visit to the ranch by Adlai Stevenson and Sam Rayburn on September 28–29 put Lyndon back in the national spotlight. The Stevenson-Rayburn visit brought a host of press people to Lyndon's frontyard, where the three of them held a press conference. Lyndon dominated the proceedings, hardly allowing Stevenson to get a word in. "I'd like to come back to Texas and either talk or listen—whatever they'll permit me to do," Stevenson said with a smile. George Reedy wrote Lyndon on the 30th: "All of the headlines carried such phrases as 'Big Three,' 'At the Summit,' 'Three most powerful men in the Democratic Party.' " The visit left the widespread impression in the Press Corps that Johnson had largely recovered. Bobby Baker wrote to say that he had seen him repeatedly on television with his "two distinguished guests." He also reported that the Republicans were in "a state of panic" over Eisenhower's illness and seemed likely to "tear each other to pieces." In the South, "Republicans and Democrats alike are universal in their opinion that you alone, as far as our party is concerned, possess the character and integrity necessary to be President." [57]

By the middle of October, Johnson had created the impression that he was as vigorous as ever and once again at the center of Democratic party activities. A stream of prominent party visitors had made the ranch into the party's "political capital," and his appearance at the Dallas State Fair on October 13, where he made a twenty-minute speech before an enthusiastic audience and toured the grounds shaking hands, convinced people that he was in good physical condition. He also considered going to Washington, D.C., for a meeting with Dulles before the Secretary left for a Foreign Ministers conference in Geneva. Even though the trip would have publicized his recovery, his doctors vetoed the plan.[58]

A meeting with Dulles would also have advanced his presidential candidacy. Throughout the fall, George Reedy sent him a series of memos on how to build support and convince the country that he was the "man in the saddle." Reedy, for example, saw the addition of Grace Tully—a symbol of New Deal liberalism—to Lyndon's staff as an opportunity to induce the representatives of minority groups in Texas—Hispanics, Catholics, Jews, and blacks—"to let their northern brethren know they have a favorable opinion of Lyndon B. Johnson." Above all, he needed to persuade people that a southerner and a man with a heart condition could be nominated and elected. If he could be seen as more of a westerner than a southerner and identified with a program off-setting anti-southern bias, it would go far to meet the first problem. If he could compile an impressive record in the first few weeks of the second session, he could show the country that he was "the same 'miracle man' he was before the heart attack."[59]

To win the nomination, Lyndon believed it essential to deny his candidacy and forestall the emergence of a "stop Johnson" movement. In late October, when a wealthy Houston supporter asked his thoughts about running, Lyndon replied: "I haven't thought about it. I am just out here getting well." A letter from John Stennis, saying he was going to come out for Lyndon for President at the beginning of November, produced a Johnson request not to do it. When columnist Joe Alsop published a report that Johnson had issued "a rallying call for a southern effort to impose a 'centrist' candidate on the Democratic party," meaning himself rather than Adlai Stevenson, Lyndon denied it. "Joe, the only rallying call I have issued since I returned to Texas . . . was to my sheep when they had to be penned the other night for some doctoring." Lyndon hoped that Alsop would "avoid creating in the public mind a set of facts which have no basis whatsoever."[60]

The most intriguing offer to help him become President came from Joseph P. Kennedy, father of Senator John F. Kennedy. During a meeting in New York with Joe and Robert Kennedy—John's younger brother—Joe asked Tommy Corcoran to carry a message to Lyndon. If Johnson would announce his intention to run for President and promise privately to take Jack Kennedy as his running mate, Joe would arrange financing for the ticket. During a visit to the ranch in October, Corcoran put the proposition before Lyndon, who turned it down. "Lyndon told me he wasn't running and I told Joe," Corcoran recalls. "Young Bobby . . . was infuriated. He believed it was unforgivably discourteous to turn down his father's generous offer." It was the beginning of a long-term Bobby Kennedy-Johnson feud that intensified as the two men gained greater power and prestige. Corcoran remembered Jack as "more circumspect. He called me down to his office. . . . 'Listen Tommy,' Jack said, 'we made an honest offer to Lyndon through you. He turned us down. Can you tell us this: Is Lyndon running without us?' . . . Is he running?" Corcoran replied. "Does a fish swim? Of course he is. He may not think he is. And certainly he's saying he isn't. But I know God damned well he is. I'm sorry that he doesn't know it." Joe Kennedy then called Johnson to ask his intentions. Lyndon said he was not a candidate.

Lyndon saw it as premature to reveal his intentions. Any commitment to run, even one made confidentially to the Kennedys, seemed certain to leak out and jeopardize chances for the strong legislative record he and Reedy believed vital to a presidential bid. "If his colleagues thought he was pushing all those programs to get a track record for a presidential race," Corcoran said, "they'd scatter every time he called a caucus." Moreover, it was entirely possible that Eisenhower would run again, and if he did, it would make greater sense for Lyndon to seek the presidency in 1960 rather than in 1956. Johnson understood that the Kennedys wanted to use him as a stalking horse for Jack's White House ambitions. Joe Kennedy made it clear to Corcoran that the ultimate aim was to make Jack Kennedy President. From the Kennedy perspective, a losing Johnson campaign against Ike, with Jack as Lyndon's running mate, was a fine way to launch Kennedy's campaign for the presidential nomination in 1960. Joe believed that Lyndon would lose to Ike, but not by the landslide which seemed the likely outcome of another Stevenson campaign. A lopsided Eisenhower victory over Stevenson and Kennedy could partly be blamed on Jack's Catholicism and could damage his political standing. But Lyndon wanted no part of the Kennedy proposal. More important, he intended to wait until Eisenhower clarified his plans before deciding.[61]

In the meantime, he advanced his candidacy indirectly. On November 21st, Lyndon went to the small town of Whitney, between Waco and Hillsboro, in central Texas, where he tried to disarm the anti-southern bias Reedy said stood in the way of his nomination and election. Speaking in a packed gymnasium before 1500 people, several hundred of whom had come from around the state to celebrate his return to political activism, Johnson gave one of the most effective talks of his career. "I had never before seen him take such complete command of an audience," Reedy said. "It was virtually a mass orgasm. People walked out of that speech dazed. The amount of emotion that he put into it and the fire. . . . It sounded like Joshua ordering the trumpets blown at Jericho." His speech was a call for "A Program with a Heart," a return to New Deal principles upon which a Democratic candidate in 1956 could lead a united party. The program consisted of thirteen points, including expanded Social Security coverage, tax breaks for the needy, federally subsidized hospital, school, road, and housing construction, 90 percent of parity to farmers, relief to depressed areas, elimination of the poll tax, water conservation, amendments to the immigration and naturalization laws, and a natural gas bill.[62]

Except for the gas proposal, the speech was pure New Deal. As Hubert Humphrey said, it was "twelve home runs and one strike out." Reedy believed that the speech established Johnson as the leading Democrat for 1956. "Its unifying quality" made the speech effective. "There was nobody in the Democratic Party that could really object to those points as a whole." The elimination of the poll tax by constitutional amendment, for example, made the proposal palatable to southerners.

The speech made Johnson's presidential ambitions all too clear and threatened to stimulate tensions between himself and other Democratic contenders. When Stewart Alsop published a column saying the speech posed a challenge to other party aspirants, Johnson wrote him: "I cannot agree with you that there are any dangers to any Democratic candidate in it." He told Adlai Stevenson: "There are some writers and so-called strategists in Washington still trying to divide and make trouble. Watch them."[63]

That Lyndon could make a speech of this sort in a small Texas town demonstrated the extent to which Texas and the South generally had been nationalized or shared the national enthusiasm for Federal domestic programs. If the idea of a southerner or a "sunbelt" candidate making a successful run for the White House still seemed farfetched in 1956, it was a prelude to what would become accepted practice in the next twenty years.

At a press conference in Washington on December 12, Johnson refused to discuss the 1956 presidential campaign or even the upcoming legislative session, saying that his return to the Leadership depended on the results of physical examinations at the end of the month. Since it was already clear to him that he would resume the Leadership, the purpose of the press conference was to demonstrate that he was ready to do so, even if on a somewhat less hectic schedule.[64]

On January 3, 1956, Johnson returned to the Senate, where Democratic and Republican colleagues greeted him with congratulations on his recovery. The reception moved Johnson, especially words of praise by Vice President Nixon. "He stuck his neck out to do that," Johnson told Reedy. Johnson expressed "deep gratitude" to Nixon for his "friendship," "kindness," and "sympathy." Nixon was pleased "to travel the 'two way street' that runs between us." There were limits to the cordiality between them, however. With Eisenhower's plans for 1956 still uncertain, it was possible that Johnson and Nixon might face each other.[65]

Johnson's first two months back in the Senate suggested that he was

content to remain Senate Majority Leader. He followed a restricted regimen that gave few hints of presidential ambitions. In January and February, he usually arrived at the Capitol at ten, spent an hour on the
Senate floor from twelve to one, ate a light lunch, napped for two hours,
returned to the floor for another two hours in the afternoon, and left for
home at six o'clock. He also left behind-the-scenes, legislative negotiations to Bobby Baker. In January, he took a ten-day holiday in Florida,
interrupted only by a speech in Miami honoring Senator George Smathers; and in February, he took another ten-day break at the Texas ranch.[66]

Ostensibly to ease the burden on himself, he asked James Rowe to
join his staff. Rowe, who had a lucrative law practice with Tommy Corcoran, offered to help one day a week. But Lyndon said it wasn't enough.
Rowe agreed to two days, maybe three a week, but Lyndon wanted him
full time. The next thing Rowe knew, everyone from Corcoran and Libby
Rowe, Jim's wife, to people on the street urged him not to let Lyndon
down. "How can you do this to Lyndon?" they all asked. "He was working on everybody," Rowe recalled. Rowe continued to resist until a
meeting at which Lyndon wept and complained: "I am going to die, and
nobody cares. You don't care. It's typically selfish." Rowe didn't realize
what "a great performance" he was watching until he gave in: "Oh,
goddamn it, all right," Rowe said. At that, Lyndon stopped crying,
straightened up in his chair and declared: "All right, but just remember
that I make the decisions, you don't."[67]

In Jim Rowe, Johnson had a brilliant attorney with rich government
experience who could facilitate his work as Majority Leader. He also
served Lyndon's presidential ambition: a symbol of FDR's New Deal,
Rowe signaled that Lyndon was sincere about fighting for the "Program
with a Heart." Rowe's presence in Johnson's office combined with passage of the "Program" or just a part of it, would go far to blunt liberal
criticism of Johnson as a southern conservative who had served oil and
gas interests, opposed advances in civil rights, and worked closely with
a Republican administration. Convinced that his political survival, Democratic majorities in the Congress, and future Democratic control of the
White House depended on these actions, Johnson resented liberal attacks on his record as politically short-sighted. As much a New Dealer
at heart as he had ever been, Johnson relished the possibility of advancing liberal Federal programs when the time was right. The second session of the 84th Congress beginning in January 1956 impressed him as
a good moment for reform legislation that would separate him and the
Democratic party from conservative Republicans.

In announcing his intention to fight for a progressive program in 1956,
Johnson remained convinced that he and the Democratic party would
fare best if their actions impressed voters as conforming to Eisenhower's
wishes. "The major problem here," Lyndon wrote Adlai Stevenson in

January, ". . . is to keep things on an even keel and to produce the kind of program upon which any of our candidates can run." This meant passing presidential proposals the Democratic-controlled Senate had turned into more liberal measures. "There were practically no circumstances under which Johnson would contenance a 'Democratic' bill," George Reedy says. "He insisted that the changes be made by striking the language of key portions of an *Eisenhower* bill and inserting Democratic language in its place. There were a number of subtleties to this concept that could not be publicly discussed. Leaving the Eisenhower name on a bill had a placatory effect upon the President, which meant that he was unlikely to intervene in the debate while it was going on in the Senate and unlikely to veto the measure. It also meant that the Senate Democrats were pitted solely against Senate Republicans and, as the Democrats were fighting only for amendments, the picture before the public was that of a Republican president and a Democratic Senate cooperating in the service of the nation while a small group of GOP partisans were trying to throw sand in the gears." [68]

At the start of the new session in January, Johnson told Democratic senators that the first session of the 84th Democratic-controlled Congress had passed 33 percent more bills recommended by the President than the first session of the Republican-controlled 83rd Congress. Johnson saw the political advantages to the Democrats in this statistic as self-evident. Moreover, when Eisenhower's January 1956 State of the Union message included recommendations touching upon 11 of the 13 points in Johnson's legislative program, it convinced Lyndon that he could achieve the aims motivating his Whitney speech—the enactment of laws that would serve the country, the Democratic party, and himself. [69]

First on his agenda was farm legislation. At the start of 1956, every major segment of the American economy was booming except agriculture. In 1955, corporate income had increased 28 percent over 1954, workers' wages had risen by 6 percent, and stock prices had jumped 33 percent, but farm prices had dropped 5 percent and farmers' income 10 percent. To meet the problem, Eisenhower proposed the creation of a soil bank. Farmers were to receive Federal payments for putting land back into ungrazed grass or forest. The Administration hoped to cut total cultivated acreage in the United States by 12 percent, reduce farm surpluses, and increase commodity prices. The White House also saw flexible price supports, which would reduce government manipulation of agricultural markets, as an essential feature of the plan. [70]

Lyndon and a majority of Democrats insisted that the soil bank be coupled with fixed price supports of 90 percent parity. The President's "proposals are designed primarily to remove agricultural surpluses," Lyndon announced. "They would do very little to meet the cost-price squeeze which is pressing so cruelly on family-size farms. In effect, the

President expresses the hope that farmers and livestock producers can somehow survive the difficulties of the present while the government— in a hesitating fashion—tackles the problems of the future. This is cold comfort." Hubert Humphrey asserted that Eisenhower had turned down all suggestions for helping farmers until he had heard the word "bank," which was something the Republicans could favor. White House threats to veto a fixed-support bill didn't intimidate Lyndon, who led a 90 percent parity measure through the Senate. And though Eisenhower vetoed it, Lyndon had the satisfaction of standing up for a New Deal tradition. The Democratic National Committee invited him to answer Ike's veto in a nationally broadcast speech in which he was able to make clear distinctions between the Democratic and Republican farm programs. Although conflict over the farm bill contradicted bipartisanship, Lyndon considered the issue one which the country and the Democrats could not afford to give ground on.[71]

The Democrats and Lyndon fared much better on a Social Security bill. In 1954, an election year, Eisenhower had responded to the political clout of senior citizens by favoring increased Social Security benefits. In 1955, the House had passed a new Social Security measure reducing the retirement age for women from 65 to 62 and providing benefits to totally disabled persons at the age of 50 instead of 65. The latter provision would mean the transformation of Social Security from a retirement plan to "a vehicle for broad social welfare schemes," including Federal health insurance financed by the Social Security system. Although the Eisenhower administration was ready to support a Social Security bill in 1956, it opposed the disability reform as too far reaching.[72]

Since Ike would find it difficult to veto Social Security reform in an election year, Lyndon decided to fight for the bill. The fact that it would benefit disabled Americans, bring Federal health insurance for the elderly closer to realization, and give Democrats a political victory made the measure particularly appealing to Lyndon. "I happen to believe passionately in Social Security," he wrote labor leader George Meany. ". . . I went through the Depression and saw what it did to our older people. A country that is as great as ours does little enough for them." When the bill came before the Senate Finance Committee, the American Medical Association persuaded Robert Kerr of Oklahoma, the Committee's chairman, to drop the disability provision. Using a letter from Elizabeth Wickenden, an expert on Social Security, Johnson persuaded Kerr and Walter George of Georgia that support for the disability provision would allow the Democrats to go into the election with a Social Security issue that "clearly differentiated them from the Republicans."

Although Lyndon persuaded most of the Democrats to support the reform, the outcome was uncertain. He spent four twelve-hour days on the Senate floor during the closing phase of the battle to push the bill through the Senate by 47 to 45. His margin of victory came from conservative Republican George W. (Molly) Malone of Nevada and liberal Democrat Earle Clements of Kentucky. Malone swapped his vote on the Social Security law for passage of a tungsten subsidy that aided Nevada interests and helped Malone's chances for reelection in 1958. Under pressure from the tobacco and medical lobbies in his state, Clements had opposed the bill. With the vote tied 46 to 46, however, he agreed to cast an aye vote, giving Lyndon his two-vote victory. Although Eisenhower was reluctant to load on to the "Social Security System something that I don't think should be there," he signed the bill.[73]

Lyndon had other victories as well for his "Program with a Heart." The Congress passed a health bill aiding medical research and increasing grants for hospital construction; approved school construction and public housing bills; enacted water conservation laws; and passed a public roads measure providing $33 billion for the construction of an interstate highway system over thirteen years. The last was more Eisenhower's program than Johnson's, but Lyndon counted the highway bill as a victory for the public well-being, especially in the South, where the interstate highway resulting from the law "brought isolated counties without access to markets or distribution centers into the national economy." The Johnson "Program" however, had more misses than hits. There was no farm, tax, depressed area, or immigration reform, while the school, medical, housing, and water bills fell well short of Lyndon's initial proposals.[74]

His greatest difficulties came over civil rights and natural gas deregulation. A constitutional amendment eliminating poll taxes was unrealistic, and Johnson had proposed it as a way to placate party liberals without antagonizing southern conservatives. The civil rights issue confronted him again in March 1956 when 101 congressmen and senators signed a Southern Manifesto pledging to resist the *Brown* decision integrating public schools. Lyndon, along with Albert Gore and Estes Kefauver—both of Tennessee—were the only southern senators who refused to sign. Senator Richard Neuberger, liberal Democrat from Oregon, described Lyndon's absence from the Manifesto, as "one of the most courageous acts of political valor I have ever seen . . . in my adult life." Johnson himself mentioned it "many times" to Hubert Humphrey. "He was very proud of the fact that he didn't sign it," Humphrey said. "Also, he used it." Indeed, Johnson believed it politically essential to separate himself from southern segregationists if he were going to run for President. He also believed that southern efforts to hold back integration were a disservice to the region. In his view, the South could never come into the mainstream of American economic and political life until it freed itself from the burden of racial segregation.

At the same time, however, Johnson took pains to appease southern racists. He announced that he had not been asked to sign the Manifesto because as Majority Leader he needed to stand above the battle. He told the Texas press: "I am not a civil rights advocate," and said that "the solution of the problem cannot be found on the Federal level. . . . It's my hope that wise leaders on the local levels will work to resolve these differences." [75]

Johnson saw a Senate fight over civil rights legislation in 1956 as a losing proposition for the country, the Democrats, and himself. But pressure in the first months of the year to consider some kind of legislation was irresistible. In late 1955, when Emmett Till, a black teenager from Chicago visiting Mississippi, was dragged from his relatives' home, beaten, mutilated, and murdered for allegedly whistling at a white woman, it provoked demands for Federal action. In the winter of 1955–56, when a non-violent black protest against segregated seating in Montgomery, Alabama, buses led to shootings and bombings of blacks that the police ignored while arresting protestors, pressure grew for Federal intervention. Eager to court the black vote in an election year and pressed by Attorney General Herbert Brownell to act, Eisenhower introduced a bill calling for a bipartisan commission to investigate civil rights abuses, a new Justice Department division to prosecute civil rights violators, additional powers to enforce voting rights, and amendments to existing civil rights laws to facilitate the protection of citizens. [76]

In July, after a three-month struggle, the House passed a watered-down version of the bill by a decisive margin. With the Senate slated to adjourn in four days for the presidential nominating conventions, consideration of the House bill seemed certain to tie up pending legislation, including Social Security reform and a foreign aid bill. It also promised to agitate North-South divisions among the Democrats and undermine Johnson's standing with one or the other wing of the party. Adlai Stevenson, Eleanor Roosevelt, Hubert Humphrey, Wayne Morse, and Jim Rowe, all prominent party liberals, shared the conviction that a civil rights debate in the summer of 1956 could only divide the Democrats and serve the Republicans. "As you know, I am an old 'Civil Rights' man myself," Rowe wrote Lyndon. "However, on this one you are so clearly right that I myself should like to shoot [Paul] Douglas," who was leading the fight for a debate on the House bill. Nor was there much interest or sympathy in the press for civil rights legislation. Since only a few prominent northern liberals were pressing the issue and since no one expected a bill to pass, journalists saw its advocates as playing "a political shell game." Reedy urged Johnson to tell the press that the Administration had no real interest in getting a bill through, but was eager "to cause [Democrats] the maximum of trouble with the minimum of achievement." [77]

Johnson sent the civil rights bill to the Judiciary Committee, where James Eastland, its chairman, buried it. Doing this, though, required considerable maneuvering on Johnson's part. Under normal Senate procedure, a bill coming from the House received two readings on the floor and then went to an appropriate committee. To bring the civil rights bill directly to the floor for debate, Douglas planned to accompany the bill from the House to the Senate, where Herbert Lehman and he would prevent its going to Eastland's Committee. Lyndon arranged instead to have the bill sent out a side door to the Senate before Douglas arrived in the House. While Lehman—who was tricked into leaving the floor—was absent, Lyndon had the bill read and sent to Eastland's Committee. Douglas and Lehman then tried to have the bill discharged. Since this could only be voted on at the start of a new Senate day, Lyndon recessed the Senate each afternoon instead of adjourning it, preventing the start of a new legislative day. When Douglas forced a vote on adjournment, he lost by 76 to 5, winning the support of only one other Democrat and three Republicans.[78]

Johnson's greatest embarrassment in the session occurred over a natural gas bill. He wanted to deliver gas deregulation to cement his political hold on the Southwest. In January, he took up a gas bill Sam Rayburn had steered through the House in 1955. A majority coalition of conservative Democrats and Republicans favored quick passage. The debate ran along predictable lines. Liberals complained that this was a special interest law that would injure consumers and lump Democrats with Republicans as the tool of big business. Lyndon and others argued that oil and gas were as entitled to free enterprise as any other American industry and that deregulation would serve the national interest by expanding energy production and reducing dependence on foreign supplies.[79]

At the beginning of February, however, the gas bill became entangled with charges of improper lobbying. Heavy-handed pressure by representatives of the oil industry who swarmed into Washington aroused the indignation of opponents. When Republican senator Francis Case of South Dakota announced that the offer of a $2500 reward from a lobbyist for support of the bill had decided him to vote against it, the issue was no longer simply the merits and demerits of gas deregulation. George Reedy at once urged Lyndon to delay a vote until a Senate investigation had cleared the air. The Case speech had raised questions about the integrity of the Senate, and any one voting for the bill would probably be subject to "vicious cartoons and columns" which could damage his reputation for years to come. Lyndon set up a select committee chaired by Walter George to look into Case's allegations. At the same time, however, he resisted proposals that liberal senator Thomas Hennings of Missouri, chairman of the subcommittee on Privileges and Elections, be allowed to conduct a broader investigation of lobbying for the bill. Moreover, on February 6, three days after Case's speech, Lyndon drove the gas bill through the Senate 53 to 38.[80]

Johnson's victory was temporary. Although Eisenhower was sympathetic to the goals of the bill, he felt compelled to veto it. He confided to his diary that the Case episode was "the most flagrant kind of lobbying that has been brought to my attention in three years," and he complained of the "great stench around the passing of the bill" that had raised his blood pressure. Publicly, he declared that "private persons . . . have been seeking to further their own interests by highly questionable activities. These include efforts that I deem to be so arrogant and so much in defiance of acceptable standards of propriety as to risk creating doubt among the American people concerning the integrity of governmental processes." Eisenhower and the Republicans were so clearly identified with the oil and gas industry that the White House risked little by the veto. Since this was a Democratic bill, a veto had the advantage of tarring the Democrats with allegations of corruption.[81]

Lyndon's reputation with liberals and the general public suffered from his actions in behalf of the bill. Drew Pearson, in particular, went after him in a series of columns, calling him "the real godfather of the bill" and the recipient of many favors from George Brown of Brown & Root, "the head of a big gas pipeline company." In three successive columns, Pearson disclosed the IRS investigation of Brown & Root's campaign contributions to Johnson's 1941 Senate race. In another column, Pearson described Brown & Root's unfair labor practices and violations of Federal labor laws. He quoted a Senate report saying that there was "no room for a general contractor like B & R . . . on Federal projects." Nevertheless, Lyndon had helped them win contracts to build air-naval bases in Spain.

Pearson also jumped on Johnson for watering down a clean elections bill sponsored by Senator Hennings. Pearson and organized labor complained that Johnson's amended bill failed to limit campaign contributions and expenditures or to require adequate reporting. They particularly objected to the exclusion of primaries and conventions from the restrictions included in the bill. To head off further debate and damage to his reputation, Johnson allowed the bill to die a quiet death in the Senate.[82]

Lyndon had plunged ahead with the gas bill to secure his political base in Texas. He knew that Democratic party divisions in the state had undermined Sam Rayburn's presidential ambitions. Gas deregulation would assure Lyndon of statewide support and help him control the Texas delegation to the 1956 Democratic National Convention.

Only Governor Alan Shivers, who had split the party in 1952 by supporting Eisenhower, stood in his way. Shivers intended to control the

1956 delegation and, if need be, again support Ike over Adlai Stevenson. Shivers, in fact, was a closet Republican. Early in 1956, when Eisenhower discussed possible running mates with Leonard Hall, Republican party national chairman, they included Shivers. But land and insurance scandals in Texas worked against him. "Shivers could not be elected to anything," Hall told Ike.

Holding the same view, Johnson and Rayburn decided to challenge Shivers head-on for control of the Texas Democratic party. On March 7, Rayburn released a telegram to the press urging Lyndon to become the chairman of the Texas delegation to the National Convention as well as the state's favorite son candidate. Lyndon accepted in a speech on April 10. Shivers, seeing himself in a fight to save political ideas he had espoused for years, struck back hard. He compared Rayburn to Santa Anna, the Mexican general who had opposed Texas independence, and he identified Johnson and Rayburn with "ultra Liberal" organizations like the NAACP, the ADA, and the CIO. He demanded that Johnson state his positions on states' rights, Federal aid to education, Federal control of Texas's natural resources, and Stevenson's candidacy for another presidential race. "It's War Among Texas Democrats," one national news magazine announced. Rayburn and Johnson supporters answered: "Do you want a live Senator or a dead Governor?" Working non-stop for a week, Johnson won a three-to-one victory at statewide precinct conventions in early May and control of the state party convention at the end of the month.[83]

Before the state convention at Dallas was to open on May 22, Johnson returned to Washington, where he received a hero's welcome arranged by Walter Jenkins and George Reedy. They got a thousand people to meet his plane waving signs "Love That Lyndon" and "The USA Needs LBJ." Southern senators said his victory had boosted his chances of becoming the Democratic nominee. With Eisenhower having announced a decision on March 1 to run for reelection, however, the Democratic nomination seemed less appealing than it did the previous autumn when Ike was unsure of his plans. Nevertheless, the possibility of becoming the party's nominee was an honor that political calculation couldn't discourage Lyndon from considering. "I'm going to have first call on you to be my Secretary of State," Johnson told retiring Senator Walter George.[84]

Events at the state party convention in May weakened whatever prospects Lyndon might have had. His objective there was not only to be designated delegation chairman and favorite son candidate but also to identify himself as a practical moderate who successfully opposed party extremists—Shivercrats on the right and liberals or "Red-Hots," as he called them, on the left. Although a majority of liberal delegates made Johnson confident that he would win his principal objectives, he foresaw difficulties on secondary issues. On the evening before the convention opened, when he urged liberals not to provoke additional acrimony with Shivercrats by ousting them from the State Democratic Executive Committee, he met prolonged boos and cries of "Throw 'Lyin'-Down Lyndon' Out." To ensure a victory on this question, Johnson instructed John Connally to lobby the delegates and floor managers not to "leave the floor except to go to the bathroom—and don't go there very often. . . . Just remember, they'll screw us nine ways from Sunday if they see an opening." Although Connally held delegates on the Executive Committee in line, the liberals persuaded the convention to bypass it by setting up a Democratic Campaign Committee. They also embarrassed Johnson by rejecting Mrs. Lloyd Bentsen, Jr., his choice for national committeewoman, and selecting Mrs. Frankie Randolph, a liberal opponent. Losing control of the convention late in the day when many of his supporters went home, Lyndon complained that "we got double-crossed, outmaneuvered (a little) and out-stayed when it counted." "The middle of the road . . . doesn't always rise to support with the same enthusiasm and vigor as the extremists," was another of his observations.[85]

Lyndon's refusal to acknowledge his candidacy or run in state primaries was even more important in weakening his possibilities for the presidential nomination. Avoiding the primaries did not necessarily bar someone from becoming the nominee. Adlai Stevenson, for example, was very reluctant to enter them. "If the party wants me, I'll run again," he had told a supporter in the fall of 1955, "but I'm not going to run around like I did before and run to all those shopping centers like I'm running for sheriff." In the end, however, he felt compelled to make a substantial effort in some of the states. After losing to Kefauver in New Hampshire and Minnesota, Stevenson ran successful campaigns in Florida, New Jersey, Oregon, and California. When Kefauver subsequently announced his withdrawal from the race and his support of Stevenson, Adlai approached the Democratic Convention in Chicago as the clear front runner.[86]

Throughout the spring, despite his unwillingness to make an open bid for the nomination, Lyndon nurtured vague hopes of winning and took indirect steps to advance his candidacy. In May, Jim Rowe urged him to overcome his image as "a professional politician who spends all his time with professional politicians." He proposed that Lyndon hold a luncheon for Hugh Gaitskell, the leader of the British Labour party, and include some of the liberal senators. In June and July, Lyndon began making formal plans for the convention, choosing John Connally to make a nominating speech and arranging for a campaign headquarters and a floor demonstration to follow the nomination. His activities encouraged journalists to believe that he was doing more than "merely corralling the Texas votes for Adlai Stevenson." In late July, when NBC television offered a campaign roundup, the reporter suggested that people keep their eyes on Johnson at the Democratic convention in August. He "is the man to whom both camps of the Democratic party [southern conservatives and northern liberals] look, to play the role of a contemporary Henry Clay—to be the great compromiser at Chicago." Should he withhold his support from Stevenson, the journalist predicted, he might force the selection of a compromise candidate, possibly himself. Shortly after, when a reporter asked him, "Are you just a favorite son, or are you a serious candidate?" Lyndon replied: "I'm always serious about everything I do." [87]

As the convention neared, other journalists predicted that if Stevenson didn't make it on the first ballot, the nominee might be Lyndon Johnson. On August 11, after Harry Truman declared that Stevenson couldn't beat Eisenhower and urged support of New York governor Averell Harriman, Lyndon's chances seemed even better. Jim Rowe and George Reedy advised him that he was "now in the driver's seat" to shape the outcome of the convention. Adlai Stevenson and Jim Finnegan, his campaign manager, were also respectful of Lyndon's influence. Finnegan and Stevenson believed they would win on the first ballot, but they were not sure. After Truman's announcement, they conferred with Jim Rowe in Chicago, who reported to Lyndon that they tried to learn "what you wanted, whether you were a serious candidate, and what you planned to do." Rowe couldn't tell them. Stevenson emphasized his desire not to get at cross purposes with Lyndon, and Finnegan asked if Johnson might be interested in the vice presidency. [88]

With all this going on, Lyndon flew to Washington for a meeting of congressional leaders with the President on August 12. The nationalization of the Suez Canal by Egypt's President Nasser and a Franco-British threat of retaliation had provoked a crisis. During the trip, Lyndon tried to convince Sam Rayburn that he could get the nomination. Rayburn was unconvinced: Lyndon's "getting all steamed up over this presidency thing. It's all sewed up," Rayburn told a Johnson aide after they got off the plane in Chicago. ". . .That damn fool Lyndon thinks he's going to be nominated president," Rayburn told a group of reporters. Nevertheless, on August 12, Lyndon held a press conference to announce his candidacy, and privately told one journalist that he was "going to come out of this convention as the deadlock choice."

Stevenson and Finnegan came to see him. Finnegan emphasized that they had the nomination locked up, and if Lyndon and the South did not come on board, they would have little influence over the upcoming campaign. Finnegan was making the same point to northern delegates, saying that if the southerners put Stevenson over the top, they would end up with more influence than the North. After two days at the convention, Lyndon saw he had no chance, and told Stevenson that he might trade the Texas votes for "something on civil rights that will not hurt my people too much." Stevenson agreed to think about it, but Finnegan said, "No. . . . If we don't give the crowd in the North that, they are going to use machine guns. The answer is no." Later, Johnson told Richard Russell: " 'I was . . . making some real progress with Adlai. I took my knife and held it right against him. All of a sudden I felt some steel in my ribs and I looked around and Finnegan had a knife in my ribs.' He laughed, and Russell said, 'Finnegan is a pro,' and that was it." [89]

Despite Stevenson's almost certain first-ballot victory, Lyndon went forward with his favorite-son candidacy. John Connally, in a nominating speech, described this "son of the hill country of Texas" as "the solid foundation stone upon which the strength of the Democratic Party has been rebuilt" and as a man who could draw "Democrats from all sections . . . together in a common effort for the nation's welfare." The first ballot gave Stevenson the nomination with 905½ votes to 210 for Harriman, 80 for Lyndon, and 45½ for Stuart Symington. By refusing to release Texas and Mississippi delegates who voted for him, Johnson scored points with Texas conservatives who opposed Stevenson. To secure his hold on Texas and other southern conservatives, Johnson had also persuaded Richard Russell to spend a day and a half with him at the convention, where they would be seen sitting, talking, and eating together.

None of Johnson's close advisers could ever say with certainty what he had hoped to accomplish in Chicago. But he was probably aiming at 1960. On the eve of the convention, Rowe had urged against seeking either the presidential or vice-presidential nomination in 1956. Since Eisenhower was likely to win big that year, Lyndon would only lose by being on the ticket. Rowe proposed instead that he now "hold himself apart" and devote the next four years to winning the nomination and the White House. Rowe also urged him to take his distance from the South and become a national candidate. Lyndon saw the wisdom of Rowe's advice, except on one point. Before he could make himself into more than a "southern" candidate, he needed to secure his base in the South. He partly did this by having Russell with him at the convention, challenging Stevenson for the nomination, and describing the deal he tried to cut on civil rights. [90]

When a fight for the vice-presidential nomination erupted at the convention, Lyndon did a balancing act which ingratiated him with both wings of the party. Lyndon initially told Stevenson that he had no interest in the vice presidency, and would not lobby for any other candidate. After Stevenson had won the nomination, however, Lyndon, encouraged by Richard Russell and Tommy Corcoran, sent Jim Rowe to tell Adlai that he wanted the job. In their conversation with Rowe, Stevenson and

Finnegan were noncommittal. Lyndon responded by telling Adlai that "no Texan wants to be vice president." Stevenson then added to the confusion by deciding to let the delegates choose his running mate. Johnson and Rayburn opposed the plan, believing it would lead to a Kefauver candidacy unacceptable to the South. Stevenson, however, insisted on it.

Lyndon encouraged several senators to think that he favored them. John Kennedy later said that "Maybe Hubert thought that Lyndon was for him and maybe Symington thought the same thing and maybe Gore thought that too and maybe Lyndon wanted them all to think that. We never knew how that one [Johnson] would turn out." Under Lyndon's prodding, Texas voted for Gore on the first ballot, who came in third behind Kefauver and Kennedy. Southerners, including Texans, were opposed to Gore as too liberal. Johnson then told Humphrey that he would try to swing the delegation to him. While this raised Johnson's stock with Hubert, it got no where in the Texas delegation. Lyndon then swung his state to Kennedy, announcing on the second ballot: "Texas proudly casts its fifty-six votes for the fighting sailor who wears the scars of battle. . . ." Although Kefauver gained the nomination on a third ballot, Lyndon had shrewdly satisfied southerners by opposing Estes and northerners by backing Gore, Humphrey, and Kennedy in succession.[91]

After the Democratic national convention, Johnson returned to Texas, where he faced fresh challenges to his control of state politics. The Democratic primary for governor in July had pitted liberal Ralph Yarborough against conservative Price Daniel, who wanted to exchange his U.S. Senate seat for the governor's chair. When neither man won a majority on July 28, they entered a run-off campaign that Daniel won by 3500 votes. The race was so close that it took two additional weeks to sort out the result, which Yarborough described as a "stolen election."[92]

Publicly, Lyndon expressed no preference, but favored Daniel behind the scenes. The FBI subsequently received information about irregularities in south Texas counties which a state judge refused to let the Texas attorney general investigate. If the Bureau tried to look into the charges, one FBI official told another, "Lyndon Johnson would be advised of this matter within six hours and would have the investigation stopped." The inquiry went no further and the report was filed in a folder containing derogatory information about Johnson. The file had been opened on April 10, the day Lyndon announced his decision to fight Shivers for control of the May convention. Toward the end of the year, U.S. Attorney General Brownell, who had supported Shivers in his fight against Johnson and Rayburn, asked the FBI to find out whether the Internal Revenue Service had investigated the Johnsons. A check with the IRS in Washington and the FBI office in San Antonio revealed no investigation, and the special agent looking into the matter advised that "even

. . . a discreet request" to a local IRS office in Texas would likely get back to the Johnsons. J. Edgar Hoover wanted nothing more done.[93]

Johnson's dominance of the state Democratic convention in September confirmed Bureau assumptions about his influence in Texas. His control of the convention, however, required a nasty fight which made it "one of the 'bloodiest' in state history." "We had a mean, rough, violent State Convention," Lyndon said a week after it met. Later Congressman Jake Pickle remembered that the meeting required "police protection in the front and on the inside" and lasted seventeen or eighteen hours from nine a.m. until two or three the following morning. Although the liberals had a majority of delegates, they worried that Johnson and Rayburn would seize control of the proceedings and give control of the State Executive Committee to Price Daniel. They were right. Lyndon stocked the Credentials Committee with allies who seated conservative county delegations over the protests of liberals complaining of Johnson's "big steal." He brought a sheriff's posse into the convention to keep the "Red Hots" in line, and used Texas congressmen to pressure delegates into voting as he wished. When El Paso County judge Woodrow Wilson Bean promised to deliver the votes of his liberal delegates to Johnson if they were seated, Lyndon agreed. When Bean couldn't deliver, though, Johnson, pounding Bean's chest with a finger, gave him "a three-minute lesson in integrity," and promised to ruin him. The Credentials Committee then unseated Bean's delegates. By the close of the meeting, Lyndon had thoroughly routed the liberals, electing a conservative Executive Committee and passing a Price Daniel platform.[94]

As a reporter put it, "In the spring he [Johnson] defeated the Texas Democratic conservatives and in the fall the liberals." Now, as the national election campaign began, he believed support of the ticket was essential to maintaining Democratic congressional majorities. Johnson sent word to conservative Virginia senator Harry F. Byrd that "if you would simply say that you are going to vote for the ticket . . . Texas would be found in the Democratic column. . . . Control of the committee chairmanships in the House and the Senate . . . may be at stake if some effort is not made for the ticket." At the end of August, when Bobby Baker reported that he had helped Loyal Democrats in his home state of South Carolina defeat "Dixiecrats" proposing opposition to Stevenson and Kefauver, Johnson told Baker "[I am] just as proud of you as I can be."[95]

Johnson himself promised Stevenson and Finnegan to do everything he could to help the ticket. "I have absolutely no misgivings whatsoever about backing your candidacy to the hilt," he wrote Stevenson, "and . . . whatever lies within my power to do will be done." Lyndon's offer was "most gratifying and comforting" to Stevenson, who partly relied on Johnson "to take care of the South." Up to a point, Lyndon did what he could. He attended a meeting with Stevenson and Kefauver at Santa Fe, New Mexico, to discuss strategy for the Southwest; he spoke at fund-raising dinners in Norfolk, Virginia, and Baltimore; he accompanied Kefauver on a tour of several Texas communities; and he spoke in eight Texas cities and on statewide radio for the Democratic party.[96]

Lyndon had few, if any, illusions about beating Eisenhower, but he thought the Democrats could keep control of Congress. Consequently, his principal appeal in the campaign was not for Stevenson and Kefauver, who were largely omitted from his speeches, but for the Democrats. The Republicans, Johnson declared, were "unfit to handle the reins of the Government." The GOP had "only one real interest in the President . . . to secure Old Guard control of the Congress and the Executive agencies." The "Democratic Party is the only organization through which all Americans . . . can work together to solve our common problems. The Republican Party is not—and cannot be—an instrument for the common good. Its heart belongs to the big business interests of the Northeast and the Middlewest." "It is chained to Wall Street and the grain pit in Chicago."[97]

Lyndon also made special efforts to help Democratic Senate candidates. He assigned George Smathers of Florida to chair a Democratic Senatorial Campaign Committee. Smathers soon complained that the job was giving him "saddle sores, a swayed back, fallen arches, and other assorted ills." But with Lyndon's help he managed to raise campaign funds for distribution to party candidates. Johnson took a special interest in Alan Bible in Nevada, whom he had convinced to run for reelection, Wayne Morse in Oregon, Warren Magnuson in Washington, and Frank Church in Idaho. The outcome of the Senate races was gratifying. The Democrats maintained their 49 to 47 margin, and Lyndon looked forward to another two years as Majority Leader.[98]

The results in the presidential election generally and in Texas in particular were less satisfying. Eisenhower trounced Stevenson by 10 million popular votes out of 61 million cast and by 457 to 73 in the electoral column. Stevenson carried only seven southern states. Texas was not one of them: Ike won by an even larger margin than he had in 1952. Stevenson had not bothered to come into the state, and Texas liberals blamed Lyndon for Ike's decisive victory. Although one close observer of Texas politics believed that the state "would have gone for Eisenhower no matter what the issues or how much money was spent," he could not convince liberals that Johnson wanted to win the state for Stevenson. Mindful of the political climate in Texas, Lyndon had taken his distance from Stevenson in the state campaign, partly by distributing a syndicated column praising Lyndon and attacking Adlai. Johnson remained convinced that a strong base in Texas for himself depended more on an accommodation with conservative sentiment than with less popular liberal views.[99]

Despite the Texas vote for Eisenhower, Johnson emerged from the 1956 election as the Democratic party's dominant national figure. While the Eisenhower landslide had buried Stevenson, it had left the Democratic congressional majorities intact and made Rayburn and Johnson the party's undisputed leaders. More than ever, a successful presidential bid by Lyndon seemed to be a realistic possibility. But nothing could be taken for granted. Lyndon needed some kind of track record in foreign affairs and an accommodation with party liberals if he were to make an effective bid for the 1960 nomination.

In September, George Reedy had already emphasized Johnson's need to convince the public of his knowledge of foreign relations. Egypt's nationalization of the Suez Canal and unrest in Poland and Hungary generated by the publication of Soviet leader Nikita Khrushchev's speech to the Twentieth Communist Party Congress denouncing Stalin had heightened American interest in world affairs. In response, Johnson had decided to attend the NATO meeting in Paris in November. During the fall, a Soviet invasion of Hungary and a combined Israeli-British-French attack on Egypt, which Eisenhower denounced, had given foreign policy an additional urgency. On November 14, as he began a two-week trip to Europe for the NATO talks, Johnson issued a statement saying he would visit defense installations in Germany and would work to strengthen the mutual defense system which had been "severely strained by recent developments." [100]

In the midst of these two crises, Johnson saw bipartisanship as more essential than ever. At a White House briefing for congressional leaders about the Middle East and Hungary on November 9, Johnson accepted what the President and CIA Director Allen Dulles said without comment. Four days later, when he visited Secretary of State Dulles in the hospital, where he was being treated for cancer, Lyndon "expressed his determination to try to preserve a united front on foreign policy." He warned that the Administration "would not have an easy time with the Democratic membership of the [Foreign Relations] Committee." He suggested frequent informal breakfast meetings with him and Mike Mansfield of Montana, the Senate's new Democratic Whip. This "would be an excuse for ignoring some of the more senior members (Democrat) of the . . . Committee and that we might in this way maintain a degree of bipartisan unity on foreign policy which might not be obtainable otherwise." It would also serve Lyndon politically by giving him the limelight among Democrats on foreign affairs.[101]

When Lyndon returned from Europe at the end of November, he confronted a challenge to his authority from Democratic party liberals. "While Johnson saved the necks of his fellow senators," they said, "he was primarily and directly responsible for keeping the Democrats out of the White House." Johnson's bipartisanship or failure to fight any significant battles with Eisenhower had made it impossible for Stevenson to campaign effectively against the President. Liberals called for a legislative program in the next congressional session that would set the Democrats apart from the Republicans. Six Democratic senators led by Hubert Humphrey issued a sixteen-point manifesto of what Democrats would try to pass in the opening session of the 85th Congress. At the same time, Paul Butler and the Democratic National Committee set up a seventeen-member Advisory Committee "to coordinate and advance efforts in behalf of Democratic programs and principles."[102]

Lyndon believed that the Humphrey-Butler programs would defeat rather than advance Democratic legislation in the Congress and lead to Democratic electoral defeats in 1958 and 1960. Whether the Humphrey manifesto represented the majority will of Senate Democrats remained to be seen, Lyndon told Hubert. He, Sam Rayburn, and other Democratic members of Congress would not participate in the Advisory Committee, Johnson told Butler, because it "would only cause delays and confusion" in the "already very difficult legislative process." The American people would not appreciate the attempt of non-elected officials to encroach upon the powers of the representatives they elected to legislate for them, Lyndon told the press.[103]

When Butler decided to establish the Advisory Committee without congressional members, Lyndon anticipated an ongoing battle with liberals for party control. Jim Rowe agreed. Unless Johnson found an issue on which he could fight Eisenhower and unite Democrats behind him, he told Lyndon at the end of December, "he will be subjected to increasing cross fire." The only issue Rowe saw was foreign policy, and here "the good of the country coincide[s] with the political needs of Lyndon Johnson." Rowe recommended that Johnson take the lead in conducting an investigation into "the bumbling and the fumbling" by the Administration in dealing with the crises in the Middle East and Eastern Europe. Ike's insistence on Anglo-French withdrawal from Egypt at the same time he did nothing to punish Soviet aggression against Hungary was unpopular with Democrats and Republicans alike.

Although Lyndon wouldn't abandon bipartisanship on the Suez and Hungarian problems, he agreed with Rowe that his political future partly rested on taking some greater distance from the Eisenhower White House which could mute tensions with liberals. These political considerations would have a large impact on Johnson's leadership of the 85th Congress. In 1957–58, politics and public need would produce landmark legislation affecting the country for years to come.[104]

15

The Liberal
Nationalist

"AT the start of 1957 Lyndon believed that his presidential prospects for 1960 depended on steering a middle course between liberals and conservatives without alienating either of them. Like FDR in 1932, he would have to be "a chameleon on plaid." "Yesterday was my first day back in the office after arriving in Washington and they have begun to hit at me from all sides," Lyndon wrote George Brown on January 3. He had been anticipating renewed tensions with liberals, but he now found himself under the gun from conservatives who could deny him the Majority Leadership. If only one of the forty-nine Democrats defected, Vice President Nixon would have given Republicans control of the upper house. "The Republicans planned to organize the Senate any time they had forty-eight Senators present who would vote for Republican organization," William Knowland told Johnson.[1]

Hopes of turning the Democrats' two-seat advantage into a tie partly rested with freshman Senator Frank Lausche of Ohio, a conservative five-term Democratic governor, whom Eisenhower had considered making his running mate in 1956. Lausche had encouraged rumors that he would vote with the Republicans to organize the Senate. When he failed to show up at the Democratic caucus on January 3, it added to fears that he might bolt the party. "I don't know if I'll be the majority or minority leader," Lyndon told his colleagues. Lyndon knew, however, that Lausche would have no clout in either party if he joined the Republicans, and so Lyndon ignored him. Although Lausche lent some drama to the vote on Senate organization by passing on the first roll call, he cast his ballot with the Democrats on the second.[2]

Allan Shivers represented another conservative threat to Lyndon's

Leadership. With Price Daniel slated to resign from the Senate on January 15 to become governor of Texas, Shivers had the power to make an interim appointment. If he chose a Republican, the Democrats would lose their majority until Texas, as seemed likely, elected another Democrat. Shivers, however, saw no point in making an empty gesture by appointing a Republican. Eisenhower, who was eager to keep Lyndon as Majority Leader, agreed: "I'm sure you're going to get a lot of pressure to appoint a Republican, with the situation in Washington like it is," the President told Shivers. When Shivers said that he didn't think he could do that, Ike replied: "Well, I'm glad to hear you say that." When Shivers appointed William A. "Dollar Bill" Blakley, a wealthy reactionary Democrat from Dallas, it temporarily relieved Johnson's anxieties about Texas politics. Responding to the news of Blakley's appointment, Lyndon declared: "Shivers is tough. He'll grab the flag and take his folks somewhere. I like that in a leader."[3]

Johnson was content to have a conservative Texas Democrat as his Senate colleague. The unappealing alternative was a Republican, who would overturn his Majority rule or a Democrat who would join the liberal opposition. With twenty-three Democrats and only one Republican announcing for Daniel's seat in a special spring election, Johnson feared that the Republican might win. He also worried that conservatives by splitting their votes between the Republican and Martin Dies, the leading Democratic conservative in the race, would give Ralph Yarborough, a prominent liberal Democrat, the seat. Lyndon, Rayburn, and Governor Daniel tried to convince Dies to quit the race in favor of Lieut. Governor Ben Ramsey. When they couldn't, conservatives, fearful of a Yarborough victory, unsuccessfully urged a change in the Texas election law that would have required a run-off if none of the candidates received a majority. Lyndon, who viewed Yarborough as more acceptable than the Republican, lent no public support to the measure. Yarborough's election with 38 percent of the vote in April did not make Johnson happy, but it was better than Yarborough's defeat by a Republican. Such an outcome would have been blamed partly on Lyndon and cost him politically with Democratic party liberals.[4]

And he already had enough differences with liberals, which he was struggling to overcome. Their tensions were less over legislative goals than political tactics. The liberals saw public differences with Eisenhower and the Republicans as a necessary prelude to increased congressional majorities in 1958 and a return to the White House in 1960. Lyndon saw the means to these ends through continuing bipartisanship and an emphasis on greater Democratic understanding of what served the national interest.

But unable to sell liberals on his means for achieving Democratic gains, he sought other ways to blunt their antagonism. At the end of December, Jim Rowe had urged him not only to separate himself from the Eisenhower foreign policy but also to court Phil and Kay Graham, publishers of the *Washington Post*, Adlai Stevenson, and Harry Truman. Rowe wrote that although it was "untrue," there was a "growing public impression that you are the leader of the Southern Conservatives. This had long worried me and I know it worries you too." Johnson replied on January 2: "I have invited Stevenson and Truman up to my office and we will have a little friendly session." He had already seen the Grahams at his Texas ranch, and they gave Rowe the impression that Lyndon had done "a remarkable selling job there: They wasted an hour of my time telling me what a remarkable man you are."[5]

Rowe and liberal Chester Bowles, Truman's ambassador to India, were especially eager for Johnson to announce a foreign policy separate from Eisenhower's. Rowe warned that a bipartisan White House briefing on January 1 on a "new" Middle East policy would leave Lyndon and other senators with little information for making critical judgments. Bowles told Johnson that improving Democratic prospects in the next four years was compatible with an opposition foreign policy. The Democrats either could point to shortcomings in Eisenhower's policies or force the White House into a "genuine partnership" on foreign affairs, meaning the appointment of Democrats to key policymaking positions. A full partnership would receive wide public support and "would strengthen our position as we looked to the elections of 1958 and 1960."[6]

Johnson was reluctant to abandon the bipartisanship that he believed had served the country and congressional Democrats during Ike's first term. But pressure from liberals, a defense of congressional prerogatives, and genuine differences over Middle East policy pushed him into conflict with Ike. On January 1, Eisenhower and Dulles briefed twenty-nine representatives and senators on the Eisenhower Doctrine. They described a "vacuum" in the Middle East which Eisenhower wanted the United States to fill before the Soviets did. He sought congressional authorization of a special economic fund and the possible use of military force to counter Soviet moves. Johnson said that he hoped the President's Doctrine "would be the product of a consensus . . . despite the possibility of many honest differences." Other congressional leaders questioned authorizing what was already in the President's power. They also worried about military actions without United Nations approval. Eisenhower, who wanted strong congressional support for his Doctrine, ended the four-hour meeting with a plea for non-partisanship and Executive-congressional cooperation that would serve the security of the United States.[7]

Nevertheless, Congress was cool to Eisenhower's request on January 5 for an endorsement of his Doctrine. Former Secretary of State Dean Acheson called it "vague, inadequate, and not very useful." Congressional Democrats viewed it as an unpopular commitment of money and armed support for Arab states. Rayburn and Richard Russell introduced substitute resolutions backing "the preservation of the independence and integrity of the states of the Middle East," but eliminating any specific promises of economic and military aid. Although Johnson was conspicuously quiet in public about the President's proposal, he worked behind the scenes to force a compromise. He believed that Congress must give Eisenhower part of what he asked or risk undermining U.S. prestige in the Middle East and the capacity to deal firmly with Moscow. Lyndon insisted that economic aid to the Arabs come from regular foreign aid monies. Further, instead of authorizing the President to send troops to the Middle East, Lyndon wanted Congress to declare that the United States "is prepared" to use force if the President "determines the necessity thereof." Although the White House objected to the changes, the Senate followed Lyndon's lead.[8]

Lyndon also attacked Eisenhower's support of U.N. sanctions against Israel. When the Administration couldn't persuade Israel to withdraw from the Gaza Strip in Egypt or Sharm el Sheikh at the southern tip of the Sinai peninsula, the White House threatened to support a U.N. resolution against governmental and private assistance to Israel by member states. The proposal met stiff bipartisan opposition in the United States. "If I were Lyndon Johnson, I would take credit for something that is going to happen anyway—and that is to come out against the United Nations talk about sanctions against Israel," Jim Rowe wrote Johnson. Lyndon was reluctant to weaken the Administration's hand in dealing with Israel by expressing congressional opposition. But with Knowland and House Democratic Majority Leader John McCormack already doing it, he seized the chance to help himself with "the group in the North," where he was, as Rowe put it, "not too popular."[9]

On February 11, Johnson wrote Dulles urging opposition to U.N. sanctions against Israel. Since the United Nations was taking no action against Moscow for its invasion of Hungary or against Egypt for attacks on Israel from Gaza, he hoped the Administration would oppose any U.N. action against Israel. Jim Rowe passed a copy of the letter to Phil Graham at the *Washington Post* and to Drew Pearson, but the *New York Herald Tribune* published it before they could. The press, radio, and television gave Johnson's letter "excellent coverage," and Bobby Baker urged him to make it "available to every Jewish friend you have in this country."

Lyndon now milked his opposition to the Administration's position for everything he could. He won unanimous endorsement from the Senate Democratic Policy Committee, and at a White House meeting on February 20, he complained that his letter had become the property of the press without his knowledge, implying that the State Department had

leaked it against his wishes. Although it was transparent that only Johnson would profit from publication of the letter, the Administration's alleged leak to the press added to the public view of Johnson as at odds
with the White House. At the end of the February 20 meeting, Johnson,
speaking for his congressional colleagues, told the press that "our views
have not been changed."[10]

Dulles's written response to Johnson's letter became another opportunity for Lyndon to publicize his differences with the Administration
and score points with liberals. Two days after the White House meeting,
Dulles sent an Assistant Secretary of State to hand deliver a reply to
Johnson. By this means Dulles hoped to avoid another press leak. After
the messenger called Lyndon's office to alert him to his mission, however, Johnson told a Senate colleague, who gave the story to a journalist.
Before Dulles's messenger arrived, the journalist asked Lyndon if he
could see the letter. Feigning outrage that a reporter knew about the
letter before he received it, Johnson refused to accept it until Sam Rayburn, at the Administration's request, intervened. Johnson's posturing
on the invented issue threw Dulles on the defensive and gave Lyndon
added notoriety as a Majority Leader capable of strong opposition to the
President.[11]

Yet Johnson's opposition was more symbolic than substantive. At the
beginning of March the Israelis gave in to Administration pressure and
withdrew from Gaza. The following day Lyndon defeated Russell's
amendment to the Eisenhower Doctrine eliminating funds for economic
and military assistance. "It was the hardest thing he had ever done,"
Johnson told Dulles, "because Russell had . . . consistently supported
him . . . for the Democratic Leadership." On March 5, the President's
proposal with the changes in language Johnson had included passed by
a vote of 72 to 19. Eisenhower signed the Resolution on March 9. It
provided a congressional endorsement of presidential authority in foreign affairs that Johnson later saw as a precedent for asking congressional backing to deal with a Communist threat to South Vietnam.[12]

Johnson's fight with the White House over Middle East policy netted
him little gain with liberals. Marietta Tree, a prominent New York liberal, complained to Jim Rowe in February that Johnson "never develops
any issues that will help the Democratic Party." Lyndon had George
Reedy prepare an answer to "that woman" describing "the issues that
have been sharply and clearly defined." Reedy emphasized Johnson's
differences with Ike on public power, Social Security, tax relief, price
supports for farmers, and the recent clashes over Israeli sanctions and
the President's Middle East Doctrine. But, Reedy said, Stevenson's failure to capitalize on these issues in the 1956 campaign and inattention
to what Johnson had been doing made liberals "blissfully unaware" of
his differences with the Administration.

Johnson's critics, however, had been paying more attention than Reedy acknowledged. They understood that bipartisanship rather than aggressive opposition to the White House had largely shaped Johnson's actions. Yet they gave him little credit for helping Democrats win control of Congress, and exaggerated the belief that clear-cut opposition by congressional Democrats during Ike's first term could have changed the outcome of the 1956 race. After two losing presidential campaigns, however, frustrated liberals wanted a more aggressive approach to a Republican President who would not be able to run again in 1960.[13]

A debate over the 1958 budget afforded Lyndon another chance to do "something constructive for our country and . . . relieve some of the pressure from the extreme liberal side of our party." The issue posed serious problems for Republicans and Democrats alike. Despite much talk by Eisenhower of reducing government outlays and balancing budgets, pressures for military spending, foreign aid, and domestic programs serving special interests and buoying the national economy had nearly doubled the federal budget from the Truman years and increased the national debt by billions of dollars. Consequently, when Eisenhower proposed $73.3 billion in spending for fiscal 1958, Secretary of Treasury George Humphrey warned that continued spending of this "terrific amount" over a long period of time would lead to "a depression that would curl your hair." Eisenhower himself echoed Humphrey's concern: "If Congress can cut the budget, it is their duty to do it."[14]

Lyndon and his fellow Democrats saw the President's invitation as an opportunity to do the country and their party some good. But Johnson understood that cutting expenditures without injuring vital needs and interests was no simple task. In March he wrote Republican senator Styles Bridges of New Hampshire, who was in the hospital: "The calendar is jammed; the Committees are working full blast. Half of my mail says the budget has got to be cut—and the other half wants more dams, more schools, and the greatest and strongest air force ever. Move over, friend, so I can share a nice cozy hospital bed."

Budget cuts also had little appeal to party liberals. Historian Arthur Schlesinger, Jr., told Lyndon: "There is obviously a great temptation to get cheap headlines in the Republican press by coming out strong for 'economy' . . . But for Democrats to take this position is really madness. It will persuade nobody. . . . It makes neither political, moral, nor economic sense." It failed the political test because Democrats "would never win a national election as the party of retrenchment." It made no moral sense as long as so many children, elderly, and sick people were suffering neglect. And it was economically unsound because the budget represented only 17.5 percent of the GNP, the lowest percentage since 1939. "There is nothing less likely to inspire public confidence in our party," Schlesinger concluded, "than for one wing to denounce Eisenhower for the size of his budget while the other wing denounces him for doing so little to provide services for the people." [15]

Lyndon fully agreed that "the Democratic Party will never win a national election as the party of 'retrenchment, economy, and inadequate public services.'" Yet he found himself "faced with a practical problem." He had to find some means to handle the public outcry for less Federal spending. He proposed a campaign against waste and extravagance that "would be helpful to our party and helpful to our country." Yet Lyndon knew that an attack on waste would be largely symbolic. Moreover, he saw little actual room to reduce defense and foreign aid, the two expenditures people most wanted cut. To be sure, he led the public charge against both segments of the budget, helping reduce the $38.5 billion earmarked for defense by over $2 billion and foreign aid by nearly a billion; but the total reduction of some $4 billion was only a little over 5 percent of the budget, and even a good part of that was restored later in emergency authorizations. Besides, Lyndon's behind-the-scenes discussions with Ike and Dulles reflected his conviction that the Congress should largely meet the President's requests in both categories. He told Dulles that he favored a foreign aid cut of only $300 million and that if he accomplished this, he "would be entitled to a 'citation.'" He also said that he "was bucking the same sentiment that had driven" Tom Connally of Texas and Walter George of Georgia out of the Senate. He emphasized the need for "greater efforts to educate public opinion." [16]

The budget battle nevertheless gave Lyndon an irresistible chance for some political posturing that could ingratiate him with all factions of the Democratic party, especially the liberals. In 1956, Eisenhower appointed Under Secretary of Labor Arthur Larson head of the United States Information Agency (USIA). Larson, a former Rhodes Scholar and dean of the University of Pittsburgh Law School, had published a book pleasing to the President, *A Republican Looks at His Party*. He praised Eisenhower's approach to government as "Modern Republicanism" and made the case for being liberal in human affairs and conservative in fiscal matters. Eisenhower himself called it "dynamic conservatism," being "conservative when it comes to money and liberal when it comes to human beings." Adlai Stevenson took this to mean "that you will strongly recommended the building of a great many schools to accommodate the needs of our children, but not provide the money." Neither Eisenhower nor Larson was very clear on just what "dynamic conservatism" or "Modern Republicanism" meant, but it was designed to set Ike off from the Republican Old Guard and give his party a mass appeal that could blunt the popularity of the Democrats. Eager to make the case for the Republicans as representative of mainstream America, Larson attacked the Democrats in a speech in Hawaii on April 16, 1957, as unAmerican.

"Throughout the New and Fair Deals," he said, "this country was in the grip of a somewhat alien philosophy imported from Europe." [17]

The following day the House of Representatives reduced Larson's USIA budget from $144 to $106 million for fiscal 1958. Now a member of the Senate Appropriations Committee, Lyndon was chairman of the subcommittee responsible for the USIA budget. He relished the chance to go after "Mr. Modern Republican," as Democrats derisively called Larson. Johnson announced on the eve of the USIA budget hearings that the House may have cut too little. For four days beginning on May 2, Johnson took Larson apart. "Of all the agency heads, you are asking for the most money to be restored to the funds cut by the House," Johnson said at the outset. "We look to you as the distinguished *author* and *spokesman* for your party to enlighten us." Larson, who had only been at USIA for three months and had an imperfect understanding of its operations, was a poor witness. He stumbled through many of the questions, provoking sneers and laughter from the senators and subcommittee clerks. "I really felt sorry for Arthur Larson," George Reedy recalled. "Like dressing a kid in a Little Lord Fauntleroy suit and sending him up the back alley in the neighborhood where I grew up. Ooh! He really stepped in with his chin wide open. It was rather merciless. In retrospect that was something of a hatchet job which was performed on the agency, but Democrats were pretty damn mad at Larson." [18]

At the end of the hearings, Lyndon's subcommittee reduced the USIA budget by an additional $15 million, saddling it with a 38 percent cut. The Appropriations Committee approved and the Senate went along by a vote of 61 to 15. Eisenhower, who had gone on television to oppose excessive budget cuts in vital defense programs, was furious. He wrote Lyndon: "As for the USIA . . . I am very disappointed that . . . you found it desirable to reduce rather than to increase the pressure of our effort. . . . It is . . . difficult for me to understand why this vital weapon in our arsenal would be blunted at this critical juncture in world affairs." Johnson ordered Reedy to draft a "tough" reply to Eisenhower. He did. "It is my belief that unless steps are taken to put this agency on a basis where all Americans can be proud of it, that it will be difficult to persuade Congress next year to grant even as much money as it did this year." Although the Conference Committee raised the agency's budget $6 million to $96 million, Lyndon had scored political points with most members of his party. [19]

Still, he had found no galvanizing issue that convinced fellow Democrats, and especially liberals, that he was the man to lead their party in 1960. *New York Times* columnist James Reston had pointed up Lyndon's dilemma in April, when he said that "there is a gap on Capitol Hill," where "the Majority Leadership is decelerating." Though Phil Graham of the *Washington Post* told Walter Jenkins that "this is absolute crap," he nevertheless urged Lyndon to persuade Stewart Alsop to write a column that made it sound like Johnson "is the goddamned end on foreign relations." In early June, after Soviet Premier Nikita Khrushchev had accepted an invitation from CBS for an interview to be broadcast in the United States, Johnson publicly proposed an "open curtain" program of regular uncensored radio and television exchanges between the U.S. and the U.S.S.R. When Lyndon began getting credit for a new idea, Eisenhower and Dulles insisted that this was something they had been trying to arrange since November 1955. Dulles told a press conference that Johnson's proposal was essentially one "we have been pressing . . . off and on, for the last 18 months." [20]

When newspapers reported that Johnson resented Dulles's remarks, the Secretary went to see him at his Senate office. The meeting was entirely friendly: Johnson said that he had read Dulles's comments and found "nothing derogatory" in them. Johnson or someone close to him gave a different version of the meeting to columnist Jack Anderson. As Anderson reported it to Drew Pearson, Johnson angrily told Dulles that "if the State Department had been pressing for an 'open curtain' since 1955 . . . it had been a well-kept secret." He also complained that Dulles had been "petty in his press conference crack and seemed to be more interested in trying to prove that he was 18 months ahead of Johnson than in doing something about the problem." Johnson was trying to maintain good relations with the Administration at the same time he encouraged a public picture of himself as ahead of it on foreign affairs. His friendly private exchange with Dulles demonstrated his continuing commitment to bipartisanship while press accounts of sharp differences with him on Soviet-American relations served Lyndon's political ends. [21]

Whatever the gains from his budget and foreign policy fights with the Administration, Lyndon knew that he needed some more dramatic public achievement if he was to advance his national political fortunes for 1960. The issue he had fixed on at the beginning of 1957 had been civil rights. During 1956 the Supreme Court had ordered integration of the municipal bus systems in Columbia, South Carolina, and Montgomery, Alabama. In February 1957, *Time* put Martin Luther King, Jr., on its cover and praised him as the leader of the Montgomery movement and organizer of a Southern Leadership Conference seeking desegregation through non-violent means. It was clear to Lyndon that pressure from southern blacks made change in the region inevitable. Renewed pressure for legislation that would implement the *Brown* decision on school desegregation and enforce black voting rights made these matters ripe for action in Congress. With the House likely to pass a bill, as it did in 1956, the Senate would be the focus of attention. If he could lead a major civil rights bill through the Senate, it would be the first Federal legislative advance in this field in eighty-two years. Such an achievement would have multiple benefits; not the least of which would be a boon to his presidential ambitions. A civil rights bill credited to Johnson would help transform him from a southern or regional leader into a national spokesman.

Men as politically removed from one another as Richard Russell and Jim Rowe shared the understanding that Lyndon could not become President unless he did something significant to protect black rights in the South. "We can never make him President unless the Senate first disposes of civil rights," Russell told George Reedy in the fall of 1956. Jim Rowe advised Johnson: "Your friends and your enemies . . . are saying that you are trapped between your southern background and your desire to be a national leader. . . . If you vote against a civil rights bill you can forget your presidential ambitions in 1960." Rowe urged him to "get all the credit for . . . a compromise . . . , with the emphasis in the South on compromise, and emphasis in the North on getting a bill." [22]

The importance of civil rights was impressing itself on Republican presidential aspirants as well. Nixon and Knowland, who had unimpressive voting records on civil rights, suddenly became champions of legislative advance. [23]

Several other considerations influenced Lyndon's support of a civil rights law in 1957. A noticeable shift of black votes from Democrats to Republicans in the 1956 elections gave the issue a political urgency Lyndon and other Democrats had not felt before. Further, Democratic unity required that southerners and northerners find a way to compromise on the question and mute it as a divisive force in party affairs. Administration sponsorship of a civil rights bill in 1956 demonstrated that the South could no longer rely on Republicans to block reform. As George Reedy told Johnson, "The South is now *completely without allies.* In this situation, the South can stave off disaster only by appealing to those men who wish to see a civil rights bill enacted but *who are willing to listen to reason.*" Reedy urged an alliance between southern and moderate western Democrats like O'Mahoney of Wyoming, Clint Anderson of New Mexico, and Mike Mansfield of Montana to put across "reasonable and prudent legislation." [24]

Arthur Schlesinger, Jr., gave Lyndon another reason to support a civil rights bill. He thought such a law would remind voters that the Democrats had not abandoned their "determination to use affirmative government as a means of serving the people and enlarging their rights and opportunities." Lyndon agreed: "I believe . . . that it is going to be difficult to obtain affirmative action until the Civil Rights issue is disposed of in some manner," he replied. ". . . There must be action on it, because . . . it is a road-block to the positive, constructive steps from which our party does gain advantages. . . . I hope that we can find a just and equitable solution that will enable us to put an end to the present internecine warfare."[25]

Lyndon also believed that the future well-being of the South depended on Federal civil rights legislation that reduced racial strife. This was something he had known since the thirties when he had used the NYA and New Deal agricultural and housing laws to ease the suffering of black Texans and give them a greater measure of economic equality with whites. Harry McPherson, a liberal Texas attorney on his staff in the late fifties, believed that "Johnson felt about the race question much as I did, namely, that it obsessed the South and diverted it from attending to its economic and educational problems; that it produced among white Southerners an angry defensiveness and parochialism; that there were, nevertheless, mutually rewarding relationships between many Southern whites and Negroes; and that it should be possible to remove the common guilt by federal law while preserving the private values."[26]

Doris Kearns reached a similar conclusion about Johnson's view of how segregation hurt the South. Johnson told her that by 1957 "the Senate simply had to act, the Democratic Party simply had to act, and I simply had to act; the issue could no longer wait." Inaction would injure the Senate's prestige, erode black support for the Democratic party, and "brand him forever as sectional and therefore unpresidential." Moreover, he believed that southern opposition to civil rights legislation made it impossible for the region "to act on its most fundamental problem—economic growth. Johnson argued, and he probably believed, that the South was on the verge of new possibilities for rapid expansion. However, the realization of these possibilities was far from certain. Decisions made by the leadership and people of the South could determine whether it would become one of the most prosperous areas of the country or whether it would remain an economic backwater. . . . Among the most significant determinants of Southern prospects would be the willingness of Southern leadership to accept the inevitability of some progress on civil rights and get on with the business of the future, or its continued insistence on conjuring the ghost of Thaddeus Stevens."[27]

Johnson's sympathy for greater racial equality also moved him to support civil rights reform. To be sure, he could talk comfortably to other southerners in the vernacular. "Sam, why don't you all let this nigger bill pass?" he asked Rayburn during 1957. Even as late as 1965, when, as President, he appointed the first black Associate Justice to the United States Supreme Court, he privately used the same pejorative term to describe his appointee. When a young Texas attorney joining his staff suggested a fine but obscure black federal judge for the position, Johnson said, "Son, when I appoint a nigger to the court, I want everyone to know he's a nigger." The attorney never heard him speak about blacks that way again and felt that Johnson was playing a part and trying to create a kind of rapport between two "good old Southern boys" at their first meeting.[28]

This posturing aside, Johnson, according to Harry McPherson, was "your typical Southern liberal who would have done a lot more in the field of civil rights early in his career had it been possible; but the very naked reality was that if you did take a position . . . it was almost certain that you would be defeated . . . by a bigot. . . . But Johnson was one of those men early on who disbelieved in the Southern racial system and who thought that the salvation for the South lay through economic progress for everybody." George Reedy echoes the point: "The man had less bigotry in him than anybody else I have ever met. Much less than I had. As a kid, I was brought up in an Irish section of Chicago where we'd get out and beat up all the Polack kids whenever we could, or all the Italian kids. . . . And I grew up thinking that dumb Swede was one word. . . . But Johnson had none in him. . . . He had others, but not racial, ethnic, or religious prejudices." And liberal Democrat Clark Clifford, who got to know Johnson well in the fifties, feels that Johnson's sincerity could be in doubt on some matters but not racial equality. He looked at blacks and Hispanics, "looked at their lives, and saw they really did not have a chance. They did not have a decent chance for good health, for decent housing, for jobs; they were always skating right on the edge, struggling to keep body and soul together. I think he must have said to himself, 'Someday, I would love to help those people. My God, I would love to give them a chance!' "[29]

In December 1956, Johnson had decided to pass a civil rights law. At the end of the month, journalist Robert S. Allen published a column titled "Lyndon Pushes Civil Rights." His source was someone of "unquestioned friendship and loyalty" to Johnson. In January, rumors circulated in Washington that "Johnson had told the Southerners in no uncertain terms that a bill was going through and that they had better drop their customary 'corn and pot liquor' arguments and address themselves to its merits." He also assured Clint Anderson that a bill would pass in 1957.

Johnson denied he was doing anything of the kind. He told Bob Allen that Allen had been misinformed, and he answered inquiries from Texas about his interest in passing a civil rights bill as having "no foundation whatever. . . . I am strongly and irrevocably opposed to forced integration of the races." During the first months of 1957, after the White House had reintroduced its 1956 civil rights bill, Lyndon made several trips to Texas "to do an awful lot of base-touching" to discourage the idea that he was betraying Texas and the South by lining up with proponents of a law.[30]

But that is exactly what he was doing. And more: he was orchestrating its passage. Between January and June the House proceeded deliberately on a bill, passing the Administration's proposal on June 18. While Lyndon gave no public indication during this time of how he would respond to House approval, he was actively preparing the Senate for the event. He began holding a series of conversations with Richard Russell about the need to avoid a filibuster that the South might lose. With the Republicans backing Eisenhower's bill, it was entirely possible that a two-thirds majority might be assembled to vote cloture. Johnson persuaded Russell to accept the likelihood of a bill and to work instead to transform it into a measure more acceptable to the South than the one proposed by the White House.

Russell and Lyndon agreed to two major changes in Eisenhower's bill. First, they aimed to eliminate Section III, which would allow the Federal government to take a more active part in integrating southern schools. Russell described it as "a cunning device" to use "the whole might of the federal government, including the armed forces if necessary, to force a co-mingling of white and Negro children." Second, they wished to ensure that anyone cited for contempt of court in a civil rights case would receive a jury trial. Such an amendment would have the practical effect of nullifying the law: white juries, the only kind southerners then had, would not convict other whites for violating black rights. With these revisions, the bill would turn into a voting rights law which would be largely unenforceable. In Lyndon's view, the South would buy the bill not only because it would be a weak law but also because conservative southern senators found it difficult to justify blatant constitutional violations of black voting rights. They were Constitutionalists who could not fight a voting rights measure with the same fervor they battled school desegregation or fair employment practices. Civil rights advocates would accept the measure as a limited, symbolic, but nevertheless important, first step toward greater Federal protection of black rights.[31]

Getting a bill passed required a series of behind-the-scenes maneuvers largely arranged by Johnson. When the House bill arrived in the Senate on June 18, its advocates fought to put it on the calendar for floor debate or keep it from going to Eastland's Judiciary Committee where it would once again be buried. On June 20, Republican Minority Leader Knowland and liberal Democrat Paul Douglas joined forces to win the procedural fight by a vote of 45 to 39. Johnson, knowing proponents of the bill would win, sided with the southerners and insulated himself from criticism in Texas that he had joined the civil rights camp.

More surprising, four liberal western senators—Wayne Morse, Warren Magnuson, Mike Mansfield, and Jim Murray—voted to give Eastland the bill. They were trading their votes on civil rights for southern votes on public power. They had promised to help Johnson and Russell on civil rights in return for passage of a bill financing the Hells Canyon

Dam on the Snake River in Idaho. In 1956, private power advocates had prevailed by 51 to 41 in turning back the Hells Canyon bill. The westerners seized the opportunity to switch conservative southern votes to their side. Howard E. Shuman, Paul Douglas's legislative assistant, remembered how Morse changed his position on sending the rights bill to the Judiciary Committee. Although he had signed the petition to put the bill on the calendar, he reversed course during the debate, declaring that "good procedure was as important as good substance." The *quid pro quo*," Shuman says, "was that the Southerners allowed the Hells Canyon bill to come out." The southern maneuver to keep the civil rights bill from coming to the floor failed, but they honored their commitment anyway by helping pass the Hells Canyon bill, 45 to 38, on June 21. Five southerners, Russell, Eastland, Sam Ervin, Russell Long, and George Smathers, all of whom had previously voted against the dam, now favored it.[32]

Compared with the previous year, when Johnson gave no appreciable support to Hells Canyon, he now pulled out all stops. Johnson relied on a southern-western coalition to finance the dam and pass a civil rights bill without a filibuster, Frank Church of Idaho recalled. "He knew the western interest in Hells Canyon, and it was through his intervention with key southern senators, I'm sure, that enabled us to pass the bill." Although the westerners did not make specific commitments to back changes in the civil rights bill Lyndon and Russell deemed essential, they had an unspoken, gentlemen's agreement to do just that.[33]

On July 2, Richard Russell began the debate on the civil rights bill with a speech attacking all of Section III authorizing "the reimposition of post-Civil War Reconstruction" and part of Section IV sanctioning trials by Federal judges without juries to punish defiance of the law. The speech was revealing less for what Russell said than what he didn't say. His attack was not on the entire bill but on two of its principal provisions, signaling that their elimination could lead to passage of a watered-down bill. To George Reedy "the question then became the kind of bill that should be passed rather than whether a bill should be passed." When Reedy made this point to Johnson, he did not argue with him. Nor did Johnson seem "downcast by the speech." In fact, he gave Reedy "the distinct impression that he knew about it before it took place," and endorsed it as part of a Russell-Johnson strategy for passing an amended bill.[34]

Johnson and Russell got unexpected help from Eisenhower on the next day. At a press conference, when the President was asked to comment on opposition to his bill, he replied that he wished only to protect and extend the right to vote. Was he willing to rewrite the bill to limit it to voting rights? a reporter asked. He refused to answer, "because I was reading part of that bill this morning, and there were certain phrases I didn't completely understand. So, before I made any more remarks on that, I would want to talk to the Attorney General and see exactly what they do mean." "It was a stunning confession of ignorance," Eisenhower biographer Stephen Ambrose writes. Ike "had been pushing the bill for two years . . . and yet now said he did not know what was in it. Eisenhower's admission was an open invitation to the southern senators to modify, amend, emasculate his bill, and they proceeded to do just that." On July 10, Russell visited Eisenhower at the White House to ask support for amending the bill. The President expressed his willingness "to listen to clarifying amendments to the Bill as it stands." The President's secretary noted in her diary: "He is not at all unsympathetic to the position people like Senator Russell take; far more ready than I am, for instance, to entertain their views. He always says 'I have lived in the south, remember.' " The President also expressed himself as adamant on the right to vote, however, which was just what Russell and Johnson wanted to hear.[35]

Lyndon responded to these developments by emphasizing the need for reasonableness and compromise. On July 11, he described the debate in the Senate as "of great value to our country," and inserted a *New York Times* editorial in the *Congressional Record* urging that the bill be restricted to voting rights. "It would in no way prejudice the inexorable forward march of school desegregation in the South to make it clear that this bill deals exclusively with voting rights, which is what almost everybody had thought all along it deals with," the *Times* said. "Integration of schools is quite another matter . . . it is the part of wisdom to take one step at a time and concentrate now, in this law, on the basic right of a free ballot."

Eisenhower's remarks at another press conference on July 17 gave further impetus to those who wished to limit the bill to voting rights. Asked if "it would be a wise extension of federal power at this stage to permit the Attorney General to bring suits on his own motion, to enforce school integration in the South," the President replied that action without any request from local authorities was not a good idea. "I personally believe if you try to go too far too fast in laws in this delicate field that has involved the emotions of so many million Americans, you are making a mistake."[36]

Eisenhower's comments convinced Senate liberals that it would be difficult to keep an unamended Part III in the bill. The opinions of several Washington attorneys, including former Secretary of State Dean Acheson and FDR advisers Ben Cohen and Jim Rowe, that Part III was unconstitutional reinforced this view. "It [Part III] would be hopeless confusion—just madness," Acheson told Johnson. ". . . We have got to convince these damn fool Northern liberals not to nail their flag to the mast. They are defending the wrong thing [in Title III]." But the liberals' strategy was to compromise only after forcing a vote on Part III. When Gerry Siegel, one of Lyndon's staff attorneys, privately proposed a revised Title III that Russell had already agreed to, Paul Douglas and liberal attorney Joe Rauh refused to consider it. The liberals wanted to vote for the original Part III, and if it was defeated they would then support a modified version.[37]

But they never had the chance. After listening to the floor debate for two days, Clinton Anderson of New Mexico, a civil rights supporter, suggested to Johnson that Part III be removed from the bill. It would ease southern fears of Federal military intervention to enforce school desegregation and would allow the Senate to pass a voting rights bill. Lyndon, who was "very receptive" to the idea and "very, very anxious to help," urged Anderson to find a moderate Republican co-sponsor who commanded bipartisan respect. When Anderson won the agreement of Vermont Senator George Aiken to help, it allowed Lyndon to put together a moderate-southern coalition which eliminated Title III on July 24 by a vote of 52 to 38. Lyndon was delighted: "The United States Senate has demonstrated that it can handle an emotion-charged issue with restraint and with moderation," he wrote Mississippi governor James Coleman the next day. "I am confident at this point that the end result will not be punitive, but will be constructive."[38]

Some hard work to put across a jury trial amendment remained. Johnson now worked around the clock, sleeping in his office and getting fresh clothes from Lady Bird each morning. To impress upon civil rights supporters his eagerness for a bill, he invited Eleanor Roosevelt, who was visiting Washington, to come see him at the Capitol. He sent his car with Grace Tully, FDR's secretary, to bring her to his office. During their meeting, he told the former First Lady, who felt he had been slow to act on civil rights, "I'm here every night all night, day and night, but where are all the liberals?" Tully remembered Mrs. Roosevelt as "so interested" in what Johnson had to say. But, like other liberals, she had mixed feelings about the jury trial amendment.[39]

Although liberals worried that a jury trial in cases arising out of civil rights violations would mean certain acquittal for southern offenders, some of them found the argument for a trial by jury irresistible, especially when Lyndon, supported by distinguished liberal attorneys like Ben Cohen and Abe Fortas, offered civil rights advocates certain concessions. Relying on an argument set forth by a Wisconsin law professor in a liberal magazine, the *New Leader*, Johnson agreed to omit jury trials in civil contempt cases but require them in criminal contempt proceedings. To draw labor support, he had the amendment include a requirement for trial by jury in criminal contempt cases involving unions. Major segments of organized labor, led by George Meany of the AFL and John L. Lewis of the UMW, agreed to support a bill that would ensure jury trials in criminal contempt cases resulting from violations of labor injunctions. Meany and Lewis hoped that the amendment would help protect labor from the indiscriminate use of injunctions by arbitrary judges. Walter Reuther of the CIO, however, opposed the amendment as nothing more than a means to continue denying black southerners the right to vote.[40]

To answer this assertion, Johnson had Frank Church offer yet an additional amendment, guaranteeing "the right of *all* Americans to serve on [Federal] juries, regardless of race, creed or color." On the evening of August 1, just before the final vote on the jury trial amendment, Lyndon advised Church when to offer his "addendum; and he staged and timed that drama at the end of the long debate . . . in such a way as to attract maximum attention to this modification of the amendment, in the hopes that it would pull over . . . undecided votes." Although the addition pulled some swing votes to Lyndon's side, it temporarily made some of the southerners waver. Richard Russell felt "sold down" by Clint Anderson and Johnson. On August 2, he complained in a handwritten memo to himself that he had "allowed himself to be stampeded by Clint Anderson on threats of reviving Part III." With ten senators who had voted to eliminate Part III ready to vote against jury trials and nine who had supported retention of Part III prepared to back jury trials, "a little shaking and the house could come down." Anderson himself tried to impress on Russell how weak his commitment to the jury trial amendment was by saying that he would vote for it "only to please L.B.J." [41]

The Administration fought hard to block the jury trial provision. Knowland and Vice President Nixon pressed Republican senators to stick by the White House, holding out offers of patronage to bring some of the waverers into line. Lyndon also pulled strings. After the jury trial amendment had been introduced, he felt the need for some "histrionics" supplied by Rhode Island's John Pastore. "Now you just watch the little Italian dancing master and see what happens here," Johnson told some of his aides. Pastore got up and started arguing against jury trials for criminal contempt. But a few minutes into his speech, he suddenly asked, "Wait, is that right?" And after analyzing what he had said, he concluded that he was wrong and came out strongly for the proposed amendment. Lyndon also promised Republican senators from Kansas and Maryland the right to fill newly created Federal district judgeships in return for their votes. Knowland, who thought he could count on thirty-nine Republicans, in fact had only thirty-three on his side. Late in the evening of August 1st, after it was clear that Johnson had enough votes to win, Nixon told him in the Senate cloakroom, "You've really got your bullwhip on your boys tonight, Lyndon." "Yes, Dick," Johnson answered, "and from the way you've been trying to drive your fellows, you must have a thirty-thirty strapped to your hip, but it's not doing you any good." Nixon acknowledged that Johnson had won for the time being, but predicted that the long run would produce a different result. Shortly after midnight on August 2, at the end of a fourteen-hour legislative day, the Senate voted 51 to 42 for inclusion of the jury trial provision. The following day senators gave unanimous consent not to introduce additional amendments.[42]

White House opposition jeopardized final passage of the bill. Nixon described the Senate action on the jury trial amendment as "a vote against the right to vote," and declared it "one of the saddest days in the history of the Senate." Reports described the President as "bitterly disappointed" and "damned unhappy," while House Minority Leader Joe Martin said the bill was "dead for the session." In response, civil rights advocates expressed "bitter disappointment" over the Senate changes in the bill, but urged its passage nevertheless as providing "some progress in this area." On August 7, the Senate voted 72 to 18 to pass the amended bill. But House members of a conference committee refused to accept the Senate changes. They won agreement to jury trials in criminal contempt cases only when a judge's sentence exceeded a $300 fine or 45 days in jail. Strom Thurmond of South Carolina staged a record-setting twenty-four-hour eighteen-minute filibuster against the compromise bill on August 28–29. He embarrassed other southern senators and momentarily deterred final passage of a bill most of them saw as a victory over civil rights advocates. Thurmond's action provoked Richard Russell to describe it as "a form of treason against the people of the South." Passing both houses on August 29, the President signed the bill into law on September 9.[43]

Johnson was closely identified with the law, which received a mixed reception. Critics objected to the bill as a sham, a false promise of increased opportunity for southern blacks to vote. Eleanor Roosevelt complained that Lyndon was "trying to fool the people" with a law she called a "mere fakery." Republican and Democratic civil rights advocates echoed her complaint. Eisenhower's Deputy Attorney General William Rogers compared the law to "handing a policeman a gun without bullets." Prominent black leaders Ralph Bunche and A. Phillip Randolph thought it would have been better to have no bill or considered it worse than no bill at all. Senator Paul Douglas said the bill "was like soup made from the shadow of a crow which had starved to death." To Joseph Rauh of the Americans for Democratic Action, "Johnson's triumph was so tarnished that it proved his unfitness for national leadership." Johnson's critics had a point. The 1957 law did little to increase black voting and nothing to protect other civil rights. Two years after the bill had become law, for example, there were only 205 black voters on the rolls in four Alabama counties with large black populations, and not a single southern black had been added to the voting rolls.[44]

Nevertheless, at the time, many civil rights proponents considered the bill a significant advance on where the Congress and the country had been. Benjamin Cohen called it "a great, historic event . . . the first time in over three-quarters of a century that the Senate has taken positive action on a civil rights bill." The theologian Reinhold Niebuhr saw the law as "a great triumph of democratic justice . . . because it . . . made some progress in reconciling a recalcitrant South to a higher standard of justice." Black civil rights leader Bayard Rustin thought it was a weak but "very important" law "that would establish a very important precedent." Civil rights leaders "were right in claiming that it contained only limited substance . . . ," George Reedy said. "But they failed to recognize the irrelevancy of the point. The act was a watershed. . . . A major branch of the American government that had been closed to minority members of the population seeking redress for wrongs was suddenly open. The civil rights battle could now be fought out legislatively in an arena that previously had provided nothing but a sounding board for speeches. . . . In less than a decade, a body of civil rights legislation was placed on the statute books to a degree that outstripped anything conceived in 1957." Reedy was right. The 1957 law was more symbol than substance, but it worked a radical change in legislative behavior: enacting an effective civil rights bill was no longer out of reach.[45]

Lyndon himself called the law "a great step forward." He saw it as an inducement to Americans everywhere to recognize that "nothing lasting, nothing enduring has ever been born from hatred and prejudice—except more hatred and prejudice." One columnist believed that Johnson had made himself "a—if not the—principal spokesman of the Democratic party in the country. Because he voted for and is an architect of the right-to-vote law, he is the first Southern Democratic leader since the Civil War to be a serious candidate for Presidential nomination and, if nominated, to have a fair chance of winning." Bobby Baker wrote him: "Your labors are being recognized in the American press. It is gratifying to know that the record made by you is acceptable to the great majority of Americans."[46]

Texas, however, was a different story. "Johnson did his party a great favor by his engineering of the Civil Rights Bill of 1957," a columnist for the *Dallas News* wrote, "but he did himself no good at all in Texas." This journalist was convinced that if strife over desegregation continued during the next three years, Johnson might not even be a delegate to the 1960 national convention, let alone a candidate for reelection to the Senate.

To check the slide in his Texas popularity, Lyndon spent part of the fall speaking across the state. He also took pains to deny that he was likely to abandon his Senate seat in 1960 for a presidential campaign. When Bobby Baker asked Lyndon's permission to visit southern government officials in the fall and "explain to them what you did to save the South from disaster," Johnson was receptive on the condition that Baker describe him as having no presidential ambitions. At the same time, however, he continued building bridges to Democratic party liberals as a prelude to a presidential bid. A victory for William Proxmire in a Wisconsin Senate race in August, the first liberal Democrat in the state to win a seat in the upper house since the early New Deal, was fresh evidence to Johnson of growing liberal influence in the party.[47]

Johnson's hope that the civil rights law would mean a significant advance in southern race relations received a sharp jolt from a crisis in Little Rock, Arkansas. On September 3, Governor Orval Faubus had called out the National Guard to prevent the integration of Central High School. After a Federal court enjoined Faubus from using the Guard to keep black students from attending the school, Faubus withdrew the troops. In response, howling mobs appeared at the high school on September 23 and 24 to prevent attendance by nine black pupils. On the 24th, Eisenhower federalized the Arkansas Guard and sent additional Federal troops to enforce the law.

Southern political leaders were outraged. Senator Eastland called it "an attempt to destroy the social order of the South"; Richard Russell complained of "highhanded and illegal methods," "Hitler-like storm-trooper tactics," and "bayonet-point rule." Although the black students were able to attend the school and the crisis slowly faded during the next month, it showed that the 1957 Civil Rights Act had done little to advance the cause of reasonable race relations in the South. "I only hope that the magnificent work that you accomplished last summer has not been destroyed by the events in Arkansas," the historian C. Vann Woodward wrote Lyndon. "I confess that those events make me less hopeful for the future of the Democratic party as well as for a solution to the integration problem."[48]

During the conflict, Lyndon tried to keep a low profile. Gerry Siegel, George Reedy, and Jim Rowe all advised Johnson not to "be involved either directly or indirectly." Lyndon saw the political wisdom in their advice, but he worried that the lack of constructive leadership or solutions would injure the entire nation. "The Arkansas situation is deeply disturbing," he wrote Dean Acheson. ". . . It is difficult to see a terminal point to a situation which is basically intolerable, and I am afraid that this country is headed for some real moments of trouble." "The task of responsible leadership . . . is to avoid irreconcilable positions," he wrote Chester Bowles. "The emotional tensions that have been created cannot be confined to one part of the country." Publicly, Johnson deplored the use of troops to maintain law and order and counseled self-restraint and prudence. When matters had calmed down in October, Jim Rowe urged him to become an intermediary between Faubus and

Eisenhower. But the White House, which also considered discussing the situation with Johnson, sent him word that any conversation would "bring a bombardment for a statement . . . and this naturally had some of the potentialities of a trap." Convinced they were right, and seeing no political gain for either the nation or himself, Lyndon allowed the crisis to run its course without intervention on his part.[49]

A crisis over a Soviet-launched man-made earth satellite, *Sputnik I*, became Johnson's principal public concern during the last months of 1957. The successful Soviet space launch sent a tremor of fear through the American Congress, press, and public. Although the device weighed less than 200 pounds and carried no military or scientific equipment, the country saw it as a demonstration of Soviet superiority in missiles and scientific education. Eisenhower assured the country that the satellite did not raise any apprehensions in him and that he saw nothing "significant in that development as far as security is concerned." But the country was unconvinced. Despite the President's assertion that the United States held the lead in a race for intercontinental ballistic missiles (ICBMs), Americans, spurred by Soviet boasting, now feared that Moscow had the capacity to send nuclear warheads across the ocean to strike their homeland. The Soviet accomplishment initiated a sharp debate in the United States, where "interservice rivalry, underfunding, complacency, disparagement of 'egghead' scientists, inferior education, lack of imagination in a White House presided over by a semiretired golfer, and a general lethargic consumerism" received blame for America's second-class status in space.

Democrats attacked the Eisenhower administration for allowing the United States to fall behind the Soviets. Senator Stuart Symington of Missouri took the lead. He urged Richard Russell to hold hearings by the Armed Services Committee: "If this now known superiority over the United States [in missiles] develops into supremacy, the position of the free world will be critical. . . . The future of the United States may well be at stake." Symington was eager to advance America's missile program, to blunt criticism of his failure as Truman's Air Force Secretary to make missiles a priority, and to become a leading presidential candidate.[50]

Lyndon also saw the potential for enhancing his candidacy. "The issue *[Sputnik]* is one which, if properly handled, would blast the Republicans out of the water, unify the Democratic party, and elect you President," George Reedy wrote him. "Eye think you should plan to plunge heavily into this one." Johnson saw the political advantage to himself and the Democrats in seizing the space issue. But he feared a witchhunt that might further undermine confidence in the country's military strength and reveal the Administration as unable to meet the Soviet challenge. He believed that a restrained, less partisan investigation than the one

Symington had in mind would better serve the country and himself.

Richard Russell agreed. After hearing from Symington, Russell asked Johnson to gather information from the Defense Department on the state of America's missile program before deciding on an appropriate course of action. The Pentagon was eager to cooperate. "We very much appreciate the way you are approaching this," Ike's Secretary of Defense Neil McElroy told Johnson on October 21. ". . . If through your efforts it is kept out of partisan politics, it will be for the good of the public and we want to work with you." Yet McElroy had no illusions about the politics involved. As one assistant told him, "No sooner had *Sputnik*'s first beep-beep been heard—via the press—than the nation's legislators leaped forward like heavy drinkers hearing a cork pop."[51]

On November 3, the Soviets launched a second, much heavier satellite carrying a dog. Two days later, Lyndon told Dulles that "the country was scared. Something had to be done. He himself was not panicky and did not want to engage in a search for a scapegoat but did feel that there was a need for a searching and constructive inquiry by Congress. If he did not initiate it, it would be done by Symington and that would be much worse." On the same day, he told Styles Bridges that Dick Russell was very upset. Russell felt that Johnson and Bridges should use the Preparedness subcommittee for an investigation. It would keep Symington from raising a lot of hell that would not be in the national interest. Johnson also said that he was putting together a top-notch staff that included attorneys Ed Weisl and Don Cook and three prominent scientists from Harvard, Rice Institute, and Cal Tech. Johnson advised Bridges to tell the press that he was "in complete agreement with Senator Johnson and that this should be a national investigation instead of a partisan one; that we are going to ask the people in charge to tell us . . . how we can regain the leadership." Before the subcommittee began its hearings on November 25, Johnson urged the importance of nonpartisanship on its six other members—Democrats Kefauver, Stennis, and Symington and Republicans Bridges, Flanders, and Saltonstall.[52]

Johnson set up a series of ground rules to insulate the investigation from becoming too political. First, the only guilty parties in the inquiry were Joe Stalin and Nikita Khrushchev. Second, the Committee's only interest in the past would be as a guide for future action. Third, the inquiry's sole objective was securing the defense of the United States. And fourth, the party identification of witnesses was irrelevant; what mattered was their knowledge on how the United States could produce better missiles at a faster rate. "Johnson and Russell will run a good investigation. It will serve a useful purpose," John Steele told his editors. "Democrats won't hesitate to take advantage of any political hay that may be made by Administration mistakes (and there's no reason why they shouldn't). But it is not, repeat not, being conceived as a political witch-hunt. Johnson knows that a good investigation is the only kind that will satisfy anyone, and in the end bring credit to anyone. . . . Here, as downtown, there is a sense of urgency, of consideration of the national interest." [53]

During the two months of hearings, Lyndon largely stuck to his design. Other members of the subcommittee, except for Symington, followed Johnson's lead. And when Symington became too partisan, Johnson sat on him. Symington's extended and sharp examination of Secretary McElroy, for example, moved Johnson to press him to finish. "All I would like to do is get a chance to ask my questions," Symington responded. "Certainly there is no disposition to . . . keep you from having a reasonable length of time," Johnson said. But "we do have plans to conclude the hearings."

Yet Lyndon himself was not simply a selfless patriot. He also took partisan advantage of the hearings, but in more subtle ways. The facts emerging from the investigation demonstrated the Administration's ineptness in mounting an effective missile and space program. It also allowed Lyndon to identify himself as the country's leading congressional advocate of a stepped-up effort in space. He dominated the hearings, introducing witnesses, leading cross-examinations, and making himself the principal spokesman to the press. When an attempt to launch an American missile on December 6 ended in failure, Lyndon declared: "How long, how long, oh God, how long will it take us to catch up with the Russians' two satellites?"

On January 7, 1958, the day before the President gave his State of the Union message, Lyndon delivered his own State of the Union address to the Democratic caucus. He appealed for an end to budget constraints that had inhibited the development of an effective space program. Without directly criticizing the White House, he identified the Democrats with a greatly expanded space effort that would serve the national defense. "Control of space means control of the world," he declared. *Sputnik* represented the greatest challenge to America's national security in its history. Similarly, after the conclusion of the hearings on January 23, he persuaded the subcommittee to issue seventeen recommendations for advancing America's space program. They did not have the sort of partisan bite Symington wanted, but they identified Johnson and the Democrats as pushing the Administration into what seemed essential for the national well-being.

Johnson's handling of the *Sputnik* crisis, journalists Evans and Novak said, was "a minor masterpiece." Without involving himself in a direct collision with the President, Lyndon used the space issue to damage the White House and benefit himself and the Democrats. Yet at the same time, he served the nation by propelling it into the space age. [54]

The two-month investigation from November to January represented only the first phase of Lyndon's effort to make the country the world's leader in space. He believed it essential to set up a permanent Federal space agency and a standing congressional committee. By February, however, other pressing national matters were competing for his attention. "Speaking solely from a selfish point of view, I believe you have gained all you can on space and missiles," Jim Rowe wrote him on the 5th. " . . . You have received a tremendous press, increased your national stature and got away scot-free without a scratch. . . . I think you should now turn . . . to the obvious new issue which is unemployment." George Reedy remembered that Lyndon did just that. With a recession and large-scale unemployment developing that winter, Johnson "just plain lost interest" in the space issue. Gerry Siegel and Reedy "had one devil of a time" keeping his attention focused on space. "We'd shove the bills into Johnson's hands and get him to introduce them, and shove the speeches in his hands and get him to make them," Reedy said.[55]

At the same time, Lyndon had resumed the breakneck pace that had preceded his heart attack. In January 1958, John Steele noted that Johnson's serious heart attack of two years ago had been all but forgotten as he "whirled through days and nights of activities seemingly without end." He is "a man of frenzied action and intensity." A current Capitol Hill quip was: "Light a match behind Lyndon and he'd orbit." At one o'clock in the morning on January 7 he worked on a speech in the back of his limousine as he headed for home. By seven-thirty the next morning he was back at work in bed as he "consumed (he consumes never really eats)" breakfast, Steele said. Having already scanned three newspapers, he "was alternately working the four telephone lines running into his home."

By 9:05 a.m., he was in his "splendidly ornate, crystal chandeliered, green and gold Capitol office." After studying some morning papers and listening to a news broadcast, he conferred with two Senate colleagues, and then discussed arrangements for the Democratic party caucus scheduled for ten. As he headed down the corridor toward the party meeting, he issued a stream of orders to "a harried secretary who padded behind him." For two hours he held sway at the party conference. A "torrent" of words followed in a half-hour press conference, which ended abruptly when "he loped from the room and over to the Senate floor for the year's opening session" that lasted only eleven minutes. He wolfed a hamburger for lunch while he described plans for the coming session, and then joined Vice President Nixon at midafternoon on the Capitol steps to greet 1200 visiting steelworkers. Next in succession came a meeting with Texas members of the delegation, a taped television interview, a conference with counsels for the Space Investigating subcommittee, and work on "a mountain of correspondence, with two girls . . .

flying in and out of the office," and "fevered scratching of signatures and postscripts on the mail . . . broken by a flow of telephone calls." At seven he changed into formal dinner wear for a speech at the Women's National Press Club. "Still churning and with an important managing editor in tow for a quick chat," he drove off to dinner at a downtown hotel.[56]

"Rest and relaxation seem to be painful to Johnson," another journalist wrote. "He will stride into a Washington cocktail party, his impressive 6-foot-3, 185-pound figure a whirlwind of movement. . . . LBJ lives his life at top speed. Recently he finished a speech on the Senate floor, and came charging through the cloakroom doors with aides and reporters tugging at his coat tails. Johnson crashed past them to shake hands with half a dozen Texas college students. . . . The students got one minute and 30 seconds. Then Johnson tore off toward the elevator. He chattered rapidly with a reporter on the way up to his office. . . . Flinging open the door, Johnson hurried inside, and without breaking stride, simultaneously shook hands with an important visitor and ushered him along to a private office, meanwhile calling to a secretary, 'Get me Senator Green!' " Columnist Joseph Alsop told him in March, "You are the exemplar of Justice Holmes's remark that the main purpose of man is to function. . . . I hope you won't mind my saying that . . . you have been over-expending yourself," Alsop added. Lyndon knew it: "With all of the things that are going on," he wrote Ed Clark in April, "I cannot add to my schedule without also putting through a bill for a 28-hour day." But he could not restrain himself. "Lyndon burns his energies with a reckless abandon," Steele said.[57]

Yet for all the competing demands on his time, Lyndon continued to make the creation of a space agency a high priority. On February 6, he led a resolution through the Senate setting up a Special Committee on Space and Astronautics which was to frame legislation for a national space program. On the 20th, he became chairman of the 13-member committee, and on April 14, he and Styles Bridges co-sponsored the Administration's bill creating a National Aeronautics and Space Agency (NASA).

Although Reedy and Siegel, Ed Weisl, and Cyrus Vance, one of Weisl's law partners, attended to most of the details of the Special Committee's work, Lyndon played a significant part in shaping NASA's organization. He was eager to give the military a large say in the country's space effort, but he saw good reasons for putting the program in civilian hands. If the task had been assigned to one of the military services, it would have created a budgetary imbalance between them. It seemed wiser to create a civilian-controlled space agency that could call on all three services for support. It also made good political sense. Lyndon and the White House knew that peaceful rather than military uses of space were more palatable to domestic and foreign opinion. He received his most favorable publicity when identified with the international aspects of outer space, aides told Johnson. In historian Walter A. McDougall's words, "The space program was a paramilitary operation in the cold war, no matter who ran it," but civilian control headed off a significant imbalance between the services and met the political needs of American officials at home and abroad.

Two other goals for the space program eluded Lyndon. He wanted the legislation to include a nine-member Space Council that would set comprehensive space policy and designate specific programs. But Eisenhower, who thought it would become another National Security Council, urged that the Space Council be a purely advisory body. After Lyndon acceded to Ike's wishes at a White House meeting on July 7, the way was cleared for the measure to become law on July 29. Lyndon also wanted senators to dominate a joint congressional space committee. But House members led by Majority Leader John McCormack refused, and separate committees were created.[58]

During the first half of 1958, at the same time he helped develop the space program, Johnson worked to overcome a severe recession. By December 1957, many of America's basic industries were operating at less than 70 percent capacity and unemployment was increasing rapidly. By February, the steel and auto industries were using only half of their productive facilities, and over five million people, 7 percent of the workforce, were looking for jobs. With the Administration inclined to let the downturn run its course, Lyndon and fellow Senate Democrats mapped out an anti-recession program that could relieve economic distress and pave the way for Democratic victories in the 1958 and 1960 elections. Although Democrats never lost sight of the political gains from fighting the recession more actively than the White House, fears of a more serious crash and genuine compassion for the unemployed primarily moved them to act.[59]

In February, Senate Democrats described an anti-recession program in a series of public speeches. John Sparkman urged more public housing, Paul Douglas freer foreign trade, Bob Kerr wider unemployment relief, Albert Gore a new Public Works Administration, and Jack Kennedy increased unemployment compensation. Lyndon outlined a ten-point program at a dinner honoring Harry Truman. Behind the scenes, Lyndon and fellow Democrats debated means of overcoming the slowdown. They divided between a tax cut and increased spending on a variety of public programs. Convinced that tax-cut legislation would provoke a debate on the "right kind" of cuts and take longer to affect the recession than public works programs, which would add houses, hospitals, roads, and schools to the national assets, Lyndon favored increased Federal spending.[60]

In conjunction with Sam Rayburn, who saw tax reductions as difficult to reverse and likely to unbalance the Federal budget more than expanded public programs, Lyndon led several spending measures through the Senate: $1.8 billion for housing, $1.5 billion for flood control, $1.8 billion for highways, and money for fifteen more weeks of unemployment compensation and a three-year extension of the Hill-Burton Hospital Construction Act. The Senate also authorized expenditure of $5 billion in appropriated but unspent monies on reclamation projects and military construction, and barred Agriculture Secretary Benson from reducing parity payments from 1957 levels.[61]

The Senate's actions produced less economic relief than Lyndon hoped. Eisenhower was unsympathetic to most of what the Senate did. He feared that "under the guise of legislation to relieve unemployment, the nation would get strait-jacketed into something terrible for years to come. The Democrats, he said, were promoting a philosophy of centralizing power and responsibility in the Federal government, and they were doing it in a way that appeals to people." He also complained that "if the Federal government went into the countercyclical business on a huge basis, there would be inflation such as the country had never had before. So, he felt, it was imperative to channel hysteria and demagoguery into areas where 'we' can exert some reasonable control." Although he feared being "tagged as an unsympathetic reactionary fossil," he opposed any tax cut and vetoed the farm and flood control bills, saying, "I cannot overstate my opposition to this kind of waste of public funds."[62]

Despite the vetoes, which the Democrats couldn't override, the overall record of the 1958 congressional session pleased Lyndon. Many Senate watchers agreed that the list of bills was "really impressive." A *Newsweek* reporter described the session as "Lyndon Johnson's Congress" and said that "it is one of the most productive in history." Allen Ellender of Louisiana wrote Lyndon: "The last session was most productive— as a matter of fact I don't know of any session in my twenty-two years as a senator in which more was accomplished." In addition to establishing NASA and passing the anti-recession bills, the Senate reorganized the Defense Department, renewed the Reciprocal Trade Act, expanded access to government documents through a Freedom of Information Act, made the Small Business Administration a permanent agency, authorized the largest expenditure in U.S. history for medical research, nearly $300 million, increased social security benefits, extended Federal assistance programs for school construction, provided $1 billion over seven years for loans and graduate fellowships under a National Defense Education Act, admitted Alaska to the Union, and reformed labor union practices to eliminate racketeering.[63]

Lyndon also won the applause of liberals for blocking conservative legislation designed to limit the powers of the Supreme Court and the

Federal government in general. Ever since the 1954 *Brown* decision, southerners had favored legislation that would reverse one or more of the Court's decisions. In 1958, conservative Republicans took up the cause in response to Court rulings against state anti-subversion laws, especially one in Pennsylvania, where the state had preempted the right of the Federal government to punish a Communist organizer for sedition. H.R. 3, a bill that gave state laws equal standing with Federal laws unless the latter had excluded state action, had passed the House by a wide margin in April. Lyndon had bottled up this and other anti-Court bills in the Democratic Policy Committee until the end of the session in August. But pressured by powerful conservatives, Lyndon told the Committee: "I guess we are going to have to give them their day on these Court bills." On August 19 and 20, under Lyndon's watchful eye, the Senate killed off two of them by narrow votes of 41 to 39 and 49 to 41.

Lyndon then called up H.R. 3. To his distress, Paul Douglas offered an amendment endorsing the recent Supreme Court decisions holding racial segregation unlawful in public education and transportation. Douglas's injection of the civil rights issue aroused partisan feelings that Lyndon had tried to quiet. Although managing to sidetrack the Douglas amendment, Lyndon and the liberals failed to table the bill, 39 to 46. A second attempt also fell short, 40 to 47. Richard Russell, who had voted for the bill but knew "what a benighted mess it would cause," whispered to Lyndon: "You'd better move to adjourn. They're going to pass this god-damned bill." Lyndon did just that. Walking over to Hubert Humphrey, who was a floor manager for the bill, Lyndon said: "You boys screwed it up. You thought you knew how to beat it and you didn't." Launching into an explanation of where Hubert had gone wrong, Lyndon abruptly stopped when he found himself surrounded by reporters and assistants. "Let's go upstairs," he exclaimed. "I don't know all these people." On the way, he invited George Reedy and Anthony Lewis, Supreme Court reporter for the *New York Times*, to join them. The next morning Lewis described for Harry McPherson, a Johnson aide, the late-night discussion. McPherson "could sense Johnson's pleasure in describing the art of making a majority. What an opportunity: to defeat a bad bill, save the Court, and win the embarrassed thanks of the Senate liberals!"

To save some senators from having to vote openly against H.R. 3, Johnson changed the discussion from an up or down motion to one sending the bill back to committee. Several senators, under pressure from Lyndon, now changed their votes or stayed in the cloakroom. With Bobby Baker's final count standing at 41 to 40 against Johnson's motion, Lyndon convinced Republican Wallace Bennett of Utah, a staunch conservative, to switch his vote. Warned that there would be a 41 to 41 tie that would force Vice-President Nixon to decide the issue and injure his presidential prospects, Bennett helped kill the bill by 41 to 40. Hubert Humphrey told Lyndon that he had performed "a miracle." "What you really are is a great American. . . . FDR would have been proud of you. You have his touch and his political genius." [64]

With the session at an end in late August, Lyndon looked forward to a well-deserved rest in Texas. But his mother's death from cancer on September 12 at the age of seventy-eight blighted his autumn recess. Her passing triggered bitter-sweet memories of his childhood and "made me realize that I have a permanent source of inspiration which I do not think will ever desert me." Her death, combined with his fiftieth birthday on August 27, aroused in him feelings about his own mortality and an almost compulsive need to hang onto his youth. George Reedy says that he now developed "a pattern of conduct that indicated beyond a doubt a desire to revert to childhood. He intermingled, almost daily, childish tantrums; threats of resignation (which I realize in retrospect were the equivalent of the small boy who says he will take his baseball and go home); wild drinking bouts; a remarkably nonpaternal yen for young girls; and an almost frantic desire to be in the company of young people." He would assemble with younger members of his staff "—especially in Texas when the Senate was out of session—and spend hours basking in their company, obviously at peace with the world." [65]

Reedy also believes that his behavior had something to do with an approaching crossroads in his career. By September 1958 he had entered the small circle of men from whom the nation picks its chief executives. The possibility of being his party's nominee and becoming President evoked in him a divided response. An impulse to flee responsibilities he may have felt inadequate to master warred with a desire to achieve the highest ambition he had held for years. The prospect of Democratic victories in 1958 and 1960 gave an immediacy to this tension he had not felt before. With 12 Democratic and 20 Republican seats up for grabs in the Senate, prospects for an increased Democratic majority seemed very good. Continuing unemployment, the "missile gap," farmer discontent in the Midwest, Republican support of integration in the South, Republican sympathy for anti-union, right-to-work laws in industrial states, and a cloud over the Administration from the influence peddling of Sherman Adams, Ike's Special Assistant who had been forced to resign in September, gave Democrats a decisive advantage in the congressional elections. [66]

Lyndon played a major role in the campaign. With the help of George Smathers and Earle Clements, he ran the Senate Democratic Campaign Committee, which provided money and sage advice to party candidates. He greatly contributed to the belief in a "missile gap" through the space hearings and by endorsing a Drew Pearson book, *USA—Second Class Power*, as containing "shocking revelations" and "many alarming facts" about our decline in military strength. He made campaign appearances in eight states, including West Virginia, Tennessee, New Mexico, and Texas. But he was particularly helpful in Indiana, Wyoming, Utah, and Nevada, where his presence aided Vance Hartke, Gale McGee, Frank Moss, and Howard Cannon, all non-incumbents, to win last-minute, come-from-behind victories.

The elections produced stunning Democratic gains: the Democrats' margin in the Senate increased by 28 seats from 49–47 to 64–34, while the House showed a nearly two-to-one advantage, 282–153. No party in American history had ever won so many Senate seats in a single election. Even before the ballots had been cast, Frank Church, liberal from Idaho, had been forecasting a Democratic sweep, "for which, I think, you are entitled to a major share of the credit. Your brand of constructive leadership has strengthened the Party, even as it has served the best interests of the country." Hubert Humphrey agreed: "The election is a great victory for you, the Democratic party, &, I Believe, the country. Responsible performance by the Democrats in Congress . . . under your leadership has paid off." [67]

Other liberals were less enthusiastic about Johnson's leadership. And with the new Senate taking a decidedly liberal tilt, challenges to Lyndon's authority promised to be a central feature of the 1959 session. Five of the fifteen new Democrats elected to the Senate were liberals and the other ten were moderates. To head off a potential "liberal revolt," Johnson announced a twelve-point legislative program on November 7 that would "clean up" problems left over from the last session and meet liberal demands for an agenda different from the Administration's. Prominent Democrats, including Clark Clifford, Senator Theodore Green of Rhode Island, and Hubert Humphrey, were eager to assist Johnson in putting across his program. By contrast, the White House saw the increase in liberal strength and Johnson's legislative agenda as promising increased deficits, higher inflation, and an unstable dollar that would jeopardize the country's economic development and long-term security. On November 18, when Eisenhower pressed these points on Johnson at a White House meeting that included Treasury Secretary Robert B. Anderson, Lyndon predicted that his proposals for expanded domestic programs would cost only $1.8 billion and could be financed largely from savings on foreign aid. [68]

Lyndon also hoped to "quiet" the liberals by giving them responsibilities that would make them more practical and less idealistic. Hubert Humphrey and Mike Mansfield had been two cases in point. Four days after the election, Johnson told a journalist that the new senators were "progressive, reasonable, capable, able men. . . . Men of that caliber know how to cooperate for constructive action. Predictions that Democrats are going to split up are a dime a dozen after every election. But the record of the past six years has been a record of harmony and achievement and I see no reason to believe it will be any different now." When John Steele visited Lyndon at his ranch five days later, on November 13, he found him in an expansive mood. The Democrats elected to the Senate were not liberals or conservatives, Lyndon said, but "men who would get things done for their constituents." After taking a call from Gale McGee, a forty-three-year-old history professor just elected in Wyoming, Lyndon said: "You see, all these new men are reasonable. . . . They're moderates, they're not extremists of the right or the left. . . . They [the pundits] talk about . . . the troubles I'll have with a big majority. . . . Believe me things were tough when we had only a two-vote edge, how can they be as tough when we have a decent majority?"[69]

Jim Rowe, however, warned Lyndon against being so complacent. The twelve-point program was realistic and practical, Rowe told him, but the Democratic party in Congress would have to do "considerably more in the next two years." The party would have "to move if it is to survive." The same was true for Lyndon, who needed to "make a determined effort to give the 'Northern liberals' something. . . . You know there has been this undercurrent of emotion against your leadership in the last six years. I think it is unfair, and rather stupid, but . . . it is much stronger today than it has ever been in the past."[70]

Joe Clark, Democratic senator from Pennsylvania, gave meaning to Rowe's warning at the end of 1958. A Main Line aristocrat and reform mayor of Philadelphia for eight years, Clark had worked hard to get along with Lyndon after coming to the Senate in 1957. But Johnson's overbearing personality, salty language, and "opportunism" drove Clark into opposition. Convinced that progressive senators would never get their due in the party or the chance to shape national affairs unless they reduced Johnson's power, Clark sent Lyndon a letter on November 18 urging additional seats and more influence for northern liberals on the Senate Democratic Policy Committee and the Steering Committee. Although Clark's letter embarrassed Lyndon when it found its way into the press, he refused to meet Clark's demand.[71]

However respectful liberals were of Johnson's capacity for deal-making and practical results, his unwillingness to push harder for a more substantial progressive agenda remained a source of antagonism. Differences in style and manner added to the tension. Liberals saw him as too highhanded or overbearing and too self-aggrandizing or hungry for power and control. "I despised the guy" from the early days in the Senate, Clark said. "He was a hypocritical s.o.b. . . . He was a typical Texan wheeler-dealer with no ethical sense whatever, but a great pragmatic ability to get things done." Doris Fleeson, the liberal columnist, distrusted Johnson's professions of public service. She saw him as subordinating the interests of his party and country to his personal ambitions, and his overpowering style irritated her: told that another journalist had written a favorable piece about Johnson to keep Lyndon talking to him, she responded, "How could you stop him?" Critics also joked about a sixty-foot flagpole at Johnson's ranch flying Old Glory, the ensign of the Lone Star state, and a personal pennant with LBJ set in the middle of five white stars on a blue field. Antagonism to his grandiosity expressed itself in quips on the eve of the 1958 and 1959 State of the Union messages: Lyndon Johnson "will resent Ike's interference in governmental affairs"; "Senator Lyndon Johnson entered the House chambers to a sustained rising ovation. He was accompanied by the President." [72]

John Kennedy entertained audiences in 1958 with the story that the Good Lord in a dream told him he would be the Democratic party's nominee and would then be elected President. He told Stu Symington about his dream, who said it was funny that he had the same dream himself. When they both told Lyndon their dreams, he said, "That's funny. For the life of me I can't remember tapping either of you two boys for the job." [73]

In the winter of 1958–59 Johnson critics focused on his appetite for office space that moved the *Chicago Tribune* to dub him "the Maharajah of Texas." The newspaper reported that eighteen new senators with comparatively cramped quarters were "wistfully eyeing" Johnson's "expanding official domain." It consisted of twenty palace-size rooms, "most of them ornately decorated and thickly carpeted." In addition to offices occupied by his Preparedness and Space committees, a private room off the gallery just over the Senate floor, and the Majority conference room on the second floor of the Capitol, Lyndon took over a seven-room suite across from the Senate floor, which he was having renovated at a cost of between $100,000 and $200,000 of taxpayers' money. Decorated in royal green and gold with crystal chandeliers and plush furniture, the offices became known as the "Taj Mahal" or the "Emperor's Room." The inner chamber featured a lighted, full-length portrait of Lyndon leaning against a bookcase and two overhead lamps projecting "an impressive nimbus of golden light" as Lyndon sat at his desk. Some Capitol Hill employees derisively referred to him as "Mr. President." To accommodate him, three elevator operators were required to come to the deserted Capitol on Sundays to run the automatic elevators, should he appear. Similarly, operators of the underground railway between the Capitol and the Senate Office Building no longer stopped working at 6 p.m., as had been customary, but remained on duty until Lyndon went home. No other senator enjoyed that privilege. [74]

Yet for all the antagonism to him, no one could deny that he had become one of the country's most formidable political figures with a powerful claim on the presidential nomination of his party. In the summer of 1958, when M.I.T. economist Walt W. Rostow saw John Kennedy in Washington, the Massachusetts senator said that "the Democratic Party owed Johnson the nomination. He's earned it. He wants the same things for the country that I do. But it's too close to Appomattox for Johnson to be nominated and elected. So, therefore I feel free to run." Similarly, Adlai Stevenson considered Johnson "as the best qualified Democrat for the presidency from the standpoint of performance and ability, but plagued with a grave weakness: he was a Southerner." [75]

Although Johnson made blanket denials in 1957–58 that he was a candidate, few people believed him, and many assumed that despite certain handicaps, his ability, drive, and energy might well carry him to the nomination and the White House. In the spring of 1957, when Arthur Schlesinger, Jr., and Hubert Humphrey told liberal attorney Joe Rauh that Johnson had convinced them that he wasn't running, Rauh said: "Anybody who will believe that will believe anything." And John Steele felt that even without a direct organized effort by Lyndon, he might be nominated anyway: "There is no vestige of a Johnson-for-President organization," Steele told his editors. " . . . But Lyndon has strong sinews of strength running through the South, the Southwest, the West up to the California line, and now in Indiana, Missouri, touching here and there in Illinois, south of Chicago. If such a line was to be consolidated with a Southwestern alliance at its heart, if there was a convention deadlock . . . Lyndon Johnson could find himself the nominee." [76]

No one was more aware of his prospects than Lyndon. He may have been ambivalent about running, but part of him yearned to do it. "He'd wake up in the morning wanting to be president, by the time the afternoon came along I think he'd have changed his mind again," Reedy said. " . . . Nobody with the intense ambition that Lyndon Johnson had—and it was intense—could totally divorce himself from a desire to be president." And although he refused to set up any formal organization in November 1958 to serve his ambition, he nevertheless took steps to advance his candidacy. [77]

Mindful of how important a successful track record in foreign and defense affairs was to a candidate, Lyndon launched a two-pronged effort after the Democratic election victories to demonstrate his competence in international relations. With multi-national exploration of outer space on the agenda for discussion at the United Nations, Ambassador Henry Cabot Lodge proposed that Lyndon "drop in" to see him during the debate. It promised "a lot of good publicity" for Lyndon, and it would ease doubts about American foreign policy created by the election results. Seizing upon Lodge's proposal, Johnson had Mike Mansfield of the Foreign Relations Committee approach the Administration about a Johnson speech on the subject. "It is going to give everybody in the world the impression that Johnson is moving in to take over the running of foreign policy," Dulles initially said. ". . . It is obvious J[ohnson] attaches the greatest importance to this. Let's don't fool ourselves here. They are beginning to build up for 1960." After discussing it with the President, however, Dulles agreed to have Lyndon speak, telling him "if it is handled right, it can be very good. We can't obviously have two people trying to run foreign policy at the same time as it would be in a . . . mess," Dulles also told Lyndon. "But the UN has always been a bipartisan delegation with members of Congress. . . . If we handle it right, it can be constructive." In his speech on November 17, Johnson emphasized the unity in the U.S. government and between the parties on studying the outer space problem. Moreover, he urged the eighty-one members of the U.N. to commit themselves to a similar kind of cooperation on dedicating outer space to peaceful purposes. The speech received wide publicity and positive reviews.[78]

The following week Johnson met in Acapulco with Mexican president-elect Adolfo Lopez Mateos. The original suggestion had come from Lo-pez Mateos in the spring of 1958 before he had been elected president. Lyndon was receptive to the idea, but the State Department had thought it impolitic before the Mexican elections. In November, before Lopez Mateos's inauguration, the contacts were renewed and a meeting arranged. Although Lopez Mateos never made clear why he wanted the meeting, Johnson got the impression that the Mexican "wanted to meet someone in the American government whose career paralleled his own so thoroughly." No doubt Lopez Mateos found an affinity for Lyndon in their shared childhood experiences in rural sections of their countries and in their initial common interest in being teachers. But the Mexican president probably saw Johnson as the most likely American leader to succeed Eisenhower and wished to initiate a relationship that could be used to good effect during their respective presidential terms.

For Lyndon, the meeting meant a chance to emphasize his interest in and skill at improving American relations with Mexico. Yet he took pains in a subsequent press conference to declare that only the President of the United States could speak for America. At the same time he wished to demonstrate his capacity to serve as a Chief Executive, he worked to discourage views of himself as an avowed presidential candidate. He was sure that such a conviction would work against his nomination by impairing his effectiveness in the 1959 congressional session. As earlier, he believed that his success as Majority Leader was essential to any campaign he might mount to become President.[79]

His impulse was to build on what he had accomplished in 1957–58. It was impressive. He had marked out a record of liberal nationalism and party advantage in those two years that eclipsed anything achieved by any previous Majority Leader. The civil rights bill, with all its limi-tations, was a landmark law which broke an eighty-year pattern of talking the issue to death. It was an incomplete structure, a symbolic rather than a material advance on black voting rights and the freedom to participate on an equal basis with whites in the nation's political and economic life. But it was an opening wedge, a step toward the equality and opportunity black Americans had been denied since emancipation almost a century before. The Space Agency was also a major advance for the nation. It institutionalized the country's commitment to the exploration of the universe. Although the lure of military advantages partly fueled the willingness to invest in so costly an enterprise, scientific investigation of a new frontier became a fixed, vital part of the agency's work.

When Democrats, led by Lyndon, coupled these gains with their concern for a healthy domestic economy, it translated into huge gains at the ballot box. The challenge to him at the end of 1958 was not to declare his candidacy but to enlarge his record as Majority Leader before acknowledging his presidential bid.

16

The Making of a
Vice President

F ROM the fall of 1958 to the Democratic convention in July 1960
the struggle for the party's presidential nomination was front-page news.
At the beginning of 1959, political pundits agreed that Senators Hubert
Humphrey, Lyndon Johnson, John Kennedy, and Stuart Symington, New
York governor Averell Harriman, and Adlai Stevenson were the front
runners. The start of the year was a crucial time in the fight for the
nomination. Jim Rowe urged Lyndon to launch a campaign at once.
Lyndon said he couldn't get the nomination and wouldn't run. Rowe
didn't believe him, or at least thought he was ambivalent. "He wanted
the thing. I think he wanted it so much his tongue was hanging out.
Then this other part of him said, 'This is impossible. Why get my hopes
up? I'm not going to try. If I don't try, I won't fail.' " For several months
Rowe had refused to take no for an answer. He told Lyndon that he was
"preeminently qualified" to be President, compared him to FDR, and
described his reluctance to run as a disservice to the country and himself. But Lyndon wouldn't budge, and in January 1959, Rowe gave up
and joined the Humphrey campaign.[1]

Lady Bird believed that Lyndon had decided against running. "If he
had really yearned for the presidency, he would have been working for
it two years ahead of time," she said in July 1963. "He couldn't work
for it and be Majority Leader . . . that is absolutely a full-time thing."
Yet she also acknowledged that Lyndon's intentions remained something of a mystery to her. "And how do you plumb the depths of anybody's heart, really, even your own husband's," she asked.[2]

Doubts about winning gave Lyndon some hesitation. But he had been
in the race since 1956. His refusal to mount an organized public cam-

paign was part of a strategy for getting the nomination. "Lyndon Johnson is a very complicated man," Arthur Schlesinger, Jr., stated in 1971. "He might have said to Jim Rowe, 'I'm not planning to do it,' and at the same time have said to himself that it would be highly useful to have Jim Rowe working for Humphrey in case the Humphrey thing collapsed." In other words, Rowe would keep Humphrey's campaign going as a means of undermining John Kennedy, who had emerged as *the* front runner by January 1959. In addition, by rejecting Rowe's pleas and freeing him to work for Humphrey, it encouraged the view that Lyndon really wasn't a candidate.[3]

Johnson believed that an open bid for the nomination in 1959 would have defeated him. He told Rayburn: "All this talk about my candidacy is destroying my leadership. I'm trying to build a legislative record over there. The Senate already is full of presidential candidates. If I really get into this thing, they'll gang up on me and chop me up as leader so that I'll be disqualified for the nomination." Attacks on him as a "dictator" also influenced his strategy. He believed that an aggressive campaign would strengthen the image of him as power hungry. His best chance for the nomination would be if it publicly sought him rather than the other way around.

Lyndon's strategy was to stay in the Senate, where he would continue to build a record of accomplishment, and let the other candidates kill each other off. He partly took his cue from an analysis Jim Rowe had sent him in October 1958. Kennedy was "way ahead of everyone," but a combination of liberals, "eggheads," labor, Protestants, and southerners would probably stop him. Stevenson had reached the same conclusion, and he intended to stay out of the battle, maintain good relations with everyone and become the logical alternative in a deadlocked convention. Lyndon had a similar plan. There was to be no overt campaign, only an indirect effort which would make him the choice of a divided party.[4]

Lyndon cautiously promoted his candidacy in the first half of 1959. Onetime Senate Majority Leader Ernest McFarland "told him if he didn't tell me not to, I was going to go out and try to do some work for him. He didn't tell me not to." McFarland reported this to Sam Rayburn, who said: "Well, you've gotten more out of him than anybody else has." In May 1959, McFarland attended the western states Democratic meeting in Denver, where he "spread the word of Johnson's availability," saying that Johnson "definitely will be a candidate for the nomination." When Congressman Adam Clayton Powell of New York told him that he had filmed a television interview endorsing his candidacy, Lyndon did not object. Between February and June, Johnson accepted speaking engagements in Connecticut, New York, Pennsylvania, Massachusetts, and Rhode Island, where in John Steele's words, Lyndon was "emerg-

ing—or trying to—as a national figure." Georgia senator Herman Talmadge remembers Lyndon's telling him "what fine receptions" he received in these areas. "Lyndon, you're not going to get fifty delegates in
the five most populous states in the Union," Talmadge predicted. Lyndon bet him a hat that he would.

In the spring of 1959, Lyndon arranged changes in Texas election
laws that advanced primaries from July and August to May and June
and allowed a candidate to run for two national offices at the same time.
Were Lyndon renominated for the Senate in the spring, he could still
become the party's presidential or vice presidential nominee in the summer and run for both offices simultaneously.[5]

During 1959 Lyndon believed his strategy was working. In March,
Reedy told him that columnists accepted his denials as "genuine and
sincere," but he continued to be "in the Presidential picture. . . . You
are the only national Democratic leader who has a record of achievement. You are the only national Democratic leader who has displayed
the moral fiber that a President must have." At the beginning of May,
John Steele believed that Johnson could become the nominee in a deadlocked convention.[6]

Lyndon attributed his viability as a candidate to his identification as
a political moderate, a pragmatic southwesterner capable of good working relations with Americans across the political spectrum. In a time of
intense racial and sectional strife, Johnson saw himself as perhaps the
only political leader who could substantially ease black-white and North-
South tensions. Moreover, as a visceral New Deal liberal who had worked
effectively with southern and western conservatives and Eisenhower
moderates, he thought he could accommodate the various special interests in the nation as no politician had since FDR. Finally, as a consistent
advocate of a strong defense, he viewed himself as someone around whom
the nation could rally in foreign affairs. He believed that the party and
country would turn to him as a consensus builder, a moderate nationalist who could more effectively hold the nation together and address its
domestic and international problems than any politician, Democrat or
Republican, on the national scene.

He signaled his determination to hold to a middle ground in a speech
to the Democratic caucus on January 7. In response to liberal demands
for action, he chided the Administration's "laggard government" with
its "deficit of vigor . . . and . . . will." He called for "new tools of
government" that would modernize the country's budget process and tax
structure and save it from inflation, poverty, "educational blight," "medical
mediocrity," "social depression," and unequal standards of freedom,
opportunity and equality. Yet the speech was little more than a rhetorical bow in the direction of liberals and was balanced by an appeal for

"fiscal solvency" and "financial prudence," Eisenhower watchwords. "Our first responsibility is responsibility itself," Lyndon said.[7]

To give substance to his rhetoric of moderation, he proposed a change in Senate rules that positioned him between northern liberals and southern conservatives. The issue was Rule XXII requiring a two-thirds vote of the full Senate to invoke cloture against a filibuster. Convinced that the increased number of Senate liberals would press for more substantial civil rights reform, southerners wanted no reduction in their ability to sustain a filibuster. Eager to press the civil rights fight, liberals wanted to allow a majority of senators to end debate after fifteen days.

Lyndon's middle ground was a revised rule permitting two-thirds of senators present and voting to end a filibuster. In fact, as most liberals understood, Johnson's "compromise" represented only a small modification of the rule, which southerners could live with. "There are rumors going around that the Southerners are merely making a few short speeches for the record and that they agreed to the compromise right from the beginning," Jim Rowe wrote him on January 10. "In many ways Thurmond and Talmadge will be your best friends if they will really 'growl' for a few days." On January 12, fourteen southerners voted against the Johnson proposal, but it was token opposition for political consumption at home. Privately, John Stennis praised Johnson's "matchless leadership," and Fulbright advised a constituent that "the fight over the filibuster turned out to be much more acceptable to the South than any of us expected. Lyndon Johnson was at his very best and has convinced everyone that he really is a political genius, not that this endears him to our Northern friends."[8]

A 72 to 22 vote, including eight freshmen on the majority side, convinced some that Johnson was "now more thoroughly master of the Senate" than ever. In an article in the *Saturday Evening Post* on January 24, Stewart Alsop described Johnson as "the second most powerful man in the nation," perhaps even the "most powerful man, because he loves to exercise power and President Eisenhower does not."[9]

Yet Lyndon had less control over the Senate and less power than advertised; the Rule XXII fight had stimulated strong liberal opposition. UAW officials had joined Paul Douglas and Wayne Morse in complaining openly about Johnson's tactics. Opposition from freshman Ed Muskie of Maine had been more subtle. At an initial meeting, Johnson had advised him to delay his vote on significant issues until they got to the M's in the roll call. Later, when Lyndon had pressured Muskie to support his Rule XXII "compromise" and asked how he would vote, Muskie replied: "Well, Senator, I think I'll follow your advice and just wait until they get to the M's." Bobby Baker let it be known that Johnson had described Muskie as a "chickenshit" and Lyndon then assigned him to three second-line committees. Wayne Morse objected: "Those of us who do not follow you blindly must expect to travel a rocky political road in the Senate, but I wish to assure you it will not only be our tires which get punctured." [10]

William Proxmire of Wisconsin gave substance to Morse's warning the following month. Angry at being denied appointment to the Finance Committee, which he believed stemmed from his vigorous opposition to the oil depletion allowance, Proxmire attacked Johnson's "dictatorial" leadership in a speech on the Senate floor. He complained that at no time in the Senate's history had power been "so sharply concentrated. . . . The typical Democratic Senator has literally nothing to do with determining the legislative program and policies of the party." The annual party caucuses were a sham, "not a single matter of party business [was] discussed." Dick Neuberger of Oregon immediately rose to Lyndon's defense. "You are biting the hand that feeds you," Neuberger said. "Everything you've got in the Senate was given to you by Lyndon Johnson. . . ." "Well," Proxmire said later, "Senator Neuberger made my point. Senator Johnson sure did make the committee appointments, he did indeed decide what legislation would come up and . . . everybody in the Senate knew that if you wanted to get things done you had to do it through the leader or he could stop you." [11]

Proxmire received a lot of private support for his criticism of Johnson, but sympathetic senators called him at his home rather than in his office. "They were afraid the lines might be tapped." Although they asked Proxmire to keep their names out of it, they said: "You're right. Keep it up, give it to him. But there was nothing open about that because frankly they were afraid of him. They feared his power." Some journalists joined in the complaint and political cartoonists had a field day. Herblock portrayed "King Johnson" on his throne with a spear knocking off his crown, and Johnson saying, "Methinks, milord, that the peasantry is getting restless."

Proxmire's attack had little overt effect. The Senate was the scene of a David and Goliath drama, one Washington publication reported. Only it didn't work out the way the Bible has it: "Instead of Goliath being slain, it was David who was slain." Senator Russell told Proxmire that his "position reminded him of a bull who had charged a locomotive train. . . . 'That was the bravest bull I ever saw, but I can't say a lot for his judgment.' " [12]

Johnson was more stung and upset than Proxmire realized. He told Neuberger that he "would never forget" his action and hoped that "God Almighty takes good care of you." Initially, he revealed his anger only to close associates, who counselled him to ignore Proxmire. Lyndon was too angry to be convinced, however, and had to be dissuaded from resigning the Leadership and asking the party caucus for a vote of confidence. He feared that the charges would hurt his presidential prospects. He shared the conclusion of several newspapers that Proxmire's attack was really an attempt of liberals to undermine his candidacy, which it did.[13]

Civil rights reform also frustrated him and hurt his reputation for mastery during the 1959 session. Convinced that another major civil rights bill would lead to unproductive acrimony in 1959, he wanted to leave the issue alone. Several considerations, however, changed his mind. In December 1958, Dean Acheson urged him to take the lead in finding a way out of the impasse on "the school and voting questions" in the South. "The present trend of the North-South division will tear our country and our party apart," Acheson warned. He felt that Johnson was "the one man in the Democratic Party whose rare gifts of leadership . . . make possible the solution of this seemingly insoluble problem." Then Horace Busby reminded him that "the South stands on the verge of one of the greatest economic expansions in history. . . . The only factor that can now stand in the path of Southern growth would be a refusal of the South itself to admit the realities of the modern world. If the South insists on endlessly fighting the Civil War in seeking to freeze conditions of a bygone age, this expansion will not take place." With liberals and the White House planning to introduce separate civil rights bills, Lyndon decided to sponsor one of his own.[14]

On January 20 he proposed a bill that provoked opposition from conservatives and liberals alike. It extended the life of the Civil Rights Commission through January 1961; established a federally sponsored independent conciliation service to mediate racial conflicts; granted subpoena rights to the Attorney General in voting cases; and made shipping explosives across state lines for use in bombing churches and schools a violation of Federal law. One southerner expressed disbelief that Johnson would sponsor such a bill and sell "the South down the river." "Everything proposed in my bill can be supported by reasonable men," Johnson replied. He did not believe in letting "the extremists take over," but in presenting "a reasonable proposal around which men of all sections of the country could rally." Roy Wilkins of the NAACP disagreed. He called Johnson's bill "a sugar-coated pacifier" which would do nothing about "the paramount domestic issue of desegregation of the public schools."

A steady drumfire of opposition and competing liberal and Administration bills that went well beyond what he proposed moved him to consider withdrawing or rewriting his bill. In the end, he did neither. With the Senate Judiciary Committee refusing to act on any of the bills, Lyndon and Republican Minority Leader Everett Dirksen declared civil rights dead in the 1959 session. They promised to resume consideration of the issue early in 1960.[15]

Lyndon's failure to make progress on civil rights was representative of what occurred during the 1959 session. Believing that the most liberal Congress since New Deal times had a mandate to push for significant reforms, he had announced himself in favor of major progressive measures. He told reporters that he and Rayburn would use the Democratic majorities to pass a package of reform bills not seen since FDR's Hundred Days in 1933. At the same time, he proposed the creation of a Temporary National Economic Commission similar to one set up under FDR in 1938 to study how "the full potential of our economy . . . can be realized for the greater benefit of all our people." "I would like to have your best thinking on . . . how we should proceed," Johnson wrote liberal columnist Drew Pearson. He wanted Pearson's advice on how to make "broad, horizon-opening" studies that would avoid "rabbit-chasing." [16]

During the first month of the session, Johnson urged passage of major housing, airport construction, and depressed areas or area redevelopment bills. The programs were to cost nearly $1 billion in 1960, with additional outlays in future years. Eisenhower told Republican legislators that "every sort of foolish proposal will be advanced in the name of national security and the 'poor' fellow. . . . We've got to convince Americans that thrift is not a bad word." Agitated by the prospect of a $12 billion deficit in 1959, Ike threatened to veto all budget-busting bills and meet any congressional override with a proposal for new taxes. With new Republican Leaders, Charles Halleck of Indiana in the House and Everett Dirksen of Illinois in the Senate, promising to enforce party discipline over reduced Republican ranks and woo enough conservative Democrats to block congressional overrides, Ike promised to use his "veto pistol" whenever necessary. Eisenhower took his fight for a balanced budget to the people through news conferences and congressional messages; he saw political advantage for 1960 in labeling the Democrats the spendthrift party.[17]

The political threat was not lost on Lyndon. At a Democratic party gathering in New Mexico on January 24, he described the White House as the big spender and praised Democrats for cutting appropriations proposed by Ike in 1958. Lyndon gave substance to his words by resisting liberal proposals for additional spending on housing and urban renewal and by reducing the allocations in the housing and airport bills before they passed the Senate on February 5 and 6. His support of the housing bill now took on a defensive tone: "Some of us want to put a few roofs over people's heads," he said. ". . . It does not mean I am a spender because I want to vote for a housing bill." Further, in a statement on the Senate floor on February 17, he attacked the "distorted picture" of "one branch of the government fiercely determined to 'hold the line' on spending and another branch determined to spend and spend and spend." He pointed out that the President wanted to limit expenditures on domestic social programs, but proposed to increase spending on mutual security, civil defense, the USIA, fish and wildlife services, and State Department salaries.[18]

Johnson tried unsuccessfully to maneuver between congressional liberals and a conservative White House. To appease Ike, who vetoed the housing bill and won an override fight, Lyndon led a second, less expensive measure through the Congress. But again to no avail. It angered liberals and provoked another White House rejection, which the Senate once more sustained. Only a third housing law costing roughly half of the original was able to get past Ike's veto gun. Likewise, an airports bill ended up with only about one-quarter of the initial funding to ensure Ike's signature. The depressed areas bill passed the Senate by only three votes, 49 to 46, but died in the House. Other bills, including agricultural supports, unemployment compensation, and water conservation, emerged with shrunken appropriations, which in the case of the farm and water bills still did not insulate them from presidential vetoes. At the end of the session, Johnson announced that the Congress had cut $1.3 billion from the President's proposals and a total of $10.6 billion in the five years between 1955 and 1959.[19]

None of this gave Lyndon an advantage over Ike in the struggle to appear as a great economizer. In a CBS television interview, one reporter told Johnson that people around the country saw the President as having won "most of these major [congressional] battles" in the last session. "Did you think there was a new Eisenhower as there is a great deal of talk about?" another panelist asked Johnson. "No, no," he replied. Yet in private, Lyndon acknowledged that Eisenhower's strategy in the 1959 session had ended his "unbelievable success" as Majority Leader. One Johnson aide said: "Very frankly, it had just an absolutely frustrating effect on him. He was frustrated in his desires to do things. . . . There was a Herblock cartoon at the time that showed Eisenhower—in his usual grinning countenance that Herblock put on him— sitting behind his desk. And there's Rayburn and Johnson in front of his desk with their hat[s] in their hand[s], bowed over. And Eisenhower is saying, 'You may tell the men that they can keep their horses and plows.' He really just beat them down."[20]

Johnson's watered-down domestic reforms not only failed to appease Ike or increase public approval of Democrats as economizers but also provoked liberals. In June the Democratic Advisory Committee (DAC) under Paul Butler urged "the Democratic majority [in Congress] to use its power and give the nation a significant program of constructive legislation regardless of Republican opposition." Butler now also directly attacked Johnson, declaring publicly that "Democrats in the South and Southwest cannot, or should not, or will not be nominated for the Pres-

idency." In July, some of Johnson's liberal Senate colleagues began circulating a chart showing how "anti-liberal" Johnson was compared with
John Kennedy, Hubert Humphrey, and Stuart Symington in his votes
on urban renewal, unemployment compensation, and tax reform. Americans for Democratic Action took up the attack by announcing that Rayburn and Johnson had "snuggled into the strait jacket offered them by
the administration. Instead of accepting the challenge to meet the country's needs, the leadership made divided government work by the simple
expedient of surrendering to the President." [21]

The attacks incensed Johnson. He believed that half a loaf—some
housing, some urban renewal, some airport construction, some area redevelopment—was better than none, and considered the liberal strategy
of all-out conflict with the White House as unwise and unconstructive.
"It is not going to be the Congress that paralyzes the President and the
country by approving legislation certain to be vetoed," Johnson said.
". . . Nothing is going to be gained by getting nothing." Moreover, it is
bad politics advocated "only by those more interested in nominating a
candidate than in electing a nominee." As for the voting records of himself and the three other senators, he told Jim Rowe: "If the votes that
you sent me represent the test of 'liberalism,' then the day has really
arrived when pigs have got wings and fly." [22]

Johnson had reason to be frustrated. For all his compromises with
southern conservatives and the Eisenhower administration, he had done
more for liberal advance as Majority Leader than Kennedy, Symington,
or even Humphrey. He was also right about a greater liberal interest in
winning the nomination than in looking ahead to the 1960 election.
While liberal sentiment was on the rise in the country after nearly seven
years of conservative rule, it was by no means the dominant national
temper, as the Democrats would see in the 1960 campaign.

Although Johnson was disdainful of the DAC, which he called an
"impotent group," he knew it carried considerable weight in the Democratic party and could not be dismissed by a contender for the 1960
presidential nomination. Johnson now searched for new ways to overcome liberal criticism. In a series of staff conferences, he pressed his
aides to come up with new ideas and programs. And when they didn't,
he chewed them out for not being inventive or ingenious enough.

He fell back on rhetoric. In April, at an AFL-CIO unemployment
conference, he lambasted the Eisenhower administration for favoring a
balanced budget over the needs of 4.5 million jobless Americans. "The
best way to balance the budget is to put 4½ million Americans back to
work," he declared. On May 30th, Memorial Day, he celebrated the
achievements of Roosevelt and the New Deal in a speech at FDR's grave
in Hyde Park, New York. Genuinely moved by the occasion, he spoke
from the heart, making it, in Eleanor Roosevelt's words, "the most suc-

cessful Memorial Day Service that had ever been held" at Hyde Park. In June, he promised to keep the Congress in session until it enacted a dozen progressive bills liberals were advocating, even if it meant staying on the job until November. But the results fell well short of what he promised, and left him at odds with the White House for trying to do too much and with liberals for failing to do enough.[23]

A genuine regard for his legislative leadership and contribution to Democratic electoral success tempered liberal attacks on him. Newspaper stories in Oregon that Wayne Morse "would blast" Johnson if he came into the state in 1960 evoked a sharp denial from Morse. It is "an absolute falsehood," Morse announced on the Senate floor. When Drew Pearson publicly asserted that Joe Clark didn't think Johnson deserved to be Majority Leader, Clark asked for a retraction. "Johnson is the best Democrat to lead our Party in the Senate," Clark said. "I have voted for him twice as Majority Leader and would again if an election were held tomorrow." Other senators, including several liberals, answered Paul Butler's attacks on Johnson. "We are paying Butler $35,000 a year to try to destroy the Democratic Party while [Republican National Chairman] Thurston B. Morton would . . . do it free," Herman Talmadge of Georgia said. Johnson's defenders emphasized his record of accomplishment as Leader and the Democrats' political gains flowing from it.[24]

The liberal attack on Johnson was overdrawn. For all the limitations of the 1959 session, it had accomplishments which, as in earlier sessions, were largely his doing. One was the retirement of ninety-one-year-old Theodore F. Green from the chairmanship of the Senate Foreign Relations Committee and his replacement by J. William Fulbright of Arkansas, a well-regarded expert on foreign affairs. Fulbright's reputation partly rested on his wartime sponsorship of American participation in the U.N. and of the program named after him for the international exchange of scholars.

By 1959, Green was too old to manage so important an assignment. Failing hearing, eyesight, and memory had made him excessively dependent on aides for the management of Committee affairs. He had difficulty finding the way from his office to the Committee's hearing room without guidance, and once there, had problems identifying colleagues without a seating chart prepared by the Committee's chief clerk. On one occasion, when Stuart Symington sat in an absent member's seat, Green addressed him by the wrong name. "My name is . . . Symington," the irritated Senator replied. Green would hold press briefings to discuss closed-door Committee meetings. After a few questions, he would leave and the Committee's Chief of Staff would tell the journalists "what happened as distinct from what Senator Green remembered." Green would get up in the Senate and "mumble-stumble" his way through a set speech written for him.

The *Providence* (R.I.) *Journal* ran an editorial urging Green to give up his chairmanship. To get him to comply, Lyndon commiserated with him over the unfairness of the newspaper's advice, but pointed out that only by resigning could he hope to insulate himself from future attacks. Green then asked to be relieved of his chairmanship. At a meeting of the Foreign Relations Committee, when Lyndon praised Green lavishly and expressed regrets over his resignation, Green decided to reconsider. Lyndon then announced a short recess. "Go with him," Johnson whispered to the Committee's Chief of Staff. "Don't let him change his mind!" As two aides worked on Green, Johnson told Committee members that Green was sick and tired and that if he weren't relieved of his duties, he might not be with us much longer. When Green announced his determination to stick by his decision, everybody breathed a sigh of relief.[25]

Johnson also took pride in the Senate's action on statehood for Hawaii. Statehood for Alaska and Hawaii had been before the Congress for several years. Eisenhower had favored admission for Hawaii but not Alaska. Hawaii seemed more likely to be a Republican state than Alaska, and proposals for its admission embarrassed Democrats by agitating their North-South split. Southerners saw Hawaii's large Asian population as reason to keep it out of the Union. Ike also thought that Alaska did not have enough population to become a state. By 1958, however, majorities in both houses favored statehood for Alaska but not Hawaii. Rayburn and Johnson convinced Hawaii's advocates to support Alaska's admission first, predicting that Hawaii would not be far behind. They were right. Alaska's statehood in 1958 opened the way to Hawaii's admission in the spring of 1959. Congressional action came in the form of what Representative, and later Senator, Daniel K. Inouye called "a pure and simple civil rights bill. . . . The argument against the statehood bill, although not said so loudly and publicly, was that if Hawaii became a state you would have representation by a strange looking people. As one senator said, 'How would you like to be sitting next to a fellow named Yamamoto?' It was this type of atmosphere in which Lyndon Johnson operated, and he was able to convince those who were opposed to this type of movement to soften their voices and weaken their resistance—and it went through."[26]

Lyndon believed that Hawaii's admission partly represented an opportunity to score propaganda points in the Cold War. The United States was showing the world that it "practices what it preaches." Lyndon did not wish to leave it at that, however. He believed that Hawaii was a standing symbol of interracial harmony among Americans that could encourage racial peace in the South and improve America's image in the under-developed regions of Asia, Africa, and the Middle East. To heighten domestic and foreign consciousness of Hawaii's racial accord,

Johnson proposed the creation of an East-West Center at the University of Hawaii in Honolulu that would attract students and faculty from both East and West. When several senators asked for State Department recommendations, Lyndon agreed to a study before a Center was created. Nevertheless, he considered this first step toward an East-West Center a significant achievement of the 86th Congress.[27]*

In Johnson's book, however, the primary accomplishment of the 1959 session was labor reform. The law represented not only a triumph over racketeering in labor unions but also gave Lyndon a political victory in the race for the 1960 nomination. In 1958, in an attempt to improve his presidential prospects, John Kennedy had joined New York's Republican senator Irving Ives in sponsoring a bill to restore rank and file control to unions that had fallen under the influence of organized crime. With no legislative achievements to speak of during his first Senate term, Kennedy needed a major success. As a member of the Labor and Public Welfare Committee, he was able to take advantage of sensational revelations about union corruption coming from a special Rackets Committee headed by John McClellan of Arkansas. Kennedy backed a mild reform bill that did not add to Taft-Hartley limitations on unions. Lyndon played the central role in leading the Kennedy-Ives bill through the Senate by an 88-to-1 vote. According to Ives, had it not been for Lyndon's leadership, "there would have been no labor bill passed by the Senate." He beat back efforts of conservative Republicans to undermine unions and exploited political pressure for labor reform to win almost unanimous backing for the Kennedy-Ives law.[28]

On the surface, Lyndon's support of Kennedy's 1958 bill is difficult to understand. Kennedy's emergence as the leading candidate for the Democratic presidential nomination puzzled Lyndon. "It was the goddamnedest thing," he later told Doris Kearns, "here was a whippersnapper, malaria-ridden and yellah, sickly, sickly. He never said a word of importance in the Senate and he never did a thing. But somehow . . . he managed to create the image of himself as a shining intellectual, a youthful leader who would change the face of the country. Now, I will admit that he had a good sense of humor and that he looked awfully good on the goddamn television screen and through it all he was a pretty decent fellow, but his growing hold on the American people was simply a mystery to me."[29]

Nonetheless, Lyndon seemed ready to help him add to it, but only up to a point. By aiding Jack, he created a rapport with him and Joe Kennedy that could be turned to good advantage if and when Jack's campaign faltered. Lyndon had already taken steps along that path when he supported Jack for the vice presidency in 1956 and elevated him to a

*Federal legislation creating the Center was passed in 1960.

seat on the Foreign Relations Committee in 1957. After he gave Foreign Relations to Jack over Kefauver, who had four years seniority on him, Lyndon said: "I kept picturing old Joe Kennedy sitting there with all that power and wealth feeling indebted to me for the rest of his life, and I sure liked that picture." Helping Jack pass his labor bill in 1958 added to the impression that Lyndon was supportive of Kennedy's ambitions. But Lyndon could afford to be generous with his help. Labor reform was a popular cause that also aided him and Democrats generally. Lyndon correctly anticipated, however, that Kennedy-Ives would fail in the House, where a coalition of pro-business and pro-union representatives considered the bill either too mild or too harsh. A Senate-passed bill that did not become a law would be of little value to Kennedy in a national campaign.[30]

The 1959 session challenged Lyndon to find a fresh means of helping Kennedy pass a labor law that would not serve his presidential campaign. Kennedy made it easy for him by asking Lyndon's permission to be floor manager of his own bill. Although Lyndon usually insisted on this prerogative, he granted Jack's request. Nor did he move to bail Kennedy out when John McClellan attached a Bill of Rights to the original measure that labor leaders believed would make unions unmanageable. With some of the usually reliable members of the "Johnson network" voting with McClellan, the Bill of Rights passed 47–46. When a reconsideration produced a 46–46 tie, vice President Nixon cast a decisive positive ballot. "Although the outcome was scarcely detrimental to Johnson," Evans and Novak write, "it wounded two potential political opponents." Labor leaders blamed Nixon for voting against them and Kennedy for exposing them to anti-labor restrictions he could not defeat.[31]

Unanticipated difficulties arose, however, when Richard Russell showed Lyndon that McClellan's Bill of Rights would allow the Federal government to enforce integration in unions and open the door to more rigorous Federal enforcement of school desegregation. Under pressure from southern senators, the Senate reconsidered and largely eliminated McClellan's amendments. Lyndon now received the thanks of organized labor for helping remove provisions that "would have drastically hampered the legitimate activities of the labor movement." But the passage of Kennedy's original bill in only slightly altered form also meant a boost for his national standing, which Lyndon wished to prevent. With Lyndon's encouragement, however, the House blocked Kennedy's bill. Backed by pro-business forces and the White House, Georgia Democrat Phil Landrum and Michigan Republican Robert Griffin sponsored an anti-union bill that curbed picketing, secondary boycotts, and racketeering. Sam Rayburn made every effort to defeat the bill, but lost the fight 229 to 201. He was particularly incensed at Texas Democrats, who voted 16 to 4 for Landrum-Griffin. Rayburn believed that Johnson encouraged Texas congressmen to vote for the bill by warning them that a vote against it would ruin them in Texas.[32]

Although Lyndon was careful not to support Landrum-Griffin openly, his actions behind the scenes leave no doubt of his efforts. In a telephone conversation with Eisenhower, who favored the measure, Lyndon said that they were pretty close together on the labor bill. Further, after the House passed its bill, Lyndon wanted the Senate to concur in the House version without going to conference. But precedent dictated otherwise. Finally, after the conference approved a slightly modified Landrum-Griffin bill, to which Kennedy refused to lend his name, Lyndon had an aide write a memo saying that "the final bill was unquestionably strict. . . . But it cannot be argued successfully that the bill was unfair." Lyndon's sleight of hand had produced a labor bill that stood him in good stead nationally but embarrassed Kennedy. Small wonder that a newsletter to Texas constituents celebrated the result: "If the Congress had done nothing more than pass the anti-racketeering law, it would deserve a place in history. This measure was aimed at thieves and hoodlums, while safeguarding the legitimate rights of our people."[33]

Lyndon faced another challenge to his presidential candidacy in a Senate struggle over Ike's nomination of Lewis Strauss to be Secretary of Commerce. Strauss was a retired rear admiral who had served a five-year term as chairman of the Atomic Energy Commission. Imperious, arrogant, and aggressively conservative, Strauss had come into sharp conflict with liberal senator Clinton P. Anderson of New Mexico, the chairman of the Joint Atomic Energy Committee. Strauss's arbitrary identification of physicist J. Robert Oppenheimer as a security risk, resistance to a greater oversight role for Congress in the development of atomic energy, and outspoken opposition to public power put him at political odds with Anderson. The two men were also bitter personal enemies. When Anderson complained about Strauss's excessive secrecy in dealing with Congress, Strauss said Anderson had "a limited understanding of what is involved." Sensitive about his lack of formal education and any slight to his intellect, Anderson never forgave Strauss his remark. Strauss believed that Anderson would block his reappointment to the AEC, so he accepted appointment as Secretary of Commerce.[34]

The hearings and debate on Strauss's confirmation lasted for three months beginning in mid-March 1959. At the outset, few anticipated his rejection. In the Republic's 170-year history, only seven Cabinet nominees had been denied confirmation, and none since 1925. Personal, political, and institutional forces now came together to make Strauss the eighth. Strauss was his own worst enemy. He was self-righteous, condescending, and evasive in testimony before the Senate Commerce Committee, and he won its support by only a 9-8 vote.

Although not a member of the Committee, Anderson effectively took up the cudgels against Strauss. Anderson complained that Strauss had consciously misled and shown contempt for Congress as chairman of the AEC. Senators found substantial appeal in Anderson's defense of congressional prerogatives; they were angry about presidential vetoes that embarrassed the Senate. Anderson lobbied aggressively for Strauss's defeat. "One of [the] ablest presentations of a weak case I have ever heard," Richard Russell noted on his calendar after seeing Anderson in May. "Had picked record with a fine tooth comb and had every little conflict—inconsistency. . . . Said he would filibuster if necessary and implied threat on LBJ Rule being charged if they got away with it." Russell thought that Anderson's performance was "Rather Strange," and he was "sure [that] LBJ 'sicked' him on me."[35]

Initially, Lyndon was convinced that Strauss would be confirmed. When senators began to line up against him, however, it put Lyndon on the spot. He told Gale McGee, who was an outspoken foe of confirmation, that "I gave him a great many hours of sweating, meaning having to come to grips with a very delicate question that he had just as soon not have been in the firing line about." Earle Clements told Lyndon that his vote would carry four others with him and determine the outcome in a closely divided Senate. Lyndon saw good political reasons to vote against Strauss. Ultra conservatives would not object to Strauss's defeat, Texas oil man H. L. Hunt told Johnson. More important, opposition to Strauss would align Lyndon with party liberals. It also would represent a pay back to Ike for uncompromising opposition to a liberal Congress.[36]

Lyndon refused to take a public stand on the issue until June 19, the day of the vote. Privately, however, he worked to ensure a majority against confirmation. Kennedy and Symington, who shared Lyndon's sensitivity to the liberals in their nomination campaigns, shifted ground at the last minute and followed Johnson's lead. So did Neuberger and Fulbright, though the latter agreed only to be absent and not vote for Strauss. The final count showed 47 Democrats and 2 Republicans opposed and 32 Republicans and 14 Democrats in favor. The two anti-Strauss Republicans were populist William Langer of North Dakota and Margaret Chase Smith of Maine. Langer's vote surprised no one, but Smith's did. Angry at the White House for forcing her into an override fight for pork barrel legislation affecting Maine and indebted to Lyndon for numerous favors, Smith shocked Republican colleagues with her vote. When he heard her say, "No," Barry Goldwater of Arizona shouted "Goddam!" and pounded his desk.

The 49-46 vote enraged Eisenhower, who called it the most shameful thing that had happened in the Senate since the attempt to remove President Andrew Johnson from office. Ike said, "this is the most shameful day in Senate history." Lyndon tried to appease Ike by telling journalists that "the Senate merely exercised its constitutional responsibility. If the President lets it go at that, there is no need for any cold war." But with Democrats jousting for advantage in the presidential nomination fight and the parties already focused on the 1960 election campaign, political warfare was unavoidable.[37]

The close of the congressional session in September revived questions about Lyndon's intentions in the 1960 campaign. Publicly and privately he continued to deny his candidacy. Asserting that his health would not permit him to run and that a southerner could not get the nomination or be elected, he refused to acknowledge that he was in the chase. Other political leaders didn't believe him. Adlai Stevenson thought he was a candidate; Republican senator Styles Bridges detected a "very active" candidacy; and Jack Kennedy said that Lyndon was "running very hard." Jack sent his brother and campaign manager Bobby Kennedy to John-son's ranch to ask him directly. Lyndon said he wasn't running and wouldn't oppose or help Jack, but urged against a third nomination for Adlai. During the visit, Johnson insisted that they hunt deer. Bobby was knocked to the ground and cut above the eye by the recoil of a powerful shotgun Johnson had given him to use. Reaching down to help the thirty-four-year-old Bobby up, Lyndon said: "Son, you've got to learn to han-dle a gun like a man." The incident was an indication of Johnson's small regard for Jack Kennedy's claim on the White House.[38]

People close to Johnson at this time believed that his heart condition and fear of defeat inhibited him from an all-out fight for the nomina-tion. These concerns account in part for Johnson's undeclared candi-dacy. But, more important, his non-candidacy continued to serve his political ends. He thought an announced bid for the presidency would make him the immediate front runner and the object of a powerful, and probably successful, stop-Lyndon movement. He saw no other Demo-crat with an equal claim to the nomination and White House. Stevenson had had his chances, and party leaders would shun him. Humphrey was too closely identified with the liberals to be an effective national candi-date. Symington lacked the sort of track record that would inspire the party and country to make him President. That was even more the case with Jack Kennedy, however appealing his style and personality. Lyn-don told Bobby Baker that he knew ten times more about running the country than Jack did. "That kid needs a little gray in his hair," Lyndon said. He simply couldn't take Kennedy all that seriously. He called him a "playboy" and a "lightweight," who was "smart enough," but had shown little capacity for the sort of hard work required of an effective President or the kind of President Lyndon hoped to be.

Johnson's obtuseness about Kennedy speaks volumes about Lyndon's limited understanding of how important style was in a presidential can-didate and successful White House occupant. Franklin Roosevelt's patrician bearing, Harry Truman's plain spoken honesty, Dwight Eisenhower's benign, nonpartisan demeanor, and John Kennedy's charm and intelligence served to endear each of them to great numbers of Americans. Johnson's deserved reputation for crudeness and wheeling and dealing cast a long shadow over his many legislative achievements and undercut his chances of winning a majority of Democrats and the nation's voters to his side.

Lyndon's Puritanism and grandiosity also played him false. Convinced that he had earned the nomination and would make the best Democratic candidate, he assumed that the party would come to him without an all-out public effort on his part.[39]

In private Lyndon was aggressively running for President. At the beginning of August, newspapers reported that when Ike was asked about possible Democratic candidates, he omitted Lyndon from his list. Although none of the people he mentioned—Frank Lausche, Spessard Holland, John Stennis, and Sam Rayburn—could be seen as serious candidates, Lyndon was incensed, and told a fellow Texan, Treasury Secretary Robert Anderson, "I have had about all I can have of this." When a White House aide urged Ike to make amends, he replied that "Johnson had made some comments much worse about him." At a White House social gathering, Lyndon "sat in almost complete silence. . . . When the President turned to Johnson, he answered only in monosyllables." Lyndon was not placated until the President telephoned to apologize for any misunderstanding.[40]

In September, after Congress adjourned, Lyndon laid plans "to build up his . . . stature . . . in the foreign field." He began by meeting Soviet leader Nikita Krushchev on September 15 at the Capitol. Eager to rival Vice President Nixon, who had made headlines by way of a "kitchen debate" with the Soviet chairman in Moscow in July, Johnson reported to the press that Krushchev told him, " 'I have read your speeches. And I don't like any of them!' " On September 16, Robert Anderson approached Secretary of State Christian Herter about a Johnson trip to Canada and Latin America for mutual defense and good-will talks. Anderson emphasized that Lyndon had assured him of his non-candidacy, saw this as a chance to promote bipartisanship, and wished to make the journey before the Congress reconvened in January, but after Mexican president Lopez Mateos visited his ranch in October.

Although Herter was receptive to the idea, Johnson decided instead to confine his travel to the western United States, where he could woo party leaders, tour defense facilities, and speak out on "survival issues— aid to education, *adequate* national defense and . . . planned use of our economic power in relation to foreign policy." The trip, which took Johnson to Missouri, Kansas, Nebraska, Iowa, and Arizona, aimed to enlist support of western senators in "the Johnson for President campaign" and keep it from becoming "a southern monopoly."[41]

In the fall, he worked to ensure that a mail fraud conviction against George Parr did not jeopardize his political future in Texas or nationally. Parr was in a position to hurt Johnson politically if he raked up charges about the 1948 campaign. In return for Parr's continuing silence, Lyndon arranged to have Abe Fortas and Paul Porter handle Parr's appeal to the U.S. Supreme Court. Fortas and Porter kept Lyndon informed of progress in the case by phone messages to Walter Jenkins. Anything in writing about their reports unnerved Lyndon, who on at least one occasion told Jenkins to "burn your memos up on phone calls." Jenkins didn't, but the Fortas-Porter work on the appeal, which Parr won the following spring, was kept secret.[42]

In October, Lyndon made a series of public statements that encouraged speculation that he was running. The *Dallas Morning News* reported that while "he is not a candidate now, he is definitely 'available.'" He did not refute the *Morning News* report during a national television interview. A few days later he told a radio audience that "anyone who loves his country has to be careful about saying that he would refuse to serve his country." In November and December, Lyndon gave his blessing to nation-wide Johnson-for-President clubs. "I hear what some of my friends are doing, and I see what they are doing," he told the *Christian Science Monitor* on November 14. " . . . The people usually have a way of selecting the person they think best qualified. I have no doubt but what wise judgments will prevail."[43]

Lyndon still believed that the best way to convince people of his unmatched suitability for the White House was to excel in 1960 as Majority Leader. Jack Kennedy disagreed: "Johnson had to prove that a Southerner could win in the North, just as I had to prove a Catholic could win in heavily Protestant states." But Lyndon refused to declare his candidacy and enter state primaries. His strength was not on the hustings, where a John Kennedy and a Hubert Humphrey could outshine him. If his speaking style in the South and Southwest could be described as "a master performance of native American political art," it was seen in "the cynical North and the citizen West" as "cornball." Entering primaries might be disastrous for his campaign. His hope rode on letting Kennedy, Humphrey, Symington, and Stevenson fragment the convention. The floundering Democrats would then turn to the master consensus-builder, the Senate Majority Leader who had arranged so many unholy alliances in support of legislation serving the national interest. Lyndon understood that he might be wrong, that one of the other candidates could defy the odds and win on a first ballot. But he felt it was the best strategy someone with his background, style, and record could devise.[44]

The 1960 congressional session, however, made it difficult for him to sustain the image of a masterful Senate Leader. In early January, liberal Democrats attacked Lyndon's "one-man rule" by proposing that all

Democratic Senators rather than just the leader select the party's Senate Policy Committee, and that the Committee formulate a legislative agenda for submission to all Democratic senators. The formal resolution, which received newspaper headlines as a challenge to Lyndon's leadership, incensed him. He told Reedy that "everybody in the Senate could go commit a biological improbability. . . . Screw 'em all, I'm sick and tired of this kind of nonsense," he said. He complained that the Policy Committee hadn't "done any wrong. This is nothing but a reflection on me. . . . I don't think I ought to be subjected to this kind of torment." Lyndon accurately predicted that the resolution would be voted down, as it was, 51 to 12.[45]

Despite his victory, Lyndon felt compelled to accommodate liberal sentiment. He wished to use the session to advance a program of "responsible moderation" that knits people together and translates into practical gains. Liberals wanted to heighten the contrast in an election year between Democratic and Republican support of domestic reform. Convinced that he could not win the Democratic nomination without softening liberal opposition to himself, Johnson outlined a bold program of reform legislation that seemed unlikely to pass: Federal aid to education; medical care for the aged; an increased minimum wage; a bill to ensure housing for every American; income equity for farmers tied to distribution of surplus produce to the needy; a depressed areas bill; water conservation; abolition of the poll tax; and a new civil rights law.[46]

During a six-month session Congress enacted only a civil rights law. And the rights bill was more an expression of the "responsible moderation" Lyndon favored than a major attack on racial discrimination. He believed that anything more than a narrowly focused statute would increase rather than reduce racial and sectional tensions, further divide the Democratic party, and jeopardize its chances of recapturing the White House. He favored a compromise measure that genuinely granted blacks their constitutional right to vote and eased sectional tensions by demonstrating that the South would not be treated as "a conquered outlaw province." He urged a bill that would be a victory for "moderation," "common sense," "fair play," and, above all, the "nation." He also hoped that it would serve his presidential ambitions by once again demonstrating his talent for creating unity and harmony where there had been division and acrimony. Johnson told a group of civil rights leaders in January that he would try to pass a civil rights bill because it "is the moral responsibility to protect every person's constitutional rights." "Our nation has been living with this . . . in one form or another ever since . . . [it] was founded," he told a North Carolina journalist in February. "I do not believe that we can continue indefinitely without coming to some sensible resolution."[47]

Johnson cut several corners to pass a bill. To avoid having another civil rights act bottled up in the Judiciary Committee, he invited senators to attach proposals protecting constitutional rights to a House bill leasing army property to a Missouri school district. His tactic also would allow Senate provisions on civil rights to go directly to the House floor rather than to the conservative House Rules Committee. Southerners denounced Johnson's maneuver as a lynching of orderly Senate procedure and called him a traitor to his region. Johnson said privately that it was the only kind of lynching Senator Russell had ever objected to.[48]

Johnson's opposition to a filibuster further incensed southerners. Speaking in two-hour shifts and issuing frequent quorum calls, eighteen southern senators brought the upper house to a standstill. To break the filibuster, Lyndon kept the Senate in continuous, around-the-clock session. But it didn't work. Only two senators could hold the floor four or six hours at a time. One of them would give a long prepared speech and the other would spell him with long involved questions while the speaker would rest or go to the men's room. At the end of their four- or six-hour stint, one of them would call for a quorum. With their southern colleagues absenting themselves, civil rights supporters had to produce fifty-one senators to force a new two-man team of opponents into another round of talk. To reduce the time between speeches when filibusterers could rest, Lyndon arranged to have rights advocates on constant call, sleeping and eating in their offices. But the effect was to wear out the senators trying to break the filibuster rather than its supporters. The filibuster ended when the southerners were ready to accept a watered-down law.[49]

Some liberals believed that Johnson conspired with Richard Russell to pass a weak civil rights bill that would have a limited impact on the South and help Johnson win the presidential nomination. Lyndon's refusal to support a liberal proposal for cloture enflamed their suspicions. They were largely justified. In February, when Herman Talmadge of Georgia wanted to know where Lyndon stood on the civil rights issue, he asked Richard Russell. Further, in March, at the height of the congressional debate, when a black-owned newspaper in Pittsburgh asked Johnson where he stood on the deprivation of fundamental rights, Lyndon asked Russell's advice on how to reply. Russell persuaded him to remove a phrase denouncing ultra-liberal and southern obstructionist senators, because it "would do no good in the North and would hurt in the South." He urged him instead to "stick as closely as possible to Constitutional rights on the grounds that no man can possibly be hurt on such a stand."[50]

The southerners' willingness to abandon their filibuster knowing a rights bill would pass also suggests a Johnson-Russell deal. Johnson believed that unless he could end the filibuster and produce a compromise bill, it would "destroy me." From Russell's perspective, a law principally focused on voting rights with an ineffective provision for court registration of black voters was an acceptable "compromise." Southerners and "ardent advocates of civil rights" called the measure a victory for the South. Lyndon, Dirksen, and the Eisenhower administration, however, described the law as "a step forward." Moreover, some liberals took satisfaction from the fact that the bill's main provisions on voting rights had been preserved and that this was the first time a rights bill had been passed in spite of a filibuster. The *New York Times* reported praise for Johnson's efforts and said that his campaign for the Democratic presidential nomination "is expected to benefit from the result."[51]

By the spring of 1960, Lyndon's fight for the nomination was an open secret. After helping organize the Johnson-for-President clubs at the end of 1959, Walter Jenkins had begun coordinating a state-by-state campaign. In January and February, he discussed Johnson's candidacy with local party leaders in eighteen states in every part of the country. Although Jenkins was the point man, no one doubted that Lyndon was behind the whole thing. "It looks like out here in the west things are not going too well for the Senator from Massachusetts," Jenkins's contact in New Mexico reported. "I want to talk with the Senator [Johnson] when he comes out here to the Western Conference. . . . I want to ask the Senator just how he wants me to do this job behind the scenes. I have no pride of authorship; all I want to do is get the job done."[52]

Publicly, Lyndon had restated his unwillingness to run. "I have been asked about my Presidential candidacy from Phoenix, Arizona, all the way to Washington, D.C.," he announced on January 6. "My answer has been the same in every instance. I am not running for anything other than a successful session of this Congress and United States Senator from Texas." Yet he left the door ajar by declaring: "I do not pretend to know what I will be doing next summer or next fall. The only thing of which I am certain is that the Democratic nominee will have my support." He also continued to emphasize his role as a responsible national leader who got things done. Nonpartisanship for the sake of the nation was essential in both foreign and domestic affairs, he declared in a speech on January 21. "Responsibility," he told a Democratic audience on the 23rd, "builds America up—it does not try to slow America down. . . . And, I say to you, the people of America are for responsibility." He pointed to victories in the last three congressional elections as evidence of his assertion.[53]

At the same time, he continued to encourage a picture of himself as ambivalent about running. Early in January, he had met with Jack and Bobby Kennedy. There is no record of their conversation. But it left Jack Kennedy uncertain about Lyndon's intentions. Shortly after, when Kennedy rode a train from New York to Washington with Leslie Carpenter, a Johnson friend and Texas journalist, Kennedy "spent the whole time trying to find out what I knew about whether Lyndon Johnson was actually going to be more than a favorite son candidate in the Los Angeles convention." Sam Rayburn and Richard Russell helped Johnson obscure his intentions. They knew he was running, and publicly and privately talked up his candidacy. But they said that Johnson had refused to follow their advice and become a candidate.[54]

At the beginning of March, Reedy summed up Johnson's strategy. Jack Kennedy was the clear front runner. He was piling up the most delegates through a well-organized state-by-state effort. Yet there was a "better than even chance" that he wouldn't have enough to win the nomination at the convention and that the party would then turn to Lyndon Johnson. It was pointless, Reedy asserted, to aim at winning more delegates than Kennedy. That was now highly unlikely, if not impossible. Instead, Johnson needed to maintain his "status" as a responsible national leader who stood above sectional interests and principally served the national well-being.[55]

Johnson reflected Reedy's advice in a conversation with Massachusetts congressman Thomas P. (Tip) O'Neill in March 1960. " 'Now I realize you're pledged to the boy'—referring, of course, to Jack Kennedy," O'Neill remembers Lyndon saying. " 'But you and I both know he can't win. He's just a flash in the pan, and he's got no record of substance to run on. Will you be with me on the second ballot?' During the entire conversation, he never once mentioned Jack Kennedy by name. It was always 'the boy.' " When O'Neill predicted that Kennedy would win the nomination on the first ballot, Johnson "couldn't believe what he was hearing."[56]

Other politically sophisticated observers shared O'Neill's conviction. In mid-February, Jim Rowe sent Lyndon an analysis of the nomination fight based on his observations during recent trips around the country. "The contest for the Democratic presidential nomination is just about over." Although party pros would like to maneuver Kennedy into second place on the ticket, he was getting too strong to be denied the top spot. The "only possibility for upsetting Kennedy: Johnson, if he can take the West by storm. There is much Johnson sentiment, particularly in the Rocky Mountain States, but it's going untended. His strategy of keeping out of the primaries is fine; his neglect of the West is disastrous." Eliot Janeway told Jenkins that Johnson's impulse to make his candidacy an "inside job" was a poor idea. "I think he better come out and be a candidate. . . . Either you are running for President or you are not. . . . You ought to call off this cloak and dagger business and just tell the people."[57]

Yet at the same time, Lyndon received numerous indications that his strategy was achieving good results. He had reports that neither Symington nor Humphrey had good prospects for the nomination. Moreover, he heard that he was doing well in New York, Kansas, Oregon, New Mexico, Oklahoma, and "even New Jersey." One Dallas friend was willing to lay five-to-four odds that Lyndon would be the nominee. In response to these reports, Lyndon put the best possible face on things. When journalist Dick Berlin informed him that California's governor Pat Brown had a deal with the Kennedys, Johnson "just pooh poo'd the idea. You know Lyndon—" Berlin told Jenkins, "he believes what he wants to believe."[58]

By the end of March, however, even George Reedy, who had been consistently optimistic, began to have second thoughts. He suggested in a memo he asked Johnson to destroy that they might want to consider doing "a hatchet job" on Kennedy. The focus of the attack was not to be Kennedy's religion or youth, his assumed weaknesses, but Joe Kennedy's efforts to buy the presidency. *"Americans would bitterly resent the concept that the White House is a plaything to be handed out as a Christmas present."*[59]

Lyndon had not seen dirty tricks as yet necessary to beat Kennedy for the nomination. At the beginning of April, he had some hope that Hubert Humphrey would beat Jack in the Wisconsin primary on April 5 and in West Virginia on May 10, where 95 percent of the state was Protestant. Lyndon knew that no one could accumulate enough delegates through the primaries to win the nomination, but they were a test of how a candidate might fare in a general election. And for Kennedy, who needed to show that his religion was not a bar to winning Protestant votes, Wisconsin and West Virginia were major obstacles on the road to the nomination. Kennedy beat Humphrey by a narrow margin in Wisconsin, but his victory did more to focus attention on than dispose of the religious issue. Kennedy's support had come principally, Reedy told Lyndon, from Catholic districts and Humphrey's from Protestant ones. Kennedy will need to win across the board in West Virginia if he is to bury the issue.[60]

Lyndon tried to help Humphrey beat Kennedy in West Virginia and derail Jack's drive for the nomination. Humphrey had said that if he lost in Wisconsin, he would withdraw from the race. But convinced that Wisconsin represented a moral victory for him and encouraged by the Johnson people, Humphrey went into West Virginia.

Lyndon's principal supporter in the state was its junior Senator Robert C. Byrd. At the beginning of April, Byrd announced his support of Lyndon for the presidency and declared that party leaders around West Virginia shared his sentiment. In response, Jack Kennedy came to see Lyndon on April 8. According to what Johnson told *New York Times* columnist Arthur Krock, Kennedy asked him "to get Senator Bob Byrd 'out of West Virginia.' I reminded him that this is Byrd's own State and I couldn't get him out of it if I were foolish enough to try." Johnson then reminded

Kennedy of all the favors he had done for him. Lyndon also told Krock that he thought "Kennedy's request about Bob Byrd and his complaints against Humphrey in West Virginia are the consequence of 'campaign fatigue' and 'most unfortunate.' " In fact, Kennedy's pressure on Lyndon was a response to Byrd's support of Humphrey. On April 22, for example, Byrd gave Humphrey a detailed memo on the political complexion of West Virginia's various counties and suggested a strategy for beating Kennedy in the primary.[61]

But Humphrey, Byrd, and Lyndon were unable to combat Kennedy's West Virginia campaign. After polls showed Humphrey with a commanding lead three weeks before the election, the Kennedy people pulled out all the stops. In a state whose politics one journalist described as among the "most squalid, corrupt and despicable" in the Union, the Kennedy campaign outbid Humphrey for the support of local bosses, released documents implying that Humphrey was a World War II draft-dodger, and outspent and outmaneuvered Humphrey in the use of television. Kennedy confronted the religious issue head on, disarmed anti-Catholic sentiment, and won the election by a decisive margin.

Lyndon had tried to boost Humphrey's campaign at the last minute by traveling to Clarksburg, West Virginia, for a Jefferson-Jackson Day Dinner on May 7th. Although stressing the differences between Democrats and Republicans in his address and predicting that any of the Democratic candidates would beat the Republican nominee in November, Lyndon had emphasized the domestic social programs for which the party stood and with which Hubert was so closely identified. Lyndon's appearance had done little more than add credibility to Kennedy's assertion that Humphrey could not win the nomination and was nothing more than a stalking horse for unannounced candidates. Lyndon said privately, he "had tried so hard" in West Virginia," and "had failed."[62]

After West Virginia, with Humphrey dropping out of the race, Lyndon believed that Kennedy was probably unstoppable and that only some new aggressive strategy might deadlock the convention. Jim Rowe remembered that Johnson called him after West Virginia and asked, "What are the possibilities? Are any left?" Rowe replied: "Kennedy has got this. There is only one way to stop him that I can see. That's for Adlai to give a signal and for you to get behind Adlai. If you two get together, you might stop him. I don't think you can, but nobody else can." Johnson had a meeting scheduled with Stevenson for the following week, and said he would talk to him about it. After Adlai saw Johnson, he called Rowe, who repeated what he had told Lyndon. "Well, I can't do that," Stevenson said. "Well, the horse race is over," Rowe replied.

Stevenson's resolve, however, was not as strong as he led Rowe to think. Diary notes on Johnson's conversation with Stevenson described their meeting as "very friendly and cordial." Lyndon suggested that "he

and the Governor ought to let their people be more active for them."
When Johnson said "he resented all the pressure coming from Kennedy
. . . Stevenson said he did, too." Newton Minow, a Stevenson political
adviser, learned after 1960 that Stevenson had a couple of meetings with
Johnson in which Lyndon kept saying, " 'Now, listen Adlai, you just
hang loose here. Don't make any commitments. You may still get it.
Don't help that kid, Kennedy. You just stay neutral.' And I believe that
Governor Stevenson, at some point, made a commitment to him that he
would do so." Kennedy certainly thought so. On May 24, when Arthur
Krock told him that "Stevenson was running hard for the Democratic
nomination," Kennedy said, "And how!" reflecting his "irritation that
Stevenson is encouraging support for his nomination among Democrats
whom Kennedy felt would otherwise be for him." [63]

Lyndon now adopted a two-pronged strategy in the eight weeks before the convention met in Los Angeles. He seized every opportunity to
undercut Kennedy and question his suitability for the White House. And
he stepped up the campaign to win delegate support: on the first ballot,
if possible, but also on subsequent ballots should the convention deadlock.

The attack on Kennedy in the three weeks after West Virginia included assertions that he had bought the election there and was doing
the same in Oregon. At the same time, Lyndon used a nationally televised news show to make light of Kennedy's primary victories. We
wouldn't want to nominate a President based on what four or five or
even eight states did in primaries with limited voter participation, he
declared.

The attack on Kennedy also focused on his religion as a roadblock to
the White House. On May 24, when Drew Pearson asked Johnson if
New York party boss Carmine DiSapio had been to see him about a
block-Kennedy effort, Lyndon answered: "None of these big city leaders
in New York, New Jersey, or Illinois want Kennedy. Most of them are
Catholics, and they don't want a Catholic heading up the ticket." Johnson backers also questioned Kennedy's sincere commitment to traditional Democratic policies for helping the disadvantaged. Kennedy's
vote-buying in West Virginia had taken advantage of a poverty-stricken
people, one Johnson supporter wrote Pearson. If Kennedy is elected to
the White House, he will "forget to remember West Virginia in December as he courted her in May." At the end of the month Lyndon, while
Arthur Krock sat in his office, called a farm spokesman in St. Paul,
Minnesota. "You and I have got a lot in common, and I don't think you
and your people have any with Boston," Lyndon said. "Thus the Democratic Band of Brothers," Krock noted in a memo. [64]

In that same meeting, Johnson told Krock that the Kennedy campaign
was making unfair attacks on him and he might have to respond. De-

spite all he had done to " 'build up' " Kennedy, " 'Kennedy's people' were constantly 'circulating lies' about his attitude as leader toward the Labor Relations Act of 1959 and other bills in which Kennedy had a special interest. '. . . I told Kennedy about this sniping from his camp the other day and afterward he sent me a copy of a memo to his staff forbidding this activity (thereby conceding it was going on). But today a reporter, who is practically a Kennedy hired hand, asked me a needling question based on an untruth about my scheduling of the minimum wage bill, and my staff informed me he got this version from the Kennedy people. I am going to have to tell Kennedy that if this underhand sniping keeps up I will take steps to protect myself.' " With Lyndon now the most formidable challenger to Kennedy in the last weeks of the nomination campaign, the two camps entered into a bare knuckles fight.[65]

Lyndon was particularly eager to draw comparisons between himself and Kennedy, which would show that "Sonny Boy," as Johnson and some of his Senate friends called him, was not presidential timber. Reedy told Johnson that the Catholic issue had "completely diverted public attention from the real issue of whether Kennedy should be President of the United States."

The shooting down of an American U-2 spy plane over the Soviet Union and collapse of an Eisenhower-Khrushchev Summit scheduled for May 15 allowed Johnson to compare himself and Kennedy in foreign affairs. Kennedy, eager to counter assertions that he was too young and inexperienced to cope with the Soviets and preserve world peace, spoke out forcefully on the Administration's reaction to events. He criticized the White House for allowing such a flight so close to the Paris Summit, giving out false statements, and failing to express regret about the incident and preserve the conference. Lyndon stressed the need for national unity, and echoed Republican attacks on Kennedy as a naïve appeaser by asking audiences: "I am not prepared to apologize to Mr. Khrushchev—are you?" Lyndon underscored his small regard for Kennedy's expertise in foreign policy by excluding him from a telegram he, Stevenson, Rayburn, and Fulbright sent Khrushchev urging him to reverse a decision to postpone the Summit meeting until after the November elections.[66]

At the same time, the Johnson campaign made a greater effort to win delegates and generate enthusiasm for his nomination. Behind-the-scenes work went forward in states across the country; Lyndon spoke in Indiana, Oklahoma, Delaware, Idaho, Washington state, both Dakotas, and California during the last two weeks of May; John Connally prepared to open a Johnson for President Headquarters in Washington, D.C.; and Lyndon gave additional broad hints of his intention to run. Still convinced, however, that it would do more harm than good to acknowledge his candidacy before the eve of the convention, Lyndon refused to announce. Nevertheless, he continued to receive ample encouragement that he would come out on top. The Summit difficulties had enhanced his appeal considerably, Lyndon was told. Averell Harriman sent word that Johnson was just the sort of experienced and judicious leader the country was ready to support.[67]

In June, the Johnson campaign belatedly took the form of a full-scale nomination drive. At the start of the month, the conservative Scripps-Howard newspaper chain announced its support of Lyndon's candidacy; Sam Rayburn declared that Johnson would receive the support of 500 delegates at the convention, giving him "a great chance to be nominated"; and Lyndon traveled to New Jersey and upstate New York to woo delegates. On the 11th, the Johnson campaign circulated a private memo showing that on a first ballot Lyndon would win 526½ of the 761 votes needed for the nomination. His total was to rise to 618 on a second ballot, and to 802 on a third. Eight days later at a press conference in Des Moines, where he had gone to court the Iowa delegation, he told a reporter asking if he were a candidate: "I certainly didn't travel out here just to look for botanical specimens."

The campaign now prepared a "confidential background sheet" on each delegate to the convention. Jack Anderson told Drew Pearson: "Your friend the Senate leader is always thorough. . . . He had instructed his aides to find out the delegates' Texas contacts, business associates, relationships with Democratic Senators and Congressmen. He also leaves space for a 'suggested approach.' All the better to bring pressure on delegates." On June 24, a full-page ad appeared in major newspapers urging Johnson to run. At the end of June, he won a 67-to-25 vote to recess rather than adjourn the Congress until August. Since Lyndon would have a large say in the actions of the rump session and its record might have an impact on the November elections, Lyndon hoped the decision to recess would give him added leverage with convention delegates.[68]

To no one's surprise, on July 5, Lyndon formally announced his candidacy. He predicted that he would win on the third ballot. He explained that he had not been able to declare his candidacy while Congress was in session. As Majority Leader, he could not miss the hundreds of votes other active candidates missed. As for the nomination, the issue before the convention was experience and capacity to lead. World Communism would show "no mercy for innocence, no gallantry toward inexperience, no patience toward errors." Whatever Democrats might think of Johnson's candidacy, Eisenhower favored his nomination. He privately told Arthur Krock that he couldn't understand how the Democrats could consider nominating an " 'inexperienced boy' " like Kennedy, "or for that matter Symington or Stevenson. 'Lyndon Johnson . . . would be the best Democrat of them all as President from the viewpoint of responsible management of the national interest.' " [69]

In Los Angeles for the opening of the convention, Johnson declared that Kennedy's bandwagon was moving in reverse. Three weeks ago he had been claiming the support of 710 delegates, but now he seemed only to count on 600 first-ballot votes. Despite his brave words, Lyndon had known for over a month that his chances of defeating Kennedy were poor. At the beginning of June, Jim Rowe had told him: "I can't see much indication that it is not all over in Kennedy's favor." State-by-state analyses tended to confirm Rowe's supposition, and the Kennedy camp predicted a first-ballot victory. Although Johnson advised people not to count him out, he admitted that "those wanting to bet the favorite, 'had better put their money on Jack.' " [70]

During the final weeks before the convention, Johnson had hoped that his campaign could tarnish Kennedy's image enough to defeat him. He saw the need for the sort of hardball politics Kennedy had used in West Virginia, and others, including Kennedy, were now trying to use against him. Drew Pearson, for example, recorded that conservative *Time* publisher Henry Luce had "secretly assigned ace reporter Herbert Solow to dig up the facts about . . . Johnson's radio and television holdings. Solow came back with the report that . . . the Johnson radio-television empire had prospered while Johnson served on the Senate Appropriations Subcommittee which votes out funds to the Federal Communications Commission. But Solow's story never appeared in *Time* or *Life*. Luce's top political editor, Jim Shepley, has now gone to work for Vice President Nixon, and the Solow manuscript on Johnson may be used in the campaign—if Johnson should win the Democratic nomination." Lyndon believed that the Kennedy people were feeding anti-Johnson stories to Pearson in retaliation for Johnson's attacks on Jack's youth and immaturity. Pearson himself felt manipulated by the Kennedys. He took a full-page ad in a Los Angeles newspaper that was later distributed to convention delegates describing how the Kennedy campaign managed and suppressed the news. Joseph Kennedy, Jack's father, got into the act when he stopped in Las Vegas on the way to Los Angeles to bet a substantial sum on Jack's nomination. His objective was less to win money than to ensure that the gambling odds favored Jack and added to the bandwagon psychology at the convention. The Kennedy campaign also raised questions about whether a man with a heart condition was fit for the presidency. [71]

In June and July, Johnson supporters went after Kennedy for failing to take a stand against Joe McCarthy, his absenteeism in the Senate, and hiding health problems that might make him unsuited for the White House. The Johnson campaign seized upon Eleanor Roosevelt's comment about Kennedy's Pulitzer Prize-winning book, *Profiles in Courage*, in reference to Kennedy's response to McCarthy: "A man cannot be President who understands what courage is, and admires it but has not quite the independence to have it," Mrs. Roosevelt said. The disquieting thought about Kennedy, Johnson people asserted, is that he "never really saw exactly what McCarthyism represented." [72]

The attack on Kennedy's over-all Senate performance was more aggressive. Johnson "field workers" received detailed comparisons of Johnson's and Kennedy's attendance and voting records. "Where Was Kennedy?" the Johnson campaign memo asked, and demonstrated that the Massachussets senator had a long history of missing important quorum calls and votes on major bills. The memo concluded that "Senator Kennedy has seemed almost to abdicate his senatorial responsibility." Instigated by Johnson, Republican senator Hugh Scott of Pennsylvania published an open letter to Kennedy on June 19 sarcastically briefing Kennedy on events in the Senate. "Well, we don't want to bore you, Jack," Scott wrote. "If you have time, drop in and if not, just send one of the other Kennedys down." As Lyndon put it to John Steele, "Jack was out kissing babies while I was passing bills, including his bills." Johnson also told Steele, "I don't think I'm absolutely qualified to be President, but when I look at the other boys (always boys), when I look at Jack and Stu and Adlai, I think I'm better qualified than they are. I'm a doer, I've passed the bills, I've minded the store." [73]

Nothing incensed the Kennedys more than the Johnson campaign revelations about Jack's health. On July 4, India Edwards, a prominent Democrat for Lyndon, and John Connally publicly urged an evaluation of Kennedy's health and revealed that he had Addison's disease, a malfunctioning of the adrenal glands. The use of cortisone since 1950 had made the disease less than life-threatening, but the Kennedys refused to acknowledge Jack's affliction for fear it would raise doubts about his capacity to serve as President. Bobby Kennedy publicly denied that Jack had "an ailment classically described as Addison's Disease." Jack released a medical report saying his "health is excellent." The revelation enraged the Kennedys, who called it "despicable tactics." India Edwards believed that the episode made Kennedy's "Irish Mafia," particularly Bobby, hate her. Although Lyndon publicly took the high road, saying none of us would be in the race without a clearance from his doctor, he savaged Kennedy in private. "Toward Kennedy he is contemptuous," John Steele said. "Did you hear the news?" Johnson asked Republican congressman Walter Judd of Minnesota when they met in a Senate elevator just before the Democratic convention. "What news?" Judd replied. "Jack's pediatricians have just given him a clean bill of health!" Johnson described Kennedy to Peter Lisagor of the *Chicago Daily News* as a " 'little scrawny fellow with rickets.' " " 'Have you ever seen his ankles?' " Johnson asked. " 'They're about so round,' and he traced a minute circle with his finger." [74]

By the time the convention began in earnest on the evening of July 11, Lyndon knew that Kennedy had the nomination locked up. Two days before, after seeing Hubert Humphrey and Governor Robert Meyner of New Jersey, Johnson had told an aide, "It is all over with. It is going to be Kennedy by a landslide." As he and Jim Rowe ate dinner in Johnson's suite at the Biltmore Hotel and watched Frank Church give the keynote speech, Lyndon said: "I don't see how we can stop this fellow [Kennedy], do you?" Rowe agreed. So did Sam Rayburn, who according to Tommy Corcoran, "knew the jig was up." [75]

Although Lyndon had few illusions left, he would not go quietly. He was angry at losing to someone he felt had less legitimate claim on the nomination than he did. "I can't stand to be pushed around by that forty-two-year-old kid," he told Adlai Stevenson. In the last two days before the nomination, Johnson gave little overt indication of a man who was whipped. He enlisted the support of Minnesota senators Hubert Humphrey and Eugene McCarthy, who declared themselves for Stevenson as a way to keep Lyndon's nomination alive. Indeed, McCarthy, who was encouraged to believe that he would be Johnson's running mate, gave a brilliant nominating speech for Stevenson that touched off the noisiest and most emotional demonstration of the convention. Lyndon also spoke to several delegations to appeal for their support and used the opportunity to strike out at Kennedy. Privately, Johnson's people raised the Catholic issue, "muttering 'the Holy Ghost this, the Holy Ghost that.' It was about as smart as opening a Kosher deli in Cairo," Tommy Corcoran said. Publicly, Lyndon compared the Kennedy and Johnson records as senators and attacked Joe Kennedy for wanting, as Ambassador to Britain, to appease Hitler: "I wasn't any Chamberlain-umbrella policy man," Johnson told the Washington state delegation. "I never thought Hitler was right." [76]

In a last-ditch effort to turn the tide against Kennedy, Johnson challenged him to a debate before the Massachusetts and Texas delegations on the afternoon of July 12. Confident of winning the nomination and eager to show his regard for Johnson, whom he saw as a potential running mate, Kennedy accepted. Lyndon used the occasion to attack Kennedy's voting record on farm legislation and civil rights. Johnson noted that Kennedy had voted six out of eight times for Eisenhower's stingy farm support programs, and pointed out that "some Senators" had missed all fifty quorum calls and voted on only eleven of the forty-five roll call votes on the 1960 civil rights bill. Kennedy deftly turned aside Johnson's attack, saying he didn't see any need for a debate with Lyndon "because I don't think that Senator Johnson and I disagree on the great issues that face us." His answer to Lyndon's recounting of Senate attendance records amused the audience and defused the issue. Since Lyndon was not specific about what senators were absent, "I assume that he was talking about some of the other candidates and not about me." Kennedy praised Lyndon's "wonderful record in answering those quorum calls," and declared himself "strongly in support of him for majority leader and . . . confident that in that position we are all going to be able to work together." [77]

On the night of July 13, after Kennedy won the nomination on the first ballot, 806 to Lyndon's 409, Kennedy was not happy at having to choose a running mate in twenty-four hours. But he already had given the question some thought. Several weeks before the convention, Theodore Sorensen and other campaign advisers had given him lists of potential vice-presidential nominees. Johnson's name headed several of the lists, but Kennedy did not think Lyndon would give up the Senate Leadership. "I wouldn't want to trade a vote for a gavel, and I certainly wouldn't want to trade the active position of leadership of the greatest deliberative body in the world for the part-time job of presiding," Lyndon had said. Consequently, Kennedy had focused on getting someone from the Middle West or Far West. After overtures to Humphrey, which were spurned, Kennedy had told Clark Clifford at the end of June and again in Los Angeles that Stuart Symington was his first choice. [78]

Meanwhile, the Kennedy campaign had assured labor leaders and liberal delegates they were wooing that Lyndon would not be on the ticket. On Monday, July 11, however, columnist Joe Alsop and *Washington Post* publisher Phil Graham urged Kennedy to pick Johnson. "He immediately agreed, so immediately as to leave me doubting the easy triumph," Graham remembered, "and I therefore restated the matter, urging him not to count on Johnson's turning it down but to offer the VPship so persuasively as to win Johnson over. Kennedy was decisive in saying that was his intention, pointing out that Johnson would help the ticket not only in the South but in important segments of the Party all over the country." Informed by Graham of his exchange with Kennedy, Jim Rowe dismissed it as transparent bait to push Johnson out of the race. Lyndon also refused to take the news seriously, saying "he supposed the same message was going out to all the candidates." Yet Graham took his conversation with Kennedy at face value, and instructed the *Post* to publish a story on Tuesday saying "the word in Los Angeles is that Kennedy will offer the VPship to Lyndon Johnson." [79]

Graham and Alsop weren't the only ones active in Lyndon's behalf. According to Arthur Krock, Governor David Lawrence of Pennsylvania, speaking for Mayor Richard Daley of Chicago and Carmine DiSapio of New York, recommended that Kennedy put Johnson on the ticket. On Tuesday night, after the Kennedy-Johnson "debate," Tommy Corcoran also urged Kennedy to take Johnson as his running mate. Catching Jack in an elevator, Corcoran said it was the best way to bring the party together, win the South in November, and avoid being beaten on the "Catholic issue," which would rule out another Catholic candidate "for generations." After the day's events, in which Lyndon had attacked Joe Kennedy and struck out in his debate with Jack, Kennedy doubted that Lyndon would run with him. While Corcoran held open the elevator door, "which was spastically trying to close on my foot," Jack said, " 'Stop kidding, Tommy. Johnson will turn me down!' " When Corcoran asked Kennedy to "let me see if he'll take it," Jack "smiled, nodded and said, 'Tommy you have peculiar abilities.' "[80]

That morning, in the Massachusetts delegation's hotel suite, Tip O'Neill had found House Majority Leader John McCormack talking with Sam Rayburn and Texas congressman Wright Patman. When O'Neill reported that Kennedy estimates gave him fifty more votes than needed for the nomination, Rayburn said, "Well, if Kennedy wants Johnson for Vice President . . . then he has nothing else he can do but to be on the ticket." Rayburn gave McCormack and O'Neill his phone number, and asked them to tell "Jack Kennedy that if he wants me to talk to Lyndon Johnson, I'll tell him exactly that. . . . If Jack Kennedy is interested in Lyndon Johnson being the vice-presidential nominee, you have him call me and by golly, I'll insist on it." That evening, O'Neill related the message to Kennedy on the sidewalk in front of Chasen's Restaurant in West Hollywood, where Kennedy had gone for a reception. "Of course I want Lyndon Johnson," Kennedy said. ". . . The only thing is, I would never want to offer it and have him turn me down; I would be terrifically embarrassed. He's the natural. If I can ever get him on the ticket, no way we can lose. We'd carry Texas. Certainly I want him. I'll call Sam Rayburn. You tell Sam that I'll call him after the convention tonight." O'Neill gave Rayburn the message at the convention later that night. O'Neill didn't see Rayburn again until they returned to Washington. When they met in the House lobby, Sam said, "Well Tom . . . I guess we played a part of history that will never get in the history books."[81]

On Wednesday night, after Kennedy's victory, Tommy Corcoran went to see Lyndon. "If Jack offered you the vice presidency, would you take it?" Corcoran asked. "He won't give it to me," Lyndon replied. Corcoran asked Lyndon's permission "to work out the option." "Only if Sam goes along with it. He hates Kennedys." Corcoran went to Rayburn, who said, "No, I won't go along with it. I wouldn't trust Joe Kennedy across the street. He'll doublecross us sure as hell." Corcoran claims that he then convinced Sam that Lyndon's only real future was in the number two spot on the ticket.

But Corcoran had no substantial impact on either Johnson or Rayburn. They had already agreed that Lyndon should join Kennedy on the ticket. But they did not want people, then or later, to see that they were eager for Lyndon's nomination as Vice President. They wanted everyone to think that they had to be dragooned into taking the second spot. In his later recounting of the decision, Johnson depicted both Rayburn and himself as having to be convinced to accept Kennedy's offer. According to Johnson, Rayburn told him on the night of the 13th, after Kennedy's nomination, that "he thought Kennedy was going to ask me to run with him, and he said, 'Don't get caught in that trap. Don't accept.' . . . I sure as hell didn't want to do it," Johnson himself said. "A Vice President is generally like a Texas steer. He has lost his social standing in the society in which he resides."[82]

In a variation on this theme, in 1965, Johnson told Arthur Krock that at 2 o'clock on the morning of July 14, Rayburn called to tell him it would be "idiotic" to accept. But nine hours later, after supposedly being convinced by two fellow Democrats that Lyndon's absence from the ticket would result in a Nixon presidency, Rayburn urged Johnson to take Kennedy's offer. "I am a damn sight smarter than I was last night," Johnson quoted Rayburn. It is inconceivable that as astute a politician as Rayburn needed instruction on what Johnson's presence on the ticket would mean.[83]

In addition to Rayburn's conversation with McCormack and O'Neill, there is other evidence that Lyndon was eager for the vice-presidential nomination if he couldn't get the top spot. In March 1960, as Johnson and several friends had driven in his limousine to a wedding in New Jersey, they discussed Kennedy's qualifications for the presidency. When everyone agreed that Jack had the class, education, instincts, and guts to do the job, Lyndon suddenly said: "A fellow from my part of the country couldn't be anything more than another John Nance Garner." Johnson seemed to be thinking about what he could make of the vice presidency. As with the Majority Leader's post, could he make it into something more than it had traditionally been? In June, Bobby Baker had "cautioned" Ted Sorenson "not to be so certain that his boss would reject a Kennedy-Johnson ticket." At the same time, Reedy gave Johnson a memo justifying a decision to take the vice presidency. Further, on July 5, when a reporter pressed him to say if he would consider taking the vice presidency, he replied: "I would never reject something that hasn't been offered to me. . . . I have been prepared throughout my adult life to serve my country in any capacity where my country thought my services were essential." Clark Clifford says that on the night of July 13, after Kennedy's nomination, Rayburn urged Jack to take Lyndon as his running mate. Eliot Janeway remembers that Johnson "was very anxious to get out of the Majority Leadership. Johnson would have paid for the vice presidency."[84]

Johnson in fact had good reason to want the vice presidential nomination. In Arthur Schlesinger, Jr.'s view, Johnson had "a deep sense of responsibility about the future of the South in the American political system. He used to lament the fact that so much southern political energy was diverted from constructive political channels to the defense of the past . . . fighting for lost causes. If the Democratic party did not give a southerner a place on the ticket in 1960, it would drive the South even further back on itself and into self-pity, bitterness and futility. He may well have seen in the Vice-Presidency a means of leading the South back into the Democratic party and the national consensus." [85]

It was also clear to Johnson that he could no longer control the Senate as he had in 1955–58. In 1959 and 1960, party liberals and Eisenhower's assertiveness had undermined Johnson's effectiveness as Leader. "Johnson felt he had lost control," Janeway says. "He had lost emotional control of the Senate. And he was very bitter against a good third of the Democratic caucus." Theodore F. Green of Rhode Island told Tommy Corcoran that "Lyndon was finished as an effective majority leader. . . . If he went back, Green said, they might give him the title again but they wouldn't follow him." Lyndon didn't need Janeway or Green or Corcoran to tell him what he already knew. His best days as Majority Leader had passed. If Kennedy won the presidency, the White House would set the legislative agenda and Lyndon would be little more than the President's man in the Senate. If Kennedy lost the election, Lyndon would be left to cope with another assertive Republican President, as Ike had been in 1959–60, and hostile Democratic liberals, who would surely say that Lyndon's bipartisanship or failure to publicize differences between Democrats and Republicans had contributed to a Nixon victory. If he ran with Kennedy and they lost, he could still go back to the Senate and be in a stronger position than ever to seek the presidential nomination. Should Kennedy and he win, Lyndon might use his political magic to convert the vice presidency, as with the Senate Leadership, into something more than it had been before. [86]

Johnson and Rayburn tied the idea of expanded vice-presidential powers to a picture of Lyndon as reluctant running mate. If Kennedy had to convince him to run, Johnson was in a better position to ask for commitments in return. When Sam Rayburn told Corcoran that Joe Kennedy would "doublecross us sure as hell," he was referring to the possibility that Kennedy would renege on a promise to make Lyndon an influential Vice President. According to Alfred Steinberg, Kennedy promised Rayburn that he would "give the Vice President important domestic duties and send him on trips abroad." Corcoran told Rayburn that after the Kennedy-Johnson ticket won, Lyndon could say: " 'I'm your vice president, I'm the re-elected Senator from Texas. I'll gladly be your vice president if you'll make it worth my while. I mean to do a job, not to be a ceremonial presiding officer of the Senate.' " If the Kennedys tried "to trap Lyndon as a figurehead," Corcoran proposed that Lyndon resign the vice presidency and Sam, as Speaker of the House, become Vice President. It was a fantastic suggestion and Rayburn dismissed it: " 'Jesus Christ,' he said—and his whole bald head got red. 'Get behind me; I won't go.' "

Lyndon and Rayburn weren't prepared to be as Machiavellian as Corcoran, but they wished to convert Lyndon's ostensible reluctance to run into enhanced influence for him as Vice President. The picture of him as reluctant running mate served two other purposes. It helped appease Lyndon's Texas friends who felt betrayed by Johnson's decision to join the ticket. Johnson and Connally had raised a lot of money for Lyndon in Texas by saying he was running for President and would not accept the vice presidency. Some of Lyndon's Texas supporters viewed it as humiliating for Johnson to play second fiddle to Kennedy. Had Johnson shown himself as eager for the vice presidency, it would have caused an irreparable breach with some of his Texas backers. John Connally says that some of them never forgave him anyway. Johnson's insistence that Kennedy talked him into running was also a matter of pride. It reflected Lyndon's difficulty in being second to anyone and his conviction that a Johnson-Kennedy ticket would have been more appropriate and just.[87]

It is impossible to reconstruct the exact sequence of events on July 14 leading to Johnson's selection as the vice-presidential nominee. "The full story of how Kennedy selected Johnson as vice president will never be told," Myer Feldman, a special counsel to President Kennedy, said. When Feldman asked the President what the true story of the selection was, Kennedy replied: "Well, you know, I don't think anybody will ever know." It is certain that Jack called Lyndon at about 8 A.M. on the morning of the 14th and asked to come see him at 9:30. Johnson offered to come up to Kennedy's room but Jack insisted on coming down. He arrived at about ten and invited Lyndon to join the ticket. According to Robert Kennedy, Jack had no expectation that Johnson would accept. "The reason he went down and offered him the nomination is because . . . there were enough indications from others that he wanted to be offered the nomination. But he never thought he'd take the nomination. . . . He never dreamt that there was a chance in the world that he would accept it. When he came back, he said, " 'You just won't believe it.' I said, 'What?' And he said, 'He wants it.' And I said, 'Oh, my God!' He said, 'Now what do we do?' . . . We spent the rest of the day—and we both promised each other that we'd never tell what happened—but we spent the rest of the day alternating between thinking it was good and thinking that it wasn't good that he'd offered him the vice presidency—and how could he get out of it."[88]

Robert Kennedy's recollections are difficult to credit. Jack's conversations with Graham, O'Neill, Corcoran, and Rayburn must have persuaded him that Lyndon had serious thoughts of taking the vice presidency. Further, given Jack's comments to O'Neill that he would be terribly embarrassed if Johnson rejected his offer, Kennedy must have been confident that Lyndon would accept.

That Jack and Bobby hesitated considerably over the next six hours before Jack announced Johnson's selection is more credible. When they informed principal campaign advisers, all hell broke loose. Kenneth O'Donnell was "so furious" that he "could hardly talk. I thought of the promises we had made to the labor leaders and civil rights groups. . . . I felt that we had been doublecrossed." O'Donnell told Kennedy it was "the worst mistake" he had ever made; he was going against all the people who had supported him. When labor leaders Walter Reuther, Arthur Goldberg, Jack Conway, and Alex Rose met with Jack, Bobby, and O'Donnell that morning, Bobby was "very distressed," O'Donnell "looked like a ghost," and Jack was "very nervous." Jack was defensive: he explained that Johnson "would be so mean as Majority Leader—that it was much better having him as Vice President where you could control him." Jack also said that he offered Johnson the job but couldn't "see any reason in the world why he would want it." Jack Conway told Bobby, "If you do this, you're going to fuck everything up." Afterward, Goldberg and Reuther talked about a floor fight to block Lyndon's nomination. Bobby Kennedy called John Kenneth Galbraith, who was just getting into bed after being up all night, and asked him to get back to the convention hall to help quiet rebellious delegates.[89]

Meanwhile, Lyndon also had to convince some political allies that he should take the vice presidency. He asked John Stennis, Governor Buford Ellington of Tennessee, Robert Kerr of Oklahoma, Price Daniel, Clinton Anderson, George Smathers, and Ed Weisel, among others, to talk with him about going on the ticket. Kerr, Daniel, and Anderson were opposed. "I'll go get my long rifle," Kerr said. ". . . If you accept, I'll shoot you right between the eyes." "We can't carry this boy [Kennedy]," Daniel said. Anderson told Lyndon: "You're young. You'll be elected some day yourself. Don't take a chance on getting messed up now." Warned not to trade the powers of the Majority Leader for the emptiness of the vice presidency, Lyndon replied: "Power is where power goes." Sam Rayburn took Kerr into the bathroom. When they emerged, Kerr said, "Lyndon, if Jack Kennedy asked you to be his running mate, and if you don't take it, I'll shoot you right between the eyes."[90]

Facing more serious opposition than Lyndon, the Kennedys, according to Robert's recollection, tried to get Johnson to withdraw. Between two and four in the afternoon, Bobby Kennedy remembered seeing Lyndon twice: first, to feel him out, and then to propose his withdrawal. Bobby had no clear memory of the first meeting, but the second was etched sharply in his mind. He and Lyndon sat alone on a couch in Johnson's room. Bobby told him what he and Jack agreed he should say: "There was going to be a lot of opposition, that it was going to be unpleasant, that we were going to have trouble with the liberals." Jack "didn't think that he wanted to go through that kind of unpleasant fight. But [JFK] wanted to have him play an important role, and he could run the party—the idea being that . . . he could get a lot of his own people in, and then, if he wanted to be President in eight years or something, he would have the machinery where he could run for President or do whatever he wanted." Bobby remembered how Johnson turned on this sad look, and "I thought he'd burst into tears. I don't know whether it was just an act or anything. But he just shook, and tears came into his eyes, and he said, 'I want to be Vice President, and if the President will have me, I'll join with him in making a fight for it.' " Kennedy said, "Well, then, that's fine. He wants you to be Vice President if you want to be Vice President."[91]

Phil Graham and others remembered the Bobby Kennedy visits differently. They recalled that when Bobby showed up the first time, he saw Sam Rayburn. Bobby suggested to Sam that Lyndon be Democratic National Chairman instead of Vice President. "Rayburn is reported to have given Bobby a long look and answered 'Shit.' " Lady Bird and Graham persuaded Lyndon not to see Bobby. Instead, they agreed that Graham call Jack, and say that Lyndon would only take the nomination if Jack "drafts" him. Kennedy told Graham that "he was in a general mess because some liberals were against LBJ." He was in a meeting about the matter just then, and he asked Graham to call back for a decision in three minutes. When Graham got back to him, Kennedy said, "It's all set. . . . Tell Lyndon I want him." Graham did and left to make another call. Shortly after, Lyndon summoned Graham "to say that Bobby Kennedy had been back down to see Rayburn some twenty minutes before (say, roughly, 3:00) and had said Jack would phone directly. No call had come and LBJ was considerably on edge." At 3:30, Graham telephoned Kennedy. When told what Bobby had said, he promised to call Lyndon at once. "He then again mentioned opposition to LBJ and asked for my judgement." Graham advised that southern gains would more than offset liberal losses, and argued against any change in plans. Kennedy "agreed about the finality of things."[92]

Johnson took Kennedy's call sitting on a bed. Kennedy read a press release about the vice presidency to Johnson. Lyndon's only response was: "Do you really want me?" Kennedy said, "Yes," and Lyndon said, "Well, if you really want me, I'll do it."

Shortly after 4:00, while he was trying to reach Bobby Kennedy about seconding speeches for Lyndon, Graham received another summons from Johnson. He found Lyndon "in a high state of nerves . . . about to jump out of his skin. He shouted at me that Bobby Kennedy had just come in and told Rayburn and him that there was much opposition and that Lyndon should withdraw for the sake of the Party." Prodded by Rayburn, Graham called Kennedy again. " 'Jack,' I said, 'Bobby is down here and is telling the Speaker and Lyndon that there is opposition and Lyndon should withdraw.' 'Oh,' said Jack, as calmly as though we were discussing the weather, 'that's all right; Bobby's been out of touch and doesn't know what's been happening.' " Kennedy then asked that Lyndon make a statement right away, adding that he had just finished making his. After a brief conversation with Lyndon, Jack asked to speak with Bobby, "who walked in looking dead tired. . . . As Graham left the room, he heard Bobby say, 'Well, it's too late now,' and half slam down the phone." Looking as if they had just survived a plane crash, Lyndon and Lady Bird stood in the entrance hall of their suite still reluctant to make a statement to the press. With much bravado, Graham told Lyndon: "Throw your shoulders back and your chin out and go out and make that announcement." As Graham watched them "rising to stand on some chairs . . . their faces metamorphosed into enthusiasm and confidence." [93]

Phil Graham believed that Bobby Kennedy had acted on his own in trying to keep Johnson off the ticket. Bobby later disputed Graham's conclusion. He said that Graham's account on this point "flabbergasted" him. "Obviously, with the close relationship between my brother and me, I wasn't going down to see if he would withdraw just as a lark on my own." In 1964, the journalist Theodore White said he was "certain that Robert Kennedy was *not* acting on his own, but had been snarled by a confusion of communications and messages in a turbulent day." Jim Rowe agreed. He told Merle Miller: "My own theory is that Bobby had left Jack Kennedy's suite to tell Johnson that there was a hell of a lot of pressure against him. While he was gone, Graham called Jack and then Jack called Lyndon. But Bobby didn't know that Jack had just called and made the final commitment. It was just a matter of bad timing, but Johnson thought that Bobby was out to get him, to do him in." White and Rowe were probably right. But after Lyndon had gone into the corridor to announce his candidacy and Bobby had finished speaking to Jack, he said to Rowe: "Jim, don't you think it is a terrible mistake? It should have been Symington or [Henry] Jackson [of Washington]." Rowe replied: "You can't win with either Symington or Jackson. . . . The only two fellows that can help you are either Johnson or Humphrey." But Rowe's response didn't register on Bobby, who said: "Well, if we weren't so tired, this wouldn't have happened." As Jack later told Myer Feldman, we will never know the full story of how Johnson became the vice-presidential nominee. [94]

On the evening of the 14th, Lyndon's name went before the convention. Liberal delegates, particularly from Michigan, were still threatening to object. Phil Graham dissuaded liberal attorney Joe Rauh from nominating Minnesota's Orville Freeman. The balloting began, and when the roll call reached Massachusetts, John McCormack proposed a voice vote on Johnson's nomination. Eager to avoid embarrassing objections, the Kennedys arranged with McCormack and Governor LeRoy Collins of Florida, the convention chairman, to suspend the rules and permit the voice vote. When Collins put the proposition to the delegates, the shouted "ayes" and "nays" seemed about evenly divided. But Collins declared that two-thirds of the delegates had concurred and Senator Lyndon B. Johnson had been nominated for the vice presidency by acclamation.[95]

The next day, before delivering their acceptance speeches, Kennedy and Johnson met with black delegates at the Biltmore Hotel. Although the Kennedys had encouraged the convention to approve the most liberal civil rights plank in Democratic party history, liberals saw Johnson's selection as evidence of backtracking or an intention to accommodate the South. To dispel the belief that Kennedy was adopting a "Southern strategy," Lyndon assured black delegates that he was "going to run on the platform that this convention adopted. . . . I assure you from the bottom of my heart that I have done my dead-level best to make progress in the field of civil rights—that I have done it against great odds, both in the Senate and at home, at times." He promised that if they were elected in November, "you will find . . . that you have made more progress in 4 years than you have made in the last 104 years. . . . I want to campaign from coast to coast on the platform of this convention."

Liberal theologian Reinhold Niebuhr told Arthur Schlesinger, Jr., that if the Democrats had nominated a northern liberal for Vice President after adopting so strong a civil rights plank, it would have "confirmed the South in its sense of isolation and persecution. But the nomination of a southern candidate who accepted the platform, including the civil rights plank, restored the Democrats as a national party and associated the South with the pursuit of national goals."[96]

In the six weeks before the traditional Labor Day start to the presidential race, Kennedy and Johnson made campaign plans. The Kennedys wanted Lyndon to focus on the South and West and Jack on the industrial states. Johnson was to be a "regional candidate" who would "solidify the South . . . attract the conservatives and . . . give an atmosphere of soundness" to the ticket. Johnson's advisers urged him instead to be a "national candidate" who went into all sections of the country and faced elements in the party and the electorate that viewed him with suspicion. Likewise, they felt that Kennedy should go into the South and meet the religious issue head on. Jim Rowe particularly pressed the idea of Johnson as a national candidate, arguing that if they lost the 1960 election, Johnson would then be in a better position to win the presidency in 1964. Rowe also urged Johnson to have his own campaign staff. This would allow them "to handle" Bobby Kennedy, who had developed a reputation as a "ruthless son of a bitch." He had no compunctions about ripping into governors, mayors, or any other high official that dissatisfied him. Rowe wanted to keep Bobby at arm's length, and he believed that John Connally, who could "be fully as 'hard nosed' as Bobby," should become Lyndon's campaign manager.[97]

At the end of July, Lyndon went to the Kennedy Compound at Cape Cod to discuss campaign strategy and the congressional session beginning on August 8. Some of Kennedy's aides privately criticized Johnson's overbearing manner and verbosity during the two days of talks, but Kennedy considered the meeting a success. Lyndon's ebullience at a joint press conference, in which he did most of the talking, pleased Kennedy, who felt it dispelled talk of any incompatibility between them. Johnson encouraged the picture of mutual congeniality in a press release to Texas papers: Texans like Johnson and New Englanders like Kennedy shared a sense of pride, tradition, and fearlessness that Texans would see for themselves when Kennedy came to the Lone Star state.[98]

The press handout reflected a decision that Kennedy would campaign in the South. But it spoke principally to the belief that Lyndon had to do a selling job for the ticket in the South without alienating northern liberals. Sometime during the two-day meeting, Kennedy had asked Robert Troutman, Jr., a prominent Georgia Democrat, to invite leading southern Democrats to an informal meeting with Lyndon in Nashville. Kennedy explained that Lyndon was coming there to tell a convention of Young Democrats that "though he was a Southerner . . . he had to be more an American than a Southerner." It "had some racial connotation at that time and it was a very sensitive thing," Troutman said later. In his speech, Lyndon stressed his determination to speak "as an American to Americans—whatever their region, religion or race."[99]

Troutman arranged to have between fifteen and twenty-five leading southern Democrats, including governors, senators, and congressmen, come to Nashville. Lyndon's private talk with these southern politicians differed from what he said publicly. Republican congressman Walter Judd heard that behind closed doors Lyndon told his southern friends: " 'You should vote for Kennedy and me despite all this bunk about ending racial segregation, the Supreme Court decision on integration of the schools, busing and the rest. You have to elect Kennedy in order to have me in the administration so I, your fellow-Southerner, can defeat his integration proposals.' "

Bill Moyers, a young staff member, later described Johnson as "a man of time and place" who "felt the bitter paradox of both." During the 1960 campaign, he gave Moyers "a vivid account of that southern schizophrenia he understood and feared. We were in Tennessee. During the motorcade, he spotted some ugly racial epithets scrawled on signs. Late that night in the hotel, when the local dignitaries had finished the last bottles of bourbon and branch water and departed, he started talking about those signs. 'I'll tell you what's at the bottom of it,' he said. 'If you can convince the lowest white man that he's better than the best colored man, he won't notice you picking his pocket. Hell, give him somebody to look down on, and he'll empty his pockets for you.' "[100]

During his visit to Nashville, Johnson asked Troutman to help him persuade Georgia senators Richard Russell and Herman Talmadge to support the Democratic ticket. With tears in his eyes, he described his affection and regard for Russell who had done so much for his career. As for Talmadge, Johnson described him as beholden to me for having tried to help him accomplish everything he ever wanted. When Troutman recited "chapter and verse" what Johnson had told him, Russell was amused at Lyndon's selling job, but indicated that he intended to sit out the election. Talmadge was more responsive to Lyndon's plea and publicly welcomed Kennedy and Johnson to Georgia when they campaigned there separately in the fall.[101]

In early August, Lyndon fixed his attention on the three-week congressional session that occupied him for the rest of the month. Although he promised to pass some "important needed legislation," including minimum wage, medical care for the aged, education, and housing bills, the session was a complete wash out. A coalition of Republicans and conservative southern Democrats, backed up by threats of Eisenhower vetoes, blocked passage of the Kennedy-Johnson legislative agenda. According to Theodore Sorensen, it embarrassed and embittered the Democratic candidates. Although they viewed the session as a setback in the campaign, it in fact proved to be of little consequence in the election. Indeed, just as Lyndon had overestimated the impact of his effective Senate Leadership on his bid for the presidency, so Kennedy and Johnson exaggerated the importance to voters of the rump meeting of Congress.[102]

At the beginning of September, people were more concerned about Kennedy's religion than the record of the 86th Congress. By early August, Johnson had received so much mail questioning a Catholic's suitability for the presidency that he had asked the Kennedy campaign for suggestions on a reply. Texas friends also predicted a tough fight for the state and said religion was the main problem. "We are just catching hell on that issue," one observer told Walter Jenkins. A telephone survey of 35,000 people in Houston, Dallas, and El Paso showed Richard Nixon, the Republican nominee, with a 52-48 percent lead over Kennedy. And this did not include a survey of rural areas, where "unrest" among Baptists and Church of Christ folks would make the Republican advantage even greater.[103]

The Reverend Dr. Norman Vincent Peale and one hundred and fifty other Protestant clergyman made Kennedy's religion the principal issue of the campaign on September 9. They announced that a Roman Catholic President would be "under extreme pressure by the hierarchy of his church" and "duty bound to admit to its direction." Lyndon responded that it was well to get this matter out in the open, where everyone can see it. He decried applying a religious test to office holding in the United States, and warned that it meant tearing up the Bill of Rights and the Constitution. It would ultimately lead to the exclusion of members of other faiths from the presidency. If Kennedy had been qualified to serve in the Armed Forces, where he had risked his life saving crew members of his PT boat, and in the House and the Senate, he was also suited to be President.[104]

As in West Virginia, Kennedy needed to confront the issue himself. Although Lyndon compared it to going through a minefield, in which Kennedy would have to watch his every step, Johnson urged him to accept an invitation to speak before the Greater Houston Ministerial Association on September 12. Arriving in Texas that morning, Kennedy and Johnson spoke in El Paso, Lubbock, and San Antonio. At the Alamo in San Antonio, signs saying "We want the Bible and the Constitution" and "We don't want the Kremlin or the Vatican" greeted them. Johnson embarrassed the pickets with the observation that when Jack Kennedy was saving those Americans [on PT-109], they didn't ask him what Church he belonged to." Ticking off the names of McCafferty, Bailey, and Carey as among those who died in the Alamo, Kennedy said, "But no one knows whether they were Catholic or not. For there was no religious test at the Alamo."[105]

Kennedy spoke to the ministers that evening at the Rice Hotel in Houston. As Theodore Sorensen remembered it, "a sense of tension and hostility hung in the air." Kennedy gave "the best speech of the campaign and one of the most important in his life." He declared his commitment to separation of church and state and opposition to public funding of church schools and ecclesiastical instruction to public officials on public policy. He said he did not speak for his church on public matters and his church did not speak for him. Before a state-wide television audience, Kennedy then answered a "barrage" of less than friendly questions. His poise and directness disarmed many critics and largely, though not entirely, freed him from the religious issue for the rest of the campaign. He even felt free to joke publicly about the matter. When Nixon chastised Harry Truman for telling southern Republicans to go to hell, Kennedy promised to wire the former President "that our side [must] try to refrain from raising the religious issue."[106]

Nixon and the Republicans shrewdly kept the issue alive by continually deploring efforts to discuss it. Throughout the rest of the cam-

paign, especially in the South, Lyndon hammered on the religious bigotry behind the opposition to Kennedy. He also attacked Nixon for failing
"to publicly repudiate those raising" the religious question and say that
he didn't want their support. White House counsel Bryce Harlow told
Nixon that he was "being religioned right out of this campaign." While
Nixon wouldn't discuss the matter directly, "Lyndon is talking religion
at every stop, all over the country . . . And you're just flat losing the
campaign on religion, and that's wrong. You should attack it, the hy-
pocrisy of it. . . . It's a calculated stance. Kennedy can't talk it. Lyndon
can and Lyndon's talking it." [107]

A lot of Johnson's calculated talk on religion came in a five-day whistle-
stop tour of the South beginning October 10. Former President Harry
Truman, who had used the back platform of a train so effectively in the
1948 campaign, urged Lyndon to do the same thing. Starting in Virginia, Johnson's tour covered 3500 miles across eight states, where he
gave sixty speeches. The eleven-car train, the *LBJ Victory Special*, or
"Cornpone Special," as some journalists dubbed it, was met by governors, senators, congressmen, and other state and local officials who shared
the back platform with Lyndon for a few stops along the way. The trip
was good political theater. Aides to Texas congressmen dressed in cov-
eralls positioned themselves throughout the crowd in Culpepper, Virginia, and led the cheers for Johnson. Lindy Boggs, wife of Louisiana
Congressman Hale Boggs, led an advance team of five other women
dressed in blue blazers, white pleated skirts and blouses, and red hats.
They flew from city to city to meet the train, where their presence helped
discourage opponents from more overt displays of antagonism to Kennedy and Johnson. Using southern songs played over loudspeakers and
homespun speeches to disarm audiences, Lyndon celebrated Democratic achievements, decried Nixon's unreliability, and compared the attack on Kennedy's Catholicism to prejudice against the South. [108]

Hecklers with signs declaring "LBJ Is a Friend of Socialism" and
"The *Yellow* Rose of Texas" showed Lyndon the limits of his influence
in the South. He worried especially about Texas, where the election was
a toss-up. At the end of September, he wired Fort Worth newspaper
publisher Amon Carter, "I need you as I have never needed you before."
Former congressman Lloyd Bentsen told Walter Jenkins that Texas
Democrats were broke and weren't getting money from their usual
sources. In mid-October, Lyndon told John Connally he was "deeply
disturbed about Texas. . . . We just must not win the nation and lose
Texas. Imagine when we win how the next Administration will look upon
us." [109]

Jim Rowe remembered that Johnson "was wound up tight like a top
and I think the ever haunting fear of losing Texas never left him for a
second." Johnson's tension over the outcome of the campaign spilled

over into private tirades at his staff. Two weeks after the election, Rowe told Hubert Humphrey that "privately, he [Lyndon] was pretty awful. The worst in him came out in the back rooms and why his staff did not kill him I do not know. They almost did several times." Almost anything could touch him off: a disappointingly small crowd, a tight speaking schedule, a schedule with too much free time, an encounter with someone he didn't like, a podium that didn't meet his exact specifications for reading a speech or being seen by his audience, a failure of the loudspeaker system, a missing change of clothes, or practically anything that other less temperamental or intense personalities would have ignored. Johnson was "a man of some violence, a very violent temper, and no person, even though he was volunteering his services, wanted to have that temper vented on him," one aide on the campaign trail in 1960 recalled. When Johnson tried to bully Kennedy into rushing to make an appointment with Sam Rayburn, Jack told him: "I believe you're cracking up. If you do, where do you want me to send it?" Johnson's behavior so incensed Jim Rowe that he told him he was "a Mogul emperor. He didn't like that a damn bit." After the election Rowe and Johnson "just more or less drifted apart." [110]

Yet whatever the difficulties with him in private, "he ran a tremendous public campaign," Jim Rowe said. He celebrated "the Boston-Austin Axis," the union of North, South, and West; attacked Nixon and religious prejudice; praised Kennedy; pressured southern Democrats into working for the ticket; and mustered all possible support in Texas. Johnson gave the Kennedys reason to feel that they had chosen an effective running mate. [111]

No single incident in the campaign involving Johnson did more to help the ticket than the public abuse of Lyndon and Lady Bird by rightwing opponents in Dallas four days before the election. Lyndon confronted a mob of angry protestors at a downtown hotel on November 4. Led by Dallas congressman Bruce Alger, Texas's only Republican representative, they carried signs denouncing Johnson as a Carpetbagger controlled by Yankee Socialists. As Lyndon and Lady Bird walked across the street from the Baker to the Adolphus Hotel and then through its lobby to an elevator, the crowd, partly of Junior League women, "the Mink Coat Mob," some called it, verbally and physically assaulted the Johnsons, hitting Lady Bird on the head with a picket sign and spitting at them.

Although Lyndon was genuinely outraged by the abuse, he immediately saw the political advantage in Texas and throughout the South in the televised pictures of a shrieking mob assaulting an unprotected vice-presidential candidate. Indeed, as they inched forward through the crowd, Johnson asked the police to leave: " 'If the time has come when I can't walk through the lobby of a hotel in Dallas with my lady without a police escort, I want to know it.' " When Lady Bird lost her temper and started to answer one of the hecklers, "Mr. Johnson kind of put his hand over her mouth and stopped that and brought her right along." The Johnsons could have made their way through the Adolphus lobby in five minutes, one observer recalls. But they "took thirty minutes . . . and it was all being recorded and photographed for television and radio and the newspapers, and he knew it and played it for all it was worth." Bill Moyers said that Johnson "could never have calculated that scene or fixed that situation or arranged for it. He didn't know how he was going to carry Texas. . . . If he could have thought this up, he would have thought it up. Tried to invent it. But the moment it happened, he knew." He used the incident to tar the Republicans as extremists and persuade Richard Russell to do some last minute speaking for the ticket in Texas and South Carolina.[112]

On November 8, Kennedy won the presidency by 112,881 votes out of 66,832,818 cast. The electoral college showed a more decisive margin of 303 to 219. Seven of the old Confederate states—Alabama, Arkansas, Georgia, Louisiana, North and South Carolina, and Texas—went Democratic. Florida, Tennessee, and Virginia voted Republican, while Mississippi gave a plurality to an independent segregationist ticket. Texas favored Kennedy and Johnson by only 46,233 votes out of 2,311,670 cast. At the same time, Lyndon won his Senate race against Republican John Tower, but by only 56.5 percent to 43.5 percent, 1,210,000 to 936,000 votes.

Kennedy's effectiveness in a series of debates with Nixon, his sympathy call in October to Mrs. Martin Luther King, Jr., over her husband's unjust jailing in Georgia, and his attractiveness as a political leader alongside of Nixon were decisive elements in the election. But no one in the Kennedy camp discounted the importance of Lyndon's contribution, especially in the South, where he skillfully emphasized all the Democrats had done for the region without publicly using racist appeals to win white votes. When Robert Kennedy called Lyndon to say that he was going to call the Georgia judge urging that King be given bail, Lyndon replied, "Tell Jack that we'll ride it through down here some way, and at least he's on the right side." As Joseph Kennedy had predicted immediately after Jack had chosen Johnson as his running mate, "Don't worry, Jack. . . . Everyone will be saying that this was the smartest thing you ever did." If it was not the smartest, it certainly was one of the shrewdest. It is doubtful that a midwestern running mate would have given him the help he needed in the South.[113]

Lyndon responded to their victory with mixed feelings. He was exhilarated by the important part he played in the campaign, and particularly at having helped put Texas in the Democratic column for the first time since 1948. Yet he also had a sense of frustration at being elected Vice

President rather than President. On election night, after he knew they had won, he "looked as if he'd lost his last friend on earth. . . . I don't think I ever saw a more unhappy man," one of his secretaries recalls. He expressed his distress and rivalry with Kennedy during a telephone call: " 'I see you are losing Ohio,' " he said to Jack. " 'I am carrying Texas and we are doing pretty well in Pennsylvania.' " "Doesn't that sound like him?" Jim Rowe told Hubert Humphrey.[114]

Everyone who knew Lyndon well would have agreed. He was a difficult, overbearing personality who struggled with inner demons that drove and tormented him. He had to be the best, outshine all the competition, and win at almost any cost. However small or large the stakes—whether jousting for control of student government in college, running for Speaker of the Little Congress, the U.S. House of Representatives and Senate, or building a radio and TV empire—the premium was on winning by fair means and foul. He balanced his actions against the knowledge that other political leaders and businessmen did similar things. Indeed, he never could have carried off his tainted political and financial gains in an atmosphere of genuine civic virtue. His electoral and business practices were not all that exceptional in the thirty years after he entered the public arena in 1931. What set him apart from others, however, was the extent or degree of his skulduggery. When he broke campaign spending laws, stuffed ballot boxes, cut a political or business deal, it was always just a bit more, a little larger than what others were ready to do.

Yet Johnson also knew that backroom dealings were not the only means by which Texas and American politics generally proceeded. He saw plenty of politicians and businessmen who were above board, had fine careers, earned a solid living, and enjoyed an inner peace and the respect of their fellow citizens. But being a successful politician or earning an ample living or holding the regard of compatriots was not enough for him. He needed to have the best career, to be among the richest, to be revered rather than respected. It was a case of unbounded ambition or of needing to make up for some inner want, some sense of unrelenting deprivation that drove him forward to ever larger things. As a man of exceptional intelligence and insight into others, he must have occasionally puzzled over his own private struggle—his incessant reach for prominence and wealth. Yet it was never enough to hold him back. He convinced himself that no one played by the rules, and up to a point he was right. But he exaggerated the stealth and unscrupulousness of public officials as a way to rationalize his own improprieties.

The fact that he had turned his power and influence to good for many across Texas, the South, and the entire United States also eased his conscience. In the twenty-five years from 1935 to 1960 Johnson left an indelible mark on American life. His work at the National Youth Administration resulted in public structures and schooling and training for young people that enriched the lives of thousands of Texans. The dams on the Lower Colorado River, which he did so much to build, provided flood control, conservation, and public power, the electricity for farms and small towns that ended much of the drudgery of rural life in south-central Texas. The public works projects he helped fund in the thirties, forties, and fifties expanded the economy and produced airports, hospitals, roads, post offices, and school and university facilities that served all Americans. The low-cost housing, of which he was such a warm advocate, sheltered millions of the country's least affluent citizens. The expanded Social Security benefits and increased minimum wage and farm subsidies that he consistently favored made a significant difference to the elderly, unskilled workers, and farmers. The Civil Rights Act of 1957, which he led through the Senate, was a prelude to the greatest advances for black Americans in the country's history. The admission of Hawaii to the Union, for which he deserves considerable credit, fulfilled longstanding American commitments to equal treatment and rights for all citizens. The creation of the National Aeronautics and Space Administration, which was as much his doing as that of any government official, promised to expand the frontiers of human understanding for as far into the future as anyone could see. Johnson, the most powerful Majority Leader in Senate history, in one of the striking ironies of his career, democratized the upper house by reducing the importance of seniority in its organization and governance.

If Lyndon Johnson demanded and took much, he also gave much in return. No elected Federal official worked harder than Johnson and few held a deeper concern for the national well-being. However powerful the self-serving impulses that led him into unsavory deeds and pragmatic alliances with oil interests and anti-labor and anti-black conservatives, he had a genuine commitment to New Deal, Fair Deal programs, the liberal nationalism of the thirties and forties, that transformed America. He was particularly instrumental in encouraging Federal programs that raised living standards in the South and weakened racial segregation, a system he considered unjust and incompatible with the region's movement into the mainstream of American economic and political life.

The origins of the war on poverty and Great Society programs can be found in the convictions and actions governing much of Johnson's behavior in the thirty years before he became President. Likewise the origins of Johnson's foreign policies, particularly his judgments on Vietnam and the means by which he led the country into the war, can be traced partly to the pre-presidential years described in this volume. Although his actions abroad would differ in both degree and kind from those of his predecessors, his reactions to what FDR, Rayburn, Truman, Eisenhower, and Dulles did in response to external threats form an indis-

pensable backdrop to Johnson's White House years. Roosevelt's maneuvering to build up U.S. forces, 1937–41, Rayburn's highhandedness in
driving the draft renewal law through the House in 1941,Truman's assertion of executive power in taking the country into the Korean fighting
in 1950, the Eisenhower-Dulles actions to topple Arbenz in Guatemala
in 1954, and Ike's requests for congressional endorsements of potential
military moves in Asia and the Middle East made indelible impressions
on Johnson that later shaped his thinking about overseas affairs.

As the Vice President elect in 1960, Johnson hoped to provide a measure of leadership uncommonly associated with that largely symbolic
office. He knew how little his predecessors had accomplished in what
John Adams called "the most insignificant office that ever the invention
of man contrived or his imagination conceived." But as a congressional
secretary, an NYA administrator, a congressman, and a senator, he had
achieved things others had not thought possible. He aimed to convert
the vice presidency into a vehicle for gains the country would not soon
forget. And should the presidency be within his reach after a vice-
presidential term, he would challenge the country to fulfill its boldest
dreams. For Lyndon Johnson, politics had been a difficult, sometimes
dirty business. But most of all, it was a vocation in which a fallible man
could rise from the obscurity of the Texas Hill Country to the second
office of the land and along the way do extraordinary things.

Sources

Manuscript Collections

Alabama Department of History and Archives, Montgomery,
    William B. Bankhead Papers

Eugene C. Barker Texas History Center, Austin,
    John C. Granbery Papers
    Lyndon B. Johnson Biographical File and Scrapbooks
    Maury Maverick, Sr., Papers

Baylor University, Waco, Texas
    Ruth Shick Montgomery Papers
    Pat Neff Papers

Boise State University, Boise, Idaho
    Frank Church Papers

Cornell University, Ithaca, New York
    Irving M. Ives Papers

Dakota State College, Madison, South Dakota
    Karl E. Mundt Papers

Dwight D. Eisenhower Library, Abilene, Kansas
    Christian Herter Papers
    John F. Dulles Papers
    Dwight D. Eisenhower Papers
     Diaries on microfilm
     Papers As President: Administrative Series
     Papers As President: Ann Whitman Diary Series
     President's Official Files
     President's Personal Files
    White House Office: Office of the Staff Secretary:
     Legislative Meeting Series
    White House Office: Office of the Staff Secretary: L. Arthur Minich

Federal Bureau of Investigation, Washington, D.C.
Thomas G. Corcoran Wiretaps
J. Edgar Hoover Official and Confidential Files
Lyndon B. Johnson: Main File

Federal Communications Commission, Washington, D.C.
Records of Radio Station KTBC, Austin, Texas
Records of Radio Station KVET, Austin, Texas
Records of Television Station KTBC, Austin, Texas
Records of Television Station KWTX, Waco, Texas

Herbert Hoover Library, West Branch, Iowa
Bourke Hickenlooper Papers
Herbert Hoover Papers
Post-Presidential Items
Lewis L. Strauss Papers

Lyndon B. Johnson Library, Austin, Texas
John D. Coffer Papers
Family Correspondence: Rebekah B. Johnson Papers
Arthur E. Goldschmidt Papers
Lewis L. Gould Papers
Welly K. Hopkins Papers
Department of Interior Files, Record Group 48, Microfilm
from the National Archives
Lyndon B. Johnson Papers
Appointment File, Diary Back Up
House of Representatives Papers
LBJ Archives: Congressional File
LBJ Archives: Famous Names
LBJ Archives: Selected Names
LBJ Archives: Subject File
House of Representatives Scrapbooks on Microfilm
Materials from the Franklin D. Roosevelt Library on Microfilm
Navy Unofficial Personnel File
Notes and Transcripts of Conversations
Pre-Presidential Confidential File
Pre-Presidential Diary, January 1959–March 1961
Pre-Presidential Memo File
Senate Papers
Senate Political Files
Statements of Lyndon B. Johnson
White House Central Files
White House Famous Names
World War II Diary
Luther E. Jones, Jr., Papers
Richard M. Kleberg Papers
Richard M. Kleberg Scrapbooks, 1931–1933, Microfilm
Gene Latimer Papers
Lower Colorado River Authority Papers

Charles Marsh Papers
National Youth Administration Papers
Dorothy J. Nichols Manuscript
Office Files of White House Aides: Walter Jenkins
Office Files of White House Aides: Mildred Stegall
Wright Patman Papers
Drew Pearson Papers
Southwest Texas State University Papers
John L. Steele Papers
Alvin J. Wirtz Papers

Library of Congress, Washington, D.C.
Joseph and Stewart Alsop Papers
Association of Former Members of Congress Papers
Tom Connally Papers
Thomas G. Corcoran Papers
William O. Douglas Papers
James A. Farley Papers
Harold L. Ickes Manuscript Diaries and Papers

Minnesota Historical Society, St. Paul, Minnesota
Hubert H. Humphrey Papers

National Archives, Washington, D.C.
Department of the Navy Records, Military Archives Division
National Youth Administration Papers, Record Group 119

New England College, Henniker, New Hampshire
Styles Bridges Papers

Princeton University, Princeton, New Jersey
Arthur Krock Papers

Sam Rayburn Library, Bonham, Texas
Sam Rayburn Papers on Microfilm

Franklin D. Roosevelt Library, Hyde Park, New York
Harry Hopkins Papers
Henry Morgenthau, Jr., Manuscript Diaries and Papers
Eleanor Roosevelt Papers
Franklin D. Roosevelt Papers
  Official Files
  President's Personal Files
  President's Secretary's Files
James H. Rowe, Jr., Papers
Henry A. Wallace Papers on Microfilm
Aubrey Williams Papers

Southwest Texas State University Library, San Marcos, Texas
Cecil Evans Papers

Syracuse University, Syracuse, New York
Fulton Lewis, Jr., Papers

Middle Tennessee State University, Murfreesboro, Tennessee

Albert A. Gore Papers

Sam Houston Regional Texas State Library, Liberty, Texas
Martin Dies Papers

Harry S. Truman Library, Indpendence, Missouri
Tom C. Clark Papers
William L. Clayton Papers
Clark Clifford Papers
David D. Lloyd Papers
Stuart Symington Papers
Harry S. Truman Papers
Appointment Books
Official Files
Post-Presidential Office Files
President's Personal Files
President's Secretary's Files

University of Alabama, Tuscaloosa,
Lister Hill Papers

University of Arkansas, Fayetteville,
J. William Fulbright Papers
Oren Harris Papers

University of Georgia, Athens
Richard B. Russell Papers and additional papers in Winder, Georgia

University of Houston, Houston, Texas
James V. Allred Papers

University of North Carolina, Chapel Hill, North Carolina
Johathan Daniels Papers
Sam Ervin Papers

University of Oregon, Eugene
Wayne Morse Papers
Richard L. Neuberger Papers

University of Virginia, Charlottesville,
Harry F. Byrd, Sr., Papers

University of Wyoming, Laramie,
Joseph O'Mahoney Papers

Wayne State University, Detroit, Michigan
Walter P. Reuther Papers

State Historical Society of Wisconsin, Madison,
Alexander Wiley Papers

Oral Histories

Boston University Library, Boston, Massachusetts
John W. McCormack, Nov. 27, 1970

Dwight D. Eisenhower Library, Abilene, Kansas
    Herbert Brownell, 1967–68
    Edward T. Dicker, Dec. 23, 1969
    Allan Shivers, Dec. 23, 1969

Lyndon B. Johnson Library, Austin, Texas
    "A Discussion Conducted by William S. White with a Group from
        Lyndon Johnson's Days as Director of the NYA," n.d., 1968
    Robert S. Allen, May 30, 1969
    Clinton Anderson, May 20, 1969
    Robert B. Anderson, July 8, 1969
    Malcolm G. Bardwell, Oct. 17, 1968
    Levette J. "Joe" Berry, Dec. 10, 1985
    W. Sherman Birdwell, April, n.d., 1965, Oct. 21, 1970,
        February 9, 15, 1979
    Merrell Blackman, Nov. 15, 1979
    James Blundell, Oct. 29, 1974
    Charles Boatner, Dec. 17, 1968, May 21, 1969, June 1, 1976
    Paul Bolton, April 6, 1981
    Percy Brigham, April, n.d., 1965
    Albert Brisbin, Feb. 6, 1979
    Marietta Moody Brooks, Sept. 15, 1981
    George R. Brown, April 6, 1968, Aug. 6, 1969, July 11, 1977
    Richard R. Brown, July 25, 1978
    Russell M. Brown, Jan. 10, 1978
    Raymond Buck, May 27, 1969
    Cecil Burney, Nov. 26, 1968
    Horace Busby, April 23, 1981
    Robert W. Calvert, May 6, 1971
    Elizabeth Carpenter, Dec. 3, 1968
    Leslie Carpenter, Feb. 6, 1969
    Clifton C. Carter, Oct. 1, 9, 1968
    John Brooks Casparis, Jan. 7, 1982
    James E. Chudars, Oct. 2, 1981
    Frank Church, May 1, 1969
    Tom C. Clark, Oct. 7, 1969
    Earle C. Clements, Oct. 24, 1974, Dec. 6, 1977
    James P. Coleman, April 29, 1972
    Donald C. Cook, June 30, 1969, Oct. 1, 1981
    John J. Corson, July 17, 1978
    Ben Crider, Aug. 1, 1968
    Ernest Cuneo, April 23, 1970
    Price Daniel, June 5, 1970
    Jonathan Daniels, March 6, 1971
    William H. Darden, Dec. 6, 1974
    Willard Deason, April 11, 1969, Aug. 8, 10, 1978
    Helen Gahagan Douglas, Nov. 10, 1969
    Paul Douglas, Nov. 1, 1974

Clifford and Virginia Durr, March 1, 1975
Virginia Foster Durr, Oct. 17, 1967
L. T. (Tex) Easley, May 4, 1979
Georgia Cammack Edgeworth, Dec. 17, 1981
Louise Casparis Edwards, Jan. 20, 1982
Truman and Wilma Fawcett, April 21, 1971
Truman Fawcett, July 2, 1975
Sam Fore, Jr., Jan. 20, 1965
Mrs. Sam Fore, Jr., July 12, 1971
Abe Fortas, Aug. 14, 1969
Gordon Fulcher, Nov. 22, 1968
E. B. Germany, May 24, 1969
Sim Gideon, March 21, Oct. 3, 1968
Roswell L. Gilpatrick, Jan. 19, 1972
Arthur E. Goldschmidt and Elizabeth Wickenden, June 3, 1969
Elizabeth W. Goldschmidt, Nov. 6, 1974
E. Ernest Goldstein, Dec. 9, 1968
Ed Gossett, Aug. 18, 1969
Bertha Allman Graef, Oct. 20, 1982
Callan Graham, Aug. 10, 1978
Elmer Graham, April, n.d., 1965
H. M. Greene, Jan. 21, 1965
James C. Hagerty, Nov. 16, 1971
Walter G. Hall, June 30, 1969
Estelle Harbin, Nov. 10, 1977
D. B. Hardeman, Feb. 26, March 12, 1969, Jan. 19, 1977
Bryce Harlow, Feb. 28, 1979, May 6, 1979
Houston Harte, Sept. 27, 1968
Albert C. Harzke, Nov. 27, 1979
Jessie Hatcher, March 28, 1968
Brooks Hays, Oct. 5, 1971
F. Edward Hebert, July 15, 1969
Charles F. Herring, Oct. 4, 24, 1968
Lister Hill, Feb. 1, 1971
Henry Hirshberg, Oct. 17, 1968
Anna Rosenberg Hoffman, Feb. 17, 1977
Welly K. and Alice Hopkins, June 9, Dec. 1, 1977
Welly K. Hopkins, May 11, 1965, Nov. 14, 1968, June 9, 1977
Ardis C. Hopper, Nov. 6, 1979
Walter C. Hornaday, April 13, 1970
Solis Horwitz, June 9, 1969
Lorena and Allie T. Hughes, April 30, 1965
Hubert H. Humphrey, Aug. 17, 1971, June 20, June 21, 1977
Daniel K. Inouye, April 18, 1969
Henry Jackson, March 13, 1978
Robert M. Jackson, April 5, 1965
W. Ervin "Red" James, Feb. 17, 1978
Leon Jaworski, Dec. 23, 1968

Walter Jenkins, Aug. 14, 1970, May 13, Aug. 12, Sept. 16, 1982, Jan. 18,
    July 22, Sept. 22, Oct. 6, 1983, April 18, 24, 25, July 12, July 19,
    Aug. 30, 1984
Mrs. Alvin Jensen, Oct. 31, 1968
Alfred T. "Boody" Johnson, Nov. 27, 1979
Lyndon Baines Johnson, "The Hill Country: Lyndon Johnson's Texas,"
    May 9, 1966
Lyndon Baines Johnson, "Remarks to College Officials," April 27, 1970
Lyndon Baines Johnson, "Conversation with Old Friends," April 27, 1970
Lyndon Baines and Lady Bird Johnson, Sept. 18, 1972
Luther E. Jones, Jr., June 13, 1969, Oct. 14, 1977
Marvin Jones, March 22, 1969
William H. Jordan, Jr., Dec. 5, 1974
Edward Joseph, Aug. 27, 1971, Feb. 23, 1978
Carroll Keach, April, n.d., 1965, July 10, 1969
Claud Kellam, May 10, 1965
Jesse Kellam, April, n.d., 1965, Feb. 26, 1970
Mylton L. Kennedy, May 9, 1980
Leon H. Keyserling, Jan. 9, 1969
John Koeniger, Nov. 12, 17, 1981
Eugenia Boehringer Lasseter, March 10, 1981
Gene Latimer, Aug. 17, 1971, Oct. 5, 1979, Dec. 12, 1981
Ray E. Lee, Feb. 14, 1968, Feb. 8, 1979
Erich Leinsdorf, March 18, 1969
Kittie Clyde Leonard, July 27, 1971
David E. Lilienthal, June 18, 1969
Otto Lindig, March, n.d., 1965
R. J. (Bob) Long, April 19, 1972
Russell Long, Feb. 22, June 20, 1977, July 26, 1978
Stuart M. Long, August 13, 1968
J. C. Looney, October 3, 1968
Kathryn Deadrich Looney, Jan. 21, 1965
John E. Lyle, Jr., April 13, 1984
Sarah McClendon, Feb. 16, 1972
John W. McCormack, Sept. 23, 1968
Cameron and Lucille McElroy, March 11, 1981
Ernest W. McFarland, Feb. 8, 1970
Gale McGee, Feb. 10, 1969
Felix McKnight, Oct. 4, 1979
Harry McPherson, Dec. 5, 1968
Warren G. Magnuson, March 14, 1978
Leonard Marks, June 15, 1970
Cecille Harrison Marshall, Feb. 19, 1976
Joe Mashman, March 28, 1974
Newton Minow, March 19, 1971
Robert H. Montgomery, Aug. 19, 1968
Booth Mooney, April 8, 1969, March 10, 1977
Paige Mulhollan, April 23, 1969

Robert W. Murphey, Nov. 22, 1983, Feb. 8, 1984
Dorothy J. Nichols, Sept. 24, 1968, Nov. 1, 1974
Lawrence F. O'Brien, Sept. 18, 1985
Robert Oliver, June 16, Nov. 29, 1977
Frank Oltorf, Aug. 3, 1971
Thomas P. O'Neill, Jan. 28, 1976
Edith H. Parker, Aug. 27, 1979
J. R. Parten, Feb. 28, 1976
Wright Patman, Aug. 11, 1972
Drew Pearson, April 10, 1969
General Carl Phinney, Oct. 11, 1968
R. L. (Bob) Phinney, Sept. 19, 1968
J. J. (Jake) Pickle, May 31, June 17, 1970, March 1, 1971
Ella SoRelle Porter, Nov. 28, 1979
Paul A. Porter, Oct. 2, 1970
Dorris Powell, April 18, 1978
C. W. Price, Jan. 12, 1984
William Proxmire, Feb. 4, 1986
Daniel Quill, Jan. 20, May 10, 1965
Mary Rather, Dec. 10, 1974, Jan. 13, 1975
Emmette Redford, Oct. 2, 1968, March 31, April 1, 1982
George Reedy, Dec. 12, 20, 1968, Feb. 14, 1972, June 7, 1975, May 21,
    Oct. 27, 1982, May 23, May 24, Aug. 16, 17, Dec. 20, 21, 1983, June 22,
    1984
William Reynolds, June 16, 1975
Horace E. Richards, Dec. 19, 1985
Fenner Roth, Sept. 23, 1968, Oct. 11, 1978
Payne Rountree, n.d.
Elizabeth Rowe, June 6, 1975
James H. Rowe, Jr., Sept. 9, 16, 1969, May 10, 1983
Josefa Baines Saunders, Dec. 28, 1964
Arthur Schlesinger, Jr., Nov. 4, 1971
Emily Crow Selden, Jan. 10, 16, 1980
Emmett Shelton, June 15, 1982
Polk and Nell Shelton, March 2, 1968
Allan Shivers, May 29, 1970
Gerald W. Siegel, May 26, June 9, 1969, Feb. 11, June 17, 1977
Byron Skelton, Oct. 15, 1968
Margaret Chase Smith, Aug. 20, 1975
Preston Smith, Nov. 8, 1979
Robert J. Smith, May 15, 1979
William R. Smith, Nov. 9, 1983
John Sparkman, Oct. 5, 1968, June 9, 1977
Max Starcke and Dorothy Palmie Starcke, Oct. 4, 1968
John C. Stennis, June 17, 1971
O. B. Summy, April 3, 1965
Stuart Symington, Oct. 6, 1976, Nov. 28, 1977
Herman Talmadge, July 17, 1969

Antonio J. Taylor, Nov. 23, 1969
Hobart Taylor, Sr., Jan. 29, 1972
Willie Day Taylor, Nov. 29, 1968
Donald S. Thomas, Feb. 3, 1980
R. E. Thomason, Oct.–Nov. 1968
Homer Thornberry, Dec. 21, 1970
Emma Boehringer Tooley, June 2, 1978
Grace Tully, Oct. 1, 1968
Carl Vinson, May 24, 1970
Louis F. Walter, Feb. 18, 1969
Margaret Mayer Ward, March 10, 1977
Harfield Weedin, Feb. 24, 1983
Edwin Weisl, Sr., May 13, 1969
William S. White, March 5, 1969, July 21, 1978
Mrs. William S. White, Feb. 17, 1976
R. Vernon Whiteside, Aug. 1, 6, 1985
Claude Wild, May 7, 1965, Oct. 3, 1968
John Wildenthal, March 14, 1975
James W. Wilson, Feb. 26, 1971
Wilton and Virginia Woods, Dec. 6, 1979, April 20, May 4, June 10, 1982,
  April 14, 1983
Warren Woodward, June 3, 1968, May 26, 1969
Milton R. Young, July 18, 1978

John F. Kennedy Library, Boston, Massachusetts
  Myer Feldman, 1966–1968

Library of Congress, Washington, D.C.
  Association of Former Members of Congress Papers: Oral Histories
    Wallace F. Bennett, Dec. 1, 1978
    John W. Bricker, Oct. 2, 1978
    Joseph S. Clark, Oct. 2, 1978
    J. William Fulbright, March 5, 1979
    Gale W. McGee, June 8, 1979

National Park Service Library, Johnson City, Texas
  Ava Johnson Cox, Jan. 22, 1976, March 2, 1978
  Tom Crider, Aug. 11, 1976
  Joe Crofts, n.d.
  John Dollahite, April 28, 1976
  Georgia Cammack Edgeworth, Aug. 12, 1976
  Stella Gliddon, Nov. 27, 1975, May 2, 1978
  Jessie Lambert, July 9, 1976
  Joe Payne, June 14, 1976
  Josefa Baines Saunders, March 4, 1976
  Clayton Stribling, March 20, 1976

North Texas State University, Denton, Texas
  Price Daniel, May 6, 1967
  John Miller, Jan. 5, 1972
  Robert W. Murphey, April 19, 1969

H. Grady Perry, April 8, 1968
Allan Shivers, Aug. 8, 1966

Harry S. Truman Library, Independence, Missouri
C. Girard Davidson, July 17–18, 1972
Walter H. Judd, April 13, 1970, Jan. 26, 1976
Donald J. MacDonald, Aug. 3, 1970
Stuart Symington, May 29, 1981

United States Senate Historical Office, Washington, D.C.
Leonard H. Ballard, Aug. 1983–Jan. 1984
Darrell St. Claire, Dec. 1976–April 1978
Grover W. Ensley, Oct. 29–Nov. 1, 1985
Pat M. Holt, Sept. 9–Dec. 12, 1980
Stewart E. McClure, Dec. 8, 1982–May 3, 1983
Carl M. Marcy, Sept. 14–Nov. 16, 1983
Floyd M. Riddick, June 26, 1978–Feb. 15, 1979
Howard E. Shuman, July 22–Oct 22, 1987
Ruth Young Watt, July 19–Nov. 9, 1979

University of Georgia, Athens,
Richard Russell Papers: Oral Histories
David William Brooks, March 25, 1971
John T. Carlton, March 5, 1971
William Proxmire, April 20, 1971
Robert Troutman, Jr., March 4, 1971
Samuel E. Vandiver, Jr., Feb. 23, 1971

University of North Carolina Library, Chapel Hill, North Carolina
Virginia Durr, March 13–15, 1975

Interviews

Robert G. Baker, no date, telephone interview with John Brice
Horace Busby, Nov. 16, 1987, with John Brice, Washington, D.C.
Horace Busby, July 16, 1988, Washington, D.C.
Edward Clark, Dec. 15, 1986, Austin, Texas
Clark Clifford, Jan. 8, 1988, Washington, D.C.
John B. Connally, June 30, 1988, Houston,Texas; Oct. 28, 1989, Bakersfield,
California
Ava Johnson Cox, June 24, 1985, Johnson City, Texas
Elizabeth Wickenden Goldschmidt, Dec. 20, 1986, New York City
Edwin O. Guthman, Nov. 13, 1987, Los Angeles, California
Eliot Janeway, Dec. 20, 1986, New York, New York
Lady Bird Johnson, July 3, 1963 with Blake Clark, in Ruth Shick Montgomery
Papers, Baylor University, Waco, Texas
Lady Bird Johnson, July 13–18, 1983, with John Brice, Austin, Texas
Lady Bird Johnson, Dec. 15, 1986, Austin, Texas

Jake Pickle, February 10, 1986, with Christie Bourgeois, Austin, Texas
Walt W. Rostow, July 1, 1988, Austin, Texas
Arthur Schlesinger, Jr., Aug. 3, 1987, New York, New York
Larry Temple, March 29, 1989, Austin, Texas
Brian VanDeMark, April 30, July 7, 1989, telephone conversations
James W. Wilson, April 8, 1988, Austin, Texas

Unpublished Books, Papers, and Theses

Christie Lynne Bourgeois, "Lyndon Johnson's Years with the National Youth Administration," Master's Thesis, University of Texas, Austin, 1986.
Louis S. Gomolak, "Prologue: LBJ's Foreign Affairs Background, 1908–1948," Ph.D. Dissertation, University of Texas, Austin, 1989.
Rebekah Baines Johnson, "The Johnsons: Descendants of John Johnson, A Revolutionary Soldier of Georgia: A Genealogical History," in LBJL.
Edwin W. Knippa, "The Early Political Life of Lyndon B. Johnson, 1931–1937," Master's Thesis, Southwest Texas State College, San Marcos, Texas, 1967.
Deborah Lynn Self, "The National Youth Administration in Texas, 1935–1939," Master's Thesis, Texas Tech University, Lubbock, Texas, 1974.
John M. Smith, "The History and Growth of the Southwest Texas State Teachers College," Master's Thesis, University of Texas, Austin, 1930.
Arthur Stehling, "A Country Lawyer: The Story of a Lifetime in Law, Business and Politics in the Texas Hill Country," book manuscript.
Michael Stoff, "The Lower Colorado River Authority," unpublished paper.

Newspapers, Periodicals, and Annuals

Among Friends of LBJ: A Newsletter of the Friends of the LBJ Library
Atlanta Journal & Constitution
Atlantic Monthly
Austin American
Austin American-Statesman
Austin Statesman
Blanco County Record
Blanco News
Broadcasting
Business Week
College Star, Southwest Texas State University, San Marcos, Texas
Dallas Morning News
Dallas Times Herald
Fort Worth Star-Telegram
Fredericksburg Radio Post
Gillespie County News
The Houston Post
The Houston Press

Johnson City Record-Courier
"Johnson City Walking Tour," Brochure of the National Park Service,
    Johnson City, Texas
Life
Los Angeles Times
The New Republic
New York Times
Newsweek
Pedagog, Annual, Southwest Texas State Teachers College, San Marcos, Texas
People
San Angelo Standard Times
San Antonio Express
Saturday Evening Post
Time
U.S. News & World Report
Wall Street Journal
Washington Post
Washington Evening Star

Books

Ambrose, Stephen E. *Eisenhower: Soldier and Candidate, 1890–1952*. New York,
    1983.
———. *Eisenhower: The President*. New York, 1984.
———. *Nixon: The Education of a Politician, 1913–1962*. New York, 1987.
Bailyn, Bernard, *et al. The Great Republic: A History of the American People*.
    Boston, 1985, 3rd ed.
Baker, Bobby. *Wheeling and Dealing: Confessions of a Capitol Hill Operator*.
    New York, 1978.
Bearss, Edwin C. *Historic Resource Study: Lyndon B. Johnson National Historic
    Site: Blanco & Gillespie Counties, Texas*. Denver, Colorado, 1971.
———. *Furnishing Study: Lyndon B. Johnson Birthplace-Cottage*. Denver, Colo-
    rado, 1979.
———. *Lyndon B. Johnson and the Hill Country, 1937–1963: Historic Resource
    Study*. Santa Fe, N.M., 1984.
Benson, James, and Anthony Sisto, comps. *The Student Editorials of Lyndon B.
    Johnson*. San Marcos, Texas, and New Brunswick, N.J., 1968.
Berman, Daniel M. *A Bill Becomes a Law: Congress Enacts Civil Rights Legis-
    lation*. New York, 1966 ed.
Blum, John M. *The Price of Vision: The Diary of Henry A. Wallace, 1942–1946*.
    Boston, 1973.
Burns, James MacGregor. *Roosevelt: The Lion and the Fox*. New York, 1956.
———. *Roosevelt: The Soldier of Freedom*. New York, 1970.
———. *The American Experiment*. Vol. 3: *The Crosswinds of Freedom*. New York,
    1989.
Brown, Norman D. *Hood, Bonnett, and Little Brown Jug: Texas Politics, 1921–
    1928*. College Station, Texas, 1984.

Caidin, Martin, and Edward Hymoff. *The Mission*. Philadelphia, 1964.

Carleton, Don E. *Red Scare!: Right-Wing Hysteria, Fifties Fanaticism and Their Legacy in Texas*. Austin, Texas, 1985.

Caro, Robert. *The Years of Lyndon Johnson: The Path to Power*. New York, 1982.

———. *The Years of Lyndon Johnson: Means of Ascent*. New York, 1990.

Carter, Paul A. *Another Part of the Twenties*. New York, 1977.

Chafe, William H. *The Unfinished Journey*. New York, 1986.

Congressional Record, 1937–1960. Selected Volumes. Washington, D.C., 1937–60.

Conkin, Paul. *Big Daddy from the Pedernales: Lyndon B. Johnson*. Boston, 1986.

Connery, Robert H. *The Navy and the Industrial Mobilization in World War II*. Princeton, N.J., 1951.

Dallek, Robert. *Franklin D. Roosevelt and American Foreign Policy, 1932–1945*. New York, 1979.

Daniels, Jonathan. *White House Witness, 1942–1945*. New York, 1975.

Davis, Kingsley. *Youth in the Depression*. Chicago, 1935.

Dickerson, Nancy. *Among Those Present: A Reporter's View of Twenty-five Years in Washington*. New York, 1976.

Divine, Robert A., ed. *The Johnson Years*. Vol. II: *Vietnam, the Environment, and Science*. Lawrence, Kansas, 1987.

Donovan, Robert J. *Conflict and Crisis: The Presidency of Harry S. Truman, 1945–1948*. New York, 1977.

Douglas, William O. *Go East, Young Man: The Early Years*. New York, 1974.

———. *The Court Years*. New York, 1980.

Dugger, Ronnie. *The Politician: The Drive for Power from the Frontier to Master of the Senate*. New York, 1982.

Evans, Rowland, and Robert Novak. *Lyndon B. Johnson: The Exercise of Power*. New York, 1968.

Fehrenbach, T. R. *Lone Star: A History of Texas and Texans*. New York, 1968.

Feingold, Henry L. *The Politics of Rescue: The Roosevelt Administration and the Holocaust, 1938–1945*. New Brunswick, N.J., 1970.

Flynn, Edward J. *You're the Boss*. New York, 1947.

Gallup, George H. *The Gallup Poll: Public Opinion, 1935–1971*. Vol. II: *1949–1958*. New York, 1972.

Goldman, Eric. *The Tragedy of Lyndon Johnson*. New York, 1969 ed.

Goodwin, Doris Kearns. *The Fitzgeralds and the Kennedys: An American Saga*. New York, 1987.

Gould, Lewis L. *Progressives and Prohibitionists*. Austin, Texas, 1973.

———. *Lady Bird Johnson and the Environment*. Lawrence, Kansas, 1988.

Green, George N. *The Establishment in Texas Politics: The Primitive Years, 1938–1957*. Westport, Conn., 1979.

Guthman, Edwin O., and Jeffrey Shulman, eds. *Robert Kennedy: In His Own Words*. New York, 1988.

Halberstam, David. *The Powers That Be*. New York, 1979.

Hamby, Alonzo L. *Beyond the New Deal: Harry S. Truman and American Liberalism*. New York, 1973.

Hardeman, D. B., and Donald C. Bacon. *Rayburn: A Biography*. Austin, Texas, 1987.

Hebert, F. Edward. *I Went * I Saw * I Heard.* Privately published, 1946.

Heard, Alexander. *The Costs of Democracy.* Chapel Hill, N.C., 1960.

Humphrey, Hubert H. *The Education of a Public Man.* New York, 1976.

Ickes, Harold L. *The Secret Diary of Harold L. Ickes: The Inside Struggle, 1936–1939.* New York, 1954.

———. *The Secret Diary of Harold L. Ickes: The Lowering Clouds, 1939–1941.* New York, 1954.

Johnson, Rebekah Baines. *A Family Album.* New York, 1965.

Johnson, Lyndon B. *The Vantage Point: Perspectives of the Presidency, 1963–1969.* New York, 1971.

Johnson, Sam Houston. *My Brother Lyndon.* New York, 1969.

Journal, Texas House of Representatives. 1st Session, 37th Legislature, 1921.

Kalman, Laura. *Abe Fortas: A Biography.* New Haven, Conn., 1990.

Kearns, Doris. *Lyndon B. Johnson and the American Dream.* New York, 1976.

Key, V. O. *Southern Politics in State and Nation.* New York, 1949.

Kimball, Warren F., ed. *Churchill & Roosevelt: The Complete Correspondence.* Princeton, N.J., 1984.

Kinch, Sam, and Stuart Long. *Allan Shivers: The Pied Piper of Texas Politics.* Austin, Texas, 1973.

Kohl, Mary. *Ballot Box 13: How Lyndon Johnson Won His 1948 Senate Race by 87 Contested Votes.* Jefferson, N.C., 1983.

Krasnow, Erwin G., and Lawrence D. Longley. *The Politics of Broadcast Regulation.* New York, 1978.

LaFeber, Walter. *America, Russia, and the Cold War, 1945–1984.* New York, 1985 ed.

Lash, Joseph P. *Eleanor and Franklin.* New York, 1971.

Leinsdorf, Erich. *Cadenza: A Musical Career.* Boston, 1976.

Leuchtenburg, William E. *The Perils of Prosperity, 1914–1932.* Chicago, 1958.

———. *Franklin D. Roosevelt and the New Deal, 1932–1940.* New York, 1963.

———. *A Troubled Feast: American Society Since 1945.* Boston, 1973.

———. *In the Shadow of FDR: From Harry Truman to Ronald Reagan.* Ithaca, N.Y., 1983.

Lindley, Ernest K. *A New Deal for Youth: The Story of the National Youth Administration.* New York, 1938.

Louchheim, Katie. *The Making of the New Deal: The Insiders Speak.* Cambridge, Mass., 1983.

Ludeman, Annette M. *LaSalle County: South Texas Brush Country, 1856–1975.* Quanah, Texas, 1975.

Lyndon B. Johnson: A Bibliography. Vol. I. Austin, Texas, 1984.

Lyndon B. Johnson: A Bibliography. Vol. II. Compiled by Craig H. Roell. Austin, Texas, 1988.

McDougall, Walter A. . . . *the Heavens and the Earth: A Political History of the Space Age.* New York, 1985.

McElvaine, Robert S. *The Great Depression: America, 1929–1941.* New York, 1984.

McKay, Seth S. *W. Lee O'Daniel and Texas Politics, 1938–1942.* Lubbock, Texas, 1944.

———. *Texas Politics, 1906–1944.* Lubbock, Texas, 1952.

————. *Texas and the Fair Deal.* San Antonio, Texas, 1954.

McPherson, Harry. *A Political Education.* Boston, 1972.

Manchester, William. *The Glory and the Dream: A Narrative History of America, 1932–1972.* Boston, 1973.

————. *American Caesar: Douglas MacArthur, 1880–1964.* Boston, 1978.

Matthews, Donald R. *U.S. Senators and Their World.* New York, 1973 ed.

Miller, Merle. *Lyndon: An Oral Biography.* New York, 1980.

Montgomery, Ruth S. *Mrs. LBJ.* New York, 1964.

Mooney, Booth. *The Lyndon Johnson Story.* New York, 1964 ed.

————. *LBJ: An Irreverent Chronicle.* New York, 1976.

Morgan, Anne H. *Robert S. Kerr: The Senate Years.* Norman, Okla., 1977.

Morris, Roger. *Richard Milhous Nixon: The Rise of an American Politician.* New York, 1989.

Moursund, John S. *Blanco County Families.* Burnet, Texas, 1981, revised ed.

Murphy, Bruce Allen. *Fortas: The Rise and Ruin of a Supreme Court Justice.* New York, 1988.

Newlon, Clarke. *L.B.J.: The Man from Johnson City.* New York, 1964.

Nichols, Tom W. *Rugged Summit.* San Marcos, Texas, 1970.

O'Neill, Tip. *Man of the House: The Life and Political Memoirs of Speaker Tip O'Neill.* New York, 1987.

Paige, Glenn D. *The Korean Decision, June 24–30, 1950.* New York, 1968.

Polenberg, Richard. *War and Society: The United States, 1941–1945.* Philadelphia, 1972.

————. *One Nation Divisible: Class, Race, and Ethnicity in the United States since 1938.* New York, 1981 ed.

Pool, William C., *et al. Lyndon Baines Johnson: The Formative Years.* San Marcos, Texas, 1965.

Presley, James. *A Saga of Wealth: The Rise of the Texas Oilmen.* New York, 1978.

Public Papers and Addresses of Franklin D. Roosevelt: The Court Disapproves. Vol. 4. New York, 1938.

————. Vol. 8. New York, 1940.

Public Papers of the Presidents of the United States: Lyndon B. Johnson, 1963–1969. Washington, D.C., 12 vols., 1965–70.

Reedy, George. *Lyndon B. Johnson: A Memoir.* New York, 1982.

Rogow, Arnold A. *James Forrestal.* New York, 1963.

Roosevelt Presidential Press Conferences. 25 vols. New York, 1972.

Rulon, Philip R., ed. *Letters from the Hill Country: The Correspondence Between Rebekah and Lyndon Baines Johnson.* Austin, Texas, 1982.

Schlesinger, Arthur M., Jr. *The Crisis of the Old Order, 1919–1933.* Boston, 1957.

————. *The Coming of the New Deal.* Boston, 1959.

————. *The Politics of Upheaval.* Boston, 1960.

————. *A Thousand Days: John F. Kennedy in the White House.* Boston, 1965.

————. *Robert Kennedy and His Times.* Boston, 1978.

Schlesinger, Stephen, and Stephen Kinzer. *Bitter Fruit: The Untold Story of the American Coup in Guatemala.* New York, 1982.

Sherry, Michael S. *Preparing for the Next War.* New Haven, Conn., 1977.

Sitkoff, Harvard, ed. *Fifty Years Later: The New Deal Evaluated.* New York, 1985.

Solberg, Carl. *Hubert Humphrey: A Biography.* New York, 1984.

Sorensen, Theodore C. *Kennedy.* New York, 1966 ed.

Spanier, John. *The Truman-MacArthur Controversy and the Korean War.* New York, 1965 ed.

———. *American Foreign Policy Since World War II.* New York, 1980 ed.

Speer, John. *A History of Blanco County.* Edited by Henry C. Armbruster. Austin, Texas, 1965.

Stehling, Arthur. *LBJ's Climb to the White House.* Chicago, 1987.

Steinberg, Alfred. *Sam Johnson's Boy: A Close-up of the President from Texas.* New York, 1968.

———. *Sam Rayburn: A Biography.* New York, 1975.

Tananbaum, Duane. *The Bricker Amendment: A Test of Eisenhower's Political Leadership.* Ithaca, N.Y., 1988.

Texas: A Guide to the Lone Star State. New York, 1940.

Theoharis, Athen G., and John Stuart Cox. *The Boss: J. Edgar Hoover and the Great American Inquisition.* Philadelphia, 1988.

Thompson, Kenneth W. *Virginia Papers on the Presidency.* Vol. 10. Washington, D.C., 1982.

Tindall, George B. *The Ethnic Southerners.* Baton Rouge, La., 1976.

Truman, Margaret. *Harry S. Truman.* New York, 1974.

Webb, Walter P., ed. *The Handbook of Texas.* Austin, Texas, 1952.

Weeks, O. Douglas. *Texas Presidential Politics in 1952.* Austin, Texas, 1953.

White, Theodore H. *The Making of the President 1960.* New York, 1988 ed.

———. *The Making of the President 1964.* New York, 1965.

White, W. L. *Queens Die Proudly.* New York, 1943.

White, William S. *Citadel: The Story of the U.S. Senate.* New York, 1957.

———. *The Professional: Lyndon B. Johnson.* Boston, 1964.

Whitley, Edythe Rucker. *Kith and Kin of Our President: Lyndon Baines Johnson.* Nashville, Tenn., 1967.

Williams, T. Harry. *Huey Long.* New York, 1969.

Wilson, Richard W., and Beulah F. Duholm. *Bunton-Buntin-Benten-Bunting: A Genealogy.* Lake Hills, Iowa, 1967.

Wright, Gavin. *Old South, New South: Revolutions in the Southern Economy Since the Civil War.* New York, 1986.

Ziegler, Philip. *Mountbatten.* New York, 1985.

Articles

Alsop, Stewart. "Lyndon Johnson: How Does He Do It?" *Saturday Evening Post* (Jan. 24, 1959).

Baker, Richard Allen. "A Slap at the 'Hidden-Hand Presidency': The Senate and the Lewis Strauss Affair," *Congress & the Presidency.* (Spring 1987).

Barron, John. "The Johnson Money," *The Washington Evening Star* (June 9, 1964).

Billington, Monroe. "Lyndon B. Johnson and Blacks: The Early Years," *Journal of Negro History* (Jan. 1977).

Burka, Paul. "A Monumental Man," *Texas Monthly* (Jan. 1983).

Busch, Noel F. "Senator Russell of Georgia," *Reader's Digest* (Dec. 1966).

Cater, Douglas. "Lyndon Johnson, Rising Democratic Star," *The Reporter* (Jan. 20, 1953).

——. "How the Senate Passed the Civil-Rights Bill," *The Reporter* (Sept. 5, 1957).

Caro, Robert A. "Annals of Politics: The Johnson Years: A Congressman Goes to War," *The New Yorker* (Nov. 6, 1989).

Carpenter, Leslie. "The Whip from Texas," *Collier's* (Feb. 17, 1951).

Davis, Steve. "The South as 'the Nation's No. 1 Economic Problem': The NEC Report of 1938," *Georgia Historical Quarterly* (Summer 1978).

Elliott, Gary E. "A Legacy of Support: Senator Alan Bible and the Nevada Mining Industry," *Nevada Society Historical Quarterly* (Fall 1988).

Engelke, Louis B. "Our Texas Towns: Cotulla," *San Antonio Express Magazine* (Sept. 21, 1952).

Frantz, Joe B. "Opening a Curtain: The Metamorphosis of Lyndon B. Johnson," *Journal of Southern History* (Feb. 1979).

Gould, Lewis L. "Robert Caro and George Reedy on Lyndon Johnson: An Essay Review," *Southwestern Historical Quarterly* (Spring 1983).

Greenfield, Meg. "The Man Who Leads the Southern Senators," *The Reporter* (May 21, 1964).

Guinn, Jack. "Screwball Election in Texas," *American Mercury* (Sept. 1941).

Hall, Joseph S., ed. "Horace M. Hall's Letters from Gillespie County, Texas, 1871–1873," *Southwestern Historical Quarterly* (Jan. 1959).

Healy, Paul F. "The Frantic Gentleman from Texas," *Saturday Evening Post* (May 19, 1951).

Hinckley, Carolyn. "LBJ—Teacher Turned President," *Texas Outlook* (March 1972).

Huitt, Ralph K. "Democratic Party Leadership in the Senate," *American Political Science Review* (June 1961).

Hurt, Harry III. "The Most Powerful Texans," *Texas Monthly* (April 1976).

Janeway, Eliot. "The Man Who Owns the Navy," *Saturday Evening Post* (Dec. 15, 1945).

——. "Johnson of the Watchdog Committee," *New York Times Magazine* (June 17, 1951).

Johnson, Lyndon B. "Texas Turns to Its Youth," *The Texas Outlook* (Nov. 1935).

Johnston, Alva. "White House Tommy," *Saturday Evening Post* (July 31, 1937).

Kelley, Wayne. "How Russell Helped LBJ to Presidency," *Atlanta Journal and Constitution Magazine* (June 30, 1968).

——. "Senator Russell Vows to Speak His Mind," *Atlanta Journal and Constitution Magazine* (Feb. 4, 1968).

King, Larry L. "Bringing Up Lyndon," *Texas Monthly* (Jan. 1971).

Kohlmeier, Louis. "The Johnson Wealth," *The Wall Street Journal* (March 23, 1964).

Kornitzer, Bela. "President Johnson Talks about His Mother and Father, *Parade* (Jan. 5, 1964).

Kowert, Bruce. "Lyndon B. Johnson, Boy of Destiny," *The Junior Historian* (Nov. 1960).

Lemann, Nicholas. "The Unfinished War," *The Atlantic* (Dec. 1988).

Link, J. B., ed. "George W. Baines," *Texas Historical and Biographical Magazine* (1891).

McEvoy, J. P. "I've Got That Million Dollar Smile," *American Mercury* (Oct. 1938).

Miller, Hope R. "The Little Congress Speaks," *Washington Post Magazine* (Feb. 11, 1934).

Moyers, Bill. "LBJ and the FBI," *Newsweek* (March 10, 1975).

Niebuhr, Reinhold. "The Civil Rights Bill," *The New Leader* (Sept. 16, 1957).

Oates, Stephen B. "The Johnson Biographies," *The Texas Observer* (June 3, 1983).

Orum, Anthony M. "The Making of Austin: Taming the River: Part One," *The Texas Observer* (Dec. 14, 1984).

———. "Taming the River: Part Two," *The Texas Observer* (Jan. 11, 1985).

Phillips, Cabell. "Who'll Head the Ticket in '56?" *New York Times Magazine* (July 25, 1954).

Reichard, Gary W. "Democrats, Civil Rights, and Electoral Strategies in the 1950s," *Congress & the Presidency* (Spring 1986).

Ritchie, Donald A. "Making Fulbright Chairman: Or How the 'Johnson Treatment' Nearly Backfired," *Society for Historians of American Foreign Relations Newsletter* (Sept. 1984).

Rulon, Philip. "The Education of Lyndon Baines Johnson," *Presidential Studies Quarterly* (Summer 1982).

Schendel, Gordon. "Something Is Rotten in the State of Texas," *Collier's* (June 9, 1951).

Schreiber, Flora Rheta. "Lady Bird Johnson's First Years of Marriage," *Woman's Day* (Dec. 1967).

"The Senate Majority and Minority Leaders," *Senate History* (May 1985).

Shelton, Isabelle. "Lyndon Johnson's Mother," *Saturday Evening Post* (May 8, 1965).

Sparks, Andrew. "President Johnson's Georgia Ancestors," *Atlanta Journal & Constitution Magazine* (March 1, 1964).

Stilwell, Hart. "Will He Boss Texas?" *The Nation* (Nov. 10, 1951).

Toffler, Al. "LBJ: The Senate's Mr. Energy," *Pageant* (July 1958).

Waugh, Gene B. "This Man—Lyndon B. Johnson," *The Texas Public Employee* (March 1964).

Welsh, David. "Building Lyndon Johnson," *Ramparts* (Dec. 1967).

Wheeler, Keith, and William Lambert. "The Man Who Is the President," *Life* (Aug. 14, 1964).

White, William S. "Carl Vinson Has Been Unified," *New York Times Magazine* (Sept. 10, 1950).

Young, Roland. "Lone Star State Razzle Dazzle," *The Nation* (June 21, 1941).

Abbreviations in the Notes

BTHC	Eugene C. Barker Texas History Center
DDEL	Dwight D. Eisenhower Library
FCC	Federal Communications Commission
FDRL	Franklin D. Roosevelt Library
HHL	Herbert Hoover Library
HRP	House of Representatives Papers
HSTL	Harry S. Truman Library
LBJA:CF	Lyndon B. Johnson Archives: Congressional File
LBJA:FN	Lyndon B. Johnson Archives: Famous Names
LBJA:SN	Lyndon B. Johnson Archives: Selected Names
LBJA:SF	Lyndon B. Johnson Archives: Subject File
LBJL	Lyndon B. Johnson Library
LC	Library of Congress
LCRA	Lower Colorado River Authority
M	Microfilm
NA	National Archives
NPSL	National Park Service Library
NTJC	Notes and Transcripts of LBJ Conversations
NTSU	North Texas State University
OF	Official File
OH	Oral History
PPCF	Pre-Presidential Confidential File
PPF	President's Personal File
PPMF	Pre-Presidential Memo File
PPSF	Pre-Presidential Secretary's File
PSF	President's Secretary's File
PPP	Public Papers of Presidents
RBJ	Rebekah Baines Johnson
SEJ	Sam Ealy Johnson, Jr.
SHO	Senate Historical Office
SLBJ	Statements of Lyndon B. Johnson

SP	Senate Papers
SPF	Senate Political Files
SRL	Sam Rayburn Library
SWTSU	Southwest Texas State University
WHCF	White House Central Files
WHFN	White House Famous Names

Notes

Readers wishing to trace citations should use the Notes in conjunction with the Sources. I have deposited an even more detailed version of the Notes in the Lyndon B. Johnson Library, where it is available to interested readers.

Introduction: LBJ in History

1. The historian Paul Conkin has published a relatively brief, interpretive biography, *Big Daddy from the Pedernales: Lyndon B. Johnson* (Boston, 1986). *Lyndon B. Johnson and the American Dream* (N.Y., 1976) by political scientist Doris Kearns rests largely on Kearns's conversations with Johnson and provides an interesting psychological portrait of LBJ. Neither of these books can be described as a major research study. The works by the two journalists are: Ronnie Dugger, *The Politician: The Drive for Power, from the Frontier to Master of the Senate* (N.Y., 1982); and Robert Caro, *The Years of Lyndon Johnson: The Path to Power* (N.Y., 1982).

2. The Harris Poll 1988 # 97, Nov. 20, 1988.

3. Stephen B. Oates, "The Johnson Biographies," *The Texas Observer*, June 3, 1983, p. 23.

4. The anecdote may be apocryphal, but it is a good example of Johnson's reputation for manipulativeness.

5. Nicholas Lemann, "The Unfinished War," *The Atlantic*, Dec. 1988, pp. 37–56; the quote is on p. 37.

6. Richard Goodwin, *Remembering America: A Voice from the Sixties* (N.Y., 1988); Dugger, *The Politician*; Caro, *The Path to Power*, xix-xx.

7. The anecdote was told to me by James W. Wilson, an attorney and LBJ Senate aide.

8. Lemann, *The Atlantic*, Dec. 1988, p. 53; the anecdote was told to me by Professor Fred L. Israel of the City College of New York, the editor of the State of the Union volumes.

9. Russell Baker, *The Good Times* (N.Y., 1989), 281–82; Sidney Blumenthal, "The Years of Robert Caro," *The New Republic*, June 4, 1990, p. 36.

10. Merle Miller, *Lyndon: An Oral Biography* (N.Y., 1980), 418.

11. Gavin Wright, *Old South, New South: Revolutions in the Southern Econ-

comy Since the Civil War (N.Y., 1986), 199. Also see Bruce J. Schulman, *From Cotton Belt to Sunbelt: Federal Policy, Economic Development, and the Transformation of the South, 1938–1980* (N.Y., 1990); and 153 for the Faulkner quote.

12. Robert Coles's quote is in *The New Republic*, Aug. 7, 14, 1976, p. 28.

Chapter 1: The Heritage

1. Larry L. King, "Bringing Up Lyndon," *Texas Monthly*, Jan. 1971, p. 85; Bela Kornitzer, "President Johnson Talks About His Mother and Father," *Parade*, Jan. 5, 1964.

2. The lives of John and Jesse Johnson are recounted in: Rebekah Baines Johnson, "The Johnsons: Descendants of John Johnson, A Revolutionary Soldier of Georgia: A Genealogical History," an unpublished manuscript at the LBJL, 1–5, 27, 29 (hereafter cited as RBJ, "Geneal. Hist."). Andrew Sparks, "President Johnson's Georgia Ancestors," *Atlanta Journal and Constitution Magazine*, March 1, 1964; Rebekah Baines Johnson, *A Family Album* (N.Y., 1965), 87–89; Edwin C. Bearss, *Historic Resource Study: Lyndon B. Johnson National Historic Site: Blanco & Gillespie Counties, Texas* (Denver, 1971), 1–6. Also see Alfred Steinberg, *Sam Johnson's Boy* (N.Y., 1968), 3–4; Caro, *Path to Power*, 15–16; T.R. Fehrenbach, *Lone Star: A History of Texas and Texans* (N.Y., 1968), 81–88.

3. RBJ, "Geneal. Hist.," 66; Bearss, *Historic Resource Study*, 7–8; John S. Moursund, *Blanco County Families* (Burnet, Tex., 1981, rev. ed.), 226–28, 231–33; Steinberg, *Sam Johnson's Boy*, 4; Caro, *Path to Power*, 8–14, 16–19, 21–23.

4. Bearss, *Historic Resource Study*, 7–27.

5. *Ibid.*, 8; Caro, *Path to Power*, 19–20.

6. John W. Speer, *A History of Blanco County*, ed. by Henry C. Armbruster (Austin, 1965), 48, 51, 56–57; Bearss, *Historic Resource Study*, 29–34, 43–47; Moursund, *Blanco County Families*, 232–33, 235–36; Joseph S. Hall, ed., "Horace M. Hall's Letters from Gillespie County, Texas, 1871–1873," *Southwestern Historical Quarterly* 62 (Jan. 1959): 336–46; Caro, *Path to Power*, 20, 25–31.

7. R.B. Johnson, *Family Album*, 107–8, 115–17. Richard W. Wilson and Beulah F. Duholm, *Bunton-Buntin-Benten-Bunting: A Genealogy* (Lake Hills, Iowa, 1967), xiv, xvii, xx, 1–3, 6–9. Edythe Rucker Whitley, *Kith and Kin of Our President: Lyndon Baines Johnson* (Nashville, 1967, privately published), 32–36.

8. Wilson and Duholm, *Bunton*, 12–16; Dugger, *The Politician*, 28–30, 407–9; Caro, *Path to Power*, 4–6.

9. RBJ, *Family Album*, 89–90; Wilson and Duholm, *Bunton*, 19; Whitley, *Kith and Kin*, 40–45; Bearss, *Historic Resource Study*, 48–49; Caro, *Path to Power*, 6–8.

10. RBJ, *Family Album*, 72–75; Bearss, *Historic Resource Study*, 39–43; Fehrenbach, *Lone Star*, 298–301; Caro, *Path to Power*, 20.

11. Bearss, *Historic Resource Study*, 34–39.

12. *Ibid.*, 48–51; RBJ, *Family Album*, 73–74; Caro, *Path to Power*, 31; Dugger, *The Politician*, 51–52, 411–12.

13. Bearss, *Historic Resource Study*, 51, 170, 174, 178–82; Otto Lindig Oral History (hereafter OH); Caro, *Path to Power*, 17, 31–32.

14. RBJ, *Family Album*, 71; Bearss, *Historic Resource Study*, 51–52; Caro, *Path to Power*, 26–27, 33; Dugger, *The Politician*, 52–55; Bernard Bailyn et al., *The Great Republic: A History of the American People* (Boston, 1985, 3rd ed.), 585.

15. RBJ, *Family Album*, 22; Steinberg, *Sam Johnson's Boy*, 3, 6; Caro, *Path to Power*, 40–41.

16. RBJ, *Family Album*, 22–23; William C. Pool et al., *Lyndon Baines Johnson: The Formative Years* (San Marcos, 1965), 22–23; Steinberg, *Sam Johnson's Boy*, 7; Caro, *Path to Power*, 41–42.

17. RBJ, *Family Album*, 23; Pool, *LBJ: Formative Years*, 23;Steinberg, *Sam Johnson's Boy*, 7.

18. RBJ, *Family Album*, 24; Pool, *LBJ: Formative Years*, 23–24; Caro, *Path to Power*, 42–43.

19. Pool, *LBJ: Formative Years*, 24–25; Otto Lindig OH; Caro, *Path to Power*, 43–44.

20. Lewis L. Gould, *Progressives and Prohibitionists* (Austin, 1973), 40; Pool, *LBJ: Formative Years*, 25–26. "Sam E. Johnson," n.d., "Johnson, Sam E. (Father)" Folder, Family Corres.: RBJ; and Caro, *Path to Power*, 44–46.

21. Dugger, *The Politician*, 56; Caro, *Path to Power*, 46; Steinberg, *Sam Johnson's Boy*, 565.

22. Caro, *Path to Power*, 46–48.

23. Steinberg, *Sam Johnson's Boy*, 9–10; Caro, *Path to Power*, 47–48. However, they incorrectly say that Sam was one of only seven votes against Bailey. For the vote, see *Texas House Journal, 1907*, 195–96. I am indebted to Professor Lewis L. Gould of the University of Texas, Austin, for calling the error to my attention.

24. Dugger, *The Politician*, 57–59; *Texas House Journal, 1907*, 204, 702–3; Pool, *LBJ: Formative Years*, 28–30; "Sam E. Johnson," Family Corres.: RBJ.

25. RBJ, *Family Album*, 109, 117.

26. J.B. Link, ed., *Texas Historical and Biographical Magazine* (1891), 480–85; also see, RBJ, *Family Album*, 96–97; and "Life and Ministry of George W. Baines," White House Central Files (hereafter cited as WHCF); Dugger, *The Politician*, 62.

27. RBJ, *Family Album*, 75–80; Pool, *LBJ: Formative Years*, 30–32; Kearns, *Lyndon Johnson*, 20; Dugger, *The Politician*, 63, 414.

28. RBJ, *Family Album*, 28–29, 99–100, 112–13; Caro, *Path to Power*, 50.

29. RBJ, *Family Album*, 25 and 29; Steinberg, *Sam Johnson's Boy*, 10–11; Caro, *Path to Power*, 51–52; Kearns, *Lyndon Johnson*, 21; Louis F. Walter OH; RBJ to SEJ, April 1, 1907, Family Corres.: RBJ.

30. Edwin C. Bearss, *Furnishing Study: Lyndon B. Johnson Birthplace-Cottage* (Denver, 1979), 10; RBJ to SEJ, April 1, 1907; Dugger, *The Politician*, 63–64; *Among Friends of LBJ: A Newsletter of the Friends of the LBJ Library*, Jan. 1, 1983, p. 7; RBJ, *Family Album*, 30; Caro, *Path to Power*, 52, 55; J.B. Saunders OH, LBJL. Also see Charles Boatner OH; Isabelle Shelton, "Lyndon Johnson's Mother," *Saturday Evening Post*, May 8, 1965, p. 96; Caro, *Path to Power*, 54.

31. RBJ, *Family Album*, 30; Bearss, *Historic Resource Study*, 174–77 and il-

lustrations; Bearss, *Furnishing Study,* 11–29 and illustrations; Steinberg, *Sam Johnson's Boy,* 11–12; Dugger, *The Politician,* 63; Caro, *Path to Power,* 52.

32. Caro, *Path to Power,* 52–53 and chap. 27.

33. Jessie Hatcher OH; Caro, *Path to Power,* 54–55. For the newspapers, which are in the Eugene C. Barker Texas History Center (hereafter cited as BTHC), Austin, see *Gillespie County News* for 1904–05 generally and the issue of Oct. 8, 1904; also see issues of the *Blanco News* for 1906.

34. RBJ, *Family Album,* 30; Caro, *Path to Power,* 54; Kearns, *Lyndon Johnson,* 22.

Chapter 2: Childhood

1. Such recollections of Rebekah and Sam can be found in many of the oral histories at the LBJL and the National Park Service Library (hereafter cited as NPSL) in Johnson City, Texas, a number of which I cite in this chapter. Source library is indicated only when more than one is involved. For the quotes, see Stella Gliddon OH; John Brooks Casparis OH; also see Philip R. Rulon, ed., *Letters from the Hill Country: The Correspondence between Rebekah and Lyndon Baines Johnson* (Austin, 1982), 37–38.

2. RBJ, *Family Album,* 17–18, and an 11 page hand-written manuscript in Family Corres.: RBJ. This manuscript has been used throughout the chapter. RBJ tried to give her accounts an objective quality by writing in the third person. In neither the manuscript nor the published *Album* did she describe a midwife as being present, and in the manuscript she states that Dr. John Blanton of Buda was present, though she only implied this in the *Album.* "I don't think Rebecca [sic] would have ever wanted anybody to say that Lyndon came with a midwife instead of a real doctor," Jessie Hatcher, her sister-in-law, said. Jessie Hatcher OH; Otto Lindig OH; and "Lindig Looks at Lyndon," *Fredericksburg Radio Post,* Nov. 11, 1965.

3. RBJ, *Family Album,* 18, and in the hand-written manuscript.

4. Bruce Kowert, "Lyndon B. Johnson, Boy of Destiny," *The Junior Historian* of the Texas State Historical Association (Nov. 1960), 10; RBJ to SEJ, n.d.; SEJ to RBJ, April 1909, Family Corres.: RBJ.

5. Hand-written manuscript; Ava Johnson Cox OH; RBJ to SEJ, n.d.; RBJ, *Family Album,* 18–19; Josefa Baines Saunders OH, LBJL; Kearns, *Lyndon Johnson,* 25.

6. Lyndon Baines and Lady Bird Johnson OH, NPSL interview in LBJL; and an NBC television interview with LBJ, "The Hill Country: Lyndon Johnson's Texas," May 9, 1966; "Notes of the President's Meeting with Ronnie Dugger," Dec. 13, 1967, Appt. File, Diary Back Up, LBJL; Kearns, *Lyndon Johnson,* 28–29; A.J. Cox OH; and J.B. Saunders OH, NPSL.

7. See Kearns, *Lyndon Johnson,* 26–27, 17.

8. "The Hill Country: Lyndon Johnson's Texas"; LBJ to Mrs. Chester C. Looney, Aug. 18, 1960, WHCF; Jessie Hatcher OH; J.B. Saunders OH, LBJL; Lyndon Baines and Lady Bird Johnson OH; interview with A.J. Cox; Caro, *Path to Power,* 67–68.

9. "The Hill Country: Lyndon Johnson's Texas"; LBJ to Mrs. Chester C. Looney; Looney to LBJ, July 2, 1964; "Miss Kate and the President," WHCF; K.D. Looney OH; Shelton, "Lyndon Johnson's Mother," *Sat. Eve. Post*, May 8, 1965, p. 97; Kearns, *Lyndon Johnson*, 26.

10. Fehrenbach, *Lone Star*, 302; Jessie Hatcher OH; Rulon, *Letters from the Hill Country*, 24.

11. Nora Aly to Pres. and Mrs. Johnson, May 20, 1964, WHCF; G.C. Edgeworth OH, NPSL. See also "Johnson City Walking Tour," a brochure of the National Park Service, LBJ National Historic Site, Johnson City; S. Gliddon OH; E. Redford OH; Otto Lindig OH; Caro, *Path to Power*, 56–58.

12. Bearss, *Historic Resource Study*, 133–64, and illustrations; Caro, *Path to Power*, 58, 62, and 95; also see Jessie Hatcher OH; J. Lambert OH; interview with A.J. Cox. LBJ's comment is in: "Notes of Meeting with Dugger," Diary Back Up; S. Gliddon OH; Wilton and Virginia Woods OH; J.B. Casparis OH; L.C. Edwards OH; RBJ to Mrs. Biggers, June 15, 1931, LBJA: SF.

13. "The Hill Country: Lyndon Johnson's Texas"; "Notes of Meeting with Dugger"; Kearns, *Lyndon Johnson*, 23–25; John Dollahite OH; Ervin Duggan to LBJ, June 7, 1968, with poem attached, LBJA:SF.

14. G.C. Edgeworth OH, LBJL; S. Gliddon OH; J.B. Saunders OH, NPSL; J.B. Casparis OH; L.C. Edwards OH; Shelton, *Sat. Eve. Post*, May 8, 1965, p. 96.

15. Larry L. King, "Bringing Up Lyndon," *Texas Monthly*, Jan. 1971, pp. 79–80; Kearns, *Lyndon Johnson*, 24–25, 33–34, 39–40; *Dallas Morning News*, June 30, 1941; A.J. Cox interview.

16. Kearns, *Lyndon Johnson*, 22; Steinberg, *Sam Johnson's Boy*, 15.

17. *Ibid.*, 13, 15; Kearns, *Lyndon Johnson*, 24; John B. Casparis OH.

18. "Notes of Meeting with Dugger"; L.C. Edwards OH; A.J. Cox OH; Kearns, *Lyndon Johnson*, 22–23; Shelton, *Sat. Eve. Post*, May 8, 1965, p. 96; S. Gliddon OH.

19. Joe Crofts OH; G.C. Edgeworth OH, LBJL; Dugger, *The Politician*, 73; Kearns, *Lyndon Johnson*, 38–39.

20. Kearns, *ibid.*, 19–20, 26; Sam Houston Johnson, *My Brother Lyndon* (N.Y., 1969), 10–11; LBJ interview with Robert E. McKay, May 21, 1965, WHCF.

21. L.C. Edwards OH; S. Gliddon OH; Steinberg, *Sam Johnson's Boy*, 14.

22. G.C. Edgeworth OH, NPSL; Keith Wheeler and William Lambert, "The Man Who Is the President," *Life*, Aug. 14, 1964, pp. 26 and 28; Kowert, *Junior Historian* of the Texas State Hist. Assoc., Nov. 1960, p. 11.

23. Jessie Lambert OH; Jessie Morris to LBJ, May 19, 1964, WHCF; E. Redford OH; J.B. Casparis OH; Steinberg, *Sam Johnson's Boy*, 16; Dugger, *The Politician*, 77; Bearss, *Historic Resource Study*, 99; *San Angelo Standard Times*, Dec 8, 1963.

24. Kittie Clyde Leonard OH; J.B. Casparis OH; King, *Texas Monthly*, Jan. 1971, p. 83; Caro, *Path to Power*, 108.

25. King, *Texas Monthly*, Jan. 1971, p. 83; Horace Busby review of Doris Kearns, *Lyndon Johnson and the American Dream*, in *Washington Post Book World*, June 6, 1976.

26. A.J. Cox OH.

27. S. Gliddon OH; Gene B. Waugh, "This Man—Lyndon B. Johnson," *The*

Texas Public Employee, March 1964, p. 8; Dugger, *The Politician*, 74; Otto Lindig OH; A.J. Cox OH.

28. See "Luzia Casparis interview by Jim Mulligan, 1979," attached to the transcript of J.B. Casparis OH; Joe Payne OH.

29. PA Biogal. File, LBJA:SF; Steinberg, *Sam Johnson's Boy*, 15; L.C. Edwards OH; Jessie Hunter to Dorothy, Jan 9, 1966, PA Biogal. File; Caro, *Path to Power*, 100–101; Rulon, *Letters from the Hill Country*, 15.

30. A.J. Cox OH; L.C. Edwards OH; Dugger, *The Politician*, 87, 94–95; John Dollahite OH.

31. S. Gliddon OH; Caro, *Path to Power*, 70–72, 76; Joe Payne OH.

32. Philip Ziegler, *Mountbatten* (N.Y., 1985), 25.

33. L.C. Edwards OH; Kittie Clyde Leonard OH; Charles K. Boatner OH; Estelle Harbin OH. Also see Miller, *Lyndon*, 14–16; Shelton, *Sat. Eve. Post*, May 8, 1965, p. 96; "The Hill Country: Lyndon Johnson's Texas"; Kornitzer, *Parade*, Jan 5, 1964; Dugger, *The Politician*, 61.

34. Rulon, *Letters from the Hill Country*, 16, 19, 28, 38.

35. G.C. Edgeworth OH, NPSL; John Koeniger OH; Homer Thornberry OH; Caro, *Path to Power*, 63–64; Dugger, *The Politician*, 83.

36. E. Redford OH; Truman and Wilma Fawcett OH; *Record-Courier*, Oct. 28, 1937; Caro, *Path to Power*, 83–84; Wright Patman OH.

37. RBJ, *Family Album*, 27; Caro, *Path to Power*, 60–61, 64–65.

38. SHJ, *My Brother Lyndon*, 17–19; Tom Crider OH; John Koeniger OH.

39. Kittie Clyde Leonard OH; A.J. Cox OH; A.J. Cox interview; S. Gliddon OH; Caro, *Path to Power*, 72–73; Dugger, *The Politician*, 73–74.

40. See Caro, *Path to Power*, 61–63; Dugger, *The Poltician*, 73.

41. See Pool, *Lyndon Baines Johnson*, 33–36; Steinberg, *Sam Johnson's Boy*, 21–24; Caro, *Path to Power*, 63–64.

42. Dugger, *The Politician*, 83–84; Caro, *Path to Power*, 79–80.

43. Dugger, *The Politician*, 84; Steinberg, *Sam Johnson's Boy*, 22–23. Also see Gould, *Progressives and Prohibitionists*, which is excellent on Texas politics in general on the progressive era and on Jim Ferguson in particular. Gould also makes some insightful observations about LBJ's political heritage from Sam Ealy on p. 132, n. 29; and in "Robert Caro and George Reedy on Lyndon Johnson: An Essay Review," *Southwestern Historical Quarterly* (Spring 1983), 63–65.

44. See Steinberg, *Sam Johnson's Boy*, 24–26; Dugger, *The Politician*, 84–85. Also see Pool, *Lyndon Baines Johnson*, 36–42; Caro, *Path to Power*, 80–83, who give greater emphasis to Sam's idealism than I do. For another special effort Sam made to ensure German support for himself, see Caro, p. 74.

45. J. Hatcher OH; Kearns, *Lyndon Johnson*, 33–34; A.J. Cox interview. "The Hill Country: Lyndon Johnson's Texas"; Dugger, *The Politician*, 84.

46. E. Redford OH; "Notes of Meeting with Dugger"; *Among Friends of LBJ*, Jan 1, 1983, p. 7; Dugger, *The Politician*, 79.

47. Kearns, *Lyndon Johnson*, 36; R.E. Thomason OH; Wright Patman, quoted in Steinberg, *Sam Johnson's Boy*, 28.

48. Kearns, *Lyndon Johnson*, 36–37.

49. Steinberg, *Sam Johnson's Boy*, 29; Caro, *Path to Power*, 75. Crider is quoted in Miller, *Lyndon*, 25. Joe Payne OH.

50. E. Redford OH; *L.C. Edwards OH; Dugger, The Politician,* 79; also see Tom Crider OH; Truman Fawcett OH.

51. Ben Crider OH; J.B. Casparis OH; Luzia Casparis interview by Jim Mulligan, 1979, attached to J.B. Casparis OH.

52. Otto Lindig OH; Dugger, *The Politician,* 98–99; J.B. Casparis OH; Steinberg, *Sam Johnson's Boy,* 30–31.

53. Joe Payne OH.

54. Kearns, *Lyndon Johnson,* 22, 42; G.C. Edgeworth OH, NPSL; S. Gliddon OH; Luther E. Jones to Eric Goldman, April 6, 1965, Luther E. Jones MSS., LBJL; Estelle Harbin OH.

55. L.C. Edwards OH; Joe Crofts OH; Truman and Wilma Fawcett OH; Caro, *Path to Power,* 109–10. Also see E. Redford OH, for more on LBJ's relations with elderly women.

56. King, *Texas Monthly,* Jan. 1971, p. 87; Kearns, *Lyndon Johnson,* 42.

57. Miller, *Lyndon,* 29. Lady Bird and Lyndon B. Johnson interview; *Time,* Feb. 5, 1973, p. 34.

58. E. Redford OH; S. Gliddon OH; Kittie C. Leonard OH; G.C. Edgeworth OH, LBJL.

59. G.C. Edgeworth OH, LBJL; Truman and Wilma Fawcett OH; Waugh, *Texas Public Employer,* March 1964, pp. 9–10, 26; E. Redford OH.

60. E. Redford OH; Dugger, *The Politician,* 98.

61. Bearss, *Historic Resource Study,* 81, 171; Caro, *Path to Power,* 85–90; Dugger, *The Politician,* 89; Miller, *Lyndon,* 26.

62. "Sam E. Johnson," n.d., listing all the laws he sponsored, in Family Corres.: RBJ; see also *Texas House Journal, 1921,* 51–52, 74–75; Wright Patman OH; "Patman Cites Klan Fight by President's Father," *Washington Post,* April 1, 1964; Miller, *Lyndon,* 23; Norman D. Brown, *Hood, Bonnet, and Little Brown Jug: Texas Politics, 1921–1928* (College Station, Tex. 1984), chap. 2 and pp. 66–67 in particular. Also see Pool, *Lyndon B. Johnson,* 43–44.

63. Dugger, *The Politician,* 91; H. Grady Perry OH; Caro, *Path to Power,* 90–97; Clayton Stribling OH; J. Hatcher OH; Welly and Alice Hopkins OH; L.C. Edwards OH; E. Redford OH; S. Gliddon OH; A.J. Cox interview.

64. See Caro, *Path to Power,* 98–99, 103, 106.

65. *Ibid.,* 100–102; "LBJ—A Student, a Cutup, and Just a Regular Guy," *San Angelo Standard Times,* Dec. 8, 1963; Kearns, *Lyndon Johnson,* 39–40; Dugger, *The Politician,* 88, 94–96; S.H. Johnson, *My Brother Lyndon,* 11–12.

66. *Blanco County Record,* May 9, 1924; Steinberg, *Sam Johnson's Boy,* 31.

67. Caro, *Path to Power,* 119–23. My supposition that LBJ went to the subcollege in the summer of 1924 rests on an "Entrance Card" he filled out in 1927 in which he recorded that he had done "credit work" at the College in 1924. The card is in the Billy Mac Jones Folder, SWTSU Papers, LBJL. Also see Alfred T. "Boody" Johnson OH; Kearns, *Lyndon Johnson,* 40.

68. SHJ, *My Brother Lyndon,* 20–22. Lyndon is quoted in Welly and Alice Hopkins OH; O.B. Summy OH.

69. Payne Rountree OH; J. Hatcher OH; O.B. Summy OH; Ben Crider OH; Mrs. Alvin Jensen OH; "Crider Tells of Childhood Days with LBJ, Trip to California," *Cloverdale Reveille,* July 2, 1964.

70. *Ibid.* Also see Tom Crider OH; John Koeniger OH; Caro, *Path to Power*, 125–27.

71. See John Koeniger OH; "Johnson Had His Ups and Downs in California," *Los Angeles Times*, II, Nov. 26, 1963; Caro, *Path to Power*, 124, 127–29; Wheeler and Lambert, *Life*, Aug. 14, 1964, pp. 28–29; Kearns, *Lyndon Johnson*, 43–44.

72. John Koeniger, OH; J. Hatcher OH; A.J. Cox interview; Dugger, *The Politician*, 103.

73. Dugger, *ibid.*; *Public Papers of the Presidents of the United States: Lyndon B. Johnson, 1963–64* (Washington, D.C., 1965), 726 (hereafter cited as *PPP:LBJ*). A.J. Cox interview. See Ben Crider OH; Dugger, *The Politician*, 104; Caro, *Path to Power*, 132–33; Brown, *Hood, Bonnet, and Little Brown Jug*, 280, 492, n. 51.

74. Caro, *Path to Power*, 129–30, 134. L.C. Edwards OH; Ben Crider OH; Brown, *Hood, Bonnet, and Little Brown Jug*, 356–59.

75. Dugger, *The Politician*, 104; Caro, *Path to Power*, 133–35; A.J. Cox interview; Caro, *Path to Power*, 135–36; Dugger, *The Politician*, 106.

Chapter 3: Student and Teacher

1. See Steinberg, *Sam Johnson's Boy*, 35, 37; Pool, *Lyndon Baines Johnson*, 6, 78–79, 89–90; Caro, *Path to Power*, 141–42, 144–45; Percy Brigham OH.

2. LBJ interview with Robert E. McKay, May 21, 1965, WHCF..

3. Truman and Wilma Fawcett OH.

4. Group interview, Southwest Texas State College faculty, Dec. n.d., 1963; David F. Votaw interview, Feb. 6, 1965, WHCF.

5. Miller, *Lyndon*, 32; Steinberg, *Sam Johnson's Boy*, 36; Kearns, *Lyndon Johnson*, 44–45.

6. Lyndon's "whole life," a later associate said, "was spent in a relentless, often tormented, drive to 'make up' for his origins and what those origins denied him. The most embittering denial was education. It was not just that his college education was mediocre. It was that those with good educations must, he seemed to believe, have understandings of a world from which he and his mind were forever excluded. The quality of his mind approached genius, yet, to him, the absence of academic certification was crippling." Horace W. Busby, "Robert Caro's L.B.J.: There Was Such a Man, Warts and All," *Los Angeles Times*, March 31, 1983. John Smith, "The History and Growth of the Southwest Texas State Teachers College," unpublished master's thesis, Univ. of Texas, Austin, 1930; Tom W. Nichols, *Rugged Summit* (San Marcos, 1970); Ella SoRelle Porter OH; Emmett Shelton OH; Pool, *Lyndon B. Johnson*, 67–87; Caro, *Path to Power*, 141–42, 801.

7. LBJ said he got a D: see *PPP:LBJ, 1965*, 818; and transcript of his record in S.T.S.U. Papers, LBJL. E.S. Porter OH; *College Star*, June 29, 1927; A.T. Johnson OH; Clayton Stribling OH; LBJ, "Remarks to College Officials," April 27, 1970, LBJL; Caro, *Path to Power*, 143–44.

8. See LBJ, "Remarks to College Officials"; Steinberg, *Sam Johnson's Boy*,

39; Pool, *Lyndon B. Johnson*, 100–101; Caro, *Path to Power*, 153; Rulon, *Letters from the Hill Country*, 16; Ben Crider OH.

9. Larry King, "Bringing up Lyndon," 84; Pool, *Lyndon B. Johnson*, 99; LBJ, "Remarks to College Officials"; Kearns, *Lyndon Johnson*, 47; Caro, *Path to Power*, 144–45; Dugger, *The Politician*, 109–10.

10. Pool, *Lyndon B. Johnson*, 99–100; Dugger, *The Politician*, 110; Caro, *Path to Power*, 145–46.

11. Dugger, *The Politician*, 110–12; Pool, *Lyndon B. Johnson*, 112–17; and editorials in the *College Star*, for June 27, 29, July 6, 21, 27, Aug. 3, 10, 17, 1927—the June and July editorials are quoted in Pool, *Lyndon B. Johnson*, 114–16; the ones for August appear in James Benson and Anthony Sisto, comps., *The Student Editorials of Lyndon B. Johnson* (San Marcos and New Brunswick, N.J., 1968).

12. See Lorena and Allie T. Hughes OH; Albert C. Harzke OH; group interview, S.T.S.C. faculty; *The Houston Press*, Dec. 12, 1963. Also see Pool, *Lyndon B. Johnson*, 97–98.

13. L. and A.T. Hughes OH; Ardis C. Hopper OH; R. Vernon Whiteside OH; E.S. Porter OH; Pool, *Lyndon B. Johnson*, 96–97; Dugger, *The Politician*, 120–21.

14. Caro, *Path to Power*, 153–56, 160; R.V. Whiteside OH; C. Stribling OH; E.S. Porter OH.

15. Caro, *Path to Power*, 154, 158; Horace E. Richards OH; Willard Deason OH; Wheeler and Lambert, *Life*, Aug. 14, 1964, p. 76; Steinberg, *Sam Johnson's Boy*, 39–40, 44; group interview, S.T.S.C. faculty; L. and A.T. Hughes OH.

16. Kearns, *Lyndon Johnson*, 53–54.

17. William E. Leuchtenburg, *The Perils of Prosperity, 1914–1932* (Chicago, 1958), 95; Paul A. Carter, *Another Part of the Twenties* (N.Y., 1977), 176–77, quoting Coolidge; Kearns, *Lyndon Johnson*, 56.

18. Steinberg, *Sam Johnson's Boy*, 43; Shelton, *Sat. Eve. Post*, May 8, 1965, p. 97; Dugger, *The Politician*, 121; Caro, *Path to Power*, 154, 802; *Houston Press*, Dec. 10, 1963; LBJ college transcript, S.T.S.U. Papers, LBJL. Three of the grades on the transcript are blacked out, but for him to have had a B- average, as he and Dean Nolle both said, these grades had to have been Cs. There were also six extension courses listed on the transcript, but the grades were not counted in LBJ's average.

19. Caro, *Path to Power*, 150–51; *Houston Press*, Dec. 11, 1963; *College Star*, July 25, 1928; Pool, *Lyndon B. Johnson*, 74–75; group interview, S.T.S.C. faculty; D.F. Votaw interview; Evans Papers, S.T.S.U. Library, San Marcos.

20. R. Vernon Whiteside OH; E.S. Porter OH; Wilton and Virginia Woods OH; Steinberg, *Sam Johnson's Boy*, 44.

21. H.M. Greene OH; group interview, S.T.S.C. faculty.

22. *Houston Chronicle*, Dec. 8, 1963; *Texas Federation News*, Dec. 1963; H.M. Greene OH; L. and A.T. Hughes OH; Claud Kellam OH; Fenner Roth OH; A.C. Hopper OH; Albert C. Harzke OH; W. and V. Woods OH; Mylton L. Kennedy OH; Pool, *Lyndon B. Johnson*, 92–96; Dugger, *The Politician*, 121–22.

23. Nichols, *Rugged Summit*, 19–20, and chap. 13, esp. p. 347; Pool, *Lyndon B. Johnson*, 74, 99–100; group interview, S.T.S.C. faculty; E. Shelton OH; F.

Roth OH; Welly and Alice Hopkins OH; Caro, *Path to Power*, 144–45, 152–53; Dugger, *The Politician*, 112–13.

24. Nichols, *Rugged Summit*, 436; Pool, *Lyndon B. Johnson*, 99; Kearns, *Lyndon Johnson*, 48; Steinberg, *Sam Johnson's Boy*, 37.

25. Nichols, *Rugged Summit*, 436; Dugger, *The Politician*, 112; Pool, *Lyndon B. Johnson*, 100; LBJ, "Remarks to College Officials".

26. A. Hopper OH; E.S. Porter OH; A.T. Johnson OH; LBJ, "Remarks to College Officials"; group interview, S.T.S.C. faculty; Nichols, *Rugged Summit*, 439–40.

27. Group interview, S.T.S.C. faculty; clipping, "Debate Tryouts Held Monday Night," attached to LBJ to Grandmother, LBJA:SF; Elmer Graham OH; G. Preston Smith OH; Merrell Blackman OH; Pool, *Lyndon B. Johnson*, 101–2; Steinberg, *Sam Johnson's Boy*, 42–43; Miller, *Lyndon*, 34–35; Dugger, *The Politician*, 113; Caro, *Path to Power*, 154–55.

28. A.C. Hopper OH; E.S. Porter OH; E. Shelton OH; group interview, S.T.S.C. faculty; Pool, *Lyndon B. Johnson*, 102–5.

29. Alfred T. Johnson OH; LBJ, "Remarks to College Officials"; Pool, *Lyndon B. Johnson*, 105; Caro, *Path to Power*, 156–59; C. Stribling OH; Levette J. Berry OH; W. and V. Woods OH; Miller, *Lyndon*, 36; E. Shelton OH; *Pedagog: 1928*, S.T.S.U. Library, San Marcos.

30. LBJ to Don H. Biggers, Feb. 21, 1927 (contents indicate it should be 1928) and "Lyndon B. Johnson: Biographical Sketch," both in LBJA:SF; Percy Brigham OH; Steinberg, *Sam Johnson's Boy*, 40, 45; Miller, *Lyndon*, 34; Dugger, *The Politician*, 110–11; Caro, *Path to Power*, 155, 163–65, 167; R. Vernon Whiteside OH; Jessie Hatcher OH; Pool, *Lyndon B. Johnson*, 139–41.

31. Caro, *Path to Power*, 172; WPA guide book: *Texas: A Guide to the Lone Star State* (N.Y., 1940), 447–48, 450–51; Walter P. Webb, ed., *The Handbook of Texas* (Austin, 1952), 424; Louis B. Engelke, "Our Texas Towns: Cotulla," *San Antonio Express Magazine*, Sept. 21, 1952; Annette M. Ludeman, *LaSalle County: South Texas Brush Country, 1856–1975* (Quanah, Tex., 1975), 32, 35; Steinberg, *Sam Johnson's Boy*, 45–46, 48; Pool, *Lyndon B. Johnson*, 137–38; Dugger, *The Politician*, 115.

32. The farmer was the father of the historian John L. Gaddis, who related this episode to me in November 1985; Caro, *Path to Power*, 167, 169–70.

33. *PPP: LBJ, 1963–64*, 309; *PPP: LBJ, 1965*, 286; *PPP: LBJ, 1968–69*, 1138–39; *PPP: LBJ, 1966*, 1349–50.

34. *PPP: LBJ, 1965*, 229–30; Kearns, *Lyndon Johnson*, 65–67.

35. On becoming principal, see Steinberg, *Sam Johnson's Boy*, 46; *Houston Post*, Jan. 27, 1964; "The Hill Country: Lyndon Johnson's Texas."

36. Carolyn Hinckley, "LBJ—Teacher Turned President," *Texas Outlook*, March 1972.

37. Durham, N.C., *Morning Herald*, Jan. 20, 1964; *Houston Post*, Jan. 27, 1964; *Texas Outlook*, March 1972; Maclovio Segovia to LBJ, Jan. 20, 1964, WHCF; an interview with Juan Rodriguez in *Pit and Pour*, April 1964; "The Hill Country: Lyndon Johnson's Texas."

38. *PPP: LBJ, 1965*, 229–30.

39. *Houston Post*, Jan. 27, 1964; *Texas Outlook*, March 1972; Rulon, *Letters from the Hill Country*, 18; Steinberg, *Sam Johnson's Boy*, 46–47; Philip Rulon,

"The Education of Lyndon Baines Johnson," *Presidential Studies Quarterly*, XII (Summer 1982): 404.

40. Dugger, *The Politician*, 116; *Houston Post*, Jan. 27, 1964; LBJ college transcript; Rulon, *Letters from the Hill Country*, 18–19; Caro, *Path to Power*, 172.

41. Rulon, *Letters from the Hill Country*, 18–19; "The Hill Country: Lyndon Johnson's Texas"; Kearns, *Lyndon Johnson*, 56–67; Caro, *Path to Power*, 161–63, 172–73, 198; *Houston Post*, Jan. 27, 1964. LBJ never acknowledged that Carol rejected him. Indeed, he reversed the roles in his later telling of what occurred (see pp. 56–60 of Kearns, who discusses how unbearable personal rejection was for him).

42. See Alfred Johnson OH; *College Star*, June 19, 1929; Fenner Roth OH; A.C. Hopper OH; Pool, *Lyndon B. Johnson*, 100, 109.

43. See LBJ college transcript and issues of the *Star* for June 12, June 19, 26, July 10, Aug. 14, 1929.

44. "The Hill Country: Lyndon Johnson's Texas"; LBJ college transcript; Alfred Nolle to M.B. Holleman, March 28, 1930, LBJA:SF; Bertha Allman Graef OH; biographical sketch in *Pedagog, 1930.*

45. The origins of the White Stars are obscured by the reliance on participants' memories. There are no contemporary written records and the recollections of the organizers conflict on exactly when and who started the organization. See the following oral histories: Horace E. Richards; Fenner Roth; Willard Deason; Albert C. Harzke; Wilton and Virginia Woods; R. Vernon Whiteside. Also see LBJ, "Remarks to College Officials"; Pool, *Lyndon B. Johnson*, 102–11; Dugger, *The Politician*, 113–14; Caro, *Path to Power*, 175–77.

46. Albert Harzke OH; Willard Deason OH; Pool, *Lyndon B. Johnson*, 106–7; Miller, *Lyndon*, 35; Kearns, *Lyndon Johnson*, 51–52; Caro, *Path to Power*, 176–78.

47. A.C. Hopper OH; LBJ, "Remarks to College Officials"; SHJ, *My Brother Lyndon*, 26–28; Kearns, *Lyndon Johnson*, 49–50; Dugger, *The Politician*, 114.

48. Caro, *Path to Power*, 178–80, 181–83; Fenner Roth OH; Albert C. Harzke OH; W. and V. Woods OH; Horace E. Richards OH; and R. Vernon Whiteside OH.

49. Caro, *Path to Power*, 180–81; R. Vernon Whiteside OH.

50. LBJ, "Remarks to College Officials"; Steinberg, *Sam Johnson's Boy*, 41; Caro, *Path to Power*, 194, 196, 189–90.

51. R. Vernon Whiteside OH; Horace E. Richards OH; Pool, *Lyndon B. Johnson*, 109–10; Kearns, *Lyndon Johnson*, 50–51; Dugger, *The Politician*, 120; Caro, *Path to Power*, 186–90.

52. Fenner Roth OH; Pool, *Lyndon B. Johnson*, 95–96; A.C Hopper OH; Lavette J. "Joe" Berry OH, who says that the reallocation of funds "didn't influence anything the football team did. . . . There was no curtailment of any athletic event I was aware of."

53. *Pegadog, 1930.* R. Vernon Whiteside OH; Ardis Hopper OH: "Even though Lyndon and I had some differences on that Council, we'd go home and talk about it, and sleep there on the same bed. There never was any animosity between us at all. . . . I kept thinking . . . well, we just argue like heck up there all the time on that Council and go home and laugh about it and continue the

argument without getting mad at each other. And he holds no grudges and neither do I." "If this White Star thing were as serious to him as it appears to be," Hopper also said, "I would be surprised if it ever was that serious to him. Because he knew Boody [Merrell Blackman] and I were Black Stars and his attitude towards us never changed."

54. Welly K. Hopkins OH; Hopkins to Emmie Craddock, Dec. 3, 1964, PPCF; W. and V. Woods OH. Also see Neff to Sam Johnson, June 7, 21, Aug. 8, 1930, and Johnson to Neff, June 18, July 10, 1930, Pat Neff Papers, Baylor Univ.; Steinberg, *Sam Johnson's Boy*, 50–53; Kearns, *Lyndon Johnson*, 69; Dugger, *The Politician*, 122–23; W. Hopkins OH; Fenner Roth OH; W. and V. Woods OH; Horace Richards OH; Hopkins to Roy Miller, Nov. 25, 1931, LBJA:SN; Caro, *Path to Power*, 202–4.

55. Steinberg, *Sam Johnson's Boy*, 54–56; Pool, *Lyndon B. Johnson*, 145–59; LBJ to George Johnson, May 19, 1930; *San Antonio Express*, "LBJ Smile Won Him Job", n.d., LBJA:SF. LBJ must have felt guilty about deceiving Barron: in an interview with Robert E. McKay, May 21, 1965, he told a self-serving story of how the Pearsall superintendent refused to hold him to a commitment he said he gave not to go to Houston and practically forced him to take the better job.

56. Steinberg, *Sam Johnson's Boy*, 56; Pool, *Lyndon B. Johnson*, 145–47; Dugger, *The Politician*, 127; McKay interview, May 21, 1965; Jessie Hatcher OH.

57. McKay interview with LBJ; Luther E. Jones, Jr. OH; Steinberg, *Sam Johnson's Boy*, 54–57; Pool, *Lyndon B. Johnson*, 147–49; Dugger, *The Politician*, 127.

58. Dugger, *The Politician*, 125; Caro, *Path to Power*, 206–7; Everett Collier to Jack Valenti, Jan. 21, 1964, WHCF; L.E. Jones, Jr. OH.

59. See Willard Deason OH; Gene Latimer OH; "Interviews on Board Bus," April 11, 1965, Gene Latimer Papers; L.E. Jones, Jr., to Eric Goldman, April 6, 1965, Jones Papers; Gene Latimer OH; Caro, *Path to Power*, 206–9.

60. LBJ scrapbook on his debating teams (the scrapbook was found by a mover in 1987 in the attic of the house on Hawthorne Street where LBJ lived in 1930–31). Also see Pool, *Lyndon B. Johnson*, 151–57; Caro, *Path to Power*, 209–11; Dugger, *The Politician*, 126.

61. Pool, *Lyndon B. Johnson*, 151, 158; Caro, *Path to Power*, 206–7, 209. "Interviews on Board Bus"; Gene Latimer OH.

62. See McKay interview, May 21, 1965; Gene Latimer OH.

63. See Pool, *Lyndon B. Johnson*, 155–58; Caro, *Path to Power*, 210–11; McKay interview with LBJ; G. Latimer OH; W. and A. Hopkins OH; Latimer to Lady Bird Johnson, March 18, 1975, Latimer Papers.

64. Pool, *Lyndon B. Johnson*, 167–71; Welly K. Hopkins OH; Dugger, *The Politician*, 127–28 and note 7 on pp. 424–25; Felix McKnight OH.

65. Welly Hopkins to Roy Miller, Nov. 25, 1931, LBJA:SN; Welly Hopkins OH; Pool, *Lyndon B. Johnson*, 159; Malcolm G. Bardwell OH.

66. Pool, *Lyndon B. Johnson*, 159–60; Kearns, *Lyndon Johnson*, 70.

Chapter 4: Kleberg's Secretary

1. LBJ to L.E. Jones, Dec. 6, 1931, L.E. Jones Papers; Estelle Harbin OH; Arthur M. Schlesinger, Jr., *The Crisis of the Old Order, 1919–1933* (Boston, 1957), 227–29.

2. Robert M. Jackson OH.

3. R.M. Jackson OH; Carroll Keach OH; Estelle Harbin OH; Russell M. Brown OH; Gene Latimer OH; Steinberg, *Sam Johnson's Boy*, 67–68; Dugger, *The Politician*, 165–66; Caro, *Path to Power*, 224; for LBJ's salary, see Memo in Box 73, LBJA:SN.

4. Schlesinger, Jr., *Crisis of the Old Order*, 248–51; William E. Leuchtenburg, *Franklin D. Roosevelt and the New Deal, 1932–1940* (N.Y., 1963), 1–3; Robert S. McElvaine, *The Great Depression: America, 1929–1941* (N.Y., 1984), 80–81, 90–91.

5. Schlesinger, Jr., *Crisis of the Old Order*, chap. 25 and pp. 224, 245; Edwin W. Knippa, "The Early Political Life of Lyndon B. Johnson, 1931–1937," M.A. thesis, Southwest Texas State University, San Marcos, 1967, pp. 8–10; Caro, *Path to Power*, 218–19.

6. *Washington Herald*, Dec. 9, 1931; *American Business Survey*, Jan. 1932; *The Southern Messenger*, n.d., clipping in Box 73, LBJA:SN; *The Washington Post*, May 24, 1934; Richard M. Kleberg Scrapbooks, 1931–33, LBJL; Luther E. Jones OH; Gene Latimer OH; Wright Patman OH; Estelle Harbin OH; Steinberg, *Sam Johnson's Boy*, 80; Caro, *Path to Power*, 219–21; Dugger, *The Politician*, 170, who quotes Jackson.

7. Caro, *Path to Power*, 223; LBJ to Jones, Dec. 6, 1931.

8. Kearns, *Lyndon Johnson*, 72–73; Marvin Jones OH; R.E. Thomason OH.

9. Estelle Harbin OH; Booth Mooney, *The Lyndon Johnson Story* (N.Y., 1964 ed.), 38.

10. Caro, *Path to Power*, 221–22, 242–43; Estelle Harbin OH; LBJ to L.E. Jones, April 18, 1932, Jones Papers.

11. Luther E. Jones OH; Estelle Harbin OH; Gene Latimer OH; Knippa, "Early Political Life of LBJ," 16–17; Steinberg, *Sam Johnson's Boy*, 76; Caro, *Path to Power*, 226, 232–35. The correspondent was Bob Jackson, who was also Congressman R.E. Thomason's secretary; his article appeared in the *Corpus Christi Caller*, *San Angelo Times*, and *The Abilene Reporter*.

12. Gene Latimer OH; Russell M. Brown OH; Luther E. Jones OH; Knippa, "Early Political Life of LBJ," 15–18; Dugger, *The Politician*, 171; Caro, *Path to Power*, 233–34.

13. Robert M. Jackson OH; Estelle Harbin OH; Knippa, "Early Political Life of LBJ," 19–20; Caro, *Path to Power*, 225–27; Dugger, *The Politician*, 170–71; Kearns, *Lyndon Johnson*, 73.

14. Estelle Harbin OH; Gene Latimer OH; LBJ to Mr. and Mrs. Latimer, Jan. 31, 1933; and "Tues. Evening, 6:30 P.M., 1933," Latimer Papers; Robert H. Harper to Vice President Johnson, March 27, 1962, LBJA:SF; Luther E. Jones OH; LBJ to Jones, April 18, 1932; Steinberg, *Sam Johnson's Boy*, 77; Caro, *Path to Power*, 229–30.

15. Gene Latimer OH; Luther E. Jones OH; Jones to Eric Goldman, April 6,

1965, Jones Papers; Dugger, *The Politician,* 170–71; Caro, *Path to Power,* 230–32, 234; Kearns, *Lyndon Johnson,* 75.

16. Caro, *Path to Power,* 235–59; Gene Latimer OH.

17. Jones to Eric Goldman, April 6, 1965; Gene Latimer OH; Luther E. Jones OH; Douglass Cater, "Waiting for Caro," *Washington Post,* March 8, 1983.

18. Luther E. Jones OH; Gene Latimer OH; Russell M. Brown OH.

19. Russell M. Brown OH; Gene Latimer OH; Mamie Kleberg letters, PPCF; Dugger, *The Politician,* 183.

20. Unidentified newspaper clipping, "Congressman Kleberg Entertains Editors and Friends on King Ranch," Nov. 1933, Kleberg Scrapbooks, 1931–33; Steinberg, *Sam Johnson's Boy,* 80–81.

21. Carroll Keach OH; Luther E. Jones OH; Gene Latimer OH; Knippa, "Early Political Life of LBJ," 28; Steinberg, *Sam Johnson's Boy,* 69–71, 79–80; Kearns, *Lyndon Johnson,* 78.

22. See Russell M. Brown OH; Knippa, "Early Political Life of LBJ," 25–27; Dugger, *The Politician,* 174; Kearns, *Lyndon Johnson,* 74–77; Robert M. Jackson OH; R.H. Montgomery OH.

23. William Manchester, *The Glory and the Dream: A Narrative History of America, 1932–72* (Boston, 1973), 26; Dugger, *The Politician,* 311.

24. Schlesinger, Jr., *Crisis of the Old Order,* 256–65; for Kleberg's views, see his speeches in Kleberg Papers; Dugger, *The Politician,* 168–69, 182; Russell M. Brown OH.

25. See Leuchtenburg, *FDR and the New Deal,* 3–4, 27–28, and n. 6 on p. 3.

26. *Ibid.,* 96–99; T. Harry Williams, *Huey Long* (N.Y., 1969), 556–58. LBJ told John Koeniger that he "never missed an opportunity to hear Huey make a speech." Koeniger OH; Dugger, *The Politician,* 168; Kearns, *Lyndon Johnson,* 92.

27. *PPP: LBJ, 1965,* I, 480–81; Williams, *Huey Long,* 692–701.

28. *PPP: LBJ, 1963–64,* I, 546, and *1967,* I, 115, 621–22; Kearns, *Lyndon Johnson,* 91; William S. White OH; Dugger, *The Politician,* 172, 183.

29. Luther E. Jones OH; Carroll Keach OH; Russell M. Brown OH; Clarke Newlon, *L.B.J. The Man from Johnson City* (N.Y., 1964), 47–48; Steinberg, *Sam Johnson's Boy,* 76–77, 92–93; Dugger, *The Politician,* 172–73; for Kleberg's votes, see Box 1, Kleberg Papers; *PPP: LBJ, 1966,* I, 608; II, 1142.

30. Arthur M. Schlesinger, Jr., *The Coming of the New Deal* (Boston, 1959), chaps. 2–4, esp. pp. 59–61; Leuchtenburg, *FDR and the New Deal,* 51–52, 72–73; Caro, *Path to Power,* 252–60.

31. Russell M. Brown OH; Robert M. Jackson OH; Luther E. Jones OH; Willard Deason OH; Gene Latimer OH; Caro, *Path to Power,* 269–71.

32. Russell M. Brown OH; Luther E. Jones OH; Robert M. Jackson OH; Steinberg, *Sam Johnson's Boy,* 76.

33. Luther E. Jones OH; Kearns, *Lyndon Johnson,* 92.

34. Bearss, *Historic Resource Study,* 122; Knippa, "Early Political Life of LBJ," 28–30; Pool, *Lyndon B. Johnson,* 173; Dugger, *The Politician,* 169; Mrs. Sam Fore, Jr. OH; Gene Latimer OH; Sim Gideon OH; Mr. S. Fore, Jr. OH; Steinberg, *Sam Johnson's Boy,* 74–75.

35. For the "communist" charge and League support, see Caro, *Path to Power,* 272–73; Steinberg, *Sam Johnson's Boy,* 74–75; *San Marcos Daily News,* March

5, 1934; Luther E. Jones OH; Gene Latimer OH; Dugger, *The Politician*, 174–75; Steinberg, *Sam Johnson's Boy*, 91–92; J. Kaaz Doyle, "Out of Step: Maury Maverick and the Politics of the Depression and the New Deal," doctoral thesis, History Department, University of Texas, Austin, 1989, pp. 157–58.

36. Hope R. Miller, "The Little Congress Speaks," *Washington Post Magazine*, Feb. 11, 1934; Russell M. Brown OH; Gene Latimer OH; *Washington Evening Star*, April 28, 1933; Steinberg, *Sam Johnson's Boy*, 78–79; Caro, *Path to Power*, 261–63.

37. William S. White OH; William S. White, *The Professional: Lyndon B. Johnson* (Boston, 1964), 109–10; Caro, *Path to Power*, 266–68.

38. Steinberg, *Sam Johnson's Boy*, 84–85; Kearns, *Lyndon Johnson*, 81; Dorris Powell OH; Lady Bird Johnson interview, Montgomery Papers, Baylor Univ.; Ruth Montgomery, *Mrs. LBJ* (N.Y., 1964); Antonio J. Taylor OH.

39. Steinberg, *Sam Johnson's Boy*, 83–84; Antonio J. Taylor OH; Cameron and Lucille McElroy OH; Lady Bird Johnson interview, Baylor Univ.; *Time*, Aug. 28, 1964; Eric Goldman, *The Tragedy of Lyndon Johnson* (N.Y., 1969 ed.), 402.

40. Steinberg, *Sam Johnson's Boy*, 85; Lady Bird Johnson interview, Baylor Univ.

41. *Ibid.*, Emma Boehringer Tooley OH; *Time*, Aug. 28, 1964; Flora Rheta Schreiber, "Lady Bird Johnson's First Years of Marriage," *Woman's Day*, Dec. 1967, p. 89; Steinberg, *Sam Johnson's Boy*, 86; Caro, *Path to Power*, 296–97.

42. Eugenia Boehringer Lasseter OH; Lady Bird Johnson interview, Baylor Univ.; Steinberg, *Sam Johnson's Boy*, 86–87; Lewis L. Gould, *Lady Bird Johnson and the Environment* (Lawrence, Kan., 1988), 10.

43. See Lady Bird Johnson interview, Baylor Univ.; Dugger, *The Politician*, 176–77.

44. *Ibid.*

45. Kearns, *Lyndon Johnson*, 80; Dugger, *The Politician*, 177–78; Schreiber, "Lady Bird Johnson's First Years of Marriage," 90–91; Emily Crow Selden OH; Caro, *Path to Power*, 294; Dugger and Caro particularly stress the idea that Lyndon's initial attraction to Lady Bird was her family wealth.

46. Lady Bird Johnson interview, Baylor Univ.; Steinberg, *Sam Johnson's Boy*, 87; Dugger, *The Politician*, 178–79; Caro, *Path to Power*, 299–300; Malcolm G. Bardwell OH.

47. The correspondence is in "A National Tribute to Lady Bird Johnson: On the Occasion of Her Sixty-fifth Birthday," Dec. 11, 1977, LBJL.

48. See Lady Bird Johnson interview, Baylor Univ.; Schreiber, "Lady Bird Johnson's First Years of Marriage," 89; Caro, *Path to Power*, 301.

49. See Lady Bird Johnson interview, Baylor Univ.; Daniel Quill OH; Henry Hirshberg OH; Cecille Harrison Marshall OH; Steinberg, *Sam Johnson's Boy*, 88–89.

50. Eugenia Boehringer Lasseter OH; Lady Bird Johnson interview, Baylor Univ.; Schreiber, "Lady Bird Johnson's First Years of Marriage," 89.

51. "First Years of Marriage," 89–90; Caro, *Path to Power*, 302–4; Steinberg, *Sam Johnson's Boy*, 255.

52. Schreiber, "First Years of Marriage," 89–91; Kearns, *Lyndon Johnson*, 83–84.

53. Russell M. Brown OH.

54. Mary Rather OH; Luther E. Jones OH; Russell M. Brown OH.

55. Dugger, *The Politician*, 179; Russell M. Brown OH; Luther E. Jones OH.

56. See Robert M. Jackson OH; Luther E. Jones OH; James P. Coleman OH; Russell M. Brown OH; Gene Latimer OH; Gov. James P. Coleman to Robert Dallek, Oct. 27, 1986; Caro, *Path to Power*, 263–65, 335–38. Caro says that Johnson "kept control of the organization through hand-picked candidates." He also says that "whispers about the way in which Lyndon Johnson had won the organization's Speakership had not died away—because with each succeeding election, invariably won by 'the Boss of the Little Congress,' they started up again." But the fact that LBJ served one term from 1933 to 1935 and Payne, his only chosen successor lost, seems to contradict these assertions. Governor Coleman's letter to me takes issue with other points in Caro's account.

57. Luther E. Jones OH; Willard Deason OH; Caro, *Path to Power*, 338–39.

58. See Steinberg, *Sam Johnson's Boy*, 93; Dugger, *The Politician*, 183; Caro, *Path to Power*, 272–90.

59. See Robert M. Jackson OH; Robert H. Montgomery OH; Malcolm G. Bardwell OH; Aubrey Williams to Maury Maverick, Sr., 1953, Maury Maverick, Sr. Papers, BTHC; Steinberg, *Sam Johnson's Boy*, 69–71, 93–94; Dugger, *The Politician*, 184–85; Caro, *Path to Power*, 333–34, 340, who stresses the part played by Sam Rayburn in LBJ's appointment. Caro describes how often Rayburn would go to the Johnson's apartment to take meals with them in 1935 and how Lyndon would kiss him on his bald head when they met in the halls of Congress. There can be no doubt that these events occurred, but it seems unlikely that much of this took place in 1935 when LBJ was still only a secretary. Moreover, the Johnsons were in Washington only from January to July. It seems more likely that this socializing and great closeness occurred after LBJ returned to Washington as a congressman in 1937. "Was he particularly close to Rayburn yet," an interviewer asked Robert M. Jackson about the period when he served as Kleberg's secretary. "No, he wasn't especially close to him. I think he was sort of getting more and more that way all the time." Jackson OH. Caro also says that Rayburn went to see FDR and got the appointment of DeWitt Kinard, the man originally selected, withdrawn and LBJ appointed in his place. But this contradicts the recollections of both Montgomery and Williams.

Chapter 5: The Making of a Congressman

1. Betty and Ernest K. Lindley, *A New Deal for Youth: The Story of the National Youth Administration* (N.Y., 1938), 8–11; Kingsley Davis, *Youth in the Depression* (Chicago, 1935), 5; Knippa, "Early Political Life of LBJ," 44–49; Deborah Lynn Self, "The National Youth Administration in Texas, 1935–1939," M.A. thesis, Dept. of History, Texas Tech University, Lubbock, 1974, pp. 1–7.

2. Joseph P. Lash, *Eleanor and Franklin* (N.Y., 1971), 536–38.

3. *Ibid.*, 539–40. *The Public Papers and Addresses of Franklin D. Roosevelt*, Vol. 4: *1935: The Court Disapproves* (N.Y., 1938), 281–82.

4. Dugger, *The Politician*, 185. Lady Bird Johnson interview, Baylor Univ.

5. Lindleys, *A New Deal for Youth*, x-xi.

6. LBJ to Aubrey Williams, Aug. 15, 1935, NYA Papers, National Archives (hereafter cited as NA); LBJ, "Texas Turns to Its Youth," *The Texas Outlook*, Nov. 1935, pp. 36–37; Knippa, "Early Political Life of LBJ," 58; Self, "The NYA in Texas," 18–19, 40–42; Caro, *Path to Power*, 346–47; Christie Lynne Bourgeois, "Lyndon Johnson's Years with the National Youth Administration," M.A. thesis, Dept. of History, Univ. of Texas, Austin, 1986, pp. 19, 30–31.

7. Steinberg, *Sam Johnson's Boy*, 94–95; Aubrey Williams to LBJ, July 25, 1935, LBJA:SN; John Corson to LBJ, Aug. 5, 1935; LBJ to Williams, Aug. 8, 1935, NA.

8. Arthur M. Schlesinger, Jr., *The Politics of Upheaval* (Boston, 1960), 351–52; Willard Deason OH; Bourgeois, "LBJ's Years with the NYA," 22–23.

9. W. Sherman Birdwell OH; Jesse Kellam OH; "Administrative Set-up, Texas," Jan. 1936, NA; Knippa, "Early Political Life of LBJ," 54–55; Steinberg, *Sam Johnson's Boy*, 95–96.

10. Richard R. Brown OH; *PPA:FDR, 1935*, 327–28; Dugger, *The Politician*, 185.

11. W. Sherman Birdwell OH; Jesse Kellam OH; Willard Deason OH; Kearns, *Lyndon Johnson*, 85; Bourgeois, "LBJ's Early Years with the NYA," 23–25.

12. Willard Deason OH; W. Sherman Birdwell OH.

13. Caro, *Path to Power*, 351–53. Willard Deason OH; Fenner Roth OH; "A Discussion Conducted by William S. White with a Group from Lyndon Johnson's Days as Director of the NYA," OH.

14. Knippa, "Early Political Life of LBJ," 79; Miller, *Lyndon*, 66.

15. Dugger, *The Politician*, 187–88; "A Discussion Conducted by William S. White . . . ," OH; Willard Deason OH; Fenner Roth OH; Albert Brisbin OH; Newlon, *L.B.J.*, 62; Bourgeois, "LBJ's Early Years with the NYA," 25–26, 63; Caro, *Path to Power*, 355–60.

16. LBJ to John J. Corson, Aug. 10, 1935; Corson to LBJ, Aug. 14, 1935, attached to Corson OH; Richard R. Brown OH; Steinberg, *Sam Johnson's Boy*, 101; Self, "The NYA in Texas," 26–27; Bourgeois, "LBJ's Early Years with the NYA," 26–28; LBJ to Corson, Sept. 30, 1935, NA.

17. Russell Ellzey to LBJ, Sept. 28, 1935; Herbert C. Henderson to LBJ, Oct. 1, 1935, NA; Self, "The NYA in Texas," 32–33; Ray E. Lee OH.

18. Lindleys, *A New Deal for Youth*, 158, 193; LBJ to C.F. Klinefelter, Aug. 20, 1935; and J.J. Corson to LBJ, Aug. 28, 1935, NA.

19. Knippa, "Early Political Life of LBJ," 58–59; H.A. Ziegler to LBJ, Sept. 27, 1935, which is part of LBJ to J.J. Corson, Sept. 30, 1935, NA; Jesse Kellam OH; Bourgeois, "LBJ's Early Years with the NYA," 31–32.

20. Willard Deason OH; W. Sherman Birdwell OH; LBJ to L.R. Alderman, Sept. 13, 1935, NA.

21. LBJ to Richard R. Brown, Oct. 10, 17, 1935; L.R. Alderman to LBJ, Oct. 14, 1935; Brown to LBJ, Oct. 22, 1935, NA; LBJ, *Texas Outlook*, Nov. 1935, p. 36; LBJ to James V. Allred, Sept. 27, 1935, and May 11, 1936, James V. Allred Papers, Univ. of Houston; LBJ, "Government Making It Possible for Young Men and Women to Attend College," *The Texas Press Messenger*, Sept. 1936.

22. H.A. Ziegler to LBJ, Sept. 27, 1935, NA; President Bradford Knapp of Texas Technological College, May 21, 1936, FDRL-M; Knippa, "Early Political Life of LBJ," 60–64; Self, "The NYA in Texas," 52–56.

23. LBJ to Aubrey Williams, Oct. 8, 1935, esp. attached Resolution, Sept. 30, 1935, NA; Self, "The NYA in Texas," 54–55, 57–60; Jesse Kellam OH.

24. See LBJ to Cecil Evans, Sept. 6, 12, 1935, Evans Papers, SWTSU; Kellam to LBJ, Sept. 28, 1935; LBJ to Aubrey Williams, Oct. 8, 1935; LBJ to Richard R. Brown, Oct. 29, 1935, NA; "Government Making It Possible," Sept. 1936, in LBJ scrapbks., BTHC; Self, "The NYA in Texas," 36, 69–72.

25. McElvaine, *The Great Depression*, 87–95; Harvard Sitkoff, "The New Deal and Race Relations," *Fifty Years Later: The New Deal Evaluated*, ed. Harvard Sitkoff (N.Y., 1985), 94–95, 98–101; Richard Polenberg, *One Nation Divisible: Class, Race, and Ethnicity in the United States since 1938* (N.Y., 1981 ed.), 24–25, 33; Bourgeois, "LBJ's Early Years with the NYA," 74–77.

26. Sitkoff, "New Deal and Race Relations," 98.

27. WPA Guide, *Texas*, 90; Bourgeois, "LBJ's Early Years with the NYA," 79, 90.

28. John J. Corson to LBJ, Sept. 17, 1935; LBJ to Corson, Sept. 22, 1935, NYA Papers, LBJL.

29. LBJ to Corson, Sept. 22, 1935; and Corson to LBJ, Sept. 26, 1935.

30. Luther E. Jones OH; WPA Guide, *Texas*, 89, 460–61: ". . . The vast majority of Mexicans south of the Nueces River exist in a system not unlike medieval feudalism." "In front of his guests, Johnson would often shout 'nigger' at me," Robert Parker, a black servant who worked part-time for LBJ in the 1940s, said. "LBJ and Me," *The Houston Post*, June 29, 1986. LBJ to Jesse Kellam, Jan. 20, 1945, LBJA:SN, in which he explained that they could have the evening out because he had "a nigger gal to watch the babies."

31. Monroe Billington, "Lyndon B. Johnson and Blacks: The Early Years," *Journal of Negro History*, V, 62 (Jan. 1977): 29–30; "Report for October 1935," NYA Admin. Reports; LBJ to Richard R. Brown, March 4, 1936; "Special Report of Negro Activities of the NYA in Texas," March 5, 1936, NA.

32. Dugger, *The Politician*, 188; Kearns, *Lyndon Johnson*, 231.

33. LBJ to Richard Brown, April 27, 1936, NA; "Government Making It Possible," Sept. 1936; Albert W. Brisbin OH.

34. Knippa, "Early Political Life of LBJ," 64–65; Caro, *Path to Power*, 346–47; W. Sherman Birdwell OH.

35. R.H. Montgomery OH; Dugger, *The Politician*, 186–87; Bourgeois, "LBJ's Early Years with the NYA," 37–38; W. Sherman Birdwell OH; Jesse Kellam OH; Willard Deason OH; Caro, *Path to Power*, 347.

36. L.E. Jones OH; LBJ to Richard Brown, July 29, 1936; Brown to LBJ, March 20, 1936; Akridge to Brown, July 14, 1936, NA; Self, "The NYA in Texas," 84–85.

37. Brown to LBJ, May 25, 1936; LBJ to Brown, July 29, 1936; L.B. Griffith to LBJ, Aug. 27, 1936, NA; James Allred to LBJ, Aug. 31, 1935; LBJ to Allred, Sept. 27, 1935; Nov. 25, 1936, with news release of Nov. 22 attached, Allred Papers; Knippa, "Early Political Life of LBJ," 68–74; "Texas, 1939" and "NYA Resident Projects: Prairie View State Normal and Industrial College," April 15, 1938, NA.

38. "Report on the National Youth Administration," June 26, 1935 to June 30, 1938; J.C. Kellam to Brown, April 13, 1937, NA; Mooney, *The LBJ Story*, 42; *Congressional Record*, 76th Cong., 1st sess., pp. 2238–39; Knippa, "Early Political Life of LBJ," 83–84; *PPP:LBJ, 1967*, I, 515–16.

39. Ellzey to LBJ, April 7, 1936; Ellzey to W.O. Alexander, April 6, 1936; Akridge to Brown, July 14, 1936; Brown to Williams, Feb. 2, 1937, NA; Bourgeois, "LBJ's Early Years with the NYA," 65–66.

40. Richard R. Brown OH; Beatrice Denmark to Brown, Feb. 9, 1937, NA.

41. Self, "The NYA in Texas," 45; Senator Tom Connally to Malvina Scheider, Jan. 21, 1936; Eleanor Roosevelt to LBJ, Jan. 26, 1936, Eleanor Roosevelt Papers, FDRL; telephone conversation, LBJ and Aubrey Williams, June 3, 1936, Aubrey Williams Papers, FDRL; Ray Lee OH; Fenner Roth OH; Steinberg, *Sam Johnson's Boy*, 98; Dugger, *The Politician*, 189; Bourgeois, "LBJ's Early Years with the NYA," 66–68; Jesse Kellam OH.

42. Wirtz to Welly Hopkins, Feb. 24, 1936, Hopkins Papers, LBJL; Sim Gideon OH; Schulman, *From Cotton Belt to Sunbelt*, 42–43; Kearns, *Lyndon Johnson*, 85–86; Dugger, *The Politician*, 190, and n. 1, p. 433.

43. *Austin Statesman*, Feb. 23, 1937; Mr. Sam Fore, Jr. OH; Daniel Quill OH; E. Shelton OH; Claude Wild OH.

44. Mary Rather OH; Steinberg, *Sam Johnson's Boy*, 105–6; Kearns, *Lyndon Johnson*, 86.

45. Steinberg, *Sam Johnson's Boy*, 101–5; Caro, *Path to Power*, 373–76. Caro focuses on Wirtz's desire for "power over other men," and asserts that "Wirtz had early seen dams as the way to get it." He places no credence in the idea that Wirtz had commitments to the New Deal, and he argues that Wirtz's support of LBJ's candidacy rested almost exclusively on his expectation of using Johnson to assure the completion of the dams, which was jeopardized by Buchanan's death and other developments. Caro does not explain, however, why Herman Brown of the Brown & Root construction firm, which had an essential financial stake in the completion of the dams, refused to support LBJ in the 1937 campaign (see p. 475).

46. *Austin American*, Feb. 28, 1937; Caro, *Path to Power*, 398–99; Ray Lee OH.

47. Steinberg, *Sam Johnson's Boy*, 106–7; "My Friend Lyndon," chapter in "Rendezvous with Democracy: The Memoirs of 'Tommy the Cork,' " Corcoran Papers, Library of Congress (hereafter cited as LC); Dr. R.H. Montgomery OH; Dugger, *The Politician*, 192–93.

48. Ray Lee OH; Steinberg, *Sam Johnson's Boy*, 108–9; Caro, *Path to Power*, 402–3.

49. Knippa, "Early Political Life of LBJ," 88; L.E. Jones OH; Mary Rather OH; W. and V. Woods OH.

50. *Austin American*, March 28, 1937; George N. Green, *The Establishment in Texas Politics: The Primitive Years, 1938–1957* (Westport, Conn., 1979), p. 14, and n. 7, p. 233; *Austin American*, March 1, 6, 1937.

51. *Austin American*, March 1, 6, 25, 1937; *Austin Statesman*, March 12, 1937.

52. Steinberg, *Sam Johnson's Boy*, 110; Caro, *Path to Power*, 404; Green, *The Establishment in Texas Politics*, 14; LBJ to Granbery, March 18, 1937., John C. Granbery Papers, BTHC.

53. "Opponents" folder, House of Representatives Papers (hereafter cited as HRP), LBJL.

54. The speeches and press release are in Boxes 1 and 331, HRP.

55. Edward Clark interview, Dec. 15, 1986; Dugger, *The Politician*, 192, 194, 196; Caro, *Path to Power*, 405. Welly Hopkins OH.

56. Hopkins to LBJ, n.d.; Hopkins to West, March 10, 1937, Hopkins Papers, LBJL; Knippa, "Early Political Life of LBJ," 143; *Austin Statesman*, March 24, 1937; Elliott Roosevelt to LBJ, n.d.; and Drew Pearson, "Washington Merry-Go-Round," n.d., in HR scrapbks., LBJL; *Austin American*, April 9, 1937; C.N. Avery to FDR, April 5, 1937; M.H. McIntyre to Avery, April 7, 1937, FDRL. Judging from a telegram he sent Farley on April 5, Elliott Roosevelt's support was apparently given without the approval of the Administration: "Congressional race is coming to a head down here as straight out fight between Lyndon Johnson who is backing father wholeheartedly on his whole program including the court issue and two other candidates who have refused to support father on that question. Would it be advisable for me to speak on behalf of Johnson. Would appreciate wire today so that I can advise them one way or other as to my acceptance." At the top of the telegram is written: "Your judgement he should not." Also see Farley's letter to Elliott Roosevelt, April 6, 1937, Farley Papers, LC.

57. E. Shelton OH; Caro, *Path to Power*, 411, 431, 433–35; "Tit-Tat-Too," a Huling, Texas, clipping in HR scrapbks., LBJL.

58. *Austin American*, March 25, 28, April 8, 1937; *Austin Statesman*, March 20, 1937; Ray Lee OH; Caro, *Path to Power*, 403–4, 428; Dugger, *The Politician*, 196.

59. Interview, A.J. Cox; *Austin American*, March 27, 1937; Caro, *Path to Power*, 428–29.

60. *Washington Post*, April 11, 1937; Caro, *Path to Power*, 409–11; Dugger, *The Politician*, 196.

61. Caro, *Path to Power*, 411–18; Kearns, *Lyndon Johnson*, 88; Ray Lee OH; E. Shelton OH; Fore, Quill, Buck, and White OH; *Austin American*, April 8, 1937; A.J. Cox interview; memos in Box 1, HRP.

62. Ray Lee OH; *San Antonio Express*, March 27, 1937; Caro, *Path to Power*, 427.

63. Claude Wild OH; Dugger, *The Politician*, 195–96; *Austin American*, April 6, 1937; LBJ speech, "Happy Days for the Liberty League," April 2, 1937, HRP.

64. E. Shelton OH; Polk and Nell Shelton OH; L.E. Jones OH; Edward Clark interview; Caro, *Path to Power*, 408–9.

65. Knippa, "Early Political Life of LBJ," 133. LBJ speech, "Happy Days for the Liberty League," April 2, 1937; "Lyndon Debates Shelton's Kinsman," *Austin American*, April 8, 1937.

66. Caro, *Path to Power*, 408; Emmett Shelton OH.

67. Fore, Quill, Buck, White OH; Claude Wild OH; Gordon Fulcher OH.

68. Ray Lee OH; and a memo of the vote by 10th District counties, April 1937, HRP.

Chapter 6: The New Dealer

1. Henrietta Pyle to LBJ, April 30, 1937, Allred Papers.

2. *Austin American*, April 27, 1937; telegrams from LBJ to Avery, Shelton, and Stone, n.d. (probably April 13, 1937); Maverick to LBJ, April 12, 1937, HRP.

3. *Austin American*, April 27, 1937; Thomas B. Love, April 11, 1937; Reese B. Lockett, April 11, 1937; memo for the trip file, April 20, 1937; Allred to McIntyre, May 6, 1937, Franklin D. Roosevelt Library (hereafter cited as FDRL); Allred to LBJ, April 27 and May 3, 1937, Allred Papers. Robert Caro says that LBJ asked for assignment to the House Agriculture Committee, but I found nothing in the materials he used or I read to substantiate that point: *Path to Power*, 446.

4. *Austin American*, May 12, 1937; Carroll Keach OH; Tom Crider OH; Dugger, *The Politician*, 200–201; Caro, *Path to Power*, 446–47.

5. *New York Times*, May 12, 1937; "My Friend Lyndon," p. 3, Corcoran Papers, LC; Edward Clark interview, Dec. 15, 1986; *Congressional Record*, 1937, vol. 82, p. 354; Steinberg, *Sam Johnson's Boy*, 119–20; Miller, *Lyndon*, 75–76, and n. 8, p. 715; Dugger, *The Politician*, 201–2.

6. Caro, *Path to Power*, 448–49; Rowland Evans and Robert Novak, *Lyndon B. Johnson: The Exercise of Power* (N.Y., 1966), 18.

7. Welly K. Hopkins OH; *Congressional Record*, 1937, vol. 81, p. 4508; *Dallas News*, May 14, 1937; LBJ to Sam Rayburn, May 13, 1939, LBJA:CF.

8. *New York Times*, May 19, 1960; p. 4 of "My Friend Lyndon," Corcoran Papers; Eliot Janeway interview, Dec. 20, 1986; Edwin Weisl, Sr. OH.

9. James H. Rowe, Jr. OH; Elizabeth Rowe OH; Virginia Foster Durr OH; Clifford and Virginia Durr OH; Arthur E. Goldschmidt and Elizabeth Wickenden OH; E.W. Goldschmidt OH; Abe Fortas OH; William O. Douglas, *Go East, Young Man: The Early Years* (N.Y., 1974), chaps. x, xi, xviii–xxi.

10. "My Friend Lyndon," 3, 4, Corcoran Papers; Douglas, *Go East, Young Man*, 327; V. Durr OH.

11. J.H. Rowe, Jr. OH; E. Rowe OH.

12. Evans and Novak, *LBJ: Exercise of Power*, 18–19; (Texas) *State Observer*, June 10, 1940; Paul Bolton OH.

13. J.H. Rowe, Jr. OH.

14. John W. McCormack OH (LBJL) and OH (Boston Univ. Library); in latter McCormack elaborated on his regard for LBJ as a political leader.

15. Steinberg, *Sam Johnson's Boy*, 121.

16. LBJ to Bankhead, Dec. 3, 1938, William B. Bankhead Papers, Alabama Archives; Eliot Janeway, "The Man Who Owns the Navy," *Sat. Eve. Post*, Dec. 15, 1945, pp. 45, 101–2; William S. White, "Carl Vinson Has Been Unified," *New York Times Magazine*, Sept. 10, 1950, pp. 12, 42, 44.

17. Steinberg, *Sam Johnson's Boy*, 137–39.

18. Alfred Steinberg, *Sam Rayburn: A Biography* (N.Y., 1975), 24–28, 130–38, 173–200.

19. *Ibid.*, 197. John W. McCormack OH (LBJL); R.E. Thomason OH; David

E. Lilienthal OH; Anna Rosenberg Hoffman OH; Edward Joseph OH; LBJ to Sam Rayburn, May 13, 1937, LBJA:CF; Caro, *Path to Power*, 333–34, 452–53.

20. Steinberg, *Rayburn*, 195–97; J.H. Rowe, Jr. OH.

21. *PPP:LBJ, 1963–64*, I, 150–51; Kearns, *Lyndon Johnson*, 89.

22. All of LBJ's votes, 1937–41, except on term insurance and reorganization, are recorded in "Voting Record of Congressman Lyndon B. Johnson," 75th, 76th, and 77th Congresses; the other two votes can be found in "Complete House Voting Record of Lyndon B. Johnson," 249, 288, LBJL.

23. Dugger, *The Politician*, 215 and 438, n. 7; Leuchtenburg, *FDR and the New Deal*, 277–80; Edward C. Eicher to FDR, Dec. 23, 1938, J.H. Rowe, Jr. Papers, FDRL.

24. Steinberg, *Rayburn*, 179; Steinberg, *Sam Johnson's Boy*, 139.

25. "LBJ Voting Record," 75th Congress; Steinberg, *Sam Johnson's Boy*, 129–30; E. Ernest Goldstein OH; "LBJ Complete House Voting Record," 11–12, 85–86, 88–89; J.H. Rowe, Jr. OH. Because LBJ was not vocal in support of liberal actions and did not introduce national legislation or take an aggressive stand on national issues, Caro sees him as an unprincipled opportunist: "He had shouted 'Roosevelt, Roosevelt, Roosevelt' to get to Congress; in Congress, he shouted nothing, said nothing—stood for nothing. Not only was he not in the van of any cause, he was not in the ranks, either." *Path to Power*, 550, 544–52. For a contrary picture, see William E. Leuchtenburg, "Lyndon B. Johnson," a chapter in *In the Shadow of FDR: From Harry Truman to Ronald Reagan* (Ithaca, N.Y., 1983), and n. 3 on p. 297 in particular, where Leuchtenburg writes that Caro depicts LBJ as "a conservative or a man of no principles. Caro has unearthed a remarkable amount of new material, but the weight of evidence, including much of Caro's own evidence, leads to a contrary conclusion." Also see Paul Burka, "A Monumental Man," *Texas Monthly*, Jan. 1983, pp. 124–29.

26. Newlon, *L.B.J.*, 76–77; Mooney, *Lyndon Johnson Story*, 51; Monroe Billington, "Lyndon B. Johnson and Blacks: The Early Years," *Journal of Negro History*, Jan. 1977, p. 32; "LBJ Complete House Voting Record," 12.

27. Henry L. Feingold, *The Politics of Rescue: The Roosevelt Administration and the Holocaust, 1938–1945* (New Brunswick, N.J., 1970), chap. 1; LBJ to Erich Leinsdorf, Aug. 4, 1939, LBJA:FN; Erich Leinsdorf OH; Erich Leinsdorf, *Cadenza: A Musical Career* (Boston, 1976), 56, 75–79; Caro, *Path to Power*, 481–82; Louis S. Gomolak, "Prologue: LBJ's Foreign Affairs Background, 1908–1948," Ph.D. dissertation, Dept. of History, Univ. of Texas, 1989, pp. 35–51, who has reconstructed these events from Jim Novy's papers and interviews; Lady Bird Johnson, *A White House Diary* (N.Y., 1970), 28. ·

28. Corcoran to M.A. LeHand, July 8, 1938, FDRL; memorandum, Nov. 11, 1939, Corcoran Papers, LC; *Austin American*, Sept. 13, 1937; *Burnett Bulletin*, June 30, 1938; *The Bartlett Tribune*, July 1, 1938; *Elgin Courier*, June 9, 1938; *Austin American-Statesman*, May 14, 1939; "Schedule of Visits of Cong. LBJ to FDR, 1937–44," FDRL; J.H. Rowe to Corcoran, June 1, 1939, Corcoran Papers; two LBJ speeches, Sept. 20–22 and Oct. 14, 1937, HRP.

29. Caro, *Path to Power*, 497–501.

30. LBJ to W.E. Stevenson, Feb. 4, 1983, HRP; "Austin Business Man" to Tom Miller, June 23, 1938, LBJA:SN; LBJ to Evans, June 11, 16, 1938, Evans

Papers; *Austin American,* April 1, 1938; *Austin Statesman,* June 23, 1938; Caro, *Path to Power,* 496–97.

31. *Congressional Record,* 1938, vol. 83, p. A 1252; Dugger, *The Politician,* 209–10; *Austin American,* Dec. 21, 22, 23, 1937, Jan. 14, 1938.

32. Leon H. Keyserling OH.

33. *Austin American,* Jan 15, 20, 21, 22, 23, 1938; LBJ to Robert Allen, May 16, 1939, LBJA:SF.

34. *Austin American,* Jan. 24, 25, 1938; *Dallas Morning News,* Dec. 17, 1939; *PPP:LBJ, 1968–69,* II, 1192–93; Miller, *Lyndon,* 87.

35. *Austin American,* March 1, 18, 1938, June 25, 26, 1939; *Austin Statesman,* March 18, 1938; *Dallas Morning News,* Dec. 17, 1939; Dugger, *The Politician,* 211.

36. Memorandum Relative to the Dams on the Colorado River, Texas: From Mary Rather, April 1, 1975, Lower Colorado River Authority Papers (hereafter cited as LCRA), LBJL; Anthony M. Orum, "The Making of Austin: Taming the River: Part One," *The Texas Observer,* Dec. 14, 1984, pp. 15 and 17; LBJ, "Must the Farmer Stay in the Lurch?" Sept 20, 1937, HRP; Steinberg, *Sam Johnson's Boy,* 104; Dugger, *The Politician,* 206; Caro, *Path to Power,* 377.

37. Memo Relative to Dams, April 1, 1975; Orum, *The Texas Observer,* Dec. 14, 1984, pp. 17–19.

38. Memo Relative to Dams, April 1, 1975: Mary Rather to Charles Corkran, April 4, 1975; Memorandum Covering Services Rendered by A.J. Wirtz, n.d., LCRA Papers; Henry T. Hunt, Memo to the Administrator, April 26, 1935, HRP; Orum, *The Texas Observer,* Dec. 14, 1984, pp. 17–19, 21–22.

39. Orum, *The Texas Observer,* Dec. 14, 1984, p. 22; Hunt to Administrator, April 26, 1935; FDR to Sec. of the Treasury, May 28, 1935; Résumé of Colorado River Dams, n.d., HRP; *Fort Worth Press,* Feb. 17, 1937.

40. Memo: LCRA: Colorado River Project, Texas, n.d., LCRA Papers; Herman Brown to LBJ, July 16, 1937, HRP; John C. Page to Burlew, June 29, 1937; Budget Officer to Hopkins, June 30, 1937, Selected Documents Relating to LBJ, Department of Interior Files, M, LBJL; LBJ to Tom Miller, July 21, 1937, HRP; *Austin American,* July 22, 1937; For LBJ's additional efforts, 1937–41, see Box 167, HRP, Dept. of Interior Files, M, LBJL, OF 402, FDRL; and Anthony M. Orum, "Taming the River, Part Two: Enter Lyndon Johnson," *The Texas Observer,* Jan 11, 1985.

41. "My Friend Lyndon," 4–5, Corcoran Papers.

42. Brown to LBJ, May 2, June 12, 1939, LBJA:SN; Dugger, *The Politician,* 276–80; Orum, *The Texas Observer,* Jan. 11, 1985, p. 15.

43. Leuchtenburg, *FDR and the New Deal,* 157–58; Schlesinger, Jr., *Politics of Upheaval,* 379–80.

44. Caro, *Path to Power,* chap. 27, and pp. 513, 515, 518 in particular.

45. Schlesinger, Jr., *Politics of Upheaval,* 379–83.

46. Sim Gideon OH; Virginia Durr OH; Russell Morton Brown OH; LBJ to Carl White, March 28, 1938, LCRA Papers.

47. The LCRA needed to sell its hydroelectric power to pay off its bonds. Whether it sold it to private utilities companies, cities, or cooperatives, however, seemed to be less of an issue for LCRA Board members than for Johnson. LBJ

to Carol White, March 28, 1938; Statement of LBJ, April 12, 1938, LCRA Papers; LBJ to Gordon Fulcher, Feb. 7, 1938, LBJA:SN.

48. LBJ to Clarence McDonough, March 16, 1938; press release, March 17, 1938; statement of LBJ, April 12, 1938, LCRA Papers. Alvin Wirtz shared Johnson's desire to bypass the private utilities and sell LCRA power to cities and cooperatives: Wirtz to LBJ, March 22, 1938, LBJA:SN.

49. "City Distribution of Cheap Power Asked of Group," *Austin American-Statesman*, May 1, 1938; Fritz Englehard to LBJ, April 26, 1938; LBJ to McDonough, May 14, 1938; McDonough to LBJ, May 18, 1938, LCRA Papers; LBJ, "Conversation with Old Friends," April 27, 1970, LBJL; Miller, *Lyndon*, 85.

50. K to McIntyre, June 3, 1938; LBJ to FDR, June 8, 1938, FDRL; LBJ, "Conversation with Old Friends."

51. "My Friend Lyndon," Corcoran Papers; LBJ, "Conversation with Old Friends"; Lady Bird and LBJ interview, Sept. 18, 1972.

52. *PPA:FDR, 1938*, 421–26; Steve Davis, "The South as 'the Nation's No. 1 Economic Problem': The NEC Report of 1938," *Georgia Historical Quarterly* (Summer 1978), 119–32; LBJ, "Conversation with Old Friends"; Lady Bird and LBJ interview, Sept. 18, 1972; Miller, *Lyndon*, 85; LBJ to McDonough, June 10, 1938; E.K. Burlew to Gray, June 9, 1938; Gray to Burlew, June 18, 1938, Dept. of Interior Files, M, LBJL; Charles Henderson to Sherman Birdwell, July 11, 1938, HRP; "Half Million Set Aside for Power Line," *Fredericksburg Standard*, June 30, 1938; "Colorado Lines Are Assured," *Mason News*, July 14, 1938; Tom to M.A. LeHand, July 8, 1938, FDRL.

53. "4 Texas Towns to Ballot on Power Plants," *Dallas Times Herald*, Sept. 24, 1938; Arthur Stehling to LBJ, June 28, 1938, HRP; Caro, *Path to Power*, 524–26; "Struggling Texas Co-ops Succeeded with LBJ Aid," *Rural Electrification*, Jan. 1964, pp. 8–9.

54. Gordon Fulcher OH; Starcke to LBJ (1938), LCRA Papers; Orum, *The Texas Observer*, Jan. 11, 1985, p. 19; George B. Tindall, *The Ethnic Southerners* (Baton Rouge, 1976), chap. 10; Arthur Goldschmidt to LBJ, Aug. 13, 1938, HRP.

55. Edwin C. Bearss, *Lyndon B. Johnson and the Hill Country, 1937–1963: Historic Resource Study* (Santa Fe, 1984), 5–7; "More than 1,000 Attend Two Meetings," *Austin Statesman*, July 26, 1938; "Johnson Cites Fight Upon CRA . . . ," *Austin American*, Aug. 25, 1938; "Johnson Appeals for . . . CRA Power," *Austin American*, Sept. 24, 1938; Orum, *The Texas Observer*, Jan. 11, 1985, p. 19.

56. Gordon Fulcher OH; Caro, *Path to Power*, 527–28; *Austin American*, Jan. 2, 1939; *Houston Chronicle*, Jan. 3, 1939.

57. LBJ to McDonough, March 24, 1939; LBJ to Wirtz, April 26, 1939; Wirtz to LBJ, April 29, 1939, LCRA Papers; Lady Bird and LBJ interview, Sept. 18, 1972; *The Weekly Dispatch*, July 28, 1939; Acting Chmn. Power Comm. to Pres. Carpenter, T. P. & L., n.d., HRP; Legal Services Rendered LCRA, n.d., 10–12, Alvin Wirtz Papers, LBJL; Wirtz to Goldschmidt, Jan. 5, 14, 1939, Arthur Goldschmidt Papers, LBJL.

58. LBJ to FDR, July 18, 1939; LBJ to FDR, Oct. 4, 1939, with attachments; LBJ to Carmody, Jan. 31, 1959, LBJA:FN.

59. H.A. Wallace to FDR, July 19, 1939; LBJ to FDR, July 29, 1939; FDR to LBJ, Aug. 2, 1939, FDRL; Harold L. Ickes Ms. Diary, July 24, 1939, LC; Caro, *Path to Power*, 501, who quotes Corcoran.

Chapter 7: National Politics

1. Ben Crider to LBJ, March 26, 1939, LBJA:SN; Ralph W. Yarborough to LBJ, June 2, 1939, LBJA:CF; Steinberg, *Sam Johnson's Boy*, 126; Miller, *Lyndon*, 89.

2. "Mirrors of Austin," (Texas) *State Observer*, June 10, 1940; Arthur E. Goldschmidt and Elizabeth Wickenden OH; LBJ to Jesse Kellam, Aug. 8, 1937, LBJA:SN.

3. Dorothy J. Nichols OH; Sherman Birdwell OH.

4. Gene Latimer OH; Sherman Birdwell OH; John F. Koeniger OH; LBJ to Bill Deason, June 16, 1937, LBJA:SN; Dugger, *The Politician*, 217.

5. John B. Connally interview, June 30, 1988; Walter Jenkins OH; Steinberg, *Sam Johnson's Boy*, 126–27; Miller, *Lyndon*, 88–89; Dugger, *The Politician*, 217; Caro, *Path to Power*, 495–96.

6. Dugger, *The Politician*, 205; Sherman Birdwell OH.

7. LBJ to Jesse Kellam, Aug. 8, 1937, LBJA:SN; Sherman Birdwell OH; Gene Latimer OH; Caro, *Path to Power*, 494.

8. "Lyndon Baines Johnson, an American Original," *People*, Feb. 2, 1987, p. 36; Jake Pickle interview with Christie Bourgeois, Feb. 10, 1986; Felix Mc-Knight OH; Dorothy J. Nichols OH; Walter Jenkins OH.

9. Sherman Birdwell OH.

10. W. Ervin "Red" James OH; L.T. (Tex) Easley OH; *People*, Feb. 2, 1987, pp. 36, 38.

11. Schreiber, *Woman's Day*, Dec. 1967, p. 91.

12. *Ibid.*, 91, 94–95; Katie Louchheim, *The Making of the New Deal: The Insiders Speak* (Cambridge, Mass., 1983), 303; Steinberg, *Sam Johnson's Boy*, 127–29.

13. Eliot Janeway interview, Dec. 20, 1986; confidential source; Laura Kalman, *Abe Fortas: A Biography* (New Haven, 1990), 196; Walter Jenkins OH: "I remember one conversation he talked about sex. I think part of it was trying to shock me maybe, an innocent young kid. But it also is kind of generally the way he felt about things. [He said] he didn't see anything wrong with people having sex outside of marriage or something of that kind. It kind of shocked me. I said, 'Well, wouldn't that bother you in your own family?' He said, 'Well, not really,' but I know that it would have."

14. Caro, *Path to Power*, chap. 25; "Charles E. Marsh, President-Maker," *Orlando Sentinel*, Jan. 1, 1965.

15. *Ibid.* Although Caro may have exaggerated the seriousness of the affair, there seems little doubt that LBJ and Alice had an extended intimate relationship; see letter from Diana Marsh to the Editor, *Atlantic Monthly*, March 1983; Joe B. Franz's review of Caro in the *Dallas Morning News*. For a more judicious estimate of the relationship than Caro's, see Conkin, *Big Daddy*, 97–99. When

I asked Edward Clark about LBJ and Alice Glass, he replied: "I never saw them screwing. But she was in that business." Interview, Dec. 15, 1986. John Connally related the weekend episode to me in an interview, June 30, 1988. Dugger, *The Politician*, 253–54; Nancy Dickerson, *Among Those Present: A Reporter's View of Twenty-five Years in Washington* (N.Y., 1976), 138–39; Emily Crow Selden OH; *People*, Feb. 2, 1987, p. 35.

16. See "Johnson Boomed for Committee Job," *Austin American*, Oct. 8, 1938; Ed Gossett OH; L.T. (Tex) Easley OH.

17. Warren Magnuson OH; Steinberg, *Sam Johnson's Boy*, 140; Margaret Chase Smith OH; George Brown OH. On March 5, 1940, in reply to a Johnson letter of February 27, 1940, in which LBJ mentioned "the ninety-six old men," Brown wrote: "I don't know whether or not you have made up your mind about what future course you want to take, but some day in the next few years one of the old ones is going to pass on, and if you decided to go that route I think it would be 'gret' to do it," LBJA:SN.

18. "I am in worse financial condition right now than anyone you know," was Johnson's answer to a request for a contribution in March 1940. "I have had three operations and four deaths in my immediate family in the last two years, and I have exhausted about all the resources I have." LBJ to John C. Granbery, March 30, 1940, Granbery Papers; Caro, *Path to Power*, xiii-xvi; George Brown OH; Conkin, *Big Daddy*, 93. Although oil and natural gas interests were beginning to have substantial power in Texas by the late thirties, an open identification with them for someone seeking statewide office was not good politics. Wilbur L. O'Daniel, the highly successful candidate for governor in 1938 and 1940, for example, was supported quietly by big oil in his campaigns, but he posed as a liberal opposed to big-business interests. See Green, *Establishment in Texas Politics*, 14–15, 25, 28.

19. Leuchtenburg, *FDR and the New Deal*, 266–72.

20. James MacGregor Burns, *Roosevelt: The Lion and the Fox* (N.Y., 1956), 412–14; *Time*, March 20, 1939.

21. *Secret Diary of Harold L. Ickes: The Inside Struggle, 1936–1939* (N.Y., 1954), 607; LBJ to James Rowe, May 17, 1939, Rowe Papers; *Austin American*, July 13, 1939; *Edinburg Review*, July 15, 1939; *Corsicana Sun*, July 21, 1939; *Austin Statesman*, July 21, Aug. 5, 1939; *Dallas News*, Aug. 5, 1939; memo to Congm. Lyndon B. Johnson, July 18, 1939, FDRL.

22. "LBJ Complete House Voting Record," 163–64; *Dallas Times Herald*, Aug. 17, 1939; Dugger, *The Politician*, 222; Robert Coles's review of Kearns's *Lyndon Johnson and the American Dream*, in *The New Republic*, Aug. 7, 1976, pp. 28–29; Paul Burka's review of Caro in the *Texas Monthly*, Jan. 1983, p. 129.

23. Ickes, *The Inside Struggle*, 688, 693–94, 699; Steinberg, *Rayburn*, 158–59.

24. *Houston Post*, July 28, 1939; *Fort Worth Star-Telegram*, July 30, 1939.

25. Ickes, *The Inside Struggle*, 653–54; *Secret Diary of Harold L. Ickes: The Lowering Clouds, 1939–1941* (N.Y., 1954), 95; Miller, *Lyndon*, 90–91.

26. FDR to Postmaster General, July 6, 1939; memo, July 15, 1939; James Rowe to LeHand, Aug. 10, 1939; FDR to Rowe, Aug. 14, 1939, FDRL; *Austin Statesman*, Aug. 30, 1939; LBJ to Birdwell, Jan 1, 1940, LBJA:SN.

27. Burns, *Lion and the Fox*, 412–13.

28. Ickes, *Lowering Clouds*, 84, 94–95, 104–5, 158; Burns, *Lion and the Fox*, 414; Steinberg, *Sam Johnson's Boy*, 145. Maverick to A.J. Wirtz, Dec. 13, 1939; Wirtz to Maverick, Jan. 6, 1940, Maverick Papers; *Houston Press*, Jan. 3, 1940.

29. Ickes, *Lowering Clouds*, 140, 145, 155–57.

30. Steinberg, *Sam Johnson's Boy*, 146–47; Dugger, *The Politician*, 222.

31. Hardeman and Bacon, *Rayburn*, 238–39; Rayburn to Burris C. Jackson, April 23, 1940; Rayburn to Homer D. Wade, April 30, 1940, Sam Rayburn Papers, Sam Rayburn Library (hereafter cited as SRL).

32. Ickes, *Lowering Clouds*, 167–69; Rayburn and Johnson to Wirtz and Blaylock, April 29, 1940, and replies of April 30, 1940, Wirtz Papers; *Austin Statesman*, April 30, 1940; *Austin American*, April 30, May 1, 1940.

33. Hardeman and Bacon, *Rayburn*, 236–38, 243.

Caro describes the Administration's embarrassment of Rayburn as inspired by LBJ and Wirtz. Caro sees this as part of a "Secret campaign [on LBJ's part] to undermine Rayburn in Roosevelt's eyes." According to Caro, Johnson wished to tar Rayburn so that he could replace him as "Roosevelt's man in Texas." He also depicts Johnson as highly secretive about what he was doing. So much so, that Garnerites like E.B. Germany did not think that LBJ was one of the principal figures in the pro-Roosevelt, anti-Garner campaign in Texas. Caro makes much of the fact that Johnson spent little time in Texas between April and June 1940, and points particularly to his apparent absence from the state Democratic convention in Waco beginning on May 28, 1940 (pp. 588–605, 618–19).

I share the conclusion of Hardeman and Bacon, *Rayburn*, 236–38, that there is "scant evidence" for the assertion that Johnson was making a systematic campaign to undermine Rayburn, which produced serious tensions between them. See my discussion later in this chapter of what happened between them. As for the assertion that Johnson kept his actions hidden, see the *New York Times* of April 6, 1940, which listed LBJ along with Miller, Ed. Clark, Maverick, and Governors James and Miriam Ferguson as leaders in a third-term draft movement in Texas. Also see *San Antonio Express*, May 17, 1940, which included a story published in many other Texas newspapers describing LBJ as one who had the "complete confidence and close personal friendship of Roosevelt" and as the man proposed by the "third-term group" as vice-chairman of the Texas delegation to the state Democratic convention. A front-page *Washington Post* story, May 1, 1940, on the compromise described LBJ as a "Roosevelt 100 per center." See the citations in note 34 below, which explain LBJ's absence as caused by the international crisis. In fact, none of the Texas Democrats in Congress came to the Waco convention because of developments in the European war.

34. *Washington Post*, May 1, 1940; LBJ to Rayburn, May 6, 1940; Rayburn to Lee Simmons, May 24, 1940; to S.F. Leslie, May 24, 1940; Leslie to Rayburn, May 31, 1940, Rayburn Papers; Maverick to LBJ, Wirtz, and Ickes, May 20, 1940, Maverick Papers; *Fort Worth Star-Telegram*, May 24, 1940; *Austin American*, May 2, 27, 28, 1940; *Austin American Statesman*, May 26, 1940; *Austin Statesman*, May 28, 1940; Steinberg, *Sam Johnson's Boy*, 148–49; Dugger, *The Politician*, 223.

35. Edith H. Parker OH; Steinberg, *Sam Johnson's Boy*, 149–51; Burns, *Lion and the Fox*, 428–30; Leuchtenburg, *FDR and the New Deal*, 317; Dugger, *The Politician*, 223–24; and Hardeman and Bacon, *Rayburn*, 239–41.

36. Robert Dallek, *Franklin D. Roosevelt and American Foreign Policy, 1932–1945* (N.Y., 1979), 218–32; Leuchtenburg, *FDR and the New Deal*, 299–300; Hardeman and Bacon, *Rayburn*, 227–28; Voting Record of LBJ, 76th Cong., 3rd sess.

37. *Austin Tribune*, June 8, 1940; Wirtz to LBJ, May 20 and June 24, 1940, Wirtz Papers.

38. Henry L. Stimson to LBJ, n.d. (1940), Charles Marsh Papers, LBJL; Robert J. Smith OH; Carl Vinson OH.

39. George Brown OH; "My Friend Lyndon," 5, Corcoran Papers; David Welsh, "Building Lyndon Johnson," *Ramparts*, Dec. 1967, p. 54; Caro, *Path to Power*, 584–86.

40. *Ibid.*, 598–99; "My Friend Lyndon," 5; "Memorandum re Lyndon Johnson—Texas Situation" (Sept. 1940), Corcoran Papers.

41. *Ibid.*; Charles Kramer to FDR, June 14, 1939, Corcoran Papers; "Memorandum for the President," n.d., 1940, HRP; Hardeman and Bacon, *Rayburn*, 247–48.

42. "Memorandum re Lyndon Johnson—Texas Situation"; Ickes to FDR, Sept. 23, 1940, FDRL; Wright Patman to Flynn, Sept. 26, 1940, Wright Patman Papers, LBJL; Harold Ickes Ms. Diary, Sept. 28, 1940, LC; *New York Times*, Sept. 24, 1940; LBJ to Corcoran, Sept. 25, 1940, HRP; Ickes to FDR, Sept. 27, 1940; LBJ to FDR, Oct. 1, 1940, FDR, M, LBJL.

43. James Rowe to LeHand, Oct. 4, 1940, Rowe Papers; Miller, *Lyndon*, 91–92; Ickes, *Lowering Clouds*, 348; Rayburn to Maverick, Oct. 16, 1940, Rayburn Papers; Drewry to FDR, Oct. 2, 1940; FDR to "Pa" Watson, Oct. 4, 1940; FDR to MacIntyre, Oct. 4, 1940; Schedule of Visits of Congm. LBJ to Pres. F.D. Roosevelt, Oct. 9, 1940, 1 p.m., FDRL; Hardeman and Bacon, *Rayburn*, 249.

44. Pearson and Allen, "Washington Daily Merry-Go-Round," Nov. 16, 1940; Robert S. Allen OH; Dugger, *The Politician*, 224.

45. Maverick to Rayburn, Oct. 5, 1940; Wayne Johnson to Rayburn, Oct. 2, 1940, Rayburn Papers; "Memorandum re Lyndon Johnson—Texas Situation" (Sept. 1940), Corcoran Papers; Ernest Cuneo OH; statement of Patrick Drewry, chmn. of the DCCC, Oct. 1940, HRP.

46. Caro, *Path to Power*, 609; Alexander Heard, *The Costs of Democracy*, (Chapel Hill, 1960), chap. 8, esp. pp. 213–16, 224–28.

47. Brown to LBJ, June 12, 1939, Oct. 19, 1940; LBJ to Brown, Oct. 21, 1940, LBJA:SN; LBJ to Swager Sherley, Oct. 21, 1940, HRP; Caro, *Path to Power*, 627–28.

48. *Ibid.*; LBJ to Rayburn, Oct. 22, 1940, Rayburn Papers; Caro, *Path to Power*, 633.

49. Hardeman and Bacon, *Rayburn*, 250.

50. Charles Roeser to LBJ, Oct. 23, 1940; LBJ to Roeser, Oct. 25, 1940, HRP; Edward Clark interview, Dec. 15, 1986; Eliot Janeway interview, Dec. 20, 1986; Hardeman and Bacon, *Rayburn*, 250–51, n. 8, 502; Miller, *Lyndon*, 92; Dugger, *The Politician*, 224–25; Caro, *Path to Power*, 634–35, 834.

51. James Rowe to FDR, Oct. 18, 1940, Rowe Papers; John B. Connally to

LBJ, Oct. 22, 1940; Memos to LBJ, PPMF; LBJ to —-, Oct. 15, 1940, with questionnaire and list attached, HRP; Caro, *Path to Power*, 629–30.

52. James L. Melton, Oct. 15, 1940; LBJ to Charles F. McLaughlin, Oct. 17, 1940; LBJ to Arthur Mitchell, Oct. 24, 1940, HRP.

53. DNC 1940 folder, HRP; James Rowe to FDR, Oct. 18, 1940, Rowe Papers; Caro, *Path to Power*, 630–31, 640–41.

54. DNC 1940 folder; Caro, *Path to Power*, 639–40.

55. LBJ to Jack Robinson, Oct. 18, 1940, LBJA:CF; LBJ to Nan Wood Honeyman, Oct. 22, 1940, and other correspondence in HRP; also see materials on Honeyman in Rowe Papers.

56. LBJ to ———, "Wire 26th"; DNC 1940 Folder, HRP.

57. LBJ to Sherley, Oct. 28, 1940; Wilton and Virginia Woods OH; Caro, *Path to Power*, 647–52, 835–36; DNC—Gen. Corresp. 1940 folder, HRP. Caro says that the oil money "this time" came not through Rayburn but Johnson. The letters he cites on p. 836 in boxes 6,7,8, and 9 of the HRP do not demonstrate that. Though the money came to LBJ, it was because Rayburn's "presumably nonpartisan role as Speaker precluded his getting too openly involved in such blatantly partisan activities as fund raising." Hardeman and Bacon, *Rayburn*, 249.

58. James Rowe to LBJ, Dec. 11, 1940, Rowe Papers; LBJ to LeHand, Nov. 4, 1940, HRP.

59. Burns, *Lion and the Fox*, 451–55; Leuchtenburg, *FDR and the New Deal*, 321–22; Caro, *Path to Power*, 654; Miller, *Lyndon*, 92–93.

60. The column of Nov. 16, 1940, is in the Welly Hopkins Papers, LBJL.

61. Campaign, Oct. 15, 1940, folder, HRP; LBJ to FDR, Nov. 14, 1940; FDR to LBJ, Nov. 25, 1940, FDRL; LBJ to Harry Hopkins, Nov. 30, 1940, LBJA:FN.

62. Robert S. Allen to LeHand, Nov. 7, 1940, FDRL; Harold Ickes Ms. Diary, Dec. 1, 7, 1940, LC; LBJ to Harry Hopkins, Dec. 2, 1940, LBJA:FN.

63. Ickes Ms. Diary, Dec. 7, 1940; Ickes to FDR, Dec. 7, 1940, FDRL; *New York Times*, Nov. 27, 1940, p. 13; Dec. 3, 1940, p. 28; Dec. 6, 1940, p. 26; Dec. 7, 1940, p. 20; Dec. 10, 1940, p. 30; Dec. 14, 1940, p. 11; Dec. 17, 1940, p. 31.

64. Dallek, *FDR and American Foreign Policy*, chap. 10, esp. pp. 252ff and 530; "The Cork Bobs Up Again," *New York Times*, May 19, 1960.

65. Ickes to FDR, Dec. 19, 1940, FDRL; Ickes Ms. Diary, n.d., pp. 5086–7, LC; Rowe to Corcoran, Dec. 18, 1940, Corcoran Papers; LBJ to John Connally, Dec. 21, 1940; LBJ to Rowe, Jan. 2, 1941, LBJA:SN; LBJ to FDR, Jan. 30, 1941; FDR to Watson, April 4, 1941, FDR, M, LBJL; Hardeman and Bacon, *Rayburn*, 253–55.

Caro says that "Johnson's work with Democratic congressional candidates had in effect added a new factor to the equation of American politics. The concept of financing congressional races across the country from a single central source was not new, but the Democrats had seldom if ever implemented the concept on the necessary scale or with the necessary energy. 'No one before had ever worked at it,' James Rowe says. 'Johnson worked at it like hell.' " *Path to Power*, 662. Caro also asserts that Rayburn and Johnson gave independent oilmen in Texas "a channel through which their money could flow to the seat of national power 2,000 miles away, to far-off Washington. Rayburn had cut them the channel. A new source of political money, potentially vast, had been tapped in America, and Lyndon Johnson had been put in charge of it. He was the conduit for their cash" (636–37).

Caro is undoubtedly correct in saying that Rayburn and Johnson were tapping new sources of money for the Democratic party, but the amounts and power Lyndon himself could command were not large enough in the winter of 1940–41 to persuade Roosevelt to give him what he wanted—a significant place in the party machinery. To be sure, the President appreciated Johnson's loyalty to him and the party, and this would be demonstrated in the events of the spring and early summer, but Roosevelt did not see Johnson's control over Texas money as so extraordinary that he was ready to make him a major party powerbroker.

66. Walter Jenkins OH; Mary Rather OH.

67. Walter Jenkins OH; J.J. Pickle OH; Wirtz to Carl White, April 12, 1941, LBJA:SN; Ickes Ms. Diary, Dec. 20, 1941, LC; Rowe to FDR, April 10, 14, 1941; FDR to Rowe, April 11, 1941, FDRL.

68. Notes on telephone call, April 11, 1941, Marsh Papers; George Brown OH; Elmer Irey to Sec. Morgenthau, Jan. 14, 1944, Henry Morgenthau, Jr., Papers, FDRL.

69. *New York Times,* Feb. 26, 1941, p. 42; Steinberg, *Sam Johnson's Boy,* 170–71.

70. Rowe to FDR, April 10, 14, 1941; Ickes to FDR, April 11, 1941, FDRL.

71. Lewis M. Dabney, Jr., to Corcoran, May 5, 1941, Corcoran Papers: "Eliot [Janeway] told me that the President was anxious to have Lyndon on the Senate Military Affairs Committee." Steinberg, *Sam Johnson's Boy,* 158–62; Miller, *Lyndon,* 98–99; "It Is Later Than We Think," LBJ speech, April 21, 1941, HRP; *Austin American,* April 22, 1941.

72. *Washington Herald, Washington Post,* and *Austin Statesman,* all April 23, 1941; *Taylor Times,* April 24, 1941; Ickes Ms. Diary, April 26, 1941, LC; FDR press conference, April 22, 1941. *Roosevelt Presidential Press Conferences* (N.Y., 1972).

73. Seth S. McKay, *W. Lee O'Daniel and Texas Politics, 1938–1942* (Lubbock, 1944), 481; Jack Guinn, "Screwball Election in Texas," *American Mercury,* Sept. 1941; "27 Candidates Seek Senate in Screwy Texas Race," *Life,* June 30, 1941; Steinberg, *Sam Johnson's Boy,* 163; Caro, *Path to Power,* 688.

74. *Washington News,* April 23, 1941; Robert H. Jackson to James Rowe, May 2, 1941, Rowe Papers.

75. Seth S. McKay, *Texas Politics, 1906–1944* (Lubbock, 1952), 346–48; Steinberg, *Sam Johnson's Boy,* 160; Miller, *Lyndon,* 99; Caro, *Path to Power,* 676–77; campaign literature in Martin Dies Papers, Texas State Library.

76. McKay, *Texas Politics, 1906–1944,* 349–51; Miller, *Lyndon,* 99; Green, *Establishment in Texas Politics,* 69–74; Dies to D.J. McRaven, May 20, 1941, Dies Papers.

77. J.P. McEvoy, "I've Got That Million Dollar Smile," *American Mercury,* Oct. 1938; McKay, *O'Daniel and Texas Politics,* preface, pp. 14–23, 31–45, and chaps. 3–4; Steinberg, *Sam Johnson's Boy,* 156–58; Miller, *Lyndon,* 95–97; Caro, *Path to Power,* 695–703. John Connally to LBJ, May 1, 1941; Connally to R. Bonna Ridgway, April 30, 1941, HRP.

78. Joe Belden articles, *Austin American,* May 11, and June 21, 1941; Patman

to Rayburn, April 16, 1941, Patman Papers; W.R. Poage to LBJ, April 28, 1941; Ray Roberts to Chief, April 28, 1941, HRP.

79. Clippings in HR Scrapbk., especially one from *Austin Statesman*, May 12, 1941; schedule of radio talks and speeches, 1941 folder; May 3, 1941 speech at San Marcos, HRP.

80. May 3, 1941 speech; Caro, *Path to Power*, 692–95; conversation among Marsh, Young, and Glass, Dec. 18, 1940, Marsh Papers; Marsh to LBJ, April 24, 1941; Lloyd Croslin to Connally and Carroll Keach, May 5, 1941, HRP.

81. Miller, *Lyndon*, 101–2; Caro, *Path to Power*, 704. "In the early days [of the campaign] when a depression was on me like a blanket, I felt like reaching for the phone and getting a kick in the pants from a gentleman from Montana." LBJ to Rowe, July 3, 1941, Rowe Papers.

82. *Austin American*, May 14, 20, 1941; Chapman to Ickes, May 14, 1941; Biddle to Ickes, May 22, 1941; Ickes to Biddle, May 23, 1941, Ickes Papers. Hoover's memorandum was not with these letters.

83. Marsh to Henry Wallace, May 15, 1941, Marsh Papers; Connally to Walter Jenkins, May 17, 1941; J.C. Looney to Everett Looney, May 9, 1941; Connally to Roy Hofheinz, May 9, 1941; Hofheinz to Gordon Fulcher, May 13, 1941; Ray Roberts to Connally, May 19, 1941; Jenkins to Connally, May 20, 1941, HRP; J.C. Looney OH; Belden poll, June 21, 1941, FDR, M, LBJL; Steinberg, *Sam Johnson's Boy*, 166–67.

84. "Things look very encouraging," LBJ wrote Mary Rather on May 26, 1941; ? to Senator, June 2, 1941, HRP; Ickes to FDR, April 25, 1941; FDR to Rowe, April 30, 1941; Rowe to FDR, May 5, 1941, Rowe Papers; James Rowe OH; Jenkins to Connally, May 23, 28, 29, 1941, HRP; memo of Ickes and Morgenthau conversation, May 22, 1941, Morgenthau, Jr., Ms. Diary; Rowe to FDR, May 10, 1941, FDRL.

85. Ickes and Morgenthau conversation, May 22, 1941, Ms. Diary; Ickes to FDR, May 29, 1941, Morgenthau, Jr., Papers; Biddle to Ickes, May 22, 1941; Ickes to Biddle, May 23, 1941; Ickes to Mayo McBride, May 26, 1941; McBride to Ickes, May 27, 1941; Wirtz to Ickes, May 24, 1941; Ickes to Wirtz, May 28, 1941, Ickes Papers; Ickes, *Lowering Clouds*, 526.

86. Roland Young, "Lone Star State Razzle Dazzle," *The Nation*, June 21, 1941, pp. 722–23; Steinberg, *Sam Johnson's Boy*, 165–66, 171–72; Caro, *Path to Power*, 698–702.

87. Connally to LBJ, May 1, 1941, HRP; Eliot Janeway interview, Dec. 20, 1986; Harfield Weedin OH; Robert P. Coon to Members of the Senate and House, Austin, June 30, 1941, HRP.

88. Memo headed, "Martin Dies," n.d., HRP; Roland Young, *The Nation*, June 21, 1941, p. 722; Green, *Establishment in Texas Politics*, 49–50, 69–70; E.G. Moseley to J.C. Puterbaugh, May 7, 1938, HRP; Malcolm Bardwell OH; Henry Hirshberg OH; Caro, *Path to Power*, 702.

89. Dugger, *The Politician*, 229–30; Elmer Irey to H.M. Morgenthau, Jr., Nov. 13, 1943 and Jan. 14, 1944, Morgenthau, Jr., Papers. Corcoran told Ickes that "he had raised every cent that had been required for the campaign in Texas," Ickes Ms. Diary, June 28, July 5, 1941, LC. "In that 1941 race we gave him everything we could, everything," Corcoran later said (Miller, *Lyndon*, 106). John

C. Granbery to LBJ, July 14, 1941, reporting accusations that LBJ had spent $384,000, Granbery Papers. Drew Pearson, "Washington Merry-Go-Round," *Washington Post,* March 26, 27, 28, 1956; Caro, *Path to Power,* 683–86, 743–53.

90. Wilton and Virginia Woods OH.

91. Band Concert and Rally—Longview, May 28, 1941, with invitations attached; "Program," n.d., HRP; *Austin American,* June 6, 7, 1941; Harfield Weedin OH.

92. Miller, *Lyndon,* 100–1; J.J. Pickle OH; Harfield Weedin OH; *Wichita Record News,* June 9, 1941; program for Corpus Christi Rally: Internatl. Revue, June 17, 1941, HRP; Steinberg, *Sam Johnson's Boy,* 173–75; Caro, *Path to Power,* 706–711.

93. Numerous newspaper clippings for May and June in HR Scrapbk., LBJL; Dugger, *The Politician,* 231–32.

94. LBJ to LeHand, May 31, 1941; Rowe to FDR, June 3, 1941; FDR to LBJ, June 3, 1941, FDR, M, LBJL. FDR also supported LBJ with public messages on parity prices for farmers and old-age pensions. LBJ to FDR, May 23, 1941; FDR to LBJ, May 26, 1941; FDR to D.C. McCord, June 21, 1941, FDR, M, LBJL; LBJ folder in Rowe Papers; Political folder, "65," Box 236, Ickes Papers.

95. Irving Caesar corresp. with the adaptations of several popular songs, HRP.

96. William O. Douglas to FDR, June 16, 1941, FDRL; Belden polls, June 8 and 21, 1941, FDR, M, LBJL.

97. Steinberg, *Sam Johnson's Boy,* 169–70; Green, *Establishment in Texas Politics,* 73–74; McKay, *O'Daniel and Texas Politics,* 481.

98. Beaumont and San Antonio clippings, June 24, 25, 1941, FDR, M, LBJL; Simeon Hyde to LBJ, June 24, 1941, HRP; McKay, *O'Daniel and Texas Politics,* 481; Steinberg, *Sam Johnson's Boy,* 168–69; Caro, *Path to Power,* 728–30.

99. FDR to LBJ, May 26, 1941; FDR to D.C. McCord, June 21, 1941, FDRL; O'Daniel folders, HRP; McKay, *O'Daniel and Texas Politics,* 470–74; Steinberg, *Sam Johnson's Boy,* 171–72, 175–76, 178–79; Caro, *Path to Power,* 711–13.

100. Miller, *Lyndon,* 103; Dugger, *The Politician,* 233; Caro, *Path to Power,* 733; Lady Bird Johnson interview, Baylor Univ.; Ickes Ms. Diary, July 5, 1941, LC; Rowe to LBJ, June 30, 1941, HRP; Marietta Moody Brooks OH.

101. Miller telegram, attached to Claude Pepper to Grace Tully, June 26, 1941, FDRL; Ickes Ms. Diary, July 5, 1941, LC; D.B. Hardeman OH; R.J. Long OH; Russell M. Brown OH; Marietta Moody Brooks OH; Robert W. Murphey OH; Dugger, *The Politician,* 333–34, who quotes O'Daniel's aide; handwritten notes attached to a memo from Brooks, July 10, 1941, Marsh Papers.

102. J.C. Looney OH; Rowe to Harry Hopkins, June 23, 26, 30, 1941, Rowe Papers; Horace Guerra to LBJ, June 18, 1941; Caro, *Path to Power,* 718–23.

103. Caro, *Path to Power,* 731–33. John B. Connally interview, June 30, 1988; Dugger, *The Politician,* 233.

104. *Ibid.,* 234–35; Miller, *Lyndon,* 104–5; Caro, *Path to Power,* 734–38; Belden to Connally, July 11, 1941, HRP; Walter Jenkins OH; John B. Connally interview, June 30, 1988. The final count favored O'Daniel by 1,311 votes out of 575,879 cast: Miller, *Lyndon,* 106.

105. Dugger, *The Politician,* 234; Caro, *Path to Power,* 739.

106. *Roosevelt Presidential Press Conferences*, July 1, 1941, Vol. 18, pp. 6–7; Ickes Ms. Diary, July 5, 1941, LC; I.E. Gross, a Texas union official, later wrote Harold Young of Dallas, who was Vice President Henry Wallace's chief aide, "I enjoyed talking to you by telephone when you called me at Emory while I was there pulling votes for Lyndon Johnson out of the east Texas sand. We didn't win, but gave them plenty of fright for a few days" (April 10, 1943), Henry Wallace Papers, FDRL.

107. Matthew F. McGuire to Rowe, July 14, 1941, with Justice Dept. reports of July 3 and 9, 1941, attached, Rowe Papers; Dugger, *The Politician*, 235. Others in Texas also opposed an investigation. Texas state senator Houghton Brownlee wrote Senator Tom Connally, July 16, 1941, about a Texas Senate committee to investigate the election: "It is my personal opinion that if a public investigation were held by this committee, that a great many of my friends and your friends would be greatly embarrassed, because there is no doubt in my mind that the laws, both state and Federal, were flagrantly violated. Furthermore, it is my personal opinion that such an investigation would create a nation-wide scandal that would cripple or injure the Democratic party in future elections."

108. "A National Tribute to Lady Bird Johnson," Dec. 11, 1977, pp. 14–16, LBJL; James Rowe OH; Miller, *Lyndon*, 106, who quotes Corcoran.

Chapter 8: Politics, Patriotism, and Personal Gain

1. Kearns, *Lyndon Johnson*, 93–94; Arthur Perry to LBJ, July 2, 1941; Claude Pepper to LBJ, July 1, 1941, HRP.

2. Dallek, *FDR and American Foreign Policy*, 262–68; Evans and Novak, *Lyndon B. Johnson*, 23–24.

3. LBJ to James Allred, Aug. 5, 1941, LBJA:SN; LBJ to FDR, July 21, 1941, FDR, M, LBJL; Rowe to FDR, July 17, 1941; "Schedule of Visits of Cong. LBJ to President F.D. Roosevelt," FDRL; *PPP:LBJ, 1965*, I, 149.

4. Dallek, *FDR and American Foreign Policy*, 248–50, 276–77; James MacGregor Burns, *Roosevelt: The Soldier of Freedom* (N.Y., 1970), 120; Walter Jenkins OH.

5. William S. White OH; Hardeman and Bacon, *Rayburn*, 265–66; *Congressional Record: House, 1941*, vol. 87, pp. 6938–39.

6. Hardeman and Bacon, *Rayburn*, 263–70.

7. Radio Address by LBJ, Louisville, Ky., Aug. 21, 1941, HRP; *Austin Statesman*, Aug. 22, Oct. 7, 20, Nov. 2, 1941; *Austin Tribune*, Oct. 9, 1941; *Austin American*, Oct. 21, 1941; *Tyler Morning Telegraph*, Oct. 23, 1941; *Houston Chronicle*, Nov. 2, 1941.

8. Brenham Banner Press, July 16, 1941; *Austin Statesman*, Sept. 29, 1941; *Beaumont Enterprise*, Nov. 11, 1941; *Amarillo Globe*, Dec. 6, 1941; LBJ, News Release to Editors, Nov. 30, 1941, HRP; Wright, *Old South, New South*, 238; Schulman, *From Cotton Belt to Sunbelt*, 94–111; LBJ, Memorandum: Price of Crude Oil, n.d.; Rowe to LBJ, Oct. 27, 1941; Rowe to Leon Henderson, Dec. 1, 1941, Rowe Papers.

9. Willard Deason to LBJ, July 25, 1941; Tom Miller to LBJ, Sept. 11, 1941;

a series of LBJ and Everett L. Looney letters between Aug. 12 and Nov. 1, 1941, and an undated statement by LBJ saying that "unless Senator O'Daniel goes down the line for the entire defense program, I will definitely be a candidate against him," LBJA:SN. Marsh Papers contain several memoranda in the fall from Marsh advising Johnson on how to arrange his next Senate campaign. *Austin American,* Oct. 16, 1941; *Yoakum Times,* Nov. 7, 1941; *Beaumont Journal,* Nov. 10, 1941; *Beaumont Enterprise,* Nov. 11, 1941; *Corpus Christi Press,* Nov. 17, 1941.

10. James Rowe to LBJ, Sept. 2, 1941, Rowe Papers; memo, Rayburn, Hon. Sam, Sept. 2, 1941; memo for Gen. Watson, Sept. 17, 1941; LBJ, "Visit Schedule," FDRL; LBJ to Tom Miller, Sept. 18, 1941, LBJA:SN; Rowe to FDR, Sept. 29, 1941; Rowe to Grace Tully, Aug. 26, 1941; draft memo, FDR to McIntyre, Sept. 5, 1941, Rowe Papers; memo, Dec. 6, 1941, PPF 6149, FDRL.

11. LBJ to Bernard Hanks, Nov. 30, 1941; LBJ to Bob Jackson, Dec. 2, 1941, HRP.

12. Connally to LBJ, Nov. 25, 1941; LBJ to Connally, Nov. 27, 1941, LBJA:SN; Marsh to LBJ, Oct. 6, 7, Nov. 5, 1941, Marsh Papers.

13. Connally to LBJ, Nov. 25, 1941; LBJ to Connally, Nov. 27, 1941.

14. LBJ to Ray Lee, Nov. 20, 1941; Connally to LBJ, Dec. 3, 1941; LBJ to Connally, Dec. 8, 1941, LBJA:SN.

15. LBJ to Bernard Hanks, Dec. 17, 1941; statement, Dec. 8, 1941, HRP.

16. Dugger, *The Politician,* 238; Steinberg, *Sam Johnson's Boy,* 189; Walter Jenkins OH; Arnold A. Rogow, *James Forrestal* (N.Y., 1963), 89–92; Alvin Wirtz to Navy Sec. Frank Knox, May 24, 1940, Wirtz Papers. Welly Hopkins and Adlai Stevenson also apparently had a hand in the appointment. Hopkins OH; Dept. of the Navy Records, Military Archives Division, NA.

17. LBJ to FDR, Dec. 8, 1941, FDR, M, LBJL; Navy Dept. announcement, Dec. 9, 1941, attached to Frank Knox to LBJ, March 2, 1943; LBJ to Robert H. Connery, Feb. 6, 1962, LBJA:SF; four memos of Dec. 16 from J.W. Barker, Navy Personnel File, LBJL. Although Johnson later claimed that he was the first member of Congress to enter the armed forces after Pearl Harbor, then Congressman Warren Magnuson entered at the same time. Dorothy Territo to Liz, Oct. 12, 1966, LBJA:SF; Warren Magnuson OH.

18. Burns, *Roosevelt: Soldier of Freedom,* 190–97; Robert H. Connery, *The Navy and the Industrial Mobilization in World War II* (Princeton, 1951), chap. xiv in general and pp. 309–11 in particular.

19. The numerous documents describing LBJ's navy work during this four-month period can be found in: LBJ Personal Papers, Navy Unofficial Personnel File; Box 73, LBJA:SF; December travel memos and Policy Memorandum folders, HRP; Forrestal folder, LBJA:FN; and LBJ folder, Aubrey Williams Papers, FDRL; LBJ to Sam Rayburn, Feb. 19, 1942, Rayburn Papers; *Memorandum,* n.d., "Policy Memorandum folder," Box 149, HRP.

Robert Caro describes LBJ as traveling up and down the West Coast with John Connally having "a lot of fun." "In spite of these little incidents," Connally told him, "we were really working." Ever ready to put Johnson in the worst possible light, Caro emphasizes only LBJ's self-indulgence and preoccupation with his political future during the first four months of 1942. "Annals of Politics:

The Johnson Years: A Congressman Goes to War," *The New Yorker*, Nov. 6, 1989, pp. 96, 98, 100–3.

20. Folders cited in note 19 above; General Report of Activities of Lt. Cmdr. Johnson in Los Angeles and San Diego, Jan. 2–6, 1942, LBJA:SF; memorandum, n.d., in Policy Memorandum folder, Box 149, HRP.

21. *Ibid.*; LBJ to Forrestal, March 5, 1942; LBJ to J.W. Barker, Feb. 21, March 23, 1942, Navy Personnel File, LBJL; LBJ to FDR, Dec. 30, 1941, FDRL.

22. LBJ folder, Aubrey Williams Papers; Policy Memorandum folder, Box 149, HRP; Arthur E. and Elizabeth Wickenden Goldschmidt OH.

23. LBJ, "Visit Schedule," FDRL; there is no record of a Jan. 23, 1942 conversation; LBJ to Cmdr. John Gingrich, Feb. 27, 1942, Navy Personnel File.

24. LBJ to Grace Tully, n.d., attached to LBJ to FDR, March 7, 1942, FDRL; Wirtz to LBJ, Feb. 23, 1942, LBJA:SN.

25. Harold Ickes Ms. Diary, Dec. 14, 1941, LC; Jonathan Daniels, *White House Witness, 1942–45* (N.Y., 1975), 28–29.

26. LBJ to FDR, March 7, 1942, FDRL; LBJ to Wirtz, March 14, 1942; Wirtz to Lady Bird Johnson, May 22, 1942, LBJA:SN; Charles Marsh to Roy Hofheinz, March 13, 1942; Marsh to LBJ, March 17, 1942; Marsh to Grace Tully, March 23, 1942; Marsh to LBJ, May 20, 21, 1942, Marsh Papers; A National Tribute to Mrs. Lyndon B. Johnson Benefiting the Friends of the LBJ Library, Dec. 11, 1977.

27. Harold Ickes Ms. Diary, April 26, 1942, LC; Wirtz to LBJ, March 6, 1942, Marsh Papers; Wirtz to LBJ, Feb. 23, 1942; Wirtz to Lady Bird Johnson, May 22, 1942; Ed Clark to Lady Bird, May 5, 1942; Lady Bird to Clark, May 6, 1942, LBJA:SN; Jake Pickle to Lady Bird, April 11, 1942; Lady Bird to Jerry Wilkie, April 15, 1942; Pickle to LBJ, n.d., HRP; J.J. Pickle OH; Lady Bird to Cecil Evans, May 22, 1942, Evans Papers. Under prodding from Marsh, who wanted him to run for the Senate, LBJ, before going to Australia in May, left signed applications with John Connally to run for both the Senate and the House. Marsh tried, unsuccessfully, to persuade FDR to back a Senate race, but Roosevelt refused; Connally filed the House papers. John B. Connally interview, June 30, 1988.

28. LBJ to "Pa" Watson, March 7, 1942; LBJ to Marvin McIntyre, March 7, 1942, FDRL; LBJ to Harry Hopkins, March 7, 1942; Thomas McCabe to Hopkins, April 23, 1942, Harry Hopkins Papers, FDRL; Marsh quoted in Dugger, *The Politician*, 240–41.

29. LBJ, "Visit Schedule," FDRL; handwritten record of LBJ conversation with FDR is recorded on a piece of his House stationery, n.d., LBJA:SF.

30. Burns, *Roosevelt: Soldier of Freedom*, 201–9, 222–23; William Manchester, *American Caesar: Douglas MacArthur, 1880–1964* (Boston, 1978), chap. 5 and pp. 277–91. FDR to Churchill, March 7, 1942, in Warren F. Kimball, ed., *Churchill & Roosevelt: The Complete Correspondence*, I (Princeton, 1984), 390–93.

31. Bryce Harlow OH; George Brown OH; Daniels, *White House Witness*, 28–29; Dugger, *The Politician*, 253.

32. *Complete Itinerary*, 5/2–7/10, 1942, Naval Career folder, LBJA:SF; typescript of President Lyndon B. Johnson's World War II diary, March 11, 1977,

pp. 1–4, LBJL; Martin Caidin and Edward Hymoff, *The Mission* (Philadelphia, 1964), 32–33, 36–38, 40–41.

33. Dugger, *The Politician*, 242–43.

34. Record of LBJ meeting with MacArthur is attached to Burdette M. Fitch to LBJ, June 23, 1942, LBJA:SF; Caidin and Hymoff, *The Mission*, 44–45.

35. *Ibid.*, 49–50; Dallek, *FDR and American Foreign Policy*, 354.

36. Caidin and Hymoff, *The Mission*, 78–80, chap. 10, esp. pp. 117–19.

37. *Ibid.*, chaps. 8–11; Dugger, *The Politician*, 243–45.

38. Caidin and Hymoff, *The Mission*, chaps. 12–15; Dugger, *The Politician*, 245–47.

39. LBJ's World War II diary, March 11, 1977, pp. 10–11; W.L. White, *Queens Die Proudly* (N.Y., 1943), 263–67; Caidin and Hymoff, *The Mission*, 184–88; Dugger, *The Politician*, 247.

40. LBJ's World War II diary, March 11, 1977, pp. 11–12; Caidin and Hymoff, *The Mission*, 189–91; Dugger, *The Politician*, 248–49.

41. *New York Times, Washington Post, Washington Times Herald*, June 12, 1942.

42. Undated memo beginning "Over the weekend I returned to Washington," Corcoran Papers; Ickes Ms. Diary, July 26, 1942, LC; Dugger, *The Politician*, 249, 251–53.

43. LBJ's World War II diary, March 11, 1977, pp. 12–14; Dugger, *The Politician*, 249–50.

44. Jesse Kellam to LBJ, July 14, 1942, LBJA:SN; Grace Tully OH; James Rowe OH; Roosevelt's directives are attached to Frank Knox to LBJ, March 2, 1943, LBJA:SF; Lady Bird to George Brown, July 3, 1942, LBJA:SN.

45. "America's Fighting Congress," 1943, 78th Congress, 1st sess., Senate Doc. No. 94; Connally to Corcoran, n.d., Corcoran Papers; Dugger, *The Politician*, 247–48.

46. LBJ to Grace Tully, July 13, 1942; Marvin McIntyre to Roberts Barrows, July 14, 1942; LBJ's "Visit Schedule," July 15, 1942, FDRL; Frank Knox to LBJ, March 2, 1943, LBJA:SF.

47. LBJ to Carroll Keach, July 15, 1942, LBJA:SN; Ickes Ms. Diary, July 26, 1942, LC.

48. Margaret Truman, *Harry S. Truman* (N.Y., 1974), chap. 8, esp. pp. 150–57; Robert J. Donovan, *Conflict and Crisis: The Presidency of Harry S. Truman, 1945–48* (N.Y., 1977), xii, xiv-xv.

49. Steinberg, *Sam Johnson's Boy*, 196–97.

50. LBJ to Forrestal, July 16, 1942, HRP.

51. On the possibility of becoming Navy Secretary, see Edward Clark to LBJ, Oct. 21, 1942, LBJA:SN; *Abilene Reporter News*, Oct. 22, 1942. Ickes Ms. Diary, Oct. 25, 1942, LC: "Lyndon insisted that the President ought to clean out the entire Navy Department in the top ranks, including Knox and his Assistant Secretaries. He thinks that Knox is putty in the hands of the admirals, and he would like to see many of the admirals demoted or retired. He has it from the inside of the Navy that his diatribes against the Navy have been anathema to the admirals, but that all of the younger officers, up to those occupying the rank of lieutenant-commander, feel that he has been right." For his radio talk, see *New York Tribune*, July 26, 1942.

52. For the speech, see Aug. 19, 1942 clipping in Box 161, Ickes Papers. The speech had little resonance: see John Connally to LBJ, Aug. 21, 1942, HRP.

53. LBJ to Rayburn, Oct. 10, 1942, LBJA:CF; LBJ and Jonathan Daniels to Marvin McIntyre, Oct. 12, 13, 1942, Jonathan Daniel Papers, Univ. of North Carolina.

54. Burns, *Roosevelt: Soldier of Freedom*, 273–81; Daniels, *White House Witness*, 54–55.

55. *Ibid.*, 73; Foster May to Marvin McIntyre, Nov. 5, 1942; LBJ to McIntyre, Nov. 13, 1942, FDRL.

56. Elmer Irey to Henry Morgenthau, Jr., Nov. 13, 1943; memo of conversation between Morgenthau, Jr., Irey, John Sullivan, and Alvin Wirtz, Nov. 12, 1943, esp. p. 5, where Irey says that the investigation "started with the regular revenue agents' examination. They stumbled across the stuff and reported to the Intelligence Unit," Morgenthau, Jr., Papers; James Rowe to Grace Tully, Nov. 20, 1942, FDRL; Drew Pearson, "Difficulties Cited in Income Probe," *Washington Post*, March 28, 1956; Welsh, *Ramparts*, Dec. 1967, p. 55.

57. Irey to Morgenthau, Jr., Nov. 13, 1943; Rowe to Tully, Nov. 20, 1942; Pearson, *Washington Post*, March 28, 1956; Caro, *Path to Power*, 742–45.

58. Miller, *Lyndon*, 128; Wheeler and Lambert, *Life*, Aug. 14, 1964, p. 78; Daniels, *White House Witness*, 98.

59. *Ibid.*, 58; Schreiber, *Woman's Day*, Dec. 1967, p. 95; Claudia Taylor Johnson, Deed of Trust records in the Lewis L. Gould Papers, LBJL; Frank Baldwin to Harold Young, Sept. 18, 1942; Young to Baldwin, Sept. 21, 1942, Wallace Papers; Edward Joseph OH; Lady Bird interview, Baylor Univ.

60. Steinberg, *Sam Johnson's Boy*, 201–2.

61. Erwin G. Krasnow and Lawrence D. Longley, *The Politics of Broadcast Regulation* (N.Y., 1978), chaps. 1–2; Steinberg, *Sam Johnson's Boy*, 202, 204; Fly to FDR, Dec. 23, 1940; James Rowe to FDR, Jan. 4, 1941, Rowe Papers, which demonstrate Administration concern about newspaper owners gaining control of so many radio stations.

62. Steinberg, *Sam Johnson's Boy*, 201–2; Dugger, *The Politician*, 268–70; Edward Joseph OH; W. Ervin "Red" James OH; Roy Hofheinz to LBJ, July 14, 1941, Corcoran Papers.

63. Clifford and Virginia Durr OH.

64. Louis M. Kohlmeier, "The Johnson Wealth," *Wall Street Journal*, March 23, 1964, p. 1; Steinberg, *Sam Johnson's Boy*, 202–4; Dugger, *The Politician*, 269–70, 447; George R. Brown OH; W. Ervin "Red" James OH; "Qualifications of Assignee," n.d. (apparently Jan. 1943), describing Lady Bird's qualifications, Records of Radio Station KTBC, FCC. Mr. James Brown, an official at the FCC, told me that there are no records of a hearing on Lady Bird's request or of any discussion by the commissioners of it. There is only an index card showing that the application was filed and approved. Telephone conversation with James Brown, Aug. 20, 1987, and index card #4, Application Record—Broadcasting, KTBC, FCC.

65. Connally to LBJ and Lady Bird, Aug. 31, 1943, two letters and attached memo, PPCF.

66. Lady Bird Johnson interview, Baylor Univ.; Miller, *Lyndon*, 131; application for the modification of license, June 25, 1943, Records of KTBC, FCC,

requesting and justifying the changes in hours, frequency, and power; approved on July 20, 1943; Harfield Weedin OH.

67. Weedin remembered that Johnson ordered him not to use his name in connection with the station (Weedin OH); Lady Bird interview, Baylor Univ.; David Halberstam, *The Powers That Be* (N.Y., 1979), 439–40; agreement with CBS, Sept. 21, 1943, Records of KTBC, FCC.

68. LBJ to Kellam, June 17, 1943; LBJ to Clark, Oct. 2, 4, 30, 1943; Clark to LBJ, Oct. 27, 1943, LBJA:SN; Edwin Weisl, Sr. OH; Dugger, *The Politician*, 271.

69. 1941–42 folder, Corcoran Papers; LBJ to Mrs. John Connally, June 14, 1944, HRP. After giving Nellie Connally a sales job at KTBC, LBJ wrote her: "If you can't talk, sell, wink customers into getting on KTBC who in the world can? Besides I am coming home in a couple of weeks to give you plenty of help."

70. Dugger, *The Politician*, 272–73; Douglas, *Go East, Young Man*, 409.

71. Elmer Irey to Morgenthau, Nov. 13, 1943, Jan. 14, 1944, and two memos of Nov. 12, 1943, Morgenthau, Jr., Papers; Wirtz to "Pa" Watson, Nov. 1, 6, 1943; Wirtz to FDR, Nov. 1, 1943; Watson to Wirtz, Nov. 5, 1943, FDRL; Drew Pearson column, *Washington Post*, March 28, 1956; Caro, *Path to Power*, 745–49.

72. *Ibid.*, 749–53; Wirtz to Watson, Dec. 27, 1943; Watson to Wirtz, Dec. 30, 1943; memorandum for General Watson, Jan. 11, 1944, FDRL; Jack Anderson to Drew Pearson, Jan. 9, 1949: memo of conversation between Anderson and LBJ, Drew Pearson Papers, LBJL; Pearson column, *Washington Post*, March 28, 1956.

73. Daniels, *White House Witness*, 76–78, 99; Ickes Ms. Diary, Feb. 21, 1943, LC.

74. Burns, *Roosevelt: Soldier of Freedom*, 422–24; *San Antonio Light*, Dec. 10, 1942.

75. Clippings from Texas and other newspapers on the speech in HR Scrapbk., and one in *The Daily Texan*, Dec. 11, 1942, raising the question about LBJ as Navy Secretary. LBJ to "Pa" Watson, Nov. 30, 1942, and attached note of Dec. 2; James Rowe to LBJ, Dec. 7, 1942, Rowe Papers; John Morton Blum, *The Price of Vision: The Diary of Henry A. Wallace, 1942–1946* (Boston, 1973), 139. Caro (*Path to Power*, 764–65) erroneously describes the speech as a demonstration of Johnson's betrayal of FDR and the New Deal. He misses the fact that the speech had Roosevelt's approval and served his purposes.

76. Richard Polenberg, *War and Society: The United States, 1941–1945* (Philadelphia, 1972), chap. 6; LBJ to Rayburn, March 25, 1942, Rayburn Papers.

77. Polenberg, *War and Society*, 19–21.

78. "Labor: Absent Without Leave," *Time*, Jan. 11, 1943; materials in Absenteeism folders, particularly the memo "Statistical Data"; also LBJ's Report of Feb. 22, 1943, to the House, Boxes 150–51, HRP. In public statements, Johnson exaggerated the statistics, see *Philadelphia Inquirer* clipping, April 1943, Marsh Papers.

79. Margaret Chase Smith to LBJ, with attached materials, Feb. 16, 1943, and clippings dated, Feb. 27, March 11, 17, and 18, 1943, HRP.

80. Absenteeism—Labor Material folder, HRP; "Miss Perkins Hits Absenteeism Bill," *New York Times*, March 11, 1943; "Labor: 'Not Present,' " *Time*, March 8, 1943; clippings of March 18, 1943 in Absenteeism folder; Mary T. Norton to Carl Vinson, March 16, 1943, HRP; Miller, *Lyndon*, 125.

81. "Answer to N.P. Alifas," n.d., HRP; James Rowe to LBJ, March 20, 1943; LBJ to Rowe, March 25, 1943, Rowe Papers; LBJ Complete House Voting Record, 226–27; Polenberg, *War and Society*, 165–69. Early in 1945, LBJ backed another "work or fight" bill introduced by Andrew May of Kentucky. It passed the House but died in a conference committee: Miller, *Lyndon*, 125–26.

82. Carl Vinson to LBJ, Jan. 26, 1943, HRP; Donald C. Cook OH; Steinberg, *Sam Johnson's Boy*, 197.

83. Gene Latimer OH.

84. Extensive materials on the work of Johnson's subcommittee, in Boxes 151–57, HRP; Carl Vinson OH; Donald C. Cook OH; Connery, *Navy and Industrial Mobilization in W.W. II*, 418–19.

85. Polenberg, *War and Society*, 193–95; Marsh to LBJ, Jan. 14, 1943, Marsh Papers; Rowe to LBJ, March 20, May 22, 1943, Rowe Papers; LBJ Complete House Voting Record, 77.

86. LBJ, "The War Today—What Tomorrow?" HRP; Polenberg, *War and Society*, 192–93; three memos of May 1, June 11, and Aug. 3, 1943, PPF 6149, FDRL.

87. Materials in the Contract-Renegotiation folder; LBJ's Address to the Texas House of Reps., Jan. 3, 1944; LBJ to Paul Bolton, Dec. 1, 1943: "When the story of this war is written, Paul, we will not be blamed for allowing too little profit. We will be cussed for allowing too much," HRP.

88. *Ibid.*; Burns, *Roosevelt: Soldier of Freedom*, 422–26; Polenberg, *War and Society*, 197–99; LBJ Complete House Voting Record, 273.

89. Material in Naval Affairs-Elk Hills folder, HRP; Donald Cook OH; Paul A. Porter OH; LBJ Complete House Voting Record, 106, which shows the date of the vote as June 14, 1944; Miller, *Lyndon*, 123–24; Dugger, *The Politician*, 259.

90. LBJ to Clark, Nov. 27, 1943, LBJA:SN; LBJ speech, "Citizens of the Tenth District," n.d., HRP.

91. Ickes Ms. Diary, Nov. 21, and Dec. 19, 1943, LC; Everett Looney to LBJ, Oct. 4, 1943; LBJ to Tom Miller, Sept. 16, 1943; LBJ to Edgar Perry, Oct. 22, Nov. 1, 1943; J.H. Blundell to LBJ, Nov. 15, 1943; Alvin Wirtz to LBJ, Jan. 26, 1944; Ed Clark to LBJ, Jan. 27, 1944, LBJA:SN.

92. Letters in Tom Miller folder, LBJA:SN.

93. LBJ Complete House Voting Record, 91–92; Polenberg, *War and Society*, 195–97.

94. Ickes Ms. Diary, April 9, 1944, LC; Paul Bolton OH.

95. Green, *Establishment in Texas Politics*, 46; Wirtz to Ickes, May 25, 1944, FDRL.

96. Green, *Establishment in Texas Politics*, 45–47; *Dallas Morning News*, May 24, 1944.

97. *Ibid.*; *Time*, June 5, 1944, p. 21.

98. Steinberg, *Sam Johnson's Boy*, 212–13, 216–17; Minutes of Texas Dem.

State Convention, May 23, 1944, FDRL; statement of LBJ, May 26, 1944, Wirtz: LBJA:SN; *Dallas Times Herald,* n.d. (? May 1944); Wirtz to Ickes, May 25, 1944; Rosenman to FDR, May 29, 1944; FDR to Rosenman, June 2, 1944, FDRL; Daniels, *White House Witness,* 227–28.

99. *Austin Statesman,* July 18, 1944; Steinberg, *Sam Johnson's Boy,* 213; Hardeman and Bacon, *Rayburn,* 295–97.

100. Steinberg, *Sam Johnson's Boy,* 213–14; Hardeman and Bacon, *Rayburn,* 297–300.

101. LBJ to James Rowe, May 11, 1944, LBJA:SN; campaign materials in Box 328, HRP; LBJ to Jesse Kellam, July 31, 1944, LBJA:SN; Steinberg, *Sam Johnson's Boy,* 214–15.

102. *Ibid.;* Dugger, *The Politician,* 261; *The Houston Post,* July 26, 1944; LBJ to Roy Miller, July 31, 1944; "They used everything in the books, Johnnie, and much that never appeared in any of the books," LBJ wrote John Connally, who was away in the Navy. "It was sponsored by money from without," July 26, 1944, HRP.

103. Memo: Texas Electors, Aug. 29, 1944; Wirtz to Edwin Watson, Sept. 9, 1944; Wirtz to FDR, Sept. 23, 1944, FDRL; Steinberg, *Sam Johnson's Boy,* 217–19; Polenberg, *War and Society,* 212–14.

104. Schreiber, *Woman's Day,* Dec. 1967, p. 95; LBJ to Paul Bolton, March 20, 1944; LBJ to Edward Cape, March 21, 1944, HRP; LBJ to Sherman Birdwell, March 14, 29, Oct. 23, 1944, LBJA:SN; Steinberg, *Sam Johnson's Boy,* 209–10.

105. LBJ to James Rowe, May 11, 1944, LBJA:SN. While admitting that LBJ helped them win the contract for the Corpus Christi air station, George Brown denied that Johnson had "a thing in the world" to do with B & R shipbuilding contracts (George Brown OH). Report of LBJ's subcommittee, Aug. 15, 1943, in Navy Investig. Brown Shipbuilding Corp, HRP; Welsh, *Ramparts,* Dec. 1967, pp. 54–55; Corcoran to George Brown, Nov. 18, 1946, with attachments of Dec. 15, 1943, showing that B & R paid Corcoran's law firm $15,000 for "advice, conferences, and negotiations in respect of the shipbuilding contracts of George and Herman Brown with the U.S. Navy," Corcoran Papers. LBJ also helped the Browns with various labor problems: Herman Brown to LBJ, Jan. 28, May 7, 1943; LBJ to Herman Brown, Feb. 1, May 8, 1943; Jack Head to LBJ, June 29, 1943, HRP; LBJ to George Brown, April 22, 1944; Brown to LBJ, April 25, 1944; LBJ to Harfield Weedin, July 27, 1944, March 19, 1945; LBJ to Jesse Kellam, Oct. 24, 1944, LBJA:SN; records of Radio Station KTBC, FCC.

106. Paul Porter OH; W. Ervin "Red" James OH.

107. Dugger, *The Politician,* 254–55; FDR to Rosenman, June 2, 1944; LBJ to Watson, June 10, 1944; FDR to Watson, n.d.; LBJ's "Visits Schedule," June 23, 1944, FDRL.

108. William S. White, *New York Times,* April 13, 1945, p. 3.

109. *Ibid.;* Max Starcke and Mrs. Dorothy Palmie Starcke OH; Leuchtenburg, *In the Shadow of FDR,* 121–23; Miller, *Lyndon,* 126–27; James Rowe to LBJ, June 16, 1945; LBJ to Rowe, July 10, 1945, LBJA:SN.

Chapter 9: The Liberal as Conservative

1. Miller, *Lyndon*, 127; LBJ to James Rowe, July 10, 1945, LBJA:SN.

2. LBJ to Sam Rayburn, April 13, 1945, LBJA:CF; LBJ to HST, April 16, 1945, WHFN; Rowe to LBJ, June 16, 1945; LBJ to Rowe, July 10, 1945, LBJA:SN.

3. Carl Vinson to LBJ, May 10, 1945, HRP; F. Edward Herbert OH; Donald C. Cook OH.

4. Cook OH; memo to Juanita, Sept. 23, 1965, with a trip itinerary attached; Vice Adm. S.M. Robinson to Carl Vinson, June 29, 1945, HRP; Rear Adm. Donald J. MacDonald OH.

5. James Forrestal to Carl Vinson, June 25, 1945, HRP.

6. Memorandum with Respect to Sub-Committee's Trip to British Isles, Europe and Africa, HRP; Donald C. Cook OH. The Committee also visited Munich and the concentration camp at Dachau. F. Ewd. Herbert, *I Went * I Saw * I Heard* (privately published diary, 1946); LBJ later claimed that he was with the committee on the Dachau trip, but Donald Cook (OH) says that Johnson was "a little indisposed" that day and he and Johnson did not go—an early example of what later became known as the "credibility gap."

7. Trip memorandum; Donald C. Cook OH.

8. D.C. Cook OH; F. Edward Herbert OH.

9. Donald C. Cook OH.

10. Donovan, *Presidency of Harry Truman*, chap. 4; trip memorandum, HRP; Donald C. Cook OH.

11. Donovan, *Presidency of Harry Truman*, chap. 12.

12. Alonzo L. Hamby, *Beyond the New Deal: Harry S Truman and American Liberalism* (N.Y., 1973), 41–85; the quotes are from pp. 41, 44–45, 83.

13. Clark to LBJ, May 23, 1945, HRP; Donald C. Cook OH; LBJ to Rowe, July 10, 1945, LBJA:SN.

14. Postwar Planning and Postwar Planning Conference folders; press release from LBJ's office, in Box 159, HRP.

15. Hamby, *Truman and American Liberalism*, 63–64; LBJ Voting Record, 79th Congress, 1st sess., votes of June 23, 30, Dec. 14, 1945; 79th Congress, 2nd sess., votes of Feb. 6, March 6, 7, 14, April 17, 18, May 9, July 1, 23, 1946; LBJ speeches, 1946, HRP.

16. Reprint of speech from the *Congressional Record*, April 13, 1946, HRP; Schulman, *From Cotton Belt to Sunbelt*, 117–18.

17. *Congressional Record*, 1946, 79th Congress, 2nd sess., pp. A827–28; LBJ to Robert Montgomery, Feb. 19, 1946, HRP; Dugger, *The Politician*, 296–97, 451, n. 1.

18. *Austin Statesman*, Jan. 10, 1946; Memo: Atomic Bomb, n.d., HRP; LBJ Complete House Voting Record; Donovan, *Presidency of Harry Truman*, 203–6; Dugger, *The Politician*, 297–98, 451–52, n. 2.

19. Helen Gahagan Douglas OH; Hamby, *Truman and American Liberalism*, 65–67, 76–79; LBJ Voting Record, 79th Congress, 2nd sess., Jan. 31, Feb. 4, 7, May 25, June 11, 1946.

20. LBJ Voting Record, 79th Congress, 1st sess., June 12, Oct. 10, 1945; 2nd sess., Feb. 21, 1946; LBJ Complete House Voting Record, 86–87, for his votes

against the FEPC in 1946; Monroe Billington, "LBJ and Blacks: The Early Years," *Journal of Negro History*, Jan. 1977, pp. 32–34; Robert Parker, "LBJ and Me," *The Houston Post*, June 29, 1986.

21. Dugger, *The Politician*, 288–89; LBJ statement, "When men leave their jobs," HRP; Steinberg, *Sam Johnson's Boy*, 221; E. Janeway to LBJ, Oct. 11, 1945; LBJ to Janeway, Oct. 31, 1945, LBJA:SN.

22. Helen Gahagan Douglas OH.

23. LBJ to Connally, April 12, 1945, HRP; Ickes Ms. Diary, April 29, Nov. 25, 1945, LC; Publicity: Johnson for Governor folder; Allred to LBJ, July 10, 1945; LBJ to Allred, July 11, 1945; memo of LBJ's conversation with Ted Taylor, Feb. 5, 1946, HRP; *The Texas Spectator*, Feb. 15, 1946, with the headline, "Poll's Outcome Keeps Johnson Out of Race"; Steinberg, *Sam Johnson's Boy*, 225–27.

24. Ickes Ms. Diary, Dec. 2, 1944; LBJ to Oriole Bailey, Feb. 7, 1946; Wirtz to LBJ, Feb. 19, 1946; LBJ to Wirtz, Feb. 23, 1946, HRP; Harry Middleton related the anecdote about the governor to me.

25. Wirtz to LBJ, Feb. 27, 1946, HRP.

26. Howard Bland to LBJ, March 29, 1946; LBJ to Bland, April 4, 1946; LBJ to Charles Green, April 5, 1946, HRP.

27. Hollers's war record in the Corcoran Papers; LBJ to Irving Goldberg, April 15, 1946, HRP.

28. Corcoran to "Dear Stu," April 16, 1946, with attached memos and Hollers's war record, Corcoran Papers. LBJ to Connally, May 13, 1946, HRP.

29. Connally to LBJ, May 15, 20, 1946, HRP.

30. Four Hollers speeches, HRP; Dugger, *The Politician*, 299–302.

31. LBJ to Dr. A.A. Ross, June 23, 1946; LBJ to Hollers, June 26, 1946, HRP.

32. *Ibid.;* LBJ to Peterson, June 25, 1946; South Trimble to LBJ, July 8, 1946, HRP; Walter Jenkins OH.

33. LBJ to Hollers, June 26, 1946; Ray Lee to LBJ, Feb. 18, 1946; T.A. Lowe, Jr. to LBJ, June 7, 1946; LBJ to Lowe, June 8, 1946, HRP.

34. W.K. Syers to Hollers, July 7, 1946; Speech-Inform. folder; KVET Lie, n.d., HRP; Stuart M. Long OH; R.L. (Bob) Phinney OH; Jesse Kellam OH; Paul Porter OH; W. Sherman Birdwell OH; Paul Bolton OH; Walter Jenkins OH; LBJ to Corcoran, 10:10 p.m. call, Feb. 21, 1946, Corcoran Wiretaps, FBI Papers; Records of KVET, March 19, 1946–July 1, 1951, FCC; Steinberg, *Sam Johnson's Boy*, 240–41; LBJ to Bob Long, July 6, 1945; LBJ to Harfield Weedin, Oct. 11, Nov. 5, 1945, LBJA:SN; Records of KTBC, May 19, 1946, FCC; "The Story of the Johnson Family Fortune," *U.S. News & World Report*, May 4, 1964, p. 41; Deason to Jenkins, n.d., 1955, with clipping from *Broadcasting* attached, LBJA:SN.

35. Harfield Weedin OH; LBJ to Edgar Perry, Oct. 22, 1943, LBJA:SN; Charles Herring OH; memo, "Personal Finances of Cong. and Mrs. Lyndon B. Johnson," n.d., PPCF; Walter Jenkins OH; press release, July 7, 1946, HRP.

36. Dorothy J. Nichols OH; Walter Jenkins OH; J.J. Pickle OH; Connally to LBJ, May 24, 1946; LBJ to Connally, June 9, 1946; LBJ to Houston Harte, June 20, 1946, HRP.

37. LBJ to Connally, June 23, 1946; LBJ schedule, July 8, 1946; Background folder, 1946, HRP.

38. LBJ to Connally, June 23, 1946; J.J. Pickle OH; "Let's Vote for Lyndon Johnson," n.d., HRP; LBJ to Allred, Feb. 18, 1944; Autry to LBJ, April 5, 1944, June 11, Sept. 24, 1945; LBJ to Autry, Sept. 26, 1945, LBJA:FN.

39. Pamphlet "I Remember . . . ," n.d., HRP; J.J. Pickle OH.

40. *Ibid.*; "The Man Who Is Doing the Job," n.d.; "Some of the Charges You May Hear," n.d., HRP; J.J. Pickle OH; Pickle to LBJ, June 19, 1946, HRP; Clark to "Jimmy" Byrnes, July 19, 1946, with attached statement; LBJ to Clark, July 20, 1946, with attached statements from Krug and Wallace; Clark to LBJ, July 29, 1946, Tom C. Clark Papers, Harry S Truman Library (hereafter cited as HSTL).

41. LBJ press release, Austin, July 1946, HRP; Corcoran to LBJ, July 29, 1946; LBJ to Elizabeth Rowe, Aug. 20, 1946, LBJA:SN.

42. Donovan, *Presidency of Harry Truman*, chaps. 19, 23, and 24, and pp. 229–30 for quotes.

43. *Ibid.*, 231, 237; Rowe to Lady Bird Johnson, Nov. 12, 1946, LBJA:SN.

44. Denton (Texas) *Record-Chronicle*, April 6, 1947.

45. Green, *Establishment in Texas Politics*, 103–7.

46. LBJ to Tom Clark, Jan. 15, 1947, Clark Papers; LBJ to W.E. Jackson, Jan. 27, 1947; LBJ to Fred Hartley, Feb. 26, 1947; Bill to Amend Fair Labor Standards folder, HRP; Donovan, *Truman Presidency*, 299–304; LBJ Complete House Voting Record, 233–34; Walter Jenkins OH; Joe B. Frantz, "Opening a Curtain: The Metamorphosis of Lyndon B. Johnson," *Journal of Southern History*, Feb. 1979, pp. 13–14; LBJ to My Dear Friend, n.d., Box 165, HRP.

47. Donovan, *Truman Presidency*, chap. 35, and pp. 352–56; R.B. Latting to LBJ, Feb. 4, 1948, HRP.

48. LBJ to Willard Deason, May 1, 1948, with attached materials; Walter Jenkins to Mrs. Oscar Maurer, Jr., March 22, 1948; LBJ to B.B. Chandler, May 5, 1948; Jenkins to LBJ, Feb. 26, 1948; LBJ to Johnny Clark, March 4, 1948, HRP; Alvin Wirtz to LBJ, Feb. 6, 1948, LBJA:SN.

49. Donovan, *Truman Presidency, 1945–1948*, 230; LBJ Complete House Voting Record, 242–43.

50. *Ibid.*; LBJ Voting Record, 80th Congress, 1st sess, pp. 1, 3–7; 2nd sess., pp. 1–3; reprint from *Congressional Record*, March 18, 1948, HRP.

51. LBJ to Forrestal, March 20, 1946; Vinson to Forrestal, April 4, 1946, LBJA:FN.

52. Correspondence in the Stuart Symington folders, LBJA:CF, and press release in Box 328, HRP.

53. Elk Hills Hearing folder, HRP; Donald C. Cook OH; HST to LBJ, Dec. 16, 1946, WHFN.

54. Donovan, *The Truman Presidency*, chap. 29; LBJ's remarks, March 6, 1947, HRP.

55. Donovan, *The Truman Presidency*, 279–85; LBJ to Wirtz, April 29, 1947; Wirtz to Aubrey Williams, April 21, 1947, LBJA:SN; *Congressional Record*, May 7, 1947 in Box 332, HRP.

56. Donovan, *The Truman Presidency*, 287–91, 342.

57. Speech—Austin Kiwanis Club, 1947, HRP.

58. Correspondence in Atomic Energy Commission folder; speech to San Antonio Rotary Club, Oct. 31, 1947, HRP; David E. Lilienthal OH; Lilienthal to Joe Frantz, May 10, 1972, attached to the OH.

59. Memos in the folders labeled Rubber and Oil in Boxes 162 and 163, HRP.

60. Donovan, *The Truman Presidency*, 357–61, 363–65; LBJ to HST, March 20, 1948; Horace Busby to LBJ, March 23, 1948, HRP.

61. HST to LBJ, March 22, 1948; LBJ to HST, April 5, 1948; statement, April 8, 1948, HRP; *Washington Post*, April 11, 1948; "Truman Linked Crises in World to Congress Lag: March Letter to Texan in House Assailed Inaction on White House Program," April 5, 1948, untitled newspaper clipping, HSTL.

62. Armed Services Comm: 70 Group folder, and Air Policy, 1948 folder; *Congressional Record*, 1948, excerpts, HRP; Stuart Symington OH; correspondence between LBJ and Symington, January to April 1948, Stuart Symington Papers, HSTL; LBJ speeches, March 15, April 14, 22, 1948.

63. Bryce Harlow OH; James Rowe to LBJ, April 16, 1948; Stuart Symington to LBJ, Jan. 26, 1948, Symington Papers; LBJ to R.W. Hedges, April 21, 1948, HRP; press release, July 29, 1948, Forrestal Folder, LBJA:FN.

64. Sherman Birdwell, Jr. OH; Kearns, *Lyndon Johnson*, 100.

65. Steinberg, *Sam Johnson's Boy*, 235–38; 1948 Campaign folder, PPCF.

66. Texas poll, Feb. 15, 1948; Pre-Campaign Attitudes of the Texas Public Toward Election of U.S. Senator, March 1–6, 1948; memorandum to Mr. Johnson, March 11, 1948; Texas poll, March 28, 1948, HRP; Connally to LBJ, March 12, 1948, LBJA:SN.

67. Maury Maverick to LBJ, April 7, 1948; LBJ to Maverick, April 10, 1948, Maverick, Sr., Papers.

68. Kearns, *Lyndon Johnson*, 100; Steinberg, *Sam Johnson's Boy*, 240; LBJ to John Connally, March 27, May 3, 1948; H.A. Ziegler to Connally, April 19, 1948; Connally to LBJ, April 22, 1948, LBJA:SN; Stuart M. Long OH; R.L. Phinney OH; J.J. Pickle OH; Steinberg, *Sam Johnson's Boy*, 239–42; Dugger, *The Politician*, 308–9.

69. *Austin American*, May 13, 1948; Steinberg, *Sam Johnson's Boy*, 242; Dugger, *The Politician*, 309–10.

Chapter 10: Texas Elects a Senator

1. Dorothy Palmie Starcke OH.

2. Seth Shepard McKay, *Texas and the Fair Deal, 1945–1952* (San Antonio, 1954), 177–78.

3. Warren Woodward OH; Charles F. Herring OH; Paul Bolton OH.

4. Warren Woodward OH; *Austin American*, May 23, 1948; Miller, *Lyndon*, 143–44; Dugger, *The Politician*, 310.

5. "Challenge of New Day," May 22, 1948, HRP.

6. Steinberg, *Sam Johnson's Boy*, 243; Miller, *Lyndon*, 144; Warren Woodward OH.

7. *Ibid.;* Stuart Symington OH.

8. *Ibid.*

9. Lady Bird Johnson interviews with John Brice, July 13–18, 1983 (hereafter cited as Lady Bird Johnson–Brice interviews), for the NBC television movie, "LBJ: The Early Years."

10. *Ibid.;* Warren Woodward OH.

11. Steinberg, *Sam Johnson's Boy*, 244; Miller, *Lyndon*, 145; Warren Woodward OH; Paul Bolton OH.

12. James Rowe to Lady Bird, May 29, 1948, LBJA:SN; Walter Jenkins OH; Warren Woodward OH; Horace Busby to Walter Jenkins, June 6, 1948; Roy Wade to LBJ, May 30, 31, 1948; Wade to Claude Wild and John Connally, n.d. (1948), PPMF.

13. Warren Woodward OH; speech by LBJ, June 7, 1948, HRP.

14. Warren Woodward to LBJ, May 3, 4, 10, 1948; Walter Jenkins to LBJ, May 23, 1948, HRP; Walter Jenkins to Overton Brooks, July 12, 1948, LBJA:CF; Walter Jenkins OH. James E. Chudars, the pilot of the Sikorsky, remembered Johnson saying that a hundred or hundred and five veterans threw in five dollars apiece to rent the helicopter for him. "But I don't think five dollars apiece would have gotten that helicopter for him." Chudars estimated that it cost $50 or $60 an hour to run the helicopter and that they were using it approximately four hours a day: Chudars OH; *Austin American,* June 6, 1948; LBJ to Grace Stewart, June 12, 1948, LBJA:SN.

15. LBJ's helicopter schedule for June 14–July 4, 1948, attached to James E. Chudars OH; press release, July 11, 1948, HRP; Mary Rather to Stuart Symington, June 25, 1948, Symington Papers; Warren Woodward OH.

16. Instructions for Advance Men, n.d., HRP; Charles F. Herring OH; J.J. Pickle OH; James E. Chudars OH; Mary Rather to Symington, June 25, 1948, Symington Papers.

17. Warren Woodward OH; Charles F. Herring OH; Carroll Keach OH; James E. Chudars OH; Joe Mashman OH.

18. Warren Woodward OH; J.J. Pickle OH; Walter Jenkins OH; Frank Oltorf OH; Joe Mashman OH; James E. Chudars OH; Roy Wade to LBJ, June 14, 1948, PPMF; press releases June 15 and July 11, 1948; Paul Bolton to LBJ, June 11, 1948; Horace Busby to Roy Wade, June 26, 1948; State Hdqtrs. to All Dist. and County Chairmen, June 19, 1948, HRP; Dugger, *The Politician*, 317.

19. Warren Woodward OH.

20. Dorothy J. Nichols OH; Claude Wild to LBJ, June 19, 1948, PPMF; press release, July 11, 1948; instructions for Advance Men, n.d., HRP; James E. Chudars OH; Frank Oltorf OH; Dorothy Palmie Starcke OH; Joe Mashman OH.

21. Walter Jenkins OH; State Hdqtrs. to All Dist. and County Chairmen, June 19, 1948; Claude Wild to All Dist., County and Women Chairmen, June 30, 1948; Horace Busby to Roy Wade, June 24, 1948; press release, July 11, 1948, HRP; James E. Chudars OH.

22. Dave McNeely's column on Robert Caro's "research for second book on LBJ," April 2, 1986, *Austin American;* Walter Jenkins OH; State Hdqtrs. to All Dist. and County Chairmen, June 19, 1948, HRP.

23. Horace Busby to Walter Jenkins, June 6, 1948, PPMF; McKay, *Texas and the Fair Deal*, 182–83. On May 21, 1948, an aide told LBJ about a conversation

with a C.T. Johnson who urged advertising in southeast Texas newspapers in the towns between Houston and San Antonio. "Told him that if you started to advertise you would have to do it in every paper in the state and it would cost a fortune. Frankly you just did not have the money to do it. However nothing prevented him from doing it for you. . . . He said that he would take care of it in the Schulenberg *Sticker*, Halletsville *Herald*, La Grange *Herald*, and Moulton *Eagle*." Walter Jenkins OH: "We tried to get committees to spend as much as they would because you didn't have to report what a committee spent. You only had to report what the candidate spent."

24. LBJ to Corcoran, Nov. 15, 1948, with Stevenson press release of Nov. 12, 1948, attached, Corcoran Papers; Claude Wild to All Dist., County and Women Chairmen, June 30, 1948, and Wild's Aug. 16, 1948, memo to the same people, HRP; C.K. Ballard to John Coffer, Oct. 8, 1948, John D. Coffer Papers, LBJL; Dugger, *The Politician*, 315, 319; Steinberg, *Sam Johnson's Boy*, 254–55; Green, *Establishment in Texas Politics*, 252, n. 1; Blumenthal, *The New Republic*, June 4, 1990, pp. 30–31.

25. George R. Brown OH; W.F. Matheny to Walter Jenkins, June 22, 1948, LBJA:SN; Walter Jenkins OH; Houston Harte OH; W. Ervin "Red" James OH; Hobart Taylor, Sr. OH; Edwin Weisl OH; memorandum, n.d. (July 1948), HRP; LBJ to General Ira Eaker, Dec. 17, 1948; LBJ to Howard Hughes, Dec. 31, 1948, LBJA:FN; Paul Porter to LBJ, May 24, 1948, LBJA:SN; Steinberg, *Sam Johnson's Boy*, 243, 254–55; Miller, *Lyndon*, 139–41; Dugger, *The Politician*, 308, 312, 315–16.

26. John Connally told me that the campaign spent between a quarter and a half million dollars: interview, June 30, 1988; James Presley, *A Saga of Wealth: The Rise of the Texas Oilmen* (N.Y., 1978), 216–19; Jenkins to W.F. Matheny, Jan. 8, May 20, June 18, 1948; LBJ to Matheny, May 5, 18, 1948; E.L. Early to Asst. Gen. Counsel, WAA, May 18, 1948; Matheny to Jenkins, June 22, 1948; Glynn Stegall to Jenkins, July 22, 1948; G.S. to LBJ, July 30, 1948; Jenkins to Glynn Stegall, Nov. 9, 1948, LBJA:SN.

27. W. Ervin "Red" James OH; Dugger, *The Politician*, 282.

28. George R. Brown OH; Welsh, *Ramparts*, Dec. 1967, pp. 56–57; Dugger, *The Politician*, 281–82.

29. Welsh, *Ramparts*, Dec. 1967, p. 56; Steinberg, *Sam Johnson's Boy*, 243; Dugger, *The Politician*, 282–87, 308; the remarks of Republican Senator William Langer of North Dakota in *Congressional Record: Senate*, 80th Congress, 2nd sess., pp. 11139–41.

30. Glynn Stegall to Walter Jenkins, July 22, 1948; G.S. to LBJ, July 30, 1948, LBJA:SN; Dugger, *The Politician*, 282; Herman Brown to Sam Rayburn, June 7, 1947, LBJA:SN. Texas Eastern won its bid for the pipelines in February 1947, but it wanted to convert a temporary right to transmit natural gas, rather than just crude oil, into a permanent one. *New York Times*, Feb. 11, 1947, 40:8; Feb. 15, 1947, 21:6; May 31, 1947, 18:4. Wolverton's Interstate and Foreign Commerce Committee held hearings on the natural gas issue in May 1947: see *Congressional Record: Senate*, 80th Congress, 2nd sess., p. 11140, in which John Schreiber, the coordinator of the solid fuel industry in New York, refers to his testimony before the Committee. LBJ to Corcoran, n.d. (content clearly indicates June 1948), Corcoran Papers.

31. *Ibid.*

32. John Connally interview, June 30, 1988; Dorothy J. Nichols OH; Charles F. Herring OH; Warren Woodward OH; Walter Jenkins OH; Joe Mashman OH; Willie Day Taylor OH; Fenner Roth OH; James Rowe to LBJ: "I have been trying to raise some money but with no great success, as you can plainly see, but I will keep trying," July 7, 1948, PPMF.

33. McKay, *Texas and the Fair Deal*, 206–8, quotes several newspapers; the song is in HRP.

34. LBJ's speeches of June 7, 25, 1948, and his press releases of June 15, 23, 30, July 11, 15, 1948, HRP; LBJ to R.L. Phinney, Feb. 15, 1949, LBJA:SN; Roy Wade to LBJ, June 7, 1948; Mary Rather to Paul Bolton, June 11, 1948, PPMF; Walter Jenkins to LBJ, May 23, 1948; Jenkins to Mary Payne, May 27, 1948; Glynn Stegall to Jenkins, July 10, 1948; LBJ to Fred Caterall, July 7, 9, 1948; LBJ to Walter E. Long, July 9, 1948; Bryan Spires to LBJ, July 13, 1948; LBJ to Walter Bremond, March 13, 1948; Jenkins to Marguerite Anderson, May 13, 1948; Jenkins to Doris Fleeson, May 17, 1948, HRP; Claude Wild OH; Warren Woodward OH; Hobart Taylor, Sr. OH; LBJ to Ricardo Jimenez, Aug. 19, 1948; Paul Bolton to John Connally, June 23, 1948, PPMF; Stuart M. Long OH; Joe Mashman OH.

35. Press release, July 21, 1948, HRP.

36. Press releases, July 14, 20, 22, 1948, HRP; Dugger, *The Politician*, 311–12.

37. *El Paso Times*, June 26, 1948, *El Paso Herald Post*, June 28, 1948, and *Marshall News Messenger*, June 29, 1948; press release, June 23, 1948, HRP; McKay, *Texas and the Fair Deal*, 200–201; Steinberg, *Sam Johnson's Boy*, 247–48.

38. Glynn Stegall to Walter Jenkins, June 29, 1948; Statement of Mr. Corcoran, July 9, 1948, PPMF; Robert Oliver OH.

39. On May 14, Lady Bird sent LBJ a message that the head of the CIO had told Albert Thomas that Stevenson had promised AFL leaders in Texas that he would vote for repeal of Taft-Hartley if elected. Mary Rather to LBJ, May 14, 1948, HRP; Booth Mooney OH; Allan Shivers OH in LBJL and North Texas State Univ. (hereafter cited as NTSU); Charles Boatner OH; Claude Wild OH; Walter Jenkins OH; McKay, *Texas and the Fair Deal*, 201; Steinberg, *Sam Johnson's Boy*, 248; Miller, *Lyndon*, 147–48.

40. Press releases, June 23, July 14, 1948, HRP. "The people are tired of politicians who sit and sit and sit and do nothing. They are tired of the Hoover type," LBJ declared in a speech on July 1, 1948, *Austin American*, July 2, 1948.

41. Frank Oltorf OH; Robert W. Murphey OH, LBJL; Steinberg, *Sam Johnson's Boy*, 238–39; Miller, *Lyndon*, 142–43; Dugger, *The Politician*, 310.

42. Green, *Establishment in Texas Politics*, chap. 7, esp. pp. 79–82, 86–87, 90, 99, and 256, n. 3; *Dallas News*, April 5, 1944; J. Frank Dobie to LBJ, May 28, 1948; James Rowe to LBJ, June 18, 1948; Campaign Songs Folder, HRP.

43. Horace Busby to Roy Wade, June 24, 1948; memo of May 17, 1948, HRP; W. Sherman Birdwell, Jr. OH; Miller, *Lyndon*, 142.

44. Allan Shivers OH, NTSU; Charles Boatner OH; Robert W. Murphey OH, LBJL; Booth Mooney OH; *El Paso Herald-Post*, June 28, 1948; McKay, *Texas and the Fair Deal*, 188–92; Steinberg, *Sam Johnson's Boy*, 249–50.

45. McKay, *Texas and the Fair Deal*, 217; Morris Roberts to All County Chairmen, July 17, 1948, HRP.

46. McKay, *Texas and the Fair Deal*, 218–19; Lady Bird Johnson interview, Baylor Univ.

47. Charles F. Herring OH; Willard Deason OH; Lady Bird Johnson–Brice interviews.

48. McKay, *Texas and the Fair Deal*, 213–14; Steinberg, *Sam Johnson's Boy*, 251.

49. McKay, *Texas and the Fair Deal*, 220–22, 225; Steinberg, *Sam Johnson's Boy*, 251–52; Arthur Stehling, *LBJ's Climb to the White House* (Chicago, 1987), 3–4.

50. Walter Jenkins OH; J.J. Pickle OH; Drew Pearson OH; Les Carpenter's story of Stevenson's Press Conf., PPMF; Miller, *Lyndon*, 148–49.

51. LBJ speech, July 29, 1948, HRP; *Austin American*, Aug. 7, 1948; McKay, *Texas and the Fair Deal*, 235.

52. *Austin American*, July 28, Aug. 7, 1948; Walter Jenkins OH; First Primary Returns folder and General Election folder, PPCF; McKay, *Texas and the Fair Deal*, 1–5, 222–24.

53. Miller, *Lyndon*, 150; Charles F. Herring OH.

54. Claude Wild to LBJ, July 31, 1948, HRP; Steinberg, *Sam Johnson's Boy*, 255–56.

55. Stehling, *LBJ's Climb to the White House*, 4–5, 77–86.

56. Claude Wild to LBJ, July 31, 1948, HRP.

57. McKay, *Texas and the Fair Deal*, 225–26; LBJ speech, Aug. 11, 1948, HRP.

58. Dugger, *The Politician*, 319–20; *Austin American*, Aug. 19, 1948.

59. Welly Hopkins OH.

60. A.F. Whitney to Tom Clark, July 30, 1948; Grace Stewart to LBJ, Aug. 2, 1948; Alvin Wirtz to Clark, Aug. 5, 1948; Clark to Ray Miller, Aug. 6, 1948, Clark Papers; Glynn Stegall to Walter Jenkins, Aug. 3, 1948, PPMF; Stegall to Jenkins, Aug. 17, 1948, HRP; Corcoran to Harold Ickes, Aug. 11, 1948, Corcoran Papers; McKay, *Texas and the Fair Deal*, 234–35.

61. *Ibid.*, 227, 229, 231; Dugger, *The Politician*, 314–15.

62. *Austin American*, Aug. 26, 1948.

63. Steinberg, *Sam Johnson's Boy*, 255–57; Lady Bird Johnson–Brice interviews; Lady Bird Johnson interview, Baylor Univ.; *Austin American*, Aug. 28, 1948.

64. *Ibid.*, Aug. 28, 29, 1948. The Bexar County vote is in PPCF; Glynn Stegall to LBJ, July 26, 1948; G.S. to John Connally, Aug. 16, 1948, HRP; LBJ to Jim Kilday, Aug. 12, 1948, LBJA:SN; Malcolm G. Bardwell OH; Stuart Symington to LBJ, Aug. 5, 1948, Symington Papers; Charles Boatner OH; Dugger, *The Politician*, 320–21.

65. General Election folder, PPCF; Dorothy J. Nichols OH; *Austin American*, Aug. 28–Sept. 3, 1948; McKay, *Texas and the Fair Deal*, 237–39; Steinberg, *Sam Johnson's Boy*, 257–58.

66. Walter Jenkins OH; John Miller OH, NTSU; Suggested Subjects for Discussion, n.d. (content clearly indicates sometime in the week before July 28, 1948), PPMF; Miller, *Lyndon*, 151.

67. Robert Murphey OH, NTSU; McKay, *Texas and the Fair Deal*, 238;

Steinberg, *Sam Johnson's Boy*, 258; Miller, *Lyndon*, 152; Dugger, *The Politician*, 326.

68. Robert Murphey OH, NTSU.

69. Dugger, *The Politician*, 328; Miller, *Lyndon*, 151–52; McKay, *Texas and the Fair Deal*, 239.

70. *Ibid.; Austin American*, Sept. 1, 1948; Dugger, *The Politician*, 328; LBJ statement, Sept. 4, 1948, PPCF.

71. Gordon Schendel, "Something Is Rotten in the State of Texas," *Collier's*, June 9, 1951, pp. 13–15, 68–71; Steinberg, *Sam Johnson's Boy*, 259–61; Dugger, *The Politician*, chap. 55; John E. Lyle, Jr. OH.

72. Callan Graham OH.

73. Schendel, *Collier's*, June 9, 1951, pp. 13–15, 68–71.

74. *Austin American*, Aug. 29, 30, 1948; Dugger, *The Politician*, chap. 56; Ed Lloyd to LBJ, Feb. 26, 1949, PPCF. Mary Kahl, *Ballot Box 13* (Jefferson, N.C., 1983), the most complete study of Box 13.

75. Steinberg, *Sam Johnson's Boy*, 261–63; McKay, *Texas and the Fair Deal*, 240–41; Price Daniel OH, LBJL; Robert L. Bobbitt to Tom Connally, Oct. 8, 1948; Glynn Stegall to John Connally, Sept. 8, 1948, LBJA:SN; Chronological Summary of Events Relative to Primary, n.d., Justice Dept. Investig folder, PPCF.

76. Voting Irregularities folders in Box 6, PPCF and in Box 126, HRP; the speech is in HRP.

77. Steinberg, *Sam Johnson's Boy*, 261; " '48 Senate election 'was stolen' for LBJ, ex-vote judge claims," *The Houston Post*, July 31, 1977.

78. *Ibid.;* Hugh Sidey, "L.B.J.: The Softer They Fall," *Time*, Aug. 15, 1977, p. 10; Russell Morton Brown OH; John E. Lyle, Jr. OH; Robert Bobbitt to Sen. Tom Connally, Oct. 8, 1948, LBJA:SN; Donald S. Thomas OH; Dugger, *The Politician*, 325–29. LBJ's caution about exposing himself to any charges of wrongdoing during the campaign is demonstrated by an episode in San Antonio. During a private dinner organized by the local machine, striptease dancers entertained the guests. LBJ immediately went to the men's room, where he climbed out the window. When Horace Busby asked why he left so suddenly, LBJ explained that he didn't want to be there if the sheriff, who was a Stevenson man, showed up. Horace Busby interview, July 16, 1988.

79. Callan Graham OH; Miller, *Lyndon*, 154–56; Dugger, *The Politician*, 330–31, 457–58, n. 1.

80. Callan Graham OH.

81. *Ibid.*

82. *Ibid.*

83. *LBJ vs. Coke R. Stevenson in the District Court of Travis County*, n.d.; Helen Sellers, Clerk of Travis Dist. Ct., Sept. 10, 1948, PPSF: Mildred Stegall; Steinberg, *Sam Johnson's Boy*, 263–64; Dugger, *The Politician*, 331, 458, n. 2.

84. McKay, *Texas and the Fair Deal*, 241; Robert W. Calvert OH. According to Walter Jenkins, the reduced 87–vote margin was the result of two reporting errors (Jenkins affidavit, Sept. 22, 1948), PPCF. Jenkins to Don Cook, Sept. 16, 1949, Senate Political Files (hereafter cited as SPF); W. Jenkins OH.

85. Robert W. Calvert OH; Steinberg, *Sam Johnson's Boy*, 264–65.

86. Robert W. Calvert OH; J.J. Pickle OH; Callan Graham OH; Steinberg, *Sam Johnson's Boy*, 265; Dugger, *The Politician*, 332.

87. J.J. Pickle OH; Stuart Long OH; Robert W. Calvert OH; Steinberg, *Sam*

Johnson's Boy, 265–66; Miller, *Lyndon*, 157; Dugger, *The Politician*, 332.

88. Stuart Long OH; Byron Skelton OH; Robert Calvert OH; Walter Jenkins OH; Allan Shivers OH, NTSU; Green, *Establishment in Texas Politics*, 111; Miller, *Lyndon*, 158–59; Dugger, *The Politician*, 332–33; Hardeman and Bacon, *Rayburn*, 339; Gus Celaya to Jim Kilday, n.d.; Kilday to Tom Clark, Dec. 8, 1948, with the notation "Relay to Lyndon's office," Clark Papers.

89. Steinberg, *Sam Johnson's Boy*, 267; Green, *Establishment in Texas Politics*, 115–16; Miller, *Lyndon*, 159–60; Dugger, *The Politician*, 333–34; Stehling, *LBJ's Climb to the White House*, 52–56; Raymond E. Buck to Alvin Wirtz, Sept. 17, 1948, PPSF: Mildred Stegall; Walter Jenkins OH; Callan Graham OH.

90. Hugh Sidey, "L.B.J., Hoover and Domestic Spying," *Time*, Feb. 10, 1975, p. 16; J.R. Parten OH; Supreme Court of Texas, *LBJ vs. Paul H. Brown, et al.*, n.d.; Robert L. Holliday to Wirtz, Sept. 17, 1948, PPSF: Mildred Stegall; handwritten notes, Sept. 20, 1948, Coke Stevenson folder, HRP.

91. Stehling, *LBJ's Climb to the White House*, 55–57; Biddle, Arnold, Porter to Wirtz, Sept. 18, 1948, PPSF: Mildred Stegall; Luther Jones to Eric Goldman, April 6, 1965, Jones, Jr., Papers; Abe Fortas OH; Miller, *Lyndon*, 161–62.

92. District Court record, PPSF: Mildred Stegall; Lady Bird Johnson–Brice interviews; Stehling, *LBJ's Climb to the White House*, 57–63; Walter Jenkins OH.

93. Luther E. Jones, Jr. OH; Jones to Eric Goldman, April 6, 1965, Jones, Jr., Papers; Stehling, *LBJ's Climb to the White House*, 63–68.

94. Luther E. Jones, Jr. OH; record in the Circuit Court, n.d., PPSF: Mildred Stegall; Paul Porter OH; Miller, *Lyndon*, 162.

95. Clark Clifford to LBJ, Sept. 14, 1948; Horace Busby to Clifford, Sept. 20, 1948; LBJ to Clifford, Oct. 15, 1948, LBJA:FN; interview with Clark Clifford, Jan 8, 1988; HST—Contacts folder, WHFN; Jonathan Daniels OH; Tom Clark OH; Steinberg, *Sam Johnson's Boy*, 270; Miller, *Lyndon*, 163–64.

96. Jonathan Daniels OH; Lady Bird Johnson interview, Baylor Univ.

97. Dugger, *The Politician*, 336; 308–page court transcript, LBJL.

98. John D. Cofer to Raymond Buck, Oct. 7, 1948, Cofer Papers, LBJL; William R. Smith OH; C.W. Price OH.

99. Abe Fortas OH; Paul Porter OH; Steinberg, *Sam Johnson's Boy*, 270–71; Dugger, *The Politician*, 336–37.

100. Steinberg, *Sam Johnson's Boy*, 270–71; Dugger, *The Politician*, 335–36; Tom Clark OH; "*Memorandum with Respect to the Texas Second or Run-Off Primary*," March 31, 1949; LBJ to Tom Clark, Nov. 8, 1948; Clark's telegram to LBJ, Feb. 1, 1949, Clark Papers.

101. Kalman, *Abe Fortas*, p. 202; *New York Times*, April 10, 1989; Bruce Allen Murphy, *Fortas: The Rise and Ruin of a Supreme Court Justice* (N.Y., 1988), 524–25, 539; William O. Douglas, *The Court Years* (N.Y., 1980), 335.

102. Glynn Stegall to LBJ, Sept. 29, 1948, HRP; LBJ to Ickes, Sept. 28, Oct. 7, 1948; Ickes to LBJ, Sept. 23, Oct. 1, 1948, LBJA:FN; Corcoran to Ickes, Oct. 6, 1948, Corcoran Papers.

103. "The Present Situation," memo, n.d. (content suggests early October); three memos; "Release," n.d., and a letter "To the Editor" following up on the ideas in the first memo; all in Horace Busby folder, HRP; John Connally to Fred Korth, Oct. 12, 1948, LBJA:SN; McKay, *Texas and the Fair Deal*, 243.

104. Porter flyer, Busby folder, HRP; Wirtz to Jimmy Allred, Oct. 19, 1948, PPSF: Mildred Stegall; Oct. 28 speech, HRP; *Dallas Morning News*, Oct. 3, 15, 18, 22, 27, 29, 31, 1948; McKay, *Texas and the Fair Deal*, 243–44.

105. Dugger, *The Politician*, 337–38; Glynn Stegall to LBJ, Oct. 18, 1948, PPMF; McKay, *Texas and the Fair Deal*, 244–45, 274.

106. LBJ to Claude Pepper, Oct. 7, 1948, LBJA:CF; Robert L. Bobbitt to LBJ, and to Senator Tom Connally, Oct. 8, 1948, LBJA:SN; Wright Patman to Sam Rayburn, Nov. 27, 1948, LBJA:CF; Donald Cook OH; Senatorial Contest Synopsis of Facts, March 25, 1949; J. Edgar Hoover to A.C. Campbell, Oct. 28, 1948; Chronological Summary of Events Relative to Primary, n.d., Justice Dept. Investig. folder, PPCF; "Memorandum with Respect to the Texas Second or Run-Off Primary," March 31, 1949, Clark Papers; Dugger, *The Politician*, 338, 462, n. 16.

107. LBJ to Sen. William Jenner, Oct. 29, 1948, HRP; *Dallas News*, Nov. 8, 1948; Corcoran to Sam Rayburn, Nov. 15, 1948; LBJ to Corcoran, n.d.; Corcoran to LBJ, Nov. 10, 1948, Corcoran Papers. The Justice Department also conducted an investigation of the election that was dropped for what it called a lack of hard evidence. See Chronological Summary of Events Relative to Primary, n.d., Justice Dept. Investig. folder and the cordial exchange of correspondence between J. Edgar Hoover and LBJ, Nov. 9 and 18, 1948, LBJA:FN.

108. Coke Stevenson, Nov. 12, 1948, HRP

109. Frank Oltorf OH; Alvin Wirtz to LBJ, Dec. 11, and memo, Dec. 15, 1948, LBJA:SN; Wirtz to LBJ, Dec. 16, 1948, PPSF: Mildred Stegall; Tom Connally statement, Jan. 3, 1949, PPCF.

110. Sen. Francis Myers (D, Pa.) statement, Jan. 3, 1949, PPCF; Wirtz to LBJ, Jan. 8, 1949; Charles I. Francis to LBJ, March 16, 1949, PPSF: Mildred Stegall; Report of Senate Subcommittee on Privileges and Elections, June 21, 1949, PPCF.

111. LBJ to Sen. J.W. Fulbright, Nov. 22, 1948, LBJA:CF; LBJ to Harold Ickes, Sept. 28, 1948, LBJA:FN; R. Vernon Whiteside OH; Dugger, *The Politician*, 341.

112. L.T. Easley OH; Jayne Andrews to LBJ, July 10, 1952, Texas Dept. of Public Safety report on Smithwick attached, LBJA:SN; Dugger, *The Politician*, 463, n. 2, 339–41, 464, n. 5.

113. *Houston Post*, July 31, 1977; Miller, *Lyndon*, 164–66.

114. Green, *Establishment in Texas Politics*, 116–17; Dugger, *The Politician*, 463, n. 1.

115. David S. Broder's review of Robert A. Caro, *The Years of Lyndon Johnson: Means of Ascent* (N.Y., 1990) in *The Washington Post: Book World*, March 4, 1990, p. 10. Broder, citing Horace Busby, relates the veterans' vote. Professor Lewis L. Gould of the University of Texas pointed out the impact of the Bentsen-Kazen race to me with supporting statistics. Gould to Dallek, Feb. 25, 1990.

Chapter 11: "The Best Possible Senator for . . . Texas"

1. Bryce Harlow OH.
2. George Reedy, *Lyndon B. Johnson: A Memoir* (N.Y., 1982); George Reedy OH.
3. Arthur Schlesinger, Jr. interview, Aug. 3, 1987; Miller, *Lyndon*, 247.
4. Bryce Harlow OH.
5. *Ibid.*
6. "Help Your Husband Guard His Heart," *Dallas Morning News*, Feb. 12, 1956, p. 9; Hubert H. Humphrey OH; Donald C. Cook OH.
7. Harry McPherson OH.
8. Horace Busby OH; Charles Boatner OH; Edward Clark interview, Dec. 15, 1986.
9. Walter C. Hornaday OH; Felix McKnight OH; Gerald W. Siegel OH; Harry McPherson OH; Reedy, *LBJ: A Memoir*, x.
10. Harry McPherson OH; George Reedy OH; Mrs. William S. White OH; Milton R. Young OH; Warren Magnuson OH; Helen Gahagan Douglas OH.
11. Reedy, *LBJ: A Memoir*, xii.
12. Mrs. William S. White OH; Harry McPherson OH; Reedy, *LBJ: A Memoir*, 21; Horace Busby OH.
13. *Ibid.*
14. Reedy, *LBJ: A Memoir*, 77; Harry McPherson OH; Kenneth W. Thompson, ed., *Virginia Papers on the Presidency*, Vol. 10 (Washington, D.C., 1982), 18–19; Darrell St. Clare OH, U.S. Senate Historical Office (hereafter cited as SHO); Mrs. William S. White OH.
15. Harry McPherson OH.
16. Margaret Chase Smith and William Lewis OH.
17. Harry McPherson OH; Edwin Guthman interview, Nov. 11, 1987.
18. Horace Busby OH; Hugh Sidey, "L.B.J.: The Softer They Fall," *Time*, Aug. 15, 1977, p. 10.
19. J.V. Daniel to Tom Connally, Dec. 30, 1948, PPSF: Mildred Stegall.
20. LBJ to Paul Bolton, Oct. 4, 1949, LBJA:SN.
21. Barefoot Sanders to Warren Woodward, Dec. 20, 1948; Woodward to Sanders, Dec. 22, 1948, LBJA:SN; memo to DP from JA, Jan. 9, 1949, Pearson Papers.
22. Everett Looney to LBJ, June 28, 1949; LBJ to Looney, July 1, 1949; Jake Pickle to LBJ, n.d.; LBJ to Pickle, July 6, 1949, LBJA:SN.
23. *Amarillo Times*, Jan. 9, Feb. 8, 1949; *Houston Chronicle*, Oct. 23, 1949; *Hilsboro Mirror*, Feb. 10, 1949; Sen. Carl Hayden to LBJ, Nov. 18, 1948; LBJ to Sen. Dennis Chavez, Aug. 25, 1949, LBJA:CF.
24. *Amarillo Times*, Jan. 9, Feb. 8, 1949; Horace Busby OH; D.B. Hardeman OH; Stuart Symington OH; Harry Hurt III, "The Most Powerful Texans," *Texas Monthly*, April 1976, p. 108.
25. *Houston Chronicle*, Oct. 23, 1949; King, *Texas Monthly*, Jan. 1971, p. 87; Eliot Janeway, "Johnson of the Watchdog Committee," *New York Times Magazine*, June 17, 1951, p. 13; Steinberg, *Sam Johnson's Boy*, 279.

26. Connally to Joe Belden, Jan. 27, 1949; Connally to Hugh Patterson, Feb. 28, 1949; Jenkins to Stuart Long, March 18, 1949, LBJA:SN; Walter Jenkins OH; Mail Survey folders, Box 58, LBJA:SF; Christine Moore to LBJ, n.d., Jan.-Aug. 1949 folder, Senate Papers (hereafter cited as SP); Steinberg, *Sam Johnson's Boy*, 278; LBJ to Jenkins, Nov. 28, 1951, SP; Booth Mooney OH.

27. Jake Pickle interview with Christie Bourgeois, Feb. 10, 1986; Gerald W. Siegel OH; Felix McKnight OH; Kearns, *Lyndon Johnson*, 131; Leslie Carpenter, "The Whip from Texas," *Collier's*, Feb. 17, 1951, p. 60; King, *Texas Monthly*, Jan. 1971, p. 87.

28. Corcoran to Jenkins, Nov. 2, 1964, Corcoran Papers; Bill Moyers, "LBJ and the FBI," *Newsweek*, March 10, 1975, p. 84; Kearns, *Lyndon Johnson*, 131–32; Horace Busby interview with John Brice, Nov. 16, 1987; Walter C. Hornaday OH; Willie Day Taylor OH; Dorothy J. Nichols, memo, n.d., Dorothy J. Nichols Papers, LBJL.

29. Harry McPherson OH; Lady Bird Johnson–Brice interviews; Jenkins to O.J. Weber, Sept. 20, 1949, LBJA:SN; Willie Day Taylor OH; Charles Boatner OH.

30. Memo on press releases, May 4, 1950, SP; Paul Bolton to LBJ, April 24, 1950, LBJA:SN.

31. LBJ to Allan Shivers, Feb. 7, 1949, LBJA:FN; Busby to Connally and Jenkins, Jan. 7, 1949, SP; LBJ to Wright Patman, Jan. 21, 1950; Mary Rather to Warren Woodward, Feb. 13, 1950, LBJA:CF; LBJ to R.L. Phinney, Feb. 15, 1949; LBJ to Jake Pickle, Feb. 10, 1950; Jenkins to Pickle, May 19, 1950, LBJA:SN; memorandum on Jake's visit, n.d., LBJA:SF.

32. Jimmy Allred to LBJ, May 2, 1950; LBJ to Allred, May 8, 1950, LBJA:SN.

33. LBJ to James Forrestal, Nov. 18, 1948, LBJA:FN; Donald R. Matthews, *U.S. Senators and Their World* (N.Y., 1973 ed.), 152–54.

34. Frank Oltorf OH.

35. LBJ to Kenneth McKellar, Nov. 13, 19, 1948; McKellar to LBJ, Nov. 22, 1948; LBJ to Alben Barkley, Nov. 13, 1948; Barkley to LBJ, Nov. 27, 1948; LBJ to Sam Rayburn, Dec. 2, 1948, LBJA:CF; Rayburn to LBJ, Dec. 8, 1948; Rayburn to Barkley, Dec. 8, 1948; LBJ to Millard Tydings, Dec. 22, 1948, Clark Papers.

36. Memo to LBJ, May 17, 1949, LBJA:SF; Walter Jenkins to LBJ, Sept. 7, 1949, SP; LBJ to Stuart Long, Nov. 20, 1950, LBJA:SN; Raymond Buck OH; Walter Jenkins OH; Wright Patman to LBJ, Aug. 2, Sept. 30, 1950, LBJA:CF; Clint Murchison to LBJ, March 18, 29, 1949; LBJ to Murchison, March 22, April 1, 1949, PPCF.

37. Robert Smith to LBJ, Oct. 24, 1949, LBJA:FN; Mary Rather to LBJ, April 13, 1949, SP; Raymond Buck to LBJ, Feb. 22, 1949, LBJA:SN.

38. E.B. Germany statement, Aug. 25, 1948, LBJA:SN.

39. H.R. Cullen to LBJ, Sept. 30, 1952, LBJA:CF; Evans and Novak, *LBJ: Exercise of Power*, 40–43; Hubert H. Humphrey, *The Education of a Public Man* (N.Y., 1976), 162–63.

40. Steinberg, *Sam Johnson's Boy*, 289–90; Hamby, *Beyond the New Deal*, 293–94, 311–13.

41. LBJ to James Rowe, March 15, 1949, SP; Horace Busby interview, July

16, 1988; John C. Stennis to Ina Smith, March 7, 1949; LBJ to Stennis, March 11, 1949, LBJA:CF; Evans and Novak, *LBJ: Exercise of Power*, 41–43; Dugger, *The Politician*, 344.

42. LBJ, "Unlimited Debate: The Last Defense of Reason," speech, March 9, 1949, SP.

43. *Ibid.*

44. Walter G. Hall OH; James Rowe to LBJ, Feb. 23, 1949; Rowe to LBJ, April 18, 1949; Lulu White to LBJ, March 9, 1949, SP; Billington, *Journal of Negro History*, Jan. 1977, pp. 37–40.

45. LBJ to Paul Bolton, March 18, 1949; LBJ to Amon Carter, March 14, 1949, SP.

46. James Rowe to LBJ, Feb. 23, 1949; LBJ to Rowe, March 15, 1949, SP.

47. Billington, *Journal of Negro History*, Jan. 1977, p. 38.

48. Charles I. Francis to LBJ, Feb. 3, 1949, LBJA:SN; Felix Longoria material, PPCF; newspaper clippings, Jan. 1949, SP; Frank Oltorf OH; Walter Jenkins OH.

49. LBJ to Rowe, March 15, 1949; LBJ to Harry V. Burns, Jan, 18, 1950; LBJ to Mary Tom Jackson, Jan. 24, 1950, SP; Wright, *Old South, New South*, 238–41.

50. LBJ to Reynold Gardner, April 4, 1949; cf. letters to D.W. Hooker, April 25, 1949, and Eewil Fernandez, May 10, 1949, SP; LBJ Senate Voting Record, 1949–62, pp. 129–30, 169, 199–201, 301, 373, LBJA:SF; Hamby, *Beyond the New Deal*, chaps. 14–15.

51. LBJ Senate Voting Record, 1949–1962, pp. 304–5, 129–30; as with rent controls, Johnson favored a more limited minimum wage law than the Administration proposed; LBJ to J. Webb Howell, April 27, 1949; LBJ to Clarence Holden, May 16, 1950, SP.

52. D.B. Hardeman OH; Harry McPherson OH.

53. Bobby Baker, *Wheeling and Dealing: Confessions of a Capitol Hill Operator* (N.Y., 1978), 34, 39–41; Bobby Baker telephone interview with John Brice.

54. LBJ to Allan Shivers, Feb. 13, 1950, LBJA:FN; E.B. Germany OH; LBJ Senate Voting Record, 1949–1962, pp. 394–96; Steinberg, *Sam Johnson's Boy*, 292–93.

55. Tom Clark OH; LBJ to Tom Clark, March 14, 1949, SP; Robert L. Bobbitt to LBJ, March 20, Oct. 8, 1948, Feb. 7, 17, 1949, Sept. 2, 1950; LBJ to Bobbitt, Dec. 27, 1948, Sept. 7, 1950, LBJA:SN; Price Daniel to LBJ, July 20, 1950; LBJ to Daniel, Aug. 1, 1950, LBJA:CF; J. Chrys Dougherty to LBJ, Nov. 21, 1950, LBJA:SN; LBJ to Allan Shivers, Dec. 18, 1950; materials in the Tidelands folder, Box 240, SP; Green, *Establishment in Texas Politics*, 108, 113, 142–43, 147.

56. Drew Pearson's columns in *The Washington Post*, March 13, 29, 1950; Harry McPherson OH; Wallace F. Bennett OH.

57. Natural Gas folders; April 1949 clippings folder, SP; LBJ Senate Voting Record, 1949–1962, pp. 325–26; Natural Gas folders in the Clark Clifford Papers contain material on LBJ's role in passing the law, HSTL.

58. Charles I Francis to LBJ, April 13, 1949, LBJA:SN; Steinberg, *Sam Johnson's Boy*, 293–94; Evans and Novak, *LBJ: Exercise of Power*, 45–46; Dugger, *The Politician*, 350–51.

59. Steinberg, *Sam Johnson's Boy*, 295–96; Dugger, *The Politician*, 351–52; memo, "Leland Olds is Not Qualified," n.d., and print of hearings, Olds folders, PPCF; John E. Lyle OH.

60. Steinberg, *Sam Johnson's Boy*, 295–96; Miller, *Lyndon*, 176–77; LBJ to Palmer Hoyt, Oct. 15, 1949, SP; HST to Edwin Johnson, Oct. 3, 1949; Edwin Johnson to HST, Oct. 4, 1949, WHFN; Anne H. Morgan, *Robert S. Kerr: The Senate Years* (Norman, Okla., 1977).

61. LBJ, "Leland Olds: The Record vs. The Propaganda," Oct. 12, 1949, SP; Evans and Novak, *LBJ: Exercise of Power*, 47–49.

62. Rauh is quoted in Frantz, *Journal of Southern History*, Feb. 1979, pp. 15–16; James Rowe OH.

63. LBJ to James R. Wood, Nov. 26, 1949, SP; LBJ to Richard Russell, Oct. 17, 1949, LBJA:CF.

64. Si Cassidy to LBJ, Oct. 26, Nov. 5, 1949; LBJ to Cassidy, Nov. 17, 1949; LBJ to E.M. Pooley, Nov. 5, 1949; Walter Jenkins to LBJ, Nov. 3, 1949, SP; Jack Anderson to Drew Pearson, Oct. 8, 1949, Pearson Papers; Hamby, *Beyond the New Deal*, 335–36.

65. Biographies of Johnson uniformly depict him as holding fixed aims for which he worked from the start of his Senate career: Steinberg, *Sam Johnson's Boy*, chap. 31; Evans and Novak, *LBJ: Exercise of Power*, chap. 3; Miller, *Lyndon*, 171–73; Dugger, *The Politician*, chap. 59; and Kearns, *Lyndon Johnson*, 102–10.

66. Baker, *Wheeling and Dealing*, 40.

67. Evans and Novak, *LBJ: Exercise of Power*, 41–42; Kearns, *Lyndon Johnson*, 103; Dugger, *The Politician*, 343.

68. Description of Russell in Current Biography (N.Y., 1949), 536–39; Noel F. Busch, "Senator Russell of Georgia," *Reader's Digest*, Dec. 1966, pp. 150–56; George Reedy OH; Harry McPherson OH; J. William Fulbright OH; *Congressional Record*, 92nd Congress, 1st sess., 1971, p. 421; Steinberg, *Sam Johnson's Boy*, 285–86.

69. Kearns, *Lyndon Johnson*, 104–5; Evans and Novak, *LBJ: Exercise of Power*, 43–44; William H. Darden OH; Baker, *Wheeling and Dealing*, 42; Miller, *Lyndon*, 172; Richard Russell to LBJ, Nov. 25, 1949; LBJ to Russell, Nov. 30, 1949, LBJA:CF.

70. Bobby Baker telephone interview with John Brice; Humphrey, *Education of a Public Man*, 133; Harry McPherson OH; Hubert Humphrey OH.

71. Humphrey, *Education of a Public Man*, 124–25, 161–62; Carl Solberg, *Hubert Humphrey: A Biography* (N.Y., 1984), 160–61; Hubert Humphrey OH.

72. Interview with Clark Clifford, Jan. 8, 1988; Evans and Novak, *LBJ: Exercise of Power*, 58–59; Steinberg, *Sam Johnson's Boy*, 298.

73. Stuart Symington OH; LBJ Senate Voting Record, 1949–1962, pp. 46–47; *Austin American*, Aug. 29, 1949; *Dallas Morning News*, Sept. 16, 1949; memo, n.d., Major LBJ Sponsored Legis. folder, SP; Louis Johnson to LBJ, Nov. 8, 1949, LBJA:FN.

74. Bernard Baruch to LBJ, Feb. 14, 1950; LBJ to Baruch, Feb. 17, 1950; LBJ to Gen. Ira Eaker, April 11, May 23, 1950; Eaker to LBJ, May 10, 1950, LBJA:FN; Steinberg, *Sam Johnson's Boy*, 300; Dugger, *The Politician*, 359–63;

Walter LaFeber, *America, Russia, and the Cold War, 1945–1984* (N.Y., 1985, 5th ed.), 96–98.

75. Glenn D. Paige, *The Korean Decision, June 24–30, 1950* (N.Y., 1968); Harsch quote, p. 194; Dugger, *The Politician,* 364–65.

76. LBJ statement on Korean Situation, June 27, 1950, statements of LBJ (hereafter cited as SLBJ); LBJ to HST, June 28, 1950; HST to LBJ, June 30, 1950, WHFN.

77. LBJ to Si Cassidy, June 28, 1950; LBJ, "Delay-Defeat-Retreat," July 12, 1950; LBJ statement, July 17, 1950, SP.

78. Steinberg, *Sam Johnson's Boy,* 303–5; Evans and Novak, *LBJ: Exercise of Power,* 55–56; LBJ, statement, July 17, 1950; LBJ to Millard Tydings, July 19, 1950, SP.

79. *St. Louis Post-Dispatch,* Aug. 4, 1950; Leslie Carpenter, "The Whip from Texas," *Collier's,* Feb. 17, 1951, p. 33; Walter Jenkins OH; Gerald Siegel OH.

80. LBJ to Louis Johnson, Aug. 2, 1950; HST to Louis Johnson, Aug. 4, 1950; HST to Emanuel Celler, Aug. 1, 1950, HSTL.

81. LBJ to Matthew Connelly, Aug. 3, 1950, with attached statement of July 31, 1950; Connelly to LBJ, Aug. 7, 1950, HSTL; LBJ visits with Pres. Truman, 1945–52, Aug. 8, 1950; memo: Visit at the White House, Aug. 8, 1950, WHFN.

82. Memorandum concerning accomplishments of Senate Preparedness Sub-comm.; summary of first thirty-six reports of Senate Preparedness Subcomm., n.d.; Executive sess.: final meeting of Preparedness Subcomm., Feb. 10, 1953, SP.

83. Donald Cook OH; memo: Visit at White House, Aug. 8, 1950, WHFN; Walter Jenkins OH; Steinberg, *Sam Johnson's Boy,* 305–7; Evans and Novak, *LBJ: Exercise of Power,* 58.

84. Memo: LBJ to HST, n.d. (content places it in Sept. 1950), HSTL; LBJ to HST, Sept. 20, 21, 1950; HST to LBJ, Sept. 25, 1950, WHFN; Steinberg, *Sam Johnson's Boy,* 309–10.

85. Clippings in Preparedness Subcomm., Sept.-Dec. 1950 folder, Box 354, and in Jan. 1951 folder, Box 2013, SP; *Business Week,* Oct. 21, 1950; *Saturday Eve. Post,* May 19, 1951; *New York Times Magazine,* June 17, 1951; *Newsweek,* Dec. 3, 1951.

86. Paige, *Korean Decision,* 141, 150–54; LaFeber, *America, Russia, and the Cold War,* 110–13.

87. LBJ to All Members of the Staff, July 29, 1950, PPMF; memo: comm. prospects for 1951, n.d., Box 346, SP.

88. LaFeber, *America, Russia, and the Cold War,* 113–20. LBJ, "Resources Defend America," Oct. 23, 1950; "What Are We Waiting For?" Dec. 12, 1950, SLBJ.

89. Lister Hill OH; Dugger, *The Politician,* 367; Steinberg, *Sam Johnson's Boy,* 316–17; Evans and Novak, *LBJ: Exercise of Power,* 52–53; Carpenter, *Collier's,* Feb. 17, 1951, p. 33.

90. Jake Pickle to LBJ, Dec. 26, 1950, Senate Political Files (hereafter cited as SPF).

91. Carpenter, *Collier's,* Feb. 17, 1951, p. 59.

92. Wayne Kelley, "How Russell Helped LBJ to Presidency," *Atlanta Journal and Constitution Magazine,* n.d., 20; George Reedy OH; Donald Cook OH.

93. Harry Byrd, Jr., "Lyndon Johnson and the United States Senate, 1948–1961," *Congressional Record—Senate*, 98th Congress, 2nd sess., March 3, 1986, pp. 1910–11.

Chapter 12: For Country, Party, and Self

1. Carpenter, *Collier's*, Feb. 17, 1951, pp. 33, 59–61; Paul F. Healy, "The Frantic Gentleman from Texas," *Sat. Eve. Post*, May 19, 1951, pp. 34, 174, 176–78; Steinberg, *Sam Johnson's Boy*, 320–21.

2. Healy, *Sat. Eve. Post*, May 19, 1951, pp. 34, 177–78; George Reedy OH.

3. LBJ to William O. Douglas, Jan. 10, 1951, William O. Douglas Papers, LC; Steinberg, *Sam Johnson's Boy*, 317–18, 320–31; Evans and Novak, *LBJ: Exercise of Power*, 54–55; Kearns, *Lyndon Johnson*, 107; Conkin, *Big Daddy*, 130; memo to LBJ on Baruch's comments, dated Jan. 3, 1950 (should be 1951), SP; HST-Contacts folder, WHFN; Miller, *Lyndon*, 182; Texas newspaper clippings in boxes 362 and 2013, SP.

4. Elizabeth Carpenter, "82nd Congress Has Broken All Investigation Records," *Amarillo Times*, Sept. 24, 1951.

5. John Spanier, *American Foreign Policy Since World War II* (8th ed.; N.Y., 1980), 61; Dugger, *The Politician*, 368.

6. William H. Darden OH; LBJ to HST, Sept. 20, 1950; HST to LBJ, Sept. 23, 1950, HSTL; George C. Marshall to LBJ, Jan. 17, 1951; Marshall to LBJ, Feb. 15, 1951, SP; Mary to LBJ, Feb. 14, 1951; Pres. Truman calls to LBJ, Feb. 15, March 10, 1951, Notes and Transcripts of LBJ conversations (hereafter cited as NTJC); *Times Review*, Cleburne, Texas, March 17, 1951; *Dallas Times Herald*, May 29, 1951; HST Appt. Books, June 19, 1951, HSTL; *The Gallup Poll: Public Opinion, 1935–1971*, Vol. 2: *1949–1958*, pp. 984, 1034, 1047; memorandum to Sen. Richard Russell listing eight Senators who want to sponsor the UMT bill, Jan. 1952, Richard Russell Papers, Univ. of Georgia; LBJ to George Cowen, March 20, 1952, and to D.N. Scott, June 14, 1952, discussing House action on UMT, SP.

7. Eliot Janeway, "Johnson of the 'Watchdog Committee,' " *N.Y. Times Magazine*, June 17, 1951, pp. 13, 26–27; summary of first thirty-six reports of Sen. Preparedness Subcomm., n.d.; final meeting of Preparedness Subcomm., Feb. 10, 1953, SP; *Austin American Statesman*, Nov. 13, 1951, *Fort Worth Press*, Nov. 14, 1951.

8. Summary of first thirty-six reports of Sen. Preparedness Subcomm. reports, n.d., SP; *Fort Worth Press*, Feb. 9, 1952; *Dallas Morning News*, March 9, 1952; *Newsweek*, Dec. 3, 1951, pp. 19–22.

9. LBJ to Ed Eastman, March 21, 1952; to H.W. Rahn, May 29, 1952; to Harold C. Stuart, June 24, 1952; George Reedy to LBJ, May 29, 1952; Ashbrook P. Bryant to LBJ, n.d., SP; Evans and Novak, *LBJ: Exercise of Power*, 58.

10. *Austin Statesman*, Dec. 6, 1951; George Reedy to LBJ, March 28, 1952, SP.

11. Dugger, *The Politician*, 369–71; LBJ to E.L. Meley, April 20, 1951, SP;

Washington Star, Oct. 11, 1951; LBJ statements of April 16, and June 1951, SLBJ.

12. *Gallup Poll: 1949–1958,* pp. 949, 951, 958, 965, 998–99, 1018.

13. Dugger, *The Politician,* 371–72; Hubert H. Humphrey to LBJ, Sept. 13, 1951; LBJ to Humphrey, Sept. 18, 1951, Hubert H. Humphrey Papers, Minn. Hist. Soc.; Eliot Janeway to Louise Evans, July 11, 1952; Janeway to LBJ, Nov. 10, 20, 1952; LBJ to Janeway, Nov. 15, 1952, LBJA:SN. Conservative Republican sympathy for Johnson's preparedness committee work is evident in the correspondence between LBJ and Iowa Senator Bourke B. Hickenlooper, Hickenlooper Papers, Herbert Hoover Library (hereafter cited as HHL).

14. John W. Spanier, *The Truman-MacArthur Controversy and the Korean War* (N.Y., 1965 ed.), Parts I and II.

15. *Ibid.,* chap. 11.

16. LBJ statement, n.d.; Warren Woodward to LBJ, April 14, 1951, SP; Walter Jenkins OH; LBJ to Mrs. D.R. Spangler, April 14, May 5, 1951; numerous letters protesting MacArthur's dismissal, SP; Phil Hopkins to LBJ, April 23, 1951, LBJA:SN.

17. Clint Murchison to LBJ, April 17, 1951; LBJ to Murchison, April 20, 1951, PPCF.

18. Spanier, *Truman-MacArthur Controversy,* chaps. 12 and 13.

19. George Reedy OH; Gerald W. Siegel OH; memo on questions for MacArthur hearings, n.d., box 341, SP.

20. *Fort Worth Press,* May 9, 1951; and the following excerpts from the hearings: "Military Situation in the Far East," Part I, May 3–14, 1951, pp. 206–16, 474–79, 704–8; Part III, June 1–13, 1951, pp. 1771–78, 2325–31; Part IV, June 14, 27, 1951, pp. 2603–8, 2647–51, SP.

21. LBJ statements, May 6, 13, 1951, SP; George Reedy OH; Spanier, *Truman-MacArthur Controversy,* 220.

22. Gerald Siegel OH; Roswell L. Gilpatric OH; George Reedy OH; Steinberg, *Sam Johnson's Boy,* 319.

23. George Reedy to LBJ, Feb. 11, 18, 1952, and other memos on public relations in boxes 412–13, SP; George Reedy OH.

24. Jimmy Roosevelt to LBJ, April 28, 1952; LBJ to Roosevelt, May 5, 1952, LBJA:CF; memo of LBJ-Under Sec. John McCone conversation, Feb. 15, 1951, NTJC; Walter Jenkins to Woodie, Dec. 21, 1951, esp. handwritten note at bottom of memo, LBJA:SN.

25. Welsh, *Ramparts,* Dec. 1967, p. 56; Wheeler and Lambert, *Life,* Aug. 14, 1964, p. 80; J.H. Blackaller to H.B. Zachry, Aug. 25, 1952, Maverick Papers. In March 1952 Johnson publicly attacked "revolting waste and corruption" in the "huge North African air base program." The Subcomm.'s 42nd report "described the large-scale waste in the construction of American air bases in North Africa"; *Dallas Times Herald,* March 20, 1952; final meeting of Preparedness Subcomm., Feb. 10, 1953, SP.

26. George Reedy to LBJ, Jan. 22, 1952, SP; *Austin American,* Sept. 13, 1951; *Austin American-Statesman,* Oct. 7, 1951.

27. Dorothy to LBJ, Jan. 11, 1951, SP; Walter Jenkins to LBJ, Feb. 9, 1951; "Mr. Corcoran called," Feb. 9, 1951, LBJA:FN.

28. Johnson-Byrd votes on major issues, 1950–56, LBJA:CF; memo, n.d., Major

LBJ Sponsored Legis. folder; Summary of LBJ Voting Record, SP; John Wildenthal OH.

29. Hubert H. Humphrey OH

30. *San Angelo Standard Times,* Sept. 29, 1951; LBJ speech, "Oil—the Lifeblood of Defense," Sept. 28, 1951; Al Buchanan to LBJ, Oct. 11, 1951; H.R. Cullen to LBJ, Oct. 12, 1951, SP.

31. *Dallas Morning News,* Oct. 12, 1951; LBJ to HST, Nov. 5, 1951; HST to LBJ, Nov. 13, 1951, WHFN; *Dallas Morning News,* March 11, 1952.

32. *Austin American,* Oct. 8, 1951.

33. Untitled clipping, April 27, 1952, attached to LBJ to R.M. Anthony, May 5, 1952, and other correspondence in Leg.: Steel [Dispute] folders, SP; LBJ Senate Voting Record, 1949–1962, p. 136; Hamby, *Beyond the New Deal,* 454–58.

34. LBJ Senate Voting Record, 1949–1962, pp. 369, 215; Helen G. Douglas OH; Hamby, *Beyond the New Deal,* 408–15, 484. Fears of Communist subversion were so great in the country between 1946 and 1952 that the FBI won funding to double its number of agents from 3,559 to 7,029; see Athan G. Theoharis and John Stuart Cox, *The Boss: J. Edgar Hoover and the Great American Inquisition* (Philadelphia, 1988), 7.

35. *Houston Post,* Nov. 11, 1951; Walter Jenkins OH; Lady Bird Johnson–Brice interviews.

36. Steinberg, *Sam Johnson's Boy,* 280–81.

37. *Ibid.,* 281–82; Gordon Fulcher OH.

38. Steinberg, *Sam Johnson's Boy,* 282–83; Margaret Mayer Ward OH.

39. Dugger, *The Politician,* chap. 62, and notes on p. 467.

40. Conkin, *Big Daddy,* 123–24; Richard Wilson's column in *Dallas Morning News,* May 17, 1966.

41. Interview with Lady Bird and Lyndon Johnson, Sept. 18, 1972; "The Hill Country: Lyndon Johnson's Texas," May 9, 1966; Conkin, *Big Daddy,* 124; George Reedy (OH) believes that the ranch gave Johnson "a refuge that he hadn't had previously. . . . The ranch was a real retreat for him. He'd go to that, I think, and spin all kinds of dreams."

42. The change in company name and the assets and profitability of KTBC are all in KTBC records for 1947–52 at the FCC. "The Story of the Johnson Family Fortune," *U.S. News & World Report,* May 4, 1964, pp. 38–45; Louis Kohlmeier, "The Johnson Wealth," *The Wall Street Journal,* March 23, 1964; Krasnow and Longley, *Politics of Broadcast Regulation,* 19–20, 118.

43. LBJ to Eddie Weisl, April 23, 1948; LBJ to Paul Raibourn, April 23, 1948, LBJA:SN; Jesse Kellam OH; Leonard Marks OH; Edward Joseph OH; Walter Jenkins OH; Gould, *Lady Bird Johnson and the Environment,* 19.

44. Sen. Edwin C. Johnson et al. to Sen. Burnet R. Maybank, May 19, 1952, SP.

45. Kohlmeier, *Wall Street Journal,* March 23, 1964, p. 12.

46. Leonard Marks OH; Willard Deason OH; Jesse Kellam OH; LBJ to J.P. Coleman, June 26, 1959; résumé of LBJ-Coleman conversation, June 30, 1959, LBJA:FN.

47. John Connally, who learned his political trade working for Johnson, told me: "I have not during my entire career reduced to writing a great many things

that I should have. . . . I never kept diaries. . . . I never dictated memos. Early on in Washington I realized that I was a very young, unsophisticated fella, and I became very wary, very early of putting everything in writing." Interview with John B. Connally, June 30, 1988; W. Ervin "Red" James OH. In 1953, after Eisenhower appointed John Doerfer, a Republican from Wisconsin, to the FCC, LBJ established a friendship with him. Arthur Perry to LBJ, July 21, 1953, PPMF, passing along a message of appreciation from Doerfer to LBJ for arranging swimming privileges for his children at the Naval hospital.

48. Gene Autry to LBJ, Sept. 24, 1945; LBJ to Autry, Sept. 26, 1945, LBJA:FN; telephone calls: Corcoran to LBJ, Nov. 5, 1945; Charles Denney to Corcoran, Nov. 30, 1945; Corcoran to Denney, Dec. 5, 1945; LBJ to Corcoran, Feb. 21, 1946, Corcoran Wiretaps, FBI.

49. Arthur Stehling unpublished manuscript, "A Country Lawyer: The Story of a Lifetime in Law, Business and Politics in the Texas Hill Country," 272–76.

50. Kohlmeier, *Wall Street Journal,* March 23, 1964, p. 12; John Barron, "The Johnson Money," *Washington Evening Star,* June 9, 1964, pp. 1 and 10; Wheeler and Lambert, *Life,* Aug. 21, 1964, p. 64; Willard Deason OH; Deason defended the LBJ monopoly by pointing to three other state capitals with one station; Gary Cobb to Oren Harris, March 4, 1958, comparing Austin to Amarillo, Oren Harris Papers, Univ. of Arkansas.

51. Interview with John B. Connally, June 30, 1988.

52. LBJ to Horace Busby, Dec. 1, 1951; George Reedy to LBJ, Aug. 14, 1952, SP; Wheeler and Lambert, *Life,* Aug. 21, 1964, pp. 64, 66.

53. Verne Young to T.J. Slowie, Dec. 19, 1951; Bill Boswell to LBJ, Jan. 31, 1952; Paul A. Walker to LBJ, March 3, 1952; Eugene L. Burke to T.J. Slowie, Aug. 11, 1952; Texas Broadcasting Co. statement, Feb. 28, 1953; LBJ to FCC, April 30, 1953; Slowie to LBJ, May 20, 1953, KWTX-TV and KTBC-TV Records, FCC.

54. Kohlmeier, *Wall Street Journal,* March 23, 1964, p. 12; Barron, *Evening Star,* June 9, 1964, p. 10; Robert F. Jones to Mary Jane Morris, April 28, 1955, with attached brief, KWTX-TV Records, FCC.

55. *Ibid.;* responses: CBS, May 5, 1955; ABC, May 9, 1955, and J.C. Kellam, May 9, 1955 to Mary Jane Morris in the same FCC file.

56. Wilford W. Naman to FCC, May 14, 1955; Mary Jane Morris to Naman, May 16, 1955, KWTX-TV Records, FCC; Kohlemier, *Wall Street Journal,* March 23, 1964, p. 12; Barron, *Evening Star,* June 9, 1964, p. 10.

57. The attorneys for KWTX saw a "conspiracy" in these events. They overlooked or ignored the possibility that it extended to some of their own clients. Boswell's letter to LBJ of Jan. 31, 1952, mentioned Wilford Naman and Hilton Howell, "with whom, of course, you are acquainted." The reply to the KWTX brief by Leonard Marks and Everett Looney, May 9, 1955, in KWTX-TV Records, FCC, did not persuade me.

58. Leonard Marks to Mary Jane Morris, June 14, 1955; Marks to Morris, Feb. 27, 1956; Morris to Marks, March 2, 1956; statements of assets, April 30, 1956, March 31, 1959, KTBC-TV Records, FCC; Kohlmeier, *Wall Street Journal,* March 23, 1964, p. 12; Barron, *Evening Star,* June 9, 1964, p. 10.

59. "Robert S. Allen Reports," *Waco Times-Herald,* March 27, 1951; LBJ and

Allen telephone conversation, March 30, 1951; LBJ's conversation with Allan Shivers, June 11, 1952, NTJC; other Smithwick materials in 1948 Campaign—Smithwick folder, PPCF and in box 7, SPF; J. Edward Johnson to Sam Houston Johnson, Dec. 11, 1952, with Feb. 1952 poll attached, LBJA:SN.

60. Green, *Establishment in Texas Politics*, chap. 10 ; Jake Pickle to LBJ, July 6, 1951, LBJA:SN; *Daily Times Herald*, Sept. 24, 1951; Allan Shivers OH, LBJL; Price Daniel OH, LBJL; Paul Bolton broadcast, April 14, 1952, LBJA:SN.

61. Harry Seay et al. to LBJ, Sept. 21, 1951; LBJ to Seay, Sept. 27, 1951, SPF; Price Daniel OH, LBJL and NTSU.

62. Steinberg, *Sam Johnson's Boy*, 324–26; Green, *Establishment in Texas Politics*, 143–45; Dugger, *The Politician*, 374–75; memos of LBJ conversations with Weldon Hall, April 22, 24, 1952, and with Allan Shivers, June 11, 1952, NTJC; Hardeman and Bacon, *Rayburn*, 361.

63. Maury Maverick to LBJ, Sept. 16, 1952, Maverick Papers; Allan Shivers OH, LBJL and NTSU; Byron T. Skelton OH; Walter G. Hall OH; Hall says that Shivers's conversation with Rayburn committing himself to support the party's nominees occurred before the convention; James P. Coleman OH; memo: "Houston Post-During National Convention 1952," Shivers folder, LBJA:FN; Green, *Establishment in Texas Politics*, 145.

64. Allan Shivers OH, LBJL; LBJ to Richard Russell, March 18, 1952, LBJA:CF; George Reedy to LBJ, May 1, 1952, SP; Sen. Ed Johnson to LBJ, June 4, 1952; LBJ to Ed Johnson, June 19, 1952, with statement attached, LBJA:CF; memo, "Dictated July 1952," David Charnay folder, Richard Russell Papers; Walter Jenkins OH; William H. Darden OH; Evans and Novak, *LBJ: Exercise of Power*, 242–43; Dugger, *The Politician*, 373 and 375, and note 2, p. 470.

65. Evans and Novak, *LBJ: Exercise of Power*, 243; Dugger, *The Politician*, 375–76; Gary W. Reichard, "Democrats, Civil Rights, and Electoral Strategies in the 1950s," *Congress and the Presidency*, Spring 1986; Hardeman and Bacon, *Rayburn*, 368–69.

66. Stephen E. Ambrose, *Eisenhower: The Soldier and Candidate, 1890–1952* (N.Y., 1983), 502–8; Edward T. Dicker OH, DDEL; O. Douglas Weeks, *Texas Presidential Politics in 1952* (Austin, 1953), chaps. 5–7; Don E. Carleton, *Red Scare!: Right-Wing Hysteria, Fifties Fanaticism and Their Legacy in Texas* (Austin, 1985), 229–30.

67. Allan Shivers OH, NTSU and DDEL; Price Daniel OH, LBJL; resolutions in Pol. Files, 1952 folder, SPF; Byron Skelton OH; D.B. Hardeman OH; Weeks, *Texas Presidential Politics in 1952*, chaps. 8 and 9; Green, *Establishment in Texas Politics*, 145–48; Hardeman and Bacon, *Rayburn*, 370–72; also see Rayburn's 1952 correspondence on Texas politics, SRL.

68. George Reedy OH; William S. White OH; Dugger, *The Politician*, 376.

69. Richard E. Berlin to Herbert Hoover, Aug. 26, 1952, Hoover Papers; LBJ to Jesse Smith, Sept. 4, 1952; LBJ to S.L. Brannon, Oct. 28, 1952, SPF; LBJ to Dr. E.O. Deal, Oct. 26, 1952, LBJA:SN.

70. LBJ press release, Aug. 28, 1952; LBJ radio speech, Oct. 13, 1952; activities of LBJ in behalf of Natl. Dem. presidential candidates in 1952, 1952—Schedule folder, SPF; Adlai Stevenson to LBJ, Aug. 30, Sept. 17, 1952; LBJ to Stevenson, Sept. 8, 1952, LBJA:FN; Rayburn to LBJ, Sept. 26, 1952; LBJ to

Rayburn, Sept. 27, 1952; J. William Fulbright to LBJ, Oct. 22, 1952, LBJA:CF; Mary Rather to LBJ, Oct. 28, 1952, SPF; Walter Jenkins OH; Mary Rather to J. William Fulbright, Oct. 16, 1952, J. William Fulbright Papers, Univ. of Arkansas.

71. Clint Murchison to LBJ, Sept. 30, 1952, SPF; Allan Shivers OH, NTSU and LBJL; LBJ speeches, Oct. 13, 17, 1952, SLBJ; Pearson statement, Feb. 5, 1954, SP; Drew Pearson OH; Steinberg, *Sam Johnson's Boy*, 330 and 338; Dugger, *The Politician*, 376–77.

72. E.L. Byers to LBJ, Oct. 6, 1952, Jan. 6, 1953; LBJ to Byers, Oct. 21, 1952; Philip E. Fox to LBJ, Feb. 13, 1953; LBJ to Fox, Feb. 17, 1953; untitled clipping, Nov. 6, 1952, with note attached, SPF; Texas poll, Dec. 7, 1952, Belden folder, LBJA:SN; *Dallas Times Herald*, Nov. 12, 1952.

73. Booth Mooney, *LBJ: An Irreverent Chronicle* (N.Y., 1976), 10–13, 16; *Business Week*, Nov. 15, 1952, p. 40.

74. Baker, *Wheeling and Dealing*, 60–61; S.H. Johnson, *My Brother Lyndon*, 82–83.

75. Evans and Novak, *LBJ: Exercise of Power*, 62–63; Steinberg, *Sam Johnson's Boy*, 338–39; Dugger, *The Politician*, 379; John T. Carlton OH, Univ. of Ga.; George Reedy OH; William H. Darden OH.

76. S.H. Johnson, *My Brother Lyndon*, 83–85; Allan Shivers OH, NTSU.

77. Ernest W. McFarland OH; Evans and Novak, *LBJ: Exercise of Power*, 63–65; Steinberg, *Sam Johnson's Boy*, 339–40; Dugger, *The Politician*, 379; Richard Russell, calendar, Nov. 10 and 17, 1952, Russell Papers.

78. Walter Jenkins to LBJ, Nov. 13, 1952, LBJA:SN; Drew Pearson, "Friction of Democrats," *Washington Post*, Nov. 20, 1952; Drew Pearson OH; telephone call to Adlai Stevenson, Nov. 20, 1952, NTJC; Kearns, *Lyndon Johnson*, 107–8.

79. Humphrey, *Education of a Public Man*, 163; Steinberg, *Sam Johnson's Boy*, 340; LBJ telephone call to Adlai Stevenson, Nov. 20, 1952, NTJC.

80. Humphrey, *Education of a Public Man*, 163–64.

81. Mary Rather to Lady Bird Johnson, Jan. 8, 1953, with Richard Russell notes of his nominating speech attached, SP; Walter Jenkins OH; Miller, *Lyndon*, 188; Humphrey, *Education of a Public Man*, 164–65; Steinberg, *Sam Johnson's Boy*, 341.

Chapter 13: Bipartisan Politics

1. Steinberg, *Sam Johnson's Boy*, 347–48.

2. Reedy to LBJ, Nov. 6, 8, 1952, SP; George Reedy OH; Hardeman and Bacon, *Rayburn*, 373, 375–77.

3. Reedy, *LBJ: A Memoir*, xiii, 92; LBJ statements, Jan. 2, 3, Feb. 3, 14, 1953, SLBJ.

4. *Washington Evening Star*, Nov. 14, 1952; George Reedy OH; *Time*, June 22, 1953, p. 20.

5. Earle C. Clements OH; George Reedy OH; Evans and Novak, *LBJ: Exercise of Power*, 64–65; Miller, *Lyndon*, 193–94.

6. George Reedy to LBJ, Nov. 19, 1952; LBJ statement, Jan. 7, 1953, SP;

Adalai Stevenson-LBJ telephone conversation, Jan. 10, 1953, NTJC; Gerald Siegel OH; Evans and Novak, *LBJ: Exercise of Power*, 72–74; Miller, *Lyndon*, 189–90; Baker, *Wheeling and Dealing*, 63–66. J. William Fulbright of Arkansas, a liberal, also wanted to be on the Policy Committee. Johnson put him off by promising to bear his request in mind when another vacancy occurred: Fulbright to LBJ, Jan. 10, 1953; LBJ to Fulbright, Jan. 12, 1953, Fulbright Papers.

7. The six appointees were Burnet Maybank of South Carolina, John McClellan of Arkansas, A. Willis Robertson of Virginia, Matthew Neely of West Virginia, John Pastore of Rhode Island, and Hubert Humphrey; LBJ statement, Jan. 7, 1953, SP; George Reedy OH; Evans and Novak, *LBJ: Exercise of Power*, 74–75.

8. Miller, *Lyndon*, 190–91; LBJ-Stevenson conversation, Jan. 10, 1953, NTJC; Reedy memo., n.d.; calendar of business, Feb. 23, 1953, SP.

9. Hubert Humphrey OH; LBJ-Stevenson conversation, Jan. 10, 1953.

10. Baker, *Wheeling and Dealing*, 64; Gary W. Reichard, *Congress and the Presidency*, p. 61.

11. Steinberg, *Sam Johnson's Boy*, 342–43; Gerald Siegel to LBJ, March 20, 1953; Dem. Pol. Comm. Minutes, March 24, 1953, SP; George Reedy OH; *Time*, June 22, 1953, p. 21.

12. Price Daniel OH, LBJL; LBJ statements: March 1, April 27, 30, 1953; suggestions for Pres.'s reply to tidelands filibusters, n.d., SP; LBJ to Joe Belden, May 2, 1953, LBJA:SN; Herbert Brownell OH, Dwight D. Eisenhower Library (hereafter cited as DDEL); *Time*, June 22, 1953, pp. 20–21; Steinberg, *Sam Johnson's Boy*, 357–58.

13. Roger Morris, *Richard Milhous Nixon: The Rise of an American Politician* (N.Y., 1989), 625–26; Drew Pearson OH; LBJ-Al Friendly telephone conversation, Jan. 19, 1953, NTJC.

14. Memorandum (26 pages) from George Reedy to LBJ, n.d. (1954), SP.

15. *Ibid.*; LBJ-Al Friendly telephone conversation, Jan. 19, 1953; telephone conversations with Sen. Leverett Saltonstall, Jan. 20, 1953, and Rhea Howard, Jan. 24, 1953; Mary Rather to LBJ, Jan. 30, 1953, recounting a conversation with James Rowe, NTJC.

16. Sam Rayburn to Corcoran, Nov. 17, 1952 (Rayburn described the Republican victory as an "Eisenhower victory" by "a nationally advertised product"), Corcoran Papers. George Reedy OH; LBJ to Joseph Alsop, Feb. 13, 1953, Joseph and Stewart Alsop Papers, LC; LBJ to Fulton Lewis, Jr., Feb. 13, 1953, Fulton Lewis, Jr., Papers, Syracuse Univ.; LBJ to Sen. Alexander Wiley (Republican chairman of the Foreign Relations Committee), Feb. 27, 1953, Alexander Wiley Papers, State Hist. Soc. of Wisconsin; John Sparkman OH; Robert B. Anderson OH; LBJ to Maverick, April 14, 1953, Maverick Papers.

17. Stephen E. Ambrose, *Eisenhower: The President* (N.Y., 1984), 46–49; LBJ statement, Feb. 2, 1953, SLBJ; L. Arthur Minnich memos, Feb. 16, 19, 1953, DDEL; memo to LBJ, Dec. 30, 1953, summarizing a call from Sen. Byrd, PPMF.

18. Draft resolution, Feb. 1953, Sen. Dem. Pol. Comm. Mins., SP; Ambrose, *Eisenhower: The President*, 47–49, 54, 65–66.

19. George Reedy OH; Dem. Pol. Comm. Mins., Feb. 24, March 4, 1953, SP; memo of Dulles call to LBJ, March 3, 1953, NTJC; Ambrose, *Eisenhower: The President*, 66–67.

20. *Ibid.*, 59–61; LBJ Senate speech, March 27, 1953, SLBJ; George Reedy's memos analyzing the meaning of the Bohlen fight for the Republicans in general and for McCarthy in particular, n.d., 1953, and July 9, 1953, SP.

21. Congressman Walter Judd of Minnesota (OH, HSTL), one of the Republican hardliners, remembered LBJ at a State Department conference on Korea convinced that "we should just continue to talk, talk, talk, and not give an ultimatum to the other side to end the fighting." Steinberg, *Sam Johnson's Boy*, 355–56; Ambrose, *Eisenhower: The President*, 30–35, 97–107.

22. *Ibid.*, 68–70; Duane Tananbaum, *The Bricker Amendment: A Test of Eisenhower's Political Leadership* (Ithaca, N.Y., 1988), chaps. 1–7.

23. Ambrose, *Eisenhower: The President*, 69; George Reedy OH.

24. Baker, *Wheeling and Dealing*, 90–91; William S. White OH; Walter Jenkins OH; Tananbaum, *Bricker Amendment Controversy*, chaps. 6–7; LBJ radio broadcast, Sept. 13, 1953, SP.

25. Tananbaum, *Bricker Amendment Controversy*, chaps. 8–9; Gerald Siegel to LBJ, Jan. 28, 29, 30, 1954, SP; G. Siegel OH; Miller, *Lyndon*, 192–93.

26. Tananbaum, *Bricker Amendment Controversy*, chap. 10; John W. Bricker OH, LC.

27. Baker, *Wheeling and Dealing*, 66–67; Steinberg, *Sam Johnson's Boy*, 359–60; Tananbaum, *Bricker Amendment Controversy*, 179–81.

28. Reedy, *LBJ: A Memoir*, 85–86; William E. Leuchtenburg, *A Troubled Feast: American Society Since 1945* (Boston, 1973), 88; LBJ to Sen. Lister Hill, March 16, 24, April 24, 1953; Julius C.C. Edelstein to Hill, March 20, 1953, Lister Hill Papers, Univ. of Alabama.

29. Steinberg, *Sam Johnson's Boy*, 351, 353; *Congressional Record: Senate*, 99th Congress, 2nd sess., p. 1911; Ambrose, *Eisenhower: The President*, 118, 164; Evans and Novak, *LBJ: Exercise of Power*, 71.

30. LBJ statement, Aug. 3, 1953; LBJ press release, Aug. 4, 1953, SP.

31. Steele to Laybourne, Aug. 7, 1953, John L. Steele Papers, LBJL.

32. Douglas Cater, "Lyndon Johnson, Rising Democratic Star," *The Reporter*, Jan. 20, 1953, pp. 34–37; George Reedy OH; Arthur Perry to LBJ, June 30, 1953, PPMF; *Abilene Reporter News*, June 11, 1953; DDE to Herbert Brownell, March 13, 1953; Jack Porter to DDE, July 20, 1953; DDE to Porter, July 27, 1953, DDEL.

33. Sam Houston Johnson, *My Brother Lyndon*, 86–87; Booth Mooney OH.

34. *Time*, June 22, 1953, p. 23; LBJ to Joe Alsop, Aug. 11, 1953, Alsop to LBJ, Aug. 14, 1953, Alsop Papers; Reedy to LBJ, June 24, 1953, SP; LBJ to Jesse Kellam, April 3, 1953; Booth Mooney to Jesse Kellam, July 7, 1953; LBJ to Val Lawrence, July 7, 1953, LBJA:SN; Reedy to LBJ, n.d., Policy Comm. folder; Reedy to LBJ, Sept. 12, 1953; Walter Jenkins to LBJ, March 23, 1953; letters in 1953 General Files and Air Force folders, SP; Pickle folder, LBJA:SN.

35. George Reedy to LBJ, June 24, 1953, and memo, n.d. (1953), SP; George Reedy OH.

36. Walter Jenkins to Jack Conn, Oct. 15, 1953; Bernice Grieder folders, SPF; J.J. (Jake) Pickle OH; Cecil Burney OH.

37. George Reedy to LBJ, n.d. (content suggests Dec. 1953), SP.

38. Estes Kefauver to LBJ, Dec. 24, 1953, LBJA:CF; Reedy to LBJ, Dec. 30, 1953; Felton Johnson and Gerald Siegel to LBJ, Dec. 22, 1953, SP; "Biparti-

san," Jan. 5, 1954, DDEL; James Rowe to LBJ, Jan. 4, 1953 (date should be 1954), LBJA:SN; LBJ address, Jan. 6, 1954, SLBJ; Evans and Novak, *LBJ: Exercise of Power*, 82–83.

39. Memo to LBJ, Jan. 7, 1954, PPMF; Reedy to LBJ, Jan. 25, 1954, SP; Steele to Williamson, Feb. 13, 1954, Steele Papers.

40. *Ibid.; Courier-Journal*, Feb. 2, 1954; DP from FB, n.d. (1954), Pearson Papers; Pearson statement, Feb. 5, 1954; Reedy to LBJ, Feb. 2, 1954, SP.

41. Evans and Novak, *LBJ: Exercise of Power*, 84–85; Hardeman and Bacon, *Rayburn*, 381–82.

42. Steele to Williamson, Feb. 13, 1954, Steele Papers; Manchester, *The Glory and the Dream*, 704–5.

43. LBJ address, May 6, 1954, SLBJ; Ambrose, *Eisenhower: The President*, 158–60.

44. Evans and Novak, *LBJ: Exercise of Power*, 85–86; Price Daniel OH, LBJL; LBJ Senate Voting Record, 1949–1962, p. 120.

45. Ambrose, *Eisenhower: The President*, 173–85.

46. *Ibid.*, 173–78; Wayne Kelley, "Senator Russell Vows to Speak His Mind," *Atlanta Journal and Constitution Magazine*, Feb. 4, 1968, p. 9.

47. LBJ address, May 6, 1954, SLBJ.

48. Ambrose, *Eisenhower: The President*, 116–18, 157–58; Steinberg, *Sam Johnson's Boy*, 384–85; LBJ Senate Voting Record, 1949–1962, p. 305; James Rowe to Arthur Goldberg, May 12, 1954, LBJA:SN

49. Reichard, *Congress and the Presidency*, Spring 1986, pp. 61–62; Texas poll, April 11, 1954, LBJA:SN; LBJ speech, May 18, 1954, SP; Ambrose, *Eisenhower: The President*, 189–92; Hubert Humphrey OH.

50. Correspondence in Old Age Assistance folder, SP; LBJ Senate Voting Record, 1949–1962, pp. 176, 201, 248, 305, 385–86, 396–97; "Johnson-Byrd Votes on Major Issues, 1950–1956," LBJA:SN.

51. Ambrose, *Eisenhower: The President*, 192–97. Stephen Schlesinger and Stephen Kinzer, *Bitter Fruit: The Untold Story of the American Coup in Guatemala* (N.Y., 1982).

52. Steinberg, *Sam Johnson's Boy*, 360; Evans and Novak, *LBJ: Exercise of Power*, 87–88; Dulles-Knowland telephone conversation, June 26, 1954; Dulles-LBJ telephone calls, June 26, 28, 1954, John Foster Dulles Papers, DDEL.

53. Evans and Novak, *LBJ: Exercise of Power*, 90–92; LBJ Senate Voting Record, 1949–1962, pp. 98–100; Hubert Humphrey (OH) remembered LBJ's collaboration with liberals on the Atomic Energy bill rather than his defeat of the filibuster. Also see LBJ to Humphrey, Aug. 14, 1954, Humphrey Papers.

54. LBJ statement, Aug. 20, 1954, SLBJ; LBJ to Fulton Lewis, Jr., May 19, 1954, Lewis, Jr. Papers.

55. Sam Low to LBJ, Jan. 22, 1954; LBJ to Edward Clark, Feb. 4, 1954, LBJA:SN; *Austin American* and *San Antonio Express*, Feb. 2, 1954; Herman Brown to LBJ, Feb. 3, 1954; LBJ to Brown, Feb. 6, 1954, LBJA:SN.

56. Clippings in Parr folders; H. Grady Harlan to LBJ, Feb. 16, 1954, PPCF; Everett Looney to LBJ, Feb. 5, 1954, LBJA:SN; George Reedy to LBJ, Feb. 24, 1954, PPMF.

57. Feb. 1954 survey of 1954 campaign, PPCF; Alex Lewis to Jake Pickle, Feb. 25, 1954, LBJA:SN.

58. Evans and Novak, *LBJ: Exercise of Power*, 83–84; Steinberg, *Sam Johnson's Boy*, 383; Miller, *Lyndon*, 196; Carleton, *Red Scare*, 261–62; George Reedy to LBJ, Feb. 12, 1954, SP; George Reedy OH.

59. LBJ radio address, Feb. 28, 1954, SLBJ; Edward Clark to LBJ, Feb. 24, 1954; LBJ to Clark, March 1, 1954, LBJA:SN; Booth Mooney to LBJ, March 9, 1954, PPMF; Paul Bolton to LBJ, March 2, 10, 25, 1954, SPF; Walter Jenkins to LBJ, April 8, 1954, PPMF; Willie Day Taylor to LBJ, April 22, 1954, SPF; Jake Pickle to LBJ, April 2, 7, 1954; LBJ to Mary Rather, April 13, 1954, LBJA:SN; LBJ to Stuart Symington, April 7, 1954; Carl Estes to Symington, April 21, 1954, LBJA:CF; George Reedy to LBJ, April 20, 21, 1954, SP.

60. Memo of Walter Jenkins–Sam H. Johnson conversation, April 30, 1954, SP; Paul Bolton to LBJ, June 8, 10, 30, 1954, SPF; LBJ to Edmunds Travis, May 10, 1954; to Richard Spinn, May 13, 1954; to Wiley Thornton, June 29, 1954, SP; Booth Mooney to LBJ, June 22, 1954, PPMF; Jake Pickle to LBJ, June 26, July 20, 1954, LBJA:SN; Miller, *Lyndon*, 196–97.

61. Dougherty, release #2, n.d.; Willie Day Taylor to LBJ, May 12, June 25, 1954; Walter Jenkins to Jake Pickle, June 10, 1954, SP; Jenkins to LBJ, June 28, 1954, SPF; L.B. Nichols to Tolson, Aug. 7, 1954, LBJ: Main File, FBI; Pat McCarran to LBJ, April 30, 1954; George Reedy to LBJ, June 15, 1954, SP; Herman Brown to Comm. on Constl. Govt., June 2, 1954; Roy Cullen to LBJ, July 7, 1954; Jenkins to Reedy, n.d.; LBJ to Cullen, July 12, 1954, LBJA:SN; Reedy to Ed. Ray, June 29, 1954, SP.

62. Willie Day Taylor to LBJ, April 30, May 31, 1954; Jenkins to Jake Pickle, June 10, 1954; Gerald Siegel to LBJ, June 15, 1954; Jenkins to Taylor, July 8, 1954, SP; Alsop column, July 6, 1954, in LBJA:SN; Alsop to LBJ, June 30, July 2, 1954, Alsop Papers.

63. Willie Day Taylor to LBJ, Aug. 5, 1954; George Reedy to LBJ, June 4, 1954, SP; Alsop to LBJ, June 30, 1954, Alsop Papers.

64. Manchester, *Glory and the Dream*, 562, 606–7; Steinberg, *Sam Johnson's Boy*, 360–63.

65. Miller, *Lyndon*, 199; Steinberg, *Sam Johnson's Boy*, 362; Hubert Humphrey to Sen. Olin D. Johnston, Feb. 18, 1954, WHFN; Maverick to LBJ, April 2, 1954, Maverick Papers.

66. Lady Bird Johnson–Brice interviews; Evans and Novak, *LBJ: Exercise of Power*, 92–93; Arthur Stehling, "A Country Lawyer," 424–25, ms. memoir.

67. Miller, *Lyndon*, 202; Hubert Humphrey OH; LBJ to Maverick, April 27, May 12, 1954, Maverick Papers; Baker, *Wheeling and Dealing*, 92–93.

68. Miller, *Lyndon*, 202–3, 207–8; George Reedy OH; Reedy, *LBJ: A Memoir*, 106–7; Hubert Humphrey OH; Henry Jackson OH.

69. Manchester, *Glory and the Dream*, 700–709.

70. Miller, *Lyndon*, 204–5; Robert G. Baker telephone interview with John Brice, n.d.

71. Manchester, *Glory and the Dream*, 709–16.

72. *Ibid.*, 716; *Austin American-Statesman*, June 13, 1954.

73. Manchester, *Glory and the Dream*, 716–17; memo of LBJ-Sen. McClellan telephone conversation, n.d. (clearly July 29, 1954); minutes of Dem. Policy. Comm. Meeting, July 29, 1954, SP; Steele to Williamson, July 30, 1954, Steele Papers.

74. Evans and Novak, *LBJ: Exercise of Power*, 93–94; Miller, *Lyndon*, 208; Baker, *Wheeling and Dealing*, 94.

75. Walter Jenkins OH; LBJ to Will Clayton, Aug. 4, 1954, William L. Clayton Papers, HSTL; Lady Bird Johnson–Brice interviews; Earle C. Clements OH; William S. White OH; Hubert Humphrey OH; George Reedy OH; Baker, *Wheeling and Dealing*, 94; Evans and Novak, *LBJ: Exercise of Power*, 94–96; Miller, *Lyndon*, 208–9; William S. White, *Citadel: The Story of the U.S. Senate* (N.Y., 1957), 127–31.

76. William S. White OH; White, *Citadel*, 128–31.

77. *Ibid.*, 127–28; George Reedy to LBJ, Nov. 29, 1954, PPMF; Evans and Novak, *LBJ: Exercise of Power*, 96–97; Miller, *Lyndon*, 209–10.

78. Evans and Novak, *LBJ: Exercise of Power*, 97; Miller, *Lyndon*, 210–11; Paul Douglas OH; Reedy, *LBJ: A Memoir*, 107–8; Franz, *Journal of Southern History*, Feb. 1979, pp. 16–19.

79. *New York Herald Tribune*, March 15, 1954; memo, "State of the Party," n.d., SPF; Cabell Phillips, "Who'll Head the Tickets in '56?" *New York Times Magazine*, July 25, 1954, pp. 13, 50.

80. Solberg, *Hubert Humphrey*, 157–59; LBJ Senate Voting Record, 1949–1962, p. 370; Humphrey to LBJ, Sept. 6, 1954; George Reedy to LBJ, Sept. 10, 1954, WHFN.

81. Stephen E. Ambrose, *Nixon: The Education of a Politician, 1913–1962* (N.Y., 1987), 347–49, 351–55.

82. *Ibid.*, 352; Hardeman and Bacon, *Rayburn*, 381–82; Steele to Williamson, Nov. 6, 1954, Steele Papers; George Reedy OH; LBJ to Sen. Theodore F. Green, Oct. 23, 1954, SP.

83. Ambrose, *Eisenhower: The President*, 217–19; Ambrose, *Nixon: Education of a Politician*, 356–57; Hardeman and Bacon, *Rayburn*, 385; George Reedy OH; Rayburn and LBJ to Eisenhower, Oct. 9, 1954, SP.

84. LBJ speech, Oct. 5, 1954, SLBJ; George Reedy OH.

85. LBJ western states' tour schedule, Oct. 13, 1954, SP; Reedy to LBJ, Oct. 11, 13, 1954, PPMF; George Reedy OH; William S. White OH; LBJ speech in Cheyenne, Oct. 17, 1954, Joseph O'Mahoney Papers, Univ. of Wyoming; Steinberg, *Sam Johnson's Boy*, 389–90; Solberg, *Humphrey*, 158.

86. Ambrose, *Nixon*, 358; Steinberg, *Sam Johnson's Boy*, 391–92; Steele to Williamson, Nov. 6, 1954, Steele Papers.

87. LBJ statement, Nov. 1954, SLBJ; Reedy memos (election eve, 1954), SP; Steele to Williamson, Nov. 6, 1954, Steele Papers.

88. *Ibid.*; Richard Nixon to LBJ, Sept. 27, 1954, WHFN; Karl Mundt to LBJ, Sept. 21, 1954, Karl E. Mundt Papers, Dakota State College.

Chapter 14: The Making of a Majority Leader

1. Matthews, *U.S. Senators and Their World*, 118–29.

2. Ralph K Huitt, "Democratic Party Leadership in the Senate," June 1961, pp. 333–37; "The Senate Majority and Minority Leaders," *Senate History*, May 1985, 1, 5–7 (a Senate Hist. Office publication). "Johnson was one of the very

few Senators willing to accept the combination of political risk and little real authority attendant on party leadership in the 1950s," Doris Kearns writes. *Lyndon Johnson*, 109.

3. LBJ-Shivers conversation, Nov. 15, 1954; George Reedy memo with telegram of Nov. 16, 1954, attached, NTJC.

4. Memorandum to LBJ, n.d. (1954), PPMF; interviews of LBJ, Jan. 7, 17, 1955, SP; C. Girard Davidson OH, HSTL; Steinberg, *Sam Johnson's Boy*, 392–94; Evans and Novak, *LBJ: Exercise of Power*, 157–60.

5. *Ibid.*, 160; Miller, *Lyndon*, 214.

6. George Reedy memo, n.d., discussing the tax cut; Dem. Policy Comm. Meeting, March 8, 1955, SP; LBJ Senate speech, March 15, 1955, SLBJ; Steele to Laybourne, March 11, 1955; Steele to Williamson, March 18, 1955, Steele Papers; George Reedy OH; Evans and Novak, *LBJ: Exercise of Power*, 160–61; Miller, *Lyndon*, 214.

7. LBJ Travel folder, 1955, LBJA:SF; DDE to LBJ, Jan, 22, 27, 1955; LBJ to DDE, Feb. 7, 1955, DDEL; Corcoran to Mrs. Johnson, Jan. 22, 1955, LBJA:FN; Booth Mooney to LBJ, Feb. 7, 1955; George Reedy to LBJ, Jan. 29, 1955, PPMF; LBJ to Adlai Stevenson, Feb. 7, 1955, LBJA:FN; LBJ to Wayne Morse, Jan. 27, 1955, Wayne Morse Papers; LBJ to Richard Neuberger, Jan. 27, 1955, Richard L. Neuberger Papers, Univ. of Oregon; LBJ to Hubert Humphrey, Feb. 2, 1955, Humphrey Papers; LBJ to William O. Douglas, Douglas Papers; John Stennis to LBJ, March 2, 1955; LBJ to Stennis, March 7, 1955, LBJA:CF; George Reedy OH.

8. Bryce Harlow OH; Evans and Novak, *LBJ: Exercise of Power*, 105.

9. Matthews, *U.S. Senators and Their World*, 147–48; Kearns, *Lyndon Johnson*, 112–13.

10. Steele to Williamson, Jan. 13, 1955, Steele Papers; Humphrey to Tom Stokes, Jan. 14, 1955, WHFN; Rayburn to LBJ, Jan. 14, 1955, Rayburn Papers. Typical of the appreciation LBJ generated among freshmen is Richard L. Neuberger to Nan Wood Honeyman, Jan. 21, 1955: "I have received excellent committee assignments and feel that the patience and understanding of Lyndon Johnson are main reasons for this," Neuberger Papers.

11. Evans and Novak, *LBJ: Exercise of Power*, 113–14; LBJ to O'Mahoney, Jan. 11, 1955, O'Mahoney Papers; LBJ to Morse, Jan. 11, 1955; Morse to LBJ, Jan. 13, 1955, Morse Papers.

12. LBJ to Kennedy, Jan. 11, 1955, WHFN; LBJ conversation with Kefauver, Jan. 11, 1955, LBJA:CF.

13. Huitt, *American Political Science Review*, June 1961, p. 338; Kearns, *Lyndon Johnson*, 115.

14. Matthews, *U.S. Senators and Their World*, 128–29; J. William Fulbright OH, LC; Stuart Symington OH.

15. Stewart E. McClure OH, SHO; Kearns, *Lyndon Johnson*, 116; Grover W. Ensley OH, SHO.

16. Huitt, *Amer. Pol. Sci. Rev.*, June 1961, p. 338; Evans and Novak, *LBJ: Exercise of Power*, 117–18; Kearns, *Lyndon Johnson*, 119–21; Mundt to LBJ, April 15, 1955; LBJ to Mundt, April 18, 1955, Mundt Papers; Margaret Chase Smith OH.

17. Huitt, *Am. Pol. Sci. Rev.*, June 1961, pp. 337–38; Matthews, *U.S. Senators and Their World*, 126–27; Conkin, *Big Daddy*, 135.

18. Evans and Novak, *LBJ: Exercise of Power*, 115–16; Miller, *Lyndon*, 212–14.

19. Kearns, *Lyndon Johnson*, 122–25.

20. *Ibid.*, 122.

21. *Ibid.*, 124; Evans and Novak, *LBJ: Exercise of Power*, 116; Miller, *Lyndon*, 213, who quotes Fulbright; Henry Jackson OH.

22. Sarah McClendon OH; Miller, *Lyndon*, 119, 124.

23. Interview with Clark Clifford, Jan. 8, 1988; Gerald Siegel OH; Kearns, *Lyndon Johnson*, 126.

24. *Ibid.*, 127–28.

25. *Ibid.*, 117–18; William Darden OH; Stewart Alsop, "Lyndon Johnson: How Does He Do It?" *Sat. Eve. Post*, Jan. 24, 1959, p. 14.

26. *Time*, Oct. 18, 1963, p. 29; Ruth Young Watt OH, SHO; George Reedy OH.

27. Baker, *Wheeling and Dealing*, 35–39, 69; Leonard H. Ballard OH, SHO.

28. Robert G. Baker telephone interview with John Brice, n.d.; Evans and Novak, *LBJ: Exercise of Power*, 108–9; Robert S. Allen OH; LBJ to Bobby Baker, Sept. 16, 1955, SP.

29. Floyd M. Riddick OH, SHO; Steinberg, *Sam Johnson's Boy*, 412; Evans and Novak, *LBJ: Exercise of Power*, 126–29; Kearns, *Lyndon Johnson*, 129–31.

30. Steele to Williamson, Jan. 6, 1955, Steele Papers; Walter White press release, Jan. 13, 1955; Hubert Humphrey to White, Jan. 13, 1955; Humphrey to LBJ, Jan. 13, 1955, WHFN; Reichard, "Democrats [and] Civil Rights," *Congress and the Presidency*, 62.

31. Ambrose, *Eisenhower: The President*, 231–35; Walter Jenkins OH; notation of a DDE telephone call to LBJ, Jan. 18, 1955, WHFN; Baker to LBJ, Jan. 26, 1955, PPCF; Reedy to LBJ, Jan. 29, 1955, PPMF; Albert Gore to LBJ, Feb. 8, 1955, Albert Gore Papers, Middle Tenn. State Univ.

32. Ambrose, *Eisenhower: The President*, 237–45; Stennis to LBJ, Feb. 8, 1955, LBJA:CF; Reedy memo, n.d. (1955), PPMF.

33. Ambrose, *Eisenhower: The President*, 237–45; Steele to Williamson, March 26, 1955, Steele Papers.

34. Evans and Novak, *LBJ: Exercise of Power*, 186–87; Reedy memo, June 21, 1955, SP; LBJ statement, Aug. 7, 1955, SLBJ; *Congressional Record—Senate*, 84th Congress, 1st sess., pp. 7638–46; memo: McCarthyism, June 21, 1955, DDE Papers.

35. Memo to: All Democratic Senators from Senate Dem. Policy Comm., n.d. (1955), Harry F. Byrd, Sr., Papers, Univ. of Virginia; memorandum, n.d. (1955), SP; LBJ statement, Aug. 7, 1955, SLBJ; *New York Times*, Aug. 3, 1955, p. 14.

36. Ambrose, *Eisenhower: The President*, 249–52.

37. Evans and Novak, *LBJ: Exercise of Power*, 162; Oil Imports and Reciprocal Trade-Oil Imports folders, SP; Steele to Williamson, May 5, 1955, Steele Papers.

38. Evans and Novak, *LBJ: Exercise of Power*, 162–63; Huitt, *Am. Pol. Sci.*

Rev., June 1961, p. 341; LBJ statement, June 4, 1955, SP; Robert Oliver OH; Hubert Humphrey OH.

39. Evans and Novak, *LBJ: Exercise of Power*, 163–65; Miller, *Lyndon*, 216–17; Steele to Williamson, June 9, 1955, Steele Papers; John Sparkman OH; Hubert Humphrey OH; memo (housing), June 8, 1955, SP; Sparkman to LBJ, June 10, 1955, LBJA:CF; LBJ Senate Voting Record, 1949–1962, p. 201.

40. Evans and Novak, *LBJ: Exercise of Power*, 100; Grace Tully to LBJ, June 22, 1955; LBJ letters denying that he was running, SPF; Reedy to LBJ, July 20, 1955; memos of June 9 and July 17, 1955, SP.

41. Al Toffler, "LBJ: The Senate's Mr. Energy," *Pageant*, July 1958, p. 102.

42. Evans and Novak, *LBJ: Exercise of Power*, 101; Steinberg, *Sam Johnson's Boy*, 404–5; Miller, *Lyndon*, 219; Baker, *Wheeling and Dealing*, 70; John Sparkman OH; Brooks Hays OH.

43. Steinberg, *Sam Johnson's Boy*, 413.

44. *Ibid.*, 414; Miller, *Lyndon*, 219; Stuart Symington OH.

45. Steinberg, *Sam Johnson's Boy*, 414; Evans and Novak, *LBJ: Exercise of Power*, 101–2; Miller, *Lyndon*, 219–20.

46. Steinberg, *Sam Johnson's Boy*, 414–15; Evans and Novak, *LBJ: Exercise of Power*, 102; Miller, *Lyndon*, 220; George Brown OH; Frank Oltorf OH; Lady Bird Johnson–Brice interviews.

47. Steinberg, *Sam Johnson's Boy*, 415; Frank Oltorf OH.

48. Lady Bird Johnson–Brice interviews; Walter Jenkins OH; George Reedy OH; Evans and Novak, *LBJ: Exercise of Power*, 103; Toffler, *Pageant*, July 1958, p. 104; Miller, *Lyndon*, 221.

49. Lady Bird Johnson–Brice interviews; Walter Jenkins OH; Lady Bird to Nellie Connally, July 16, 1955, SP; Lady Bird to Terrell Maverick, July 28, 1955, LBJA:SN; Steinberg, *Sam Johnson's Boy*, 418.

50. *Ibid.*; Walter Jenkins OH; George Reedy OH; Booth Mooney OH; Lady Bird Johnson–Brice interviews.

51. Lady Bird Johnson to Sen. Sam Ervin, July 16, 1955, Sam Ervin Papers, Univ. of N.C.; Styles Bridges to LBJ, July 6, 1955; Harry F. Byrd to Lady Byrd, July 8, 1955; Wayne Morse to LBJ, n.d., LBJA:CF; Hubert Humphrey to LBJ, July 30, 1955, WHFN; Symington speech in Senate, Aug. 2, 1955, LBJA:CF; Willie Day Taylor OH.

52. Hubert Humphrey OH; Lady Bird to Wayne Morse, July 15, 1955, Morse Papers; Lady Bird to HST, July 19, 1955, HSTL; George Reedy OH.

53. Steinberg, *Sam Johnson's Boy*, 418–19; Miller, *Lyndon*, 222–23; clipping, "Famous Fables," n.d.; *Newsweek* interview, July 22, 1955, SP; Booth Mooney to LBJ, Aug. 11, 18, 1955, PPMF; Sarah McClendon OH; LBJ to Joseph Alsop, Aug. 15, 20, 1955, Alsop Papers; LBJ to O'Mahoney, Aug. 18, 1955, O'Mahoney Papers; LBJ to Fulbright, Aug. 18, 1955, Fulbright Papers.

54. Lady Bird to Wesley West, July 27, 1955, LBJA:SN; *Houston Post*, Aug. 25, 1955; Mary Rather OH; LBJ to Stuart Symington, Sept. 14, 1955, SP; Steinberg, *Sam Johnson's Boy*, 419–20.

55. LBJ to Symington, Sept. 14, 1955, SP; Mary Rather OH; George Reedy OH; Walter Jenkins OH; Dorothy Palmie Starcke OH; Steinberg, *Sam Johnson's Boy*, 420.

56. LBJ to Hubert Humphrey, Sept. 26, 1955, WHFN; Jack Martin-LBJ telephone conversation, Sept. 25, 1955, NTJC; James C. Hagerty OH; Reedy memos, n.d. (1955), PPMF; Ambrose, *Eisenhower: The President*, 270–96.

57. Steinberg, *Sam Johnson's Boy*, 421–22; LBJ to James Rowe, Sept. 28, 1955, SP; LBJ to Charles I. Francis, Sept. 30, 1955, LBJA:SN; Reedy to LBJ, Sept. 30, 1955, PPMF; Baker to LBJ, Oct. 4, 1955, PPCF.

58. Reedy to LBJ, Oct. 11, 19, 1955, PPMF; memo, travel (1955) folder, LBJA:SF; George Reedy OH; LBJ to Bobby Baker, Oct. 10, 1955, PPCF; DDE to LBJ, Oct. 14, 1955, DDE Diaries.

59. Two Reedy memos, n.d. (1955); LBJ to Reedy with attached memo, Sept. 16, 1955, PPMF.

60. LBJ-H.R. Cullen telephone conversation, Oct. 24, 1955, NTJC; John Stennis to LBJ, Oct. 25, 1955; LBJ to Stennis, Oct. 31, 1955, LBJA:CF; LBJ to Joe Alsop, Nov. 4, 1955, Alsop Papers.

61. Corcoran's recollections of when these events occurred were murky. In a manuscript memoir, he couldn't remember the year and in a 1965 letter to LBJ, he said it was the fall of 1959. In fact, a letter from LBJ to Joe Kennedy in August 1956 makes clear that these discussions took place in October 1955. Arthur Schlesinger, Jr., and Steven Smith, JFK's brother-in-law, confirm that the Kennedys made this proposal to Johnson in 1955. A letter from Corcoran to Lady Bird and Lyndon in November 1955 indicates that he had been to see LBJ in October and that they had discussed presidential politics.

"The Boston-Texas Axis," a chap. in Corcoran's ms. memoir, Corcoran Papers; Corcoran to LBJ, Oct. 9, 1965, WHCF; Corcoran to Lady Bird and LBJ, Nov. 10, 1955, LBJA:FN; James Rowe to LBJ, Oct. 26, 1955, LBJA:SN; LBJ to Joseph Kennedy, Aug. 25, 1956, in Lyndon B. Johnson, *The Vantage Point: Perspectives of the Presidency, 1963–1969* (N.Y., 1971), 3; Arthur Schlesinger, Jr., to author, July 15, 1987; interview with Arthur Schlesinger, Jr., Aug. 3, 1987; Doris Kearns Goodwin, *The Fitzgeralds and the Kennedys: An American Saga* (N.Y., 1987), 780–81.

62. Mary Rather OH; Mary Rather to Corcoran, Nov. 27, 1955, LBJA:FN; George Reedy OH; Whitney speech, Nov. 21, 1955, SLBJ.

63. George Reedy OH; LBJ to Alsop, Nov. 28, 1955, SP; LBJ to Stevenson, Nov. 27, 1955, LBJA:FN.

64. LBJ press conference, Dec. 12, 1955, Pearson Papers; George Reedy OH.

65. Steinberg, *Sam Johnson's Boy*, 423; LBJ to Reedy, Jan. 4, 1956; to Richard Nixon, Jan. 5, 9, 1956; Nixon to LBJ, Jan. 12, 1956, WHFN.

66. Steinberg, *Sam Johnson's Boy*, 423–24; Out-of-Washington speaking engagements, 1956, LBJA:SF.

67. James H. Rowe, Jr. OH; Miller, *Lyndon*, 225–26.

68. LBJ to Stevenson, Jan. 31, 1956, LBJA:FN; Reedy, *Johnson: A Memoir*, 85–86.

69. LBJ to Joseph O'Mahoney, Jan. 11, 1956, O'Mahoney Papers; Gerald Siegel to LBJ, Jan. 5, 1956, SP.

70. Ambrose, *Eisenhower: The President*, 299–300; Gerald Siegel to LBJ, April 6, 1956, SP.

71. LBJ press releases, Jan. 6, 9, 1956, SLBJ; Russell Long OH; George Reedy

OH; LBJ to Ralph Yarborough, March 14, 1956, LBJA:CF; Rowe to LBJ, April 20, 1956, LBJA:SN; Rowe to LBJ, April 24, 1956; LBJ to Hubert Humphrey, Aug. 3, 1956, SP; Ambrose, *Eisenhower: The President*, 300–301.

72. *Ibid.*, 158, 160; Evans and Novak, *LBJ: Exercise of Power*, 169–70; Miller, *Lyndon*, 229–30.

73. Evans and Novak, *LBJ: Exercise of Power*, 170–73; Miller, *Lyndon*, 230–21; Elizabeth Wickenden Goldschmidt OH; interview with E.W. Goldschmidt, Dec. 20, 1986; Russell Long OH; George Meany to LBJ, July 18, 1956; LBJ to Meany, July 19, 1956, LBJA:FN.

74. 13–Point "Program with a Heart," Aug. 6, 1956, SP; LBJ to John F. Kennedy, Dec. 15, 1956, with attached memo: "Twenty Most Impt. Measures Passed by the Sen. in 84th Congress," WHFN; LBJ had problems with the highway bill: Steinberg, *Sam Johnson's Boy*, 434; Evans and Novak, *LBJ: Exercise of Power*, 167–69. On its importance to the South, see Schulman, *From Cotton Belt to Sunbelt*, 158.

75. John C. Stennis OH; George Reedy OH; Hubert Humphrey OH; LBJ statement, March 10, 1956, SP; *Seattle Times*, March 16, 1956; Sen. Neuberger to James A. Wechsler, April 10, 1956, Neuberger Papers; Ambrose, *Eisenhower: The President*, 306–7.

76. *Ibid.*, 304–9.

77. Reichard, *Congress and the Presidency*, 62–64; Rowe to LBJ, July 24, 1956, LBJA:SN; Reedy to LBJ, July 24, 1956, two memos—one in SP and one in SPF; George Reedy OH; Evans and Novak, *LBJ: Exercise of Power*, 134–35.

78. Steinberg, *Sam Johnson's Boy*, 434–36; Evans and Novak, *LBJ: Exercise of Power*, 135–36.

79. George Reedy to LBJ, Jan. 28, 1956, PPCF; LBJ statement, Jan. 30, 1956, SLBJ; Steinberg, *Sam Johnson's Boy*, 432–33.

80. George Reedy OH; Sen. Francis Case statement, Feb. 3, 1956; Reedy memos: Feb. 4, 7, 1956, and undated, PPCF; Steinberg, *Sam Johnson's Boy*, 433; Evans and Novak, *LBJ: Exercise of Power*, 166–67.

81. Dwight D. Eisenhower Diaries, Feb. 11, 1956; DDE press statement, Feb. 17, 1956, DDEL; Ambrose, *Eisenhower: The President*, 301–3.

82. Summary accounts of Drew Pearson columns concerning the Dem. Leader, 1956; UAW, A Legal Analysis of the Johnson-Kowland Bill, n.d., SP; James Rowe to LBJ, May 25, 1956, LBJA:SN; Rowe to LBJ, June 22, 1956, SP; Drew Pearson, *Washington Post*, March 26, 27, 28, April 13, 1956. An evaluation of LBJ's Senate voting record by the UAW for the years 1947–56, however, showed Johnson voting right on 10 of 16 bills, Walter Reuther Papers, Wayne State Univ.

83. Steinberg, *Sam Johnson's Boy*, 424–25; Evans and Novak, *LBJ: Exercise of Power*, 244–45; Sam Kinch and Stuart Long, *Allan Shivers: The Pied Piper of Texas Politics* (Austin, 1973), 168–69, 184–85; DDE Diary, Feb. 9, 1956; Rayburn to LBJ, March 7, 1956, Rayburn Papers; memo of meeting at LBJ ranch, April 3, 1956; Reedy to LBJ, memo, n.d. (1956), SPF; LBJ, TV and radio speech, April 10, 1956; Shivers press release, April 10, 1956, SLBJ; George Reedy OH: *U.S. News and World Report*, April 27, 1956, pp. 45–46.

84. Press release, May 7, 1956, SPF; George Reedy OH; Steinberg, *Sam Johnson's Boy*, 428–29. Southern feeling about an LBJ candidacy is reflected in

LBJ's Presidential file, the Russell Papers, and the LBJ folder, Byrd Sr. Papers.

85. Report of State Dem. Conv., May 22, 1956, SPF; LBJ to Homer Thornberry, May 25, 1956, LBJA:CF; LBJ to John Connally, May 25, 1956, SP; Mooney, *LBJ: An Irreverent Chronicle*, 116–17; Steinberg, *Sam Johnson's Boy*, 429–31.

86. Newton Minow OH; Miller, *Lyndon*, 238.

87. Rowe to LBJ, May 8, July 3, 1956, LBJA:SN; Reedy to LBJ, June 29, 1956; Agronsky Campaign Round Up, July 22, 1956, SPF; Booth Mooney OH.

88. Memo to LBJ, Aug. 8, 1956, SPF; Rowe to LBJ, Aug. 11, 1956, and updated memo, LBJA:SN; Reedy to LBJ, Aug. 12, 1956, SPF; Steinberg, *Sam Johnson's Boy*, 438.

89. Evans and Novak, *LBJ: Exercise of Power*, 251–53. Booth Mooney OH; Reedy to LBJ, Aug. 12, 1956, SPF; Leslie Carpenter OH; James Rowe OH.

90. Connally nominating speech, SPF; Steinberg, *Sam Johnson's Boy*, 438–39; Evans and Novak, *LBJ: Exercise of Power*, 251–52; Rowe to LBJ, Aug. 11, 1956, LBJA:SN; James Rowe OH.

91. LBJ to Stevenson, Aug. 29, 1956; Stevenson to LBJ, Sept. 1, 1956, LBJA:FN; James Rowe OH; Evans and Novak, *LBJ: Exercise of Power*, 253–55; Steinberg, *Sam Johnson's Boy*, 439–41; Miller, *Lyndon*, 242–44; Hardeman and Bacon, *Rayburn*, 403–6; Hubert Humphrey to Corcoran, Sept. 10, 1956, LBJA:FN, in which Humphrey said: "I know that Lyndon didn't let me down." In a letter to Joseph Kennedy on Aug. 25, 1956, LBJ explained his bid for the nomination as "involved [with] a local political situation here in Texas," and did not contradict "what I told you last October." He also emphasized his support of Jack for the vice presidency. LBJ, *The Vantage Point*, 3.

92. Steinberg, *Sam Johnson's Boy*, 442.

93. Price to Rosen, Oct. 18, 1956; index card to the LBJ folder, April 10, 1956–Feb. 13, 1964, noting it contained 150 pages, including "Derogatory information"; A. Rosen to Tolson, Dec. 12, 1956, with the notation: "I have advised A.G. who inquired about it," meaning the investigation of the Johnsons; A. Rosen to Director Hoover, Dec. 13, 14, 1956, Official and Confidential Files of J. Edgar Hoover, FBI.

94. LBJ conversation with Sen. John Sparkman, Sept. 17, 1956, LBJA:CF; J.J. Pickle OH; Reedy to LBJ, Sept. 4, 1956, SP; Steinberg, *Sam Johnson's Boy*, 443–45.

95. *Ibid.*, 445; W.L. Prieur, Jr., to Harry F. Byrd, Sr., Oct. 4, 1956, Byrd Papers; Walter Jenkins to LBJ, Aug. 27, 1956; LBJ to Baker, Aug. 28, 1956, PPCF.

96. LBJ to Stevenson, Aug. 31, 1956; Stevenson to LBJ, Sept. 1, 1956, LBJA:FN; LBJ conversation with Finnegan, Aug. 21, 1956; Finnegan to LBJ, Aug. 23, 1956, SPF; Reedy to LBJ, March 3, 1960, PPMF; LBJ's speaking schedule, 1956, SPF.

97. LBJ to Sen. A. Willis Robertson, Aug. 31, 1956, LBJA:CF; LBJ's speeches between Oct. 5 and Nov. 6, 1956, SLBJ.

98. Sen. George Smathers to LBJ, Sept. 6, 1956, SPF; Walter Jenkins to John Connally, Sept. 26, 1956, with letter of Sept. 19, 1956 from Smathers to LBJ, attached, LBJA:SN; Baker to LBJ, April 19, Oct. 8, 1956, PPCF; Gary E. Elliott, "A Legacy of Support: Senator Alan Bible and the Nevada Mining In-

dustry," *Nevada Society Historical Quarterly*, Fall 1988, pp. 185–87; Sen. Wayne Morse to LBJ, Sept. 13, Oct. 4, 1956; LBJ to Morse, Sept. 20, Oct. 19, 1956, Morse Papers; LBJ to Sen. Richard Neuberger, Nov. 3, 1956, Neuberger Papers; LBJ to Frank Church, Oct. 23, 1956, Frank Church Papers, Boise State Univ.; Miller, *Lyndon*, 244–45.

99. Ambrose, *Eisenhower: The President*, 370; Evans and Novak, *LBJ: Exercise of Power*, 257–58; George Reedy to Gerry Siegel, Oct. 22, 1956, SPF; Creekmore Fath to Pearson, Oct. 26, 1956, Pearson Papers; Bill Brammer to LBJ, Nov. 29, 1956, PPMF; Dean F. Johnston to Membs. of the Dem. Natl. Comm., Nov. 5, 1956, Fulbright Papers; *San Antonio Light*, Oct. 21, 1956.

100. James Rowe to LBJ: "Johnson, Eisenhower, Dulles and Foreign Policy," n.d., Corcoran Papers; George Reedy to LBJ, Sept. 15, 1956; LBJ statement, n.d., SP; Fact Sheet for European trip, Nov. 14–29, 1956, LBJA:SF.

101. Bipartisan meeting, Nov. 9, 1956, DDEL; memo of conversation with Sen. Lyndon Johnson, Nov. 13, 1956, Dulles Papers.

102. James Rowe to LBJ: "Johnson, Eisenhower, Dulles and Foreign Policy," n.d., Corcoran Papers; folder of correspondence in Humphrey Papers about Humphrey's manifesto; George Reedy's memo, n.d. (probably Nov. 1956), SP; LBJ to Sam Rayburn with attached memorandum, Dec. 3, 1956, Rayburn Papers.

103. LBJ to Hubert Humphrey, Nov. 30, 1956, SP; LBJ to Paul Butler, Dec. 11, 1956, attached to Robert Baker to Humphrey, Dec. 14, 1956, Humphrey Papers; Steinberg, *Sam Johnson's Boy*, 447.

104. Paul Butler to LBJ, Dec. 26, 1956, SPF; James Rowe to LBJ: "Johnson, Eisenhower, Dulles and Foreign Policy," n.d., Corcoran Papers.

Chapter 15: The Liberal Nationalist

1. LBJ to George Brown, Jan. 3, 1957, LBJA:SN; minutes of Senate Dem. Conf., Jan. 3, 1957, SP.

2. Steinberg, *Sam Johnson's Boy*, 448; DDE Diary, Feb. 9, 1956; George Reedy OH.

3. Steinberg, *Sam Johnson's Boy*, 448; Kinch and Long, *Shivers*, 189–90; Allan Shivers OH, LBJL.

4. Booth Mooney to LBJ, Dec. 5, 1956, PPMF; telephone conversation: Walter Jenkins and Dick Berlin, March 4, 1957, Office Files of Walter Jenkins (hereafter cited as OF:Jenkins); Green, *Establishment in Texas Politics*, 180–84.

5. Jim Rowe to LBJ, n.d. (context suggests Dec. 31, 1956), Corcoran Papers; Rowe to LBJ, Dec. 21, 1956; LBJ to Rowe, Jan. 2, 1957, LBJA:SN.

6. Rowe to LBJ, n.d. (probably Dec. 31, 1956); Chester Bowles to LBJ, Jan. 2, 1957, Fulbright Papers.

7. Notes on Presidential-Bipartisan Congressional Leadership meeting, Jan. 1, 1957; concluding remarks of President at Bipartisan meeting, Jan. 1, 1957, DDE Diary.

8. Roy H. Cullen to LBJ, Feb. 5, 1957; LBJ to Cullen, Feb. 16, 1957, LBJA:SN; telephone calls: Dulles to Sen. Knowland, Feb. 12, 14; to LBJ, Feb. 14, 1957,

Dulles Papers; Evans and Novak, *LBJ: Exercise of Power*, 188–91; Ambrose, *Eisenhower: The President*, 381–83.

9. Steinberg, *Sam Johnson's Boy*, 464–65; Evans and Novak, *LBJ: Exercise of Power*, 191–92; Ambrose, *Eisenhower: The President*, 385–87; James Rowe to LBJ, Feb. 11, 1957, SP.

10. LBJ to John F. Dulles, Feb. 11, 1957, SP; Philip Graham to James Rowe, Feb. 19, 1957; Drew Pearson to Rowe, Feb. 20, 1957, Rowe Papers; Robert Baker to LBJ, Feb. 19, 1957, PPCF; statements by LBJ in *Congressional Record on Middle East, Feb. 19, 1957, SLBJ; Bipartisan meeting, Feb. 20, 1957, DDEL*; Steinberg, *Sam Johnson's Boy*, 465–67.

11. John F. Dulles to LBJ, Feb. 21, 1957, SP; LBJ statement, Feb. 25, 1957, SLBJ; Dulles telephone call to LBJ, Feb. 25, 1957, Dulles Papers; Evans and Novak, *LBJ: Exercise of Power*, 193–95. Evans and Novak depict Johnson as the innocent victim of his own indiscretion; that he didn't realize that the leak had come through a Senate colleague. This is difficult to credit in light of how Jim Rowe orchestrated the leak on the basis of LBJ's Feb. 11 letter.

12. *Ibid.*, 195; Ambrose, *Eisenhower: The President*, 388; memo of conversation with LBJ, March 2, 1957, Dulles Papers.

13. Marietta Tree to James Rowe, Feb. 15, 1957; Rowe to LBJ, March 22, 1957; Mary Rather to George Reedy, n.d. (1957); Reedy memo, n.d (1957), SP.

14. Robert Baker to LBJ, Feb. 19, 1957, PPCF; Leuchtenburg, *A Troubled Feast*, 90–91; Ambrose, *Eisenhower: The President*, 388–91; Steinberg, *Sam Johnson's Boy*, 474–76.

15. LBJ to Styles Bridges, March 1, 1957, LBJA:CF; Arthur Schlesinger, Jr., to LBJ, April 3, 1957, LBJA:FN.

16. LBJ to Schlesinger, Jr., April 8, 1957, *ibid.*; Steinberg, *Sam Johnson's Boy*, 475–77; Evans and Novak, *LBJ: Exercise of Power*, 196–98; Ambrose, *Eisenhower: The President*, 391; LBJ to DDE, May 23, 1957; DDE to LBJ, May 28, 1957, WHFN; memos of conversations with LBJ, June 14, 15, 1957, Dulles Papers.

17. Steinberg, *Sam Johnson's Boy*, 476; Evans and Novak, *LBJ: Exercise of Power*, 198–200; Leuchtenburg, *A Troubled Feast*, 88.

18. Steinberg, *Sam Johnson's Boy*, 476–77; Evans and Novak, *LBJ: Exercise of Power*, 199–202; Paige Mulhollan OH; George Reedy OH.

19. Steinberg, *Sam Johnson's Boy*, 477; Evans and Novak, *LBJ: Exercise of Power*, 202–3; DDE to LBJ, May 28, 1957; Mary Rather to George Reedy, May 31, 1957; LBJ to DDE, June 3, 1957, WHFN.

20. Walter Jenkins to LBJ, April 19, 1957, SP; *Congressional Record—Senate*, June 13, 1957, 85th Congress, 1st sess., pp. 8034–36.

21. DDE telephone call to Dulles, June 11, 1957; memo of conversation with LBJ, June 14, 1957, Dulles Papers; Dulles to LBJ, June 21, 1957, SP; Anderson to Pearson, June 21, 1957, Pearson Papers.

22. Reedy to Michael Gillette, June 2, 1982, attached to George Reedy OH; James Rowe to LBJ, July 3, 1957, LBJA:SN.

23. Douglàs Cater, "How the Senate Passed the Civil-Rights Bill," *The Reporter*, Sept. 5, 1957, p. 9.

24. Reichard, *Congress and the Presidency*, Spring 1986, p. 67, and see n. 53, p. 77.

25. Schlesinger, Jr., to LBJ, June 17, 1957; LBJ to Schlesinger, Jr., June 21, 1957, LBJA:FN.

26. Harry McPherson, *A Political Education* (Boston, 1972), 153.

27. Kearns, *Lyndon Johnson*, 147–49.

28. Harry McPherson OH; Larry Temple was the attorney who related this incident to me, March 29, 1989, Austin.

29. Harry McPherson OH; George Reedy OH; Clark Clifford interview, Jan. 8, 1988. Just after the Senate passed the 1957 civil rights bill, Hubert Humphrey handed LBJ a note: "I was never more proud of you! Your speech was a masterpiece—more important, it came from the heart and soul. It's a genuine privilege to be included amongst your friends."

30. LBJ to Robert S. Allen, Dec. 26, 1956; Allen to LBJ, Dec. 28, 1956, SP; George Reedy OH; Reedy letter to Mike Gillette, June 2, 1982; LBJ to Gafford, and to Perry, both Feb. 25, 1957, SP; Cater, *The Reporter*, Sept. 5, 1957, p. 9; Evans and Novak, *LBJ: Exercise of Power*, 136.

31. Reedy to Gillette, June 2, 1982, attached to Reedy OH; Evans and Novak, *LBJ: Exercise of Power*, 137–40; Reedy, *LBJ: A Memoir*, 112–14; Ambrose, *Eisenhower: The President*, 406–7.

32. Steinberg, *Sam Johnson's Boy*, 468–69; Evans and Novak, *LBJ: Exercise of Power*, 138–43; Howard E. Shuman OH, SHO.

33. Frank Church OH; Russell Long OH; LBJ to Church, June 27, 1957, Church Papers. Despite Senate passage, the Hells Canyon bill was defeated in the House.

34. Reedy to Gillette, June 2, 1982, attached to George Reedy OH.

35. Ambrose, *Eisenhower: The President*, 407–8; DDE diary, July 10, 1957.

36. *Congressional Record*, 85th Congress, 1st sess., July 11, 1957, pp. A5541–42; McPherson, *A Political Education*, 145; Evans and Novak, *LBJ: Exercise of Power*, 145; Ambrose, *Eisenhower: The President*, 409–10.

37. George Reedy to LBJ, July 22, 1957, detailing a telephone conversation with Acheson, LBJA:FN; Solis Horwitz OH; Howard E. Shuman OH, SHO; Cater, *The Reporter*, Sept. 5, 1957, pp. 10–11.

38. Clinton Anderson OH; LBJ to James P. Coleman, July 25, 1957, LBJA:FN; Reichard, *Congress and the Presidency*, Spring 1986, pp. 67–68.

39. Grace Tully OH.

40. Gerald Siegel OH; Solis Horwitz OH; LBJ to HST, July 29, 1957, WHFN; Cater, *The Reporter*, Sept. 5, 1957, pp. 11–12; Steinberg, *Sam Johnson's Boy*, 471–72; Evans and Novak, *LBJ: Exercise of Power*, 146–50.

41. LBJ statement, Aug. 1, 1957; Walter Jenkins to Eli Morgan, Aug. 1, 1957, SP; Frank Church OH; Russell note [Aug. 1957]; Russell notes, Aug. 2, 1957, Russell Papers.

42. Solis Horwitz OH; Cater, *The Reporter*, Sept. 5, 1957, pp. 12–13; Steinberg, *Sam Johnson's Boy*, 472–73; Evans and Novak, *LBJ: Exercise of Power*, 150–51.

43. Cater, *The Reporter*, Sept. 5, 1957, p. 13; DDE Diary, Aug. 23, 1957; Evans and Novak, *LBJ: Exercise of Power*, 151–53; Meg Greefield, "The Man Who Leads the Southern Senators," *The Reporter*, May 21, 1964, p. 17.

44. LBJ to Eleanor Roosevelt, Aug. 12, 1957, Rowe Papers; Steinberg, *Sam Johnson's Boy*, 474; Howard E. Shuman OH, SHO; McPherson, *A Political Ed-*

ucation, 147–48; James MacGregor Burns, *The Crosswinds of Freedom* (N.Y., 1989), 322; William H. Chafe, *The Unfinished Journey* (N.Y., 1986), 157.

45. Ben Cohen to LBJ, Aug. 13, 1957, SP; Reinhold Niebuhr, "The Civil Rights Bill," *The New Leader*, Sept. 16, 1957, p. 9; Dean Acheson to LBJ, Aug. 13, 1957, SP; Miller, *Lyndon*, 258; Reedy, *LBJ: A Memoir*, 120.

46. LBJ statement, Aug. 7, 1957, SP; Roscoe Drummond in *New York Herald Tribune*, Aug. 30, 1957; Baker to LBJ, Sept. 3, 1957, PPCF.

47. *Ibid.*; Baker to LBJ, Sept. 3, 20, 1957; LBJ to Baker, Sept. 10, 27, 1957, PPCF; clipping from *Dallas News* attached to Gerry Siegel to Rowe, Sept. 23, 1957, Rowe Papers; Speaking Engagements During Fall of 1957, Travel folder, LBJA:SF; Gerald Siegel to LBJ, Sept. 23, 1957, LBJA:FN; *Boston Sunday Herald*, Sept. 1, 1957; two memos from Rowe to LBJ, with a cover note dated Aug. 15, 1957, in which Rowe urged him to make friends with "top labor leaders," David McDonald and George Meany. Rowe also advised him that if he wanted "to make a liberal noise," he should make needed improvements in an FBI bill coming before the Senate, Rowe Papers.

48. Ambrose, *Eisenhower: The President*, 414–23; C. Vann Woodward to LBJ, Nov. 6, 1957, with an article by Woodward in *Commentary* which described LBJ as having "the genius of a Henry Clay," SP.

49. Reedy to LBJ, Sept. 11, 1957, SP; LBJ to Acheson, Oct. 7, 1957; LBJ to Bowles, Oct. 8, 1957, LBJA:FN; letters in Faubus files, SP; Rowe to LBJ, Oct. 14, 1957, LBJA:SN; memorandum for the Record: Sen. Alexander Smith's appt. with DDE, Oct. 8, 1957, DDEL.

50. Ambrose, *Eisenhower: The President*, 423–27; Walter A. McDougall, . . . *the Heavens and the Earth: A Political History of the Space Age* (N.Y., 1985), 141–43; Stuart Symington to Russell, Oct. 5, 1957, Russell Papers; Evans and Novak, *LBJ: Exercise of Power*, 206.

51. *Ibid.*, 204–5; McDougall, . . . *the Heavens and the Earth*, 148–49; Russell to Symington, Oct. 7, 1957, Russell Papers; Solis Horwitz to Neil McElroy, Oct. 11, 1957; LBJ telephone conversation with McElroy, Oct. 21, 1957, SP.

52. LBJ speaking engagements, Fall of 1957 Travel folder, LBJA:SF; LBJ-Dulles telephone conversations, Oct. 31, Nov. 5, 1957, Dulles Papers; LBJ-Styles Bridges telephone conversation, Nov. 5, 1957, LBJA:CF; memo, n.d., Hearings Folder, box 355, SP..

53. *Ibid.*; Steele to Williamson, Nov. 7, 1957, Steele Papers; Robert A. Divine, "LBJ and the Politics of Space," in *The Johnson Years: Vol. II: Vietnam, the Environment, and Science*, ed. by Robert A. Divine (Lawrence, Kan., 1987), 217–22.

54. William Darden to Russell, Nov. 26, 1957, Russell Papers; Steinberg, *Sam Johnson's Boy*, 481–82; Evans and Novak, *LBJ: Exercise of Power*, 206–9; Divine, *Johnson Years*, II, 222–25.

55. Rowe to LBJ, Feb. 5, 1958, LBJA:SN; George Reedy OH.

56. John L. Steele to Lumsden, Jan. 9; to Williamson, Feb. 7, 1958, Steele Papers.

57. Toffler, *Pageant*, July 1958, pp. 103–4; Alsop to LBJ, March 18, 1958, Alsop Papers; LBJ to Ed Clark, April 19, 1958, LBJA:SN; Steele to Williamson, March 4, 1958, Steele Papers.

58. Legis. action on Space Involving Sen. Johnson, 1957–1959, Space Note-

book folder; statements by LBJ, July 15, 16, 1958; Report of Spec. Sen. Comm. on Space and Astronautics on S. 3609, SP; William Reynolds OH; Solis Horwitz OH; DDE Diary, July 7, 17, 1958; McDougall, . . . *the Heavens and the Earth*, chap. 7; Divine, *Johnson Years*, II, 226–28. In the final legislation the Agency was upgraded to an Administration.

59. Walter Reuther to LBJ, Dec. 16, 1957, Feb. 17, March 10, 1958; LBJ to Reuther, Jan. 8, March 15, 1958, LBJA:FN; Steele to Williamson, Feb. 6, 1958; "Nonpartisanship," March 4, 1958, Steele Papers; George Reedy OH; Steinberg, *Sam Johnson's Boy*, 483.

60. Steele to Williamson, March 7, 1958, Steele Papers; Arthur Schlesinger, Jr. to LBJ, March 4, 12, 1958; LBJ to Schlesinger, Jr., March 6, 18, 27, 1958; LBJ to John K. Galbraith, March 18, 1958, with *N.Y. Times* clipping, March 13, 1958, attached, LBJA:FN; LBJ to Janeway, March 26, 1958, LBJA:SN.

61. Steele to Williamson, March 6, 1958, "Lyndon Johnson Cover— XIV," and March 7, 1958, Steele Papers; Dem. Legis. Record, 85th Congress, 2nd sess., SP; Steinberg, *Sam Johnson's Boy*, 483–84.

62. DDE Diary, Legis. Leadership meeting, Supplementary Notes, March 25, 1958; Steinberg, *Sam Johnson's Boy*, 484; Ambrose, *Eisenhower: The President*, 460–61.

63. Reedy to LBJ, July 23, 1958, SP; Ellender to LBJ, Sept. 5, 1958, LBJA:CF; Dem. Legis. Record, 85th Congress, 2nd. sess, SP.

64. Minutes of Dem. Pol. Comm. meeting, July 22, 1958, SP; Hubert Humphrey et al. to LBJ, Aug. 12, 1958; Humphrey to LBJ, Aug. 21, 1958, WHFN; memorandum, n.d., the debate on Aug. 20, Sup. Ct. bills, SP; *Columbia* (S.C.) *Record*, Aug. 23, 1958; Neuberger to LBJ, Aug. 25, 1958, Neuberger Papers; Evans and Novak, *LBJ: Exercise of Power*, 178–81; McPherson, *A Political Education*, 131–34.

65. LBJ to James Rowe, Sept. 23, 1958, SP; Reedy, *LBJ: A Memoir*, 51–52.

66. *Ibid.*, 51, 54; LBJ to Clinton Anderson, Jan. 23, 1957, LBJA:CF; Steinberg, *Sam Johnson's Boy*, 493; Ambrose, *Eisenhower: The President*, 467–69, 480–82, 487.

67. Steele to Williamson, Nov. 12, 1958, Steele Papers; LBJ-Drew Pearson telephone conversation, Oct. 22, 1958, NTJC; Rowe-Jenkins telephone conversation, Oct. 23, 1958, OF:Jenkins; LBJ Out-of-Washington speaking engagements, 1958, Travel folder, LBJA:SF; undated Willie Day memos, 1958, SP; Warren Woodward OH; Gale W. McGee OH, LC; Frank Church to LBJ, Oct. 20, 1958, LBJA:CF; Steinberg, *Sam Johnson's Boy*, 493–94; Ambrose, *Eisenhower: The President*, 488.

68. Reichard, *Congress and the Presidency*, Spring 1986, p. 69, and 78, n. 63; Clark Clifford–Walter Jenkins telephone conversation, Nov. 14, 1958, OF:Jenkins; Green to LBJ, Nov. 17, 1958, LBJA:CF; Humphrey to LBJ, Nov. 12, 1958, two letters, WHFN; memo of conversation: DDE, LBJ, and Anderson, Nov. 18, 1958, DDE Diaries.

69. Memo, Nov. 8, 1958, SP; Steele to Williamson, Nov. 7, 13, 1958, Steele Papers.

70. Rowe to LBJ, Nov. 20, Dec. 4, 1958, LBJA:SN.

71. Evans and Novak, *LBJ: Exercise of Power*, 213–15. LBJ tried to discour-

age liberal "hot heads" from talking to "the Republican press" about Democratic divisions. See LBJ to Gov. Orville Freeman, Dec. 4, 1958, SP.

72. Joseph S. Clark OH, LC; Steele to Williamson, Nov. 12, 1958, Jan. 10, 1959, Steele Papers; Leonard Marks to LBJ, Jan. 8, 1959, LBJA:SN; Horace Busby to LBJ, n.d. (Jan. 1959), SP.

73. Steinberg, *Sam Johnson's Boy*, 486.

74. *Chicago Tribune*, March 9, Dec. 21, 1958; File 43, Folder 121, LBJ, Styles Bridges Papers, New England College; Anderson to Pearson, Nov. 24, 1958, Pearson Papers; Steinberg, *Sam Johnson's Boy*, 505–6; Miller, *Lyndon*, 264.

75. Walt. W. Rostow told me this anecdote, July 1, 1988, Austin. For Stevenson's view, see Evans and Novak, *LBJ: Exercise of Power*, 260.

76. Jenkins to Byron Skelton, Oct. 30, 1958, LBJA:SN; Reedy memo, n.d. (clearly November 1958), SP; Reedy OH; Mary Rather to LBJ, April 8, 1957, SP; Steele to Williamson, Nov. 12, 1958, Steele Papers.

77. George Reedy OH.

78. Lodge-Jenkins telephone conversation, Nov. 5, 1958, OF:Jenkins; Reedy to LBJ, Nov. 8, 1958; LBJ statement, Nov. 10, 1958; memo, n.d. (Nov. 1958), SP; Macomber to Dulles telephone calls, and Dulles to Lodge, Nov. 8, 1958; Macomber to Dulles, Dulles to Macomber and Herter, and to LBJ, Nov. 10, 1958; Lodge to Dulles, Nov. 18, 1958, Dulles Papers; LBJ press release, Nov. 17, 1958, SP; *N.Y. Times*, Nov. 18, 1958.

79. George Reedy OH; Roscoe Drummond, *Washington Post*, Dec. 3, 1958; material in two folders: Travel—Mexico—Nov. 1958, and Mexico Trip 1958, LBJA:SF.

Chapter 16: The Making of a Vice President

1. Rowe to LBJ, Jan. 17, 1959, LBJA:SN; James Rowe OH.

2. Lady Bird Johnson interview, Baylor Univ.

3. Arthur Schlesinger, Jr. OH; memoranda of Jan. 1959 and June 13, 1959, Rowe Papers.

4. Hardeman and Bacon, *Rayburn*, 432–33; Rowe to LBJ, Oct. 4, 1958; LBJ to Rowe, Oct. 9, 1958, LBJA:SN.

5. Ernest W. McFarland OH; memo: "Western Meeting," May 18, 1959, SP; LBJ-Adam Clayton Powell telephone conversation, March 19, 1959, NTJC; LBJ, Out-of-Washington speaking engagements, 1959, and Travel, 1959, LBJA:SF; Steele to Williamson, May 7, 1959, Steele Papers; Herman Talmadge OH; *Houston Press*, April 17, 1959; Cliff Carter to LBJ, April 18, May 30, 1959; three folders, 1959–Elec. Law, SP.

6. Reedy to LBJ, March 26, 1959, SP; Steele to Williamson, May 7, 1959, Steele Papers.

7. LBJ speech, Jan. 7, 1959, SLBJ.

8. LBJ press conference, Nov. 19, 1958, SLBJ; Rowe to LBJ, Jan. 10, 1959, LBJA:SN; Stennis to LBJ, Jan. 13, 1959, LBJA:CF; Fulbright to Pickens, Jan.

13, 1959; Fulbright to Shnable, Jan. 14, 1959, Fulbright Papers; memos, Jan. 5, 1959; Robert G. Baker to Russell, Jan. 6, 1959, Russell Papers.

9. Evans and Novak, *LBJ: Exercise of Power*, 217; Stewart Alsop, "Lyndon Johnson: How Does He Do It?" *Sat. Eve. Post*, Jan. 24, 1959; Reedy to LBJ, Feb. 5, 1959, SP; O'Mahoney to LBJ, Jan. 13, 1959, O'Mahoney Papers.

10. Steinberg, *Sam Johnson's Boy*, 494–95; Evans and Novak, *LBJ: Exercise of Power*, 215–17; Morse to LBJ, Jan. 15, 1959, LBJA:CF.

11. *New York Times*, Feb. 24, 1959, p. 1; William Proxmire OH; Sen. Robert Byrd, "Lyndon Johnson and the U.S. Senate, 1948–61," *Congressional Record—Senate*, March 3, 1986, p. 1916.

12. *Ibid.* There is a substantial body of letters in a folder marked "Johnson-Proxmire Case" in the Neuberger Papers, Univ. of Oregon, supporting Proxmire and criticizing Neuberger; W. Proxmire OH; "Washington Window," March 13, 1959, in LBJA:CF; Proxmire-Russell conversation, April 20, 1971, Russell Papers; Steinberg, *Sam Johnson's Boy*, 495–97.

13. Memo, n.d. (Feb. 1959), Neuberger Papers; Reedy to LBJ, Feb. 26, 1959; memo, n.d. (Feb. 1959), SP; memo of Rowe message to LBJ, March 11, 1959, LBJA:SN; clippings in 1959–Senate Leadership folders, SP; Charles McCabe to Ed Weisl, March 19, 1959, with clipping attached, LBJA:FN; Steinberg, *Sam Johnson's Boy*, 496–97. Bryce Harlow (OH), who handled relations with Congress for the Eisenhower White House, later said: Johnson "had as much power as they would let him have, because the power he had was at their sufferance. He ran off with nearly all of it because they let him. They reveled in it. It made them all irresponsible. 'Let Lyndon run it.' It's comfortable to have a leader like that."

14. LBJ press conference, Nov. 19, 1958, SLBJ; Acheson to LBJ, Dec. 18, 1958, Feb. 2, 1959; LBJ to Acheson, Dec. 24, 1958, Feb. 7, 1959; memo, Reedy to Busby, n.d., SP; *Congressional Record—Senate*, March 2, 1959, pp. 2805–7. Johnson reflected on the economic situation of the South in a press conference, Nov. 19, 1958. He pointed out that twenty years ago it was "our No. 1 problem." The East "monopolized 80% of the nation's capital with the south and the west about 10% each. This has now changed to 59% in the east and 20% in the south and 20% in the west." He said that the shift in conditions in the two areas and the promise of future development was one of the things that had impressed him most during 25 years in public life.

15. Margaret Hales to LBJ, Jan. 21, 1959 (mistakenly dated 1958); LBJ to Friend, Feb. 3, 1959; NAACP newsletter, Jan. 2, 1959; Reedy to LBJ, March 3, 1959; Siegel, Horwitz, and Wilson to LBJ, March 10, 1959, SP; Russell's note: "This was given me by Sen. Johnson as copy of [revised civil rights] Bill he planned to introduce on May 6, '59. He changed his mind and did not introduce it. He told me Aug. 10th he did not wish to lead fight vs. South," Russell Papers. Evans and Novak, *LBJ: Exercise of Power*, 236; Daniel M. Berman, *A Bill Becomes a Law: Congress Enacts Civil Rights Legislation* (N.Y., 1966 ed.), 33–39.

16. Evans and Novak, *LBJ: Exercise of Power*, 218–19; LBJ to Douglas, Feb. 14, 1959, LBJA:CF; LBJ to Pearson, Jan. 13, 1959, Pearson Papers.

17. LBJ Senate Voting Record, 1949–62, pp. 204–5, 292, 407–8; LBJ statement, March 23, 1959, SLBJ; Steinberg, *Sam Johnson's Boy*, 497–98; Evans and

Novak, *LBJ: Exercise of Power*, 219–21; Ambrose, *Eisenhower: The President*, 496–97.

18. Evans and Novak, *LBJ: Exercise of Power*, 221–22; Reedy to LBJ, Feb. 5, 1959, SP; LBJ Senate Voting Record, 1949–62, pp. 204–5; LBJ statement, Feb. 17, 1959, SLBJ.

19. Minutes of Dem. Pol. Comm. meeting, May 9, 1959; LBJ statement, Sept. 14, 1959, SP; LBJ Senate Voting Record, 1949–62, pp. 205–7, 407–8, 292.

20. "Face the Nation," Oct. 11, 1959, SP; James W. Wilson OH.

21. DAC statement, June 14, 1959, SP; Sen. Thomas Dodd to Paul Butler, June 8, 1959, Corcoran Papers; Rowe to LBJ, July 7, 1959, LBJA:SN.

22. Steele to Williamson, June 20, 1959, Steele Papers; LBJ to Rowe, July 13, 1959, LBJA:SN.

23. Steele to Williamson, June 20, 1959, Steele Papers; Fortas to Reedy, March 31, 1959, LBJA:SN; James W. Wilson OH; LBJ speeches, April 8, May 30, 1959, SLBJ; LBJ-Eleanor Roosevelt telephone conversation, May 28, 1959, NTJC; E. Roosevelt to LBJ, June 2, 1959, Corcoran Papers; clipping, "Robert S. Allen Reports," n.d., SP.

24. Form letter from Morse, July 21, 1959, Morse Papers; Joseph S. Clark to Pearson, July 10, 1959, Pearson Papers; statements by Maj. Membs. of Cong., June 8–July 12, 1959, SLBJ.

25. Donald A. Ritchie, "Making Fulbright Chairman: Or How the 'Johnson Treatment' Nearly Backfired," *Soc. for Historians of Amer. Foreign Rels. Newsletter*, Sept. 1984, pp. 21–28. The article largely rests on the recollections of Committee Chiefs of Staff Pat M. Holt and Carl M. Marcy, interviews, SHO.

26. Of 25 achievements by the 1959 Congress, LBJ listed Hawaiian statehood no. 1: LBJ statement, Sept. 14, 1959; Dem. Pol. Comm. meeting, Jan. 15, 1958, SP; Sen. Alexander Wiley et al. to LBJ, July 21, 1958; LBJ to Wiley, Aug. 4, 1958, LBJA:CF; Russell B. Long OH; Daniel K. Inouye OH; Sen. Frank Church to LBJ, June 5, 1958, Church Papers; Steinberg, *Sam Johnson's Boy*, 485; Ambrose, *Eisenhower: The President*, 157–58.

27. Dai Ho Chun to LBJ, April 21, 1959; LBJ to John Moody, May 16, 1959; print of S. 2135; memo, n.d.; LBJ statement, n.d.; Solis Horowitz to LBJ, June 16, 1959; LBJ statement, Sept. 14, 1959, in East-West folders, SP; Daniel K. Inouye OH.

28. Ives to LBJ, Sept. 8, 1958, Irving M. Ives Papers, Cornell Univ.; Reedy to LBJ, Aug. 5, 1958, SP; JFK to LBJ, June 18, 1958, WHFN; Huitt, *Am. Pol. Sci. Rev.*, June 1961, p. 340; Steinberg, *Sam Johnson's Boy*, 500; Evans and Novak, *LBJ: Exercise of Power*, 231–32.

29. Goodwin, *Fitzgeralds and Kennedys*, 780.

30. *Ibid.*, 790. Reedy to LBJ, April 1958, SP; Evans and Novak, LBJ: *Exercise of Power*, 232.

31. Steinberg, *Sam Johnson's Boy*, 500–501; Evans and Novak, *LBJ: Exercise of Power*, 232–33. They differ on whether Kennedy managed the bill, but the Democratic Policy Committee Minutes, April 14, 1959, suggest he did, SP.

32. Memoranda in Labor Legis. folder, SP; Solis Horwitz OH; George Meany to LBJ, May 5, 1959, LBJA:FN; D.B. Hardeman OH; Hardeman and Bacon, *Rayburn*, 431–32.

33. LBJ-DDE telephone conversation, Aug. 4, 1959, DDE Diaries; Solis Horwitz to LBJ, n.d.; memo: Hist of 1959 Legis. Agst. Labor Racketeering, n.d., SP; LBJ, newsletter, Sept. 16, 1959, David D. Lloyd Papers, HSTL; Evans and Novak, *LBJ: Exercise of Power*, 235, incorrectly describes LBJ as pushing for a conference committee but accurately describes the final result of the committee's work.

34. Richard Allan Baker, "A Slap at the 'Hidden-Hand Presidency': The Senate and the Lewis Strauss Affair," *Congress and the Presidency*, Spring 1987, pp. 1–14.

35. *Ibid.;* calendar sheet, May 20, 1959, Russell Papers.

36. Gale McGee OH; Earle Clements OH; Walter Jenkins to LBJ, May 22, 1959, LBJA:SN.

37. LBJ letters of June 1 and 18, 1959 to constituents, in which he refused to make his position known. Handwritten on the June 18 letter is: "This was the date of the vote," Lewis L. Strauss Papers, HHL; LBJ statement, June 18, 1959, SP; DDE Diary, June 19, 1959; Reedy to LBJ, June 20, 1959, SP; Steinberg, *Sam Johnson's Boy*, 503–5; Evans and Novak, *LBJ: Exercise of Power*, 228–31; Baker, *Congress and the Presidency*, Spring 1987, pp. 11–13.

38. Baker, *Wheeling and Dealing*, 42–43; Evans and Novak, *LBJ: Exercise of Power*, 262–63; John Brice, who produced an NBC television film, "LBJ: The Early Years," included this encounter between LBJ and RFK in the film. He told me that Judge A.W. Moursund described this event to him. Robert Kennedy's visit to the ranch is noted on Nov. 19, 1959, in LBJ pre-presidential diary.

39. Price Daniel to Richard Russell, Nov. 2, 1959, and Russell to Daniel, Nov. 18, 1959, in which Russell says that he had "often discussed" the 1960 Democratic nomination with Lyndon and that vocal support for a Southerner "alienates the states that are necessary to success." Russell's tack was to tell the press that he had no candidate, "but that Johnson was the strongest candidate the Democrats could nominate and the one most likely to beat either Nixon or [Governor Nelson] Rockefeller" of New York, Russell Papers. Corcoran to Mayor Robert Wagner, n.d. (clearly June 1959), saying that a 'Parade' poll of Republicans chose LBJ as the hardest Democrat to beat, Corcoran Papers; Baker, *Wheeling and Dealing*, 43.

40. DDE Diary, Aug. 3, 1959; LBJ-DDE telephone conversation, Aug. 4, 1959, NTJC.

41. LBJ pre-presidential diary, Sept. 15, 1959; Steinberg, *Sam Johnson's Boy*, 507–8; memo of conversation with Sec. of the Treas. Anderson, Sept. 16, 1959, Christian Herter Papers, DDEL; Lopez Mateos folder, SP; memo #1, Oct. 9, 1959, Corcoran Papers; LBJ, Out-of-Washington speaking engagements 1959, LBJA:SF; Reedy to LBJ, Nov. 9, 1959, SP; LBJ statements, Dec. 8, 9, 10, 1959, SLBJ; Clifton Carter OH; George Reedy OH.

42. Highlights of conversation, Dec. 4, 1959; résumé of telephone calls, Dec. 7, 1959, with LBJ to Jenkins memo attached, OF:Jenkins; Murphy, *Fortas*, 104–5; Laura Kalman, *Fortas*, 209.

43. Bill to Jenkins, n.d., a collection of statements LBJ made about his presidential candidacy between Oct. 1, 1959, and April 22, 1960, SP; telephone

calls, Nov. 2, 5, 18, Dec. 2, 3, 4, 9, 1959, OF:Jenkins; Reedy memo, n.d. (1959), SP; first pre-planning meeting of Johnson for Pres., Nov. 30, 1959; Johnson for Pres. Hdqtrs., Dec. 23, 1959, SPF.

44. Steinberg, *Sam Johnson's Boy*, 511; Theodore H. White, *The Making of the President 1960* (N.Y., 1988 ed.), 43–44, 131–32.

45. Minutes of Sen. Dem. Conf., Jan. 7, 1960; minutes of Sen. Dem. Pol. Comm., Jan. 12, 1960, SP; George Reedy OH; LBJ-Sen. Eugene McCarthy conversation, Jan. 12, 1960, NTJC; *Dallas Morning News*, Jan. 13, 1960.

46. LBJ speech, Feb. 5, 1960, SLBJ; LBJ partly relied on liberal columnist Drew Pearson for advice in drawing up this program. Pearson to LBJ, Feb. 1, 1960, Pearson Papers.

47. LBJ radio broadcast, April 11, 1960, SLBJ; Gerald Siegel OH; LBJ remarks to Clarence Mitchell and other delegates, Jan. 13–14, 1960, SP; LBJ-Bruce Jolly conversation, Feb. 29, 1960, SLBJ; E. Roddan to Tom Corcoran, Feb. 18, 1960, Corcoran Papers.

48. Berman, *A Bill Becomes a Law*, 57–61; letters to Harry F. Byrd and LBJ for Feb. 1960, Byrd, Sr., Papers; letters to LBJ and Russell for Feb. 1960, Russell Papers; clippings for Feb. 1960, SP; LBJ pre-presidential diary, Feb. 21, 1960.

49. Berman, *A Bill Becomes a Law*, 66–67; Howard E. Shuman OH, SHO.

50. Berman, *A Bill Becomes a Law*, 72, 74–77; Creekmore Fath to Pearson, Feb. 16, 1960, Pearson Papers; Dick Berlin-Walter Jenkins telephone conversation, March 10, 1960, OF:Jenkins; telephone message, Talmadge to Russell, Feb. 3, 1960, Russell Papers; George Reedy to LBJ, March 10, 1960, SP.

51. LBJ pre-presidential diary, Feb. 29, 1960; Berman, *A Bill Becomes a Law*, 125–26; Harry Byrd, Jr., "LBJ and the U.S. Senate, 1948–1961," *Congressional Record—Senate*, March 3, 1986, p. 1917; Reichard, *Congress and the Presidency*, Spring 1986, pp. 70–71; *St. Louis Argus*, April 29, 1960; *New York Times*, April 9, 1960; Harry F. Byrd, Sr., to Walter Sillers, May 26, 1960: "he [LBJ] is a man of great ability, and you can rely absolutely upon his word. . . . It was the influence of Lyndon Johnson that defeated the most iniquitous parts of the proposed [civil rights] bill," Byrd, Sr., Papers.

52. Telephone conversations for Jan. 5, 20, 25, 26, 27, Feb. 1, 13, 16, 18, 19, 24, 26, 1960, OF:Jenkins. Fred Harris-Jenkins telephone conversation, Jan. 26, 1960; Blackmon to McCrary, Feb. 3, 1960; Blackmon to Ramos, Feb. 4, 1960, SPF.

53. LBJ statement, Jan. 6, 1960; LBJ speeches, Jan. 21, 23, 1960, SLBJ.

54. LBJ, pre-presidential 1960 diary; Leslie Carpenter OH; Sam Rayburn, "On the Presidential Qualifications of LBJ," *The New Mexican*, Jan. 14, 1960, in Hickenlooper Papers; unidentified, undated (from context clearly March 1960) clipping sent by LBJ to Sam Rayburn, Rayburn Papers; summary of *Houston Post* story, March 2, 1960; Cecil R. King statement, Jan. 20, 1960; Roy Mundy to Russell, Jan. 21, 1960; Russell to Mundy, Jan. 23, 1960; LBJ to Russell, Jan. 28, 1960, Russell Papers.

55. Reedy to LBJ, March 5, 1960, SP.

56. Tip O'Neill with William Novak, *Man of the House: The Life and Political Memoirs of Speaker Tip O'Neill* (N.Y., 1987), 181–82.

57. Impressions gathered during recent trip, Feb. 17, 1960, date on attached envelope, Rowe folder, LBJA:SN; Janeway-Jenkins telephone conversation, March 17, 1960, OF:Jenkins.

58. Memo to Juanita attached to transcript of LBJ-Buford telephone conversation, Feb. 18, 1960, PPCF; transcripts of telephone conversations, March 1, 2, 9, 10, 11, 30, 1960; Berlin-Jenkins telephone conversation, March 14, 1960, OF:Jenkins.

59. Reedy to LBJ, March 21, 1960, PPMF.

60. Goodwin, *Fitzgeralds & Kennedys*, 795–97; Reedy to LBJ, April 8, 1960, SP.

61. Hubert H. Humphrey OH; Humphrey, *Education of a Public Man*, 213, where Humphrey says that "when the chips should have been down, Johnson's people refused money absolutely." LBJ to Robert C. Byrd, April 8, 1960; Dallas Badgett to Byrd, April 12, 1960; memorandum for Sen. Hubert Humphrey, April 22, 1960, with "Byrd, Sen. Bob" hand written at the top of the memo as well as Johnson's initials, SPF; LBJ pre-presidential diary, April 8, 1960; Krock notes of conversation with Sen. LBJ, May 3, 1960, Arthur Krock Papers, Princeton Univ.

62. White, *Making of the President 1960*, 97–114; Goodwin, *Fitzgeralds & Kennedys*, 797–99; LBJ speech, May 7, 1960, SLBJ; LBJ pre-presidential diary, May 9, 1960.

63. James Rowe, OH; LBJ pre-presidential diary, May 16, 1960; Newton Minow OH; private memo, May 26, 1960, Krock Papers.

64. Reedy to LBJ, May 16, 1960, SP; "Face the Nation" broadcast, May 22, 1960, SLBJ; Lee Hendrick to Drew Pearson, May 13, 1960; Pearson talk with Lyndon Johnson, May 24, 1960, Pearson Papers; Krock private memo, May 26, 1960, Krock Papers.

65. *Ibid.*

66. Steinberg, *Sam Johnson's Boy*, 522; Reedy to LBJ, n.d. (1960), SP; Theodore C. Sorensen, *Kennedy* (N.Y., 1966 ed.), 168–69; LBJ statements, May 10, 13, 18, 1960, SLBJ; LBJ et al. to DDE, May 17, 1960, WHFN; Pearson talk with LBJ, May 24, 1960, Pearson Papers.

67. W.C. Daniel to Robert Baker, May 23, 1960, Byrd, Sr., Papers; Memo: Work Needed to Be Done, May 3, 1960; Byron Skelton to Jenkins, May 3, 1960; LBJ to Skelton, May 16, 1960; Larry Jones to Irvin Hoff, May 19, 1960; Larry Blackmon to John Sparkman, May 30, 1960, SPF; LBJ-Gov. Freeman telephone conversation, May 23, 1960, and LBJ-Bill Arbogast, May 24, 1960, NTJC; LBJ statements, May 26, 27, 1960, SLBJ; calls for May 16–31, 1960, OF:Jenkins; travel, 1960, LBJA:SF.

68. *Louisville Courier-Journal*, June 3, 1960; travel, 1960, LBJA:SF; Reedy: Memo File 1960, SP; "How LBJ Will Be Nominated," June 11, 1960 (Jenkins), SPF; press conference, June 19, 1960, SLBJ; Anderson to Pearson, June 22, 1960, Pearson Papers; LBJ to Rayburn, June 24, 1960, Rayburn Papers; LBJ-Bill Minnell telephone conversation, June 30, 1960, NTJC; Evans and Novak, *LBJ: Exercise of Power*, 281–82.

69. LBJ statement, July 5, 1960, SLBJ; Krock private memorandum, July 7, 1960, Krock Papers.

70. LBJ statement, July 7, 1960; memo, June 23, 1960; Rowe-Jenkins tele-

phone conversation, June 8, 1960, SP; Steele to Harry Johnston, July 8, 1960, Steele Papers.

71. Memo, n.d., Pearson Papers; LBJ-C.J. Block telephone conversation, June 23, 1960, NTJC; Drew Pearson OH; Goodwin, *Fitzgeralds & Kennedys*, 800–801. Clark Clifford believes that a lot of the later LBJ-Robert Kennedy bad feeling stemmed from the 1960 nomination campaign when the Kennedy camp raised the issue of Johnson's heart condition, and the Johnson people replied in kind. Conversation with Brian VanDeMark, Clifford's assistant, July 7, 1989. John Connally also describes the attack by the Kennedys on LBJ's health (interv., Oct. 28, 1989).

72. "Senator Kennedy and the McCarthy Story," n.d., WHFN.

73. Bill to Jim, n.d., with "A Contrast of the Voting Records of LBJ and JFK" attached, SP; Attendance and Voting Record LBJ and JFK, n.d., SPF; Hugh Scott to JFK, June 19, 1960, LBJA:CF; Steele to Harry Johnston, July 8, 1960, Steele Papers.

74. Sorensen, *Kennedy*, 176; Goodwin, *Fitzgeralds & Kennedys*, 734–35, 745, 774–76, 788; *New York Times*, July 5, 1960, p. 19; Charlie Kress-Jenkins telephone conversation, July 5, 1960; Eliot Janeway-Jenkins, July 5, 1960; Bobby Baker-Jenkins, July 6, 1960, OF:Jenkins; Steele to Johnston, July 8, 1960, Steele Papers; India Edwards OH; Walter H. Judd OH, HSTL; Arthur M. Schlesinger, Jr., *Robert Kennedy and His Times* (Boston, 1978), 204–5.

75. LBJ pre-presidential diary, July 9, 1960; James Rowe OH; "The Boston-Texas Axis," in Corcoran ms. memoir, Corcoran Papers.

76. *Ibid.*; Steinberg, *Sam Johnson's Boy*, 524–26; Evans and Novak, *LBJ: Exercise of Power*, 286–89; Howard E. Shuman OH, SHO.

77. Transcript of recorded remarks, LBJ and JFK, July 12, 13, 1960, SLBJ; Evans and Novak, *LBJ: Exercise of Power*, 289–91; Sorensen, *Kennedy*, 176–77.

78. Sorensen, *Kennedy*, 183–84, 186; Schlesinger, Jr., *Robert Kennedy*, 206–7.

79. *Ibid.*, 207; "The Choosing of Lyndon B. Johnson (The Graham Memorandum)," pp. 407–9 of Theodore H. White, *The Making of the President 1964* (N.Y., 1965).

80. Krock private memorandum, Sept. 22, 1960, Krock Papers; "The Boston-Texas Axis," Corcoran Papers.

81. Thomas P. O'Neill OH.

82. "The Boston-Texas Axis," Corcoran Papers; "LBJ Reminisces: The 1960 Campaign," *Among Friends of LBJ Newsletter*, Jan. 1, 1983, p. 3.

83. Arthur Krock's story on page 1 of the *New York Times*, Aug. 30, 1965.

84. Evans and Novak, *LBJ: Exercise of Power*, 292–93; Sorensen, *Kennedy*, 186; Reedy to LBJ, June 14, 1960, SP; LBJ press conference, July 5, 1960, SLBJ; telephone conversation with Brian VanDeMark, Clark Clifford's assistant, April 30, 1989; interview with Eliot Janeway, Dec. 20, 1986.

85. Arthur M. Schlesinger, Jr., *A Thousand Days: John F. Kennedy in the White House* (Boston, 1965), 48.

86. Eliot Janeway interview, Dec. 20, 1986; "The Boston-Texas Axis," Corcoran Papers; John Connally interview, Oct. 28, 1989.

87. "Boston-Texas Axis," Corcoran Papers; Steinberg, *Sam Johnson's Boy*, 530; John Connally interview, Oct. 28, 1989.

88. Myer Feldman OH, JFKL; Evans and Novak, *LBJ: Exercise of Power*,

296–98; Edwin O. Guthman and Jeffrey Shulman, eds., *Robert Kennedy: In His Own Words* (N.Y., 1988), 316–17.

89. Schlesinger, Jr., *Robert Kennedy*, 208–9; Miller, *Lyndon*, 316–17.

90. *Ibid.*, 314; Evans and Novak, *LBJ: Exercise of Power*, 298–99.

91. Guthman and Shulman, eds., *Robert Kennedy*, 21–22.

92. Miller, *Lyndon*, 317–18, 725, n.6; Graham memorandum in White, *Making of the President 1964*, 411–12.

93. James Rowe OH; Graham memorandum, *Making of the President 1964*, 413–14; Miller, *Lyndon*, 319–20. In a private memorandum, Sept. 22, 1960, Arthur Krock recorded that Johnson and Rayburn construed the Bobby Kennedy visits "as a hint Kennedy wanted to withdraw his promise, and when I checked with the Johnson group they were breathing threats about what Johnson would do to Kennedy in the post-convention session of Congress and elsewhere. In this way I discovered, to my surprise, that Johnson was eager for the Vice Presidential nomination despite his attacks on Kennedy." Krock Papers.

94. Guthman and Shulman, eds., *Robert Kennedy*, 22; White, *Making of the President 1964*, 415; Miller, *Lyndon*, 319–20; James Rowe OH. Lawrence F. O'Brien, JFK's campaign manager, believes that Bobby Kennedy acted without JFK's endorsement in trying to get LBJ off the ticket: O'Brien OH.

95. Schlesinger, Jr., *A Thousand Days*, 57–58; Evans and Novak, *LBJ: Exercise of Power*, 303–4.

96. Meeting of LBJ and JFK with Negro Delegates, July 15, 1960, SLBJ; Reichard, *Congress and the Presidency*, Spring 1986, p. 72; Schlesinger, Jr., *A Thousand Days*, 58.

97. Three Rowe memos to LBJ (two for July 25 and one for Aug. 24, 1960), LBJA:SN; Schlesinger, Jr., *Robert Kennedy*, 211–14.

98. Steinberg, *Sam Johnson's Boy*, 534–35; Evans and Novak, *LBJ: Exercise of Power*, 309–12; Schlessinger, Jr., *A Thousand Days*, 62–64; memo: "Press Talk: About Kennedy-Johnson Visit, Etc.," n.d., SLBJ.

99. Robert Troutman, Jr. OH, Univ. of Ga.; LBJ, speech to Young Dems., July 31, 1960, SLBJ.

100. Walter Judd OH, HSTL; Bill Moyers, "What a Real President Was Like," *Washington Post*, Nov. 13, 1988, C5. Steinberg cites reporters who "said that behind the scenes he [LBJ] reassured Southern political leaders that the national platform's civil rights promises were not to be taken seriously." *Sam Johnson's Boy*, 543.

101. Robert Troutman, Jr. OH, Univ. of Ga.

102. Travel 1960, LBJA:SF; LBJ statement to the press, July 14, 1960, SLBJ; Evans and Novak, *LBJ: Exercise of Power*, 238–40; Sorensen, *Kennedy*, 192.

103. Jenkins-Pierre Salinger telephone conversation, Aug. 2, 1960; Jenkins-Irving Goldberg, Aug. 16, 1960; Jenkins-Ed Clark, Aug. 17, 1960; Jenkins-Byron Skelton, Aug. 20, 1960; Jenkins-Gerald Mann, Aug. 22, 1960; Mildred-Jenkins, Aug. 25, 1960; Jenkins-Tom Phinney, Sept. 8, 1960, OF:Jenkins.

104. Miller, *Lyndon*, 324; LBJ speech and press conference, Sept. 9, 1960, SLBJ.

105. Miller, *Lyndon*, 324–25; Evans and Novak, *LBJ: Exercise of Power*, 319; Sorensen, *Kennedy*, 214.

106. *Ibid.*, 215–18.

107. *Ibid.* 218; Steele to Johnston, Sept. 16, 1960, Steele Papers; Bryce Harlow OH.

108. News release, Oct. 5, 1960, Lloyd Papers, HSTL; speeches for Oct. 10–15, 1960, SLBJ; Steinberg, *Sam Johnson's Boy,* 539–41; Miller, *Lyndon,* 325–27.

109. LBJ to Amon Carter, Sept. 28, 1960, LBJA:CF; Lloyd Bentsen-Jenkins telephone conversation, Sept. 16, 1960, OF:Jenkins; LBJ to Connally, Oct. 18, 1960, SP.

110. Rowe to Humphrey, Nov. 22, 1960, Rowe Papers; James Rowe OH; James Blundell OH; William H. Jordan, Jr. OH; D.B. Hardeman OH; Steinberg, *Sam Johnson's Boy,* 541; Evans and Novak, *LBJ: Exercise of Power,* 313–15; Miller, *Lyndon,* 322–24.

111. Rowe to Humphrey, Nov. 22, 1960, Rowe Papers; Evans and Novak, *LBJ: Exercise of Power,* 315–16; Steinberg, *Sam Johnson's Boy,* 211–12.

112. Gen. Carl Phinney OH; Charles Boatner OH; Elizabeth Carpenter OH; William H. Jordan, Jr. OH; LBJ speech, Nov. 6, 1960, SLBJ; Samuel E. Vandiver Jr. OH; David William Brooks OH, Univ. of Ga.; Steinberg, *Sam Johnson's Boy,* 542–43; Miller, *Lyndon,* 330–32.

113. Steinberg, *Sam Johnson's Boy,* 544; Schlesinger, Jr., *A Thousand Days,* 58, 74. Gary Reichard points out that LBJ helped win Dixie's white votes without an anti-civil rights or a "southern strategy." *Congress and the Presidency,* Spring 1986, pp. 72–73. It has been asserted that voting irregularities in Illinois, where Kennedy won by fewer than 9,000 votes, and Texas determined the outcome of the election. Arthur Schlesinger, Jr., believes "that in Illinois one party stole as many votes as the other. When the Illinois count was challenged, the state electoral board, which was 4–1 Republican, voted unanimously to certify the Kennedy electors." *Robert Kennedy,* 220. A challenge to the result in Texas was also denied. Leon Jaworski, the attorney for LBJ and the Democrats in the case, says (OH) that the challenge "was the weakest feeblest effort you ever saw, with no real proof of any probative value as to any irregularities. The things they were talking about could as well have cost us votes as cost them votes." The judge dismissed the case. Cf. Clifton C. Carter OH.

114. Miller, *Lyndon,* 334; Rowe to Humphrey, Nov. 22, 1960, Rowe Papers.

Index